DATE DUE

THE JEWS

THEIR HISTORY,
CULTURE, AND RELIGION

THIRD EDITION

Edited by

Louis Finkelstein

CHANCELLOR

THE JEWISH THEOLOGICAL SEMINARY OF AMERICA

Volume II

HARPER & ROW PUBLISHERS NEW YORK

To

IRVING LEHMAN

(1876-1945)

Who in life and precept
integrated the ancient tradition
of the Hebrew prophets with the
spirit of American democracy

CONTENTS

IV. THE JEWISH RELIGION

ILLUSTRATIONS

MAP

CHAPTER 18

THE MODERN RENAISSANCE OF HEBREW LITERATURE

By Hillel Bavli

Foreword

During the past century and a half Hebrew literature has experienced a remarkable transformation. It emerged with newborn power from the obscurity into which it had sunk after the splendid medieval period. Quickened by the Enlightenment of eighteenth-century Western Europe, Hebrew literature soon grew receptive to new ideas and new forms, more sensitive to rising contemporary problems and conscious of its high calling to inspire and to guide the Jewish people.

In spirit, modern Hebrew literature is in close affinity with universal literature. It has drawn strength from many cultures and it bears the imprint of many environments. Italian Renaissance, French rationalism, and pseudoclassicism, German and English romanticism affected its course. This is but natural, since it has flourished in various countries.

Having assimilated the foreign influences that stimulated it, Hebrew literature before long became aware of its own traditions, and was gradually regenerated by the force of its own consciousness. In its totality, modern Hebrew literature embodies a record of the physical and spiritual life of the Jewish people. It expresses the temporal and the eternal, the national and the universal. Through it and with many voices, the social, religious and aesthetic forces that went into the making of our modern age became articulate.

The following pages attempt a summary and an appraisal of the leading tendencies and personalities through whom modern Hebrew literature, in my opinion, is best represented.

1. AIMS OF HASKALA

The predominant characteristic of modern Hebrew literature, from the middle of the eighteenth to the latter part of the nineteenth century, is generally described by the word *Haskala*, that is, Enlightenment. This very name is given to the literature of that entire age. The urge for Haskala brought about a literary revival, first in Germany, where it was short lived, then in Austria, particularly in the province of Galicia, and in Russia, including Poland and Lithuania, in which countries it was more enduring and of great significance.

Haskala aimed primarily at a studied adjustment of Jewish life to the modern world as a prelude to the social and political emancipation of the Ghetto Jew.[1a] Hence it called for drastic change in the curriculum of the Jewish school in Germany and Eastern Europe, where secular studies were completely disregarded. The translation of the Pentateuch into German by Moses Mendelssohn (1729-1786), first fruit of Haskala in Germany, was to provide a stimulus to the study of the German language and an introduction to Western culture. The study of the humanities became the coveted goal of the Haskala movement in Germany and elsewhere. There was nothing revolutionary in this idea, nor anything contrary to Jewish tradition. In fact, the leading rabbinic authority of the age, the Gaon of Vilna (1720-1797), considered the study of "worldly wisdom" essential for a deeper understanding of the Torah. Still, the vigorous effort of the Haskala movement to remove the barrier between religious and worldly culture made the ideal of secularism a contributing factor in the Hebrew literary revival.

Haskala meant also a cultivation of the aesthetic sense, a craving for beauty. Poetry above all, as a symbol of the sublime and the beautiful, became a subject of special adoration. The young poet Shlomo Loewisohn (1789-1821), a native of Hungary, gave artistic utterance to the ideal of the age. In an exalted ode, *Poetry Speaks*, written in colorful blank verse, he pictured poetry, "the offspring of beauty," as the guiding and all-dominating spirit of the universe. This majestic ode has in it something of the impassioned sublimity of Shelley's *Defence of Poetry* with its challenging final pronouncement: "The poets are the unacknowledged legislators of mankind."

Synonymous with poetry and with beauty was the Hebrew language. An ecstatic devotion to the Hebrew tongue, a sustained vision of its complete revival, inspired the entire Haskala literature. The love of Hebrew has been the expression of a great faith in the vitality of the Jewish people. The sacred tongue, long associated in the minds of most people with religious culture only, shook off the dust of antiquity and assumed a creative role for the renewal of Jewish life in all its phases.

Haskala strove to normalize Jewish life. It proclaimed the ideal of manual labor, of agricultural pursuit in particular, as a great moral catharsis, a spiritual as well as physical cure for the sorely tried Ghetto Jewry. This ideal was stressed with homiletic skill, supported by numerous quotations from ancient texts, by the pioneer champion of Haskala in Russia, Isaac Baer Levinsohn (1788-1860). Life alone with nature, a life of labor, became the theme song for many a poem, allegory and story.

In its later militant stages, the Haskala movement sought radically to reinterpret traditional Jewish values, to shatter ancient forms and patterns of thought and behavior. In short, Haskala aspired to reform Jewish life socially, religiously and aesthetically, to regenerate Hebrew literature by injecting into it the serum of reality.

The most striking characteristic of Haskala literature is the deep humanity pervading it, its abiding faith in mankind, in the triumph of reason, in human progress. A representative poet of Haskala, Adam Lebenson (1794-1878) of Lithuania, visualized Mercy, "the heavenly daughter," standing at the crossroads pleading with the passers-by to sustain her in healing humanity of its ills due to cruelty, to adversity, to catastrophe. The note of woe and mercy, the common bond of humanity, struck in his poem *Mercy*, is characteristic of the entire age, for while the immediate concern of Haskala was the Jewish people, its outlook was worldly, and its supreme ideal the universal.

2. THE RISE OF THE SCIENCE OF JUDAISM

The Haskala movement was the outgrowth of an idea. But ideas have a way of releasing strange forces, unforeseen by those with whom the ideas are original. Thus Haskala, which aimed to teach the modern Jew to observe the world about him, eventually led the thinking Jew to look more deeply into his own world.

The Age of Enlightenment, which saw a deepening of historical thinking, witnessed the emergence of the "Science of Judaism," whose main purpose was to study the Jewish past critically, with scientific thoroughness, through a systematic examination of the minutest details. The founders of the Science of Judaism, Solomon Judah Loeb (Shir) Rapaport (1790-1867) and Nachman Krochmal (1785-1840) in Galicia, Samuel David Luzzatto (1800-1865) in Italy, and Leopold Zunz (1794-1886) in Germany, the first three in Hebrew and the last one in German, applied the discipline of scholarship to vast unexplored regions of Hebrew literature, ancient and medieval. They, their disciples and followers, brought to light the inner spirit of Judaism manifesting itself in biblical and Rabbinic literature, in liturgy and homily, in the Hebrew language and Hebrew poetry. The achievements of the Science of Judaism in the past century made possible a more proper evaluation of Judaism's civilizing role throughout the ages.

To reveal the historic character of Judaism was the main objective of Nachman Krochmal and Samuel David Luzzatto, two of the boldest spirits of the Haskala age.

In his philosophic work, *Guide for the Perplexed of the Age*, Krochmal brought the history of Judaism within the orbit of world civilizations and applied the laws of change and development governing all peoples and cultures to the study and interpretation of the spiritual values of Israel. Probing into the past, Krochmal performed a twofold task: he traced the points of similarity between the historic course of Israel and that of other peoples and, above all, he indicated the distinctiveness of the Hebrew genius. "In truth," he affirmed, "the individuality of a nation as such is merely the individuality of its spirit."[2] The mark of Jewish individuality, he reasoned, is the absolute spirit, the belief in an incorporeal God Who is not predicated by any material symbolism. Therein, he concluded, is the secret of the eternity of Israel, inasmuch as the Infinite, the Absolute Spirit, is imperishable.

To Krochmal, the disciple of Maimonides and the devotee of German idealism, faith and reason, religion and philosophy complemented one another as manifestations of the spirit. Neither is adequate to retain its loftiness and purity, escaping fanaticism or skeptic materialism without the inspiration and guidance of its counterpart.

A different road was taken by Samuel David Luzzatto, the poet and critic, exegete and interpreter of medieval Hebrew poetry. Intensity of emotion rather than depth of thought was the dominant force of his personality. His writings, in both poetry and prose, are characterized by optimism and human tenderness. Unlike Krochmal, he disclaimed any philosophic, theoretical approach to Judaism and emphasized instead the humanitarian aspect, the quality of mercy, which he regarded as one of the fundamentals of Judaism.

In him faith was stronger than reason. He exalted the religion of the heart above the intellect, the primitive traditional religion with its belief in the supernatural and the miraculous. Like Judah Ha-Levi,[3a] whose poetry he interpreted so beautifully, he believed that the intuitive grasp, the ecstatic emotion could open gates of Divine Revelation which no philosophic system could. With Ha-Levi he could say: "And my heart saw Thee and believed in Thee, as though it had stood at Mount Sinai. I sought Thee in my visions and Thy glory descended and passed through my clouds."

He, too, rejected the "wisdom of the Greeks," with its emphasis upon intellectualism, and extolled Judaism, the Abramitic spirit, as he called it, with its insistence upon moral improvement, upon training of character. Challenging the rationalist views of the age, Luzzatto called for a rebirth of Judaism from within through a deepening of emotional attachment to tradition, through a heightening of national consciousness.

Krochmal and Luzzatto, for all their differences in outlook and temperament, were at one in some respects. Both saw in the Jewish individuality an emblem of indestructible nationhood. Both analyzed the problems of the past with an eye to the future, convinced that the Hebrew genius still had great contributions to make. Finally, both maintained that only in cultivating the original character of Judaism through the Hebrew language and literature, was there any hope for the spiritual revival of the Jewish people.

3. Voices from the Bible

Nowhere has the Renaissance of Hebrew literature been so pronounced as in the field of poetry. At the beginning of the nineteenth century the Hebrew muse was remarkably inarticulate. The poetic vigor of medieval Spain had long been spent. Whatever there was of Hebrew poetry was stilted, didactic and colorless. In time, however, Hebrew poetry found its voice again. In form, in color, in tone, it grew rich and broad.

There was one great voice heard in Hebrew poetry in the eighteenth century, that of Moses Hayyim Luzzatto (1707-1747) of Padua, Italy.[4a] This Messianic visionary, whose chief work lies in the fields of religious mysticism and ethics, was destined to inject new life into Hebrew literature by his poetry. His two major dramatic poems, the imaginative *Tower of Strength* and the allegorical *Praise to the Righteous*, clearly bear the marks of European pseudoclassicism. In fact the first is, in part, borrowed from the popular pastoral drama, *Il Pastor Fido*, by the sixteenth-century Italian, Guarini. Nevertheless, in Luzzatto the minor pseudoclassic strain became a major classic voice, austere and strong and melodious. Luzzatto's two love stories, with their recurring moralism in the triumph of the simple, pure heart endowed with natural piety over the cunning of the wicked and blind cruelty of the mob, combine to a rare degree romantic imagery with classic severity of composition. The occult and rational qualities of man, dreamlike vision and intellectual observation, are fused in these works. Their sublimation of nature, of simple life, their deep sense of the ethical and the aesthetic alike re-echoed strongly in later Haskala literature. The exalted blank verse of Luzzatto, couched in purest biblical style, turned renascent Hebrew literature to the Bible itself.

Literary revival very often implies the power to lend new meaning and importance to ancient lore, to revitalize the inherited and make it function again. The Haskala poets, in their quest for humanism and classic beauty, rediscovered the Bible as a source of poetic inspiration, as an instrument of cultural and social progress. Characteristically enough, the above-mentioned Shlomo Loewisohn made the first attempt in modern Hebrew literature at a literary, aesthetic appreciation of the Scriptures, in a volume on the rhetoric of the Bible.

In an introduction to his long and tedious epic on the life of Moses, Napthali Herz Wessely (1725-1805), chief spokesman of Haskala in Germany, spoke about the need for poetic commentary on the Bible. Such a commentary indeed was written by numerous gifted poets; it was, however, not merely a commentary on the Bible but also on their own lives and on the age in which they lived. Many searched deeply in the ancient Book for the elixir of creative life. From the Bible, dramatic and narrative poems borrowed characters in ancient dress—kings, prophets, peasants, shepherds—who were nevertheless sufficiently European in manner to befit the modern age. Voices from the Bible mingled with echoes from French and German poets. Collectively, this poetry constitutes a cultural phenomenon. To the Ghetto Jew, removed from nature, it brought both a glorious vision and contact with the soil.

Occasionally biblical scenes and characters reflected the poet's own personality and his inner struggles. A notable example is Micah Joseph Lebensohn (1828-1852) of Vilna. In him epic serenity and lyric ecstasy were equally strong. His short and tragic life is compressed in his noble poetry.

Romantic melancholy, worldly illusion, a passion for life, and the bitterness of approaching death, fill his verse. The search for truth and beauty and the tragedy of unfulfillment, the antinomies of reason and emotion, are the leitmotifs of his lyric poetry. They are also the very heart of his biblical epics. The striking image of youthful King Solomon drunk with love, with poetry, with faith, is a stirring image of romantic youth and high idealism. The somber figure of Kohelet, Solomon in his declining years, seared by delusions and doubts and frustrations, is, in its symbolic allusions, the poet's mocking criticism of the rationalistic trend of his age. With tense feeling, in soulful, musical lines, the poet portrays the tragic beauty of ancient characters: Moses at Mt. Abarim breathing his last while "his eye is turned toward Jerusalem"; Jael, torn between love of country and deep compassion as she is about to slay Sisera; blind and furious Samson avenging himself on the Philistines in his last heroic act; and the medieval poet Judah Ha-Levi, struck by a marauder's hand as he prays at the gates of Jerusalem. The remote past envisioned by the poet becomes an intimate personal experience.

Bible-inspired poetry reached its peak in the works of Abraham Mapu (1808-1867), a native of Lithuania. His two major historical novels, *The Love of Zion* and *The Guilt of Samaria*, the first novels in modern Hebrew literature, have in them much of the intensity and ardor of true poetry. In Mapu, the romantic novel found an accomplished artist, the biblical epic its great master.

The novels of Mapu are fantastic love stories, intricate in plot, rich in action, in intrigue and adventure, in the tradition of the romantic school. The great and magnanimous lover, the virtuous and the wicked, the nobleman and the simple peasant—all these inevitable characters are here. The righteous come to their reward, of course, and the lovers triumph over all obstacles.

The great popularity of these tales in their day was due to the many fascinating surprises in the narratives. But the real value and significance of Mapu lie in his *ars Hebraica*. Mapu transplanted the romanticism of the Occident into the soil of ancient Palestine; he saturated that romanticism with the living waters of the prophetic fountain, and raised it to a splendor and originality all its own.

Amid the squalor and horrors of Ghetto life in czarist Russia, Mapu projected a vision of ancient Judea and presented a pageant of wholesome Hebrew life rooted in its own soil, nurtured by its own culture. Jerusalem with its environs, its landscape and its populace; the countryside with its peasantry; prince, priest, prophet and plain people, customs and ritual—all assumed an illusory reality. Mapu was able to make his vision vivid by his unusual insight, by his genius for the primitive, and above all, by his marvelous sense of the rhythm and spirit of the Bible.

Reading Mapu one gets the feeling that here is not a mere studied imitation of biblical style but rather a complete self-identification with the temper and speech and outlook of biblical days. Therein, in his intuitive, creative penetration into the very accent of the Bible, lies his great cultural significance.

More than any of his contemporaries, Mapu symbolized the deep, newborn consciousness of nature and the spirit of Jewish regeneration through contact with the soil of Palestine.

4. Seeing the Present

Modern Hebrew literature was not confined merely to classic beauty and idyllic aestheticism. The scholarly and imaginative treatment of the past constituted but one phase of that literature. Another phase, predominant in the latter half of the nineteenth century, was the realistic portrayal of the present. The entire structure of Jewish life in the Ghetto was exposed to critical scrutiny. The ideal of change and revision permeated much of Hebrew prose and poetry. Finally, literature became critical of itself and examined its own character, its functions and its ideals.

One of the severe critics of the age was its most representative poet, Judah Loeb Gordon (1830-1892), a native of Vilna.

The poetry of Gordon is distinguished by its epic quality; occasionally it is colored by lyrical soliloquy. The minor romantic strain of his early poetry is the least characteristic of it. It has little of the rapture and sweet melancholy of impassioned youth. It is rational, forceful and incisive. Satirical invective is its strongest weapon.

In a series of powerful narratives Gordon portrayed Jewish society, holding up to ridicule all that seemed ugly, stagnant and unworldly. He fought the phantoms of the past: rigorous traditions, stifling prejudices, bigotry and ignorance. In historical epic, biblical monologue and contemporary tale, he inveighed against the ills and follies of the present, and called for a more liberal outlook on life, in consonance with the spirit of the time.

His epic, *Between the Lion's Teeth*, is a striking portrayal of the loss of the Judean state and the heroism of one of its defenders who met a martyr's death at the arena in Rome. The tragedy of a people is compressed in stirring scenes. Out of the past rises the piercing voice of the poet, scorning the ancient Jewish leaders and, by innuendo, the leaders of his day who, in their preoccupation with spiritual matters, failed to prepare their people for the day of trial, and have taught Israel "to be dead on earth, alive in the heavens."

A similar note is struck in the dramatic monologue, *Zedekiah in Prison*. Blinded King Zedekiah, in captivity contemplating his fate, appears as a progressive leader of the state, an advocate of labor and agriculture, in opposition to the superspiritual views of the prophet Jeremiah. But Zedekiah is merely the poet's mouthpiece. Gordon challenges those of his contemporaries who would divorce Judaism from worldly interests and activities and would confine it mainly to the archives of ancient glory.

His *Epics of the Present* are stirring narratives of tragic episodes in Jewish life resulting from a lack of adjustment of the ancient tradition to the modern environment. These "Epics" storm with protest, with indignation against the severity of Jewish orthodoxy, the static state of Jewish society, the shortsightedness of its leaders.

The influence of Gordon's poetry on Hebrew literature was far reaching. It was a dynamic factor in rousing the creative forces in Jewry to selfrenewal through a deeper attachment to the soil and the world, and through a stronger faith in the future destiny of the Jewish people.

The ideal of social and religious reform was the motivating force of the best work of Moshe Leib Lilienblum (1843-1910), a notable figure in Haskala literature.

His most colorful work, *Sins of Youth*, unfolds the ghastliest pictures of Ghetto life in Lithuania. The author's experiences are drawn with the pain and joy of self-revelation in a series of oppressive scenes: his gloomy childhood in an environment of ugly fanaticism and melancholy asceticism, his rabbinic training and youthful piety, the rising doubts and passions of adolescence, his struggles for Haskala and the fury of persecution unleashed against him. Lilienblum himself characterized his work as "a Hebrew drama without theatrical effect and unfinished, but rich in misfortune."[5] It is, in essence, a book of revolt against obsolete forms, against an ascetic tradition, against indolence and ignorance.

To Lilienblum the need for the liberalization of Judaism was prior to any social reform. Consequently, he advocated that the principle of change and inner development which once influenced talmudic literature be recognized again by the Rabbinic authorities. The legal abolition of out-dated customs and inhibitions would, he believed, strengthen Judaism from within and open the road for social and economic progress.

In the persistent call for realism, for the adjustment of religion to life, Lilienblum and many of his contemporaries showed little understanding of the emotional and romantic aspect of religion. Any mystic or legendary strain was damned by them as reactionary. Hasidism, with its imaginative, emotional approach to life, they regarded as a source of all evil; to them folklore was sheer nonsense and superstition.

The vision of the poet and the polemic of the publicist were made lively by the story of the novelist. In fact, the Haskala novel combined poetic lyricism, publicistic moralizing, and plain, realistic storytelling. Those traits are particularly evident in the works of Perez Smolenskin (1842-1885), a native of White Russia who spent his creative years in Vienna, where he founded and edited the influential Hebrew monthly *Hashahar*.

Smolenskin attempted to portray the totality of Jewish life, the various strata of society in and outside the Ghetto with a naturalness and broad sweep unknown before in Hebrew literature. Out of his rich picture gallery three collective types come to the fore.

First the forlorn souls who, like the hero in his leading novel are *lost in the ways of life*. These are the budding intellectuals, uprooted from the soil of their own traditions and maladjusted to any other milieu; they wander aimlessly like spiritual gypsies.

Next come the "pillars of society," the men of might and influence, community elders who despise and crush the poor, the exploiters, wicked obscurantists and hypocrites who attack Haskala, adventurers and scoundrels.

Alongside these characters stand the men of truth and high idealism, the torchbearers of Haskala; with them are the saintly men of deep faith and religious ecstasy.

The novels of Smolenskin are volatile and dramatic. They suffer from overmoralizing and loquacity, from an overabundance of the bizarre and extravagant. Nevertheless, for all their artistic imperfections, they contain magnificent portraits and caricatures of the age. They did for Hebrew literature what the novels of Dickens did for English literature. They are charged with the reformer's zeal and the idealist's passion, and their love is reserved for the weak, the humble, the oppressed.

The weakness of the Haskala novel lies in its inability to describe natural objects accurately, or to perceive the elements of character dis-tinctly. Vague generalization prevented the novelist from recognizing reality.

The great master of Hebrew realism was Mendele Mocher Seforim (1836-1916), *i.e.*, Mendele the Bookseller, pseudonym of S. J. Abramowitz, a native of White Russia who spent a major part of his life in Odessa.[6a] An artist in both Hebrew and Yiddish literature, Mendele is unique as a novelist. He is the type of author whom only a rich, indigenous Jewish life and culture could have produced.

Mendele the Bookseller, his leading character, is a typical Jew who, following his calling, roams the Ghetto far and wide. He is the observant eye describing all he sees. In truth, the author assures us, there are two Mendeles struggling within him. One is simple and naïve and the other critical and satirical. And we see Ghetto life through the eyes of both. The external ugliness of the Ghetto, depicted so mercilessly by Mendele, is mellowed by the spiritual grandeur and nobility of Jewish traditional life. An unrivaled painter of Jewish poverty and Jewish tragedy, Mendele is, equally, the fierce critic who satirizes the provincial backwardness of the Ghetto Jew, his rootlessness, his detachment from the soil.

Mendele is distinguished alike as interpreter of human character and painter of the visible world. His gloomy pictures of Ghetto misery are set within a framework of quiet, natural scenery.

The descriptive art of Mendele is matched by the magnificence of his style. Mendele revitalized classical Hebrew, gave it new color and marked it with the reality of a spoken, pungent vernacular. He merged biblical and Rabbinic diction, spiced it with elements of popular colloquialism, and created an instrument of powerful expression.

The acute critical sense which Hebrew literature displayed in the last decades of the nineteenth century was in time directed against literature itself. Hebrew literature became critical of its own functions and accomplishments. Style, motif, plot, craftsmanship, were subjected to critical analysis. The most representative critic of his age was David Frishman (1860-1922), a native of Poland.

Frishman made his critical debut in 1883, at the decline of the Haskala age, but the spirit of Haskala lived on in him to the end. His activities covered a number of fields—poetry, short story, essay—but it is chiefly as a critic that he is to be remembered. He detected in Hebrew literature the very faults that Gordon and Mendele exposed in Ghetto life: provincialism, ignorance, lack of perspective and good taste. In a musical biblical style approaching poetic prose, he preached the doctrine of aestheticism and universalism. "To create gradually through the good a feeling and taste for the good"—this dictum of Goethe which he repeatedly quoted served him as guide in his work. He was the inspired herald and interpreter of classic European literature and the charming translator of many masterpieces from the works of Shakespeare and Byron, Goethe and Heine and Nietzsche.

Frishman was one of the last knights-errant of Haskala; a firm believer in the ideals of humanism, and above all in the power of poetry and pure art to guide and elevate mankind.

5. THE FORCE OF NATIONALISM

In 1880 Gordon, poet of Haskala, elegized: "I am distressed for you, unfortunate poet of mine. You, too, I know, are as sick as I am. Your perfume is fouled here by stench and mud, and no wide spaces have you for the wandering of the spirit."[7] Thus the saddened poet heard the departing *Shekinah*, fugitive inspiration, speak to him. A disenchanted age was speaking through the voice of the poet.

By the end of the century, Haskala as a creative force had spent itself. The overemphasis which Haskala laid upon Western culture as a pattern of Jewish life, upon secularism and universalism as supreme ideals, inevitably brought about a shrinkage of Jewish individuality, a weakening of its moral fiber. A reaction was bound to set in. The current of assimilation that swept many of the "enlightened" Jewish youth, the rise of anti-Semitism in Germany, the outburst of pogroms in Russia, disillusioned the most ardent champions of Haskala, who had failed to realize sufficiently that the growth of a people comes primarily from within, from its own spiritual source.

A new force was emerging, shaping the course of Hebrew literature; it was the force of national orientation. Emphasis was now being laid upon the nationhood of the Jewish people, upon the uniqueness of its culture and traditions.

Perez Smolenskin, one of the chief exponents of Haskala, was among the first to expose and criticize its failures. Smolenskin charged the Haskala movement, particularly in its German phase, with a disruptive influence upon Jewish life, due mainly to its servile imitation of Western ways, without regard for Jewish individuality. The Reform movement, which denied the Messianic hope of Israel's restoration on the assumption that Israel was merely a religious community, not a nation, was an outgrowth, Smolenskin asserted, of this self-effacing imitation, leading to national suicide. The survival of Judaism as a creative force, he proclaimed, is dependent on the recognition of the Jewish people as a national entity.

The concept of nationhood, argued Smolenskin, has always been primary in Jewish consciousness. Israel never ceased regarding itself as a people. It is national consciousness that served to unify all elements in Israel, even the wayward sons, as long as they regarded themselves members of the Jewish people. The religious idea and the national concept are inseparable in Jewish history. Torah is a national as well as religious covenant. The religious precepts also attest to the national will and spring therefrom.

Nationalism, Smolenskin pleaded as did Moses Hess in his *Rome and Jerusalem,* is not in opposition to the spirit of universal progress. It is a rung in the ladder of humanity leading to its very top which is universal brotherhood.

In expounding his theories, Smolenskin laid stress upon the spiritual character of Jewish nationalism which was founded upon three basic principles: (1) Torah, the very essence of true spirituality, (2) the ideal of Israel's restoration as a people in Eretz Yisrael, and (3) the Hebrew language. But spiritual nationalism must remain pale and ineffective without a national soil. The abstract theories of Smolenskin and his contemporaries eventually were transformed into the vigorous affirmations of *Hibbat Zion,* the movement for Jewish colonization of Palestine. The rebuilding of Palestine along with Hebrew cultural renaissance became the driving forces of modern Hebrew literature.

In the peaceful quarters of Haskala, with their bright universal illusions, a dark, foreboding figure made its appearance—Jewish tragedy. Its horrible features cast their menacing shadows over story and essay and poem alike.

Leon (Judah Loeb) Pinsker's *Autoemancipation,* with its keen analysis of the Jewish problem and its diagnosis of Judophobia as a hereditary psychic aberration incurable by Haskala and emancipation, found fertile ground in Hebrew literature.

Pinsker's call for the rise of national self-respect, for a "national decision" to lay the ghost of Jewish homelessness (main cause of anti-Semitism, in his view), was in line with the fiery challenges of Smolenskin and the stern warnings of Lilienblum.

The destructive effect of homelessness, of *Galut* on Jewish character and morale was drawn in bold and dark lines. The Jewish people has to make its choice, exhorted Lilienblum in his eloquent essay *The Revival of Israel on Its Ancestral Soil,* either to live as a minority in the Diaspora, subject to endless persecution and massacre, to dissolve gradually under the corroding influence of assimilation, or to take the only honorable course—to live a normal life on the reconstituted ancestral soil.

With the rise of Hebrew nationalism another ideal emerged: the revival of Hebrew as a spoken tongue. Throughout the ages, even when it ceased to be spoken, Hebrew had been more than a mere literary language. It was and is one of the deep sources of Jewish consciousness. It is the unbroken chain linking the entire religious and cultural tradition of the Jewish people, bearing the indelible imprint of Hebrew individuality. Nevertheless, having been confined for ages to the book primarily, it lost touch with reality. The revival of Hebrew as a vernacular became the very symbol and touchstone of Hebrew Renaissance.

This phenomenal revival was accelerated by numerous factors: the amazing evolution of Hebrew literature during the nineteenth century, the creative ingenuity of such masters as Mapu, Gordon, Mendele, their contemporaries and their followers, the rise of Hebrew dailies, the work of Hebrew educators and pedagogues.

Eliezer Ben Yehuda (1858-1922) stands out as the pioneer of spoken Hebrew. In 1878 he had already formulated his view that Hebrew spiritual revival is futile unless Palestine is established as a national center. He settled in Palestine in 1881 and dedicated his life with singlehearted devotion to the revival of spoken Hebrew. As journalist, editor and philologist he had but one goal: the adjustment of Hebrew to daily life. His monumental encyclopedic *Dictionary of Ancient and Modern Hebrew* comprises the accumulated linguistic wealth of the ages and abounds in words coined by the author, current in Hebrew speech of today.

The miraculous revival of spoken Hebrew in modern Palestine is one of the great testimonies to the reality of the Hebrew Renaissance.

The ideal of national revival found its clearest expositor and interpreter in Ahad Ha-Am (born in the Ukraine 1856, died in Tel-Aviv 1927).

Ahad Ha-Am saw the national movement as the latest stage in the long evolution of the Hebrew spirit. He regarded it as the manifestation of the national will-to-live—the very blind force that asserted itself during crucial periods in Jewish history. The critical position of Judaism in the modern era that called forth the national movement as a saving force was due, in the view of Ahad Ha-Am, no less to internal than to external dangers. Judaism, which in the remote past was in a continuous state of flux and development, in conformity with the needs of each generation, is in danger of becoming atrophied. It is losing contact with life. The Jewish people is on the verge of disintegration. Not that it has lost its creative powers. But Jewish genius is diverted to strange channels and whatever it produces is marked by foreign influence. Judaism can no longer be isolated. "Not only the Jews, but Judaism, too, came out of the Ghetto wherever it came in contact with modern culture. Leaving the Ghetto walls it is in danger of losing its individuality or, at best, its national cohesiveness."[8] Only a great national ideal could save the Jewish people from stagnation. But such an ideal cannot be born in the Diaspora. It can grow only within the historical atmosphere of Judaism, where the Hebrew spirit can assert itself freely, unhampered by foreign influences.

Zionism is therefore synonymous with Judaism itself. Through Zionism, Israel declares itself to be alive. Palestine, rejuvenated by Hebrew culture, would become the mainstay of Judaism and "the true miniature of the Jewish people as it ought to be." Ultimately it would develop "not merely as a state of Jews but as a Jewish state."[9] To the Jews in the Diaspora Palestine would be a "spiritual center" embodying the spirit of Judaism at its highest. It would serve the Diaspora as a "center of imitation," symbolizing a pattern of life to be followed, uplifting Jewish morale, integrating Jewry the world over.

Since it sought the spiritual rehabilitation of Israel, Zionism would be insufficient, reasoned Ahad Ha-Am, as a mere political movement. A small state would be inadequate compensation for two thousand years of agony. The Jewish people was preserved through the ages by two great forces. It was maintained by the exalted ideals of the prophets who placed spiritual values above physical prowess and taught Israel never to be dismayed by brute power. Secondly, it was kept intact by a peculiar genius to assimilate any alien elements which threatened its existence and to utilize them for the enrichment of its own individuality. A political ideal which does not draw its support from the national culture would not be in consonance with Jewish tradition.

Consequently, the national ideal calls for spiritual regeneration, for complete Hebraization of Jewish education, for revival of Hebrew literature and Jewish learning, for activization of the prophetic teachings. Hence, the function of Hebrew literature is to illuminate Jewish past and present, to cultivate Jewish mind and consciousness to the end that national interests shall be placed above the individual good. Like Smolenskin, Ahad Ha-Am said that true nationalism is in no way contrary to the universal spirit. "Nationalism is a concrete form whereby the universal spirit reveals itself in every people in conformity with that people's circumstances, special needs and historic course."[10] Living normally on its own historic soil, engaging in all branches of human culture, developing its own national treasures, the Jewish people will rise to its highest possible level. Israel realizing itself will make its maximum contribution to the civilization of the world as it did in the past.

Rational as the theories of Ahad Ha-Am seem on the surface, they rise ultimately from the deep well of ancient faith. Judaism is viewed by Ahad Ha-Am not merely as a religion but as the sum total of all that the Jewish spirit created. Yet, in discussing the essence and destiny of Judaism, Ahad Ha-Am often assumes an air of mystery akin to religious fervor.

Throughout the same mirror of reason and faith with which he looked upon Judaism, Ahad Ha-Am beheld nationalism not as a lone episode in Jewish history but as the very core of Judaism.

Alongside the stream of clear thought emanating from the essays of Ahad Ha-Am, there was a current flowing in the opposite direction, represented by Micah Joseph Berdichevsky (1865-1922), a native of the Ukraine who spent a great part of his life in Germany.

Berdichevsky was a complex personality ever on the threshold of conflicting ideas, caught in the twilight of thought and emotion. The problem that confronted him in his youth and ever after was disturbing many of his contemporaries. It was the dilemma so magnificently presented by Mordecai Zeeb Feierberg (1874-1899) in his autobiographical story

Whither—to the deep shadows of a strangely fascinating and repelling past or to the alluring lights of European culture? The cry of a torn soul lost in a maze of conflicts is audible in many of the essays, soliloquies, and stories of Berdichevsky.

As a way out of the dilemma, Berdichevsky struggled—unsuccessfully, however—to sever the ties of the past altogether. The entire Jewish cultural history appeared to him as one continuous effort to curb the will of the individual and to impose the discipline of normative Judaism on the unwilling masses. With a touch of pagan heresy, he clamored for a transvaluation of values in Jewish history, for the abrogation of the supreme authority of the Book in Jewish life, for renewal of spirituality through contact with the soil, through life in nature.

Berdichevsky regarded as the supreme purpose of Hebrew renascence the liberation of the individual rather than the fortification of the national will, the obliteration of any prohibitive distinction between the sacred and profane, between the national and universal. Pathetically, he exclaimed: "The great world, life in all its fullness, the manifold passions, desires, instincts—everything concerns us and our own soul as it concerns any human being. We can no longer solve life's problems, nor can we live and act as our fathers did. We are children and grandchildren of the generations that preceded us, but not their coffins. It is up to us: either to be the last Jews or the first of a new people."[11]

Yet, in his wildest rebellion, Berdichevsky was tragically aware of his double loyalty: to the past and the future. Mournfully he confessed: "I would like in my innermost to unify, to create a new nation, new people; but I am torn in my soul."[12]

Berdichevsky's stories present the same ideological background as his essays. They glow with the nostalgic melancholy of afflicted souls, of lone rebels who broke away from old sanctuaries without finding new ones to replace them. Or else they glorify the ecstatic joys and primitive passions of plain people. In their simple unadorned style the tales of Berdichevsky produce a weird romantic atmosphere of ancient chronicles. Even stern reality assumes an almost legendary character. The remote becomes intimately close and a casual event is endowed with vision.

Berdichevsky represented the spirit of revolt, critical self-analysis and inquiry which pervades modern Hebrew literature. In his gropings and in his heresies, he was a spirit of liberation, calling for the reassertion of a vigorous, well-balanced Hebrew individuality as the basis of national revival.

6. POETRY OF REVIVAL

The new spirit that permeated Hebrew literature at the eclipse of Haskala and the rise of the national movement manifested itself with particular power and beauty in the domain of poetry. Within the past half century Hebrew poetry rose to its greatest heights. It became not only more expressive of Jewish life, but also more universal in character and scope.

This new era dawned with Hayyim Nahman Bialik (1873-1934), a native of the Ukraine who spent the last ten years of his life in Palestine. His poetry reads like a confession of a great heart, like the spiritual autobiography of a generation.

Bialik is a poet of intense emotions, rooted in the soil of his native village, in the "basic visions," as he calls them, of his childhood days and, equally, in the variegated culture and the tragically sublime history of his people. His poetry is a record of recurrent flights from one sphere to another—from his own "self" to nature and to his people's past and present.

The world appeared to Bialik in a state of continuous revelation. His nature poetry has a religious ecstasy. His major nature poem, *The Lake*, is a realistic description of a lake and a neighboring forest. But the lake grows into the living spirit of the universe, the all-seeing eye that absorbs everything, tree and cloud and man, and yet lives its own imperceptible, dreamy life. It is symbolic of Bialik's poetry as a whole, in which the borderland between vision and reality is indeterminate.

Nature showed to the poet not only the path to the Infinite; it also revealed his limitations in this finite world. It accentuated the abject Ghetto life and opened the dark chambers of elegy. The singer of sunshine became the poet of Jewish tragedy. His cycle of poems called forth by the pogroms in czarist Russia, in the first decade of the century, added a horrible chapter to Hebrew poetry of martyrdom. These poems unleash the pent-up furies, the protest and defiance of generations. They contain a modern version of the piercing challenge of Job: "O earth, cover not thou my blood, and let my cry have no resting place!" Jewish tragedy becomes world tragedy. Martyrdom is visualized by Bialik as an elemental force which may upset the equilibrium of the world. God Himself is pictured as being in despair. With biting irony Bialik portrays the defeat of divinity through the downfall of humanity.

Thwarted, disheartened by his people's bitter lot, Bialik took refuge in the House of Study, the Yeshiva, where the spiritual life of Israel has been nourished for generations. In a semilyrical epic, he drew the picture of a saintly Talmud student whose life is consecrated to the study of Torah. The triumph of spirit over matter, of faith over skepticism, gives the epic an inexhaustible beauty.

Bialik's ability to make vivid ancient Hebrew lore and to give it universal significance is best shown in his epic *The Dead of the Wilderness*. The poet utilized an old myth that the Israelites, who died in the wilderness upon leaving Egypt, still lie somewhere, dead in appearance only. Out of this material Bialik drew a series of bold and awesome figures. The vengeful desert, mysterious, like the force of destiny; the creatures of the desert: the eagle, the lion, the serpent and, above all, the dead of the wilderness, giants asleep, gruesome. Whoever approaches them withdraws in terror. The epic moves like a Greek tragedy, leading to inevitable doom. A storm breaks. The dead rise singing in chorus a song of rebellion. But the Supreme Will is not to be forced. The storm passes and the spell of ages remains unbroken.

In grandeur of expression, in the art of delineation and power of suggestion, the epic is as mighty and universal as the Greek *Prometheus*. The historic struggle of the Jewish people is presented against a background of splendid color and imagery that cannot but stir human fancy.

One of the definite contributions of modern Hebrew poetry is the revival of prayer, twin sister of lyric poetry. In this revival Bialik led the way.

Free of all worldly illusions, the poet communes with himself and sinks into meditation—on the visions of his childhood, on his orphanhood, on life's ambitions and frustrations, on the silent tragedies of the soul. Humbly he pays tribute, in one of the noblest of his poems, to "the meek of the world, the mute in soul who weave their lives in secret, modest in thought and in deed." With them he would unite his lot. These "princes of the spirit, who pass through the paths of life on tiptoe," exclaims the poet, "are the faithful guardians of the Divine Image on earth."

The intuitive grace of many of Bialik's poems, the purity of their accent, and their moral loftiness qualify them as high among the prayers of mankind.

The newly acquired world awareness which, alongside deepened national consciousness, is so characteristic of modern Hebrew poetry is manifested with particular effectiveness in the works of Saul Tchernichovsky (1875-1943). Tchernichovsky saw the world as one harmonious entity, a unity in multiple phenomena. He conceived the poet as the seer who envisages the essential affinity between apparently discordant elements in nature, the one who perceives, amidst a confusing multitude of sounds and voices, the intimate notes uniting mankind's remote past with the present. Tchernichovsky lived up to this exalted notion of the poet in his own works. His creative spirit drew its subject matter from many ages, from many lands and cultures, and from varied strata of the animate and the inanimate world.

Tchernichovsky has an eye and feeling for the minutest details, for the remotest scenes of nature. His *Nocturne*, his *Charms of the Forest*, are benedictions to the meanest plant, to the tiniest creature. Nature to Tchernichovsky is not merely a source of aesthetic enjoyment. It is the model, the archpattern for human conduct, a symbol of power ever renewing itself. Man cannot but follow its dictates, be imbued with its dynamic, invincible spirit, for man is "brother to the storm, to rock and to forest."

> I am unto God like hyacinth and mallow,
> Having nothing in the world but this bright sun.

These opening lines of the superb sonnet sequence *To the Sun* are an apt motto for the nature poetry of Tchernichovsky.

As a worshiper of nature and as priest of beauty, Tchernichovsky turned for inspiration to ancient Greece, "the cradle of the beautiful and mighty souls," as he calls it. Greek mythology, the abundant, harmonious life of the ancient Greeks, to whom "beauty was wisdom and wisdom beauty," exerted a deep influence on his poetry.

Tchernichovsky's emphasis on ancient Greece was due not only to his absorption in Greek culture. The poet's return to Apollo symbolized the return to the beauties and bounties of the earth from which his *Galut*-weary forebears and a cruel world had torn him. His Neo-Hellenism actually meant Neo-Hebraism—the regeneration of the Jewish people through a profound attachment to the soil, through cultivation of the aesthetic sense and a keen appreciation of the eternal values of mankind.

The path of beauty and heroism led Tchernichovsky from ancient Greece to ancient Israel. He invoked images and characters from the distant past—bold, rebellious Jewish spirits. Out of the mouths of the ancients he spoke to his contemporaries, bearing the message of revival on the soil of Palestine.

"Man," says Tchernichovsky, "is merely the image of his native environment." The poet-wanderer roaming through the world, ancient and modern, returned ever and again to his native Crimea and painted its mountains, its prairies, its historical monuments and ruins and above all its people. In a series of idylls in dactylic hexameter, he drew, with keen observation and quiet humor, intimate pictures of simple people. His characters are drawn from all walks of life: merchants, laborers, farmers, clergymen, servants, jailbirds. A bond of common humanity unites them all. Frequently, a Jew and non-Jew are paired and presented in the light of spiritual affinity. Elements of native folklore, both Jewish and Slavic, and a background of luxuriant natural scenery add spice and charm to the magnificent human panorama.

The universality of the poet's spirit is evident in his translations no less than in his original works. Among his translations are ancient Babylonian epics, all of Homer, *Oedipus Rex* of Sophocles, Anacreon, the odes of Horace, Shakespeare's *Macbeth* and *Twelfth Night*, Goethe's *Reineke Fuchs*, old Slavic epics, the Finnish *Kalevala*, Longfellow's *Hiawatha* and *Evangeline*.

This singer of the heroic and the beautiful was also the poet of the sad and the cruel. In lyric and epic poetry Tchernichovsky gave powerful expression to medieval Jewish martyrdom and to the horrors of our present age. Still, the close relationship between man and the world of beauty is not broken even in his poetry of martyrdom. Tragedy itself is softened through a portrayal of human courage, by a radiance flowing from natural phenomena. In the epic *Baruch of Mayence,* on Jewish suffering in Germany during the Crusades, some of the most memorable passages are descriptions of idyllic, rural scenes of the beauties of evening, night and dawn before the outbreak of furious persecution.

The broad humanity of Tchernichovsky, his ruggedness, his nature consciousness became more intense after he settled in Palestine in 1932. To his many lovable characters was added the image of a land rising from its ruins, renewed in vigor through toil and suffering and valor. The inborn strength of the poet, his blithe spirit, were invigorated by the soil of Palestine.

In Palestine, shortly before his death, he produced his major epic, *The Golden People,* the locale of which is Crimea and modern Palestine. The main characters are a retired deacon of the Greek Orthodox Church, whose life hobby is the nurture of bees, and a young *Halutz,* an admirer of the deacon who takes up the nurture of bees in Palestine.

The epic is a résumé of the aesthetic and social tendencies of the poet. The beehive becomes the symbol of humanity, with its feuds and class wars and social experiments. Revolting against the beehive system, the poet sings a song of individual freedom concluding with an exalted ode on the symphony of nations in which each member plays its individual instrument.

In Bialik and Tchernichovsky, Hebrew literature presented two figures whose achievements entitle them to be ranked among the foremost poets of the modern age in world literature.

At the turn of the century, Hebrew poetry was enriched by a variety of new talents. It became more diverse in content and in form. It shed new light on the inner life of the individual. It plumbed the depths of man, unraveling his psychic perplexities, exposing the darkest recesses of mind and the obscurest passions.

A poet of striking individuality is Zalman Shneour (born 1886 in White Russia, long a citizen of France, now resident in the United States). With Walt Whitman, Shneour could readily say: "I celebrate myself and I sing myself." His poetry is refreshingly bold, in utter defiance of established conventions and patterns of thought. It is a lusty hymn to the poet's ego, to the will of man, to intellectual vigor, to physical and spiritual adventure. It sublimates human passions, the blind, dark forces of man, the *fleurs du mal.* His full-blooded eroticism is, in a measure, an outcry against the ascetic traditions of his forebears.

The world appears to Shneour as a giant arena where man is forever wrestling with his own weak self, with hostile elements and with tyrant society. Shneour loves to pit the rebellious self-assertive individual against the colorless, amorphous mass. In dashing verse he exalts the ancient Roman gladiator Spartacus and his followers of all ages, whose watchword was eternal resistance.

The poetry of Shneour explores wide regions of the universe. It abounds in natural scenery of great charm. The epic *Among the Mountains*, for instance, contains marvelous descriptions of the Swiss Alps in all their wild beauty. But man holds the central place in the world of Shneour. Nature itself is deeply humanized by the poet. The very cosmos is the means for the display of man's superior qualities.

The social upheavals within recent decades impressed themselves greatly upon the poetry of Shneour. The poet sees society in dissolution, in spiritual bankruptcy, without God, without ideals. In an elegy, *At the Banks of the Seine*, he pictures modern man as emptyhearted, bored, and scared by ghosts of a dying past. "Culture with all its uproar, its smoke and flash could not drown the whisper of the dying gods." Man, godless and forlorn, is compared by the poet to a lone child who, frightened by the shadows at twilight, plays with wooden toys in order to overcome his fears "while his little heart is beating in the quiet: where is father, where is mother? O, when will they return home?"

Contemptuous fury and bitter irony are the mightiest weapons of Shneour. Their sharpest edges he reserves for the enemies of his people. In an exalted ode, *The Melodies of Israel*, he portrays the historic struggle of disinherited, exiled Israel to retain its individuality, alone among the nations. Anti-Semitism he views as the nemesis of the pagan deities subdued by the Hebraic spirit, subdued but not crushed. Thus, the inner strength of Israel is cause of its martyrdom. An outraged sense of justice, national pride, contemptuous indignation, burn in this poem of challenge to a cruel world which failed Israel, its spiritual benefactor.

The Middle Ages Are Approaching is the name of another remarkable poetic utterance of Shneour. In prophetic vein it predicted, in 1913, the decline of the era of progress ushered in by the Renaissance and the resurgence of medievalism with all its attendant horrors, chief among them the persecution of the Jews. It is a song of doom unequaled in its day for farsightedness.

There is an undertone of deep melancholy in the poetry of Shneour. "Who are you, hangman," asks the poet in his *Song of Grief*, "God, the great world, or my own self?" His is the tragic loneliness of one venturing on majestic flights of vision and thought.

The three representative poets discussed above, together with their contemporaries and successors, made Hebrew poetry the living spirit of

Hebrew revival. Modern Hebrew poetry rose to the highest calling of poetry in general, which is to expose in fullest measure the very essence of human life.

7. The New Prose

The spirit of revival asserted itself also in Hebrew fiction. The master of Hebrew prose, Mendele Mocher Seforim, whose artistic portrayals of Jewish life reached their height at the turn of the century, set an example for a rising generation of prose writers. The Mendele tradition meant a penetrating observation and minute description of the Jewish milieu, thorough craftsmanship and a classic robust style. The new realism gave to Hebrew prose a concentrated power, a precision and vividness which it lacked in Haskala days. In the wake of this realism with its insistence upon sharp delineation of the material, objective world, there was to follow a realism of the spirit based on the close observation of the inner, occult world of man. Particular respect was now paid to the manifestations and experiences of religious life. Jewish tradition, which heretofore super-critical Haskala saw in its gloomiest aspect, was viewed now from a bright angle under the influence of the national renaissance. Hasidism, long the target of rationalists, came into its own and exerted a salutary influence upon literature.[13a] This great movement of religious revival with its optimistic, enthusiastic approach to the world, to God and to the common man, with its emphasis upon the godliness and sanctity of everyday life, stirred a new spirit in Hebrew literature, softening and brightening the somber aspect of Hebrew prose.

Isaac Leibush Peretz[14a] (1851-1915), Judah Steinberg (1863-1908), Micah Joseph Berdichevsky and their followers discovered divine inspiration and artistic loveliness in ancient rites and ceremonies, in Jewish folklore in general, and, particularly, in the simple hasidic tales and miracle stories, in hasidic melodies and folk dances.

The poetic quality of hasidism is caught in the imaginative stories and monologues of Peretz, who left his mark on Hebrew and Yiddish literatures. The media of Peretz were many, even as his tendencies were divergent. In essay and short story, in verse and in prose poetry, in allegorical fantasy and in dramatic play, he touched upon the boundaries of Haskala rationalism, of social realism and symbolism. His crowning achievement, however, was his hasidic lore.

A great solemnity marks the simple characters of his stories, whose religious ecstasy turns an ordinary occurrence into a lofty spiritual experience. The common, uneducated man and the most revered saint are joined in a comradeship of piety. Peretz succeeded in reproducing the emotional climate in which religious ideas grow, in which even the irrational appears to be a natural phenomenon. His folk stories about plain Jewish people are ethical gems. Through Peretz and his contemporaries, a never-dying past reaches out toward the future.

These sympathetic views of tradition did not alter the course of the younger realists, successors of Mendele, who, with eyes on the present, depicted the less festive side of Jewish life. The small town, nerve center of Jewish life in Russia, was described from close quarters with a greater degree of truthfulness and naturalism than ever before. The average man—the worker, the artisan, the tradesman—became the central figure. The struggle for a livelihood within the Pale of Settlement, the oppressive czarist regime, the dissensions between the young and old, between the pious and young rebels, small-town episodes and character sketches constitute, by and large, the subject matter of renascent Hebrew fiction. Occasionally the dark panorama was brightened by scenic descriptions of Bessarabia, the Ukraine, Lithuania, and other regions.

All in all, a new feeling for the common run of life, a new sensitivity to man and nature, pervaded Hebrew prose. This is evidenced also in the Hebrew language which adopted the rhythm of daily life and the manifold subtleties and nuances of living speech.

Bialik, in his appreciation of the short-story writer S. Ben-Zion (1860-1932), drew the following distinction between Mendele and his disciples: Mendele "is the great artist of small details. But one thing Mendele lacked: there is no alcoholism in his writing, none of the sheer joy of life and its intoxication. Not so Ben-Zion and his colleagues, in most of whose works there is a definite quantity of that alcoholism, something of that intoxication and joy of living, in the sense of 'my heart and my flesh sing for joy.' " This is an apt characterization by one who himself was a master of realistic prose.

The stormy days of the Russian Revolution of 1905 and its aftermath of pogroms had deep repercussions in Hebrew prose as well as poetry. No one expresses the temper of this turbulent age as fully as Joseph Hayyim Brenner (1881-1921).

Brenner's novels and short stories are unpolished. The narrative is frequently broken by lyrical passages. Slight attention is given to externals, to scenic effects. The plot is of little significance. But they abound in profound studies in which the autobiographical element plays a prominent part. They are pageants, so to speak, of acute human suffering and Jewish misery. The locale of Brenner's stories varies: Russia, land of his birth, the Whitechapel Ghetto in London, where he lived from 1904 to 1908, and Palestine, where he settled in 1909 and met a martyr's death at the hands of Arabs. But the leading character in all his novels is the same introspective Ghetto-wearied individual, desperately self-analytical, lashing himself and his environment, clamoring for freedom, for personal salvation. Brenner saw nothing but decay and misery in the Ghetto. With stark realism and deep sympathy he described the wretchedness of the poor and lowly, the agonies and frustrations of a neurotic Jewish intelligentsia, the empty prattle of social reformers, the bitter despair of a maladjusted youth, broken in faith and spirit.

In Brenner's works there is no hope for Jewish life in the Diaspora. "I, the Zionist," says one of his characters in the story *From Here and From There,* "do not speak of renaissance, of spiritual revival, but of the exodus, the ideal of exodus from the Ghetto."[15]

His maturest novel, *Bereavement and Defeat,* written in Palestine, is also his saddest. In the background is old Jerusalem with its winding streets, its hospitals and poorhouses and human wreckage, the driftwood of European Ghettos. We witness the lives of the weak and the meek: forsaken creatures, ascetic scholars, dreamers and mystics, and sick souls whom not even the city of Divine healing could cure. And amidst and above all these is the solitary figure of the leading character, an index of human agony and spiritual derangement. With rare insight Brenner dissects his inner life and portrays the gradual metamorphosis of a broken spirit from hopeless despair to a moderate, philosophic affirmation of life despite its horrors. The road to individual salvation may be symbolic of the larger course of national regeneration. "The passion for redemption," says one of Brenner's unfortunates, "saved me from compromise. This love of the people and the tortures of such love are in no way smaller than the tortures of another love of some Werther."

In the stories of Uri Nisan Gnessin (1880-1913) the spiritual physiognomy of an ultra-individualist is drawn with acumen and fastidious imagery. The plot is often of the flimsiest sort; but by means of most painstaking description the author lays consciousness bare. We look into the inner life of a self-centered, half-somnambulant individual, given to metaphysical obscurities and lyrical hallucinations, completely detached from the environment and from the vexing problems of the day.

A manifold view of reality is presented by Gershom Shofmann (born 1880 in White Russia), an accomplished master of the short story. His compact and suggestive stories are among the finest products of Hebrew narrative.

Shofmann is the interpreter of life and of human character through a studied observation of small incidents and episodes. He is the great observer who explores and sees things from an oblique angle in an original manner. An isolated, trivial action, an evanescent mood, a fleeting moment become under his searching eye all important in determining the mainsprings of human behavior. His subjects represent a cross section of cosmopolitan polyglot society in its upper and lower strata: pious old Jews and young radicals, scholarly professors, and "eternal students," disinherited artists and globe trotters, Russian soldiers and officers of the czarist regime, prisoners and harlots, Viennese damsels and sturdy peasants.

The tragic position of the Jew in a strange and hostile world and, lately, the horrifying Nazi brutalities were recorded by Shofmann in sharp and gruesome pictures. In his recent volume, *Before the All-Quiet*, the stress and agony and heroic behavior of the Jewish community in Palestine are drawn in refreshing sketches that breathe quiet power and faith.

A rounded picture of small-town life, reflecting the idyllic as well as the tragic side, is given by Yitzhok Doiv Berkowitz (b. 1885 in White Russia). With clear vision and subdued lyricism, with a fine touch of wholesome humor, Berkowitz projects the image of a Lithuanian small town: austere, melancholic, impoverished, yet abundant in life, verdant amidst poverty, rich in human material and Jewish character. The underprivileged, the forlorn, silent souls are shown with compassionate understanding. A simple Jew vainly tries to express his elation over his boy's admittance to a Russian *Gymnasium*; a lonely working girl is driven by a nostalgic urge from the big city to her native town but is no longer able to adjust herself to her home environment; a country boy is subjected to ridicule and torture by big-town boys on account of his boorish ways. The quiet tragedies of these and similar characters are treated by Berkowitz with discernment and tenderness.

Coming to New York in 1915, Berkowitz became one of the builders of modern Hebrew literature in America. In his American stories and plays the small-town characters of his earlier work flourish with all their peculiarities on American soil. They are either pathetic, completely out of step with the New World, bitterly critical of American Jewish life, or else they are comic in their exaggerated efforts to parade their Americanism by denying their Jewish identity.

In addition to his original work, Berkowitz is famous for his superb translations from the works of Sholem Aleichem, the great Yiddish humorist.[16a] The tales, monologues and plays of Sholem Aleichem, portraying Jewish life in an inimitable style, were transformed by Berkowitz into Hebrew classics.

In his recent works Berkowitz reveals the influence of Palestine, where he now lives. The novel *Messianic Days* depicts modern Palestine in broad outline. Eretz Yisrael is shown through the mature vision of an intellectual physician who spent many years in the United States and through the youthful eyes of an idealistic American Jewish lad. Contemplation and quiet enthusiasm mark the entire novel. The solid, reserved portrayal of the growing Palestinian community is pervaded by a sense of wonder at the miracle that has come to pass.

The works of Brenner, Shofmann, and Berkowitz, aside from their inherent qualities, are indicative also of the changing locale of Hebrew literature.

Modern Hebrew fiction as a whole pictured the weakening and gradual disintegration of the traditional Eastern European Jewish small town under the impact of social and economic changes. In narrative and imagery it recorded Jewish life in transition.

8. Diaspora and Eretz Yisrael

The past few decades, which brought fateful changes in Jewish life, saw the shift of the main Hebrew literary center from Russia—since the Revolution of 1917 a banned territory for Hebrew culture—to rejuvenated Eretz Yisrael, and the strengthening of Hebrew literary activity in the United States.

In the interval between the two World Wars, the Hebrew center in Poland, long pre-eminent, was gradually dwindling away. Only a few literary figures remained there. Of these, Matithyahu Shoham (1893-1937) deserves special attention.

Shoham is the interpreter of Israel's spiritual history in his four biblical poetic dramas: *Thou Shalt Not Make Thee Iron Gods, Balaam, Jericho, Tyre and Jerusalem*. Through the conflicting characters of Abraham and the legendary Gog, dictatorial chieftain of the Kingdom of the North, through Moses and Balaam, the Prophet Elijah and Queen Jezebel, Shoham presents decisive struggles of Judaism with the pagan world at various stages of biblical history. In the clash of ancient personalities and ideas we hear the wrangling ideologies of our own troubled age. In a number of magnificent scenes, Shoham sublimates the liberating spirit of Judaism destined to ennoble mankind and to unite the family of nations.

During this very period, Hebrew literature formed an important colony on the American continent. Hebrew literary attempts had already been made here in the latter part of the nineteenth century. In 1871 the first Hebrew weekly in the United States made its appearance. An occasional sheaf of verse, a stray scholarly or pseudo-scholarly work, a short-lived periodical sounded the note of Hebrew culture on American soil. It was a melancholy, solitary note, at times a note of bitterness and despair, as that of Menahem Mendel Dolitzky (1856-1931), one of the pioneers of Hebrew poetry in America. During the past few decades [1946], however, Hebrew literary expression in America assumed, both quantitatively and qualitatively, the character of literature. At present, Hebrew letters in America hold the tragic distinction and responsibility of being the only Hebrew literature in the Diaspora. Literary activity is being stimulated by a regular periodic press, the weekly *Hadoar*, edited for over a quarter of a century by Menachem Ribalow, and the monthly *Bitzaron*, founded in 1939 by the Talmudic scholar and essayist Chaim Tchernowitz (1871-1949), besides various other publications.

In general, American Hebrew literature manifests traits common to modern Hebrew literature as a whole, of which it forms an integral part. Its poetry and prose, however, reveal also the impact of the American locale.

American Hebrew poetry, in the main, follows the classic tradition. Aestheticism, moral speculation, the longing for "the sublime and the beautiful" and religious exaltation are voiced in many memorable lyrics. Jewish martyrdom and the revival in the Land of Israel have inspired American Hebrew poets along with all other Hebrew writers. The Hebrew poetry of the New World has turned to the Bible and Jewish history for many of its characters. Abraham Regelson's *Cain and Abel, The Love of Hosea* by Simon Ginsburg (1891-1944), Simon Halkin's lyrical monologue, *Baruch, the Son of Neriah,* the odes to the medieval poets Gabirol and Ha-Levi by Eisig Silberschlag and Moses Feinstein's dramatic poem *Abraham Abulafia* are but a few noteworthy examples of this tendency.

The immigrant Jew, perplexed by the new American environment, struggling pathetically to retain his individuality, has found a sympathetic spokesman in the American Hebrew poet. The broad canvas of America, American natural scenery, portraits of American life and character, are woven into the very texture of American Hebrew poetry, notably in the works of Israel Efros, Ephraim E. Lisitzky, Gabriel Preil and A. Z. Halevy.

American folklore had a marked effect on the Hebrew muse. Three Hebrew epics, wide in scope, relate the story of the American Indian: *Facing the Tent of Timora* by Benjamin Nahum Silkiner (1882-1933), *Sinking Bonfires* by Ephraim E. Lisitzky, and *Silent Wigwams* by Israel Efros. Much as these epics vary in artistic achievement, they have this in common: they all depict the heroic life and struggle of the red man in his decline, all draw richly upon Indian lore, and the tragic narratives are set against a background of luxuriant scenery. In singing of the American Indian, the Hebrew poets voiced not only their attachment to American soil and American lore, but also the outcry of a small minority in the struggle for survival.

In prose, too, American Hebrew literature made some important contributions. The historical plays and tales of Harry Sackler, revolving around characters drawn from various periods of Jewish history, dramatize the course and destiny of Judaism and its heroic battle for the supremacy of the spirit. Sackler's stories combine intellectual insight and the fantasy of folklore. The biographical novels of Jochanan Twersky—*Uriel Acosta, Alfred Dreyfus*—are rich in descriptive power, pageant-like in effect. They portray character through an abundance of historical details, and accentuate environment and the *Zeitgeist.* The trilogy by Samuel Loeb Blank, a story of a Jewish family on a farm in Bessarabia, is a romantic saga about simple people and their sentimental attachment to the soil. Simon Halkin, in his analytical stories, conveys the spiritual gropings of confused Jewish individuality caught in the maelstrom of American life. Reuben Wallenrod's stories and sketches are vivid pictures of immigrant life in New York City, in the process of gradual adaptation to the American environment.

The essay in its various forms, particularly the critical essay, occupies a place of importance in American Hebrew prose.

In a class by themselves are the achievements of American Hebrew scholars in talmudic and Rabbinic literature, in medieval Hebrew poetry, in philosophy, philology, and pedagogy.

To the credit of Hebrew literature in America should be added the numerous translations in poetry and prose from English and American literature. Among the translations are those of Shakespeare's works.

Thus far Hebrew literature in America has been an immigrant product, though its leading exponents have lived in the United States from their early youth. In a sense, Hebrew literature presents a challenge to American Israel. Whether this literature is to be a permanent, growing expression or merely a transitory episode depends largely upon the cultural and spiritual course American Jewish life will take in the future.

The very center of present-day Hebrew literature is Palestine.

Eretz Yisrael has been one of the great stimuli of modern Hebrew literature, even as it was a mainstay of the Hebrew spirit throughout the ages.

Palestine in the Hebrew literature of preceding ages was principally a coveted vision of religious exaltation. The land was viewed through an ideal veil colored by biblical imagery. Only recently did it become a reality in Jewish life and letters.

The last decades of the nineteenth century were noted largely for the valiant efforts of Ben Yehuda to revive Hebrew as a spoken tongue. But at the turn of the century the growing Palestinian Jewish community became articulate. The new life on the soil of Palestine was described and interpreted romantically in the stories and adventure novels of Moshe Smilansky. He also gave a sympathetic portrait of Arab primitive life in his short stories *Children of Arabia*. The Hebrew press and periodic literature became increasingly important and influential.

The early stages of Hebrew literature in Palestine were guided by the stalwart spirits of Joseph Hayyim Brenner and Aaron David Gordon.

In his publicistic and critical writings no less than in his novels discussed in a previous chapter, Brenner unsparingly laid bare the ills and frustrations of Diaspora Jewish life. *Galut* was to him a malignant disease, a lingering moral evil. For Brenner, the Jewish problem had a very simple solution: the methodical salvation of the Jewish people, collectively and individually, through a life of labor in the Land of Israel.

This ideal of agricultural labor as a moral cure was henceforth to become a creative force in the growing literature of Eretz Yisrael. Its most zealous advocate was Aaron David Gordon (1856-1922). He came to Palestine from Russia in 1904 and by his own life, as a laborer in the fields of Palestine, personified the return of the intellectual Jew to the soil from which he had been estranged for generations. Gordon ascribed mystic qualities to labor. He saw in it an ennobling power capable of bringing man closer to nature, of revealing his higher self. Literature and all cultural activity were of value to him only if they were by-products of life, resulting from communion with nature. With many of his Haskala forerunners Gordon believed that the ideal of labor was "the great human universal ideal" which alone could revitalize the Jewish people. Moreover, the saving influence of labor, he declared, was necessary not merely as a means of becoming attached to the soil but also as the source and mainspring of a truly national culture.

Gordon's ethical personality, stamped upon his ponderous essays and meditations, became a telling factor in the new center of Hebrew literature.

The spirit of modern Palestine is at its best in its poetry. A group of poets, for all their individual differences, have jointly become the voice of a land rising above ruin. The beauty of the country, whose inner character they have perceived and with which they feel a strong kinship, has haunted many of its poets.

A representative poet of Palestinian landscape is Jacob Fichman (born 1882 in Bessarabia; in Palestine since 1912). He painted the weird beauty of Palestinian scenery in sonnet cycles and in the dramatic poems *Ruth* and *Samson in Gaza*. With subdued ecstasy he observes the effect of rain on "the ringing trees of a jubilant garden" and the magnificence of "a vine spreading green-handed on a hillock, embroidering a shadowy inscription with luminous fingers." Quietly he unites austere, multicolored Jerusalem, the picturesque ruins of Jericho and Anatoth, and the flourishing modern settlements of Deganiah and Nahalol.

Remote biblical figures become close to us through the soil of Palestine. Well may the poet apply to himself and to his generation the words he put into the mouth of Ruth: "Each contact with the ground under my feet is a holy covenant with this new home, as if all I knew and loved since my glorious childhood days till now beaconed to this small and blessed land wherein I found myself."

A longing for complete absorption by Eretz Yisrael rises like a prayer from many Palestinian poets. In the doleful, simple lyrics of the poetess Rahel (1890-1931), who as a girl toiled in the fields of Kinnereth in Galilee, the passion for Palestine takes the form of life's greatest fulfillment.

Palestinian poetry was also quickened by the pioneering spirit, *Haluziut*, which has been active in Jewish life at various intervals since 1882 and which reached its height after the First World War.

Haluziut, as a movement of liberation, is an outlet for a variety of forces. It is inspired by ages of longing and praying for Zion, by Jewish tragedy, by an inner protest and revolt against an unjust world where the Jewish people can find no security, by the hope of constructing in Palestine a righteous society, and by a Messianic ideal for human salvation and the restoration of Israel. These forces are expressed with varied emphasis and poetic form by a number of Palestinian poets.

In a series of idylls, David Shimoni (1886-1956), who first visited Palestine in 1909 and settled there in 1921, pictured the regeneration of Palestine from the beginning of the century to our day. He describes Palestine in the making, the transformation of dream and legend into reality, the enthusiastic pilgrimage of the *Halutzim,* the building of settlements and communes, the mounting hardships of daily life, the struggles of acclimatization, the toil and suffering, the bloody Arab disturbances. A host of characters come to the fore: farmers, laborers, watchmen, drivers— all of them observed by the poet-traveler tramping through the country.

The unrest and social turmoil that engulfed Europe after the First World War found strong repercussions in the poetry of Palestine.

Yitzhak Lamdan (1900-1954), who witnessed the pogroms in the Ukraine in 1919, projected in *Massada,* his blank verse epic, the background of horror and utter despair of the ravaged Russian Jewish communities, the former homes of the *Halutzim.* Massada was the last Judean fortress defended with great heroism against the Roman conquerors. Thus, modern Palestine is to the poet the last refuge and citadel of Jewry. Scenes of destruction and gloom alternate with those of renascent life in this work. In shrill, pathetic verse, in touching prayer, in buoyant choral song Lamdan sublimates the tragedy of modern Jewish life, the last hopeful act of which is Eretz Yisrael.

With ingenious metrical effect, the poetry of A. Shlunsky expresses the hurly-burly of the early twenties, the confused, jittery state of war-torn society. His work reflects the mad joy of throwing off the burdens of the past, the intoxication of working in the fields of the Emek (Valley of Jezreel), and of building a new home.

The most characteristic note was struck by Uri Zevi Greenberg (born 1894 in Galicia). His poetry is uneven in temper, as discordant as the tumultuous period in which it was produced. Mockery, blatant bravado, melancholy, passion, and lyrical solemnity—all blend in a medley of forceful expression. Greenberg's poetry flings a mighty challenge to a world that haunted and persecuted him. In stirring apocalyptic visions he predicts the coming of the Messianic age and the restoration of Israel.

A deep religious mood pervades Palestinian poetry. The revival of Eretz Yisrael is seen as a prelude to a new revelation, to the return of the prophetic spirit.

"This is the soil, the soil of madness," exclaims Avigdor Hameiri (born

1886 in Hungary) in a poem-cycle *Sinai Is Seething*: "Each clot here is aglow with bliss divine. Come hither, brother, if your soul be imprisoned, come hither barefoot, a pilgrim, and you shall see open-eyed the God of the wilderness of Sinai."

The miraculous rebuilding of the land gave wing to fancy. As of old, Jerusalem, Zion, became full of mystic significance. The eternal covenant with these hallowed names is renewed in enthralling odes. "And it matters to me," declares Uri Zevi Greenberg, "that I do not enter you, Jerusalem, with a golden prayer shawl, even as a High Priest entering your gates towards evening. And it matters to me that Jews walk in your midst without psalms on their lips and hands uplifted as candelabra." And another poet, Yehuda Karni prays: "Take me with the Jerusalem-stone and place me in the walls, daub me with plaster, and out of the wall's enclosure my pining bones will sing towards the Messiah."

Palestine as a symbol of the resurgence of the Divine Spirit is epitomized by the noted poet Jacob Cahan (born 1881 in White Russia) in his *Psalm for the Remnant of Israel*. Its concluding lines are: "Forged by the divine hammer, purged by flames divine we shall stand upon Zion's soil, our psalm in our mouth, the divine psalm, and skies will respond, all the extremes of the world, and all the peoples will respond to us."

The impress of modern Palestine is also in its prose, though to a lesser degree than in poetry. On the whole, Palestinian prose shows a growing tendency to throw off the oppressive yoke of a curbed, maladjusted life which weighs heavily upon much of Diaspora fiction. It is distinguished by a new vigor and a refreshing awareness of reality.

The joy of work in the fields, the thrill of cultivating fallow soil, of redeeming a land in ruins, the adventures and dangers of pioneering, are recurrent themes in Palestinian fiction. The individual with his personal problems and complexities becomes secondary to the larger problems of community welfare.

Immersed in the present, Palestinian prose shows sympathetic understanding not merely of the growing new life but also of old forms of Jewish life in Palestine and elsewhere.

Ancient Jerusalem looms large and inspiring. Its character, partly luminous, partly perplexing, magnificently sketched by the poet-essayist Jacob Steinberg (1887-1947), appears like a protecting genius of the country and its people.

The various communities of Jerusalem, a veritable "gathering of exiles," are pictured by a number of storytellers and novelists against the background of the mother city. The novels of Yehuda Burla (born 1886 in Jerusalem), the first important novelist Palestine produced, portray the life of Orthodox Sephardic Jews and the influence of modernity upon the younger generation, with unaffected simplicity and Oriental charm.

Similarly, the little-known Yemenite Jew has recently come into full view through the work of Hayyim Hazaz, a novelist of impressive literary stature. Thus, the literature of Palestine serves as a cultural interpreter and unifier of the tribes of dispersed Israel.

Much of Palestinian Hebrew fiction deals with Jewish life in the Diaspora. The humane stories of Asher Barash, for instance, center primarily around country life in Galicia; the compact short stories of Deborah Baron are small-town epics of Lithuania; while the expansive narratives of Hazaz give masterly pictures of Jewish life in Russia before and after the Revolution of 1917.

In recapturing the spirit of the past, Palestinian literature made notable contributions. A significant figure among these interpreters is Samuel Joseph Agnon (born 1888 in Galicia, went to Palestine in 1909).

Agnon depicts Jewish life of yesterday with an uncritical love, with grace and humor, and with something like epic fullness. He takes particular delight in describing the idyllic, harmonious side of that life, its spiritual cohesiveness and moral grandeur. His tales, couched in colorful, ornate style, brocaded with biblical and talmudic allusions, have a legendary character. They are much like old family pictures set in huge antique frames from which look down smiling, patriarchal faces.

Agnon is essentially the poet of Jewish tradition. He seems to be moving in a remote, enchanted world, which to him is very real, miraculously preserved and left altogether intact. The world is the Polish Ghetto of more than a century ago, when Jewish life was self-sufficient and followed its natural course, untouched by influences from without. There is tranquillity and contentment and good cheer in that world, despite poverty and adversity. It is a world illuminated by learning and kept warm by the exuberant spirit of genuine piety.

The Bridal Canopy, one of the major works of Agnon, is on the surface a simple story of quiet adventure—the record of a quixotic journey made through Galician Jewish communities sometime during the early part of the nineteenth century by two amiable God-fearing Jews. The importance of the work, however, lies in the particular art of storytelling which it reveals. Folk tale and anecdote, Rabbinic homily and parable are strung together and fused into one narrative. It is a veritable mine of folklore and learning, a treasure of Jewish customs and ceremonies, manners of speech and thought, superstitions and beliefs.

Another travel narrative of his, *In the Heart of the Seas,* is a profound expression of the deep-seated Jewish love for Palestine. It is a poetic description of the dreamlike adventures of a group of Galician Jews on a journey to Eretz Yisrael. The story is a monument of love to high idealism and all-conquering spirituality.

Agnon approaches the task of storytelling with deep religious ecstasy, with a spirit akin to that of one of his characters, the saintly Raphael the Scribe, who dedicated his life to copying the Scrolls of the Torah. His quaint art invokes the spirit of Jewish tradition with fresh beauty.

A novelist's or poet's interpretation of the past is very often an artistic device to advance definite ideas for the present. To the visionary, past and present are indivisible. Hence, Hebrew literature in Palestine, as elsewhere, has summoned from the past important figures to serve as heralds of the modern revival. The work of Aaron Abraham Kabak (1882-1944) is an excellent illustration of this art.

Kabak was the faithful interpreter of his own age and earlier ages. His novels and stories, whether dealing with the immediate present or with the remote past, are of a piece: they are studies of environment and of human character in its relationship to society; and they are alive with ideas, with psychological and social problems.

The revival of Israel on its own historic soil occupies a central position in Kabak's works. But this theme never stands alone. It is always associated with the ideal of general human and individual welfare. The universal, the personal are inseparable from the national.

In his first novels *Alone* and *Daniel Shaffronov*, written in Russia in the early part of the century, Kabak drew parallel characters—Jewish intellectuals who sacrificed their lives to the cause of the Russian Revolution and, on the other hand, bold idealists who champion Hebrew renaissance and Jewish rehabilitation in Palestine. Zionism becomes stronger and nobler by the juxtaposition of two remote spheres united by the ideal of liberation. Strikingly enough, *Under the Shadow of the Gallows*, the very last work of Kabak, published in Palestine in 1944 as part of his monumental trilogy *The History of a Family*, treats of the Polish insurrection of 1863; and the leading character is a Jewish youth, an enthusiastic advocate of the Polish cause.

The ideal of liberation in its triple form—universal, national, individual —was beautifully expressed by Kabak in his historical trilogy *Shlomo Molcho*. This sixteenth-century Marrano who was under Messianic illusions and who died a martyr's death, becomes in Kabak's hands the embodiment of human struggle for salvation and the symbol of Israel's deep yearning for redemption. We follow the bold dreamer on his strange and devious road through his native Portugal, through Palestine, through Germany, proclaiming the restoration of Israel. We see a lone soul in flight from a contaminating environment, from his past, from his passions and worldly ambitions, consumed by a love of God, of man and of his martyred people.

In *In the Narrow Path*, Kabak's novel on the life of the Founder of Christianity, the crucial problem is individual versus national salvation. Here nature and man vie with equal power. Picturesque Palestinian scenery and intricate human character combine in a magnificent portrayal of Jewish religious and social life at the closing period of the Second Commonwealth.

In sum, Kabak penetrates into the Jewish past and sheds upon it the brilliant light of national and universal ideas.

9. RECENT PHASES

Since the Second World War, Hebrew literature has been strongly influenced by two dominant forces: the catastrophe which overtook Jewry under the Nazi regime of terror and the heroic struggle of the *Yishuv* in Eretz Yisrael culminating in the rise of the State of Israel.

The horrors of Nazi bestialities and the tragedy of Jewish martyrdom pervade much of Hebrew literature of the given period, its poetry in particular.

Mortifying chronicles, tales of despair, lamentations and prayers, challenging defiance and protest commingle in this substantial literature of martyrdom.

Occasionally, an author takes refuge in the past, shedding from distant spheres a reflected light on the present. Thus Saul Tchernichovsky enshrined the horrors of the age in his elegiac "Ballads of Worms" chronicling in the form of folk tales tragic events of the Crusades' period, among them the martyrdom of Rabbi Meir of Rothenberg. Jacob Cahan re-created in dramatic monologue, "The Third Cry," the story of the Ten Martyrs of the ancient Roman period. David Shimoni chose a legendary character of medieval folklore, "The Wicked Armelus," half Satan, half stone, to portray the dehumanized, diabolic figure of Hitler battling the spirit of Divine Providence and human freedom symbolized by the Jewish people. Yitzhak Lamdan invoked the spirit of the Patriarchs to envision the tragic destiny of Israel in his biblical ballads, "The Covenant Between the Parts" and "For the Sun Descended." As Abraham watches the vulture coming down upon the carcasses, he muses and wonders, in the words of the poet:

> And so ever endlessly: vulture and God together
> Both of you forever on one side and I—on the other, alone?

And Jacob, communing with God in the Dream at Beth-el, is made to utter his refusal, forcefully but ineffectually, to be the Chosen One of God, "to be despised by men but beloved by God." This very note of spurning the Election of Israel as a historic target for persecution was voiced with plainspoken irony also by the poet Nathan Alterman during the same period.

Defiance and spiritual exaltation in the face of tragedy are raised to sublime heights by the novelist Asher Barash in his story "He Who Remained in Toledo." It is the story of a cultured Spanish Jew, a dealer in old manuscripts, a friend of the dignitaries of the Church, to all appearances indifferent to the faith of his fathers, who, upon the expulsion of the Jews from Spain in 1492, stays on in Toledo refusing to be converted to Christianity (as have members of his own ostensibly pious family) or to join the mass of fugitives. The words of the Psalmist "I shall not die, but live!" which he inscribes on a piece of parchment and carries with him attached to his body, like "a holy Scroll," become his watchwords and magic symbol.

This lone, proud figure, regarded by the populace as a madman, walking ghostlike through the streets of Toledo decades after the Jewish expulsion, with the death-defying words of the Psalmist on his lips, is an enduring image of moral grandeur.

The picture of an entire community meeting death with firm heart in a state of worshipful exaltation is presented by the poet Sh. Shalom as a grim chronicle in his ballad, "A Procession."

Few, if any, expressed the horrors of the age as vividly, as boldly as Uri Zvi Greenberg. His volume *Streets of the River* may be viewed as a compendium of the various aspects of Hebrew poetry of martyrdom. It contains the tender elegy, the full-throated, tempestuous lamentation, the fiery condemnation, the lashing irony, the flamboyant vision.

The very name of the volume is indicative of its character. It envisions persecution of the Jews as one great historic river with many confluent streams and the tormentors of the various ages as one many-faceted monster.

The deep gloom of horrible scenes is invariably lightened by a streak of light emanating from the consciousness pointing toward the historic destiny of Israel, heralding its ultimate triumph. "Amen," says the poet, "ours is the eternal word in the universe."

At this point, special mention should be made of the martyred poet and playwright Yitzhak Katzenelson (1886-1944). In the prison camp in Vital, France, where he was incarcerated, he wrote his stirring elegy in Yiddish, "The Song of the Slain Jewish People," a Hebrew play "Hannibal" and a number of Hebrew poems which were hidden in the ground and retrieved after the war. A bare, simple stanza from this martyr's legacy may stand as his epitaph:

> For no cause lost, destroyed in vain,
> All, all for no cause slain;
> No eye did see, no ear did hark—
> No grave, no mark.

In the dramatic poem "Between Fire and Redemption," a work in three parts by the American Hebrew poet, Aaron Zeitlin, whcih appeared in 1957, both the catastrophe and the emergence of the State of Israel are viewed from a visionary sphere. The hidden meaning of the two, the Fire of Doom and the miracle of Redemption, is probed and visualized by the poet. And indeed these two forces were actuating Hebrew literature simultaneously.

The trials and struggles of the *Yishuv*: the Arab terror, the severe British impositions, Jewish open and underground resistance, the feats of the *Maapilim*, the daring spirits who defied the British blockade, bringing in under the cover of night "illegal" immigrants—the various stages which led to the birth of the State of Israel, including the War of Liberation, are reflected in recent Hebrew literature.

The spirit of self-sacrifice which animated the *Yishuv*, the steadfastness of purpose, the resoluteness and valor which characterized the defenders of Israel—these are the common notes in the odes and prayers, elegies and ballads of such diverse poets as, for instance, David Shimoni and Nathan Alterman, Sh. Shalom and Hayyim Guri.

"It is good to live with death at you staring," is the opening line of a poem by Sh. Shalom. This consciousness of the call of destiny, accompanied by an unflinching spirit of self-reliance, is characteristic of the war literature of Israel, of its poetry and prose alike.

The chronicles, reminiscences and realistic tales, the published letters and diaries of many of the victims of the war, the numerous memorial volumes, the enormous anthology *Parchments of Fire* edited by Reuben Avinoam containing "the literary and artistic legacy of those who fell in the War for Israel's Independence"—these are destined to be documents of great human value and perennial sources of strength for Hebrew literature.

In recent years a group of native Israelis have come to the fore in Hebrew fiction and drama: Joshua Bar-Yoseph, Moshe Shamir and S. Yizhar; Yigal Mosenson, Mordecai Tabib and Nathan Shaham, to cite a few out of many. This group constitutes a creative force of considerable achievement. It grapples with the new reality of modern Israel, with life on the farm, in the *kibbutzim* and in the *maabarot*, the transistory camps for the new immigrants, the *olim*. It probes the varied social and cultural problems presented by the "ingathering of exiles" and shows a keen awareness of the Oriental Jew. It is marked by a deep consciousness of the soil and landscape of Israel, as the pictorial stories of S. Yizhar—to single out one of the group—indicate.

In the past decade [1947-1957], Hebrew fiction has been enriched by a number of works of high merit. Of great significance is the latest novel by the old master Samuel Joseph Agnon, *Yesterday and Before Yesterday*, which portrays on a broad canvas Eretz Yisrael in the early part of the century. The old *Yishuv* and the new one meet in this novel in a series of character representations and in the consummate reproduction of the particular atmosphere and milieu characteristic of the two.

Another work of distinction is the massive novel, *Yaish*, by Hayyim Hazaz, which pictures with great subtlety Yemenite Jewish life, its primitivism and piety, in Yemen and in Israel. The novel revolves around the main character, Yaish, a unique personality, and we get a clear view of his religious ecstasies and vagaries, his messianic illusions and worldly temptations, his artistic urge and ascetic eccentricities.

Of the numerous recent novels by native Israelis, two in particular stand out prominently. One is the historical novel *King of Flesh and Blood* by Moshe Shamir, a dramatic narrative depicting Judea seething with conflicting ideas and personalities during the Hasmonean period, with King Alexander Yannai as the leading character. The other work is the trilogy *Enchanted City* by Joshua Bar-Yoseph. It is a vivid, colorful portrayal of a Safed family during the course of three generations, from the middle of the nineteenth century to World War I. The guiding spirit of the novel is the "Enchanted City," the ancient city of Safed, renowned center of Cabbala, with its inhabitants, its traditions, its festivities, its scenic beauty and mystic lore.

The literature of Israel is an initial fulfillment of the hopes and visions of the moving spirits of modern Hebrew literature. It is the partial culmination of the great ideal which inspired the Hebrew renaissance: the self-renewal of the Jewish people, individually and collectively, on its own soil, and the continued growth of an indigenous Hebrew culture, in harmony with the highest aspirations of mankind.

NOTES

[1a For the emancipation movement by countries cf. above Cecil Roth, "The Jews of Western Europe (from 1648)," pp. 264-265.]

2 *More Nebukhe Hazeman*, ed. S. Rawidowicz, p. 36.

[3a Cf. above Shalom Spiegel, "On Medieval Hebrew Poetry," pp. 877-878.]

[4a Cf. *Ibid.*, pp. 883-884.]

5 *Collected Works of M. L. Lilienblum*, II, 399.

[6a Cf. below Yudel Mark, "Yiddish Literature," pp. 1207 ff.]

7 In the poem *Siluk Shekinah*.

8 *Al Parashat Derakhim*, II, 28.

9 *Ibid*, p. 29.

10 *Ibid.*, I, p. 87.

11 Collected Works of Berdichevsky, *Baderech*, II, 20.

12 *Ibid.*, I, 74.

[13a Cf. Mark, *op. cit.*, pp. 1201 ff.]

[14a *Ibid.*, pp. 1213 ff.]

15 *Mikan Umikan*, p. 39.

[16a Cf. Mark, *op. cit.*, pp. 1212 ff.]

Selected Bibliography

A

General

Halkin, Simon, *Modern Hebrew Literature*. New York, 1950. "A Study," in the words of the author, "of the socio-historical forces which have motivated Jewish life during the last two centuries" and influenced the course of Hebrew literature.

Klausner, Joseph, *A History of Modern Hebrew Literature (1785-1930)*. Translated by H. Danby, London, 1932. A brief survey of the main trends of modern Hebrew literature.

Slouschz, Nahum, *The Renascence of Hebrew Literature*. Philadelphia, 1909. Stresses the role of Hebrew literature as a civilizing factor in Jewish life and as an instrument of national emancipation.

Spiegel, Shalom, *Hebrew Reborn*. New York, 1930. A series of essays in historical perspective on leading figures and ideas in modern Hebrew literature.

Waxman, Meyer, *A History of Jewish Literature from the close of the Bible to our own Days*. New York, 1936. Vols. III and IV. Very detailed and informative.

B

Special

Studies of distinct periods or authors

Bavli, Hillel, *Some Aspects of Modern Hebrew Poetry*. New York, 1958.

Efros, Israel, *Hayyim Nachman Bialik*. New York, 1940. An essay published by the Hebrew P.E.N. Club of the U.S.A.

Ginsburg, Simon, *The Life and Works of Moses Hayyim Luzzatto*. Philadelphia, 1931.

Greenberg, Louis S., *A Critical Investigation of the Works of Rabbi Isaac Baer Levinsohn*. New York, 1930.

Halkin, Simon, "The Hebrew Literature in Palestine," in *Jewish Review* (New York), 1943, pp. 48-82.

Kabakoff, Jacob, "Hebrew Culture and Creativity in America," in the Quarterly, *Judaism*. New York, 1954.

Landau, J. L., *Short Lectures on Modern Hebrew Literature*. From M. H. Luzzatto to S. D. Luzzatto. London, 1923.

Morais, Sabato, *Italian Hebrew Literature*. New York, 1926. Some material about S. D. Luzzatto and a few of his contemporaries noted in Hebrew literature.

Raisin, Jacob S., *The Haskalah Movement in Russia*. Philadelphia, 1913. A detailed study of the social and literary forces of the period.

RHINE, A. B., *Leon Gordon; an Appreciation*. Philadelphia, 1920. A study of the life and works of the distinguished poet of the *Haskala* period.

SCHECHTER, SOLOMON, "Nachman Krochmal and the Perplexities of his Time," in *Studies in Judaism*, Series I. Philadelphia, 1896.

SILBERSCHLAG, EISIG, "Hebrew Literature in America," in *Jewish Book Annual*. New York, 1955.

SIMON, LEON, *Ahad Ha'am*. Introduction to Selected Essays of Ahad Ha-Am. Philadelphia, 1912. A critical analysis of the teachings of Ahad Ha-Am.

WALLENROD, REUBEN, *The Literature of Modern Israel*. New York, 1956. A study of Hebrew literature in Eretz Yisrael, mainly till the rise of the State of Israel.

C

Translations

The number of *adequate* translations from modern Hebrew literature is, unfortunately, very limited.

AGNON, SAMUEL J., *The Bridal Canopy*. Translated by I. M. Lask. Garden City, New York, 1937.

AHAD HA-AM, *Selected Essays*. Translated by Leon Simon. Philadelphia, 1912.

———, *Ten Essays on Zionism and Judaism*. Translated by Leon Simon. London, 1922.

BIALIK, HAYYIM NAHMAN, *Complete Poetic Works*. Translated by various translators. Edited with introduction by Israel Efros. New York, 1948.

———, *Aftergrowth and other Stories*. Translated by I. M. Lask. Philadelphia, 1939.

———, *And it Came to Pass: Legends and Stories about King David and King Solomon*. Translated by Herbert Danby. New York, 1938.

GORDON, A. D., *Selected Essays*. Translated by Frances Burnce. Boston, 1938.

GREENBERG, URI ZVI, *Jerusalem*. Translated by Charles A. Cowen. New York, 1939.

HAZAZ, HAYIM, *Moki Saʿid*. Translated by Ben Halpern. New York, 1956. A novel of Yemenite life.

MALETZ, DAVID, *Young Hearts*. Translated by Solomon N. Richards. New York, 1950. A novel of modern Israel.

SHAMIR, MOSHE, *The King of Flesh and Blood*. Translated by David Patterson. London, 1958. An historical novel of the Hasmonean period.

SHIMONI, DAVID, *Idylls*. Three selected idylls, with an essay on the poet, by Joseph Klausner. Translated by I. M. Lask. Jerusalem, 1957.

SNOWMAN, L. V., *Tchernichowsky, S. and his Poetry*. London, 1929. Selections from his poetry with biographical and critical comments by the translator.

STEINBERG, JEHUDA, *In Those Days*. Translated by George Jeshurun. Philadelphia, 1915. A story of a kidnapped Jewish conscript during the reign of Czar Nicholas I.

TCHERNICHOWSKY, SAUL, "Baruch of Mayence." Translated by Sholom J. Kahn, in *Poet Lore*. Summer, 1948.

WALLENROD, REUBEN, *Dusk in the Catskills*. Translated by Mrs. Wallenrod. New York, 1957. A novel of American Jewish life.

YAARI, YEHUDA, *When the Candle Was Burning*. Translated by Menahem Horwitz. London, 1947. A novel of Jewish life in Eastern Europe and in Eretz Yisrael during and after the First World War.

Additional translations are to be found in the following collections and anthologies:

FEIN, HARRY H., *A Harvest of Hebrew Verse*. Boston, 1934. Selections from the poetry of *Haskala* and the modern age.

FLEG, EDMOND, *The Jewish Anthology*. Translated by Maurice Samuel, New York, 1925.

SCHWARZ, LEO W., *A Golden Treasury of Jewish Literature*. New York, 1937.

—————, *The Jewish Caravan*. New York, 1925.

Israel Argosy. Edited by Isaac Halevi Levin. Jerusalem, 1952-1956.

Sound the Great Trumpet. Edited by M. Z. Frank. New York, 1955.

Tehilla and other Israeli Stories. London and New York, 1956.

The Literary Review, an International Quarterly of Contemporary Writing, published by Fairleigh Dickinson University, Teaneck, New Jersey. Israeli Number, Spring, 1958. Selections from modern Hebrew poetry and prose, including a play, "Michal, The Daughter of Saul," by A. Ashman.

CHAPTER 19

THE MYSTICAL ELEMENT IN JUDAISM

By Abraham J. Heschel

1. THE MEANING OF JEWISH MYSTICISM

There are people who take great care to keep away from the mists produced by fads and phrases. They refuse to convert realities into opinions, mysteries into dogmas, and ideas into a multitude of words, for they realize that all concepts are but glittering motes in a sunbeam. They want to see the sun itself. Confined to our study rooms, our knowledge seems to us a pillar of light; but when we stand at the door that opens out to the Infinite, we see how insubstantial is our knowledge. Even when we shut the door to the Infinite and retire to the narrow limits of notions our minds cannot remain confined. Again, to some people explanations and opinions are a token of wonder's departure, like a curfew after which they may not come abroad. In the cabbalists, the drive and the fire and the light are never put out.

Like the vital power in ourselves that gives us the ability to fight and to endure, to dare and to conquer, which drives us to experience the bitter and the perilous, there is an urge in wistful souls to starve rather than be fed on sham and distortion. To the cabbalists God is as real as life, and as nobody would be satisfied with mere knowing or reading about life, so they are not content to suppose or to prove logically that there is a God; they want to feel and to enjoy Him; not only to obey, but to approach Him. They want to taste the whole wheat of spirit before it is ground by the millstones of reason. They would rather be overwhelmed by the symbols of the inconceivable than wield the definitions of the superficial.

Stirred by a yearning after the unattainable, they want to make the distant near, the abstract concrete, to transform the soul into a vessel for the transcendent, to grasp with the senses what is hidden from the mind, to express in symbols what the tongue cannot speak, what the reason cannot conceive, to experience as a reality what vaguely dawns in intuitions. "Wise is he who by the power of his own contemplation attains to the perception of the profound mysteries which cannot be expressed in words."[1]

The cabbalist is not content with being confined to what he is. His desire is not only to *know* more than what ordinary reason has to offer, but to *be* more than what he is; not only to comprehend the Beyond but to concur with it. He aims at the elevation and expansion of existence. Such expansion goes hand in hand with the exaltation of all being.

The universe, exposed to the violence of our analytical mind, is being broken apart. It is split into the known and unknown, into the seen and unseen. In mystic contemplation all things are seen as one.[2] The mystic mind tends to hold the world together: to behold the seen in conjunction with the unseen, to keep the fellowship with the unknown through the revolving door of the known, "to learn the higher supernal wisdom from all" that the Lord has created and to regain the knowledge that once was in the possession of men and "that has perished from them."[3] What our senses perceive is but the jutting edge of what is deeply hidden. Extending over into the invisible, the things of this world stand in a secret contact with that which no eye has ever perceived. Everything certifies to the sublime, the unapparent working jointly with the apparent. There is always a reverberation in the Beyond to every action here: "The Lord made this world corresponding to the world above, and everything which is above has its counterpart below . . . and yet they all constitute a unity";[4] "there being no object, however small, in this world, but what is subordinate to its counterpart above which has charge over it; and so whenever the thing below bestirs itself, there is a simultaneous stimulation of its counterpart above, as the two realms form one interconnected whole."[5]

Opposed to the idea that the world of perception is the bottom of reality, the mystics plunge into what is beneath the perceptible. What they attain in their quest is more than a vague impression or a spotty knowledge of the imperceptible. "Penetrating to the real essence of wisdom . . . they are resplendent with the radiance of supernal wisdom."[6] Their eyes perceive things of this world, while their hearts reverberate to the throbbing of the hidden. To them the secret is the core of the apparent; the known is but an aspect of the unknown. "All things below are symbols of that which is above."[7] They are sustained by the forces that flow from hidden worlds. There is no particular that is detached from universal meaning. What appears to be a center to the eye is but a point on the periphery around another center. Nothing here is final. The worldly is subservient to the otherworldly. You grasp the essence of the here by conceiving its beyond. For this world is the reality of the spirit in a state of trance. The manifestation of the mystery is partly suspended, with ourselves living in lethargy. Our normal consciousness is a state of stupor, in which our sensibility to the wholly real and our responsiveness to the stimuli of the spirit are reduced. The mystics, knowing that we are involved in a hidden history of the cosmos, endeavor to awake from the drowsiness and apathy and to regain the state of wakefulness for our enchanted souls.

It is a bold attitude of the soul, a steadfast quality of consciousness, that lends mystic character to a human being. A man who feels that he is closely enfolded by a power that is both lasting and holy will come to know that the spiritual is not an idea to which one can relate his will, but a realm which can even be affected by our deeds. What distinguishes the cabbalist is the attachment of his entire personality to a hidden spiritual realm. Intensifying this attachment by means of active devotion to it, by meditation upon its secrets, or even by perception of its reality, he becomes allied with the dynamics of hidden worlds. Sensitive to the imperceptible, he is stirred by its secret happenings.

Attachment to hidden worlds holds the cabbalist in the spell of things more basic than the things that dominate the interest of the common mind. The mystery is not beyond and away from us. It is our destiny. "The fate of the world depends upon the mystery."[7]* Our task is to adjust the details to the whole, the apparent to the hidden, the near to the distant. The passionate concern of the cabbalist for final goals endows him with the experience of surpassing all human limitations and powers. With all he is doing he is crossing the borders, breaking the surfaces, approaching the lasting sources of all things. Yet his living with the infinite does not make him alien to the finite.

2. THE EXALTATION OF MAN

In this exalted world man's position is unique. God has instilled in him something of Himself. Likeness to God is the essence of man. The Hebrew word for man, *adam*, usually associated with the word for earth, *adamah*,[8] was homiletically related by some cabbalists to the expression, "I will ascend above the heights of the clouds; I will be like (*eddamme*) the Most High" (Is. 14:14). Man's privilege is, as it were, to augment the Divine in the world, as it is said, "ascribe ye strength unto God" (Ps. 68:35).

Jewish mystics are inspired by a bold and dangerously paradoxical idea that not only is God necessary to man but that man is also necessary to God, to the unfolding of His plans in this world. Thoughts of this kind are indicated and even expressed in various Rabbinic sources. "When Israel performs the will of the Omnipresent, they add strength to the heavenly power; as it is said, 'To God we render strength!'" When, however, Israel does not perform the will of the Omnipresent, they weaken—if it is possible to say so—the great power of Him Who is above; as it is written "Thou didst weaken the Rock that begot thee"[9] (Deut. 32:18). In the *Zohar* this idea is formulated in a more specific way. Commenting on the passage in Ex. 17:8, "Then came Amalek and fought with Israel in Rephidim," R. Simeon said: "There is a deep allusion in the name 'Rephidim.' This war emanated from the attribute of Severe Judgment and it was a war above and a war below . . . The Holy One, as it were, said:

'When Israel is worthy below, My power prevails in the universe; but when Israel is found to be unworthy, she weakens My power above, and the power of severe judgment predominates in the world.' So here, 'Amalek came and fought with Israel in Rephidim,' because the Israelites were 'weak' [in Hebrew: *raphe*, which the *Zohar* finds in the name 'Rephidim'] in the study of the Torah, as we have explained on another occasion."[10] Thus man's relationship to God should not be that of passive reliance upon His Omnipotence but that of active assistance. "The impious rely on their gods . . . the righteous are the support of God."[11] The Patriarchs are therefore called "the chariot of the Lord."[12] The belief in the greatness of man, in the metaphysical effectiveness of his physical acts, is an ancient motif of Jewish thinking.

Man himself is a mystery. He is the symbol of all that exists. His life is the image of universal life. Everything was created in the spiritual image of the mystical man. "When the Holy One created man, He set in him all the images of the supernal mysteries of the world above, and all the images of the lower mysteries of the world below, and all are designed in man, who stands in the image of God."[13] Even the human body is full of symbolic significance. The skin, flesh, bones and sinews are but an outward covering, mere garments,[14] even though "the substances composing man's body belong to two worlds, namely, the world below and the world above."[15] The 248 limbs and 365 sinews are symbols of the 613 parts of the universe as well as of the 248 positive and 365 negative precepts of the Torah. Man's soul emanates from an upper region where it has a spiritual father and a spiritual mother, just as the body has a father and mother in this world.[16] The souls that abide in our bodies are a weak reflection of our upper souls, the seat of which is in heaven. Yet, though detached from that soul, we are capable of being in contact with it. When we pray we turn toward the upper soul as though we were to abandon the body and join our source.

Man is not detached from the realm of the unseen. He is wholly involved in it. Whether he is conscious of it or not, his actions are vital to all worlds, and affect the course of transcendent events. In a sense, by means of the Torah, man is the constant architect of the hidden universe. "This world was formed in the pattern of the world above, and whatever takes place in this earthly realm occurs also in the realm above."[17] One of the principles of the *Zohar* is that every move below calls forth a corresponding movement above.[18] Not only things, even periods of time are conceived as concrete entities. "Thus over every day below is appointed a day above, and a man should take heed not to impair that day. Now the act below stimulates a corresponding activity above. Thus if a man does kindness on earth, he awakens lovingkindness above, and it rests upon that day which is crowned therewith through him. Similarly, if he performs a deed of mercy, he crowns that day with mercy and it becomes his protector in the hour of need. So, too, if he performs a cruel action, he has a corresponding effect on that day and impairs it, so that subsequently it becomes cruel to him and tries to destroy him, giving him measure for measure."[19] Even what we consider potential is regarded as real and we may be held accountable for it: ". . . just as a man is punished for uttering an evil word, so is he punished for not uttering a good word when he had the opportunity, because he harms that speaking spirit which was prepared to speak above and below in holiness."[20]

The significance of great works done on earth is valued by their cosmic effects. Thus, e.g., "When the first Temple was completed another Temple was erected at the same time, which was a center for all the worlds, shedding radiance upon all things and giving light to all the spheres. Then the worlds were firmly established, and all the supernal casements were opened to pour forth light, and all the worlds experienced such joys as had never been known to them before, and celestial and terrestrial beings alike broke forth in song. And the song which they sang is the Song of Songs."[21]

Endowed with metaphysical powers man's life is a most serious affair; "if a man's lips and tongue speak evil words, those words mount aloft and all proclaim 'keep away from the evil word of so-and-so, leave the path clear for the mighty serpent.' Then the holy soul leaves him and is not able to speak: it is in shame and distress, and is not given a place as before . . . Then many spirits bestir themselves, and one spirit comes down from that side and finds the man who uttered the evil word, and lights upon him and defiles him, and he becomes leprous."[22]

Man's life is full of peril. It can easily upset the balance and order of the universe. "A voice goes forth and proclaims: 'O ye people of the world, take heed unto yourselves, close the gates of sin, keep away from the perilous net before your feet are caught in it!' A certain wheel is ever whirling continuously round and round. Woe to those whose feet lose their hold on the wheel, for then they fall into the Deep which is predestined for the evildoers of the world! Woe to those who fall, never to rise and enjoy the light that is stored up for the righteous in the world to come!"[23]

3. THE EN SOF AND HIS MANIFESTATIONS

Mystic intuition occurs at an outpost of the mind, dangerously detached from the main substance of the intellect. Operating as it were in no-mind's land, its place is hard to name, its communications with critical thinking often difficult and uncertain and the accounts of its discoveries not easy to decode. In its main representatives, the cabbala teaches that man's life can be a rallying point of the forces that tend toward God, that this world is

charged with His presence and every object is a cue to His qualities. To
the cabbalist, God is not a concept, a generalization, but a most specific
reality; his thinking about Him full of forceful directness. But He who is
"the Soul of all souls"[24] is "the mystery of all mysteries." While the
cabbalists speak of God as if they commanded a view of the Beyond, and
were in possession of knowledge about the inner life of God, they also
assure us that all notions fail when applied to Him, that He is beyond
the grasp of the human mind and inaccessible to meditation.[25] He is the
En Sof, the Infinite, "the most Hidden of all Hidden."[26] While there is an
abysmal distance between Him and the world, He is also called All. "For
all things are in Him and He is in all things . . . He is both manifest and
concealed. Manifest in order to uphold the all and concealed, for He is
found nowhere. When He becomes manifest He projects nine brilliant
lights that throw light in all directions. So, too, does a lamp throw brilliance in all directions, but when we approach the brilliance we find there
is nothing outside the lamp. So is the Holy ancient One, the Light of all
Lights, the most Hidden of all Hidden. We can only find the light which
He spreads and which appears and disappears. This light is called the
Holy Name, and therefore All is One."[27]

Thus, the "Most Recondite One Who is beyond cognition does reveal
of Himself a tenuous and veiled brightness shining only along a narrow
path which extends from Him. This is the brightness that irradiates all."[28]
The En Sof has granted us manifestations of His hidden life: He had
descended to become the universe; He has revealed Himself to become the
Lord of Israel. The ways in which the Infinite assumes the form of
finite existence are called Sefirot.[29] These are various aspects or forms of
Divine action, spheres of Divine emanation. They are, as it were, the
garments in which the Hidden God reveals Himself and acts in the
universe, the channels through which His light is issued forth.

The names of the ten Sefirot are Keter, Hokmah, Binah, Hesed,
Geburah, Tiferet, Netsah, Hod, Yesod, Malkut. The transition from
Divine latency to activity takes place in Keter, the "supreme crown" of
God. This stage is inconceivable, absolute unity and beyond description.
In the following Sefirot, Hogmah and Binah, the building and creation of
the cosmos as well as that which divides things begins. They are parallel
emanations from Keter, representing the active and the receptive principle.

While the first triad represents the transition from the Divine to the
spiritual reality, the second triad is the source of the moral order. Hesed
stands for the love of God; Geburah for the power of justice manifested
as severity or punishment. From the union of these emanates Tiferet,
compassion or beauty of God, mediating between Hesed and Geburah,
between the life-giving power and the contrary power, holding in check
what would otherwise prove to be the excesses of love.

The next triad is the source of the psychic and physical existences—*Netsah* is the lasting endurance of God, *Hod* His majesty, and *Yesod* the stability of the universe, the seat of life and vitality. *Malkut* is the kingdom, the presence of the Divine in the world. It is not a source of its own but the outflow of the other *Sefirot*; "of itself lightless, it looks up to the others and reflects them as a lamp reflects the sun."[30] It is the point at which the external world comes in contact with the upper spheres, the final manifestations of the Divine, the *Shekinah*, "the Mother of all Living."[31]

The recondite and unapproachable Self of God is usually thought of as transcendent to the *Sefirot*. There is only a diffusion of His light into the *Sefirot*. The *En Sof* and the realm of His manifestations are "linked together like the flame and the coal," the flame being a manifestation of what is latent in the coal. In the process of the emanation, the transition from the Divine to the spiritual, from the spiritual to the moral, from the moral to the physical, reality takes place. The product of this manifestation is not only the visible universe but an endless number of spiritual worlds which exist beyond the physical universe in which we live. These worlds, the hidden cosmos, constitute a most complex structure, divided into various grades and forms which can only be described in symbols. These symbols are found in the Torah, which is the constitution of the cosmos. Every letter, word or phrase in the Bible not only describes an event in the history of our world but also represents a symbol of some stage in the hidden cosmos. These are the so-called *Raze Torah*, the mysteries, that can be discovered by the mystical method of interpretation.

The system of *Sefirot* can be visualized as a tree or a man or a circle, in three triads or in three columns. According to the last image the *Sefirot* are divided into a *right* column, signifying Mercy, or light, a *left* column, signifying Severity, the absence of light, and a *central* column, signifying the synthesis of the right and left. Each *Sefirah* is a world in itself, dynamic and full of complicated mutual relations with other *Sefirot*. There are many symbols by which each *Sefirah* can be expressed, *e.g.*, the second triad is symbolized in the lives of each of the three Patriarchs. The doctrine of *Sefirot* enables the cabbalists to perceive the bearings of God upon this world, to identify the Divine substance of all objects and events. It offers the principles by means of which all things and events can be interpreted as Divine manifestations.

The various parts of the day represent various aspects of Divine manifestation. "From sunrise until the sun declines westward it is called 'day,' and the attribute of Mercy is in the ascendant; after that it is called 'evening,' which is the time for the attribute of Severity . . . It is for this reason that Isaac instituted the afternoon prayer (*Minhah*), namely, to mitigate the severity of the approaching evening; whereas Abraham instituted morning prayer, corresponding to the attribute of mercy."[32]

The plurality into which the one Divine manifestation is split symbolizes the state of imperfection into which God's relation to the world was thrown. Every good deed serves to restore the original unity of the *Sefirot,* while on the other hand, "Sinners impair the supernal world by causing a separation between the 'Right' and the 'Left.' They really cause harm only to themselves, . . . as they prevent the descent of blessings from above . . . and the heaven keeps the blessings to itself." Thus the sinner's separation of the good inclination from the evil one by consciously cleaving to evil separates, as it were, the Divine attribute of Grace from that of Judgment, the Right from the Left.[33]

4. The Doctrine of the Shekinah

Originally there was harmony between God and His final manifestations, between the upper *Sefirot* and the tenth *Sefirah.* All things were attached to God and His power surged unhampered throughout all stages of being. Following the trespass of Adam, however, barriers evolved thwarting the emanation of His power. The creature became detached from the Creator, the fruit from the tree, the tree of knowledge from the tree of life, the male from the female, our universe from the world of unity, even the *Shekinah* or the tenth *Sefirah* from the upper *Sefirot.* Owing to that separation the world was thrown into disorder, the power of strict judgment increased, the power of love diminished and the forces of evil released. Man who was to exist in pure spiritual form as light in constant communication with the Divine was sunk into his present inferior state.

In spite of this separation, however, God has not withdrawn entirely from this world. Metaphorically, when Adam was driven out of Eden, an aspect of the Divine, the *Shekinah,* followed him into captivity.[34] Thus there is a Divine power that dwells in this world. It is the Divine Presence that went before Israel while they were going through the wilderness, that protects the virtuous man, that abides in his house and goes forth with him on his journeys, that dwells between a man and his wife.[35] The *Shekinah* "continually accompanies a man and leaves him not so long as he keeps the precepts of the Torah. Hence a man should be careful not to go on the road alone, that is to say, he should diligently keep the precepts of the Torah in order that he may not be deserted by the *Shekinah,* and so be forced to go alone without the accompaniment of the *Shekinah.*"[36] The *Shekinah* follows Israel into exile and "always hovers over Israel like a mother over her children."[37] Moreover, it is because of Israel and its observance of the Torah that the *Shekinah* dwells on earth. Were they to corrupt their way, they would thrust the *Shekinah* out of this world and the earth would be left in a degenerate state.[38]

The doctrine of the *Shekinah* occupies a central place in the cabbala.

While emphasizing that in His essence "the Holy One and the *Shekinah* are One,"[39] it speaks of a cleavage, as it were, in the reality of the Divine. The *Shekinah* is called figuratively the *Matrona* (symbolized by the Divine Name *Elohim*) that is separated from the King (symbolized by the ineffable Name *Hashem*) and it signifies that God is, so to speak, involved in the tragic state of this world. In the light of this doctrine the suffering of Israel assumed new meaning. Not only Israel but the whole universe, even the *Shekinah*, "lies in dust"[40] and is in exile. Man's task is to bring about the restitution of the original state of the universe and the reunion of the *Shekinah* and the *En Sof*. This is the meaning of Messianic salvation, the goal of all efforts.

"In time to come God will restore the *Shekinah* to its place and there will be a complete union. 'In that day shall the Lord be One and His Name One' (Zech. 14:9). It may be said: Is He not now One? no; for now through sinners He is not really One. For the Matrona is removed from the King . . . and the King without the Matrona is not invested with His crown as before. But when He joins the Matrona, who crowns Him with many resplendent crowns, then the supernal Mother will also crown Him in a fitting manner. But now that the King is not with the Matrona, the supernal Mother keeps her crowns and withholds from Him the waters of the stream and He is not joined with her. Therefore, as it were, He is not one. But when the Matrona shall return to the place of the Temple and the King shall be wedded with her, then all will be joined together, without separation and regarding this it is written, 'In that day shall the Lord be One and His Name One.' Then there shall be such perfection in the world as had not been for all generations before, for then shall be completeness above and below, and all worlds shall be united in one bond."[41]

The restoration of unity is a constant process. It takes place through the study of the Torah, through prayer and through the fulfillment of the commandments. "The only aim and object of the Holy One in sending man into this world is that he may know and understand that *Hashem* (God), signifying the *En Sof*, is *Elohim* (*Shekinah*). This is the sum of the whole mystery of the faith, of the whole Torah, of all that is above and below, of the written and the oral Torah, all together forming one unity."[42] "When a man sins it is as though he strips the *Shekinah* of her vestments, and that is why he is punished; and when he carries out the precepts of the law, it is as though he clothes the *Shekinah* in her vestments. Hence we say that the fringes worn by the Israelites are, to the *Shekinah* in captivity, like the poor man's garments of which it is said, 'For that is his only covering, it is his garment for his skin, wherein he shall sleep.' "[43]

5. MYSTIC EXPERIENCE

The ultimate goal of the cabbalist is not his own union with the Absolute but the union of all reality with God; one's own bliss is subordinated to the redemption of all: "we have to put all our being, all the members of our body, our complete devotion, into that thought so as to rise and attach ourselves to the *En Sof,* and thus achieve the oneness of the upper and lower worlds."[44]

What this service means in terms of personal living is described in the following way:

Happy is the portion of whoever can penetrate into the mysteries of his Master and become absorbed into Him, as it were. Especially does a man achieve this when he offers up his prayer to his Master in intense devotion, his will then becoming as the flame inseparable from the coal, and his mind concentrated on the unity of the lower firmaments, to unify them by means of a lower name, then on the unity of the higher firmaments, and finally on the absorption of them all into that most high firmament. Whilst a man's mouth and lips are moving, his heart and will must soar to the height of heights, so as to acknowledge the unity of the whole in virtue of the mystery of mysteries in which all ideas, all wills and all thoughts find their goal, to wit, the mystery of *En Sof.*[45]

The thirst for God is colored by the awareness of His holiness, of the endless distance that separates man from the Eternal One. Yet, he who craves for God is not only a mortal being, but also a part of the Community of Israel, that is, the bride of God, endowed with a soul that is "a part of God." Shy in using endearing terms in his own name, the Jewish mystic feels and speaks in the plural. The allegory of the Song of Songs would be impertinent as an individual utterance, but as an expression of Israel's love for God it is among the finest of all expressions. "God is the soul and spirit of all, and Israel calls Him so and says: (My soul), I desire Thee in order to cleave to Thee and I seek Thee early to find Thy favor."[46]

Israel lives in mystic union with God and the purpose of all its service is to strengthen this union: "O my dove that art in the clefts of the rock, in the covert of the cliff" (Song of Sol. 2:14). The "dove" here is the Community of Israel, which like a dove never forsakes her mate, the Holy One, blessed be He. "In the clefts of the rock": these are the students of the Torah, who have no ease in this world. "In the covert of the steep place": these are the specially pious among them, the saintly and God-fearing, from whom the Divine Presence never departs. The Holy One, blessed be He, inquires concerning them of the Community of Israel, saying, "Let me see thy countenance, let me hear thy voice, for sweet is thy voice"; "for above only the voice of those who study the Torah is heard. We have learned that the likeness of all such is graven above before the Holy One, blessed be He, Who delights Himself with them every day and watches them and that voice rises and pierces its way through all firmaments until it stands before the Holy One, blessed be He."[47]

The concepts of the cabbala cannot always be clearly defined and consistently interrelated. As the name of Jewish mysticism, "cabbala" (lit.: "received lore"), indicates, it is a tradition of wisdom, supposed to have been revealed to elect Sages in ancient times and preserved throughout the generations by an initiated few. The cabbalists accept at the outset the ideas on authority, not on the basis of analytical understanding.

Yet the lips of the teachers and the pages of the books are not the only sources of knowledge. The great cabbalists claimed to have received wisdom directly from the Beyond. Inspiration and Vision were as much a part of their life as contemplation and study. The prayer of Moses: "Show me, I pray Thee, Thy glory" (Ex. 33:18) has never died in the hearts of the cabbalists. The conception of the goal has changed but the quest for immediate cognition remained. The Merkaba-mystics, following perhaps late prophetic traditions about the mysteries of the Divine Throne, were striving to behold the celestial sphere in which the secrets of creation and man's destiny are contained. In the course of the centuries the scope of such esoteric experiences embraced a variety of objectives. The awareness of the cabbalists that the place whereon they stood was holy ground kept them mostly silent about the wonder that was granted to them. Yet we possess sufficient evidence to justify the assumption that mystic events, particularly in the form of inner experiences, of spiritual communications rather than that of sense perceptions, were elements of their living. According to old Rabbinic teachings, there have always been Sages and saints upon whom the Holy Spirit rested, to whom wisdom was communicated from heaven by a Voice, through the appearance of the spirit of Elijah or in dreams. According to the *Zohar*, God reveals to the saints "profound secrets of the Holy Name which He does not reveal to the angels."[48] The disciples of Rabbi Simeon ben Yohai are called prophets, "before whom both supernal and terrestrial beings tremble in awe."[48a] Others pray that the inspiration of the Holy Spirit should come upon them.[49] The perception of the unearthly is recorded as an ordinary feature in the life of certain Rabbis. "When R. Hamnuna the Ancient used to come out from the river on a Friday afternoon, he was wont to rest a little on the bank, and raising his eyes in gladness, he would say that he sat there in order to behold the joyous sight of the heavenly angels ascending and descending. At each arrival of the Sabbath, he said, man is caught up into the world of souls."[50] Not only may the human mind receive spiritual illuminations; the soul also may be bestowed upon higher powers. "Corresponding to the impulses of a man here are the influences which he attracts to himself from above. Should his impulse be toward holiness, he attracts to himself holiness from on high and so he becomes holy; but if this tendency is toward the side of impurity, he draws down toward himself the unclean spirit and so becomes polluted."[51]

Since the time of the prophet Joel the Jews have expected that at the end of days the Lord would "pour out His spirit upon all flesh" and all men would prophesy. In later times, it is believed, the light of that revelation of mysteries could already be perceived.

The mystics absorb even in this world "something of the odor of these secrets and mysteries."[52] Significantly, the Torah itself is conceived as a living source of inspiration, not as a fixed book. The Torah is a voice that "calls aloud" to men;[53] she calls them day by day to herself in love . . . "The Torah lets out a word and emerges for a little from her sheath, and then hides herself again. But she does this only for those who understand and obey her. She is like unto a beautiful and stately damsel, who is hidden in a secluded chamber of a palace and who has a lover of whom no one knows but she. Out of his love for her he constantly passes by her gate, turning his eyes toward all sides to find her. Knowing that he is always haunting the palace, what does she do? She opens a little door in her hidden palace, discloses for a moment her face to her lover, then swiftly hides it again. None but he notices it; but his heart and soul, and all that is in him are drawn to her, knowing as he does that she has revealed herself to him for a moment because she loves him. It is the same with the Torah, which reveals her hidden secrets only to those who love her. She knows that he who is wise of heart daily haunts the gates of her house. What does she do? She shows her face to him from her palace, making a sign of love to him, and straightaway returns to her hiding place again. No one understands her message save he alone, and he is drawn to her with heart and soul and all his being. Thus the Torah reveals herself momentarily in love to her lovers in order to awaken fresh love in them."[54]

6. The Torah—A Mystic Reality

The Torah is an inexhaustible esoteric reality. To enter into its deep, hidden strata is in itself a mystic goal. The Universe is an image of the Torah and the Torah is an image of God. For the Torah is "the Holy of Holies"; "it consists entirely of the name of the Holy One, blessed be He. Every letter in it is bound up with that Name."[55]

The Torah[55a] is the main source from which man can draw the secret wisdom and power of insight into the essence of things. "It is called Torah (lit.: showing) because it shows and reveals that which is hidden and unknown; and all life from above is comprised in it and issues from it."[56] "The Torah contains all the deepest and most recondite mysteries; all sublime doctrines both disclosed and undisclosed; all essences both of the higher and the lower grades, of this world and of the world to come are to be found there."[57] The source of wisdom is accessible to all, yet only few resort to it. "How stupid are men that they take no pains to know the ways of the Almighty by which the world is maintained. What prevents them? Their stupidity, because they do not study the Torah; for if they were to study the Torah they would know the ways of the Holy One, blessed be He."[58]

The Torah has a double significance: literal and symbolic. Besides their plain, literal meaning, which is important, valid and never to be overlooked, the verses of the Torah possess an esoteric significance, "comprehensible only to the wise who are familiar with the ways of the Torah."[59] "Happy is Israel to whom was given the sublime Torah, the Torah of truth. Perdition take anyone who maintains that any narrative in the Torah comes merely to tell us a piece of history and nothing more! If that were so, the Torah would not be what it assuredly is, to wit, the supernal Law, the Law of truth. Now if it is not dignified for a king of flesh and blood to engage in common talk, much less to write it down, is it conceivable that the most high King, the Holy One, blessed be He, was short of sacred subjects with which to fill the Torah, so that He had to collect such commonplace topics as the anecdotes of Esau, and Hagar, Laban's talks to Jacob, the words of Balaam and his ass, those of Balak, and of Zimri, and such-like, and make of them a Torah? If so, why is it called the 'Law of Truth?' Why do we read 'The Law of the Lord is perfect . . . The testimony of the Lord is sure . . . The Ordinances of the Lord are true . . . More to be desired are they than gold, yea, than much fine gold' (Ps. 19:8-11). But assuredly each word of the Torah signifies sublime things, so that this or that narrative, besides its meaning in and for itself, throws light on the all-comprehensive Rule of the Torah."[60]

"Said R. Simeon: 'Alas for the man who regards the Torah as a mere book of tales and everyday matters! If that were so, we, even we, could compose a torah dealing with everyday affairs, and of even greater excellence. Nay, even the princes of the world possess books of greater worth which we could use as a model for composing some such torah. The Torah, however, contains in all its words supernal truths and sublime mysteries. Observe the perfect balancing of the upper and lower worlds. Israel here below is balanced by the angels on high, of whom it says: 'who makest thine angels into winds' (Ps. 104:4). For the angels in descending on earth put on themselves earthly garments, as otherwise they could not stay in this world, nor could the world endure them.

"Now, if thus it is with the angels, how much more so must it be with the Torah—the Torah that created them, that created all the worlds and is the means by which these are sustained. Thus had the Torah not clothed herself in garments of this world the world could not endure it. The stories of the Torah are thus only her outer garments, and whoever looks upon that garment as being Torah itself, woe to that man—such a one will have no portion in the next world. David thus said: 'Open thou mine eyes, that I may behold wondrous things out of Thy law' (Ps. 119:18), to wit, the things that are beneath the garment. Observe this. The garments worn by a man are the most visible part of him, and senseless people looking at the man do not seem to see more in him than the garments. But in truth the pride of the garments is the body of the man, and the pride of the body is the soul. Similarly the Torah has a body made up of the precepts of the Torah, called *gufe torah* (bodies, main principles of the Torah), and that body is enveloped in garments made up of worldly narratives. The senseless people only see the garment, the mere narrations; those who are somewhat wise penetrate as far as the body. But the really wise, the servants of the most high King, those who stood on Mt. Sinai, penetrate right through to the soul, the root principle of all, namely to the real Torah. In the future the same are destined to penetrate even to the super-soul (soul of the soul) of the Torah . . ."[61]

How assiduously should one ponder over each word of the Torah, for there is not a single word in it which does not contain allusions to the Supernal Holy Name, not a word which does not contain many mysteries, many aspects, many roots, many branches! Where now is this "book of the wars of the Lord"? What is meant, of course, is the Torah, for as the members of the Fellowship have pointed out, he who is engaged in the battle of the Torah, struggling to penetrate into her mysteries, will wrest from his struggles an abundance of peace.[62]

7. THE MYSTIC WAY OF LIFE

A longing for the unearthly, a yearning for purity, the will to holiness, connected the conscience of the cabbalists with the strange current of mystic living. Being puzzled or inquisitive will not make a person mystery stricken. The cabbalists were not set upon exploring, or upon compelling the unseen to become visible. Their intention was to integrate their thoughts and deeds into the secret order, to assist God in undoing the evil, in redeeming the light that was concealed. Though working with fragile tools for a mighty end, they were sure of bringing about at the end the salvation of the universe and of this tormented world.

A new form of living was the consequence of the cabbala. Everything was so replete with symbolic significance as to make it the potential heart of the spiritual universe. How carefully must all be approached. A moral rigorism that hardly leaves any room for waste or respite resulted in making the cabbalist more meticulous in studying and fulfilling the precepts of the Torah, in refining his moral conduct, in endowing every-day actions with solemn significance. For man represents God in this world. Even the parts of his body signify Divine mysteries.

Everything a man does leaves its imprint on the world. "The Supernal Holy King does not permit anything to perish, not even the breath of the mouth. He has a place for everything, and makes it what He wills. Even a human word, yes, even the voice, is not void, but has its place and destination in the universe."[63] Every action here below, if it is done with the intention of serving the Holy King, produces a "breath" in the world above, and there is no breath which has no voice; and this voice ascends and crowns itself in the supernal world and becomes an intercessor before the Holy One, blessed be He. Contrariwise, every action which is not done with this purpose becomes a "breath" which floats about the world, and when the soul of the doer leaves his body, this "breath" rolls about like a stone in a sling, and it "breaks the spirit." The act done and the word spoken in the service of the Holy One, however, ascend high above the sun and become a holy breath, which is the seed sown by man in that world and is called Zedakah (righteousness) or (loving-kindness), as it is written: "Sow to yourselves according to righteousness" (Hos. 10:12). This "breath" guides the departed soul and brings it into the region of the supernal glory, so that it is "bound in the bundle of life with the Lord thy God" (I Sam. 25:29). It is concerning this that it is written: "Thy righteousness shall go before thee; the glory of the Lord shall be thy reward" (Is. 58:8). That which is called "the glory of the Lord" gathers up the souls of that holy breath, and this is indeed ease and comfort for them; but the other is called "breaking of spirit." Blessed are the righteous whose works are "above the sun" and who sow a seed of righteousness which makes them worthy to enter the world to come.[64]

Everything a man does leaves its imprint upon the world: his breath, thought, speech. If it is evil, the air is defiled and he who comes close to that trace may be affected by it and led to do evil. By fulfilling the Divine precepts man purifies the air and turns the "evil spirits" into "holy spirits." He should strive to spiritualize the body and to make it identical with the soul by fulfilling the 248 positive and 365 negative precepts which correspond to the 248 limbs and the 365 sinews of the human body. The precepts of the Torah contain "manifold sublime recondite teachings and radiances and resplendences,"[65] and can lift man to the supreme level of existence.

The purpose of man's service is to "give strength to God," not to attain one's own individual perfection. Man is able to stir the supernal spheres. "The terrestrial world is connected with the heavenly world, as the heavenly world is connected with the terrestrial one."[66] In fulfilling the good the corresponding sphere on high is strengthened; in balking it, the sphere is weakened. This connection or correspondence can be made to operate in a creative manner by means of *kawwanah* or contemplation of the mysteries of which the words and precepts of the Torah are the symbols. In order to grasp the meaning of those words or to fulfill the purpose of those precepts one has to resort to the Divine Names and Qualities which are invested in those words and precepts, the mystic issues to which they refer, or, metaphorically, the gates of the celestial mansion which the spiritual content of their fulfillment has to enter. Thus, all deeds—study, prayer and ceremonies—have to be performed not mechanically but while meditating upon their mystic significance.

Prayer is a powerful force in this service and a venture full of peril. He who prays is a priest at the temple that is the cosmos. With good prayer he may "build worlds," with improper prayer he may "destroy worlds." "It is a miracle that a man survives the hour of worship," the Baal Shem said. "The significance of all our prayers and praises is that by means of them the upper fountain may be filled; and when it is so filled and attains completeness, then the universe below, and all that appertains thereto, is filled also and receives completeness from the completion which has been consummated in the upper sphere. The world below cannot, indeed, be in a state of harmony unless it receives that peace and perfection from above, even as the moon has no light in herself but shines with the reflected radiance of the sun. All our prayers and intercessions have this purpose, namely, that the region from whence light issues may be invigorated; for then from its reflection all below is supplied."[67] "Every word of prayer that issues from a man's mouth ascends aloft through all firmaments to a place where it is tested. If it is genuine, it is taken up before the Holy King to be fulfilled, but if not it is rejected, and an alien spirit is evoked by it."[68] For example, "it is obligatory for every Israelite to relate the story of the Exodus on the Passover night. He who does so fervently and joyously, telling the tale with a high heart, shall be found worthy to rejoice in the *Shekinah* in the world to come, for rejoicing brings forth rejoicing; and the joy of Israel causes the Holy One Himself to be glad, so that He calls together all the Family above and says unto them: 'Come ye and hearken unto the praises which My children bring unto Me! Behold how they rejoice in My redemption!' Then all the angels and supernal beings gather round and observe Israel, how she sings and rejoices because of her Lord's own Redemption—and seeing the rejoicings below, the supernal beings also break into jubilation for that the Holy One possesses on earth a people so holy, whose joy in the Redemption of their Lord is so great and powerful. For all that terrestrial rejoicing increases the power of the Lord and His hosts in the regions above, just as an earthly king gains strength from the praises of his subjects, the fame of his glory being thus spread throughout the world."[69]

Worship came to be regarded as a pilgrimage into the supernal spheres, with the prayerbook as an itinerary, containing the course of the gradual ascent of the spirit. The essential goal of man's service is to bring about the lost unity of all that exists. To render praise unto Him is not the final purpose. "Does the God of Abraham need an exaltation? Is He not already exalted high above our comprehension? . . . Yet man can and must exalt Him in the sense of uniting in his mind all the attributes in the Holy Name, for this is the supremest form of worship."[70] By meditating upon the mysteries while performing the Divine precepts, we act toward unifying all the supernal potencies in one will and bringing about the union of the Master and the Matrona.

Concerning the verse in Ps. 145:18, "The Lord is nigh to all them that call upon Him, to all that call upon Him in truth," the *Zohar* remarks that the words "in truth" mean in possession of the full knowledge which enables the worshiper perfectly "to unite the letters of the Holy Name in prayer . . . On the achievement of that unity hangs both celestial and terrestrial worship . . . If a man comes to unify the Holy Name, but without proper concentration of mind and devotion of heart, to the end that the supernal and terrestrial hosts should be blessed thereby, then his prayer is rejected and all beings denounce him, and he is numbered with those of whom the Holy One said, 'When ye come to see my countenance, who hath required this from your hand, to tread my courts?' All the 'countenances' of the King are hidden in the depths of darkness, but for those who know how perfectly to unite the Holy Name, all the walls of darkness are burst asunder, and the diverse 'countenances' of the King are made manifest, and shine upon all, bringing blessing to heavenly and earthly beings."[71]

The lower things are apparent, the higher things remain unrevealed. The higher an essence is, the greater is the degree of its concealment. To pray is "to draw blessings from the depth of the 'Cistern,' from the source of all life . . . Prayer is the drawing of this blessing from above to below; for when the Ancient One, the All-hidden, wishes to bless the universe, He lets His gifts of Grace collect in that supernal depth, from whence they are to be drawn, through human prayer, into the 'Cistern,' so that all the streams and brooks may be filled therefrom." The verse in Psalm 130:1, "Out of the depths have I called Thee," is said to mean not only that he who prays should do so from the depths of his soul; he must also invoke the blessing from the source of all sources.[72]

8. The Concern for God

The yearning for mystic living, the awareness of the ubiquitous mystery, the noble nostalgia for the nameless nucleus, have rarely subsided in the Jewish soul. This longing for the mystical has found many and varied expressions in ideas and doctrines, in customs and songs, in visions and aspirations. It is a part of the heritage of the psalmists and prophets.

There were Divine commandments to fulfill, rituals to perform, laws to obey—but the psalmist did not feel as if he carried a yoke: "Thy statutes have been my songs" (119:54). The fulfillment of the *mitzvot* was felt to be not a mechanical compliance but a personal service in the palace of the King of Kings. Is mysticism alien to the spirit of Judaism? Listen to the psalmist: "As the hart panteth after the water brooks, so panteth my soul after Thee, O Lord. My soul thirsteth for God, for the Living God; when shall I come and appear before God?" (42:2-3). "My soul yearneth, yea even pineth for the courts of the Lord; my heart and my flesh sing for joy unto the Living God" (84:3). "For a day in Thy courts is better than a thousand" (84:11). "In Thy presence is fulness of joy" (16:11).

It has often been said that Judaism is an earthly religion, yet the psalmist states, "I am a sojourner in the earth" (119:19). "Whom have I in heaven but Thee? And beside thee I desire none upon earth" (73:25). "My flesh and my heart faileth; but God is the rock of my heart and my portion forever" (73:26). "But as for me, the nearness of God is my good" (73:28). "O God, Thou art my God; earnestly will I seek Thee; my soul thirsteth for Thee, my flesh longeth for Thee in a dry and weary land, where no water is . . . for Thy lovingkindness is better than life. My soul is satisfied as with marrow and fatness; . . . I remember Thee upon my couch and meditate on Thee in the nightwatches . . . My soul cleaveth unto Thee, Thy right hand holdeth me fast" (63:2, 4, 6, 7, 9).

In their efforts to say what God is and wills, the prophets sought to imbue Israel with two impulses: to realize that God is holy, different and apart from all that exists, and to bring into man's focus the dynamics that prevail between God and man. The first impulse placed the mind in the restful light of the knowledge of unity, omnipotence, and superiority of God to all other beings, while the second impulse turned the hearts toward the inexhaustible heavens of God's concern for man, at times brightened by His mercy, at times darkened by His anger. He is both transcendent, beyond human understanding, and at the same time full of love, compassion, grief, or anger. The prophets did not intend to afford man a view of heaven, to report about secret things they saw and heard but to disclose what happened in God in reference to Israel. What they preached was more than a concept of Divine might and wisdom. They spoke of an inner life of God, of His love or anger, His mercy or disappointment, His interest or participation in the fate of Israel and other nations. God revealed Himself to the prophets in a specific state, in an emotional or passionate relationship to Israel. He not only demanded obedience but He was personally concerned and even stirred by the conduct of His people. Their actions aroused His joy, grief or disappointment. His attitude was not objective but subjective. He was not only a Judge but also a Father. He is the lover, engaged to His people, who reacts to human life with a specific *pathos*, signified in the language of the prophets, in love, mercy or anger. The Divine pathos which the prophets tried to express in many ways was not a name for His essence but rather for the modes of this reaction to Israel's conduct which could be changed by a change in Israel's conduct. Such a change was often the object of the prophetic ministry.

The prophets discovered the holy dimension of living by which our right to live and to survive is measured. However, the holy dimension was not a mechanical magnitude, measurable by the yardstick of deed and reward, of crime and punishment, by a cold law of justice. They did not proclaim a universal moral mechanism but a spiritual order in which justice was the course but not the source. To them justice was not a static principle but a surge sweeping from the inwardness of God, in which the deeds of man find, as it were, approval or disapproval, joy or sorrow. There was a surge of Divine pathos, which came to the souls of the prophets like a fierce passion, startling, shaking, burning, and led them forth to the perilous defiance of people's self-assurance and contentment. Beneath all songs and sermons they held conference with God's concern for the people, with the well out of which the tides of anger raged.

There is always a correspondence between what man is and what he knows about God. To a man of the *vita activa*, omnipotence is the most striking attribute of God. A man with an inner life, to whom thoughts and intuitions are not less real than things and deeds, will search for a concept of the inner life of God. The concept of inner life in the Divine Being is an idea upon which the mystic doctrines of Judaism hinge. The significance of prophetic revelation lies not in the inner experience of the prophet but in its character as a manifestation of what is in God. Prophetic revelation is primarily an event in the life of God. This is the outstanding difference between prophetic revelation and all other types of inspiration as reported by many mystics and poets. To the prophet it is not a psychic event, but first of all a transcendent act, something that happens to God. The actual reality of revelation takes place outside the consciousness of the prophet. He experiences revelation, so to speak, as an ecstasy of God, who comes out of His imperceivable distance to reveal His will to man. Essentially, the act of revelation takes place in the Beyond; it is merely directed upon the prophet.

The knowledge about the inner state of the Divine in its relationship to Israel determined the inner life of the prophets, engendering a passion for God, a *sympathy* for the Divine pathos in their hearts. They loved Israel because God loved Israel, and they frowned upon Israel when they knew that such was the attitude of God. Thus the marriage of Hosea was an act of sympathy; the prophet had to go through the experience of being betrayed as Israel had betrayed God. He had to experience in his own life what it meant to be betrayed by a person whom he loved in order to gain an understanding of the inner life of God. In a similar way the sympathy for God was in the heart of Jeremiah like a "burning fire, shut up in my bones and I weary myself to hold it in, but cannot" (20:9).

The main doctrine of the prophets can be called *pathetic theology*. Their attitude toward what they knew about God can be described as religion of sympathy. The Divine pathos, or as it was later called, the *Middot*, stood in the center of their consciousness. The life of the prophet revolved around the life of God. The prophets were not indifferent to whether God was in a state of anger or a state of mercy. They were most sensitive to what was going on in God.[73]

This is the pattern of Jewish mysticism: to have an open heart for the inner life of God. It is based on two assumptions: that there is an inner life in God and that the existence of man ought to revolve in a spiritual dynamic course around the life of God.[73a]

Notes

[1] *Zohar* (to which all unspecified references in the following notes relate. The translation used is that mentioned in the Bibliography.) II, 23a.

[2] I 241a.

[3] II 15b.

[4] II 20a.

[5] I 156b.

[6] II 2a.

[7] II 15b.

[7*] III 128a.

[8] Cf. *Midrash Rabbah* (Soncino Press Edition. London, 1939), Gen. XVII; Mid. Hag. Gn. 2, 7.

[9] *Pesik*, ed. Buber, XXVI, 166b.

[10] III 65b.

[11] Gen. R., *op. cit.*, LXIX. 3; Cf. Louis Ginzberg, *Cabala*, JE, v. 3.

[12] Gen. R., *op. cit.*, XLVII. 6; LXXXII, 6.

[13] II 75a.

[14] II 76a.

[15] II 23b.

[16] II 12a.

[17] II 144a.

[18] I 164a.

[19] III 92a-92b.

[20] III 64b.

[21] II 143a.
[22] III 64a.
[23] II 220b.
[24] III 109b.
[25] II 42b.
[26] I 21a.
[27] III 288a.
[28] II 146b.
[29] *Tikkune Zohar*, 1.
[30] II 23a; cf. I, 27a; II 158a.
[31] On the concept of *Shekinah* in rabbinic literature cf. J. Abelson, *The Immanence of God in Rabbinical Literature*. London, 1912.
[32] II 21a-21b.
[33] II 26b.
[34] I 22b.
[35] I 76a.
[36] I 230a.
[37] II 120b.
[38] I 61a.
[39] II 118b.
[40] II 9b.
[41] III 77b.
[42] II 161b.
[43] I 23b.
[44] II 216a-b.
[45] II 213b.
[46] III 67a.
[47] III 61a.
[48] III 78b.
[48*] II 144b.
[49] II 154a.
[50] II 136b.
[51] I 125b; cf. I 99b.
[52] *Sefer Hassidin,* ed. Wistinetzki (Frankfort, 1924). Cf. *Zohar* I 105b.
[53] III 58a; III 23a.
[54] II 99a.
[55] III 73a.
[[55a] Cf. above Robert Gordis, "The Bible as a Cultural Monument," see also below Louis Finkelstein, "The Jewish Religion: Its Beliefs and Practices" (Chapter 42).]
[56] III 53b.
[57] I 134b-135a.
[58] III 75b.
[59] II 95a.
[60] III 52a.
[61] III 152a.
[62] III 55b-56a.

[63] II 100b.

[64] III 59a.

[65] II 218b.

[66] I 70b.

[67] II 145b.

[68] III 55a.

[69] III 40b.

[70] II 55b.

[71] II 57a.

[72] III 63a.

[73] Cf. Abraham Heschel, *Die Prophetie* (Cracow, 1936), pp. 56-87; 127-180.

[[73a] For the influence of cabbala on the philosophic thought of the Renaissance see below Alexander Altmann, "Judaism and World Philosophy," pp. 980-981.]

BIBLIOGRAPHY

Only an inkling of the vast literature of Jewish mysticism can be offered in the limits of a single chapter. It was considered proper to dwell primarily upon one phase of the Cabbala, the history of which abounds in thoughts and events. The *Zohar,* the authoritative book of the movement, was chosen as the basis of our chapter.

Ginzberg, Louis, "Cabala," in *The Jewish Encyclopedia,* III, 456-479. New York and London, 1902.

Scholem, Gerhard G., *Major Trends in Jewish Mysticism.* Jerusalem, 1941.

Waite, Arthur E., *The Holy Kabbalah.* London, 1929.

The Zohar. Translated by Harry Sperling and Maurice Simon. 4 vols. London, 1931-1934.

CHAPTER 20

JUDAISM AND WORLD PHILOSOPHY

By Alexander Altmann

It would be futile to attempt a presentation of Judaism as a philosophic system, or to speak of Jewish philosophy in the same sense as one speaks of American, English, French or German philosophy.[1] Judaism is a religion, and the truths it teaches are religious truths. They spring from the source of religious experience, not from pure Reason. There can, therefore, be no purpose in treating Judaism and world philosophy as two manifestations of the philosophic spirit, the one in a specific and the other in its generic form.

Yet while one must be careful not to confound Judaism with philosophy, one must not ignore the fact that many of the leading religious concepts of Judaism (such as the Unity and Incorporeality of God, *Creatio ex nihilo,* a universal Law for all mankind) were evolved in opposition to the mythical world view, and are therefore imbued with a high degree of rational and abstract thought.[2] They do not for this reason become in themselves philosophic, for they never lose touch with the springs of religious imagination; their whole tenor and significance remain religious. At the same time, their rational character places them in direct proximity to the Greek philosophic tradition, which grew up independently from a different stem of civilization. That tradition, too, developed in marked defiance of mythology, the traces of which it still bears in the classical, medieval and Renaissance periods.

Both the Jewish religious and the Greek philosophic traditions have, then, this in common that they are grappling, each in its own way, with the problem of mythology. It should, therefore, not be surprising if they had something to tell each other. The fact is that they did communicate with each other, and that they profited by their mutual contacts. The influence of philosophy on the development of Jewish thought, both rational and mystic, forms an important chapter in the history of the Jewish mind. World philosophy, likewise, was stimulated and enriched by the influence of Judaism. Our task will be to trace the various forms that this mutual interpenetration of Judaism and philosophy assumed in the course of history.

The importance of the contribution Judaism has made to the evolution of Western civilization can hardly be exaggerated. Ever since the entrance of the Jewish element into the world of Western thought—an entrance largely effected through the gateway of Alexandria—Judaism has become a potent factor in the intellectual realm of Western civilization. This is true in a double sense: not only has a considerable volume of Jewish thought been absorbed into that civilization through the medium of Christianity, but direct Jewish influence, too, has been strong and persistent, a fact to which E. Troeltsch has rightly drawn attention.[3]

It may be hard, in the modern age of emancipation and secularization, to separate the Jewish from general Western traits in the contributions of individual Jewish philosophers. In many cases no distinctly Jewish tradition may be traceable. Yet there can be little doubt that, in some way or other, a Jewish "quality" asserts itself. This applies not merely to the intensely Jewish Hermann Cohen, but also to thinkers on the extreme periphery of Judaism like Samuel Alexander and Henri Bergson. Alexander's "Taking Time Seriously"[4] is essentially Jewish and opposed to the Platonic-Christian tradition. Bergson's Comprehension of Reality and Being, under the symbols of purpose, creation, realization, insistence, progress, power, energy and life, has its origin in prophetic teaching, as Nathan Soederblom has emphasized.[5]

As we shall endeavor to show, there is an unbroken line of Jewish influence from the Hellenistic period down to the Middle Ages, and leading to the modern period of philosophy. We hope our historical survey will demonstrate how intimate is the fusion between Judaism and world philosophy, and how well founded is the Jewish claim that, through its contribution, Judaism has become an integral part of the intellectual and spiritual make-up of Western civilization.

1. Hellenistic Jewish Philosophy

Hellenistic Jewish philosophy derives from the influence of Stoic, Platonic and Neopythagorean thought on the Greek-speaking Jews of Alexandria in the period between the second century b.c.e. and the first century c.e. At its mature stage, it joins the movement of the Platonic "Renaissance," inaugurated by Posidonius (b. c. 135 b.c.e.), the great Stoic teacher and tutor of Cicero, who has been termed "the first Neoplatonist," although a distance of more than three hundred years separates him from Plotinus, the founder of the Neoplatonic School.[1] The revival of Platonism must have been of particular interest to Hellenistic Jews because it broke the spell of Stoic materialistic pantheism and paved the way for a spiritual concept of God, more in line with the Jewish tradition. Both the unknown author of the *Wisdom of Solomon* (first century B.C.E.) and Philo of Alexandria[1a] (*c.* 30 B.C.E.-40 C.E.) are greatly indebted to Posidonius.[2] But in many respects Philo pursues the Platonic trend much more resolutely, and with infinitely deeper appreciation, than Posidonius,[3] and it has been rightly said that he merits the title of "the first Neoplatonist" with greater justification than his Stoic master.[4]

The process of Hellenization—the universal characteristic of the epoch —produced, so far as philosophy is concerned, a frame of mind which was different in Alexandria from what it was in Rome. Whereas the Romans adopted the scientific and "humanist" outlook of Greek philosophy, and regarded themselves, unreservedly, as the disciples of the Greeks,[5] the Alexandrian Jewish writers, and the Orientals in general, were inclined to employ science and philosophy in the service of religion.[6] Cicero, through the mouth of Pontifex C. Aurelius Cato, refuses to be guided in matters of religion by the Stoic philosophers, and accepts his ancestral faith "even without proof."[7] Philo and his Jewish predecessors introduce philosophy into the very heart of religion, and try to uphold the authority of the Bible by claiming that the Greek thinkers were in fact the disciples of Moses.

Analogous claims were made by other Orientals such as the Egyptians and Persians.[8] The Christian Fathers were eager to repeat these claims at a time when they had to defend themselves against attacks from the Neoplatonic pagan philosophers. It was a favorite contention of theirs that Plato had been a disciple of the prophets. According to one particular legend, he had met the prophet Jeremiah during his stay in Egypt and received from him the Mosaic doctrine of monotheism.[9] Eusebius devotes the twelfth book of his *Praeparationes Evangelicae* to proving "the accord of Plato's doctrines with the oracles of the Hebrews."

The theory of the Hebraic origin of Greek philosophy persisted throughout the Middle Ages down to the Cambridge Platonists.[10] It is quoted approvingly by Judah Ha-Levi and alluded to by Maimonides.[11] Its chief historic significance lies in the fact that it enabled Christian thinkers in the early Middle Ages to "admit the pagan Plato to the realm of the *doctrina Christiana.*" It can hardly be assumed that Plato would have achieved the position in Christian thought which Augustine and the School of Chartres assigned to him, without the belief that he had known and used the Scriptures.[12]

At first sight, the attitude of the Hellenistic Jewish writers, who, in addition to absorbing the dominant philosophy of the age, claimed its identity with the "deeper" meaning of the Bible, seems to be a novel one in the history of Jewish thought. In reality, it is in basic accord with the earlier tradition of Jewish Wisdom literature. It exhibits the same pattern of mind, and is in fact the continuation of the older movement on a new level.

There is an unbroken line from the canonical Wisdom literature (Proverbs, Job, Ecclesiastes) to the Wisdom of Ben Sira (about 200 B.C.E.), which the author's grandson translated into Greek shortly after 132 B.C.E., and from that work to the pseudonymous Wisdom of Solomon, which was produced a little later by a Diaspora Jew of Alexandria. While Ben Sira shows no trace of philosophic influence, the Wisdom of Solomon is considerably influenced by Posidonius's *Protreptikus*.[13] It thus represents the historic link between the earlier Hebrew Wisdom movement and Hellenistic Jewish philosophy.

The pattern of thought, which underlies the whole of postbiblical Wisdom literature, is best described as a persistent effort to equate Torah and Wisdom. Whereas the canonical writers make no attempt to interpret Wisdom (*Hokmah*)[13a] in terms of specifically Jewish religious teachings and observances—their concept of Wisdom has rightly been defined as belonging to an essentially "humanist" tradition—Ben Sira[13b] is the first to affirm the identity of Torah and *Hokmah*. When the Divine Wisdom was seeking for a place on earth where she might alight and make her home, God directed her to the Temple in Jerusalem (Ecclus. 14:9-12). "Divine wisdom and the Law are coextensive and coeternal." The national possession of Israel is "a universally and eternally valid expression of truth, because it is the word of the only God, the Creator of all."[14] The same equation occurs in the Wisdom of Solomon[14a] and the Book of Baruch (probably written after 70 C.E.), and pervades the whole of Rabbinic Torah mysticism. It underlies as a preformed structural pattern the thought of Philo as well. In endeavoring to discover the sum total of Greek wisdom in the Bible, Philo merely applies the principle that the Wisdom literature had firmly established, namely, that of the identity of Torah and Wisdom. It is a natural corollary of this theory that any true wisdom found in the possession of the heathens must derive from the Bible.

The fusion of the two streams of Greek and Jewish tradition, which characterizes Hellenistic Jewish philosophy, has its *raison d'être* not merely in the particular frame of mind just described, but also in the fact that there existed certain affinities of outlook which suggested spiritual kinship. The stern rejection, from Xenophanes onward, of Homeric mythology and anthropomorphism in the Greek philosophical schools (except the Epicureans) is relative to this point. It had found classical expression in Plato's *Republic*, which banishes mythology, chiefly on account of its unethical character.[15] The tradition is upheld by the Stoa. The older school had endeavored to bridge the gulf between philosophy and mythology by employing the method of allegorical interpretation. The younger Stoa, from Panaetius onward, rejected mythology altogether. In Posidonius's telling phrase, which Augustine was to quote almost verbally, "Homer is to blame because he ascribed human qualities to the gods rather than derive divine excellencies upon man."[16] The Septuagint does not attempt to introduce philosophic concepts into its rendering of the biblical text. But it meticulously seeks to avoid anthropomorphism.[17] Aristobulus first offered allegorical interpretations of difficult passages in the Bible, and Philo follows in this tradition. His contempt of mythology is derived as much from Platonic-Stoic "enlightenment" as from the scorn which the biblical writers pour on the false pagan gods. The very term "mythology," which for Plato still retained an air of solemnity,[18] is used by him as synonymous with fancy, lie and falsehood.[19] Whereas the Stoics could afford to criticize the allegorization of myths,[20] Philo, to whom the Bible possesses undisputed authority as a divinely inspired Book, is compelled to allegorize at least those passages which, in their literal sense, appear mythical.

Another aspect which Judaism and certain trends in Greek philosophy had in common was the notion of the "moral God." As Werner Jaeger has shown, there are many facets in Plato's approach to the Divine; but primarily it is the Socratic, *i.e.*, ethical, approach: What is the nature and unity of virtue? His answer is: The divine Good, the "measure of all things." The philosopher's life thus becomes an assimilation to the Divine standard, *Imitatio Dei*.[21]

The same can be said of the Stoic ideal of the Wise, which places the practice of virtue above theoretical knowledge, and teaches that following the "unwritten law" of nature is tantamount to following God. The younger Stoa had emphasized the need for training in the arts and sciences (the so-called "Encyclical Studies"), but, as Seneca made it clear, they were not ends in themselves but steppingstones to a virtuous life.[22]

The moral character of this teaching must have struck Hellenistic Jews —and, no doubt, Palestinian Jews as well—as fundamentally akin to Judaism. The Rabbinic *Ethics of the Fathers*, and Jewish ethics in general, though not appreciably influenced by Stoic moral philosophy, show indeed many affinities in both thought and expression.[23] Philo shows himself keenly aware of this spiritual kinship. A large proportion of his philosophy is taken up by the concept of the Wise and its implications. In one of his earliest treatises he elaborates the famous Stoic paradoxes which declare the wise to be the only free, rich, noble and beautiful. He is emphatic that the Encyclical Studies are not ends in themselves, but preliminaries to virtue, "the greatest of all themes." Like the Stoics, he describes them as "handmaids" of philosophy.[24] He accepts the Platonic-Stoic doctrine of the Four Virtues,[25] but, characteristically, adds two more, piety and humanity.[26] Of great significance to him is the notion of Natural Law. He sees in the biblical figures of the Patriarchs living embodiments of that Law, and the legislation of the Torah is to him the unfolding, in all essential details, of its principles.[27] Moreover, the "ideal state," which

Plato had outlined in his *Republic* and *Laws,* he considers to be realized in the shape of the Mosaic legislation. Here he is in complete agreement with the sentiments expressed in the *Letter of Aristeas* and in Josephus's *Antiquities.*[28]

Finally, the Platonic-Stoic belief in Divine Providence as a benevolent and just power must have impressed Hellenistic Jews as yet another evidence of spiritual kinship with Judaism. Cicero makes the point that Divine beatitude is incompatible with idleness, and Seneca in his treatise *On Providence* seeks to prove the just rulership of Divine Reason in the world. It was this belief which formed one of the main planks of the Stoic doctrine *vis-à-vis* the Epicureans, who considered the gods "a privileged class of society in the universe, yet powerless to interfere with the scheme of things."[29] In Plato's *Laws* the gods are represented as sternly just rulers of the cosmos like earthly rulers, steersmen, and guards, and the same metaphors reappear in Stoic theology. Philo, both as a Stoic and as a Jew, is unable to conceive of an idle deity. To ascribe inactivity to God is to him tantamount to blasphemy. Many of the expressions he uses in describing God's world-ruling functions are borrowed from the Platonic-Stoic vocabulary.[30]

It is the great achievement of Philo not only to have grasped the essential points of contact between Jewish and Greek thought, but to have created a metaphysical system which combined important elements of the two traditions, and paved the way for Neoplatonism. Moreover, it is due to his transformation of Platonic philosophy that, as we have noted before, "Platonism could be considered as having an affinity with Judaism or with Christianity so that 'Platonic' doctrines could be made to appear as consonant with Scripture, and passages from the Bible could be interpreted in a 'Platonic' sense."[31]

In speaking of God's transcendence, Philo sometimes uses Platonic terms. God is "the measure of all things"; "the Good and Beautiful"; "the best Being"; "the first Good"; "the sun of suns."[32] No doubt, in his interpretation, Plato's Idea of the Good was meant to be identical with God, a view which has since been held by a great many scholars.[33] But Philo seems to outbid Plato when, in other passages, he calls God "better than the Good, purer than the One, and more primordial than the Monad."[34] God's essence is unknowable, and the only statement that can be made of Him is "that He is, not what He is."[35] The biblical phrase (Ex. 3:14), "I am that I am," he interprets to mean "My nature is to be, not to be spoken; no personal name may be properly assigned to the truly Existent."[36] Through him, this verse has become a *locus classicus* for scholastic ontology. He was also the first to interpret in the sense of "negative theology" the biblical passage (Ex. 33:13 ff.) in which Moses implores God to manifest His glory, and receives the answer, "Thou shalt see what is behind Me, but My face thou shalt not see." Philo explains it, like Maimonides after him, by distinguishing between the knowledge of God's "essence" and that of his "actions."[37]

Philo's negative theology is a blend of biblical and Platonic motives. Negative theology is implied in two passages of Plato (*Parm.* 142 A; *Epist.* VII 341 C-D) which, in the Neopythagorean and Neoplatonic school traditions, were understood to refer to the supreme God.[38] The passage in the *Parmenides* reads: "The one cannot have a name or be spoken of, nor can there be any knowledge or perception or opinion of it. It is not named or spoken of, not an object of opinion or of knowledge, not perceived by any being." The similarity of this utterance of Plato's to some of the Philonic passages quoted above is striking enough. Nor is there any difficulty in assuming that the *Parmenides* passage could have served as a starting point for Philo's negative theology, seeing that it reappears with but slight variation in the Neoplatonic treatise of Pseudo-Dionysius Areopagita as characteristic of the Godhead, and has had a decisive influence on the rise of medieval mysticism.[39]

On the other hand, in calling God "better than the Good and purer than the Monad," Philo goes much beyond Plato and the Neopythagoreans. His source appears to be the Jewish prophetic teaching that God is beyond comparison. "To whom will you liken Me, that I should be equal?" (Is. 40:25).[40] Philo never fails to stress the gulf that divides the created from the Uncreated. "God has no likeness even to what is noblest of things born"; "He Himself resembles none of the things which have come into being."[41] He is the absolute, transcendent Being Which, at the same time, fills the world.[42]

The most celebrated of Philo's notions is that of *Logos*. Philo knew Plato's *Timaeus* both from the original and from Posidonius's Commentary. In his own account of creation, he adopts the figure of *demiurge*; but whereas in Plato's cosmology the pattern of Ideas, the model, in whose likeness the world is framed, is independent of the Divine Craftsman, standing as it does in its own right,[43] it now becomes the "thoughts" of the God-Creator. The Ideas become the ideas of God, a concept which can also be found in Seneca,[44] and has played an important part in philosophical speculation from Plotinus down to Augustine, Anselm of Canterbury, the School of Chartres, Malebranche and Kant. As Philo puts it, "When God willed to create this visible world He first fully formed the intelligible world, in order that He might have the use of a pattern wholly God-like and incorporeal. This 'intelligible world,' 'the universe that consisted in ideas' has 'no other location than the Divine Reason which was the Author of this ordered frame.' "[45]

But Philo apparently hesitates to describe the "intelligible world" in terms of "Divine Reason." Since it is but the ideal abstract of the visible world and as such accessible to contemplation and knowledge, it cannot be identical with the Mind of God, Which is assumed to be beyond human approach. Philo, therefore, distinguishes between the hidden mystery of God and the Divine Mind in process of creation. Posidonius had already identified the Platonic *Ideas* with the Stoic *Logos*. Philo goes a step further by placing the Ideas in the Mind of God; but he makes it clear that they represent only God's relation to the world, not His essence. The *Logos* doctrine is thus introduced not so much in order to bridge the gulf between God and the world, as is often asserted, but rather to create that gulf. Philo is emphatic that those who know the *Logos* know only the "Shadow" or "Image" of God; the *Logos* is "the God of the Imperfect," and "those who regard the Image of God, the *Logos*, as His very self are like people who take the gleam of the perihelion for the sun or the halo of the moon for that luminary itself."[46]

Apart from the Stoic and Platonic elements of Philo's *Logos* concept, there is in it also the biblical notion of "angel" as well as a number of mythological features. The figure of "divine man," which goes back to Iranian mythology and plays an important part in Gnosis, is sometimes associated with the *Logos* as the Image of God.[47] Of special significance is the close affinity between the *Logos* and the biblical figure of *Wisdom*,[48] since it illustrates the historic connection between Philo and the ancient Jewish Wisdom literature. The question whether Philo's *Logos* may have derived from the biblical notion of the "Word of God" has been answered in the negative.[49] But occasionally Philo does suggest that the "*Logos of God*" through which the world was made was the "Word of God" in the biblical sense: "God spake and it was done"; "His Word was deed."[50]

Echoing Plato's famous image of the Cave (*Rep.* VII 514 ff.), Philo compares those who are unable to rise to the contemplation of the Ideas to "dwellers in perpetual night" who "disbelieve those who live in the daylight."[51] In terms which are borrowed from the descriptions of Eros in the *Symposium* and *Phaedrus*, he speaks of the "winged and heavenly yearning" for the "Forms of good" when, "smitten by its ideal beauty," the mind follows the archetypal pattern of all virtue and "beholds with ecstasy its most divine loveliness." The mind of the "genuine philosopher" is "borne upward, insatiably enamoured of all holy Natures that dwell on high."[52] Like Plato, Philo sees the motive power of philosophic Eros in the divine nature of the soul. But he gives this thought a biblical turn: the Spirit of God inbreathed into man is the force that calls him up to God. Thus Moses is "called up above" (Lev. 1:1) to behold the archetypes whereas Bezalel merely fashions the "shadows."[53] Moreover, the Platonic concept of Eros is blended with the biblical idea of the Love of God. The "delight in the Lord" (Ps. 37:4) which the Psalmist experiences is interpreted as the "ecstasy of love" and "divine frenzy" which Plato described. But whereas in Plato's view the Eros finds fulfillment only in the vision of the One pure Being to which the Mind, albeit "with difficulty," is able to rise, Philo's Love of God is an end in itself since, belonging to the order of created beings, the soul can only "love God but not behold Him." "With Lovers of God, then, in their quest of the Existent One, even if they never find Him, we rejoice, for the quest of the Good and the Beautiful, even if the goal be missed, is sufficient of itself to give a foretaste of gladness."[54]

Philo approaches the problem of "knowing God" from yet another angle. The younger Stoa had revived the Socratic maxim of "Know thyself" and interpreted the Self as the divine soul, the *daemon* in man. Then it went a stage further: "He who knows himself knows the Divine."[55] Philo gives this trend of thought a Jewish coloring: Self-knowledge reveals man's "nothingness" before God, "and the man who has despaired of himself is beginning to know Him that is."[56] But he also interprets the Socratic-Stoic maxim in a mystical sense. We have to learn "to live in the soul alone"; to migrate from body, sense and even speech in order to find God in the peace of our mind.[57] The Divine Spirit abides only in those who "having disrobed themselves of all created things and of the innermost veil and wrapping of mere opinion, with mind unhampered and naked will come to God." Their symbol is the High Priest who, once a year, in solitude enters the Holy of Holies.[58] In words and images which seem to be directly borrowed from Philo, Plotinus expresses a similar view.[59]

Philo's doctrine of the "knowledge of God" culminates in his theory of prophetic ecstasy. Plato had distinguished between three kinds of "divine frenzy": that of the prophet, the poet, and the philosopher who is transported by Eros.[60] Philo assigns the highest rank to the divine possession "to which the prophets as a class are subject."[61] The phenomenon of ecstasy—he is the first to introduce the term in its technical sense into philosophic literature[62]—can therefore be studied best in the prophet. Philo does not distinguish between the ecstatic character of early Hebrew prophecy (Nebiism) and its classical form.[62a] To him all prophecy, including that of Moses, is ecstatic. It means that "the mind is evicted at the arrival of the divine Spirit."[63] This view seems to be borrowed from Posidonius.[64] But Philo's concept has a depth of its own. Prophetic inspiration he describes as something akin to the mystical experience of illumination from above. In its most elaborate form, this view is expressed in Philo's mystical theory of the "Light Stream" which emanates from God and is perceived by the "Eye of the soul," a theory which is deeply steeped in Greco-Egyptian mythology and cannot be pursued here.[65] But the concept of an illumination from above has its root in Philo's own experience of "inspiration" which he occasionally describes with remarkable psychological insight.[66]

A matter of particular interest is Plotinus's indebtedness to Philo. Whereas it is generally admitted that the forerunners of Plotinus bear unmistakable traces of Philonic influence, scholars have been reluctant to agree that the same is the case with Plotinus himself.[67] Yet this conclusion can hardly be avoided. Numenius, who stands midway between Philo and Plotinus, knew and appreciated Philo's work. It was he who said, "Either Philo platonizes or Plato philonizes." Traces of Jewish doctrines, probably through Philo's mediation, have also been found in Ammonias Saccas, the teacher of Plotinus and Origen, whose personality seems to have impressed itself deeply on his disciples.[68] Origen is decisively influenced by Philo.[69] Should, then, his fellow student, Plotinus, have had no knowledge of the Jewish thinker, as some scholars have ventured to suggest? In fact, H. Guyot's painstaking study has revealed abundant evidence of Plotinus's indebtedness to Philo. Guyot's conclusion is that Plotinus had read Philo and made use of his writings, notwithstanding the fact that he nowhere mentions his name.[70] This view has been endorsed by Fritz Heinemann who sees in Philo the most important factor, next to Plato himself, in the evolution of Neoplatonism.[71]

Philo's share in the development of the Neoplatonic doctrine is matched, if not surpassed, by the influence he has exercised on Christian theology. It is widely assumed that the *Logos* in the Fourth Gospel is indebted to Philo, but it may as well be that we move here in the general atmosphere of nascent Gnosis or are faced merely with a simple and straightforward exegesis of text of Genesis.[72] Philonic influence is, however, clearly attested in patristic literature, both in Greek and in Latin, where Philo is not only an accepted authority in the field of allegorical exegesis, but also highly regarded on account of his *Logos* doctrine. His influence is recognizable as early as in the Apologists of the second century c.e. and gains depth in the Christian Platonists of Alexandria (Clement, Origen). The very preservation of his writings is due to the ample use to which they were put by the Church Fathers who even came to consider their author a convert to Christianity, a legend which was propagated by Eusebius. As late as in the fourth century, St. Ambrose and St. Jerome show close acquaintance with his teachings. So numerous are the echoes and reminiscences of Philo scattered through the writings of St. Ambrose that very often successful attempts have been made to reconstruct from the works of Ambrose the much-corrupted text of Philo.[73] Literal borrowings from Philo have been found in Nemesius of Emesa (*c.* 400), and an analysis of John of Damascus's (d. *c.* 749) famous *De fide orthodoxa* leads to the same result.[74]

The question as to how far Jewish mysticism and philosophy are shaped by the legacy of Philo constitutes one of the most fascinating problems of modern research in the history of Jewish thought. It seems that Philo's influence in this respect is much wider and more effective than previously assumed. A number of Philonic motifs are echoed not only in talmudic and midrashic literature,[75] but, as Samuel Poznański has shown, extend to the Jewish sectarians in Persia and Babylonia in the tenth century c.e. The angel doctrine of Nahawandi (middle of ninth century) and of the Maghariya sect is closely akin to the *Logos* of Philonic tradition. The "Alexandrian" whose writings Karkassani records among the books of the Maghariya is identical with Philo.[76] From these circles the *Logos* concept has traveled to the early Jewish mystics in medieval Germany.[77] Moreover, traces of Philonic influence can be found in the Jewish Neoplatonists of the Middle Ages (Gabirol, Judah Ha-Levi).[78] Seeing that the cabbala is evolved chiefly from Neoplatonic sources—in some measure through the mediation of Gabirol[79]—it can be stated that Philo has a certain share in its evolution. A comparison, moreover, of the basic doctrines of cabbala and Philo's philosophy reveals striking resemblances to which Erwin R. Goodenough has drawn attention. David Neumark's endeavor to reclaim Philo as a Jewish philosopher of considerable influence on Jewish thought[80] has been increasingly vindicated.

2. MEDIEVAL JEWISH PHILOSOPHY

Medieval Jewish philosophy is an offspring of the Arabian culture, which, as a result of the Hellenization of Islam, took its rise under the Abassid caliphs in the ninth century c.e. The fascinating story of the transmission of Greek science and philosophy to the Middle Ages cannot be told here in any detail. Only the salient points need be recalled in order to help us to appreciate the character of medieval Jewish philosophy, and the role it was destined to play in that process of transmission.[1]

At the time when Saadia Gaon[1a] inaugurated medieval Jewish philosophy, the homogeneous unity of the ancient Hellenistic civilization, which had embraced the Middle Eastern and European centers of culture, had ceased to exist. It had broken up into three, more or less distinct, civilizations, *i.e.*, the Latin, Byzantine and Islamic spheres. Of the three, the one least connected with the ancient legacy of Greece was the Latin West. The sources of Greek thought available to Latin readers in the early Middle Ages were, apart from a few translations of original texts, such accounts and casual references as could be found in the works of Latin writers, like Cicero, Seneca, Macrobius and the Latin Fathers. The development of Western thought would have taken a different course had Boethius (*c.* 470-*c.* 525) been allowed to carry out his great project of translating into Latin the whole of Plato's and Aristotle's writings. Unfortunately, his execution by order of Theodoric in 524 deprived the Latin West of an opportunity that was not to recur until the thirteenth century.

The result was that medieval Christian philosophy in the Latin West remained almost exclusively dependent on the Platonic and Neoplatonic traditions which were reinforced by the authority of Augustine, the dominant figure in Latin Christianity. From the end of the Academy (forcibly closed by Justinian in 529) until John Scotus Erigena (*c.* 810-*c.* 877) there is an almost complete gap in the philosophy of the West. From the ninth century onward, the writings of Pseudo-Dionysius Areopagita give a powerful impulse to Latin thought through a series of translations reaching down to the Renaissance period. Scotus Erigena, the first Christian scholastic, bases his thought chiefly on the Neoplatonic mysticism of Pseudo-Dionysius. Then there is a further gap from Scotus to Béranger de Tours (d. 1088) and Anselm of Canterbury (1033-1109). The Christian scholasticism of the thirteenth century (Albertus Magnus, Thomas Aquinas) bears the full impress of the influx of the writings of Aristotle and of the Arabian Commentaries and is greatly indebted to medieval Jewish thought, notably Gabirol and Maimonides.

In Eastern Christianity, the legacy of Greece had remained much more alive than in the Latin West. Synesius, bishop of Ptolemais (*c.* 410), had been brought up in the Neoplatonic School of Alexandria, and Nemesius of Emesa is deeply steeped in Neoplatonic thought. The closing of the Platonic Academy in Athens by Justinian did not disrupt the continuity of the philosophic tradition. Not only did pagan Neoplatonists, such as Simplicius, devote themselves to the writing of learned commentaries on Aristotle—thus following a line of activity which had already been in vogue among earlier members of the school (Plutarch, Syrianus)—but Christian scholars were no less eager to develop the study of Plato's dialogues and Aristotle's lecture courses. John Philoponus (485-555) is outstanding among Christian commentators on Aristotle in the sixth century.

Moreover, Neoplatonism penetrated into Christian theological speculation through the influence of Pseudo-Dionysius Areopagita, a Christian thinker of the school of Proclus (410-485), the great pagan Neoplatonist at Athens. The pious fraud that ascribed the mystical teachings of Proclus's disciple to Paul's convert at Athens (Acts 17:34), facilitated their absorption into Christian thought. John of Damascus, the spokesman of the Eastern Church, shows himself deeply influenced by the negative theology of Pseudo-Dionysius. As he spent part of his life at the Umayyad court, it is probable that through his intermediacy negative theology was transmitted to Islamic and Jewish thought. As has been stressed by Wensinck, a great deal of Stoicism also was absorbed into the rising Islamic and Jewish philosophy through his mediation. The philosophic interest evinced by Christian scholars in Alexandria was shared by the Syriac Church, which sponsored the translation from Greek into Syriac of a large number of Greek pagan and patristic works. It is against this background of the Eastern Christian tradition in the early Middle Ages that the magnificent rise of Islamic culture must be viewed.

The Arab conquest of the Eastern centers of learning did not put an end to the continuity of the ancient civilization. On the contrary, thanks to the remarkable tolerance and generosity displayed by the Islamic rulers, it led to a powerful revival of Greek science and philosophy. Under the patronage of the Caliph Mamun (813-833), a school for translations was established in Bagdad. The Arabic Nestorian Hunain ibn Ishak, the head of the school, was possibly in personal contact with the Byzantine civilization. His excellent knowledge of Greek enabled him to base his translations on the original texts of the manuscripts, of which he possessed a large collection. In the tenth century, when the knowledge of Greek had faded in Arab lands, translations into Arabic were based on Syriac intermediate renderings. A very considerable part of the scientific and philosophic literature of classical and Hellenistic Greek thought down to the Neo-platonists was thus made accessible to the Islamic world. It included complete translations of many of Plato's *Dialogues*; Galen's *Synopsis of Plato*; practically the whole corpus of Aristotle's writings, together with their more important commentators; over a hundred medical and philosophic works of Galen; several Plato commentaries by Proclus, and parts of Porphyry's *History of Philosophy*.

Then there are two outstanding Neoplatonic works which made their reappearance in disguise: the "Theologia Aristotelis," a Syrian forgery, which is a recast of the last portion of Plotinus's *Enneads*; and the "Book on the Pure Goodness" (*Liber de causis*), which is based on Proclus's *Elements of Theology*.

It was inevitable that the acquisition of this vast treasure of Greek thought should initiate a period of profound scientific and philosophic activity. While the Latin West was confined to a small segment of the Greek legacy, the Islamic world, being in almost complete possession of the ancient tradition, assumed the leadership in the cultural sphere. The Jews living under Islamic rule took a prominent part in all branches of science,[2] and soon evolved a philosophic movement of their own, which persisted throughout the Middle Ages and reached down into the Renaissance period.

For nine centuries—from Philo to Saadia (882-942)—Jewish philosophic activity had ceased. Alexandrian Jewry had lost its creative impulse, and the Academies of Palestine and Babylonia felt little inclination toward philosophy;[3] only faint traces of Platonic, Neopythagorean and Stoic thought, probably through the intermediacy of Philo, can be found in talmudic and midrashic literature. Even so, they proved to be of some importance for the subsequent evolution of medieval Jewish philosophy. But they do not represent any philosophic effort. What there existed of speculative endeavor in the religious field was attracted by Gnostic thought, the influence of which is reflected in apocalyptic literature, scattered talmudic and midrashic references, the ecstatic hymnology of *Hekalot* mysticism and kindred mystical tracts.[4]

The first systematic treatise of Jewish mysticism is the *Sefer Yezirah* (Book of Creation)—written probably between the third and sixth centuries —which approaches the problem of cosmology from a background of "late Hellenistic, perhaps even late Neoplatonic mathematical mysticism" combined with Rabbinic *Merkaba* speculation.[5] In the view of Leo Baeck, the book is a Jewish version of Proclus's Neoplatonic philosophy and, in a way, a Jewish parallel, in miniature, to the writings of Pseudo-Dionysius.[6] Whether or not Baeck's thesis is correct—G. G. Scholem doubts it[7]—the *Sefer Yezirah* seems to have originated from some Neoplatonic or Neopythagorean source, as is evidenced by the terminology employed; it suggests, as Scholem points out, a paraphrase of some Greek text.[8] When Jewish philosophy re-emerged in the tenth century, the authority of the book, which claimed the Patriarch Abraham as its author, was already established. The first literary attempt of the newly awakened philosophic impulse is Saadia's Commentary on the *Sefer Yezirah* (931 C.E.). It would, however, be mistaken to infer from this fact that medieval Jewish philosophy inherited the Gnostic and mystical traditions of the period intermediate between Philo and Saadia as an essential feature of its character. These traditions play some part in medieval Jewish thought, particularly when they are reinforced by similar trends in the Islamic tradition, but, on the whole, medieval Jewish philosophy is cast in a rationalistic mold.

The rationalistic bent of medieval Jewish philosophy is largely inspired by the intellectual climate of Islamic thought, but has a temper and quality of its own which derives from the rational character inherent in the Jewish religion. It must also be borne in mind that many of the problems with which Islamic religious philosophy was confronted for the first time as a result of the influx of Greek thought were not entirely new to Jewish thinkers. Judaism had already faced them, in some measure, at a previous stage in the history of Jewish thought, when it had its first experience of the Hellenistic civilization. The process of rationalization through which Islam was passing had long before left its impress on the body of Jewish thought. Thus, the nature of the Law—a problem on which the Arabian theologians fought violent battles—is defined by Saadia in accordance with an earlier talmudic distinction between rational and revelational laws, a distinction which clearly reflects the Greek concept of the Written and Unwritten Laws. Another instance is the "purification of the idea of God," which had, in Judaism, already resulted in the Philonic and targumic avoidance of anthropomorphic references to God. Here and in many other fields of speculation, medieval Jewish philosophy had only to link up with the Jewish theological tradition.[9] Moreover, the "humanist" element preserved in the canonical Wisdom literature offered some authoritative basis for speculative thought.

In its initial phase, medieval Jewish thought is not yet committed to any particular philosophic system, but reflects, with rational theology as its focal point, the influence of the various schools of Greek philosophy that had become known through the fresh translations. Its Arabic model is the movement of Kalam, which had been stimulated, to some extent, by the theological discussions in the Eastern Church, particularly by John of Damascus. As M. Schreiner has emphasized, some credit for the rise of Kalam is due to the influence of Jewish thought.[10] Through the intermediacy of Origen, the legacy of Philo plays a not inconsiderable part in the development of Kalam. As has been pointed out, John of Damascus preserved a great deal of Philonic thought. The word "Kalam" denotes, in the first place, speech, and later assumed the meaning of dogmatic theology; it is, however, significant, as Wensinck points out, that the *mutakallimun* (speakers, disputants) were by their very name characterized not as theologians but as rationalists and philosophers, which is a clear indication of the rationalistic direction that Islamic theology took from its inception.[11]

Saadia Gaon, the outstanding representative of Jewish Kalam,[11a] follows in his *Book of Doctrines and Beliefs* the lead of the Mutazilite wing of Kalam, with which the movement of Islamic Kalam gradually came to be identified. But unlike some of the Karaite[11b] adherents of Kalam (Josef al-Bassir, Joshua ben Yehudah) he is not merely a Mutazilite clothed in a Jewish garb. His dependence on the Mutazila, though far from inconsiderable, has often been overstated. He freely employs Platonic, Aristotelian, Stoic, and Neoplatonic elements of thought as they suit his trend of argument. He shows himself intimately acquainted not only with Greek philosophy, but also with Gnostic schools, Indian thought, and Christian theology. Despite his eclecticism, Saadia was able to give a powerful lead to subsequent Jewish philosophy, and to imbue it with the rationalistic and "humanist" traditions that he had absorbed through his invigorating experience of the rising Islamic culture, nowhere struggling harder to find its true expression than in the bewildering atmosphere of Bagdad in the tenth century with its immense variety of religious sects and philosophic schools.[12]

Saadia emphatically states that the doctrines of the Jewish religion can be verified by rational inquiry. There is, in his view, no conflict between Reason and Revelation. Speculative reason is able to work out, by its own independent effort, the truths of revelation. Yet revelation is necessary for pedagogical reasons. Since the process of rational inquiry involves time and is exposed to error, man has to be guided by the authority of revelation before he is able to rely on the results of his speculation. But while defending the need for Divine Revelation, Saadia is no less insistent in his demand that man should try to understand rationally what religion teaches him. He implies that the duty of philosophizing is a religious commandment. His distinction between rational and revelational laws in the Torah was accepted by Jewish Kalam philosophers and Neoplatonists such as Josef ibn Saddik. It was rejected, on Aristotelian grounds, by Maimonides, but has been of considerable importance for the evolution of the doctrine of natural law. Its identification of natural and rational law, which goes back to the Stoa, is upheld by Thomas Aquinas and Hugo Grotius.

Saadia's arguments for Creation, which are deduced from the principles of Aristotelian physics, follow the Kalam. By refuting the various cosmologies in vogue at his time and by stressing the significance of the biblical concept of *Creatio ex nihilo*, he clearly showed the incompatibility, at this vital point, of Jewish and Platonic-Aristotelian thought. His viewpoint was adopted by practically all Jewish philosophers in the Middle Ages.

Equally important is his doctrine of the Divine attributes. The conception of God as Creator implies the three attributes of Life, Power and Wisdom, which are not separate aspects of the Divine Essence, such as the Christian notion of trinity suggests, but really one and identical with the essence of God.

The philosophy of Kalam remained the guiding star for Oriental Jewry. Samuel ben Hofni (d. 1013),[12*] Gaon of the Academy of Sura (Babylonia) like Saadia, is deeply influenced by Kalam. The same applies to Nissim ben Jacob, of Kairouan in North Africa, and to a lesser degree to Hai Gaon (d. 1038), the last rector of the Academy of Pumbedita (Babylonia).

The Karaites, in particular, follow in their theology the pattern of Kalam in its Mutazilite form. As late as in the fourteenth century Karaite Kalam is still prevalent, and reaches its culminating point in Aaron ben Elijah, whose work, *Tree of Life*—written in 1346—attacks Maimonides from the standpoint of Kalam.[13] It may be noted that the Latin West became acquainted with Islamic Kalam chiefly through the account given of it by Maimonides, who strongly rejects its principles and method of argument. Leibnitz, *e.g.*, knew the Kalam theory of continuous creation from Maimonides's *Guide*. In his (unpublished) dialogue, *Pacidius Phillethes seu prima de motu philosophia*, a Mutakallimun appears at the end of the discussion, a hymn in praise of God's continuous creation.[14]

The second phase of medieval Jewish philosophy is characterized by the influence of the Islamic tradition of Neoplatonism, and by al-Kindi's, al-Farabi's and Avicenna's attempts to combine it with Aristotelianism. As Renan has shown, Aristotle's authority dates from the last phase of Neoplatonism when, after the closing of the Academy, the Neoplatonic professors devoted themselves almost exclusively to the study of Plato's great disciple.[15] They tried to prove his concord with Plato, and this tradition is followed by al-Kindi and al-Farabi. The former, in his *Liber de intellectu*, pretends to discuss the intellect "secundum sententiam Platonis et Aristotelis"; and one of the latter's works is entitled *Concordance of Plato and Aristotle*.[16] This tendency is not confined to the medieval Islamic tradition, but is also characteristic of early Latin thought; Boethius intended to show the essential concord between Plato and Aristotle.[17]

A recent discovery, by M. Guidi and R. Walzer, of an Introduction to Aristotle by al-Kindi[18] has thrown some light on his ultimate Greek source. He is, as Walzer suggests,[19] apparently nearer to some Christian variant of Proclus's Athenian Neoplatonic school than to the Neoplatonic Christian school of Alexandria, with which al-Farabi, and through him Averroës, are ultimately connected. The introduction of Divine Revelation into an otherwise predominantly Aristotelian system of thought constitutes the main evidence for the link between al-Kindi and Proclus. There are parallels to al-Kindi's theology in Christian theologians like John of Damascus. Al-Farabi, on the other hand, had his immediate spiritual ancestors in Alexandria and is obviously nearer to classical Greek philosophy than al-Kindi. Walzer assumes his ultimate Greek source to be the Christian Neoplatonist, Synesius, who tried to reconcile philosophy and Christian faith by interpreting the dogma as "a sacred and mysterious allegory," which the philosopher need not take too seriously; he held himself free to "be a priest, fond of wisdom at home and fond of myths outdoors." His belief in the supremacy of philosophy as the final arbiter over the truths of revelation makes him indeed a forerunner of Averroës through the intermediacy of al-Farabi. Saadia, though a contemporary of al-Farabi (d. 950), is not yet touched by the Neoplatonic Aristotelianism of the Islamic thinker, nor should it be possible to derive his thought from the influence of al-Kindi.

The first Neoplatonist in medieval Jewish philosophy is Isaac ben Solomon Israeli (*c.* 850-950), whose *Book of Elements* and *Book of Definitions*—both preserved in Hebrew and Latin translations, the Arabic originals having been lost—are largely inspired by Aristotle and Galen. His definition of philosophy as *imitatio dei* follows the Neoplatonic commentators of Aristotle, and may have been adopted under the influence of Nemesius.[20] In medieval Jewish philosophy Israeli's reputation as a philosopher was considerably less than his fame as an author of medical writings. Christian Schoolmen were, however, impressed by his importance as a philosopher as well.

Of great significance in the history of both Jewish and Christian medieval thought is Solomon ibn Gabirol[20a] (*c.* 1020-1050, possibly 1070), the first Jewish philosopher in Spain. His writings became known to the Latin world through the translation of the *Mekor Hayyim (Fons Vitae)*[20b] by Dominicus Gundissalinus in collaboration with Avendeath, a baptized Jew of Toledo (*c.* 1090-*c.* 1165). Owing to the corruption of Gabirol's name into Avicebron or Avicembrol, he was considered by the Scholastics to have been a Christian. His philosophy is less faithful to Aristotle than al-Kindi's, al-Farabi's, and Avicenna's, and makes an original attempt to break the dualism inherent in the Aristotelian concept of the universe. Its key notions are the unity of matter as the common element subsistent to all being and the concept of form as the principle of differentiation. Fundamentally, there is no gulf between the spiritual and the material since both share in the same matter. All created beings, including the angels, are composed of matter and form. From the Will of God proceeds the dynamic activity of form and from His essence the element of matter.

Gabirol's Neoplatonism is derived chiefly from Plotinus and Proclus, most probably also from Philo. His position in the world of Arabian and Jewish thought has been rightly compared to that of Duns Scotus in Latin Scholasticism.[21] His work exercised a profound influence on the Schoolmen of the thirteenth and fourteenth centuries, notably on Albertus Magnus and Duns Scotus.[22] It also influenced Jewish Neoplatonists like Abraham ibn Ezra (*c.* 1092-1167) and the Jewish mystics of Gerona in the thirteenth century.[23] His great hymn, *The Royal Crown*, which expresses the essence of his philosophy in the language of religious exaltation has found its way into the Jewish liturgy.

The most popular of medieval Jewish thinkers is the Neoplatonist Bahya ben Joseph ibn Pakudah whose book *The Duties of the Heart* (written between 1080 and 1090) has become the standard work of Jewish moral philosophy. The "duties of the heart," such as sincerity of faith, humility, and love of God, should inspire the "duties of the limbs," *i.e.*, the ceremonial observances. There is a sprinkling of asceticism in Bahya's ideal of the devotional life, which is due to the influence of Islamic mysticism and has its ultimate source, as I. Heinemann has shown,[24] in Hermetic literature. The much-debated question as to whether or not Bahya was influenced by al-Ghazzali (1059-1111), the great Islamic philosopher and mystic, seems to be decided in the negative. The passages which Bahya has in common with al-Ghazzali are based on an earlier Christian source, as has been evidenced by D. H. Baneth.[25]

The influence of Islamic mysticism, chiefly in the form given to it by the "Faithful Brethren" of Basra, is also pronounced in the treatise *On the Nature of the Soul*, which has been wrongly attributed to Bahya, and probably belongs to about the same period. In describing the descent of the soul through the celestial spheres and zones of elements until it reaches earth and enters the body, the book shows itself to be strongly influenced by Gnostic sources, especially of Hermetic origin.[26] Similar views were expressed, within the orbit of Latin thought, by Macrobius in his Commentary on the *Somnium Scipionis* (third-fourth century).[27]

Abraham bar Hiyya, of Barcelona (beginning of the twelfth century), the first medieval Jewish philosopher who wrote his works in Hebrew, adopts the usual Neoplatonic triad of World, Soul, and Intellect, but adds to it two more stages, *i.e.*, the Worlds of Light and Dominion (Speech). The latter is possibly a variant of the *Logos*, as Julius Guttmann has suggested.[28]

Of great interest is Abraham bar Hiyya's attempt to establish a Jewish philosophy of history, which goes back for its sources to talmudic, Gnostic, Christian, and Islamic concepts. The periods of the world historic process correspond to the seven days of Creation; man's corruption through the fall of Adam has been remedied in one particular line of the descendants of the First Man, *i.e.*, the "chosen people" of Israel, in whom the rational soul is preserved in its original purity.[29] This concept is decisively influenced by the Islamic version of the Gnostic Anthropos myth, and has been adopted by Judah Ha-Levi.[30]

Joseph ibn Saddik (d. 1149) combines Neoplatonic, Aristotelian and Mutazilite teachings in his *Microcosm*, which may have been inspired by Nemesius of Emesa, the Christian Neoplatonist of the fifth century.[31]

Judah Ha-Levi, the celebrated poet[31a] and thinker (*c.* 1085-*c.* 1141), is hardly a Neoplatonist in the strict sense, and could be termed a Jewish follower of Kalam with some justification. Like al-Ghazzali, his Islamic counterpart and model, he seems to have passed through a more or less radically philosophic phase, from which he emerged as a mystic and theologian rather than a philosopher.[32] His famous dialogue, *Kuzari*, is a glowing tribute to Judaism. It bears, in the Arabic original, the title *Book of Arguments and Proofs in Defense of the Despised Religion*, and is almost contemporary with Abelard's *Dialogue between a Jew, a philosopher, and a Christian* (written about 1141). Judah Ha-Levi, like al-Ghazzali, places the intuitive knowledge of the prophet above the speculative knowledge of the philosopher. The "God of Aristotle" is the God of rational theology, a mere "First Cause"; the "God of Abraham" is the personal, living God of religious experience, the God of revelation. The prophet is endowed with a suprarational disposition which enables him to reach the "angelic" stage, and to commune with God.

It appears that at about the middle of the twelfth century the Aristotelian component of Jewish Neoplatonism became predominant, a tendency which Judah Ha-Levi's attack upon Aristotelianism was intended to combat. The first work, in which the new trend of thought found expression, Abraham ibn Daud's *The Exalted Faith*, did not appear until a few decades after *Kuzari*. But, as Julius Guttmann surmises, Judah Ha-Levi's polemic

A PAGE FROM THE *Guide to the Perplexed* OF MAIMONIDES

The first draft in the author's handwriting in the original Arabic, Part I, Chapter III, a discussion of two biblical terms and their theological implications.

This fragment, from the Geniza manuscripts in the Elkan N. Adler Collection of The Library of The Jewish Theological Seminary of America, was identified by Morris Lutzki. (Together with other Maimonides autographs, it is included by him in the *Alexander Marx Jubilee Volume.*)

would have been pointless if the new trend toward a more consistent Aristotelianism had not been fairly strong as early as in his day.[33] It is no easy matter to draw a hard and fast line to demarcate the new Aristotelianism from the earlier type of Neoplatonism, which had also been shot through with Aristotelian elements. Both Abraham ibn Daud and Maimonides, who represent the new phase of development, still contain a great deal of Neoplatonism, if this term is at all permissible in denoting the peculiar character of early medieval thought. Raymond Klibansky has made the point that the medieval Platonic tradition as a whole is much too complex to be described indiscriminately as either Platonism, as was formerly, or Neoplatonism, as is now the rule.[34] It is much easier to distinguish between the Neoplatonic Aristotelianism of Abraham ibn Daud and Maimonides, on the one hand, and the strict Aristotelianism of Averroës, on the other.

Although Maimonides (1135-1204) was a younger contemporary of Averroës, there is no evidence that Maimonides was acquainted with the works of the Islamic philosopher at the time when he wrote the *Guide of the Perplexed*.[34a] He mentions Averroës at some later date in a letter to Samuel ibn Tibbon, but from Maimonides's previous silence it appears that the *Guide* was written "in complete ignorance of the works of Averroës." Moreover, "on all the points at issue between Avicenna and Averroës, Maimonides follows the views of the former and restates them without the slightest suggestion of his knowledge of the views of the latter."[35]

Maimonides, like his predecessor, Abraham ibn Daud (d. *c.* 1180) recognizes in Aristotle the principal philosophic authority. His proofs for the existence of God follow the Aristotelian pattern. In addition, he develops an argument, first suggested by Avicenna, which postulates, on logical grounds, a necessary being whose existence follows from its essence, and is transcendent to all contingent being. This necessary being is an absolute unity. Following the Neoplatonic tradition of "negative theology," Maimonides explains in his famous doctrine of attributes that no positive statement, except that of existence, can be made of God. Two kinds of attributes only are admitted, those of "negation," which exclude imperfections from God, and those of "action," which describe His relation to the world. The latter, which include God's moral attributes, matter most from the aspect of religion. Maimonides's conflict with Aristotle concerns the problem of Creation. The alternative between the Aristotelian doctrine of the eternity of the world and the Jewish concept of *Creatio ex nihilo* is tantamount to the choice between an impersonal God, from Whom the world emanates by necessity, and a personal God, endowed with will, Who creates the world freely. Neither of these doctrines can be rationally demonstrated, and the decision is therefore to be left to the authority of prophecy. Maimonides argues against Aristotle that the law of causal necessity which operates within the created world does not apply prior to creation. God remains in control of the physical laws of nature. The possibility of miracles is thus safeguarded, but Maimonides tends to allegorize the miracles narrated in the Bible.

The core of Maimonides's philosophy is his theory of prophecy. The prophet is superior to the philosopher, but not, as Ha-Levi had it, on account of a suprarational disposition. There exists no faculty higher than the rational, but as a result of supreme intellectual training and moral conduct a person whose mind is concentrated on "God and the angels" may receive flashes of intuition, which illumine both the rational and imaginative faculties of his soul and give it insight into metaphysical truths denied to the discursive thinking of the ordinary philosopher. The over-powering vision of the prophet requires for its expression the use of symbolic images. Hence the pictorial character of prophetic speech and the necessity to interpret it allegorically. In addition to being a perfect phi-losopher, the prophet is also the lawgiver of the ideal state, and thus represents Maimonides's version of Plato's "philosopher-king," following the precedent of al-Farabi and, ultimately, of Philo.

Maimonides's *Guide*, the most important work of Jewish philosophy, achieved a notable synthesis of Judaism and Neoplatonic Aristotelianism. It exercised a powerful influence on Jewish philosophic thought and, to some extent, also on Jewish mysticism (Abraham Abulafia),[36] although Maimonides's treatment of cosmology and theology hardly contains the mystic themes attributed to it in cabbalistic thought.[37] Through its popular presentation in his famous code (*Mishne Torah*),[37a] the essential outline of Maimonides's philosophy became accessible to large sections of the community. His statement of the "Thirteen Principles" of the Jewish faith,[37b] formulated in his Commentary on the Mishna, was the first attempt of its kind and gave rise to a prolonged discussion. It soon found its way into the Daily Prayer Book. Of considerable importance is Maimonides's influence on the Christian Schoolmen of the thirteenth century (Albertus Magnus, Thomas Aquinas, Duns Scotus).[38]

The last phase of medieval Jewish philosophy is dominated by the more radical Aristotelianism of Averroës. Maimonides's endeavor to bridge the gulf between Aristotle and the Bible by whittling down their differences had not won the day, as is evidenced by the embittered controversy that divided Jewry during the thirteenth century.[39] In the end, the orthodox opponents of Maimonides helped to swell the rising cabbalistic movement, while the rationalists accepted the lead of Averroës.

The Jewish struggle over the legacy of Maimonides's rationalism is, in a way, an echo of the great controversy that had arisen in the Christian world of the Latin West.[40] There had grown up in the university of Paris a school of Averroists, whose philosophic doctrines were considered to be contrary to the teaching of the Church. It was Thomas Aquinas's endeavor to vindicate the truths of Christianity against heretical teachings of the Averroists, and Maimonides furnished him, in some respect, with the methods to be employed in achieving a synthesis between Aristotle and the Bible. The famous altarpiece by Francesco Traini, in St. Catarina at Pisa, and many similar paintings depict the triumph of Thomas over Averroës, who lies prostrate before the Christian philosopher.[41] Characteristically enough, Averroës wears the Jewish badge upon each shoulder.

There is poetic truth in his presentation as a Jew, seeing that Jewish commentators and translators had a large share in making Averroës known to Latin Christianity. As has been pointed out by Steinschneider, the preservation of Averroës's Commentaries on Aristotle is due almost entirely to Jewish activity. Averroës's popularity among Jews is best illustrated by the fact that of his extensive writings almost all were translated into Hebrew, some of them more than once, and that a host of Hebrew commentaries were written on them.

The influence of Averroës's teachings on Jewish thought varies in degree. Isaac Albalag (thirteenth century) represents, like Siger of Brabant, and John of Jandun on the Christian side, the more extreme form of Averroism, which is known as the doctrine of the double truth. Jewish Averroists of a more moderate outlook are Samuel ibn Tibbon, the translator of Maimonides's *Guide*, and Jacob Anatoli (1194-1256), the chief representative of the Hebrew translators in Sicily, who translated Averroës into Hebrew; Joseph Caspi (1279-*c.* 1340); Hillel ben Samuel of Verona (d. *c.* 1291); Moses ben Joshua of Narbonne (d. 1362); and Judah Messer Leon (fifteenth century).

The outstanding Jewish Averroist of the late medieval period is Levi ben Gerson (Gersonides, 1288-1344), whose *The Wars of the Lord*—by its cabbalistic opponents mockingly called "The Wars against the Lord"[42] —attempts the reconciliation of Judaism and philosophy on a strictly Aristotelian basis. Gersonides abandons the Neoplatonic concept of the unity of God, which excludes positive attributes, and affirms, like Thomas Aquinas, that positive terms may be attributed to God. Creation means that the plurality of forms, which is contained in God, is released and imparted to the *prima materia,* the substratum of becoming. Gersonides thus upholds the concept of creation in Time, but not in the sense of *Creatio ex nihilo.* The activity of God is spent in the act of creation; the governance of the world is regulated by natural causality. Prophecy is knowledge of causal necessity applied to a concrete situation.

The extreme rationalism of the Averroists is made the target of attack by Hasdai ben Abraham Crescas (*c.* 1340-1410), which recalls Judah Ha-Levi's criticism of Neoplatonic Aristotelianism three centuries earlier. Crescas's religious philosophy is based on a *reductio ad absurdum* of

Aristotelian metaphysics as a whole. His critique of Aristotle demolishes such basic Aristotelian notions as Matter, Space and Time, and foreshadows the approaching Renaissance. Pico della Mirandola quotes him extensively, and Spinoza, possibly also Giordano Bruno, are indebted to him. Crescas's demonstration of the infinity of Space and Time renders Aristotle's proof for the existence of God (that of the "Prime Mover") invalid. But even an infinite world requires as its ground a necessary Being. Creation need not be interpreted as an act in Time, but must be understood as *Creatio ex nihilo*. Like Gersonides, Crescas admits positive attributes of God. But God is essentially not a pure intellect; He is essentially pure love. It follows that man achieves communion with God not through knowledge but through love. Prophecy is a result of such communion in love.

Crescas's successors continue more or less the Aristotelian tradition of Jewish philosophy, but the steady deterioration in the political fortunes of Spanish Jewry during the fifteenth century is reflected in a decline of the philosophic spirit and in a trend toward religious dogmatism.

Simon ben Zemah Duran (1361-1444) reverts essentially to the position of Maimonides, and resumes the discussion of "principles" of faith. He reduces them to three, *i.e.*, Existence of God, Revelation, Reward and Punishment, principles which Averroës had declared to be essential to all revealed religion, and from which, in the opinion of Duran, the whole system of Judaism could be derived.

Joseph Albo (d. 1444) makes Duran's triad the basis of an elaborate dogmatic system. His philosophy seeks to harmonize the essential elements of earlier Jewish thought, notably Maimonides and Crescas. In combining Saadia's and Maimonides's views on natural law, he distinguishes between natural, conventional, and divine laws. Hugo Grotius knew his work, and may have derived from it his distinction between rational and revelational laws.

The last great Spanish-Jewish thinker is Don Isaac Abrabanel (1437-1509), whose philosophy marks a complete return to religious dogmatism in the garb of philosophy. In his son, Judah Abrabanel (Leone Ebreo, *c.* 1460-*c.* 1521), the philosophic impulse comes to life again through his contacts with the leaders of the Platonic Academy of Florence. His *Dialoghi d'Amore*[42a] was the most successful philosophic work of the Italian Renaissance, and transmitted its spirit to other countries as well. Medieval philosophy had ignored the aesthetic elements of Plato's philosophy. In Leone's concept of the universe God is the source of both truth and beauty, and the universe a living organism animated by love. Leone's theory of knowledge is essentially Averroistic.[43]

Elijah Delmedigo (1460-1493), another Jewish philosopher of the Italian Renaissance, translated Averroës's writings, at the request of Pico della Mirandola, from Hebrew into Latin. His *Examination of the Faith* strikes a balance between the doctrine of the double truth and the philosophic interpretation of religion, as attempted by Maimonides.[44] Delmedigo is the last Jewish Averroist of importance.

From the thirteenth down to the end of the fifteenth century, Averroism had been the dominating influence in Jewish philosophy, but concurrently, Christian Scholasticism had also begun to exercise some influence on a number of Jewish philosophers, in both Spain and Italy. Hillel of Verona makes ample use of Averroës's refutation by Thomas Aquinas, without, however, following Thomas in his complete rejection of Averroës. Gersonides's scholastic method obviously emulates the procedure in vogue among Christian Scholastics. Certain Christian traits are also unmistakable in Crescas's thought, and Judah Messer Leon, too, exhibits some dependence on Christian Scholasticism. The transition of medieval Jewish philosophy from the Arabian to the Latin sphere of influence is reflected in the abandonment of Arabic in favor of Hebrew as a medium of expression for Jewish philosophy. The replacement of Arabic by Hebrew coincides with the gradual recession of Islam from Spain. A new terminology and style was created in the Hebrew tongue, which proved itself plastic enough to express in lucid and graceful terms the subtle notions and distinctions of philosophic speculation. Harry A. Wolfson has pointed to the interesting fact that Jewish thinkers, especially the commentators, introduced into the study of philosophy an attitude toward texts and a method of interpretation similar to that adoped by Rabbinic scholars toward the Talmud, and continued in the Rabbinic novellae upon the Talmud. The French school of the Tosafists, which began to flourish in the twelfth century, marked the climax of this development in the Middle Ages, and undoubtedly led to the introduction into the philosophic literature of the form of novellae upon standard texts, "resembling the talmudic novellae in their external literary form even to the extent of using the same conventional phrases by which questions and answers are introduced." Crescas's work is an instance of that type of novellae literature in medieval Jewish philosophy.[45]

While medieval Jewish philosophy, in its latest phase, is somewhat indebted to Christian Scholasticism, the latter movement owes a great deal to Jewish philosophic activity, especially to the Jewish translators who helped to make Aristotle and Arabian philosophy accessible to the Latin West. The rediscovery of the lost works of Aristotle, as well as the newly established contacts with the philosophic speculations of Arabians and Jews, revolutionized the outlook of Latin Christianity.[46] The result was the recognition of philosophic truth as independent of Divine Revelation, and the rise of Christian Averroism with its radical separation of philosophy and faith. The new development was made possible chiefly through the translations from the Arabic into Latin, a process in which intermediate Hebrew translations formed an integral part.

One must, however, not underrate the significance of the translations made by Christian scholars in the twelfth and thirteenth centuries from the original Greek into Latin. As Klibansky has emphasized, the intellectual development of the Latin West was not completely unrelated to that of the Greek world. It is most likely that the close political and economic connection between East and West from the earlier Middle Ages was accompanied by a marked influx of Byzantine ideas into the Occident.[47] Thus Greek patristic literature was translated into Latin in the twelfth and thirteenth centuries. The translation of Aristotle's *De anima* from the Greek into Latin is older than the Arabic-Latin one which was made by Michael Scot in 1217. Whereas Thomas of York interprets Aristotle invariably *secundum expositionem Averrois*—following as he does the Arabic-Latin translations—Thomas Aquinas quotes the *exemplaria Graeca*. Most of the Aristotelian works used by him had been rendered from the Greek into Latin, or had been revised, by William of Moerbeke, who had also translated Simplicius's Commentaries on some of Aristotle's works.[48]

But the important activities of the Christian translators, notably William of Moerbeke, Robert Grosseteste, and Gerard of Cremona, were amply supplemented by the works of their Jewish opposite numbers. They were in that age the chief intermediaries between the Islamic and Latin civilizations. A more detailed description of this aspect of medieval Jewish effort has been given by Charles and Dorothea Singer in *The Legacy of Israel*.[49] The motives that prompted Jewish translators were varied. We know of generous Jewish patrons of literature such as Meshullam of Lunel, who was, perhaps, the first medieval Jewish Maecenas of his kind, and of Benveniste ben Solomon ibn Labi (fourteenth century). A number of Christian rulers such as Frederick II, his son Manfred, Robert of Anjou, and Don Pedro III, sponsored translations of Greek, Arabian and Jewish works into Latin. The ultimate motive, however, was, according to Moritz Steinschneider, a genuine interest in the spread of learning,[50] and due credit must be given to the numerous Jewish translators who, through their work, saved many of the literary treasures of the past from oblivion.

3. MEDIEVAL JEWISH PHILOSOPHY IN ITS BEARING ON THE WORLD

The final disintegration of the close-knit unity of medieval Scholasticism must be considered a natural process, seeing that the elements of which it was composed were of a heterogeneous nature. Renaissance and Reformation liberate the religious spirit of the biblical tradition; Machiavelli renews the Roman concept of power; Grotius, Descartes and Spinoza rediscover, on the basis of Stoic thought, the autonomy of reason in the spheres of both practical and theoretical philosophy. This natural process, by which the three principal elements of the Latin civilization break away from their more or less artificial harmonization, has far-reaching effects on the evolution of the modern world. Human energies are set free which for centuries had been harnessed to the labors of subtle reconciliation. The abounding vitality of the Renaissance, which Burckhardt so vividly describes, is a direct result of this release of energy. Important changes take place in the social and political spheres, in the development of commerce and industry. The new discoveries and inventions of the period greatly enhance man's self-consciousness. The individual citizen begins to assert his human rights *vis-à-vis* feudal pressure and ecclesiastic regimentation. The idea of religious tolerance emerges as one of the leading concepts of the modern age.[1, 1a]

It would be idle to pretend that in this complex and universal process, which extends from the Renaissance down to the Enlightenment of the seventeenth and eighteenth centuries, Judaism, or for that matter medieval Jewish thought, played a dominant role. The inferior social and political status of the Jews in the period concerned renders any such assumption meaningless. It would, however, be equally mistaken to ignore the contribution of Judaism, and medieval Jewish philosophy in particular, to the development of the modern outlook. As we shall see, this contribution is marked and has a quality of its own. It assumes considerable depth in the religious field; many of the heterodox movements of the Middle Ages, including the Reformation in its various forms, owe a great deal to Judaism. But Jewish influence extends to the purely philosophical realm as well.

At first sight, it may seem paradoxical to attribute to medieval philosophy any significance for the evolution of modern thought. Are we not justified in contrasting medieval Scholasticism with the free spirit of inquiry that characterizes modern philosophy? In answering this objection, it may be pointed out that, notwithstanding its "modern" outlook, modern philosophy is much more indebted to medieval thought than is commonly realized. It did not, like Minerva, spring full grown—from its father's head—clad in glittering armor, and chanting a triumphant song of victory. Rather, did it arise as a result of a long process, stretching from the Renaissance down to the philosophy of Enlightenment in the eighteenth century. Throughout this period of transition and growth, the medieval legacy was never extinct; on the contrary, it formed the ever-present background of thought and exercised an appreciable influence. How considerably Descartes is shaped by Christian Scholasticism has been demonstrated by Etienne Gilson, and re-emphasized by Jacques Maritain in his fascinating book on Descartes.[2] A parallel case is Spinoza, who is as much heir to medieval Jewish philosophy as Descartes is to Christian. As Manuel Joel, Leon Roth and Harry A. Wolfson have shown—the latter with overwhelming evidence—medieval Hebrew literature is a basic element in Spinoza's thinking.[3]

With Leibnitz, the most erudite man of his century, the position is essentially the same. He is steeped in medieval thought, both Christian and Jewish. We owe to a French baron, A. Foucher de Careil, the publication of two manuscripts by Leibnitz, one containing a précis of, and observations on, Maimonides's *Guide*; the other commenting on a contemporary attempt to harmonize Spinoza and the cabbala.[4] Judging from his opening remarks in the first of the two manuscripts, Leibnitz was very much impressed by the profundity of Maimonides, of whom he says that he was "a distinguished philosopher, mathematician, physician and expositor of Holy Scripture" (*"fuit in philosophia, mathematicis, medica, arte, denique, sacrae scripturae intelligentia insignis"*). His acquaintance with both Maimonides and the cabbala are not without influence on his own philosophy, as Foucher de Careil and, more recently, Joseph Politella have shown.[5] Needless to say, he is even more thoroughly familiar with the Christian Scholastic tradition. In answering John Toland's *Christianity not Mysterious* he reverts to the Scholastic thesis that nothing is allowed in theology which is contrary to reason, but that what is above reason is not therefore excluded.[6]

Spinoza and Leibnitz are by no means isolated instances of medieval Jewish influence on seventeenth-century thought. In 1629 the appearance of Buxtorf's Latin translation of Maimonides's *Guide* (replacing the older translation by Justinian) had given rise to an intensified study of the Jewish philosopher.[7] Leibnitz drew his knowledge of Maimonides from this translation.[8] In addition to Leibnitz, Hugo Grotius, John Selden, Pierre Bayle, John Spencer, and the Cambridge Platonists read Maimonides.[9]

The cabbala, too, exercised considerable influence.[9a] As early as in the Renaissance period, cabbalistic thought had fascinated thinkers like Pico della Mirandola, the first Christian student of the cabbala, at whose suggestion Pope Sixtus IV had arranged the translation into Latin of Recanati's cabbalistic Commentaries on the Pentateuch, and of other works besides.[10] The cabbala held a special attraction for Milton, some of whose most original notions Denis Saurat has traced back to the *Zohar*. Saurat's arguments have been disputed by Martin Alfred Larson, but without venturing to pass a verdict on this very intricate problem it does appear that there is a considerable measure of evidence for Milton's indebtedness to the cabbala.[11] It also seems from Harris Francis Fletcher's work on *Milton's Rabbinical Readings* (Urbana, University of Illinois Press, 1930) that Milton made ample use of Rabbinical commentaries on Scripture.

The role of cabbala in the philosophy of the Cambridge Platonists (Henry More, Cudworth) has not yet been sufficiently clarified.[12] Ernst Cassirer, in his excellent monograph on *The Platonic Renaissance in England and the School of Cambridge* (Berlin, 1932) ignores it entirely, but there can be little doubt that cabbalistic influence was pronounced. On the other hand, one must not be misled by the use of the word "cabbala" in the works of this school, seeing that, *e.g.*, Henry More's *The Defense of the Threefold Cabbala* (London, 1662) lavishly employs that term without offering a single quotation from cabbalistic writings. His philosophy is a curious mixture of Plotinus, patristic thought, Descartes, Rabbinic exegesis and medieval Jewish philosophy. He is familiar with Maimonides, whom he calls "the most rational of all the Jewish Doctors."[13]

Of great significance is Maimonides's influence on John Spencer, whose famous work, *De legibus Hebraeorum ritualibus et eorum rationibus* (first published in Cambridge, 1685) elaborates Maimonides's historical interpretation of the ceremonial laws in the Bible. To the rationalists of the seventeenth century the ceremonial laws appeared most awkward, if not offensive. Spencer is glad to use the historical argument and thus to maintain the "wisdom" of the Divine Lawgiver. Robertson Smith said of Spencer's work that "it created the foundations of the science of comparative religion." As Julius Guttmann remarked, this title to fame can be claimed, in the first place, by Maimonides.[14] The subject excited great interest, which did not abate in the eighteenth and the early nineteenth centuries. Pierre Bayle's review of the second edition of Spencer's work (1688) thoroughly approves of the author's aim to show that one need not resort, for the solution of all difficulties, to the inscrutable Will of God, but could demonstrate the reasonableness of the ceremonial laws of the Bible by reference to historical circumstances.[15] In the eighteenth century, Moses Lowman, the author of *A Rational of the Ritual of the Hebrew Worship; in which the wise designs and usefulness of that Ritual are explain'd, and vindicated from objections* (London, 1748) seeks to apply the "principles of true religion stated by Herbert of Cherbury" to the Mosaic law in order to show "their real virtue and worth," but in fact goes back to Maimonides, whom he calls "the most learned and judicious Hebrew Doctor."[16] He also wrote *A Dissertation on the Civil Government of the Hebrews* (London, 1740).

As late as 1827, James Townley published a book entitled *The Reasons of the Laws of Moses from the "More Nevochim" of Maimonides with notes, dissertations, and a life of the author* (London). It shows how persistent was the interest in Maimonides's interpretation of biblical law. Townley quotes Clavering, bishop of Peterborough, the ardent admirer of Maimonides, who had said, "The memory of Maimonides has hitherto flourished and will continue to flourish forever." His references, in the preface of the book, to earlier publications on the subject, accessible to English readers, again show how deep and widespread was the interest in the discussion that Maimonides had started. He mentions, apart from

Lowman, Fergus's *On the Reasonableness of the Laws of Moses*; Michaelis's *Commentaries on the Laws of Moses* (4 vols., translated from the German by Smith); and Woodward's *On the Wisdom of the Egyptians*, which tries to refute the opinions of John Spencer.[17]

A great deal of medieval Hebrew literature had been translated into Latin, and thus made accessible to a wider public of scholars. As an interesting example we may quote the edition both of the Hebrew original and of its Latin translation of Maimonides's *Hilkot Aboda Zara* under the title *R. Mosis Maimonidae De Idololatria Liber, cum interpretatione Latina & Notis Dionysii Vossii* (Amsterdam, 1641). But it appears that the knowledge of Hebrew among scholars and philosophers was fairly widespread. The humanists of the Renaissance had rediscovered not only the Greek, but also the Hebrew language. In the seventeenth century it was quite fashionable to quote from Hebrew Rabbinic and philosophic literature in the original language. The works of Hugo Grotius and John Selden are steeped in Hebrew learning. The same applies to Paul Fagius, Sebastian Muenster, Joseph Scaliger, John Buxtorf, Wilhelm Schikard and others.[18] Wilhelm Schikard's *Mishpat ham-Melek, Jus Regium Hebraeorum, e Tenebris Rabbinicis erutum & luci donatum* (1625) is another instance of interest in the biblical legislation, and betrays great Hebrew erudition.

Rather significant, from a philosophic point of view, is William Wollaston's *The Religion of Nature Delineated* (London, 1722). The book, whose first two editions appeared anonymously, ran into eight editions, and enjoyed an exceptionally wide circulation. Queen Caroline, who held the author in great esteem, commissioned John Clarke to translate its learned notes with their quotations in Latin, Greek and Hebrew into English. A French translation of the work by Garrigne appeared at The Hague in 1726.[19] This scholarly and well-reasoned book, which shows also great gifts of literary grace, is in very large measure influenced by medieval Jewish philosophy, particularly by Maimonides. The "Religion of Nature" which it advocates is but a replica of Maimonides's negative theology, but makes also ample use of other Jewish writers, such as Saadia, Abraham ibn Ezra, Joseph Albo, and medieval commentators as well as talmudic and midrashic sources. The notes abound in Hebrew quotations side by side with quotations from Plato, Cicero, and Chrysostom; the latter's hatred for the Jews, so violently expressed in his Sermons, did not save him from being cited in close proximity with Jewish writers.

The foregoing literary survey will have made it plausible that acquaintance with medieval Jewish thought in the postmedieval period down to the nineteenth century was significant enough to influence the development of philosophy. The next question we have to answer concerns the nature of that influence.

Wilhelm Dilthey sees the two principal aspects of the evolution of modern thought in what he terms European pantheism, on the one hand, and the idea of a universal, natural religion, on the other. In masterly fashion, he traces the history of European pantheism from Nicholas Cusanus over Giordano Bruno to Spinoza and Hegel, Schelling and Goethe. In even greater detail, he describes the line of development that leads from the "universal theism" of the Renaissance philosophers to the Natural Law School (Grotius and Selden) and the movement of Deism in the seventeenth century, and, further down, to the concept of natural religion in the eighteenth century philosophy of Enlightenment. Dilthey is emphatic that in both these lines of development great influence is exercised by the legacy of Stoic thought which the Renaissance had rediscovered.[20] He may have overrated the role played by the Stoic revival.[21] There can, however, be little doubt that from Francis Petrarch (b. 1304) onward the awakening interest in human character and temperament creates a literature which goes back for its model to the Roman Stoics (Cicero, Seneca, Marcus Aurelius, Epictetus). From Petrarch and the Florentine writers, the movement spreads to Vives, Cardano, Scaliger, Telesio, Montaigne, and reaches its climax in the scientific anthropologies of the seventeenth century.

It is from this literature with its new awareness of the human will and that will's immanent power that the philosophy of the age receives its most stimulating impulse. It strengthens the belief in the moral autonomy of man, and helps to disrupt the Christian dogma of original sin; it stands diametrically opposed to the asceticism and defamation of the body which characterizes the Middle Ages. To live in the full consciousness of power and beauty, to be sensitive to the passions and affections operating in private and political life, this was the overwhelming experience that manifested itself in the new literature on man.[22] It went hand in hand with a pantheistic trend in metaphysics as we meet it in the Platonism of the Florentine Academy. In all this development a great deal of Stoicism asserts itself. It penetrates the Platonism of the age, and communicates to it the monistic and pantheistic tendency of the Stoa. It infuses the spirit of humanism into the general outlook of the period. In a way, the whole movement represents a revival of ancient paganism, all the more pronounced for its rehabilitation of Epicurus. Thinkers such as Giordano Bruno and Laurentius Valla are marked by a decidedly pagan outlook, not to speak of Machiavelli.[23]

But whilst Dilthey is justified in stressing the Stoic and generally pagan background of Renaissance philosophy, it must be pointed out that the transition from the Scholastic philosophy of the Middle Ages to modern thought is not one from Christianity to paganism. The philosophy that emerges as the new European philosophy is still Christian, though shorn of some of the dogmatic elements of Christianity. As Erich Przywara remarked, the absolutist philosophies of the modern age are "de-theologized theologies." Hegel's system cannot be divorced from his theological background.[24] Descartes's rationalism is a kind of secularized Scholasticism,[25] and Spinoza's logical schematism is "shot through and enlivened by a religious awe in presence of the Infinite, which must be traced, not so much to his system and its effect, as to his upbringing in a Jewish family and to a transference to *Deus-substantia* of the psychological attitude that an orthodox Jew would manifest toward the Creator-God of Judaism."[26] Franz Rosenzweig put the position in a nutshell when he said that Descartes, Leibnitz, Kant and Hegel were no longer pagan Greek philosophers, but Christian heretics. In them, a new, postmedieval, synthesis between biblical religion and Greek philosophy is achieved.[27] Our thesis is that this new humanist synthesis is decisively aided and promoted by the influence of medieval Jewish philosophy, in which the humanist trend had been much stronger than in Latin Christianity.

The humanist element, as represented by the Stoic tradition, which the Renaissance rediscovered for the Latin West, had been at the bottom of medieval Jewish philosophy right from its inception. One of the essential differences between Jewish and Christian medieval thought lies in the fact that, while both share in the Neoplatonic and Aristotelian traditions, the Stoic legacy had been much more alive in Judaism than in Latin Christianity. It had remained a potent factor also in the Eastern, Greek Church, as is evidenced by the writings of Clement, Origen, Nemesius of Emesa, and John of Damascus; all of whom are greatly indebted to Philo. It is due to the Philonic heritage that the humanist tradition was much stronger in the Eastern than in the Western Church.[28] John of Damascus seems to have exercised some influence in the rise of Arabian Kalam, and in this way, besides other channels, Stoic notions may have made their entrance into Islamic theology and philosophy.[29] It was S. Horovitz who first drew attention to the Stoic elements in Kalam,[30] and the matter is at present (1946) being further investigated.[31] The evidence available is enough to suggest that Stoicism played a decisive role in the evolution of Islamic philosophy. Medieval Jewish Scholasticism which takes its rise from the Arabian Kalam, bears, from the outset, eloquent testimony to this fact.

That medieval Jewish philosophy is influenced by the pantheistic trend of the Stoa can hardly be denied. We know that the Philonic *Logos* plays some part in Gabirol's and Judah Ha-Levi's thought.[32] The affinity of Philo's *Logos* to the Stoic *Logos* is obvious, and it appears that the pantheistic outlook which informs Gabirol's attack upon Aristotle is inspired not merely by the intrinsically Jewish concept of unity, but by Stoicism as well. Gabirol sees in matter the matrix of all being, both corporeal and spiritual.[33] It is interesting that, while Duns Scotus adopted his notion of *materia universalis*, Roger Bacon rejected it as leading to pantheism.[34] There is some truth in this observation, but remarkably enough, medieval Jewish thinkers such as Abraham ibn Ezra[35] and the mystics of Gerona, showed themselves amenable to this pantheistic trend of thought, which also dominates some of the cabbalistic systems.[36] As Gerhard Scholem remarks, Spinoza could have claimed Moses Cordovero as his spiritual ancestor.[37] It is the Stoic legacy, in addition to its Neoplatonic tradition, that is largely responsible for the monistic outlook of cabbala. Renaissance Neoplatonism differs from original Neoplatonism chiefly on account of the influence of the cabbala. The Renaissance view that matter, the flesh and nature are not a degradation, but an expression of the Divine, is first brought forward by Pico della Mirandola as derived from cabbalistic thought.[38]

In this connection, mention must be made of a further contribution of medieval Jewish philosophy to the emergence of the modern view of the universe. Giordano Bruno rediscovered the infinity of space, and thus helped to lay the foundations of the new European pantheism. He was preceded by Hasdai Crescas (*c.* 1340-1410), whose critique of Aristotle anticipates, in all essentials, the Renaissance view.[39] Crescas's arguments are largely determined by his immanent criticism of the absurdities to which Aristotle's concepts of matter and space lead. But they are also guided by the influence of positive Jewish teaching. He quotes the famous Rabbinic dictum which calls God "the Place of the World,"[40] an utterance which Philo and, following him, John of Damascus, had paraphrased, and which played an important part in cabbala.

Two things are implied in this concept. It breaks with the idea of God's transcendence in a spatial sense, so characteristic of the medieval view of God beyond the spheres; and it gives a new meaning to space as a metaphor for the Infinite. The infinity of God becomes the symbol of space. It is in this sense that Newton understood the Rabbinic utterance that had become known to him through the Cambridge Platonists.[41] His famous phrase which describes space as *sensorium Dei* thus goes back to Jewish influence. Space is no longer a mere attribute of body or motion. Newton's absolute space has since been replaced by Kant's phenomenal space and by the functional space of modern physics, but this development was initiated, or at least heralded, by Crescas's critique of Aristotle, which was extensively quoted by Pico della Mirandola, and probably known to Giordano Bruno.[42]

The Stoic element in medieval Jewish thought is even more pronounced when we come to consider the medieval Jewish contribution toward the development of the Natural Law School and of the modern view of religion. The idea of natural law and natural religion is deeply ingrained in medieval Jewish thought. Saadia declares that human reason is able to work out the truths of revelation, by its own independent effort, provided it avoids the pitfalls of impatience and error. There is no essential difference between the truths of reason and those of revelation. The problem is thus not so much one of reconciliation as one of explaining why revelation is at all necessary. Of his three answers to this question, the most significant is the one which assigns to revelation a pedagogical function; it foreshadows Lessing's theory of revelation as an educational force in the history of the human race.[43] Saadia's view is influenced by the Kalam concept of natural religion (fitra) which, in turn, goes back to Stoic sources, as has been shown by Arent Jan Wensinck. It is reason, divinely implanted in man, that enables him to work out his own salvation.[44]

Saadia's concept of *rational laws* as distinct from *revelational laws* arises from the same consideration.[45] It is adopted not only by the Jewish followers of Kalam, but also by Jewish Neoplatonists like Joseph ibn Saddik.[46] Its rejection by Maimonides is in line with the Aristotelian tradition which reserves the aspect of rationality to theoretical truths only.[47] As Leo Strauss has shown, Judah Ha-Levi, too, admits the existence of a law of reason as the framework of every code, and identifies it with the law of nature. It includes the indispensable minimum of morality required for the preservation of any society, and the demands of natural piety as well.[48] Joseph Albo, toward the close of the medieval period, speaks of "two divine laws existing at the same time," the reference being to the Noachic and Mosaic revelations. With the Talmud he affirms that "The pious of all nations have a share in the world to come."[49] No doubt, the biblical concept of the Noachic laws with its implication of a basic morality common to all mankind greatly facilitated the acceptance by medieval Jewish thinkers of the Stoic notion of natural law.

It is not surprising that the evolution of the idea of natural law and religion in the sixteenth and seventeenth centuries should have followed the Stoic pattern, as Dilthey emphasized, seeing that medieval Jewish philosophy had preserved the Stoic legacy so effectively. It is no mere coincidence that the elaboration of natural law by Grotius and Selden goes hand in hand with biblical exegesis and makes frequent reference to medieval Jewish sources. Grotius quotes Saadia's distinction between rational and revelational laws, but seems to attribute it to Maimonides.[50] He knew Albo, and may have derived his knowledge from that source.[51] What seems to have most impressed both him and Selden is the tolerant outlook implied in the concept of the Noachic law. "Among the Hebrews there were always living some strangers, persons devout and fearing God. . . . These, as the Hebrew Rabbis inform us, were obliged to observe the laws given to Adam and Noah, to abstain from idols and blood, and other things that were prohibited; but not in the same manner to observe the laws peculiar to the Jewish people."[52]

Selden, in the preface to his great work, *De Jure Naturali et Gentium, juxta Disciplinam Ebraeorum, Libri septem* (1665), draws attention to the novelty, introduced by him, of identifying the *Jus Naturale et Gentium* with the Noachic laws. The frontispiece of the book shows a group of bearded men, one of whom, obviously a Jew, wears headgear. The group is assembled round an altar of stone which bears the Hebrew inscription, *Mizvot Bene Noah* ("the commandments for the descendants of Noah"). Two tablets of stone are leaning against the altar, the one containing the First, the other the Second Commandment. The Jew points with his finger to the tablet, on which the words *Lo Yihyeh Leka* ("Thou shalt have no other gods besides Me") are clearly visible. He seems to insist that in addition to the seven Noachic laws the concept of the Unity of God is entitled to universal acceptance.

One may say that the frontispiece chosen by Selden is symbolic of a trend of thought that can be traced throughout the periods of the Renaissance and Enlightenment. The universal theism and, arising from it, the concept of natural religion draw much of their inspiration from Jewish sources. Nicholas Cusanus opens the long and impressive series of humanists who advocate a universal religion of reason. As we shall see, in most of them medieval Jewish thought represents an important element. His adoption of Maimonides's doctrine of negative attributes compels Cusanus to give a new interpretation to the Christian concept of trinity as denoting not the essence, but the activity of God.[53] This transformation of the Christian dogma enables Cusanus to plead for a universal religion; he feels that both Jews and Mohammedans could accept his modified notion of trinity. In his *De pace fidei*, he claims that all religions are essentially one.

Georgios Gemistos Plethon (1385-1450), the spiritual begetter of the Florentine Academy, radically upholds the unity of God, and rejects the doctrine of trinity outright. His concept of the Divine Will is influenced by Gabirol. As Gennadios reports, he was a disciple of the Jew Elissaios. His religion of humanity has many affinities to Judaism.[54] His avowed aim was "the foundation of a universalist theism as a new religion, different from Christianity."[55]

Marsilius Ficinus, the leader of the Florentine Academy, is likewise free from dogmatism, and deeply touched by medieval mysticism, including cabbala. He knew Gabirol, and his concept of love, in which Platonic and biblical motifs are blended, may owe some inspiration to Crescas.[56]

Pico della Mirandola, tutored in medieval Jewish thought by Elijah del Medigo, and introduced into cabbala by Johanan Aleman, sees in cabbala a confirmation of Christianity; but, in fact, little is left of Christian dogmatism in his universalist theory of salvation through knowledge of God.[57]

It is in this atmosphere of humanism that Leone Ebreo, the Jewish Renaissance philosopher, finds his spiritual home. Had he remained in Spain, where Catholic Christianity was firmly entrenched, he would probably, as Carl Gebhardt suggests, have shunned closer contact with the Gentile world. In Italy he entered into an environment that was dominated, not by exclusiveness, but by a keen desire to absorb the humanist ideas of ancient paganism and of Jewish as well as Islamic thought. In his *Dialoghi d'Amore*, the most successful literary work of the Renaissance —it was translated into several languages and transmitted the spirit of the age to the whole of Europe—Leone boldly underlines the fact that he writes as a Jew for the non-Jewish world; something revolutionary, and surely indicative of the new universalism that the Renaissance had created.[58]

In France, Jean Bodin had a deep understanding of Judaism, and a good knowledge of medieval Jewish thought.[59] He lavishly quotes Philo, Saadia, Maimonides and other Jewish thinkers. In 1593 he wrote his *Hetaplomeres* which purports to be a religious disputation in Venice between a Catholic, a Lutheran, a Reformer, a Jew, a Mohammedan, a representative of natural religion, and a pagan universalist. Both Solomon, the Jew, and Toralba, the spokesman of natural religion, do credit to Judaism. Solomon is a full-blooded Jew, convinced of the superiority of Judaism; stressing the unity and incorporeality of God; and placing the emphasis on practical morality rather than on theology. Toralba represents natural religion in terms of the Adamitic and Noachic revelations. He rejects the Christian dogmas of incarnation and trinity. He subscribes to Solomon's objections against the dogma of original sin. Thus, in Bodin's view, Judaism and natural religion go very well together.

It is not clear which of the conflicting religions Bodin accepted for himself. Dilthey thinks that he suspended judgment, and was prepared to recognize the relative truth of each religion, provided it fulfilled the condition of tolerance. Readers of the *Hetaplomeres* in the seventeenth century, however, accused Bodin of being inclined toward Judaism. His treatment of Solomon is indeed exceedingly sympathetic, and Judaism is portrayed as much more consistent than Christianity.[60]

The universal theism of the Renaissance was attacked by the Reformation. Luther vigorously renewed the Christian dogma of original sin and the exclusiveness of the Christian claim to holding the key to salvation. He denounced Erasmus's courageous plea for the freedom and essential goodness of the human will. But the evolution of the modern spirit could no longer be suppressed. The development of modern thought follows in the footsteps, not of Luther, but of Erasmus, Reuchlin, and Sebastian Franck.[61] They are the heralds of the philosophic movements of the seventeenth century; and they are shaped by the legacy of the Renaissance in which so much of the biblical and medieval Jewish heritage had come to life again. From Erasmus there goes a straight line to Coornhert, the great Dutchman who helped to make Holland the home of freedom of conscience and speech; to the heterodox movements of Socinianism and Arminianism, and to the Deists.[62]

Another school of modern speculative theology, which culminates in Friedrich Schleiermacher, arises from the mystical tradition of medieval and Renaissance philosophy,[63] and is also somewhat indebted to medieval Jewish thought, seeing that its spiritual ancestors (Eckhart, Cusanus) were influenced by Maimonides.[64] It is inspired by the same universalist theism which we met in the Renaissance.[65]

The sixteenth and seventeenth centuries are filled by a longing for religious peace and tolerance, for the establishment of natural religion, and for freedom of conscience.[66] But the hopes cherished for the establishment of a universal religion of reason remained unfulfilled. The heterodox movements suffered defeat. The Cambridge Platonists were unable to stem the advance of Puritanism and orthodox Calvinism. Nevertheless, Cassirer assures us, the labors of these thinkers did not remain without result; they paved the way for the "Enlightenment" of the eighteenth century, in which the struggle between Luther and Erasmus was resumed and decided in favor of the latter.[67] The weapons for this struggle had been forged in the seventeenth century. Bayle's Dictionary became the arsenal of the whole philosophy of Enlightenment. Bayle was emphatic that religion was primarily morality, and that the literal sense of the Bible must be discarded if it offends against the moral sense.[68] This seems a modern version of Maimonides's exegetical rule that Scripture must be interpreted in conformity to reason. Bayle knew Maimonides, whose doctrines of free will and providence he quotes.[69] Bayle's work is followed up by Voltaire, who declares that religion is to be judged according to its moralizing influence, and postulates tolerance as "the fundamental claim of reason" and "the very essence of the philosophic spirit."[70]

A similar tendency prevails in English Deism. John Locke attempts to prove the *Reasonableness of Christianity*. Toland's *Christianity not Mysterious* and Tindal's *Christianity as Old as the Creation* make the point that the essential criterion for the genuineness of any revelation is its universality and independence of time and space. Universality belongs to the moral law only. Religion is the knowledge of our moral duties *qua* divine laws. The primacy of practical reason is the guiding principle in all these moralistic interpretations of religion, a tendency which may have been fostered from Jewish sources. Maimonides's negative theology culminates in the idea of God as the Divine standard for man's practical duties. In the famous last chapter of the *Guide*, the "hidden God" of the mystic becomes the "revealed God" of the moralist. We do not know the essence of God, but we know His moral attributes. Ultimately, the God of theology and the God of ethics are one, but as Maimonides's thesis implies, the idea of God as the "moral God" is meaningful in itself. The significance of morality is independent of metaphysics. This separation, in a sense, of ethics from ontology is the first step in a direction which was to be followed by the philosophers of modern Enlightenment down to Kant.

The influence of Deism was decisively broken by Hume's analysis of human nature, which destroyed the rational basis of natural religion. According to Hume, the *raison d'être* of religion is neither logical nor ethical, but psychological; religion arises from the emotional states of hope and fear and other psychic phenomena which lie at the root of even the higher religions. Natural religion has thus to be discarded; what remains is, in the phrase which forms the title of Hume's book, a "Natural History of Religion."[71]

This radical attack upon the rationality of religion did not make its influence felt during the eighteenth century; least of all in Germany, where the influence of Leibnitz's harmonizing tendency prevailed. It left room for the claims of both reason and revelation. Leibnitz, as we have noted before, knew and admired Maimonides, whose synthesis of faith and reason he must have felt to be akin to his own trend of thought.

Moses Mendelssohn follows in the footsteps of Leibnitz. The basic ideas of religion—the existence of a personal God and the immortality of the individual soul—are universal possessions of mankind by dint of their reasonableness. They need not wait for revelation to be announced, since they are manifest at all times and everywhere. In his famous phrase, Judaism is not a revealed religion, but a revealed law. Mendelssohn's importance as an apostle of tolerance in the eighteenth century is considerable, and enhanced by his friendship with Lessing, who essentially shared his outlook. The difference between him and Lessing concerns the nature of reason in relation to history. Mendelssohn believes in the constancy and immutability of reason; Lessing holds it to be dynamic, not static. It is only in the historical process that the fullness of reason manifests itself. Man's failures are necessitated by the dialectic nature of the historical process, and it is for this reason that we must be tolerant and sympathetic toward them.[72]

While Lessing is heir to the humanist tradition and a herald of Hegel, Mendelssohn is in intimate touch with both the humanist tradition and the legacy of medieval Jewish thought, particularly Maimonides. It is a testimony to the persistence of Maimonides's influence that Moses Mendelssohn could consider himself a disciple both of the medieval Jewish thinker and of the rationalists of his period. An interval of almost three centuries separates Mendelssohn from the close of medieval Jewish philosophy. During that long interval Jewish philosophic activity had almost completely ceased. Yet when, after this period of silence, broken only by Spinoza, Mendelssohn opened the new era of modern Jewish philosophy, he took up his position in a manner which suggested that he was in complete accord with the tenor both of his time and of medieval Jewish philosophy. That he was able to do so is in large measure due to the influence that medieval Jewish philosophy, posthumously, as it were, had exerted on the evolution of modern thought.

Our analysis would be incomplete if we omitted reference to Spinoza's great contribution to European thought which began to exercise its influence from the late eighteenth century onward. The revival of interest in Spinoza in the nineteenth century means that a great deal of the medieval Jewish legacy which he preserved came to be appropriated by modern thought. The "Jewishness" of Spinoza consists in much more than in his knowledge of medieval Jewish philosophy and the influence it had on the processes of his thinking. It is of the very essence of his approach to the problems of philosophy. Santayana hardly exaggerates when he calls Spinoza's pantheism a faithful expression, in logical terms, of the biblical concept of the omnipotence of God.[73]

There is at work in Spinoza's thought a Jewish passion for unity which the medieval systems had failed to satisfy. As H. A. Wolfson has shown, the medieval attempt to derive the material world from a God wholly spiritual, can hardly be regarded as successful.[74] Spinoza certainly refused to regard it as such, and although his concept of *Deus sive Natura* destroys the biblical notion of the personality of God, it preserves the religious fervor of the biblical spirit. As Frederick Pollock put it, "God has not been reduced to nature, but Nature exalted to God."[75] Moreover, in full conformity with Judaism, Spinoza stresses the activity of God. "It is as impossible for us to conceive of God as non-existing as to conceive of him as not acting" (Eth. II, 3 sch.). It is this concept of God as the active source of all things, as the power that pervades and animates the universe, which so deeply impressed Jacobi, Herder and Goethe.

There has been a great deal of controversy as to the indebtedness of Goethe to Spinoza. But dispute could only arise through a mechanistic interpretation of Spinoza's system, an interpretation which is historically wrong and certainly in flagrant contradiction to Herder's and Goethe's views of Spinoza.[76] They rightly saw in Spinoza's Substance the *ens realissimum*, the active power of the universe. They welcomed enthusiastically the radical pantheism of this new "world religion," as Jacobi termed it, as an expression of the monistic trend of the age. Neither Descartes's nor Leibnitz's pluralistic systems could satisfy the overwhelming yearning for unity that had taken hold of the post-Kantian schools of Idealism. Both Hegel and Schelling are deeply influenced by Spinoza.

There is yet another aspect of Spinoza's Jewish quality. He comes to philosophy, as Leon Roth observes, not from physical science or mathematics or logic, but from the problem of conduct as an eminently practical problem.[77] He is primarily a moralist, and for that matter, a Jewish moralist. His saying that "Blessedness is not the reward of right living, but the right living itself" is reminiscent of a famous passage in the Rabbinic *Ethics of the Fathers*.[78] His advice not to pursue the things perishable—riches, honor, sensual pleasures—but to love the object that is eternal and infinite, recalls a well-known passage at the end of Maimonides's *Guide*. Spinoza's concept of *Amor Dei Intellectualis* derives from the same source. Like Maimonides, Spinoza affirms that man is the more perfect the greater the object of his knowledge and love, a phrase which seems to be echoed in a beautiful utterance of Kierkegaard: "Not one shall be forgotten who was great in the world; but each was great in his own way, according to the greatness of the things he loved. For he who loved himself became great for himself, and he who loved others became great through his devotion, but he who loved God became greater than any of these."[79]

Spinoza's ethics has met with fierce opposition, and was rejected by Herbart and others as irreconcilable with the moral consciousness. But Nietzsche showed deep insight into the Jewish character of Spinoza's attitude when he remarked that Spinoza had restored to the world its innocence.[80] Spinoza's view is the complete antithesis to the doctrine of original sin, which from Augustine over Luther to Pascal, Kierkegaard and Karl Barth has dominated the Christian consciousness.

EPILOGUE

Modern Jewish philosophy reflects the fundamental change in outlook that characterizes modern thought in general. It no longer seeks to harmonize the truth of revelation with those of authoritative pagan thinkers, but is concerned with the significance of the Jewish religion as a manifestation of the human spirit, and its place within the larger framework of thought, be it conceived as universal reason, the dialectic of the mind, the system of culture, or the human existence as such.

The rise of Kantianism accentuated the division between the theoretical and practical spheres, which Spinoza and Mendelssohn had accepted. The destruction of rational theology, cosmology and psychology, which Kant had accomplished, made religion wholly dependent on ethics, and fundamentally, an expression of practical reason. Kant's ethical and religious philosophy proved exceedingly attractive to Jewish thinkers.[1] Moritz Lazarus (1824-1903) interprets Judaism as a system of ethics in the light of Kant's "categorical imperative." Hermann Cohen (1842-1918), the founder of the Marburg school of Neokantianism, develops a Jewish religious philosophy from the premises of his own system. The idea of

God is indispensable both to theoretical and to practical reason. Moreover, it establishes the necessary link between the two spheres by assuring the final realization of man's moral destiny within the natural order of being.[2] Cohen emphatically rejects Spinoza's pantheism because it destroys the autonomy of ethics. Prophetic Judaism has freed the concept of God from its mythical associations, and medieval Jewish philosophy has been following in this tradition.

Hermann Cohen's *The Religion of Reason from the Sources of Judaism* (published posthumously in 1919) goes much beyond the strict limits of his system of "pure ethics" in order to do justice to the essentially religious character of Judaism. It is the historic merit of Cohen to have refuted Spinoza's presentation of Judaism as a political legislation without universal religious significance, a view which Kant adopted from Spinoza. Cohen took up the challenge and vigorously renewed the Jewish claim to spiritual leadership.[3]

The idealist movement in the early part of the nineteenth century had inspired Solomon Formstecher (1808-1889) and Samuel Hirsch (1815-1889) to recast the systems of Schelling and Hegel, respectively, in order to assess the true significance of Judaism within the dialectic process of history. Nahman Krochmal's (1785-1840) philosophy of Jewish history is influenced by Hegel, and helped to create the new science of Jewish historical research. Of particular profundity is the more recent elaboration of Schelling's "positive philosophy" and its combination with modern existentialism by Franz Rosenzweig (1886-1929).[4] God, man and world are irreducible entities. The idealist attempt to derive everything from one single principle is mistaken. Philosophy can only seek to interpret the interrelations which exist between God, man and world. They are brought out in full by the terms Creation, Revelation and Redemption. Not the formal truths of logic in their timeless, abstract character are really vital and relevant, but the truths brought out in the relationships of human beings with God and with one another, truths which spring from the presentness of time. Rosenzweig's "philosophy of speech"—the "New Thinking," as he terms it—is indebted to Eugene Rosenstock-Huessy.[5] It plays a notable part also in Martin Buber's (b. 1878) thought. His book, *I and Thou*—complemented by *Between Man and Man* (1947)—has exercised considerable influence on modern theology and social philosophy.[6]

NOTES

[1] Cf. Julius Guttmann, *Die Philosophie des Judentums* (Munich, 1933), pp. 9-11; Felix Weltsch, "Mahi Pilosofiah Yehudit?" in *Eyoon*, ed. S. Ucko, Vol. I (Jerusalem).

[2] Cf. Hermann Cohen, *Die Religion der Vernunft aus den Quellen des Judentums* (Leipzig, 1919).

[3] Cf. E. Troeltsch, *Gesammelte Schriften*, IV (1925), 820-821; Albert Lewkowitz, *Das Judentum und die geistigen Stroemungen des 19. Jahrhunderts* (Breslau, 1935). On the "Hebrew Consciousness" as an essential element of Christianity cf. John MacMurray, *The Clue to History* (London, 1938).

[4] Cf. Samuel Alexander, *Space, Time and Deity* (1920); *Spinoza and Time* (1921).

[5] Cf. Nathan Soederblom, *The Living God* (Oxford University Press, 1939), p. 311, n. 1.

I

[1] Cf. W. W. Jaeger, *Nemesios von Emesa*, Quellenforschungen zum Neuplatonismus und seinen Anfaengen bei Poseidonios (Berlin, 1914).

[1a] Cf. below Ralph Marcus, "Hellenistic Jewish Literature," pp. 1107 ff.]

[2] Cf. I. Heinemann, *Poseidonios' Metaphysische Schriften*, I (Breslau, 1921), II (1928).

[3] Cf. I. Heinemann, in *Monatsschrift fuer Geschichte und Wissenschaft des Judentums* (Breslau), Vol. 64, (28), 1920, pp. 101-122.

[4] Cf. F. Heinemann, *Plotin, Forschungen ueber die plotinische Frage, Plotins Entwicklung und sein System* (Leipzig, 1921), p. 8.

[5] Horace's famous line (*Epist.* II, 156-157) is typical of the Roman attitude in this respect.

[6] H. H. Schaeder, "Der Orient und das griechische Erbe," in *Die Antike*. ed. W. W. Jaeger (Berlin, 1928).

[7] Cicero, *De natura deorum*, III, ii; cf. K. Kerényi's interpretation of this passage in *Die antike Religion* (Amsterdam, 1942), pp. 123-126.

[8] Cf. Theodor Hopfner, "Orient und griechische Philosophie," in *Beitraege zum "Alten Orient,"* No. 4 (Leipzig, 1925).

[9] Cf. Hopfner, *loc. cit.*, p. 8, n. 1.

[10] Cf. Solomon Munk's article in *Dictionnaire des Sciences Philosophiques*, ed. A. Franck (Paris, 1875), II, 834 ff.; J. Burnet, *Early Greek Philosophers* (London, 1920), pp. 17-19.

[11] Cf. Kuzari, I, 63, II, 66; *Moreh Nebukim*, I, 71.

[12] Cf. Raymond Klibansky, *The Continuity of the Platonic Tradition during the Middle Ages* (London, 1939), p. 34.

[13] Cf. I. Heinemann's work quoted above, I, 136 ff.

[13a] On *Hokmah* and the Wisdom literature, cf. above Robert Gordis, "The Bible as a Cultural Monument," pp. 808 ff.]

[13b] Cf. above Elias J. Bickerman, "The Historical Foundations of Postbiblical Judaism," pp. 95 ff.]

[14] Cf. J. Coert Rylaarsdam, *Revelation in Jewish Wisdom Literature*, (Chicago, 1946), p. 38; chapters I and II of this book give a valuable survey of the historical development of Jewish Wisdom literature.

[14a] Cf. Marcus, *op. cit.*, pp. 1101-1103.]

[15] Cf. W. W. Jaeger, *Paideia, The Ideals of Greek Culture*, II (Oxford, 1944), pp. 213, 217.

[16] Cf. I. Heinemann, *loc. cit.*, p. 117; Augustine, *Confessions*, I, 16.

[17] Cf. J. Freudenthal, in *The Jewish Quarterly Review* (London), Vol. 2, 1890, pp. 205 ff.

[18] Cf. Kerényi, *loc. cit.*, p. 18.

[19] Cf. *De Cher.*, 125; *De Gig.*, 58-59; *De Post*, 2-9.

[20] Cf. Cicero, *De natura deorum*, III, xxiv ff.

[21] Cf. Jaeger, *loc. cit.*, p. 415.

[22] Cf. I. Heinemann, *loc. cit.*, p. 76, n. 2.

[23] Cf. J. Bergmann, "Die stoische Philosophie und die juedische Froemmigkeit," in *Judaica, Festschrift zu Hermann Cohens Siebzigstem Geburtstage* (Berlin, 1912), pp. 145-166.

[24] Cf. *De Congr.*, 11 ff.; I. Heinemann, *op. cit.; Monatsschrift*, Vol. 64 (28), 1920, pp. 18 ff.

[25] Cf. *De Mut.*, 153; *Leg. All.*, L. 63.

[26] Cf. *Philo.* Loeb Classical Library, ed. F. H. Colson-G. H. Whitaker, VIII, x-xi. It was Panaetius who first introduced the concept of *humanitas* into philosophical ethics. Cf. R. Reitzenstein, *Werden und Wesen der Humanitaet im Altertum* (1907).

[27] Cf. *De Abr.*, 5; also in many other places. Cf. E. R. Goodenough, *By Light, Light, The Mystic Gospel of Hellenistic Judaism* (1935), pp. 72-94.

[28] Cf. Leon Roth, *Paganism,* Ahad Ha'am Memorial Lecture, 1934 (Jerusalem, 1934).

[29] Cf. A. H. Armstrong, *The Gods in Plato, Plotinus, Epicurus,* in *Classical Quarterly* (London), Vol. 32, 1938, pp. 192-195.

[30] Cf. *De Dec.*, 53; *Quod Deus,* 30.

[31] Cf. R. Klibansky, *loc. cit.*, pp. 33-34.

[32] *De Somn.*, II, 193; *De Post.*, 21; *De Fuga,* 131; *De Sacr.*, Ab. 92; *De Sacrifiant,* 4.

[33] Cf. J. A. Stewart, *Plato's Doctrine of Ideas* (Oxford, 1909), p. 59; a brilliant advocacy of this view has been recently put forward by W. W. Jaeger, *loc. cit.*, pp. 285-286; p. 414, n. 39b.

[34] Cf. *De Vita Contempl.*, 2; *De Praem.*, 40.

[35] Cf. *De Praem.*, 39; *Quod Deus,* 62.

[36] Cf. *De Mut.*, 11; *De Post.*, 167.

[37] Cf. *De Mut.*, 9; *De Post.*, 169.

[38] Cf. E. R. Dodds, *Proclus, The Elements of Theology* (Oxford, 1933), pp. 310 ff.

[39] Cf. Raymond Klibansky, *Plato's Parmenides in the Middle Ages and the Renaissance,* Medieval and Renaissance Studies, I.2 (London, 1943), pp. 284-286.

[40] Cf. Emile Bréhier, *Les Idées philosophiques et religieuses de Philon d'Alexandrie* (Paris, 1925), p. 73.

[41] *De Gig.*, 42; *De Somn.*, 75; *Leg. All.*, II, 1.

[42] Cf. *De Conf.*, 136; *De Post.*, 14; 20; 30; *De Fuga,* 75.

[43] Cf. F. M. Cornford, *Plato's Cosmology* (London, 1937), pp. 34 ff.

[44] Cf. *Ep.*, 65, 7.

[45] *De Op.*, 16; 20.

[46] Cf. *Leg. All.*, III, 96; 207; *De Somn.*, I, 239.

[47] Cf. Goodenough, *loc. cit.*, p. 366; R. Reitzenstein, *Zwei religionsgeschichtliche Fragen* (1901), pp. 83-92.

[48] Cf. Goodenough, *loc. cit.*, pp. 22 ff., 58, 161, 273.

[49] Cf. Leopold Cohn, "Zur Lehre vom Logos bei Philo," *Judaica, Festschrift zu Hermann Cohens Siebzigstem Geburtstage* (Berlin, 1912).

[50] Cf. *De Sacr.*, Ab. 8; 65; *De Fuga,* 95.

[51] Cf. *Quod Omn.*, 5; *De Migr.*, 10; 13; *De Ebr.*, 136.

[52] Cf. *De Ebr.*, 136-137; *De Plant.*, 24-5.

[53] Cf. *De Plant.*, 26-27; one will notice the etymological interpretation of the name "Bezalel" (In the shadow of God).

[54] Cf. *Phaedrus*, 247c; *De Plant.*, 39; *De Mut.*, 7; *De Post.*, 21.

[55] Cf. I. Heinemann, *loc. cit.*, pp. 69-70.

[56] Cf. *De Somn.*, I, 60; *De Sacr.*, Ab. 55; *Quis. Rer.*, 74; elsewhere he affirms that from the spiritual nature of the mind we may infer God's own spirituality, and that in this sense self-knowledge leads to the knowledge of God. Cf. *De Mig.*, 192-193.

[57] Cf. *Quis Rer.*, 71.

[58] Cf. *De Gig.*, 52-53.

[59] Cf. *Enn.*, VI, 9. 11; W. R. Inge, *The Philosophy of Plotinus* (1929), II, 146.

[60] Cf. *Phaedrus,* 244.

[61] Cf. *Quis Rer.*, 249.

[62] Cf. the article "Ekstasis" in G. Kittel, *Theologisches Woerterbuch zum Neuen Testament.*

[62a] Cf. Gordis, *op. cit.*, pp. 795 ff.]

[63] Cf. *Quis Rer.*, 265.

[64] Cf. I. Heinemann, *Monatsschrift*, Vol. 64 (28) 1920, pp. 26 ff.

[65] Cf. Goodenough, *loc. cit.*

[66] Cf. *De Migr.*, 35.

[67] Cf. Charles Bigg, *The Christian Platonists of Alexandria* (Oxford, 1913), pp. 123, 242; Thomas Whittaker, *The Neo-platonists* (Cambridge, 1918), p. 33; Inge, *loc. cit.*, I, 37.

[68] Cf. F. Heinemann, "Ammonias Sakkas und der Ursprung des Neuplatonismus," in *Hermes, Zeitschrift fuer Klassische Philologie,* ed. R. Heinze and A. Korte, Vol. 61 (Berlin, 1926), p. 11, 21-25.

[69] Cf. P. Aloisius Lieske, S.J., *Die Theologie der Logos-mystik des Origenes* (Muenster i.W., 1938).

[70] Cf. H. Guyot, *Les Reminiscences de Philo le Juif chez Plotin* (Paris, 1906).

[71] Cf. F. Heinemann, *Plotin*, pp. 6-9, 189.

[72] Cf. Carl Siegfried, *Philo von Alexandria als Ausleger des Alten Testaments* (Jena, 1875), pp. 317-321. R. Bultmann, *Zeitschrift fuer Neutestamentliche Wissenschaft*, Vol. 24 (1925); F. C. Burkitt, *Church and Gnosis* (Cambridge, 1932), pp. 92-99.

[73] Cf. Otto Bardenhewer, *Patrology*, transl. Thomas J. Shahan (Freiburg i. Breisgau, 1908), pp. 431-436; Hans Lewy, "Neue Philontexte in der Ueberarbeitung des Ambrosius, mit einem Anhang: Neu gefundene Philonfragmente,"

in *Sitzungsberichte d. preuss. Akademie der Wissenschaften, Phil.-Hist. Klasse,* 1932, pp. 1-64.

[74] Cf. Jaeger, *Nemesius of Emesa,* pp. 139-143; John of Damascus, *De fide orthodoxa,* ed. Migne, col. 852 (quoted by A. J. Wensinck, *The Muslim Creed* [Cambridge, 1932], p. 69); *De Somn.,* I. sec. 65-70.

[75] Cf. J. Freudenthal, *Hellenistische Studien,* vol. 1, (Breslau, 1874), I, 67 ff.; Leo Baeck, "Zwei Beispiele midraschischer Predigt," in *Monatsschrift,* Vol. 69, 1925, pp. 258 ff.

[76] Cf. W. Bacher, *The Jewish Quarterly Review,* Vol. 7, 1894, p. 703; S. Poznański, *Revue des Etudes Juives* (Paris), Vol. 50, 1905, pp. 12-23.

[77] Cf. G. G. Scholem, *Major Trends in Jewish Mysticism* (Jerusalem, 1941), pp. 113-114.

[78] Cf. M. Bieler, *Der Goettliche Wille (Logosbegriff) bei Gabirol* (1933); I. Heinemann, *Zion,* Vol. 9, p. 168.

[79] Cf. G. Scholem, *"Ikbotav shel Gabirol ba-Kabbalah,"* in *Meassef Sofre Erez Yisrael,* 5700 [1940].

[80] Cf. David Neumark, *Geschichte der juedischen Philosophie des Mittelalters,* Vol. 2, 1 (1910). pp. 465-467.

2

[1] Cf. for the following account R. Klibansky, *The Continuity of the Platonic Tradition during the Middle Ages* (London, 1939); R. Walzer, "Arabic Transmission of Greek Thought to Medieval Europe," in *Bulletin of the John Rylands Library* (Manchester), Vol. 29, No. 1 (1945), pp. 160-183; Thomas Whittaker, *The Neo-Platonists* (Cambridge, 1918), pp. 154-215; Etienne Gilson, *La Philosophie Au Moyen Age* (Paris, 1944); A. J. Wensinck, *The Muslim Creed* (1932); *The Legacy of Islam,* ed. Sir Thomas Arnold and Alfred Guillaume (Oxford, 1931); A. Mez, *Die Renaissance des Islams* (1922).

[1a Cf. above Judah Goldin, "The Period of the Talmud," pp. 194 ff.]

[2] Cf. J. Finkel, "An Eleventh Century Source for the History of Jewish Scientists in Mohammedan Lands," in *Jewish Quarterly Review,* N.S. 8 (1927-1928), pp. 45 ff.; S. Poznański, "Die juedischen Artikel in Ibn al-Qifti's Gelehrtenlexikon," in *Monatsschrift fuer Geschichte und Wissenschaft des Judentums,* N.F. 13 (49), 1905, pp. 41 ff.

[3] Cf. N. N. Glatzer, *Geschichte der Talmudischen Zeit.* (Berlin, 1937), pp. 167-169.

[4] Cf. G. G. Scholem, *Major Trends in Jewish Mysticism* (Jerusalem, 1941), pp. 39-74; see also the present writer's articles, "Gnostic Themes in Rabbinic Cosmology," in *Essays in honour of the Very Rev. Dr. J. H. Hertz* (London, 1942), pp. 19-32, and "The Gnostic Background of the Rabbinic Adam Legends," in *Jewish Quarterly Review.* N.S. Vol. 35, No. 4 (1945), pp. 371-391; also "Kedushah Hymns in the Earliest Hekalot Literature (from an Oxford Manuscript)," in *Melilah,* ed. Edward Robertson and Meir Wallenstein (Manchester, 1946), II, 2-24.

[5] Cf. Scholem, *loc. cit.,* p. 75.

[6] Cf. Leo Baeck, "Zum Sepher Jezira," in *Monatsschrift fuer Geschichte und Wissenschaft des Judentums*, N.F. 34 (70), 1926, pp. 371-376.

[7] Cf. Scholem, *loc. cit.*, p. 363, n. 128.

[8] Cf. Scholem, *loc. cit.*, p. 75.

[9] Cf. *Saadya Gaon, The Book of Doctrines and Beliefs, Abridged Edition, Translated from the Arabic, With an Introduction and Notes*, by Alexander Altmann (Oxford, 1946), pp. 17-18.

[10] Cf. M. Schreiner, *Der Kalam in der juedischen Literatur* (Berlin, 1895).

[11] Cf. Wensinck, *loc. cit.*, p. 79.

[11a Cf. below Abraham S. Halkin, "Judeo-Arabic Literature," pp. 1137 f.]

[11b On Karaism cf. Goldin, *op. cit.*, pp. 191 f.]

[12] Cf. *Saadya Gaon, loc. cit.*, pp. 12-14.

[12*] Cf. Jacob Mann, "The Last Geonim of Sura," *JQR*, N.S., XI (1920-1921), p. 419.

[13] Cf. Julius Guttmann, *Die Philosophie des Judentums* (Munich, 1933), pp. 85-96.

[14] Cf. A. Foucher de Careil, *Leibniz, la Philosophie Juive et la Cabale* (Paris, 1861), pp. 33-40.

[15] Cf. E. Renan, *Averroes et l'Averroisme*, pp. 92-93, quoted by Thomas Whittaker, *loc. cit.*, p. 183.

[16] Cf. R. Klibansky, *loc. cit.*, pp. 16-22; Gilson, *loc. cit.*, pp. 346-347.

[17] Cf. R. Klibansky, *loc. cit.*, p. 22.

[18] Cf. M. Guidi and R. Walzer, "Uno scritto introduttivo allo studio di Aristotele," in *Reale Accademia Nazionale Dei Lincei* (1940).

[19] Cf. R. Walzer, *Arabic Transmission*, etc., pp. 174 ff.

[20] Cf. Gilson, *loc. cit.*, p. 73.

[20a On his poetry cf. above Shalom Spiegel, "On Medieval Hebrew Poetry," pp. 876-877.]

[20b Cf. Halkin, *op. cit.*, p. 1139.]

[21] Cf. C. R. S. Harris, *Duns Scotus* (Oxford, 1927), p. 231; W. Kahl, *Die Lehre vom Primat des Willens bei Augustinus, Duns Scotus und Descartes* (Strassburg, 1886), p. 55 (quoted by C. R. S. Harris).

[22] Cf. C. R. S. Harris, *loc. cit.*, *passim*.

[23] Cf. Julius Guttmann, *loc. cit.*, pp. 135-136; G. Scholem, "Ikbotav shel Gabirol ba-Kabbalah," in *Meassef Sofre Eretz Yisrael*, 5700 [1940].

[24] Cf. I. Heinemann, "Die Lehre von der Zweckbestimmung des Menschen im griechisch-roemischen Altertum und im juedischen Mittelalter," in *Bericht des Juedisch-theologischen Seminars* (Breslau, 1926), pp. 37-48.

[25] Cf. D. H. Baneth, "The Common Teleological Source of Bahye ibn Paqoda and Ghazzali," in *Magnes Anniversary Book* (Jerusalem, 1938) pp. 23-30.

[26] Cf. Julius Guttmann, *loc. cit.*, pp. 126-128.

[27] Cf. Gilson, *loc. cit.*, p. 116.

[28] Cf. Julius Guttmann, *loc. cit.*, p. 383, and his Introduction to *Abraham bar Hija, Megillat ha-Megalle*, ed. A. Poznański and Julius Guttmann, (Berlin, 1924); see also G. Scholem, *Monatsschrift*, N.F., 39 (75), pp. 172 ff.

[29] Cf. Julius Guttmann, *loc. cit.*, pp. 130-131.

[30] Cf. R. A. Nicholson, *Studies in Islamic Mysticism* (Cambridge, 1921); H. H. Schaeder, "Die islamische Lehre vom Vollkommenen Menschen," in *Zeitschrift der Deutschen Morgenlaendischen Gesellschaft*, N.F. 4 (79), 1925, pp. 192 ff.; see also the present writer's articles, "Saadya's Theory of Revelation: its Origin and Background," in *Saadya Studies*, ed. E. I. J. Rosenthal (Manchester, 1943), pp. 22-25, and "The Climatological Factor in Yehudah Hallevi's Theory of Prophecy," in *Melilah*, Vol. 1, ed. E. Robertson and M. Wallenstein (Manchester, 1944), Vol. I, p. 16.

[31] Cf. Gilson, *loc. cit.*, pp. 72 ff.

[31a Cf. Spiegel, *op. cit.*, pp. 877-878.]

[32] Cf. Leo Strauss, "The Law of Reason in the Kuzari," in *Proceedings of the American Academy for Jewish Research*, XIII (1943), pp. 52, 62.

[33] Cf. Julius Guttmann, *loc. cit.*, p. 153.

[34] Cf. R. Klibansky, *loc. cit.*, p. 36.

[34a Cf. Halkin, *op. cit.*, pp. 1143-1144; also see below Charles Singer, "Science and Judaism," pp. 1389 ff.]

[35] Cf. H. A. Wolfson, *Crescas' Critique of Aristotle* (Cambridge, Harvard University Press, 1929), p. 323.

[36] Cf. G. G. Scholem, *Major Trends of Jewish Mysticism*, pp. 124 ff.

[37] Cf. the present writer's article, "Das Verhaeltnis Maimunis zur juedischen Mystik," in *Monatsschrift*, N. F., 44 (80), 1936, pp. 305 ff.

[37a Cf. Halkin, *op. cit.*, pp. 1134-1135.]

[37b Cf. below Louis Finkelstein, "The Jewish Religion: Its Beliefs and Practices," p. 1755.]

[38] Cf. Jacob Guttmann, "Der Einfluss der maimonidischen Philosophie auf das christliche Abendland," in *Moses Ben Maimon*, ed., W. Bacher, M. Brann, D. Simonsen (Leipzig, 1908), Vol. 1, pp. 135 ff.; E. Koplowitz, *Die Abhaengigkeit Thomas von Aquins von R. Moses ben Maimon* (1935).

[39] Cf. Joseph Sarachek, *Faith and Reason: The Conflict over the Rationalism of Maimonides* (Williamsport, Pa., 1935), Vol. I.

[40] Cf. J. L. Teicher, "Maimonides, Christian Theology and the Jewish Opposition," in *Journal of Theological Studies* (Oxford, 1942), XLIII, pp. 69 ff.

[41] Cf. *The Legacy of Israel*, ed. Edwin R. Bevan and Charles Singer (Oxford, 1928), p. 265.

[42] Cf. M. Joel, *Lewi ben Gerson (Gersonides) als Religionsphilosoph* (Breslau, 1862), p. 12.

[42a Cf. Spiegel, *op. cit.*, pp. 880 f.]

[43] Cf. Carl Gebhardt, *Leone Ebreo, Dialoghi d'Amore* (1929), p. 51.

[44] Cf. Julius Guttmann, "Elia del Medigos Verhaeltnis zu Averroës in seinem Bechinat ha-Dat," in *Jewish Studies in Memory of Israel Abrahams* (New York, 1927), pp. 192 ff.

[45] Cf. H. A. Wolfson, *Crescas' Critique of Aristotle*, pp. 24-31.

[46] Cf. C. R. S. Harris, *loc. cit.*, p. 70, and *passim*.

[47] Cf. R. Klibansky, *loc. cit.*, p. 20.

[48] Cf. Martin Grabmann, *Mittelalterliches Geistesleben* (Munich, 1926), pp. 16-18, 276-295.

[49] Cf. *loc. cit.*, pp. 173 ff.

[50] Cf. M. Steinschneider, *Die hebraeischen Uebersetzungen des Mittelalters und die Juden als Dolmetscher* (Berlin, 1893), pp. xvi-xx.

3

[1] Cf. Wilhelm Dilthey, *Gesammelte Schriften* (Leipzig and Berlin, 1921), Vol. II; Jacob Burckhardt, *The Civilization of the Renaissance in Italy*, Transl. by S. G. C. Middlemore (London-New York, 1928 [9th impression]).
[[1a] Cf. above the chapter by Cecil Roth, "The Jews of Western Europe (from 1648)."]

[2] Cf. E. Gilson, *Etudes sur le Rôle de la Pensée Mediévale dans la Formation du Système Cartésien* (Paris, 1930); Jacques Maritain, *The Dream of Descartes*, Transl. by M. L. Andison (London, 1946).

[3] Cf. Leon Roth, *Spinoza* (London, 1929); H. A. Wolfson, *The Philosophy of Spinoza*, 2 vols. (Cambridge, Mass., 1934).

[4] Cf. A. Foucher de Careil, *Leibniz, la Philosophie Juive et la Cabale* (Paris, 1861); The first part of this work contains "Leibnitii observationes ad Rabbis Mosis Maimonidis librum qui inscribitur Doctor Perplexorum." By the same author: *Refutation inédite de Spinosa par Leibniz* (Paris, 1854); contains "Leibnitii Animadversiones ad Georg. Wachteri librum de recondita hebraeorum philosophia."

[5] Cf. Foucher de Careil, *Leibniz*, pp. 33, 37, and *passim*; Joseph Politella, *Platonism, Aristotelianism and Cabalism in the Philosophy of Leibniz* (Philadelphia, 1938), pp. 13-16; 25-26; 29-34.

[6] Cf. F. H. Heinemann, "Toland and Leibniz," in *Philosophical Review* (New York, 1945), pp. 437 ff., 443.

[7] Cf. David Kaufmann, "Der 'Fuehrer' Maimûni's in der Weltliteratur," in *Gesammelte Schriften*, Vol. II, ed. M. Brann (Frankfort a.M., 1910), pp. 174 ff.

[8] Cf. Foucher de Careil, *Leibniz*, p. 2; David Kaufmann, *loc. cit.*, p. 175.

[9] For evidence see further below in the text.
[[9a] For the tenets of Cabbala cf. above the chapter by Abraham J. Heschel, "The Mystical Element in Judaism."]

[10] Cf. Israel Abrahams, "Pico della Mirandola," in *Hebrew Union College Jubilee Volume* (Cincinnati, 1925), pp. 317 ff.

[11] Cf. Denis Saurat, *Milton, Man and Thinker* (London, 1944); M. A. Larson, *The Modernity of Milton* (Chicago, Ill., 1927).

[12] Certain attempts in this direction have been made by Flora Isabel MacKinnon, *Philosophical Writings of Henry More*, ed. with Introduction and Notes (New York, 1925); Politella, *loc. cit.*

[13] Cf. Henry More, *The Defense of the Threefold Cabbala* (London, 1662), p. 80.

[14] Cf. Julius Guttmann, "John Spencers Erklaerung der biblischen Gesetze in ihrer Beziehung zu Maimonides," in *Festschrift Professor David Simonsen* (Copenhagen, 1923), pp. 259 ff.

[15] Cf. Pierre Bayle, *Oeuvres Diverses*, I (1727), 537.

[16] Cf. *loc. cit.*, pp. 3, 27.

[17] Cf. *loc. cit.*, pp. iii-iv, vii.

[18] Cf. the list of Christian talmudical scholars given by John Selden in his *De Jure Naturali et Gentium, juxta Disciplinam Ebraeorum, Libri septem* (1665), pp. 34-35.

[19] Cf. *British Museum Catalogue of Printed Books* (London, 1884); *Dictionary of National Biography*, ed. Sidney Lee (London, 1909); *Nouvelle Biographie Générale*, ed. Firmin Didot Frères (Paris, 1866).

[20] Cf. Dilthey, *loc. cit.*, pp. 107-108, 315-316, and *passim*.

[21] Cf. Leo Strauss, *The Political Philosophy of Hobbes* (Oxford, 1936), p. 4.

[22] Cf. Dilthey, *loc. cit.*, pp. 16-89.

[23] Cf. Dilthey, *loc. cit.* pp. 326 ff.; J. H. Whitefield, *Petrarch and Renascence* (Oxford, 1943).

[24] Cf. Erich Przywara, S.J., *Analogia Entis* (Munich, 1932), p. 41.

[25] Cf. Maritain, *loc. cit.*

[26] Cf. F. C. Coplestone, "Pantheism in Spinoza and the German Idealists," in *Philosophy*, Vol. XXI, No. 78 (1946), p. 45.

[27] Cf. The present writer's article, "Franz Rosenzweig and Eugen Rosenstock-Huessy: An Introduction to their Letters on Judaism and Christianity," in *Journal of Religion* XXIV (1944), (Chicago, Ill.), p. 262.

[28] Cf. W. W. Jaeger, *Humanism and Theology* (The Aquinas Lecture, Milwaukee, 1943); R. Walzer, "Arabic Transmission of Greek Thought to Mediaeval Europe," in *Bulletin of the John Rylands Library* (Manchester), Vol. 29, No. 1, pp. 168-171.

[29] Cf. A. J. Wensinck, *The Muslim Creed* (Cambridge, 1932).

[30] Cf. S. Horovitz, "Ueber den Einfluss der griechischen Philosophie auf die Entwicklung des Kalam," in *Jahres-Bericht des Juedisch-theologischen Seminars* (Breslau, 1909).

[31] Cf. Simon Van den Bergh, *Epitome der Metaphysik des Averroes* (Leyden, 1924); an annotated translation of Averroës's *Destructio destructionis*, by the same author, is to be published by the trustees of the Gibb Memorial Fund, Oxford. It will deal with the influence of Stoic thought on Moslem theology, which Van den Bergh thinks to be very considerable. (Letter to the present writer.)

[32] Cf. M. Bieler, *Der goettliche Wille (Logosbegriff) bei Gabirol* (1933); I. Heinemann, *Zion* (Hebrew), Vol. 9, p. 168.

[33] Cf. Julius Guttmann, *Die Philosophie des Judentums* (Munich, 1933), pp. 105 ff.; Abraham Heschel, "Der Begriff des Seins in der Philosophie Gabirols," in *Festschrift fuer Dr. Jakob Freimann* (Berlin, 1937); by the same author: "Das Wesen der Dinge nach der Lehre Gabirols," in *Hebrew Union College Annual*, Vo. XIV, 1939, pp. 359 ff.

[34] Cf. C. R. S. Harris, *Duns Scotus* (Oxford, 1927), I, 126 ff.

[35] Cf. Julius Guttmann, *loc. cit.*, pp. 135-137.

[36] Cf. G. Scholem, "Ikbotav shel Gabirol ba-Kabbalah," in *Meassef Sofre Eretz Yisrael*, 5700 [1940].

[37] G. G. Scholem, *Major Trends in Jewish Mysticism* (Jerusalem, 1941), pp. 249, 402.

[38] Cf. Denis Saurat, *Milton*, p. 231.

[39] Cf. Julius Guttmann, "Chasdai Creskas als Kritiker der aristotelischen Physik" in *Festschrift Jakob Guttmann* (Leipzig, 1915), pp. 28-54; H. A. Wolfson, *Crescas' Critique of Aristotle* (Cambridge, Harvard University Press, 1929), pp. 34-37.

[40] Cf. H. A. Wolfson, *loc. cit.*, pp. 123, 201.

[41] Cf. Flora Isabel MacKinnon, *Philosophical Writings of Henry More*, pp. 293-295; see also Leibnitz, *Nouveaux Essais sur l'Entendement*, II, 17 (ed. C. J. Gebhardt, Vol. V, Berlin, 1882, pp. 136). Leibnitz attacks the doctrine of real space as "an idol of some modern Englishmen," "Since space," he writes to Samuel Clarke, "consists of parts, it is not a thing which can belong to God" (Collection of Papers, Leibnitz to Clarke, 3rd paper).

[42] Cf. H. A. Wolfson, *loc. cit.*, pp. 34-37.

[43] Cf. the present writer's article, "Saadya's Conception of the Law," in *Bulletin of The John Rylands Library* (Manchester), Vol. 28, No. 2 (1944), pp. 320 ff., 331.

[44] Cf. A. J. Wensinck, *loc. cit.*, pp. 214-216.

[45] Cf. the present writer's article quoted above.

[46] Cf. S. Horovitz, "Die Psychologie bei den juedischen Religionsphilosophen des Mittelalters von Saadia bis Maimuni," in *Jahres-Bericht des Juedisch-theologischen Seminars* (Breslau, 1906), p. 159.

[47] Cf. the present writer's article quoted above, p. 334.

[48] Cf. Leo Strauss, "The Law of Reason in the Kuzari," in *Proceedings of the American Academy for Jewish Research*, XIII (1943), 47 ff.

[49] Cf. Joseph Albo, *Sefer Ha-Ikkarim*, ed. Isaac Husik (Philadelphia, 1929), IV, 355.

[50] Cf. Hugo Grotius, *The Rights of War and Peace, including the Law of Nature and of Nations* (transl. A. C. Campbell), 3 vols., 1814, Book I, ch. I, 9. See Leo Strauss, *loc. cit.*, p. 48, n. 4.

[51] Cf. the present writer's article quoted above, p. 335.

[52] Cf. Hugo Grotius, *loc. cit.*, Book I, ch. I, 16.

[53] Cf. Albert Lewkowitz, *"Das Judentum und die geistigen Stroemungen der Neuzeit,"* in *Bericht des juedisch-theologischen Seminars* (Breslau, 1929), p. 44-49.

[54] Cf. Lewkowitz, *loc. cit.*, pp. 16-21.

[55] Cf. Dilthey, *loc. cit.*, p. 45.

[56] Cf. Lewkowitz, *loc. cit.*, p. 26.

[57] Cf. Lewkowitz, *loc. cit.*, pp. 26-32.

[58] Cf. Leone Ebreo, *Dialoghi d'Amore* (ed. Carl Gebhardt), pp. 35-37; 94-96.

[59] Cf. Jacob Guttmann, "Ueber Jean Bodin in seinen Beziehungen zum Judentum," in *Monatsschrift fuer Geschichte und Wissenschaft des Judentums* (1905), pp. 477 ff.; Lewkowitz, *loc cit.*, pp. 72-86.

[60] Cf. Dilthey, *loc. cit.*, p. 147.

[61] Cf. Dilthey, *loc. cit.*, pp. 73 ff.

[62] Cf. Dilthey, *loc. cit.*, p. 77.

[63] Cf. Dilthey, *loc. cit.*, pp. 77, 80, 109.

[64] Cf. Lewkowitz, *loc. cit.*, p. 45; Joseph Koch, "Meister Eckhart und die

juedische Religionsphilosophie des Mittelalters," in *Jahresbericht der Schlesischen Gesellschaft fuer vaterlaendische Kultur* (Breslau, 1928).

[65] Cf. Dilthey, *loc. cit.*

[66] Cf. Dilthey, *loc. cit.*, pp. 90-108.

[67] Cf. Ernst Cassirer, *Die Philosophie der Aufklaerung* (Tuebingen, 1932), pp. 182-188.

[68] Cf. Cassirer, *loc. cit.*, p. 223.

[69] Cf. Pierre Bayle, *Oeuvres Diverses*, III, 792.

[70] Cf. Cassirer, *loc. cit.*, p. 225.

[71] Cf. Cassirer, *loc. cit.*, pp. 238-244.

[72] Cf. E. Cassirer, "Die Idee der Religion bei Lessing und Mendelssohn," in *Festgabe zum Zehnjaehrigen Bestehen der Akademie fuer die Wissenschaft des Judentums* (Berlin, 1929), pp. 22-41.

[73] Cf. George Santayana in his Introduction to Spinoza's *Ethics,* in Everyman's Library, ed. Ernest Rhys (1910).

[74] Cf. H. A. Wolfson, *The Philosophy of Spinoza*, I, 79 ff.

[75] Cf. Pollock, *Spinoza* (1912), p. 331; the phrase is quoted by Leon Roth, *loc. cit.*, p. 72.

[76] Cf. F. H. Heinemann's Review of Franz Koch's "Goethe und Plotin," in *Deutsche Literaturzeitung*, 1927, No. 11.

[77] Cf. Leon Roth, *loc. cit.*, p. 43. On Spinoza's "Jewishness" see also A. E. Taylor's *The Faith of a Moralist* (1932), p. 221.

[78] Cf. *Abot*, IV, 2.

[79] Cf. Soeren Kierkegaard, *Fear and Trembling,* transl. by Robert Payne (Oxford, 1939), pp. 13-14.

[80] Cf. Friedrich Nietzsche, "Zur Genealogie der Moral," in *Nietzsches Werke*, Taschen-Ausgabe (Leipzig, 1905), VIII, 377-378; David Baumgardt. "Spinoza und der deutsche Spinozismus," in *Kant-Studien* (Berlin), Vol. XXXII, No. 1 (1927), p. 191.

EPILOGUE

[1] Cf. Julius Guttmann, "Kant und das Judentum," in *Schriften herausgegeben von der Gesellschaft zur Foerderung der Wissenschaft des Judentums* (Leipzig, 1908).

[2] Cf. Siegfried Ucko, *Der Gottesbegriff in der Philosophie Hermann Cohens* (Berlin, 1929).

[3] Cf. Franz Rozenzweig, "Ein ungedruckter Vortrag Hermann Cohens ueber Spinozas Verhaeltnis zum Judentum," in *Festgabe zum Zehnjaehrigen Bestehen der Akademie fuer die Wissenschaft des Judentums* (Berlin, 1929), pp. 42-68.

[4] Cf. Else Freund, *Die Existenzphilosophie Franz Rosenzweigs.*

[5] Cf. the present writer's article, "Franz Rosenzweig and Eugen Rosenstock-Huessy: an Introduction to Their 'Letters on Judaism and Christianity,'" in *Journal of Religion* (University of Chicago Press), Vol. XXIV, No. 4, 1944, pp. 258 ff.

[6] Cf. Karl Heim, *God Transcendent: Foundation for a Christian Meta-*

physic, transl. by E. P. Dickie (London, 1935); John Baillie, *Our Knowledge of God* (Oxford University Press, 1939); Helen Wodehouse, "Martin Buber's *'I and Thou,'*" in *Philosophy* (London) Vol. XX, No. 75, 1945, pp. 17-30; Buber's influence is particularly noticeable in J. H. Oldham's writings.

BIBLIOGRAPHY

The suggested readings are listed below under headings which correspond to those used in the body of the chapter.

ALEXANDER, SAMUEL, *Space, Time and Deity.* 2 vols. London, 1920.

———, *Spinoza and Time.* London, 1921.

COHEN, HERMANN, *Die Religion der Vernunft aus den Quellen des Judentums.* Leipzig, 1919.

GUTTMANN, JULIUS, *Die Philosophie des Judentums.* Munich, 1933.

LEWKOWITZ, ALBERT, *Das Judentum und die geistigen Stroemungen des 19. Jahrhunderts.* Breslau, 1935.

MACMURRAY, JOHN, *The Clue to History.* London, 1938.

SOEDERBLOM, NATHAN, *The Living God.* Oxford, 1939.

WELTSCH, FELIX, "Mahi Pilosofiah Yehudit?" in *Eyoon* (ed. S. Ucko), Vol. I. Jerusalem.

HELLENISTIC JEWISH PHILOSOPHY

Since this bibliography was prepared in 1946, Professor Harry A. Wolfson's monumental work on Philo has appeared. It was therefore added to the original list. However, it has not been possible otherwise to bring the bibliography up to date.

BACHER, W., "Qirqisani, the Qaraite, and his Work on Jewish Sects," in *Jewish Quarterly Review,* Vol. VII. London, 1894.

BAECK, LEO, "Zwei Beispiele midraschischer Predigt," in *Monatsschrift fuer Geschichte und Wissenschaft des Judentums,* Vol. 69. Frankfort a.M., 1925.

BERGMANN, J., "Die stoische Philosophie und die juedische Froemmigkeit," in *Judaica,* Festschrift zu Hermann Cohens Siebzigstem Geburtstage. Berlin, 1912.

BIELER, MAJER, *Der goettliche Wille (Logosbegriff) bei Gabirol.* Breslau, 1933.

BIGG, CHARLES, *The Christian Platonists of Alexandria.* Oxford, 1913.

BRÉHIER, EMILE, *Les Idées philosophiques et religieuses de Philon d'Alexandria.* Paris, 1925.

BURKITT, F. C., *Church and Gnosis.* Cambridge, 1932.

COHN, LEOPOLD, "Zur Lehre vom Logos bei Philo," in *Judaica, op. cit.*

CORNFORD, F. M., *Plato's Cosmology.* London, 1937.

DODDS, E. R., *Proclus, The Elements of Theology.* Oxford, 1933.

FREUDENTHAL, J., "Are there Traces of Greek Philosophy in the Septuagint?" in *Jewish Quar. Rev.*, Vol. II, 1890.

———, *Hellenistische Studien*. Breslau, 1874. Vol 1.

GOODENOUGH, E. R., *By Light, Light, The Mystic Gospel of Hellenistic Judaism*. New Haven, 1935.

GUYOT, H., *Les Reminiscences de Philo le Juif chez Plotin*. Paris, 1906.

HEINEMANN, F., "Ammonias Sakkas und der Ursprung des Neuplatonismus," in *Hermes*, Zeitschrift fuer Klassische Philologie. Vol. 61. Berlin, 1926.

———, *Plotin, Forschungen ueber die plotinische Frage, Plotins Entwicklung und sein System*. Leipzig, 1921.

HEINEMANN, I., "Philons Lehre vom Heiligen Geist und der intuitiven Erkenntnis," in *Monatsschrift*, Vol. 64, 1920.

———, *Poseidonios' Metaphysische Schriften*. Vol. I, Breslau, 1921; Vol., II, 1928.

HOPFNER, THEODOR, "Orient und griechische Philosophie," in *Beitraege zum "Alten Orient,"* No. 4. Leipzig, 1925.

INGE, W. R., *The Philosophy of Plotinus*. London, 1918. Vol. II.

JAEGER, W. W., *Nemesios von Emesa*, Quellenforschungen zum Neuplatonismus und seinen Anfaengen bei Poseidonios. Berlin, 1914.

———, *Paideia, The Ideals of Greek Culture*. Oxford, 1944. Vol. II.

KERENYI, K., *Die antike Religion*. Amsterdam, 1942.

KITTEL, G., *Theologisches Worterbuch zum Neuen Testament*, 3 vols. Stuttgart, 1933-1935-1938. The article "Ekstasis."

KLIBANSKY, RAYMOND, *The Continuity of the Platonic Tradition during the Middle Ages*. London, 1939.

LEWY, HANS, "Neue Philontexte in der Ueberarbeitung des Ambrosius mit einem Anhang: Neu gefundene Philonfragmente," in *Sitzungsberichte d. preuss. Akademie der Wissenschaften*, 1932.

LIESKE, P. ALOISIUS, *Die Theologie der Logos-mystik des Origenes*. Muenster, i.W., 1938.

MUNK, SOLOMON, "La Philosophie chez les Juifs," in *Dictionnaire des Sciences Philosophiques*. Paris, 1875.

NEUMARK, DAVID, *Geschichte der juedischen Philosophie des Mittelalters*. Berlin, 1910. Vol. 2, 1.

POZNAŃSKI, S., "Philon dans l'ancienne littérature Judéo-Arabe," in *Revue des Etudes Juives*, Vol. L. Paris, 1905.

REITZENSTEIN, R., *Werden und Wesen der Humanitaet im Altertum*. Strassburg, 1907.

ROTH, LEON, *Paganism*. Ahad Ha-Am Memorial Lecture. Jerusalem, 1934.

RYLAARSDAM, J. COERT, *Revelation in Jewish Wisdom Literature*. Chicago, 1946.

SCHAEDER, H. H., "Der Orient und das griechische Erbe," in *Die Antike*. Berlin, 1928.

SCHOLEM, G. G., "Ikbotav shel Gabirol be-Kabbalah," in *Meassef Sofre Eretz Yisrael*, 5700 [1940].

———, *Major Trends in Jewish Mysticism*. Jerusalem, 1941.

SIEGFRIED, CARL, *Philo von Alexandria als Ausleger des Alten Testaments.* Jena, 1875.

WHITTAKER, THOMAS, *The Neo-platonists.* Cambridge, 1918.

WOLFSON, HARRY A., *Philo: Foundations of Religious Philosophy, Judaism, Christianity and Islam.* 2 vols. Cambridge, 1947.

MEDIEVAL JEWISH PHILOSOPHY

ALTMANN, ALEXANDER, "The Climatological Factor in Yehuda Hallev's Theory of Prophecy," in *Melilah,* ed. E. Robertson and M. Wallenstein, Vol. I. Manchester, 1944.

———, "Das Verhaeltnis Maimunis zur juedischen Mystik," in *Monatsschrift,* N. F. 44 (Vol. 80), 1936.

———, "Gnostic Themes in Rabbinic Cosmology," in *Essays in Honour of the Very Rev. Dr. J. H. Hertz.* London, 1942.

———, "The Gnostic Background of the Rabbinic Adam Legends," in *Jewish Quarterly Review,* N.S. Vol. 35, No. 4, 1945.

———, "Kedushah Hymns in the Earliest Hekalot Literature (from an Oxford Manuscript)," in *Melilah, op. cit.*

———, *Saadya Gaon, The Book of Doctrines and Beliefs.* Abridged edition, translated from the Arabic with an Introduction and Notes. Oxford, 1946.

———, "Saadya's Theory of Revelation: its Origin and Background," in *Saadya Studies.* ed. E. I. J. Rosenthal. Manchester, 1943.

ARNOLD, SIR THOMAS, and GUILLAUME, ALFRED (eds.), *The Legacy of Islam.* Oxford, 1931.

BAECK, LEO, "Zum Sepher Jezira," in *Monatsschrift,* N.F. 34 (70), 1926.

BANETH, D. H., "The Common Teleological Source of Bahye ibn Paqoda and Ghazzali," in *Magnes Anniversary Book.* Jerusalem, 1938.

FINKEL, J., "An Eleventh Century Source for the History of Jewish Scientists in Mohammedan Lands (Ibn Sa'id)," in *Jewish Quarterly Review,* N.S. 18, 1927-1928.

FOUCHER DE CAREIL, A., *Leibniz, la Philosophie Juive et la Cabale.* Paris, 1861.

GILSON, ETIENNE, *La Philosophie Au Moyen Age.* Paris, 1944.

GLATZER, N. N., *Geschichte der Talmudischen Zeit.* Berlin, 1937.

GRABMAN, MARTIN, *Mittelalterliches Geistesleben.* Munich, 1926.

GUTTMANN, JACOB, "Der Einfluss des maimonidischen Philosophie auf das christliche Abendland," in *Moses Ben Maimon.* eds. W. Bacher, M. Brann, D. Simonsen. Leipzig, 1908. Vol. 1.

GUTTMANN, JULIUS, *Die Philosophie des Judentums.* Munich. 1933.

———, "Elia del Medigos Verhaeltnis zu Averroes in seinem Bechinat ha-Dat," in *Jewish Studies in Memory of Israel Abrahams.* New York, 1927.

HARRIS, C. R. S., *Duns Scotus.* Oxford, 1927.

HEINEMANN, I., "Die Lehre von der Zweckbestimmung des Menschen im griechisch-roemischen Altertum und im juedischen Mittelalter," in *Bericht des juedisch-theologischen Seminars*. Breslau, 1926.

Joel, M., *Lewi ben Gerson (Gersonides), als Religionsphilosoph*. Breslau, 1862.

Klibansky, R., *The Continuity of the Platonic Tradition during the Middle Ages*. London, 1939.

Koplowitz, E., *Die Abhaengigkeit Thomas von Aquins von R. Moses ben Maimon*. Kallmuenz, 1935.

Mez, A., *Die Renaissance des Islams*. Heidelberg, 1922.

Nicholson, R. A., *Studies in Islamic Mysticism*. Cambridge, 1921.

Poznański, S., "Die juedischen Artikel in Ibn al-Qifti's Gelehrtenlexikon," in *Monatsschrift*, N.F. 13 (49), 1905.

Renan, E., *Averrhoës et l'Averrhoisme*. Paris, 1852.

Sarachek, Joseph, *Faith and Reason: The conflict over the Rationalism of Maimonides*. Williamsport, Pa., 1935. Vol. I.

Schaeder, H. H., "Die islamische Lehre vom vollkommenen Menschen," in *Zeitschrift der Deutschen-Morgenlaendischen Gesellschaft*, N.F. 4 (79), 1925.

Scholem, Gerhard, "Reste neuplatonischer Spekulation in der Mystik der deutschen Chassidim und ihre Vermittlung durch Abraham bar Chija," in *Monatsschrift*, N.F. 39 (75), 1931.

Schreiner, M., *Der Kalam in der juedischen Literatur*. Berlin, 1895.

Steinschneider, M. *Die hebraeischen Uebersetzungen des Mittelalters und die Juden als Dolmetscher*, 2 vols. Berlin, 1893.

Strauss, Leo, "The Law of Reason in the Kuzari," in *Proceedings of the American Academy for Jewish Research*, Vol. XIII. New York, 1943.

Teicher, J. L., "Maimonides, Christian Theology and the Jewish Opposition," in *The Journal of Theological Studies*, Vol. XLIII. Oxford, 1942.

Walzer, R., "Arabic Transmission of Greek Thought to Mediaeval Europe," in *Bulletin of the John Rylands Library*, Vol. 29, No. 1. Manchester, 1945.

Wensinck, A. J., *The Muslim Creed*. Cambridge, 1932.

Whittaker, Thomas, *The Neo-Platonists*. Cambridge, 1918.

Wolfson, H. A., *Crescas' Critique of Aristotle*. Cambridge, Mass., 1929.

Medieval Jewish Philosophy in its Bearing on the Modern World

Abrahams, Israel, "Pico della Mirandola," in *Hebrew Union College Jubilee Volume*. Cincinnati, 1925.

Altmann, Alexander, "Saadya's Conception of the Law," in *Bulletin of the John Rylands Library*. Vol. 28, No. 2, 1944.

Baumgardt, David, "Spinoza und der deutsche Spinozismus," in *Kant-Studien*, Vol. XXXII, No. 1. Berlin, 1927.

Bayle, Pierre, *Œuvres Diverses*. La Haye, 1727. Vol. I.

Burckhardt, Jacob, *The Civilization of the Renaissance in Italy* (transl. by S. G. C. Middlemore). London and New York, 1928.

CASSIRER, ERNST, "Die Idee der Religion bei Lessing und Mendelssohn," in *Festgabe zum Zehnjaehrigen Bestehen der Akademie fuer die Wissenschaft des Judentums*. Berlin, 1929.

———, *Die Philosophie der Aufklaerung*. Tuebingen, 1932.

COPLESTONE, F. C., "Pantheism in Spinoza and the German Idealists," in *Philosophy*, Vol. XXI, No. 78. London, 1946.

DILTHEY, WILHELM, *Gesammelte Schriften*. Leipzig and Berlin, 1921. Vol. II.

FOUCHER DE CAREIL, A., *Leibniz, la Philosophie Juive et la Cabale*. Paris, 1861.

———, *Refutation inédite de Spinosa par Leibniz*. Paris, 1854.

GEBHARDT, CARL, (ed.), Leone Ebreo, *Dialoghi d'Amore*. Heidelberg and London, 1929.

GILSON, E., *Etudes sur le Rôle de la Pensée Mediévale dans la Formation du Système Cartésien*. Paris, 1930.

GROTIUS, HUGO, *The Rights of War and Peace, including the Law of Nature and of Nations* (transl. A. C. Campbell). 3 vols. Washington, 1901.

GUTTMANN, JACOB, "Ueber Jean Bodin in seinen Beziehungen zum Judentum," in *Monatsschrift*, 1905.

GUTTMANN, JULIUS, "Chasdai Creskas als Kritker der aristotelischen Physik," in *Festschrift Jakob Guttmann*. Leipzig, 1915.

———, *Die Philosophie des Judentums*. Munich, 1933.

HARRIS, C. R. S., *Duns Scotus*. Oxford, 1927.

HEINEMANN, F. H., "Toland and Leibniz," in *Philosophical Review*. New York, 1945.

HESCHEL, ABRAHAM, "Das Wesen der Dinge nach der Lehre Gabirols," in *Hebrew Union College Annual*, Vol. XIV. Cincinnati, 1939.

———, "Der Begriff des Seins in der Philosophie Gabirols," in *Festschrift fuer Dr. Jakob Freimann*. Berlin, 1937.

HOROVITZ, S., "Die Psychologie bei den juedischen Religionsphilosophen des Mittelalters von Saadia bis Maimuni," in *Jahres-Bericht des Juedisch-theologischen Seminars*. Breslau, 1906.

———, "Ueber den Einfluss der griechischen Philosophie auf die Entwicklung des Kalam," in *Jahres-Bericht, ibid.*, 1909.

JAEGER, W. W., *Humanism and Theology* (The Aquinas Lecture). Milwaukee, 1943.

KAUFMANN, DAVID, "Der 'Fuehrer' Maimûni's in der Weltliteratur," in *Gesammelte Schriften*, Vol. II, ed. M. Brann. Frankfort a.M. 1910.

KIERKEGAARD, SOEREN, *Fear and Trembling* (transl. by Robert Payne). Oxford, 1939.

KOCH, JOSEPH, "Meister Eckhart und die juedische Religionsphilosophie des Mittelalters," in *Jahresbericht der Schlesischen Gesellschaft fuer vaterlaendische Kultur*. Breslau, 1928.

LARSON, M. A., *The Modernity of Milton*. Chicago, 1927.

LEIBNITZ, G. W., *Nouveaux Essais sur l'Entendement* (ed. C. J. Gebhardt). Berlin, 1882. Vol V.

LEWKOWITZ, ALBERT, "Das Judentum und die geistigen Stroemungen der Neuzeit," in *Bericht des juedisch-theologischen Seminars*. Breslau, 1929.

MacKinnon, Flora Isabel, *Philosophical Writings of Henry More*. New York, 1925.

Maritain, Jacques, *The Dream of Descartes* (transl. by M. L. Andison). London, 1946.

More, Henry, *The Defense of the Threefold Cabbala*. London, 1662.

Politella, Joseph, *Platonism, Aristotelianism and Cabalism in the Philosophy of Leibniz*. Philadelphia, 1938.

Roth, Leon, *Spinoza*. London, 1929.

Saurat, Denis, *Milton, Man and Thinker*. London, 1944.

Scholem, G. G., *Major Trends in Jewish Mysticism*, Jerusalem, 1941.

Strauss, Leo, *The Political Philosophy of Hobbes*. Oxford, 1936.

Taylor, A. E., *The Faith of a Moralist*. London, 1930.

Van den Bergh, Simon, *Epitome der Metaphysik des Averroes*. Leyden, 1924.

Whitefield, J. H., *Petrarch and Renascence*. Oxford, 1943.

Wolfson, H. A., *Crescas' Critique of Aristotle*. Cambridge, Mass., 1929.

———, *The Philosophy of Spinoza*. 2 vols. Cambridge, Mass., 1934

Epilogue

Altmann, Alexander, "Franz Rosenzweig and Eugen Rosenstock-Huessy: an Introduction to Their 'Letters on Judaism and Christianity,' " in *Journal of Religion*, Vol. XXIV, No. 4. Chicago, 1944.

Baillie, John, *Our Knowledge of God*. Oxford, 1939.

Freund, Else, *Die Existenzphilosophie Franz Rosenzweigs*. Leipzig, 1933.

Guttmann, Julius, "Kant und das Judentum," in *Schriften herausgegeben von der Gesellschaft zur Foerderung der Wissenschaft des Judentums*. Leipzig, 1908.

Heim, Karl, *God Transcendent: Foundation for a Christian Metaphysic* (transl. E. P. Dickie). London, 1935.

Rosenzweig, Franz, "Ein ungedruckter Vortrag Hermann Cohens ueber Spinozas Verhaeltnis zum Judentum," in *Festgabe zum Zehnjaerhrigen Bestehen der Akademie fuer die Wissenschaft des Judentums*. Berlin, 1929.

Ucko, Siegfried, *Der Gottesbegriff in der Philosophie Hermann Cohens*. Berlin, 1929.

Wodehouse, Helen, "Martin Buber's 'I and Thou,' " in *Philosophy*, Vol. XX, No. 75, London, 1945.

CHAPTER 21

A PHILOSOPHY OF JEWISH ETHICS

By Mordecai M. Kaplan

Introduction

The wide range of subject matter discussed in this book as germane to Judaism* testifies to a far broader conception of Judaism than the conventional one which would limit it to a particular set of religious dogmas, practices and institutions. The very fact that religion as such occupies only one section of the book, whereas the greater part of the book is devoted to a variety of subjects such as law, poetry, art, science, literature and social welfare, implies that Judaism is a many-faceted, dynamic civilization, the civilization of the Jewish people. Once we realize this truth about Judaism, we naturally come to the conclusion that it is impossible to understand Judaism without knowing a great deal about the Jewish people. A knowledge of its history, sociology and demography is indispensable for an understanding of Judaism. These considerations indicate the approach in this chapter to the study of Judaism as a contribution to world ethics.

A comparative study of the different ethical systems, or normative patterns of human conduct, reveals an infinite variety of practices approved by some peoples and condemned by others. But the underlying distinctions of right and wrong, and the accompanying inner inhibitions that we associate with conscience, can be found in every human society, even the most rudimentary. Even those high principles which are often referred to as the consummation of ethics are not monopolized by any one religion, culture or ethical system.

Judaism, however, is unique in being the first civilization consciously and deliberately to recognize the primacy of the ethical good in human life. It is unique in being the creation of a people which was the first to dedicate itself to the furtherance of what we generally speak of as the good life. Whatever acceptance and prevalence the good life owes to Judaism are the result of the fact that for centuries there has lived a people which did not merely produce a few religious leaders or thinkers who uttered some startling and inspiring ideas of ethical import, but which had the

* When this chapter was written, the title of the book was to have been *Judaism and the Jews*, as explained in the Preface.

highest interests and purposes of its entire population organized around the assumption that the ethical idea is fundamental to living as human beings. Judaism's contribution to the good life was made possible because Judaism, not merely as a religion but as the living historical civilization of the Jewish people, is the product of a new and original emphasis on the place of the ethical in human life. What that emphasis was, it is the purpose of this chapter to set forth.

1. THE RELATION OF ETHICS TO RELIGION

Human beings in their mutual relations feel and act on the basis of what they expect of one another. These expectations, which assume a certain uniformity in human behavior, may be divided into natural and ethical. A natural expectation is one formed on the assumption that the person, with whom we have dealings, will feel and act toward us on the basis of the power we possess to help or harm him, to satisfy his wants or to cause him pain. We expect, for example, that one who owes us money should pay his debt. This is a natural expectation, provided we are in a position to enforce payment. But if, despite our inability to enforce our claim and his ability to deny it, we still expect him to pay his debt, we are entertaining an ethical expectation. No human society could exist for any length of time if it had to depend entirely upon coercion. No social machinery can be so devised as to exert pressure ubiquitously. There are numerous occasions when the individual can manage to elude all law enforcement. This would mean that on all such occasions, if we could not rely on people to act ethically, we would never know what to expect of them. Such a state of uncertainty would lead to anarchy and chaos in social life.

The tendency in present-day apologetic literature of religion is to convey the impression that the combination of ethics and religion is an original contribution of the Judeo-Christian tradition. The truth is that all human societies in one way or another look to their gods as the chief guardians of moral behavior. It could not be otherwise, since no external authority can possibly be adequate as a means of getting people to live up to moral requirements. A god's gaze is always assumed to be capable of penetrating the most secret recesses of the heart. To quote but a few instances—in describing the ancient Mexican religion, Andrew Lang says that "the prayers, penances and confessions . . . indicate a firm belief that even these strange deities 'made for righteousness,' loved good, and, in this world and the next, punished evil."[1] In the mythology of the Inca race the sun god is represented as addressing the parents of that race, as follows: "My children, when you have brought the peoples of these lands to our obedience, you should have care to maintain them therein by the laws of reason, of piety, of clemency and equity. . . . In this you will follow my example, for, as you know, I cease not from doing good to mortals . . ."[2]

James Henry Breasted devotes his entire book *The Dawn of Conscience* to proving the unmistakable emergence of a moral order among the Egyptians as far back as five thousand years ago. One of the tomb reliefs of the Memphite cemetery reads: "I did that which men loved and the gods approved, that they may make my eternal house (tomb) endure and my name flourish in the mouths of men."[3] Likewise the inscription on the tomb of the first known great explorer, Harkhup of Elephantine, bears testimony to the assumption, present in all human societies, that God demands obedience to the moral law. That inscription reads: "I desired that it might be well with me in the great God's presence."[4] Similar examples of this intimate bond between morality and religion could be multiplied *ad libitum*.

It is tempting to evaluate the character of a civilization on the basis of its ethical maxims. Even so high an authority as Breasted yields to that temptation. "As a young orientalist," says Breasted, "I found that the Egyptians had possessed a standard of morals far superior to that of the Decalogue over a thousand years before the Decalogue was written."[5] In this he speaks not as a scientist but as a special pleader. If ever there was a case where comparisons are odious it certainly is this one. There are times when it is far more scientific to be puzzled by what is unique in a phenomenon than to see in it only the familiar. The truth is that there is nothing in any ancient civilization which can compare with the ethical implications of believing in a God Whose claim to allegiance and obedience is based on His having redeemed a people from bondage to a tyrant, or that can compare with the duty on the part of an entire population to set aside one day in seven to physical and spiritual recreation. No text should be torn out of its historical context, even in preaching, much less in objective science.

To ascertain Judaism's contribution to world ethics it is necessary to ascertain the historical background of mankind at the time that the influence of Judaism made itself most felt. That was unquestionably the case when the classic world order began to break up. It is, furthermore, necessary to establish the particular context of Judaism as a whole, in order to discover what in its ethic was distinctive and therefore most likely to strike the attention of the Gentiles who came in contact with it.

2. THE DIMENSION OF THE ETHICAL

The study of human life has by this time made it clear that man's deliberate efforts to better his lot and to improve himself lie in more than the one dimension of those vital needs, or vitalities, which man shares with other living beings. As manifestations of physical and mental life, the vital needs are manifestations of power, for life is inherently power. Those needs are governed by nature or necessity; yet in satisfying them, man must reckon with something more than their inherent necessity. Always something asserts itself that clearly lies outside that dimension. So insistent have been those transnatural factors in human life that they have succeeded in winning recognition for themselves as constituting the human differential. All living beings are, to be sure, governed by natural forces or impulses. These may even be the source of those higher developments in man that mark him off from the rest of creation; but only in man do those natural forces or impulses achieve self-consciousness. Self-consciousness introduces a new quality into the content of human life. That new quality impels man to live in other dimensions beside the one of the vitalities or of power. One such dimension is that of the rational, or the universal, and the other is that of the spiritual, or the eternal. The dimension of the rational may be said to give *form* to the content of human life; the dimension of the spiritual may be said to give to it *purpose*.

To the dimension of the rational or the dimension of the universal belong all the interests and values that center around truth, or the knowledge of reality for its own sake, together with all those interests and values which center around moral goodness, or the practice of the right for its own sake. Since in ancient times the development of reason was for the most part limited, except in the case of Hindu and Greek philosophers, to the interests and values of moral goodness, the term "rational" will here be used interchangeably with "ethical," and *vice versa*. To the dimension of the spiritual, or the eternal, belong the three groups of interests and values that center respectively around (1) personality, or the self as a responsible being, (2) the social group, which is the medium of man's physical and mental life and growth, and which evokes his loyalty, and (3) the totality of things, or cosmos, as divine, or as contributing to man's salvation or self-fulfillment, and as evoking his piety.

The significant fact about any human society, from the most rudimentary to the most civilized, in which the integrative forces are stronger than the disintegrative, is that the rational and the spiritual values not only figure in the mutual relations and expectations of its members but are also regarded as original and autonomous instead of as derived from, or ministering to, the vitalities. To be sure, health, prosperity and social approval are generally considered rewards for ethical conformity, and for deference to the interests of personality, society and God; but those rewards are only incidental. In fact, the rationality or spirituality of any act is impugned as soon as it is believed to be motivated by the prospect of reward.

From the foregoing we can realize what is meant by the universality of ethics and religion. The diversities in ethical and religious thought and practice result from the differences in the opportunities to achieve knowledge and social contact with other groups and ways of life. The scope of life possible to a rudimentary society like that of a nomad tribe which wanders from oasis to oasis is far narrower than that possible to an urban community which engages in trade and commerce. That narrowness is bound to be reflected in its ethics and religion. Except when under the influence of some individual or collective passion, human beings normally reckon, according to their lights, with the rational and the spiritual interests. So long as any human group is sufficiently integrated to know itself as a unit, and is not subject to extraordinary pressure or influence, it manifests an unmistakable regard for rational and spiritual considerations. Every normal society reflects some sensitiveness to the universal values of reason and to the eternal values of the spirit.

3. When Ethical Values Are Questioned

Societies of men—families, tribes, clans, federations of clans, and city-states—have always been in a condition of flux, due to the pressure of populations on the food supply. In the struggle for existence, the weaker societies are broken up by the stronger. The survivors of the weaker society, finding their inherited way of life unable to provide them with the necessary protection and maintenance, become reconciled to their conquerors' way of life. But there are societies which fall victim to disintegration, not as a result of direct assault from without but of intrigue and struggle within. Then the very assumptions on which social solidarity is based begin to be questioned. Those assumptions will generally be found to belong to the ethical and the spiritual dimension of life.

Such a questioning attitude, however, never achieved the articulation and self-consciousness potent enough to act as a disruptive force on a large scale until the appearance of the Greek Sophists. Their activity was part of the general disintegration of the Greek spirit. The scientific progress, which had prepared the way for them, became in their hands a means of undermining all faith in the rational and spiritual foundations of society. By making a business of training young men for political careers, they succeeded in developing in those who were to be entrusted with authority a cynicism toward the very moral values that were essential to conscientious exercise of power. The morally corrosive influence of the Sophists reached down to the period of the Roman Empire and had no small share in its final disintegration.

Skepticism, whether intellectual, ethical or spiritual, thrives on social decay. Its procedure generally consists in proving that the higher values, which are upheld as the special distinction of man, are in effect nothing more than indirect or disguised means of gaining power over others. The yearning for truth and the passion for righteousness are shown to be merely a form of self-delusion. The undermining of faith in the intrinsic reality and worth of man's higher values is aided by the prevalent diversity in laws, customs and moral expectations. That diversity was played up by the Sophists as evidence that all ethical standards were nothing more than subjective and without any inherently obligatory character. The very ideal of justice became in their hands a mere honorific term for the cunning exercise of power which the strong wielded over the weak, or for the vindictive urge of the weak against the strong. Such reasoning led to the nihilism that threatened to paralyze man's efforts to transcend his selfishness.

The initial impulse to counteract this menace of moral nihilism came from Socrates. He succeeded in transmitting to subsequent generations the deep conviction that there ought to be a way of recapturing the faith in fundamental principles of truth and goodness as universally valid and as independent of their partial and distorted embodiments in actual life. Three schools of thought, the Platonic, the Aristotelian and the Stoic, which flourished during the Greco-Roman period, sought to retrieve the recognition of the inherent otherness of rational and spiritual values, an otherness that renders their essence independent of all considerations of power. Thus Plato discovered the nature of the idea as something other than any of its embodiments. He maintained that the highest idea of all, the Idea of the Good, was identical with God. Aristotle saw the danger of assigning complete otherness to the good and true; it was likely to lead to a final separation of the idea from the tangible realities of existence. He tried, therefore, to hold on to Plato's discovery without having to sever connections with the dimension of power and the vitalities in which we live and have our being. The Stoics attained the clearest and most emphatic enunciation of duty, and the consciousness of the "ought" as the very essence of reason which men share with cosmic reason. They expressed their intuitive awareness of the distinctive ethical dimension by stressing duty as an imperative of reason. Their emphasis upon the originality, independence and otherness of the ethical is so much like Judaism's assumption concerning the nature of the good life that Philo of Alexandria[6a] was able to regard Stoicism as little more than a Greek version of the teachings of Moses.

With the prominent role of the great philosophic schools in those days, and especially with the great influence wielded by the Stoics in high social and governmental circles, one would imagine that they should have succeeded in checking the progressive social disintegration and the moral disorientation of their day. Their learning had a marked influence on Roman jurisprudence, but their teachings had no effect on the inner life of those who controlled the destinies of the state. It did not even touch the masses, which were becoming increasingly demoralized. The military campaigns carried on by Rome contributed to the supplanting of vast populations. The number of human beings transported and sold into slavery and thus left culturally and spiritually rootless kept growing. The intellectualized ethics of the philosophic schools had no message for these forgotten people. The Stoics became, as it were, private chaplains of the well-to-do, with never a thought for the underprivileged who constituted the bulk of the population.

4. THE WESTERN WORLD SAVED FROM MORAL DISINTEGRATION BY JUDEO-CHRISTIAN TRADITION

Within this mass of confused and disintegrating humanity, the Jewish people appeared as a strange and inexplicable phenomenon. Despite the most cruel blows of fate, this pe ple clung desperately to its group life and managed to survive by virtue of its confidence in its way of life as the only one certain to bring salvation to mankind. The Jewish people lived in a state of dispersion far beyond the borders of its own land; yet all its scattered communities regarded themselves as bound together by a common destiny. So contagious was the example of the Jews that many Gentiles, noting the inner sense of security that Judaism afforded its adherents, joined the Jewish people.

Before long a new wave of religious enthusiasm swept from Palestine to all Jewish communities in the Diaspora, in the form of the Christian gospel. That gospel not only retained the confidence the Jews had had in their own way of life, as well as the original emphasis upon the primacy and the divine character of the ethical, but it also possessed the irresistible vigor and impetus of a new revelation. Thus did the long stored-up moral energy of the Jewish people sweep across the Western world like a tidal wave. In the same way that Paul saved the personality of Jesus from oblivion, so did Christianity save the ethical emphasis of Judaism from being confined to the Jewish people. In both instances, however, transmission of values from one civilization to another resulted in their refraction.

The fact, however, that the Judeo-Christian way of life called forth astonishment and admiration among the spiritually uprooted and disoriented in the Greco-Roman world does not mean that they had a clear idea of what was most significant in that way of life. They were scarcely aware of the distinctive character of the ethical teachings and ideals in the Judeo-Christian tradition. They did not weigh the ethical precepts of Judaism or Christianity against those of Stoicism. They merely found in that tradition an answer to the question that then troubled all who sought some means of overcoming their sense of frustration: What is salvation, and how can one attain it? The conviction that accompanied the answer given by Judaism and Christianity brought into sharp relief the ethical teachings that were included in the answer. In a world in which all ethical values and assumptions were in danger of being swept away, the sincerity with which the Jewish people affirmed the divinely revealed nature of its own way of life, provided the only safe anchorage.

No philosophy, however consistent and edifying, could hope at that stage of human development to restore the confidence in the inherently independent and underived character of the difference between right and wrong. Philosophic thinking had destroyed that confidence. Only supernatural revelation could restore it. The Jews were the only people who, at that critical period in the life of Western mankind, were convinced that God had revealed to them the true way of life. Moreover, the ardent conviction that the God Who had revealed to them their way of life was the only true God, reinforced the validity of the claim that their way of life was divinely revealed and therefore unquestionably true. By affirming the oneness of God and prohibiting the worship of Him under any conceivable image, Judaism was able to hold its own against the philosophies of the day, not only in the ethical aspect of reason but also in the metaphysical. This rendered its teachings acceptable to the sophisticated as well as to the unlettered. The same is true of Christianity. Accordingly, *the service that the Jewish people rendered to human civilization may be said to consist in having restored confidence in the original and underived character of the ethical values and in their independence of the considerations of expediency and self-interest.*

Undoubtedly the assertion that the Ten Commandments were spoken by God at Sinai, taken literally, conveys a fact which is in conflict with the modern man's outlook. But a knowledge of the workings of the ancient mind and of the way it was wont to report its profoundest experience has taught us to penetrate beneath the surface of a tradition and to get the functional significance of that tradition, from the standpoint of the attitudes and behavior it was intended to call forth. There is a large area of feeling and experience for which even the most articulate lack the right expression. Suppose an ancient people, untutored in philosophic speculation, had the irresistible intuition that the ethical values stemmed from a source other than that of individual expediency—by no means incredible—how could they put that intuition into words other than those recorded in the Jewish tradition? As what else than a revelation from God could they possibly describe this experience of compelling certainty? The sense of inner compulsion which a highly important truth always carried with it led the ancients to ascribe that truth to a source which belonged to a different dimension of being from that of normal experience. Such a source could only be Divine Revelation.

5. Moral Values Given Foundation of Certainty by Judaism

In the light of these considerations, Judaism's contribution to world ethics consists in having reaffirmed the objective character and cosmic significance of the difference between good and evil, right and wrong, at a most critical juncture in the history of Western mankind. That affirmation by itself did not determine the content of the ethical values. It did not, for example, actually answer the question whether slavery and polygamy were morally right or wrong. But it helped to re-establish the certainty that a moral standard was part of the very nature of reality, and that to function as human beings we must always strive to approximate it in all our relations with one another.

Because the modern era is also one of social confusion and disintegration, there has been a recrudescence of the nihilist notion that the only function of power is to be successful, regardless of the claims of reason and spirit. The first sensational formulation of such nihilism in modern times is to be found in Machiavelli's *The Prince*. It finally attained rodomontade swagger in Nietzsche. Many thinkers have sought to restore the rational foundations of ethics, but none with as much acumen as did Kant. His great contribution to the understanding of the nature of the moral law consists in the rediscovery of its intrinsic rationality and worth, independently of any empirical consequences to which its application may lead. He stresses again and again the need of its being observed for its own sake and not for the sake of happiness or any other good. In describing the moral law as a categorical imperative, which is the expression of the autonomy of the practical reason, Kant definitely assigns to it a different dimension from that in which man lives out his vital needs and powers. This fact, which Kant points out as true of the moral law, is what human beings normally experience in the form of intuition, and what the Jewish people with its tradition, which it regarded as divinely revealed, helped to conserve for Western civilization. But what the Jewish people accomplished no individual thinker or school of philosophers could have accomplished.

How liable human beings are to lose their normal intuition concerning the objective and underived character of the moral law, has been amply demonstrated in the 1930's by the spread of fascism. Fascism is essentially moral nihilism. In its lethal effect on human life it outstrips by far the moral nihilism of the philosophic hedonists, who declare that pleasure is the only criterion of the good. According to fascism, virtually the only thing worthwhile in human life is the possession of power over other people's lives and happiness. Nietzsche's nihilism can be practiced only by the individual who possesses extraordinary cunning and prowess. But fascism goes much further and makes it possible for every Tom, Dick or Harry to act out the tendency to nihilism. This tendency is no less innate than the tendency to reckon with the moral law, even as the death-wish is as innate as the will-to-live. If mankind will recover from its contemporary partial relapse into moral nihilism, it will be only through some extraordinary reassertion of its will-to-live. Some rightly choose to call such a reassertion a manifestation of Divine Grace.

6. THE AREA OF HUMAN RELATIONS THE PRINCIPAL OBJECT OF JEWISH ETHICS

From the standpoint of ethical theory, it may be sufficient to establish the autonomy, the otherness or the different dimensionality of the moral law of ethical values. But from the standpoint of everyday living and the betterment of human relations, it is necessary to know to which of the needs or vitalities of human life the moral law is to be applied. This involves specifying the particular vital functions which are most prone to moral evil, or to the violation of the moral law. If we divide the vitalities into two main areas, one harboring the physical desires and the other the various strivings and ambitions which function through the mutual relations of human beings, the tendency in certain ages and civilizations, like the Hindu and the medieval Western, has been to regard the physical hungers as man's chief stumbling block. This has been especially true in relation to the sex hunger.

Judaism, on the other hand, may be said to have been the first civilization to insist that the field of human relations is the area most in need of being brought within the dimension of the moral law. The tendency of the strong and the clever to exploit the weak and the simple is, in the estimate of Judaism, the source of man's undoing. To be sure, Judaism abounds in taboo and restrictions intended to restrain the physical hungers from running riot. But whatever provision it makes for such restraint it does essentially in the same spirit as modern society provides for the social health of the community, as a kind of hygienic measure. Only to the extent, however, that human relations are implicated in those physical hungers do those hungers become subject to moral law.

Since the main evil in the area of human relations, which has ever brought in its wake chaos and disaster to human life, is the lust to dominate (directly, when one is strong enough to do so, or indirectly by identifying oneself with the leader or his mob in whom such strength resides), that is the evil against which Judaism principally invokes the moral law. This distinctive note in the ethics of Judaism is quite unmistakable. A summary of the ethical teachings in Israel's Torah might well be the famous scripture in Zechariah: "Not by might nor by power but by My Spirit, saith the Lord of Hosts" (Zech. 4:6), or even the less well known scripture in Samuel: "For not by strength shall man prevail" (I Sam. 2:9).

7. THE ETHICAL IMPLICATION OF TORAH AS A CONSTITUTIVE PRINCIPLE OF PEOPLEHOOD

"Torah" is often used, in a limited sense, to designate the Pentateuch together with the mass of Rabbinic tradition based on it. As such "Torah" consists of the Written and the Oral Law.[7a] The term "Torah" may also be used in a wider sense, to designate all that we understand by Judaism. To grasp, however, the essence of what that term conveys in this wider sense, it is necessary to study carefully what it represents in its more limited sense. The Torah as the Written and the Oral Law is not a book or a code but a people-making instrument. It was the charter of the Jewish people. This function of Torah throws much light upon Judaism's contribution to what has been described as "the ethical seriousness in our Western culture." As an idea, therefore, "Torah" may be said to represent the principle that made the Jews into a people.

Rab Saadia[8a] uttered a most penetrating truth when, in referring to the Jews, he said, "The only thing that makes us into a people is the Torah." By that he probably meant to negate the idea that it was kinship, blood or race that made the Jews into a people, and to affirm the fact that the particular pattern of living or way of life unfolded in the Torah formed the bond of ethnic unity. There is another possible negation involved in Rab Saadia's statement. It may justly be interpreted as implying that the constitutive principle of Jewish peoplehood is not the power the group has over its individual members, as in the case of all other peoples, but the opportunity which the Jewish group affords the individual Jew to share the way of life promulgated in the Torah. This amounts to saying that, in so far as the Jews felt that the Torah was the constitutive principle of their peoplehood, it precluded the machinery of state from being that principle.

The state as a political entity is essentially the organization of the force inherent in a nation. A state-constituted nation is therefore the product of force, regardless of moral law as such. The machinery of the state has all too often been directed against the underprivileged within the nation itself as well as against other nations. Franz Oppenheim, in his book *The State*, proves that, historically, the state is the product of the same *force majeure* which enables the invader to conquer and take away the lands and goods of the conquered. It is therefore intrinsically the antithesis of morally constituted organization. Those who compiled the Torah, and had it adopted as the basis of Jewish unity, had no such sociological awareness of the origin and true character of the state, yet intuitively they must have sensed these facts about the state.

Likewise, the spiritual leaders of the Jewish people seem to have been eager to prevent Israel from being completely identified with the state and dependent upon it for survival. To mention only a few striking examples of this negative attitude: the early preference for divinely sent instead of popularly chosen leaders, the resistance which the prophet Samuel is said to have displayed toward the people's demand for a king, the Torah's casual reference to the appointment of a king as optional instead of as an expected procedure, the prophet Hosea's allusion to the institution of kinghood as irritating to God, and above all, the greater judicial and legislative authority which Pharisaism[9a] conferred upon the spokesman of the Torah than upon the representatives of the state. All these instances point to a conscious deprecation of organized force as the basic principle of peoplehood. The ethical implications of that attitude to the state are, indeed, far reaching. The significance of this attitude in our day may be inferred from the fact that it is the very antipode of that implied in the Hegelian conception of the state as "the Divine Idea as it exists on earth." What that conception implied, and what happened when it was acted on by some nations, was frankly expressed in the well known epigram of H. V. Treitschke: "The essence of the state is in the first place power, in the second place power, and in the third place, once more, power" (*"Bundesstaat und Einheitstaat"*).

Since, according to the idea of "Torah," the authority of the people as a whole over the individual who is a member of it does not stem from the collective force which it can bring to bear upon him, that authority must stem from another source. That source is none other than the Will of God, which the people mediates for the individual. Torah thus came to represent the articulation of the Will of God as it manifested itself, first, in the career of the people and, secondly, in the particular way of life to which the people was committed. The Jews thus evolved the principle that the basis of society, or its main cohesive influence, was not the power the strong might wield over the weak, but the common submission of both strong and weak to the Will of God. The Will of God is not the will of a mighty potentate who can intimidate human beings into obedience, but the principle of righteousness conceived in cosmic terms and become articulate in the people's philosophy of life and in the precepts and commandments that set forth the norms that guide its life.

The unity which the Jewish people, through its Torah, held up as the only kind that may legitimately bind men together, coincides with what Josiah Royce interpreted to be the motivating influence of all ethical living. Royce identified loyalty to a cause as the most potent factor for the good life. He defined a "cause" as *"some conceived, and yet also real, spiritual unity which links many individual lives into one, and which is therefore essentially superhuman, in exactly the same sense in which we find the realities of the world of reason to be superhuman.* Yet the cause is not, on that account any mere abstraction. It is a live something. 'My home,' 'my family,' 'my service,' 'mankind,' 'the church,' 'my art,' 'my science,' 'the cause of humanity,' or once more 'God's Will'; such are the names for the cause . . . This cause is not a mere heap or collection of human beings; it is a life of many brethren in unity . . . Such a principle does not mean, 'lose yourself,' or even simply 'sacrifice yourself.' It means 'Be as rich and full and strong a self as you can, and then with all your heart and your soul and your mind and your strength, devote yourself to this cause, to this spiritual unity, in which individuals may be, and (when they are loyal) actually are, united in a life whose meaning is above the separate meanings of any or all natural human beings.' "[10] Every word in the foregoing passage brings out most sharply the implications of that section of the Torah known as the *Shema*, which it has been the sacred duty of every Jew to read twice daily. There everyone in Israel is invoked to love God with all of his being and to express that love by being ever mindful of God's behests and communicating them to his children. The love of God which the Israelite is called upon to foster is the exact equivalent of the loyalty to a cause which Royce so warmly urges as indispensable to salvation.

8. THE RATIONALE FOR THE GOOD LIFE SUPPLIED BY THE TORAH NARRATIVE

How did the Will of God, according to the Torah, reveal itself in the career of Israel? In answer, the Torah unfolds the panorama of the creation of the world and the spread of mankind, and it indicates the place of Israel in that panorama. This gives to the Torah a function which very few suspect, since to most people Torah is only a synonym for law. That function is to convey to the individual an orientation that is expected to motivate loyalty to his people and love for his God, and to arouse in him an eagerness to perform God's Will as revealed in His people's code of law and ethics. This means that on a par with legal and ethical precepts is the narrative that serves as their background and rationale. The Jew is not expected to obey God's Will blindly. Such obedience might be prompted by fear, or by the awareness of God's overwhelming power. That would destroy the very essence of the ethical deed. A deed is ethical, as has been shown, only to the extent that it is a free act. It is a free act when motivated by the love of God. The reason for loving God, which the Torah advances to the Jew, is not the success or prosperity he might enjoy, or share with his people, but the divinely guided career and the God-appointed destiny in which he should participate as a member of that people. This accounts for the importance the Torah attaches to having the Jew oriented as definitely as possible concerning the place of his people in God's world.

Seldom are the foregoing facts regarded as having any ethical significance. The truth, however, is that Judaism has made a far greater contribution to the good life by means of this indirect emphasis upon the need,
on the part of every individual, for an ethico-spiritual orientation to life
as a whole than if it had developed in elaborate form some abstract argument concerning the nature of the moral good. Judaism could not have
stressed more strongly the principle of the dignity of the human person
than by this recognition of the right of the individual to know the general
pattern and meaning of life and the place of his own group in that pattern.
It is like honoring a soldier who is a mere private with information not
only about the tactics of the battle but also about the strategy of the war.

*The comprehensiveness of the narrative portion of the Torah and the
brilliance with which its significant points are highlighted have probably
done more to foster both cosmic and group consciousness, first in the
Jews and then in the adherents of Christianity and Islam, as a rationale
for ethical attitudes and conduct, than all the systematic thinking of the
philosophers.* It matters not that, from a scientific viewpoint, the narrative
of the origin and early beginnings of Israel is on the whole legendary.
That very fact is perhaps all the more reason for regarding the narrative
section of the Torah as ethically significant, because it points to the existence
of definite ethical assumptions as having shaped, if not actually having
created, the narrative material.

In this discussion only the merest mention can be made of what renders
the Torah narrative so conspicuously important, from the standpoint of
the good life. The career of Israel is there shown to owe its beginnings to
God's purpose of having a people that would fulfill His Will. What God
wills concerning man is clearly stated in the reason given for God's choice
of Abraham as the founder of a people: "For I have known him to the
end that he may command his children and his household after him, that
they may keep the way of the Lord, to do righteousness and justice" (Gen.
18:19). That choice fell upon Abraham because he happened to be the
first human being to obey God implicitly. He fulfilled the Divine behest
to be *tamim* ("simple" or "perfect") which, to judge from the various
contexts in which that term is used, implies acting in a spirit of implicit
obedience to God. Thus Abraham is represented as the foil, setting off by
contrast the character of Adam, who symbolizes man in general and who
in the allegory of the Garden of Eden is represented as having through
his sin brought toil, suffering and death on the human race. How far
Abraham was willing to make God's Will the dominant purpose of his
own life is indicated by the unquestioning faith he displayed—a faith
which God "accounted it to him as righteousness" (Gen. 15:6)—and the
readiness to sacrifice his only son at God's bidding. His very self-surrender
to the Will of God, which is synonymous with righteousness and justice,

impells him paradoxically enough to take God to task for threatening to carry out a seeming act of injustice. "Shall not the Judge of all the earth do justly?" (Gen. 18:25) asks Abraham, when learning of the doom that was to befall the wicked cities of Sodom and Gomorrah.

The descendants of Abraham were to grow into a people that was to live not by might nor by strength but by the spirit of God, or the spirit of righteousness. How was that to be compatible with the realities which called for the acquisition of a land? All the habitable lands the ancients knew of had already been occupied. No new people could have arisen without displacing some existing people. Such displacement could not apparently take place without involving the unrighteous use of force. The Torah resolves this dilemma by pointing out that the peoples which inhabited the land of Canaan had made themselves unworthy of it, by reason of their moral corruption. During Abraham's life, however, and for a number of centuries after him, the iniquity of the Amorite was not yet full (Gen. 15:16). His descendants had therefore to wander about for a long time. When they finally did find temporary domicile, they had to pay for it by becoming slaves in a land that was not theirs (Gen. 15:13), and by submitting to harsh treatment. All this, in order not to commit the injustice of dispossessing a people before it had become completely undeserving of its land! However dangerous we now know such rationalization of conquest to be, nevertheless, in its unsophisticated form, it undoubtedly expresses a new kind of group sensitivity to ethical values.

To proceed with the Torah narrative: in the meantime the events, which culminate in the redemption of the Israelites from Egypt and the revelation of the laws by which they are to order their lives, help to emphasize the ethical implications of God's relation to man. That relation was experienced by the Israelites in their miraculous redemption from Egyptian bondage. From beginning to end, that redemption, as well as the journeying through the wilderness and the final occupation of the land, is depicted as having been made possible entirely through God's intervention. Everywhere in the telling of those stories we note the unmistakable purpose of stressing the weakness and the helplessness of the Israelites and their complete dependence upon God.

The key to the understanding of the narrative portions of the Torah and of the other books of the Bible is to be found in statements like the following: "The Lord will fight for you and ye shall hold your peace" (Ex. 14:14), or, "(Beware of saying to yourselves), 'My power and the might of my hand hath gotten me this wealth'" (Deut. 8-17). The sin to which the Torah ascribes Israel's wanderings in the desert is not the sin of having worshiped the Golden Calf, but that of having refused to rely upon God's power to enable them to overcome the strongly fortified

natives of Canaan. That refusal implied that the Israelites had not abandoned the prevalent assumption that whatever force man wielded was
entirely his own, and being his own he could do with it what he pleased.
This, according to the Torah, is man's cardinal sin. The one unvarying
theme in all of ancient Judaism's teachings concerning Israel's career is
the deprecation of the possible claim that whatever success Israel achieved
in its struggle for existence, for freedom, or for possession it owed to its
own prowess. All such success must be ascribed only to God.

The power of God is always directed against strong peoples which act
insolently. They generally defy God's Will, which is essentially the same
as what we mean by the moral law. This fact stands out most conspicuously
in the case of the redemption from Egypt. As is well known, that event
figures as the main point of reference in Israel's religious career. It is the
seminal or archetypal event in its history. From it the Jew is expected to
draw the principal inspiration for fulfilling God's Will. The commemoration of it is given as a rationale for the Sabbath. It is the main rationale
for the Passover festival, which had been transformed from a nature
festival to a historical one, and which came to be celebrated with far greater
éclat than the two other pilgrim festivals. The main experience of God's
intervention in Israel's career is thus associated with an event in which
God redresses the wrong done to those who have been oppressed and
rescues them from the power of their oppressor. This fact could not but
contribute to the conception of God as the champion of the weak against
the strong. That conception of God is a corollary of the intuition that the
distinction between right and wrong belongs to a different dimension of
existence from that of the physical vitalities and powers.

9. POWER ENTRUSTED BY GOD TO MAN FOREVER SUBJECT TO ABUSE

It is doubtful whether the comparative study of religion can yield a
parallel instance of such unmitigated insistence on treating force or power
as something with which it is dangerous to entrust man. It is as though
traditional Judaism affirmed of power, whether exercised over things in
the environment or over other human beings, what the ancient Greeks
said about fire, when they spoke of it as stolen from heaven by Prometheus.
In common with the rest of the world, the Jews naturally identified power
as the very essence of Godhood. On the other hand, they fully realized
that man's avoidable sufferings were, for the most part, the result of the
abuse of power. That is the abuse described in Scriptures as violence, a
term for that which caused God to regret that He had created man (Gen.
6:6).

In the Middle Ages many mystics believed that by proper invocation of
the different appellations of God and His angels they might achieve con-

trol over nature. Those who held that belief realized fully the dangers their very success might bring on them and on the rest of the world. They feared that they might become so intoxicated with their newly acquired power as to use it for selfish ends. They therefore prescribed numerous restrictions which would permit only those of pure and unselfish character to engage in mystic lore, and they themselves underwent the most exacting routines in self-discipline. In our own day likewise, we have come to dread the possible consequences of entrusting the knowledge of modern science and invention to all and sundry. Remembering the possible abuses of force, we are afraid to consent even to the enforcement of international peace.

Fear of the abuse of force led all those who had a hand in the shaping of the Jewish consciousness—priests, prophets and sages—to emphasize the existence of a sharp antithesis between force and spirit, between power and moral law. That was one of the ways in which the ancients tried to articulate the profound intuition that spirit and moral law constituted a different dimension of existence from, and were entirely other than, considerations of utility or expediency which have to do with whatever force or power man has at his command. When Plato discovered the fact that ideas as such belonged to an entirely different order of existence from the things we know through the senses, he was able to articulate that fact only by emphasizing the impassable gulf that divided ideas from things. Had he not gone to extremes in stressing the otherness of idea, philosophy would probably have made little progress. Similarly, if Judaism had not gone to extremes in maintaining that force was incommensurate with spirit, or that power could not be equated with moral law, man would never have understood why all his achievements in the domain of power turn to dust and ashes, unless they are based on the moral law and unless they conform to the demands of the spirit.

10. TORAH LAW AS A MEANS OF CHANNELING POWER INTO MORAL CONDUCT

But if Judaism had stopped at the deprecation of man's use of power, it would have done what many other civilizations and religions tried to do when they sought to prevent man's involvement in material things and physical desires. Instead it sought to channel man's use of force within a way of life according to the Will of God. The way of life detailed in the Torah includes for the most part such laws, customs and mores as were on the whole common to the ancient civilizations of the Nile and the Euphrates. In the form in which those laws are found in the traditional Torah, they are the result of modification, first, as a result of differences in local conditions that obtained in Eretz Yisrael and, secondly, as a result of a uniquely ethical outlook on life. The general effect of thus directing whatever power man legitimately possesses into the channel of law has been to foster what may be considered the most important ethical principle underlying the use of power. That principle is that the exercise of power must be accompanied by the assumption of a commensurate degree of responsibility. Responsibility is modern man's equivalent for the traditional concept of Divine law for man.

It may well be that even despite the ethical refinement of the law and custom which had thus come down from Israel's prehistoric days, or would have been taken over from other civilizations, the laws and customs still fall below accepted standards of the best in modern life. That fact, however, is entirely irrelevant from the standpoint of Judaism's role in the ethical development of mankind. *That development was determined not by the particular content of the law but by the spirit that permeated the law.* The laws in the Torah dealing with slavery assume the institution of slavery to be normal, and in addition discriminate between a Hebrew and a Gentile slave in a manner that would now be regarded as definitely unethical. There are, to be sure, many laws which, even in the light of the highest standards of what is best in our own day, are ethically unimpeachable. But this method of appraising each particular law to determine how much of it is standard and how much is above standard is misleading from the standpoint of the question: How did the Torah influence the ethical consciousness of the Western world? That influence does not derive from any particular law or laws, but from the spirit that permeates all of them. We should, therefore, recognize that spirit and analyze its essential character if we want to know in what way the Torah as law contributed to world ethics.

The purpose to be served by the laws of the Torah is unmistakably set forth again and again. That purpose is declared to be that of rendering Israel a holy people. During the preparations for the theophany on Mt. Sinai, Moses was commanded to tell the Israelites that they were to be "a Kingdom of priests and a holy nation" (Ex. 19:6). In the very midst of what is known as the "Book of Covenant," which contains most of the laws that have served as the basis of civil jurisprudence in traditional Judaism, we read, "And ye shall be holy men unto me" (Ex. 22:30). The collection of laws known as the "Holiness Code"[11a] is called such because of the opening behest, which seems to represent the spirit intended to animate the whole of that code: "Speak unto all the congregation of the children of Israel, and say unto them; ye shall be holy; for I the Lord your God am holy" (Lev. 19:2). That the keeping of the commandments is to be the means of rendering Israel holy is stressed in numerous passages (cf. Lev. 22:31; Num. 15:40; Deut. 14:2, 14:21, 23:15, 28:9).

11. Holiness in God and Man as Harmonious Synthesis of Power and Goodness

The meaning of holiness has been explored by students of both rudimentary and highly developed religions. They have invariably found that holiness was used in two senses, a physical and an ethical. In addition, they have found that "holy" and "divine" are generally used interchangeably. A god is a holy being, and a holy being is one that possesses something of the attribute of godhood. These discoveries of the scientific study of religious phenomena do not justify us in interpreting those phenomena as though those who were aware of them were students of religion. But they do help us penetrate into the religious consciousness of the ancients and reconstruct their ways of thought and their emotional responses.

These two conceptions of holiness as physical and as ethical are found in the Bible, though it is not always easy to draw the line between them. When God was about to descend on Mt. Sinai, He ordered Moses to warn the Israelites not to go near the mountain, lest they be stoned or shot through. When Uzza touched the Holy Ark for fear that it might fall off the wagon, as the cattle which drew it slipped, he was smitten. In both instances, holiness is conceived as a powerful physical force that shocks the human being to death when he ventures too close to it. However, there are equally unmistakable evidences of the use of the term "holiness" in a spiritual or ethical sense, as when God is said to have blessed the Sabbath and to have hallowed it (Ex. 20:11). The nature of the commandments imparted to Israel, after they are urged to be a holy nation, is entirely of a spiritual and an ethical character. The same is true of most of the behests in the Holiness Code.

The inference to which the foregoing facts point is that the purpose of the Torah, in that phase of it which deals with law, is to answer the question that its narrative section raises: Since whatever power man wields, and that reveals itself in his desires and ambitions, is not his own but entrusted to him by God, to Whom it actually belongs, how is man to know whether he employs it as he should? The answer furnished by the Torah is the following: The only way you can be sure that you are employing properly the God-given power entrusted to you is by using it in accordance with the prescribed testimonies, judgments and statutes. In the words of the Torah itself, "And ye shall remember all the commandments of the Lord and do them; and that ye go not about after your own heart and your own eyes, after which you use to go astray: that ye may remember and do all my commandments and be holy unto your God" (Num. 15:39-40).

The assumption is that the laws or commandments emanate from the moral or spiritual dimension in the nature of God, a dimension of holiness which is other than the one of force or power. The prophet Isaiah says: "The Lord of Hosts is exalted through justice, and God the Holy One is sanctified through righteousness" (5:16). A further assumption is that the nature or holiness of God is such that the dimension of force and the dimension of goodness abide in Him in perfect harmony, though those two attributes exist in Him on a scale beyond human computation. To the degree that they exist in man in a state of harmony, man is godlike, or holy. To achieve that godliness, or holiness, he has to obey the law of God. When man deliberately transgresses or ignores God's law, the assumption is that he does so because he imputes to himself all or most of the power he needs for the fulfillment of his desires and ambitions. If he credits himself with, and takes glory in, all the power he happens to possess, he dispenses with worship entirely; if he leaves some margin to supernatural sources, he tends to worship God in the wrong spirit, or to worship false gods.

If space allowed, it would have been interesting to note how differently the Greek philosophers developed the aim of God-likeness as the animating principle of ethical behavior. All that need be mentioned at this point is that the meaning of God-likeness is necessarily determined by that in human life which is considered as of supreme value and, therefore, as a reflection of divinity. To the Greek thinkers, a life of contemplation was of supreme value. Therefore to be Godlike meant to them to be like God in the ability to see life as it really is, to excel in *theoria*. For the creators of Judaism, what mattered most was the existence of a people that ordered its life in accordance with the principle of holiness, as it was assumed to exist in God. The apotheosis of Torah implies that the harmony of power and goodness is achieved by a people when it organizes its life around laws which have as their purpose the striving to be holy, even as God is holy.

12. The Significance of the Archaic Character of Torah Law

As a result of the tendency to incorporate ancient forms of thought into our own universe of discourse, we may be using the same words as did the ancients, but we seldom speak the same language. Ancient concepts taken out of their original context are desiccated and devitalized and have about as much of the original taste to the intellectual palate as dried-out vegetables have to the physical. Thus the traditional doctrine of the Torah as divinely revealed loses its functional significance when dissociated from the ancient universe of discourse and, in losing that significance, is reduced to a theological dogma devoid of any ethical connotation. To recapture what the conception "divinely revealed" meant in its original setting, we have to find in our own universe of discourse some conception that bears as close a resemblance to it as possible in terms of pragmatic significance. Such a modern analogy, it seems, is offered by the conception "back to nature." If that is true, a second ethical implication of the Torah as divinely revealed becomes apparent, the first being the one discussed above, namely, the otherness and autonomy of the moral law.

With the aid of that analogy we can understand what motivated those who compiled the various writings which go by the name of Pentateuch. They who "handled the Torah" (tofse ha-torah, Jer. 2:8) were people who seemed to have sought out whatever ancient fragments contained law or narrative which they regarded as furthering the purpose of giving moral and spiritual character to Israel's life as a people. They took for granted that the archaic laws, which were part of the original tribal life of Israel, were inherently more moral and spiritual than those which obtained in their own day. This was in line with the prevalent tendency to idealize Israel's sojourn in the wilderness as having been a period when the people was assumed to have been governed by the very presence of God in its midst (Ex. 25:8). In the words of Jeremiah: "Thus saith the Lord: I remember for thee the affection of thy youth, the love of thine espousals; how thou wentest after me in the wilderness, in a land that was not sown" (2:2). Since the archaic laws in the Torah were known to have come down from what were already then olden times, and were viewed as the embodiment of the ethical principles by which power was to be regulated, they were inevitably regarded as having emanated from God. By the time those laws were integrated into Israel's Torah they were for the most part already obsolete. But they served the all-important purpose of emphasizing the need of submitting every exercise of human power to the Will of God as manifest in the law of righteousness. It is, indeed, significant that the prophetic writings close with the words: "Remember ye the law of Moses My servant, which I commanded unto him in Horeb for all Israel, even statutes and ordinances" (Mal 3:22).

13. TORAH AS BACKGROUND OF PROPHECY IN ISRAEL

Only on the assumption that the Jews had been sensitized to moral and spiritual interests through the medium of Torah, which, in outline at least, was a forerunner of the Torah as we have it, can we view the prophetic contribution to Judaism in its proper perspective.[12a] The biblical scholars, who have assumed that the prophetic writings represent the emergence of a new spiritual force completely alien to the environment in which it appeared, make far greater demands upon credulity than the traditional view which looks upon the prophets as having functioned entirely in line with long existing ethical trends. It is inconceivable that the prophets would resort to violent denunciation of their people's ignorance of God's true character, or that they would engage in bitter condemnation of the social injustice that prevailed among their contemporaries, unless those whom they addressed might be expected to know better and to act more ethically. Already Hosea alludes to some kind of Torah which God had written for Israel, but which had remained a dead letter (8:12). In the parable of the vineyard, Isaiah states that after all that God had done for the House of Israel and the men of Judah, "He looked for justice, but behold violence" (5:7). Apparently those whom Isaiah addressed must have been familiar with the stories we read in the Pentateuch and with the laws that form part of the traditional Torah. Otherwise his bitter denunciation would have been entirely unwarranted. Only people familiar with the story of Sodom and Gomorrah could have grasped the invective implied in being called "Rulers of Sodom and people of Gomorrah" (1:10). Only on the assumption that new moons, Sabbaths and holy convocations were strictly observed—which indicates the existence of priestly Torah—has Isaiah's reference to their futility any meaning.

We must therefore conclude that not only do the prophets themselves owe their passion for righteousness to a moral climate which had been deliberately fostered, but that their very mission must be understood as an application to new and bewildering situations of the ethical principles which were accepted in their day as of long standing. Moreover, only this intrinsic relation between Torah and Prophecy can account for the fact that the writings of the prophets attained a canonicity second in authority and sanctity only to that of the traditional Torah. Such canonicity is another one of those unique elements in Judaism which have had a greater influence on the world than even some of its most important ethical principles. We can well understand that anciently recorded tradition or law should be raised to the status of a high ethnic possession. But that a collection of the most vehement censure of a people's policies and way of life should be given the same high rank as its organic law marks a new stage in the ethical development of human societies.

Such moral censures abound in the writings of all great civilizations, but they merely point to the existence of a few moral critics who refused to reconcile themselves to the evils of the life around them. Their protests generally remained voices in the wilderness. In the case of Israel's prophets, however, their most denunciatory charges against their people were incorporated into the body of that people's sacred writings. Thus the trait of group self-criticism came to be an ethical requirement or expectation. This is something entirely new in the ethical consciousness of mankind and should be set down as a further contribution of Judaism to world ethics. A long time will probably elapse before nations, churches or even lesser groups will be able to overcome their collective vanity and acquire the ability to submit to criticism. Without such ethical maturity, collectives are bound to neutralize whatever virtues or moral excellences some of their individual members may attain. "Moral man in immoral society" is not merely the title of a book; it describes the present universal condition of man.

14. THE ETHICAL IMPLICATIONS OF THE PROPHETIC CONCEPTION OF GOD

There is an integral relation between the spirit of prophecy and the spirit of Torah. This is evident from the fact that the main provocation for the prophets' rebuke is the people's failure to live up to the fundamental teaching of the Torah. The people is denounced for not acting on the principle that whatever power man possesses is entrusted to him by God, and must be employed in accordance with God's ethical traits which find expression in His laws. This underlying principle of the Torah may be viewed either as derived from or as the source of the Jewish conception of God. According to that conception, God combines in Himself in perfect harmony infinite power and unqualified righteousness. In the conduct, however, which the prophets beheld in people about them, and in the political intrigues carried on by the governments of Israel and Judah, this conception of God was consistently ignored. God was regarded in much the same light as the other peoples regarded their respective deities. He was to them the main source of power, and was therefore to be appealed to and, if need be, even cozened, in the hope that He would grant some of that power to them for the fulfillment of their own wants. In this attitude toward God, all moral issues were ignored. The sacrificial cult and the ritual practice were observed with meticulous care, but all those laws which sought to protect the weak against the strong were completely overlooked.

This is the refrain of so much of the prophetic writings that one typical passage from the Book of Jeremiah should suffice to illustrate the point:

Trust ye not in lying words, saying: "The temple of the Lord, the temple of the Lord, the temple of the Lord, are these." Nay, but if ye thoroughly amend your ways and your doings; if ye thoroughly execute justice between man and his neighbor; if ye oppress not the stranger, the fatherless, and the widow, and shed not innocent blood in this place, neither walk after other gods to your hurt; then will I cause you to dwell in this place, in the land that I gave to your fathers, for ever and ever. Behold, ye trust in lying words, that cannot profit. Will ye steal, murder, and commit adultery, and swear falsely, and offer unto Baal, and walk after other gods whom ye have not known, and come and stand before Me in this house, whereupon My name is called, and say: "we are delivered," that ye may do all these abominations? Is this house, whereupon My name is called, become a den of robbers in your eyes? Behold, I, even I, have seen it, saith the Lord. (Jer. 7:4-11.)

In this indictment we hear echoes of the Ten Commandments which must have been generally known at that time.

In all the prophetic indictments, the worship of false gods, as well as of the true God in the wrong spirit, is an outstanding charge. As in the Torah, so in the prophets, unethical conduct is always closely associated with idolatry. The reason for this association of ideas can easily be surmised. Unethical conduct was considered as stemming from the failure to use, according to prescribed law, the power that God entrusted to man. This failure is part of the general tendency of man to view as his own whatever power he happens to possess and to resort to some deity for whatever additional control he may want to exercise over things or fellow men. When an Israelite sought superhuman aid in that spirit, he was bound either to misconceive the character of Israel's God or to turn to other gods. There are two ways in which men appeal to Deity, either as a power that sanctions and grants their uncriticized wants—such is the popular conception—or as a power helping them to discover and fulfill their true but unrecognized needs—such is the prophet's conception of God.

The foregoing pattern of ideas seems to underlie the characteristic attitude of the prophets toward the political intrigues and maneuverings of the royal households both in Israel and in Judah. The prophets took very literally and very seriously both the historical perspective and the way of life which were regarded as constituting "the Torah of God." They were certain that, if the Israelites had lived in accordance with the true way of life as formulated in that Torah, they would have been secure from attack and invasion by foreign foes. The fundamental principle of all the ancient narratives expressed in the verse, "The Lord will fight for you, and you shall hold your peace" (Ex. 14:15), is at the basis of the unvarying political policy of the prophets.

Thus in denouncing the alliance with Egypt, Isaiah says:

Woe to the rebellious children, saith the Lord, that take counsel, but not of me; and that form projects, but not of My spirit, that they may add sin to sin . . . it is a rebellious people, lying children, children that refuse to hear the teaching of the Lord, that say to the seers, "See not" and to the prophets. . . . "Cause the Holy One of Israel to cease from before us." Wherefore saith the Holy One of Israel: Because ye despise this word and trust in oppression and perverseness and stay thereon . . . For thus said the Lord God, the Holy One of Israel: In sitting still and rest shall ye be saved, in quietness and in confidence shall be your strength; And ye would not (30:1-15).

The prophet condemns the resort to military force and diplomatic intrigue, instead of relying upon God's miraculous power, as a grievous sin. God, however, cannot come to the aid of His people unless they conform to His law of righteousness. If they want to avoid disaster they must repent of their evil ways. "Therefore," continues Isaiah, "will the Lord wait, that He may be gracious unto you, and therefore will He be exalted that He may have compassion upon you; for the Lord is a God of justice; happy are all they that wait for Him" (30:18).

It is amazing with what persistence Judaism held on to the twofold principle until modern times, first, that the miraculous manifestation of Divine power is the only means of man's salvation and, secondly, that God would manifest His power as soon as man would repent and submit to God's law of righteousness. The pietist movement known as Hasidism,[13a] which flourished in Eastern Europe during the nineteenth century and still numbers many adherents, proves that Judaism, in some Jewish circles, still prefers to rely upon Divine miracle, in disregard even of the realities of life, rather than trust to man's initiative. So fearful is Judaism of man's use of power. Such a defiance of the realities of life flared up almost two thousand years ago, when the Jews experienced the full weight of the Roman yoke. In those days there was a much better chance for such defiance to spread and to become the rallying cry for multitudes of men than there is today. Among the Jews as a people, this determination to live by the letter as well as the spirit of the Torah and the prophets led to the gradual severance of their inner life from the state. This made it possible for R. Johanan ben Zakkai[14a] and his successors to reconstitute the Jews into the *Kenesiah,* or the synagogue. In addition to being a people, Jews were now also the *Kenesiah.* At the same time, among a small section of Jewry, the renewed determination to live by the teachings of the Torah and the prophets found embodiment in the Messianic movement of Jesus of Nazareth, the movement which Paul succeeded in developing into Christianity and which found embodiment in the *ecclesia,* or church.

The foregoing twofold principle, which is at the basis of both traditional Judaism and traditional Christianity, seems at first to belong to the domain of theology, in that it expresses a particular view with regard to God's way with man. But viewed functionally, it is a most revolutionary ethical idea. It accentuates what is involved in the problem of human conduct and men's relation to one another. It makes clear that human nature tends to be corrupted by the possession of power. Consequently, the only way to overcome that tendency is to subordinate the use of power to the moral law. *This cardinal doctrine concerning power furnishes the best clue to Judaism's contribution to world ethics.*

The prophets did not have to create this cardinal doctrine. They absorbed it from the tradition of Torah, which had been of long standing. Without the prophets, however, that tradition would have died out; they put new life into it by emphasizing the potency of the moral law, and its categorically imperative character. Jeremiah refers more than once to the moral law as integral to the very constitution of the universe and of man. Such reference implies that only by conforming to the moral law can man be true to his innermost essence. Thus Jeremiah tells his people to stand by the ways and look and ask for the ancient paths: "Where is the good way, and walk therein and ye shall find rest for your souls" (6:16). Elsewhere we read: "Yea the stork in the heaven knoweth her appointed times, and the turtle and the swallow and the crane observe the time of their coming, but My people know not the ordinance of the Lord. How do ye say 'We are wise, and the Law of the Lord is with us?'" (Jer. 8:7). Man's distinction, accordingly, is in the achievement neither of worldly wisdom, strength nor wealth, but in the realization of the moral law as inherent in the very nature of God. "Thus saith the Lord: Let not the wise man glory in his wisdom, neither let the mighty man glory in his might, let not the rich man glory in his riches; but let him that glorieth glory in this, that he understandeth, and knoweth Me, that I am the Lord who exercise mercy, justice, and righteousness, in the earth" (Jer. 9:22-23).

15. The Three Cardinal Principles of Prophetic Ethics

A further contribution which Judaism has made to world ethics through the prophets is the specific formulation which the moral law received at their hands. That formulation helps to identify and motivate the particular laws or expectations which embody the moral law. Such a formulation of the moral law is that given by the prophet Micah who was a contemporary of Isaiah during the latter half of the eighth century (B.C.E.). "What the Lord doth require of thee; only to do justly, and to love mercy, and to walk humbly with thy God" (Mic. 6:8).

When we study the history of the various attempts to formulate ethics into a normative science, free from a religious or theological basis, we note very little, if any, advance on the theories to be found in Plato's and Aristotle's writings. The reason for the failure to make any headway in ethical theory is that it is as difficult to motivate the good life by means of reasoning based on other than intrinsic grounds, as it is to prove the worth-whileness of life itself by means of such reasoning. Two outstanding modern thinkers recognized this truth, each in his own way, Immanuel Kant and M. Guyau. How, then, is the good life to be motivated? Judaism's answer has been: By sharing the life of a people which is consecrated to the furtherance of the good life as defined by the prophet Micah. Not intellectual speculation concerning the good life, but the actual experiencing of it in the give-and-take of human intercourse can motivate it and channel out for it the proper laws, customs and moral standards.

The good life as an object of experience may be described, in terms of the modern universe of discourse, as doing the best of which we are capable and being at our best in both prosperity and adversity. Evidently everything depends upon what we mean by "best." According to the prophet Micah, to do one's best is to practice justice and lovingkindness, and to be at one's best under all circumstances is to walk humbly with God. What this implies may be inferred from what Judaism regards as the central problem of human conduct. We have seen that problem to be, how to prevent man from misusing the power entrusted to him by God. The laws given in the Torah, which are regarded as commanded by God, are intended as specific means of solving that problem. It should not be difficult to group those laws under the categories of justice, lovingkindness and walking humbly with God. By noting how each of these three categories is related to the problem of power, we can get at the ethical purpose underlying virtually all the laws in the Torah.

a. Justice

Justice is that aspect of human behavior which seeks to prevent anyone from being deprived of that measure of power with which God has entrusted him. This, of course, assumes that the power so entrusted is to be used in accordance with God's Will. It is obvious that the ultimate in the defiance of God is the fratricide associated with the name of Cain, because murder is an absolute and irrevocable extinction of a human life, which is the sum total of the power entrusted to a human being. To destroy a human life is thus also an act of *lèse majesté* against God, in whose image man is made (cf. Gen. 9:6), or whose harmonious combination of power and goodness must be reflected in human life. To inflict suffering upon a fellowman without justification is to rob him of such power as God has bestowed upon him. To deprive anyone of whatever rightly belongs to him is to deprive him of legitimate power, and therefore to commit an act of injustice. Whatever abilities we naturally possess and whatever is necessary to enable those abilities to function are ours by *divine* right. Justice thus precludes all manner of oppression, exploitation and deceit, as well as all forms of theft, slander and assault. Moreover, native and alien are alike in respect to justice.

The foregoing prophetic conception of justice limits its scope merely to negating what is wrong. This limitation stands out in strong contrast to the conception of justice in Greek ethics. In Greek ethics, justice is conceived as coextensive with the good life as a whole, whereas in Jewish ethics it occupies only one of three areas of the good life, the other two being lovingkindness and walking humbly with God. In Greek ethics, justice is essentially an aesthetic aspect of human behavior; it is harmony and sense of proportion. It is the harmony and proportionate functioning of conflicting tendencies and interests within the individual himself and among those of different individuals. Plato studied justice as it might be realized in the state, because it could be seen there on a sufficiently large scale to illustrate the principle of harmony in the individual.[15] Justice, to be sure, is a quality pertaining both to the state and to the individual. But in neither instance is it conceived as being conformity to a human or divine standard which is autonomous or independent of aesthetic or utilitarian considerations. The fact that justice is approached from a purely humanist standpoint enables one to examine it analytically and to differentiate it into such categories as distributive and corrective justice. But when justice is removed from the religious synthesis in which it is seen in Judaism it ceases to have that new dimensionality, or that otherness, which renders any extraneous sanction superfluous or irrelevant. From the standpoint of power as God's gift to man, justice as the obligation to do nothing that might rob man of that gift is inherently understandable.

b. Lovingkindness

Lovingkindness, from the standpoint of its effect on the power to which man is entitled, is the particular behavior in human relations which elicits and activates that power in others. To love one's neighbor as oneself is to call forth in him the fullest use of whatever powers God has endowed him with. All consideration shown to the unfortunate, all humane treatment of those who are dependent, all provisions for the needy enable human power, otherwise unused, to come into play, and therefore belong to the category of lovingkindness. So also does the act of forgiveness. When, instead of bearing a grudge against our neighbor, we air our grievance frankly and come to an understanding with him (Lev. 19:17) we help him to make use of his legitimate powers; whereas, if we vent our anger upon him, we are bound to inhibit his use of them.

To express the basic intuition that justice and lovingkindness constitute a dimension of reality which is self-existent, other and underivable from the dimension of the vital needs, Judaism projects them into the very being of God. God is, accordingly, represented throughout all stages of Judaism as a God of both justice and lovingkindness. In His capacity as a God of justice, He is the author of those laws which tell man what he must do to guard against depriving his fellow man of the power wherewith God has endowed him. In that same capacity, God punishes those who transgress His laws. In His capacity as a God of lovingkindness, He not only teaches man how to conduct himself so as to elicit the best in his fellow, but He also calls upon the transgressor to repent. When man repents, God forgives, and by His forgiveness enables man to use his own powers as God would have him do. A frequently repeated principle in the Rabbinic writings is the application of *imitatio dei* to the divine attributes of lovingkindness ascribed to God. Commenting on the verse in Ex. 15:2, Abba Saul, who read it to mean, "I will be like Him," added: "Be thou like Him. Just as He is gracious and compassionate, so be thou gracious and compassionate."[16]

c. Humility

"To walk humbly with God," the third item in Micah's summary description of the good life, is rendered most significant, like the other two items, in the light of the central problem of human conduct and human relations. How we bear ourselves amid the vicissitudes of fortune, which affect the amount of power over which we have control, determines our character and our share in the good life. Prosperity, or the possession of all those instruments which augment one's power, easily turns one's head and gives rise to a sense of self-sufficiency and insolence. Such an attitude must lead to the disregard of God's laws of justice and lovingkindness. This is a danger to which nations are even more subject than individuals. "Jeshurun waxed fat, and kicked— Thou didst wax fat, thou didst grow thick, thou didst become gross— And he forsook God who made him, And contemned the Rock of his salvation" (Deut. 32:15).

The villain in the divine drama of human life, as portrayed in Jewish Scripture, is not a demonic or satanic being which tempts man to defy God, but man himself who, having come into great power through conquest, wealth or fame, tries to play the god. He is the *rasha*, the wicked one. The *rasha* acts as a foil to God's purpose with man. He tries to thwart that purpose by denying God, either openly or in his heart, and he attempts to order the world according to his own arrogant will-to-power. "For the wicked [the *rasha*] boasteth of his heart's desire, and the covetous vaunteth himself, though he contemn the Lord. The wicked [the *rasha*], in the pride of his countenance saith: 'He will not require' . . . His ways prosper at all times . . . He saith in his heart: 'I shall not be moved' " (Ps. 10:3-6). At the very opposite pole of the wicked one (*rasha*) is the humble one (*ani* or *anav*), who walks humbly with God. When Abraham interceded with God in behalf of Sodom, he said: "I am mere dust and ashes." His humility was not confined to his attitude toward God. It also found expression in his attitude toward Lot, to whom he said: "Let there be no strife, I pray thee, between me and thee" (Gen. 13:8), although as the head of the clan Abraham might well have resorted to the prerogative of authority and power. Likewise it is said of Moses, when he was assailed by Miriam and Aaron, that he was "very meek [*anav*] above all the men that were upon the face of the earth" (Num. 12:3).

To walk humbly with God, however, is a virtue which is by no means intended to be limited to a life of prosperity. It has its place also under conditions of adversity. Misfortune, whether due to natural causes or to human viciousness, leaves one bereft of power. It often leads to bitterness and despair, which are bound to lead to moral deterioration of the sufferer. Such an attitude is a kind of inverted pride and rebellion against God. The Sage whose words are recorded in the Book of Proverbs prayed that he be tempted neither to deny God by reason of prosperity nor to repudiate Him by reason of adversity (Pr. 30:8). But not always are men spared either temptation. Occasions of adversity are by far the more prevalent. The advice to walk humbly with God even under those circumstances is, therefore, always timely. When Job sat upon the ash heap and scraped himself with a potsherd, his wife said to him: "Dost thou still hold fast thine integrity? blaspheme God, and die." His answer to her is Judaism's conception of walking humbly with God in time of adversity: "Thou speakest as one of the impious women speaketh. What? shall we receive good at the hand of God, and shall we not receive evil?" (Job 2:8-10) In the Book of Psalms we get an insight into the soul of the humble one who, despite suffering, knows how to walk humbly with God.

16. GOD IN HISTORY AS VIEWED BY THE PROPHETS

The prophets express the conviction that had the Israelites followed the principles of justice, lovingkindness and walking humbly with God, as embodied in God's Torah, they would have enjoyed peace and security. They were equally certain that invasion, enslavement and exile were God's punishment for the violation of these principles by relying upon the manipulation of power politics, and by mere lip worship to God and His law. The political and social crises which began to come in fast succession, as one or another of the neighboring empires or of invading hordes threatened to overwhelm Israel, led the prophets to achieve a larger world orientation than had been possible under the dispensation of Torah. Torah had taught Israel's spokesmen to think in historical terms, but their mental horizon scarcely extended beyond the immediate neighboring peoples. The events amid which the prophets lived changed all that. The rise and fall of empires had to be fitted into the traditional conception of the God of Israel, the God Who is the source of all power, and whose main attributes are justice and lovingkindness. This led the prophets to give universal scope to their ethical intuitions and assumptions.

The main concept by which the prophets succeeded in universalizing the ethical teachings of Judaism was that of "the day of YHWH."[17a] This concept, it appears, was originally promulgated by the zealots of YHWH and the "success prophets" of an earlier era. It was used by them as a slogan of victory for mobilizing the armed forces in battle against the enemies of Israel. The great prophets, however, reinterpreted the concept of "the day of YHWH." They employed it as a means of getting their people to think in terms of world events as a manifestation of God's power, a power that is not arbitrary or subject to whim, but one dominated by justice and love. Thus did the ethical principles pass beyond the stage of individual reflection or inspiration. Had they remained in this stage, they would have been of as little influence as those of the philosophers. Only by being given the impetus of a profoundly moving religious idea—such as that which enabled men to behold the hand of God in the shaping of human history—did those ethical principles finally permeate the consciousness of the greater part of mankind.

In the course of time, the concept of the Day of YHWH came to express the hope that God would establish His Kingdom on earth. This assurance grew out of the deep conviction according to which the world was inherently so constituted that, despite the prevalence of evil and the repeated setbacks in man's moral progress, the good life would be achieved by man in ever-increasing measure. The prospect of such a future is always needed, but never more than in times of crisis like our own.

It is not too much to say that Judaism's contribution to world ethics consists in having called attention to the truth that, for men to learn the art of living together, the one problem they must seek to solve is how to tame their will-to-power. To discover the specific character of that contribution we have to interpret the ethical teachings of Judaism as they functioned in solving that problem. The conclusions we then arrive at are: First, that Judaism has always affirmed in the most vigorous fashion the inherent truth and the categorical and imperative character of the moral law, apart from all considerations of expediency, aesthetic interest or any other source of validation. The fact that it promulgated that principle at a morally crucial period in ancient times enabled it to save Western mankind from moral disintegration. Secondly, as a result of this intrinsic and underived character of the moral law, the problem of the good life cannot be *why* we should live the good life, but *how* we should live it. It is no more possible to prove why we should live the good life than why we should live at all, especially when life bears down hard on us. The answer that Judaism gives to the question of *how* to live is contained in Micah's description of the good life as consisting of justice, lovingkindness and walking humbly with God. This summary, properly understood, points to the only possible means of taming our will-to-power.

The assumption of traditional Judaism, that the specific laws and social arrangements which incarnate justice, lovingkindness and walking humbly with God were supernaturally revealed to ancient Israel, is for many no longer tenable. But, interpreted functionally, that assumption implies that *all* human laws and social arrangements must be subjected to the moral test of being effective as a means of taming man's will-to-power. Otherwise they are only pretentious disguises for selfish exploitation of power and its antisocial use.

Never since the days of Rome's decline and the disintegration of the classic order has mankind been so threatened, as it is today, by moral nihilism. Never since then has it been in such need of the reaffirmation of the moral values as the only means of saving human life from impending doom. Together with all other bodies which are in a position to forestalled a world cataclysm, the Jewish people, by reason of its great moral tradition, can play once again an important role in the salvation of mankind.

NOTES

[1] See the article "Ethics and Morality," by H. B. Alexander in the *Encyclopedia of Religion and Ethics* (New York, 1912), Vol. V, p. 440.

[2] *Ibid.*, p. 441.

[3] J. H. Breasted, *The Dawn of Conscience* (New York, 1939), p. 124.

[4] *Ibid.*, p. 126.

[5] *Ibid.*, p. xi.

[6a] Cf. above Alexander Altmann, "Judaism and World Philosophy," pp. 955 ff.; also cf. below Ralph Marcus, "Hellenistic Jewish Literature," pp. 1107 ff.]

[7a] Cf. above Robert Gordis, "The Bible as a Cultural Monument," pp. 790 ff.; also cf. below Louis Finkelstein, "The Jewish Religion: Its Beliefs and Practices," p. 1739.]

[8a] Cf. above Judah Goldin, "The Period of the Talmud" (135 B.C.E.-1035 C.E.), pp. 194 ff.]

[9a] Cf. *Ibid.*, pp. 117 ff.]

[10] Josiah Royce, *Sources of Religious Thought* (New York, 1914), pp. 199-201.

[11a] Cf. above William Foxwell Albright, "The Biblical Period," pp. 11-12.]

[12a] Cf. Gordis, *op. cit.*, pp. 795 ff.]

[13a] Cf. below Yudel Mark, "Yiddish Literature," pp. 1200 f.]

[14a] Cf. Goldin, *op. cit.*, pp. 146 f.]

[15] *The Republic*, 368-369.

[16] Shabbat, 133b.

[17a] On the use of the Tetragrammaton YHWH, cf. above Elias J. Bickerman, "The Historical Foundations of Postbiblical Judaism," pp. 96-97.]

BIBLIOGRAPHY

ARISTOTLE, *Nicomachean Ethics*. London, 1926.

BREASTED, JAMES H., *The Dawn of Conscience*. New York and London, 1933.

COHEN, ABRAHAM, *The Teachings of Maimonides*. London, 1927. Ch. XI.

FINKELSTEIN, LOUIS, *The Pharisees*. Philadelphia, 1938. Chs. X, XIV-XVIII.

HASTINGS, JAMES, (ed.), *Encyclopedia of Religion and Ethics* (New York, 1910-1922): "Righteousness," Vol. X, pp. 777-811, "Conscience," Vol. IV, pp. 30-47, "Ethics," Vol. V, pp. 415-436.

HERFORD, R. TRAVERS, *Pharisaism*. London and New York, 1912. Ch. VI.

LAZARUS, MORITZ, *The Ethics of Judaism*. Philadelphia, 1901.

MOORE, GEORGE F., *Judaism in the First Centuries of the Christian Era*. Cambridge, 1927-1930. Vol. II, pt. V.

PORTER, N., *Kant's Ethics*. Chicago, 1886.

ROYCE, JOSIAH, *The Sources of Religious Thought*. New York, 1914.

SCHECHTER, SOLOMON, *Aspects of Rabbinic Theology*. New York, 1909. Ch. XIII.

STRONG, T. B., "Ethics," *Dictionary of the Bible* (James Hastings, ed.), New York, 1902. Vol. I, pp. 777-789.

CHAPTER 22

JUDAISM AND SOCIAL WELFARE

By Israel S. Chipkin

1. JEWISH PHILANTHROPY IN AMERICA

The record of Jewish social welfare activities in the United States adds an illustrious chapter to the long and varied history of the Jewish people in the field of social service. It is surely worth noting the character of American Jewry's contribution to the sacred and deeply rooted tradition of *Zedakah,* Jewish benevolence, especially since the beginning of World War I. The unprecedented measure of giving, and the multiplication of services rendered by American Jews to their needy brethren during this period, not only have added honor to their own generation but have exalted and intensified their tradition. Despite sharing fully with fellow citizens of all faiths, in all war responsibilities and joint war relief collections during and between the two World Wars, American Jews superbly discharged their added obligations toward their fellow Jews in the United States, in the war-ridden countries and in Palestine (now Israel).

A. OVERSEAS SERVICES

From January, 1939, to the end of 1953, the United Jewish Appeal will have collected from American Jewry well over $900,000,000. In the year 1948 alone, it collected approximately $148,000,000. The end of the European war in May, 1945, disclosed the abysmal horror and tragedy that had overtaken world Jewry. American Jewry, therefore, set as its annual United Jewish Appeal goals sums between $150,000,000 and $250,000,000.[1] All this money has been used to rescue Jews from Nazi brutality and to aid them in their lands of sojourn and settlement, especially in Israel. The United Jewish Appeal[2] included the Joint Distribution Committee, an agency in existence since World War I, providing relief and rehabilitation to Jews overseas; the United Palestine Appeal (today called United Israel Appeal), comprising most Zionist organizations helping to reconstruct Palestine (now Israel) as a Jewish homeland; and the National Refugee Service (now the United Service for New Americans),[3] an agency created to help the settlement of Jewish refugees in America. To these rescue and relief agencies should be added such organizations as Hadassah, which, besides its several services in Palestine (now Israel) has rescued thousands of children through the Youth *Aliyah* to Israel; HIAS, which has been helping European Jewish emigrants abroad and in the United States for many years, even before World War II; ORT, which for many years before the Second World War helped Jews in Europe, in South America, and elsewhere to train for trade occupations and agriculture; OSE, which, with funds from the United Jewish Appeal, continued its hygiene and medical services among Jews abroad; the Vaad Hahazalah of the Orthodox Rabbinical Union, which sought to rescue rabbis, and later other Jews also, from concentration camps in Europe. These agencies, too, spent added millions of dollars during these years for their respective services.[4] No attempt is made here to describe in detail the many and difficult services rendered by the agencies mentioned, nor to list all the organizations that have sent funds abroad. It is well, however, to remember that since World War I, in addition to what organizations sent, American Jews have privately sent increasingly large sums (amounting to many millions) to their relatives in Europe, Palestine, and elsewhere.

If there be anything more significant than the funds made available for rescue, relief, and settlement purposes, it is the kind of services rendered and the qualifications of the persons who rendered them. Whether it be medical supplies, food, or shelter for young and old; whether it be negotiating with enemy or friendly governments, or hiring rescue ships, or transporting refugees over continents, or resettlement and rehabilitation work—the men and women appointed to these tasks were of the highest caliber, expert or especially trained in their tasks. If ever a task was performed with intelligence, lovingkindness, and in keeping with the Jewish tradition *Pidyon Shebuyin* (Ransom of Captives) —the supreme form of Jewish benevolence[5]—it was in the work of these agencies.

B. CIVIC-PROTECTIVE SERVICES

Other services, not directly related to the rescue and rehabilitation work of the overseas agencies, and which may be called civic-protective in character, were undertaken by another group of agencies. The national agencies in this group alone spent, during the year, 1952, a total of approximately $6,000,000, in addition to what the local agencies spent. Their services can be classified into two groups, those dealing with the plight and rights of Jews overseas and those dealing with anti-Semitism within the United States. The four major agencies in this field were the American Jewish Committee, the American Jewish Congress, the B'nai B'rith, and the Jewish Labor Committee. These organizations united for a while with seven other organizations, religious and Zionist in character, to form the Joint Emergency Committee for Jewish affairs. Independently and together these agencies aroused American public opinion against Nazi atrocities against Jews in Europe, obtained expressions of sympathy and protest from President Roosevelt and the Congress, pleaded with American and Allied governments for rescue and settlement of Jewish refugees, and preserved civic rights for Jews in North Africa. To supersede and replace this Joint Emergency Committee, there was organized the American Jewish Conference, which consisted of the representatives of national agencies and local communities. In all there were 502 representatives to this Conference—375 chosen by local, state or regional elections, and 127 by major national organizations. The American Jewish Committee, which originally joined the Conference, later withdrew to carry on its independent efforts. While this Conference undertook political measures to help rescue Jews in Europe, its major activities were dedicated to the preparations for the Peace Conference with a view to protecting Jewish rights in Europe and the Jewish Commonwealth in Palestine. Together with those of the American Jewish Committee, its representatives attended the United Nations San Francisco Conference in April, 1945, as observers, where they fought successfully for the protection of the rights of Jews within Europe and Palestine and for the interpretation of the principles of freedom, equality, and justice within the United Nations Charter.

Despite attempts to unite their efforts, each of the four major civic-protective agencies mentioned above carried on its independent programs for combating the anti-Semitism spread by the Nazis in the United States and elsewhere, and for disseminating among the Christian population enlightened information about Jews. Christian groups and individuals and even social science experts were frequently enlisted by these agencies. Their respective programs were eventually co-ordinated in some measure through the intervention of the National Council of Jewish Federations and Welfare Funds acting on behalf of the civic-protective efforts of local Jewish Community Councils. This co-operative or co-ordinating body is called the National Community Relations Advisory Council[6] and includes representatives of the four national agencies mentioned above as well as those of the Jewish War Veterans and the national religious bodies, the Union of Orthodox Jewish Congregations of America, the United Synagogues of America, and the Union of American Hebrew Congregations, and twenty-eight local communities and regional bodies (1953).

In all these branches of activity, outstanding Jewish leaders and trained personnel were employed, while the types of services engaged in by these agencies ranged from diplomacy and university research work to the publication of literature, the production of movies, and the calling of conferences of Christians and Jews.

The striking fact about the overseas, Palestine, and civic-protective agencies is the measure of organization and co-operation achieved by them within their own scope of national activity under the stress of emergency. Their activities reach practically into all organized communities of any size in the country.

C. THE NATIONAL JEWISH WELFARE BOARD

The two World Wars brought forth a special form of Jewish social service, namely, service to the Jewish men and women in the armed forces and to the Jewish war veteran after his discharge. This service grew out of the activities of the Young Men's Hebrew Associations and Jewish Centers, and led to the organization during World War I of the National Jewish Welfare Board. Between the two wars, the Board developed a rich social and educational program for youth and adults through its many Jewish Centers located in every section of the country. World War II and postwar events forced the expansion of the Board's normal Army and Navy activities to meet the emergency and extraordinary needs of a global war and a cold war.

1. Wartime Services

To co-ordinate and intensify the war efforts of many Jewish organizations, the Jewish Welfare Board established co-operating advisory committees representing these organizations. To help the government obtain Jewish chaplains needed in the armed services, it established a Committee on Religious Activities of the Army and Navy Committee of the Jewish Welfare Board. In this Committee were represented the Orthodox, Conservative, and Reform rabbinical organizations. About 200 chaplains served in the American Army of World War II as compared with only twenty-six in World War I. Twenty-four Jewish chaplains served in the American Navy in World War II as compared with only one in World War I, and one Jewish chaplain served in the Merchant Marine during World War II whereas there was none in the previous war. Since the end of World War II the Committee has established a permanent corps of 100 full-time chaplains scattered over twenty-one countries and a corps of 250 part-time chaplains serving domestic installations.

To supplement the personal, religious, and social services rendered by Jewish chaplains in the armed services at home and abroad, there were many National Jewish Welfare Board workers. These workers also acted as the liaison between Jewish communities and nearby camps, and comprised the Jewish workers and committee members of the United Service Organizations, an interfaith welfare agency established with the help of the United States government to serve in the camps and in communities visited by the men and women on furlough. The facilities of about 280 Jewish Centers were made available to these men and women. Through its officers and workers, the National Jewish Welfare Board frequently made possible contact with families of men and women in the armed forces, and also contact with Jewish home, community, and festival life in the temporary locations of the soldiers. Through the co-operation of many Jewish religious and educational organizations, and through its own efforts, the National Jewish Welfare Board supplied these men and women with numerous pamphlets and booklets, lectures and courses, dealing with historical, idealistic, religious, and cultural aspects of Jewish life. Through its Women's Division, consisting of representatives of the major national women's organizations, devoted to other religious, social, educational, and Zionist work, the Jewish Welfare Board obtained a host of workers in all Jewish communities to help in the many services required by the men and women in the armed forces.

Those services included also aid to the sick and disabled, inside and outside the hospitals, and to the returning veterans, who can turn to the National Jewish Welfare Board, as an accredited agency of the government's Veterans' Administration, for personal or group assistance to help them get re-established in normal civilian life.

There is yet another service rendered by the National Jewish Welfare Board to the community as a whole, rather than to the individual. Through its committee on public relations, in which the several civic-protective organizations are represented, and with their co-operation, it collects and distributes information among Jews and non-Jews concerning the number of Jews in the armed services (their number exceeds their proportion in civilian life) and concerning the valiant services rendered by them as fighting men. With the help of the Bureau of War Records, it published two volumes entitled *American Jews in World War II*.

The size and number of the services rendered during World War II by the National Jewish Welfare Board can perhaps be measured by the size of its budget, which rose between 1940 and 1945 from approximately $150,000 to approximately $2,000,000. To this sum should be added $2,500,000 of the government-sponsored United Service Organizations money spent by the Jewish Welfare Board, as well as hundreds of thousands of dollars spent by local Army and Navy Committees affiliated with the Jewish Welfare Board, but not financed by it. Since the ending of wartime hostilities in Germany and Europe, it has continued its services to the American armed forces wherever they are found, and extended them to Korea when the United States troops entered that area of war activity.

2. Peacetime Services

The measure of Army and Navy services by the Jewish Welfare Board corresponds in war or in peace to the needs of the country, and is of course dictated by the program and policies of the American government. In peacetime, however, the major activities of the National Jewish Welfare

Board are directed toward Jewish youth and adults in the many Young Men's and Young Women's Hebrew Associations, Jewish Centers, camps, and kindred institutions throughout the country.

In 1953[7] there were 351 Centers affiliated with this Board. Their total membership was 530,000, their aggregate attendance about 12,000,000, and their total annual expenditures amounted to about $13,500,000. The buildings of these institutions alone amounts to about $90,000,000. A host of social, recreational, vocational, educational, religious, and personal services are rendered by these institutions to their respective memberships. They are the services that help to socialize, "Judaize," "Americanize," and normalize the interests and activities of the young and old who visit these buildings. The activities help to introduce the individual to his Jewish and civic responsibilities.

The J. W. B. is also sponsor to such national activities as Jewish Book Month, Jewish Music Month, and the National Jewish Youth Conference. On the international scene, it has opened the first Jewish Center in Jerusalem, and since World War II has created a World Federation of Y. M. H. A.'s, including Jewish Centers in Europe, the Americas, Australia, and South Africa.

D. COMMUNITY WELFARE AGENCIES

The total funds contributed and the combined services rendered by the several overseas, civic-protective, and war-service agencies take on even greater meaning when we note the following fact: until 1942 they represented less than half the sums raised and the professional services rendered locally by the respective institutions and communal agencies within Jewish communities in the United States. In 1944 these Jewish agencies expended for local Jewish welfare and cultural needs about $26,000,000. To this sum might be added another estimated $25,000,000 spent by close to 4,000 congregations for religious and educational work. In 1953, these local agencies spent an estimated total of $47,000,000, and the religious and educational agencies, another estimated total of $50,000,-000.

Outstanding among the local Jewish agencies in each community is the central fiscal body, known as the Federation of Jewish Charities or the Jewish Welfare Fund. In some communities, both types of central agency exist side by side. The former collects funds for local welfare needs, the latter collects funds for overseas and American national agencies. The most important fact about these central agencies is that they are communal in character. As such, they help not only to reach the Jews in the community for support of Jewish social welfare activities, but in a measure also to co-ordinate and advance the standards of these activities. Such communities also have a Jewish Community Council, which helps not only to obtain more popular support for the central fiscal agency but also to express public opinion concerning its activities. The largest Federation of Jewish philanthropic societies for the support of local social welfare services is the one in New York City, which celebrated its thirty-fifth anniversary in 1952. In the variety and significance of its services it is typical of other Federations and Welfare Funds in smaller communities, and also serves as a standard for them. A report of its organization and activities will help to give some account of the social services rendered by such an agency.

The New York City Federation of Jewish Philanthropic Societies[8]

As its name implies, the New York City central fiscal agency is a Federation of many philanthropic societies. In 1942, it included 116 societies. This Federation was organized in 1917. Prior to that, its affiliated societies raised a total of $1,429,260. In the year following its organization, in 1918, it raised a total of $2,868,000. In 1942, twenty-five years later, it raised a total of $7,710,000. In 1944 it raised more than $10,500,000. In 1945 it launched a building repair, and expansion fund with a goal of $30,000,000. In 1949 it raised $24,000,000, including a Building Fund for $13,000,000. In 1952, it spent over $17,000,000.

In 1917, the first year of its campaign activity, a total of 27,000 individual gifts were received by Federation. In 1942 more than 265,000 individual gifts were received by Federation. In 1944 this figure rose to 285,000. It has been estimated that in pre-Federation days the cost of collections for the several societies amounted to between 25 and 30 per cent of the total raised; in 1942 it cost Federation about 8 per cent of the total raised. Equally important is the fact that about 8,000 persons were actively engaged as volunteers in the collection of these funds. Another interesting fact reported by Federation is that, while it had received about $321,000 a year in legacies during recent years, legacies for the individual societies affiliated with Federation have during these years totaled about $360,000 a year. In other words, legacies to individual institutions have not suffered because of legacies to Federation.

Three significant facts are revealed in these figures: (1) The sums collected have increased tremendously. (2) Efficiency and scientific approach have marked both the collection and the distribution of funds. (3) A communal, co-operative attitude has been developed among volunteer contributors and workers (collectors).

The first fact, the increased collections, is, of course, important, but it is only a consequence of the second and third facts, namely, efficiency and communal endeavor. To quote the official report, those who founded Federation sought "to effect orderliness and the elimination of competitive and duplicating effort in the financing of local institutional life." But they also "foresaw Jewish philanthropies as being no longer the preoccupation of the wealthy few, but the possession and concern of widening circles of Jewish life . . . they envisioned institutions, freed from problems of money raising, as being enabled to concentrate on the raising of standards of their functional services, the advancement of skills, techniques and medical services in their respective fields."

It is difficult to assay briefly the relative merits of Federation's two great contributions to Jewish philanthropy: its communal approach and its advancement of the standards of the services rendered by its affiliated societies.

The results of its communal approach are described in its own report: "in the earlier days, we had a number of bands of devoted individuals: today we have a community." It demonstrated that every Jew in the community, regardless of economic status, can be a contributor to Jewish philanthropy, that a businessman or a laborer, a business concern or a labor union, can be trained to make a contribution to Jewish charity, can assume a regular annual obligation in its budget; that such contributions can be increased manifold under the stress of communal needs and public opinion, and that voluntary, democratic giving can become a reliable source for the progressive growth of Jewish social welfare services.

The value, variety, and progressive character of these services can be judged from the following figures: In 1942, the hospitals affiliated with Federation gave 662,000 days of free ward care to 62,418 patients, or one-third of all free ward cases given by all voluntary hospitals in New York City. In the first twenty-five years of its existence, Federation distributed among its affiliated societies a total of $96,000,000. Of this sum, $33,000,000 was given to hospitals and medical services, $18,000,000 for family welfare work, $17,000,000 for work with children, $11,000,000 for neighborhood centers, $6,000,000 to check juvenile delinquency, $4,000,000 for Jewish education, $4,000,000 for employment and vocational guidance services, $2,000,000 for care of the aged, and $1,000,000 for "fresh air" work.

More impressive than the quantitative aspect of the services rendered by Federation societies is their qualitative aspect. These services reflect the broader humanitarian approach to social welfare and the expanding knowledge in medicine, psychology and education. Not only have Federation institutions and their professional staffs kept abreast of advancing standards in science and in social practice, but they have themselves made notable contributions in both these areas. For example, out of an affiliate hospital of Federation has come the method of blood transfusion, a discovery which made blood banks possible during the war and other emergencies. Another Federation hospital was the first to devote its efforts to the care and treatment of chronic diseases. Still another of its hospitals gave medicine the five-day treatment of syphilis. Out of Federation co-ordinating activities has come the integration of child care services and the substitution of the foster home for the institutional asylum in the care of the orphan and dependent child. Because the state is gradually assuming the responsibility for material assistance to citizens and families in need, the character of Jewish family case work has shifted toward emphasis on self-reliance, self-respect, and self-knowledge on the part of the client. Federation's institutions for the aged have developed an individualized code for the aged, which takes care not only of the sick but also of those who can be maintained in usefulness to themselves and to others. Here, its institutions have been among the first to utilize occupational therapy. In the field of juvenile delinquency, its affiliated societies have been among the first to apply group therapy and child guidance with a view to preventing antisocial behavior of the child or the adolescent. To all these services should be added those of the Joint Purchasing Corporation developed by Federation, which has made possible not only great savings in money but high quality of merchandise.

No less important than the standards achieved by its affiliated societies in their respective fields of service are the standards achieved by Federation in its organization of the various elements in the community for the purpose of raising funds. Involved are thousands of organizational details and months of careful planning by hundreds of chairmen and committees representing three hundred groups of workers, who have to discover "the right solicitor to visit the right prospect." These groups are distributed among four main divisions: the trades division, the women's division, the neighborhood division, the division of fraternal, benevolent, and labor organizations. Nothing less than phenomenal progress has been made in educating those groups to participate in and to increase their gifts to Federation campaigns. It is thus that the wider democratic and communal basis is being laid for the disorganized and unco-ordinated group life of two million Jews in New York City.

The secret of Federation's growth and success is ascribed by its leaders to the "faith" which the community in New York City kept "with its Hebrew traditions and heritage" and to the "democratic, free spirit of America" with its "tradition of neighborliness."

"More important than size is the spiritual meaning of Federation. It is an important link, a guiding light in the way of life that we as Jews are building in America as an expression of our deepest ideals and highest aspirations—and as a solidifying influence in our group life . . .

"In Federation, the openhanded tradition of America is intertwined and harmonized with the basic Jewish spiritual principle of *Zedakah*. Through Federation these cherished ideals find practical expression in the busy day-to-day life of the metropolis in kindly deeds to fellow men."

2. COMMUNITY RESPONSIBILITY FOR JEWISH SOCIAL SERVICE A HISTORIC PRACTICE

The magnitude and the high professional standards of social service rendered by American Jewry during the past thirty years may be unprecedented in Jewish history, but the variety of service and the sense of communal responsibility that made the standards possible have their origin in Jewish religious teachings and historic traditions, to which the leaders of the New York City Federation properly pay their respects. The dicta of the Rabbis that all Israel are brethren, and therefore bear a special responsibility to each other, have had greater influence on American Jewish charitable endeavor than the legend about Peter Stuyvesant, who is said to have exacted a promise from the Jews seeking admission into New Amsterdam that they would always look after their own needy brethren.

A. IN THE UNITED STATES

The size, the character, and the organization of Jewish charitable endeavor in America have reflected the size, the character, and the organization of Jewish group life in this country. When the Jewish population was small, all Jewish social life was more intimate and family-like. Jewish activity was organized about the synagogue through which social services were discharged. With the coming of larger numbers of German Jews during the nineteenth century, we find the establishment of special institutions to take care of increased needs and to provide specialized services. Such institutions were the Mt. Sinai Hospital in New York City (1852), a Jewish Hospital in Cincinnati (1850), the Hebrew Education Society in Philadelphia (1849), the B'nai B'rith House for the Aged and Infirm in New York City (1848), the Orphan Asylums of B'nai B'rith in New Orleans (1855), in Cleveland (1863), and San Francisco (1871), the New York City Orphan Asylum (1860), the Hebrew Benevolent Society in New York City (1822), the Hebrew Sheltering and Guardian Society in New York City (1879), and the Montefiore Home for Chronic Invalids in New York City (1884).

In New York City there existed for a time two Benevolent Societies, one organized by Jews of Spanish-Portuguese origin and one by Jews of German origin. These societies combined in 1860 to become the United Hebrew Charities, which in more recent years became the Jewish Social Service Association. This organization was previously a family relief society, but soon had to assume many functions that were later to become the specialized services of other agencies. Not only did it distribute money, clothing, coal, food, medicines; it also conducted employment bureaus, loan bureaus, nurseries, workrooms for the unskilled, and provided widow pensions, transportation, etc. After 1881 the United Hebrew Charities became responsible for the East European immigrants with all their attendant problems. It can readily be seen how the resultant volume and variety of services would overwhelm this agency, and how the need for more specialized institutions would be felt in the community. The next thirty years, therefore, saw the rise of numerous hospitals, orphanages, homes for the aged, societies for the prevention and care of delinquents, immigrant societies, trade schools, loan societies, religious schools, agricultural societies, settlement houses and Y.M.H.A., etc.

After 1910, the New York City community began to feel the need for the co-ordination of all these different agencies, their various services and their many appeals for support. A movement toward a Federation of these agencies developed in New York City, as well as in other cities. In New York City, such a Federation was finally established in 1917, and with it was re-established the communal approach to Jewish philanthropy.

A change in the character of social service followed the growth of the Jewish population. The sense of intimacy that existed in the early settlement days between the beneficiary and the synagogue agency disappeared. Organized charity had to be placed on a responsible communal and professional basis. The paid agent had to replace the volunteer. Relief had to be administered not only from the point of view of the recipient but also from the point of view of the community. Scientific standards of service became necessary. The prevention of poverty and pauperism, and the rehabilitation of the poor to the point of self-support, became a responsibility of the community.

B. IN EUROPEAN COUNTRIES

This sense of communal responsibility and this historic growth of charitable agencies are to be found in other Western European countries, too, where large centers of Jewish population developed. Already at the beginning of the eighteenth century we find Jewish charitable societies in existence in London, Paris, and Berlin. By the middle of the nineteenth century there were in those cities Jewish specialized agencies: hospitals, orphanages, family relief societies. In those cities and in their respective countries, we find again the Jewish sense of community responsibility and organization asserting itself. Thus, in London, the Jewish Board of Guardians helps and conducts hospitals, orphanages, almshouses for the poor and the aged, an institution for deaf and dumb, a training school for nurses, an institution for animals, low-rent housing projects, loans, workrooms, apprentice boys, immigrants, youth activities. In Paris there is a similar Federation of social agencies known as the *Comité de Bienfaisance de la Ville Paris,* which has been in existence since 1809; one of its off-shoots was the *Alliance Israélite Universelle.* The social services rendered by the Comité's affiliated agencies resemble very much those of the institutions mentioned above. In Berlin and Germany generally, the comparable central co-ordinating agency was the *Deutsch-Israelitische Gemeindebund.* It represented more than elsewhere a union of congregations. This is due primarily to government regulations. Here, too, there was a variety of institutions and social services supported by the Jewish community and supervised by a central community agency.

When we come to East European communities, we find smaller Jewish populations within the cities and towns, poorer facilities, and less scientific standards, but a stronger influence of Jewish religious tradition and a more natural community consciousness. Here the force of Jewish social service and community management resemble more the historic practices and original traditions which Jews carried with them from country to country from as far back as Biblical times than do the institutions and methods of contemporary Jews in Western countries.

3. EARLY FORMS AND TRADITIONS OF JEWISH SOCIAL SERVICE AGENCIES

In many European towns today there are institutions which date back to medieval and even mishnaic times. During the Middle Ages, Spanish and Italian Jews displayed special talent for organization. Thus, in Rome the community operated through four central agencies. There were (1) the *Ozer Dalim,* or the Society for Aid to the Poor, (2) the *Gemilut Ha-Sadim,*[9] or the Society for Free Burial, (3) the *Moshab Zekenim,* or the Society for the Home for the Aged, (4) the *Shomer Emunim,* or the Society for Faith and Worship.

In East European towns the synagogue (*Bet Ha-Keneset*) and its House of Study (*Bet Ha-Midrash*) were the centers of Jewish communal life. Alongside this institution there was usually a *Talmud Torah* for poor children and a *Hekdesh,* an agency set aside as a hospital, as a shelter for the aged, for the stranger and for the poor. Such were the purposes served by the *Hekdesh* in Cologne in the eleventh century. Frequently there were communal hostelries or soup kitchens, sometimes known as *Tamhui,* to serve warm food to the needy. For travelers there was in some places the *Pandok,* situated on the highway for the purpose of offering food and shelter to the wanderer and the homeless.

In many larger East European towns or cities separate societies existed, each looking after the fulfillment of one or another branch of charity. Among them were (a) the *Malbish Arumim,* to clothe the naked, (b) *Talmud Torah,* for the education of poor children, (c) *Ha-Knasat Kallah,* to provide poor maidens with a dowry, (d) *Maot Hittim,* to provide matzah and wine to the poor for Passover, (e) *Bet Yetomim,* for the

care of orphans, (f) *Bikkur Holim,* for visiting the sick, including con-
valescent women who have given birth, (g) *Moshab Zekenim,* for the
care of the aged, (h) *Hesed Shel Emet,* for free burial, (i) *Pidyon
Shebuyim,* for the ransom of captives and refugees. In addition to these
special societies there was the central charity fund known as *Kuppah Shel
Zedakah,* the Charity Fund, and more recently as *Zedakah Gedolah,* or
the great charity fund.

Israel Abrahams in his *Jewish Life in the Middle Ages* reports that
these societies multiplied in number toward the sixteenth and seventeenth
centuries. As Jews suffered because of epidemics, massacres during the
Crusades, and the plunder of oppressive rulers or Mediterranean pirates,
the need for group help became greater and greater and gradually replaced the usual services practiced among them within the Ghetto walls.
Quoting Hermann Vogelstein and Paul Rieger (*Geschichte der Juden in
Rom*), Abrahams refers to the existence of eleven separate and distinct
societies for the promotion of educational and religious aims alone, besides
such organizations as the women's societies, the Palestine societies, and
others. He finds listed in *Meil Zedakah,* a historic treatise by Elijah ben
Solomon Halevi of Smyrna (seventeenth century), at least seventy titles of
charitable acts covering personal services to be rendered, occasions to be
celebrated or remembered, public charities to be maintained, and other
miscellaneous purposes. Many of these titles later became the titles and
purposes of societies formed. Cecil Roth reports that in Rome, in the
Ghetto period, there were not less than thirty of these benevolent societies
in a population not exceeding 5,000.

All writers concerning Jewish social service in the Middle Ages stress
the personal character of the services rendered. The act of *Zedakah*
involved a religious obligation, a gift of self rather than of mere alms.
The sick were cared for not only by the community and the doctor, but
by their neighbors. Visiting the sick, poor or rich, was a religious as
well as a social service act. It became customary to make formal visits
to the sick immediately after the Sabbath morning services in the synagogue. Almost a complete code of bedside manners gradually developed,
which showed a remarkable understanding of the physical and psychological needs of the patient. Naturally, care of the poor sick involved more
personal attention and interest by many neighbors. Eventually this interest
and attention led to the formation of a special "visiting the sick" society.
In many instances, the services of the physician were available gratis, but
subsequently his services, too, were made possible by a special society or by
the community as a whole, through its central funds.

What has been said of services to the sick can be said of services to the
deceased and to his bereaved family. Providing for proper burial and for
the comfort of the grief-stricken survivors was considered among the chief

religious obligations of every Jew and of the community as a whole. Sometimes special guardians were appointed to take care of the material and spiritual needs of orphans. Hence, there was much personal "social" and communal service offered. Similar illustrations can be cited for other forms of charity, which involved personal services and were later performed by groups or societies organized for these specific purposes. Incidentally, personal service, or the "society" (*Hebrah*) service which replaced it, was extended to non-Jews as well as Jews, although contributions from non-Jews, except royalty, were accepted reluctantly, if at all.

Another characteristic of personal and social service during the early Middle Ages was relief in kind rather than of alms. This was a practice which can be traced back to talmudic times. Giving a person shelter in one's home, sharing one's (Sabbath) food and clothing, providing matzot and wine for the Passover, gifts for the Sabbath and festival occasions, added to the personal interest, joy, and religious significance of the act of *Zedakah*. This fact may also help explain in part why house-to-house begging was discouraged even within Ghetto walls. (It was definitely forbidden to go begging of non-Jews outside the Ghetto.) Only the community collectors were originally permitted to make such house-to-house collections, which, of course, involved money rather than personal services or goods. Gradually the restrictions on house-to-house begging in the Ghetto were relaxed, but begging in front of synagogues or by children was forbidden. Usually house-to-house begging was done on Fridays, so that the recipient might prepare for the Sabbath day. Incidentally, it is well to remember that in addition to the respect that was due him as a matter of religious obligation, the *Schnorrer* in the Ghetto had his own pride, too. He knew that just as the rich man shared his earthly goods with him, he, the poor, contributed to the rich man's measure of religious grace, of divine reward, in the world to come. From a religious point of view, the beneficiary was only collecting his portion of God's goods entrusted to the benefactor. The benefactor, on the other hand, was privileged to perform a mitzva, thus adding to his own religious and social merit. In this mutual attitude of beneficiary and benefactor there is another reflection of the intimacy and family relationship involved in the personal and social services in the Ghetto community of the Middle Ages. Of course, the behavior of the *Schnorrer* or the *Nagid* (rich man) sometimes led to arrogance and abuse. To prevent or correct such behavior, the Rabbis in the Talmud had long before expounded religious teachings and developed a tradition in favor of work and self-help, and Jewish communities in Palestine and elsewhere had issued a system of regulations to supervise the collection and distribution of alms.

As previously noted, Israel Abrahams reports that gradually, and as conditions in the medieval Ghetto deteriorated, the personal character of social service yielded to *Hebrah* (society) service. By the thirteenth century, philanthropic societies for various purposes appeared. Many of these societies were offshoots of the synagogue, which in most places served as the central community agency for all religious and social services. Eventually, these societies began to perform their functions as semi-independent organizations.

Israel Abrahams reports further that for many, many years during the Middle Ages personal services and *Hebrah* services existed side by side, and that many traditional forms of service still persisted. Thus, for example, the *Kuppah* and the *Tamhui* existed in many places, *Tamhui* providing casual relief, the *Kuppah* regular relief.

During those centuries, there was one form of relief which became the paramount obligation of the individual and the whole community. This relief was directed toward protecting the wandering Jew. Expulsions of Jews from their homes and lands and the capture of Jews for ransom purposes made all Jews conscious of their special responsibility to one another. As a result, we find individual homes, synagogues, and even privately owned inns open to Jewish wayfarers. Entertaining strangers or the poor on a Sabbath day in private homes was extended as a weekday practice in order to accommodate refugees. Communal agencies opened community hostelries of their own, sometimes called *Hekdesh*, or "hospitals," or paid community innkeepers for the hospitality to such unfortunate strangers. As the number of Jewish captives for ransom purposes increased, not only did the number of special societies for *Pidyon Shebuyim* increase, but entire communities became responsible for the ransom of their leaders and brethren. For such purposes communities sometimes had to appropriate accumulated legacies. Frequently transportation, too, was provided by these communities.

Thus external forces helped to intensify the traditional sense of community responsibility among Ghetto Jews.

Another important mitzva of individual Jews and of Jewish communities in the Diaspora was support of Palestine Jewry and its institutions. Communities set aside special funds and fund-raising activities for the Holy Land. Salo W. Baron reports a record[10] (1648) showing Continental Jewry sending $30,000 annually to Palestine for the benefit of Ashkenazic Jews. The *Halukah* (distribution) system in Palestine seems already to have been established previous to that date. In Northern Europe, the Polish Council of Lithuanian Jews received private and synagogue collections for transfer to Palestine. In Southern Europe, Venetian Jewry taxed its community members at least one-half ducat annually on behalf of Palestine.

Reference has been made to the *Kuppah* (money collections) and *Tamhui* (food collections). Both these practices or institutions go back to mishnaic times. The word *Kuppah* means box. Every community in

Palestine had a *Kuppah,* or charity box. Even the Temple had one. It contained the contributions for the poor. The poor who were permanent residents received money every Friday to cover fourteen meals for the whole family and for purchase of clothing. Transient poor received money for one meal for the day and for three meals on the Sabbath. The *Tamhui* was a kind of free community bowl kitchen to serve meals for immediate relief.

In the early centuries in Palestine the trustees of the *Kuppah* were known as *Gabbai Zedakah.* These men were chosen from among the most respected citizens. Rabbi Akiba[11a] occupied such a post.[12] Later these trustees were also known as *Parnasim* (providers). These trustees decided on the personal merits and the worthiness of the applicants and their claims. Usually there were three trustees in charge of a *Kuppah.* Two tax or alms collectors were appointed with power to assess people or seize property as penalty for failure to contribute. Collections had to be made by the two members working together.[13] Collections for the *Kuppah* were made weekly, for the *Tamhui* daily. For food collections there were three collectors. The rate of collections was as follows: thirty days' residence in a town obliged an individual to contribute to the *Kuppah;* three months' residence obliged him to contribute to the *Tamhui;* six months' residence obliged him to contribute clothing, *Kesut;* nine months' obliged him to contribute to the burial fund.[14] Women, children, and even the poor contributed.[15] No contributions were accepted from idolators except from royalty, in which instance it was distributed to the non-Jewish poor.[16]

So far as the recipients from the *Kuppah* were concerned, women were given precedence over men, students over the ignorant regardless of rank. Non-Jewish poor, too, were aided. "We support the poor of the heathen along with the poor of Israel and visit the sick of the heathen along with the sick of Israel. . . ." Only transgressors of the Law could not claim assistance.[17]

The *Kuppah,* the central relief agency of the Palestine community, became the widely accepted charity fund of European Jewish communities. Maimonides states that "we had never seen or heard of a Jewish community which does not have a *Kuppah.*"[18] Many traditions, practices, and responsibilities of the Palestine *Kuppah* were carried forward into European Jewish communities. Their central agencies, too, had the power to assess contributions and to collect them, and they appointed official collectors and overseers. In some places these powers received government sanction. Funds for these central agencies were collected from various sources. Some moneys were derived from periodic assessments on individual members of the community which, in many instances, included the poor, too. These collections took place weekly or monthly or three times a year. Some funds were received from voluntary donations commemorating happy or sad events, private or public; the gifts might be offered in the synagogue during or after prayers, they might come from the symbolic selling of the Torah Scroll, from legacies, tithes, or individual incomes. Women and children also were accustomed to make voluntary contributions. In addition, there were collections from fines imposed for transgression of community regulations. Sometimes communities even borrowed funds against future revenue. It is important to note that overseers and collectors of these central agencies were duly elected or licensed persons. Only the most honored persons were selected for these positions. Usually collectors as well as distributors of charitable funds worked in teams of two, and there was an official accounting offered. Sometimes there were traveling collectors from other communities, especially Palestine. They, too, had to have their credentials.

Concerning the government and powers of the central agencies in Jewish communities, Baron[19] reports that, while the law governing Jewish communities in Babylonia or Palestine or elsewhere seems extremely ambiguous, everywhere a governing body, evidently elective, seems to have exercised all rights in the name of the whole community. (In Palestine, this Council was called *Heber Ha-Ir*.) Although, as previously indicated, the synagogue building was used for all kinds of purposes, including school, asylum of homeless and aged, and other charitable activities, "expenditures for cult and philanthropy were usually defrayed from a common exchequer." "The community rather than the congregation was the basic unit of organization." In larger cities the Jews erected sufficient synagogues to accommodate worshipers in all neighborhoods, but the community, embracing all congregations, controlled the administration of justice, tax collections, and general charity. In Rome the cemeteries did not belong to the congregations but to the community as a whole. In Spain the communities maintained Talmud Torahs (Valladolid, 1432) and set aside the income from taxes on meat and wine for the payments of teachers' salaries. In the final analysis, the community as a whole took the chief responsibility for the care of the sick, the aged, the orphan, the destitute, the captive, the needy in Palestine, and all other similar philanthropies.

Cecil Roth reports that "in the eighteenth century, one in every three of the Jewish population in Germany, England and Italy was dependent upon his coreligionists for relief. . . . But their cry for assistance was never in vain." He quotes Emperor Julian in the fourth century, who refers with admiration to the example of the Jews, "in whose midst no beggars were to be found." Concerning this fact, Baron makes the following comment: "However large the communal debts, it is apparently true that no Jew seems ever to have died of hunger while living in a Jewish community." But he deplores the fact that such communal responsibility and congregational integration no longer exist in our times, for he adds that "in the United States of America, Italy and France, the full independence of each congregation, although undoubtedly conducive to keeping alive the members' interest in congregational affairs, became co-responsible for a state of anarchy not to be found in any other sector of Jewry." He is ready to allow for "both the uncurtailed vitality" of the small local association, and for "self-restraint by necessary powers of co-ordination, consultation and supervision of the central agencies."

The fully developed medieval program of social service and its modern counterpart, although calculated to meet the specific needs prevalent at a particular moment, did not come into being because of the exigencies of the moment but stems from a tradition which is as old as Jewish history—a tradition which has its origin in Biblical commandments and injunctions, which was elaborated and enriched by Rabbinic interpretation and application. The original Biblical expressions and their rabbinic reformulation have become to the Jew teachings of Torah, which must be scrupulously observed and adhered to under all conditions of life. It would be well, therefore, to pause briefly in order to examine these teachings of Torah which undergird the traditions of Jewish social service.

4. TEACHINGS OF TORAH UNDERLYING THE TRADITIONS OF JEWISH SOCIAL SERVICE

The traditions of Jewish social service are derived from the original conception of *Zedakah*, which means righteousness. In accordance with this conception, an act of *Zedakah* is therefore not an act of grace or of liberality, but an act of duty toward one's fellow men.

A. BIBLICAL SOURCES

Zedakah—A Divine Command

The concept of *Zedakah* as righteousness, as duty, and as personal debt is perhaps best formulated in the Biblical passages in Deut. 15:7-11:

If there be among you a needy man, one of thy brethren, within any of thy gates, in thy land which the Lord thy God giveth thee, thou shalt not harden thy heart, nor shut thy hand from thy needy brother; but thou shalt surely open thy hand unto him, and shalt surely lend him sufficient for his need in that which he wanteth. . . . Thou shalt surely give him, and thy heart shall not be grieved when thou givest unto him; because that for this thing the Lord thy God will bless thee in all thy work, and in all that thou puttest thy hand unto. For the poor shall never cease out of the land (interpreted by

Rashi as meaning in those lands where the will of God is not heeded); there-fore, I *command* thee saying: *"Thou shalt surely open thy hand unto thy poor and needy brother in thy land."*

At the same time, God promises the Israelites that "there shall be no needy among you . . . *if only* thou diligently hearken unto the voice of the Lord thy God to observe to do all this commandment" (Deut. 15:4, 5).

This sense of duty to share God's bounty with the poor is responsible for the reminder to the Israelite that when he rejoices in a festival he must share his joys with the poor, the stranger, the orphan, the widow, his laborers, and the Levite (the public servant) (Deut. 16:11, 14). It is this sense of duty, of debt, and of gracious giving that is summarized in Pr. 19:17 as follows: "He that is gracious unto the poor lendeth unto the Lord, and his good deed will He repay unto him."

The duty and demand for righteous conduct are emphasized in the Pentateuch over and over again. "He doth execute justice for the father-less and widow, and loveth the stranger" (Deut. 10:18, cf. Ex. 22:21-23). At the end of each three-year period, the poor, the orphan, the widow, the stranger are entitled to the annual tithes in accordance with their respective needs, which injunction if complied with will be rewarded with God's bounty (Deut. 14:28, 29). Similar instructions are directed to owners of fields, who are enjoined to leave to the poor, the orphan, the widow and the stranger the corners of the fields they harvest (*Peah*), the gleanings of the harvest (*Leket*), the forgotten sheaf (*Shikhah*), and the growth of the seventh year (*Shemitah*) (Deut. 24:19-21; Lev. 19:9, 10; Ex. 23:11). Again, this duty and righteous conduct is illustrated in the Biblical injunction concerning a loan on a pledge to a poor man. The pledge must be returned if the poor man needs it so that he may "bless thee; and it shall be righteousness (*Zedakah*) unto thee before the Lord thy God" (Deut. 24:12, 13).

Zedakah and Its Rewards

Numerous other texts may be added from the Pentateuch and from other books of the Bible. The Book of Proverbs is replete with references to the reward for *Zedakah* and to the punishment for failure to pursue *Zedakah:* "Treasures of wickedness profit nothing; but righteousness (*Zedakah*) delivereth from death" (10:2); "Righteousness (*Zedakah*) exalteth a nation; but sin is a reproach to any people" (14:34); "Whoso stoppeth his ears at the cry of the poor, he also shall cry himself, but shall not be answered" (21:13); "He that followeth after righteousness (*Zedakah*) and mercy (lovingkindness, *Hesed*) findeth life, prosperity and honor" (21:21).[20] The passages reaffirm the Divine command con-cerning acts of righteousness by the individual and by the nation, the equality of the rich and poor before God, the blessings that follow obedience, and the retribution that follows the failure to share God's bounty with the poor and the weak.

Man and His Possessions Belong to God

Similarly, the Psalms are full of praise for the righteous and of demands for just and kind behavior to one's fellow man. Man is reminded by the psalmist that all wealth belongs to God, that "the earth is the Lord's, and the fulness thereof; the world, and they that dwell therein" (24:1). (Cf. Lev. 25:23: "And the land shall not be sold in perpetuity; for the land is Mine." Cf. also I Chron. 29:11-14.)

Righteousness, Justice, Lovingkindness

Psalms, too, is replete with passages in which the spirit of giving is stressed (cf. 33:5) and in which *Zedakah*, righteousness, is associated with justice and lovingkindness. "Happy are they that keep justice, that do righteousness at all times" (106:3) is a refrain that occurs innumerable times in nearly all the psalms. Justice and righteousness are always associated. It is the *doing* of righteousness that is stressed, and it is lovingkindness, trust in and gratitude to God, with which this justice and righteousness is practiced.

When we come to the prophets, it is difficult to select passages, for what are the prophetic writings if not a protest against wrongdoing, a call to nation and individual to practice social justice, righteousness, and loving-kindness toward one's fellow man, especially toward the poor, the weak, and the unfortunate? Can there be any more thunderous denunciation of wrongdoing and a greater promise of righteousness than that contained in the first chapter of Isaiah? "I cannot endure iniquity along with the solemn assembly . . . when ye make many prayers, I will not hear. Your hands are full of blood. . . . Cease to do evil; learn to do well; seek justice, relieve the oppressed, judge the fatherless, plead for the widow." Speaking of the city of Jerusalem, he cries out, "How is the faithful city become a harlot! She that was full of justice, righteousness lodged in her, but now murderers. . . . Every one loveth bribes, followeth after rewards, they judge not the fatherless, neither doth the cause of the widow come unto them. . . ." Her only hope is that "Zion shall be redeemed with *justice* and they that return of her with *righteousness*." It is only then that Isaiah sees the grand vision when the law will go forth out of Zion and war shall be no more. When the prophet brings comfort to his people (Is. 60-61), he sees them all righteous and they will inherit the land forever. He brings good tidings to the humble, promises "to bind up the broken hearted, to proclaim liberty to the captives, and open the eyes of them that are bound" (61:1). Elsewhere (58:6, 7) he asks what is the fast day for, except to help "loose the fetters of wickedness . . . to deal thy bread to the hungry . . . bring the poor . . . to thy house . . . to cover . . . (the naked) and that thou hide not thyself from thine own flesh?"

Echoes of the voice of Isaiah and of his thought and expressions can be found in all the prophets, especially Micah, whose crystallization of the Law of God is very familiar. "What doth the Lord require of thee, only to do justly, and to love mercy (lovingkindess), and to walk humbly with thy God" (6:8). Jeremiah puts the same thought somewhat differently: "Did not thy father eat and drink, and do justice and righteousness? Then it was well with him . . . *Is not this to know Me?* saith the Lord" (22:15-16, cf. 9:22 f.). Jeremiah continues his outcry against injustice. "Execute ye justice and righteousness, and deliver the spoiled out of the hand of the oppressor . . . do no wrong . . . to the stranger, the fatherless, nor the widow. . . . Woe unto him that buildeth his house by unrighteousness, and his chambers by injustice; that useth his neighbor's service without wages and giveth him not his hire" (22:3, 13).

Amos, like Isaiah, denounces the Temple sacrifices, the solemn assemblies, and the meaningless prayers. "Take thou away from Me the noise of thy songs"; he cries out, "and let Me not hear the melody of thy psalteries. But let justice well up as waters, and righteousness as a mighty stream" (5:23-24). Malachi describes God's wrath "against those that oppress the hireling in his wages, the widow, and the fatherless, and that turn aside the stranger . . . and fear not Me" (3:5). It is Malachi who has given us the famous dictum "Have we not all one father? Hath not one God created us? Why do we deal treacherously every man against his brother, profaning the covenant of our fathers?" (2:10)

Zedakah, Mishpat, Hesed, Emet

All through the Biblical writings we find *Zedakah* (righteousness) associated with *Mishpat* (justice) and *Hesed* (kindness). Similarly, the word *Hesed* is very frequently associated with the word *Emet* (truth). Hosea describes God's controversy with the inhabitants of the land "because there is no truth, nor mercy, nor knowledge of God in the land" (4:1). Like the other prophets, he quotes God as saying "For I desire mercy and not sacrifice" (6:6). "Keep mercy and justice and wait for thy God continually" (12:7). This association of *Zedakah* and *Hesed* is also found in one of our penitential prayers, "Our Father, our King, be gracious unto us and answer us for we have no good works of our own: Deal with us in *Zedakah* and *Hesed* and save us."

In all these Biblical quotations and throughout the books of the Bible, the concept of *Zedakah is presented as a divine commandment, an act of duty, a prerequisite of justice, a deed of righteousness and love, a deed of kindness and gratitude, a prescription of truth, a promise of peace and prosperity; but not as an act of special grace or liberality on the part of one man to his fellowman.*

Ephraim Frisch in his *Historical Survey of Jewish Philanthropy* makes the following summary comments about Biblical teachings concerning charity:

> On the whole, it may be said, that in the attempt to induce men to be charitable, the writings of the Prophets appealed to the highest ethical motives, the Book of Deuteronomy gave philanthropy the deepest emotional touch, the Psalms invoked aid to the distressed on the most fervent religious grounds and the Wisdom literature met the demand of the most practical utilitarianism. Everywhere the love of one's fellowman as brothers of the same paternity— God, ran alongside as a concurrent determining force. . . . The Biblical period did not develop a comprehensive system of philanthropy, in our modern meaning of the word, but it had in it the germ of such a system. It exercised a profound, determining influence on all future benevolent thought and endeavor. It was the main current in the stream of Jewish charity and thereby helped water the soil of kindness and uplift among human kind generally.

B. THE RABBINIC CONCEPTION OF ZEDAKAH[21]

To the Biblical concept of *Zedakah,* the Rabbis added their own refinements and interpretations. What the Rabbis are concerned with particularly is the spirit of the giver and the recipient. They expected humility and the attitude of sharing on the part of both, since both rich and poor are the children of God to whom all material possessions belong.

From the Psalmist's declaration that the earth "and the fulness thereof, the world, and they that dwell therein" are the Lord's (Ps. 24:1) the Rabbis deduced that all wealth belongs to God and that it is obligatory to share with those who are less fortunate. "Give unto Him of what is His, seeing that thou and what thou hast are His."[22] As a corollary of this teaching, they concluded that poor and rich, being alike children of God, are to regard one another as brothers and that God, Father of both rich and poor wants one to help the other, and in this way to make the world a household of love.[23]

Rabbis Stress Lovingkindness in Zedakah

The Rabbis accepted the mandatory aspect of *Zedakah* but sought to stress the aspect of *Hesed* which the Bible associated with it. Hence they developed a concept of giving which they called *Gemilut Ha-Sadim,* which literally means the payment of acts of lovingkindness. Such could be practiced by rich and poor in terms of personal services and personal encouragement as well as of material assistance. "Greater than *Zedakah* is *Gemilut Ha-Sadim* and the act of *Zedakah* can be valued only by the measure of *Gemilut Ha-Sadim* which is contained therein."[24] Here again we note that an act of kindness by one man to another is a matter of obligation and debt, not an unexpected act of special grace. "*Gemol Dalim*," the Talmud says, playing with the letters *Gimmel Dalet* (third and fourth letters of the alphabet), "pay kindness to the poor."[25] *Gemilut Ha-Sadim* is an act of divine grace and therefore must come from a heart full of love for one's fellow man. It is interesting to note that the term *Gemilut Ha-Sadim* is now used to designate the granting of a loan without interest to help a man establish himself economically.

In this spirit the Rabbis required both the giver and the recipient to be God-fearing men. They sought to remove false pride from the heart of the recipient and advised him not to refuse aid when he was in need.[26] On the other hand, the community was ordered not to hurt the feelings of the recipient, to provide him in accordance with his needs and previous social status, and to do so in utmost secrecy.[27] "A man who gives charity in secret is greater than Moses, our teacher."[28] "It is better not to have given at all than to have given in a manner which humiliates."[29]

In the Mishna Peah (8:7, 8, 9) minimum standards are laid down for the giving to the poor.[30] The Rabbis were also considerate of the givers. While the Bible asked for tithes, or a tenth of one's income, for charity, they counseled the giver not to give away more than one-fifth of his possessions lest he become dependent himself.[31] They even indicated priority in obligations. "A man's family, his poor relations and his townsmen," they stated, "have prior claims on one's giving."[32] This list of priorities, which is probably the basis for the expression "charity begins at home," is worked out in great detail.[33]

Reverent Regard for the Unfortunates

But it was the manner of giving, the attitude and the motivation, that seemed to give the Rabbis the most concern; thus they called attention to the Psalmist's statement: "Happy is he that *considereth* the poor" (Ps. 41:21) and pointed out that the word is *considereth*, not *giveth*.[34] Charity should be given joyously. If a man has nothing to give, he should at least seek to comfort the poor one. "He who receives his fellow man with a cheerful countenance, even though he has not given him anything is credited as if he had given him most precious gifts."[35]

Hospitality to the poor was considered one of the most worthy of Jewish practices. The estimate by the Rabbis of this practice can be judged from the following quotations: "Let thy house be open wide and let the poor be members of thy household."[36] "Greater is the reception of the wayfarers than the reception of the *Shekinah*" (Divine Presence).[37] "Whoever busies himself in the study of Law alone (without engaging in acts of loving-kindness) is like one who recognizes no God."[38] In this connection it is interesting to note that the Rabbis remembered Abraham for his hospitality and ascribed a special meaning to the tamarisk he planted at Beer-sheba. The Hebrew word for this tree consists of three letters, *aleph, shin, lamed*. By using these letters as an acrostic, they got three words: *eating, drinking, lodging:* the courtesies a gracious host offers the wayfarer.[39]

The Rabbis, too, like the Biblical teachers, dwell on the blessings that follow acts of *Zedakah*, and on the retributions that follow the failure to perform these acts, as may be gathered from the following aphorisms: "More than the master of the house does for the poor man, the latter does for the former."[40] "If a man is anxious to give charity, the Holy One, blessed be He, furnishes him money with which to give it."[41]

Society Preserved through Zedakah

But it is not only the individual who profits by his performance of *Zedakah*. The whole people and the world "share in the benefits derived." "Whoever practices *Zedakah* and *Mishpat* (justice), it is as though he fills the whole world with *Hesed* (lovingkindness)."[42] Thus we come again to the Rabbinic emphasis on the practice of lovingkindness. Such importance did they attach to it that they regarded *Gemilut Ha-Sadim* as one of the three pillars upon which society (the social order) rests, the other two being Torah and Worship.[43] The basis for organized communal charity may have been derived from the high regard of the Rabbis for secret giving, when the benefactor and the beneficiary did not know each other.[44]

Degrees of the Spirit in Giving

These various qualities of giving were later summarized by Maimonides (twelfth century) in the form of a scale.[45a] He listed eight kinds of givers. Foremost is he who assists the poor man to become self-supporting by helping him to establish himself in some profitable occupation, and, if necessary, by advancing him money for that purpose.[46] Second is he who gives secretly, so that he and the recipient know not each other. Third is he who gives secretly to a poor man whom he knows, but the recipient knows not the giver. Fourth is he who gives to a poor man *he* does *not* know, but the poor knows who is the giver. Fifth is he who gives before he is solicited. Sixth is he who gives after he is solicited. Seventh is he who gives inadequately but with good grace. Eighth is he who gives inadequately and with bad grace.[47]

Man Needs Sense of Independence

The Rabbis were very sensitive to man's feeling. They knew that a man was most at ease when he did not have to depend on others for his livelihood, even if they were his own children. "A man takes greater delight in one measure of his own than in nine measures he might receive from his fellow man."[48] This sensitivity is embodied in one of the prayers in the Grace after Meals, when the participants in the meal say, "We beseech You, O God of our Fathers, that You cause us not to be in need of the gifts of flesh and blood, nor of their loans, but make us dependent only on Your hand, which is full, open, holy and ample, so that we may not be ashamed or embarrassed." For these reasons and for others, the Rabbis made sure to counsel man not to regard any work beneath his dignity. "Flay a carcass in the market place, if necessary," they said, "receive thy wage, and do not say, I am a great man, and it is beneath my dignity to do such a thing."[49]

Labor Dignifies Man

This understanding of man's need for independence helped the Rabbis to stress the great importance of work, for the health of man and society. "He who enjoys the labor of his hands," they said, "is greater than he who fears God."[50] "Make thy Sabbath a weekday and do not be reduced to need the help of human beings."[51]

In this manner they sought to exalt labor to a position of religious merit. "Both work and Torah," they said, "were bestowed upon Israel through a covenant with God."[52] "He who engages in work causes the *Shekinah* to dwell among Israel."[53] Thus Rabba ordered his pupils to absent themselves from school during certain seasons of the year so that they might attend to agricultural duties. The Rabbis went to all ends to emphasize the dignity of labor. They found in its creative principle a divine quality.

Zedakah Emphasizes Democratic Concept of Man

Whence did the Rabbis derive their concern for the sensibilities of the poor man, the recipient of *Zedakah* or of *Gemilut Ha-Sadim?* Of course, their original source of instruction and inspiration was the Bible. Read again the quotation from Deut. 15:7-11, on the manner in which loans should be made during the sabbatical year. Their own interpretations of Biblical teachings were, in addition, influenced greatly by the democratic conception of the origin of man. Not only was man created in God's image, but all men are descended from one ancestor. All men are therefore brothers who must practice loving deeds toward one another. "Be a lover of thy fellow creature," they said.[54] Because man was created in the image of God, the life and dignity of every human being are sacred. So high a value did the Rabbis place on human life that they regarded the life of the human being equal to the whole creation. Therefore, "when one saves a human life, it is as if he had saved the whole world, and counterwise, when one destroys a human life, it is as if he had destroyed the whole world."[55]

Zedakah Emphasizes Mutual Responsibility between the Individual and the Community

This respect for human life and human dignity was expressed not only in the relationship between man and man, but also in the relationship between man and the community. The Rabbis counseled man to "obey all the king's laws except those that would lead to a renunciation of God and Torah."[56] Except for this limitation, they told him to pray for the government,[57] to accept the law of the land he dwelt in as binding,[58] and not to separate himself from his obligations toward or participation in the community.[59] On the other hand, they had some special advice for the selection of leaders for the community. "A leader of a community must not be appointed," they said, "without first consulting the people of the community."[60] And those "who occupy themselves in the affairs of the community must do so in the name of Heaven,"[61] not for ulterior purposes.

Zedakah Emphasizes Equal Treatment of the Non-Jew

The attitude of the Rabbis concerning a Jew's obligation to his fellow man is further expressed in their description of the relationship between the Jew and the non-Jew. They demanded equal treatment for the poor of the Gentiles. "We need to support the poor of the Gentiles," they said, "together with the poor of Israel, visit the sick of the Gentiles together with the sick of Israel . . . and give proper burial to the dead of the Gentiles as to those of Israel, because of the ways of peace." This sentiment had already been expressed in the Bible, when the Israelites were enjoined not to prevent the *stranger* from enjoying gleanings, forgotten sheaves, and the corners of the field (Lev. 19:9).[62]

In days of persecution, the Rabbis reminded Jews that "God judges Gentiles by the best of them."[63] They insisted that "The righteous of all peoples shall inherit the bliss of the hereafter."[64] The instruction to keep God's statutes, which "if a man do, he shall live by them" (Lev. 18:5), applies to the Gentiles as well as to the Jews. "A Gentile who obeys the laws may be compared to the High Priest."[65] For a Jew to sin against a Gentile is considered a more serious offense than to sin against another Jew. "Stealing from a Gentile is a more serious offense than from an Israelite, because it involves the profanation of God's name (*Hillul ha-Shem*)."[66]

Divine Merit and Group Distinction Achieved Only through Conduct and Sacrifice

The Rabbis made sure to remind the Jews that even their sufferings did not make them a superior people, emphasizing a thought frequently expressed in the Scriptures that the law given to Israel is the law of mankind (cf. II Sam. 7:19). And Moses is said to have expounded this law in seventy languages. If Israel sought the merit of being called "The Guardian of the Torah," they would have to achieve it through conduct, at times even through suffering. The Holy One, blessed be He, bestowed three gifts upon Israel—Torah, Eretz Yisrael, and the world to come, none of which is obtained except through suffering[67] (cf. Pr. 3:12: "Whom God loveth, He correcteth").

Teachings Derived from Biblical and Rabbinic Sources

Enough quotations have been cited above from Biblical and Rabbinic sources to make evident that the concept Zedakah is not just an act of charity or almsgiving to the poor and handicapped on the individual's or society's part; it is rather a fulfillment of a divine commandment, a source of spiritual vitality to the individual and to the community. This meaning is perhaps best illustrated by the Biblical interpretation of Abraham's faith in God, which is accredited to him as an act of Zedakah (Gen. 15:6) because it was prompted by a spiritual impulse and not by external compulsion. This concept of Zedakah is further elaborated in greater detail in a series of Rabbinic codes and ethical writings[68] during the Middle Ages which have served the individual Jew and his community as moral guides and religious laws.

The larger significance of the Hebrew concept of Zedakah, as interpreted by Biblical and Rabbinic sources, is well summed up by Maurice Thorner in his study of this subject, when he says: "Zedakah, righteousness, the watchword of the Law and of the prophets, is the biblical solution to the problem of poverty . . . when individual unrighteous conduct and social injustice will cease, poverty, a resulting condition from these, will also cease. . . . Charity (Zedakah) will help to restore social and moral equilibrium which has been disturbed by corruption and injustice."

From his Biblical and Rabbinic studies Thorner observes a further significance to the Hebrew attitude toward charity. He finds, on the one hand, an "abundance of Hebrew terms for the poor, picturing a conception of physical and moral suffering" and, on the other, "a paucity of distinct terms for the conception of wealth." He therefore concludes that "not property but humanity, especially the weaker and less fortunate part thereof, was the chief care of the ancient Hebrews."

"Social righteousness and humanitarian considerations are the very core of Jewish religious learning and behavior. Their permanent foundations and structures have been erected in the teachings of the Bible and the Rabbis."

CONCLUSION

When Maurice Thorner speaks of *Zedakah* as the Biblical solution to the problem of poverty, he anticipates the modern approach to philanthropy as stated by Boris Bogen, one of the pre-eminent Jewish social workers in recent times. "The tendency of modern philanthropy," he said, "is toward the elimination of the causes predisposing to dependency, rather than toward palliative measures affecting the symptoms of distress alone." Bogen finds the causes of poverty in economic maladjustment, in ignorance, in political disability, in exploitation of labor and immigrants, in slums, and in the ills of modern civilization.

In seeking the causes of and offering a solution to the problem of poverty in our own day, this Jewish social worker is echoing the teachings of a long line of prophets and Sages, who have created a religious tradition and a philosophy for Jewish social service.

Whatever may have been the historic experience of the people of Israel out of which the Biblical and Rabbinic teachings were crystallized as a way of life, these teachings were further tested and refined in the post-Rabbinic, medieval, and modern European civilizations through which the Jewish group maintained itself.

These teachings were again subjected to a supreme test during the past thirty-five years when two World Wars threatened the very existence of Jewish group life. This time American Jewry sustained the test. Horrible, inhuman treatment of their brethren overseas by a pagan world only strengthened the traditions of social righteousness, humanitarianism, and brotherhood within the Jewish group in America. Individuals and communities rallied to their social obligations, animated by the religious teachings of their forebears, and inspired by the historic examples of previous generations of Jews. The result has been a more organized Jewish community life, a greater measure of united action, a larger degree of individual and group responsibility toward the relief of Jewish sufferers in Europe and the re-establishment of Jewish group life in Palestine (now the State of Israel).

With World War II ended, and the European Jewish community practically wiped out, American Jewry becomes heir to all the cultural and spiritual wealth of historic Israel. Whatever be the blessings of peace to the world, American Jewry found that the vestiges of war, hatred, and betrayal against Israel were still prevalent. Jews had still to ransom refugees, to rescue suffering brethren from concentration camps and from lands behind the Iron Curtain, to fight enemies from within and from without, to secure the State of Israel for its inhabitants and for all Israel, and to safeguard great religious teachings which may yet someday save the world from utter destruction.

To meet this supreme challenge, American Jewry undertook two colossal peacetime acts of *Zedakah*. One was to raise in one year $250,000,000 for immediate aid to world Jewry. The other was to raise in three years a loan of $500,000,000 through the sale of Israel Bonds, in order to help re-establish the State of Israel on a self-supporting basis. Thus American Jewry manifested by deeds its own practice of *Gemilut Ha-Sadim* which leads to self-help, the highest form of the Jewish concept of *Zedakah*, and its own faith in the Jewish teaching that *Zedakah Tazil Mimavet* (Righteousness will save the Jews and the world from destruction).

In 1948, the Jews in Palestine proclaimed the re-establishment of the State of Israel, the third historic Jewish commonwealth in the land. It was immediately recognized by our own United States of America and by the Soviet Union. In 1949, the State of Israel was admitted into the United Nations. Since that time, this new State has become a refuge for all oppressed Jews, to which they have flocked in the hundreds of thousands. During the first five years of its existence, the number of Jews in the State of Israel increased from 650,000 to 1,500,000.

Without physical resources, and surrounded by enemies, the new Israelis accepted suffering and self-denial in order to make possible the influx of brethren from all parts of the world. Despite their own poverty, they set up social welfare agencies, security agencies, and a system of free compulsory education for all children, Jewish and non-Jewish. They accepted for themselves advanced measures of labor legislation, and granted religious and cultural rights to minorities. Supported by world Jewry, they have demonstrated miraculous self-help in agriculture, industry, and social adjustment. They have become a citadel of free democracy in the Middle East. Once more the people of Israel in the land of Israel have set an example to inspire all Israel with the ideals and traditions of social justice inherited from former generations of prophets, teachers, sages, and martyrs. Together with its American brethren, Israeli Jewry has accepted the responsibilities for all the cultural, religious, and philanthropic ideals inherited from common ancestors and evolved through historic Judaism.

NOTES

[1] In 1946, the United Jewish Appeal collected $102,000,000. In 1947, it set a goal of $170,000,000; in 1948, of $250,000,000.

[2] Between 1948, when the State of Israel was established, and 1953, the U.J.A. spent about $268,000,000 in Israel and $212,000,000 in other countries. A good deal of J.D.C. funds, too, were spent by J.D.C. in Israel for the benefit of refugee Jews settling there.

[3] The National Refugee Service became United Service for New Americans in 1947.

[4] For 1952 alone, these agencies were reported by the Council of Federations and Welfare Funds to have spent more than $16,000,000 for Israel and other countries.

[5] Baba Batra 8b.

[6] Recently the B'nai B'rith and the American Jewish Committee have withdrawn from this joint Advisory Council. Efforts are being made to bring them back (1953).

[7] Nineteen hundred and fifty-four marked the 100th anniversary of the founding of American Jewish community centers. The first Y.M.H.A. was established in 1854 in Baltimore.

[8] See article in *American Jewish Year Book*, Vol. 45, pp. 117-134.

[9] In more recent years, this title has been reserved for free loan societies.

[10] *The Jewish Community*, II, 340.

[[11a] Cf. above Judah Goldin, "The Period of the Talmud (135 B.C.E.–1035 C.E.)," pp. 155 ff.]

[12] Mishna Maaser Sheni 5:9; Kiddushin 27a.

[13] Mishna Peah, 8.7.

[14] Baba Batra 8a.

[15] Baba Batra 8a; Baba Kamma 119a.

[16] Baba Batra 106.

[17] Gittin 61a.

[18] Mattenot Aniyim 9:3.

[19] *Social and Religious History of the Jews*, I, 283 ff., 291, 435 ff.

[20] Cf. Pr. 17:5, 19:1, 22:2, 22-23. The last passage is particularly characteristic. It, like Deut. 10:18 referred to above, stresses that God executes judgment for the poor: "Rob not the weak, because he is weak, neither crush the poor in the gate; for the Lord will plead their cause and despoil of life those that despoil them."

[21] See *Everyman's Talmud*, Rev. Dr. A. Cohen (Dent & Sons, Ltd., London), for an excellent account and quotations of Rabbinic teachings. See also S. Schechter, "Notes of Lectures on Philanthropy," in *Studies in Judaism* (Third Series).

[22] Abot 3.8.

[23] Tanhuma Shemot (ed. Buber), p. 43a.

[24] Sukkah 49b.

[25] Shabbat 104a.

[26] Yer. Peah 8; Lev. R. 34-1.

[27] Ketubot 67b; Shabbat 118a.

[28] Baba Batra 9b.

[29] From the phrase, "Thou shalt give to *him*" (Deut. 15:10) it is deduced that a gift to the poor must be made privately, with no one else present; and as an illustration reference is made to a chamber in the Temple in Jerusalem where peculiarly scrupulous persons deposited their charitable donations in secrecy, while with equal privacy the impoverished members of good families drew from this fund their sustenance (G. F. Moore, *Judaism*, II, 167; see Tos. Shekalim 2, 16; Ket. 67b).

[30] See translation of these paragraphs by Ephraim Frisch in his *Historical Survey of Jewish Philanthropy*, pp. 49-58.

[31] Ketubot 50a.

[32] Baba Mezia 71a.

[33] Seder Eliyahu, p. 135.

[34] Yer. Peah 8:8; Lev. R. 34:1.

[35] Abot of Rabbi Nathan 13; cf. Baba Batra 9b.

[36] Abot 1.5.

[37] Shabbat 127a.

[38] Aboda Zara 17b.

[39] Gen. R. 54:8.

[40] Lev. R. 34:8.

[41] Baba Batra 9b.

[42] Sukkah 49b.

[43] Abot 1.2.

[44] Baba Batra 10b, top.

[[45a] Cf. below Louis Finkelstein, "The Jewish Religion: Its Beliefs and Practices," p. 1747.]

[46] Shabbat 63a, bot.

[47] Yad Hahazakah-Mattenot Aniyim 10:7-13.

[48] Baba Mezia 38a.

[49] Baba Batra 110a; Pesahim 113a.

[50] Berakot 8a.

[51] Pesahim 113a.

[52] Abot of Rabbi Nathan 11.

[53] *Ibid.*

[54] Abot 1:12.

[55] Mishna Sanhedrin 4:5.

[56] Tanhumah Noah 10.

[57] Abot 3.2.

[58] Baba Kamma 113a.

[59] Abot 2.5.

[60] Berakot 55a.

[61] Abot 2.2.

[62] Cf. Mishna Gittin 5.8.

[63] Yer. Rosh Hashana 57a.

[64] Tosefta Sanhedrin 13.2.

[65] Sifra (ed. Weiss) 86a.

[66] Tosefta Baba Kamma 10.15.

[67] Berakot 5a.

[68] See appended Bibliography.

BIBLIOGRAPHY

ABRAHAMS, ISRAEL, *Jewish Life in the Middle Ages*. Philadelphia, 1911, Chapters 17-18, Private and Communal Charity.

Articles in *American Jewish Year Book* (New York):

    a. "Jewish Social Welfare in the United States," H. L. Lurie. Vol. 47.

    b. "Overseas Relief," Geraldine Rosenfield. Vol. 46.

    c. "Zionist and Pro-Palestine Activities," Samuel Dinin. Vol. 46.

    d. "Overseas Relief," B. Pelcovitz. Vol. 45.

    e. "Jewish Social Welfare in the United States," M. Freund. Vol. 45.

    f. "New York Federation, After Twenty-Five Years," A. Medalia. Vol. 45.

    g. "Federation for the Support of Jewish Philanthropic Societies of New York City," I. E. Goldwasser. Vol. 20.

    h. "Federation Movements in American Jewish Philanthropy," Joseph Jacobs. Vol. 17.

    i. "The Jews of America 1654-1787," A. M. Friedenberg. Vol. 28.

    j. "Federation in the Changing American Scene," B. M. Selekman. Vol. 36.

    k. "Twenty-five Years of American Aid to Jews Overseas, A Record of the Joint Distribution Committee," J. C. Hyman. Vol. 41.

    l. "The Jewish Welfare Board—Twenty Years Old," Cyrus Adler. Vol. 39.

    m. "Jewish Social Research in the United States," Hyman Kaplan. Vol. 22.

    n. "Jewish War Relief Work," H. Schneiderman. Vol. 19.

    o. "Jewish Community Organization in the United States," M. J. Karpf. Vol. 39.

    p. "Jewish Community of New York City." Vol. 11.

    q. "B'nai B'rith, A Century of Service," B. Postal. Vol. 45.

    r. "Statistics of Jews and Jewish Organizations 1850-1937," H. S. Linfield. Vol. 19.

    s. "Sketch of the History of the Jews in the United States." Vol. 4.

Articles on Charity and Hospitality in *The Jewish Encyclopedia*. New York and London, 1901.

BARON, SALO W., *A Social and Religious History of the Jews*. New York, 1937.

    Vol. I. Diaspora Community, pp. 99 ff.

            Ethnic Exclusiveness and Humanitarianism, pp. 119 ff.

            Self-Government, pp. 281 ff.

    Vol. II. Within Ghetto Walls, pp. 86-117.

            Communal and Religious Transformation, pp. 387 ff.

            Jewish Communal Planning, pp. 432 ff.

    Vol. III. Index Under Charities, Community, Poor Laws, Social Teachings, Social Control, International Conference on Jewish Social Work.

————, *The Jewish Community, its History and Structure to the American Revolution*. Philadelphia, 1942. Vol. II, Chapter XVI, Social Welfare.

BOGEN, BORIS D., *Jewish Philanthropy*. New York, 1917.

COHEN, A., *Everyman's Talmud*. London, 1934.

    (Especially recommended.)

CRONBACH, ABRAHAM, *Religion and Its Social Setting*. Cincinnati, 1933.

DUKER, A. G., "Structure of the Jewish Community," in *The American Jew— A Composite Portrait*, ed. by Oscar I. Janowsky. New York, 1942.

EPSTEIN, MORDECAI, *Aspects of Jewish Life and Thought*. New York, 1922. Chapter on Jewish Charity.

FEINBERG, LOUIS (transl.), *Shulhan Arukh*. New York, 1915.
Section on Charity.

FINKELSTEIN, LOUIS, *Jewish Self-Government in the Middle Ages*. See Index, Charity Fund, Orphans and Talmud Torah, pp. 91 to 98, 264, 324, 351, 358, 371.

FLUEGEL, MAURICE, *The Humanity, Benevolence and Charity Legislation of the Pentateuch and the Talmud*. Baltimore, 1908.

FRISCH, EPHRAIM, *An Historical Survey of Jewish Philanthropy*. New York, 1924. (Especially recommended.)

HEILPRIN, ISRAEL, *Pinkas Vaad Arba Haaratzot* (Hebrew). Jerusalem, 1945. See index Zedakah.

KAPLAN, MORDECAI M., *Judaism as a Civilization*. New York, 1934. Chapters 21, 27, 30.

KOHLER, KAUFMANN, "The Historical Development of Jewish Charity," in *Hebrew Union College and Other Addresses*. Cincinnati, 1916.

LICHENSTEIN, MORRIS, *Judaism*. New York, 1934. Chapter 4.

List of Rabbinic Leaders and Ethical Writings during Middle Ages (see Ephraim Frisch's *Historical Survey of Jewish Philanthropy*. Chapter VII).

   a. Maimonides (12th century): *Mishna Torah (Yad Ha-Hazakah)*, section entitled "Mattenot Aniyim."

   b. Jacob b. Asher (14th century): *Tur, Yoreh Deah, Hilkot Zedakah*.

   c. Joseph Caro (16th century): *Shulkhan Aruk, Hilkot Zedakah*.

   d. Aaron b. Joseph Halevi of Barcelona (13th century): *Sefer Ha-Hinuk* (Book of Pedagogy).

   e. Judah He-Hasid (12th century): *Sefer Hasidim* (Book of the Pious).

   f. Isaac Aboab (13th century): *Menorat Ha-Maor* (The Lamp of Light).

   g. Moses of Przemysl (16th century): *Matteh Moshe* (The Staff of Moses).

   h. Elijah b. Solomon Abraham Hakohen of Smyrna (18th century).

   i. *Meil Zedakah* (The Mantle of Charity).

   j. Rabbi Bachya ibn Pakudah, Saragossa, Spain (11th century): *Hobot Ha-Lebabot* (Duties of the Heart) (1040) translated from Arabic by Judah ibn Tibbon (1161-1180).

MOORE, GEORGE FOOT, *Judaism in the First Century of the Christian Era*. Cambridge, 1927-1930. Vol. II, part V, Chapter VII, Private and Public Charity.

NEWMAN, LOUIS I., and SPITZ, SAMUEL, *The Talmudic Anthology*. New York, 1945. Pp. 49-68.

ROTH, CECIL, *The Jewish Contribution to Civilization*. Cincinnati, 1940. Chapter XII.

SCHECHTER, SOLOMON, *Studies in Judaism* (first series). New York and London, 1896. P. 167.

———, *Studies in Judaism* (third series). Philadelphia, 1924. Section on Jewish Philanthropy.

———, *Some Aspects of Rabbinic Theology*. New York, 1909. P. 112.

THORNER, MAURICE, *Poor and Rich in the Old Testament with a Study of Zedakah in the Bible and Rabbinical Literature*. New York, 1905.

CHAPTER 23

HELLENISTIC JEWISH LITERATURE

By Ralph Marcus

1. INTRODUCTION

The name "Hellenistic" is given by students of classical civilization to the period of about three centuries following the conquests of Alexander the Great in the Near East. The Greek noun *hellenistes* commonly meant a non-Greek speaker of Greek or imitator of Greek fashion; "Hellenistic" is therefore an appropriate term for an age in which Jews, Egyptians, Syrians, Iranians and other Oriental peoples were united—so far, at least, as their wealthier urban classes were concerned—in a common pattern of Greek-Oriental culture with more or less important variations of local color.

Students of European history usually consider the lower limit of the Hellenistic period to be 30 B.C.E. because by that time the Roman Empire under Augustus had consolidated its control over the Greek-Oriental kingdoms of Egypt, Syria and Asia Minor. But the orientalist and the historian of Western culture are inclined to extend the lower limit another few centuries because the official and educated classes in the large cities of the Near East continued to be Greek rather than Roman in speech and culture long after the Hellenistic kingdoms had been incorporated as provinces of the Roman Empire. In the case of the Jews this is true even of the Diaspora communities in Italy and other parts of Europe.

While each age has, of course, its peculiar significance in the perspective of world history even for those who assume that historical development is continuous in most spheres of social activity, that significance may seem to later ages to be clearer in one form of culture than in others. Thus, the Hellenistic age is especially interesting to us because it saw the birth and early nurturing of a world-consciousness in philosophy, law, religion and politics. This cosmopolitanism, to use a term coined by the Stoic philosophers or possibly by the Jewish philosopher Philo under Stoic influence, was only partially realized in such forms as Jewish-Christian ethics, Roman law, Greek ethnography, pagan astrology and Gnosticism; but these forms of universalism or cosmopolitanism were sufficiently developed in the Hellenistic age to provide thought and impulse to action for many centuries afterwards.

2. THE SEPTUAGINT

While the scribes of the Second Commonwealth were collecting and ordering the sacred books, many Jews both in Palestine and in the Diaspora were circulating didactic or historical or apocalyptic writings, some of them under the names of patriarchs or prophets, in order to obtain greater authority for their works. These books, even those written in Hebrew or Aramaic, were not admitted into the canon of Sacred Scripture by the Rabbinic scholars of the early talmudic period for one of two reasons: either the Rabbis thought that they had been written after the close of the Persian period, when prophetic inspiration was supposed to have ceased, or else they regarded them as unorthodox in content. In a few cases, however, such postprophetic books were admitted into the canon; for example, the Book of Daniel, which represents itself as a work of the Babylonian period, and perhaps the Book of Ecclesiastes, ascribed to Solomon.

But the noncanonical Hebrew and Aramaic writings were translated into Greek and circulated among the Jews of the Diaspora. Some of these writings in their Greek version were included in manuscripts of the Greek Bible, and were preserved either as sacred or as edifying books by the Christian church. In a few cases the original Hebrew or Aramaic text, or one based on the original, has been preserved by Jewish scribes, for example, the Wisdom of Ben Sira and the Book of Tobit. But in the case of most of these so-called apocryphal or pseudepigraphic books, we have only the Greek version, handed down by Christian scribes.

Although this chapter does not discuss the apocryphal writings composed by Palestinian Jews in Hebrew or Aramaic, they have been mentioned because of their being preserved in Greek and included in manuscripts of the Greek Bible. We must now turn our attention to this translation, which is extremely important and interesting in its own right.[1a]

This great monument of Hellenistic Jewish literature is called the Septuagint, meaning "seventy" in Latin, because there was current among early Christian scholars of Western Europe the story, first told by a Hellenistic Jewish writer (see below on the Letter of Aristeas), that seventy-two elders were sent from Palestine to Alexandria in Egypt to translate the Law of Moses from Hebrew into Greek. In the course of time the title "Translation of the Seventy-two" was simplified into "the Seventy" and was extended to include the translation of the prophetic and hagiographic portions of the Hebrew Bible.

The Septuagint is of great importance for several reasons. In the first place, it is a valuable control of the traditional Hebrew text of the Bible, known as the Masora. The earliest complete Hebrew manuscript of the Bible dates from the tenth century c.e., whereas the principal manuscripts of the Greek Bible date from the fourth and fifth centuries c.e. (There are considerable papyrus fragments written still earlier but they agree very closely with the chief manuscript, *Codex Vaticanus*.) Moreover, the Greek translations of the various books of Scripture were made from unvocalized Hebrew texts. Thus they sometimes yield a reading of a form or the meaning of a root which makes better sense than that of the masoretic text.

In the second place, this early translation, having been made by competent scholars with some knowledge of early Palestinian exegesis, is of great aid in interpreting some obscure passages in the Hebrew. There is also a strong probability that in some passages the Hebrew text was altered by the Palestinian scholars for theological or legalistic reasons, and since the Greek version was made from an earlier text than that handed down to us by the Palestinian authorities, it sometimes enables us to recover the original meaning of the biblical passage.

In the third place, the Septuagint was the source of a number of secondary versions made for the early Christian churches in Europe and the Near East such as the Coptic, Ethiopic, Armenian, Slavonic, Gothic and Old Latin. (The Old Latin has not been entirely replaced by Jerome's translation, called the Vulgate, which became the official Bible of the Roman Catholic Church by decree of the Council of Trent in 1546.) Thus through the Septuagint the contents of the Hebrew Bible became known to the peoples of Europe and Western Asia and contributed greatly to the forming of their beliefs and institutions.

In the fourth place, the Greek Bible played a considerable part in the gradual transformation of Greek philosophy into the theology of the Church Fathers and into the influential body of thought known as Neoplatonism. These in turn exerted an immeasurably great influence on medieval Scholasticism, Christian, Jewish and Moslem. For example, it would be difficult to overrate the importance for following centuries of the synthesis effected between the Platonic theory of the creation of the world by a beneficent spirit, the Demiurge, as described in the *Timaeus*, and the account of the creation given in the first two chapters of the Greek Genesis. Such syntheses are presented by the Jewish philosopher Philo and by the Christian philosopher Chalcidius in his Commentary on Plato's *Timaeus*.

As we shall deal with Philo below, it may suffice to remark here that his great work of harmonizing Greek philosophy with Judaism, which deeply influenced Christian theologians, perhaps all the way down to Dante, would have been almost impossible if he had not had at his disposal an official Greek translation of the Hebrew Bible, which he regarded as no less inspired than the original text.

The most important fact about the Septuagint for those who are interested in the history of European civilization, as well as in Judaism, is that the existence of this version was indispensable to the rise of Christianity. The earliest Christian apostles to the Gentiles would probably have had much less success in converting Jews of the Diaspora and "God-fearing" Gentiles to Christianity if they had not had an authoritative Greek text of the Jewish Scriptures with which to support their claim that Jesus of Nazareth, whom they called the Lord Christ, was the Messiah whose coming had been predicted by the Hebrew prophets. The quotations from the Old Testament found in the writings of Paul and the Apostolic Fathers agree closely with the text of the Septuagint, although in some cases, of course, the Christian writers quote from memory or alter the wording to suit their apologetic purposes.

For the several reasons given above we may fairly say that the Greek translation of the Bible by the Jewish scholars of Alexandria was one of the most important translations ever made.

Before turning to the original Hellenistic Jewish writings, let us briefly consider some of the stylistic aspects of the Septuagint. Its vocabulary and inflections were not very different from those of contemporary pagan writings composed in the language used by the vast majority of people in the Hellenistic period, the so-called "common" Greek dialect or *Koiné*. But because the Septuagint was a translation from Hebrew and dealt with concepts and ways of living and speaking peculiar to Jewish Palestine, its Hebraic style and special usages of many terms must have made it seem a strange and un-Greek book to such Gentiles as may have chanced to read it or hear it quoted. Many Hebrew idioms, to be sure, were adapted to Greek usage, but most of them were taken over literally, with curious results to the Greek style. The various books of the Bible differ in this respect. Some of the narratives in the Greek versions of Samuel and Kings, for example, read fairly smoothly, while the Greek Book of Ecclesiastes is so literal as to be almost unintelligible to one ignorant of the Hebrew original.

On the whole, the Greek Bible is a poor specimen of literary Greek, not because of the linguistic incompetence of the translators but because their primary concern was to produce a faithful rendering of the Hebrew for Greek-speaking Jews. There are occasional surface Hellenizations, such as allusions to well-known mythological figures and the use of Greek metrical forms in parts of the Book of Proverbs. But beneath these superficial adaptations there is a thoroughly Jewish, even Hebraic, spirit in the Septuagint. Those Jews in the Diaspora whose reading was confined to the Greek Bible were in no danger of being seduced by the charm of Greek literature.

3. HISTORICAL LITERATURE

When we turn to the historical literature of the Jews originally written in Greek, we must not expect to find anything like the relatively scientific spirit of inquiry and concern for factual accuracy that we admire in such Greek historians as Thucydides and Polybius. Rather we shall find that most of the historical writing preserved to us is heavily weighted with self-conscious pride in Jewish cultural achievements and might more justly be called apologetic or hortatory than historical. Some of it is merely historical fiction.

1. *Demetrius, Eupolemus and Artapanus*

Let us begin by briefly discussing three (probably) Alexandrian writers of whose works we have only fragments preserved in the ninth book of the Evangelical Preparation of the Church Father Eusebius, written about 300 C.E. Eusebius took these excerpts from a *Universal History* compiled by Alexander Polyhistor, a Greek encyclopedist of the first century B.C.E.

Some time near the end of the third century B.C.E. a Jew named Demetrius wrote a history of Israel in brief chronological form. The extant fragments deal with some of the events in the lives of Jacob and Moses and with the number of years that elapsed between the Israelite deportation to Assyria and the writer's own date, the reign of Ptolemy IV. Although Josephus held Demetrius to be a Gentile, the author's painstaking attempt to fix the exact dates of Jewish history makes it more likely that he was a Jew. Neither the style nor the content of the remaining fragments is of exceptional interest.

More promising are the fragments of Eupolemus, who wrote a *History of the Jews* about the middle of the second century B.C.E. Whether he lived in Egypt or Palestine is not known. Some scholars identify him with the Eupolemus mentioned in I Macc. 8:17 as an envoy sent to Rome by Judas Maccabeus; they do so partly on the ground that Eupolemus the historian seems to have used a Hebrew as well as a Greek text of Scripture. But there is no reason why an Alexandrian Jew should not have known Hebrew in addition to Greek. On the whole, it is more probable that Eupolemus wrote in Egypt than in Palestine.

Like most of the Hellenistic Jewish historians known to us Eupolemus embellished his work with legendary material showing the Jews in the most favorable light. He tells us, among other things, that Moses was the first Sage and the first to introduce writing among the Jews; the Phoenicians took it from the Jews and the Greeks took it from the Phoenicians. The most extensive fragment preserved by Eusebius tells of the building of Solomon's Temple and includes the imaginary correspondence between

Solomon and Vaphres (biblical Hophra). We may cite from this the reply made by the Egyptian king to Solomon's request for assistance, which was obviously designed to impress Gentile readers with the greatness of the Hebrew king.

King Vaphres to the great king, Solomon, greeting. I have read your letter with great pleasure, and I and all my court regard as memorable the day of your accession to the throne, for you are a worthy man and one favored by a very great god. In accordance with your request I have sent you eighty thousand men from the following districts, etc.

Eupolemus, as we can see from this brief excerpt, was not an impartial historian of the Jews. But his partiality was moderate in comparison with that of his near-contemporary Artapanus.

On internal evidence it is clear that Artapanus wrote in Alexandria, but when he lived is more difficult to determine further than that he was active before the first century B.C.E., since he was known to Alexander Polyhistor, who flourished about 100 B.C.E.

Artapanus bettered the example of rationalistic Greek historians who taught that the popular gods were only deified men who had made useful discoveries in art and science. He went so far as to assert that Moses was none other than the Greek Museus and the Egyptian Hermes (Thoth). Not only were the Jews a distinguished people of Syrian origin, and not the descendants of plague-carrying outcasts from Egypt, as their enemies charged, but Moses had even given the Egyptians the elements of their culture. It seems strange to us that a Jewish writer should have attributed the origin of Egyptian idolatry to Moses, but perhaps, as some scholars have suggested, Artapanus meant to pass off his work as that of an Egyptian priest (some of whom, like Artapanus himself, bore Persian names after the conquest of Egypt by Cambyses). It is probable that Josephus in his narrative of Moses in the *Antiquities* used the writings of Artapanus, thinking him to be a pagan author.

A translation of part of the longest extant fragment of Artapanus may serve to show his inventive powers.

After the death of Abraham [a slip for "Jacob"] and his son and also Mempsasthenoth, the king of Egypt, the latter's son Palmenoth succeeded to the throne, but he proved to be unfriendly to the Jews. He first built Kessan and erected a temple there, and then built a temple in Heliopolis. He had a daughter named Merris, whom he married to a certain Khenephres, king of the region above Memphis; at that time there were several kings in Egypt. Merris, being childless, secretly adopted a Hebrew child whom she called Moses. By the Greeks he was called Museus. This Moses was the teacher of Orpheus. When he reached manhood he devised many things useful to mankind; he invented boats and stone-laying machines and Egyptian weapons and instruments for irrigation and war. He was also the founder of philosophy.

Moreover, he divided the country into thirty-six nomes, and to each of these he assigned the worship of a particular god. To the priests he gave the sacred writing [hieroglyphs]. Now these gods were cats and dogs and ibises. He also assigned to the priests separate estates. All these things he did in order to make Khenephres's rule more secure, for before that time the unruly populace had expelled some of their kings and installed others in their places or reinstalled the dethroned ones. Because of all these achievements Moses was loved by the common people and was granted divine honors by the priests under the name of Hermes ["interpreter"] because he had interpreted the sacred writings.

2. II Maccabees

The Second Book of Maccabees is no mere variant of the First Book of Maccabees even though their contents are in part the same. The differences between them are more interesting and significant than the similarities. I Maccabees was originally written in Hebrew; II Maccabees is a Greek epitome of an original Greek work in five books composed by an otherwise unknown Jason of Cyrene (in North Africa). I Maccabees covers a period of forty years, 175-135 B.C.E., from the persecution of Antiochus Epiphanes to the death of Simon and the winning of Judea's political independence; II Maccabees covers a period of only fifteen years, 175-161 B.C.E., from the persecution of Antiochus Epiphanes (or a little earlier) to the victory of Judas Maccabeus over Nicanor. I Maccabees is a rather matter-of-fact account of the military achievements of the Hasmonean family; II Maccabees is a partly legendary account of the Jewish heroes and martyrs whose noble deeds were achieved with the miraculous help of God. It is largely because of the exalted tone and picturesque marvels of II Maccabees that it has won a more favored place in biblical literature than the more sober and historical I Maccabees. The heroic loyalty to ancestral tradition of the old man Eleazar and the mother with seven sons, in spite of the tortures inflicted on them by the Syrian king, became a classical example of martyrdom that was imitated in the vast literature of persecution of both Jews and Christians.

To the historian of Judaism and Christianity the book is especially important because in addition to various statements about the observance of the Sabbath and other practices that may be said to reveal a Pharisaic point of view, it contains what are probably the earliest explicit references to the resurrection of the body. This particular belief became one of the few cardinal dogmas of Pharisaism. It is stated in several passages of the book. In 7:9 one of the martyred youths says to the king before dying under torture:

You braggart, you release us from this present life, but the King of the world will resurrect us to an eternal new life because we have died for His laws.

Again in 12:43-44 we are told that Judas made a sin-offering in Jerusalem because of his belief in resurrection.

For if he had not expected that those who had fallen would rise again, it would have been superfluous and foolish to pray for the dead.

Incidentally, this last passage is one of several which have made II Maccabees one of the biblical writings most esteemed by Roman Catholic theologians.

As a characteristic example of the author's (or perhaps epitomator's) love of the marvelous and his rhetorical inventions we may select the following passage, 3:24-28, concerning the Divine punishment visited on the Syrian official Heliodorus for attempting to rob the treasury of the Temple in Jerusalem.

But no sooner had he and his guards arrived before the treasury than the Lord of our fathers and Master of all authority gave a great manifestation, so that all those who had come with him in their recklessness were smitten by the power of God and paralyzed and routed in terror. For there appeared to them a horse bearing a terrible rider and adorned with most handsome trappings, which rushed swiftly on Heliodorus and struck him with its forefeet. And its rider appeared in golden armor. And two youths also appeared to him, remarkably strong and most handsome in form and splendid in dress. These stood on either side of him and flogged him continually, showering many blows upon him. Suddenly he fell to the ground and was overwhelmed by great darkness, and so his men seized him and placed him on a litter—the same man indeed who had just entered the treasury we mentioned before, with such pomp and so great a retinue they now carried off because he was unable to help himself. Thus did they clearly recognize the sovereign power of God.

The author's ability to use simpler but more effective rhetoric is illustrated by his account of the death of the aged martyr Eleazar, 6:30-31:

As he was about to die under the blows, he said with a groan, "The Lord with His holy knowledge knows that though I might have escaped death, I endure dreadful pains in my body, being flogged, but in my soul I am glad to suffer this through fear of Him." And so he died, leaving in his death an example of nobility and a memorial of virtue not only to the young but also to the greatest part of his nation.

3. III Maccabees

The Third Book of Maccabees is found in most manuscripts of the Septuagint and in the Greek editions of the Apocrypha but it is not included in the Vulgate version or in the King James version, and is therefore less known to English readers than are I and II Maccabees. The word "Maccabees" in its title is misleading since the book is concerned with the Jews of Egypt and has nothing to do with the Hasmoneans; still there is a certain appropriateness in connecting this book with the two books of the Maccabees since it bears an obvious resemblance to II Maccabees in conception and style and also to some extent in the incidents related.

III Maccabees supposedly dates from the reign of the Macedonian king of Egypt, Ptolemy IV Philopator, 221-203 B.C.E. It relates that Ptolemy, after defeating the Seleucid king Antiochus III at Raphia on the Egyptian-Palestine border in 217 B.C.E., attempted to enter the Temple of Jerusalem and was miraculously kept therefrom (like Heliodorus in II Maccabees). On his return to Egypt the wrathful king decreed that his Jewish subjects were to suffer the loss of some of their religious and political privileges unless they should register as worshipers of the Ptolemies' patron god Dionysos. On seeing that the vast majority of Jews remained loyal to their religion, he had Jews brought from the country to Alexandria and imprisoned in the Hippodrome to be trampled to death by intoxicated elephants. Through Divine intervention the elephants turned against the persecutors of the Jews, and King Ptolemy, being convinced that the Jews enjoyed Divine protection, repented of his hostility and allowed them to return home safely and to take vengeance, not on Greek or Egyptian persecutors, be it noted, but on Jewish apostates. The story and atmosphere of the book remind one strongly of II Maccabees, the Letter of Aristeas and the Book of Esther.

When the book was actually written and to what incident in Jewish history it refers is difficult to determine. The incident of the exposure to trampling by drunken elephants is practically the same as that described by Josephus in his *Against Apion* as having taken place in the reign of Ptolemy VII Physcon, almost a century after the time of Ptolemy IV Philopator; moreover, the political troubles of the Jews hinted at in the book seem to belong to the time of Ptolemy Physcon rather than to that of Ptolemy Philopator. On the other hand, the description of the battle of Raphia and other details of the official acts of Ptolemy Philopator indicate that the author had a good knowledge of the events of his reign. The various problems of date and composition are best solved by assuming that an Egyptian Jewish writer of the first century B.C.E. has combined events of the reigns of two different kings and has added picturesque details suggested by the Book of Esther and II Maccabees to make up a well-knit piece of historical fiction. Several scholars have argued that III Maccabees was written in the Roman period and really alludes to the persecution of the Jews in Alexandria (and Palestine) by the Roman emperor Caligula, but, for reasons which cannot be given here, the present writer believes that the book was written in the first century B.C.E. to encourage the Jews of Palestine and Egypt to hope for Divine intervention in the face of an invasion of Palestine by the Ptolemaic sovereigns Cleopatra and Ptolemy VIII Lathyrus during the reign of Alexander Janneus.

The book is written in quite respectable and sometimes rather polished

Greek. As a story it is continuously interesting and even exciting. Not the least skillful device of the author is the succession of pointed references to God's power to save the Jews from their enemies. As a whole the work has less of the miraculous than II Maccabees but is no less orthodox in doctrine. The following brief passage illustrates its style and theology:

6:16-21. And just as Eleazar was ending his prayer, the king came to the Hippodrome with the beasts and his whole insolent force. And when the Jews beheld this, they cried out to heaven so that the adjacent hollows re-echoed their cry and caused an uncontrollable wailing among all the host. Then the greatly glorious, almighty and true God manifested His holy countenance and opened the gates of heaven, from which two glorious angels of terrible aspect descended, being visible to all except the Jews. And these stood over against them and filled the army of their adversaries with confusion and fear and bound them with immovable fetters. And a trembling fell upon the king's body, and forgetfulness of his heavy-handed arrogance came upon him. And the beasts turned round against the forces that followed them and began trampling on them and destroying them.

4. Josephus

The late Henry St. John Thackeray began his discussion of Josephus in his admirable Stroock Lectures on the historian by reminding his audience that there was a time in his country (England) when almost every house possessed two books, a Bible and a Josephus in the old eighteenth-century version of William Whiston. The same thing might be said of Presbyterian Scotland and Puritan New England and of other Protestant countries of Europe with their various vernacular translations of Josephus. But translations and paraphrases of Josephus were popular long before Whiston's English translation was made. Great numbers of Jews from the early Middle Ages down to recent times have eagerly read the Hebrew *Yosippon*, which is to a large extent a paraphrase of Josephus's *Jewish War*, while the Latin paraphrase ascribed to Hegesippus found great favor among Christian Latinists. Few pagan historians of classical antiquity have been more widely read or quoted than Flavius Josephus, the Palestinian Jew, whose Greek works on the history of his people and their war with Rome and eloquent apology for Judaism have done much to atone for his adherence to the Roman cause when his country was conquered by Vespasian and Titus.

Joseph, son of Matthias, later called Flavius Josephus, claims, in his *Life*, to have been of priestly and Hasmonean descent. He was born in 37 or 38 c.e. in the year when Caligula became emperor. He tells us that he was so precocious a student of the Jewish law that learned Rabbis consulted him when he was only fourteen. He studied the doctrines of the various Jewish schools and even retired to the wilderness for three years of ascetic training with a certain Bannus.

At the age of nineteen Josephus became a member of the Pharisaic party. In 64 c.e. he sailed to Rome and succeeded, with the help of a Jewish actor and the Empress Poppea, in liberating some priests who had been sent to Nero for trial. Josephus's visit to Rome impressed him with the hopelessness of a Jewish revolt against Rome which the extremists were planning. However, during the interval between the defeat of the Twelfth Legion under Cestius in the autumn of 66 and Vespasian's arrival in Palestine in the spring of 67 Josephus became an important figure in the revolt.

What his private attitude was toward the Romans and the exact nature of the commission entrusted to him by the authorities in Jerusalem are matters of doubt. In his earliest work, the *Jewish War*, Josephus states that the responsible leaders appointed him commander of the Jewish forces in Galilee.[2a] In the *Life*, written some thirty years later, he writes that he and two other priests were chosen to induce the rebels in Galilee to lay down their arms and to leave the decision of war to the authorities in Jerusalem; only afterwards was he made supreme commander of the forces in Galilee. Those scholars are probably right who prefer the later account and hold that in the *Jewish War* Josephus has exaggerated the importance of his appointment in order to impress Roman readers. At any rate, it appears from both works that he fought without conviction though he may have shown resourcefulness and military skill.

After the fall of the town of Jotapata, which had held out against the Romans for more than a month, Josephus with a few companions escaped to a cave, and persuaded them not to kill him to prevent his capture or surrender but to draw lots to determine the order of their mutual self-destruction. "He, however—" the evasive writer tells us, "should one say by fortune or by the providence of God?—was left alone with one other, and anxious neither to be condemned by lot nor, should he be left to the last, to stain his hand with his countryman's blood, he persuaded this man also under a pledge to remain alive." Brought before Vespasian, Josephus predicted that the Roman general would become emperor (as the Roman historian Suetonius also attests) and thanks to this prediction was liberated from bonds when Vespasian was acclaimed emperor by his troops in July, 69 c.e. During the last two years of the war Josephus served as interpreter and mediator. At the end of the war he was given a piece of land outside Jerusalem and some sacred books; he also obtained the liberation of several of his friends.

The last thirty years or so of his life the Jewish careerist spent in Rome, enjoying for about a third of this time the patronage of the imperial family. But life was not wholly pleasant for him during his residence in Rome, for he was constantly subject to the criticism of his coreligionists as a deserter or as a falsifier of his part in the war. Whatever the justice of these charges, we must be sincerely grateful to Josephus for having left us the four works which have so greatly enriched our knowledge of Jewish and Greco-Roman history.

The earliest extant work, the *Jewish War* or *Capture* (of Jerusalem) as Josephus himself probably meant it to be called, was clearly written soon after 70 C.E. at the suggestion of the Roman government in order to discourage further opposition by the Jews and other peoples living in Parthian territory. Our Greek text is apparently a second edition of the book, the first presumably being closer to the original draft, now lost, written in Aramaic. Parenthetically I may say that it is a very doubtful assumption that the Slavonic version is a translation of the original Aramaic text rather than a secondary translation of the Greek. Various references to Christianity or Jewish prophecies of the Roman period, which are found in the Slavonic version, are probably additions made by Byzantine scribes.

The *Jewish War* has a rapid survey of Jewish history in the Hellenistic-Roman period in the first book, largely based on the *Life of Herod* by Nicholas of Damascus, and in the remaining six books dramatically narrates the course of the Jewish war against Rome and its aftermath. Josephus not only drew on his personal experience but also used the military journals of the Roman commanders Titus and Vespasian and other official Roman documents. For these reasons the work has the greatest value as a historical source. At the same time, like most ancient histories, it contains a number of rhetorical embellishments, especially in the speeches attributed to the leading actors, and various echoes of Greek writers, notably the tragic poet Sophocles. Also it naturally reflects the prejudices and private interests of Josephus himself. With the help of a well-trained Greek collaborator the Jewish historian was able to produce a work of considerable literary skill both in construction and in style. We may safely conjecture that educated Romans found considerable pleasure in reading it.

Of even greater interest to students of Judaism and Christianity is Josephus's second great work, the *Jewish Antiquities*, divided into twenty books like its partial prototype, the *Roman Antiquities* of Dionysius of Halicarnassus. The *Jewish Antiquities*, written during the reign of Domitian after Josephus had lost his royal patrons, was put out with a different motive from that which prompted him to publish the *Jewish War*. The later work was designed not to celebrate the achievements of the Romans but to acquaint them with the history of the conquered Jewish people and to show that the Jews had a glorious past worthy of the respect of their Roman conquerors.

The first ten books of the *Jewish Antiquities*, covering the history of the Jews from the patriarchal period to the Babylonian Exile are in the main a paraphrase of the Greek version of the biblical narratives from Genesis to Daniel. Josephus's paraphrase of the Septuagint is no mere stylistic variation of the biblical text. He has incorporated numerous legendary and homiletic additions, most of them from Alexandrian writers (including Philo) and Palestinian tradition. Recent studies have shown that in addition to the Greek Bible Josephus used the Hebrew original and an Aramaic version closely resembling the extant Targums of Onkelos and Jonathan. The *Jewish Antiquities* is, of course, a valuable check on the Septuagint text, but more than that, it is of great importance as one of the earliest specimens of Jewish biblical exegesis.

The second half of the *Jewish Antiquities* covers the period from the return of the exiles to Judea in the reign of Cyrus to the term of the last procurator before the outbreak of the war against Rome. For the history of the Persian period and the Hellenistic period down to the reign of Hyrcanus, Josephus has used as his chief sources the Books of Ezra and Nehemiah, Esther, the Letter of Aristeas and I Maccabees, supplemented by handbooks of Greek history written by Gentile historians. For the Hasmonean, Herodian and procuratorial periods he is chiefly dependent on Jewish tradition and on the works of the Greek historians Nicholas of Damascus and Strabo and some unknown Roman historians. His quotations and paraphrases of Nicholas and Strabo make up a considerable part of the fragments preserved of their lost works.

The *Jewish Antiquities* is not only our chief and in part our only source for the history of the Jews in Palestine and in the Diaspora during the Hellenistic and Roman periods but it is also a valuable source for some otherwise poorly documented episodes of Seleucid and Roman history; for example, it gives us the most detailed account we possess of the assassination of the Emperor Caligula and the accession of Claudius. Where the *Jewish War* and the *Jewish Antiquities* overlap, as in the reign of Herod the Great, a comparison of the two accounts reveals significant differences of arrangement and political attitude, and thus throws light on Josephus's methods and motives. Not the least interesting portions of the parallel passages in the *Jewish War* and the *Jewish Antiquities* are those dealing with the Jewish schools or parties, Pharisees, Sadducees and Essenes.[3a] Although Josephus, following the example of Nicholas of Damascus, who wrote for Gentile readers, has converted social and theological differences among the Jewish parties into matters of philosophy, his discussion of their doctrines and controversies must be recognized as one of our principal sources for the history of Judaism in the early talmudic period.

There is another reason why the *Jewish Antiquities* was studied and prized by Christian scholars after the time of Eusebius; in Book XVIII there occurs a brief passage about the life and death of Jesus, the so-called *Testimonium Flavianum*, which is the only extant explicit mention of the founder of Christianity, outside the New Testament of course, dating from the first century of the Common Era. A vast literature exists dealing with the problem of the genuineness of this passage. Almost no modern scholar regards the testimony to Jesus's miraculous powers and resurrection as genuine in its present form; a few scholars believe that it is a Christian revision of an original reference to Jesus that was quite neutral in tone; most scholars believe, with greater justice, that the entire passage is a Christian interpolation.

We have already mentioned the *Life*, published as an appendix to the second edition of the *Jewish Antiquities*. It was probably written to answer the criticisms of the *Jewish War* made by a rival Jewish historian, Justus of Tiberias. Besides being valuable as an account of Josephus's activities as commander of the Jewish forces in Galilee (see above), it provides us with our only though sketchy account of Josephus's entire career.

The latest work of Josephus, *Against Apion*, in two books, has a greater scope than the title indicates, since Apion was only one of several Greek writers whose calumnies against the Jews Josephus undertakes to refute. This little treatise is not only a persuasive and eloquent refutation of the various charges, some of them patently absurd, some more insidious, which were brought against the Jews by Egyptian and Greek anti-Semites and sometimes by more impartial Gentile historians, but it is also an inspired defense of the Mosaic Law and a triumphant vindication of Jewish morality and culture. Few champions of Judaism have more successfully presented their case; and so, this earliest reply to literary anti-Semitism must be regarded as ample atonement for any sins Josephus may have committed against his people as a military leader.

There are far too many quotable passages in Josephus's four works to make it easy to choose any single one in this brief sketch, but I cannot resist quoting part of the conclusion of the *Against Apion* in Thackeray's translation:

I would therefore boldly maintain that we have introduced to the rest of the world a very large number of very beautiful ideas. What greater beauty than inviolable piety? What higher justice than obedience to the laws? What more beneficial than to be in harmony with one another, to be a prey neither to disunion in adversity nor to arrogance and faction in prosperity; in war to despise death, in peace to devote oneself to crafts or agriculture, and to be convinced that everything in the whole universe is under the eye and direction of God? Had these precepts been either committed to writing or more consistently observed by others before us, we should have owed them a debt of gratitude as their disciples. If, however, it is seen that no one observes them better than ourselves, and if we have shown that we were the first to discover them, then the Apions and Molons and all who delight in lies and abuse may be left to their own confusion.

4. JEWISH PROPAGANDA IN GENTILE GUISE

The basic instincts and broad patterns of social behavior were not very different, whether among Jews or Gentiles, in the Hellenistic age from those of present-day peoples, but some of their conventions were dissimilar enough from our own to evoke surprise in a modern person when first he learns of them. The ancient attitude toward plagiarism and literary borrowing, for example, was much less proprietary than it is today. The same is true of their attitude toward the practice of foisting one's own work on the great names of classical tradition. Bearing this in mind, we should not be too greatly scandalized by the fact that some Jewish apologists composed works in prose or verse designed to show Jews in a favorable light, and published them as the writings of real or imaginary Gentile authors, just as Christian writers of the fourth or fifth century forged a correspondence between the Roman philosopher Seneca and the Apostle Paul. The present section deals with the best known works or fragments of this kind which have come down to us. In all probability they are only a small part of the entire body of this literature.

1. *Pseudo-Hecateus*

Among the Gentile historians of the time of Alexander the Great and his immediate successors whose works have been preserved only in excerpts by later writers of antiquity was a certain Hecateus who wrote, among other things, a *History of Egypt* including passages on the Jews. Some portions of this book have been preserved by the Greek historian Diodorus Siculus, who flourished under Augustus. There is no reason to doubt the genuineness of these passages. But there are other passages cited by Josephus and early Christian writers, supposedly from Hecateus's book *On the Jews* or *On Abraham*, which are generally regarded as extracts from a Jewish work passed off as Hecateus's and therefore known today as excerpts from Pseudo-Hecateus. Recently, however, some scholars have convincingly argued that the suspected passages in Josephus's *Against Apion* are really from the genuine Hecateus, and it is likely that as our knowledge increases through the discovery of new evidence, the extent of the assumed pseudepigraphic material will have to be considerably reduced. But the strong probability remains that other fragments from "Hecateus," for example, in Clement of Alexandria and Eusebius, are from Pseudo-Hecateus, the Jewish apologist, whose real name and date are unknown to us. That even in antiquity there was some suspicion of the supposititious character of passages quoted from Hecateus's book *On the Jews* is indicated by a statement in Origen that the author is so attached to this nation because of its wisdom that Herennius Philo [a Hellenized Phoenician, who flourished about 100 c.e.] in his work *On the Jews* in the first place expresses doubt whether the work is by the historian, and in the second place says, if it really is his work, that he has been ravished by Jewish persuasiveness and won over by their doctrines.

It is perhaps Pseudo-Hecateus, not the genuine Hecateus, who is quoted in the Letter of Aristeas (§5) as saying that pagan writers have refrained from discussing Jewish history because of the great sacredness attaching to it.

2. *The Letter of Aristeas*

Although the Letter of Aristeas was highly esteemed and used by such early Jewish writers as Philo and Josephus (and, of course, by Christian theologians), it was not until the sixteenth century that the liberal Italian Jewish scholar Azariah de'Rossi rescued it from the neglect into which, because it was written in Greek, it had fallen among his coreligionists. De'-Rossi's Hebrew translation and discussion of the Letter of Aristeas are included in his critical history of Jewish tradition, called *Meor Eynayim*.

The Letter of Aristeas purports to be a letter written to a certain Philocrates by his brother, a court official of Ptolemy II Philadelphus (285-247 b.c.e.). It narrates the events leading up to the translation of the Hebrew Pentateuch into Greek made by the Palestinian scholars whom the king invited to Alexandria at the suggestion of the royal librarian, Demetrius of Phalerum. The account of the translators' methods takes up only the last twelfth of the book; the preceding sections describe the emancipation of Jewish captives in Egypt by royal command, the invitation to Eleazar, the High Priest in Jerusalem, to send scholars to Alexandria for the work of translation, the presents sent to the Temple in Jerusalem by Ptolemy, the impressions made on Aristeas by the Temple and the city, and the splendid reception given to the Palestinian scholars on their arrival in Alexandria; then comes a long philosophical discussion, in the form of question and answer, between the king and the Jewish Sages on matters of politics and morality.

Even a casual reading of this fascinating book reveals that the author was not, as he pretends, a Ptolemaic official narrating a series of historical events but a Hellenistic Jew writing a sort of historical novel (or novelette) about the translation of the Law and embellishing it with apologetic passages skillfully employing the devices of Greek philosophical literature.

The problem of the date has long exercised the ingenuity of scholars but the weight of learned opinion today favors a date not long after 200 b.c.e. Such a date would account for some slight errors about the history and court etiquette of Ptolemy II's reign made by the generally well-informed author as well as for his use of certain forms and phrases known to be current in Egypt in the early part of the second century B.C.E. It may be conjectured, though it would be difficult to prove, that in addition to giving a laudatory description of Jewish customs for the edification of Gentiles, the author had the more specific purpose of alleviating any suspicions entertained by the Ptolemaic ruler of his time that the friendly relations between the Jewish communities of Alexandria and Jerusalem might trouble the political situation in Egypt.

To the Jewish and Christian historians of antiquity the most important part of the Letter of Aristeas was that which told how the Law was translated into Greek. Josephus was content to paraphrase this account but other ancient writers, like the Christian Fathers, Ireneus, Clement and Epiphanius, repeat the picturesque invention of Pseudo-Justin that the seventy-two translators mentioned by Aristeas were placed in thirty-six cells and by Divine inspiration separately produced versions that were found to be in absolute agreement. The original account (§§301-309) reads in part as follows.

Three days later Demetrius [the royal librarian] took the men and passing along the sea wall of seven stadia to the island, crossed the bridge and went to the northern part. Here he called them together in session in a house built on the seashore; it was very splendid and located in a quiet place. He then encouraged them to carry out the work of translation, for everything had been well provided that was needed for this purpose. So they began their task, making their results agree by comparing them, and what was agreed upon was duly written down with the approval of Demetrius. The session lasted until the ninth hour [3:00 P.M.] After this they were dismissed to attend to their bodily needs, and everything they wanted was freely supplied to them. In addition they were given the same daily provisions as the king; Demetrius attended to this, having been ordered by the king so to do. Early every day they appeared at court and paid their respects to the king, after which they went back to their own place. And, as is the custom among the Jews, they washed their hands in the sea in order to pray to God and then began to read and translate the passages given to each. . . . And it so happened that the work of translation was completed in seventy-two days, as though this had been arranged of set purpose. When the work had been completed, Demetrius called the Jewish populace to the place where the translation had been made, and read it to all in the presence of the translators, who received a great ovation from the populace on the strength of the great benefits for which they had been responsible.

To a modern reader there are other equally interesting passages that deserve quotation, but lack of space forbids giving more than a part of the section (§§ 128-171) that contains the earliest moral allegory of some of the ritual prescriptions of Mosaic Law, such as was later richly developed by Philo.

For though in general all things are alike in their physical principles, being governed by the same power, in every case there is a deep reason why we abstain from the use of some things and enjoy the use of others. This I will summarily explain by one or two examples. For you must not get the degrading notion that it was out of respect for mice and weasels and such creatures that Moses showed such care in his legislation. Rather did he draw up all these solemn prescriptions for the sake of righteousness and to aid in attaining holiness and the perfecting of character. For all the birds we use [for food] are tame and distinguished by their cleanliness and feed on grain and pulse, such as pigeons, turtledoves, moorfowls, partridges, geese and other such birds. But the birds that are forbidden you will find to be wild and carnivorous and to dominate others by their strength and wrongfully prey on the tame birds mentioned above. . . . He therefore used them as examples, calling them "unclean," to show that those for whom the Law was ordained should practice righteousness in their souls and not dominate anyone in reliance upon their own strength nor deprive others of anything, but steer their lives by what is right, just as the tame birds mentioned above consume various kinds of pulse growing in the earth, and do not dominate their kindred species in order to destroy them.

3. *Pseudo-Phocylides*

Among the Greek moralistic poets of whose works only a few fragments have come down to us was a certain Phocylides of Miletus who lived in the sixth century B.C.E. Evidently he was a writer of considerable authority in later times, for a Jew of the Hellenistic period chose Phocylides as the pagan poet on whom to foist his own composition consisting of 230 hexametric verses in classical Greek style and with a content chiefly based on the moral prescriptions of Mosaic Law.

This crypto-Jewish work in Greek form is the more interesting for its failure to denounce pagan idolatry or to praise specific Jewish customs, as did outspoken Jewish Hellenists like Philo and the author of III Maccabees. Pseudo-Phocylides is so careful to conceal his Jewish origin that he presents only the most universalistic features of biblical morality and piety. This concealment, it is safe to say, is due to his technique of propaganda and not to expediency or timidity. Of course, there is a bare possibility that the author was not a Jew but a pagan admirer of the Greek Bible, or even a crypto-Christian. But in view of the assured Jewish character of similar works, it is far more probable that the author was Jewish. A few specimen lines (8-11, 84-85) are here translated in rough approximation of the Greek style and dactylic meter:

First honor God, and next after Him honor those who begot thee.
Deal out justice to all men, and twist not judgment to favor.
Turn not away the poor without right, and respect not men's persons.
Be not a wicked judge lest God in turn some day condemn thee.

Flee from false witness, and justice alone be what thou desirest.
Let no one take from the nest all the birds that are sheltered within it,
But set the mother bird free, and some other day thou'lt have her fledglings.

4. The Wise Menander

Most famous of the writers of the comedy of manners in the Hellenistic world was the Attic poet Menander, who flourished in the generation after Alexander the Great. His numerous plays were not only imitated and adapted by the two great Roman comedy writers Plautus and Terence but continued to influence Roman satirists of the imperial age, and like the plays of Shakespeare, became a part of the general culture of the Western world after their author had died. Echoes of Menander's informal philosophy are found even in the New Testament, for example, "evil communications corrupt good manners" in I Cor. 15:33. Moreover, wise and witty sayings were culled from the numerous works of Menander (of which, unfortunately, only fragments have survived) and included in anthologies of maxims from the Greek poets and philosophers.

It was probably the Attic Menander who was in the mind of the author or editor of a collection of gnomic sayings, probably in the iambic meter of six feet used for this purpose in Greek literature, of which a Syriac translation was found in a seventh-century manuscript of the British Museum, bearing the title *The Wise Menander Said*. Thirty years after its publication by J. Land in 1862, another scholar, Frankenberg, showed that these verses, about a hundred and fifty in number, closely resembled sayings in biblical Wisdom literature, and thus, he argued, they represent the work of a Jewish writer of the Roman period. But since the collection contains a number of genuine sayings of Menander and other pagan writers, it is probable that the Greek original of this Syriac translation was a Jewish pseudepigraph, designed to convey Jewish ideas in a form that would appeal to Greek readers, particularly because of the prestige that was attached to the name of Menander. The following few verses are given in a translation that attempts to suggest the meter probably used in the lost Greek original of the Syriac text.

> Fear God, and honor too thy father and thy mother.
> Mock not old age, for thou thyself wilt come to it.
> If from his youth thy son emerge both meek and wise,
> Teach him the scribal art and wisdom; these two things
> Are good to learn and bring clear eyes and flowing tongue.
> What's hateful to thee, unto friends seek not to do.

In the expression "scribal art and wisdom" the reader will immediately recognize an allusion to Dan. 1:17.

5. *The Sibylline Oracles*

Among the ancient legendary givers of oracles and prophecies the mysterious women called Sibyls enjoyed great prestige in the Hellenistic-Roman period. Most high school boys of past generations were familiar with the story, told by Virgil in the sixth book of the *Aeneid*, of Aeneas's visit to the Cumean sibyl who foretold to him the future trials and triumphs of the Roman people and prepared him for his descent into the nether world. But the Cumean sibyl was only one of several whose prophecies, recorded in Greek hexameters, were widely circulated in the early days of the Roman Empire. Besides the Greco-Roman sibyls of Cumae in Italy, of Erythrae in Asia Minor, of Libya, of Delphi in Greece, there were also Oriental sibyls, Hebrew, Persian and Chaldean. Sometimes they were considered separate figures, sometimes the Persian and Chaldean sibyls were identified with the Jewish sibyl, Sabbe or Sambathe, the daughter of Berossus (Berossus actually having been a Babylonian historian of the third century B.C.E. who translated cuneiform records into Greek).

The extant manuscripts of Sibylline Oracles represent a collection made in the fifth or sixth century C.E., which contains several thousand verses, divided into fourteen or fifteen books. They are ostensibly pagan prophecies of the dire calamities about to overtake the Gentile world, but actually they are in large part Jewish and Christian compositions in pagan disguise, meant to warn their readers to repent of their sins and to recognize the truth of Jewish or Christian teaching. Some of the Jewish oracles probably date from the second century B.C.E. It is hardly necessary to state that they were not genuine predictions of things to come but, like many apocalyptic writings, were prophecies after the event.

It is not always easy to distinguish the Jewish from the Christian portions because the original Jewish prophecies were imitated or revised by Christian writers. However, there is general agreement that we have basically Jewish material in most of Books III, IV and V and in parts of later books. Many events of Jewish history in the Hellenistic-Roman period are alluded to in these supposed prophecies, but the language is often so poetically obscure and the symbolism so vague that it is not always possible for modern scholars to be certain of the exact incidents described. From the less ambiguous passages we can be fairly sure that the Jewish author or authors included a rapid survey of Jewish history from the reign of Antiochus Epiphanes to the decades following the destruction of the Temple of Jerusalem by the Romans in 70 C.E. Clearly Jewish is the tone of those passages in which the sibyl denounces pagan idolatry and immorality, announces the coming of a Messianic age and the punishment of the godless, and consoles the righteous with promise of Divine help.

Unfortunately there is not sufficient material to enable us to estimate how deep an impression was made upon pagan readers by these crypto-Jewish Sibylline Oracles, but it is safe to say that Virgil was influenced by them in writing his *Fourth Eclogue,* which describes the coming golden age of Roman imperialism. Occasional echoes of Messianic imagery in later Greek and Latin literature suggest that these Jewish verses in Greek form had considerable effect in forming certain types of pagan literature during the early centuries of the Roman Empire. Whether they had a more practical effect in winning pagan converts to Judaism can only be conjectured.

Of the large number of verses of undoubted Jewish origin, the following few are selected as representative; they are given in metrical translation suggesting the form of the Greek meter employed (Book III, 36-39, 46-52).

> O generation delighting in blood, crafty, evil and godless,
> Men who lie and are double-tongued and evil of nature,
> Stealing other men's wives, idolators, craftily plotting;
> Evil lurks in your breasts, like a maddening gadfly pursues you.
> But that day will come when Rome will rule over Egypt,
> Though it be still delayed, and then the almighty kingdom
> Of the eternal King will appear to mankind in glory.
> Then will the holy prince come and on earth bear the scepter
> Throughout all aeons forever, as time hurries onward.
> Then shall the wrath inexorably descend on the Latins,
> And by a pitiful fate Three will bring Rome into ruin.

5. EPIC AND DRAMA

Until quite recent times it was generally thought that the Jews of the Greek-speaking Diaspora were almost completely unaffected by the artistic impulses of their Greek neighbors. However, the excavations of synagogues decorated with mosaic and painted representations of human, animal and floral figures have caused us to revise our opinions concerning the lack of pictorial art among the Jews of the Hellenistic-Roman period. By contrast, philologists have long been aware that among Greek-speaking Jews there were persons of literary talent who showed skill in adapting the language and style of Greek epic and dramatic poetry to biblical themes. Unfortunately the works of all but three of such writers have been completely lost, and of the three whose poetry has escaped oblivion only scant fragments have survived in the ninth book of the *Evangelical Preparation* of Eusebius, the same writer who has preserved fragments of the Hellenistic Jewish prose writers mentioned above. For this reason it may be something of a surprise to the general reader that in the Hellenistic age there were Jews who wrote epics and dramas in Greek about the sacred history of Israel.

1. *Philo the Elder* (*Philo Epicus*)

The Jewish epic poet Philo was not, of course, the philosopher Philo of Alexandria (on whom see below) but was probably the same person whom Josephus, in his *Against Apion*, refers to as Philo the Elder and couples with the Hellenistic Jewish historians Demetrius and Eupolemus. Since Josephus and Eusebius depend for their information about Philo the Elder upon Alexander Polyhistor, who flourished about 100 B.C.E., it is clear that the poet must have written as early as the second century B.C.E.

According to Eusebius, Philo wrote an epic called *On Jerusalem*, but the learned Church Father has seen fit to quote only three fragments amounting in all to twenty-four lines. It is also unfortunate that the few extant verses are written in the recondite and labored style of Alexandrian epic poets and are somewhat difficult to understand. The following is a verse-translation of a five-line fragment on Joseph, quoted by Eusebius from the fourth book (we must amend ms. "fourteenth" to "fourth"). From the position of this fragment and the statement of Clement of Alexandria that Philo wrote about the kings of Israel, we may conjecture that the epic covered twenty-four books, like the *Iliad* and the *Odyssey*.

> For them a blessed abode did the great world leader establish,
> He, the Most High, of old for the children of Abram and Isaac
> And of the child-blessed Jacob. Thence came Joseph the dreamer,
> Prophet of God, who wielded the scepter over all Egypt,
> And revolved in his mind the secrets of time in the floodtide of fortune.

2. *Theodotus*

About Theodotus, the author of an epic *On the Jews*, we know as little as about his contemporary Philo Epicus. The forty-seven hexameter verses cited by Eusebius in the ninth book of his *Evangelical Preparation* from Alexander Polyhistor are concerned with the Israelites' conquest of Shechem and the revenge taken by Simeon and Levi for the seduction of Dinah. From the fact that the extant fragments narrate only this episode and that Shechem is called a "holy city" some scholars have inferred that Theodotus was a Samaritan rather than a Jew. But "holy city" is a stock epithet in Greek epic poetry, and there is no trace of anti-Jewish feeling in the poem, such as one would expect in a Samaritan work; moreover, the poem stresses the impiety of the Shechemites. We shall therefore probably be right in considering Theodotus a Jewish writer.

Theodotus writes in a simpler and more Homeric style than Philo Epicus, who, as we saw, preferred the artificial manner of contemporary

Alexandrian poets. In respect of the Hellenistic elements in this Jewish work it is interesting that Eusebius reports the author as saying that the city got its name from "Shechem son of Hermes." But in spite of Theodotus's use of the language of Greek mythology we must, I think, agree with the German editor Ludwich in regarding "Hermes" as a corruption of *Hamor* (Greek *Emor*), since Shechem is so designated in the poem itself as in the Greek version of Genesis, on which the extant fragments are based (ch. 34).

The following few lines from the passage describing Jacob's coming from Mesopotamia to Palestine (here called Syria) may suffice to give an idea of the style:

> Then Jacob made his way to the kine-bearing land of Syria,
> Leaving behind the stream of the wide, onrushing Euphrates,
> For he had come from there, leaving the bitter reproaches
> Made by his very own kin, though gladly had Laban received him
> Into his home, who was cousin to him, and sole ruler
> Over all Syria . . .

3. Ezekiel the Tragic Poet

Epic poetry was not the only field of Greek literature cultivated by the Jewish writers of Alexandria. Centuries before Christian monks and clerics produced dramas based on biblical themes, a Jewish poet named Ezekiel wrote tragedies on these subjects. Considerable fragments, amounting to over two hundred lines, from one of his dramas on the Exodus have been preserved by Eusebius in that precious ninth book of his *Evangelical Preparation*, again from the lost compilation of Alexander Polyhistor.

Ezekiel has taken the story of Moses and the Israelites' flight from Egypt from the Greek version of the Book of Exodus, and has given it dramatic form on the lines of classical Greek tragedy, especially under the influence of Euripides. There are, however, some deviations from the pattern of Attic drama, such as more frequent changes of scene and the omission of choral passages. Unity of action is obtained by making Moses the central figure in all the scenes. The meter used in the extant fragments is the iambic trimeter, regularly employed in the dialogue of Attic plays.

Modern scholars disagree on the question whether Ezekiel's *Exodus* was meant to be presented in an Alexandrian theater or merely to be read as a closet drama. The latter is more likely, not merely because of the technical problems presented by frequent changes of scene but also because it is difficult to believe that Jews would have attended a theatrical performance of a sacred legend in which God Himself was one of the actors. Nor is it much more likely that there would have been a Gentile audience for such a play. But it would be foolish to speak dogmatically on this subject in the present state of our knowledge about the everyday life of Jews in the Hellenistic Diaspora.

It is also probable that Ezekiel wrote this drama about Moses and the Exodus not merely for the instruction or encouragement of Jews who had a Greek secular education but also for Gentiles whom he might hope to impress with the power of Israel's God to save His people from persecution. For translation I have selected part of the dialogue between God and Moses concerning the miracles which God wishes Moses to perform with his staff (based on Ex. 4:2-7). The language here is simple, rapid and almost prosaic:

GOD: What is this thing in thy two hands? Speak quickly now.
MOSES: It is a staff with which to strike both beasts and men.
GOD: Cast it upon the ground and quickly move away.
        For 'twill become a serpent dreadful to behold.
MOSES: See, I have thrown it down. O Lord, be gracious now.
        How dreadful! What a monster! Do Thou pity me!
        I shudder at the sight and tremble in every limb.
GOD: Fear naught, but stretch thy hand and take its tail,
        And once more it will be a staff just as before.
        Now thrust thy hand into thy bosom and draw it out.
MOSES: Thy bidding I have done. My hand is white as snow.
GOD: Now thrust it back again. 'Twill be just as before.

6. WISDOM LITERATURE AND PHILOSOPHY

Like the other nations of the ancient Near East the Israelites treasured the admonitions and counsels of their wise men concerning right behavior toward God and fellow man. These sayings, though written in language more prosaic, more reflective and less emotional than that used by the prophets, were no less religious in content, if we give to the word "religion" the more inclusive meaning that it had in antiquity. Sometime during the early part of the period of the Second Commonwealth, a collection of such wise sayings was published under the title the Proverbs of Solomon, though in fact a large part of the collection dates from a period after Solomon, and a few of the thirty-one chapters are actually a translation of Egyptian Wisdom literature written long before Solomon's time.

This Book of Proverbs became the model for Palestinian writers of the Hellenistic period, like the authors of the Book of Ecclesiastes and the Wisdom of Ben Sira,[4a] who further developed the ancient theme that "the beginning of wisdom is the reverence of God." In their choice of subjects to moralize about and their concern to identify *Hokmah* (Wisdom)[5a] with Torah (Revealed Law), they closely followed traditional lines of moral and religious speculation.

Among the Jewish thinkers of the Greek Diaspora, however, the contact with Greek philosophy and theology, however superficial it may have been in some cases, led them to give a more logical or systematic or metaphysical form to their expositions of Judaism. This is not to imply that the talmudists of Palestine were less acute in argument or less rational in ethics than the Greek philosophers or Hellenistic Jewish theologians. It is only to state the innocuous truism that the formal aspects of our Western intellectual traditions go back to the Greeks, and that it was the Greek philosophers, particularly those of the Hellenistic period, who created the terminology and methodology of our scientific thinking.

1. *The Wisdom of Solomon*

Of the three Hellenistic Jewish philosophical works that have survived in addition to the extensive remains of Philo, only the Wisdom of Solomon (which is also, of course, apologetic and eschatological in content) adheres to the pattern of Wisdom literature established by the Book of Proverbs. What distinguishes it most conspicuously from this and other Hebrew books of like nature, such as Ecclesiastes and Ben Sira, is its occasional use of Greek philosophical terms and forms of argument and its partial adoption of Greek notions of the pre-existence and immortality of the soul and of the Divine powers. In some passages, as in the catalogues of virtues and sins, its rhetoric reminds one of that of the Stoic diatribe, a kind of street-corner sermon.

On the other hand, it is clear from the frequent use made of biblical doctrines, imagery and phrases that the author must have been familiar with the Scriptures, probably with the Hebrew text as well as with the Greek translation. In this connection we are reminded that the book was well known to the apostle Paul whose own teaching was an even more subtle blend of Jewish and Hellenistic ideas and turns of expression. Perhaps it was Paul's admiration for the Wisdom of Solomon that caused the early Christian church to regard it as one of the most important books in the Apocrypha.

While there is an undeniable unity of tone and vocabulary throughout the nineteen chapters of the book, the subject matter is rather obviously divisible into three parts. Chapters 1-5 deal with future rewards and punishments for good and evil conduct and briefly allude to the part played by Wisdom in promoting righteousness. Chapters 6-10 form an eloquent dissertation on Wisdom which, as an effluence of God's power, has preserved the righteous throughout Israel's history. This section takes as its point of departure the famous passage in the Book of Kings in which Solomon prays for wisdom rather than riches and power, at least according to later tradition. In this part of the book Wisdom corresponds fairly closely to the Rabbinic personification of Torah as well as to the Stoic *Pronoia*, or Providence. Chapters 11-19 sketch Israel's earlier history and

in Rabbinic fashion demonstrate how Israel's enemies have been punished
on the principle of "measure for measure"; for example, the various
plagues that afflicted the Egyptians were appropriate to the injuries they
had done the Israelites. These chapters also present a well-reasoned
argument against idolatry, having especially the Egyptians in mind, and
give a quasi-anthropological account of the origins of this practice, which
though more tolerant is not less effective than the prophetic denunciations
of idol worship.

With the technical problems of the date, composition, authorship and
original language of the Wisdom of Solomon we have not space to deal at
length. It must suffice to say that the weight of evidence supports those
scholars who believe that most if not all the book was composed in Greek
by an Alexandrian Jew who probably spoke or at least read Hebrew as
well as Greek. Though several distinct subjects are treated, perhaps based
on different sources, the writer has combined them in such a way as to
give the work the stamp of single authorship. The date of composition or
final editing cannot be fixed exactly but was probably near the beginning
of the Common Era. Some scholars of an earlier period conjectured that
the philosopher Philo was the author of this apocryphal book, but this
conjecture is no longer taken seriously.

With many interesting and eloquent passages to serve as quotations
from a book which has had so great an influence on Christian thought,
it is an ungrateful task to select a very few as illustrative of its doctrine
and style. It is hoped that the following three passages are sufficiently
representative.

In 3:1-5 we have, in answer to the age-old query of why "the good die
young," a testament of faith that the righteous do not die but pass on to
eternal life. This belief is found also in Philo and Rabbinic literature
but there it is perhaps less poetically expressed.

> The souls of the righteous are in the hand of God,
> And no torment will touch them.
> In the eyes of the thoughtless they seem to have died,
> And their departure is reckoned as an evil,
> And their going hence as a disaster.
> But they are at peace.
> For if in the sight of men they have been punished,
> Their hope is full of immortality.
> Being chastised a little, greatly will they be rewarded.
> For God has tested them and found them worthy of Him.

When, in 6:17-20, the author commends to earthly rulers the study
and practice of Wisdom, he attempts to show that Wisdom alone leads to
kingship by using the *sorites*, or chain argument, favored by the Stoics.
Thus he combines Stoic logic with the spirit of Judaism to make the point,

central in the teachings of Plato and later Greek political thinkers, that kings should be philosophers.

> For her [Wisdom's] beginning is the most sincere desire for instruction,
> And the concern for instruction is love.
> Love is the keeping of her laws,
> And observance of the laws is assurance of incorruption.
> Incorruption brings men close to God.
> Thus does the desire for Wisdom lead men to kingship.

The last passage for which there is room here is part of a breathless catalogue, in 7:22-23, of the various beneficent aspects of versatile Wisdom. In this catalogue some commentators have found a striking similarity to a list of the attributes of wisdom or virtue made by the Stoic philosopher Cleanthes.

> For in her there is a spirit intellectual and holy,
> Only-begotten, of many parts, subtle,
> Mobile, delicate, undefiled,
> Clear, harmless, loving good, keen,
> Undeterred, beneficent, humane,
> Firm, sure, without care,
> All-powerful, all-seeing,
> Pervading all spirits
> That are intellectual, pure and subtle.

This spirit of Wisdom, the chapter continues, is a breath of God's power and a reflection of eternal light, which has passed into the holy souls of all generations and made them friends of God and prophets. Nowhere in Jewish literature except in Philo, who is more elaborate and sophisticated, does one find so appealing a fusion of Greek and Jewish teaching concerning the part played by Wisdom in human affairs.

2. *Aristobulus*

We have seen, in the brief discussion of the Letter of Aristeas, that that book contains some passages of a philosophical nature, but as they are merely incidental to the book's apologetic purpose, the author is hardly to be classed as a professional philosopher. Among the Alexandrian philosophers who preceded Philo, however, there is one writer of whose work extensive enough fragments have been preserved to enable us to form some notion of the more strictly philosophical literature produced by Philo's coreligionists.

This writer was Aristobulus who was, according to the Church Father Clement of Alexandria, a contemporary of Ptolemy VI Philometor who reigned 181-145 B.C.E. Some scholars place Aristobulus in the Roman period and some hold him to have been a Christian, but so far no convincing evidence has been offered to refute the traditional date. More doubtful is the accuracy of Clement's statement, echoed by Eusebius, that Aristobulus belonged to the Peripatetic, or Aristotelian, school of philosophy. What is clear from the extant fragments is that he attempted to harmonize the Law of Moses with the teachings of Greek philosophy in a work which bore the title *Interpretation of the Law of Moses,* or *Interpretation of the Sacred Laws.*

This harmonization Aristobulus sought to achieve partly through an allegorical explanation of the anthropomorphic allusions to God in the Pentateuch (that is, allusions to the eyes, arms, countenance, walking, etc., of God); partly by quoting Greek verses falsely attributed to Homer, Hesiod and other real and mythical poets who supposedly supported the statements of Scripture; and partly by attempting to show that Pythagoras, Plato and other Greek thinkers drew their theological doctrines from Moses. From these passages it appears, on the plausible assumption that Christian tradition correctly placed Aristobulus in the second century B.C.E., that he was a forerunner of Philo with respect to harmonizing Greek philosophy with Judaism. Whether he was Philo's equal in learning, subtlety and literary skill it would not be fair to decide, in view of the little we have from his pen compared with the extensive Philonic literature that has come down to us. From the few fragments that we have, however, it does seem that he was inferior to Philo in all three respects.

The following selections from the excerpts found in the ninth and thirteenth books of Eusebius's *Evangelical Preparation* may give some idea of the peculiar combination of ingenious interpretation and elusive phrasing that seems to characterize Aristobulus's writing.

For often what our lawgiver Moses wishes to convey when he is using language proper to other matters, by which I mean their appearances, he expresses by physical qualities and the forms of great things[?]. Now those who are able to think clearly admire the wisdom and divine inspiration for which the prophet is celebrated. To their number belong the philosophers we have mentioned and many others, especially poets who have taken notable arguments from him, for which they are admired. But to those who do not share his power and understanding and attend only to what is literally set down, he does not seem to be interpreting anything of great import. I will begin by taking each of the passages in question and explaining it so far as I am able. And if I do not find the truth or convince you, do not attribute the lack of sense to the lawgiver, but to me who am unable to make clear exactly what was in his mind. Now the arms are something that is clearly and commonly understood by us. And when you as king send out your forces with the intention of achieving something, we say that the king has a "great arm," for the word used is referred to the force which you possess. This is the very thing alluded to in our law by Moses when he says, "God brought you out of Egypt with a mighty arm."

The second fragment explains the passage in Genesis that describes how God rested on the seventh day after creating the world.

It is consistent with this that God created the whole world and, because daily life is a difficult experience for all, gave us the seventh day as a day of rest. Thus it may physically [*i.e.*, philosophically] be called the genesis of light, since by this all things are perceived. The same metaphor may be applied to Wisdom, for all light comes from her. And some of the Peripatetic school have said that she fills the part of a lantern, for those who steadily follow her will remain unconfused throughout the whole of life. But still more clearly and beautifully did one of our ancestors, Solomon, say that she existed before heaven and earth. And this is in harmony with what has been said before. For the interpretation of the statement in the Law that God rested on this day is not, as some have understood it, that God no longer continued to create but that He made an end of ordering things so that they were ordered as they were for all time. For [Scripture] indicates that in six days He made heaven and earth and all things in them that He might reveal what the various times were and foretell the order of their precedence. For once having ordered them, He preserves them and does not alter their positions. This He has made clear to us in the Law in order that we may have the principle of the number seven before us, and through this have knowledge of things human and divine. For the whole world of things that are born and grow revolves through periods of seven. And this seventh day is called the Sabbath which translated means "rest." Both Homer and Hesiod, who used our [sacred] writings as a source, have indicated that it is holy.

At this point Aristobulus introduces a number of spurious verses from Homer, Hesiod and the mythical Linos to show that the ancient Greeks also held the seventh day to be holy.

3. *IV Maccabees*

It was probably sometime near the beginning of the Common Era that an Alexandrian Jew with an intimate knowledge of Greek philosophy, especially that of the Stoic Posidonius (early part of the first century B.C.E.), and a formidable Greek vocabulary composed a sort of sermon or lecture on the theme: reason can control passion. This argument is illustrated by examples taken from Jewish history, especially of the Maccabean period.

Though this book, commonly known as IV Maccabees, is included in three of the oldest and most important manuscripts of the Greek Bible, it was (mistakenly) regarded by Eusebius, Jerome and other early Church Fathers as the work of Flavius Josephus; for this reason it is not found in the Latin Bible and consequently is not counted among the apocryphal books of the English and other modern versions of the Bible. IV Maccabees seems to have been entirely unknown to the Jews until modern times but it is not impossible that it was used, perhaps at second hand by the

author of the medieval Hebrew work *Yosippon*. Christian writers, on the
other hand, greatly admired the book, and the famous Erasmus made a
revision of the Latin version.

Like Aristobulus and Philo, the author of IV Maccabees is chiefly concerned to show that the great virtues of the Platonic-Stoic tradition are to
be attained by observing the Law of Moses. The larger part of the book,
chapters 4-18, is a glorification of the triumph of reason over passion
achieved by the martyrs of the Maccabean period, Eleazar, and the mother
and her seven sons, whose defiance of Antiochus Epiphanes had earlier
been told in II Maccabees.

Chapter 1 is a philosophical introduction that reminds one forcefully of
the treatises on reason and passion that are found in the writings of Cicero
and Seneca, who, like the writer of IV Maccabees, were greatly influenced
by Posidonius. The theme of the book is admirably announced in verses
13-17 of this chapter.

We are inquiring, then, whether reason is sovereign master ["autocrat" in
Greek] of the passions. But let us define what reason is and what passion is,
and how many forms of passion there are, and whether reason has power
over all of these. Reason, then, is thought [or "mind"] based on correct
principles, which chooses above all else a life of wisdom. Wisdom, moreover,
is the knowledge of things human and divine and their causes. And this is
education [or "culture"] acquired from the Law, through which we religiously learn things divine, and for our profit learn things human.

As historical examples of self-control in the face of great provocation or
desire the author, in chapters 2 and 3, cites the cases of Moses when
angered by Dathan and Abiram, of Jacob when incensed with Simeon and
Levi at their cruel treatment of the Shechemites, and of David when his
soldiers risked their lives to bring him water after an all-day battle with
the Philistines (here our book considerably alters the account given in II
Samuel and I Chronicles). In this last instance it gives a vivid impression
of David's thirst and of the bravery of the soldiers who sought to bring
him water.

But he [David], although burning with thirst, considered that the drink,
being equivalent to blood, was a great danger to his soul. He therefore opposed his reason to his desire and poured the drink as a libation to God. For
the temperate mind is able to conquer the constraint of passion and to quench
the fires of goading desire and to wrestle victoriously with the pains of the
body, however overpowering they may be, and by the excellence of reason to
spurn the bid for power made by the passions. But now the opportune moment
calls us to narrate the story of temperate reason.

With this introduction the narrator launches into the story of the persecution of the Jews by Seleucus IV and his brother (here called son)

Antiochus Epiphanes. In general the narrative follows the contents and order of II Maccabees, but there are many variations in detail and a more extended and philosophical treatment of the martyr episodes. In II Maccabees, for example, the aged Eleazar nobly meets death under torture with a comparatively few defiant words; in IV Maccabees, how-ever, he makes a longer and more didactic speech. Though here the details of the torture and his suffering are realistically and horrifyingly described, the author does not hesitate to represent the aged martyr as taking time to make a philosophical defense of the Mosaic Laws. With a quotation of part of his eloquent address (5:33-38) this brief account of IV Maccabees may fittingly be concluded.

I will not belie thee, O Law, that wast my teacher, nor will I abjure thee, dear Continence, nor will I bring shame upon thee, O wisdom loving Reason, nor deny thee, honored Priesthood and knowledge of the Law. Neither shalt thou, O mouth, defile my revered old age or the years I have spent in living according to the Law. Pure shall my fathers receive me, nor do I fear thy [Antiochus's] torments even unto death. For over impious men thou mayest tyrannize, but neither by words nor by deeds shalt thou be master over my pious reason.

4. *Philo*

Of the Hellenistic Jewish writers whose works have come down to us in part or whole none is so intrinsically worthy of study or, with the possible exception of Josephus, so important in the Western tradition of learning as Philo of Alexandria. Throughout the whole period of scholarship since the Renaissance there has been a continuous and intensive study of his writings by theologians and exegetes. But it has been only during the past few decades that Philo has begun to achieve recognition as a creative or at least historically productive philosopher,[6a] and there has been an ever-increasing number of books and monographs devoted to this aspect of his work. Some indication of the attitude that prevailed half a century ago among historians of ideas is given by the fact that the great German historian of Greek philosophy, Eduard Zeller, in the fourth edition of his magisterial *Philosophie der Griechen* (1903) gives only half as much space to Philo as to Plotinus, and treats Philo as a theologian rather than as a philosopher. By the time this chapter has been published there will have appeared two substantial volumes from the pen of Professor Harry A. Wolfson of Harvard University which will seek to rehabilitate Philo as an original philosophical thinker and to give him his rightful place in the history of that discipline.[7a]

We are not concerned here, however, with the problem of whether Philo was primarily a theologian or a philosopher, since the distinction between theology and philosophy had far less, if any, meaning for the intellectuals of Philo's time than for us. What is of greater importance in this connection is the fact that his writings have a threefold value in the study of philosophy. In the first place, they furnish us with a body of thought with which to compare the theology and ethics of Paul and of the Rabbis of Palestine and thus enable us to arrive at a more just estimate of the intellectual climate in which Christianity arose. Second, on closer scrutiny they are revealed as the source of a great part of the synthesis of Hellenism and Judeo-Christian tradition that was effected by the Greek Church Fathers (many of whom liberally quoted or paraphrased Philo's interpretations of Scripture). Third, it was Philo more than any single predecessor of Plotinus who, as Zeller admits (iii. 2.89), gave the first powerful impetus to that fusion of Greek and Oriental thought known as Neoplatonism, which in turn became the inspiration of one of the chief currents of medieval Scholasticism and even of some modern idealistic philosophies.

Apart from the philosophical aspects of Philo's works one must notice the gratifying fact that among religious historians of today there has arisen a new appreciation of the poetry and mystical insights of Philo, which are so pervasive an element in his writings that some scholars have gone so far as to argue that he was primarily a mystic who used Judaism merely as an outer form in which to clothe an esoteric personal religion. Such a view, however, is a distortion of his whole manner of thought and expression and does not correspond to what we know of his practical activity. It is far more reasonable to regard Philo as the most gifted and versatile of those pious Hellenistic Jews who sought to find the highest truths of Greek philosophy, science and religion in the laws of Moses. Like Aristobulus, Pseudo-Aristeas and others, Philo tried to show that a life lived in accordance with the Jewish tradition was not incompatible with the attainment of Greek culture but that Judaism was as full and rich a doctrine as Platonism or Stoicism or Orphism or any combination of pagan beliefs. He further tried to prove that even the rigorous discipline and ceremonial requirements of the Mosaic Law might lead to a devout and unworldly inner life of piety and contemplation.

The little we know of Philo's life is based on a brief paragraph in Josephus and occasional personal remarks in his own writings. He was a resident of Alexandria and must have been born about 20 B.C.E., since he speaks of himself as "an elderly man" at the time of his mission to Rome in 40 C.E. The wealth and prestige of his family are indicated by the facts that his brother Alexander was an important tax official of the Roman government and that one of his nephews, a son of Alexander, was married to a daughter of King Agrippa I, while another nephew, named Tiberius Julius Alexander, was at one time Roman procurator of Judea and later a Roman prefect of Egypt and one of the leading Roman generals who took part in the siege of Jerusalem. Whether Philo quarreled with his brother's son because of his completely anti-Jewish attitude we do not know. Neither do we know whether Philo was throughout his life as active a political figure in the Alexandrian Jewish community as was his apostate nephew in the Roman government. We do know, however, that Philo was head of the Jewish legation sent from Alexandria to Rome in 40 c.e. to protest to the mad Emperor Caligula against the pogrom instigated by Egyptian and Greek anti-Semites and abetted by Roman officials. Incidentally, there is no trustworthy evidence to support the Christian story that while in Rome Philo met the Apostle Peter.

From incidental statements in his writings we learn that, though Philo scrupulously observed Jewish ritual, he attended the Greek theater, athletic contests and chariot races. Moreover, in addition to his firsthand knowledge of the more external aspects of Greek culture, Philo had a wide and deep knowledge, which would have been remarkable even in a Gentile scholar, of Greek poetry and philosophy.

Though we no longer possess the whole of Philo's work, to judge from the catalogue of his writings given by Eusebius we do have a large part of it, amounting to some thirty complete treatises and a large number of fragments. His writings have been variously classified by modern scholars on the bases of chronology, content and motivation (whether addressed primarily to Jews or to Gentiles). The following classification closely follows that made by Leopold Cohn, one of the greatest Philonic scholars of modern times.

I. Writings of Purely Philosophical Content.

These include four treatises: *On the Eternity of the World; That Every Good Man is Free; On Providence* (preserved partly in Greek, wholly in Armenian); *Alexander,* or *That Animals Have Reason* (preserved only in Armenian).

II. Interpretation of the Pentateuch (chiefly Genesis and Exodus).

This body of work is subdivided into three classes.

A. The Allegorical Commentary on Genesis. This is a running commentary on Gen. 2-41, consisting of sixteen treatises, concerned chiefly with the first half of the biblical book.

B. Questions and Answers on Genesis and Exodus. This is a briefer running commentary, preserved only fragmentarily in Greek and much more fully in Armenian. The Armenian version has preserved most of the original six books on Genesis and two of the original five on Exodus.

C. A Historical-Exegetical Commentary on the Mosaic Law. This is not a running commentary, except on the biblical narrative of the Creation, but a systematic treatment of the ethics of the Pentateuch, partly arranged under types of morality symbolized by the Patriarchs and Moses. This systematic work contains the following treatises: *On the Creation of the*

World; On Abraham; On Joseph or *The Statesman; On the Special Laws* (of the Decalogue) in four books with various subtitles.

III. Historical-Apologetic Writings. These include: *On the Life of Moses* in three (originally two) books; *Hypothetica* (preserved only in fragments); *Apology for the Jews* (preserved only in fragments); *On the Contemplative Life* (of the Therapeuts); *Against Flaccus* (the anti-Jewish governor of Egypt); *The Legation to Gaius*. The last two treatises once formed part of a larger work in five books dealing with the Divine punishments visited upon the persecutors of the Jews.

It would be foolish to try to give in the limited space at our disposal even an outline of Philo's metaphysical and ethical and theological doctrines, to say nothing of his views on education and politics. It must suffice to state summarily that Philo, like some of his Alexandrian Jewish predecessors, used whatever Greek philosophical theories were convenient for adaptation to his allegorical interpretation of the Bible, of which the Greek text was regarded by him as no less inspired than the Hebrew original. Thus, to give a few obvious examples, he makes consistent use of the Platonic doctrine that the immaterial ideas are superior to sense-perceived matter, that the world was created as a perfect thing by a benevolent God, and that the ills of human life arise from the victory of sense and passion over reason. From Plato and the Stoics he borrowed the formulation of the idea (though not the idea itself) that reason must control the senses and that through reason, which is a spark of the Divine in man, we can come closer to God. Philo was the first philosopher known to us who achieved any degree of success in harmonizing the idea of an eternal immaterial God with the God of Jewish history, and in showing how a transcendent God came into contact with a material world subject to the changes of time and with the human personality. Philo solves these problems, to his satisfaction and that of many of his Neoplatonic and Christian readers, by assuming that there were intermediaries between God and the world, these being hypostatized physical and moral powers emanating from God Himself. The first intermediary power was the *Logos*, which Philo poetically describes as the eldest son of God (but not in the sense that the Gospel of John has in making the pre-existent Word of God identical with Jesus). The *Logos* in turn produced from itself other powers of God, the royal power and the beneficent power, which remind us of the two *Middot* or attributes of God in Rabbinic theology, the attribute of mercy and the attribute of justice. Like the Rabbis, Philo connects one power with the name "Lord" and the other with the name "God," but differs from them in connecting mercy with "God" and royalty with "Lord" instead of the reverse. The history of the idea of a *Logos*, or immaterial principle, pervading the material world is too complex to be more than mentioned here. But it may be of interest to note that the

Logos plays somewhat the same role in Philo's theology that Torah does in Rabbinic theology.

What is probably of more interest to a casual reader is the ingenuity of Philo's allegorical interpretation of Scripture and his amazingly consistent use of biblical symbols to describe the unresting pilgrimage of the soul to the eternal truth of a God beyond space and time. His great allegory of the patriarchal history and the Mosaic Law is a kind of *Divine Comedy*. Though it is written in prose and without formal literary unity, it has the architectonic quality of Dante's great poetic synthesis of medieval theology and history.

Not only do the more obvious "properties," to borrow a theatrical term, such as the Patriarchs and the sacred cult objects serve Philo as symbols of moral and religious ideas, but even the most neutral and common things mentioned in the Pentateuch, such as rivers, mountains, plants and animals, are all made to play a meaningful part in this dramatic composition. His ability to create a consistent theological pattern out of bits of natural lore, folklore, Pythagorean number-mysticism and a vast assortment of materials constantly astonishes and sometimes wearies the faithful reader of his works.

Just as there is something Dantesque in the sustained dramatic intention of his allegory, so there is something Proustian in the psychological acuteness of his observation of human actions and in the overrich complexity of his discourses on morality and history. Some fifty years ago Claude Montefiore published in the *Jewish Quarterly Review* a delightful anthology of choice passages from Philo that deserves reprinting in more convenient form. The reader who has access to the files of that periodical is urged to read the whole of Montefiore's *Florilegium Philonis*. The following few passages, chosen independently by the present writer, are given not with a view to making a miniature anthology of the most appealing passages in Philo but merely to illustrate some of his characteristics.

The first selection is from Philo's later and briefer commentary on Genesis and Exodus, called *Questions and Answers* (preserved only in Armenian except for a few score incomplete paragraphs). This particular passage, from Book II:42, takes the biblical verse, Genesis 8:11, part of the story of the flood, and draws from it, as a magician might from a plain hat, a variety of colorful interpretations. The verse reads, "And the dove returned again to him at eventide; holding an olive-leaf, a dry branch" ("dry branch" is Philo's interpretation of the "plucked branch" of Scripture). Let us see how Philo skilfully transforms each of these simple words into complex symbols.

All these are chosen symbols and tests: The "returning again," the "at evening," the "bearing an olive-leaf," the "dry branch," the "oil" and the "in its mouth." But the several symbols must be studied in detail. Now the return is distinguished from the earlier flight. For the latter brought the report of a nature altogether corrupt and rebellious and one destroyed by the flood, that is, by great ignorance and lack of education. But the other repents of its beginning. And to find repentence is not easy but a very difficult and laborious task. For these reasons it comes at evening, having passed the whole day from early morning until evening in inspection, in word by passing through various places, but in actuality by looking over and inspecting the parts of its nature and in seeing these clearly from beginning to end. And the third symbol is "bearing a leaf." The leaf is a small part of a plant. However, it does not come into being without the plant. And similar to this it is to begin to repent. For the beginning of improvement gives a slight indication, as if it were a leaf, that it is to be guarded and can also be shaken off. But there is great hope that it will attain correction of its ways. The fourth symbol is that the leaf was of no other tree than the olive. And oil is the material of light. For evil, as I have said, is profound darkness, but virtue is a most radiant splendor. And repentance is the beginning of light. But do not think that the beginning of repentance is already in blossoming and growing things, but only while they are still dry and arid do they have a seminal principle. Wherefore the fifth symbol is that when it [the dove] came, it bore a "dry branch." And the sixth symbol is that the dry branch was "in its mouth," since six is the first perfect number. For virtue bears in its mouth, that is, in its speech, the seeds of wisdom and justice and altogether goodness of soul. And not only does it bear these gifts but it also gives a share in them to outsiders, offering water to their souls, and watering with repentance their desire for sin.

An aspect of Philo's thought which has no parallel in extant Hellenistic Jewish literature is his frequent use of the terms and ideas used in the pagan mystery-cults which professed to enable the initiate to be reborn and by divesting himself of earthly encumbrances to come into ecstatic union with a savior-god such as Dionysos or Osiris or Mithra. Philo's conception of mystical union with the Divine was less physical and emotionally primitive than that found in even the most spiritualized pagan mysteries, partly because Philo's God was less personal and more transcendent than Greek-Oriental gods, and partly because his healthy Jewish instinct or training kept him from too exalted or irrational a flight into unreality. The dangers of substituting pure symbolism for a life of active and traditional piety enriched by symbolism are pointed out in one of the more frequently quoted passages from Philo, *On the Migration of Abraham* (89 ff.), which reads in part:

There are some who take the literal laws as symbols of intellectual matters, and while they are overscrupulous about the latter, they carelessly neglect the former. Such men I for my part would blame for their offhandedness. They ought to give attention to both things . . . We should have to neglect the holy service of the temple and a thousand other things if we gave thought only to the things revealed in their deeper sense. Rather should we look on these [outward] things as resembling the body, and the other [inner] things as resembling the soul. Now just as we have to take thought for the body as the dwelling-place of the soul, so we have to pay attention to the letter of the laws, for if we keep them we shall have a clearer notion of the things which they symbolize, and at the same time we shall escape the blame and reproach of the multitude.

What seems to a modern reader most salutary in his writing is his adherence to a doctrine that while the senses are not to be completely suppressed they are to be constantly controlled by reason and that through this same reason the soul can be possessed by a mystical rapture. It is no mere use of picturesque quotation but sober truth to say that long before Spinoza the unique beauty of "the intellectual love of God" was celebrated by Philo. The following passage, from the *Sacred Allegories* (i. 39 ff.), illustrates Philo's belief that the soul achieves mystical rapture not by intoxication or other disturbances of normal behavior, as in the pagan mysteries, but by submerging the senses in a flood of reason, a flood that wells up from the hidden sources of the Mosaic Law rightly understood and practiced. The passage is a commentary on Gen. 2:7, "And God formed man by taking clay from the earth and breathed into his face the breath of life; and the man became a living soul."

Philo comments as follows:

There are two kinds of men, one the heavenly man, the other earthly . . . We must account the man made of earth to be mind in the process of being mixed with body but not already mixed. This earthly mind is in reality corruptible except that God breathes into it a power of true life . . . God projects the power that comes from Him through the mediating breath [or wind] till it reaches the subject. And for what other purpose is this than that we may obtain a conception of Him, for how could the soul have conceived of God if He had not breathed into it and seized it through His power? . . . For the mind imparts to the irrational part of the soul a share of that which it has received from God, so that the mind is besouled by God while the irrational part is besouled by the mind. For the mind is, as it were, the God of the irrational part, just as Scripture does not hesitate to speak of Moses as "a God to Pharaoh."

Of Philo's poetic metaphysics we have a good example in the treatise *On Creation* (20 ff.), where he compares the creation of the world through the instrumentality of the *Logos* with the planning of a city by an architect using charts which set down the ideal city he has in mind and from which he proceeds to build the actual city. The same idea of the divine architect is found in Plato's *Timaeus* and in the Rabbinic work *Bereshit Rabbah*, but Philo's metaphor is more sustained and more vivid. A part of the passage in Philo reads as follows:

Similarly one must think about God, that when He was minded to found the great city [*i.e.*, the world], He first conceived of the types of its parts, and from these He wrought an intelligible [*i.e.,* ideal] world, which He used as a model for the sensible [*i.e.,* visible] world. And just as the city formed within [the mind of] the architect has no place outside him but has been engraved in his soul as by a seal, so also the world of ideas would have had no other place than the Divine *Logos* which made this ordered world.

It is a great pity that lack of space makes it impossible to comment on many other aspects of Philo's work and to illustrate these by quotations. Perhaps this brief study can best be concluded with a quotation from the treatise *On the Change of Names* (39 ff.), which shows that this mystical thinker was not concerned solely with his own salvation but was also constantly mindful of his fellow man.

These men are possessed by a divine madness and live a wild and solitary life. But there are others who are familiars of a gentle and tame wisdom. They practice piety eminently and do not despise human things. This is attested by the oracle in which it is said to Abraham out of the mouth of God (Gen. 17:1), "Be well-pleasing before Me." "This means 'not to Me only but to My works also [*i.e.,* other human beings], while I as judge watch and oversee thee' " . . . And so Moses in his exhortations gives this charge (Deut. 12:28), "Thou shalt do what is well-pleasing before the Lord thy God," which means that you should do such things as shall be worthy to appear before God and which he will see and approve; such deeds are likely to be well-pleasing to our fellows as well.

NOTES

[1a Cf. above Elias J. Bickerman, "The Historical Foundations of Postbiblical Judaism," pp. 97-101.]

[2a Cf. above Judah Goldin, "The Period of the Talmud (135 B.C.E.-1035 C.E.)," p. 143.]

[3a Cf. *ibid.,* pp. 116-117.]

[4a Cf. Bickerman, *op. cit.,* pp. 95-96, 97-99.]

[5a Cf. above Robert Gordis, "The Bible as a Cultural Monument," pp. 808-813.]

[6a Cf. above Alexander Altmann, "Judaism and World Philosophy," pp. 955 ff.]

[7a In 1948 the Harvard University Press published Professor Wolfson's two volumes, *Philo: Foundations of Religious Philosophy in Judaism, Christianity, and Islam.*]

BIBLIOGRAPHICAL NOTE

A

The English reader will find the books here discussed most conveniently edited and translated in the following works:

The apocryphal and pseudepigraphic books are well translated and provided with instructive introductions and notes by various scholars in R. H.

Charles (ed.), *The Apocrypha and Pseudepigrapha of the Old Testament*. 2 vols. Oxford, 1913.

The best English translation of Josephus is that in the Loeb Classical Library, London, of which seven volumes have appeared to the present time: Vols. 1-4 were translated by the late Henry St. John Thackeray. Vols. 5-7 by Ralph Marcus.

The best English translation of Philo is also that in the Loeb Classical Library, of which nine volumes have appeared: Vols. 1-5 were translated by F. H. Colson and G. H. Whitaker; Vols. 6-9 by F. H. Colson; Vols. 11-12 by Ralph Marcus.

The fragments of the Hellenistic Jewish writers will be found in the work of Wallace N. Stearns, *Fragments from Graeco-Jewish Writers*. Chicago, 1908.

B

The following books will be of interest to those wishing to have more detailed discussions of some of the writers here treated.

NORMAN BENTWICH, *Philo Judaeus of Alexandria*. Philadelphia, 1910. Though now antiquated in some respects, this book is still useful because of its abundance of information and its excellent judgment. Moreover, it is written in attractive style.

ERWIN R. GOODENOUGH, *Introduction to Philo Judaeus*. New Haven, 1940. The author, a well-known Philonist of Yale University, always writes in a stimulating and illuminating way though not all of his views are to be accepted.

CLAUDE G. MONTEFIORE, "Florilegium Philonis, in *Jewish Quarterly Review*, VII, pp. 481-545. London, 1894-1895. The excellence of this anthology has already been mentioned.

ROBERT H. PFEIFFER, *Introduction to the Old Testament*. New York, 1941. A comprehensive and authoritative, though somewhat technical, study of Old Testament literature with valuable chapters on versions of the Bible and excellent bibliographies, including apocryphal literature.

HARRY A. WOLFSON, *Philo: Foundations of Religious Philosophy, Judaism, Christianity and Islam*. 2 vols. Cambridge, 1947.

Since this bibliography was prepared in 1946, Professor Harry A. Wolfson's monumental work on Philo has appeared. It should therefore be added to this original list.

CHAPTER 24

JUDEO-ARABIC LITERATURE

By Abraham S. Halkin

Judeo-Arabic literature comprises works composed in Arabic, almost always in Hebrew script, by Jewish authors who lived in lands where Arabic was the dominant language. More specifically the title is applied to the output of authors from, roughly, the ninth to the thirteenth century. But if one were to write a comprehensive history of Judeo-Arabic literature, one would extend the limits at both ends, to the sixth century and to our own time, respectively.

The most striking aspect of this literary activity is its variety of subject matter and its novel approach. Jewish creativity, which for centuries had confined itself to religious themes, so that even purely literary material was clothed in a religious garb, developed a catholicity of expression which included medicine, mathematics and other sciences, philosophy, history. Under the same impetus, secular poetry and belles-lettres appeared in Hebrew. Even within the field of religion new disciplines were introduced. Investigation of Hebrew grammar was pursued far more seriously than at any time in the past, commentaries were written to explain the Bible text and systematic codification of the law occupied the minds of great talmudists.

Before we undertake to account for this efflorescence it is important to know something of the environment within which the literature developed, to appreciate the economic, political and cultural conditions under which the Jews labored. They lived in a world which was predominantly Moslem in religion and Arabic in vernacular. Judged by any standard and, particularly, by the conditions prevailing in non-Moslem regions, this world was quite comfortable.[1a] Upon the payment of a special tax, collected from all *Dhimmis* (non-Moslems who were permitted to live by their faith), they were not harassed on religious grounds, nor did they, save for isolated occasions, suffer from any serious disability. They were privileged to engage in all economic activities, including services in the administration. They were not segregated and thus came in contact with the non-Jewish population. Moreover, politically they benefited from the characteristic concept of the state in medieval times, especially in Moslem lands. The Islamic state was a theocracy, and its head a representative or successor (caliph) of the prophet. The Koran, which is the revealed Book of the followers of Mohammed, was the source of all Islamic law. Like Judaism, it did not distinguish between a civil and an ecclesiastical law, different from each other in origin. Both were derived from the same religious sources. To be a member of the Moslem body politic was a privilege which only adherents of that faith could enjoy. Non-Moslems lived under the protection of the dominant group as a result of a special agreement between the sovereign church-state and them. The state was organized along religious lines. The dominant group possessed the right to administer the state and to regulate its affairs. But the tolerated religious minorities, in addition to the guarantee of the right of domicile, of earning a livelihood, and of the safeguarding of life and limb, were also granted internal autonomy. All matters in which the state had no direct interest would be regulated within these units by their duly authorized administrators, in conformity with the laws of the particular group. As a result, it was possible for a non-Moslem individual not only to share in the rights and privileges that belong inherently to a human being, but also to identify himself with his own group and participate in its life and functions.

Undoubtedly, the political theory of the Islamic state, or even its application, did not eliminate difficulties or friction among the several sections of the population. We know of a considerable amount of animosity, of literary polemics, of religious persecutions, and of occasional outbreaks of violence. In Jewish writings we read complaints of the state of exile, and yearnings for the restoration of Zion and the realization of Messianic hopes. While such themes were to some extent conventional, they certainly indicate some dissatisfaction with conditions as they were. The pathetic terms in which the highly placed and wealthy Jewish public official, Hasdai ben Shaprut, expresses his readiness to come and kneel before the distant Jewish king of the Khazars, or the pitiful plaints of oppression by Christians and Moslems which resound so loudly in the writings of the Jewish poets of Spain, certainly reveal an awareness of being alien and the existence of difficulty and trouble. Yet, in general, life under Moslem rule was as comfortable a one as the Jews have ever had under foreign domination, and the average individual probably found little to complain of on religious grounds.

The Arab-speaking world within which the Jews lived was the most cultured center of medieval times. Having absorbed through conquest the civilized centers of Christianity and Zoroastrianism—within which Greek culture, in modified form, no doubt, had previously continued its existence after the classical period—the Arabs became disciples, and set about learning what the two civilizations of East and West had to offer. A wave of translations marks the ninth and tenth centuries, in the course of which scientific and philosophic writings of the ancients were rendered into

Arabic. Thanks to the interest of enlightened caliphs, the efforts of zealous translators, and the gratitude of a substantial body of readers and students, the Arabic-reading public fell heir to the scientific and philosophic thought of the Greeks, the Syrians, the Persians and the Hindus. The new cultural possessions served as the groundwork for a ramified and intensive pursuit of study and enlightenment among the Moslems. In the wake of the translated texts, original works in Arabic followed in the same fields, and thus the Greek cultural tradition, with all its modifications, found its redeemer and heir in the lively activity in which the Moslems were now engaged. In all this literary productivity neither ethnic nor religious boundaries interfered. Although literary polemics abounded along both national and religious lines, the efforts of the numerous men of letters, of diverse national and religious origin, all contributed to the enhancement and enrichment of Arabic literature. As a result, during the centuries when Western, and even Eastern, Christendom passed through the so-called Dark Ages, the vast Moslem empire, particularly after its decentralization into several states, housed learning and enlightenment. Indeed, the eventual awakening of Christian Europe, the age of Scholasticism, and the subsequent Renaissance are indebted to the impetus given by Islam.

The Jewish communities in the Moslem countries had, of course, a long cultural history behind them. In Mesopotamia, Palestine, Egypt, North Africa and Spain, all now dominated by rulers who professed Islam, the Jews possessed, to a greater or lesser degree, the Rabbinic literature produced over the many centuries from the beginning of the Common Era or earlier to the rise of Islam. With all allowance made for external influences in the centers where this literature was created, it cannot be denied that it bears a native Jewish stamp. It is Jewish in spirit, in emphasis, in form. The successive additions to the cultural treasures, visible as the effect of foreign ideas and environments may be, are all—with the possible exception of the esoteric literature of that period—genuinely Jewish, natural and logical outgrowths of the earlier strata to which they are added.

As time passed, these Jewish communities found themselves increasingly within a milieu which, religiously, was akin to their own and, culturally, challenged their self-sufficiency. As no hard and fast social, economic or political boundary lines separated them from their Moslem countrymen, they responded to the lure and challenge of the larger world within which they were continuing their Jewish existence. They gradually abandoned Aramaic, which had been their vernacular, and became speakers of Arabic; they studied works in Arabic; nor did they limit themselves to translations from other languages into it. They also read and learned original writings in poetry, history and grammar. They even studied the Koran. In a word, they went through a profound process of adaptation to the environments.

As a result, the cultural history of the Jews in Moslem countries necessarily followed new paths. New interests and problems engaged the intellectuals, and they found expression in a multitude of works written in Arabic and Hebrew. The Moslem world is not the only instance in Jewish history where the Jewish way of life encountered another which it regarded with interest and was impelled to emulate. Both before and after there were occasions when Jews came in contact with a civilization which had much to offer and from which they gladly took. There have been environmental conditions other than the Moslem where Jews looked to the environment with respect and felt themselves called upon to defend and justify their adherence and loyalty to their way of life before themselves and the larger world. Yet, if we exclude modern Hebrew and Yiddish literatures, which have their own causes and explanations,[2a] and cannot therefore figure in this generalization, the Arabic period is the only one where this contact resulted in a lasting and positive contribution to the Jewish cultural heritage, and produced works which have been recognized and revered by Jews of other days and other lands.

For an explanation of this phenomenon it is necessary to dwell briefly on the character of the civilization that developed within Islam. It has already been stated that Greek culture came into this world from the outside. Its presence confronted the adherents of Islam with the problem of adjustment. Greek ideas of God, of man, of the world, and of their relation to one another, were not at all like the basic conceptions in the Koran or the subsequent literature that elaborated upon it. And while the majority of Moslems knew little about the imported ideas and cared less, and, on the other hand, some individuals may have been so completely captivated by them as to divorce themselves entirely from the traditional faith, a large number of intelligent and honest people found themselves in the throes of an inner conflict. The situation paralleled to an extent that which existed for Hellenistic Jewry.[3a] This section in Islam was driven by the philosophic discussions and doctrines of Greek origin not only to ponder and analyze religious dogmas and problems which were either nonexistent in the native Moslem world or definitely stated and put beyond question but also to agree with a good deal of what was taught by the ancient philosophers. But when this happened, a reconciliation was made necessary between what was rationally acceptable to them and what they received on faith. The result was a theology which made some concessions to philosophic method and discipline, and a philosophy which nominally paid homage to religion, but essentially adhered to the truths it inherited from the classical environment. It cannot be truthfully said that the compromise was a success, when objectively studied; it may even be doubted whether a compromise is possible. But it worked for a time, and in one form or another it won adherents.

The experiences of the Moslems were an inestimable boon to the Jewish communities in that world. The issues they later had to face were almost identical with those confronting the dominant group of that time. The problem that both groups were called upon to solve was to establish peace and harmony between two truths: the truth of religion and the truth of philosophy. The product of the peace was not a real synthesis in which the two components were integrated. Whether religion was the core and philosophy the veneer, or *vice versa,* it was not difficult to discern the dichotomy, the dualism that remained, although the two were seemingly poured into one mold. Moreover, the compromise was not one which was adopted by all adherents of Islam. Many remained the same simple believers their forefathers had been, hostile to the encroachment of philosophy on their precious holdings. But some saw clearly the logical conclusions to which philosophic speculation led, and remained faithful to them, even if they were ready to pay lip service to the accepted tenets of the faith, and appreciated the benefits it bestowed on the uninitiated. All this facilitated the problem of the Jews. The dominant civilization remained a religious one. This naturally made the Jewish religion secure among its followers. There was no group with which one could have identified oneself without involving one's religion. There was no trend away from the religious outlook to a secular point of view which left religion, or the lack of it, to the conscience of the individual. As for that section of Jewry which, like its counterpart in Islam, was faced by a problem of reconciliation, it, too, profited by the discernible dichotomy in the Moslem compromise. All that it was necessary to do was to replace the Moslem component in the theology with the Jewish one. For better or worse, whatever fate the Moslem achievement would enjoy within its domain would be shared by the Jewish one within its realm. In this way a guarantee of survival and vitality was provided for the Jewish way of life by the experiences of the Moslem way of life.

Thus it happened that the encounter of Judaism within the world of Islam with the Greek tradition was a positive beneficial influence. It acted as a leaven, stimulating activity in fields not hitherto cultivated and suggesting new directions and points of view in previously pursued activities. It opened the eyes of Jewish students to secular subjects: to medicine, to mathematics, to history. It aroused Jewish interest in secular poetry and in literary prose. It fostered a rational approach to religious prescriptions, whether of creed or of deed. It instilled a love of style and form, of systematization and organization. It added much, very much that was new to Jewish culture, but it did not shake the foundations of Judaism. Jewish civilization became much more variegated, much more diverse, but it remained Jewish. Not only were the authors and creators of that culture thoroughly Jewish in their background and in their knowledge of

Jewish literature, or in their profession of their Jewish faith and in their observance of its commandments, but they also exhibited their Jewishness in their writings. Even in books which were totally devoid of Jewish content, such as books on medicine or on some other science, an introduction was included in which the gratitude to God and other items testified to the author's group and religious affiliation. In addition, an occasional reference to a biblical or talmudic matter indicated the religion of the author.

The adaptation, beneficial as it was, also produced some negative effects. Of necessity it failed to discriminate between emulation and imitation. The positive gains also showed an obverse side which was not so commendable. The new vistas that opened before them through the acquisition of Arabic led to an attitude toward Hebrew which was not quite wholesome. One writer actually seeks to justify the composition by Saadia Gaon of a work in Hebrew. Another keeps harping on the relative poverty of Hebrew as compared with Arabic. The admiration of Moslem achievements or, perhaps more correctly, the trend of assimilation, led to some surprising and distasteful manifestations. The Koran was transcribed in Hebrew characters, evidently for people who could not read Arabic script. A fortune book exists in Hebrew which lists Mohammed as one of the Prophets. Other strange facts indicate similarly the relaxation of the Jewish way of life, sometimes all the way to "the dogmatic barrier between Judaism and Islam," and occasionally even beyond that.

The tensions and strains within Islam in its process of adjustment, the rationalism that penetrated from without and was so disturbing yet so persuasive, the individual investigations and interpretations of religion that, in this realm, are very significant, marking as they do the assertion of the individual in the face of sacred tradition, even if nominally it is within the framework of that tradition—all these found their parallels within Judaism in thought and in literature as well as in deed. The condition generated a sectarianism which produced little and insignificant schisms, and also a large and threatening party like the Karaites. It gave rise to many questionings, doubts and perplexities to which the works of medieval Jewish philosophers bear witness, and an intellectualism which at least in some cases was tantamount to a rejection of the cardinal principles of Judaism. At any rate, this intellectualism is potentially at least always a threat to the wholehearted, sincere and unquestioning faith of the simple believers. It may even be that the behavior of the Jews of Spain some centuries later, in the catastrophes of 1391 and subsequently,[4a] so strikingly different from the martyrdom of the Franco-German Jews in 1096 or 1348, has its explanation in this "liberalism." These and other alarming signs and effects are true enough; but they do not alter the fact of the rich and ramified productivity that is the subject of this chapter.

In their writings, the Jewish authors who lived in Islamic lands em-

ployed two languages. Poetry and a small part of their prose were composed in Hebrew. But the bulk of the prose and a little of the poetry were
written in Arabic. The quality of the language is generally colloquial. It
becomes apparent, from a study of the work, that the authors paid but little
attention to the artistic aspect of their composition, and did not strive to
imitate models in style and eloquence, as did their Moslem contemporaries.
Their language is clearly akin to the speech of the environment, except
for the peculiarly Jewish expressions and the Hebrew words and phrases
that found their way into Arabic as they have into every other language
spoken by Jews. By the use of the vernacular even in tracts on law or commentaries on the Bible the Jews in Moslem countries distinguish themselves from their contemporaries in Christian lands who did not employ
their daily language for writing, and resemble Jews in modern times in
Western countries who likewise utilize the language of the land for
specifically Jewish works. (It may be said in passing that the similarity
between the two civilizations manifests itself in other aspects as well, as
any comparison will show.) This unhesitating readiness to write in a
language other than Hebrew demonstrates of course an identification with
environment which was not reached in other lands, and a rather remarkable
lack of consciousness of the importance of the medium of expression. That
the problem presented itself to them is evident from the regrets and
protests over the neglect of Hebrew voiced by individuals who themselves
composed works in Arabic. They were also undoubtedly familiar with a
Rabbinic word of praise for the Jews in ancient Egypt who were redeemed
because they had not abandoned their language. Yet they continued to use
Arabic. Reasons have of course been advanced, such as, for example, the
desire of the author to reach the widest audience possible. This may be
true in one instance or another, but we ought not to exaggerate its
applicability. There is no reason to assume that the masses in Islamic
countries were more interested in matters intellectual than in other
centers at other times, or that the authors were so democratically minded
or so unaware of the cultural gradations as to strive to reach everyone.
Maimonides specifically declares in the introduction to his *Guide* that he
does not desire to have his work on philosophy fall into the hands of the
masses, or even of the whole intellectual group within them. Moreover,
one may venture the assertion that the readers who were mature and
sufficiently interested to read and study these books could read Hebrew
with the same fluency as Arabic. Another reason which has been offered
may again be partly true though it is not cogent. The inadequacy of
Hebrew for expressing what they had to, allegedly prompted authors to
fall back on Arabic. But this argument, too, is not strong. Had the desire
existed, the way would have been found. It was found by translators into
Arabic who had to adapt their language to the logic and the syntax of

Greek and had to coin a new vocabulary. It was found by later translators from Arabic into Hebrew who succeeded in developing a terminology and a style to meet the exigencies of the undertaking, and it could have been found by the authors themselves. Again Maimonides may be cited, who, in the first part of his major Hebrew work on Jewish law, gives an eloquent example of his facility in Hebrew, a facility which is unquestionably superior to that of his subsequent translators. The most probable explanation is that they did it because it was the most natural and the most effortless thing to do. Furthermore, they probably did not feel that in compositions on science the language selected preserved an ideological importance as in the case of artistic creations.

The almost consistent use of Hebrew in poetry also is an interesting problem. The naturalness of which we spoke should certainly have asserted itself in their poetic writings, in which the individuality of the writer comes to the fore. It is hardly correct, however, to suggest, as has been done, that the lyric character of poetry made the use of Hebrew imperative because the poet was compelled to sing in the language with which he felt himself most intimate. It simply goes against the facts to assume that Arabic, which they spoke from birth and used in all situations, was less their most intimate vehicle than Hebrew, which was an externally acquired medium. The explanation is to be sought more plausibly in the character of their poetry. It was considered by the people of the time as an art which approached perfection in proportion to its excellence in externals: rhythm, rhyme, language and various skills in the handling of the language. Technique, in other words, was the most important endowment of the artist, and his poetic talent an additional gift. It is to be remembered that, unlike their prose, the poetry of the Jews was grounded in an old tradition, much older than the impact of Islam. The origins of medieval poetry[5a] are to be sought in the liturgical compositions of earlier days. Since those were all written in Hebrew, a precedent was established which was maintained in later days not only in sacred but also in secular compositions. Furthermore, Moslem poetry, more perhaps than any other genre of their literature, was regarded by Moslems as a national expression, a genuinely Arab creation. It was the preferred vehicle for showing off the glory of Arabic and singing the praises of the Arabs. Jews very likely reacted by displaying a pride in their language, in its glories, its antiquity and its tradition. There may also have been involved a religious issue. The Koran was accepted by Moslems as a literary masterpiece, and although the models were pre-Islamic poets, the holy book was neverthless respected as an ideal. One of the dogmas of orthodox Islam is that the Koran is a miracle, both because of its revelation and because of its inimitable style. It provoked among the Jews a natural desire to lean on their greatest literary masterpiece, to draw on the Hebrew Bible, and to benefit from its perfection.

Among the basic productions in Judeo-Arabic literature we must undoubtedly include the translation of the Bible. Apart from its significance as a barometer of the conquest of Arabic, to the loss of Hebrew and Aramaic, comparable to a similar phenomenon in other countries—Hellenistic Egypt or the English-speaking communities—it is further important as evidence of the interest in the Bible which led to a large output of studies connected with it and the Hebrew language. The written translations were probably an outgrowth of oral traditions with their local variations. Hence the similarity in terminology among several translations which otherwise show some divergences. The best known version is that of the great and many-sided scholar Saadia ben Joseph al-Fayyumi (882-942),[6a] who, though actively participating in Jewish affairs of his day and even assuming leadership, nevertheless wrote on many subjects. He seems to have rendered almost all, if not all, of the Bible into Arabic, even if to date a comparatively small portion of his work is known. While he may have been prompted by certain apologetic motives, such as the desire to display proudly before the non-Jewish world the grandeur of Jewish Scriptures—achieved by the apparent employment of Arabic script in his version—or the wish to make the Bible palatable to intellectuals who might have objected to some rationally unacceptable items in the Sacred Text, his primary goal seems to have been to render this necessary service to a public which had no access to the Bible other than through Arabic. In his work he strove consistently to present a smooth-reading, logically arranged text. With this in mind, he took certain liberties with the original, inserting words and phrases, eliminating repetitions, and occasionally offering somewhat free renderings. He was particularly aware of the need of modifying all references to God which might hurt the sensibilities of a rationally minded person, such as himself, who conceived of God in a highly philosophic and abstract manner. And while he believed that the chief duty of a translator or a commentator was to adhere to the literal text, he asserted unequivocally that a free translation or interpretation was required whenever the literal text appeared contrary to sensual experience or to reason, to another specific statement in the Bible or to authoritative tradition. Besides Saadia's we possess remnants or complete versions by other translators, both Rabbanite and Karaite, but there is little point in either listing or characterizing them.

However, a bare translation provides only a meager understanding of biblical literature. Apart from the need for an interpretation of difficult passages, which should be fuller and longer than a translation, there were other factors which made commentary writing on the Bible a necessity.

The Bible, which was accepted by Judaism as its guide in life, was, as is known, interpreted and thus expanded by the Rabbis in order to yield that vast harvest which is termed the Oral Law. While no commentator could venture to include in his commentary all the Oral Law that he believed to be implicit in the Bible, he undoubtedly regarded it as his duty to interpret biblical passages in the spirit of Rabbinic Judaism, particularly where the failure to do so might lead to a wrong conclusion. Care also had to be exerted to take note of and refute unorthodox explanations that were circulated in large quantity by the Karaite sect, which was virile and aggressive in the ninth and tenth centuries.[7a] One may cite in illustration a discussion between Saadia and a Karaite regarding the meaning of "an eye for an eye." Saadia not only renders it "the value of an eye for an eye," as expected—since this is Rabbinic—but seeks to demonstrate that it is the only rationally tenable interpretation. The Karaite, on the contrary, disputes his rendering. The celebrated medieval polygraph, Abraham ibn Ezra, who reports this debate, realizing that no rational proof is possible, concludes with this comment: "We are unable to explain the laws of the Torah correctly unless we depend on the words of the Sages. For in the same way that we have received the Written Law from the ancients we have also received the Oral Law. There is no difference between them." This point of view necessitated a reinterpretation of the Bible in at least its prescriptive portions. The need of commentaries was felt on still another ground. The Bible, which is central in Jewish life, and regarded as the last word in truth, was not unnaturally viewed by each age as the repository of whatever it accepted as valid. In other words, as the scientific and philosophic truths developed and changed from age to age, the adherents of these evolving truths were always intent on finding them in the Bible. Since the period during which Judeo-Arabic literature was written was strongly under the influence of Greek thought in its medieval garb, it strove to read its beliefs and doctrines into the Bible. This, too, made commentary writing a basic need.

The outstanding commentator who wrote in Arabic is the previously mentioned Saadia. He composed either complete commentaries or selected notes probably on the whole Bible. These products, to the extent to which they are known to us, are masterpieces in their field. It is evident that Saadia's chief aim was to clarify. With this in mind he appended introductions to the various books, in which, from a philosophic point of view, he undertook to elucidate the purpose of the book, its method, its teachings and its plan. In his commentaries on the first half of the Five Books of Moses (it was completed by Samuel ben Hofni, see below) he is much more prolix than in the other books. The reason for it lies in the central position of the Torah in Jewish life and the consequent need for elaboration. In addition to the obvious task of explaining what is not clear, he also supplied grammatical notes whenever a knotty language problem arose, he sought to rationalize incidents and events which taxed men's credulity, and endeavored to raise the level of what sounds mythical to a philosophic plane. He is particularly ardent, in his Pentateuch commentary, in his defense of Rabbinic tradition, and in its counterpart, the attack on the Karaites, the opponents and critics of that tradition. In his commentaries on the other books he is noticeably briefer and sparser so that his explanations are in the form of occasional notes and not of a full commentary.

Another important commentator who lived in the Orient is Samuel ben Hofni, head of the Sura Academy (d. 1013).[8a] He prepared an Arabic translation of the Pentateuch, generally more literal than Saadia's, completed Saadia's commentary on the Pentateuch and wrote a commentary on it, and perhaps also on other books of the Bible. He was lengthy in his explanations, giving little attention to linguistic matters, but elaborating on various topics related to the verse or subject under discussion. He was an exponent of rationalism in his exegesis, but he accepted the halakic interpretation of the Bible and believed, contrary to Saadia's view, that all laws could be arrived at rationally. Unlike his critical attitude to the wonders related in the Talmud, he conceded the literal truth of the biblical miracles. But his rationalism forced him to approach certain biblical matters in a manner which aroused opposition. He rejected astrology and necromancy, and hence considered the success of the Witch of Endor a clever trick, and the performance of Joseph's cup the result of some mechanism with which it was equipped. He explained all dreams naturally, even those which were prophetic in character. By the same sober reasoning, however, he also shunned the discovery of the philosophy of his day in the words of the Bible.

Moslem Spain from the eleventh century on overshadows the Orient as a center of Jewish activities, and the Bible commentators of that period were almost all residents of Spain. Judah ibn Balam (c. 1080) wrote commentaries on most if not all of the Bible. An interesting light is shed on his conception of the function of a commentator by this statement of his: "I acceded to his request [i.e., of the man who asked him for an explanation of the ambiguous and difficult words which occur in the Bible], knowing that this undertaking involves three requisites: (1) that I render each word by the most approximate equivalent which Arabic furnishes; (2) that I cite in evidence other texts in the Bible where the same root is employed or, if such are not available, support from the ancients or from Aramaic or Arabic; (3) that I explain the inflection and syntax of the word. . . . As an additional favor to him I shall mention, besides, some interpretations which belong there and which come to mind, whether they are taken from others or derived from my own reasoning." While he does not display much originality in his explanations, his commentaries are valuable because of their eclectic character. We find numerous grammatical notes as well as exegetic comments. He had a faculty for conciseness and organization of his material. He was critical of Saadia, whom he accuses of violence to the Arabic in his translations. He was rather free in condemnation of others, and was not restrained in his remarks. He sometimes attacked his master, Jonah ibn Janah to whom he is indebted for a great deal, much of it without due acknowledgment. His chief target was his contemporary Moses ibn Chiquitilla, whom he criticized for his excessive rationalism. But it is his merit that he did not hesitate to admit his inability to give an adequate explanation of a word or phrase when such was the case.

Moses Ha-Cohan ibn Chiquitilla is unfortunately represented to modern scholarship by relatively few remnants culled from others who cited his explanations. He seems to have written commentaries on the bulk of the Bible, but unlike those of his younger contemporary, ibn Balam, whose works have survived in large part, ibn Chiquitilla's seem to have perished. From the little that remains it is possible to draw certain conclusions regarding his method. He attempted to apply all prophetic predictions to the immediate time of the Prophet rather than to a distant Messianic future. Accordingly, not only general prophecies but apparently Messianic sayings were related to the time of the Prophet who spoke them. The oracles of Isaiah, for example, in which he looks forward to an age of universal peace, refer, according to ibn Chiquitilla, to the time of King Hezekiah. He also made every effort to explain miracles rationally. In an apparently oral dialogue between himself and ibn Balam he denied that at Joshua's bidding the sun and moon ceased their revolutions, "for it is impossible for perpetual motion ever to be interrupted," and explained that the miracle consisted in the continued reflection of the sun even after its setting. By virtue of his enlightened approach to his work he did not hesitate to assign to sections of the Bible dates which run contrary to tradition. He believed that the chapters in Isaiah from 40 on form a separate section. While it may not be warranted to credit him with the recognition of a "Second Isaiah," he sensed the difference between the two portions of the book. He recognized a number of psalms to be of exilic date. In short, it may be stated that ibn Chiquitilla is a clear example of the rational, enlightened spirit of the Jewish-Arabic age as it manifested itself in exegesis.

But the rationalism that characterizes the commentaries of Saadia or ibn Chiquitilla was carried much further by a school of exegetes which adopted the views of Aristotelian philosophy. The beginnings of this extreme intellectualism were made by men who wrote in Arabic. Indeed, the Nestor of this school was the great Maimonides, who, without devoting much of his time and energy to the field of exegesis, indicated the lines it was to follow. The method employed by this school is that known as allegory, *i.e.*, the presumption that the Bible stated abstract truths and concepts in the form of stories, of personalities or of other figures of speech. Its tradition is old and venerable, going back to Rabbinic times, but its consistent application and, perhaps, the assumption that it is the real purport of the Bible, is the contribution of the disciples of Maimonides. The master himself is wrongly credited with an interpretation of Psalm 45, originally apparently a wedding song, which converts the entire chapter into a philosophic discourse. A few remarks by him on some verses in the Song of Songs make it clear that this booklet was conceived by him as a highly philosophic allegory of the Soul and the Active Intellect. The latter interpretation was executed in detail in the lengthy Arabic commentary on the book by Maimonides's contemporary, Joseph ibn Aknin. However, the full results of this method of exegesis became evident in a series of commentaries written in Hebrew by admirers of Maimonides who lived in Provence or in Italy.

The Orient likewise produced a commentator who was an ardent disciple of Maimonides, but his exegesis was by no means one-sidedly allegorical. Joseph ben Tanhum of Jerusalem (d. after 1260) wrote a commentary probably on the entire Bible, and his work is still extant, in whole or in part, or is at least attested for all the books except Ezra and Nehemiah. Besides the expected aid that it offers toward an understanding of the text, his exegesis is rich in discussions of realia, medicine and physics, geography, chronology and philosophy. He displays independence of mind remarkable for his age. In chronological matters he occasionally disagrees with the calculations of the universally accepted Seder Olam and suggests that the Bible sometimes gives round numbers rather than the exact extent. He recognizes copyists' errors in the transmission of names or numbers, and introduces emendations, although not explicitly. He treats the Aggada[9a] more critically than most of his colleagues. The attention he pays to the aesthetic beauty of the biblical rhetoric and to its stylistic traits is a marked feature of his approach. In this he was probably influenced by Moses ben Ezra (see below). Notwithstanding his rationalism, he nevertheless indulges in allegorical interpretation to a considerable degree. His commentary was preceded by a comprehensive introduction, with a separate title, in which he discoursed on grammar, and on other matters such as the relation of the Aggada to the literal meaning, the attitude toward Midrash[10a] and philosophical and ethical problems.

The desire to understand the Bible led to a necessary interest in Hebrew grammar, and its study resulted in notable advances. Its importance was appreciated by those who undertook to elucidate the Scriptures, as is illustrated by the large quantity of grammatical discussion and analysis in the works of the commentators, and also by those who, noting the increasing employment of Hebrew in liturgical and secular poetry, were ardent in their desire to see the language used correctly.

Like the study of the Bible, the investigation of grammar commenced in the Orient. Saadia made his contribution to this as to other fields. There were many who wrote on it, Karaites as well as Rabbanites, mostly in Arabic and some in Hebrew, but in this necessarily sketchy analysis we shall confine ourselves to three men, each of whom made a distinguished and specific contribution. Judah ibn Kuraish of North Africa, who apparently flourished during the first half of the tenth century, addressed an Epistle to the community of Fez in which he reprimanded them for neglecting to read the Aramaic version of the Pentateuch and the Prophets. He relates that when he pointed out to them how many obscure words and passages in the biblical text could be elucidated through Aramaic, and how closely related the two were, they realized the importance of the study of Targum. This experience impelled ibn Kuraish to compose his Epistle in which he would give a list of the numerous biblical and mishnaic words that have Arabic and Aramaic cognates. Of the latter about one-half has survived, but the comparisons with Arabic are lost. He attempted to account for the similarity by the physical proximity of the speakers of these languages and the common ancestry of the people who spoke them. We thus have in his Epistle the first recognition of the importance of comparative study in language, a fundamental of philological research in our day. It is noteworthy that, although the Jewish interest in Hebrew received an impetus from Arabic, the emphasis on comparative linguistics is original with them. Unlike the Arabs whose needs were adequately filled by their one language, the Jews utilized all the three and eventually came to realize their interrelation.

The man who laid the foundation of Hebrew grammar as we know it today, a veritable genius in philology, is Judah ben David Hayyuj of Fez. He was born about the middle of the tenth century and came to Spain early in life, spending the rest of it in Cordova, where he passed away early in the eleventh century. In two basic works on verbs containing weak and double letters, he established the principle that *all* Hebrew verb roots are composed of three radicals, whether they appear in every inflected form of the root or not. Before him, scholars had been inclined to argue from forms in which only one or two of the root letters appeared that such roots consisted of only one or two radicals. Hayyuj discovered both the triliteral scheme and the morphological changes that govern the "irregular" verbs. In his introduction he relates that he was pained to discover wrong verbal forms in the works of poets. He realized that if this procedure were not checked it would lead to a complete breakdown of the linguistic structure of Hebrew. He undertook, therefore, through a systematic analysis of the classes of weak verbs, followed by an alphabetic arrangement of them according to their classes, to fix and regulate the proper treatment of each root both in the interpretation of the biblical text and in the creation of new forms in contemporary compositions.

After Hayyuj discovered the principles underlying the Hebrew verb and noun, his achievements were summarized and further developed by his outstanding disciple, Jonah ibn Janah, who flourished in the first half of the eleventh century. In a comprehensive work, called *al-Tankih*, which comprises a grammar and a lexicon, he covers the various questions pertinent to Hebrew grammar, and also lists most of the roots with their definitions and illustrations of their forms as they occur in the Bible. He explains that he resented the supercilious attitude to Hebrew and to its proper use, and was annoyed to find that, whereas the Arabs devoted so much energy to the study of their language, the Jews paid but little attention to theirs. His grammar, called *Sefer Ha-Rikmah* (*Florilegium*), reviews the principles of the organs of speech, the distinction between radicals, auxiliary letters and affixes, the laws of mutation of letters, inflection of nouns and verbs and numerous other topics. It also includes valuable material on the syntax of the language. Although Janah did not deal with the subjects discussed by Hayyuj, his grammar, together with two or three of his minor works, can well serve as textbooks even for the modern scholar. His work marks the pinnacle of grammatical achievement. His successors, whose writing was almost entirely in Hebrew, not only failed to surpass him but lost ground by comparison with him by introducing views which were wrong yet were adopted for centuries. His dictionary also is exceedingly helpful. Assuming a general knowledge on the part of his readers as well as an acquaintance with his earlier contributions, he did not compile as complete a lexicon as modern standards require. But it is valuable for the light it sheds on vague and doubtful points, and the attention it pays to shades of meaning.

Other Hebrew-Arabic dictionaries were compiled, both before and after Janah's time. Hai Gaon (see below) wrote *al-Hawi* (the Compendium), a dictionary of biblical and Rabbinic Hebrew. Only fragments of it have been recovered thus far. From these we learn that he discussed under one heading words made up of similar groups of letters even if the order of the letters differed. His definitions were brief, but he seems to have elaborated where he felt it necessary. An early lexicographer, his etymologies are often faulty. The Karaite David ben Abraham al-Fasi (tenth century) composed a biblical dictionary which is really a concordance. Following a strictly alphabetical order—vitiated, however, by his belief in the existence of one- or two-letter roots—he gives the meaning of the vocables, often adding explanatory comments of grammatical, philosophical or other nature. Three centuries later, the commentator Tanhum of Jerusalem issued his *Adequate Guide*, which was designed to serve as a convenient handbook in Arabic for the vocabulary of Maimonides's Hebrew code, *Mishne Torah*, and for that section of the mishnaic terminology which was not utilized by the codifier. He felt that notwithstanding the existence of the *Aruk*, an eleventh-century talmudical dictionary, his work was needed because the former was rare, too compendious and of defective arrangement, due to its faulty understanding of grammar. Although Tanhum did not carry out his program fully, his work is useful because of the Arabic translation of the words, and also because by applying the triliteral system it accomplished for mishnaic Hebrew what Hayyuj and Janah did for its biblical phase.

Unlike the fields of biblical exegesis and philology, which were comparatively recent developments and, directly or indirectly, owed their existence to the stimulus received from Islam, the study of Talmud does not seem to have been interrupted from the time when it was first initiated. When the talmudic text was compiled, edited and declared closed, its study continued, although little material is traceable to the years 500-750. At any rate, the earlier works in Halaka during the Moslem period—responsa and codifications—were written in the Aramaic dialect which we find in the Talmud. But Arabic encroached on this field as well and challenged the supremacy of the former, and actually almost superseded it. Both the language and the method of presentation eventually attest the influence of the environment. A greater interest in systemization, in summaries, introductions and lexicography characterizes many of the halakic works in Arabic.

Once again the first outstanding author is Saadia. He enjoyed an illustrious reputation throughout the Middle Ages when his works were better known. From his extant writings, from fragments and from quotations found in books by later authorities, it is clear that he was an absolute master in Rabbinics, which he conceived to be not something additional and posterior to the Bible but an integral part of the one great unity, of Judaism, which dates from the time of Moses. His output was voluminous. He compiled compendia on legal subjects such as ritual slaughter, incest, documents and inheritance. He may have written an Introduction to the Talmud, of which, if the conjecture is correct, we still have his discussion of the thirteen hermeneutic principles for the study and expansion of the biblical law. He is also credited with either a commentary on, or a translation of the Mishna, or both. He seems to have compiled a Book of Commandments which, to judge from a recently discovered fragment, was a comprehensive list and analysis of the precepts of Jewish law. He is also the author of Responsa on various subjects. All the surviving halakic writing, and doubtless also the lost material exhibit the same system, logical order and comprehensive treatment that characterize his output in other fields. It is indeed unfortunate that so little of his contributions to Halaka has been preserved, probably because it was not translated into Hebrew.

Another Oriental talmudist who wrote in Arabic was Hefes ben Yasliah.

He probably lived after Saadia, but like those of the latter, his works also suffered a sad fate. Only fragments have survived. He compiled a comprehensive compendium of Jewish law called *Book of Precepts*, which he organized according to some plan into at least thirty-six sections. His method was to state the biblical source of the law and follow it with development and ramification in Rabbinic literature. But, ambitious and comprehensive as this program was, he went beyond it. He wrote a lengthy introduction in which, among other things, he expounded his plan and criticized the method and arrangement used by predecessors. In the body of the book he often digressed into lexicographic, philosophic and other fields, all of which undoubtedly enhanced both the quantity and the quality of the book. The extant portion includes about fifty precepts of probably 613, if, as appears probable, he followed the traditional pattern of listing that number. His influence was widespread, his book having been utilized by philologists like ibn Janah, exegetes like ibn Balam and halakists and philosophers like Bahya ben Pakudah and Maimonides.

Samuel ben Hofni (d. 1013), the most important Gaon of the Sura Academy after Saadia, seems to have employed Arabic in all his halakic writings. His output was so voluminous that a mere list of his works occupied two notebooks. He composed an Introduction to the Talmud in 145 chapters of which considerable fragments have survived. It included the history of the Talmud as well as an analysis of its method and terminology. In addition to a Book of the Laws, which may have presented a philosophic treatment of rational and traditional law and their sources, he wrote a large number of tracts on legal subjects, such as contracts, partnership, agency, court procedure, marriage and others. He seems to have participated in the lively religious polemic of his time, contributing a work which apparently dealt with the disputed problem of whether the Mosaic dispensation could be abrogated, as the Moslems contended.

Samuel's son-in-law, Hai Gaon (d. 1038), who became head of the Academy of Pumbedita after his father, the equally renowned Sherira (d. 1006), author of the famous epistle on the history of the Oral Law, wrote a number of volumes in Arabic on subjects of Jewish law. Of these, which included discussions on oaths, judges, pledges, loans and others, only fragments, if anything, have remained, either in Arabic or in Hebrew translation. The only complete item extant—in a Hebrew recension—is on purchase and sale. He is further credited with commentaries in several talmudic tractates. He also corresponded extensively, as did his predecessors and successors, replying to inquiries in the Bible, Talmud, law, prayer and worship, faith and reason and other subjects. From his responsa it can be concluded that he sought to interpret the Aggada rationally, eliminating the anthropomorphisms, and characterizing some miraculous incidents as dreams or visions of the mind's eye. He emphasized that one cannot rely on Aggada alone. His comparative broad-mindedness is illustrated by his request of aid from a Christian patriarch in the explanation of some biblical words.

By the end of the tenth century the Orient, generally speaking, yielded to the Spanish-Jewish center and the Franco-German Jewish communities, and the stream of halakic compositions continued in the West. However, on our way from the older to the newer homes of Jewish culture, we must linger with the North African settlement of Kairouan where, since the tenth century, a prosperous and intellectually alert Jewish community was in existence. Home of scholars in various fields, such as medicine, astronomy, philosophy and philology, its renown rests on its great Talmudists. Outstanding among them was Nissim ben Jacob, who flourished in the eleventh century. One of his major works, written in Arabic, is *The Key to the Locks of the Talmud*. Covering the entire Talmud, its aim was to shed light on indefinite and unsupported statements in this vast compendium by quoting the support and proof from where it may be found and by citing the *locus classicus* of all the Halakas that are stated elsewhere in the Talmud as accepted truths. A considerable portion of this voluminous work is still extant. His other major work, *A Secret Scroll*, is a compilation in Hebrew and Arabic of discussions of halakic and aggadic matter in Rabbinic literature. This work enjoyed wide circulation. Nissim also left us an interesting work which plainly ascribes its origin to the influence of Arabic literature. Its probable title was *Stories of the Sages, Being a Worthy Compilation for Comfort*. In the Introduction we are told that it was written for his father-in-law when the latter lost a son. Its purpose was to provide a book of Jewish content in place of the writings of "heretics," that is, Moslems, which his father-in-law would have read. It belongs to a type of literature which is known in Arabic by the name of "Comfort After Distress," and was calculated to distract people in their hour of sorrow. It is the popular counterpart of a more serious class of consolation literature which was produced by Jews, Christians and Moslems alike in the Middle Ages.

In Spain, the versatile Samuel Ha-Nagid (d. 1056),[11a] son-in-law of the preceding, statesman, poet and philologist, also excelled in talmudic studies. He is the author of an Arabic *Introduction to the Talmud* of which a considerable fragment is available in a Hebrew version. In this section he defines various technical terms and their implications and also establishes principles to determine whose opinion is to be accepted in case of controversy. It is evident that the Introduction was marked by a systematic and scientific approach. He also compiled a Code, which he called *Major Laws*, as a token of gratitude to God for having delivered him from his hostile captor. Too little is known of the work to enable us to characterize it, but in his poem, in which he tells us of his resolve to undertake this labor, he declares that it is his purpose to confound the Karaites. He also states there that Hai Gaon's works will be his chief guide.

The outstanding eleventh-century scholar is Isaac ben Jacob al-Fasi (d. 1103), but his main work is in Hebrew and Aramaic. His legacy in Arabic consists of some responsa and elucidations. The same is true of Joseph ibn Migas, for, although he also achieved great fame, his Arabic writings consist only of some responsa.

However, all these men are overshadowed by the truly gigantic achievements in Halaka[12a] of Moses ben Maimon, or Maimonides (d. 1204). Possessed of a vast erudition and an extraordinarily logical mind, he made an inestimably great contribution to Halaka. His first major work, chronologically, is a commentary on the complete Mishna, which he compiled while still a young man. His method of explanation is by the use of paraphrase. In each small unit—or Mishna, as it is called—he defines the difficult words and then summarizes its contents. Sometimes the definitions are woven into the paraphrase. In addition to the lucidity of the interpretation, evident throughout, and particularly in the order of *Toharot* (Laws of Cleanliness), his work is remarkable for the introductions and digressions of which there are several. It begins with a lengthy preface on the place of the Mishna in the Oral Law and on the plan followed by Rabbi Judah, the compiler of the Mishna, in the arrangement of the material. Besides this relevant matter it contains a statement on the author's views regarding the objectives of the world's creation and his assumption that all creation was meant to serve the intellectually and morally superior. He has brief introductions to the various tractates, and occasional notes within the body of the tractate in which he strives to put the reader in a position to understand the discussion in the text, a very helpful device in view of the practice of the Mishna to plunge into a subject in the belief that the reader is equipped to follow. To the ethical tractate of *Abot,* Maimonides wrote a lengthier preface in which he stated his views of the soul, its aspects, and the ethical and psychological principles that ought to guide an individual's life. Sometimes, as in the case of the chapter in the tractate of Sanhedrin which lists those who are and those who are not deserving of a portion in the world to come, he also prefaced an introduction on the subject, and, in the course of it, stated the thirteen articles of faith that are incumbent on the Jew. These, despite vigorous opposition, became virtually the accepted creed of the Jewish people.

Maimonides's greatest work in Halaka is his *Mishne Torah,* a compendium of the entire body of Jewish Law, both the part that is always operative and applicable and the part that is pertinent only in a Jewish state, or in Palestine, or when the Temple is in existence. This work, however, was written in Hebrew, the only one of his major works in that language. But he prepared a kind of outline of it in Arabic, which is known by its Hebrew name of *Sefer Ha-Mizvot*. Its purpose is to list the 613 laws that are traditionally regarded as Sinai-given. Before listing them, he enters into a lengthy discussion of the correct method in selecting the laws that properly form part of the 613. He points out errors and inconsistencies in the lists of his predecessors, stressing particularly the need to discriminate between a Mosaic and a Rabbinic ordinance. The work is characterized by the same strict logic that is evident in all his writings.

From the sketch of Maimonides's halakic writings we turn to consider important epistles left by him and by his father. The latter is the author of a pious and warm *Letter of Comfort* to the many Jews in the Moslem world who, as a result of the grievous persecutions by the Almohades in the middle of the twelfth century, were troubled and almost despaired of redemption. In the epistle, Maimon emphasizes that the promise which God made, supported as it is by the Bible and, notably, by the prophecy of Moses, whom the author characterizes in the most glorifying and adulatory terms, will most certainly be fulfilled. In connection with his exhortation he offers an edifying interpretation of Psalm 90, and recommends it as reading for those who are in difficulty.

From Maimonides's pen we possess a letter addressed to the same circle of readers, but more practical in its purpose and significance. He was deeply angered by the verdict of a contemporary Rabbi who ruled that crypto-Jews were apostates from Judaism. He felt rightly that the psychological effect of this ruling on the victims of the persecution would be disastrous, and he undertook to refute it. In his tract he makes a fine distinction between genuine and apparent conversion, and between the outward acceptance of Christianity and that of Islam. He offers the Jews sound advice to do everything possible to rid themselves of the duplicity by leaving the country, but at the same time he is passionate in his encouragement to the Marranos and in his desire to allay their fears.

Another writing, known as the *Epistle to Yemen*, also deals with persecution, this time in Arabia Felix. The contention of a converted Jew that Islam superseded the Mosaic dispensation, and the claim of another individual that he was the Messiah confused the Yemenite Jews and made a difficult life more difficult. Again Maimonides stepped in to bolster up failing spirits, to restore reason to well-meaning enthusiasts, and to keep alive in every Jew's heart the faith that he was following the right road, and the hope that salvation was not far.

Family talent was not exhausted by Maimon and his illustrious son. Abraham, the son of Moses, wrote a commentary on the Pentateuch, and a compendious work on Judaism, its principles, character, requirements and rewards. David, the son of Abraham, compiled a very readable commentary on the *Ethics of the Fathers*.

At least passing notice should be taken of a prayer book arranged by the indefatigable Saadia Gaon. In his usual manner he converted even this task into an important contribution. It comprises the laws of prayer in general, the regulations for the special occasions of the year, the ordinary prayers for private and public recitation, and a considerable body of liturgical poetry by him and by others. All this adds up to a very impressive performance, which is enhanced by the independence of mind that Saadia displays here as elsewhere.

A unique representative in Jewish literature of a genre which is extremely common in Arabic is found in a work produced by the renowned poet Moses ibn Ezra. As its florid Arabic title is a little hard to render, we may identify it by the title given it in its recent Hebrew translation: *The Poetry of Israel*. In response to a request for information, the author discusses such topics as the natural propensity of the Arabs toward poetry, the reason for the superiority of Spanish-Jewish poetry to that of other Jews, and the history of Hebrew poetry. His longest chapter is devoted to a discussion of the art of Hebrew poetry. In it he lists the various devices for enhancing the aesthetic appeal of verse and illustrates them by example from the Bible and later works. In this manner, as indicated previously, ibn Ezra displays an appreciation of the literary beauty of the Bible, which was generally overlooked until modern times. The charm of the work lies in its rambling, informal and intimate style, which puts the reader at ease. Ibn Ezra does not hesitate to digress, whether for the length of a chapter, as in his essay on the credibility of dreams, or for shorter stretches. This style of writing, generally known as *Adab*, is a very prominent feature of Arabic literature.

It is in the field of philosophy or, more correctly, religious philosophy or theology that the spirit of Judeo-Arabic literature reveals itself most fully. For one thing, the concern with the problems that form the substance of theological speculation marks a new departure. There was, it is true, Philo in Alexandria who wrote on philosophy. There are, it is true, numerous questions touched on in Rabbinic literature which properly belong to the realm of theology. But Philo's work and conclusions were not directly absorbed into the stream of Jewish thinking even if its influence may be discovered in one Rabbinic statement or another. Philo's work was not sufficiently rooted in Jewish lore, for his knowledge of that lore was deficient, so that extrinsically, let alone intrinsically, it had the appearance of an alien product.[13a] And the Rabbinic manner of dealing with its problems, by finding its support in a biblical verse, or reconciling two seemingly contradictory verses, however definitely it may represent an earnest desire to understand a certain problem or to solve a certain difficulty, cannot be called formal theology. Nor can the mystical speculations that were influenced by Gnosticism be regarded as theology, even if they concerned themselves with the celestial sphere, God and His throne, or the angels. The theological literature that was produced in the period under consideration is the effect of factors which played a major role in that period, characterized by qualities inherent in it, and permeated by an attitude peculiar to it.

Basically the impact that brought about this theological activity came from Greek and Oriental philosophy. The Jews, however, became conscious of this influence in the Moslem milieu and in an Arabic version. Within this milieu they discovered not only some of the original writings of Plato and Aristotle with their Neoplatonic commentators, but also the clash and the consequent compromise evolved in the Christian church; the polemics between the Christians and the Moslems, or between Oriental religions and the Moslems; the questionings and the doubts within the Moslem world; the rational, antireligious challenge and attacks by various people; the anti-Jewish arguments from several quarters; and certain centrifugal, disruptive tendencies which had developed in the Jewish community under these several influences. As a result, the theological or philosophical inquiries and analyses that abound in Judeo-Arabic may be reasonably regarded not as a luxury but as a necessity. Of course, it may not have been a necessity for those who remained entirely unaffected by the lively discussions and disputations, but it was a necessity for those who felt the challenge, either in their own lives or in the lives of fellow Jews whom they wished to set aright.

For purpose of simplification it is best to classify the Jewish philosophic writings, like their Moslem parallels, into three categories. One of these is known as Kalam.[14a] Its underlying physical premise is that all existence is composed of atoms, which form the substance, characterized by certain properties, which are called accidents. The latter are constantly changing since their duration is only momentary. As no object can be conceived without its properties and these are constantly created, it follows that all existence must have been created, and in this way it establishes creation. It further argues that this created world must have been fashioned by an outside force, namely, God. Among the Jewish philosophers who employed the system of Kalam, not all adopt the atomic theory. The most notable among them, Saadia Gaon, does not incline to it, preferring a variety of the Aristotelian conception of matter and form. They all, however, share in common the view that God's existence is proved by establishing the fact of creation and thus necessitating a creator. The Jewish philosophers, following the Mutazilites, one of the two schools of Moslem Kalam, are inclined to deny that God possesses attributes which stand in the same relation to Him as do properties to substances. Again, like their Moslem models, they devote much attention and space to God's justice, discussing under this heading revelation and prophecy, reward and punishment, good and evil, freedom of the will, the problem of the suffering of the righteous, and so forth. The best known work of this type is the *Book of Beliefs and Doctrines* by Saadia Gaon. He accounts for his composition of the book by explaining that as a result of the philosophic currents, doubts and perplexities and criticism have been engendered in the minds of many Jews, which threaten their loyalty to the faith. He defines our sources of knowledge, counting, in addition to the three channels of perceptual, conceptual and rationally necessary, also historical, or information reported from others. This last means, by the aid of which, as is known, so much of our knowledge is attained, serves Saadia to confirm the other source of truth, revelation. For, although he is convinced of the divine character of the Bible, and also of the complete identity of true revelation and reason, he is scientist enough to seek to demonstrate the veracity of the tradition regarding revelation, so that it might not be challenged on the basis of method. Moreover, he is rationalist enough, despite his unshaken faith in the truth of the Bible, to concede that whenever the biblical text contradicts reason the text is to be interpreted so as to obviate that contradiction.

His method in elucidating the verities of the Jewish faith in the light of reason is on two levels. In the case of a large part of the Jewish creed, he works on the assumption that it is rationally demonstrable. In this manner he proves, for example, that reason compels the belief in creation, in the existence and unity of God, in revelation, in reward and punishment, and in freedom of the will. In the case of some specifically religious articles of faith, such as the purely traditional laws, the graphic description of the procedure in the world beyond, the resurrection, Messianic times and the like, he feels it his task to prove that they are not contrary to reason. It is interesting to note that Saadia succeeds in preserving the entire religious legacy, even to details which are really incidental, from the attack of rationalism.

There were other able Kalam theologians among both Rabbanites and Karaites, with more or less original contributions. But while among the latter Kalam remained the accepted system to the end of the philosophic writing activity, Rabbanite philosophers turned from it to other systems, to Neoplatonism and to Aristotelianism with Neoplatonic coloring.

In the view of Neoplatonic philosophy, the cardinal difficulty is that of reconciling the composite, corruptible world, in which evil and wickedness inhere, with its Creator, the perfect and unique God. Its basic principle, formulated in order to resolve that difficulty, is emanation, that is, the doctrine that the entire universe, including the sublunar world, stems from God not by an act of creation but by a series of evolutions. God, as it were, separated part of Himself from Himself, without however, diminishing Himself in any way, and this part, in turn, evolved another from itself, and the next as well, and the next, until the celestial, as well as the terrestrial, world came into being. Taken over by some Jewish philosophers, it confronted them with the task of integrating this conception with the Jewish doctrine. The work of Philo, the first-century Neoplatonist, who, in his Greek writings, sought to identify the Jewish and the philosophic teachings, left little or no effect on Jewish thinking except, perhaps, through indirect channels. Medieval thinkers who favored this view were compelled to find their own solutions. The celebrated Jewish physician Isaac ben Solomon Israeli (d. *c.* 950), for example, made room for the belief in creation by apparently excluding the terrestrial world from the system of emanations and regarding it as an outcome of a *fiat* by God.

On the other hand, the most important and profound Jewish Neoplatonist, Solomon ben Judah ibn Gabirol (d. *c.* 1050),[15a] the renowned poet and ethical writer, whose philosophic work *The Fountain of Life,* originally written in Arabic, is extant only in a Latin translation, was evidently so firmly convinced of his view of the universe that he made almost no concession to Jewish beliefs, but chose rather to write philosophy pure and simple with no effort at reconciliation and no utilization of alleged proof from biblical or Rabbinic texts. Believing that matter, which he defined as that aspect of an object on which the form is impressed, underlies every existing thing, he assumed the existence of Universal Matter. Parallel to it, he postulated the existence of Universal Form, which is what distinguishes one object from another. This dualism which, in his view, extends from the lowest to the highest entities in the universe, could not be accounted for by the usual Neoplatonic explanation that as the emanations receded further from their source they became more composite, coarser, more material and corruptible. Since, in his opinion, matter is at least as noble as form, and is found in the celestial and in the intellectual worlds, he was obliged to trace both to God, their primary source. As he did not resort to creation, he endeavored to obviate the difficulty by assuming an intermediate force between God and the world. This force, which he calls the Will, he defines but vaguely (perhaps, as a statement in his *Fountain of Life* has been understood, because he discussed it separately in a no longer existing work), and students are perplexed as to its nature and to its capacity to serve as the source of both matter and form. However, notwithstanding some difficulties in his system he is acknowledged by modern scholars as an original and deep thinker. Although among Jewish philosophers his theories did not spread widely, owing to the domination of Aristotelianism among them, he exerted a far-reaching influence on Christian theologians such as William of Auvergne and Duns Scotus, who adhered to his views, and even on opponents such as Albertus Magnus and Thomas Aquinas.

Ibn Gabirol is also the author of a popular and none too profound ethical work, *On the Improvement of the Qualities of the Soul*. Starting with the assumption that physically man is the most harmonious of all creatures, and intellectually he is on a par with the angels, he teaches that man, a microcosm, should strive to preserve in the exercise of his qualities the same harmony which is so evident in his counterpart, the macrocosm. In an original, if forced, distribution of ten cardinal virtues and ten cardinal faults among the five senses, four to each, he urges control and discipline of these, counseling the practice of the Aristotelian golden mean. The work abounds in biblical citations, as also in sayings of Greek philosophers. Of the latter, ibn Gabirol compiled a collection called *The Choice of Pearls*, which enjoyed much popularity.

Bahya ben Joseph ibn Pakudah (d. *c.* 1100), author of the *Duties of the Heart*, is correctly described as a religious thinker rather than as a philosopher. Philosophically, as evident from his proof of the existence of God, he stands on Kalam ground. In his ideals, however, and the means to attain them, he is firmly rooted in Jewish tradition, although he is also beholden to Neoplatonism and to Moslem asceticism, which is itself deeply colored by the latter. The ideal he urges is the attainment of the stage in which the individual experiences a love of God. It is reached when man has realized God's greatness and providence, on the one hand, and man's insignificance and helplessness, on the other. The means required to reach that are given in the chapters of the book and their contents can be surmised from the headings, which include God's unity, consideration of creation, trust in God, humility, penitence, love of God and others. Bahya's work in its Hebrew version has become one of the most popular Jewish books and was studied by Jews even in cultural centers where philosophy did not gain a foothold.

Although certain Neoplatonic influences may be discovered in his system of philosophy, the most beloved medieval Jewish poet, Judah Ha-Levi (d. *c.* 1140), is the most independent and original thinker of the Jewish-Arabic period.[16a] Like his older contemporary in the Moslem world, Abu Hamid al-Ghazali, he was aware of the inadequacy of metaphysical reasoning, and, in his book called *Al Khazar* with its subtitle, the "Arguments and Proofs in Behalf of the Disparaged Religion," he followed another road. Ha-Levi was far from being an antirationalist. On the contrary, to the extent to which he believed its reasoning valid, he utilized the method and conclusions of philosophy. Moreover, it was his purpose to make his own doctrine rationally demonstrable. But he objected to the position taken by philosophy on matters which, in his mind, were within the domain of religion and hence superrational. He did not feel that its evidence for the existence of God was adequate. He resented its conception of God as an inactive, disinterested force, and its indifference to religious works or to the relative validity of one religion as over against another. He disagreed entirely with the conceit of philosophers that by their efforts or methods they could attain the rank of prophecy, or the true knowledge of God, and the bliss which that elevated state bestows on man. The precious gifts that living with God brings to man are acquired not by man's intellect but by knowing and doing what God has taught. The basic capacity to lead such a life is bestowed by Him. It is "a Divine matter," as Ha-Levi calls it, a special talent or quality which God grants. Historically, Ha-Levi finds, following the story of the Bible, the "Divine matter" became the heritage of Israel. Moreover, Ha-Levi, alone among medieval Jewish philosophers, regards Palestine as an essential factor in the destiny of Israel. It is the only land where Israel, endowed with the Divine matter, can, in an almost biological sense, grow and prosper, in the same way as fruits and vegetables will grow only in the appropriate soil and climate. This special quality of the Jewish people is what gained for them the revelation of God and the rank of prophecy. The revelation on Mt. Sinai, an undoubted fact, as judged by medieval standards of historical knowledge, is at once the firmest proof of the existence of God, the most valid evidence of the election of Israel, and the clearest statement of the correct and only method of attaining the coveted degree of God's favor and love. Thus, in Ha-Levi's view, the Jewish religion as it was developed and practiced by the Rabbis, rather than any philosophy, is the proved way to follow, and the Jewish people, rather than any self-appointed group of elect individuals, are humanity's most privileged species. Their present sad state is due to their sins and, particularly, to their failure to return to the appropriate soil when the opportunity was afforded. It is significant that the Jewish spokesman (the book is in the form of a dialogue between a pagan king who is eventually converted to Judaism and a representative of the Jewish faith) concludes the discussion with the decision to settle in Palestine, so as to find for himself the proper place in which he can best live the fullest Jewish life. Because of its religious fervor and its passionate defense of Israel and its Law, the book enjoyed tremendous popularity among the Jews.

Medieval Aristotelianism and Neoplatonism were not so sharply divided as in ancient times. The latter, though it postulated the emanation of the entire universe from God, recognized a dualism of matter and form in the sublunar world and, in the philosophy of ibn Gabirol, this dualism is evident in the entire universe. Aristotle's teachings, on the contrary, were suffused with a strong Neoplatonic coloring because, through a bibliographic error, part of a work by the Neoplatonist Plotinus was accepted as a writing of Aristotle. As a result, medieval Aristotelianism also speaks of emanation, and the dualism that is so fundamental in the master's teachings is at first confined to the terrestrial world, and is no longer a universal principle. It also considers the bliss that comes from a union with God rather than from a knowledge of God, as the goal of man.

Yet certain differences remained or became more emphasized. The dualism of matter and form, as the two extreme poles of existence, was much more prominent in Aristotelianism, and eventually matter was excluded from the process of emanation. Not only God, pure form, and the source of all form, is eternal and pre-existent, but also pure, formless matter. In Aristotelianism, one could talk with even less justice than in Neoplatonism of an act of creation, in view of the eternal coexistence of both matter and form. Aristotelianism further taught that God is Thought thinking Itself, creating the problem of what God knows of the world. The soul was regarded by it as the form of the body rather than an emanation of the Universal soul of Neoplatonism, and immortality became a more difficult problem. The theory of knowledge, too, although influenced by the Neoplatonist view of the action of the Active Intellect on a passive human mind, regained much of Aristotle's contention that it is dependent on perceptual knowledge and the abstraction of the latter, giving a new importance to logic and to natural philosophy.

Moreover, in the problem facing medieval Moslem and Jewish philosophers, the reconciliation of philosophy and religion, Aristotelianism proved to be a formidable system to bend and adapt. For despite the apparent similarity between reason and faith in their recognition of God, of purpose in the Universe, of a variety of immortality, of a discipline to which man must subject himself, the divergences nevertheless remained distinct. The God of Aristotle, even in his medieval definition, is most impersonal and inactive; the philosopher's purpose of the Universe is the result of a natural order which necessarily proceeds from certain eternally functioning laws, and is not subject to any direct control or voluntary regulation; its immortality a vague abstraction in place of the richly colored belief of religion; its discipline an intellectual rather than a moral system. It left little room for prophecy or revelation; it had no need of what were called traditional, or revealed, laws. In general, it was intellectual, rational, rigid and antagonistic to the irrational, romantic and intuitive, which religion brings with it.

Of the two outstanding Jewish Aristotelians, Abraham ibn Daud (d. c. 1180) did not achieve great importance because he was justly overshadowed by his superior successor Maimonides. Although ibn Daud justified the composition of the book *The Noble Faith* as a solution to the issue of the freedom of the will, he does not treat the latter more prominently than other philosophic problems. He gives a lengthy exposition of the physical world in preparation for the proof of the existence of God, and of the psychological world as background for the proof of the belief in immortality. He adopts the Aristotelian argument in proof of the existence of the First Cause, but for him, as for Moslem Aristotelians, it is not only the first cause of motion, but also the first cause of existence, and God the Creator. The contradiction between this and the theory of universal emanation, superimposed upon Aristotelianism, he solves by rejecting the latter, because it does not fit his Judaism; yet he adopts some of the teachings of emanation, such as the development of the terrestrial world out of the superlunar. In his teachings regarding the soul, he argues, like his Moslem predecessor ibn Sina, that, although it may be regarded as the form of the human body, the postulate that the form perishes with the object does not apply to it. It is obviously an independent, immaterial force in the body, and as such, immortal even if the body is mortal. This immortality, however, is limited to the intellectual part of the soul, which receives its knowledge from the Active Intellect. Its highest degree is prophecy, but it is unique in that it receives knowledge concerning the future. He goes even further and sees in prophecy, contrary to its apparently natural origin, a mission from God by which He instructs the less gifted, and even limits this gift to Israel and to Palestine. He predicates complete freedom of the will for man, and obviates the difficulty of accepting this freedom in the light of God's omniscience by limiting God's foreknowledge just as His omnipotence is limited from including human actions. In his ethical teachings, he naturally identifies the doctrines of Plato and Aristotle, which were joined by medieval philosophers, with the teachings of the Torah. While, in Aristotelian fashion, the knowledge of the celestial world is the goal of man, his main ideal is to know God, and through knowledge to gain the love of God, which is the highest happiness of man.

By his comprehensive work in philosophy called *Guide for the Perplexed*, and by the dominant position he held in Jewish and in general philosophy for the three centuries following his, Maimonides came to be recognized as the outstanding medieval Jewish thinker.[17a] While he assumed as fully as his predecessor that philosophy and religion teach the same truth, he was far more conscious than ibn Daud of the disagreements of the two sources of truth, much more conscientious in threshing the difficulties out, and much more desirous of arriving at a valid synthesis. He opens his work, which is divided into three parts, with a penetrating analysis of words and phrases in the Bible which at first glance are anthropomorphic and anthropopathetic. He disposes of them by predicating that such expressions, when applied to God, have a different meaning, and that their purport is to indicate the effect of God's work or providence in the Universe. From this he proceeds to a keen study of the vexing question of God's attributes, and takes the position that whereas we have the right to describe God by adjectives which indicate our reactions to Him, such as merciful, sovereign and the like, we have no right to apply to God any term which will imply that a certain characteristic is inherent in Him. He is so singularly One, so uniquely Himself, that any statement regarding His essence impugns His Oneness. The best we can do is to speak of Him negatively or to

understand that when we say anything positive of Him we merely mean to
imply that He is not the opposite. When we say, for example, that He is
existent, we assert that He is not nonexistent, not that His essence possesses
the attribute of existence. What it really amounts to is that all of God's
attributes are really He, and not distinguishable from Himself. The
concept, however, is so difficult to understand that Maimonides justly
admits that we have no way of knowing God except in a moment of
illumination.

Only after the author has stated his views of God's attributes, and
critically refuted the philosophy of Kalam, does he turn to the question
of God's existence. His purpose is to make the proof of the existence of
God independent of the problem of the world's creation, so that if the
latter should prove to be nondemonstrable, the belief in the existence of
God would not thereby be affected. With this in view, he utilizes the
Aristotelian argument of the First Mover, Who is the cause of all motion
in the Universe, and is God. He also employs an argument from Moslem
Aristotelians, distinguishing between the universe which is possibly existent, that is, might or might not exist, and God, Who is necessarily
existent, implying that God is not only the Prime Mover, but also the
First Cause of the Universe. By these proofs Maimonides establishes
God's existence, simplicity and eternity. After developing the system
of emanations which came into Aristotelianism, he turns to the problem of
creation versus eternity. After a lengthy and intricate examination of the
pros and cons of both, he concludes that neither is demonstrably certain,
and therefore decides in favor of creation by bringing the religious belief
as an arbiter.

In his interpretation of prophecy, Maimonides shares with Aristotelian
philosophy the view that it results from the close natural relation between
the potential prophet and the Active Intellect. However, he recognizes
that a naturally endowed prophet requires God's Will before he can
prophesy, and that the figurative form in which prophecies are delivered
is the result of the imaginative faculty of the soul in addition to the intellectual. The prophet, although he is necessarily a philosopher, is
superior to the latter in that he succeeds in acquiring that knowledge of
God which comes through illumination alone. Maimonides also makes
an exception for Moses, declaring him to have been a prophet *sui generis*.
In this way he makes Moses unique and similarly his revelation or the
Torah. They are not higher degrees of certain types but single examples in
their fields. The purpose of prophecy is to bring a certain amount of
necessary information to the masses who are not equipped to acquire it
by their own initiative.

Maimonides, as we have seen, diverges from strict Aristotelianism in
the problems of creation and of prophecy. He also shows his independence
in the assertion that the miracles related in the Bible are true and that

they formed from eternity part of God's plan of the universe, and that God knows every human action. Maimonides at the same time preserves the freedom of the will by arguing that God's foreknowledge is essentially different from the human, and the apparent contradiction between freedom of the will and knowledge is not true of God. There are, however, important religious principles regarding which Maimonides follows the Aristotelian view more closely. He defines the rational soul as the part that acquires knowledge from the Active Intellect, and limits immortality to it alone. He relates providence to the same Active Intellect and man's share in providence in proportion to his share in the knowledge which can be acquired from it. Although he recognizes the importance of moral living, it is only a means to a higher end, the intellectual perfection toward which man should strive. This makes Torah and religious living not ends in themselves but means to a loftier goal. Maimonides makes a strong effort to find a rational explanation for the laws of the Torah, and endeavors to show that traditional laws whose reasons are not apparent are either pedagogical in aim, in that they strengthen certain moral qualities within us, or a reaction to the habits and practices of the times when the Torah was revealed, whether as a concession to them or a rejection of them. The highest perfection is that which can be reached by the philosopher. In a famous example of Maimonides in which he likens the Object of human striving, as he conceives it, to a king within a palace, and the several classes of people to groups who seek to stand before the king, the talmudists are not successful in entering the palace. It is the philosopher who comes closest to Him. It should be noted that this highest bliss is not a union with God in any mystical sense but a supreme state of knowledge and the love that results from it.

After the departure of Maimonides from Spain in 1148, as a result of the religious persecutions instituted by the fanatical Moslem sect known as the al-Muwahhidun (Almohades), he lived in the Orient and produced his greatest works there. His son Abraham compiled an ethical work called by the translator of a part of it *The Highway to Perfection,* and his disciple Joseph ibn Aknin is similarly the author of an ethical treatise *The Hygiene of the Soul.* From his grandson's pen we have an interesting commentary on the *Ethics of the Fathers.* Since then, down to the present, Judeo-Arabic literature has continued in lands where Arabic has remained the spoken and written language, but its significance, save for some few exceptions, is minor, and its importance is local.

In Spain, Arabic writing practically ceased among the Jews after Maimonides. The period of intense religious zeal was finally succeeded by sweeping victories celebrated by the Spanish Christians, who were bent on freeing their land from Moslem hold. The thirteenth century saw the almost complete liberation of Spain. With the fall of Islam and the domination of Latin and Spanish, Judeo-Arabic production virtually came to an end. Subsequent creations were usually written in Hebrew. It may be added in passing that Hebrew played a significant role at this stage in the transmission of Moslem lore to the Western world. Many works were rendered into Latin not from their original Arabic but from the Hebrew version, either prepared for Jewish consumption and utilized by a Latin translator, or deliberately made for retranslation by a man who did not know Latin for a man who did not know Arabic.

But the gradual elimination of Arabic as the vernacular of the Jews in Spain did not simultaneously result in the elimination of the written monuments from Jewish life in Christian countries, not to speak of the Moslem world. Even before that time came, an interest in Judeo-Arabic literature was aroused among the Jews in neighboring Provence and Italy. Already in the twelfth century we find Judah ibn Tibbon busily engaged in Provence in translating grammatical and philosophical books into Hebrew at the request of Jewish intellectuals. This activity was maintained in succeeding generations by members of his family and others in Spain, Provence and Italy, until a considerable portion of the Judeo-Arabic legacy became available in Hebrew. Many works were unfortunately neglected, and of these some were preserved in libraries as silent witnesses of an outlived era in Jewish life, and others irretrievably lost. We should not, however, overlook the numerous Hebrew works written by men who were still conversant with Arabic, in which more or less of the lore of the ancients is preserved. Several of the translations, particularly in philosophy and ethics, made their way even into the German-Polish center, which knew little of, and was interested even less in, the diversified Jewish productivity that had flourished in the Moslem environment. Indeed, it is an irony of fate that some originally Arabic works enjoyed a far better fortune than many, if not most, of the originally Hebrew works which did not deal with Halaka or exegesis. The reaction against secular literature that was especially prevalent in northern Europe and Poland hit belles-lettres hardest, and it is remarkable to record that poets and storytellers who deliberately preferred to write in Hebrew even when the vogue was to employ Arabic were the men whose creations were the least sought after, so that they became the easiest prey of the ravages of time and bookworms.

The work pursued so actively in Moslem Spain was taken up in the Hebrew language in Spain, Provence and Italy. In the first two centers until the expulsion, and in Italy even after, individuals continued to write poetry and literary prose and to study science and philosophy. This work maintained the tradition so nobly begun under the Moslems, and although, as was the case of the authors who functioned in Italy, the Renaissance that was experienced by that land unquestionably left its mark on Jewish creativity, the activity was the continuation of the literary life begun under Judeo-Arabic stimulation and, what is just as important, the subject-matter and even the artistic devices were clearly modeled after the products of that period. Above all, however, the noteworthy fact is that the interest in belles-lettres, in science, in philosophical and theological problems, and the general concern with the world beyond their own kept alive and furthered a stimulus begun in Spain and bequeathed to these lands. And just as in its day Jewish Spain was distinguished from other European Jewries by this diversity of culture,[18a] so Italian Jewry was alone in Europe in the cultivation and preservation of the secular studies. Northern and eastern Europe remained virtually as unaffected by either the legacy of Spain or its extension in Italy as it had been centuries before when southwestern Europe went through a rich development. Only when the European Enlightenment began to show its effects in central and eastern Europe, and Jews were stirred to ask more of life politically as well as culturally, did they develop an interest in secular literature.

On the threshold of this transformation stands the great eighteenth-century Italian-Jewish poet and mystic Moses Hayyim Luzzatto.[19a] Scholars are divided on whether to consider him the father of the new wave of cultural creativity, which was imminent in Germany, Austria and Russia, or the last of the era in Italy, whose beginnings go back to the twelfth century. This uncertainty regarding the individual carries a symbolic significance. One is hardly entitled to claim that modern Hebrew literature is indebted to Judeo-Arabic writings, but one can say with full justice that it is a link in the golden chain that was first forged in biblical times, and, after a long interruption, resumed in the Moslem world, whence it has continued steadily to our day. Indeed the contribution of the Judeo-Arabic period lies not alone in the rich legacy of works which exerted a profound influence on subsequent Jewish thought, but in that it kindled a light which, sometimes glowing brilliantly, sometimes merely flickering, continued to burn until it gained a new brilliance in modern Hebrew literature. Traveling by way of Provence, Italy and Holland, medieval literature found a fertile soil in eastern Europe, where Jewish life pulsated at its strongest in the nineteenth century, and there it once again began a rich and variegated activity which continues right to the present in several Jewish centers and, most notably, in Palestine.

NOTES

[[1a] Cf. above Judah Goldin, "The Period of the Talmud (135 B.C.E.-1035 C.E.)," pp. 181 ff.]

[[2a] Cf. above the chapter by Hillel Bavli, "The Modern Renaissance of Hebrew Literature," and the one below by Yudel Mark, "Yiddish Literature."]

[3a Cf. above Elias J. Bickerman, "The Historical Foundations of Post-biblical Judaism," pp. 93 ff.]

[4a Cf. above Cecil Roth, "The European Age in Jewish History (to 1648)," pp. 233 f.]

[5a Cf. above the chapter by Shalom Spiegel, "On Medieval Hebrew Poetry."]

[6a Cf. Goldin, *op. cit.*, pp. 197 f.]

[7a Cf. *ibid.*, pp. 191 f.]

[8a On the Sura Academy, cf. *ibid.*, pp. 177-178.]

[9a Cf. *ibid.*, pp. 161 f.]

[10a Cf. *ibid.*, pp. 148-149.]

[11a Cf. Spiegel, *op. cit.*, pp. 875-876.]

[12a Cf. Goldin, *op. cit.*, pp. 159-160.]

[13a Cf. above Alexander Altmann, "Judaism and World Philosophy," pp. 957 ff.; also Ralph Marcus, "Hellenistic Jewish Literature," pp. 1107 ff.]

[14a Cf. Altmann, *op. cit.*, pp. 968-969.]

[15a Cf. Spiegel, *op. cit.*, pp. 876-877.]

[16a Cf. Altmann, *op. cit.*, pp. 972-973; for his poetry see Spiegel, *op. cit.*, pp. 877-879.]

[17a Cf. Altmann, *op. cit.*, pp. 973 f.]

[18a Cf. Roth, *op. cit.*, pp. 223-224, 234.]

[19a Cf. Spiegel, *op. cit.*, pp. 883-884.]

BIBLIOGRAPHY

HALPER, BEN-ZION, "Jewish Literature in the Arabic Language," (Hebrew) in *Ha-Tekufah*, XXIII, 262-275. Warsaw, 1925. And XXIV, 359-388. Berlin, 1928.

KARPELES, GUSTAV, *Geschichte der juedischen Literatur* (3rd. ed.) Berlin, 1920-1921. Vol. I, 398-448.

STEINSCHNEIDER, MORITZ, *Die arabische Literatur der Juden*. Frankfort a.M., 1902.

———, *Jewish Literature from the Eighth to the Eighteenth Century*. London, 1857. Pp. 59-203.

WAXMAN, MEYER, *A History of Jewish Literature from the Close of the Bible to Our Own Days*. New York, 1930-1941. Vol. I, pp. 155-375.

ZINBERG, ISRAEL, *Geschichte fun der literature bei Yiden* (Yiddish) (History of Literature among the Jews). Wilna, 1929, Vol. I.

ARNOLD, SIR THOMAS, and GUILLAUME, ALFRED (eds.), *The Legacy of Islam*. Oxford, 1931.

FRIEDLAENDER, ISRAEL, "Jewish Arabic Studies," in *Jewish Quarterly Review*, new series, I, pp. 183-215; II, pp. 481-516; III, pp. 235-300. Philadelphia, 1910-1912.

O'LEARY, DE LACY, *Arabic Thought and its Place in History*. London, 1922.

TRITTON, A. S., *The Caliphs and Their Non-Muslim Subjects*. London, 1930.

CHAPTER 25

ISRAEL IN IRAN
(A Survey of Judeo-Persian Literature)

By Walter J. Fischel

INTRODUCTION

The history of Persia from its very beginning until today, from Cyrus the Great to the Pehlevi dynasty—a history covering twenty-five centuries equally divided by the Arab conquest of the year 642 into a pre-Islamic and an Islamic period—has seen an uninterrupted and continuous association between Iran and Israel. Israel has been living on Iran's soil from the dawn of the first Persian Empire on, as an inseparable part of Iran's national destiny and development. Jews were the eyewitnesses of all the historical events in Persia under every dynasty—the Achamenids, Parthians and Sassanids, the Omayyads and the Abbassids, the Seljuks, Mongols, Safavids and Kajars, under every ruler, Caliph, Sultan, Il-khan, Emir or Shah. Jews were the contemporaries of all the manifold religious movements and sects that were born on Persian soil, such as Zoroastrianism, Manicheism, Shi'a, Sufism, Bahaism; they were companions of the great classical poets, of a Firdusi, Hafiz, Sa'adi, Jami, and of all the other great Persian masters of art, literature and philosophy who made their everlasting contributions to world culture.

Did this twenty-five centuries old association of "Iran and Israel" produce any literary works of value on the part of the Persian Jews? What is the literary heritage of Persian Jews that has come down to us as a result of twenty-five hundred years of Iranian-Jewish association? Have Persian Jews left a cultural legacy, a literature which bears the distinct stamp of Israel in Iran and which could be regarded as a typical and specific contribution of their own in the sphere of Jewish and Persian culture and scholarship—in the Islamic period?

In other words, did this association of twenty-five hundred years between Israel and Iran produce any lasting values in the realm of culture and scholarship?

EARLY INTELLECTUAL CO-OPERATION BETWEEN MOSLEM AND JEWISH SCHOLARS

The first recorded appearance of Persian Jews in the cultural sphere after the Arab conquest took the form of sectarian and heterodox movements. More than any other group of Oriental Jewry it was the Persian Jews who had been affected by the intellectual commotion which the conquest of the Arabs and the collision of victorious Islam with older religious systems and movements on Persian soil had produced. It was, as has been recognized, in conjunction with and parallel to the sectarian movements in Persia and as their reflection that Persia became also the birthplace of Jewish sects, the home of pseudo-messianic rebels and heretics. All the various manifestations of Jewish sectarianism in early Islam are geographically as well as spiritually, to a large degree, products of the Persian Shiite environment, and bear very clearly the marks of Shi'a Islam. As the names and the origin of their spokesmen already indicate, Abu 'Isa came from Isfahan, his disciple Yudghan from Hamadan, Mushki from Qum, Hivi from Balkh, Abu 'Isa ben Levi, the friend of Ibn ar-Rawendi, from Ahwaz.

Even the Karaite movement,[1a] though basically different from these sectarian groups, was led by personalities who sprang from Persian soil, such as Benjamin from Nehavend, and Daniel ben Moses from Qumis, and many of their adherents, according to Qingisani, were to be found in Khorasan, in Jibal, Fars, Tustar and other parts of the Eastern Caliphate.

The leaders of these sectarian movements and their followers were mostly "a community of simple-minded, uneducated Jews, removed from the Babylonian center of talmudic learning," and therefore an easy prey to Messianic and heterodox ideas. They were described as "barbarian and ill-bred people, destitute of intellect and knowledge," and were condemned as "more ignorant than the rest of the Jews." In the light of statements of that kind, though they actually referred only to the sectarians, it was maintained that Persian Jews as a whole had ceased to be a cultural factor, that they had exhausted themselves and remained in a state of lethargy and intellectual stagnation. This assumption, however, can hardly be justified.

Despite their legal status as nonbelievers and hence separated from the Mohammedans, Persian Jews did not live in a spiritual vacuum. They were by no means mere eyewitnesses and observers. They may have lived physically in a Ghetto, but they shared the cultural and intellectual climate of their time and of all times, and were continuously affected by the cultural and religious conditions and conflicts in the world of their neighbors. The very rise of these sectarian movements, irrespective of

A PAGE FROM A JUDEO-PERSIAN MANUSCRIPT

From the Adeshir Book by the poet, Shahin, written in the 14th century in Hebrew in Persian characters. This manuscript was copied c. 1650.

In this illustration Shah Bahman (in the center) is being told of the disappearance of his son, Shero Bahman, according to Jewish tradition, especially by Shahin, was identified with Artaxerxes of the Book of Esther, and Shero was supposed to be the son of Vashti. (This information is given by Professor Walter J. Fischel.)

their merits, proves this interrelationship and interdependence of Iran and Israel.

This sectarianism was, however, but one manifestation of that interrelationship. It can hardly be overlooked that Jewish scholars from Persia and Khorasan actively participated in the intellectual trends of the "Golden Age" in the ninth and tenth centuries. One has only to glance through the famous literary depository, the *Fihrist*, or other contemporary Islamic sources, to realize how interwoven the intellectual activities of Jews and Moslems were and how numerous were the bonds that connected Israel and Iran.

Persian Jews could hardly have sunk as low as has been believed, when among them translators, scientists, poets, mathematicians and astronomers were found who served the rulers and their court, or who readily gave help and information whenever called upon. It is only because of the general anonymity of the process of cultural revival in Islamic society in the Middle Ages that more names of Jewish scholars from Persia and Khorasan have not been preserved.

It must also be noted that when the Old Testament and the history of Israel became the object of investigation by Persian scholars—as was already the case with Arab authors, such as Mas'udi—they called on Jewish scholars for authoritative advice and authentic information.

Largely responsible for this kind of intellectual co-operation, for the development of a sort of "Hebrew scholarship" among Persian scholars, was the so-called *"Shu'ubiyya"* movement. This movement, in the ninth and tenth centuries, was a literary reaction among Persian and other non-Arab Moslems against the claim of the Arabs concerning their racial, literary and linguistic superiority over non-Arab peoples. The leaders of this movement challenged this contention and tried to prove the equality of all Moslems or even the superiority of the non-Arab Moslems in the field of literary and linguistic accomplishments. It was this attitude that stimulated non-Arabs, composed of Syrians, Greeks, Copts, Persians and others, to stress the specific values of their own national and religious culture and to emphasize their own particular contribution in the fields of science and literature.

It is not without interest to mention that one of the most active promoters of these Shu'ubite, Iranophile tendencies was Abu Ubayda Mu'amar b. al-Muthanna (d. 825), a scholar whose grandfather was allegedly a Jew from Persia.

These endeavors, especially on the part of Moslem scholars of Persian origin, led to an interest in comparative studies of religion and culture. They satisfied their urge for knowledge of the culture of ancient peoples by getting into direct touch with the living representatives of ancient civilization. Stimulated by these Shu'ubiyya tendencies, some of the outstanding scholars, such as the historian Hamza al-Isfahani and the scientist, al-Biruni, consulted with Jewish scholars in order to understand the Jewish past.

This Hamza al-Isfahani (d. 963), by origin and education deeply rooted in Iranian civilization, devoted his energy to the acquiring of knowledge about the Bible and the Jewish past. Just as he derived his knowledge of other religions through personal contact with their respective representatives, he sought information concerning the Bible through the method of direct and personal contact with Jewish scholars. In his *Annals* he expressly mentions a book on Jewish chronology by an otherwise unknown Pinhas ibn Bata al'Ibrānī, which he had consulted with the help of a Jew. He refers also to the personal contact he had with a Jew by the name of Zidkiya, from whom he obtained a historical sketch of biblical chronology. Nor does he omit reference to another Jewish scholar, of whom he said, "I met in Bagdad in the year 921, one of the Jewish scholars who claims to know the books of the Torah by heart. I heard from one of his disciples that he could recite twelve books of the Prophets."

Al-Biruni (d. 1048), who might be regarded as the greatest of Moslem-Hebraists and who is justly considered the most original and profound thinker that Islam has produced in the realm of physical and mathematical science, derived his knowledge of Judaism by this very method of personal consultation with Jewish scholars. He drew his knowledge of Judaism not only from books of his predecessors, among whom that of al-Eranshahr must have figured prominently, but also, like Hamza al-Isfahani, from learned Jews whom he consulted during his travels through Persia, Khorasan and elsewhere. He recognized his indebtedness to Jewish scholars more than once and mentions the oral and written Jewish sources he had used. He pays tribute to a Jewish scholar by the name of Jacob ben Musa al-Nikrisi, of Jorjan, in the southeastern corner of the Caspian Sea, as one of his collaborators, and gives quotations also "in the name of a Jew who is considered a wise and learned man." He undoubtedly met with other Jewish scholars, Rabbanites or Karaites, who co-operated with him, and it was probably due to such co-operation that he also had access to such Hebrew written books as *Seder Olam* and *Megilat Taanit*. That his informants were Persian-speaking Jews is evident from the manner in which the many Hebrew terms and words which he mentions in his studies, notably in his *Chronology of Ancient Nations*, are vocalized and transliterated in his works.

Al-Biruni is, however, not the only one who offers proof of the cultural interchange between Israel and Iran. The study of the Bible and of Judaism, as well as other religions, was stimulated also by a movement, quite different from that of the *Shu'ubiyya*, namely, the *Isma'ili* movement.

The leaders of this branch of Shia Islam, in their attempt to propagate their ideas concerning the seventh Imam among all religions and creeds, and in their endeavor to bind together Arabs and Persians, Christians and Jews, and, indeed, all mankind, regarded as necessary the study of the holy books of other religions, including the Old Testament.

Nasir-i Khusraw (d. 1083), traveler, poet and scholar, one of the most colorful figures of eleventh-century Persia, was one of those Isma'ili missionaries who included in his studies the religion and history of other peoples. This keen observer of foreign lands and peoples put his impressions in his Persian-written *Safer-nama,* which is not only the first diary of a traveling philosopher known in the Persian language, but also the first and earliest Persian description of Palestine of the eleventh century. Nasir-i Khusraw noticed the flocking of the Jews to the Wailing Wall in Jerusalem and states: "From all the countries of the Greek, and from other lands, the Christians and the Jews come up to Jerusalem in order to make their visits to the Church of Resurrection and the Synagogue . . . that is there."

In Tiberias he noticed "a mountain upon which has been built in hewn stone, a castle, and there is an inscription in Hebrew characters, stating that at the time it was cut, the Pleiades stood at the head of the zodiacal sign of the Ram." This passage in his diary may allow the assumption that he was able to read the Hebrew script. Indeed, in his *Autobiography,* he mentions Hebrew among the various languages he had studied.

The interest of Isma'ili leaders in Hebrew and the Bible found an even clearer expression in the work of al-Kirmani (d. 1013), the chief missionary of the Isma'ili movement in Persia in the eleventh century. He inserted into his Arabic-written work on the *Imam,* Hebrew and Syriac Bible passages, which he quoted, not in translation, but in transliteration. We must assume in this, as in previous cases, that he derived his knowledge of Hebrew from co-operation with Jewish scholars who, in view of the specific pronunciation and transliteration of the Hebrew words, were undoubtedly Persian Jews.

Kirmani does not stand alone in this usage of Hebrew quotations and transliterations. The interest in comparative religious studies led more than one Moslem scholar to acquaint himself with the Hebrew Bible and other aspects of Jewish life. Shahrastāni of Ghazna (d. 1153), one of the outstanding Moslem historians of religion in medieval Islam, had a forerunner in Abu Ma'ali Mohammed ibn 'Ubaidallah (d. 1092), a Sunni Moslem. His *Bayyan al Adyan* (Treatise on the Religions), written as a result of a theological disputation at the court of the sultan in Ghazna, is not only the most ancient treatise on comparative religion in the Neo-Persian language, but also the first which does not limit itself to Islam alone, and encompasses all the religions of the world.

This Persian scholar dealt also with the various Jewish sects and beliefs, the institution of the Exilarchate,[2a] the Hebrew names of God in the Bible. Of particular interest in his account of the Jewish religion is his insertion of the first three words of the Pentateuch in their Hebrew form in Persian transliteration. As in the case of Kirmani and al-Biruni, these quotations undoubtedly presuppose direct contact and co-operation with Jewish scholars in Khorasan, though Abu Ma'ali does not reveal his source of information.

The existence of Jewish scholars among Isma'ili groups, such as the Assassins in medieval Persia, is well attested by the Jewish traveler, Benjamin of Tudela, who states: "There are learned men among the Jews of these lands."

This intellectual help which Persian Jews had rendered to Mohammedan scholars, this mutual borrowing, giving and taking through direct personal contact, must be regarded as an important factor, as a constructive and creative contribution of Persian Jews to the learning of their times. It undoubtedly serves as a barometer of the degree of their cultural assimilation and sheds light on one phase of the relationship between Israel and Iran.

The question, however, must still be asked, whether the century-long association of Israel and Iran has produced something more tangible and feasible than this intellectual co-operation indicates, and whether Jews have produced any literary works of their own in the language of the Persian Jews. In other words, did a Judeo-Persian literature develop?

In the first centuries after the Islamic conquest a Persian literature of the Jews could hardly be expected. Just as there was no literary production in the Persian language by Persian Mohammedans, so in these first centuries there could be no literary production in the Persian language by Persian Jews. It may be recalled that the Arab conquest of Persia in 642 meant not only the end of the political and national independence of Persia for many centuries to come; the military conquest of Persia was at the same time accompanied by a religious transformation leading gradually to the triumph of Islam over Zoroastrianism, to the replacement of Ormuzd by Allah, of Zoroaster by Mohammed, of the Avesta by the Koran, of the Fire-Temple by the Mosque.

But this religious transformation of Persia led also to a linguistic conquest which brought about another fundamental change in the cultural structure of Persia. With the introduction of Islam, Aramaic—then the lingua franca of the East—was superseded by the Arabic language and Arabic alphabet. This linguistic conquest, more effective than the religious one, ultimately made Arabic, the language of the conqueror, the only instrument and vehicle of expression by any creative Persian mind for centuries to come.

The Jews within Persian territory were also fundamentally affected by the victorious march of the Arabic language. Their literary productivity, if any, would no longer be expressed exclusively in Hebrew or Aramaic, but in Arabic. For the Jews in the realm of the Caliphate Arabic indeed became the language of conversation and literary production.

If we define Judeo-Persian literature as works composed by Persian Jews in the Persian language and written in Hebrew characters, then this type of literature could be expected to come into existence only when the Persian language had penetrated so deeply into the daily life of Persian Jews that they could use it for literary expression: when they had attained such a degree of cultural assimilation to their surroundings that they could become productive and creative in this language.

Early Judeo-Persian Documents

No attempt is made here to describe the various stages in the penetration of the Persian language into the daily life of Persian Jews. Nevertheless, it is evident that after the conclusion of the Talmud an ever-increasing infiltration of Persian into Jewish circles took place. Indications of this process are the presence of Persian linguistic elements in the late responsa literature; the use of Persian by Jewish scholars, especially Hai Gaon, to explain difficult Hebrew, Aramaic or Arabic words; the frequent occurrence of Persian words in the works of Karaite scholars of Persian origin. Moreover, some early documents have come to light which reveal the actual use of Persian by Persian Jews.

The earliest document that attests to the use of modern Persian by Jews is a fragment of a Persian business letter, only recently found at Dandan-Uylik, near Khotan, in Chinese-Turkestan—comprising thirty-seven Persian written lines in Hebrew characters by a Jewish merchant, probably of the early eighth century. This letter represents the sole specimen of early Hebrew script and at the same time the earliest available document in modern Persian of any sort. Also extant are four signatures in Persian with Hebrew characters by Jewish witnesses on a copper plate referring to a grant for a Christian church on the coast of Malabar (early ninth century), as well as a letter in Judeo-Persian from Ahwaz in Khuzistan of the year 1020.

We may assume that as a result of the revival of Persian language and literature from the end of the tenth century on, Persian became even more definitely established as the language of the Jews within the orbit of Persian culture. The statement of Judah ibn Tibbon that "most of the Geonim in the Dispersion under the rule of Ishmael in Babylon, Palestine and Persia were speaking Arabic, and likewise all the Jewish communities in those lands were using the same tongue . . . and whatever commentary they wrote on the Bible, Mishna and Talmud, they wrote in Arabic" was no longer applicable to Persian Jews of that time. This is confirmed by the fact that the Jewish leaders in Bagdad in the twelfth century found it necessary to use Persian in their correspondence with the Jewish communities in Persia. The *Igrot* of Rabbi Samuel b. Ali, the Gaon of Bagdad, which reveal so many details concerning the internal religious and cultural life of Jews in Babylonia and Persia, include a letter written by the Gaon Salomon of Bagdad in 1152 to a Jew in Hamadan by the name of Safi. This letter contains not merely Persian words, but is written almost entirely in the Persian language. It may well be that but for the fragmentary character of the correspondence we would have much more evidence for the ever-increasing assimilation of Persian Jews to the Persian language and culture in the twelfth century.

But these documents and letters, indicative of the new trend as they may be, can hardly be classified as literary products. In view of the absence of any literary records in Judeo-Persian until the thirteenth century, it seems that the Jews of Persia had not yet attained that degree of assimilation which would have enabled them to be creative in the Persian language. It took, as we shall see, another century for the spiritual energies, accumulated by the Persian Jews over centuries, to be released, and for conditions to be ripe for the birth and growth of a genuine Judeo-Persian literature.

The Genesis of Judeo-Persian Literature

It is significant that the first fruits of a genuine Judeo-Persian literature became visible only at a time when Persia again had acquired the leading place in the cultural life of the East, and when Persia as a whole was in a position to make its most valuable contributions in the Persian language to science, history and literature. This was not under the rule of the Caliphate but under the Mongol Il-khan rule over Persia, from the middle of the thirteenth century on.

For the understanding of the background out of which grew the Judeo-Persian literature, it must be recalled that the Mongol conquest of Persia brought about a decisive transformation in the life and culture of Persia as well as in the position of the Jews in Persia. After the victorious march of Hulagu and the fall of Bagdad in 1258, Islam lost its dominant position in the eastern provinces of the Caliphate and became just one religion among others. With this, the Islamic concept of the *Ahl adh-dhimma,* the Protected People, was deprived of significance. The Mongols regarded all men as belonging to one and the same stock and did not differentiate between believers and nonbelievers, Christians, Jews, pagans. This change in the religious attitude under Hulagu Khan and his immediate successors meant for the non-Moslems in Persia, for Jews and Christians alike, a considerable improvement of their status, and afforded them a few decades of the greatest political and religious freedom ever experienced in Persia before or after.

At no time in the centuries-long association between Israel and Iran have Persian Jews been as prominent in public life as in the thirteenth and fourteenth centuries. They had by that time attained that degree of assimilation which enabled them to become court officials, court physicians, court astronomers and, above all, political leaders, viziers of the great Mongol Persian Empire.

It was particularly under the Il-khan ruler Arghun (1281-1289), a grandson of Hulagu, that Persian Jews appeared almost suddenly on the stage of history and began to participate actively in the political and cultural life of Persia. This awakening of Persian Jewry under the Mongols, the freeing of their intellectual energies, found its dramatic expression in two ways, politically and culturally.

The political rise of Persian Jewry in the thirteenth century is connected with the names of Sa'ad ad-Daula and Rashid ad-Daula.

The rise of Sa'ad ad-Daula, a Jew from Abhar in Persia, from the position of a physician to the Il-khan Arghun to the highest possible political office, that of vizier, prime minister, is one of the most spectacular chapters in Persian Jewish history. Though this appointment of a faithful Jew as vizier for a heathen ruler over a region predominantly Moslem was short-lived, and ended in a catastrophe for Sa'ad ad-Daula and the whole upper strata of Jewish officialdom in Babylonia and Persia, Sa'ad ad-Daula can be regarded, after biblical heroes Esther and Mordecai, Ezra and Nehemiah, as the most important Jew ever to play a decisive role in the political life of Persia.

Rashid ad-Daula, too, attained the rank of vizier, serving in continuous succession three Il-khan rulers. He was a Jew from Hamadan, who, at the age of thirty, turned Moslem. His Jewish descent, long controversial, is now definitely established, not only by his familiarity with Jewish customs and his knowledge of the Hebrew language, but by his own confession shortly before his tragic end. Unlike Sa'ad ad-Daula, however, Rashid ad-Daula entered the annals of Persian history not only as a vizier but also as a famous scholar, as a writer on medical sciences, and above all as one of the greatest historians Persia ever produced. His great historical work *Jami-i Tawarikh,* is described as "unquestionably one of the most important historical works in the Persian language"; it opened a new epoch in Persian historiography.

It was in this very atmosphere, in which Persian Jews could play such a leading role in public life and make their contribution to the culture of their country, that signs became evident of an intensified interest in the Jewish past and of a Jewish cultural awakening. There arose Jewish scholars, rooted in Persian-Islamic culture, who not only began to apply their abilities to public services but who tried to cultivate their own Jewish heritage and to promote Jewish literary values in their own language, in Persian written in Hebrew characters. It was due to these circles that a genuine Judeo-Persian literature came into existence which found its expression mainly in three fields: in Bible translations and Bible research, in Hebrew transliteration of classical Persian poetry, and in composition of original Judeo-Persian poetry.

Judeo-Persian Bible Translation

This circle turned its attention first of all to the Bible text and attempted to produce a correct translation into Judeo-Persian. Despite the long association between Iran and Israel, no translation of the Bible into Persian by Jews had been known until then. The discussion in talmudic literature of the use in the synagogues of Bible copies in foreign characters, in transliteration or in translation—especially the question of the reading of the Book of Esther in Greek, Coptic, Elamite or Median—may allude to the existence of such transliterated or translated biblical books. The numerous biblical quotations in Pehlevi literature in the ninth century, especially in the polemic works called *Dinkard* and *Shikand* suggest an existing translation in Pehlevi. It is impossible to decide from which source these Bible quotations were taken. Possibly they were based on versions common among Jewish communities in the times of the Sassanids. It may be that the Mazdeans obtained their Bible knowledge through Christian writers or, perhaps, through the medium of Mohammedan scholars, for it was just in the time of the author of *Shikand* that the knowledge of the Old Testament became rather widely known among Mohammedans, because of the Mohammedan polemics against the *Ahl al-Kitab*, the People of the Book. The assertion of Theodoret, the Syrian bishop of the fifth century, that there existed an old Persian translation of the Bible, or the view of Maimonides that an old Persian translation was extant long before Islam, cannot be substantiated; in any event, no record of such a translation has come down to us.

The first Judeo-Persian Pentateuch translation that has become known outside Persia goes back to the sixteenth century. The publication of the Jewish Polyglot Bible, in 1546, by Eleazar b. Gerson Soncino in Constantinople, contained, side by side with the Hebrew original, the Targum and the Arabic version of Saadia Gaon, as well as a Judeo-Persian translation of the Pentateuch in Hebrew characters. The author of this Judeo-Persian translation was Jacob b. Joseph Tawus, a Jewish scholar from Persia, who apparently functioned as a teacher at the Jewish Academy in Constantinople, established by the Jewish physician of Sultan Sulaiman, Moses Hamon (1490-1576).

It is astonishing that this Judeo-Persian product, the first printed work in modern Persian of any sort, remained rather unnoticed and failed to attract the attention of the Jewish scholarly world of that time. Only when over a century later, in 1657, the Tawus version was transliterated from its Hebrew alphabet into Persian characters by Thomas Hyde, and incorporated into the famous London Polyglot Bible of Bishop Bryan Walton, was interest aroused in this new field of Persian and Jewish literature. It was long believed that this Judeo-Persian Pentateuch translation was not only the oldest but also the only literary achievement of its kind produced by Persian Jews until then. Yet this Tawus Pentateuch translation, though the first to become known and the first to be printed, was far from opening a new field in the literary achievement of Persian Jewry. According to our present state of knowledge it seems actually to stand at the end of a long chain of Bible translations, and represents only the culmination in Judeo-Persian Bible studies, which had been going on for several centuries.

The available manuscript material, housed in European libraries, establishes that the oldest Judeo-Persian Pentateuch version dates back to the year 1319; the manuscript, now in the collection of the British Museum, has as its translator or copyist a certain Joseph b. Moses. Also other manuscripts, which are now known—particularly that which the Italian traveler Giambattista Vechietti[3] brought back from Persia at the beginning of the seventeenth century, now in the Vatican; as well as other manuscripts in the collections of Paris, Petersburg and London—though they may have been copied in the seventeenth century, all go back to copies or originals which can be "not earlier than the thirteenth century, and not later than the fourteenth century," as Salomon Munk had already observed.

At what exact time Persian Jews started to occupy themselves with Bible translations cannot be established. The references in Ibn Ezra's Bible commentary to two Jewish scholars of Persia, Yehuda Ha-Parsi and Moses ben Amran Ha-Parsi, indicate only the interest of Persian Jews in biblical exegesis. It is also impossible to localize the particular communities where these activities were fostered, though Isfahan, Hamadan, Shiraz, Yezd and Lar figure prominently as places of origin of the Judeo-Persian Bible manuscripts. These questions can be answered only on the basis of a future comparative study of all available Judeo-Persian Bible manuscripts; though it can be assumed that in view of the uniformity of style, the general use of Aramaisms, and the choice of the same Persian equivalents, the version of Tawus and all the other manuscripts may belong, if not to the same translator, at least to one and the same school of translators, which must have flourished as early as the fourteenth century.

The activities that centered around the Bible led in the course of time to the translation of all the canonical books of the Bible, and even of some books of the Apocrypha, copies of which are preserved in various libraries.

The translations of the books of the Bible into Judeo-Persian were supplemented in the fourteenth and fifteenth centuries by Bible commentaries and lexicographical studies. Only a few fragments of this branch of Judeo-Persian literature (such as a Judeo-Persian commentary on Ezekiel and a commentary on Samuel, *Amukot Shemuel*) have been preserved.

The study of the Bible by Persian Jews led also to the composition of lexicographical treatises for the understanding of the language of the Bible. Already in the earliest Judeo-Persian Pentateuch of 1319 reference is made to a certain Abu Sa'id. He is said to have composed a treatise concerning difficult words in the Bible and their meaning. Manuscripts such as *Biur Milot Ha-Torah*, *Perush Ha-Milot* and similar treatises indicate the interest Persian Jews always had taken in the lexicographical field. Two real Bible dictionaries composed by Persian Jews have come down to us which are of particular importance. The earlier of these, a vocabulary of the Bible, Talmud, Targum and Midrash with Persian translation, called *Sefer Ha-Melizah*, was finished in 1339 by Salomon b. Samuel, who hailed from the city of Urgenj in Transoxiana. It must have been quite popular, since it was copied by a Jew of Merv and from there came into the possession of a Jew of Samarkand.

The other Hebrew-Persian dictionary, *Agron* (fifteenth century), covering the vocabulary of the Bible in its Hebrew and Aramaic elements, originated in northern Persia. Its author was Moses b. Aron of Shirwan. Both these dictionaries attest to the spiritual interests of Jewish communities in the remote regions of central Asia as well as in the equally unknown settlements of northern Persia, and indicate that Jewish scholars, well acquainted with Rabbinical literature, occupied themselves with Bible studies of that kind.

Historical and Philological Importance

These early Judeo-Persian Bible translations, commentaries and lexicographical works are of interest in more than one important aspect. Historically they show that Jews in medieval times in Persia and even in the remote settlements in Transoxiana were far from being altogether as isolated from the rest of the Jewish world, as was hitherto believed. The authors of these works seemed to be well acquainted with the leading Rabbinical authorities of western Europe, and show to an astonishing degree the penetration of European Bible exegesis into their works. The Judeo-Persian Bible translations, from the very first available manuscript of 1319 on, indicate that the Persian Jewish scholars remained faithful to the Rabbinical traditional method of Bible exegesis and that they used as sources not only the Targum but also the works of Rashi, David Kimhi, ibn Ezra. It was to them that Persian Jews looked for guidance and advice in their search for the understanding of the Bible text. There can be no doubt that Rashi's commentary was well known to the Jewish scholars of Persia. In the dictionary of Salomon b. Samuel, Rashi is expressly referred to as "Salomon the Frenchman"; and how closely the anonymous author of *Amukot Shemuel* followed in his Persian commentary that of Rashi is indicated by the fact that he incorporated into his work whole portions of Rashi's commentary, along with its French explanations. Rashi and, no less, David Kimhi were freely used by the school of translators of the Bible into Judeo-Persian and many of their interpretations have been incorporated into the Judeo-Persian translation of the Pentateuch and Prophets. How, and through what channels, the works of the Jewish scholars from Europe reached the Persian Diaspora, how they were transmitted and received, has still to be determined.

The philological and linguistic value of these old Judeo-Persian texts is of no less importance than the historical one. They enable us to establish the specific nature and structure of the dialect spoken by the Jews in Persia, with all its linguistic peculiarities. The archaic flavor of the vocabulary, the many ancient phonetic, lexical and grammatical forms, the retention and conservation of many old words and forms of the Persian language not to be found in the oldest Persian documents, the strange combination and amalgamation of Semitic and Indo-European linguistic elements, have made these Judeo-Persian literary productions a rich and important source for Iranian lexicography. The systematic utilization of these products will undoubtedly continue to yield important results for Persian philology, and will enrich Iranian lexicography. This has been recognized by Semitists and Iranists, foremost among them Paul de Lagarde, who stated: "From now on nobody can claim to know the Persian vocabulary who has not utilized from the very beginning to the very end these Judeo-Persian translations."

Classical Persian Poetry in Hebrew Transliteration

With all the devotion of the Jews of Persia to their own religious and cultural heritage, and despite their efforts to cultivate and translate into Judeo-Persian the literary values transmitted to them from the Bible down to the poetry of a Judah Ha-Levi,[4a] a Salomon ibn Gabirol,[5a] an Israel Najara and others, Persian-speaking Jews manifested (as we shall see) a special interest in the classical poetry of Persia. This Persian poetry must have made a lasting impression on them; for they share with their Mohammedan neighbors a deep admiration for the great masters of classical Persian poetry: for Firdusi, Nizami, Rumi, Sa'adi, Hafiz and others. The Jews probably knew by heart many verses by these poets and tried to familiarize themselves, as well as wider Jewish circles, with these literary products. However, there was one great obstacle to this objective: the Arabic alphabet used in writing the Persian language.

Although Jews in Islamic countries learned the language of their neighbors, whether Persian, Arabic or Turkish, they never completely

surrendered to that language. Jews in the Islamic world would not adopt
the alphabet of their neighbors. Whatever they wrote in Persian, private
correspondence, poetry, or prose, they wrote mostly in Hebrew characters.
Thus, Persian Jews deliberately excluded themselves from Persian literature in general and maintained a graphic independence with their Hebrew
script—however complete their assimilation to the language of their
neighbors may otherwise have been. Jews regarded the Hebrew characters
as so integral a part of their religious and national heritage that the use
of a foreign alphabet and one of a religiously different group would have
been considered as a sign of conversion, an act of betrayal, yes, as a breach
of religious loyalty. It was probably this reason which made Judeo-Persian
literature in all its manifestations a kind of literary Ghetto, removed from
general Persian literature; and this accounts for the fact that in the annals
of Persian literature Judeo-Persian productions remain unnoticed and
unknown. It was probably because of the association of the Arabic alphabet
with the religion of Islam that Christian Syrians also preferred to write
their Arabic mother tongue in Syrian letters, just as the Armenians and
Greeks used their respective characters for their writings in the Turkish
language.

The refusal of Persian Jewry to employ the Arabic alphabet for their
writings and literature did not, however, prevent them from attempting
to popularize Persian poetry among their fellow Jews. To overcome the
graphic problem the method adopted was to transliterate or transcribe the
content from the Persian into the Hebrew script. Thus some of the most
important works of Persian authors were put into Hebrew dress; they were
transferred into Hebrew characters with strict and exact retainment of the
language, rhyme and meter of Persian poetry.

To these remarkable efforts we owe a new branch of Persian literature,
which led a kind of independent existence though parallel to the general
body of Persian literature. That this task of bringing some of the literary
products of Persia into the Hebrew camp was carried out is evidence,
indeed, of a great love of Persian poetry by Persian Jews and of their
liberal spirit. Through this process of transplanting, Persian-speaking
Jews were enabled to participate in the cultural achievements of their
surroundings.

The few manuscripts so far known bear testimony that all the various
types of Persian classical poetry were selected to be put into Hebrew
characters. In this form we have *Khosroe and Shirin* and *Haft Peikar* by
Nizami (d. 1202), the exponent of romantic poetry; Jalal ad-Din Rumi
(d. 1273), the most eminent Sufi poet Persia has produced, was represented by parts of his *Mathnawi*. Sa'adi (d. 1291), the exponent of
didactical poetry, entered Judeo-Persian literature with some parts of his
Gulistan. The *Diwan* of Hafiz (1390), the master of lyrical poetry, was

entirely transliterated. So, too, the whole of *Yussuf and Zuleika* of Jami
(d. 1414), the last great classical poet of Persia. Even part of the *Diwan*
of Saʿib of Isfahan (d. 1678), the prominent court poet of the post-classical
period, and many other minor poets, were made accessible in Hebrew
transliteration. In this way also Persian prose became part of Judeo-Persian
literature. Stories by Farid ad-Din ʿAttar from Nishapur (1157-1201) and
stories by other, later Persian authors were translated or transliterated.

It is worth mentioning that the *Rubaiyat* of Omar Khayyam, so famous
in Europe through FitzGerald's English translation, did not find a
transliterator, as far as we know; but translation into modern Hebrew
has repeatedly been made in recent years.

In connection with the Judeo-Persian manuscript of Saʿadi's *Gulistan*,
it is interesting to see that the refusal of Persian Jews to use anything but
Hebrew characters continued well into the nineteenth century. In this
manuscript one poem appears in Persian-Arabic script, but the Jewish owner
or copyist, uneasy about the presence of these verses in Persian characters
in an otherwise purely Hebrew transliteration, felt the need for an
explanation or apology, for he adds that "a Moslem official of the
governor, by the name of Jemjid of Ghilan, inserted this poem of Saʿadi in
the Persian script, in the year 1833."

The interest in Persian poetry in Hebrew transliteration seems to have
been alive in some Jewish communities of Persia until recent times. Joseph
Wolff, a visitor to Meshhed in 1831 was surprised to find there "a sort of
Judaized Sufis with translations of Koran, Hafiz, Rumi into Hebrew . . .
many of them had actually imbibed the mystery of the Persian Sufis. We
heard them instead of singing the hymns of Zion reciting in plaintive
strains the poetry of Hafiz and Firdusi and the writing of Masnavi . . .";
and it sounded like a great discovery when, in 1888, an English observer
wrote that "the Jews of Persia have the 'Diwans' of Hafiz, Saʿadi, the
Khamsa of Nizami and the prose and metrical works of other popular
Persian authors in their own character."

How this process of transliteration was carried out, if and to what degree
an intellectual co-operation between Jewish and non-Jewish Persian scholars
was established, in what particular communities and at what exact time and
by whom this type of Judeo-Persian literature was produced, can hardly
be established on the basis of the limited material available.

It would be illuminating if the criterion according to which the authors
of these transliterations selected their material could be established. Was
it no more than the individual translator's or copyist's taste and love of
poetry? Was the "Jewish element" in the classical Persian poetry perhaps
an attraction? This can hardly be assumed, since the Persian authors and
poets—except for Saʿadi—mention astonishingly little of the Jews and
Judaism of their own time and place, and contain only allusions and hints

to biblical heroes and symbols, to Moses, Sinai, Torah, synagogue and the like. It is much more likely that the special attraction of these works came from the philosophy behind the poetry, which was the philosophy of Sufism, the doctrine of equality of all religions, with its general human appeal, with the removal of confessional ties and its drifting from Islamic anchorage. It is a philosophy which found eloquent expression in verses such as

> Rites and Creeds count for little with God
> Who dwells neither in Mosque nor Church nor Temple
> But in the pure heart . . .

or in verses by Jalal ad-Din Rumi:

> I adore not the cross nor the crescent
> I am not giaour or a Jew
> East nor West, Land nor Sea is my home
> I have no kin nor with angel nor gnome
> I am wrought nor of fire nor of foam
> Soul and body transcending
> I live in the soul of my loved one anew.

Such a view could hardly fail, despite the deep-rooted attachment of Persian Jews to their own heritage, to make a strong impression on their minds. There is even documentary evidence from the Jews in the Arabic-speaking environment of Bagdad and Egypt which attests as early as the tenth century to the penetration of Sufic thoughts into Hebrew circles as evidenced from fragments of the *Genizah*. Hebrew transliterations from Sufic thoughts of Hallaj, the famous mystic of the tenth century, of Ghazali (d. 1111), the greatest of the Islamic theologians, and later material prove an early encroachment of Islamic Sufism and it is not unlikely that these Persian transliterations of Sufic thought into Hebrew represent the result of the same tendency.

Judeo-Persian Miniatures

Persian Jews combined with their admiration for Persian poetry the love for the pictorial art and miniatures of their neighbors. It should therefore not be surprising to find that to these Hebrew transliterations of a Nizami, Sa'adi, Hafiz, Jami and to the Judeo-Persian poetry of a Shahin and Imrani, colored illuminations were added which in color, technique, representation of figures, are hardly distinguishable from those illuminations in pure Persian poetical works. These miniatures could well be regarded as typical Persian artistic products were it not for the explanations added in Hebrew characters. Of these miniatures in Judeo-Persian manuscripts twelve large illustrations in Nizami's *Khosroe and Shirin* and miniatures in his *Haft Peikar* are outstanding, as well as illuminations in

Jami's *Yussuf and Zuleika* and the thirty-one illuminations in a Shahin manuscript.

Again, many questions arise from these illuminations. We do not know whether this pictorial art was cultivated by Jewish artists or only the Hebrew explanations were the work of a Jew; whether there was a school of Jewish artists in existence specializing in this field; and if so, how far, if at all, co-operation went between Jewish and Persian scholars and artists. An interesting example of co-operation in this field between Jewish scholars and religious leaders of Persia is provided by a manuscript of Bible illustrations dating back to the time of Shah Abbas I and preserved now in the Morgan Library in New York. It was in 1607 that there arrived in Isfahan from Cracow an ambassador on behalf of Pope Clement VIII, who wished to solicit the tolerance of the Shah toward the Christians in Persia and also to ask for his aid in a war against the Turks. As a present from the Polish cardinal of Cracow, this ambassador submitted a manuscript of Bible illustrations containing eighty-six full-page miniatures of Old Testament illustrations. These illustrations, probably from the middle of the thirteenth century, had at the bottom an explanation in Latin made in Naples about 1300. Shah Abbas I, after receipt of this manuscript, gave orders "to take an expert mulla [clergyman] to the Christian missionary and to get from him the meaning of each picture and insert it below in the Persian tongue."

Owing to unknown circumstances, probably after the destruction of Isfahan in the Afghan-Persian wars in 1722, these illustrations came back via Cairo to London where they were for sale in 1833 and were later, in 1916, purchased by J. Pierpont Morgan of New York. It must have been quite surprising to find that these illustrations contained not only the explanatory text in the original Latin and the Persian translation as ordered by Shah Abbas, but also Hebrew transliterations of the Persian text at the margins of each miniature. Whether the Shah had ordered a Persian Jew to add explanations in Hebrew or a Jew who got possession of the illustrations added the Hebrew to the Persian and Latin of his own initiative can hardly be decided. The fact, however, sheds light on the existence of Jewish copyists and scribes in Isfahan, the residence of Abbas I, and may serve to indicate a close contact between Jewish and Persian scholars.

A clear proof of intellectual co-operation in Isfahan of the eighteenth century is furnished by a Persian source, namely, the famous "Memoirs" of Sheik Mohammed Ali Hazin (1692-1779), *Tadhkirat al Ahwal*. This Persian traveler and scholar was very eager to obtain reliable information from representatives of the various religions and established contact with a learned Jew in Isfahan. About this we read in his book: "Among the Jewish inhabitants in Isfahan, who, as they believe, have been dwellers in that town since the time of Moses, there was one named Shuaib, the most learned of his brethren. I gained his confidence and took him to my house. From him I learned the Bible and its interpretations which were written out for me, and informed myself of the truth of all that they maintain."

Judeo-Persian Poetry

These productions of Judeo-Persian literature in the field of Bible studies and the Hebrew transliterations of classical Persian poetry are, however, not the only expressions of the literary awakening of Persian Jewry which can be traced back to the times of the Mongol Il-khans' rule over Persia in the thirteenth and fourteenth centuries. The creative abilities and intellectual vitality of Persian Jews opened another field of Judeo-Persian cultural activity. Under the influence of classical Persian poetry, there arose Jewish poets who, closely following the patterns of Persian verse, began to compose poetry devoted to Jewish subjects.

The man who can be hailed as a pioneer of Judeo-Persian poetry, as the first Jewish poet in the Persian language so far known to us, first in time and in importance, was Maulana Shahin. Scanty as are the data concerning his life, we know that he was born at the end of the thirteenth century in Shiraz, the seat of a large Jewish community, and wrote during the rule of the Mongol Il-khan Abu Saʿid al-Behadur (1316-1356), to whom he dedicated his first work.

Inspired by a keen desire to promote a knowledge of the Jewish past among his fellow Jews, Shahin applied the form, meter, structure and language of Persian classical poetry, particularly of Firdusi and Nizami, to the biblical narrative. His lifework represents nothing less than a poetical commentary on the Bible, a poetical paraphrase of the Pentateuch, known as *Sefer Sharh Shahin al Ha-Torah*, written in Persian with Hebrew characters, and divided into a "Book of Genesis," a "Moses Book," an "Ezra Book" and an "Ardeshir Book." It is an *Epos of the Jewish Past* in Persian, shaped after Firdusi's *Epos of the Iranian Past*. By selecting Jewish themes as the subject of his poetry and by celebrating the heroes of the Bible, particularly Moses, in a way typical of Persian classical poetry, Shahin has put the past of Israel in Iranian garb, and has thus produced the most typical literary expression of the association between Israel and Iran. He must have been conscious of the originality of his achievement, for he speaks of himself as having kindled a new lamp in composing this work to tell everyone of the greatness of Moses.

In making biblical themes and heroes the content of his poetry, Shahin combined Persian art and form with Israel's religion and history. He used three heterogeneous sources and combined them into one organic entity. Along with a thorough knowledge of the Bible and Rabbinic literature (Talmud, Midrashim) he, the Persian Jew of the fourteenth century, showed an amazing mastery also of the Koran and Islamic tradition, and an equally great knowledge of classical Persian poetry. His work testifies to his wide Jewish knowledge and consciousness, and reveals the degree of assimilation and absorption of the cultural values of his environment.

It seems that with his *Epos* Shahin satisfied the particular taste of his countrymen; it must have enjoyed great popularity. He lives on in the memory of Persian Jews as "our Master," "Maulana" Shahin, as the founder of Judeo-Persian poetry, as the Firdusi of the Jews. It is indicative of his popularity that manuscripts of his works were widely spread among many Jewish communities throughout the Persian-speaking Diaspora, to Shiraz, Teheran, Bukhara, Balkh, Samarkand and elsewhere, where they were read and studied in synagogues and at home. Yet Shahin's work might have fallen into oblivion and been entirely forgotten were it not for a Jewish scholar from Bukhara, Simon Chacham, who, at the beginning of the twentieth century rescued part of Shahin's literary heritage, the Genesis Book and the Moses Book, by publishing it in Jerusalem.

It was in the very birthplace of Shahin, in Shiraz, that two centuries later a successor in the person of the Jewish poet Imrani appeared. Inspired by Shahin's poetical paraphrase of the Pentateuch, Imrani made the post-Mosaic period of the Bible, the historical books from Joshua to Kings, until the time of Solomon, the object of his poetical presentation. Closely following the example set by Shahin, in method, form and language, combining also (though to a lesser degree) Islamic and Persian sources with the biblical narrative, Imrani in 1523 wrote his *Fath Nama* (The Book of the Conquest) which, due to its resemblance in style, was erroneously attributed to Shahin.

Imrani is also the author of *Ganj Nama* (The Book of Treasures), composed in 1536; it is a poetical paraphrase of the Mishna treatise *Pirke Abot*, which is used, however, only as a frame for themes of general meditation and religious contemplation.

Evidently that type of Judeo-Persian poetry initiated by Shahin and followed by Imrani was quite popular, for it was continued by another Jewish poet called Yehuda Lari; of his *Makhzan al-Pand* (The Treasure House of Exhortation) only a small part (151 verses) has come down to us.

It is not surprising that neither Shahin nor Imrani nor Lari, so typically Persian in their compositions, entered the annals of Persian literature. By using Hebrew characters for their poetry, they prevented it from becoming known to their Persian Moslem neighbors.

Under the Safavid Dynasty (1502-1736)

The Safavids, the new dynasty which ruled for more than two centuries, put Persia on entirely new foundations, very different from those of the Il-khan rulers. By introducing Shi'a as the state religion, by establishing a powerful hierarchy of the clergy, and by regarding all nonbelievers as ritually unclean, the Safavid rulers effected a change in the political and cultural climate, and this change had far-reaching repercussions on all aspects of Jewish life.

To illustrate the changed atmosphere, it might suffice to mention the attitude of Shah Tahmasp (1524-1526) toward the famous English traveler and merchant, Anthony Jenkinson. Upon arrival in Kazvin, then the capital of the Safavids, with a letter from Queen Elizabeth of England, he was immediately ordered to depart: "Oh thou unbeliever," said the Shah, "we have no need for friendship with the unbelievers!" Or again, Shah Isma'il II (1576-1577) hesitated to mint new coins of silver or gold because he could not bear the idea that these coins, which had on their obverse the Mohammedan confession of faith, should be touched by and fall into the hands of nonbelievers. Another shah threw a golden ring into the sea when he heard that it had been made by a Christian goldsmith. Shah Sefi II (1667-1694), at the advice of his chief minister, changed his name into Sulaiman, "in order to prevent that the Jews, having practiced some sorcery upon his person . . . have any power over him."

A change for the better was effected only through Shah Abbas I (1587-1629), the outstanding Safavid ruler. He introduced extensive reforms to weaken the theocratic basis of the state which his predecessors had built up, to free Persia from the fetters of its all-too-powerful Shi'a clergy, and to put an end to the political, economic and cultural isolation of Persia. Shah Abbas, realizing that the most urgent requirement for Persia was increased population and economic ties with the outside world, fundamentally changed the policy of the state toward non-Moslems and foreigners. Far from being antagonistic toward Europeans and nonbelievers, as his predecessors had been, he encouraged the immigration of foreigners, merchants, settlers and artisans from neighboring countries such as Armenia, Georgia, Turkey, as well as from Europe. By granting freedom of religion and special privileges and facilities to all who were ready to come to his territory, he was able to succeed in this purpose. It was his liberal and tolerant attitude that made Persia at that time the meeting place of European envoys, emissaries, diplomats, merchant-adventurers, missionaries —all eager to obtain commercial, political or religious concessions and privileges. Never before in the history of Persia's relationship with the outside world were the ties between Persia and Europe, economically and politically, closer.

This close relationship between Persia and Europe did not fail to have its effect on Judeo-Persian literature. It was because of this contact that the literary activities of Persian Jews became known for the first time to the outside world. Jewish history is particularly indebted to the Italian diplomat and traveler, Giambattista Vechietti (1552-1619), for having brought to Europe knowledge of Judeo-Persian literature (in the form of Judeo-Persian manuscripts). On behalf of Pope Gregory XIII, toward the end of the sixteenth century (1584), Vechietti went to the East entrusted with a double mission, to conciliate the Patriarch of Alexandria and to enlist the assistance of the Persians in the Pope's fight against the Turks. Unlike other envoys and diplomats of that time, Vechietti combined with his diplomatic pursuit a great interest in old manuscripts and versions of the Bible. It is of utmost significance that it was the city of Lar from which some of his material originated. It is expressly stated that in 1601 he commenced the revision of the Persian translation of the Pslams and other biblical books in Lar.

Lar was not only the home of a Jewish poet but must have been the seat of a school of scribes, translators and copyists who devoted themselves with great zeal to the cultivation of Jewish traditional values and to translating or copying books of the Holy Scripture into the Persian language, written, however, in Hebrew characters. Not a few of the Judeo-Persian manuscripts found today in European libraries and containing translations of the prophets Isaiah, Jeremiah and Ezekiel as well as of Joshua, Judges, Samuel, Kings, Ruth, Ezra and Nehemiah, Chronicles and the translations of apocryphal books such as Tobit, Judith, Bel and the Dragon, Megilat Antiochus and others, can be traced in their geographical origin to Lar, where in the first decade of the seventeenth century they were either translated or copied by a zealous group of Jewish scholars.

Under Shah Abbas II (1642-1666)

The second part of the seventeenth century was, for the Jews of Persia, a time of great suffering and persecution. The conception of the ritual uncleanliness of the Persian Jew, which led to the introduction of a special headgear for all Jews in Persia and to a crusade against secret, cabbalistic Hebrew books, culminated under Shah Abbas II in the forced conversion of all the Jews in Persia, a catastrophe which brought them to the very brink of destruction. This persecution, a tragic parallel to the Inquisition of Spain centuries earlier,[6a] regarded as "more cruel than that of the time of Ahasuerus and Haman, more terrible than that of the time of Hadrian," came as an unexpected blow. The Jews were thrown "into dreadful consternation when all of a sudden an edict from the king [Abbas II] was issued and published in every place in Persia, commanding them on pain of death to abjure the Jewish religion and profess thenceforth that of Mohammed."

The available sources describe in great detail how the Jews were compelled to abandon their religion, how the synagogues were closed, how they were forced to eat meat boiled in milk in order to emphasize their break with Jewish tradition, how they were now called *Jadid al-Islam* and were taken to the mosque and instructed in their new religion. The heroic resistance of the Jews led to the phenomenon of "Marranos," or Anusim, and for years they lived a dual religious life, in secret remaining Jews while confessing Islam officially. Only when it became evident, after almost seven years of forced conversion, that "whatever pretenses the Jews made to Mohammedanism, they still practiced Judaism, so that it was necessary to permit them again to become bad Jews because they could not make good Mussulmans," did the vizier and leaders of the Shi'a clergy allow them to return to their former religion.

In such an atmosphere of hatred and intolerance, when all the energies and efforts of Persian Jews had to be concentrated on physical survival, one could hardly expect any kind of literary activity on their part. The kind of Judeo-Persian literature that was nevertheless produced bears all the marks of the time and mirrors the grim and tragic reality of Jewish life.

It was in the city of Kashan that the torch of Jewish learning was rekindled in the seventeenth century and it was there that the martyrdom of Persian Jewry found its literary expression in a Judeo-Persian chronicle entitled *Kitab-i Anusi: The Book of the Events of the Forced Conversions of Persian Jewry to Islam;* its author was the Jewish poet Babai ibn Lutf from Kashan, himself not only an eyewitness, but a victim of the events. The poet began his work in the very midst of the persecutions under Shah Abbas II in the year 1656 and his chronicle covers the events from 1617 down to his own time. His account is one of the most important sources we possess for this or for any other period of the history of the Persian Jews. From no other source in Persian or in any other language do we obtain such an interesting glimpse into the inner life of the Jewish communities in Persia of the seventeenth century. His work is a mine of information in regard to their political persecution, their life as Marranos, their geographical distribution and economic structure, their religious customs, superstitions, places of pilgrimage and names.

It sheds a most interesting light on the relationship between the authorities, the shah, the vizier, the governors, the clergy and the Jews; at the same time it reveals the pettiness and jealousy, the lack of unity and leadership in the Ghettos of the Persian Diaspora, faults which in no small measure were responsible for the Jews' political sufferings.

The chronicle reflects also the personality of its author. He must have been a deeply religious Jew who interpreted the tragedy that had befallen his people as a punishment for their own sins, for the neglect of Torah and mitzvot, and for disunity among their leaders. "In the period of the Flood there was a Noah, in another period there arose an Ezra, in our time there is no leader," he exclaims; and adds, "We have neglected the five books of Moses, therefore God has delivered us for five years to Islam; we have abandoned the Torah, now we are forced to learn the Koran; we neglected the fast days, now we must fast the whole month of Ramadan, we did not visit the synagogue, so God caused us to go to the mosque."

In language and form, in the arrangement of facts, in the symbolism and in the metaphors, this chronicle, though written in Hebrew characters, is typically Persian. It bears witness to the great influence that Persian classical poetry, especially Hafiz and Sa'adi, no less than Shahin and Imrani, had exerted on this Jewish poet of the late seventeenth century.

Despite its unique historical importance and its reliability, by no means lessened through its poetical form, its place within the annals of Jewish historiography has hardly been given due recognition. Yet this Judeo-Persian chronicle could adequately be called the *Emek Ha-Bakha* or the *Shebet Yehuda* of Persian Jewry, for it made Jewish life in an Islamic country, and particularly the Galut within the Shi'a Islamic world, its main theme.

Babai ibn Lutf, whose chronicle describes the events from 1617 to 1656, found a continuator in his grandson Babai ibn Farhad, also of Kashan. In language, form, meter, symbolism and in the presentation of facts, his chronicle closely follows the work of his grandfather, leads to the events that occurred sixty years after Babai ibn Lutf's report, and covers the sufferings and persecution of Persian Jewry during the troubled times of the Persian-Afghan wars up to 1725.

Among other literary productions of that time, mirroring the martyrdom of Persian Jews, mention should be made of a Judeo-Persian poet by the name of Mashiah b. Raphael and also of Mulla Hizkijahu of Isfahan, whose elegies reveal the heroism, endurance and courage of the victims of the forced conversion.

Sabbatai Zevi

The sufferings of Persian Jewry at that time were intensified by the disappointment caused through the Sabbatai Zevi episode.[7a] As in Turkey, so in Persia Sabbatai Zevi aroused tremendous excitement, and Persian Jewry, always in an attitude of Messianic expectation and yearning for the deliverance from the yoke of the *Galut*, was then in a perfect mood to receive the message of the new Messiah with the utmost inner readiness. The only reference so far known to the reaction of Persian Jewry to Sabbatai Zevi illustrates this readiness. From the French traveler J. Chardin, an eyewitness of the events in 1666, we hear:

I remember, when I was in Hyrcania in 1666, just at the time when the Jews of Turkey made so much ado about a false Messiah by the name of Sabbatai Zevi—that also the Jews of Hyrcania believed like the others that the redeemer for whom they had so vainly waited so long, had arrived. They left their houses, went out in the fields, covered themselves with sack and ashes, fasting and praying for the appearance of the Messiah.

The governor of the province sent to them asking: "What are you doing, you poor devils, thus to abandon your work, instead of thinking of paying your taxes?" "The taxes, sir," they answered, "we shall not have to pay any more, our redeemer has arrived." They negotiated with the governor of the province to allow them to offer their prayers without interruption, for the time being—if within three months the redeemer would not appear with a strong hand in Persia, they would very promptly pay the taxes they owed.

Jewish Colony in China

At the beginning of the seventeenth century, in the time of the Safavids, another center of Jewish settlements appears on the horizon of Jewish history. This is the Jewish community in Kai feng Fu in China, of which nothing was known before then.

Its romantic discovery in 1607 by European missionaries, its history as revealed by stone inscriptions and the question of its origin—did the original immigrants penetrate into China along the sea route via India, or along the land route via Khorasan and Turkestan?—cannot be dealt with here. Mention of these Jews is justified, however, because their liturgy and literature show a distinct Judeo-Persian influence.

Persian touches in the writings of these Chinese Jews are very numerous. They divide the Pentateuch into fifty-three sections as do the Persian Jews and, like them, count twenty-seven letters of the Hebrew alphabet by treating the final letters as separate consonants. The instructions in their prayer books are given in Persian, they call their religious leader, their rabbi, with the Persian word *Ustadh*; a Hebrew inscription in their synagogue contains lines in the Persian language; to a Chinese manuscript of Genesis a colophon in Judeo-Persian is attached, and in their prayer books "the rubrics are all in Persian and most of the Pizmonim therein also exist among the Persian Jews." The manuscript of their Pesach Haggada contains verses translated into Judeo-Persian.

All this indicates that this Chinese Jewish colony was liturgically and linguistically under the influence of the Jews of Persia.

Nadir Shah (1736-1747) and Judeo-Persian Literature

The dynastic struggles, the anarchy and revolts that fill the pages of the history of Persia in the eighteenth century, following the overthrow of the Safavids by the Afghan dynasty in 1722 under Mahmud, made the whole of Persia a vast battlefield. While Persia faced the Afghan invaders from the east it had to encounter the Turkish invaders from the west and the Russians from the north. This was hardly a time for cultural concentration and relaxation. "At a time when the Mohammedans fought against each other, how much less safe were the Jews?" exclaimed the Jewish chronicler, Babai ibn Farhad, of that period. These dynastic changes and struggles meant for the Jews only "that they fell into the hands of new oppressors."

From out of this chaos there arose a man who at least for a short while brought back to Persia order and stability; he also has a particular significance for the Jews and Judeo-Persian literature. The man was Nadir Shah. Not only was he one of the greatest military geniuses of the East (he restored Persia's military power and extended her frontiers far into India and Afghanistan) but he was at the same time a kind of religious reformer and thinker. With his ascent to power, he abolished Shi'a Islam as state religion, which it had been under his Safavid predecessors, and replaced it with Sunna Islam. Motivated by religious as well as political considerations, he not only aimed at a unification of Sunna and Shi'a but' fostered the idea of a universal religion, comprising Islam, Christianity, Judaism and Zoroastrianism. It was with this purpose in mind that he arranged public religious disputations in which the various religious representatives participated and in which the Shah showed an amazing degree of tolerance. As his court physician he appointed the Jesuit Father Louis Bazin. Nadir Shah took a great interest in the holy books of all religions and it is reported that he ordered the translation of the New and the Old Testament into Persian. He sent a mulla to Isfahan to collect such Jews, Armenians and Franks as were considered necessary for this translation. The translation of the New Testament was started in May, 1740, with the help of Roman Catholic missionaries and Orthodox Armenian monks, while the translation of the Old Testament was entrusted to Jewish rabbis. Also the Koran was ordered to be translated into Persian. Of the Old Testament only the Pentateuch and the Psalms seem to have been completed, by a Jew from Isfahan, Baba ben Nuriel, copies of which are preserved.

Nadir Shah's importance for the Persian-speaking Jews manifested itself not only in his tolerant attitude but also in the establishment of a new Jewish settlement, out of which a center of Judeo-Persian culture emerged. This settlement was in Meshhed, his own residence.

Meshhed, the holy city of Shiites in Persia, seat of the mausoleum of Imam Riza, the most important place of pilgrimage for the Shi'a Moslems, was to become, under Nadir Shah, an important strategic point for the protection of the eastern borders of his empire. In order to increase its permanent population and not to have to rely on the fluctuating elements, the pilgrims, he transplanted groups of people from other corners of Persia to this city. Through this shifting of population, Meshhed became the seat of a Jewish community, which originated in Kazvin, in nothern Persia. Prior to Nadir Shah there were no Jews in Meshhed, for its holy character excluded nonbelievers from this part of Persia. Neither the Safavid rulers nor the population with its religious fanaticism would have permitted their holy city to be "contaminated" even by the mere presence of Jews. Only Nadir Shah, a man with strong Sunna convictions, a foe of the Shi'a, and bent on religious reforms, could dare, despite the opposition of the Shi'a clergy, to establish a Jewish community in such a city.

Without going into the development of the community thus created, we have evidence that it prospered economically as well as culturally. The exponent of the literary activities carried on here was Siman Tob Melamed, a poet and philosopher, the spiritual leader through whom Meshhed entered the annals of Judeo-Persian literature. Melamed is the author of *Azharot,* a collection of liturgical poetry in Judeo-Persian, parts of which were written in Persian, as well as Aramaic and Hebrew. The poems often carry his name in acrostic. Though his songs became a great source of inspiration for the Jews of Meshhed and other communities in central Asia and exerted great influence on their liturgy, his fame lies in his philosophical-religious book, *Sefer Hayat ar-ruh,* a kind of commentary to Maimonides's teachings, dealing with Israel's *Galut* existence and ultimate salvation. The work is strongly influenced by the ethical and Sufic ideas of Bahya ibn Pakudah's *Hobot Ha-Lebabot.* For more than a century kept as a manuscript, this *Sefer Hayat ar-ruh* found a redeemer in an Afghan Jew, who printed it in Jerusalem in 1898.

The tradition of Siman Tob Melamed was carried on even after the forced conversion of the whole community in 1839, which led to the phenomenon of *Jadid al-Islam,* Marrano Jews in an Islamic version, still in existence today, as observed by the present writer during his stay in that city in 1936. Among the leading figures of this community, which secretly remained Jewish though officially Moslem, Mordecai ben Raphael Aklar, known as Mulla Murad, stands out prominently through his many contributions to Judeo-Persian literature. He translated into Judeo-Persian the prayer book for weekdays and Sabbath known as *Oneg Shabbat.* There is also incorporated a Hebrew poem by another Jew from Meshhed, Solomon ben Mashiah. This poem describes the tragic events that led to the forced conversion of the community. Apart from his *Oneg Shabbat,* Mulla Murad translated into Judeo-Persian *Selihot, Piyyutim,* the *Haggada shel Pesah.* These were published in Jerusalem after he succeeded in settling there, and there he died a few years ago, having served two generations as the secret *Rav* of the community in Meshhed.

Bukhara

Towards the end of the seventeenth century the center of gravity in the field of Judeo-Persian activities shifted to an area which until then had remained a rather unknown spot on the map of the Jewish Diaspora in

Asia, namely, Bukhara. Bukhara, once an important center of Islamic culture in central Asia and a rallying point of Islamic scholars and scientists, must have had a Jewish community from early days. However, the origin of the community is shrouded in great obscurity. The Jewish traveler of the twelfth century, Benjamin of Tudela, refers only to Samarkand and to the leader of its Jewish community, Rabbi Obadya Ha-Nasi. The earliest authentic reference to Jews in Bukhara comes from an Arab chronicler of the thirteenth century, Ibn al-Fuwati, who reports that in 1240 a Mohammedan ordered the killing of all the Christians and Jews then living in Bukhara. It seems, however, that the Jews survived this threat, as also the vicissitudes which must have come upon them in consequence of the Mongolian invasion and the rule of Timur. Bukharian Jews entered the arena of Jewish history, however, only toward the end of the seventeenth century. They then gained prominence through their literary achievements in the field of Judeo-Persian literature which, discovered only in the nineteenth century, has shed an entirely new light on this least known group of the "Remnants of Israel" in Asia.

Remote from the dynastic quarrels and civil wars on Persian soil, spared also the afflictions and persecutions that swept over their brethren in Persia, the Jews of Bukhara could devote themselves with a greater degree of leisure to literary activities in their own language than their brethren across the border. Their literary heritage shows that they possessed Jewish scholars, poets and translators, who, with great scholarly and intellectual perfection, cultivated the field of Judeo-Persian poetry in their own particular dialect.

The outstanding contribution to Judeo-Persian literature by these Jewish scholars of Bukhara was made by the poet Maulana Yussuf Yahudi (1688-1755). An exponent of that branch of Persian poetry in Hebrew characters which goes back to Shahin and Imrani and which in previous centuries was deeply appreciated by Persian Jews, he became the author of a famous ode, *Mukhammas,* devoted to the praise and glory of Moses, and of *Haft Braderan* (The Seven Brothers), based on the Midrash of the martyrdom of the seven brothers and their mother. These works, together with his hymns in honor of biblical heroes such as Elijah, as well as other poems bearing his name in acrostic, some of which are bilingual and trilingual, form even today an integral part of the spiritual heritage of the Persian-speaking Jews of Bukhara. His *Tafsir* to *Megilat Antiochus* deserves particular mention.

Yusuf Yahudi was not less fruitful as translator. Many of the *Zemirot* of Israel Najara, which are incorporated in the collection of the Judeo-Persian songbooks, such as *Yismah Yisrael,* were introduced into Judeo-Persian literature by Yusuf. He must have inspired many of his contemporaries, since in his time a "School of Jewish Poets" was established in Bukhara and they, following his example, composed Judeo-Persian poetry.

Among these Bukharian poets was Benjamin ben Mishal, known also as Amina, who not only published *Megillat Ester* in Judeo-Persian translation in metric form but also translated into Judeo-Persian some poems by Salomon ibn Gabirol, such as *Azharot* and *Yigdal*. It is quite likely that a Daniel Apocalypse, *Daniel Nama*, of a Khodja Bukhari (1705) goes back to this Amina.

Of the many other Jewish poets of that circle, whose names are preserved in acrostics, special mention should be made of Elisha ben Samuel, also known as Mulla Raghib, who translated into Judeo-Persian the romantic story of "Balaam and Joseph," after the Hebrew version of Abraham ben Chisdai, under the title *Shah-Zadeh and the Sufi* (The Prince and the Dervish).

One of the finest poetical products in the Bukharian Jewish dialect came from the Jewish poet ibn Abu-l-Kheir. In his famous *Khodaidad* he narrates the tragic story of a Jewish merchant by the name of Nathaniel (Khodaidad) who, refusing to become a Mohammedan despite all the promises and temptations of the Mohammedan ruler and his Mohammedan neighbors, died a martyr. In making this touching and moving event the object of his poem, the author gives an interesting picture of the religious and political conditions in which the Jews of Bukhara lived in the second part of the eighteenth century, under the rule of the Emir Masum (1788). At the same time this work furnished a most authentic contribution to the linguistic peculiarities of the Persian poetry of Bukharian Jews (publ. by Salemann 1897).

This Bukharian-Jewish school of poets seemed to have had a great share in the popularization also of Persian classical poetry, and cultivated that branch with particular eagerness.

Toward the end of the eighteenth century Bukharian Jews seem to have ceased their creative activity; at any rate we have little knowledge about them. However, their cultural development was decisively influenced by a *shaliah*, a messenger from Morocco, R. Joseph b. Maman al-Maghrebi, who is credited with a revival of religious and cultural life of the Bukharian Jews, which led them at the end of the nineteenth century to emigrate to Palestine, where, as we shall see, they again began to play a decisive and active role in the promotion of Judeo-Persian literature.

Afghanistan

The literary activities of the Jews in centers such as Meshhed and Bukhara seem to have inspired Jews in Afghanistan, about whom hitherto little was known. Though Afghanistan, as part of medieval Khorasan, entered Jewish history in the ninth century particularly through Hivi al-

Balkhi of the city of Balkh, and through Jews from Maimaneh, Merv, and Ghazna, Afghanistan Jewish life fell into oblivion until Judeo-Persian literary evidence in the nineteenth century shed, unexpectedly, new light on these long-forgotten Remnants of Israel.

The history of the Jews in Afghanistan in the nineteenth century is closely connected with that of the Jews of Persia, particularly of Meshhed. Here it can only be stated that no other event so considerably affected the map of the Jewish Diaspora in Asia and also in Afghanistan as the destruction of the community in Meshhed. As a result of the forced conversion, many of the Jews of Meshhed fled and found a haven of refuge not only in Bukhara and Samarkand, but also in the territory of Afghanistan, in Herat, Maimaneh, Kabul and Kandahar, where the more tolerant Sunna Islam allowed them to live as Jews. These fugitives created new Jewish settlements or increased already existing ones, bringing a new spirit to the stagnant cultural life of Afghanistan Jewry. The origin of Afghanistan Jewry of the nineteenth century, from Meshhed, is well attested by one of the leading rabbis of Herat, Mulla Matityahu Garji: "Our forefathers used to live in Meshhed under Persian rule but in consequence of the persecutions which occurred against them my forefathers came to Herat to live under Afghan rule."

Without any contact with the outside world, Afghanistan Jews led a religious and cultural life of their own and produced liturgical and religious poetry in Judeo-Persian and in Hebrew which can be regarded as a valuable contribution to Judeo-Persian literature. It was in particular the Garji family, successively the leading rabbis of Herat, who wrote commentaries on the Bible and on the Psalms such as *Sefer Hanukkat Zion, Sefer Minhat Shmuel, Sefer Tehillim, Sefer Oneg Shabbat* and others.

These and other literary treasures would have remained unknown but for the migration of Afghanistan Jews to Jerusalem where, thanks to another Jewish family from Herat, the Shauloff brothers, much of the literature of the Afghan Jews was published. Through the initiative of the Shauloffs, deeply devoted to their own literature, the *Sefer Hayat ar-ruh* by Siman Tob Melamed was published as well, thus symbolizing the close ties that bound Jews from Meshhed with Jews from Afghanistan.

Jerusalem: The Center of Judeo-Persian Activities

Judeo-Persian literature experienced an unforeseen development toward the end of the nineteenth century, not in Persia itself, however, but in Jerusalem. This was due to a wave of immigration of Persian-speaking Jews from Bukhara, Turkestan, Afghanistan and Persia into Palestine. Almost parallel with the *Hovevei Zion* movement from Russia,[8a] but probably without direct contact, a great number of Persian-speaking Jews, imbued with a passionate love for Zion, set out for Palestine and in a continuous stream poured into the Holy Land. They came from Teheran and Shiraz, from Hamadan, Yezd and Isfahan, from Kashan and Meshhed, from Herat and Kabul, from Bukhara and Samarkand and from many other centers of Jewish settlements in the Middle East. They settled in Tiberias and Safed, in Haifa and Jaffa (Tel-Aviv); but the bulk of these lovers of Zion went to Jerusalem and established there a colony of Persian-speaking Jews. It was particularly the Jews of Bukhara who went exclusively to Jerusalem; in 1889 they established a "Society of the Lovers of Zion" and built, in 1893, a *Shekhuna*, also called *Rehovot*; the present Bukharian quarter of Jerusalem, which in the course of time became the focal point of the settlement of Persian-speaking Jews.

The establishment of this Jewish-Persian colony in Jerusalem not only opened a new chapter in the history of the urban colonization of that city, but inaugurated a new epoch in the history of Judeo-Persian literary activities. The leaders of the Persian-speaking colony in Jerusalem, though content with having attained the realization of their long hoped-for return to the Holy Land, were eager to help their brethren, in both a spiritual and a physical sense, who still remained in the lands of their origin. They intended to create stronger ties between "Zion and Iran," between Jerusalem and the Remnants of Israel in the remote Oriental Diaspora, by offering them religious education and inspiration. With this consideration in mind the leaders of that Persian-speaking colony embarked on a unique enterprise, with far-reaching results for the cultural level of each of the Persian-speaking groups. The enterprise was the establishment in Jerusalem of a publishing center, a printing press, for Judeo-Persian literature, intended to rescue the literary legacy that Persian Jews had brought with them in the form of manuscripts. These works were to be printed and distributed among all Persian-speaking Jews, in Palestine and abroad. Though the press was established partly as a token of gratitude for having reached the land of their hopes, partly to honor the memory of their forefathers, it was destined to bring about a decisive change in the history of the Judeo-Persian literature, not yet recognized in its far-reaching effects. Though Jerusalem was not the first place of Judeo-Persian printing activities, and some Judeo-Persian books had been previously published by European scholars as well as by Bukharian Jews (particularly in Vienna and Vilna by the latter)—not to mention the first Judeo-Persian print of any time in Constantinople in 1546—Jerusalem became the exclusive center of Judeo-Persian printing activities. From then on all the liturgical and literary needs of Persian-speaking Jews were satisfied from Jersualem and its Judeo-Persian press.

It can hardly be attempted nor is it intended here even to enumerate the results of these printing and publishing activities in Jerusalem during two decades; their extent and quantity would preclude such a survey. Almost everything that was thought fit to strengthen the religious and literary interests of Persian-speaking Jews was printed and published. Every field of Jewish literature, Bible, Bible commentaries, prayer books for every occasion, Rabbinical writings, Mishna and *Zohar*, religious philosophy, medieval Jewish poetry, *Piyyutim, Selihot, Pizmonim,* Midrashim, historical narratives, anthologies of songs and stories—all this was translated into Judeo-Persian, printed and distributed. Even secular literature from other than Jewish sources, such as parts of the *Arabian Nights,* and a part of Shakespeare's *Comedy of Errors,* which appealed greatly to the imagination of the Oriental Jew, found its way to the translators and printers.

Thus for the first time the Jewish world at large began to realize the quantity and quality of a hitherto unknown branch of Jewish literature.

It is of great significance that these Judeo-Persian publishing activities represented a collective effort, a co-operative endeavor of all the various groups of Persian-speaking Jewry; Jews of Bukhara joined hands with the Jews of Persia and Afghanistan and participated in the greatest common cultural enterprise in the history of Oriental Jewry.

Among the many outstanding figures of the various Persian-speaking communities, although many of them would deserve special reference, only two, one from Samarkand and one from Bukhara, can be presented here.

Solomon Babajan b. Pinchasof of Samarkand, an editor, author, translator and publisher, entered the field of Judeo-Persian publications with his translation of Job, which was followed by Judeo-Persian translations of Judah Ha-Levi's *Mi Kamokha,* Solomon ibn Gabirol's *Keter Malkhut* and other liturgical and religious poetry. However, his greatest service to Judeo-Persian literature was closely connected with the *Hibbat Zion* movement of Oriental Jews. A great part of the literary output in Jerusalem was clearly aimed at the furthering of the ideals of Zion and at promoting the knowledge of the Hebrew language among those Jews who remained in Central Asia. A typical expression of this tendency was the Judeo-Persian translation of *Ahabat Zion,* with all its romantic biblical background; so, too, the translation of the *Hatikvah* into Judeo-Persian was attached to many of the Judeo-Persian publications.

However, this tendency was manifested also in lexicographical and linguistic treatises intended to familiarize the Persian-speaking Jews with the Hebrew language and to enable them to attain a sound knowledge of Hebrew, if and when they began to immigrate into Palestine. This trend is evident in a Hebrew-Persian-Russian dictionary, *Sefer Kitzur Ha-Millim,* by David b. Jacob Chwailof, published in 1907 in Jerusalem; it contained about five thousand words in Persian, with their Russian and Hebrew equivalents in Hebrew transcription. The whole edition of this linguistic guide was sent to Bukhara for distribution among the Jews, many of whom, under the influence of Russia, were familiar with the Russian language.

A more interesting and even more curious document is the *Sefer Millim Shisha* by Solomon Babajan b. Pinchasof of Samarkand (Jerusalem, 1909), a dictionary in six languages (all in Hebrew characters) with which the author intended to provide a linguistic equipment for all those Jews of Central Asia who intended to come to Palestine. In the brief Hebrew preface to this little language guide the author says: "I have composed it for the use of our Jewish brethren who intend to go to Jerusalem, to enable them to learn all the languages necessary—without too much trouble and effort."

As such necessary languages in addition to Persian there appear Russian, French (later, in the second edition Ladino), Arabic, Turkish and Hebrew. That this "philological Baedeker" was in great demand and fulfilled its purpose is borne out by the fact that it went into two editions, the second of which appeared in 1912.

When the history of this *Hibbat Zion* movement among Oriental Jews comes to be written, it will be recognized how important a role Zion played in the thoughts and feelings of central Asiatic Jews, and how Jerusalem, thanks to these literary endeavors, has become in a very real sense a spiritual reservoir and cultural center for Persian-speaking Jews and for Oriental Jews in general.

Simon Chacham

Judeo-Persian publishing activities in Jerusalem are intimately connected with the name of a great Jew from Bukhara, Simon Chacham. Born in 1843 in Bukhara, to which his father, Eliahu, had emigrated from Bagdad, he received a thorough Jewish education and became deeply rooted in Jewish tradition. Simon Chacham then went in 1890 to Jerusalem, to join the rapidly increasing colony of Bukharian Jews. It was in Jerusalem that he began his manifold activities as author, translator, editor and publisher.

With the establishment of the Judeo-Persian printing center in Jerusalem, he brought to press for publication not only his own literary compositions and translations but also many of the manuscripts written by his Bukharian countrymen and by Persian authors.

The long, impressive list of Judeo-Persian publications which are due to the initiative of Simon Chacham, to his functions as editor, translator or author, contains almost everything which could meet the religious and liturgical needs of his fellow Jews. Without intending to give here a full bibliography of his works and a detailed description of his contribution, special mention should be made of his Judeo-Persian translation of the biblical novel *Ahabat Zion* by Abraham Mapu. It appeared in Jerusalem in 1908, and became immediately such a popular book among Oriental Jews that a second edition was printed in 1912. Simon Chacham was himself so enthusiastic about this novel that he concluded his translation with the following words: "Whoever reads this book only once, has certainly not yet comprehended it; he who reads it twice has only slightly understood its contents; only he who reads it thrice will fully grasp its meaning and penetrate into the depths of its ideas; but even he who reads it a hundred times until he knows it by heart will certainly wish to read it a hundred and one times."

A special service was rendered by Simon Chacham in publishing part of the *Epos of the Jewish Past* by Maulana Shahin of Shiraz of the fourteenth century; to this work he added his own poetical compositions. Of great service, too, was his publication of the Judeo-Persian translation of the *Shulhan Aruk*, under the title *Likutei Dinim*, prepared by his countryman Abraham Aminoff, the leading rabbi of the Bukharian colony of Jerusalem. These and many other publications were thus preserved and saved from oblivion through the literary efforts of Simon Chacham and his collaborators.

The crown and glory of his literary contributions, however, is his translation of the Hebrew Bible into the Judeo-Persian dialect of the Bukharian Jews. It was a custom among the Jews of Bukhara to have the Bible explained, in schools and especially in the synagogue, orally, by a *meturgeman*, or translator, on the basis of a commentary which had been orally transmitted. This oral method created in the course of centuries differences of text versions and explanations, departing from the traditionally accepted interpretation, and not always faithful to the text of the Bible. In order to eliminate further confusion in this respect, Simon Chacham wished to create "a fixed coin"—a written text of the *tafsir* (commentary) in the dialect of his fellow Jews.

He was motivated also by another factor; he saw in Jerusalem the Remnants of Israel from the four corners of the earth, each using the prayer book and the Bible in his own language and dialect. The Ashkenazim had their Yiddish, the Sephardim their Spaniol, the Yemenites and Maghribis their Arabic; "Why do we Persian-speaking Jews of Bukhara not possess a translation in our own dialect as well?"

Proud of the culture and language of his country of origin, Simon Chacham desired to make the Bible again a popular work by creating a written standard, authorized Judeo-Persian translation. He knew, of course, of the existence of the Pentateuch translation of Jacob b. Joseph Tawus (1546), but this version could hardly be used for his educational purposes; no copies were available and the versions differed from the specific Bukharian dialect; nor could the Bible edition of the Christian missionaries be used—for obvious reasons. The translations of some parts of the Bible into Judeo-Persian, such as the Psalms (1883), Proverbs (1885), Job (1895), *Shir Ha-Shirim* (1896 and 1904), did exist, but a complete Bible translation for the daily use of Bukharian Jews was lacking, and it was this consideration which prompted Simon Chacham to embark on this great enterprise. His *tafsir*, started in 1906, appeared in successive volumes, along with the Hebrew text, Targum Onkelos and Rashi, and, but for his death in 1910, the whole translation would have been accomplished. He completed the Pentateuch, and the Prophets up to Isaiah 41:9, and it was for his collaborators to complete the translation of the whole Bible.

With this monumental achievement Simon Chacham entered the ranks of the great Jewish Bible translators. What Saadia Gaon did for the Arabic-speaking Jews,[9a] what Moses Mendelssohn did for the German-speaking Jews,[10a] Simon Chacham did for the Persian-speaking Jews of Bukhara. With all his merits as editor, author, translator and promoter, it is his Bible translation that made him pre-eminent in the history of Judeo-Persian literature.

Europe and Judeo-Persian Literature
1. Elkan N. Adler, the Great Collector of Judeo-Persian Manuscripts

In the same period when, through the collective efforts of Persian-speaking Jews, Jerusalem was made the center of Judeo-Persian literary activities, European scholars, Jewish and non-Jewish, began to turn their attention to this branch of literature. It was not only Jerusalem but also Europe that saved the literary heritage of the Jews of Persia. Because of the close contact between Europe and Persia in the nineteenth century, an ever-increasing number of Judeo-Persian manuscripts reached the leading libraries of Europe. Short descriptions of Judeo-Persian manuscripts began to be included in the printed catalogues of libraries, such as Parma, Vatican, Paris, Petersburg, London, Oxford, Berlin, apart from private collections.

To judge from these catalogues European libraries possessed approximately fifty-five Judeo-Persian manuscripts.

A real conception of the size of Judeo-Persian literature was, however, revealed to Europe only when almost parallel with the discovery by Solomon Schechter of the *Genizah* in Cairo, an unexpectedly large collection of Judeo-Persian manuscripts was brought to Europe. The man who, more than anyone alse, has enriched our knowledge of the size of Judeo-Persian literature, was Elkan N. Adler. The travels of Elkan N. Adler to Persia and Bukhara, in the years 1896 and 1897, were revolutionary in the history of the collection of Judeo-Persian literature.

Seldom has a journey to the Middle East yielded such far-reaching results for Jewish literature and scholarship in general. While other Jewish travelers to Persia, in the nineteenth century, brought back impressions and observations on Jewish life and conditions, Adler was one of the few who, in addition to this, brought back the literary records of the peoples he visited in far-off lands. He returned from his travels with treasures hitherto unknown and hidden, with over one hundred Judeo-Persian manuscripts which changed fundamentally the prevailing conception as to quantity and quality of the literary productivity of the Persian-speaking Jews.

The collection that Adler brought from Persia and Bukhara to Europe corrected also our knowledge as to the character of Judeo-Persian productions. Most of the manuscripts in European libraries were translations of books of the Bible or of the Apocrypha, and the impression was created that their works were mostly of a religious character. The collection of Adler, however, revealed an all-embracing literature, not only translations, but also original works, not only religious literature, but literature of a secular character, poetry and prose, liturgy and philology; Adler's collection showed that no sphere of literary endeavor had been neglected by Persian Jews in their own language. Though European libraries have been continuously enriched since Elkan Adler with new Judeo-Persian manuscripts, Adler's collection has remained the outstanding single contribution to the field. With the acquisition of Elkan Adler's manuscript collection by The Jewish Theological Seminary of America, in 1923, this great treasure has found its home in New York and will enable scholars to utilize this greatest of all Judeo-Persian manuscript collections.

2. Wilhelm Bacher (1850-1913), the Great Investigator of Judeo-Persian Manuscripts

The efforts of bringing Judeo-Persian manuscripts from Persia and Bukhara to Europe, as manifested in Adler's collection, were supplemented by similar efforts in the field of the investigation and exploration of the Judeo-Persian texts, in the libraries of Europe. Already in the nineteenth century scholars, Semitists and Iranists, such as Salomon Munk, Hermann Zotenberg, Alexander Kohut, Ignazio Guidi, Paul de Lagarde, Theodor Noeldeke, Carl Salemann and Hermann Ethé, to mention but a few, had turned their attention to some of these Judeo-Persian manuscripts. A number of texts, ranging from small excerpts to complete versions, were published during that century, and language and contents have been made the object of these investigations.

Yet none of the scholars has made the study of Judeo-Persian literature so much his own and has so cultivated this new field of literary history of the Jews, as Wilhelm Bacher. While Simon Chacham could be regarded as the greatest *translator* and *publisher* of Judeo-Persian literature, and while Elkan Adler figures as the greatest *collector* of Judeo-Persian manuscripts, Wilhelm Bacher ranks undoubtedly highest among the *investigators* of Judeo-Persian literature.

Wilhelm Bacher, whose very first publication was a dissertation on the Persian poet Nizami (1871), was well equipped for the task of investigating the Judeo-Persian manuscripts. In 1895 he published his first contribution in that field in a Hebrew-Persian dictionary from the fifteenth century. With the availability of Elkan Adler's collection his interest was particularly stimulated and from then until his death in 1913 there passed no year in which he did not write numerous and valuable studies on the Judeo-Persian literature and language; there appeared in those years a continuous flow of publications that made him the undisputed authority in the field.

Elkan Adler's Judeo-Persian manuscript collection would hardly have received its proper evaluation had not Wilhelm Bacher made it one of his main tasks to utilize it exclusively.

There are undoubtedly still hidden treasures of Judeo-Persian literature in the countries of the East, in all the places in which Persian Jews settled (Jerusalem, Afghanistan, Bukhara, Turkestan, etc.); only after a systematic search for them and their description and publication, together with those in European and American libraries, will it be possible to appraise fully the literary production of Persian Jewry and to understand more fully the relationship between Israel and Iran.

Judeo-Persian Literature under the Qajar Dynasty (1796-1925)

In the nineteenth century, under the Qajar dynasty, the cultural life of Persian Jews reached its lowest level. The persecution and humiliation caused by the unchecked rule of fanatical masses, incited by a no less fanatical clergy, brought the Jews, deprived of any help or support, to the very edge of physical and moral dissolution.

In addition to the political pressure against them, there were other forces which threatened their existence as Jews, particularly the Christian missionary activities and the Bahai movement.

In the nineteenth century various Christian missionary societies in England and America embarked on a policy of spreading the gospel not only among the Nestorian Syrians in northern Persia, but also among the Jewish communities throughout Persia and Central Asia. Being fully aware of the deplorable political and social conditions of the Jews in Persia, who, as a result of centuries of persecution by the Shiite fanatics, were weakened in body and in spirit, the Christian missionaries expected to find a fertile soil in the Jewish Ghettos of Teheran, Hamadan, Isfahan and other communities.

That the Jews of Persia as a whole were by no means willing to forget their past and their religion and to follow the new message is borne out by a unique literary product which manifests very clearly the reactions of the Jews to these missionary efforts. The literary expression of the reaction is a *Toledot Yeshu* manuscript, the well-known medieval treatise on the life of Jesus; the Judeo-Persian translation was made in 1844. In translating that polemic treatise into Judeo-Persian, the author was no doubt motivated by the desire to combat the activities of the Christian missionaries of that time and to furnish a weapon of defense to the Persian Jews in their discussions with the Christian envoys. Apart from being the first literary instance that introduced the person of Jesus into Judeo-Persian literature in a polemic and apologetic way, it may even have appealed to the story-loving mind of the Persian Jew as a fantastic and interesting tale. This *Toledot Yeshu* manuscript indicates the kind of writing Persian Jews could produce in the nineteenth century, writing that bears the mark of apology and defense; indeed, Judeo-Persian literature became chiefly a weapon in the fight of Persian Jews for survival.

One of the main tasks of the Christian missionary activities was the distribution of pamphlets and stories with Christian tendencies, which, however, had to be rendered into Hebrew script in order to be read by Jews. For this they needed the help of Jewish converts to Christianity. Fully aware of the linguistic peculiarities of the Jewish population in Persian-speaking countries, the Christian missionaries started preparations as early as 1840 for the translation or transliteration of books of the New Testament into Persian with Hebrew characters. According to the British and Foreign Bible Society, "authority from Calcutta was given to issue an edition of Henry Martyn's translation of the New Testament with Hebrew characters for the use of the Jews in the northeast and southwest of Persia, whose language was Persian but who wrote it only in their traditional script." Thus, in 1847 the first Persian translation of the Gospels, transliterated into Hebrew characters, was printed in London to be distributed among the Jews of Persia.

The London Society also took steps to publish the Old Testament, particularly the Pentateuch, into Judeo-Persian. This task was entrusted to a Jewish convert, Mirza Nurallah of Teheran; he became one of the most active figures in the Protestant mission in Persia.

At the request of the British and Foreign Bible Society, Nurallah prepared, on the basis of the Persian version of the Pentateuch as published by Bruce, a transliteration of the Five Books of Moses into Hebrew characters. This was printed in London in 1895 and then distributed among the Jewish population in Persia.

Nurallah was supported in his efforts by another Jewish convert, Mirza Khodaidad with whose help the entire Old Testament in Persian translation, transcribed in Hebrew characters, was completed in 1907. For lack of any other Judeo-Persian translation of the Bible in print, it was, curiously enough, this Bible translation which penetrated into the Jewish homes and helped to make the Jew acquainted again with his own Bible.

It is symptomatic of the cultural level of the Jews in that century that to a large degree they ceased to be the creators of a literature of their own, and that others, non-Jews or former Jews, took the lead in creating Judeo-Persian writings for specific propaganda purposes.

This state of affairs is furthermore illustrated by the activities of another religious movement, born on Persian soil, which turned its attention toward the Jews, namely, the Bahai movement. This movement, Babism or Bahaism, a reaction to Shi'a Islam, had no small appeal to certain strata of Persian Jews who were attracted by the fact that this movement had abolished the influence of the clergy and the conception of ritual uncleanliness and treated all the various religious groups on an equal footing. A special apostle was entrusted with the task of winning over the Jews of Persia to that movement. Most prominent as a Bahai apostle was Mirza Abu'l Fadl of Gulpaigan, whose book *Istidlaliyya* was translated and transliterated into Hebrew for propaganda purposes. Other pamphlets, written in Persian with Hebrew characters, as well as the correspondence in Judeo-Persian between a Bukharian Jew Azizullah and a Bahai leader, preserved in the library of Edward G. Browne, are literary manifestations of the effect of the Bahai movement on Persian-speaking Jewry.

The Revival in Teheran

That Persian Jewry did not succumb to the dangers that engulfed it in the nineteenth century became evident in the first quarter of the twentieth century. Thanks to the establishment of schools in the main cities of Persia by the *Alliance Israélite Universelle,* thanks to a more liberal spirit in public life as expressed by the first constitution given to Persia under Muzaffar ad-Din Shah (1909), thanks to a closer contact with the Persian-speaking colony in Jerusalem, and last, but not least, thanks to the renaissance of Jewish life in Palestine, as the result of the Balfour Declaration, a new awakening began also among the Jews in Persia.

This awakening had a particular bearing on Judeo-Persian literature: it led to the transfer of Judeo-Persian printing activities from Jerusalem to Teheran and for the first time in history, made a Persian city, Teheran, the center of a Hebrew printing press, and with it of Judeo-Persian literature.

The first expression of the cultural renaissance of the Jewish youth in Persia was the founding of a "Society for the Promotion of the Hebrew Language" in 1917. Motivated by the endeavor to halt the stagnation and decline of Jewish life, to combat assimilation, ignorance and indifference, this society in 1918 published as the first fruit of its activities a work entitled *Sefer Hizug Sefat Eber*, a textbook for modern Hebrew. The author was Salomon ben Cohen Zedek of Teheran, a leader of the community and a Persian government official. In more than 170 pages the fundamentals of Hebrew grammar with reading and translation exercises from and into Persian are given. The work is the first attempt of its kind; and it is typical that it concludes with the Hebrew and Persian text of the *Hatikvah*.

This society published also the first *History of the Zionist Movement* in the Persian language in Hebrew characters (Teheran, 1920) by Aziz ben Yona Naim, giving a survey of the Zionist movement and the organizations and colonies in Palestine. The numerous biblical quotations from Isaiah and the Psalms in that history indicate the strong religious and Messianic character of Persian Jewry's conception of Zionism.

This Jewish circle published also a Jewish newspaper in the Persian language, *Ha-Geulah*, and later another paper called *Ha-Hayyim*, which became the mouthpiece of the Jewish renaissance movement in Persia. Some poems of the Hebrew poet Hayyim Nahman Bialik,[11a] were first translated into Persian in these periodicals by Aziz ben Yona Naim. The only other Judeo-Persian newspapers of which we have any knowledge were *Rushnai*, published in Samarkand, and *Rahamim*, published in Bukhara.

The leading figure in this group, which tried to revive Jewish consciousness among the Persian Jews, was Mulla Eliahu Hayyim More, the "most intelligent and cultured rabbi in the whole of Persia." He is the author of three important works on Jewish tradition, history and philosophy in Judeo-Persian, namely, *Sefer Derek Hayyim* (Teheran, 1927), *Sefer Gedulat Mordecai* (Teheran, 1924), *Sefer Yede Eliyahu* (Teheran, 1927), which have exerted a tremendous influence on his generation. Though blind from his early youth, this rabbi represented the most important factor in the efforts to lead Persian Jewry toward a Jewish revival. It is due to him that a new Jewish school, Koresh, was founded in Teheran in 1931, that modern Hebrew was incorporated into the curriculum and that new textbooks such as *Sefer Ha-Mathil* (Teheran, 1933-1934), modeled after Palestinian textbooks, and new prayer books for the Sabbath and holidays, were published to satisfy the religious needs of the Jewish youth.

In these activities a leading role was played also by the brothers Berukim in Teheran, who became the publishers of Hebrew-Persian and Hebrew books.

The political consequences of World War II for Persia have interrupted the process of regeneration and rejuvenation of the Jewish communities. The sound beginnings, aiming at a revival of Persian Jewish life, however, had already opened for the Jews in Persia as well as for all the communities in central Asia new perspectives of the revival of the cultural life of "Israel in Iran."

NOTES

[1a Cf. above Judah Goldin, "The Period of the Talmud (135 B.C.E.-1035 C.E.)," pp. 190-194.]

[2a Cf. *ibid.*, p. 175.]

3 For further details on Vechietti, see below pp. 1168 f. and also the *Enciclopedia Italiana*. Vol. XXXIV.

[4a Cf. above Shalom Spiegel, "On Medieval Hebrew Poetry," pp. 877-879.]

[5a Cf. *ibid.*, pp. 876-877.]

[6a Cf. above Cecil Roth, "The European Age in Jewish History (to 1648)," pp. 237 ff.]

[7a Cf. above Roth, "The Jews of Western Europe (from 1648)," p. 260.]

[8a Cf. above Itzhak Ben-Zvi, "Eretz Yisrael under Ottoman Rule, 1517-1917," pp. 677, 687.]

[9a Cf. Goldin, *op. cit.*, pp. 197 ff.; cf. also above Abraham S. Halkin, "Judeo-Arabic Literature," pp. 1124 ff.]

[10a Cf. Roth, *op. cit.*, pp. 261-262.]

[11a Cf. above Hillel Bavli, "The Modern Renaissance of Hebrew Literature," pp. 907 f.]

BIBLIOGRAPHY

With this study a first attempt is made to survey the main and typical literary productions in Judeo-Persian, to place them in their historical background and to interrelate them with the trends manifest in the general Persian cultural development.

A more detailed treatment of the subject with full documentation and annotations is given in the author's book, *The Jews in Persia, Their History and Literature,* now in manuscript.

Therefore, a brief selected bibliography will suffice here. Technical reasons prevented a more consistent transliteration of the Arabic, Hebrew and Persian words.

ADLER, ELKAN N., *Ginze Paras u-Madai . . . The Persian Jews, their Books and Ritual.* London, 1899.

BACHER, WILHELM, "Les Juifs de Perse au XVII et au XVIII Siècles." Strassburg, 1907.

————, "Judaeo-Persian Literature," in *The Jewish Encyclopedia.* New York and London, 1905. Vol. VII, pp. 317-324.

———, *Zwei juedisch-Persische Dichter, Schahin und Imrani.* Budapest, 1907-1908.

BARTHOLD, V. W., *Mussulman Culture.* Calcutta, 1934.

BLOCHET, EDGARD, "Catalogue des Manuscrits Persans de la Bibliothèque Nationale." Paris, 1905.

BROWNE, EDWARD G., *A Literary History of Persia.* Cambridge (Eng.), 1902 ff. Vols. I-IV.

CURZON, G. N., *Persia and the Persian Question.* 2 vols. London, 1892.

DARLOW, T. H., and MOULE, H. F., *Historical Catalogue of the Printed Editions of Holy Scriptures in the Library of the British and Foreign Bible Society.* London, 1911, Vol. IV, p. 1209.

ETHÉ, HERMANN, "Neupersische Litteratur," in *Grundriss der iranischen Philologie,* ed. Wilhelm Geiger. Strassburg, 1896-1904.

FISCHEL, WALTER J., "Judeo-Persian," in *Universal Jewish Encyclopedia.* New York, 1942. Vol. VI, p. 256.

———, "Literature, Judeo-Persian," in *Universal Jewish Encyclopedia.* New York, 1942. Vol. VII, pp. 96-98.

———, "Persia; from the twelfth to the twentieth century," in *Universal Jewish Encyclopedia.* New York, 1942, Vol. VIII, pp. 464-465.

———, *Jews in the Economic and Political Life of Medieval Islam* (Royal Asiatic Society Monographs). Vol. XXII. London, 1937.

———, "The Region of the Persian Gulf and its Jewish Settlements," in *Alexander Marx Jubilee Volume.* New York, 1949.

———, "Jews and Judaism at the Court of the Moghul Emperors in Medieval India," in *Proceedings of the American Academy of Jewish Research.* New York, 1949.

———, "Secret Jews of Persia: A Century-old Marrano Community in Asia," in *Commentary.* New York, January, 1949.

———, "The Jews under the Persian Kajar Dynasty (1795-1925)," in *Jewish Social Studies.* New York, 1950.

———, "New sources for the history of the Jewish Diaspora in Asia in the 16th century," *Jewish Quarterly Review,* Philadelphia, April, 1950.

———, "The Bible in Persian Translation: a Contribution to the History of Bible translation in Persia and India," in *Harvard Theological Review,* Cambridge, 1952, pp. 3-45.

———, "Isfahan: The Story of a Jewish Community in Persia," in *Joshua Starr Memorial Volume.* New York, 1953, pp. 111-128.

———, "Azerbaijan in Jewish History," in *Proceedings of the American Academy for Jewish Research,* New York, 1953, pp. 1-21.

———, "The Leaders of the Jews of Bokhara," in *Jewish Leaders,* ed. Leo Jung. New York, 1953, pp. 535-547.

FRIEDBERG, BERNHARD, *Bet Eked Sefarim* . . . Antwerp, 1928-1931.

GRAY, LOUIS H., "The Jews in Pahlavi Literature," in *The Jewish Encyclopedia.* New York and London, 1905. Vol. IX, pp. 462-465.

GUIDI, IGNAZIO, "Di una versioné persiana del Pentateuco," (Reale Accademia dei Lincei) Rendiconti. Rome, 1885.

KOHUT, ALEXANDER, *Kritische Beleuchtung der persischen Pentateuch-Ueberstezung des Jacob ben Joseph Tavus.* Leipzig, 1871.

LAGARDE, PAUL DE, "Persische Studien," in *Gesellschaft der Wissenschaften. Abhandlungen.* Goettingen, 1884.

LEVY, REUBEN, *Persian Literature; an introduction.* London, 1923.

LOCKHART, LAURENCE, *Nadir Shah; a critical study based mainly upon contemporary sources.* London, 1938.

MARGOLIOUTH, GEORGE, "Persian Hebrew Mss. in the British Museum," in *Jewish Quarterly Review,* VII, pp. 119-120. London, 1894.

MENASCE, JEAN DE, *Skand-Gumanik Vicar, Une Apologétique Mazdéenne du IX Siècle.* Freiburg, 1945.

MINORSKY, VLADIMIR, "Early Hebrew Persian Documents," in *Journal of the Royal Asiatic Society.* London, 1942, pp. 181-194.

MUNK, SALOMON, "Notice sur Rabbi Saadia Gaon et sa Version Arabe." Paris, 1838.

NICHOLSON, R. A., (ed. and tr.), *Jalal al-Din Rumi: Selected Poems from the Divani Shamsi Tabriz.* Cambridge, 1898.

ROSENTHAL, FRANZ, "A Judaeo-Arabic Work under Sufic Influence," in *Hebrew Union College Annual,* XV, pp. 434-484. Cincinnati, 1940.

SALEMANN, CARL, *Judaeo-Persica; 1 Chudaidat.* Petersburg, 1897.

———, *List of Oriental Mss. Presented to the Asiatic Museum.* Petersburg, 1898.

SELIGSOHN, MAX, "The Hebrew-Persian Mss. of the British Museum," in *Jewish Quarterly Review,* XV, pp. 278-301. London, 1903.

YAARI, ABRAHAM, *Sifre Yehudei Bukhara.* Jerusalem, 1942.

ZOTENBERG, HERMANN, *Catalogue des Manuscrits Hébreux de la Bibliothèque Nationale.* Paris, 1866.

CHAPTER 26

YIDDISH LITERATURE

By Yudel Mark

The Five Periods in the History of Yiddish Literature

Language is one of the principal elements distinguishing the Ashkenazic Jews from the Sephardic. The language of the Ashkenazim is Yiddish; that of the Sephardim, Judesmo (Ladino). Prior to World War II more than 10,000,000 persons, about two-thirds of all the Jews in the world, spoke or at least understood Yiddish.

Yiddish was born when emigrants from northern France, who spoke their own variation of old French, settled in a number of cities on the Rhine (later moving eastward) and adopted the German dialects of the area. In adopting these dialects, they adapted the new language to their old speech patterns and created a unique mixture of German dialects, caused by their wandering from one town to another. In addition, Hebrew had a continuing influence on the new dialect from the very beginning, because it (together with Aramaic) was the language of religion and scholarship. As a result, lexical, syntactical, and even morphological elements of Hebrew-Aramaic were amalgamated into Yiddish. This process of language formation began almost a thousand years ago. Later, the Slavic tongues (Czech, Polish, Ukrainian, Russian) exerted an influence on Yiddish. Thus Yiddish has to be considered a result of a fusion of the above-mentioned linguistic elements. It developed many unique characteristics due to the cultural isolation of the Jews.

Yiddish literature is only slightly younger than the Yiddish language and accompanied Ashkenazic Jewry wherever it moved. When Ashkenazic Jews arrived in sixteenth-century Italy, it became, for a short time, a center of Yiddish literary work. When an Ashkenazic community flourished in seventeenth-century Amsterdam, it became a center for the printing of Jewish books; there theatrical art in Yiddish was developed and the first Yiddish newspaper founded. When the focus of Jewish life shifted to the Slavic countries, they in turn became centers of Yiddish literature. Yiddish literature came to the United States of America with the East European immigrant masses, and the same is true in the Argentine, South Africa, and

Australia. Yiddish literature will be found on all the continents, wherever there are Ashkenazic, Yiddish-speaking Jews.

The history of Yiddish literature, which is almost eight hundred years old, may be divided conveniently into five periods:

I. The period of oral and manuscript literature—from the beginning to the close of the fifteenth century.

II. The folk book period—the sixteenth and the first half of the seventeenth century.

III. The period of relative decline—the latter half of the seventeenth and first half of the eighteenth century.

IV. The latter half of the eighteenth century to 1864 (the year Mendele Moicher Sforim began writing in Yiddish).

V. The past ninety years (1956).

The first three stages, up to the middle of the eighteenth century, represent the period of old Yiddish literature, reflecting as they do a life governed by tradition, stable, and relatively distinct from the surrounding Christian community, despite ever-present influence from the outside. The past ninety years (1956) may also be further subdivided into two periods: the first fifty years, to World War I, and the past forty years.

1. The Period of Oral and Manuscript Literature

A. THE OLD YIDDISH LITERATURE

From the outset, Yiddish literature was limited to a modest role. It was not meant to serve as the vehicle for scholarship; that was the prerogative of Hebrew. Yiddish was to provide recreational, light reading matter for the people of all social strata. At the same time however, it became a means of instructing those who had no access to Hebrew literature— women and the barely literate men. For hundreds of years the title pages of Yiddish works often carried this note: "Beautiful and instructive for Women and Girls" (for it would not have done to advertise that it was for the untutored!). Women were thus the avowed readers of Yiddish literature. A serious and scholarly man was often ashamed to be discovered frittering away his time with a work meant only to entertain.

It would be a mistake to compare the relationship between the literature in Yiddish and Hebrew with that between the vernacular and Latin literatures of Europe. For among the Jews almost every man was literate and the number who understood Hebrew was always incomparably greater than the number of educated medieval Christians who knew Latin. There was another significant difference: all didactic literature in Yiddish was either a direct outgrowth of Hebrew literature or influenced by it. Until very recent times the bond between the two literatures was so strong that one may justifiably speak of one literature in two languages (this, incidentally, was the view of Mendele Moicher Sforim, Baal-Machshoves, and Samuel Niger).

Yiddish literature, like many another, is related to folk lore, in this instance the folk lore of an ancient and sorely tried people. This folk lore is, on the one hand, didactic, full of tales of holy men, religious parables, and scholarly aphorisms and, on the other, recreational, full of general human themes. The didactic literature is based on traditional elements; the recreational works drew on the German heroic epic, chivalric tales, European folk songs and folk plays. For a short time there was a direct influence on Yiddish literature from Italian; indirectly there was influence even from Provençal.

While all the works based on general literature were often popular they were never held in high esteem by the people. Pious folk disparaged this literature, permitting its use only at celebrations, weddings, feasts. There were also periods when some rabbis expressly opposed the literature, because of its alien themes. This opposition stimulated the creation of devotional works which would be as absorbing as the secular adventure stories. As a result, the quality of the didactic literature improved.

B. THE SCRIBES AND THE SINGERS

There are extant some one hundred manuscripts containing about 150 works. Most of the manuscripts were lost as a result of the many expulsions and persecutions, and therefore our picture of the first period of Yiddish literary history is necessarily incomplete. Either the earliest manuscripts are concerned with popular medicine or they are translations of prayers and parts of the Bible.

Because handwritten works were expensive, only wealthy women could afford them. They would order scribes to prepare little anthologies for specific occasions. These scribes were not always mere copyists; they were also translators, adaptors, and even authors of original material. The scribes—or "servants of pious wives," as they called themselves—were often supported by their patronesses. These anthologies were conglomerations of songs, stories, amusing sketches, translations or new renditions of Biblical passages, important religious rules to be observed by women, and sundry helpful hints on proper conduct.

The principal disseminators of old Yiddish literature were the bards (singers) and jesters (fools), the comedians of their day. The bards sang ballads and selections from long metrical works or gave readings. Like the German *Spielmann*, or minstrel, they recounted sagas of heroism and of unusual events. The whole technique of the Yiddish bard—the tunes and stunts and terms—as well as a considerable portion of his repertoire, was adopted from the German minstrel. Almost all the better known works of the *Spielmann* reached the Jewish audiences, generally in some modified form. For example, passages referring to Christianity were either eliminated or replaced by Jewish allusions; the original work was abridged and thus made more compact; brutal scenes were somewhat humanized and made less offensive; chivalric details were omitted. Sometimes the changes were even more profound: Jewish motifs and details would be introduced and the elements of tragedy might be heightened the more effectively to arouse sympathy.

Much more interesting than the variations on foreign themes are the troubadour romances based on Jewish sources: generally, biblical stories adorned with midrashic and fanciful detail. The principal work of this genre is the *Shmuel-Bukh* (fourteenth or possibly fifteenth century), an adventure novel about David. It is a magnificent Davidiad containing details of chivalric combat, with scenes and episodes reminiscent of knighthood romances. Another such popular work was the eighty-stanza poem called *Akeydas Yitskhok*, or *Yiddisher Shtam* (*The Sacrifice of Isaac, or Jewish Descent*). With delicate lyricism and religious pathos it tells of Abraham's struggle with Satan as Isaac was being led to the sacrifice.

Not many lyrics have survived from this early period—and these only of the professional scribes and troubadours. Of the lyrics extant we find three types: (1) religious songs in praise of God and in honor of the Sabbath and the holidays; (2) didactic poems underscoring the Jewish view of life; (3) poems on general moral and folk-loristic themes.

This lyric material is also closely connected with the beginnings of Jewish drama, the humorous skits and didactic monologues and dialogues performed for the most part in the homes of the wealthy on festive occasions and during the Purim or Hanukkah holidays. Such a work was the popular *Dance of Death*; it may date back to the Spanish-Jewish period. Apparently the *Purimshpil* was already developing during this period; those we know, however, have come down to us from a later period.

C. THE RELIGIOUS POPULAR TALES

In the period between the Crusades and the sixteenth century many new legends were developed. New tales were told of the lives of great personalities. There are whole cycles of legends on men like Rabbenu Gershom, Rashi, and Rabbi Judah Hasid. Every community had its local tales. These folk stories reflect life under constant threat of expulsion, the blood libel, the pogrom, and, withal, the faith that all these dangers will be surmounted. Irrespective of the language in which they were first recorded, all these stories were developed in Yiddish.

2. THE PERIOD OF THE FOLK BOOK

A. LITERARY UPSWING IN THE SIXTEENTH AND THE FIRST HALF OF THE SEVENTEENTH CENTURY

1. *Elijah Bochur and the Bouva Story* (Bova Bukh)

The invention of printing gradually made the scribe superfluous and diminished the importance of the bard and the jester. Their tales could now be read and they had hundreds of thousands of readers. Unlike the previous period whose figures are anonymous, the great writers and folk teachers are distinct personalities. By far the most interesting figure of the first half of the sixteenth century is Elijah Bochur (1468?-1549).

Elijah Bochur's fame rests principally on his Hebrew scholarship; but he was interested in Yiddish too, and his poetic works were written exclusively in this language. His two great Yiddish novels are the *Bova Bukh* and *Paris un Viene*[1] (the latter never became popular). Both works are free adaptations of Italian romances and both are written in the Italian *ottava rima* stanza. The *Bova Bukh* became a most popular parody of the *Spielmann* novel. The author is playful and ironic; his jumbling of elements of Jewish folkways with stories of knightly exploits is grotesque. In short, he makes merry with the old claptrap of the troubadour's art.

The popular, short fantastic tale gave rise to a rich repository of novelle, legends and prose versions of the poetic works of the preceding period. The *packn-treger* (book peddler) who bore his library upon his back was the special agent who disseminated this literature, trudging all the way into the twentieth century with his bag of diverting merchandise.

Typical of the sixteenth century is the brief prose tale or novella based usually upon folk lore, Hebrew literature or foreign themes. Yet there were also some completely original works, the pearl among these being the anonymous *A Tale of Brie and Zimre*,[2] a glorification of that abiding love which is stronger than death.

2. *The Story Book and the Moralistic Tracts*

The story book (*Maase-Bukh*) of the latter sixteenth century (the oldest printed edition extant is dated 1602) is a compilation of the earlier *belles-lettres* and the cradle of later folk tales. This *Maase-Bukh*, which exerted a powerful influence on the style and content of Yiddish prose tales up to the modern period, is a collection of talmudic legends and medieval folk tales embellished with new particulars. If the *Maase-Bukh*, blending naiveté and deep faith with color, fantasy, and dramatic suspense, may be classified as didactic literature, it is the gem of that literary genre, displacing such frivolous works as the *Cow Book* (*Kuh Bukh*) and the earlier items in the bard's repertoire.

Although glossaries, like the *Mirkeves Hamishne* (Cracow, 1534), by Reb Asher Anshil, and translations of the Pentateuch, intended as aids to the teacher (*melamed*), never became folk books, they did start a trend which led to the *Woman's Pentateuch*. The so-called morality books, which showed great development during this period, applied the ethical principles of Judaism to everyday life. Whereas its prototype, the Hebrew morality book, is briefly formulary, severe and dryly apropos, the Yiddish version is more picturesque in style and less moralizing in tone. Aimed at the two-fold audience of the untutored man and the woman reader, it contains a parable at every step, illustrates the moral by an epigram and arouses interest by means of a story. Although the goal is to influence the conduct of the reader, the method is nevertheless to entertain him. The oldest Yiddish moralistic work handed down to us is the *Seyfer Mides* (*Book on Behavior*, Izni, 1542). Some morality books were meant only for the female reader, such as *Brantshpigl* (*Burning Mirror*, Basle, 1602). Later the most popular of these works was the *Lev Tov* (*Good Heart*), by Reb Isaac ben Elyokum of Posen (Prague, 1620), which was addressed to both men and women and is fervently religious.

3. The Woman's Pentateuch and the Special Prayers

Literal translations of the books of the Bible, removed as they were from the sphere of everyday life, failed to gain especial favor, and it was not until several efforts, such as the translation of the Pentateuch by Reb Isaac ben Samson, had been made that the most widely read and influential work of all Yiddish literature, the *Tseno-Ureno* (*Go Out and See*) by the Polish Jew, Jacob ben Isaac Ashkenazi (1550-1628), appeared. Ostensibly a translation of the Pentateuch, the *Haftoros* and the Five Scrolls, it is actually a unique mosaic of commentary, legend, allegory, epigram and ethical observation. The author drew upon the entire popular literary heritage from the canonization of the Bible to his own day, choosing those stories which related to the passages of the Pentateuch he was paraphrasing. Directed to the feminine reader, the work became a kind of woman's Bible which has been the source of Jewish knowledge for generations of mothers, who, Sabbath after Sabbath, have absorbed its Cabbala-flavored philosophy of life.

The *Tseno-Ureno*, reflecting the triumph of individual interpretation over literal translation, the prominence of the woman's role in everyday Jewish life and the paramount influence of Polish ritual over the more worldly Germanic, overshadowed all previous works in Yiddish and affected the life of the general population more deeply and more lastingly than any other.

Although Yiddish, like Aramaic before it, had become the language of the Jewish religion, the attempt (characteristic of the Reformation era), such as that of Joseph Bar Yokor (1544) to inaugurate a Yiddish prayer book, was not successful. However, the prayers of entreaty called the *tkhines* voluntarily added to the canonized Hebrew prayer did become popular. This supplementary prayer is concrete, speaks for a single individual and concerns a specific situation. Humbly pious and for the most part femininely delicate, many of these prayers were composed by women. The oldest collections we know are dated 1590 and 1599, while others were composed as late as the middle of the nineteenth century.

This special prayer, in reality a prose poem, expresses the religious lyricism so strongly developed in this period. A number of these Yiddish religious poems were incorporated into the Hebrew religious ceremonial. Of the numerous poets mention is made of "the pious Reb Jacob" of Teplitz and the poetesses Rebecca Tiktiner and Toibe Pan of Prague.

Some secular works were invested with a religious quality, such as the biting epigrams and doggerel of the misogynist Seligman Ulma, *Tsukhtspigl* (*Mirror of Manners*, Hanau, 1610). Although less completely developed, "wine, women, and song" poetry did make its appearance—the collection of Isaac, son of Moses Wallich of Worms (end of sixteenth century).

During the latter half of the sixteenth century Prague was the center of Yiddish poetry and the home of the most popular poet of the time, Solomon Zinger. He was famous for his wit and the few of his lyrics that are known today are distinguished for their humor and forcefulness.

The outstanding poetic form was the historical epic, describing and commemorating some important occurrence in the life of the community such as a pogrom, a fire or an epidemic. The historic poem followed a set pattern, opening with a passage in praise of God, recounting the main events in considerable detail, and ending with a prayer for the speedy advent of the Messiah. An example of such a poem is the *Vints-Hans-Song* by Elchanan, son of Abraham Heln (Frankfort on the Main, 1616), describing the anti-Semitic attack organized by Vincent Fettmilch, the expulsion of the Jewish community and its return. This scroll of Vints was read every year in Frankfort during observance of the local Purim.

The historical works in prose, of which the most popular was the *Yosifon* (Zurich, 1546) an adaptation of Josephus's *Antiquities,* followed the pattern of the earlier didactic morality books which did not separate fact from legend. Banishment and persecution are the principal themes of these historical works, such as the Yiddish translation of the *Tribe of Judah,* which recounts the expulsions from Spain and Portugal.

Descriptions of journeys are similar to the story books. Most popular and most fantastic of these travelogues was *The Regions of Eretz Israel* (Lublin, 1635), which was publicly burned by Jesuits in Warsaw. This book later was republished under the title *Path of Holiness*.

Although the stories and legends of the time were rich in dramatic detail, they did not become the bases for dramatic works. For this period we know only of Purim plays and of a rollicking comedy called *A Play About Deaf Yeklein, His Wife Kendlein and His Two Sons Fine* (end of sixteenth century).

3. THE LATTER HALF OF THE SEVENTEENTH AND FIRST HALF OF THE EIGHTEENTH CENTURY

The Sabbatai Zevi movement[3a] gave a kind of ascetic and mystical overtone to Jewish life in eastern Europe, which also became increasingly conservative. While these tendencies are reflected in the literature, no new forms were evolved or great works written to supplant the old favorites. The only center of a freer life was Amsterdam.[4a] There during the 1680's two antihomiletic translations of the Bible were made (by Blitz and Witzenhausen), entirely contrary to the spirit of the times.

However, the focal book of the period was not the Bible but the *Zohar*, the holy book of the Cabbala.[5a] Indicative of the interest in Jewish mysticism is *The Work of the Lord* (Frankfort on the Main, 1691), a collection of fifty stories about its heroes from the founder (?) Reb Simon ben Jochai to Reb Isaac Luria. The morality book *Nakhlas Tsvi*, known as "*Taytsh Zohar*" (Frankfort, 1711), by the Cracow Cabbalist Zevi Hirsh Chotscz also became popular. In the main the Cabbalists addressed themselves to the male reader, appealing to the emotions of the ordinary man of the people, and in doing so took a strong stand against the intellectual aristocracy of the talmudic scholars. Zevi Hirsh Koidanover, in his *Kav Hayosher* (Frankfort, 1705) inspires pious fear in the hearts of his readers, threatening them with punishment for their sins in the hereafter. Closely akin to the spirit of this stern work are the translations from the Hebrew of the early morality books, of which one of the best known is the gentler and more mystical Khoives Halvoves (*Duties of the Heart*, 1716). A work of this period, which foreshadowed the Hasidism of a later era, was Elchanan Kizkhhan's *Simkhas Hanefesh* (*Soul's Delight*, Frankfort, 1707).

A. POETIC AND NARRATIVE WORKS OF THE PERIOD

Laments over proscriptions and expulsions, usually entitled "new" (e.g., *A New Lament upon the Destruction in Worms; A New Lament over the Expulsion from Tannhausen*) were the most important poetic works. Their titles are ironic, for their themes are as old as the Diaspora, the form set by tradition and the only changes, those of place, year and detail of horror.

The tradition of "Sacred Poems" continued, as exemplified by Aaron ben Samuel of Eggershausen's collection entitled *Gentle Prayer or Powerful Medicine for Body and Soul* (Fuerth, 1709). Containing poetic variations of the traditional prayers along with new and original songs of praise, the work was printed in square letters like those of the authorized prayer book, instead of in "woman's script" used for Yiddish translations of Hebrew books, and consequently was banned by the rabbis.

Folk songs were the source for much vibrant poetry, such as numerous lyrics of the "one kid" variety and paraphrases of the "Who Knows One?" verses. The most important piece of satiric expression of the times is the anonymous *Description of Ashkenaz and Pole* in which Polish, German and Czech (Prague) Jews are compared. Motifs of social protest also occur in some of the laments.

The narratives, such as the humorous story about the bigamist, *A Nice New Song About What Happened in Hamburg* (Amsterdam, 1675), still follow the verse form of the "singer" or "bard." However, the "story book" pattern is used with increasing frequency, as in *The Story of Miracles*, a collection of twenty-five popular legends of Worms, by the sexton of the community, Jeptha Yuspa ben Naftoli. A curious work is the *Story of West India* in which the new and foreign literature of adventure is combined with the old fount of Jewish legend. Quite characteristically Jewish is the travel romance entitled *Amsterdam Story* which describes the experiences of a rabbi who set out to comb distant lands in search of the Lost Ten Tribes of Israel.

The best prose work of this period, however, remained in manuscript. The splendid memoirs of Glikl Hamil (of Hameln, near Hamburg) written between 1691 and 1719, tell the life story of a prominent woman, well acquainted with old Yiddish literature. The work gives an account of the contemporary way of life, of family and economic affairs, of important historical events, and of private joys and sorrows. In her entries Glikl revealed a gift for accurately observing life and still greater facility for narration.

The great events of the period aroused an interest in history manifested by a Yiddish translation of *Yeveyn-Metsule*, an account of the holocaust of 1648-1649. Menachem ben Solomon Amelander's original historical work, *Remnants of Israel* (Amsterdam, 1741), an account of Jewish history from the destruction of the Second Temple to the author's own time, enjoyed great popularity.

Of the travelogues worthy of note is the early eighteenth-century work *A Description of the Travels of Abraham Levi*. Sabbatai Bass's geographical work, *Ways of the World*, contains, in addition to directions for reaching a number of large cities, prayers to be said en route. This period also witnessed the appearance of many popular medical works, account books and collections of model letters.

Amsterdam, center of Yiddish book production, was also the home of the first Yiddish newspaper, *Di Dinstogshe Kurantn* and *Fraytogshe Kurantn* (*Tuesday and Friday Courant*), a semiweekly publication which compared favorably with contemporary Dutch papers.

Despite the growth of religious feeling during this period and despite the Jews' seclusion from the rest of the world, the Yiddish theater was well liked both as a temporary stage for Purim players and *yeshiva* students and as the theater of professional actors. A number of plays from the first half of the eighteenth century have come down to us, such as *The Sale of Joseph, The Sacrifice of Isaac, David and Goliath, The Exodus from Egypt, King Solomon's Verdict, Sodom and Gomorrah*.

4. THE SECOND HALF OF THE EIGHTEENTH AND THE FIRST HALF OF THE NINETEENTH CENTURY

A. THE DECLINE OF YIDDISH LITERATURE IN WESTERN EUROPE

Yiddish literature, like the Yiddish language, had its beginnings in Western Europe. For hundreds of years there had been a lively interchange of books and authors between West and East, when, at about the middle of the eighteenth century, a cleavage became apparent.

The period began with the abandonment of the spiritual Ghetto by the Yiddish intelligentsia of the West and its involvement in the capitalist system, which Jews helped to erect. In contradiction to its intended function, the Enlightenment movement became one of increasing assimilation, as evidenced by the use of the derogatory term "jargon" to describe the Yiddish language. For the first time Jewish scholars took pains to disparage their own language in the eyes of their people. Thus literary art in Yiddish declined rapidly; it was, however, preserved in Eastern Europe, where it later came to fruition.

In the West we find only epigonian works in the spirit and style of the foregoing period: historical poetry, chronicles, memoirs (such as the recollections of Aaron Isaacs, the first Jew in Sweden), translations of world literature (like that of *Robinson Crusoe* published in Metz in 1764). A unique work that attempted a compromise between tradition and Enlightenment, but which remained in manuscript, was *Love Letters* by Itsik Vetslar. We have only two plays of the Enlightenment school in Yiddish, both belonging to the late eighteenth century and both excellent literary creations in the style of the bourgeois drama—*Reb Hennach* or *What's to be Done with It* by Isaac Eichl and Aaron Wolfson's *Frivolity and False Piousness*. The final remnants of Western Yiddish literature in the nineteenth century are the dialect parodies of Joseph Herts and the lampoonery and playlets of Morits Gotlib Saffir.

Of the many periodical publications not one was long-lived. The *Dirnfurter Privilegirte Tseytung*, a semiweekly (1771-1772), was directed primarily to the Jews of Poland. In Amsterdam the new scholarly community of the Enlightenment and followers of the revolutionary movement published the periodical *Diskurs* (*Discourse*, 1797-1798). Amsterdam, the most stable center of Yiddish literature in the West, was also the birthplace (1784-1802) of the Yiddish operatic theater of Jacob Dessoier, himself the author of various *Zingshpiln*. In Vienna the musical comedies of David Leib Biderman were produced during the 1830's and 1840's.

B. HASIDIC LITERATURE

Hasidism, which brought a stream of joyousness and exaltation into the life of the ordinary man, made greater use of Yiddish than had earlier religious movements. Famous Hasidic rabbis frequently prayed in Yiddish and gave expression to their teachings in that tongue, thus enriching and refining the language. The Hasidic movement also gave impetus to a renascence of popular creativity: stories, poetry, parable, apothegms, and adages. The popular tale acquired a new hero, the Hasidic rabbi, while the former hero, the *Lamed Vov*, took on new importance. Thus inspired, Jewish popular fancy expressed itself in a whole series of marvelous tales which became part of the "literature of praise" of the Hasidic rabbis, the most popular being *Shivkhey Besht* (*Praises of the Besht*, 1815). In this manner a new holiday spirit entered the soul of the people and the heavens moved a little closer to earth.

The allegories and stories of the Baal Shem Tob (the Besht) himself gave the impetus to Hasidic literature. His skill in relating these tales raised them to the level of recited Torah. His disciples, in retelling these anecdotes, always added embellishments of their own, thus laying the foundation for a new and widespread oral tradition among the less educated and even the untutored Jews. The courts of some Hasidic rabbis became centers of artistic creativity in poetry, music, and the dance. The Maggid of Mezeritsh was a fine fabulist. Reb Levi Yitzkhok Barditshever was an outstanding allegorical poet. His prayers reveal the rather unusual union of exalted pantheism, a sense of intimacy with the Creator, and a feeling of the importance of the individual.

One of the greatest Jewish narrators of all time was the mystic dreamer Reb Nachman Brahtslever (1772-1810). A great-grandson of the Besht, rocked in the cradle of Hasidism, he lived more in a visionary realm than in his actual environment, against which he rebelled. While some of the elements of his fantasies are taken from the folk tale, and even from universal motifs, the essential construction, the winged scope, the delicate form, and the ethical-mystical ideas are all completely original. His romanticism, so characteristic of the period, is deeper and more revealing than the vague longings of the *Weltschmerzler*, imbued as it is with the fervor for serving God.

One group of his stories is realistic, containing details of everyday life, while the majority of his tales are of the cloth of free fantasy interwoven with lyricism. After Reb Nachman's death, his colleague and pupil, Nosn Nemirover, published the stories (which his disciples believed disclosed the secrets of the Torah and of life) in a collection entitled *Sipurey Maasiyes* (*Narrative Tales*, 1815). The disciple recorded the sayings of his master verbatim, regarding every word as a holy utterance. Thus we have an accurate picture of the style of Reb Nachman, whose wonderful personality left so deep an impression upon his followers that they never acknowledged another leader—they remained the "dead Hasidim." Up until the outbreak of World War II, they made annual pilgrimages to his grave in Uman and always conducted themselves differently from all other Hasidim.

In the *Narrative Tales* we see a link in the chain of the centuries-old narrative tradition begun with the *Maase-Bukh* and to be continued in the works of Isaac Leibush Peretz.

At the same time that the West European Jew was beginning to assimilate and cease creating anything in Yiddish, East European Jewry was being influenced by the Hasidic movement to delve deeper into itself, to amass new vitality, and to bring to the fore new works of art in Yiddish letters, music and dance.

C. THE LITERATURE OF THE ENLIGHTENMENT, TO THE MIDDLE OF THE NINETEENTH CENTURY

The movement for enlightenment (*Haskala*) followed two roads from West to East: the principal one, through Galicia to southern Russia and Poland; the other, directly to Lithuania. The *Haskala*, embracing the intelligentsia and the merchant class, aimed to free the individual from the restraints of tradition by educating him and by remodeling Jewish life on a freer foundation so that he might deserve and achieve emancipation.[6a] But the *Haskala* also brought with it from Germany the desire to forget Yiddish and adopt the language of the land. However, the more realistic of the enlightened readily realized that they had to make use of Yiddish in order to spread their beliefs. Another point of difference, and a more fundamental one, was the clash (which continued throughout the nineteenth century) between the elements opposed to Yiddish and those cultured East European Jews who loved the rejected masses and were devoted to their language. Two closely related trends are characteristic for the *Haskala* literature in Yiddish. One is indicated by works designed to instruct and propagate the ideas of the *Maskilim* (followers of *Haskala*), and the other by polemic works which were critical of the old way of life. The instructive works were a modern continuation of the morality books, while the polemic works consisted almost entirely of satires. The dramatic form was used by the *Maskilim* only as a means of faithfully recording daily events and for the purpose of debate. The narrative form is also rich in realistic detail but it is often exaggerated and interrupted by journalistic digressions.

Oddly enough it was a Geman Jew, Moses Markuse, a physician in the small towns of Poland and Lithuania where he was stranded, who wrote a most unusual book, *Seyfer Refues* (*The Book of Remedies*), highlighting the differences between the *Haskala* of the East and that of the West. The work, a mixture of popular medicinal practice and Enlightenment ideology, reveals a great love for the common man. At the same time, *Maskilim* made new translations into Germanized Yiddish of works from other languages, such as Kampe's *Discovery of America*, with a view toward contributing to the education of the people. This version by the Lithuanian *Maskil*, Mordecai Aaron Ginsburg, was not particularly successful but that of an Uman merchant, Chaim Chaikl Hurvits, *Tsofnas Paneach* (1817), was immensely popular. The language of this work, based as it was upon spoken Yiddish, represents a definite departure from the old literary language, which had become too archaic and Germanic.

The theoretician and chief protagonist of this new trend, which was making rapid headway, especially among the *Maskilim* of Galicia and Podolia, who used it in revising earlier Yiddish works, was Mendl Leffin, or Mendl Satanover (1749-1826), as he was known, a dominant figure in the Enlightenment and a link between the Berlin *Haskala* and that of Galicia and southern Russia. He proposed to translate the Bible into the idiomatic Yiddish of his Ukrainian dialect, intending, as did Moses Mendelssohn,[7a] to turn the people toward the Bible. Satanover hoped to do this by relating the Scriptures to Yiddish in contradiction to the endeavors of Mendelssohn. Satanover's plan was not realized because of disputes which arose concerning it, and only the Book of Proverbs was published (1814), several other sections circulating in manuscript. The whole project was not completed until the twentieth century through the translation by Yehoash in the United States. However, the new Yiddish literary language, based upon everyday spoken vernacular, was strengthened. Approximately at the same time the practice was established of using square characters for printed Yiddish instead of the cursive "woman's script."

At the beginning of the nineteenth century the new forms and ideas worked their way into the model-letter pamphlets which for generations had served as texts for learning Yiddish style, as well as the writing of the language itself. Illustrative is Levin Lion D'Or's *Nayer Kinstlecher Brivnshteller (New Artistic Letter Writer*, Vilna, 1825), which went through ten editions.

The *Maskilim* directed their sharpest satire against the Hasidim and the courts of their rabbis. In 1815 the rabbinical judges of Lemberg excommunicated the local *Maskilim* and by way of comment there appeared the excellent anonymous *The Duped World*, a Tartuffian comedy of much wit. Undoubtedly the author belonged to the circle of Mendl Satanover, as did Joseph Perl, wealthy merchant of Tarnopol, who authored in Hebrew and in Yiddish the satiric *Megale Tmirin*. Consisting of 151 letters of twenty-six correspondents, this work is an imitation of the humanist *Epistolae Obscurorum Virorum*. Another author of the same circle wrote the satirical story, *The Greatness of Reb Volf of Charni-Ostrow*.

The ill and poverty-stricken Isaac Baer Levinson, known as the "Philosopher of Kremenetz" and the "Mendelssohn of Russian Jewry," wrote a social satire attacking the injustice of the community to the poor masses. Entitled *Hefker Velt (Heedless World)*, this work marks the beginning of the militant social writing of the nineteenth century. "Rivol," as he was known, also wrote a satirical poem, *Purim Play*. The Polish *Maskil*, Efraim Fishlzon, composed a three-act comedy, *Theater of Hasidim*, an anti-Hasidic satire in the form of arguments. The anonymous derisive poem, *Troubles of the Teachers*, gives a sad picture of traditional education. The above-mentioned works are important for their social message rather than for their artistic merit.

In addition to the hindrances imposed by the Russian government, the fact that they were but scattered groups, prevented the *Maskilim* from developing a journalistic press. In 1823-1824 the weekly *Observer on the Vistula* was published in Warsaw; its language being quite Germanic, the publication did not long survive. It was not until the revolution of 1848 that a Yiddish weekly, called *Zeitung*, made its appearance in Lvov, Galicia; it was published again in 1863 as the *Yudishe Zeitung*.

D. ISRAEL AXENFELD AND SOLOMON ETTINGER

Almost all the *Haskala* writers mentioned thus far also wrote in Hebrew and regarded their Hebrew works as the more important. Now we turn to two writers of the first half of the nineteenth century who wrote exclusively in Yiddish.

Israel Axenfeld (1787-1866), an Odessa lawyer, was the first great storyteller of the Enlightenment. Although as a youth he had been a Hasid, indeed a colleague of Reb Nosn Nemirover, he devoted all his literary talents to combating "Baal-Shemism" and Hasidism. In the main, the naturalist in him triumphed over the satirist, and his characterizations, patterned as they were after actual persons, are vital if primitive. Yet he lacked the power for synthesis so necessary in a truly great realistic writer. The *Maskilim* read his many novels and stories in the manuscript form used in the days before the invention of printing. He was more fortunate in getting his dramatic works published and his play, *The First Jewish Recruit,* was performed with evident success on the Yiddish stage of the 1920's and 1930's. Axenfeld's sketches of milieu are still interesting today as source materials and his influence upon Mendele Moicher Sforim (see below) was considerable.

Although Galicia and southern Russia produced most of the writers of this period, the most important talent came from Poland. Solomon Ettinger (1800-1856), who has been called "the great-grandfather of modern Yiddish literature," wrote in Yiddish not for the purpose of spreading cultural or social ideas but for art's own sake. He was the first to attempt to refine Yiddish, to create new words and polish his style. The first lyricist per se, he described nature and his own moods even though they were subjective and pointed no moral. His clever allegories and good-humored epigrams are lively and witty; the poetic descriptions of character types lack the sharpness of the *Haskala* satire. Ettinger pioneered in the kind of literature that focuses upon the individual and his feelings rather than upon the group and its problems, and widened the scope of Yiddish literature, linking it with that of Europe.

Ettinger's masterpiece is the dramatic comedy *Serkele (Little Sarah)*, a story of character and environment in which the central figure is a capable woman who dominates her household and is unscrupulous in her drive for wealth and power. Although Ettinger did borrow a few secondary details from the militant comedies of David Eichl and Aaron Wolfson, his plot, technique, and characters were his own and became the prototypes for later works, such as Jacob Gordin's *Mirrele Efros* (see below) and the plays of Abraham Goldfaden. Ettinger's works, censored by the czarist regime, did not appear until after his death.

E. THE FIFTIES AND SIXTIES OF THE NINETEENTH CENTURY

The first nineteenth-century Yiddish author to enjoy a reading public numbering in the tens of thousands was the Vilna *Maskil,* Isaac Meir Dyk (1814-1893). His hundreds of realistic short stories and more romantic novels were especially popular in Lithuania and were always to be found in the itinerant peddler's pack. His intention was to enlighten and instruct the people, refine their ways, and teach them German by using many German expressions in his writings, translating them into pure Yiddish. Dyk's style often reminds us of that of the morality book. He addresses himself to the "dear lady reader" and discourses with her about child education, the dangers of luxurious living, purity in family life, the value of living off the soil and of educating oneself. Isaac Meir Dyk is a combination of the maggid and the modern storyteller, embodying the old tradition and at the same time foreshadowing the realistic literature of a later period.

The theoretician among the conservatives of the *Haskala* was Eliezer Tsvi Tsveifl, whose aim it was to combine the positive elements of Orthodoxy and Hasidism with the newer teachings of the Enlightenment. He not only sought to interest his colleagues and disciples at the rabbinical school of Zhitomir in writing in Yiddish, but was the author of some good stories himself, such as *The Fortunate Maftir* and the half-literary, half-journalistic *Life's Punishments*. Influenced by Mendl Satanover, he in turn affected Mendele Moicher Sforim and was the first to give impetus to the Neo-Hasidism of the late nineteenth and the early twentieth century.

The radical wing of the *Haskala* was distinguished by the fighting spirit of Abraham Gotlober, who had led the difficult life of a wanderer. His comedy, *The Veil, or Two Weddings in One Night*, shows the influence of Ettinger's *Serkele*. Of principal importance to Yiddish literature are his poems, such as *The Poor Yisroilik*, which was exceedingly popular and topically characteristic of the Enlightenment. His humorous Yiddish version of Schiller's *Song of the Bell* became the *Song of the Sabbath Pudding*. Incidentally, Schiller was the German writer most popular with the *Maskilim*, and there are several curious versions in Yiddish of his aforementioned *Song of the Bell*, the most felicitous of which is Hirsh Reitman's *The Kittel* (*The White Prayer Mantle*).

Alongside the poetry of the more intelligent *Maskilim* there existed the folk lyrics in the old tradition of the bards. During the middle years of the nineteenth century there were two great poets of the people: the wandering, bohemian Berl Margolies, known as Berl Broder, and the more colorful and refined Wolf Ehrenkrants, who went by the name of Velvl Zbarzher.

In the city of Brody, the center of trade and of the *Haskala*, Berl Broder established a cabaret troupe for which he created the repertory. These "Singers of Brody" became very popular and made guest appearances all over Galicia, southern Russia, and Poland, spreading Broder's merry yet melancholy songs of the fate of the common man as well as his lyrical nature poems. The collection, entitled *Shirey Zimro* (*Song Poems*), was published in 1860.

Velvl Zbarzher sang of wine and love, of the eternal yearning for peace, and of the pettiness of life in the wine cellars of Rumania and Bessarabia, in Vienna and Constantinople. Motifs of the intellectual *Haskala*, the mundane details of everyday life, old lyric balladry, and modern writing—

all were interwoven in the works of these two poets, the last in the many generations of bardic singers.

With the exception of the little-theater performances by the Singers of Brody and by sporadic companies in Warsaw (1838-1839; 1866-1870), there had not developed a permanent professional Yiddish theater. However, this did not prevent the writing of a number of dramatic works, some of them rather effective, such as *The Town Community,* by Wolf Kamrash; Joel Berish Falkovitch's *Reb Chaim the Rich* and *Little Rachel, the Singer; Heaven-Made Match* by Hirsh Reitman; Isaiah Gutman's *The Three Cousins* and *Kolboynik (The Rascal).* Such works were read aloud at small gatherings and performed by amateurs.

By the middle of the nineteenth century there was a large reading public thirsty for new books. The lack of a Yiddish press, barred by the Russian government, retarded the development of Yiddish literature. In 1862, however, the *Koil Mevasser (The Voice of the Messenger)* appeared in Odessa, and from that time forward Yiddish journalism developed very rapidly. Many talented new writers appeared and the earlier authors became more strongly established as their works were reprinted.

At about this time important changes occurred in Jewish life, with the emancipation of the Russian peasant in 1861, the migration from the small towns to the big cities, the development of commerce and trade in which the Jews took a more active part, and the rise of the working class, struggling for a freer and a better life—all related to the rapid advance of Yiddish literature.

5. THE NEW YIDDISH LITERATURE

A. MENDELE MOICHER SFORIM, HIS CONTEMPORARIES AND DISCIPLES

The central figure in Yiddish literature in the last three decades of the nineteenth century is Mendele Moicher Sforim. The major trend is his trend: the realistic. The major achievement is his, too: the establishment of form, style, technique, and modern literary language. All the literati may be grouped about him: those who walked with him and those who followed, the ones who opposed him and the ones who wrote during his time but belonged to that of his predecessors. We begin with the last mentioned.

The most important in the line of Yiddish authors linking the folk song with individual poetry is the Vilna-born Michl Gordon (1823-1892), who criticized the traditional way of life in his works. In a rhythmic and lucid style he created ballads of milieu such as *The Divorce, The Beard, After the Wedding.* And in pained elegiacs he bemoaned his impoverished life (*My Years, My Lifetime, My Last Day*). His brother-in-law, the great Hebrew poet, Yehuda Leib Gordon, touched upon social themes of the

Enlightenment in his Yiddish poems collected under the title *Sikhas Khulin* (*Commonplace Talk*, 1886). The Vilna poet, S. Y. Katsenelenbogen, treated of the most diverse topics with delicate lyricism which revealed the influence of Heine and the Russian poets, and paved the way for the poetry of Frug.

The most popular song writer was the last bard of Yiddish poetry, Eliokum Tsunzer (1835-1913). Didactic and moralizing, Tsunzer propagandized for the Enlightenment and later for Zionism. In his ballads, as in those of the bards, personification is common (*The Ferryboat*). Sung first at celebrations in well-to-do homes, his songs found their way to the masses and *The Plow, The Aristocrat, The Nineteenth Century* became extremely popular. More polished and more individual is the poetry of Abraham Goldfaden (1840-1908), author of romantically nationalistic poems and skilled in the art of versification. (On his operettas, see below.) There also belong in this line of writers Samuel Bernstein, poet and writer of comedies, and Ludwig Levinson, author of the very comical *Vaybershe Kniplekh* (*Women's Savings*).

We may now turn to the central figure, the grandfather of modern Yiddish literature. Sholem Jacob Abramovitch (1835-1917) was born in the small town of Kapulye in the province of Minsk. After several years of the hard life of a *yeshiva* student, he became the companion of a wandering beggar. But in Kamenets Podolsk he met Abraham Gotlober, who influenced him to take up cultural pursuits. For a time he lived in Barditchev, but was obliged to leave because of his work *Die Takse* (*The Meat Tax*) in which he exposed the local clique of "do-gooders." He struggled in Zhitomir and finally settled in Odessa, where he became the director of a Talmud Torah. When he began writing in Yiddish (1864) he took the name Mendele Moicher Sforim,[8a] which is more than just a pseudonym: through his works there passes the figure of an elderly Jew who rides about with his wagonful of books providing the people with prayers of supplication and lament, all the time smiling good-naturedly as he observes life around him. This figure helped to narrow the distance between the author and his readers. Mendele Moicher Sforim, inspiring love and admiration, was the first to establish a really intimate relationship between the Yiddish writer and his public.

During the first twenty years of his creative life, Mendele was a fighting satirist. Becoming more tranquil with the passage of time, he turned from satire to humor, from social crusading to memorializing a bygone way of life. True to the teachings of Eliezer Tsvi Tsveifl, he did not oppose Hasidism and never wounded the religious feeling but directed his social satire against those in power who wrong the people (*The Little Man, Die Takse*), against economic injustice (*The Wishing Ring, Fishke the*

Lame), against the helplessness of the small town and its ignorance of the world (*The Travels of Benjamin the Third*).

The motifs of the *Haskala* gain depth in his work, personified as they are by a gallery of realistic figures. Mendele is a perfectionist and does not hesitate to rewrite his works, improving and adding to them. In *Die Takse* (see above) he not only mentions the clique of exploiting benefactors, but also gives us the autobiographical figure of Shloime Wekker, forerunner of the revolutionary movement among the Jews of Russia.

In the symbolic *Klyatshe* (*The Nag*, 1873) we have, ten years before its active acceptance, the manifestation of a national idea which did not become current until the eighties, as well as a penetrating socioeconomic critique of the *Haskala*. Thus the author also occupies an outstanding place in the history of Jewish social consciousness. This parallel development of literary art and social awareness is a fundamental characteristic of the years between 1864 and 1914, the period of the greatest advance in Yiddish literature.

In making Kabtsansk (*kabtsen*-Hebrew: poor man) his typical town and Gloopsk (*gloop*-Slavic: foolish) his typical city, Mendele is a synthesist. His broad canvases depict the most ordinary small-town happenings and present the house of study and the house of the poor, the home and the public bath, the weekday and the Sabbath, the philosophy of life and the merest grimace. It is curious, however, that this richly detailed picture of Jewish life has a definite limit in time. Anything later than the 1870's escapes Mendele's brush. In the main he relies upon his memory, so that it is not surprising that his autobiography, *Schloime, Son of Reb Chaim*, is also a splendid objective novel.

Since Mendele is extremely exacting in his realistic portrayals of a rather static life, his plot structure suffers. This careless attitude toward plot development became characteristic of the entire realistic school in Yiddish literature. (Is this perhaps due to the influence of the Russians?) But his masterful descriptions of various ordinary types, specifically Jewish in flavor, and his wonderful pictures of nature have a beauty which has never been surpassed.

Mendele is primarily responsible for the standardization of modern literary Yiddish. Eschewing the use of his own dialect, he was the first to strive consciously toward a synthesis of the Lithuanian and Ukrainian dialects and to include words and usages from earlier works. Mendele is the hub of the whole nineteenth century: as a social satirist, as the creator of a plastic yet statically synthetic realism, as the molder of a new style, he embodies the sum total of the Enlightenment movement. His antecedents, Mendl Satanover and his circle, lived at the beginning of the nineteenth century and his influence extends far beyond its close.

Appearing at the same time as Mendele's writings in the *Voice of the*

Messenger, was *The Polish Boy* (in the second edition, *The Hasidic Boy*), a satirically biting autobiographical novel by Isaac Joel Linetski (1839-1916), whose indictment of Hasidic practices was the strongest ever written. The work created a great furor, but Linetski showed no further development and accomplished nothing with his anti-Mendele position.

Temporary success was enjoyed by *The Dark Young Fellow*, a sensational, melodramatic novel by Jacob Dinnezon (1856-1919). At first Dinnezon was opposed to Mendele in principle, claiming that the latter was too refined and too indifferent to the receptive capacity of the mass of Jewish readers. Although Dinnezon's themes are inclined to be those of primitive folk lore, the triumph of Mendele's artistic approach is apparent. In *Hershele* and *Yossele*, which appeared in the nineties, Dinnezon did preserve his sentimentalism, but it is subtler, revealing the influence of Mendele.

The less educated reader, in particular the women of the lower social strata, could not enjoy the Mendele literature. To fill the need of this audience, there appeared during the seventies and eighties colorful and unrealistic novels of improbable romances between a *yeshiva* student and a princess or a count and a servant maid, with detailed descriptions of their misfortunes before the inevitable happy ending, thus affording the reader a chance for a good cry.

Dozens of such novels were written by Shomer (pseudonym of Nokhem Meyer Sheikevitch), founder of a whole school of hack writers (Blohstein, Buchbinder, *et al.*). These Shomerians challenged, so to speak, the disciples of Mendele Moicher Sforim: There, let us see you create artistic works that will be intelligible as well as entertaining to all. Sholem Aleichem quite consciously took up the gauntlet and emerged the victor.

B. PIONEERS IN POETRY, DRAMA, CRITICISM

Before proceeding to Mendele's disciples, we pause for those who performed his task, that of laying the foundation for future development, in the fields of poetry and drama. Among the poets, there were Simeon Frug (1860-1916) in Russia and Morris Rosenfeld (1862-1923) in the United States.

Brought up on Russian poetry and himself a recognized Russian-Jewish poet, Simeon Frug achieved mastery in fashioning facile, rhythmic Yiddish verse despite his complaint about the crudity of the underdeveloped language. Raised in a Jewish colony in southern Russia, he was close to the land and his lyrical descriptions of nature have a directness and matter-of-factness quite foreign to Yiddish poetry. A Zionist, Frug lamented the bitterness of the Dispersal and dreamed in his poetry of the happy future when everyone would sit under his own fig tree. He made many paraphrases of the Bible and drew upon folk lore in his ballads. Nor is social pathos foreign to him. He is many-faceted but none of his faces is really distinct.

Immeasurably more profound and more effective is Morris Rosenfeld. He lifted social poetry to new heights. The socialist Morris Vintshefski (1856-1932), the anarchists David Edelstadt (1866-1892) and Joseph Bovshover (1872-1915), and many other poets of lesser stature had depicted the difficult life of the workingman. But theirs was a poetry aimed at arousing its readers to the social struggle and only indirectly expressed deeply personal experiences. However, in Morris Rosenfeld's social poetry are the very sighs and pain of the worker.

Himself a sweatshop slave, Rosenfeld went through the many metamorphoses of the Jewish immigrant in England and the United States. He portrays the worker lashed to the sewing machine, spending his strength without any brighter prospects for the morrow, crying out his protest in anguish and despair. National motifs of Jewish homelessness and the dream of deliverance also are prominent in his rough-hewn, glowing verses. The breadth and depth of his poetic creativeness, the range and frequent unexpectedness of his imagery, more than compensate for certain roughnesses of diction. Rosenfeld was the first Yiddish poet to attract foreign readers and to have his works translated into many languages.

Both Frug and Rosenfeld, pioneers in Yiddish poetry, so different in expression, paved the way for later poets who drew upon the formal elements of the one and the sincerity of the other.

Abraham Goldfaden, the founder of the first modern professional Yiddish theater, was at the same time its manager, director, composer, and playwright. He had evinced all these talents as early as 1876, in Jassy, where he laid the cornerstone for the rapid development of the theater. His operettas, setting a pattern for the Yiddish theater, which aims primarily to entertain and only secondarily to educate its audience, were of two types: comedies which make sport of the negative elements in Jewish life (for example, *The Two Simpletons, The Sorceress*) and nationalistic-romantic plays (for example, *Shulamis, Bar-Kokbha*).

The comedies contain grotesque and entertaining exaggerations and are in the tradition of the Purim play and the wine cellar art of the Singers of Brody, but also include themes of the Enlightenment and telling portrayals of mores. The dramas are melodramatically sentimental interpretations of Jewish history, combining elements of heroism and buffoonery. Tuneful melodies played no small part in making Goldfaden's operettas great favorites. The negation of Mendele's realistic approach and the catering to the popular taste, first evident in Goldfaden's works, opened the way to the banalization of his own method by such hacks as Joseph Lateiner, "Professor" Hurwitz, Shomer, and others who, in the United

States particularly, brought empty melodrama and quite vulgar operetta to the theater.

The early nineteenth-century Yiddish movement is linked with Mendl Satanover; but after the pogroms in Russia during the eighties, came the upheaval in social ideology and men turned from the Enlightenment to Zionism and nationalism. Part of the Jewish intelligentsia turned "homeward" and became more interested in the life of the masses, allying themselves more closely with those leaders of popular thought who had never strayed. At that time there were those, called the "Jargonists," who quite consciously wanted to strengthen the position of Yiddish. Thanks to this movement, such writers as I. L. Peretz, David Frishman, Simeon Frug, *et al.*, were attracted from the Hebrew and Russian literatures to the Yiddish. Simultaneously, interest in folklore increased, attempts were made to set up a uniform orthography and works of previous years were reprinted.

A number of new writers appeared on the scene: Moishe Aron Shatskes, with his excellent, mildly satirical *Before the Jewish Passover;* Paltiel Zamoshin, author of the short verses *Pictures of Life;* and "Yaknehoz," with his pleasant descriptions of small-town life. In almanacs such as the *Yiddishe Folks-Bibliotek* (*Jewish People's Library*) by Sholem Aleichem and Mordecai Spector's *Der Hoyzfraynd* (*Home Companion*), literary criticism first appeared. The young Sholem Aleichem wrote a very keen and witty critique of Shomer's novels; Joshua Honon Ravnitsky analyzed literary works instead of merely judging them; Joseph Judah Lerner introduced the positivist approach.

C. SHOLEM ALEICHEM AND ISAAC LEIBUSH PERETZ

Mordecai Spector (1858-1925) and Sholem Aleichem made their literary debuts at the same time and in the same weekly publication, the *Yiddishe Folksblat* (*Yiddish Folk Paper*) of 1883. Spector was faithful to Mendele's technique of detailed description, but his style is almost as colorless as the lives of his poor characters. His novels (*The Jewish Peasant, The Humble and the Needy, Reb Treitl*) and numerous stories are humorous and sentimental. With calm resignation and great insight he portrays the fate of the downtrodden. There is in Spector's work a deep sympathy for the poor man but no indication of any way out of his lot nor of any spiritual elation.

Sholem Rabinovitch (1859-1916), who took the pen name Sholem Aleichem, was born in the warm and fertile Ukraine. A difficult adolescence followed his idyllic childhood and it was not until he became private tutor in the home of a Jewish landowner, whose daughter he later married, that things began to go well for him. For a short time after the death of his father-in-law he conducted a successful business but subsequently lost his fortune and began to live by his writing. Illness sent him to Switzerland and Italy. Whenever he came to a Jewish ghetto city to give readings of his works, he received a great ovation, for he was the most popular of all Yiddish writers. The final years of his life were spent in New York City.

Sholem Aleichem began by writing realistic short stories and novels (*Stempeniu, Yossele Solovay*). In these early works he stood, so to speak, on the shoulders of Mendele, from whom he adopted many qualities of language and style. His originality came to the fore in *Kleine Mentshelech mit Kleine Hasoges (Little People with Little Ideas)*, where he first portrayed Kasrilevke, the composite town of poor but cheerful Jews with its happy-go-lucky Kasrillik. Later on in *Menachem Mendl*, his Kasrillik begins to wander, lands on the exchange and becomes a "speculator." Sholem Aleichem's vocabulary contains the wealth of idiom and the picturesqueness of expression found in spoken Yiddish, and his style ceases to be that of Mendele but becomes nervously dynamic. Instead of dwelling upon every detail, he sketches only a few particulars, usually the most humorous. At times he tends to become grotesque, but at his best he is a master of characterization.

Sholem Aleichem writes with especial tenderness of simple folk and of children. In the series of sketches, *Tevye the Dairyman*, we have the naïve yet deeply philosophical laborer who has intuitively absorbed the Jewish faith and its unshakable affirmation of life. In the children's stories, such as the *Song of Songs*, there is an additional individual lyricism which gives them much charm. In *Motl Paysie, the Cantor's Son*, a bright child gives an account of the life of a group of immigrants across the sea "in the golden land." The longer novels that first appeared as newspaper serials (*Wandering Stars, The Bloody Joke*) show only in part the excellence of his pen. And in the autobiographical novel *From the Fair* the writer abandons his favorite monologue form and writes in the third person. Of his dramatic works, the most performed were *Tsezeit un Tseshpreit (Scattered Far and Wide)*, concerning the life of a Jewish family about the year 1905, and *Dos Groise Gevins (The Great Winnings)*, where Shimmele Soroker, the main character, is a simplified Tevye the Dairyman.

Sholem Aleichem's genius has both breadth and depth. His characters are drawn from every class, although the background is always characteristically Jewish, whether it be Kasrilevke or the Lower East Side of New York. While writing of spiritual and emotional experiences in a seemingly cursory fashion, he is in reality plumbing the depths of an inward struggle. Thus Sholem Aleichem is interesting not only to the folk-lorist or the ethnographer, but also to the psychologist. His writing gives pleasure to the simplest reader who relishes the aphorisms and the humorous situations, while the most discriminating will find a philosophical depth and a symbolism of character rare in the works of other writers.

Everyone who read Yiddish at the turn of the century read Sholem Aleichem and even those who could not read knew of him, as it was customary to read his works aloud at celebrations and family gatherings. His unrivaled popularity is due largely to his humor, a humor which is many-sided: fresh, carefree laughter, tearful smiles, subtle wit, and grotesque exaggeration. Particularly characteristic of Sholem Aleichem is his treatment of sad and even tragic events with a kind of levity which springs from the faith that man can overcome any adversity. He gives us the comfort of a laughter which does not belittle the values of life but rather serves to emphasize them.

The genius for humor of the sorely tried Jewish people, formerly manifested in jest and epigram, shone in Sholem Aleichem's works through hundreds of characters, four of which are outstanding: Kasrillik, Menachem Mendl, Tevye the Dairyman, and Motl, the Cantor's Son. These figures came to be regarded almost as members of the reader's own family. Indeed, the extent of the influence of Sholem Aleichem upon the daily life of the East European Jew can hardly be exaggerated.

The third member of this trio of classicists, Isaac Leibush Peretz (1852-1915), affected his readers and society in quite another manner. Born in the Polish city of Zamosc, Peretz showed great intellectual ability as a youth. To earn his livelihood, he first practiced law and then worked for the Warsaw Jewish community. By his own efforts he became thoroughly versed in European literature. He was past middle age and had already written many Hebrew verses before his writings appeared in Yiddish.

At first there were succinct, realistic short stories and during the period of the *Yontev Bletlech* (*Holiday Folios*), he devoted himself to works of the Enlightenment and to the popularization of scientific material. His poetry is strongly influenced by that of Heine and Chamisso; his *Haskala* motifs are sarcastic and militant; his portrayal of the lot of women and children, sentimental and romantic.

However, it was not until the nineties, when he took up Hasidic themes, that Peretz reached the height of his career. His Hasidic stories in which he idealized the rabbis, painting them as the model men of the future, helped initiate a neo-Hasidic trend in Yiddish and Hebrew literature. But Peretz did not seek the "Sabbath and the Holy-day" Jew only among the great. He wrote the series *Silent Souls* and other tales of the "thirty-six saintly Jews" where the hero—a woodcutter, a water carrier, or a confused youth—plumbs the profoundest depths of the soul. Thus Peretz went from the realistic to the romantic, from the romantic to the symbolic. His drama *The Golden Chain* embodies the basic process of development of every religion and stresses the continuity of the age-old chain of Jewish culture. His last symbolic drama, *A Night at the Old Marketplace*, is a pessimistic summation of his own achievements, for Peretz was not satisfied to create a work of art for its own sake, but wanted to use his talents to refine the soul of his generation.

The conflict between the way of life of the Jewish radical and that of the towering personalities of the traditional past is revealed in Peretz's works. In feverishly sharp and impressionistic *feuilletons,* he champions true freedom of thought and at the same time stresses the traditional quest for God and the belief in the chosenness of the Jewish people—tenets which found new strength in the years bridging the nineteenth and twentieth centuries. While Peretz's literary technique is West European, it also stems from the folk tale and there is a direct line from the stories of Nachman Brahtslever with their romantic symbolism to the works of Peretz.

During the last fifteen years of his life, Peretz was not only the dominant literary figure of the great center in Warsaw but was also the leader of those who hoped to modernize Jewish life through the use of Yiddish and to effect a national cultural renaissance in all the lands of the dispersion. He was one of the leaders at the language conference at Czernowitz (1908), where Yiddish was proclaimed "a national language." Near the end of his life he helped establish Jewish schools for refugee children and died while composing a poem for a children's home

Almost all the young authors whose writings appeared in Peretz's publications or who made their debuts in the early years of the twentieth century were influenced by Peretz, whose attitude toward them was fatherly and encouraging. When the younger writers bestowed upon him the honorary title of "Father of Modern Yiddish Literature," they were expressing their esteem and affection for him.

The constellation of Mendele, Sholem Aleichem, and Peretz is a happy combination of mutually complementary temperaments. Mendele criticizes yet memorializes what is characteristic and typical of his age; Sholem Aleichem brings us the comical and the humorous with no apparent motive; Peretz evokes the exotic past as a model for the future. Mendele is static, the other two are dynamic. Sholem Aleichem definitely draws upon Mendele, while Peretz is tangential. Mendele and Peretz demand concentration from the reader; Sholem Aleichem is universally familiar and satisfying. All three created a new centripetal force linking, through literature, the present and the past, the intellectual and the untutored, the Jew of one region and the Jew of another.

D. THE EXPANSION OF YIDDISH LITERATURE TO 1914

Until 1914 the whole of Yiddish literature in Russia reflected the influence of Mendele, Sholem Aleichem, and Peretz.

In the United States other forces were at work: (1) The "green" immigrant needed to become organized and literature took on the character of propaganda; (2) the low cultural status of the newcomers led to semiliterate writing which impeded the development of the artistic; (3) a great, new power arose in the form of a free Yiddish press.

It is curious that Russian literature exercised a lesser influence upon Yiddish literature in Russia than it did upon Yiddish writing in America. Some of the more important American prose writers are Z. Libin (pen name of Israel Hurwitz), who, with restrained warmth faithfully records the life of the Jewish worker; Leon Kobrin, who dwells upon the problems of the individual, particularly the sexual; Bernard Gorin, who, for the most part, portrays the old country; Abraham Cahan, whose stories are dominated by socialist propaganda; Tashrack (Israel Joseph Zevin), who depicts the difficulties in the adjustments the immigrant has to make to his new environment.

In addition to this socially aware writing, such as that of Morris Rosenfeld (see above), we have the popularly oriented songs of Joseph Jaffe, the tender, idyllic poesy of Jacob Adler, M. Sharkanski's fine rhythm. While the Yiddish theater had been banned in Russia in 1883, it developed rapidly in America. The Tolstoian Jacob Gordin raised the level of the theater, producing more than sixty plays, many of which were based on foreign themes, and others that were original plays of milieu which were extremely successful (*Mirrele Efros; God, Man and the Devil*).

In Europe the seventeen years from 1897 to 1914 saw remarkable social progress. The philosophies of Zionism, socialism, and autonomism were hotly debated; parties organized; new ideas on the march. Yet the Jewish press in Russia was banned until 1903 when *Fraynd* (*The Friend*) appeared in Petersburg, to be followed by Yiddish newspapers in Odessa, Warsaw and other provincial cities. Life was particularly stormy from 1904 to 1906. There was a temporary mood of despair immediately after the failure of the 1905 revolution, but hopes soon rose and the Yiddish movement was strengthened.

The most important literary publications were *Literary Monthlies* (1908), edited by Samuel Niger, Shmaryohu Gorelik and A. Veiter (pen name of Meyer Davenishsky); *Der Pinkes, Yearbook of the History of the Yiddish Literature and Language, Folklore, Criticism and Bibliography* (1913); and the monthly magazine, *Jewish World*, also edited by Samuel Niger. Most of these publications appeared in Vilna, seat of the modern

Kletskin Publishing House. The Warsaw publishing firms were modernized as well, and the output of books was great.

Again during this period a group of Hebrew writers were attracted to Yiddish literature: Hayyim Nachman Bialik translated his *Poems of Grief and Wrath* into Yiddish and wrote directly in that language; Jacob Fichman composed delightful children's songs; Judah Steinberg painted idyllic pictures of Hasidic life; Miche Yosef Berdichevsky wrote of ordinary people. Zalman Itzkhok Onoikhi, who created the character of the philosophizing Hasid in his *Reb Abbo,* was one of the many new writers.

Folk lore was very popular and Sholem Aleichem discovered a Jewish Beranger in a Kiev lawyer, Mark Varshavski (1848-1907), whose *Genuine Folksongs* are so widely sung that many are amazed to learn that *Oif'n Pripetchok Brennt a Fierl* comes from his pen. The most prominent of the folk-lorists was Shloime Anski (1863-1920). His *Dybbuk* became popular in a later period and influenced both the Yiddish and Hebrew theaters. The work of Reb Mordkhele (Chaim Tschemerinski, 1862-1917), with its diverting allegories and satirical poetry, is also based upon an unusual familiarity with the popular idiom.

The career of Abraham Reisen (1874-1953), who wrote both poetry and prose, illustrates the fact that the influence of the folk song is more lasting than that of the folk tale. His poetry shows the impact of the folk song while his short stories have a European and Peretz-like flavor. Reisen's poems are short, unaffected melodic revelations of mood with distant echoings of *Weltschmerz,* filled with great sympathy for the lonely and the oppressed. His lucid style found great favor and Reisen early became one of the most popular poets.

Abraham Liesin (1872-1938), who was a contemporary of Reisen, individualized social-revolutionary poetry. Yehoash (pen name of Jehoash Shloime Blumgarten, 1871-1927) began with romantic nationalistic ballads, fables and lyrics. Both these poets reached their peak in later years and we shall return to them.

The Lithuanian-born David Einhorn wrote with resignation of the decline of the small town in *Quiet Songs,* while his *Jewish Daughters* introduced idyllic love motifs. His work has unusual individuality of tone and pleasant rhythm. The work of the Galician Shmuel Yakov Imber is more turbulent, more erotic.

Although the development of poetry during this period was rapid, the principal advance took place in narrative prose. In this field we have a threesome to start: Abraham Reisen, Sholem Asch, and Hersh David Nomberg. Reisen's short stories deal with daily problems and simple spiritual conflicts. They are often just barely humorous, often lyrical with compassion for man who, after all, is not so highly developed as is sometimes believed.

The perennially enamored Sholem Asch is quite different; he began by singing the praises of the small town. (Samuel Niger has called him the "Prophet of the Soil.") But he soon turned to the problems of the big city, to the life of the new immigrant in America, and to the underworld, creating a series of interesting novels. We shall return to him.

Hersh David Nomberg (1876-1927) introduced psychological analysis in portraying the dissatisfied, introverted intellectual. The clarity of style and masterly construction of his stories give him a prominent place in Yiddish literature, although he wrote little and in a single vein.

The earthiness of the writings of Itshe Meyer Veisnberg (1881-1937) is in direct contrast to Sholem Asch's idyll of the small town. Veisnberg, himself a workingman, describes the worker's life with unrelenting realism, stressing the crude and the brutal. Jonah Rosenfeld (1880-1944), also a laborer, began with realistic stories but went on to psychological analysis. Lamed Shapiro painted impressionistic portraits of nature and his powerful stories of pogroms are impregnated with the spirit of vengeance. Itzkhok Doiv Berkowitz, son-in-law of Sholem Aleichem and his splendid translator into Hebrew, portrayed ordinary people in extraordinary circumstances. Toward the end of the period appeared David Bergelson, delineating moods and highlighting the tragedy of the young woman in *Nokh Aleman* (*It's All Over*).

The drama developed much more slowly than *belles-lettres*. David Pinski, who began in the nineties with stories of the laboring classes, is the author of plays which demonstrate the conflicts arising out of the breakup of the patriarchal-religious family relationship. Sholem Asch created a sensation with his *God of Vengeance*. He also attempted historical drama and contemporary comedy. Peretz Hirshbein (1880-1948), himself the organizer of a dramatic troupe, first wrote realistic plays, turned to Maeterlinckian dramas of mood, and finally found himself among simple country folk and their rustic surroundings. There is less continuity in Yiddish drama than there is in poetry and prose. The thread Goldfaden had spun was broken, and a definite rift between the professional theater and the literary drama became apparent. The devotees of this more cultivated theater (including the semisymbolic plays of A. Veiter) are definitely characteristic of the Yiddish cultural life of this period.

Literary criticism was especially popular and was written not only by the editors of periodicals, but also by many literary minded people. Yet there was no outstanding literary critic before Baal-Machshoves (Isidor Eliashev, 1873-1924). With strict aesthetic standards he became the servant of Jewish letters, giving encouragement to almost every beginner. A follower, in principle, of the school of Hippolyte Taine, Baal-Machshoves nevertheless employed the environmental method, especially in the interpretation of realistic works. From Yiddishist circles emerged Samuel Niger, who early proved a talented critic. His work is characterized by detailed analysis particularly of the relationship of the writer to his surroundings. (More of him later.)

After 1905 the stream of immigration brought to America many authors who had already won fame in the old country, as well as young writers who had taken their first steps in the literary field. In 1908 there evolved from among these the group known as "the Young," militant beginners dissatisfied with the status of literature on the Continent, and calling for its independence of social ideologies. They published collected *Writings* (edited by David Ignatoff), in which they followed the course and even anticipated the literary development in Eastern Europe. The principal works of these "Young" were not to appear until 1914.

In summary, the fifty years between 1864 and 1914 witnessed the development of a worldly, many-sided Yiddish literature; principally realistic yet with more than a tinge of romanticism, it showed tendencies toward modern symbolism as well. Although centered in Russian Jewry, there was a parallel development of Yiddish literature in America. With its unshakable affirmation of life and its intimate family spirit, this literature was an instrument of social progress and a mighty force for unifying the scattered Jewish people.

E. YIDDISH LITERATURE IN AMERICA, 1916-1956

World War I rent asunder Russia's Jewish community of 6,000,000. The settlements in the Soviet Union, in Poland, and the small center of the Baltic countries and Rumania became completely distinct. The hegemony of Jewish life was transferred to the American center.

A kaleidoscope of literary groups, trends and forms, such as had never been known before, developed in New York, and to a lesser extent in other North American cities such as Montreal, Chicago, and Los Angeles. While social motifs were characteristic of literary endeavors of the late nineteenth and the early twentieth centuries, national consciousness has marked the writings of the past forty years (1916-1956). Negative traits, too, became apparent such as the rift between the reader and the ultra-modern author, the language assimilation of the younger generation, the halting of immigration, thus raising the average age of the reading public with little prospect of building for the future. All these factors could not help but influence the writer and his work.

Especially important was the development in the field of poetry with the appearance of a variety of temperaments, styles and themes. The two elder poets, Yehoash and Liesin, renewed their creative activities. The imagery of Yehoash became richer and more satisfying, Apollonian in its lyrical restraint. Abraham Liesin, the most nationalistic of Yiddish poets, is inspired by the *Kiddush Ha-Shem* motif and relives his youth in mystical songs of remembrance. Younger than these two were the ever-changing and very prolific Hayim Rosenblat (1883-1956) and the constant, introspective Joseph Rolnick (1878-1955). The poetry of Nokhum Yood is clear and musical.

Theoretically, Zisha Landau (1889-1937) is an antisocial aesthete but actually he celebrates the joys of everyday life in his delicate, mildly imagist songs. Mani Leib (1883-1953), influenced by the Russian poets, particularly Fett and Alexander Block, writes tender, romantic lyrics, as well as charming children's poems and ballads based on folk motifs. Israel Jacob Schwartz is equally fond of the European background of his pious rabbi father and the American environment of his children. He introduced American themes in his long poem *Kentucky*, as well as in a number of shorter works. He is also an untiring translator of both old and new Hebrew poetry.

Most impassioned of the modern Yiddish poets is Moishe Leib Halperin (1886-1932). Torn between an inborn romanticism and the cynicism of a chaotic world, he incorporates the disillusionment of the postwar generation and the spiritual "otherness" of the immigrant, who, to the very end, is unable to come to terms with his environment. The feminine poetry of Anna Margolin was subtle and passionate. The poetry of Reuben Aizland was complacent and resigned.

Faithful to the teachings of Peretz, that ethics is the goal and aesthetics but the means, is H. Leivick[9a] who voices the sorrow and unrest of our generation. In his great symbolic dramas, *The Golem* and *The Comedy of Redemption*, are unfolded the problems of world deliverance and the struggle for progress. During long years of serious illness his poems dealt with death and destruction, but his *Songs of Paradise* are touched with the joy of life. In these last years he expresses deep wrath and sorrow over the devastation of Europe. He became one of the principal poets of lamentation after the Hitler holocaust (in his volume *In Treblinke Bin Ikh Nit Geven* and in scores of later poems). A prolific poet, despite his limited themes he is outstanding because of the nuances and inferences that create variety in his leitmotiv. His last volume of poems is called *A Leaf On An Apple Tree*. Leivick is most honored among the Yiddish poets now living.

Ten years after "the Young" came the group known as *Inzikhistn*, "the Introspectionists" (after their magazine, *In Zikh, Within Oneself*). Urbane intellectuals, they espoused free verse, abstraction, allusion and metaphor. Aaron Leyeles (Aaron Glanz), N. B. Minkoff, and Jacob Glatstein headed this group. Mark Schweid introduced modern poetry in difficult verse. Jacob Glatstein was an ultramodern bold experimenter with language in the first period of his poetic creativity; of late his poetry has been less revolutionary in form and more profound in spirit, as witnessed by the book *Shtralndike Yidn*. The poetry of Leyeles also became more profound (*A Yid Oifn Yam*).

Quite distinct was the realistic "Proletpen" group, whose spiritual home was the Soviet Union. Only the capricious, bitterly sarcastic poems of Moishe Nadir (1885-1943) rose above the average monotony of their writings.

The feeling of instability, the anxiety about the course of the development of Jewish life in America, Hitler's persecutions and devastation of Europe—all these factors had the effect of strengthening traditionalism. Poetic form acquired simplicity and purity and ever recurrent were themes from the Old World. This traditionalism is apparent in the works of almost all the Yiddish-American poets, one of the outstanding being Menachem Boraisho (1888-1949), whose face turned toward the past in his great work *Der Geyer* (1943), one of the outstanding creations in Yiddish poetry. In Jacob Itzkhok Segal's (1896-1954) mellow lyrics we hear the echoes of one's grandmother's *Tkhines* (prayers). Ephraim Auerbach concludes that *The Old Spring Is Pure;* he drinks from it and dwells in *The Tents of Jacob*. Benjamin Jacob Bialostotzki and Naftoli Gross (1895-1956) also are part of this trend.

The versatile L. Feinberg is facile in his prolific verse both in describing his own *Doomed Generation* and when he glorifies the Tannaim. B. Lapin (1887-1953), a painstaking translator of poetry, earned recognition through the last collection of his original poems, *The Full Jug*. We must also mention the unique A. Lutzky, the intellectual Eliezer Greenberg, the imaginative Aleph Katz, and the younger Berish Weinstein who depicts his old home town Reishe and his American environment in epic verse.

Yiddish poetry in America for the past forty years presented a multicolored gallery of temperaments, a symphony of different tones, and a richness of themes. (Scores of names have been omitted for lack of space.)

Many stories and novels were serialized in the Yiddish press. Undoubtedly the most popular narrative writer was Sholem Asch, whose particular strength lies in the scope of his canvas and in his vivid mass scenes. He is guided by a deep faith in man and by real affection for his characters. His trilogy *Three Cities: Petersburg, Warsaw, Moscow,* depicting scenes of Jewish life before, during, and after World War I, enjoyed great success. His finest talents came to the fore in *Salvation*. Asch's *The Nazarene* and *The Apostle* gave rise to considerable controversy. The American scene is represented in many of his novels, beginning with *Uncle Moses* and concluding with *Grossman and Son*. His latest historical novels are *Moses* and *The Prophet*.

Israel Joshua Zynger (1893-1944) limited his subject matter to life in Poland in the recent past. Like Balzac, he portrayed the bitterness of the "Human Comedy," but even more coldly and more naturalistically than did the French master. His principal novels are *Yoshe the Calf, The Brothers Ashkenazi, Comrade Nachman,* and *The Karnovski Family*.

Zalman Shneour (1887-1959), Hebrew poet and Yiddish author, became known largely by way of the New York newspaper *Forward,* and is therefore included among the American writers, although it is difficult to ascribe him to any one country. In his stories he delights in physical prowess and is prone to linger over erotic passages. Shneour's series *Jews of Shklov* was very popular and his favorite hero is the young butcher, Noah Pandre. Among his numerous novels the outstanding is the historical *Napoleon and the Rabbi.*

Master of the short story is Joseph Opatoshu (1887-1954), who has a special affinity for the physical. In his trilogy (*In Polish Woods, 1863, Alone*), which treats of Jewish life in Poland in the mid-nineteenth century, there is an added romantic undertone. He turns easily from Old World themes to both Jewish and Christian life on the American continent. He wrote historical novels and novelettes (*A Day In Regensburg, The Last Insurrection*). His diction is scrupulously refined. More the painter than the storyteller was Issac Raboi (1882-1948), who introduced both the Far West (*Mr. Goldenberg*) and New England (*A Strip of the Sea*) to Yiddish literature; Samuel Niger described Raboi's novels as "masses of arrested lyricism."

The playwrights David Pinski and Peretz Hirshbein wrote a number of novels. David Ignatov (1885-1954) attempted to record the history of the American Jewish intelligentsia in his novels. Boruch Glassman (1893-1945) dwelt on the psychology of the lonely and the maladjusted; Shin Miller depicts the disintegration of Jewish life in America and in the Soviet Union. B. Demblin is one of the few Yiddish writers who protrays non-Jewish types as well (*West Side*). Although the skeptical Moishe Nadir undertook to "de-create" the silly world and "disenchant" foolish man, an unexpected warmth is to be found in his stories. The previously mentioned Jonah Rosenfeld and Lamed Shapiro (1878-1948) continued and refined their techniques of short-story telling, enriching their themes with American subjects. Jacob Glatstein combined creative writing and factual reporting in his *When Yash Went Away* and *When Yash Returned.* The charming Leon Elbe excelled in the field of literature for children. I. Metzker, who started out as a children's writer, gave us the idyllic *Grandfather's Fields.* We conclude this brief review of *belles-lettres* by mentioning the names of L. Brusiloff, M. Y. Shelubsky, and the young M. Dluzhowsky.

In America as in Europe, the drama does not keep pace with poetry and prose. In this field, David Pinski tends to be symbolic and abstract; Peretz Hirshbein refined his idyllic folkplays (*Green Fields*); Hersh Sackler found his characters in the romantic popular tale. Leon Kobrin (1873-1946) wrote dramas of everyday life (*The Country Fellow* from the old country, *Riverside Drive* in the New World). H. Leivick's *Rags* represents the real drama of the immigrant; *When the Poet Became Blind* relates the tragedy of a Yiddish poet in America. More recently he dramatized the revolt of the Warsaw ghetto (*The Miracle of the Ghetto*), then turned to the afflictions of the post-Hitler era in *The Wedding at Fernwald*, and finally returned to his previous symbolic style in *In The Days of Job*.

In America, too, almost all poets and publicists engaged in literary criticism but none of them approximated the influence exerted by Samuel Niger (1883-1955), whose diligence and sincerity made him the guardian as well as the judge of Yiddish literature. Of the multitude of critics, we mention Alexander Mukdoni, impressionistic and discerning; Borukh Rivkin, obscure and casuistical; Joel Enteen, warm and straightforward; Abraham Cahan, for many years the very influential editor of the *Forward*; Hillel Rogoff, now the editor of this sixty-year-old newspaper; Jacob Glatstein, who writes pointed weekly reviews in *Yiddisher Kempfer*; the connoisseur of poetry, A. Tabachnik; and the expert of character depiction, Schloime Bickel of the *Day-Morning Journal*. The literary historian, the late N. B. Minkoff, was secretary of the *Zukunft* editorial collegium. (Other members: H. Leivick, A. Meness, and Jacob Pat.)

In the broad field of the essay, distinction has been won by Haim Zhitlovsky, leader of the nationalistic-socialist intelligentsia; Abraham Coralnik, sensitive aesthete; Haim Greenberg, editor of the *Yiddisher Kempfer*; and Abraham Liesin, for many years editor of the *Zukunft*.

What makes Yiddish literature in America American? Much more fundamental than the subject matter is the influence of life in the New World upon the writer who began to see the old country in a different light, and to interpret the problems of the Jew in a way which stamps his work as peculiarly American.

F. YIDDISH LITERATURE IN POLAND BETWEEN THE TWO WORLD WARS

The second most important center of Yiddish literature was Poland, whose 3,500,000 Jews had been rooted in Polish soil for some 800 years. Geographically close to Russia, Polish-Yiddish literature was separated as by a wall from that of the Soviet Union. Of the two, it was the Polish center that was in contact with America.

In Poland, Yiddish literature was closely connected with the diversified communal activities and the firmly patterned everyday life. Yet it also reflected the dissensions and the gnawing uncertainty about the future. World War I destroyed the established order; the older generation of writers died out; the younger men, who had come to Warsaw from the provinces and felt insecure in their new environment, were caught up in the crosscurrents of a belated *Haskala*, radicalism, and nationalism. This milieu gave rise to an antiaesthetic and antisocial expressionism particularly among those poets of the magazine *Khalastre* (*The Bunch*). To this group belong the prose writers Ozer Varshavski, who, in his *Smugglers,* gave an angry picture of wantonness during the war period, and Avrom Moishe Fuchs, who skillfully portrayed shady characters from the dregs of humanity.

The leader of a group of poets from Lodz was Moishe Broderzon, whose rhythmic poetry illustrated his primary interest in form; but underneath his playfulness there lurked a corroding pessimism. Two Lithuanian poets introduced a fresh, youthful romanticism: Leib Neidus (1890-1918), who was a master at versification, and Moishe Kulbak, who wrote impetuous, unaffected, and somewhat modernistic poetry.

The strongest and most enduring poetic stream was fed by tradition, by a pessimistic sentimentalism, and by a universal yet specifically Jewish restlessness. Some sought solace in mysticism and a fancied traditionalism.

The traditional and the mystical are basic qualities of the creative works of Aaron Zeitlin, son of the God-seeking publicist Hillel Zeitlin, who was put to death by the Nazis. The mystic and moralist, Israel Shtern, always had a premonition of martyrdom and actually perished with those martyred by Hitler.

The well of folk lore is mirrored in the lucid, prayerlike poems of Miriam Ulinover, who drew all *From Grandmother's Treasure,* as she called one of her poetry collections. An original combination of the grotesque and the romantic is found in the bohemian carelessness and the anguished sentimentality of the poems by Itsik Manger. The poetess Kadya Molodovski found herself in singing of the lives of the poor. Just before the war, Yechiel Lehrer, also one of the martyred, produced the long poem of day-to-day life, *My Home.* The "Young Vilna" group was very much under American influence. Outstanding among them are Chaim Grahde and A. Sutskever, who were able to save themselves only to lament the devastation of Vilna, but not of Vilna alone. To the same group belonged the energetic Shmerke Kocherginski (who met an accidental death in Argentina in 1954) and the very young Hirsh Glick, author of the inspirational "Hymn of the Partisans."

Of the multitude of talented writers, the poetess Rokhl Korn, the poets I. Rubinstein and Nokhom Bomse (d. 1954), and the literary critic Rokhl Auerbach survived. The elder Yitskhok Katzenelson, who died a martyr's death, left for posterity the unforgettable *Song of the Slaughtered Jewish People.*

Mention has already been made of the narrative writers who left Poland for America. Among those remaining in Poland were Zelig Segalovitch, who depicted either capricious female characters or himself in his popular novels; Joshua Perle, who had a great love for the land of the Vistula; Efraim Kaganovski, who portrayed the poverty-stricken and the underworld of Warsaw; the tragically fated Simeon Horontchik (1889-1939), whose long novels deal with the lives of working people. In the works of Isaac Bashevis (brother of Israel Joshua Singer) are to be found purity of form and vividness of imagery. His *Satan of Gorei* depicts the aftermath of the Sabbatai Zevi movement. Just prior to World War II there appeared some powerful young writers of small-town life.

In general the drama (*Dybbuk* has already been mentioned) departed from gray reality. Jacob Pregger builds upon the folk tale (*The Temptation, Simcho Plachte*), as does Aaron Zeitlin; Alter Kacyzne uses the story of the "true proselyte" of Vilna in *The Duke;* Jekheskal Moishe Neiman gives us the idyll of *The Sabbath Fruit,* while Fishel Bimko's *Thieves* dramatizes the exotic underworld.

Of the more than one hundred periodicals flourishing at that time, *Book World, Jewish World, Art and Life, Literary Leaves,* and *Weekly* were among those devoted to literature. Some of the many critics and essayists were Nachman Maisil, editor of *Literary Leaves;* the philosophizing Yekheil Yeshaye Troonk and Leon Finkelstein; the enthusiastic Zalmen Raizen, compiler of the four-volume *Lexicon of Yiddish Literature, Press and Philology;* the historian Isaac Shipper and the philologist Noah Prilutsky.

With the advent of Hitler, the deeply rooted Polish Jewish community faced extermination. Yet its spiritual strength was inexhaustible and in the Ghettos of Vilna and Warsaw, in the shadow of the concentration camps, Jews conducted literary meetings and celebrated the anniversaries of famous authors. Some writers fled to the Soviet Union, others came to the United States, but a painfully large number perished with their readers.

G. YIDDISH LITERATURE IN THE SOVIET UNION

In 1915 the Czarist regime forbade the use of the Yiddish alphabet in the printing of periodicals and books. Immediately following the March Revolution of 1917 and during the first years of the October Revolution (1917-1921), literary creation was relatively unhampered. Gradually the situation changed: one had to become "proletarian" or remain silent.

Yiddish literature in the Soviet Union became a "Soviet" literature and no longer regarded itself as part of world Yiddish literature. Quite deliberately the leaders of this controlled Jewish life did everything possible to separate the Jews of the Soviet Union from the Jews of the rest of the world. Even the orthography was changed radically and Yiddish writers avoided phrases and expressions which stemmed from the *heder* or were associated with religious Judaism. It was not until the Popular Front of the thirties that this isolationist policy began to weaken.

In addition to the geographical isolation there was a spiritual departure from the earlier literature. A writer who walked *In Step* (a typical name for a literary collection) received greater material compensation than did the average Yiddish writer elsewhere. He also had an audience, for the reading and discussion of literary works became a routine part of club activities. However, the writer always had to fulfill a "social assignment": to defend one point of view, to oppose another. Thus he felt that his writing filled a definite need. It is impossible to understand the fluctuations of Yiddish literature in the Soviet Union without taking into consideration the constant political changes.

Even more so than elsewhere, poetry in the Soviet Union is the most important form of expression. An example of the revolutionary romanticism of the civil war period is the work of Osher Shvartsman (1890-1919). The deeply nationalistic David Hofstein influenced almost all Soviet-Yiddish poets with respect to poetic form. Peretz Markish, in his long, versified novels, depicted the struggle against the vestiges of the old order. Leib Kvitko is modest and refined. Somewhat younger than those mentioned are Itsik Feffer and Izzi Charik; the former, faithful to the Soviet regime, earned official recognition while the latter was a victim of the purges. Yet both sing with joy of the new life and glorify the fatherland.

Yiddish prose in the Soviet Union has developed much more slowly. The novels and stories dealing with the revolution are, to quote David Bergelson, "scarcely finished literary works with their roughness of style and characterization." In the twenties social progress was the principal theme; later it was praise of the champions of production and of the victory over saboteurs. In addition to following the "party line," Yiddish writers glorified the establishment of new Jewish colonies and the development of Biro-Bidjan.

David Bergelson stands head and shoulders above his Soviet colleagues. One of the finest stylists in Yiddish literature, his chief power lies in describing environment and mood. At first he saw the revolution as *A Measure of the Law* and later accepted it fully; his characters conform to the new order. In his great autobiographical novel, *Beside the Dnieper*, he gives a graphic account of his childhood and youth. The novelist *Der Nistor* (the Anonymous) (Froyim Kahanovitch), who stood apart from the others, won renown with his novel, *The Mashber Family*. A return to classicism is found in the stories of Itsik Kipnis, whose idyllic *Months and Days* aroused much controversy. Moishe Kulbak painted a pleasantly humorous portrait of a lower-class family in his *Zelmenians*. The Yiddish theater was well developed in the Soviet Union, but not the art of the drama.

No field of letters was so completely under the influence of Soviet dogma as that of literary criticism. Moishe Litvakov, editor of *Emes* (Truth), was the overseer of political *kashrut* (yet he died in prison). The excellent analyst, Nochum Oislender, was the freest and the most interesting of his colleagues. Israel Tsinberg spent many years on his ten-volume *History of Literature Among the Jews*, which was being printed in Poland but remained unfinished. The author is presumed to have died in a Soviet prison.

Western Russia with its dense Jewish population was the first to suffer Nazi attack. Most of the writers of Minsk and Kiev fled deep into Russia, thus avoiding the fate of their fellow Jews. During World War II, the restrictions on Soviet writers were eased, and they were permitted to deviate from the previously imposed limitations as to how and what they could write. As a result, the Yiddish writers began to write on Jewish themes. Even Itsik Feffer, whose poetry was a paean of praise to Stalin, published material on Jewish national themes. During this period Jewish national trends were evident in the works of both Peretz Markish and David Bergelson, as well as in the works of the writers from Poland which were published in the U.S.S.R. Literary activity was centered in the Jewish Anti-Fascist Committee, which published the Yiddish periodical *Eynikeyt*.

The end of the war saw a change in government policy which dealt a death blow to Yiddish literature in the Soviet Union. In 1948, almost all the Yiddish writers—there were at least 200 of them—were arrested, accused of treason, and sentenced to long terms of servitude in the Siberian slave labor camps. In 1952, Stalin ordered the execution of the most important writers. Of those who were not executed the vast majority died in prison. Only a few could survive the hardships of the labor camps, and these remained prisoners until Khrushchev repudiated Stalin and his policy. These survivors, however, were not permitted to return to literary activity after their liberation. Nothing has been published in Yiddish in the Soviet Union since 1948.

Such is the tragic end of that part of Yiddish literature which sought in vain to adapt itself to a tryannical political order. Its writers died martyrs' deaths.

H. THE UNIVERSALITY OF YIDDISH LITERATURE

The past forty years saw such a rapid development of Yiddish literature, and the emergence of so many colorful writers, that in order to survey it, it was necessary to divide it geographically into the three major centers. Actually, however, it remained a single integrated literature, just as it had been in the past.

We dealt first with the most important center—America—and then with Poland. To complete the picture of America we now report on the writers from Poland who escaped just before, during, and after the war.

After years spent in Eretz Yisrael, Z. Segalovitch, the most embittered poetic lamenter of the Hitler holocaust, came to the United States, where he died in 1949. Aaron Zeitlin, whom we have already mentioned, wrote more profound Jewish poetry. The destruction of the whole Zeitlin family affected the work of this outstanding Yiddish and Hebrew poet, and he, now in America, seeks to understand the religious and moral significance of the great tragedy. I. Bashevis became one of the most important novelists.

His novel, *The Mushkat Family*, the series of short stories, *My Father's Rabbinic Court*, and other works give evidence of further development of his scope and talent. E. I. Troonk published a multivolume work on Poland, which gives a picture of the lives of two generations, based on a background of his own life and family. After years in London, the poet Itsik Manger settled in America. The poetess Kadia Molodovski achieved maturity and tragic profundity. Chaim Grade, who was productive during the years of war and wanderings, published his volume of poems entitled *My Mother's Will*, and wrote other poems which describe life among the religious Jews in his old home. Recently, he has become a respected writer of prose. *My Mother's Sabbaths* received great recognition. Mordecai Shtrigler wrote a number of novels dealing with the horrors of Hitler's extermination camps.

Generally it must be kept in mind that since the forties, in all Yiddish literature, and poetry particularly, there has been one basic theme—the terrible destruction of European Jewry. Both those who barely survived and those who lived in safety created a whole literature based on this unprecedented tragedy of the Jewish people. In this respect no other literature, including the Hebrew, can compare with the Yiddish literature of the past fifteen years.

Yiddish literature was never limited to the three great centers of America, Poland, and the Soviet Union. Wherever there were Yiddish-speaking settlements there appeared literary works of all kinds to meet the great demand of the large reading public.

In Rumania between the two World Wars there was a Jewish population of about 1,000,000. Despite persecution which obstructed the development of the Yiddish press and the expansion of cultural societies, a number of vigorous talents appeared. The best allegorist is Eliezer Steinbarg (1880-1932), who introduced social motifs into the fable, giving them, a witty, typical Jewish flavor. The refined and cultured Moishe Altman created a unique novel, *Medresh Pinkhos*, and wrote interesting short stories (*Blendenish*). The stage director Jacob Shternberg was a modernistic poet. Beside the authors already mentioned from Bessarabia, we must single out the poet Jacob Gropper, a native of Moldavia.

Lithuania, with Kuanas as the principal center, teemed with young poets and authors. Outstanding was the poet Jacob Gotlieb. There were literary groups in Latvia, too, and even in the small settlement of Estonia.

The Argentine, with its 400,000 Jews, is the second largest Jewish community in the New World. With its great daily newspapers and a flourishing cultural life, it has distinguished itself in the short fifty years of its history by an unusual interest in *belles-lettres*. In his truly artistic memoirs, Mordecai Alperson has told of the hardships of thirty years of Jewish colonization. Moishe Pintshevski was the first to write Yiddish poetry in which the South American landscape is described. The energetic Jacob Botashanski is prominent in the field of the essay, memoir, and literary criticism. Jacob Rollanski is one of the prominent journalists. The most important poet is Kehos Kliger. Argentina is the only country where a Yiddish magazine devoted to philosophy is published. It is called *Davke* and is edited by Shloyme Suskovitch. During the past ten years Argentina has become the center of Yiddish publishing activities, and hundreds of volumes by Yiddish writers the world over have been published there. The most active publishing group has been the Central Association of Polish Jews.

Other Jewish communities in Latin America publish various periodicals to which local writers contribute; most prominent among these communities are Uruguay and Mexico. The relatively new Mexican Jewish community also engages in the publication of books, and has a number of groups interested in Yiddish literature and literary activities. Among the Mexican Yiddish writers Jacob Glantz is the most prominent poet and Meir Corona the local novelist.

In Palestine, where Hebrew is the official language, there was an energetic group of Yiddish poets and narrative writers who gave expression to the joys and sorrows of the pioneers. In 1937 the collection entitled *Writings of Eretz Israel,* appeared in Tel-Aviv. During this period the prominent poet was I. Papernikov. After the holocaust and after the establishment of Israel, many Yiddish writers settled in the new Jewish state. This led to the rise of a considerable center of Yiddish literature in Israel. The works of poets and prose writers are often published there. Some writers concentrate around the Yiddish newspaper in Tel-Aviv. The most important literary journal is the quarterly, *The Golden Chain,* edited by Abraham Sutzkever, who has excelled in his poetry of the holocaust and in his newer poems which extol the land, the people, and the events of the State of Israel. The fine narrative writer Joshua Shpigel; the enterprising Moishe Grossman, who publishes a new magazine *Heimish;* the prose writer Mendl Man; and many other young writers now live in Israel.

The other continents, too, are represented in Yiddish literature. The community in South Africa has its publications and literati, among them the novelist I. M. Sherman, and the poets David Fram and David Volpe. Before World War II, Australia had a very small Jewish community, but despite this it added new names to the field of Yiddish letters, as noted in the *Australian Yiddish Almanac* (Melbourne, 1937). After the war, many refugees emigrated to Australia, and two newspapers are now published there. Among those active in Yiddish literature is the exacting literary critic, I. Rappaport. Even in Paris, where the Yiddish-speaking community did not take root, there is energetic publishing activity. The unique multi-volumed novel of a Russian-born Orthodox Jew, Sambatien, appeared there, among many books of poetry and *belles-lettres.*

It has not always been easy to describe a roving writer as belonging to a particular country, and in the case of the following men it is impossible to do so: Leib Malach, who wrote a drama, *Mississippi*, a novel of South America, *Don Domingo's Crossroad*, and highly literary reports of his many travels; Melach Ravitch, wandering ambassador of Yiddish poetry (now in Montreal), whose *Continents and Oceans* embraces most of the world, and whose *Poems and Ballads* displays a great variety of subject matter; Daniel Charney (of Vilno, Berlin, Paris, and since 1940 in hospitals and sanitariums of this country), whose penetrating memoirs are distinguished by humor. These three prove that Yiddish literature transcends all boundaries.

Despite the geographical dispersion, one sees a similarity of literary development linking one land to another and the present with the past. Although weakened by language assimilation, Yiddish literature has, nevertheless, revealed in recent times a breadth of vision and a sense of responsibility for the course of development of the whole Jewish people, which is striving to clarify for itself and for the world its spiritual physiognomy.

NOTES

[1] These are names of individuals, not cities.

[2] These are names of individuals.

[3a] Cf. above Cecil Roth, "The Jews of Western Europe (from 1648)," p. 260; cf. also above Walter J. Fischel, "Israel in Iran (A Survey of Judeo-Persian Literature)", pp. 1171-1172.]

[4a] Cf. Roth, *op. cit.*, pp. 253-254.]

[5a] Cf. above the chapter by Abraham J. Heschel, "The Mystical Element in Judaism."]

[6a] Cf. above Hillel Bavli, "The Modern Renaissance of Hebrew Literature," pp. 893 ff.]

[7a] Cf. Roth, *op. cit.*, pp. 261-262.]

[8a] Cf. Ben Zion Dinur, "The Historical Foundations of the Rebirth of Israel," p. 598.]

[9a] H. Leivick's first name was Leivick, and second name was Halper, but he has become known as H. Leivick.]

BIBLIOGRAPHY

BIRNBAUM, SOLOMON A., "Literature, Yiddish," (A & B, I, II) in *The Universal Jewish Encyclopedia*. New York, 1942, Vol. VII, pp. 125-129. A very brief account of the history of Yiddish literature to the end of the nineteenth century; the discussion is merely of types of works, so the development of the literature as a whole is lost sight of.

GASTER, MOSES, "Yiddish Literature in the Middle Ages," in *Essays by Diverse Hands*. London, 1927.

MARK, YUDEL, "Yiddish Literature," in *Encyclopedia of Literature*, J. Shipley, editor. New York, 1946, Vol. II, pp. 1026-1045.

——, *I. L. Peretz, His Life and Works*. New York, 1952.

MINKOFF, NOKHUM BORUKH, "Literature, Yiddish" (B, III), "The Twentieth Century," in *The Universal Jewish Encyclopedia*, Vol. VII, pp. 129-135. Too formalistically schematized into three schools: impressionism, expressionism, traditionalism. For this reason the distinctness of the three principal centers (America, Poland, Russia) is not recognizable.

——, in collaboration with Judah A. Joffe, "Old Yiddish Literature," in *The Jewish People Past and Present*. New York, 1952, Vol. III, pp. 145-164.

NIGER, SAMUEL, "Yiddish Literature in the Past Two Hundred Years," in *The Jewish People Past and Present*. Vol. III, pp. 165-219.

——, "Yiddish Culture in the United States," *ibid.*, Vol. IV, pp. 264-307.

——, "New Trends in Postwar Yiddish Literature," in *Jewish Social Studies*, Vol. I, No. 3. New York, July 1939, pp. 337-358. A very good review of trends in the modern literature.

PINÈS, M., *Histoire de la littérature judeo-allemande*. Paris, 1911. This work is based mainly on that by L. Wiener, below.

ROBACK, ABRAHAM A., *The Story of Yiddish Literature*. New York, 1940. With a great deal of love for Yiddish literature and with a tendency to apologetics, this book gives a brief picture of ancient and later Yiddish literature and dwells principally on the contemporary; it presents many facts, not always free of inaccuracy but without a clear scheme. The bibliographical notes on pp. 403-420 are valuable.

——, *I. L. Peretz, Psychologist of Literature*. Cambridge, Mass., 1935.

——, *Curiosities of Yiddish Literature*. Cambridge, Mass., 1933.

SAMUEL, MAURICE, *The World of Sholem Aleichem*. New York, 1943. An excellent introduction to East European Jewish life.

——, *I. L. Peretz, Prince of the Ghetto*. New York, 1948.

WAXMAN, MEYER, *A History of Jewish Literature from the Close of the Bible to Our Own Days*. 4 vols. New York, 1930-1941. Vol. II, pp. 613-615; Vol. IV, pp. 463-566, 996-1047. The author provides many facts, but the attitude is as to a foreign matter and not free of inaccuracies.

WIENER, LEO, *The History of the Yiddish Literature of the 19th Century*. New York, 1899. Written with love for Yiddish literature but without a thorough knowledge of its history to the middle of the nineteenth century, this book has interesting passages only concerning the middle and the second half of the century; unfortunately, there are a number of inaccuracies.

HOWE, IRVING, and GREENBERG, ELIEZER, *Treasury of Yiddish Stories*. New York, 1954.

LEFTWICH, JOSEPH, *The Golden Peacock, an Anthology of Yiddish Poetry*. Cambridge, Mass., 1939.

BIALOSTOTZKY, B. I. (ed.), *Dovid Edelshtat Gedenk-Bukh tsum Zekhtsikstn Yortseit*. New York, 1953.

BOROKHOV, BER, "Di Bibliotek fun Yiddishn Filolog"—400 Yor Yiddisher Shprakhforshung, *Pinkes*. Vilna, 1913.

ERIK, MAX, *Vegn Alt-Yiddishn Roman un Novele*. Warsaw, 1926.

———, *Die Geshichte fun der Yiddisher Literatur fun die Aeltste Zeiten bis Haskala-Tekufa*. Warsaw, 1928.
A very valuable book for the older literature but with an exaggerated evaluation of the importance of the "bardic" period.

GLATSTEIN, JACOB, *In Tokh Genumen*. New York, Vol. I, 1947; Vol. II, 1956.

JOFFE, JUDAH A., *Elia Bokhur*. Vol. I. New York, 1949.

MEISEL, NAKHMAN, *Forgeyer un Mittsaitler*. New York, 1946.

MINKOFF, N. B., *Elia Bokhur un zain Bovo-Bukh*. New York, 1950.

———, *Glikl Hamil*. New York, 1952.

———, *Zeks Yiddishe Kritiker*. Buenos Aires, 1954.

———, *Pionern fun Yiddisher Poezye in Amerike*. 3 Vols. New York, 1956.

———, and NIGER, SAMUEL, "Literatur bei Yiden," in *Algemeine Enziklopedie*. New York, 1942. Vol. III, Cols. 1-174.

NIGER, SAMUEL, *Geklibene Shriftn*. New York, 1928. Vol. III.

———, *Sholem Aleichem*, New York, 1928.

———, *Mendele Moicher Sforim*. Chicago, 1936.

———, *Dertseylers un Romanistn*. New York, 1946.

———, *H. Leivick, 1888-1948*. Toronto, 1951.

———, *I. L. Peretz, Zain Lebn, Zain Firndike Perzenlekhkeit*. Buenos Aires, 1952.

RAIZEN, ZALMEN, *Fun Mendelssohn bis Mendele*. Warsaw, 1923.
An anthology, with introductory articles, concerning a number of writers of the second half of the eighteenth and the first half of the nineteenth century.

———, *Lexicon fun Yiddisher Literatur, Presse un Philologie*. 4 vols. Vilna, 1926-1929.
A very good, almost always trustworthy source of information; fairly long accounts of all the more important writers.

RIVKIN, B., *Grunt-Tendentsn fun der Yiddisher Literatur in Amerike*. New York, 1948.

SHATZKY, JACOB, *Elia Bokhur*. Buenos Aires, 1949.

———, *Simkhas Hanefesh*. New York, 1926.

SHIPPER, ISAAC, *Geshichte fun Yiddishe-Kunst un Drama fun die Aeltste Zeiten bis 1750*. 2 vols. Warsaw, 1923-1925.
A very valuable monograph.

SHTIF, NOKHUM, *Die Aeltere Yiddishe Literatur*. Kiev, 1929.
An anthology with brief biographies and characterizations of the writers.

SHULMAN, ELIAS (Elijah), *Geshikhte fun der Yiddisher Literatur in Amerike, 1870-1900*. New York, 1943.

SHULMAN, ELIEZER, *Sefat Yehudit-ashkenazit vesifrata*. Riga, 1913.
A brief and good review of the old and the *Haskala* literature, without, of course, the related facts that have accrued during the past fifty years.

TSINBERG, ISRAEL, *Die Geshichte fun Literatur bei Yiden*. Vilna, 1935-1937.
Vol. VI and parts of VII and VIII. Very good articles concerning the ancient and later literature, with many details of the lives of the writers and of their times.

WEINREICH, MAX, *Bilder fun der Yiddisher Literatur-geshichte, fun die onheybn bis Mendele Moicher Sforim*. Vilna, 1928.
Excellent detail studies of the older literature.

WIENER, M., *Zu der Geshikhte fun der Yiddisher Literatur in 19. Yorhundert*. 2 vols. New York, 1945.

CHAPTER 27

THE ROLE OF EDUCATION IN JEWISH HISTORY

By Julius B. Maller

The survival of Jews and Judaism is in a large measure due to the continuous emphasis, throughout Jewish history, upon the transmission of ideas and practices from old to young and from one generation to another.[1] The educative process, an integral part of all varieties of religion and culture, was at the very core of Judaism and the Jewish way of living since biblical times.

The quest for an understanding of the meaning of life and the sustained effort to pass that meaning on from generation to generation have eternally motivated Jewish endeavor. This searching for knowledge, which in its practical aspect we call education, served as a central factor in Jewish life. The chief preoccupation of the Jewish Sages of all time was learning and teaching—Torah and Talmud.

During the First and Second Commonwealth, for approximately a thousand years of Jewish self-government—with one brief interruption, the Babylonian Exile—the process of developing the way of the good life and teaching it to the people was the major responsibility of the nation's judges, priests, and prophets. After the conquest of Palestine by the Roman legions and the forced dispersal of the Jews, *The Book* became the portable homeland. The loss of territorial unity strengthened the urge to preserve spiritual continuity. Community of ideas took the place of the physical community; indeed, the Jews became known as "the People of the Book." The transmission of a complete system of ideas became the bulwark against disintegration, and education moved to the head of the Jewish table of values.

To be sure, the educational concepts did not develop in the Jewish community isolated from the world. The ideas of Jews about education were influenced by, and in turn exerted influence upon, the educational theories of Egypt, Phoenicia, Babylonia, Persia, Greece and Rome. Because of the relative inaccessibility of original Jewish sources, the Jewish contribution to the conceptual aspects of modern education is not generally recognized in textbooks on the history of education. Classical Jewish education is often described as a direct outgrowth of Greek education or it is relegated to obscurity in discussions of education during early Christianity. What must be recognized is that education was so much a part of Jewish thought and way of living that it was taken for granted; Jewish Sages considered it hardly necessary to set down an articulated plan of its principles and practices. In a similar sense, the advanced conceptions of social ethics, abundant in Jewish classical writings, were not preserved as an organized system but rather as dynamic expressions on proper life.

The present chapter will be concerned primarily with the development of educational concepts as revealed in classical Jewish sources. The organizational aspects of the school, the curriculum and administration are discussed in another chapter.[1a]

Some Basic Educational Concepts

Certain fundamental concepts of education found in the records of earlier eras continued to be stressed through subsequent periods of Jewish history. Among the basic concepts that appear to have been accepted in Jewish lore, the following may be noted:

(1) An abiding faith in the efficacy of education, that human character is modifiable and improvable. (2) Learning and doing must be integrated; knowledge of ethics must be expressed in proper conduct. (3) Education is a continual process, to be carried on literally from the cradle to the grave. (4) Environment is an important factor in the educative process. (5) Education, to be most effective, must start with the very young. (6) Individual differences among pupils must be recognized; tests reveal differences in knowledge and convictions. (7) The process of education must be gradual from the known to the unknown, from the simple to the complex, and from the immediate to the remote. (8) Responsibility for education rests with the parents and the community. (9) Training for work is regarded as both essential and honorable. (10) The teaching of history illustrates the continuity and meaning of Jewish experiences.

Jewish teaching emphasized above all else that study is essential and worth while and must be brought to the people for guidance in everyday affairs. The emphasis was definitely on the pragmatic aspects of education. The Greek concepts of contemplation or dialogue as forms of diversion and enjoyment were uncommon in Jewish lore.

The Biblical Period

The concept of one God, invisible, imageless, and ruler of human destinies, tolerated no compromise with the primitive tribal practices of paganism. The explicit concept of the unity of God and the implicit corollary of the unity of mankind were so ingrained in all Jewish thought that subsequent conceptions of life and education naturally sprang from it.

Religion, as introduced in the period of the Bible, was a synthesis of theological concepts and ethical precepts which man had to obey in order to live as a social being. Failure to fulfill Divine commandments was considered the cause of human misfortunes and national disasters. This is not to say that the lofty concepts of morals and monotheism were either fully understood or accepted by the Hebrew masses. The Hebrew leaders were constantly aware of the tendency to relapse into paganism and immorality and they spared no effort to counteract that tendency and to educate the people in the way of the good life. In every book of the Bible this concern for education and the application of ethical principles is emphasized. The people were repeatedly admonished not to forsake Divine laws, but to pass them on from one generation to another.

Thus education, which was at once religious and national, served to bind the people together and aided in their survival through centuries of invasion, servitude and oppression, under the Egyptians, the Babylonians, the Persians, the Macedonians, the Syrians and the Romans. "If ever," declares a Swiss educator, "a people has proved the power of national education, it is the Jewish people."[2]

The Scriptures are the primary source for many of the educational theories that recur throughout Jewish history, many of which are as acceptable now as they were in the days of the Jewish commonwealth.

Mankind as a group, born of the common flesh and blood, and subject to the universal desires, aspirations, temptations and weaknesses, is considered to be capable of improvement, therefore of learning. All men are exhorted to seek out wisdom, to know its blessings.

> Happy is the man that findeth wisdom,
> And the man that obtaineth understanding . . .
> Her ways are ways of pleasantness
> And all her paths are peace (Prov. 3:13, 18).

> Get wisdom, get understanding . . .
> Yea, with all thy getting get understanding . . .
> I have taught thee in the way of wisdom . . .
> Take fast hold of instruction, let her not go;
> Keep her, for she is thy life (Prov. 4:4, 13).

Knowledge of the Law and observance of it were held to be of equal importance. The bonds of the nation were strengthened through the educative principle, which demanded proper ethical behavior.

And Moses called unto all Israel and said unto them: "Hear, O Israel, the statutes and the ordinances which I speak in your ears this day that ye may learn them and observe to do them" (Deut. 5:1).

And thou shalt teach them the statutes and the laws and shalt show them the way wherein they must walk and the work that they must do (Ex. 18:20).

The concept that learning was a continuing process, functioning at all times and in all places, was stressed from the very beginning of the history of the nation.

And ye shall teach them your children, talking of them, when thou sittest in thy house, and when thou walkest by the way and when thou liest down and when thou risest up (Deut. 11:19).

This book of the law shall not depart out of thy mouth, but thou shalt meditate therein day and night (Josh. 1:8).

The early Hebrews recognized the importance of proper associations and of the home influence on the young person.

He that walketh with wise men shall be wise; but the companion of fools shall smart for it (Prov. 13:20).

My son, hear the instruction of thy father and forsake not the law of thy mother (Prov. 1:8).

They knew that the proper time to start education was when the child was very young.

Train up a child in the way he should go, And even when he is old, he will not depart from it (Prov. 22:6).

While accepting the fact that all human beings are capable of learning and improving, the scholars of the time also pointed out that individual differences in students must be taken into account.

There are the stories of Jacob and Esau, and Isaac and Ishmael, to illustrate different personality types.

Even a child maketh himself known by his doings whether his work be pure and whether it be right (Prov. 20:11).

The Prophets, who were closely concerned with the instruction of the people, understood the necessity for using gradual methods of imparting knowledge.

Whom shall one teach knowledge?
For it is precept by precept, precept by precept, line by line, line by line, here a little, there a little (Is. 28:10).

In the teachings of the Prophets the emphasis was upon behavior.

And what the Lord doth require of thee: only to do justly, and to love mercy and to walk humbly with thy God (Mic. 6:8).

The Concept of Testing

There are several biblical references to the concepts of testing devices.

For example, the ability to pronounce a Hebrew word properly was used as an identification test.

> When any of the fugitives of Ephraim said, "Let me go over," the men of Gilead said unto him, "Art thou an Ephraimite?" If he said, "Nay," then they said unto him, "Say now Shibboleth," and he said, "Sibboleth," for he could not frame to pronounce it right (Judg. 12:5-6).

(It is interesting to note that this word "shibboleth" found its way into other languages to signify a watchword or the test word of the party.)

Another example of the application of a performance test is found in the recorded manner by which the bravest three hundred soldiers were selected by Gideon from an army of 32,000 men (Judg. 7:5-6).

Tests of courage and of implicit faith are also mentioned abundantly. Abraham's willingness to sacrifice his son and the trials and tribulations of Job are striking illustrations.

The Postbiblical Period

The restoration of a Jewish community in Palestine after the Babylonian Exile brought a number of important changes in the educational concepts of the Hebrew people. Gradually the role of the prophet diminished; the priest and the Levite concerned themselves more and more with the religious functions of the Temple. Education was stressed as never before, and its function was entrusted to the scribe.

The scribes were scholars, without official designation or office, who steeped themselves in the study of Sacred Wisdom and imparted their knowledge to disciples. This institution—the teacher and his circle of students—became the characteristic mark of Jewish life for centuries. The power of the scribe was inherent not only in his learning but in his leadership in the community.

Teaching, no matter what the subject, was based on the continuity of tradition. Instruction meant conveying the dicta and interpretations of preceding scholars. There was room for originality and some Sages forged new paths in law and commentary; but no break with tradition was tolerated. Teachers and disciples approached their intellectual labors with avidity and devotedness. They were regarded as the elite of the nation, men who considered the learning of the Law as the very purpose of life. The great masters won general recognition and their opinions became authoritative.

A new system of schools gradually came into being. Young children studied the Scriptures in a lower school called the *Bet Ha-Sefer;* the youth, particularly those showing intellectual ability, studied at an institution of higher learning known as the *Bet Ha-Midrash.* And for the mass of the people there arose the *Bet Ha-Keneset,* a democratic institution where members of the community participated in discussions concerning interpretations of the Written and Oral Law. A *Bet Ha-Keneset* could be organized by any ten people. Non-Jews were welcomed at such groups. At meetings every Sabbath a portion of the Scriptures was read and later discussed by the participants. Later still, prayers were introduced at the meetings, such as the *Hallel* after the reading of the Scripture portion. Eventually the *Bet Ha-Keneset* became a house of prayer and in its final metamorphosis was known as the synagogue, from the Greek term for *Bet Ha-Keneset* (House of Assembly).

A succession of teachers carried on the study and interpretation of the holy writings. The scribes interpreted the Bible in its application to daily life and evolved a system of traditions which later was expounded and codified in the Mishna.[3a]

This compilation of traditional lore, the Mishna, was the work of over a hundred scholars called *Tannaim*. They were succeeded by generations of *Amoraim*, commentators on the set tradition. The work of all these generations of scholars was eventually collected in one body of decisions and opinions that formed the Gemara. The Mishna and the Gemara were combined to form that collection of thought and law known as the Talmud.[4a]

The popularization of education fostered a high regard for learning and the learned man. The illiterate became an object of disrepute and was called *am ha-aretz*, a term used to designate a grossly ignorant person.

Early in the century (*c.* 65 B.C.E.), preceding the fall of the Jewish state, Simeon ben Shatah, a president of the Sanhedrin, established schools of advanced studies for young men in every district of the country. Later in the same century Joshua ben Gamala[5a] instituted elementary schools for boys of six to seven years of age. Teachers were appointed for all the schools, which were supported by the communities. Thus, in a sense, free public education was introduced in the Jewish community.

It was toward the end of that century that a new development took place in Jewish cultural and spiritual life. For the first time in the history of the Jews, an intellectual center of Judaism was established outside Palestine, in Babylonia. This development was not without its drawbacks. The Palestinian schools were an integral part of the whole country, in close contact with the people's political, social and economic life, and were influenced and guided by their needs. In Babylonia the Jewish schools as well as the Jewish community were not completely integrated with the larger community. They lacked the vitalizing influence and leaned toward a rigid interpretation of the Law and tradition.

Throughout this period of Jewish history there is ample evidence that the educational concepts of earlier times were in practice and that new ones emerged and were accepted by the people.

The concept that all were capable of being educated and that education was necessary for all appears in the writings of the postbiblical period.

As water is free for all, so is the Torah free for all. As water is priceless, so is the Torah priceless. As water brings life to the world, so the Torah brings life to the world. As water brings a man out of his uncleanness, so the Torah brings a man from the evil way into the good way. As wine does not remain good in vessels of gold and silver, but only in cheap earthenware vessels, so the words of the Torah remain pure only with him who makes himself lowly. Like wine, the words of the Torah rejoice the heart. As wine grows better by keeping, so the words of the Law become better as a man grows older.[6]

Take care of the children of the poor, for it is they who advance learning.[7]

The precept that learning and doing must be closely associated is mentioned repeatedly.

An ignorant man cannot be saintly.[8]

He whose works exceed his wisdom, his wisdom endures; but he whose wisdom exceeds his works, his wisdom does not endure.[9]

For children, religious education was bound up with ritual practice:

At the Passover Seder the son asks the father the four questions and if the son lacks understanding his father teaches him.[10]

Which is greater, study or doing? Rabbi Akiba answered: Study. The majority agreed that study is greater, for study leads to doing.[11]

The value of educational continuity is expressed in several places.

Say not when I have leisure I will study; perchance thou wilt never have leisure.[12]

The Torah says: "If thou forsakest me for a single day I shall forsake thee for two days."[13]

The Sages saw the home environment and companions as important educational factors.

Let thy house be a meetinghouse for the Sages and sit amid the dust of their feet and drink in their words with thirst.[14]

The younger the child the more impressionable he is; starting education at an early age was accepted as necessary.

He that learns as a child, to what is he like? To ink written on new paper. He that learns as an old man, to what is he like? To ink written on paper that has been blotted out.[15]

The Sages of the Mishna classified students according to their differences in the following manner:

Some hear [perceive] with facility and lose with facility. Some hear with facility and lose with difficulty. Some hear with difficulty and lose with facility. Some hear with difficulty and lose with difficulty.[16]

The element of attrition in the educational process was well recognized:

It is the custom of the world that a thousand people go in to study the Bible, a hundred complete it satisfactorily; one hundred proceed to [the study of] Mishna, ten of them complete it satisfactorily; ten advance to the study of the Talmud, only one completes it successfully.[17]

As a rule, the rabbis of the Mishna advocated a system of gradation in education. They cautioned against introducing advanced studies at an early age.

At five years one is fit for the Scripture, at ten years for the Mishna, at thirteen for the fulfilling of the Commandments, at fifteen for the Talmud.[18]

Later scholars insisted on the same principle.

Just as water descends drop by drop until it becomes a stream, so it is with the words of the Torah—a man studies two laws today and two laws tomorrow until it becomes like a living spring[19]

Members of the Jewish community took cognizance of the common responsibility for education.

He who teaches his neighbor's son Torah, it is as if he had begotten him.[20]

Form groups for the purpose of study, for Torah can be acquired only in a group.[21]

Education for work was considered both honorable and necessary.

Just as a man is required to teach his son Torah, so is he required to teach him a trade.[22]

The Sages emphasized that correct pedagogical methods require respect for the personality of the pupil, guiding him to knowledge rather than forcing him. The attitude of the teacher to the pupil must be sympathetic and considerate.

An impatient man cannot teach.[23]

Let the honor of thy disciple be as dear to thee as thine own.[24]

If you see a student who finds his studies as difficult as iron it is because his teacher does not take the proper attitude toward him.[25]

As with perfume, any one who desires may be made fragrant by it, so the scholar should be willing to teach any one who desires to profit by his learning.[26]

Examples of Testing

In the Talmud we find references to a situational test used in determining the normality and concomitant responsibility of a young child. The subject was presented with the choice between nuts and pebbles. If he made the proper choice his sense of responsibility was established.[27]

An interesting test was used to determine the legibility of a written text of the Scriptures. (The law required that each word in the Scroll be of unmistakable legibility.) In case of doubtful legibility of a word it was shown to a child who was "neither wise nor foolish" (the concept of average). If he read the word correctly, it was declared legible.[28]

Period of the Geonim

The academies of Palestine and Babylonia, which were closed for a brief time in the sixth century, were reopened in 589 c.e. under the supervision of the Geonim (heads of the academy).[29a] The period has been described by Professor Louis Ginzberg as the "Middle Age of Jewish history or the dark age, dark in the sense of obscure. No period in the history of postexilic Israel is more momentous than this and none so obscure."

In this era the Talmud became a comprehensive guide of Jewish conduct in everyday life and the leadership of Babylonian Jewry became well established. Attempts at interpreting talmudic Judaism in the light of Greco-Arabic philosophy gained currency among Jews.

While knowledge of the period is scant, certain writings of the scholars of the time reveal a good deal about the spread of education, the standing of the teacher in the community and the general concern for education. It is evident that the educational principles prevailing during the talmudic period were also advanced under the leadership of the Geonim.

The form of academic conference known as the *Kalla*, established in talmudic time, continued throughout the Geonic period. The *Kalla* assembled twice a year, in the spring and the fall when farmers could leave their work, and were open to all who desired advanced education in Jewish lore. The meeting place was usually the *Yeshiva* and hundreds of students would gather to listen to the wisdom of the Sages, and to discuss a portion of the Talmud. In addition to serving as a free school of higher education, the *Kalla* was able to reach out to the various communities through the students who came to study from all sections of the country. It also helped to extend education to distant communities which were not represented at the *Kalla* through written responses prepared by the Soferim, signed by the Geonim and sent to those communities.

The parents' responsibility for education was made clear.

If thou shalt bear sons and daughters . . . purchase for them books according to the best of your ability, and arrange to provide a teacher for them at a tender age.[30]

The Middle Ages

The dissolution of the Roman Empire after the barbarian invasion spelled the beginning of the decline of that civilization. Learning virtually disappeared; the monastery became the sole place of study, the monk the only literate person. In eastern Christian states learning survived in some centers but was limited to theological disputations or historical and legal writings.

Historians point out that intellectually the Jews suffered no medieval relapse into ignorance, that they were more educated than those among whom they lived, and that even the ordinary Jew knew the Scriptures better than the churchman of that time. The Jews contributed in large measure to the rebirth of civilization in Europe, disseminating Greek culture as interpreted by the Arabs. Jews were prominent in the Spanish cultural revival and in the early renascence in Provence and in Sicily under Frederick II.[31a]

Jewish communities scattered along the Mediterranean shores and in northern Europe, by the medieval period, had developed an educational system which was an integral part of their everyday life. Education was closely allied with religious thought. A Jewish community without a school was as rare as one without a house of worship. The most respected man in the community was the scholar; there was no greater disgrace than to be an ignoramus. Families took pride in the education of their children and were honored to have scholars in their midst.

In small communities the rabbi was usually the most learned man of the group, respected not only because of the authority vested in him, but also because of his erudition. Study, to the medieval Jew, was as important as prayer. The synagogue was more than a refuge from persecution and misery; it was a place where the Jew engrossed in study envisioned a world of truth and justice.

In the progressive Arab countries, educational facilities were easier to organize; education made greater advances and developed a wider scope than in Christian Europe. Under the Arabian influence, in Syria and Palestine and, to a lesser extent, in Babylonia, philological studies of the Hebrew language were greatly in vogue. Two systems of punctuation to represent vowels were devised. The exegetical and homiletical intrepretations of the Bible were developed in Palestine; in Babylonia the rationalist interpretation continued to prevail. The great academies in Palestine and Babylonia functioned throughout the medieval period, existing in Babylonia until the beginning of the eleventh century.

In Arabic Spain and in the Jewish communities of Provence and Italy the curriculum of studies in Jewish homes and schools included, in addition to the Bible and the Talmud, secular subjects, such as philosophy, mathematics, geometry, astronomy, medicine, poetry and music. This varied curriculum contributed to the growth of Jewish poetry and philosophy in Spain during that period. Digests of the Talmud were prepared for use by the students. Grammar was taught with the aid of especially prepared books.

In northern France, Germany, and other central European countries, the Jews confined their studies to religious matters. Education was based exclusively on the Bible and the Talmud.

Scattered as the Jewish communities were among so many countries, no fixed pattern prevailed. In general, however, the training of children started in the home, continued in an elementary school, and from there the pupil was sent to a religious academy or college, over which a famous scholar presided. Practical training began with active participation in holiday services and ceremonies.

In Germany there were schools for advanced learning of almost monastic discipline. There were also "wandering students," young men who traveled from academy to academy so that they might study with all the great scholars of the time. The teacher's task was not only to educate but to inculcate in his students a respect for the traditions and their application to daily life.

Teachers were paid by the parents when they gave private instruction at home and by the communities when they taught at a community school. The talented children of parents who could not afford to contribute to their children's education were educated at community expense. Funds for schools were raised through a special school tax. Education was practically compulsory in every Jewish community and school attendance started with a solemn ceremony when the child was very young, at the age of four or five. School was conducted throughout the year, being closed only on the Sabbath and holidays. Eventually the old principle of volunteer instruction was discarded and teaching became a profession, remuneration for which varied in different communities.

An extensive literature on education was produced during the medieval period by Jewish scholars in many lands. Education being an accepted value, most of the writers concerned themselves with the enrichment of the prevailing standards. They discussed methods of arousing public interest in educational values and how to improve pedagogical techniques; they recommended subject matter for various age groups. There was general agreement on the principle that study was not to be undertaken merely for the enjoyment of knowledge. Professions and trades were recognized as necessary for maintaining a place in society, and professional or vocational training was encouraged. Learning was considered the basis of ethical conduct in everyday matters.

During the medieval period some deviation from the rationalist interpretation of the Bible and Talmud took place; a reaction which was in a sense brought about by the oppressive conditions of the time. Nevertheless, intellectual activity never ceased. Many of the outstanding medieval Jewish scholars lived through tragic events; many died, victims of persecution, but the continuity of education remained unbroken.

Rashi (1040-1105) lived through the Crusades and witnessed the destruction by fire and sword of the central European Jewish communities. His monumental commentary on the Bible and Talmud did much to facilitate the study of Jewish lore. Rabbi Meir of Rothenburg (1220-1293) died in jail as a hostage; he was the author of a stirring poem commemorating the burning of twenty carloads of invaluable Jewish books and manuscripts in Paris (1242): "They cast thee as one despised and burn the wealth of God Most High." Ibn Tibbon (1120-1190) and Moses Maimonides (1135-1204) fled the savage pogroms of the Almohades (1146). Joseph ibn Caspi suffered under the Pastoureaux pogroms (1320). Solomon Alami survived Fernando Martinez's cruel campaign to baptize or exterminate the Spanish Jews.

The didactic poem, *Mussar Haskel*, attributed to the last Gaon, Hai ben Sherira (d. 1038),[32a] outlined the principles of education conceived as a continuation of the tradition going back to biblical times. Study, according to ben Sherira, had no other purpose than the acquisition of knowledge and sound judgment. The course of study included virtually all the known sciences of the period: religion, Divine law, philosophy, mathematics, medicine, and calendar computation. A man of education was taught to be gentle, seeking to comprehend the unknown. He was expected to rise early in the morning, have a book in his hand at all times, and ask questions of those who were more learned than himself. He was to be guided by the learned man so that he, too, might become an educational leader.

Judah ibn Tibbon fled from the fanaticism of the Almohades to Lunel, France, where he practiced medicine.[33a] He was the founder of a family of scholars and translators who brought to Europe a knowledge of Arab civilization and Arab studies of the Greek philosophers. In his treatise, *Father's Admonition*, written in the form of a will to his twelve-year-old son, ibn Tibbon combined his ideas on education with rules for the good life. He advised his son to devote himself to science and religion. He agreed with al-Ghazzali that there were only two sciences, ethics and physics, and he urged his son to excel in both.

Ibn Tibbon was a lover of books and he advised his son on how to care for his library. His son was told to have two or three copies of some books so that he could lend them to friends who could not afford their own. He was also urged to make a systematic catalogue of the books and twice a year collect those he had lent to others. Ibn Tibbon wrote: "My son, make thy books thy companions, let thy cases and shelves be thy pleasure grounds and gardens. Bask in their paradise, gather their fruit, pluck their roses, take their spices and their myrrh. If thy soul be satiate and weary, change from garden to garden, from furrow to furrow, from scene to scene. Then will thy desire renew itself, and thy soul be filled with manifold delight!"

Moses Maimonides, a renowned physician, had great influence on the promotion of secular studies among Jews,[34a] but he had little interest in poetry and history. He advised young men to study languages, philosophy, and the sciences.

Jacob Anatoli (b. *c.* 1194) represented the early renaissance in southern France. A fervent admirer of Maimonides, he interpreted the Bible according to the master's method, rationally, philosophically and allegorically. He deplored the fact that the Rabbis of his time neglected the study of the Bible for talmudic dialectics. He insisted that scientific investigation was essential for comprehension of religion. He advocated the study of languages and secular sciences. He fought against fanaticism, whether Jewish or Christian, and urged his fellow Jews to accept truth from Jew and non-Jew alike. He was perhaps the first scholar to define the differentiating characteristics of the Greek, the Roman and the Jewish cultural genius. The first is exemplified by the pursuit of wisdom; the second, the pursuit of power; the third, the pursuit of morality. In his book, *Malmad Ha-Talmidim*, he outlined methods of study.

Joseph ben Judah Aknin (1160-1226) was the foremost educator of his age. In his book, *Healing of the Soul,* he, like most of the contemporary writers on ethics, devoted a chapter to education. He set high standards for teacher requirements. A teacher had to know his subject so thoroughly that he could detect errors in fundamental premises. The teacher's attitude to his pupil was likened to that of a father to his child; a friendly and pleasant manner was considered an essential quality in a teacher. A teacher was required to conduct himself according to ethical principles and by precept and example to encourage his pupils to do the same. The elementary curriculum was to include reading, writing, and grammar. At the age of fifteen the pupil was to start the study of the Talmud, followed by the secular sciences. Poetry and music were to be taught, as were natural sciences, practical mechanics and medicine.

Judah ben Samuel Abbas, who lived in the thirteenth century, published a treatise on ethics and religion, the *Illumination of the Path.* One chapter treats the problems of pedagogy. Abbas advised starting the education of the child at the age of three, so that by the age of thirteen he would have mastered the Bible and the Hebrew and Aramaic languages. According to Abbas's schedule, when the pupil reached the age of eighteen he should have mastered the Mishna, the Talmud and the commentaries of Maimonides and Rashi. After that came the study of philosophy and secular sciences.

Shemtob ben Joseph Falaqera (1225-1290) wrote, among other works, a didactic treatise in the form of a dialogue on the importance of scientific study, contending that an understanding of religion actually required a knowledge of science.

Imanuel ben Solomon (1268-1330), who was a friend of Dante, advocated the study of secular subjects before religious subjects. His interpretation of the Bible was allegoric and mystical.

Joseph ibn Caspi (1297-1340), born in France, was an admirer of Maimonides, a traveler and a well-educated man. In keeping with the custom of the time, he wrote an ethical will and a guide for his son, *Book of Admonition, and Guide to Knowledge*. The guide outlined a program of study leading to the good life. He emphasized that good deeds were more important than acquisition of knowledge.

His schedule of study was arranged so that until the age of fourteen the pupil was to learn the Scriptures and the Talmud. After fourteen he was to add the study of mathematics and astronomy, and also the moralist writing contained in such books as *Proverbs*, the mishnaic *Fathers* and Aristotle's *Ethics*. At the age of eighteen there was to be a general review and then natural sciences were added to the curriculum. At twenty, the student could start on metaphysics.

Solomon Alami wrote his *Letter of Admonition* in 1415, interpreting the Fernando Martinez massacres in Spain as God's punishment for the moral and religious laxity of the Jewish community. He was bitterly opposed to the trend, then popular, of integrating Greek philosophy with interpretation of the Laws of Moses. He reproached the talmudists for indulging in hairsplitting arguments, the modernists for cloaking the Torah in Greek philosophy, and the wealthy for neglecting to observe religious tradition. Alami set up technical rules for writing manuscripts and for methods of study. He stressed the true purpose of study, acquisition of knowledge. He declared that man must use his wealth to acquire knowledge and not his knowledge to acquire wealth.

Throughout the Middle Ages, it was evident that Jewish thought was following a pattern of continuity from earlier times. Such basic concepts as the necessity for universal education and the ability of man to improve through it became rules for living. The method of imparting education was improved and the scholars devoted much time to the practical aspects of education.

There are many references to the principle of learning through participation. The Passover Seder is centered around participation by the young who ask the traditional four questions. Every element in the ritual is arranged to provoke such questions by the children. On other holidays, too, provision was made for children's activities.

On the festival of Sukkot the children would make decorations for the *sukkah* and at the end of the festival they would amuse themselves with the burning of the covering of the *sukkah*.[35]

On the days of Hanukkah and Purim they would make them happy with small gifts and they would also use them as messengers to give gifts to poor people in order to accustom them to the giving of charity and good deeds.[36]

The children were asked to carry the prayer books for their parents to the synagogues. There, small benches were set aside for them upon which they sat to listen to the prayers.[37]

On Friday after the afternoon prayers the parents would send their children from the synagogue to their mothers to let them know that it was time to kindle the Sabbath lights.[38]

Study of the Torah was recognized as a lifelong process which must never be halted.

How long is a person required to study Torah? Till the day of his death . . . Some of the greatest of the wise men of Israel were wood choppers, others water drawers. Some even blind, and nevertheless they engaged in the study of Torah day and night.[39]

Differences in ability were recognized both in teaching methods and in the planning of the curriculum.

He who teaches children and finds that one is sharper than his companions should not remain quiet [but rather] he should say to their parents, these require separate teachers (and these again require separate teachers) even though he will lose money if they are separated. If he sees that he succeeds in the study of the Bible but not in the study of the Talmud he should not force him to study Talmud. He should teach him that which is suited to his knowledge. As soon as a man sees that his son is not deemed worthy (or rather cannot grasp) Talmud, he should teach him important laws and Midrash and Bible.[40]

And the rabbi would proceed to ask questions and each would answer according to his ability and each student would proceed to derive deeper understanding through discussion with his neighbor.[41]

The medieval scholars adhered to the principle that the simple must precede the complex for the educational process to work.

First they would teach the children to recognize the letters, then to join them together. Afterwards to read the words and then the sentences and after that the portion.[42]

In order that he should understand the language of the Talmud it is necessary for him to study the Bible in its Aramaic translation. Then he ought to start reading the first prophets to help him understand the arrangement of their words and letters and subjects. Each sentence should be read first in Hebrew and then in his own language.[43]

Community responsibility for education was acknowledged by the Rabbis of the time.

The salaries of the teachers in the small villages which cannot be paid by individuals are to be paid by the community as a whole.[44]

We make a rule that in all cities and in all communities each one shall be required to provide for the study of Torah.[45]

In suggesting methods of study, the Sages cautioned the people to respect the dignity of the student; they urged the teacher to inspire and guide rather than coerce.

He should treat his students the way he treats his own children as it is written "thou shalt teach thy children." . . . He should teach them according to their ability to grasp the arrangements of the subject matter, until he teaches them to reach the stage of perfection.[46]

The Jewish Community in Eastern Europe

The migrations of Jews from western to eastern Europe occurred in the centuries following the Middle Ages. In Russia and Poland, and in neighboring countries, where the vast majority of Jews settled, education continued to be the consuming interest of the Jewish communities.

The educational institutions that grew up in east European countries were similar to those in other countries from which the Jews came. At the beginning of the sixteenth century there was a huge wave of immigration from Bohemia into Poland, and the Jews who came from Bohemia and Germany brought with them their language, which developed into Yiddish, as well as their culture and communal organizations.

In the autonomous Jewish community in Poland, education was practically compulsory for children from six to thirteen years of age, and under the supervision of the authorities. The *Kahal* prescribed the curriculum of the *heder*, at times in great detail, even mentioning the commentaries to be used in the teaching of the Bible and the number of pupils per teacher. Jewish authority also regulated the kind of teachers, decided upon the relationship between teachers, provided free education to orphans and vocational education to those children who became of age and did not show the required abilities to pursue studies in the Talmud and the Codes.

In 1639 we find a provision in the record book of the Council representing the chief communities in Lithuania in which the rabbis are enjoined to examine the young men in the community to see whether they are continuing their studies. The students are advised that even after they start to study Mishna and Talmud they must not drop the study of the Bible until they know it thoroughly. The teachers are also warned against proceeding to teach Mishna before the children know the Bible.

In Poland, Jewish autonomy produced remarkable results in education. As late as 1790 the great Polish masses were unschooled, while the Jewish masses had community-supervised schools and practically all Jewish children were exposed to some education. The educational requirements of the Jewish school were rather high, although few of the schools trained their students for the rabbinate. The ideal of the Polish Jewish mother was that her son should be a man of learning.

The educational institutions consisted of the *heder* and the *Yeshiva*. The curriculum of the *heder* included the Bible with its Hebrew commentaries, Hebrew prayers and other Hebrew books. The *Yeshiva* developed the lay scholar and the learned rabbi; it emphasized a knowledge of the sources of Jewish literature. To the extent that the Pentateuch, Mishna, and especially Talmud and the Codes were the means of regulating the life of the Jewish people, their study had functional value, preparing its students for life in the Jewish community.

The *Haskala*, the movement toward enlightenment,[47a] which started in Germany, was associated with hopes of emancipation and had some effect upon the curriculum of the *heder* and Talmud Torah, particularly in the revival of Hebrew language. The *Haskala* movement in Russia intensified the Jew's feeling of difference from the Russian culture and Jewish nationalism followed. It resulted in a modern educational institution as a counterpart to the government schools, the *heder Metukkan*, which did not attempt to adjust the Jewish child to the Russian culture but aimed rather at imbuing him with a love for his own national culture.

Examinations

In the *heder*, the examination given orally played an important role. It was usually given on Thursday of each week and covered the material studied during the week. It served as a strong motivation for study and only the most capable students were expected to answer the questions with proficiency.

In the home, too, it was customary for the father to examine his son every Friday night or Saturday afternoon.

Modern Times

The treatment of the Jewish contribution to educational theory in modern times is beyond the scope of the present article.

The intermingling of Jews and non-Jews and the universal acceptance —if not practice—of educational values make it difficult to differentiate between Jewish and general concepts of education.

Emancipation in western Europe saw the gates of education open to Jews. The Jews flocked to the university with a zeal and consuming devotion nurtured for ages. Moses Mendelssohn[48a] and his colleagues, who strove to make German culture palatable to Jews, were eminently successful because they appealed to the Jewish yearning for knowledge and passion for learning. The same applied to Jewish communities in other west and north European countries and, in more recent years, in the United States.

Throughout the history of the Jews, from biblical days to modern times, education was the key to survival and the very basis of adjustment.[49]

NOTES

[1] Acknowledgment is made by the author of valuable assistance by Blanche Bernstein and Geraldine Rosenfeld of the staff of the Library of Jewish Information, American Jewish Committee, and many suggestions by Leo Shpall and Mark Solitenberg.

[1a] Cf. below the chapter by Simon Greenberg, "Jewish Educational Institutions."]

[2] F. Dictes, *Geschichte der Erziehung und des Unterrichtes,* Leipzig, 1871.

[3a] Cf. above Judah Goldin, "The Period of the Talmud," pp. 164-166.]

[4a] On the Palestinian and Babylonian Talmuds, cf. *ibid.,* pp. 169, 172 and 179-181.]

[5a] Cf. Greenberg, *op. cit.,* p. 1261.]

[6] Sifre Deut. Ekeb 48.

[7] Nedarim 81a.

[8] Abot 2.6.

[9] Abot 3.10.

[10] Pesahim 10.4.

[11] Kiddushin 40b.

[12] Abot 2.5.

[13] Berakot, end.

[14] Abot 1.4.

[15] Abot 4.20.

[16] Abot 5.15.

[17] Lev. R.2.

[18] Abot 5.21.

[19] Shir Ha-Shirim Rabba 1.2.

[20] Sanhedrin 19b.

[21] Berakot 63b.

[22] Kiddushin 29a.

[23] Abot 4.12.

[24] *Ibid.*

[25] Taanit 8a.

[26] Erubin 54a.

[27] Gittin 64b.

[28] Menahot 29b.

[29a Cf. Goldin, *op. cit., pp.* 186-189.]

[30] Ascribed to R. Hai, cited in Asaf, *Mekorot Letoldot Ha-Hinuk Be-Yisrael,* II, p. 8.

[31a Cf. above Cecil Roth, "The European Age in Jewish History (to 1648)," *passim.*]

[32a Cf. above Abraham S. Halkin, "Judeo-Arabic Literature," p. 1132.]

[33a Cf. below Charles Singer, "Science and Judaism," p. 1393.]

[34a Cf. above Alexander Altmann, "Judaism and World Philosophy," pp. 973 ff.; cf. also Singer, *op. cit.,* pp. 1389-1393.]

[35] Maharil, *Minhagim* (Customs), (14th-15th century), sec Sukkoth.

[36] *Ibid.*

[37] *Responsa of Maharam* (Meir ben Gedalia of Lublin), (17th century).

[38] *Eben Ha-Ezer,* by Rabbi Eliezer b. Nathan of Mayence, (12th century), #342.

[39] *Mishneh Torah,* Hilkot Talmud Torah, (Laws of Teaching the Torah), Maimonides, (12th century).

[40] Judah ben Samuel Ha-Hasid, *Sefer Hasidim* (Book of the Pious), (13th century), ed. Wistinetzky, par. 823-825, p. 209.

[41] Elijah Capsali, *Chronicles,* (16th century), cited in Asaf, *op. cit.,* II, p. 104.

[42] Isaac ben Moses of Vienna, *Or Zarua,* (13th century).

[43] Judah ben Samuel, *Yair Natib* (Will Light the Path), (17th century), cited in Asaf, *op. cit.,* II, p. 29.

[44] Mayer Ha-Levi Abulafia, in *Or Zaddikim* (Light of the Righteous) by Judah ben Manoah Said, (13th century), cited in Asaf, *op. cit.,* II, p. 52.

[45] Abraham Benevista, *Takkanah,* (15th century), cited in Asaf, *op. cit.,* II, p. 81.

[46] Joseph ben Judah ibn Aknin, *Tabb al-Nufus* (Healing of the Souls), (13th century), cited in Asaf, *op. cit.,* II, p. 37.

[47a Cf. above Hillel Bavli, "The Modern Renaissance of Hebrew Literature," pp. 893 ff.]

[48a Cf. above Roth, "The Jews of Western Europe (from 1648)," pp. 261-262.]

[49] The markedly positive attitude toward education among Jewish youth in the United States was revealed in a research study by the writer based on an attitude test given to several hundred Jewish college students. One part consisted of a series of words to which the students were to indicate positive or negative attitudes. The word "education" showed the highest incidence of

positive attitudes, with only one per cent of negative attitudes. See "The Personality of Jewish College Students" by Julius B. Maller, *Jewish Education,* III, No. 2. The author is preparing a larger work on patterns of adjustment in contemporary Jewish life with special reference to the State of Israel.

BIBLIOGRAPHY

[The editor gratefully acknowledges helpful suggestions for the present edition and especially this chapter from Dr. Shlomo Marenof of Brandeis University.]

ABRAHAMS, ISRAEL (ed.), *Hebrew Ethical Wills*. Philadelphia, 1926.
    V. The Gate of Instruction attributed to Maimonides.
    VII. Guide to Knowledge by Joseph ibn Caspi.
    III. A Father's Admonition by Judah ibn Tibbon.
———, *Jewish Life in the Middle Ages*. London, 1896. Pp. 340-356.
ASSAF, S., *Mekorah le-Toledot ha-Hinnuk,* Vols. I-IV, Tel-Aviv and Jerusalem, 1925-1942.
BARON, SALO W., *The Jewish Community*. Philadelphia, 1942. Vol. II, Ch. XIII.
BERTHOLET, ALFRED, *A History of Hebrew Civilization,* translated by A. K. Dallas. London, 1926.
COHEN, ABRAHAM, *Everyman's Talmud*. London, 1937.
DRAZIN, NATHAN, *History of Jewish Education from 515 B.C.E. to 220 C.E.* (with a Bibliography). Baltimore, 1940.
FUNK, S., *Die Entstehung des Talmuds*. Leipzig, 1910.
GAMORAN, EMANUEL, *Changing Conceptions in Jewish Education*. New York, 1924.
GOLLANCZ, SIR HERMANN, *Pedagogics of the Talmud*. Oxford, 1924.
GUEDEMANN, M., *Das juedische Unterrichtswesen waehrend der spanisch-arabischen Periode*. 3 vols. Vienna, 1888.
———, *Quellenschriften zur Geschichte des Unterrichtswesens und der Erziehung bei den deutschen Juden*. Berlin, 1891.
GUIGNEBERT, CHARLES, *The Jewish World in the Time of Jesus,* translated by S. H. Hooke. London, 1938. "The Law," "The Scribes," "The Synagogue."
LEIPZIGER, HENRY M., *Education of the Jews*. New York, 1890.
MARCUS, SAMUEL, *Die Paedagogik des israelitischen Volkes*. 2 vols. Vienna, 1877.
MORRIS, N., *The Jewish School*. London, 1937.
NEUMAN, ABRAHAM A., *The Jews in Spain*. Philadelphia, 1942. Vol. II, Chs. XV-XVI.
SCHUERER, EMIL, *A History of the Jewish People*. Edinburgh, 1893. Vol. II, "The Scribes," "School and Synagogue."
STRACK, HERMANN L., *Introduction to the Talmud and Midrash*. Philadelphia, 1931.
TSCHARNO, Y., *Studies in Education in Israel (Letoldot Ha-Hinuk beyisrael)*. Jerusalem, 1939. Parts I-II, the Biblical and Talmudic Periods.

CHAPTER 28

JEWISH EDUCATIONAL INSTITUTIONS

By Simon Greenberg

I. INTRODUCTION

Educational activity performs two functions. It broadens the range of man's knowledge and skills, and transmits this knowledge and these skills from one generation to another, or from one man to his fellow.

Educational activity is inherent in human societies on all levels of development. One society is distinguished from another, however, not merely by the quality of its intellectual inquisitiveness and the character of its accumulated knowledge and skills. Intellectual and spiritual progress are equally reflected by the institutions a society creates or adapts in order consciously to increase its knowledge and skills, consciously to transmit them to the group as a whole.

Until comparatively recent times the educational institutions of all peoples of the world were each concerned almost exclusively with the transmission of the skills, the knowledge and the traditions of its own particular group. Educational institutions were not expected to be centers for the discovery of new knowledge or channels for the transmission of truth and beauty and wisdom, regardless of their source of origin.

In the following pages we shall attempt to sketch only in briefest outline the history of the main types of educational institutions created by the Jewish people from the earliest times to the present. Another chapter in the work is devoted to the educational philosophy underlying the work of these institutions, and to the pedagogic principles adopted to achieve their goal. While a certain amount of duplication is inevitable, because it is virtually impossible to discuss any aspect of an educational institution without some reference to its philosophy and curriculum, this chapter will seek to limit itself primarily to the external history of the institutions, to the occasions that brought them into being, and to the conditions that enabled them to function.[1a]

The recorded history of the Jewish people extends over a period exceeding three thousand years and is divided into rather well-defined eras. Moreover, Jewish life took on differing forms in the various countries in which it existed. We might, therefore, treat our theme either chronologically or geographically. However, since many of the educational institutions existed during more than one era and in more than one land, we chose to present chronologically the story of the individual institution as it developed and changed from one era to another and from country to country.

II. THE HOME

The home is mankind's universal educational agency. It was but natural that within the family fathers should transmit a knowledge of their occupations to the sons and mothers teach their daughters the skills required for homebuilding. Thus, while there are no specific references in the Bible to this particular matter, we have every reason to assume that Jewish sons learned from their fathers how to plow, plant, care for vineyards, tend sheep, the art of the potter and the warrior and the other arts in ancient Israel.

But the home was not used by all groups with equal awareness and effectiveness for transmitting the spiritual and ethical teachings and the treasured historic memories of the group. The biblical record clearly indicates that among the Jews the home was at a very early period *consciously* employed for such educational purposes. Responsibility for transmitting the group's spiritual heritage to one's children is specifically enjoined upon parents, particularly the father. Abraham is known "of the Lord" in order that "he may command his children and his household after him, that they may keep the way of the Lord, to do righteousness and justice" (Gen. 18:19). A well-defined body of instruction is to be transmitted. "And these words which I command thee shall be upon thine heart and thou shalt teach them diligently unto thy children." The family is commanded to practice prescribed ceremonies for the express purpose of perpetuating the knowledge of great historic events and for stimulating the inquisitive mind of the child. His questions provide a natural setting for the father to explain and emphasize some precious traditions of the group. "And it shall come to pass, when your children shall say unto you: What mean ye by this service? that ye shall say: It is the sacrifice of the Lord's passover, for that He passed over the houses of the children of Israel in Egypt, when He smote the Egyptians and delivered our houses" (Ex. 12:26-27). In the same spirit every Jewish family was commanded to dwell in booths for seven days "that your generations may know that I made the children of Israel to dwell in booths, when I brought them out of the land of Egypt" (Lev. 23:43). The festivals and ceremonies were not and are not merely means of worshiping the Lord. They were and are the re-enactments of great historic moments in the people's past, not only to stimulate appropriate religious sentiments but also to preserve and transmit precious group memories. While the parents are commanded consciously to teach their children, the children are urged to take to heart the instructions of their parents. They are not only to "honor thy father and thy mother" (Ex. 20:12) but also to obey the instruction of the father and not to reject or neglect the teaching of the mother (Pr. 1:8).

The records do not indicate the extent to which parents gave formal instruction at regular intervals to their children. But it seems fair to imply that in the case of intellectually and spiritually alert parents that type of instruction was not entirely lacking. Hannah's relation to her son Samuel, the careful training given to Samson by his parents, a mother's recorded instruction to her son (Pr. 31:1-9), the care with which Job is reported to have supervised the religious life of his children (Job 1:5)—these and other indications justify the assumption that there were parents in early Israel who performed their duties as teachers with a high degree of seriousness.

During the days of the Second Temple, when Judaism, under the leadership of the scribes and Sages, acquired the traditional forms associated with Rabbinic or normative Judaism, the home became a far more effective educational agency. From the moment the child learned how to speak the father recited the morning and evening prayers with him; and as the child developed the father trained him in the performance of the mitzvot. Even though elementary schools were plentiful, the Rabbis stressed the father's duty that he himself teach his son, for a "child's true father is he who teaches him Torah." In addition, it was incumbent upon the father to teach his son a trade or profession, even how to swim, for lack of a trade may lead him to a life of violence and inability to swim may endanger his life.

In observing how the mother conducted the household, children learned the detailed dietary laws and the manner of daily Jewish living. They saw her welcoming the Sabbath every week not only by numerous and arduous labors in the kitchen; they also saw her dressing her home, herself and her children with particular attention, and kindling the Sabbath lights. The father's *kiddush*, recited over a cup of wine or two loaves of bread to usher in the Sabbath or the festival meal, the washing of the hands before meals, the grace after meals, the celebrations of holidays, major and minor festivals, particularly the unique and remarkable Passover eve Seder service, the fast days of the Jewish year—these and a host of other religious observances inculcated piety and faith in the growing child's heart, and acquainted him with the noblest spiritual and historical experiences of his people.

If the Jewish girl until very recent days was most often not sent to receive formal instruction in a school, it was not merely because of a widespread attitude that a girl needed no formal education. It was due rather to the feeling that her mother and home training could provide her with all the instruction she needed to live a good and pious Jewish life. Until very recent times, the expectation was, by and large, fully realized. And because the Jewish home was so effective an educational institution, the Jewish school could devote itself exclusively to the formal teaching of the sacred texts, leaving instruction in personal religious matters to the home.

For two thousand years and more, the Jewish home continued to be the most effective institution for educating the Jewish child. The social and economic forces that, after the French Revolution, tended to minimize family and home influence among Western peoples, had even more disastrous effects upon Jewish life. In addition, the vast migrations of millions of East European Jews to the West severed Jewish family life from its moorings in a well-organized community with an established public opinion. Today in America and throughout the Western world, therefore, the home as a Jewish educational institution, though still important, does not approach in effectiveness the Jewish home of Eastern Europe before World War I, or of any part of Europe before the French Revolution.

The breakdown of the Jewish home as an effective, primary Jewish educational agency in the Western world has placed enormous responsibilities upon the other educational agencies of the Jewish community. All educators are agreed, however, that the best school cannot possibly substitute for the home. At present, particularly in America, the reconstitution of the Jewish home as an effective educational agency for rich religious life represents one of the greatest challenges to Jewish educators and religious leaders.

III. THE SYNAGOGUE

Next to the home the synagogue was and is the most democratic and universal Jewish educational institution affecting the lives of old and young, men and women.[2a] Our records give us no clear picture of the place, the age or the circumstances under which it came into being. But it is safe to say that the element of instruction played at least as great a part in the founding of the synagogue as did prayer. Many unique and specifically educational features were combined in the synagogue almost from its very inception; these have remained an integral part of it to our own day.

The first and probably the oldest of these is the reading from the Scriptures. The Bible relates that Moses, after having written the Torah, commanded the priests, the Levites and all the elders that "when all Israel is come to appear before the Lord thy God in the place which He shall choose, thou shalt read this law before all Israel in their hearing. Assemble the people, the men and the women and the little ones, and thy stranger that is within thy gates, that they may hear, and that they may learn, and fear the Lord your God" (Deut. 31:11-12). While this reading was to take place on Sukkot, it was apparently to be held in every community throughout the land and not only in Jerusalem, for the women, children and strangers were not commanded to make the pilgrimage to Jerusalem, but they were commanded to hear the reading. Such a reading of Scripture before a vast throng is recorded as having taken place on various occasions before the establishment of the Second Temple.

The revolution introduced by Ezra into the religious life of the post-exilic Jewish community made the Torah at once the core and the foundation of the community's spiritual life. Scripture readings gradually became a fixed feature of the gatherings on the Sabbath and on Monday and Thursday, the two market days when the peasants came into town. Reading Scripture in itself, however, could not serve the educational purpose adequately. Hence, there was added either a translation into the vernacular or a religious message based upon the passage that was read. In time, the Five Books of Moses were divided into sections, so that the whole Pentateuch might be read from beginning to end on the Sabbaths once in three years or once every year. To the readings from the Pentateuch, passages from the Prophets were later added. Today in every traditional synagogue the Pentateuch is completed once a year through weekly Sabbath readings. The portion read is no longer orally translated into the vernacular, for in most synagogues the congregation is provided with a printed text and translation. This scriptural reading is still the central feature of the traditional Sabbath synagogue service. Many have objected to it because of the time it requires and its noninspirational quality as read in many synagogues today. Nevertheless, it continues to hold its place in the vast majority of the synagogues of the world; and it continues to exercise, though far less effectively than it might, the educational function of instructing the congregation in the contents of the Pentateuch.

In addition to the Scripture reading the synagogue became the center where spiritual leaders of the people regularly delivered their message of inspiration or information. In biblical days the prophet addressed the people in the courtyard of the Temple. On various occasions the prophet would be visited at home by his followers in order to be blessed or instructed by him. In Babylonia Ezekiel's home was apparently the rendezvous for the pious who wanted to hear a Divine message. Ezekiel's complaint that many of his listeners came to be entertained rather than instructed, sounds very modern indeed.

When a knowledge of the Torah became the *sine qua non* for spiritual leadership among the Jews, it was but natural that the message of the leader should become associated with the Torah and more particularly with the portions read on any given occasion. Until modern times that message would most often be delivered in the synagogue on the Sabbath afternoon immediately preceding the afternoon service. In more recent times a message or sermon in the vernacular based on the weekly pentateuchal portion has become a permanent feature of the Sabbath morning service in well-nigh all synagogues, particularly in America. This message is inspirational and informative and serves as a significant educational medium.

But the sermon and the Scripture readings are not the only direct educational features of the synagogue service. The traditional prayer book itself contains many educational features ordinarily not associated with a liturgy. In the first place, Judaism considers study as being superior even to prayer as a means of worshiping God. Hence passages of an ethical and historical nature from the Talmud are incorporated into the prayer book. The prayers are modified for various occasions of the year, so that the festival celebrated, or the historic occasion remembered, is given its meaning and interpretation. The synagogue liturgy does not stress merely the *individual's* relation to God, the *individual's* needs and hopes, and the *individual's* longing for Divine salvation. Equal emphasis is placed upon the *group's* relation to God, upon the *group's* needs and hopes, upon the *group's* yearning for collective salvation.

Moreover, the synagogue by its organization and form of worship has been a mighty force making for democracy within the Jewish community. Any ten male adults may conduct a regular service. Anyone among them may be their reader or preacher. There is a complete absence of anything like a clerical hierarchy. Knowledge and piety alone are the paths to leadership. Where a congregation diverges from these principles, it does so not because of the requirements of ritual or liturgy. On the contrary, it does so in violation of those requirements and merely as a concession to the human limitations of those who compose that particular congregation.

The synagogue's role as a Jewish educational agency is by no means exhausted by the above-mentioned activities. The synagogue building has always been a center of study for either children or adults. But that aspect of the synagogue's contribution to Jewish education we shall discuss later under the general subject of schools.

Thus, through its liturgy, scriptural reading, sermon and organization, the synagogue was, next to the home, the most significant educational agency in the life of the Jewish people. Together with all other religious institutions throughout the world, the synagogue's influence as a house of prayer has perceptibly waned in modern times. Other aspects of it have, however, taken on new vitality in our day. Moreover, among the Jews no other institution has as yet been created to take its place, nor to approach it even in its present weakened condition, as an influence for the moral, ethical and religious education of the people.

IV. THE ELEMENTARY AND SECONDARY SCHOOL

A. IN BIBLE TIMES

The Bible contains no direct reference to the existence of schools for either children or adults. But there can be little doubt that educational activity in biblical times was not limited exclusively to the home. There undoubtedly were men who taught children other than their own either as pupils or as apprentices. Bezalel and Oholeav, the artists who built the Tabernacle and all its vessels, were endowed by the Lord not only with the skill of their own hands, but also with the ability "to teach" others. The children of the royal family most likely had their own private teachers. The elders of Samaria seem to have trained Ahab's seventy sons. Moreover, members of the court apparently studied the dominant language of the age, as well as the Hebrew language. The ability to write—no mean achievement in ancient times—was apparently quite prevalent among Israelite children.

Priests and Levites are spoken of most frequently as the teachers of the people. King Jehoash was instructed by the priest Johoiada, Jehoshaphat, King of Judah, sent officers, together with priests and Levites, to teach throughout the Land of Judah. The Bible refers to "teacher," "instructors" and "wise men," who acted as teachers. These presumably had some fixed place and time for teaching. That the priests and Levites received some kind of systematic and formal instruction must be taken for granted. The priest had to be thoroughly acquainted not only with an elaborate and complicated sacrificial system but with the equally intricate laws of Levitical purity and physical health. The Levites had to be proficient as assistants to the priests and as members of the Temple choir. They could not possibly enter upon their duties without thorough previous instruction. The advanced age at which they started to perform their duties in the Temple, the priest at thirty and the Levite at twenty-five, probably reflects the extended period of training they had to undergo.

The early prophets appear also to have had schools or at least groups within which they trained the novitiates and developed their own spiritual powers.

However, the elementary school for the education of all Jewish children did not come into its own until well toward the end of the Second Commonwealth.

B. From the Second Commonwealth to Modern Times

The following short talmudic passage gives us the most significant information available regarding the establishment of Jewish elementary schools:

However, that man is to be remembered for good, and his name is Joshua ben Gemala [*c.* 64 c.e.]; for were it not for him Torah would have been forgotten in Israel. For at first he who had a father was taught Torah by him, and he who had no father did not study Torah. It was then decreed that teachers of children should be appointed in Jerusalem. However, he who had a father, the father would bring him to Jerusalem and have him taught, while he who had no father, would not come to Jerusalem to study. It was then decreed that teachers of the young should be appointed in every district throughout the land. But the boys would be entered in the school at the age of sixteen and seventeen and if the teacher would rebuke one of them, he would resent it and leave. Thus it was until Joshua ben Gemala decreed that teachers of children should be appointed in every district and every city and that boys of the age of six and seven should be entered.[3]

It is obvious from the above passage that the elementary school had a very long development behind it by the time Joshua ben Gemala instituted his reform. Simeon ben Shatah (first century B.C.E.)[3a] is credited with the decree requiring children to go to a *Bet Sefer,* a school, while another passage has it that Ezra was the one who sought to "set a scribe next to a scribe," that is, to multiply the number of schools in the community. The chief educational contribution of Jewish religious leaders of the Second Commonwealth was the principle that a basic elementary Jewish education must be provided by the community for every Jewish boy regardless of his social or economic status. The goal thus set was probably never fully attained, no more than any modern society with laws for universal compulsory elementary education has attained its goal. But it can be said without fear of serious contradiction that except for periods of communal disintegration or impoverishment following mass persecutions and plagues, or accompanying the pioneer efforts of recently established Jewish settlements, universal elementary education for boys was more fully attained among Jews up to the end of the eighteenth century than among any other contemporary group. The Rabbis forbade a Jew to live in a community which had no elementary school teacher. Every community having at least ten Jewish families could be compelled by law to maintain a teacher in its midst although not all of the ten families may have had pupils for him. It was, moreover, a widespread practice during these centuries for a family living in isolation to invite a teacher to become a part of the household in order to teach the children. An authority of the fourth century suggests that only if a Jewish child were captured as an infant and raised among non-Jews could he grow up without an elementary

Jewish education. This is most likely an exaggeration, as are the traditions about the hundreds of elementary schools in Jerusalem before its destruction in 70 c.e.,[4a] and the thousands of elementary schools in Bethar before the failure of the revolt of Bar Kokbah (c. 135 c.e.).[5a] But none can gainsay the fact that the elementary Jewish school in which Jewish children learned how to read Hebrew and translate the Pentateuch has been the most widespread institution of the Jewish community for the past two thousand years.

I. THE BET HA-SEFER AND THE BET HA-KENESET

From the very beginning there was a very close relationship between the school and the synagogue. The synagogue premises were the meeting place of the school, and synagogue functionaries very often acted as teachers. The elementary school was referred to in talmudic times as a *Bet Ha-Sefer* (Aramaic—*Bet Sifra* or *Bet Mikra*), House of the Book, or *Bet Ha-Keneset* (Aramaic—*Be Kenishta*), the House of Gathering. The second name is most likely derived from the place where the school met. The first name may indicate the subject matter taught, namely, the Bible, or perhaps the fact that instead of meeting in the synagogue the school met in a special community building or in a private home, and was the private enterprise of the teacher.

2. THE BET TALMUD

Secondary education, which consisted in study of Rabbinic texts—particularly the Mishna—and in an introduction to the method by which the Oral Law was discussed and developed, was provided by the *Bet Talmud*, and Talmud school. The relationship between it and the *Bet Sefer* is indicated by the Rabbinic dictum that a boy should start to study Bible at five, Mishna at ten and Talmud at fifteen, and by the remark that out of every thousand pupils who started to study Bible only one hundred continued with the study of the Mishna.

3. THE HEDER AND THE TALMUD TORAH

The twofold aspect, private and communal, of the Jewish elementary school has characterized it throughout the centuries. The duty to educate the Jewish child never became the exclusive responsibility either of the community or of the father. Circumstances determined which of the two assumed the responsibility in any particular instance. The average Jewish parent made great sacrifices to pay for his child's education. Together with other parents he could make his own arrangements with a private teacher. But when a child had no parents or when the parents were too poor to pay, the community would step in and either pay all or part of the child's tuition to a private teacher or else, where the number of indigent

children warranted it, a community school supported by voluntary contributions and self-taxation would be established.

Among the Jews of Eastern Europe the private elementary school
for children was called a "heder" (a room). It took its name from the
fact that it usually met in one of the rooms of the teacher's home. There
a group of fifteen to twenty-five children of varying ages, usually below
thirteen, would meet during the whole day. Within each heder there was
a minimum of gradation. But there was gradation among the various
hedarim serving a community. The most elementary heder catered to
children who were beginning to read and write Hebrew and to translate
sentences from the Pentateuch. Above that was the heder supervised by a
rabbi who taught only those prepared to master the translation of the
Pentateuch and selected passages from Rashi's Commentary. The highest
Heder introduced the student to the Talmud and prepared him to go on
to the *Yeshiva*.

The curriculum, the school year, the financial arrangements varied
but little from community to community. They were governed by the
prevailing cultural standards, by well-established traditions or by special
communal enactments.

The communally supported school was called the Talmud Torah, a
house for the study of the Torah. It offered the same opportunities to the
children of the poor as the heder did to the others. In rare instances, as in
the case of the Amsterdam Talmud Torah of the seventeenth century, it
was by far superior to the private heder, having a comparatively rich,
graded curriculum, a staff of well-equipped teachers, and catering to all
children of the community, not merely to the poor. The Talmud Torah
often occupied a structure of its own, though just as often it would meet
on the synagogue premises.

Both of these educational institutions continued to flourish in Eastern
European Jewish communities as late as the twentieth century. They
disappeared in Russia only with the Russian Revolution and continued
among the Jews of Poland until the 1939 debacle, which overwhelmed
Polish Jewry.

4. MODERN JEWISH SCHOOLS AND THE RISE OF SECULAR EDUCATION AMONG
   JEWS

The heder and the Talmud Torah held undisputed sway in Jewish
communities throughout the world until the end of the eighteenth century.
These schools, though they taught some elementary arithmetic and the
reading and writing of Judeo-German, were otherwise devoted exclusively
to religious subject matter. Whatever secular education was attained by

Jewish individuals here and there was the result of private instruction or personal initiative and persistence. Moreover, all government schools were either closed to Jews or were boycotted by them. In the second half of the eighteenth century a perceptible change occurred. The activities of Moses Mendelssohn (1729-1786)[6a] and his colleagues resulted in the organization (1778) in Berlin of the first Jewish free school which included German and French, as well as Hebrew, in its curriculum. The Edict of Toleration issued by Emperor Joseph II of Austria in 1781 was enthusiastically greeted by German Jewish intellectuals, and elaborate programs for the reform of Jewish education were proposed by them. Modern Jewish schools, sponsored by the government and supported by special taxes levied upon the Jewish community, were established particularly among the Jews of Galicia. While Jewish intellectuals welcomed the schools, the Jewish masses rightly suspected that the schools intended not merely to impart information but also to wean Jewish children away from Judaism and the Jewish people. Though a Jew was appointed inspector, and though some hundred such schools were opened after 1790, resistance of the Jewish masses and other factors led to their close in 1806.

Somewhat the same situation was repeated in Russia, where in 1844 a special decree permitted Jews to open their own modern schools to be supported by special taxes upon the Jewish community. The Russification and proselytizing aspect of these schools was so pronounced, however, that after ten years of functioning only a little more than three thousand Jewish pupils were attracted by them. A change in the Russian government's attitude in 1857 eliminated the element of religious proselytization from these schools, and Jews flocked to them in large numbers. But such was the zeal for Russification, which inspired even the Jewish supervisors of the schools, that before long the distinctly Jewish subjects were practically excluded from the curriculum. By that time Jewish students and parents could discern little or no difference between these Jewish government schools and the general government schools. As a result, Jewish youth turned to the general school, which had been open to them since 1804 but had been almost unanimously boycotted by Jews heretofore. By 1873 it became apparent that, from the government's point of view, the special Jewish elementary and secondary schools were no longer necessary, and they, plus the two government-sponsored rabbinical seminaries, were closed. Jewish youth was coming in increasing numbers to the general Russian government schools; within twenty years, from 1853 to 1873, the percentage of Jews in the total student body rose from 1.25 to 13.2. By 1880 Russian educators started to advocate and apply a *numerus clausus*.

a. The "Heder Metukan" and Modern Jewish School Systems in Eastern Europe

Until the last quarter of the nineteenth century all efforts to bring secular education to the Jews, whether sponsored by Jews themselves or by non-Jews, were inspired primarily by the desire to assimilate the Jew into the general population. By about 1885 a change of attitude became discernible in the ranks of Jewish intellectuals. The high hopes entertained by Jews that complete civil and social emancipation would automatically follow the secularization and modernization of Jewish life, were rudely shattered by one unhappy event after another. At the same time, a renewed spirit of self-respect was awakened within the ranks of those Westernized or modernized Jews who were deeply and irrevocably attached to Judaism and to the Hebrew language and literature. Zionism and modern Hebrew literature made remarkable headway among all classes of the Jewish community. The Yiddish language and literature simultaneously experienced an unprecedented development. All this inner cultural revival was bound before long to be reflected in the community's educational activities. A new modern Jewish school appeared, the Heder Metukan, the modern progressive heder. The language of instruction was Hebrew. There was less emphasis on religious piety and on Rabbinic literature, but there was a positive attitude toward the Jewish religion and toward all the spiritual and cultural treasures of the Jewish people. The hope for a re-established Jewish state in Palestine was at the heart of this educational activity.

Though these new schools increased in number and flourished, they never replaced the heder and the Talmud Torah, which remained predominant within Eastern European Jewry until 1914.

5. ELEMENTARY AND SECONDARY JEWISH EDUCATION IN SOVIET RUSSIA

The Soviet government soon after it was firmly established effectively outlawed the heder, the Talmud Torah and every other Jewish educational institution devoted to the preservation of the Jewish religious heritage or of the Hebrew language and culture. In their place, regular government supported schools using the Yiddish language as a medium of instruction were established in neighborhoods with preponderantly Jewish populations. The curriculum in these schools followed the curriculum of all other government schools of similar grade, except that Yiddish literature and some elements of Jewish history were taught. Since Jewish children had the choice of attending either these schools or other government schools, the percentage of the Jewish children in the Ukraine and White Russia attending Jewish schools rose to the high point of sixty-four per cent in 1932 but declined steadily since then.

Moreover, Jewish citizens of the Soviet Union today may not and do not maintain supplementary schools in which their young children can legally and systematically achieve some knowledge of the tenets of Judaism, or of the grammar and literature of the Hebrew language. No official information is at present available regarding the number of Jewish children attending Yiddish-language schools, and consequently receiving some instruction in Jewish history and Yiddish literature. We do know, however, that, with the exception of a Yiddish daily which is reputedly appearing in Biro-Bidjan, no other Yiddish periodical is now being published in all of the Soviet Union. We know, too, that so basic and elementary a religious need as a Jewish calendar indicating the religious holy days and festivals, is not available to Jews in Soviet Russia at the present time.

6. ELEMENTARY AND SECONDARY JEWISH EDUCATION IN POLAND BETWEEN THE TWO WORLD WARS

Despite the depressed economic position of Polish Jewry between the two World Wars and the patent anti-Semitic policies of the government, elementary and secondary Jewish education achieved much during those hard years. The minority rights granted to Polish Jewry by the Treaty of Versailles included the power of self-taxation for educational purposes. Funds thus made available were in themselves not sufficient to maintain the schools. Tuition fees, voluntary contributions and help from abroad supplemented government funds. Unfortunately, Polish Jewry could not unite on any one educational program. Three main national groups competed for the child. These schools paralleled the regular Polish government school in hours of sessions and in general subject matter. However, they added distinctly Jewish subjects to their curricula. The largest unit consisted of the Jabne-Mizrachi religiously and Zionistically oriented schools, claiming some fifty-six thousand pupils in 1936. Next to them came the Tarbut schools, with Hebrew as their language of instruction and Zionism as their chief ideological orientation. In 1938 forty thousand pupils attended three hundred Tarbut schools. The smallest of the three groups consisted of the Yiddish-language schools with their antireligious and antinational, or anti-Zionist, approach. In 1934-1935, some sixteen thousand pupils were registered in their classes. Obviously, a very large percentage of the Jewish children of Poland's prewar 3,300,000 was not found in any of these school systems. Many of them preferred to attend the regular Polish government schools and get their Jewish education either in a heder or from a private teacher. Horeb, a non-Zionist fundamentalist religious group, claimed in 1934-1935 to have sixty-one thousand boys in the hedarim and Talmud Torahs affiliated with it, and twenty thousand Jewish girls in its Bet Jacob schools. In addition, there undoubtedly were many private hedarim and local Talmud Torahs independent of all nationally organized groups. The heder and Talmud Torah thus continued to play an important role in Polish Jewry up to 1939.

7. ELEMENTARY AND SECONDARY JEWISH EDUCATION IN THE UNITED STATES

a. The Heder in the United States

The heder and the Talmud Torah were brought to this country by Jewish immigrants from Eastern Europe. The heder, however, deteriorated rapidly in America. Without a well-formulated and clearly articulated public opinion to supervise it, the heder became the happy hunting ground of numerous ill-prepared, maladjusted individuals who brought it into disrepute despite many self-sacrificing and noble private teachers who established hedarim a generation ago in American Jewish communities. While some thirty years ago a majority of Jewish boys in America were still receiving their religious education in such private "rooms," the number attending them today is well-nigh negligible.

b. The Talmud Torah in the United States

The Talmud Torah followed a unique course of development in this country. Since, in the beginning, American Jewry almost unanimously gave wholehearted and enthusiastic support to the American public school system, Jewish education was conceived as being supplementary to it both in curriculum and in hours of instruction. Schools maintained by the Jewish community were to limit themselves exclusively to distinctly Jewish content and were to meet during hours other than those when the public school was in session. The Talmud Torah, therefore, started its sessions at four o'clock in the afternoon on weekdays and nine o'clock on Sunday mornings. The pupil was expected to attend five two-hour sessions. Moreover, influenced by the example of the American public school, builders of the American Jewish community of the first two decades of this century sought to make the Talmud Torah the communally supported Jewish elementary school for all Jewish children, boys as well as girls, rich as well as poor. Organizationally and physically it was to be completely dissociated from the synagogue. Many imposing Talmud Torah structures were built by Jewish communities throughout the land in the first quarter of the twentieth century. Graded courses of instruction were developed by well-trained modern pedagogues. Central bureaus of education attempted to guide and co-ordinate the activities of the schools and tens of thousands of Jewish children flocked to their classes.

But Jewish life in the United States was destined soon to take a course which halted the growth of the Talmud Torah along the lines originally anticipated. As the wealthier and more Americanized Jewish families moved out of the congested areas to new neighborhoods, they organized their Jewish communal life around the synagogue. The school in which their children were to receive a Jewish education was an integral part of the synagogue and the congregation. In addition, the conflict among the religious and social ideologies struggling for supremacy within the Jewish community resulted in the establishment of a variety of weekday afternoon school systems. Finally, the number of parents willing to subject their children to ten hours of weekly afternoon or evening instruction steadily diminished. The Talmud Torah, therefore, was not able to fulfill the role originally conceived for it by American Jewish educators. It is still an extremely important educational factor, but it no longer dominates the scene as it did a generation ago. The bureaus of Jewish education of the larger Jewish communities of the land no longer give their exclusive attention to it. The leaders of these bureaus strive incessantly to make the bureaus serve all Jewish schools regardless of their religious or social ideologies.

c. The Congregational Schools

1. The Sunday School

Jewish elementary education in the United States has in the past two decades shown a definite tendency to come under congregational auspices. It was thus at the beginning of American Jewish history.[7a] The first communal Jewish school was organized in America by Congregation Shearith Israel in New York (1731). Since no other schools were then available to Jewish children, the Shearith Israel school taught secular as well as Jewish religious subjects. The following century witnessed attempts by other congregations, individually or in co-operation with one another, to establish similar day schools. All these attempts came to an abrupt end with the rise of the American public school. At first these congregations made efforts to maintain weekday afternoon schools for Jewish instruction. But, following the dominant tendency of American Protestantism at the time, most of the congregations soon limited the religious instruction of their children to Sunday morning. Since not all Jewish families were affiliated with synagogues, communally sponsored Jewish Sunday schools were also organized for the children of the poor and the unaffiliated. The Philadelphia Sunday School Society organized by Rebecca Gratz in 1838 was the most effective and proved to be the most long-lived of such communally maintained Jewish Sunday schools. It celebrated the centenary of its existence in 1938 and is still functioning vigorously. The overwhelming number of Sunday schools today are, however, integral parts of well-established synagogues. Every synagogue organized by American-born or Americanized Jews considers an elementary school to be an indispensable part of its function. Most Reform congregations consider their responsibilities for the Jewish education of their children fulfilled by maintaining a Sunday school only. But even the Orthodox and Conservative congregations, which usually strive for a more intensive elementary Jewish education, maintain Sunday departments meeting from one and a half to two and a half hours each Sunday morning. These departments are intended for children who cannot or will not take more intensive instruction, or for boys and girls still too young to carry the more exacting curriculum.

2. The Congregational Weekday School

Many Reform Jewish congregations, all Conservative, and the comparatively small number of Orthodox congregations that sponsor elementary schools have found Sunday morning instruction completely inadequate for the transmission of the Jewish religious and cultural heritage. Many of the members of the present Conservative congregations were formerly the main supporters of the communal Talmud Torah. Hence, these congregations have organized weekday afternoon schools, and require their children to attend from four and a half to six and a half hours per week divided into three to five sessions including Sunday morning. The curriculum of these schools is very similar to that of the communal Talmud Torah, the chief emphasis being upon the study of Hebrew, primarily for the sake of understanding the prayers and the Pentateuch. Jewish history and the Jewish religious calendar are the other principal subjects of instruction.

Each of these congregational schools is in theory and can in fact be a law unto itself. However, national organizations with which the individual congregation is affiliated maintain commissions on education which publish textbooks and suggest curricula. The same is done by various local congregational organizations and city bureaus of Jewish education. It is but natural for the individual congregation to seek help and guidance from these central bodies. Some measure of uniformity in educational goals and procedures has thus been attained.

While many of the congregational schools are open only to children of members of the congregation, there is a tendency to depart from this unhappy procedure and to admit any child on the payment of a fixed tuition fee ranging from ten dollars per year up. Most congregations also admit at reduced rates or free of charge those children whose parents cannot afford to pay the regular rates.

3. Other Jewish Weekday Afternoon Schools

Religious, national and social ideologies have given rise to other types of Jewish weekday afternoon schools, which appeal to a comparatively small group within the Jewish community. Though these schools differ among themselves in ideological minutiae relating to attitudes on general social problems and Zionist aspirations, by and large they agree on two basic matters. The first has to do with the Yiddish language. All schools previously discussed adopt a neutral or negative attitude toward the preservation of the Yiddish language in America. These schools, on the other hand, have a positive attitude toward the Yiddish language and make it the chief subject of instruction. Some have a positive attitude toward the Hebrew language also. But most of them have a neutral and some a definitely negative attitude toward it. Secondly, the curricula of all these schools display a neutral or definitely negative attitude toward all religious instruction. Recently a marked change has become evident in the attitude toward the Jewish religion, and particularly toward Jewish customs, holidays and festivals. Ways are being sought to reintroduce these into the school curriculum as "folk ways" and Jewish cultural values rather than as religious observances. But some seek to go further than that and are rethinking their attitude toward religion itself.

4. The Jewish Day School in the United States

We noted above that the rise of the American public school found practically the whole of American Israel committed to it. In more recent years various factors have modified that unanimity. In the first place, the expectation that Sundays and weekday afternoons would offer ample opportunity for adequate instruction in Jewish religious and cultural subjects has by and large not been realized. These schools have not produced men and women thoroughly at home in the Hebrew language and familiar with even a considerable portion of the Hebrew Scriptures, of Rabbinic literature and of modern Hebrew literature. Though there are those who maintain that this failure is to be attributed to factors other than the hours of instruction, others consider the time element the root of the evil. Hence, they seek to create schools in which a greater number of hours during the morning and early afternoon can be devoted to Jewish studies. The proponents of the Jewish day school also find that the separation of church and state is not as complete in the public schools as it should be. Not only are Christian religious festivals such as Christmas and Easter celebrated with great impressiveness in most public schools, but attendance on Jewish religious holidays is very often definitely encouraged.

Moreover, among a group of progressively minded Jewish parents there is the desire to effect a more complete integration between the general and the Jewish education of their children than that which attendance at two separate schools makes possible. Thus there have come into being all-day Jewish elementary and secondary schools providing a rich curriculum of Jewish subjects in addition to the regular school curriculum. The distribution of the hours of study devoted to the various subjects differs from school to school.

The schools organized by the progressively minded parents, usually called academies, are maintained completely out of the tuition fees or special additional contributions made by the parents, though in all instances the meeting place of the school is provided free or for a minimum rental by a congregation. These schools also give the fewest number of hours weekly to Jewish subjects, though even this minimum is more than the maximum offered by the weekday congregational school. They have the further obvious advantage of preferred hours and highly trained teachers.

Most of the other all-day schools, usually referred to as *Yeshibot Ketanot*, junior *Yeshibot*, started with devoting the whole of the morning and most of the afternoon to Jewish religious studies. General studies were taught only after public school hours, so that the services of public school teachers might be obtained at a minimum expense. The law and the parents compelled most of the schools to shorten their teaching day and to distribute their time more judiciously among the various subjects. The average all-day school now meets practically during the same hours as the public school and divides its time about evenly between Hebrew and secular subjects. Financially, the schools are maintained only in part by tuition fees. The balance of the budget is met by special campaigns conducted by the individual schools and by one national campaign whose proceeds are shared by the co-operating schools in proportion to their efforts. Many of these schools have well-equipped dormitories to accommodate numerous out-of-town students. In 1945 there were approximately nine thousand Jewish children attending sixty-five all-day schools, concentrated mostly in New York City but found also in twenty-five other Jewish communities. But the number of all-day schools has been steadily increasing as the smaller Jewish communities throughout the country are being stirred to organize such schools.

8. JEWISH ELEMENTARY AND SECONDARY EDUCATION IN PALESTINE

a. Introduction

The Jewish population of Palestine assumed significant proportions numerically and spiritually soon after the expulsion of the Jews from Spain. It declined, however, in both respects during the eighteenth and the first half of the nineteenth century. The Damascus blood libel of 1840 and Sir Moses Montefiore's repeated visits to the Holy Land brought Palestine,[8a] as well as all of Oriental and Turkish-governed Balkan Jewry, into the orbit of general Jewish interest. The awakened concern of the emancipated Western European Jewries of France and England in their brethren of the Orient was reflected also in educational endeavors in their behalf. Heretofore, the heder and the Talmud Torah were alone in the field of Jewish educational activity throughout these regions. Nor were these institutions in too flourishing a state. In 1867 through the initiative of the *Alliance Israélite Universelle*, the first modern school for Jewish children in the Balkans was opened in Adrianople. In 1937 ninety-five schools with a reported pupil enrollment of 47,822 were maintained and subsidized by the *Alliance* in the Balkans, North Africa and the Near East. Of these, five were in Palestine, among them the outstanding agricultural school at Mikveh Israel, founded in 1870. English Jewry followed some time later with the organization of a few modern schools in Palestine and the Orient. At the beginning of the Twentieth century, German Jewry through the *Hilfsverein der Deutschen Juden* also entered the field and by 1914 had established or aided some fifty schools catering to about seven thousand pupils. Each one of these groups did worthy work.

b. *Effects of the Zionist Movement*

However, the remarkable revolutionary change in Jewish education in Palestine resulted wholly from the activities of the Zionist movement and its national and international agencies. Impressive beginnings were made even before World War I in establishing the Herzliah Gymnasium in Tel-Aviv, the Bet Sefer Reali, Hebrew Secondary School, in Haifa, and the schools in the small and struggling Jewish settlements of that era. By 1914 there was no longer any doubt that Hebrew was to be the language of the modern Jewish community of Palestine and of its school system. When after World War I the Palestinian Jewish community reorganized itself within the political framework of the Balfour Declaration and the League of Nations mandate, one of its first and chief concerns was the creation of a national system of Jewish education, which should reflect not the economic impoverishment and cultural backwardness characteristic of 1920 Palestine as a whole but the high cultural aspirations and the rich spiritual history of the Jewish pioneers who came to rebuild Jewish life in the land of their fathers. The Jewish community in Palestine resolved on complete autonomy in its educational work. The lure of larger government educational subsidies did not succeed in breaking this resolution. Since the resources of the Jews of Palestine were at the time extremely limited, and since the Palestine government appropriated only a small percentage of its meager budget for educational purposes and out of that gave a ludicrously small subsidy to Jewish education, the bulk of the educational budget of the modern Jewish schools in Palestine up to 1927 was met by the Zionist Organization. The Vaad Leumi, the nationally and democratically elected, politically recognized, representative body of Palestine Jewry then assumed sole responsibility for the educational budget of the schools affiliated with it. The government subsidy was gradually increased though never represented more than about twenty-two per cent of the total educational budget. Nor did the sum granted by the government to Jewish schools represent a percentage of the total educational budget of the government equal to the percentage paid in taxes by the Jews of Palestine or to the percentage of the Jewish school population within the total school population of the country. Furthermore, the authority of the Vaad Leumi was not complete, for Jews could choose to remain outside its authority and organize separate Jewish communities. Despite these legal and financial handicaps, the Education Department of the Vaad Leumi dominated elementary and secondary education in Palestine. The budget for the schools under its supervision was met out of the parents' tuition fees and special educational taxes wherever the community had the legal right to levy them, the government subsidy, and the general funds made available to the Vaad Leumi by the Zionist movement through the Jewish Agency for Palestine.

Three distinct educational systems were united under the Vaad Leumi's supervision. The largest of these was composed of the schools organized, directed and completely controlled by the Educational Department of the Vaad Leumi itself. These were usually referred to as the General Zionist Schools. They corresponded very closely to the American public schools in philosophy and curriculum. Religion as such was not formally taught in them. The Bible and Rabbinic literature formed part of the curriculum and Jewish national and religious holidays were observed and celebrated. In 1943 there were 181 such schools with a pupil population of 38,936.

The second group of schools were under the direct supervision of the Mizrachi, the Orthodox branch of the World Zionist Organization. The curriculum of these schools and the general atmosphere pervading their classrooms and administration represented the intense religious interests of their sponsors. Much more time was given to Rabbinic literature and to Bible study in their curriculum. In 1943 there were 84 such schools with an enrollment of 14,486.

The third group was composed of the schools organized and sponsored by the Palestine Labor and the left-wing Zionist groups. They were found chiefly in the communal or co-operative colonies founded in the last quarter of a century, and in urban centers occupied by members of these groups. While the Bible was taught and Jewish holidays were celebrated, Rabbinic legal literature was hardly touched. A neutral or negative attitude toward religion pervaded the ideology and the pedagogy of these schools. Their outstanding characteristic was an emphasis upon vocational training, upon the history of the labor movement throughout the world and upon the most progressive pedagogic methods. The 218 schools of this group taught 14,561 students in 1943.

The 65,983 pupils of the schools thus united in the Education Department of the Vaad Leumi represented approximately two-thirds of the total Palestine Jewish child population of school age. Of the remainder a goodly number of girls of the Oriental or older Jewish communities in the country received no formal education of any kind, some 24,000 attended either a heder, a modern private school, or a school sponsored by some other Jewish body, while some 1,200 were in the schools of the Christian missionaries. It is a strange fact that many a poor pious Jewish parent did not hesitate to send a daughter to acquire a general elementary education in a Christian missionary school, where no tuition fee was required and where occasionally some article of clothing or other assistance was given.

Judged by modern standards, the schools of the Vaad Leumi undoubtedly represented the best organized, most adequately financed and staffed, most efficiently supervised, best housed, pedagogically and educationally best planned elementary and secondary school system ever maintained by any Jewish community in all of Jewish history. The schools formerly under the supervision of the Vaad Leumi are now, 1949, part of the Education Department of the State of Israel. The rapid expansion, transformation, and modernization of the schools within Israel are keeping pace with the many other extraordinary events that have taken place there in so kaleidoscopic a manner since the State came into being on May 14, 1948.

c. Elementary and Secondary Schools for Vocational Training

The vocational and technical school was the last to appear within all modern school systems. Among the Jews agitation for such schools first appeared at the beginning of the nineteenth century. But no practical step was taken to create such schools until the late sixties and early seventies in Russia. Because of the government's attitude, these sporadic attempts soon petered out. In 1880 the ORT, an organization for advancing trades and agriculture among Jews, was established. Its chief aim was to support existing handicraft schools, establish additional ones, and subsidize those seeking vocational training in a school or as apprentices. But all ORT's efforts were impeded by government restrictions. Only in 1905 was a charter finally granted, after which its activities among the Jews of Russia rapidly advanced. Since then ORT has been functioning on a world-wide scale, helping the Russian Jews after the revolution to retrain themselves within the new economic framework of Soviet Russia, creating retraining opportunities for victims of the Nazi persecutions, whether in concentration camps or as refugees, and establishing schools in Poland, in the Near East and in other Jewish communities for vocational training of their youth.

In Palestine the vocational and technical school has been assuming increasing importance within the Jewish educational system. The Mikveh Israel Agricultural School, established in 1870, proved to be the most successful institution of its type. In 1943 there were seven well-established agricultural schools, in addition to a number of girls' training farms and the agricultural courses given to refugee youth in labor co-operative and collective settlements. Since 1932 there has been a marked increase in the attention given to industrial education. The report of the survey of the Vocational Training Committee of the Jewish Agency for 1943 listed ten such schools including a nautical school with a total enrollment of 1,105 pupils.

V. JEWISH INSTITUTIONS OF HIGHER LEARNING

A. BIBLE TIMES

Just as poetry preceded prose in the history of literature, so organized institutions for higher learning preceded elementary and secondary schools. This was true in Israel, as well as among other peoples. We noted above that, though the Bible makes no mention whatsoever of elementary schools, it does speak of "schools" of prophets. Moreover, the Bible's reference to the manner in which people came to listen to Solomon's wisdom, which surpassed that of all the other wise men of old, would indicate that these wise men had schools very much like those of the Greek philosophers of later generations. King Hezekiah's men who copied the proverbs of Solomon (Pr. 25:1) were most likely members of some kind of academy of the learned maintained by the royal house, in order to preserve the cultural treasures of the people. The scribes and secretaries of the government,[9a] the Levites and priests of the Temple, surely had to be trained somewhere for their work.

B. THE SECOND COMMONWEALTH

For a period of some 150 years, very little is known of the inner or outer life of the Jewish community that re-established itself in Palestine after the activities of Ezra and Nehemiah.[10a] But when with Alexander's conquest of Palestine the Jewish community of the Holy Land reappears in the light of history, it seems to possess a well-established and well-organized authoritative religious body. This was the *Keneset Ha-Gedolah*, the Great Synagogue. Scholars differ on the exact nature of this body, its composition, its function, and its history. We do know, however, that one of its guiding principles was "to increase the number of students." The reference is obviously not only to children but also to adults. From what we know of the character of this body, it may be safe to assume that the *Keneset Ha-Gedolah* exercised the threefold functions of court, legislature and center of higher learning and research.

The *Keneset Ha-Gedolah* was superseded by the Sanhedrin. Considerable controversy and conjecture also surround every aspect of the history, the composition and the functioning of the Sanhedrin. But all agree that in one manner or another it, too, functioned as a legislative, judicial and educational institution. The various parties and schools of thought which multiplied in the Jewish community during the century immediately preceding the destruction of the Temple (70 C.E.) had their own centers of discussion and learning. But the conflicting viewpoints were all reflected in the seventy-one elders who composed the Sanhedrin.

C. THE ACADEMY AND THE BET MIDRASH

When the Temple was destroyed by the Romans, the authority formerly lodged in the Sanhedrin was transferred by the towering personality of Johanan ben Zakkai to the academy he founded at Jabneh.[11a] This academy, and the others which succeeded it in Palestine, continued to exercise the function of courts, legislatures and universities. They administered the law, they amended it when necessary, legislated when necessary, and continued ceaselessly to explore the hidden recesses of the Torah, in order to bring to light some previously unnoticed moral or legal implication. The Talmud records indicate that the question, "What new thought was expressed at the session of the academy today?" was frequently asked by members who had been absent. The intimate contact maintained by the academy, by virtue of its judicial and legislative functions, with the daily life of the members of the community kept its purely intellectual pursuits from departing too far into the realms of the impractical and theoretical.

The members of these academies most often supported themselves. But many were maintained out of the treasury of the patriarchate or through the generosity of individuals.

As the body of knowledge and tradition increased, various schools of interpretation and of methods of study inevitably appeared. It was but natural that similarly minded scholars should have a common meeting place for study and discussion. Moreover, outstanding teachers and scholars attracted younger men seeking knowledge of the Torah. The most natural place for such gatherings of scholars or of teachers and pupils was some room in the local synagogue, though a special structure for such purposes, usually near the synagogue, was undoubtedly frequently used. The place where these scholars, individually or in groups, pursued their studies was called a Bet Midrash, a house for studying and interpreting the Torah, to distinguish it from the Bet Tefilah, the room used primarily for prayer, or the *Bet Sefer*, the place used for instructing the young. One room could at various times of the day be used for any one of the three purposes. Apparently, however, in the early days of the Bet Ha-Midrash, scholars would not use it for prayer, but would leave off their studies and join the congregation in the synagogue. The stress laid upon study by the rabbis is perhaps best reflected in the law that a synagogue structure may be turned into a Bet Ha-Midrash but a Bet Ha-Midrash may not be sold for exclusive synagogue use, for one is permitted to elevate an object from a lower to a higher state of sanctity, but not to reduce it from a higher to a lower state.

The Bet Ha-Midrash required practically no financing. Its meeting place was supplied either by the synagogue or by voluntary contributions for the erection of a special structure. Its teacher was not a paid officer, its students were self-supporting adults, and its curriculum of studies was determined completely by the interests and desires of the participants.

The Bet Ha-Midrash remained an integral part of the synagogue throughout the ages. Practically every synagogue had a room, usually the basement, containing a library of Hebrew books including the Bible and its commentaries, the various Midrashim—homiletic interpretations of Sacred Scripture—and the Talmud and its commentaries. In the long-established communities of Eastern Europe this room would buzz with activity from early morning till late at night. Busy laymen would meet here daily in the morning or the afternoon to spend a fixed period in study either by themselves or with a companion, or with a larger group under the leadership of the rabbi or of one of their own more learned lay companions. The most advanced studied the Talmud, others studied the Mishna, while the less learned devoted themselves to the Midrashim or the Pentateuch with its commentators, especially Rashi.

American synagogues, by and large, still have a library of Hebrew books, but the men to study them are unfortunately no longer available, except in very rare instances. The modern Bible class, or study circle, meeting usually about fifteen to twenty times during the year under the leadership of the rabbi, is a very pale reflection of the intense advanced Jewish studies carried on in the Bet Ha-Midrash of some of the smallest Jewish communities of Eastern Europe up to 1939.

The discussions that took place in the academies and the Bate Midrashim until about the middle of the second century c.e. developed the vast storehouse of law and tradition that Judah the Nasi drew upon when in the second half of the second century he edited the Mishna. His compilation did not include everything that was said and taught. What he had omitted, others collected and edited. But his work, because of its intrinsic excellence and his own great personality, became almost immediately popular and authoritative, and formed the chief text for the studies in the academies of the following centuries. The Palestinian academies continued to exist and to exercise great influence throughout the Jewish world until about the fifth century. The discussions and decisions of the last two hundred years of their existence were included in the Palestinian Talmud.

D. THE BABYLONIAN ACADEMIES

With the beginning of the third century, Babylonian academies started to challenge the schools of Palestine in erudition, in creativity, and later even in authority.[12a] The greatest of the Babylonian academies was founded by Rav in Sura about the year 219. It continued to function with only brief occasional interruptions until approximately the thirteenth century. The second academy founded at about the same time by Samuel at Nahardea, was transferred by Judah ben Ezekiel in 260 to Pumbedita. There it also continued to flourish with some intermission for about eight hundred years. These two academies were the recognized leaders of Jewish religious and cultural life throughout the world from the fifth to the eleventh century. The discussions, opinions and reflections of the members and the leaders of these academies during the first three centuries of their existence form the contents of the vast treasure trove of law, history, morals, ethics and folklore, known as the Babylonian Talmud. The heads of each of these two academies from the end of the sixth century on bore the title of Gaon. Jewish communities throughout the world turned to successive Geonim for religious guidance and leadership and students came to them from great distances to study. In the beginning, the Babylonian Jewish community itself was in a position to maintain these academies through taxation and voluntary contributions. But with the deterioration of the Jewish position in the eastern Mohammedan world, the academies found it necessary to send messengers to Jewish communities throughout the Diaspora for additional support.

E. THE KALLA

A unique feature of the activities of these academies was the *Kalla*. Twice a year during the month of Ellul, the month preceding Rosh Ha-Shanah and the High Holy Day season, and during the month of Adar, preceding the Passover festival, thousands of students and scholars would come to the academies from all parts of the Diaspora and spend the month in study and discussion. The talmudic tractate analyzed during the month's session of the *Kalla* was one which had been announced at the end of the previous *Kalla* gathering and had thus been studied by the participants during the preceding five months. During the *Kalla* sessions difficult passages in the tractate would be explained, the text corrected, the diligence of the students tested, important legal decisions rendered and the subject to be studied in preparation for the next session announced. Little imagination is required to recognize the tremendous influence such semi-annual gatherings of large numbers must have had in stimulating and directing scholarly pursuits and thus influencing the spiritual and intellectual life of Jews in the remotest communities.

F. THE TARBITZA

In connection with the *Kalla* sources frequently mention the *Tarbitza*. The exact nature of this institution has not been established. Some are of the opinion that the *Tarbitza* was for those who were not sufficiently well-prepared to attend the *Kalla* sessions. At the *Tarbitza* gathering each student studied whatever tractate he preferred.

G. THE YESHIVA

The most widespread institution for higher Jewish learning developed by the Jews on the European continent was the *Yeshiva*. It was a natural outgrowth of the Babylonian academy and the Bet Ha-Midrash. No European *Yeshiva* ever attained the stature of any of the Babylonian or Palestinian academies. The European *Yeshibot* did not prove to be intellectually as bold and as creative as their predecessors, nor did they enjoy the same authority either within the Jewish community or in relation to the non-Jewish authorities. However, their outstanding leaders and students equaled their predecessors in mental acumen, in depth and breadth of erudition, in piety, and in lives of exemplary holiness and singleness of devotion to the study of Torah.

The only requirement for entrance into a *Yeshiva* was talmudic knowledge and the ability to follow the more involved talmudic debates. Exceptionally brilliant youngsters of ten or twelve could, therefore, sit side by side with men twice and three times their age to listen to the lecture and participate in the debate that followed. The Talmud and all its commentaries constituted practically the exclusive subject of study, though in some *Yeshibot*, moral and ethical texts also were read and discussed for brief periods weekly or daily. Every sizable Jewish community sought to have a *Yeshiva* in its midst and every rabbi coveted the honor of having a *Yeshiva* under his guidance. A description of the Jewish community in Poland before the massacres of 1648 relates that there was not a Jewish community of fifty families or more which did not have at least one *Yeshiva* with some thirty students.

After the Chmielnicki massacre of 1648, a period of intellectual deterioration set in for almost a century. By the middle of the eighteenth century, Polish Jewry had recovered from the disastrous effects of the massacres. There was a great revival of higher learning, particularly in Lithuania. It reached its high-water mark in the personality of the Gaon, Elijah of Vilna (1720-1797), intellectually a giant and spiritually a saint. In 1803 his student, Hayim of Volozhin, organized the *Yeshiva* of Volozhin, which for over a century exercised considerable influence on Jewish life. Other outstanding *Yeshibot* arose in impressive numbers during the subsequent century and a half until 1939. These *Yeshibot* attracted thousands upon thousands of students. As long as the Jewish communities had the legal right to impose and collect taxes, *Yeshibot* received their support, at least in part, from such taxes and from the billeting of some of their students in local Jewish homes. For the past hundred and fifty years, they were maintained exclusively by self-imposed meat or slaughtering taxes and by additional voluntary contributions, not only of money but of meals and lodging for students.

The East European *Yeshiva* devoted itself exclusively to Jewish studies. Because of the weakening of the religious bonds evident among those Jews who had acquired a secular education, secular studies, even the reading of modern secular Hebrew literature, were excluded from and forbidden by the *Yeshiva*.

The *Yeshiva* consisted most often of little more than one or two large rooms with tables at which the students sat, or with individual lecterns at which the student stood while studying his text. Except for the hour or two each day when the headmaster or other teacher gave his lecture, examined the students or discussed the text with them, each student studied aloud by himself or with a companion. Because most students at a *Yeshiva* came from a distance and dormitories and dining rooms were provided by only a few of the larger and more adequately supported modern *Yeshibot*, sleeping quarters and food were frequently arranged for in the homes of local families. Poor students were often supported by meager grants from the treasury of the *Yeshiva* or the community. Householders, however, considered it a great deed of piety to offer one daily meal or more to a *Yeshiva* student or a bed in which he could spend the night. As a result, a student frequently ate his meals each day at a different home and had various sleeping quarters for his use, including the bench in the *Yeshiva* on which he sat and studied during the day. The privations under which the average *Yeshiva* student pursued his studies are thus easily imagined and have been frequently described. Nor did the *Yeshiva* grant a rabbinic title or degree to all its students. Comparatively few desired or attained this distinction. The primary aim of the *Yeshiva* was to produce *Talmide Hakamim*, Disciples of the Wise, learned Jews who would live their lives in accordance with the laws of the Torah and set aside daily periods for its study all the days of their lives. Such was the intensity of the thirst for knowledge and such the devotion to Torah that despite the hardships the *Yeshibot* never lacked students. They produced a veritable galaxy of exceptionally learned and saintly rabbis and of highly erudite laymen for the Jewish communities of Eastern Europe.

H. The Yeshiva in the United States

Until very recently the traditional *Yeshiva*, which proscribed all secular knowledge and concentrated all its attention on talmudic studies, was nonexistent in the United States. The American Jewish day school which called itself a *Yeshiva* and is now spoken of as a *Yeshiva Ketana*, a junior *Yeshiva* (because it caters to boys of elementary and high school age), of necessity included the American public school curriculum in its studies. It never directly or indirectly discouraged or prohibited its students from pursuing further studies at a college or a university. As a matter of fact, the Isaac Elchanan Yeshiva founded in 1896,[13a] one of the oldest and today the best known of the *Yeshibot* in America, was the first to add the regular high school to its curriculum (in 1919) and hoped from the very beginning to be able to grant the regular bachelor's degree to its qualified students. That hope became a reality when in 1928 the Yeshiva College was organized, and in 1948 it was granted university status, thus becoming the first *Yeshiva* in Jewish history to make the regular college and secular postgraduate studies an integral part of its program. Nor is there a ban on modern secular Hebrew literature. Indeed, in the Teachers' Institute which was incorporated into the over-all organizational structure of the Isaac Elchanan Yeshiva in 1921, Hebrew is the primary language of instruction and modern Hebrew literature one of the main subjects of study. While many American *Yeshibot* do not consider the college degree a prerequisite to the granting of a rabbinic degree and ordain men as rabbis only on the basis of their talmudic and general Jewish knowledge, the attitude toward secular studies reflected in the American *Yeshiva* is a far cry from what it was in the East European *Yeshiva*.

We noted above the increased number of Jewish all-day schools on the elementary and secondary level in America within the past two decades. The unparalleled catastrophes which in five years' time completely destroyed Polish Jewry and every one of its educational centers brought many of the deans, faculty members and students of the Polish *Yeshibot* to this country. They at once set about with their customary energy and self-sacrifice to organize *Yeshibot* here. Their labors have not been unproductive. The *Yeshibot* thus far established have had no lack of students. Moreover, there is little likelihood that the attitude of the *Yeshiva* leaders in America toward secular studies will be what it was in Eastern Europe a generation and more ago.

I. Rabbinical Seminaries

Until the middle of the nineteenth century, the *Yeshibot* produced the men who were called to rabbinical leadership of Jewish communities. But Jews who had themselves acquired secular knowledge and who were culturally part of the Western world required differently trained men as their religious leaders. Hence, for the first time in Jewish history there were established schools whose express purpose was to prepare men for the modern rabbinate. The seminaries of necessity reflected the theological views of the groups who organized and maintained them. During the past hundred and fifty years Western Jewry divided itself religiously into three main groups, usually distinguished as the Orthodox, the Conservative, and the Reform. Seminaries to serve the needs of each of them were first founded in Germany. In 1854 the Conservative Jewish Theological Seminary of Breslau was founded by Zechariah Frankel. In 1872 two seminaries were opened in Berlin, the Reform *Hochschule fuer die Wissenschaft des Judentums* and the Orthodox Rabbinical Seminary in Berlin.

No seminary for the training of modern rabbis was opened by the Jews of Eastern Europe. Between 1844 and 1873 there were two rabbinical schools sponsored by the Russian government. Their graduates, known as "government rabbis," were never regarded by the Jews as religious leaders. Jews in Eastern Europe by and large either remained orthodox in their religious outlook or became agnostics or nonbelievers.

In the United States the first rabbinical school, the Hebrew Union College, was opened by Reform Jews in 1875 under the leadership of Isaac M. Wise.[14a] During its seventy-five years of existence, the school has graduated some five hundred rabbis. It maintains a large library, has a distinguished faculty, and has published many scholarly volumes. The well-equipped and spacious buildings include a dormitory for students. A bachelor's degree is a prerequisite for entering upon the rabbinic course. The college is maintained by income from an endowment fund, supplemented by contributions from individuals, Reform congregations and community chests.

In 1886 The Jewish Theological Seminary of America[15a] was founded in New York City by Sabato Morais, rabbi of Congregation Mikveh Israel of Philadelphia. In 1902, it was reorganized under the presidency of Solomon Schechter. Though the Seminary as such consistently refuses to identify itself as a school for the training of rabbis for any one group or party in Israel, nevertheless, because of the character of its faculty and its avowed traditional leanings, it is generally referred to as the school of the Conservative, or Historical, party. Since its reorganization the seminary has graduated some four hundred rabbis. A bachelor's degree is a prerequisite to its four-year rabbinical course. The seminary's scope of activities has steadily broadened. Its imposing buildings erected in 1930 in the Morningside Heights educational center, include the Jacob H. Schiff Library building housing the largest collection of Judaica ever gathered by Jews; the Unterberg building with quarters for the Teachers Institute of the Jewish Theological Seminary, organized in 1909, and the Seminary

College of Jewish Studies. In addition, the Brush Dormitory building, including a spacious lounge and dining hall, offers dormitory quarters for the students.

The Jewish Museum, housed in the former home of Mr. and Mrs. Felix M. Warburg, at Ninety-second Street and Fifth Avenue, is an integral part of the Seminary. So is the University of Judaism in Los Angeles, whose classes began in the autumn of 1947.[16a]

The Seminary's budget is met by income from endowments and by special annual contributions from individuals, Conservative congregations and community welfare chests.

The Isaac Elchanan Yeshiva described above is the best known institution preparing rabbis for modern American Orthodox congregations. It, too, is housed in a spacious building with dormitories and library and has a Teachers' College affiliated with it.

In 1922 the Hebrew Theological College of Chicago was founded. Its graduates are prepared to serve Orthodox communities. The other *Yeshibot* also qualify their graduates to lead this type of congregation.

In 1922 Dr. Stephen S. Wise founded the Jewish Institute of Religion in New York to train rabbis for any of the religious groups in Israel. The Institute permits complete freedom to its faculty and student body in all theological and ideological matters. Its students and graduates choose whatever Jewish theology or ideology appeals most to them and seek to serve congregations most congenial to their point of view. The Institute also requires a bachelor's degree of those applying for matriculation. Its financial support comes from contributions of individuals and of community welfare funds and of congregations served by its graduates. In 1948, the Jewish Institute of Religion and the Hebrew Union College merged under the name of Hebrew Union College-Jewish Institute of Religion.

At the present time (1948) the United States is the only country with modern seminaries training rabbis for groups other than those who are orthodox in the traditional sense of that word.

Jewish teachers' training schools also first appeared in the nineteenth century in Germany. The Kassel community opened such a school in 1810, Muenster in 1827, Berlin and Hanover in 1859, and Wuerzburg in 1864. The last of these was the only one which continued after 1926.

In Russia the first teachers' school was opened in Grodno in 1907. Other similar schools were founded later, particularly in Poland, to serve the needs of the various school systems existing there between 1920 and 1939. The Soviet government also provided teachers' training schools to prepare teachers for its Yiddish-language schools.

The first modern teachers' training school was opened in Palestine in

Jerusalem by the Ezra Verein in 1905. Similar institutions were organized by the various groups affiliated with the Education Department of the Vaad Leumi. The development of teachers' training schools is one of the most pressing problems facing the Education Department of Israel.

In the United States the first teachers' training school, Gratz College, was opened in Philadelphia in 1895. Its establishment was made possible by a bequest of Simon Gratz. The school has been functioning uninterruptedly since it was opened. In 1909, the Teachers Institute of the Jewish Theological Seminary was organized and since 1931 has been permitted to grant the graduates of its regular department the degree of Bachelor of Jewish Pedagogy. By special arrangement, its students take some of their courses at Columbia's Teachers College. In 1921, the Teachers' College formerly maintained by the American Mizrachi organization became a part of the Yeshiva College. Other teachers' training colleges were founded in various communities, such as the Baltimore Jewish College, the Chicago School of Jewish Studies, the Boston Jewish College and others. Few of these schools limit themselves exclusively to the training of teachers for the Sunday or weekday schools. They have extension departments for the education of adults and some have high school departments to prepare students for the more advanced studies.

J. Dropsie College

Unique among Jewish institutions of higher learning is Dropsie College,[17a] founded in 1907 in Philadelphia with funds bequeathed by a Philadelphia lawyer, Moses Aaron Dropsie. Under the presidency of Cyrus Adler the college was organized as a postgraduate institution granting only the Ph.D. degree in the field of Hebrew and Cognate Studies. It occupies attractive quarters, has an excellent working and reference library and a distinguished faculty. In its student body and among its graduates, Jew and Christian, men and women, are represented. More recently the college has expanded its program to include a postgraduate department in Jewish Education and an Institute on the Near East.

K. The Hebrew Institute of Technology

In 1912 a Russian Zionist, Wolf Wissotzky, with the help of Jacob H. Schiff, the Jewish National Fund and the Hilfsverein established the Hebrew Institute of Technology in Haifa. It was at this school that the language question came to a head. Many of the school's supporters wanted German to be the language of the institution. After a long and bitter struggle, the pupils, teachers and the Palestine Jewish community succeeded in making Hebrew the official language of the school. After World War I the institution was taken over by the Zionist Organization and reopened with increased facilities in 1925. Today it is the most advanced school for the training of engineers of all types found in the whole Near East. In its field it occupies relatively the same position that the Hebrew University occupies in the field of the humanities, sciences and free professions.

L. THE HEBREW UNIVERSITY IN JERUSALEM

The most rapidly developing Jewish institution of higher learning of our day is perhaps the Hebrew University in Jerusalem. Its organization was suggested at the first Zionist World Congress in 1897. Its cornerstone was laid by Dr. Chaim Weizmann in the presence of Lord Allenby, conqueror of Jerusalem, in July, 1918, while the din of battle still clearly resounded on Judea's hills. In December, 1924, the first regular classes of the university's Institute of Jewish Studies began their sessions and on April 1, 1925, Sir Arthur James Balfour in the presence of Sir Herbert Samuel, the British High Commissioner of Palestine, Dr. Chaim Weizmann, and Dr. Judah Magnes, first president of the university, officially opened and dedicated this new center of Jewish and universal learning.

The university began as a research institution. The first undergraduate department was opened in 1928 with a four-year course given by the faculty of Humanities and leading to the degree of Master of Arts. Since then the faculty of Natural Sciences has been offering a four-year course leading to the degree of Master of Science. Courses qualifying graduates of the Hebrew University or other universities for the degree of Doctor of Philosophy have also been arranged.

Since its opening, the university has become the greatest modern institution of higher learning throughout the Near East. Some fifteen different departments and institutes now exist. The foundations have been laid for a first-rate modern medical center. During the war the various scientific laboratories maintained by the university made invaluable contributions to the welfare of the fighting forces of the United Nations stationed throughout the Near East.

The student body of the university now numbers over a thousand men and women of all creeds and races, and the faculty includes some of the best known names in all fields of study. Many of them, forced out of European universities by the Nazi regime, have found in the center of learning on Mt. Scopus an opportunity to continue their teaching and research.

Given an extended period of peaceful development, the Hebrew University is destined to exert tremendous influence upon the cultural life of the whole of the Near East as well as upon the cultural life of the Jews of Palestine and the Diaspora.

NOTES

[1a Cf. above the chapter by Julius B. Maller, "The Role of Education in Jewish History."]

[2a Cf. below Louis Finkelstein, "The Jewish Religion: Its Beliefs and Practices," pp. 1766 ff.]

3 Baba Batra 21a.

[3a Cf. above Judah Goldin, "The Period of the Talmud (135 B.C.E.-1035 C.E.)," pp. 120-121.]

[4a Cf. *ibid.*, pp. 141 ff.]

[5a Cf. *ibid.*, pp. 153-155.]

[6a Cf. above Cecil Roth, "The Jews of Western Europe (from 1648)," pp. 261-262.]

[7a Cf. above Moshe Davis, "Jewish Religious Life and Institutions in America (A Historical Study)," pp. 491 ff.]

[8a Cf. Roth, *op. cit.,* pp. 271-272.]

[9a Cf. above Elias J. Bickerman, "The Historical Foundations of Post-biblical Judaism," pp. 97-99.]

[10a Cf. above William Foxwell Albright, "The Biblical Period," pp. 50 ff. and Bickerman, *op. cit., passim.*]

[11a Cf. Goldin, *op. cit.,* pp. 146-149.]

[12a Cf. *ibid.,* pp. 175 ff.]

[13a Cf. Davis, *op. cit.,* p. 524.]

[14a Cf. *ibid.,* pp. 516-517, 532-533, and on Isaac M. Wise, pp. 500 f.]

[15a Cf. *ibid.,* pp. 522-523, 534-537.]

[16a Cf. *ibid.,* pp. 562-563.]

[17a Cf. *ibid.,* pp. 545-546.]

BIBLIOGRAPHY

CHIPKIN, ISRAEL, *Twenty-five years of Jewish Education in the United States.* New York, 1937. Reprint from American Jewish Symposium of the Jewish Day School.

DRAZIN, NATHAN, *History of Jewish Education from 515 B.C.E. to 220 C.E.* Baltimore, 1940.

DUSHKIN, ALEXANDER, M., *Jewish Education in New York City.* New York, 1918.

GAMORAN, EMANUEL, *Changing Conceptions in Jewish Education.* New York, 1924.

GREENBERG, LOUIS, *The Jews in Russia.* New Haven and London, 1944. I, Chs. IV-VII.

KAPLAN, MORDECAI M., *The Future of the American Jew.* New York, 1948. Chapter XXVI.

MORRIS, NATHAN, *The Jewish School—an Introduction to the History of Jewish Education.* London, 1937.

NARDI, NOAH, *Education in Palestine.* New York, 1945.

SCHARFSTEIN, ZEVI, *The History of Jewish Education in Modern Times* (Hebrew) (*Toldot Hahinuch Beyisrael bedorot haachronim*). New York, 1945. I.

SHERRILL, LEWIS JOSEPH, *The Rise of Christian Education.* New York, 1944. Chs. I-IV.

TSCHARNO, Y., *Education Among the Jews.* (Hebrew) Jerusalem, 1939. (*Toldot Hahinuch Beyisrael*).

CHAPTER 29

THE JEWISH CONTRIBUTION TO MUSIC

By Eric Werner

Preface

Laudamus veteres, sed nostris utimur annis.

Any attempt to evaluate the Jewish contribution to the world of music will, at the very outset, be confronted by a number of controversial premises. These premises must first be clearly defined or at least circumscribed. Hence, we shall distinguish in the following pages between the musical contributions of Judaism, and those of individual Jews. In a few cases these accomplishments coincide, but certainly not always. Furthermore, it would be a misuse of an otherwise fruitful method to abstract certain elements of style from the works of composers like Mahler, Mendelssohn and Schoenberg—to name only a few—and then to pose these personal mannerisms as general criteria in a discussion of Judaism's musical accomplishments. Aside from the purely hypothetical character of all conclusions arrived at in this way, we must bear in mind two important, yet antithetic facts:

The musical contributions of Judaism lie chiefly in the realm of collective and anonymous *folk music*, the basis of its musical culture. On the other hand, individual composers of Jewish birth concerned themselves, naturally, with the *art music* of their time and environment. Considered together, it is obvious that the former aspect (folk music) far surpasses and outweighs the latter (individual works of art). Yet we must not disregard the efforts of individual composers and musicians, for they form a characteristic part of that involved mosaic known as the Jewish-Gentile symbiosis. It must be remembered that these composers speak for themselves rather than for the Jewish group.

This study endeavors to implement such general theses with essential and concrete details.

The Time of Royal Singers

Judaism originated in the Near East and migrated to the West. So simple a fact accounts for the unique position of Jewish culture, the gigantic bridge spanning the gulf between Orient and Occident. This bridge was to bear the traffic of Babylonian astronomy, as well as Greek philosophy, songs of the desert along with legalistic discussions of the academies.

Even in biblical times the Jewish people must have enjoyed an outstanding reputation as a musical nation. That is known from Jewish sources as well as from those of their hostile neighbors. An Assyrian document tells us that King Sennacherib demanded and received as tribute from King Hezekiah many Jewish musicians, male and female.[1] During the Exile, the Babylonians mockingly asked the Jewish captives to entertain them with music they brought out of Palestine. "Sing us one of the songs of Zion!" (Ps. 137). Musicians as tribute, and interest in a vanquished enemy's folk music, was unusual indeed.

Nor is it a coincidence that the idolized King David became the patron saint of Jewish music. Even if only a small fraction of the psalms attributed to him are in fact his, he would still tower above all ancient rhapsodists, except possibly Homer. David is the perfect embodiment of that unforgettable age of seers, poets and rhapsodists, which so many subsequent centuries ardently admired. Quite aside from the many legends that adorn his story in the Bible, the historical facts remain clearly to demonstrate his significance for the history of music. It was he who organized the cult music of the Levitical orders, as we learn from various biblical passages. If we understand I. Sam. 19:18-20 correctly, David combined in his person the gift of the professional prophet with that of the born poet and musician. We are entitled to assume that he was actually the author of Psalm 18, which is included *in toto* in II Sam. 22. Here is a psalm quite detached from the style of primitive folk song, as the Hebrew text will reveal. This would mean that with David artistic poetry and art music entered the history of Judaism. A great king, a brilliant soldier, and a highly gifted poet and musician! Small wonder that posterity saw in him the ideal of all pious men. Byzantine Christianity identified him with Jesus, the "faithful shepherd," and with Orpheus, the divine singer.

The biblical period, in general, created an abundance of musical forms and institutions which, later on, through Christianity, became the adored and incessantly imitated standards of Western civilization. The principal form, of course, was the psalm and the principal institution was the musical service of the Temple in Jerusalem.

A Sacred Ensemble

The literary parallelism so characteristic of the Psalms demands a corresponding musical rendition. Here is the origin of the manifold formal types we encounter in the Psalter. In the simple solo psalmody, one person alone sings its prayer (Ps. 3-5). In the response psalm, the congregation answers the chanting soloist with short and concise formulae (Ps. 48, 100, 118). The antiphon has two groups chanting alternately (Ps. 136, 148), while in the refrain psalm a refrain verse is sung by a group and inter- jected into the singing of the full text, as rendered by a soloist (Ps. 135: 1-3). The very acclamations "Hallelujah" and "Amen" and even the often misunderstood "Selah," have themselves become texts of thousands of compositions, following the call "Sing unto the Lord a new song!" We shall see later how, through constant use of the Psalter by Christians and Jews, the parallelism of the Psalms (which all translations retained) con- tributed greatly to the universality of certain musical forms.

Perhaps even more important than the psalm forms was the ideal of Temple music. It was here that a permanent example was set, and music became an integral and indispensable part of solemn worship. Up to this very day, the conception of cult music, as first represented in the Temple, has closely associated the art of music with the spirit of true religion. Musical services are described in the passages of II Chron. 15:16-24; 16: 4-7; 25:1-7, and the minute, meticulous organization of such services became the ideal of cult music for all Christianity. Many Popes—latterly Pius XI—in decrees and constitutions have praised the musical service of the Sanctuary as the model *par excellence* of all truly sacred song.

Two facts pertaining to the Psalms and the music of the Temple should not be forgotten, for they disclose the continuity of musical practice and rendition: the usage of the so-called *contrafact*, and the function of the organ.

A contrafact is the use of a familiar melody for a new text. Thus, the anthem, *America* (*My Country, 'tis of Thee*) is a contrafact of the older *God Save the King*; the hymn beginning "Rock of ages, let our song praise Thy saving power," is a perfect contrafact of the older *Maoz Tzur*. This practice is long established in the history of liturgy. Upon the idea of the contrafact the Roman Church built many of its greatest hymns and sequences. Martin Luther made quite a point of his policy "to take the songs from the streets and to use them [with sacred texts] in the church. Why should the devil have all the fine tunes?" The use of the contrafact is probably as old as mankind, yet the first records of its being employed are found in the Psalms. Some of them bear superscriptions which have nothing whatever to do with their contents, *e.g.*, Psalm 22, "To the chief musician upon the 'Hind of the Morning,' a psalm of David"; or Psalm 56, "To the chief musician upon 'Mute Dove far away' by David"; and so on. These odd superscriptions gave the first lines of folk songs, then familiar to the Psalmist. They indicated that the respective psalms were to be sung to particular tunes which, unhappily, have long since been lost.

The organ was used regularly in the Second Temple and is called *Magrepha* in talmudic literature. The tractate *Arachin* gives us a fairly good description of the *Magrepha*. We learn that it was an instrument somewhat between a siren and a primitive organ with ten pipes. It seems that its sound was powerful enough to be heard far outside of Jerusalem proper. Just how this organ worked is not quite clear. We know that it cannot have been operated by water power, for the Greek water organ, *hydraulis*, is mentioned in the Talmud, and its use in the Temple was expressly prohibited.

All these facts come to us from a time which rarely recorded the names of inventors, composers or organizers. Thus almost all Jewish musical contributions of this period are necessarily anonymous. However, they are not, for this reason, any less important. Quite the contrary! They must be considered the core of Jewish musical lore.

The Establishment of Musical Tradition

If, in a rather rough simplification, we call the biblical period one of naïve creativity, we must consider the following thousand years—(200 B.C.E. to 900 C.E.)—as the epoch of creative reflection. The external events that give meaning to these terminal dates are the beginning of Hellenism[1a] and the decline of the Gaonate (the Babylonian talmudic academies).[2a] These years encompass the period when Judaism lived in close relationship with the Greeks, the Romans, the Persians and the Arabs. The civilizations of these peoples were, at that time, not too distantly related to the Jewish orbit. Then, about 900 C.E., the great Jewish migrations from the Near East westward began. To the cultural history of Judaism this event is of even greater importance than the catastrophe of the Temple's destruction in the year 70 C.E. and the severance of Christianity from the mother religion at the Council of Nicea in 325 C.E. For as long as Israel lived and worked among kindred civilizations the perpetual problem of its culture, the problem of positive and negative assimilation, was not essentially acute. Jewish contributions to music during that period grew organically out of the germ cells firmly implanted in previous centuries. Especially noteworthy is the fact that cultic music flourished proudly, resisting the fate that had doomed the Sanctuary itself.

A direct remnant of that glorious Temple music was the melismatic element. This is the technical term for expanded coloratura singing. We know this technique to have been a distinctive feature of Temple worship and it has never since ceased to be characteristic of the Jewish chant. Melismatic practice was borrowed by the church; it became a principal attraction of its music in the famous Jubili or Alleluias, of which we shall hear more later. The idea to envelop, as it were, the priestly blessing in a rich array of musical ornaments was probably common to all Semitic peoples, but it was through Judaism that the practice became so characteristic of all devoutly exalted music. To this very day, certain parts of the Jewish prayers, especially the *Avoda* of the Day of Atonement, are adorned with these ancient forms of pious ecstasy.

We see in this illustration how some melisms are built up to quite impressive chain coloraturas. Such an effect can be achieved only when certain musical motifs are retained and varied. This principle of motif technique conquered the music of the church and thereby the music of the Occident. There is no doubt that the ancient Greeks, and probably the Egyptians too, knew the technique and made full use of it. But it so happened that it was through the Bible and the Judeo-Christian liturgy that this form structure became common property and was eventually systematized by musical theory.

How does a motif penetrate the memory and imagination of the listener? Obviously, it must bear certain characteristic features either in melody or in rhythm. (Harmony is excluded, since it came into being much later.) Apparently, the melodic element is by far the most effective "carrier," being easily variable, in contradistinction to rhythm, which soon loses its identity through variation. Frequent recurrence of the same motifs leads eventually to the establishment of so-called modes. The basic term "mode" is best explained as a melodic pattern which consists of two or three motifs and retains its identity through all kinds of variations.

Traditional music of the synagogue is based upon numerous modes, well known to every cantor. Most of old Jewish melodies are derived from these basic modes of the tradition. One example may illustrate this important point:

Magen - Abot - Mode

Vayekulu

The numbers indicate the "standing tones" of the mode.

'Va - ye - ku - lu ha - sho... o - retz; vekol tze - vo - om, va - ye - kal.. ha - shvi - i me - lach - to
a - shero - so, va - yish - bos ba - yom hash vi - i mi - kol me - lach - to a - sher o - so.

Sephardic Tune for the Tal-prayer

after Idelsohn

Lech le - sha - lom ge - shem u - vo le - sha - lom tal ki rav le - ho - shi - a u - mo - rid ha
tal a - shir shi - ra - ti ve - a - sim di - vra - ti v'ag - bi - ra se - fa - ti le - tzur ye - shu - a - ti.

Hatikvah

Spanish Cancion
("Virgen de la Cueva")

after Idelsohn

German Catholic Hymn
("Der Himmel jetzt frohlocken soll" 16th Century)

The first is the bare framework of the so-called *Magen Avot* mode, termed after the responsorial prayer on Friday evening; the following three tunes are melodies based upon that mode. First, is the *Vayekulu* of the Friday evening service, second the well-known "*Tal*" and *Hallel* of the Sephardic Jews, third, the familiar *Hatikvah* tune. It is easy to recognize the *Hatikvah* as just an extended version of the older *Hallel* and *Tal* tune. (Is any further evidence required to dismiss the widespread notion that the *Hatikvah* was borrowed from Smetana's *Moldau?* As a matter of fact, we have here one of the many "itinerant tunes" that permeate the folk music of several European and American nations.)

The principle of modality, common to the music of the entire Near East, is not a result of theoretical speculation but of the incessant reiteration or variation of living melodies, which, in the course of centuries, finally crystallized into a series of melodic skeletons. These skeletons were adorned with individual embellishments, melisms and other accessories. The finished (individual) product is a modal melody. Every musician knows some modes from his studies in counterpoint, where the so-called *church-tones* usually form his raw material. Both Jews and Greeks bequeathed their systems of modality to the incipient church, which combined them into magnificent musical synthesis.

Here the question arises: Who promoted this remarkable development? Fortunately, we can answer this question exactly and in detail, supported by many ancient sources. The institution of the cantor (*hazan*) is old and venerable. Although his functions changed somewhat in the course of centuries, it was the *hazan* who, from the sixth century to the end of the nineteenth, originated innovations of the liturgical music, and yet strove assiduously to preserve elements of the old tradition. It was definitely to the *hazan's* credit that in the period between 400 and 1000 the music of the synagogue attained an organic unity.

In the most critical part of this period—during the Babylonian Gaonate —it must have been a commanding personality, indeed, who with the full weight of his authority supported the *hazanim*. This man, according to various old sources, seems to have been R. Yehudai Gaon, a great Rabbi of the eighth century in Babylonia. It was he who officially introduced the "ternary" form (ABA) into the sphere of our religious music. He recommended that the opening eulogy (*berakah*) and the closing eulogy (*hatimah*) be chanted in the same mode, the prayer between them in a different, but "not too divergent" tune. We know also that he introduced the chanting of the *Kol Nidre* into the synagogue. Moreover, two ancient documents state that the "first *hazanim* received the authentic tradition from him." The ternary form, a part of that tradition, prevailed in European art music from the late Middle Ages down to Bach and Handel, thereby assuming an importance which cannot be overrated. In written form it occurs first in the *ballades* of the French *trouvères* (twelfth century). Its recommendation and sanction by Yehudai Gaon, three centuries earlier, should therefore be appreciated to a far greater extent than heretofore. Be it noted, Yehudai's endorsement of the ternary form was the first utterance (to my knowledge) of a rational and artistic sense of form in medieval music, and it was the music of the synagogue to which it was first applied.

Attempts at Musical Notation

At about the same time (eighth-ninth century) the problem of musical notation was at least temporarily solved by Jewish scholars and musicians. Art music was almost nonexistent and instrumental music had been forbidden since the fall of the Temple. What remained was a traditional chanting of the prayers and the cantillation of the scriptural lessons, according to certain ancient modes. The Rabbis felt the urgent need of a codified system, consisting of mnemonic signs which would facilitate the study and ensure the preservation of those modes. These symbols did not purport to give a precise code of musical notation; such was incompatible with other aims of these rhetoric signs. Actually, they had to serve grammatical, exegetic and musical purposes simultaneously. Consequently, the individual marks—the accents or the *teamim* of Scripture—do not indicate *single tones*, as does modern notation, but each sign stands for a *whole musical phrase*. These semimusical devices existed since the sixth century in rudimentary form; their perfection was accomplished around 900 by the masoretes.[3a] The modes of cantillation that these accents symbolize are, of course, much older, and some of them might go back to the time of Jesus and even earlier. It should be emphasized that this rather primitive kind of notation has little musical value without the indispensable support of oral tradition and personal teaching. Yet, through personal instruction, the system has worked very efficiently, as the following facts demonstrate. In 1518 the great Christian scholar Johannes Reuchlin, with some assistance by Jews, managed to transliterate the ancient Jewish signs into the musical notation of his time. Since that day this procedure has been emulated by a good many scholars whose musical transcriptions show but negligible differences from each other. Moreover, when we compare our contemporary practice of scriptural cantillation with Reuchlin's text, we find that in all essential points there has been little change in the more than four hundred years that have elapsed since Reuchlin.

Where did these mysterious signs or accents originate? A definite answer has, thus far, not been furnished, but all indications point to southern Syria, where early Christianity, Judaism and other sects faced the same problem, *viz.*, how to preserve the musical modes of the public recitation of the Scriptures. Hence it is not surprising that both the Eastern and the Western Church employed a system closely akin to the Jewish. Out of the system of the Roman Church evolved slowly, in the course of many centuries, our modern musical notation. Thus, while we may say that Judaism was one of the pacemakers of our notation, we must add that its own markings remained in a somewhat primitive state. The illustration on the next page shows the similarity of the so-called ekphonetic signs of the Greek Church compared to Hebrew scriptural accents.

THE CHURCH SINGS HEBREW TUNES

The musical interrelation between synagogue and church, while not entirely unknown, is still frequently overlooked or disregarded. Yet, it was through the church that Judaism made its lasting, its strongest and its most characteristic musical contribution. As a matter of fact, it is no exaggeration to state that about sixty per cent of the Gregorian chant, the authentic music of the Catholic Church, is of Jewish origin. Considering the tremendous authority of the Roman Church in all musical matters up to the eighteenth century, it is not difficult to appreciate the indirect Jewish legacy to the music of the Western world. Nor is this a recent discovery or claim; the attitude of the church on this question is quite unequivocal. The principle covering all ecclesiastical activities has been expressed in these terms: The Christian church is the sole legitimate heir of the synagogue both *de jure* and *de facto*. This statement, repeated innumerable times by the Church Fathers, explains why the church has always made open claim that both its liturgy and its music are of Hebrew origin.

Aside from theology, the outstanding musicologists all agree upon the close connection between early Christian and ancient synagogue music. Most outspoken are two great authorities on the Gregorian chant, Peter Wagner and Father Dechevrens, both priests. The latter goes so far as to maintain that "the Gregorian chant is the music of the Hebrews, and there is for the totality of the Roman Catholic melodies but one modal system, not that of the Greeks, but that of the sacred nation of the Hebrews."

FORMS OF CHURCH MUSIC

The central elements of the Christian liturgy, *viz.*, the Psalms, the Doxology, the Thrice Holy and the Lord's Prayer, all originate in the Hebrew language. With the exception of the Lord's Prayer, they form the core of synagogue liturgy to the present day. However, they were not used to the same extent in the service of the Temple.

Early Christianity, a movement of the poor and the meek, was born in the rural sections of the country, and opposed the rigid service and the hierarchy of the metropolitan Temple in Jerusalem. This was an institution

8–9th century

EARLY MEDIEVAL GREEK	EKPHONETIC NAME	LATIN NEUMES	HEBREW NEGINOT IN THE ('א'ס'ת–BOOKS)	
(symbol)	ὀξεῖα	Acutus (Virga)	Tifha	(symbol)
(symbol)	βαρεῖα	Gravis	Legarmeh	(symbol)
(symbol)	ὑπόκρισις	Quilisma descendens	Darga or Shalshelet	(symbol)
(symbol)	καθίστη	Circumflexa	Zarqa	(symbol)
(symbol)	κρημαστὴ ἀπ' ἔξω	Flexa	Atnach	(symbol)
(symbol)	συρματική =περισπωμένη	Circumflexa	Zarqa-silluq	(symbol)

Later development
11th–12th Centuries

EARLY MEDIEVAL GREEK	BYZANTINE	LATIN NEUMES	HEBREW NEGINOT ('א'ס'ת)	
(symbol)	ὀξεῖα	Virga	Tifha or Yetib	(symbol)
(symbol)	ὀλίγον (ἴσον)	Virga iacens	————	
(symbol)	κρημαστή ἀπ' ἔξω	Flexa or clivis	Atnach	(symbol)
(symbol)	κρημαστή ἀπ' ἔζω	Podatus	Shofar or babylonian Tifha	(symbol)
+	τέλεια	Punctus	Sof Pasuq	(symbol)

The most frequent combinations of accents at the close of sentences are:

I. (symbol) + = (symbol)

II. (symbol) + = (symbol) (∧)

of the priestly aristocracy, whereas Christianity concentrated upon the ideology of the Kingdom of Heaven and did not recognize the rule of priestly dynasties. It was the forms of synagogue worship that presented the pattern for the liturgy of the young church. Hence the Christian hostility to instrumental music through the first eight centuries. For the Temple employed a large priestly orchestra and a trained choir, while the provincial synagogue had available only a lay cantor and no accompaniment, except congregational response.

Five forms of musical liturgy, all born of the Hebrew genius, constituted the worship of the synagogue and later became integral parts of the ecclesiastical service: Simple Psalmody, Response, Antiphone, Litany and Lesson.

The *simple psalmody* was the usual chanting of the Psalms by one precentor; here the congregation did not participate actively. The *response* divides one or several verses in halves, of which the first part is rendered by the cantor, the second by the congregation; *e.g.*:

CANTOR: Blessed be the name of the Lord;
CONGREGATION: Forever and ever.

Or:

CANTOR: Praise ye the Lord, to whom all praise is due;
CONGREGATION: Praised be the Lord, to whom all praise is due forever and ever.

The *antiphon* divides not only the verses, but also the performers into two groups; *e.g.*:

    1st GROUP: O give thanks unto the Lord, for He is good.
    2nd GROUP: For His mercy endureth forever.
    1st GROUP: So let Israel now say:
    2nd GROUP: For His mercy endureth forever.

In this special example the second group reiterates the same verse, which is not necessarily the general practice; this refrain-antiphon is a type closely related to the *litany*, in which the cantor chants a short stanza, and the entire congregation responds with one or two refrain verses; *e.g.*:

CANTOR: Give us thy protection; deliver us from danger; grant us joy and honor as the closing hour draws nigh.
CONGREGATION: O Lord, we stand in awe before thy deeds (or:) Help us, O Lord.
CANTOR: All their sins forgiving, show favor to thy chosen as the closing hour draws nigh.
CONGREGATION: O Lord, we stand in awe before thy deeds (or:) Help us, O Lord.

All these are poetic forms, inviting music, and therefore all Christian churches made full use of such structures. The reasons for retaining the cantillating rendition of the lesson, as practiced frequently in the Roman and regularly in the Greek Church, are less of a practical and more of a traditionalist nature. Here emphasis is laid upon the continuity with the spirit and expression of the Near East, the cradle of every church. Usually the cantillation as practiced in the church is more primitive than that of the synagogue. But there is one remarkable exception: In the Lamentations, which are chanted during Holy Week, Catholicism has preserved what is probably its oldest stratum of Jewish origin. The numbers of the verses are sung in Hebrew to this day, and the body of the verse is cantillated in a tune which has many a parallel in synagogue tradition. This mixture of psalmody and cantillation is a form characteristic of the most ancient and venerable portions of Catholic liturgy. In the examples on the next page, a few analogous cantillations and melodies are given, together with the tune of the Lamentations.

THE WORDLESS HYMN

Most of the Church Fathers, especially St. Augustine, considered the Hallelujah and its solemn rendition the pinnacle of ecclesiastical music. From earliest Christianity, the Hallelujah displayed a propensity toward disembodiment, that is, to being sung without the actual word "Hallelujah," even without its consonants. Such obviously mystic, ecstatic practice led first to the omission of the consonants, and later the vowels A E U I A were replaced by those of the doxology: E U O U A E-*seculorum amen.* This "wordless hymn" was called Jubilus and praised as the kind of glorification most appropriate to the Divine Being.

There are many indications that triumphant laudation of this manner, too, is of Jewish origin. The Talmud speaks most eloquently about the glorious chanting of the Hallel, of which the Hallelujah is the very epitome. Numerous passages compel us to infer that the wordless hymn was an ancient Jewish custom. During the Middle Ages a number of Rabbis raised their voices against wordless chanting, a practice they deemed cabbalistic and devious. In the sphere of Hasidism,[4a] however, the form of the wordless hymn achieved new and vigorous life. Among the Hasidim it was called *Niggun,* and many of these ecstatic, wordless tunes have come down to us. They were frequently composed by the Hasidic *Saddikim* (Saints) as means to attain the highest transport, *hitpashtut hagashmiut,* disembodiment. Innumerable are the tales in which, through the *Saddik's* musical intercession, fallen souls were purified, sick ones healed, and frenzied men soothed and led back to sanity. The famous

The Mode of Lamentations in the Roman Church

Lamentations I, 1.

A — — — leph quo-mo-do se-det so-la ci-vi-tas ple-na po-pu-lo:

fac-ta-est qua-si vi-dua do-mi-na Gen-ti-um.

Some Catholic and Jewish Chants in Comparison

(1) Lamentations — Yemenite Jews, after Idelsohn

Na-ha-mu, na-ha-mu 'a-mi, yo-mar esh-kol ko-fer, le-na-hem nimtzo ko-tub ba-se-fer.

(1a) Lamentations III, 1. — Gregorian (Naples version)

E-go vir vi-dens, pau-per-ta-tem me-am, in vir-ga indignatio-nis e-ius.

(2) Tonus Peregrinus Ps. 114. — Gregorian

In exitu Israel ex E-gyp-to, Domus Jacob de po-pu-lo bar-ba-ro.

(2a) Sephardic — after Consolo and Aguilar

Ka-ra-ti shim-cha A-do-nai mi-bor tach-ti-yot.

(3) Ps. 81, 1. — Yemenite Jews, after Idelsohn

cf. with A

La-me-na-tze-ach al ha-gi-ttit, mi-ze-mor l'-A-saph.

(3a) Ps. 45, 2. — Gregorian

Eruc-tavit cor meum ver-bum bo-num, di-co e-go: lin-gua mea...ca-la-mus scribae.

(4) Priestly Blessing. — Yemenite Jews, after Idelsohn

cf. with A

Ye-vo-re-che-cho A-do-nai

(4a) Invitatorium Sixti Toni (Ps. 95, 1-2) — Gregorian

Ve-ni-te exsultamus Do-mi-no, prae-oc-cu pamus..fa-ciem e-ius.

(5) Barchu of the High Holidays. — Ashkenazic Jews

(5a) Hymnus: Iste confessor. — Gregorian

I ste con-fess-or, Do-mi-ni co-leu-tes.

Saddik Shneour Zalman indicated clearly his preference for wordless tunes, stating: "The songs of the soul . . . consist of tones only, dismantled of words."

Such conceptions of the ethical power of music, whose roots are as old as mankind itself, display a striking affinity to the musical philosophy of the Church Fathers. In the latter milieu, the rich synthesis of Hebrew and classic spirit tended toward Neoplatonism. In the Hasidic realm, the infiltration of mystic lore into traditional Judaism likewise created an atmosphere of esoteric speculation. These two philosophies of religion, although separated by a millennium, ran parallel in many respects.

MUSICAL PHILOSOPHY IN JERUSALEM AND ATHENS

All too often we forget that man not merely experiences emotions but insists upon contemplating them as well. Music, acclaimed as the most expressive of the arts, was early to become a favorite subject of these reflections. Now, some ideas on music were to a certain degree common to all peoples of the Near East. When we probe into the earliest history of these notions, we find that they originated in a magical conception of music. The art supposedly possesses powers which surmount the ordinary faculties of man. Countless legends of the magic of music show clearly the primeval functions of music. Such ideas are met with all over the world, and they found their way even into the guarded enclosure of biblical lore, as may be seen in various narrations, *e.g.*, in the stories of the battle of Jericho, David and Saul, Elisha before the king, and so on.

Greek philosophy sublimated the magic ideology and explained the powers of music in a more rational way. According to the Greek theories, each musical mode, each tune even, is endowed with a particular *ethos* of its own, expressing its character and, conversely, attuning the listener to its individual spirit. When this principle merged with certain Oriental ideas on the harmony of the spheres and the basically cosmic order of music, a grandiose, universal concept was established which influenced the entire theory of music up to the eighteenth century.

Some of the Church Fathers championed this Greek philosophy of music and added biblical, that is, Jewish elements to it. With Clement of Alexandria, of the late second century, this *ethos doctrine* assumed a very practical character. He ordered the devout and faithful Christians not to emulate, in their chants, the sensuous tunes of the voluptuous and decadent Greeks. Christians should praise God in a classical mode of ancient Greece which was, according to him, identical with the Hebrew mode of certain psalms. This *Tropos Spondeiakos*, for which Clement found most eloquent words of praise, has come down through the writings of Greek music theorists. Being identical with ancient Jewish tunes, it is

almost the only concrete source from which we may draw reliable information on Jewish music in the time of Jesus and shortly afterward.
Indeed, while investigating this mode, the writer found certain old Jewish
parallels to the originally Greek melody. In the illustration on the next
page, the mode, as we know it from Greek sources, is compared with some
Hebrew chants. The similarity is obvious. Moreover, we can perceive how
this mode made its way into the traditional and authentic music of the
Roman and the Greek Catholic Church.

TRANSFUSION OF TUNES

In what way were Hebrew melodies carried over into the Christian
cult? All sources tell us that the road over which the liturgical music
traveled westward was paved by Judeo-Christians, the Apostles and their
disciples. The bearers of the Jewish musical tradition in the Diaspora were
the lay ministers and cantors of the great communities in Asia Minor
and Greece. These men sympathized openly or secretly with the new
Messianism of Christianity and, when they joined the new church, brought
with them as gifts their old "hymns, psalms and spiritual songs," as St.
Paul called them. In Palestine, the situation was somewhat different.
There the Christian community consisted almost exclusively of Jews, and
the transition from the old to the new ritual was a slow, gradual, organic
process—going on for centuries—as we learn from the Acts of the Apostles,
and Eusebius's *History of the Church*. Although the entire problem
bristles with difficulties, it is possible to state that for the liturgical texts
created before the eighth century more than half the corresponding tunes
are of Jewish origin. The church borrowed from the synagogue up to the
ninth century. Then the relationship gradually reversed itself and, at
the time of the Renaissance and later, Jewry was heavily indebted to the
church for many of its melodies. Nor was Jewry entirely unaware of the
age-old interrelation of church and synagogue music. The famous Jewish
poet, Immanuel of Rome, wrote: "What does the art of music say to the
Christians? 'Indeed I was stolen out of the land of the Hebrews' " (Gen.
40:15).

JEWISH TUNES IN WESTERN MOLD

The first wave of the great Jewish migration westward broke on the
shores of North Africa, Spain, southern France, and Italy. Soon two
spiritual centers took shape in Spain and northern France. In these
countries two forms of intellectual activity evolved, attracting like magnetic fields all neighboring communities until they included, respectively,
a good deal of the Arab countries and the entire Rhineland.[5a] Each cultural

Tropos Spondeiakos

center developed a poetic and musical style of its own, in many respects differing from the other. Not only divergent physical and moral climates account for this bipartition of an originally uniform tradition. Various other factors contributed to the partition. What hitherto had been a whole—the music of Jewry in general—now began to break up into art and folk music. That this cleavage did not result in two completely different styles, as it did four centuries later in European music, was due to the unifying force of a new musical element.

This binding force was what we have come to call the technique of the "leading motif." Although the designation is borrowed from Richard Wagner's vocabulary, the practice was many centuries older, and was a remarkable contribution to European musical structure. The basic idea is to associate a particular holiday, or a particular text characteristic of this holiday, with a special tune or mode, which is used on no other occasion [*neima* or *lahan*]. This principle of leading motifs, assigned to special days or texts, evoked in the listeners clearly defined associations and emotions, even when the tune was detached from its original text or ritual environment. Thus, every Jew will immediately be reminded of the Day of Atonement when he hears the *Kol Nidre*, and, what is more, he will respond emotionally to this experience. The Christian, too, knows certain hymns which are reminiscent of particular occasions and produce corresponding sentiments. It can be proved that this practice of musical association, or leading motif, was borrowed from the medieval synagogue and has since pervaded the liturgies of all churches.

The same centuries (twelfth-fourteenth) also witnessed the opposite interaction, namely, the filtration of Spanish and German elements into Jewish tradition. This musical exchange resulted, especially in the Rhineland, in the creation of some of the most beautiful and noble Jewish melodies. A later generation, ignorant of their syncretistic origin, named these tunes *Missinai, i.e.,* brought from Mt. Sinai, in praise of their outstanding significance and value.

An example of each (see next page) may illustrate these converse trends. First we have the leading motif, originating in Judaism, entrenching itself in the practice of the church. The opposite direction is shown in a Jewish melody of the same time, demonstrating the adoption of German and French elements.

The Sanctus is a rather late addition to the Gregorian chant and serves as a leading motif for a whole Mass of the Virgin. The *Tal Kaddish* of our illustration is broken up into its constituent parts, some of which have their roots in German folk song, others in the *chansons* of the *trouvères* in northern France. It should be noted that these foreign elements have undergone a considerable transformation, having been adapted to the basic Jewish background and admirably integrated into an organic unit.

Olenu of the High Holidays

(2) Sanctus of the IX Mass, of the Virgin

(3) Derivation from (1) Abot of Musaph of the High Holidays

Bo - ruch at - to A - do - nai. etc.

Tal-Kaddish

After M. Sonntag's version (1852) Some motives from songs of Minnesingers and Trouvères

Yis _ _ _ ga - dal, ve - yis _ _ _ ka -

dash, shme _ _ _ ra - bo be - ol - mo di - vro-chiru

se ve - yam - lich mal - chu - se, etc. ve - ime - ru O - men

Some Parallel Passages in Medieval Music

Philip de Vitry (ca. 1320) (transposed)

In the - a - tris cla - mi - tat quod Ra - tio hae - si - tat.

Wizlav von Ruegen (d. 1325) Jena Ms; (transposed)

He - re ghot, giph dem vor - scamp - ten.

The Spanish-Arabic center was not quite so rich in fine melodists, but here intellectual life concerned itself strongly with the theory and philosophy of music. Of numerous writers who speculated on the essence of music, we mention only a few who seem to have been studied by Christian theorists: Shem Tob Falaqera (c. 1225-1295), Moses Abulafia (c. 1250), Isaiah ben Isaac (fourteenth century), and foremost of all, R. Levi ben Gerson (Ralbag), who, as he states, "was requested by the famous master of musical theory, Monseigneur Philippe de Vitry, to demonstrate a certain postulate of that science" (1342). The treatise referred to does indeed give the mathematical foundation of Vitry's new system of musical notation. With the exception of Gersonides, all Jewish theorists of music show the overwhelming influence of Arabic ideas.

Only recent years have brought to light the oldest extant musical documents of Judaism. The first is a hymn upon the death of Moses, a poem by Amr ibn Sach'l of the eleventh century. The composer of the hymn is unknown. The manuscript originated in the thirteenth century and is written in what are called *neumes*, the notation developed by the church and then in general usage. As deciphered, their melodic line shows close kinship with the Gregorian chant.[6] The manuscript is in the possession of the Library of The Jewish Theological Seminary.

The second, about two hundred years later, comes from the Spain of 1460-1480. Here is a masterly motet for three parts, written over a text which contains Latin, Hebrew and Arabic words. As yet its wording has not been fully deciphered. It seems to be a composition for the liturgy of the "New Christians," *i.e.*, the Marranos, who had publicly embraced Christianity but in their hearts and even in some of their customs remained devout and faithful Jews.[7a] The most remarkable feature of this manuscript is the juxtaposition of an ancient Jewish tune—which corresponds to the text (a *Kedusha*, Sanctification)—with a Gregorian hymn, set against the Hebrew tune. One is inclined to believe that the Marrano composer used the extremely enigmatic language as well as the Gregorian tune to camouflage the Jewish character of the piece before the eyes of the dreaded Inquisition.

THE DECLINE OF ANONYMOUS COLLECTIVITY

Approaching the dawn of the sixteenth century, we cannot fail to notice a gradual, but clearly discernible decline of general creativity in the Jewish world. Yet it cannot be said that, from the sixteenth century on, the number of Jewish thinkers or artists decreases or that their accomplishments do not measure up to those of previous generations. Actually, what was languishing was not the creative power itself, but its agency. While anonymous and collective expression of the Jewish group diminishes, individual contribution grows stronger. Judaism had, in the previous ages, conserved its creative vitality through its excellent faculty of transformation and active assimilation. Speaking of music, it had absorbed many elements of non-Jewish origin, but, capable of complete integration, it had assimilated them, as a plant assimilates air and light into its system. The spirit of the Renaissance, with its emphasis upon the individual, filled the intellectual air of Southern and Western Europe, and its Jewry was not untouched by it. On the contrary, where the opportunity arose, Jews responded powerfully and positively to the new conception of man and his intellectual freedom. Italy, fatherland of the Renaissance and of its frequent concomitant, political tolerance, offered the first opportunity for spontaneous creation by musicians of Jewish birth. The contributions of Judaism cease, those of Jews begin and accumulate. No wonder, then, that the fruits of this new era testify to the irresistible attraction of authors to the culture of their environments, and the gradual loss of Jewish cultural autonomy. Creative power of the individual still remains intact, but in its expression the traditional Jewish substance wanes and weakens.

JEWISH COMPOSERS IN NORTHERN ITALY AND VENICE

The dukes of Mantua and Ferrara, the dynasties of Gonzaga and Bardi, patronized contemporary composers more readily than did the equally music-minded, but conservative courts of the church. Moreover, in a number of cases, the Gonzagas demonstrated a tolerance with regard to Jews which surpassed by far the friendly indifference that was general among Italian nobility. Thus, we find at their court in Mantua a number of Jewish musicians with the high standard of ability demanded by their times. Some of them may be mentioned: Abramo d'all Arpa Ebreo (1525-1566); Isacchino Massarano (1560-1599); Davit da Civita, a composer of madrigals (about 1615), and Allegro Porto, likewise a composer of vocal pieces. The first Jewish composer to reach truly historic stature was Salomone Rossi il Ebreo (1565-1628). For more than forty years he served as court musician at Mantua, and the great number of his compositions demonstrates a prolific creativeness by no means common even in those times. Rossi's significance for the history of music has been clearly established by the great historian, Hugo Riemann, who says: "Rossi is one of the most important representatives of the *stile nuovo* [style of the late Renaissance] in the instrumental field; he was perhaps the first who cultivated the trio-sonata, and his way of treating this form has remained exemplary for a long time . . ."

Rossi was a descendant of an old aristocratic family which traced its ancestry back to King David. As a composer, he enjoyed a great reputation among his contemporaries. Monteverdi, then Italy's outstanding master, held him in such high esteem that he accepted him as collaborator in the writing of portions of the oratorio *Maddalena*. The fields of vocal and instrumental music were tilled by Rossi with equal diligence. He wrote chamber music, suites, madrigals, operatic pieces and music for the church and for the synagogue.

In the Jewish realm, he set a precedent by introducing into the synagogue, hitherto the jealously guarded court of archaic tradition, the style and the technique of his time. This meant four- to eight-part polyphonic choruses without accompaniment, full of the enchanting beauty of the late Palestrina style, and of the same admirably rounded form. It is understandable that soon a sharp reaction against so revolutionary an innovation arose, the more so since, fifty years before, orthodox Catholic circles had raised very similar objections against Palestrina's music. At that time the Council of Trent granted to Palestrina the needed artistic latitude. Now the famous Rabbi Yehuda Leon de Modena, in the company of certain other rabbis, went out of his way to sign an official opinion that there could not be a prohibition of choral art music in the synagogue.

Rabbi Leon de Modena deserves our attention in more than one respect. His incredible versatility—he admits that he succeeded in mastering more than thirty occupations—brought him into closer contact with the general spirit of his time than was heretofore considered befitting a rabbi. A well-trained musician, he founded the first artistic choir in synagogal history, a group of fine singers, named by him *Bezochrenu et Zion* (In Remembrance of Zion). The concerts of this choral society, which he conducted, attracted wide circles of the Venetian nobility.

Rabbi de Modena induced Rossi to write a set of thirty-three liturgical pieces for his synagogue, all of them choral compositions from three to eight parts. The music, though noble in style and beautiful in expression, shows but little trace of Jewish tradition. It deviates in no way from the then current idiom of the Venetian school.

Yet the chain of tradition was not completely broken in northern Italy. Strangely enough, it is other than a Jewish source which documents this fact. The interest in synagogue music displayed by Venetian noblemen in de Modena's time was a contributing factor in the appearance of a famous musical work eighty years later. The *Estro Armonico Poetico*, a collection of fifty psalm compositions for chorus and orchestra, became Benedetto Marcello's *magnum opus*. This talented non-Jewish composer included eleven melodies of Jewish tradition, quoted together with their original Hebrew texts. He made use of these tunes as *cantus firmi, i.e.,* as nuclei for his own compositions, intending thus to add a certain flavor of authenticity to them.

Intonazione degli Ebrei tedeschi
sopra
Maoz Tzur

From B. Marcello's
"Estro Poetico Armonico".
Two Hebrew Intonations

(1) Ma - oz Tzur ye - shu - a - ti le - cha na - eh le - sha - be - ach

le - et ta - chin mat - be - - ach mi - tzar haun - na - be - - ach,

as eg - mor be - shir miz - mor, cha - im - Kat ha - mis - be - ach.

Intonazione degli Ebrei Spagnuoli
sopra
Shaar Asher Nisgar

Sha - - ar a - sher - - - nis - gar

Ku - - - mah pit - - cha

hu u - tzvi a - sher ba - rach e - - - lay

shli - cha - - - - - - - - - hu.

The first part of our illustration is an old German-Jewish tune of
Maoz Tzur which displays a certain kinship to the Gregorian chant; but
in this case it is wise to exercise utmost caution before assuming Jewish
authorship, for here the synagogue seems to have borrowed from the
church. The second part shows an old Sephardic song, which, in sharp
contrast to the simple German march rhythm, has the intricate, rhythmical
pattern usually found in classical Arabic music. Marcello indicated in all
eleven cases whether the origin of the piece was Sephardic or Ashkenazic.

The *Maoz Tzur* quoted above is definitely older than the melody with which we are familiar today. Our familiar melody consists of three different German folk songs, the last of which was written around 1620.

In his preface to the *Estro*, Marcello gives a brief history of music in the Bible, expounding the manifold merits of Jewry in the field of musical endeavor. He concludes: "It seems to me most probable (which some Jews assiduously confirm) that the melodies quoted in this work lingered in the memories of the first Jews exiled from Palestine, and that they handed down these tunes by oral tradition to succeeding generations." We see here that Marcello included the traditional tunes for their authenticity and age, not for their beauty. This is the attitude of a scholar, rather than of an artist. In his scholastic concern for the music of the Bible, Marcello by no means stood alone. Since Reuchlin and Boeschenstein edited the first musical transcription of scriptural cantillation, the active interest of theologians had produced many an attempt at reconstructing the ancient, long-forgotten tunes and chords of the Temple.

CHRISTIAN THEOLOGY AND THE MUSIC OF THE BIBLE

A concomitant result of these studies was a revival of the dormant interest in Jewish customs, ritual and history. The masoretic accents of Scripture, as the hypothetical basis of synagogal chant, soon became a favorite topic of Christian scholars. Polyhistors like Bottrigari, Valdensis, Muenster, theologians like Athanasius Kircher, Vitringa, August Pfeiffer, musicologists like Burney, Forkel and the famous Gerbert, all struggled with the problem of scriptural accents, synagogal chant and the Temple music of old.

Their learned endeavors in the field of biblical music were closely watched by many contemporary composers. Time and again we meet the suggestion to reconstitute the music of the Protestant Church after the pattern of an imaginary Temple cult. These intentions frequently led to tortuous and not always unbiased arguments. Thus we need not be astounded to find titles of music collections like *Musae Sioniae, Hymnodia Sionia, Fontana d'Israel* (J. H. Schein, 1586-1630), etc.

Efforts of the scholars to bring the ancient music of Judaism into clear relief were matched by the accomplishments of composers, engaged in the gigantic work of interpreting Scripture in the musical idioms of *their* time. This mutual stimulation reached its glorious climax in the works of Johann Sebastian Bach, George Frederick Handel and a host of lesser, yet still shining luminaries of musical history.

While Judaism cannot claim a share in those extraordinary accomplishments, we should understand that it was the spirit of Hebrew literature as recovered by Protestant ardor that functioned as a catalytic agent, so to speak, between the forces of religion and those of music. Alas, this creative phenomenon was then—in the midst of the eighteenth century— totally remote from the Jewish people.

TWILIGHT BEFORE THE EMANCIPATION

During the decades preceding Emancipation, we notice signs of cultural and spiritual decline in all Jewries of Europe. Not a few Jews, attracted by the glamour of European civilization and eager to participate in it, were convinced that they would have to abandon their ethnic and religious identities before entering the larger world. This might explain why, of the few Jews connected with the history of music shortly before 1800, not one remained faithful to his religion. On the other hand, these individuals demonstrated by their remarkable understanding of all things musical that their original Jewish background, far from being an obstacle, actually deepened their appreciation of the intensive musical culture of their time.[8] We mention here only two converted Jews who made significant contributions to European music: Lorenzo da Ponte and Adolf B. Marx.

Da Ponte (1749-1838), the librettist of Mozart's *Marriage of Figaro*, *Don Giovanni* and *Così fan tutte*, was a Jew of Trieste who, early in life, adopted Christianity and became a priest—"Abbate," as he called himself. Not taking his ecclesiastical vows too seriously, he led the life of a Casanovalike adventurer. Nevertheless, he was a brilliant and, in some respects, an ingenious poet, who fully understood Mozart's genius; and he merits ample credit for the excellent dramatic structure of *Figaro* and *Don Giovanni*.[9]

Marx (1794-1866), son of a wealthy physician, friend of Felix Mendelssohn, founded the *Berliner Allgemeine Musikalische Zeitung*, and later was appointed professor of the history of music at the University of Berlin. He was one of the first representatives of modern musicology, a keenly logical student of musical theory and an outstanding teacher. His creative attempts, the oratorios *Moses* and *John the Baptist*, were failures. His chief merit lies in his clearly defined methodology and in his championship of the great contemporary composers.

These two personalities can be considered typical exponents of the centrifugal forces within Judaism, before the great wall collapsed, that wall which hitherto had separated the old people from its neighbors.

OUTSTANDING JEWISH COMPOSERS IN FIVE GENERATIONS

It is not the purpose of this study to present a complete list of Jewish musicians since 1800. (This must remain the thankless task of a special bibliography to be compiled by an apologete.) Since the musicians of Jewish birth cultivated the style and the forms determined by their environment, it is impossible to trace a consistent line of organic development in their works. Therefore it seems of doubtful value to apply the rigid method of musicology. The general import of these composers has been fully expounded in books on musical history and in monographs.

Instead of a long dull list or a strictly historical disquisition we shall present thumbnail sketches of eight of the most significant Jewish composers, representative of the five generations since Emancipation.

First Generation: Giacomo Meyerbeer (1791-1864)
                          Felix Mendelssohn-Bartholdy (1809-1847)

An anecdote in lieu of a preface: Abraham Mendelssohn, Moses Mendelssohn's son and Felix's father, was a prototype of the radical assimilationist whose only link with Judaism was forged by his generous philanthropy. Nonetheless, Felix's teacher, old Zelter, Goethe's friend, announced the forthcoming visit of his twelve-year-old pupil to the Olympian of Weimar with the jest: "Indeed, it would be 'some ting raire' [spelled in Yiddish slang *eppes Rores*] if a Jew's son would become an artist." Then he added wistfully, "It is true, he is a Jew's son but not a Jew."

Meyerbeer, son of Jacob Herz Beer, founder of the first Reform synagogue of Berlin, was essentially a showman of genuine dramatic instinct and explosive power. Yet, Richard Wagner, his flatterer to his face and most vicious critic under pseudonyms, was right when he stated that Meyerbeer's music seeks mere effect, and it is "effect without cause." On the other hand, the merits of Meyerbeer in the fields of orchestration and operatic style are undeniable. Often his melodies lack *noblesse*, and his style goes too eagerly after the current fashion. Still, in the history of opera he was a powerful influence to which even his violent critic, Wagner, was heavily indebted, as *Rienzi* and *Tannhaeuser* demonstrate most clearly.

In sharp contrast to the theatrical Meyerbeer, Mendelssohn represented the introvert and aristocratic type of artistry fostered by romanticism. His propensity toward retrospection led him to the study of the great masters of the baroque, chiefly Johann Sebastian Bach. He ardently championed the work of that greatest of all Protestant composers and conducted the first performance of his *St. Matthew's Passion* after the composer's death. By that signal action he started the revival of Bach's then almost forgotten art. In spite of his somewhat archaic inclinations, Mendelssohn was a composer of distinct originality. The ingenious *Midsummer Night's Dream*, especially the overture written in his seventeenth year, the fiery *Violin Concerto*, his once tremendously popular *Songs without Words* display supreme mastership. No less famous are his oratorios, especially *Elijah* and *St. Paul*. The latter work may, with good reason, be considered his declaration of faith, glorifying the message of Christian universalism.

His fine organ compositions, cantatas and choruses are not so well known, perhaps because of a certain lack of genuine power conditioned by his aristocratic tendencies. Only German racial theorists were able to discover traces of Jewishness in his music. Although from the Jewish point of view such a demonstration would not be unwelcome, there is no real basis for such a thesis. As organizer and first director of the famous Leipzig conservatory, he established the most renowned musical academy of Central Europe. Teacher, organizer, reviver, creative composer, all his activities made him a truly venerable figure in German cultural history—up to 1933.

Second Generation: Jacques Offenbach (1819-1880)

Son of the meritorious cantor, Isaac Judah Eberscht of Cologne, Offenbach showed little if any interest in the musical legacy of his ancestors. He is not unjustly called the "father of the modern operetta." Actually this title reflects but one facet of his complex personality. He was essentially of a polar nature—demonic satirist as well as demonic tragedian. His masterpieces of musical satire, contemporary with and akin to the drawings of Daumier, hold up a merciless mirror to the corruption of the Second French Empire. To this category belong his sharp-witted *Orpheus in Hades, Beautiful Helen, The Duchess of Gerolstein* and many others. The tragic genre is represented only by his unforgettable *Tales of Hoffmann,* his last work. The mocking satirist shed a tear, and it became the fairest memory of him. A charming jester all his life, he showed the profound side of his music only shortly before death took the pen from his untiring hands. While most of his operettas have long since been forgotten, a few live on vigorously, and many of his catchy and witty melodies have lost nothing of their charm in eighty years.

Third Generation: Gustav Mahler (1860-1911)

None of the three composers mentioned thus far can be considered as an embodiment of Jewish ideas or ideals. This is certainly regrettable. The case of Mahler, however, borders on the tragic and must be understood as a woeful symptom of the inner disintegration of the Jewish community. This is so, not only because of the monumental stature of Mahler's genius, which towers far above that of all other Jewish composers, but chiefly because his real spiritual sources ran deeply in emotional and intellectual Jewish terrain.

In many respects he must be viewed as a living anachronism: a prophet burning with the ethical fanaticism of an Amos, a God-seeker of the ecstatic *Saddik* type. A sensitive spirit uttering the words "I shall die to live again for God," though unaware of the Psalmist's similar exclamation, a composer who mysteriously shows distinct kinship with Hasidic tunes,

Mahler, an embodiment of the noblest concepts of Judaism, was entirely estranged from his own people, his own faith!

And yet he felt something of the cleavage in the depths of his being. His ardent love for German folk song, which bore splendid fruit in his first four symphonies, did not fully satisfy his searching soul. He had to go back to medieval poetry (*veni creator spiritus*) and to the mysticism of the second part of Goethe's *Faust*. And in the end he sought and found the real source of his feelings in the poetry of the ancient Far East. In his farewell to life, the immortal *Song of the Earth*, he sings: "I will go home to my abode. No more of roaming far away. Still is my heart, awaiting now its hour."

His influence upon the following generations was extraordinary. Not even now (1946), thirty-five years after his death, can we really measure the full impact of his genius upon modern music. Suffice it to say that no contemporary composer of·stature has been left wholly untouched by Mahler's style and technique.

Fourth Generation: Arnold Schoenberg (1874-1951)
                        Ernest Bloch (1880-1959)

Both of these composers, while vastly different from each other, bear the imprint of Mahler's influence. Schoenberg, the most controversial figure in modern music, shows the keenly logical and technical discipline of a true heir of Mahler, while Bloch represents the "voice crying in the wilderness" of modern musical business; he has not compromised with the concessions generally made to the purely ephemeral demands of the musical market. There is common ground between Bloch and Schoenberg. Both are primarily concerned with the autonomy of melody, and their techniques, despite differences, render harmony almost as a function and a development of melody. Both composers stand today in the forefront of contemporary music. Schoenberg's work began with the consistent disintegration of Wagner's Tristan style and led him to the borders of tonality and beyond them. He was probably the first "atonal" composer, a designation which Schoenberg himself justly abhors. It is interesting to state that this composer has recently found his way back to his people, as the works *Moses* and *Kol Nidre* demonstrate.

Bloch was early attracted by Jewish conceptions: his cello rhapsody *Shelomo* (1912), his great Sabbath liturgy for the synagogue, his inspired *Baal-Shem* suite, his symphony *Israel*, all bear proud witness to Bloch's love of Judaism. He was the first musician of real stature, after the Emancipation, publicly and unmistakably to identify himself with Israel's cause.

Fifth Generation: Darius Milhaud (1891-   )
                      George Gershwin (1898-1937)

The social and musical background of these two composers, even their geographic preconditioning, could not be more completely antithetic. Milhaud is the product of the complex, refined and sometimes decadent tradition of western Europe, Gershwin, the son of plain eastern Jewish immigrants. And yet, in one respect, they are alike: in their love for the folk song of the common man. Both composers erected monuments to the musical lore of their native countries: Milhaud in his numerous Provençal pieces, Gershwin in his *Porgy and Bess,* glorifying Negro lore of the deep South. It was Gershwin's merit to span the gulf between "classical" and "popular" music. By incorporating jazz elements into serious music and by introducing the "classical" technique into popular and dance music, he enriched both realms. Alas, his early death interrupted a promising development; and in the absence of a legitimate heir, the gulf between serious and popular music is widening again. Yet Gershwin's masterpiece, his *Porgy and Bess,* the first truly American opera, will live on as long as America loves her own songs.

Milhaud, the descendant of an old Avignon family, entered on his career soon after the First World War as a strong anti-Wagnerian. A member of the "Group of Six," in the early twenties, he assiduously followed its motto: "Return to simplicity." Later, to his own advantage, he left that narrow path. Moreover, he has become increasingly conscious of his Jewish musical heritage. He has written articles on Jewish folk song, and, what is more, his artistic work has been greatly enriched by this interest. His *Zions-Hymn,* his exultant psalms, his magnificent *Israel Lives* and many other compositions put him in the first line of living composers. That the three greatest living composers of Jewish birth are paying heed and homage to their people's musical tradition is a gratifying sign of the trend of our times.

Thus, lightly etched, we behold the eight most significant Jewish composers since the Emancipation. To say that their importance cannot equal that of a Bach or a Mozart is no indictment or disparagement of their accomplishments. We need only stop for a moment to remember that for fifteen hundred years the Jewish people was excluded from the general growth of music. Nonetheless, this small minority was able in the course of a hundred and fifty years to produce a score of outstanding musicians whose efforts well-nigh reach the highest attainments of creative genius.

On the other hand, not all Jewish composers have wrestled with the highest ideals. The history of popular music, of the operetta, of the "hit song," is replete with Jewish names. It depends upon the reader's system of values as to whether or not he considers this a matter of pride. Musical art may not have experienced any serious advance through their efforts; yet these composers have certainly brought many joyous hours to millions.

Since Offenbach, literally hundreds of operetta composers have flooded the markets of America and Europe with their products. We mention only a few names of that numerous host: Oscar Straus, (1870-1954), E. Kalman (1882-1953), L. Fall (1873-1925), L. Ascher (1880-1942), Sigmund Romberg (1887-1951), Jerome Kern (1885-1946), Irving Berlin (1888-   ). These are genuine talents, and each of them is being imitated and "emulated" by scores of followers. The fashions of popular music change often and unexpectedly. Yet, this kind of composition follows paths of its own, and what was good business yesterday may be a loss tomorrow. Thus, purely commercial music had a course of its own, somewhat removed from the principal thoroughfares of the realm of serious music.

Interpretive Musicians

Even more numerous and at least as well known as the composers are the names of Jewish interpretive musicians. A few outstanding instrumentalists might well be mentioned, for in many cases they have enriched the musical life of entire generations and countries. We list here only those outstanding artists who have influenced the whole course of their art.

Conductors: Ferdinand von Hiller (1811-1885), intimate friend of Felix Mendelssohn, highly meritorious conductor in western Germany, gifted composer and writer. It is interesting to note that this convert had to find an outlet for his Old Testament nostalgia in his oratorios, though none of them attained lasting success.

Hermann Levi (1839-1900), the famous champion of Richard Wagner's work. He was the first conductor of *Parsifal* (!), presumably the reward for his unswerving loyalty to Wagner, in spite of the master's anti-Semitic writings and opinions.

Gustav Mahler (1860-1911), the famous composer. Here it must suffice to note that he was the first representative of a type of conducting since his day frequently imitated. He was an obsessed, demonic idealist, often given to despotic fanaticism. To be sure, he was not an endearing conductor, but proved nonetheless, an ingenious and altogether faithful interpreter of the composer's intentions.

Leo Blech (1871-1958), general music director of the Berlin State Opera, the prototype of fine craftsmanship and reliable solidity.

Bruno Walter (1876-   ), inspiring champion of Bach, Mozart and of the works of his mentor and teacher, Gustav Mahler.

Arthur Bodanzky (1877-1939), disciple of Mahler, conductor at the Metropolitan Opera, a fascinating conductor of fiery temperament.

Fritz Reiner (1888-   ), at present director of the Pittsburgh Symphony; another of the Mahler heirs.

Otto Klemperer (1885-   ), revolutionary director of the Kroll-opera, Berlin; at his best as opera conductor; protagonist of contemporary music.

Eugene Ormandy (1899-   ), director of the Philadelphia Symphony;

a conservative interpreter of a slightly didactic, but intelligent and inspiring nature.

Leonard Bernstein (1918-), the youngest in the galaxy of prominent conductors; as a composer displaying creative interest in Jewish matters; for example, his symphony, *Jeremiah*.

Most of these conductors come from Central or Western Europe. When we turn to violinists and pianists, virtuosi of the concert stage, we find the overwhelming majority to be of Eastern Jewish origin. One reason for this seems to lie in the fact that the tradition of Jewish fiddlers (*klezmorim*) in the Eastern countries was still alive in the middle of the nineteenth century, whereas it was completely forgotten and obsolete in Central and Western Europe. These fiddlers functioned as dance bands, and as teachers, furnishing the cultural life of East European Jewry with a strongly artistic element.

Violinists

Most of the outstanding violinists of the past hundred years were directly or indirectly disciples of the two superb teachers of violinistic style: Joseph Joachim (1831-1907), the intimate friend of Brahms, eminent artist and teacher, finally director of the States Academy of Music of Berlin; and Leopold von Auer (1845-1925), the unforgettable master who transplanted the best European tradition to America. Of renowned violinists there are only three who developed outside the orbit of these two great pedagogues: Arnold Rosé (1863-1946), concertmaster of the Vienna State Opera and primarius of a famous string quartet; Fritz Kreisler (1875-), the well known interpreter of the works of the classics. His antagonistic, or at best indifferent, attitude toward contemporary music stands in sharp contrast to the style of the third of this group, Joseph Szigeti (1892-), the versatile advocate of modern literature for the violin. Bronislaw Huberman (1882-1947), most inspiring and noble interpreter of serious music, a virtuoso of first magnitude, but ruthless enemy of virtuosity for its own sake, was a *rara avis* among violinists. He had, moreover, the great merit of having founded the Palestine Orchestra at the time Hitler ousted the Jewish members of German orchestras. Huberman defended, proudly and unyieldingly, the honor of Jewish musicians in a revealing correspondence with Wilhelm Furtwaengler, then director of the Berlin Philharmonic Orchestra. As an artist he belongs in the Joachim orbit.

Of Auer's disciples we mention here Mischa Elman (1891-) and Jascha Heifetz (1901-), the great virtuosi; Yehudi Menuhin (1916-), one of the younger among the eminent violinists, may be considered a spiritual grandchild of Auer, since his training lay in the hands of Auer adepts.

Pianists

The briefest list of pianistic artists reflects the countless facets of the development of European style. Paraphrasing a Latin bon mot: *Quot digiti tot styli!* Beginning with Ignace Moscheles (1794-1870), the elegant friend and epigone of Mendelssohn, there is not one field of piano playing where men of Jewish extraction have not carved out their more or less significant niches. Joseph Fischhoff (1804-1857) and Stephen Heller (1814-1888) belong to the adherents of the Schumann-Chopin romantic school. Anton Rubinstein (1829-1894), friend and champion of Liszt and Wagner, seems to have been of a nature not unlike Mahler's, though scarcely of his depth. Theodor Leschetitzky (1830-1915), master teacher, and Leopold Godowski (1870-1931), both had a flair for virtuoso style, occasionally neglecting the more rigid demands of classic diction. Moritz Moszkowski (1854-1925), a fine pianist and composer of charming miniatures, and Moritz Rosenthal (1862-1946) are both exponents of late romanticism. So was Ignace Friedman (1882-1947), the great interpreter and editor of Chopin's work, one of the noblest artists of our time. In certain contrast to these neoromanticists stands the figure of Arthur Schnabel (1882-1951), stanch champion of Mozart, Beethoven and Schubert, at the same time a radical modern composer. To the same ultraclassic category belongs Rudolf Serkin. A remarkable attempt at synthesizing the virtuoso style of the Liszt school with the more severe idiom of the classicists is undertaken by the ingenious and brilliant Vladimir Horowitz (1904-   ). Modern and ultramodern music has found its faithful and subtle interpreter in Eduard Steuerman (1902-   ).

As for vocalists, their number is legion. We will not even begin to list them, for in a very real sense the evaluation of singers is largely a matter of personal taste. Nor did singers contribute independently to music's development, being more often the instruments of composers and conductors than autonomous interpreters. Of some significance were the singers of the stage; their story belongs rather to the history of the theater than to that of music.

The Science of Musicology and Its Jewish Students

In antiquity and the Middle Ages music was considered more as a science than an art, and its study was part of the *quadrivium educationis,* together with algebra, geometry and astronomy. This connection with the astronomic-mathematical branch of natural science came to an end when humanism and the Renaissance proclaimed the freedom of the individual and his scientific research. The forms of the opera and of the oratorio, with their emphasis upon spontaneous emotions of the individual, stressed the purely *artistic* side and disregarded the scientific approach of musical endeavors. The ensuing centuries and their characteristic ideologies raised this emotional attitude (at least, where secular music was concerned) to an almost antiscientific individualism. On the other hand, it was emotional romanticism, with its archaic tendencies, that gave new impetus to musical science. The history of music was given a solid standing in the academic curricula of Germany, Austria and, later, of France and England. Mendelssohn and his school consistently cultivated the music of past centuries, especially of the baroque period. Thus, it was hardly a coincidence that Mendelssohn placed A. B. Marx as the first professor of musical history at the University of Berlin. Marx was the forerunner of a group of distinguished musicologists, of whom not a few were of Jewish birth. Bypassing Eduard Hanslick (son of a Christian and a Jew), Richard Wagner's deadly adversary, the name of Guido Adler (1855-1942) and his Vienna school will for all time be linked with the establishment of musicology based upon sound historic-philological methods. This venerable Nestor of musical science had trained a host of younger scholars, of whom E. Wellesz is of outstanding significance. The Berlin school, meanwhile, had produced such able students as the late O. Abraham, one of the founders of comparative musicology, and Curt Sachs, of New York University (d. 1959), the greatest authority on musical instruments and their history and at the same time a foremost scholar in the field of the music of antiquity. A specialist in Asiatic music was the late Robert Lachmann, who also published some studies on the music of Oriental Jews. The universalistic tradition of the Riemann school is upheld by so profound a scholar as Alfred Einstein, of Smith College (d. 1952). We should add here the pioneers of the science of Jewish music, Eduard Birnbaum (1855-1920) and Abraham Z. Idelsohn (1882-1938) who, while in every respect universal scholars, applied the methods of general musicology to the particular problems of the music of Judaism and synagogal tradition. They set an inspiring example for the Jewish musicologists of today.

Epilogue

"History is change."
(J. Burckhardt)

A critical evaluation of the Jewish contribution to world music must, of necessity, expound its results in restrospective terms. Nor is it the historian's task to prophesy, however wide the vistas he has opened. The present moment, however, still belongs to the historian; and from this narrow point between past and future we may venture to estimate accomplishments yet to come. We may expect significant attainments in music only where a valuable musical tradition is already in existence. Thus, Jewish contributions may be looked for in Russia, America, perhaps in

Western Europe and Palestine. Individual creations of Russian or French Jews will be acclaimed—and claimed—by their native countries, and the Jewishness of the composers will be of little, if any, significance. Not quite so simple is the American situation, where composers of international stature have drawn originality and power from the eternal sources of their Jewish tradition. Nevertheless, they will remain exceptions rather than become the rule.

Palestine, on the other hand, has no art-music tradition of long standing; but it is building one speedily and, once this prerequisite of musical culture is fulfilled, we may expect significant contributions. Vigorous Jewish life in the Holy Land has already generated a remarkable musical folklore. Art music takes longer than the fifty years Hebrew folk song has had for its new life; a certain intellectual and spiritual homogeneity is likewise required. When this standard will be reached Palestinian compositions will be considered, rightly or wrongly, as the typical output of the Jewish spirit, as an accomplishment characteristic of Judaism, rather than of the personal style of its particular composer. This, then, may become the beginning of a chapter yet unwritten: the role not of Jews, but of Judaism in modern music.

NOTES

[1] *Keilinschriftliches Textbuch zum Alten Testament,* 3rd ed., Leipzig, 1909, p. 45.

[1a] Cf. above the chapter by Elias J. Bickerman, "The Historical Foundations of Postbiblical Judaism."]

[2a] Cf. Judah Goldin, "The Period of the Talmud," pp. 186, 200-201.]

[3a] Cf. above Robert Gordis, "The Bible as a Cultural Monument," pp. 785-786.]

[4a] Cf. above Yudel Mark, "Yiddish Literature," pp. 1201-1202.]

[5a] Cf. above Cecil Roth, "The European Age in Jewish History (to 1648)," *passim.*]

[6] This oldest document of Hebrew music has been recorded according to the transcription of the writer and its first public rendition is part of the record-album, "Israel Sings," available at the Union of American Hebrew Congregations.

[7a] Cf. Roth, *op. cit.,* pp. 236 f.]

[8] This was especially the case of the *Hazanim*: composers and singers with the ability of a Wolf Bass, Leon Singer (Leoni), A. Beer, etc., absorbed and integrated the musical style of their time.

[9] Da Ponte spent the last thirty years of his life, a miserable pauper, in this country; his American activities deserve new treatment in the light of late research. (Krehbiehl's meritorious study of that subject ought to be revised and enlarged.)

SELECT BIBLIOGRAPHY

This is not a complete bibliography; such an undertaking would easily fill a large volume. Only such works are mentioned here as are based upon original research and contain numerous bibliographical notes.

FRIEDMANN, ARON, *Lebensbilder beruehmter Kantoren*. Berlin, 1921-1927.

HOEEG, CARSTEN, "La notation ekphonétique," in *Monumenta Musicae Byzantinae*. Copenhagen, 1935.

IDELSOHN, ABRAHAM Z., *Jewish Music in Its Historical Development*. New York, 1929.

———, *Thesaurus of Oriental-Hebrew Melodies*. 10 vols. New York and Berlin, 1921-1933.

The Jewish Encyclopedia, New York and London, 1901. Articles on Jewish Music, Accents, Psalms, etc.

SACHS, CURT, *The Rise of Music in the Ancient World, East and West*. New York, 1943.

SALESKI, GDAL, *Famous Musicians of a Wandering Race*. New York, 1927.

SCHONBERG, JAKOB, *Die traditionellen Gesaenge des israelitischen Gottesdienstes in Deutschland*. Nuernberg, 1926.

WAGNER, PETER, *Einfuehrung in die Gregorianischen Melodien*. Leipzig, 1921, Vol. III.

WERNER, ERIC, and SONNE, ISAIAH, "The Philosophy and Theory of Music in Judaeo-Arabic Literature," in the *Hebrew Union College Annual*, XVI, 251-319. Cincinnati, 1941.

WERNER, ERIC, "Preliminary Notes for a Comparative Study of Catholic and Jewish Musical Punctuation," in the *Hebrew Union College Annual*, XV, 335-367.

———, "Manuscripts of Jewish Music in the Edward Birnbaum Collection," in the *Hebrew Union College Annual*, XVIII, 397-429.

———, "Prolegomena to a Bibliography of Jewish Music," in *Historia Judaica*, pp. 175-188. New York, 1944.

ZUNSER, ELYOKUM, *A Jewish Bard* (Autobiography), edited by A. H. Fromenson. New York, 1905.

CHAPTER 30

JUDAISM AND ART

By Rachel Wischnitzer

In contrast to the general conception of gods in antiquity, Israel saw in the Deity not simply one aspect of nature in preference to others, or an incorporation of a number of gods. The God of Israel transcended the world scene. He was the cause of events in nature and in history. And, being invisible, He could not be identified with any form in "heaven, earth or sea."

The attribute of invisibility was thus fundamental to the Jewish conception of God. To identify Him with any material form whatever would be to confuse the Creator with His creature.

Graven and molten images are usually associated in the Bible with idol worship; but it is quite conceivable that attempts were occasionally made by some dissidents to fashion images of the God of Israel, too. Therefore, the invisibility of God had to be stressed over and over again. When Deuteronomy recalls the circumstances of the Revelation it repeatedly insists that "Ye heard the voice of words, but ye saw no form; only a voice" (4:12). "For ye saw no manner of form on the day that the Lord spoke unto you in Horeb out of the midst of the fire" (4:15).

It is from the imagery of Creation that the Second Commandment (Ex. 20:3-4) drew its vocabulary. Nothing of the created, visible world can possibly represent God, and since "likenesses" of the visible world actually are worshiped in various cults as manifestations of God, they are particularly distasteful.[1]

The Second Commandment in the Book of Exodus reappears in chapter five of Deuteronomy without changes. In chapter four, however, the issue of image making and idol worshiping is taken up more specifically, and there the principal concern of the Lawgiver appears to be over figures "male or female" (Deut. 4:16), not "heaven, earth and sea" and "what is in them." William F. Albright[2] has suggested that the Lawgiver, in pointing to figures, wished to denounce the infamous bloody rites associated with the Canaanite god Baal and the goddess Ashthoreth. The sun was proclaimed the principle of life in Egypt; sex was the principle of life adored in the Asiatic cults. The statues of the human-bodied gods in wood and stone cast a magic spell upon the soul of the people and this spell had to be broken at all cost. Hence again and again it is pointed out that these statues can neither see nor listen to the worshiper, for they are only the works of human hands (Deut. 4:28).

Next the Lawgiver enumerates the animals, birds, snakes and fish (4:17-18). Significantly last come the celestial spheres. The sun, moon, stars and the host of heaven are individually mentioned, the astral cults strictly forbidden. But there is no reference to images associated with the astral cults. The astral cults consisted chiefly in stargazing and incense burning on altars raised on roofs. What was prohibited was "lifting up thine eyes unto heaven" (Deut. 4:19) for purposes of adoration, a practice obviously less offensive than the sanguinary ritual connected with some image cults. The motivation for the prohibition of astral cults reveals the new attitude clearly. Ikhnaton had conceded the celestial Nile as a common possession to all mankind, but the two other Niles, the actual river and the subterranean stream on which the sun was supposed to travel by night back to the east, he reserved as the exclusive property of the Egyptian Empire. But the Lawgiver tells us that the celestial bodies were "divided" by the Lord "unto all nations under the whole heaven" (4:19) and do not belong to the religious sphere of any particular nation.

The attitude of Judaism toward the arts was also affected by the changing function of the arts themselves.

The symbolic significance of an image is not an inherent quality of the image. If in the eighth century B.C.E. ivory plaques with portrayals of Egyptian deities—Horus, Re, Isis, Nephtys—and various symbols were used in Samaria as inlays in furniture, we can be sure that the owners of such furniture did not bother about the significance of the ivory carvings. The few panels that have survived the destruction of Samaria and have been excavated appear to be Phoenician ware. The Phoenician carvers who copied Egyptian models probably did have a vague idea of the subjects depicted, but the Israelite customers in Samaria hardly knew what or whom the small inlay figures were meant to represent.[3] It is interesting to note that the Prophet Amos, when denouncing the upper classes of Samaria for reclining on "beds of ivory" (3:15; 4:4), probably aimed at idleness and luxury rather than the impropriety of the Egyptian figure decoration of the couches. He does not even mention the carvings.

With this in mind, we can better comprehend the cultural background of King Solomon's time (second part of the tenth century B.C.E.) and more easily evaluate the significance of the decoration of the royal palace and the Temple of Jerusalem built by the King.[3a]

The ivory throne in the palace hall was overlaid with gold and flanked by lion statues (I Kings 10:18-20). Lion figures standing guard at a palace gate or a throne were no objects of worship in the Near East; rather they

were intended to exalt the authority of the ruler. The winged cherubim
in the Holy of Holies of the Temple, carved in wood and paneled with
gold (I Kings 6:23 ff.; II Chron. 3:10), were placed on top of the Ark as
its crowning part (I Kings 8:6 f.). There is no indication that these
cherubim were regarded as cult objects. The interior walls of the main
hall of the Temple, the Sanctuary, were decorated with a relief of alter-
nating cherubim, palm trees and open flowers (I Kings 6:29; II Chron.
3:7). There is no suggestion in the Bible that these wall reliefs were
associated with any ritual.

Edward B. Tylor has pointed out that the motif of cherubim flanking
a palm tree in the Solomonic Temple was derived from Assyrian art,
where the palm tree is found flanked by winged human or animal figures.[4]
The design is familiar from the ancient Assyrian seals and later wall reliefs
in royal palaces in Nineveh. Tylor has been able to interpret the scene.
The winged male figures on either side of the tree, carrying a basket and
what was supposed to be a fir cone, actually are pollinating the date palm.
The fertilization of the date tree in the Near East was described by
Herodotus, Theophrastus and Pliny the Elder in his *Natural History*.
The Assyrians apparently saw in the achievement of their palm growers
an evidence of the assistance of supernatural forces and therefore represented the gardeners as fantastic beings, winged, eagle-headed men, griffins
or winged horses. The palm tree became converted into a ceremonial
object, a kind of standard set with palmettes or palm-leaf clusters, a
symbol of the Tree of Life. Behind the picture there may have been the
idea of an actual liturgical performance.

We must determine just what was the relationship of the cherub-palm
motif of I Kings 6:29 to the Assyrian ceremonial scene. Since we know
that the Temple was built with the help of Tyrian artisans, we have to
take into account Phoenician influences in the elaboration of the motif.
In Phoenician art the Assyrian "gardeners," who are treated as winged
sphinxes, appear in most conventionalized postures, while the tree is
simplified and considerably reduced in its form—so much so that it seems
rather doubtful that the subject meant the same there as in the original
conception. The Phoenician limestone seal from Megiddo[5] may give us an
idea of what the design of the cherub-palm tree decoration was like in the
Temple at Jerusalem. Since the eatable date fruit is not frequently mentioned in the Bible, we are probably not wrong in assuming that the
original meaning of the motif had been lost.[6]

Not before talmudic times do we find reference to the motif of the cultivation of the date palm, that is, to its artificial fertilization. Max Gruenbaum[7] cites Pesahim 56a and records the romantic story of the barren palm
tree in Chamtan, wistfully "looking" toward Jericho, which was known
from biblical times as the palm city (Deut. 34:3; II Chron. 28:15). A palm

grower, the story goes, advises the people how to make the tree bear fruit. Josephus (*Bell. Jud.* IV:8:3) mentions a syrup of a palm fruit, apparently dates, produced in Jericho. The question is, however, was the date a popular foodstuff in biblical times in Palestine? Even more important, what role did fertilization of the date tree play in popular imagination in biblical times? It seems that the poet's mind was inspired by the general symbolism of a tree, its growth, its blossoming, its fruitfulness and beauty, rather than by any specific aspect of its cultivation.

The national tree was the olive. It is this tree which the prophet Zechariah uses as a political metaphor in his fifth vision. The king, Zerubbabel, and the High Priest, Joshua, who are expected to establish firmly the new commonwealth after the return of the exiles in 519 B.C.E., are seen as two olive trees flanking a seven-branched candlestick and furnishing it with oil (4:3 ff.). Here the original Oriental conception underlying the picture can easily be recognized, but the olive substitutes for the date palm.

It is the olive tree again which is used as a metaphor in Psalm 52:8, where the righteous is compared with a "leafy olive-tree in the house of God." In Psalm 92:12 the righteous is promised that he shall "flourish like the palm tree" and the cedar. The reference to the Temple is repeated: Those "planted in the house of the Lord . . . shall flourish in the courts of our God. They shall still bring forth fruit in old age" (vss. 13, 14).

The metaphors used in the Psalms show that the tree had become the symbol of the godly. The cult of the reproductive capacities of mother nature, practiced in Assyria, has been sublimated in Palestine into a figure of speech serving to exalt the faithful. The palm tree flanked by cherubim on the reliefs of the Temple at Jerusalem represents one of the stages in this process of spiritualization; perhaps it is the direct prototype for the literary figure.

H. T. Obbink, the Utrecht scholar,[8] has similarly attempted to explain the purpose of the "golden calves" of Jeroboam. Contrary to the palm-and-cherub reliefs in the Temple, the golden calves erected in the sanctuaries of Beth-el and Dan are expressly said to have been intended as cult objects. Jeroboam, when proclaimed king of the seceded Northern Kingdom after Solomon's death, promptly restored the two ancient sanctuaries in order to prevent pilgrimage to Jerusalem (1 Kings 12:26, 27) and gave each sanctuary a golden calf. Suspecting a disparaging tendency on the part of the Judean recorder toward the schismatic king, Obbink doubts that the bulls were actually intended as cult statues. He believes rather that they were meant as supports for the invisible YHWH comparable to the cherubim of the Temple at Jerusalem. For prototypes he points to Near Eastern bull statues used as pedestals for deities.

We know statues of the Sumerian-Acadian Anu and the ancient Semitic god Hadad were represented standing or walking on animals. Hittite deities are found standing on pedestals set on the back of a lion or a bull.

But would a wingless animal of the pedestal type be likely to suggest to the worshiper the invisible presence of God and thus be comparable in its effect to the cherubim of the Temple at Jerusalem? The cherubim set up on the top of the Ark were regarded as flying creatures of the heavenly region, rather than as supports set up on the ground. God communed with Moses "from between the two cherubim" (Ex. 25:22). He "sitteth between the cherubim" (Ps. 99:1). The conception of an uplifted position, a raised throne, seems to be fundamental to the image of the cherubim. It is this idea of an exalted position which inspired the comparison of Tyre, before its fall, with a cherub (Ez. 28:14, 16).

If, then, Jeroboam wished to imitate the cult of Jerusalem he would not have chosen as a model the wingless pedestal type of bull. The suggestion of the Divine Presence produced by a pair of cherubim was hardly possible with a wingless bull. There is, however, a different category of bulls, which fits better into the picture: it is the winged bull of Assyrian art, which can be visualized as a flying creature although it stands on the ground. But George Ernest Wright has pointed out that those huge Assyrian bulls are practically nonexistent in Palestine and Syria.[9]

Assyrian art became an influence in Jewish imagery much later, when the Jews were brought into direct contact with Mesopotamian civilization. It was noticeable in Zechariah's vision and, earlier, in Ezekiel's vocabulary. "By the river of Chebar" in Babylonia, Ezekiel had his vision which carried him back to Jerusalem into the Temple. The Lord appears to the prophet on a "seat" (Ez. 1:1 ff.) placed above four creatures which resemble the cherubim in their function, but possess distinct features of their own. Although winged, these creatures are also wheeled and thus suggest a chariot which can be driven on the ground. The "chariot" actually goes down and up in the interior of the Temple.

While the appearance of the Temple cherubim is not described in the Bible (we can imagine them either as winged sphinxes of Phoenician art, or as winged ethereal angel-like figures of Egyptian divinities, of which a Phoenician version is seen in the ivories of Samaria)[10] Ezekiel's "living creatures" are elaborately described as hybrid figures combining characteristics of a man, a lion, a bull and an eagle. The mystical quaternion implies that Ezekiel had speculated on the meaning of the colossi set up at the gates, and actually carrying the arches of the portals of Assyrian palaces. Assyria at that time was no longer a foe, but a comrade in misfortune, for she had been conquered by the Babylonians a decade before. The composite animals combining the body of a lion and a bull with the head of a man and the wings of an eagle appeared to Ezekiel as similar to the cherubim of the Temple, and the qualities symbolized by the four creatures, the strength of the lion, the virility of the bull, the swiftness of the eagle and the intelligence of man, seemed to offer a key to the comprehension of the mystical nature of the cherubim.

Flying and moving on the ground, Ezekiel's creatures are a blending of two conceptions. The seat of the Lord of Ezekiel's vision is an uplifted throne and at the same time a chariot, a *Merkabah* riding on the floor of the Temple.

The personifications of the four ideal qualities survive in a somewhat modified form in the well-known saying in *Pirke Abot* (V:20): "Be fierce as the leopard, swift as the eagle, fleet as the deer and strong as the lion to perform the will of thy Father in heaven." Originally symbolizing the qualities of faithful doormen guarding royal palaces, the Assyrian animals became converted in Ezekiel's vision into drivers of the Lord's throne-chariot and finally symbols of the pious Jew. The process of spiritualization is strikingly similar to what we observed in the development of the date tree motif.

What do these shiftings in symbolism mean in terms of Jewish art?

On a fragment of a Jewish marble sarcophagus from Rome (in the Berlin Museum)[11] we see a seven-branched candlestick flanked by palm-trees and liturgical symbols, the *etrog*, the *lulab* and some dishes. Ernst Cohn-Wiener, who dated the sarcophagus in the second century C.E., associated it with Zechariah's vision of the leaders of the Restoration. The interpretation is tempting and might be correct in a general sense. However, there are more than two trees flanking the Menorah on the relief, and if we set the date in the late third or fourth century C.E., which is more plausible, a vaguely Messianic interpretation will appear more proper. The *etrog* and *lulab* may allude to a Messianic Feast of Tabernacles in which the pious hopes to have his part.

In a sarcophagus found in a Jewish catacomb on the site of the Villa Torlonia[12] in Rome, the palm-tree motif is abandoned; the Menorah stands alone in the center, flanked by the symbols of Tabernacles. These symbols remain the permanent companions of the candelabrum in Jewish art.

The four animals of *Pirke Abot* became extremely popular in Jewish art. We know them chiefly from the folk art of the eighteenth and nineteenth centuries; they are common in the carved or painted decoration of Torah shrines and *almemars* in Poland, and appear printed on paper flags which children used to carry in the synagogue processions on Simhat Torah. In Germany they were frequently embroidered or painted on linen wrappers of the Torah Scroll.

However, the practice of portraying the four animals symbolic of the pious must be of older origin, since they appear in the magnificent *Arha*

Turim codex of the Vatican (Cod. de Rossi 555) executed by a scribe, Isaac ben Obadiah, in 1436 in Mantua.[13] The manuscript is beautifully illuminated by a first-rate artist of the school of Pisanello. The style, the color scale, the facial types and costumes are extremely close to what we find in the paintings and drawings of this great master of the Italian *quattrocento*.

Among the four larger miniatures of the manuscript there is a synagogue scene with the worshipers in the background and the reader at the *almemar* in the foreground. To the right of the desk, members of the congregation are seen taking out the Scroll from a beautifully carved Torah shrine. In the corner rectangles of the painted frame that encloses the scene are displayed the four animals, the leopard, the eagle, the deer and the lion, in the sequence adopted in *Pirke Abot*, and each animal is accompanied by the appropriate clause written on a scroll. It was a particularly fine idea to frame the synagogue scene with the symbols of piety.

Ezekiel's throne-chariot of God gave rise to esoteric speculations which constitute what is known as the lore of *Maasse Merkabah*. We do not know when the first attempt at pictorial representation of Ezekiel's vision was made by Jews. According to the Talmud (Rosh Hashanah 24b) it is forbidden to portray the four living creatures together. However, the interest in the subject was so great that it could not be entirely ignored. In the thirteenth century prayer book of the Bodleian Library in Oxford (cod. 2373) the *Merkabah* is pictured as an illustration to the portion recited at Pentecost (Mahzor Shabuot).[14] The Divine chariot is treated as a portal carried by two of the fabulous creatures, a twin bull and a twin lion. The eagle and the man are displayed inside the portal, where they are accompanied by other fantastic animals. The inclusion of the *Merkabah* symbolism in the prayer book for Pentecost was not arbitrary since the first chapter of the Book of Ezekiel where the chariot vision is recorded constitutes the *Haftarah* for the first day of Pentecost.

The association with Pentecost brought about an interesting modification in the conception of the *Merkabah*, for in the miniature the "man" of the Ezekiel vision is Moses. Since Pentecost is the Feast of Commemoration of the "Giving of the Torah," the reference to Moses is quite justified, all the more as Moses is depicted in the monologue of the Torah in the prayer book for Pentecost, as the ideal man superior to any biblical figure. In order to emphasize the central motif of the festival, the Revelation on Sinai, the Giving of the Torah is represented on the top of the picture, above the Divine canopy.

The four mystical creatures appear again, this time associated with the prayers for the Day of Atonement. In this conception the portal is literally the "Open Gate of Mercy." In a miniature of the early fourteenth century

Mahzor of the Breslau University Library, the Gate of Mercy is designed as a portal with open wings.[15] The four Merkabah figures are painted on the capitals and bases of the archway which have the form of round medallions. The motif of the archway still retains a relation to the throne-chariot concept, a relation pointed out in the medallions in which the living creatures are displayed. The medallions are meant, of course, to recall the wheels of Ezekiel's vision.

The four wheels, or medallions, enclosing the four mystical figures eventually lose every relationship with the portal which still gave the illusion of a canopied throne. In the *Mahzor* of the Leipzig University Library (second half of the fourteenth century) the four medallions stand unmotivated in a rectangular frame.[16] Rendered in a sort of short-hand style, the four creatures are merely intended to remind us of the Temple, as the text deals with the Temple tax. A pair of scales for weighing the *shekalim* is shown beside the medallions. Beasts and grotesques complete the picture.

The evolution of the chariot motif in Jewish medieval book illustration reveals, then, a tendency to dissolve the visual forms, already considerably disintegrated owing to the talmudic prohibition and the vagueness of *Merkabah* philosophical conceptions. They become immerged in patterns of beasts, foliage and interlaces. The animal decoration of Romanesque and Gothic art afforded a congenial vocabulary for these unrealistic elaborations.

After a glimpse into medieval prayer-book illustration, which uses the nostalgic visions of the Babylonian Exile[16a] as a hieratic background for synagogue liturgy, the contrast with Jewish art in antiquity becomes particularly striking. The climate of the Middle Ages seems much closer to the exalted mood of the Babylonian deportees than to the more realistic attitude of the Jews of the Hellenistic period. The beginnings of the synagogue are still shrouded in obscurity, and we do not know much about the trends in Jewish art before the third century B.C.E. when, suddenly, we meet with synagogue inscriptions.

Judaism was confronted with Hellenism all over the Diaspora, in the West and in the East, and some aspects of Hellenistic culture were necessarily felt by the Jews to be a challenge to their beliefs.[16b] Clashes between what we may call two strongly opposed conceptions of life were unavoidable. It should not be overlooked, however, that a steady process of dissociation of Hellenism from mythology was taking place, a process which made art, in some of its phases at least, tolerable to uncompromising monotheism. Typical of the more realistic and humane approach toward life were, for instance, the late Hellenistic Pergaminian sculptures in Athens, which portray enemy warriors as men endowed with a sense of dignity and pride rather than as mythological monsters.

In Roman art the scope of interests reaches further and portrait, landscape, idyllic animal scenes, subjects of current history, become increasingly important. Reliefs showing the emperor distributing largess to the populace, publicly displayed, were used as means of political propaganda.

Since art, therefore, was shifting toward secular aspects, the Jewish position had to be reconsidered. Jews had their own political concerns, too, and it may be gathered from Rabbinical writings that they were actually re-examining their historical experience in the light of contemporary events, and their discussions of an ideal leader reflected most real political aspirations. And along with the acuteness of political thinking a keener understanding of the culture and the arts of the surrounding population developed.

There is a story in the Mishna which can be regarded as typical of the new attitude. Rabban Gamaliel, the Patriarch (died before 114 c.e.), we are told, once attended the *termae* of Aphrodite at Acco. When asked how he could reconcile his conduct with the Jewish attitude toward pagan art, the Sage dismissed the question with a joke: "I did not come into her domain," he said, "she came into mine," for nobody will maintain that the bathhouse was built for Aphrodite, while it can be said that the statue was set up as an adornment of the bathhouse (Aboda Zara 44b). The debate is striking, for it reflects a most uninhibited attitude of the leading groups of Jewry toward an art which obviously was felt to be no longer a temptation to the Jewish believer.

In discussing the precedent established by the Palestinian Patriarch, a Jewish authority in Babylonia, Rabbah b. bar Hanah (latter part of the third century), ruled that a statue set up for decorative purposes—as may be the case in a large city—would not be objectionable. What was to be avoided were images in smaller places which were likely to be worshiped by the populace (Aboda Zara 41a). The distinction made in this decision is clear. To the educated classes in the big centers, art no longer meant crude idol worship.

Within the more sophisticated Roman civilization, then, emerges a Jewish art. The most important monument of Jewish antiquity is no doubt the synagogue at Dura-Europos on the middle Euphrates in Syria dated by inscription 245 c.e.[17] The entire walls of the synagogue have been found covered with biblical scenes. Dura was a Roman city of recent standing captured from the Persians. The population lived in expectation of a recapture. This actually happened before the decoration of the synagogue was completed. Nothing could possibly reflect more faithfully the feelings of the Jews of Dura than the paintings of their prayer house with their special emphasis on the good old Persian king, Ahasuerus, portrayed seated on Solomon's lion throne (the famous throne which, according to

Rabbinical views, nobody was worthy of inheriting, except possibly the Persian king), and a most detailed rendering of Ezekiel's "Vision of the Dry Bones," showing the scattered tribes reunited and gathered under one king, the resurrected King David.[18] The meaning of the biblical episode portrayed was unmistakable to the members of the congregation who knew that Davidic descendants were still alive, out of reach of the Roman invaders and under the protection of Sapur.

Were these extraordinary paintings unique?

From the mosaic decoration found in synagogues of the fourth to sixth centuries in North Africa[19] and Palestine it can be inferred that this representational art, biblical in content, talmudic in interpretation, was fairly well spread over a large area. The Jerusalem Talmud (Aboda Zara 3, 42d) records that the Samaritans made images of Jacob and Joseph, regarding the latter as their direct ancestor. It would thus appear that in the art of the Jews of the ancient period all the different traditions due to the Judaic, Israelitic and mixed popular elements were represented. The Samaritans revered Joseph as their ancestor and emphasized his story in their art, the synagogue of Dura likewise cherished the memory of Joseph, but was anxious to stress the unity of the nation, the emblem of which—the Temple of Jerusalem—was depicted above the Torah niche. This emblem is common to the floor mosaics of the synagogues at Naaran[20] and Bet Alpha[21] in Palestine, as well as to the gold glasses from Jewish catacombs in Rome. (A fine specimen of the latter can be seen at the Metropolitan Museum in New York.)[22]

It would take us too far afield to discuss the decoration of the ancient synagogue in detail. One more motif should be mentioned, however, because of its controversial character: the signs of the Zodiac, the *mazalot*. The ceiling tiles of the Dura synagogue were decorated with these signs, the floor mosaics of Palestinian synagogues display them. What was the attitude of the Rabbinical authorities toward this pictorial motif, intended to evoke the image of heaven?[23] On the whole, it would appear that they were opposed to its use. However, in the Babylonian Talmud (Aboda Zara 42b) we have a curious concession: pictures of the planets are permissible, but not those of the sun and moon. And the same source (43a) records that Rabban Gamaliel "had a picture of lunar diagrams in his upper chamber in the form of a chart hanging on the wall." There are other talmudic references to astronomical studies carried on by the Rabbis. The prohibition of images has no apodictic character in the sources of the time. What we have in the Talmud are records of discussions, of debates. Thus, in the Babylonian Talmud (Aboda Zara 41a) we find side by side two strictly opposed statements. According to one opinion, all images are prohibited; according to another, an image is not prohibited except when the figure holds a staff or a bird in its hand. What is discussed here is pagan rather than Jewish art, and in particular statues of divinities. Jewish art is also referred to and, significantly, without comment. In the Jerusalem Talmud it is related that "at the time of Rabbi Johanan (third century C.E.) they began to have paintings on the walls and the Rabbis did not hinder them." Are we to suppose that the paintings on the walls were meant to be synagogue paintings? In a fragment of the Jerusalem Talmud (Aboda Zara 3.3) preserved in the Public Library in Leningrad[24] we read: "In the days of Rabbi Abun [first half of the fourth century C.E.] they began to depict designs of mosaics and he did not hinder them." Pavement mosaics referred to in this text can safely be taken to be synagogue mosaics, since such mosaics have actually been excavated in Palestine and the Diaspora.

From the point of view of Judaism it is important to discover that the art practiced by Jews was a national, popular art dedicated to problems of Jewish interest. This art offered a counterpart to the Rabbinical interpretation of Jewish history and Jewish behavior. Art, a companion of literature, shared in the responsibility for the cultural and political education of the community.

Although the Rabbinical leaders seem on the whole to have tolerated art with some misgivings or, at best, without taking issue for or against it, in the case of the Dura murals—of which thirty panels have survived—we have to assume an active part of the spiritual head of the congregation in the planning of the decoration. The murals reveal throughout an intimate knowledge of the vast field of tradition.

As for style, the paintings have the "descriptive" quality of late Roman art, particularly of the provinces. What the synagogue artist was striving for was to convey the meaning, the point of a story, rather than to give the illusion of figures moving and acting in a three-dimensional space. Pompeian paintings had that plastic, illusionistic quality, but it was from later, more vehemently meaningful art that medieval Bible illustration developed. Christian art students evaluate the Dura synagogue paintings particularly from that point of view.

Examining the synagogue mosaics, we notice in the sixth century a tendency to depict liturgical objects rather than figure scenes, and a more conventional, rigid style which reflects restraint, introversion, an attitude due to the deteriorating political and social status under Byzantine domination. There are also to be taken into account general ideological trends, the controversy provoked in the Christian church by the Monophysite doctrine, and later on, in the seventh century, the powerful propaganda of Islam. How the mere threat of an Arab avalanche could affect the cultural policy of a country may be gathered from the bloody iconoclastic campaign initiated by Leo the Isurian in Byzantium. Aiming at the power of the monastic orders, the emperor, who was of Asiatic origin and spoke Arabic, had understood the signs of the times and knew how to make use of the new slogan.

The East was definitely becoming iconoclastic, and we can safely assume that Jewish art adjusted itself without misgivings to the uncompromising attitude of Islam, which agreed with the moods prevailing in the Jewish community. The *hadit*, in which the Prophet is reported to have declared that those to be punished most severely on the Day of Judgment are the portrayers, was probably approved by the Jews, although they had never denounced art so harshly.

In the earliest preserved Hebrew manuscripts of the tenth and eleventh centuries, executed in Syria, Palestine and Egypt, the process of ornamentalization and geometrization of real objects of the visible world is found to be completed, and the pictures of the seven-branched candlestick and the Temple utensils appear in Bible illumination, immerged in ornamental design.[25] Nothing is left of other representational topics and the skill of the artist exerts itself in penmanship. Dedications to patrons in huge gold lettering on diapered backgrounds became an outstanding feature of the magnificent parchment codices, and the masoretic notes of the Bible— a running grammatical commentary—in minuscule writing were arranged in marginal and full-page ornamental pieces.

The synagogue walls were decorated in a similar style and were hung with textiles; so, for example, the prayer house in which Maimonides prayed. It is reported that he felt distracted by the ornamental designs on tapestries and synagogue walls and therefore covered his eyes at prayer in order to achieve greater concentration.[26]

Meanwhile, in the European settlements, beasts and birds and all sorts of plants began to creep into the interlaces of the arabesques of the Jewish manuscript decoration. The synagogues were affected by a similar change of style.

The new departure seems to have been made first in the treatment of the masoretic notes, which were now written in animal and floral outlines. Rabbi Judah ben Samuel of Speyer and Regensburg condemned this practice in his *Sefer Hasidim* (twelfth century).[27] A scholar is bound to pay strictest attention to a clear disposition and legibility of the text, while the scribe is too readily inclined to neglect the text for the sake of an elegant flourish. Much of the friction between the writers and the scribes in the Middle Ages was due to this basic conflict. No concerted efforts were made to restrain art in book or synagogue decoration, however, and we cannot even speak of a united front of the Rabbinical authorities on this question.

Very significant is the fact that one of the great authorities of the twelfth century, Ephraim ben Isaac, Rabbi of Regensburg, declared himself a partisan of art.[28] He was consulted by R. Joel b. Isaac Ha-Levi of Bonn about some textiles used in the synagogue, the design of which—birds, fish and horses—seemed to him controversial; and R. Ephraim ruled in favor of animal decoration, pointing to its absolute harmlessness at a time when animal worship was no longer a problem.

The role of animal symbolism in Hebrew manuscript illumination has been touched upon in our discussion of the *Merkabah* motif. We cannot deal with this problem at any length. Suffice it to say that the famous medieval animal book, the *Physiologus,* was much influenced by the Bible and is even traced by some scholars to a Jewish source.

To understand the interest in animals, their habits and appearance, we must also take into account the role of hunting in the Middle Ages. Legend has it that Rabbi Judah ben Samuel spent his youth at archery and at the age of eighteen realized that he wished rather to study Jewish lore.[29] We cannot take this tale too literally; however, it reveals an interest in this sport, at least on the part of the recorder and his public. We do know that Rabbi Ephraim ben Isaac discussed hunting with hound and falcon in a matter-of-fact way, without any unfavorable comment.[30]

It seems that objections to animal decoration appear only after a certain period of toleration, and not as a warning against a newfangled fashion. Thus, Rabbi Isaac ben Moses Or Zarua of Vienna (*c.* 1200) recalled the verdure decoration—foliage with birds—of the Meissen synagogue from his boyhood days. In his old age he felt compelled to disapprove of that sort of thing.[31]

In the Cologne synagogue a controversy was started over some stained-glass windows which Rabbi Eliakim ben Joseph (first half of the twelfth century) wished removed.[32] His attack is particularly interesting because the Cistercian Order had prohibited stained-glass windows in their churches in 1134. The interdict aimed at the luxurious indulgence in colored glass, and was a measure of self-imposed restraint of the senses, proper for a fraternal community. Bernard of Clairvaux (d. 1153) particularly condemned animal decoration (*Patrologia Latina,* vol. 182, cols. 913 ff.). But what was in order for a monastic association was hardly right for a community of men, women and children, and we have Rabbi Judah ben Samuel's words to show that this was actually the Rabbinical view. "Do not say," he warned, "that you want to put on the hairy cloth of the Christian monk, for this would be a sinful way, as you have to deny yourself only what the Scriptures forbid you to enjoy."[33] In fact, Rabbi Eliakim's attitude was dictated by "political anxiety," rather than by religious scruples. He was fearful lest the Jews be accused of worshiping the lions and snakes depicted on those windows, the more so as the windows happened to be on the side the congregation faced at one particular prayer. It may be recalled that the Second Crusade had swept over the Jewish settlements in 1146 and the victims of the first, of 1096, were not yet forgotten. Although the Rabbi tried to associate his objections with some reservations voiced here and there in the Talmud, it was evident that these references were meant only to add some dignity to a restriction provoked by a situation beyond his control.

The last refuge of the artist was the book, for it was less exposed to the public eye than the synagogue. It is true that the Rabbinical authorities did not directly favor book decoration, not to speak of illustration; however, it is significant that while Rabbi Meir of Rothenburg (d. 1293) mildly criticized the animal-and-bird decoration of the prayer books, he did not base his criticisms on religious considerations.[34] The considerable number of prayer books from the thirteenth and fourteenth centuries decorated in this manner is proof that there was no marked opposition to be reckoned with. Perhaps the best evidence of the rather tolerant attitude prevalent is found in the illustrated prayer book (Breslau University Library) executed by a disciple of the Rothenburg Sage.[35]

It is with a sense of profound respect that we examine the huge medieval prayer books, the Bibles and the smaller Haggadas admirably written and illuminated on parchment and exquisitely bound.

Attempts at Bible illustration are found in all the types of Hebrew writings: here it may be an Esther scene, there the "Giving of the Law," or "Abraham in the fiery furnace," an episode from postbiblical literature.[35a]

Continuous biblical picture cycles are rare, however, and there is not one Bible illustrated throughout. Strange to say, an illustration beginning with Adam and Eve is found in Haggadas rather than in Bibles, the most beautiful of them (Codex Add. 27210 of the British Museum) exhibiting an immaculate thirteenth-century French Gothic style.[36] The somewhat later Haggada of the Sarajevo Museum, executed in Spain, opens with the scenes of the six days of Creation—each day represented by the disk of the earth showing the successive improvements, and the seventh day illustrated by the Lord seated on a bench and enjoying His rest.[37] Such a thing would not be possible in a Bible. The Haggada was allowed some measure of freedom and informality. There must have been a certain reluctance to illustrate the Bible codex throughout either because of the immensity of such a task or for religious reasons. At any rate, the most magnificent Bible codex, (Cod. Kennicott I of the Bodleiana completed in La Coruña in Spain in 1476) shows only a few figures: David, Phineas, Balaam and Jonah.[38] Its decoration is chiefly animal and floral.

This particular attitude toward Bible illustration may account for the behavior of Moses Arragel, the Rabbi of Guadalajara, who in 1430 compiled a Castilian translation of the Old Testament for the Order of Calatrava of which he was a vassal.[39] When asked to supervise the work of the illustrators also, Arragel declined, referring to the Decalogue. Did he fear to be involved in problems of interpretation? Possibly so, although in the Bible commentary he furnished he shows an admirable tact in giving credit to Christian and Jewish exegesis alike and siding with none.[40] The alternative is that he honestly opposed Bible illustration as something even the most liberal-minded Jew could not wholeheartedly approve.

With the expulsion from Spain (1492)[40a] the fine Hebrew manuscript production of that country was brought to a standstill. The deterioration of the position of the Jews in Germany throughout the fifteenth century was accompanied by a marked decline in the quality of their books, and the sketchy colored drawings found in their manuscripts of that time reflect haste and carelessness. In Italy alone Hebrew book illumination and, especially, illustration remain on a high level during the fifteenth and sixteenth centuries and show an unparalleled variety and wealth of vocabulary and finesse of execution.[40*] In this art, with its emphasis on balance and mellowness of color—an Italian contribution—there is to be noted also a considerable strain of influences imported by refugees from Spain and Germany.

It has often been said that the Jews had experienced no renaissance, and some students of Jewish history are inclined to extend the medieval period down to the Enlightenment and Emancipation of the eighteenth century. However, the attitude of the Jews toward art in the Renaissance seems to have outgrown the medieval pattern to such an extent that a consideration of that period in distinct terms seems imperative.

The retarding elements that make themselves noticeable during the later Middle Ages in book illumination in Germany and even in Spain are not to be discounted in the appreciation of manuscripts produced in Italy, furthermore, most important is the role of the printed book and the new techniques of illustration, the woodcut and the engraving.

The Jewish scribe and illuminator had no permanent contact with his Christian colleagues, monks or laymen organized in guilds. In the printing presses, however, Jews and Christians were bound to work together. The Jews, frequently forbidden to run presses, had their books printed in Christian printing shops, where Jewish composers had to be employed for Hebrew prints.

The practice of the printers for economy's sake to use the same cuts for various publications and to exchange cuts among themselves, had an effect upon Hebrew printing, too. The new border pieces, title pages and even illustrations turned up in the Hebrew books; and we are not surprised to discover in the Mantua Haggada of 1560 a woodcut from Holbein's Lyons Bible of 1538 as an illustration for the "son who does not know how to ask questions," and Michelangelo's Jeremiah of the Sistine ceiling in the Vatican as one of the Rabbis of Bene Berak.

If this is plagiarism, then we also have to dismiss as plagiarism the famous Renaissance church, St. Francesco in Rimini, since Alberti used the Roman gate of Rimini as a model for the church façade. What we are driving at is not to demonstrate that the whole Renaissance movement was imitative, but to point out the enthusiastic interest in research, in copying and reproducing in various techniques and adapting to various purposes of art works greatly valued. Jews and Christians alike were carried away by this artistic enthusiasm. Jewish and Christian artisans alike reproduced on faïence dishes the biblical scenes of the Loggias in the Vatican painted by pupils of Raphael. Adorned in addition with Passover symbols and illustrations from a Venetian Haggada (first printed in 1609), the Jewish plates were used for the *Seder* meal.[41] Holbein, Michelangelo, Raphael had thus become the teachers of the budding Jewish artist. And later developments were to show how these new influences affected his outlook and sensitivity.

Unfortunately the rapprochement so conspicuous in the keen interest in Hebrew language and literature among the humanists, and the emergence of the Jewish author in Italian literature—one may recall the *Dialoghi d'Amore*, a philosophical treatise by Leone Ebreo,[41a] the son of the Sephardic refugee from Spain, the great Isaac Abrabanel—did not last. That rapprochement was built on an unstable political foundation, and who could better sense the changing "climate" than a native, Italian Jew? It was the poet and grammarian Samuel Archevolti (d. 1609) who uttered the all-familiar warnings. It was clear to him that the first target for anti-Jewish attacks would be refugees, and he was alarmed by what in their customs might irritate the native Jew-baiters. There was that German synagogue at Venice with its quaint interior decoration, nothing particularly disturbing since the Ashkenazic rabbis tolerated it, but somehow inappropriate, perhaps outmoded, not in line with the fashion of the day. Archevolti objected to the "trees and plants" in that decoration, more suited for an inn or a theater, he thought, than a prayer house.[42] He went so far as to admit that he really worried lest the non-Jews accuse Jews of worshiping those images. Had not Apion, centuries earlier, slanderously accused the Jews of worshiping an ass's head?

Another story may illustrate the sense of insecurity and frustration typical of the Jews in the later sixteenth and the seventeenth century. The Jews of Ascoli, when expelled in 1569, went to Pesaro. Among the things they took with them was their synagogue Shrine. In 1639 Rabbi Moses of Trani raised the question whether the lions that adorn the Shrine were compatible with the Jewish view of plastic arts.[43] The rabbi could not know, of course, that someday lion statues carved in the round would be excavated on the site of antique Palestinian synagogues. (I refer to the finds in Chorazin and Kfar Birim.)[44] So he decided in the negative. His view was adopted by Rabbi David ibn Abi Zimra.[45] The argument brought forth was the usual reference to the diverting effect upon the worshiper. However, Abraham Joseph Solomon Graziano of Modena, the great book collector, was of a different opinion. He pointed out (c. 1670) that the lions set at the foot of the Shrine could not be well seen from the seats of the congregation and were hardly liable to disturb anyone. Graziano's liberal attitude calls for an explanation. It was Graziano's own great-grandfather, we learn, who had moved the Ascoli Shrine to Pesaro. This Shrine meant something to the man. He gave vent to his indignation in marginal remarks jotted down in his copy of Rabbi Joseph Caro's *Shulhan Aruk*. That is where David Kaufmann found them.[46]

Archevolti's summons to refrain from decorating synagogues was confirmed by the rabbinical court at Safed with some reservations regarding already existing decorations which were not to be obliterated.[47] Every new wave of persecution was followed by pious exhortations to abstain from display of any sort which might bring discredit upon the community. But no wholesale condemnation of art was pronounced by any responsible body in the name of the synagogue.

The Renaissance had released the forces of the individual, Jew and Christian alike, and there was no way back into the narrowness and isolation forced upon the Jews in the Middle Ages. Here and there emerges a name of a Jewish artist associated with some unusual achievement.

Meanwhile in the East, too, there were stirrings. In the medieval period, Western artistic trends had been carried eastward and synagogues of Worms, Regensburg and Cracow were built upon the same scheme. During the Renaissance, Italy began to export to the whole European continent architects, masons, painters, sculptors, many of whom went to Poland and Russia; some occasionally built or remodeled a synagogue. From the blending of these Italian influences with native elements in the Carpathian region, the Ukraine, Lithuania and White Russia, a Jewish folk art developed, which after the Chmielnicki pogrom (1648) was carried by emigrants from Eastern Europe back to the West.[48] Medieval animal decoration was revived in modest country synagogues of the East in terms of a provincial *baroque*. This was actually a survival of a tradition, some links of which were lost. Folk art has a long memory. In this Eastern European synagogue decoration we meet the biblical leviathan, the *behemot*, the hieratic eagle, the fabulous snake of medieval descent, the unicorn familiar from Hebrew illuminated manuscripts in the West as well as from Christian art, the four animals from *Pirke Abot*, and the view of the restored Jerusalem. Regardless of the origin of these pictorial devices—from peasant folk art, imported Oriental textiles, engravings and woodcuts from West and East—the common source of this imagery was the prayer book, with its traditional symbolism.

In a period, then, when Jewish art in central Europe stagnated, a new wave of folklore and artistic conceptions from the East was driven to Moravia, Hungary and farther westward down to the Fuerth region where, scattered in villages and townlets, lived the remnant of German Jewry.

In the seventeenth century there emerged the free republic of Holland, whereto Jews, Sephardic and Ashkenazic, flocked seeking refuge from religious persecution.[48a] Amsterdam superseded the Italian centers of Hebrew printing, and it was again through the medium of the book that Jewish art received its new stimulus.

The Marranos from Portugal, who in Holland returned to their old faith, had a more liberal conception of art, and because of their higher living standard there was among them a certain need for outer display. Family portraits belonged to the amenities of life; and we see Jews portrayed by Dutch artists.

Jewish artists soon began to attempt portraiture also, and it was characteristic of their background that their first attempts in portraiture were intended for books. Thus, in the seventeenth century appear author portraits, designed and sometimes engraved as well by Jews for frontispieces. To be sure, these were portraits of scholars and community leaders. We would hardly expect portraits of women or children in such a dignified and serious company. However, Aaron Chaves, much ahead of his time, designed in the second half of the seventeenth century a portrait of Daniel Levi Barrios with his wife, son and daughter, which was to be appended to a poetical paraphrase of the Bible written by Barrios.[49] The portrait was allegorical and the text was only a version of the Bible; nevertheless, the Portuguese community of Amsterdam refused to give its approbation to the publication of the book.

The Ashkenazim were even more particular about portraits. The portrait of Rabbi Zebi Ashkenazi in the eighteenth century had to be drawn clandestinely, without the rabbi's knowledge. His son, Rabbi Jacob Emden, had serious misgivings about this portrait. He also disapproved of the portrait medal cast for Eleazar Shmelka, the Ashkenazic rabbi of Amsterdam.[50] As late as 1837 Rabbi Akiba Eger in Posen had to be portrayed clandestinely.[51] However, there was a great demand for portraits of prominent rabbis. Whether Adamus Wagner's portrait of Rabbi Jonathan Eybeschuetz (d. 1767), signed and dated 1770, was painted after a drawing from life we do not know. The portrait was exhibited in the Akiba Eger Exhibition in Berlin in 1937.[52] The well-known engraving is a slightly modified version of that portrait. Among others the engraved portrait of Rabbi Ezekiel Landau (d. 1793) should be mentioned. Engravings were later superseded by lithographs. The Jewish Museum in

Berlin had one of the largest collections of portraits of rabbis and scholars, some of considerable artistic value.

The Sephardic community in Amsterdam may be regarded as having practically initiated that type of portraiture among Jews, although some attempts had already been made in Italy. After all, Salom Italia, who engraved portraits of J. J. A. Leon Templo [Jacob Jehudah Leone][53] and of Manasseh ben Israel, came to Holland from Italy. In Amsterdam there was a larger field and a greater demand to tempt an artist.

The Ashkenazic community of Amsterdam, more concerned with religious needs, produced a new illustrated Haggada which was to play a considerable part in the development of Jewish folk art. Compiled for the Ashkenazic and Sephardic ritual, this Haggada was published in 1695 under the patronage of Moses Wesel, an Ashkenazic Jew. The engravings were picked from the immense work of Matthaeus Merian of Basel, who had illustrated a Luther Bible and other popular publications.[54] Children particularly delighted in the many-figured and lively pictures, and it is noteworthy that for Goethe and Heine the Merian pictures were associated with the most cherished childhood memories. However, Heine knew them only from his Haggada—a handwritten and hand-painted version of the Amsterdam Haggada. He never suspected their origin. It is worth reading what he says about those lovely pictures, in his *Rabbi of Bacharach*. Executed in 1723 by Moses Judah Loeb, son of Benjamin Wolf Broda from Trebitsch, Moravia, this Haggada was dedicated to Lazarus von Geldern, Heinrich Heine's great-grandfather.[55] (The Haggada was in the possession of Dr. Heinz Frank in Amsterdam, a refugee from Cologne, when I saw it in 1936.)

The von Geldern Haggada is one of the numerous versions of the Amsterdam print, produced in the eighteenth century. The artists hailed mostly from Moravia, Bohemia and Hungary. In simplifying the composition of the scenes, Judaizing the facial types and costumes, these artists added a popular, provincial flavor to the pictures. Never blindly copying their model, they often introduced scenes or traits of their own invention, thus expanding the picture cycle and adapting it to the tastes and fashions of their own generation. Therefore, those eighteenth-century versions of the Amsterdam Haggada, neatly copied on parchment and illustrated with brightly gouache miniatures, have to be evaluated on their own merit. They offer a remarkable attempt to depict the "Jewish scene." They are in fact the first Jewish genre pictures created by Jewish artists, domestic interiors enlivened with a pot of flowers on the window sill and a bird in the cage, showing charming women, lovely children, men, old and young, gathered around a table, scenes not borrowed from Merian nor necessarily original inventions, yet ably compiled and sometimes exquisitely painted.

With these self-taught, obscure, provincial painters the puritanic spell was broken and Jewish art was at last liberated from its limitations imposed by history rather than "Law."

The painters born on the threshold of the nineteenth century,[56] the miniature-portrait painter Jeremias David Alexander Fiorino of Kassel, the well-known Moritz Oppenheim who was active in Frankfort, and Eduard Magnus, born in Berlin, all have something of the sweetness and lyricism of the Haggada painter of the eighteenth century, despite their formal training, the different background and broader outlook. Their subjects may be Jews or non-Jews; the painters do not engage in any ambitious projects likely to involve them in conflicting situations.

With closer participation in the cultural life of their countries, however, Jewish artists began to join groups organized to carry out definite ideological programs, such as the German Nazarene group in Rome, adherence to which brought about the conversion of the painter brothers, Johannes and Philipp Veit, grandsons of Moses Mendelssohn. Eduard Bendemann, who painted biblical compositions in the classicist vein, also realized soon that he needed a larger audience than Jews could offer and acted accordingly.

The problem of the Jewish artist was that of a man who cannot find an outlet for his activities within his ethnic group and sees himself drawn to the more powerful national audience. At least in Germany, this meant, in the first half of the nineteenth century, desertion of the ancestral faith.

In Austria, Hungary, Poland and Russia things matured more slowly, and serious conflicts could be more easily avoided. In the second half of the century, we meet in these countries an art which caters to the tastes of a cultivated Jewish middle class. This art was dedicated to the Jewish motif, which, as the century wore on, lost most of its lyrical character and struck a more bitter accent.

It is indicative of the social awareness of the promoters of Jewish art in Eastern Europe that a pupil of the sculptor Mark Antokolski, the late Boris Schatz, set out to found in Palestine a school of arts and crafts, the Bezalel School at Jerusalem. The idea of reactivating artistic crafts, metal and woodwork, rug weaving, embroidery and penmanship, had much in common with the program of William Morris. Characteristically, the work of Abel Pann, the outstanding painter of the Bezalel group, was close in style to that of the English Pre-Raphaelites. Whatever the merits of the individual artists associated with the Bezalel movement, they laid the foundation for a freer and more creative art in the future.

A Sephardic Jew, Camille Pissarro, a native of the Antilles, became in the seventies, in Paris, the first exponent among Jews of an experimental type of art, a member of a small group of pioneers which coined its own vocabulary.

Some people may see the significance of the impressionist movement started by Pissarro and his friends in the deheroization of man and the devaluation not only of "studio nudes," but of subject matter in general; others may see that significance in the abandoning of the academic principles of composition and the revolutionizing of painting techniques.

To the Jewish artist this movement meant a release from the sense of inferiority, from the constant awareness of his modest artistic heritage. Here at last was an art which did not claim a noble ancestry; it was a democratic art fitting into modern society, and an art in which the Jew was given a fair chance of achievement. And he accomplished a good deal.

The generation that holds the field now, and which made its first appearance during the First World War, has found a stronger and more universal response than any previous generation. The Jewish artist, like the Jewish writer, addresses himself in our time to the world, to all men. And it would appear that with art surrendering its claim to divinity and exclusiveness, the fight is actually won—for it was this claim to divinity which the Second Commandment had fought.

NOTES

[1] G. E. Wright, "How did early Israel differ from her neighbors?" in *Biblical Archaeologist,* VI, No. 1 (Feb. 1943), pp. 6 ff.

[2] W. F. Albright, *From the Stone Age to Christianity* (Baltimore, 1940), p. 206.

[3] J. W. and G. M. Crowfoot, *Early Ivories from Samaria* (London, 1938), p. 12.

[[3a] Cf. above Albright, "The Biblical Period," pp. 27-31.]

[4] E. B. Tylor, "The winged figures of the Assyrian and other ancient Monuments," *Proceedings of the Society of Biblical Archaeology,* June, 1890, p. 391.

[5] Ernst Cohn-Wiener, *Die juedische Kunst* (Berlin, 1929), Fig. 23.

[6] G. Dalman, *Arbeit und Sitte in Palaestina* (Guetersloh, 1939), VI, 107 ff.

[7] M. Gruenbaum, *Gesammelte Aufsaetze zur Sprach- und Sagenkunde,* ed. Felix Perles (Berlin, 1901), pp. 202-203.

[8] H. T. Obbink, "Jahwebilder," in *Zeitschrift fuer die Alttestamentliche Wissenschaft und die Kunde des nachbiblischen Judentums* (Giessen, 1929), Vol. 47, p. 267.

[9] G. E. Wright, "Solomon's Temple Resurrected," in *Bibl. Arch.,* Vol. IV, No. 2 (May, 1941), p. 28.

[10] J. W. and G. M. Crowfoot, *op. cit.,* pp. 18 and 24.

[11] W. H. Beyer and H. Lietzmann, *Die juedische Katakombe der Villa Torlonia* (Berlin, 1930), plate 28 and p. 44 where erroneously described under No. 27.

[12] *Ibid.,* plate 26a; see also p. 44.

¹³ Erno Munkácsi, *Miniatuermuevészet Itália koenyvtáraiban, heber Kodexek* (Budapest), publication of the Jewish Museum, n.d., Plate VI. 18. The codex was previously in the Derossiana in Vienna and is described in Hans Tietze, *Die illuminierten Handschriften der Rossiana in Wien-Lainz* (Leipzig, 1911), pp. 110-111.

¹⁴ Rachel Wischnitzer-Bernstein, *Symbole und Gestalten der juedischen Kunst* (Berlin, 1935), pp. 27-31, fig. 20.

¹⁵ *Idem.,* "The Messianic Fox," in *Review of Religion,* Vol. V, No. 3 March, 1941, p. 260, plate I.

¹⁶ Robert Bruck, *Die Malereien in den Handschriften des Koenigreichs Sachsen* (Dresden, 1906), pp. 219-225, fig. 138. The manuscript is summarily described without any attempt at interpreting the illustrations.

[¹⁶ᵃ Cf. Albright, *op. cit.,* pp. 45 ff.]

[¹⁶ᵇ Cf. above Elias J. Bickerman, "The Historical Foundations of Postbiblical Judaism," pp. 93 ff.]

¹⁷ H. F. Pearson, C. H. Kraeling, M. Crosby, J. J. Obermann, A. Pagliaro and C. C. Torrey, *Excavations at Dura-Europos.* Report of Sixth Season, Preliminary Report on the Synagogue at Dura (New Haven, 1936).

¹⁸ R. Wischnitzer-Bernstein, "The Conception of the Resurrection in the Ezekiel Panel of the Dura-Synagogue," in *Journal of Biblical Literature,* Vol. LX, No. 1 (March, 1941), pp. 43-55; *idem,* "The Samuel Cycle in the Wall Decoration of the Synagogue at Dura-Europos," *Proceedings of the Amer. Acad. for Jewish Research,* XI (1941), 85-103. For a more detailed discussion of the Dura synagogue paintings see the writer's book *The Messianic Theme in the Paintings of the Dura Synagogue* (Chicago, 1948), with bibliography, pp. 117-124. See also W. G. Kuemmel, "Die aelteste religioese Kunst der Juden," *Judaica,* II, 1 (Zurich, April, 1946), pp. 1-56; A. Grabar, *Martyrium, Recherches sur le culte des reliques et l'art chrétien antique,* 2 vols. (Paris, 1946, Plates, 1943); H. Riesenfeld, *The Resurrection in Ezekiel XXXVII and in the Dura-Europos Paintings* (Upsala Universitets Arsskrift, 1948).

¹⁹ R. Krautheimer, *Mittelalterliche Synagogen* (Berlin, 1927), pp. 68 ff., figs. 14 and 15.

²⁰ E. L. Sukenik, *Ancient Synagogues in Palestine and Greece* (London, 1934), pp. 28-31, fig. 5.

²¹ *Ibid.,* pp. 31-35, fig. 8.

²² Wischnitzer-Bernstein, "The Sabbath in Art," in A. E. Millgram, *Sabbath, The Day of Delight* (Philadelphia, 1944), pp. 324-327, fig. 19; for a discussion of gold glasses cf. *Idem,* "Die Messianische Huette in der juedischen Kunst," *Monatsschrift fuer Geschichte und Wissenschaft des Judentums,* XXX, 5 (Breslau, 1936), pp. 381 ff.

²³ For the interpretation of the meaning of the Zodiac motif see Karl Lehmann, "The Dome of Heaven," in *Art Bulletin,* College Art Association of America, Vol. XXVII, No. 1, (New York, 1945), pp. 1-27.

²⁴ J. N. Epstein, (ed.), *Tarbiz,* (Hebrew), Vol. III, No. 19, pp. 15 ff. (Jerusalem, 1931-1932). Cf. also Sukenik *op. cit.,* p. 27.

[25] Vladimir Stassof and David Gunzburg, *L'Ornement Hébreu* (Berlin, 1905). (Plates with summary description.)

[26] Leopold Loew, *Graphische Requisiten und Erzeugnisse bei den Juden* (Leipzig, 1870-1871), Pt. I, p. 34. See also Alfred Freimann, *Responsa of Maimonides* (Jerusalem, 1934) 20 and p. 19.

[27] Sefer Hasidim, (ed. Berlin) 709. Quoted in D. H. Mueller and J. von Schlosser *Die Haggadah von Sarajevo*, with appendix by David Kaufmann, "Zur Geschichte der juedischen Handschriften-Illustration" (Vienna, 1898), p. 257.

[28] Loew, *op. cit.*, p. 33; *Germania Judaica*, I. Elbogen, A. Freimann and H. Tykocinski (eds.) (Breslau, 1934), Vol. I, pt. 2, pp. 289-290.

[29] *Germania Judaica, op. cit.*, p. 293.

[30] *Ibid.*, p. 290.

[31] David Kaufmann, "Art in the Synagogue," in *Jewish Quarterly Review*, IX, 264, (London, 1897).

[32] Carl Brisch, *Geschichte der Juden in Coeln und Umgebung aus aeltester Zeit bis auf die Gegenwart* (Cologne, 1879), I, 39; see also *Germania Judaica, op. cit.*, p. 199.

[33] Loew, *op. cit.*, p. 17.

[34] *Ibid.*, p. 34; Bruno Italiener, *Die Darmstaedter Pessach Haggadah* (Leipzig, 1927), p. 18,

[35] Wischnitzer-Bernstein, "The Messianic Fox," *op. cit.*, p. 263.

[35a On illuminations of Judeo-Persian biblical manuscripts cf. above Walter J. Fischel, "Israel in Iran (A Survey of Judeo-Persian Literature)," p. 1165.]

[36] Rachel Wischnitzer, "Illuminated Haggadahs," in *J.Q.R.*, Vol. XIII, No. 2, p. 206 (London, 1922).

[37] Mueller and Schlosser, *op. cit.*, plate fol. 2.

[38] Wischnitzer, "Une Bible Enluminée par Joseph ibn Hayyim," in *Revue des Études Juives*, Vol. LXXIII, 146, p. 166. (Paris, 1921).

[39] Samuel Berger, "Les Bibles Castillanes," in *Romania*, XXVIII, 522 (Paris, 1899).

[40] Max Golde, "Die synagogale Kunst im Mittelalter," in *Menorah*, V. 571-584 (Frankfort am Main, 1927).

[40a Cf. above Cecil Roth, "The European Age in Jewish History (to 1648)," pp. 234 ff.]

[40*] Wischnitzer, "Les Manuscrits à Miniatures de Maimonide," *Gazette des Beaux-Arts*, VI, pér. T. XIII, 869 (Paris, July-August, 1935), pp. 49 ff.

[41] Wischnitzer-Bernstein, "Studies in Jewish Art," in *J.Q.R.*, N. S., Vol. XXXVI, No. 1, pp. 58-59 (Philadelphia, 1945).

[41a Cf. above Alexander Altmann, "Judaism and World Philosophy," pp. 975-977.]

[42] Kaufmann, "Art in the Synagogue," *op. cit.*, pp. 264, 265, 266.

[43] *Ibid.*, p. 258.

[44] Illustrated in E. L. Sukenik, *The Ancient Synagogue of Beth Alpha* (Jerusalem, 1932), figs. 36 and 37.

[45] Kaufmann, *loc. cit.*

[46] *Ibid.,* pp. 255 ff.

[47] *Ibid.,* p. 266.

[48] Some aspects of these eastward and westward trends were discussed in: E. Lissitzky, "The Synagogue of Mohilev," in *Rimon* (Hebrew), III, 9-12 (Berlin, 1923); *idem,* in *Milgrom,* (Yiddish) III, 9-13 (Berlin, 1923); E. Toeplitz, "Wall Paintings in Synagogues of the XVII and XVIII Centuries," in *Rimon, op. cit.,* pp. 1-8; *idem,* in *Milgrom, op. cit.,* pp. 1-7; *idem,* "Malerei in den Synagogen" (Besonders in Franken), in *Beitraege zur juedischen Kulturgeschichte* III, 3-16 (Frankfort am Main, 1929). See also Wischnitzer, "Mutual Influences between Eastern and Western Europe in Synagogue Architecture from the 12th to the 18th Century," in *YIVO Bleter* (Journal of the Yiddish Scientific Institute), Vol. XXIX, No. 1, pp. 3-51 (New York, 1947). *Idem.,* in English, in *YIVO Annual,* II-III, 1947-1948, pp. 25-68. G. K. Loukomski, *Jewish Art in European Synagogues* (London, 1947).

[[48a] Cf. above, Cecil Roth, "The Jews of Western Europe (from 1648)," pp. 253-254.]

[49] F. Landsberger, "New Studies in Early Jewish Artists," in *Hebrew Union College Annual,* XVIII, pp. 304 ff., fig. 7 (Cincinnati, 1944).

[50] Loew, *op. cit.,* p. 39.

[51] A. Kronthal, "Juedische Bildnismaler der Posener Biedermeierzeit" in *Jahrbuch fuer juedische Geschichte und Literatur,* XXX, 214-215, (Berlin, 1937).

[52] *Akiba Eger Ausstellung* (Catalogue by R. Wischnitzer-Bernstein and E. Pessen, Jewish Museum, Berlin) Hanukkah, 1937, No. 31.

[53] *Encyclopaedia Judaica,* X, p. 792. "Leon Templo, Jakob Jehuda Arje ben Abraham (1603-1675) owed his name, Templo, which he transmitted to his descendants, to his model of the Temple of Solomon which caused a sensation in its time and stimulated a whole literature."

[54] Wischnitzer-Bernstein, "Von der Holbeinbibel zur Amsterdamer Haggadah," in *Monatsschrift fuer Geschichte und Wissenschaft des Judentums,* Vol. LXXV, Nos. 7 and 8, pp. 1-18 (Breslau, 1931). For Van Dyck's influence on Jewish illustration: *Idem,* "The Esther Story in Art," in Philip Goodman, *The Purim Anthology* (Philadelphia, 1949), pp. 234 ff.

[55] Elizabeth Moses, "Juedische Kult-und Kunstdenkmaeler in den Rheinlanden," in *Rheinischer Verein fuer Denkmalpflege* (Duesseldorf, 1931), I, 99-200.

[56] For a survey of modern Jewish art see Karl Schwarz, *Die Juden in der Kunst* (Vienna and Jerusalem, 1936, 2nd ed.); *idem, Ha-Umanut Ha-Yehudit Ha-Hadashah Beeretz Yisrael* (Jerusalem, 1941); Franz Landsberger, *A History of Jewish Art* (Cincinnati, 1946). Helen Rosenau, *A Short History of Jewish Art* (London, 1948); for discussion of modern synagogue architecture, Wischnitzer-Bernstein, "The Problem of Synagogue Architecture," *Commentary,* III, 3 (New York, March, 1947), pp. 233-241.

BIBLIOGRAPHY

ALBRIGHT, WILLIAM FOXWELL, *From the Stone Age to Christianity.* Baltimore, 1940.

BERGER, SAMUEL, "Les Bibles Castillanes," in *Romania,* Vol. XXVIII. Paris, 1899.

BEYER, H. W., and LIETZMANN, H., *Die juedische Katakombe der Villa Torlonia.* Berlin, 1930.

BRISCH, CARL, *Geschichte der Juden in Coeln und Umgebung aus aeltester Zeit bis auf die Gegenwart.* Cologne, 1879. Vol. I.

BRUCK, ROBERT, *Die Malereien in den Handschriften des Koenigreichs Sachsen.* Dresden, 1906.

COHN-WIENER, ERNST, *Die juedische Kunst, ihre Geschichte von den Anfaengen bis zur Gegenwart.* Berlin, 1929.

CROWFOOT, J. W. and G. M., *Early Ivories from Samaria.* London, 1938.

DALMAN, G., *Arbeit und Sitte in Palaestina.* Guetersloh, 1939.

GOLDE, MAX, "Die synagogale Kunst im Mittelalter," in *Menorah,* Vol. V. Frankfort am Main, 1927.

GRABAR, ANDRÉ, *Martyrium, Recherches sur le culte des reliques et l'art chrétien antique.* 2 vols. and plates. Paris, 1946.

GRUENBAUM, M., *Gesammelte Aufsaetze zur Sprach- und Sagenkunde* (Felix Perles, ed.). Berlin, 1901.

ITALIENER, BRUNO, *Die Darmstaedter Pessach Haggadah.* Leipzig, 1927.

KAUFMANN, DAVID, "Art in the Synagogue," in *Jewish Quarterly Review,* Vol. IX. London, 1897.

KRAUTHEIMER, R., *Mittelalterliche Synagogen.* Berlin, 1927.

KRONTHAL, A., "Juedische Bildnismaler der Posener Biedermeierzeit," in *Jahrbuch fuer juedische Geschichte und Literatur,* Vol. XXX. Berlin, 1937.

KUEMMEL, W. G., "Die aelteste religioese Kunst der Juden," in *Judaica,* II, 1. Zurich, 1946.

LANDSBERGER, F., "New Studies in Early Jewish Artists," in *Hebrew Union College Annual,* Vol. XVIII. Cincinnati, 1944.

———, *A History of Jewish Art.* Cincinnati, 1946.

LEHMANN, KARL, "The Dome of Heaven," in *Art Bulletin,* College Art Association of America, Vol. XXVII, No. 1. New York, 1945.

LISSITZKY, E., "The Synagogue of Mohilev," in *Rimon,* Vol. III (Hebrew) and *Milgrom,* Vol. III (Yiddish). Berlin, 1923.

LOEW, LEOPOLD, *Graphische Requisiten und Erzeugnisse bei den Juden.* Leipzig, 1870-1871.

LOUKOMSKI, G. K., *Jewish Art in European Synagogues.* London, 1947.

MOSES, ELIZABETH, "Juedische Kult- und Kunstdenkmaeler in den Rheinlanden," in *Rheinischer Verein fuer Denkmalpflege und Heimatschutz,* Heft I, Duesseldorf, 1931, pp. 99-200.

MUELLER, DAVID H., and SCHLOSSER, JULIUS VON, *Die Haggadah von Sarajevo.* Vienna, 1898.

MUNKÁCSI, ERNO, *Miniatuermuevésvet Itália koenyvtáraiban, heber Kodexek.* Publication of the Jewish Museum. Budapest, n.d.

OBBINK, H. T., "Jahwebilder," in *Zeitschrift fuer die Alttestamentliche Wissenschaft und die Kunde des nachbiblischen Judentums,* Vol. XLVII. Giessen, 1929.

PEARSON, H. F., and others, *Excavations at Dura-Europos*. Report of Sixth Season, Preliminary Report on the Synagogue at Dura. New Haven, 1936.

RIESENFELD, HARALD, *The Resurrection in Ezekiel XXXVII and in the Dura-Europos Paintings*. Upsala, 1948.

ROSENAU, HELEN, *A Short History of Jewish Art*. London, 1948.

SCHWARZ, KARL, *Die Juden in der Kunst*. 2nd ed. Vienna and Jerusalem, 1936.

——, *Ha-Umanut Ha-Yehudit Ha-Hadashah Beeretz Yisrael*. Jerusalem, 1941.

STASSOF, VLADIMIR, and GUNZBURG, DAVID, *L'Ornement Hébreu*. Berlin, 1905.

SUKENIK, ELEAZAR L., *The Ancient Synagogue of Beth Alpha*. Jerusalem, 1932.

——, *Ancient Synagogues in Palestine and Greece*. London, 1934.

TIETZE, HANS, *Die illuminierten Handschriften der Rossiana in Wien-Lainz*. Leipzig, 1911.

TOEPLITZ, E., "Wall Paintings in Synagogues of the XVII and XVIII Centuries," in *Rimon*, Vol. III, and *Milgrom*, Vol. III. Berlin, 1923.

——, "Die Malerei in den Synagogen," in *Beitraege zur juedischen Kulturgeschichte*, Vol. III. Frankfort am Main, 1929.

TYLOR, E. B., "The Winged figures of the Assyrian and other ancient Monuments," in *Proceedings of the Society of Biblical Archaeology*. London, 1890.

WISCHNITZER (-BERNSTEIN), RACHEL, "Une Bible Enluminée par Joseph ibn Hayyim," in *Revue des Études Juives*, Vol. LXXIII, 146. Paris, 1921.

——, "Illuminated Haggadahs," in *Jewish Quarterly Review*, Vol. XIII, No. 2. London, 1922.

——, "Von der Holbeinbibel zur Amsterdamer Haggadah," in *Monatsschrift fuer Geschichte und Wissenschaft des Judentums*, Vol. LXXV, Nos. 7 and 8. Frankfort am Main, 1931.

——, *Symbole und Gestalten der juedischen Kunst*. Berlin, 1935.

——, "Les Manuscrits à miniatures de Maimonide," *Gazette des Beaux-Arts*, VI, per T. XIII, Nr. 869. Paris, July-August, 1935.

——, "Die Messianische Huette in der juedischen Kunst," *Monatsschrift fuer Geschichte und Wissenschaft des Judentums*, LXXX, Nr. 5. Breslau, 1936. Pp. 377-390.

——, "The Messianic Fox," in *Review of Religion*. Vol. V, No. 3. New York, 1941.

——, "The Conception of the Resurrection in the Ezekiel Panel of the Dura-Synagogue," in *Journal of Biblical Literature*. Vol. XL, No. 1. Philadelphia, 1941.

——, "The Samuel Cycle in the Wall Decoration of the Synagogue at Dura-Europos," in *Proceedings of the American Academy for Jewish Research*, Vol. XI. New York, 1941.

——, "The Sabbath in Art," in A. E. Millgram, *Sabbath, the Day of Delight*. Philadelphia, 1944.

WISCHNITZER (-BERNSTEIN), RACHEL, "Studies in Jewish Art," in *Jewish Quarterly Review*. N.S. Vol. XXXVI, No. 1. Philadelphia, 1945.

———, "Mutual Influences between Eastern and Western Europe in Synagogue Architecture from the 12th to the 18th Century," in *YIVO Bleter*, Vol. XXIX, No. 1. New York, 1947. (Yiddish.)

———, "The Problem of Synagogue Architecture," in *Commentary*, III, 3. New York, March, 1947. Pp. 233-241.

———, "Mutual Influences between Eastern and Western Europe in Synagogue Architecture from the 12th to the 18th century," in *YIVO Annual*, II-III. New York, 1947-1948. Pp. 25-68. (English.)

———, *The Messianic Theme in the Paintings of the Dura Synagogue*. Chicago, 1948.

———, "The Esther Story in Art," in Philip Goodman, *The Purim Anthology*. Philadelphia, 1949. Pp. 222-249.

WRIGHT, G. E., "How did early Israel differ from her neighbors?" in *Biblical Archaeologist*, Vol. VI, No. 1. New Haven, 1943.

———, "Solomon's Temple Resurrected," in *Biblical Archaeologist*, Vol. IV, No. 2, 1941.

CHAPTER 31

THE CONTRIBUTION OF THE JEWS TO MEDICINE

By Arturo Castiglioni

It is very difficult to consider Jewish medicine a chapter with a character all its own in the history of medicine in general.[1a] Our sources for Jewish medicine in antiquity are few and rare. There are available no medical writings which go back to ancient times; there is not even a collection of medical prescriptions or medical stories such as we have for the Egyptians and the Babylonians. The two works that are the sources for the study of Jewish history, the Bible and the Talmud, are chiefly books of laws in which medical subjects are dealt with only incidentally, only in so far as they concern the legislator. In the Talmud some laws on medical matters or problems are discussed, but always from the religious, moral or legal point of view, and evidently medical men have not at all or rarely been consulted. The Rabbis had some general knowledge of medicine, and this was the basis for their judgment or their views.

Jewish medicine of antiquity, at least what has come down to us in the texts of the sacred books, was dominated by the theocratic principle that governed the moral, social and political life of the people. It is easy to understand that this small people, which for centuries was subject to terrible wars, conquests and the influence of mighty neighbors, should in the evolution of its medicine also reveal the results of these circumstances. Unlike Egyptian or Greek medicine, therefore, Jewish medicine cannot be described as something distinctly itself. The first Jewish physicians of whose literary activity we know (seventh or eighth century c.e.) belonged to the world of Arab culture and wrote generally in Arabic, and the most ancient medical work in Hebrew is a collection of prescriptions by the Jewish physician, Sabbatai ben Abraham Donnolo, who lived in Italy in the tenth century and wrote also a mystical commentary on the Book of Creation.

It is even more difficult to speak of Jewish medicine in the period after the destruction of the Temple,[1b] when the bulk of the Jewish people lived in exile. A decisive influence in their medicine was surely the essential character of their religion, and the law which constitutes its basis. This influence is manifest even in the evolution of the thought and activity of the physician, of the hygienist, of the scholar. But the great evolution in medical science, the shift in the Greek schools from magic and dogmatic medicine to clinical medicine and the revolutionary changes in medical doctrine and practice in recent times were not brought about by Jewish scholars; nor did they play any characteristic role in this evolution. The science and scientific activity of the Jews became a part, sometimes more, sometimes less important, of the cultural life of the people in whose midst they lived. Single great scholars accomplished remarkable work, single schools had an important part in the education of scholars and practitioners; it is, however, impossible to say that these scholars or these influences derived from a special character of the Jewish people or of the Jewish mind, and as such stimulated definite action in one or another direction. For many centuries the Jews were concentrated in the Mediterranean countries. Here their medicine had its most important development. A remarkable period of this development is connected with the Arab conquest of the Mediterranean countries. The Jews were the great intermediaries of the Mediterranean; for centuries all commercial goods as well as the treasures of literature and science passed through their hands. The Jewish physicians were philosophers and subtle reasoners, able practitioners, expert diagnosticians and excellent students of botany and pharmacology. They won most important positions at the courts and as teachers, and from this time originate the fame they enjoyed and the role they played in the schools of the Renaissance, especially in Italy, France and Spain. In the following centuries, however, the battle of the European Jews against persecution made their participation in scientific activities difficult and often impossible.

With the emancipation of the Jews in many European countries and the progressive internationalization of science, Jews became more active in medicine and other sciences but no longer did their work have a peculiar character. In later times Jewish scholars held a prominent place as teachers and practitioners, and they made an important contribution to scientific progress. But this contribution cannot be distinguished from that of other great scholars with whom the Jews were in constant contact and from whom they adopted the fundamental concepts and systems of medicine.

We believe, therefore, that this chapter, which attempts to survey the role the Jews played in the history of medicine, may be divided into four parts. The first will be devoted to the medicine of the Bible and Talmud; the second, to the evolution of medicine among the Jews in the Middle Ages and their influence on Arabic medicine; the third, to the role Jewish scholars played in the schools of the pre-Renaissance and Renaissance periods; and finally, a short account of medicine among the Jews in the modern period.

It is not our intention to write the history of the great physicians and scholars and to give their biographies: this has been done in many works at different times and from different points of view. We shall try as far as possible to trace the history of the ideas, the evolution of medical thought, either as it was influenced by the Jews or as it exerted its influence on them, and to give a picture of the role the Jewish scholars and practitioners played in the history of medical science.

The fundamental concept that distinguished the medicine of biblical Israel from that of all other ancient peoples is this: Scripture declares it as a basic doctrine that the One God is the source of life and health; He is also, however, the source of all disease, which comes as a punishment and reproof. "I kill, and I make alive; I have wounded, and I heal" (Deut. 32:39). The animistic concept, the belief in malignant demons, universally accepted among peoples in protohistoric times, was suppressed and all magical practices were forbidden. This is the principle clearly expressed in all canonic books.

The Jewish concept of pathology reveals, however, the belief in a supernatural cause. Humbert states correctly that the origin of disease was attributed by the Jews equally to the Will of God, or to human malediction, or to a fault committed by ancestors (as in the threat of Divine punishment up to the third and fourth generations). As defenses against the hostile influence of individuals, prayers and spells were used. Sigmund Mowinckel and Adolphe Lods have shown that many of the invocations of the Psalms are to be regarded as simple incantations, and that such curses as "Let their eyes be darkened that they see not . . . Let them be blotted out of the book of the living" (69:24, 29) are procedures analogous in their form and scope to the magic preserved in the Assyro-Babylonian texts. According to the earliest narratives, it is not always the One God Who strikes. The plague is carried by an angel of God, who strikes 185,000 Assyrians in one night (II Kings 19:35). The "destroyer" smites the firstborn of Egypt (Ex. 12:23) and the "adversary," one of the *Bene Elohim,* inflicts malignant ulcers on Job. Angels and malignant demons appear here and there in the sacred books; one of these demons devours the limbs of the dead (Job 18:13).

The concept that tends to attribute chief importance to the blood and a preponderant role in general to the humors is of Sumerian origin. In Scripture, too, will be found the influence of the Egyptian pneumatic concept, that the spirit is the center of life (see Gen. 7:22 "in whose nostrils was the breath of the spirit of life").

In the development of the Jewish concept there is a manifest tendency and practical necessity to concentrate authority and power in the hands of the priestly caste, not because the priests are believed to possess by themselves the power of healing but because they are the interpreters or intermediaries of the will of the One God.

Note the fundamental difference from the medicine of other peoples.

The Jewish priest never plays the role of a physician; he gives his advice according to the religious Law and can help with his prayers. He may be, and really is, an adviser and an expert friend, but he never believes or boasts that he is a healer. When King Asa consulted physicians instead of calling for the help of God through His priests he was promptly punished: he "slept with his fathers" (II Chron. 16:12, 13).

According to this conception it is to God that the sick appeals for the cure of his ills; before Him man prostrates himself to invoke salvation. From the belief in the healing power of God followed the duty to obey all Divine precepts with a scrupulousness no less thorough than that of other nations in their use of magical prescriptions, and to carry out rules of sanitation with the same exactness and fervid faith that had to accompany all religious practices. This was the cause for the rapid development of sanitary legislation, what we may call the first codification of hygienic regulations, among the Jews.

In this recognition of a supreme Divine law and in the abolition of magic beliefs and practices lies the importance of the monotheistic concept for the evolution of medicine in Israel. All the medical practices described in ancient Egyptian and Babylonian texts are originally magic practices, though they may sometimes be rooted in experience; they belong to the religious rites of strange gods and are, therefore, forbidden to the people of Israel. Medicine is poorly represented in early Jewish literature because whenever the magic medicine of Babylonia and Egypt appeared in ancient Judea it was rigorously proscribed and suppressed. Nevertheless, it cannot be denied that in Israel, as among others, some of these practices persisted through the centuries, and it is interesting to see the traces of these practices in the biblical literature. In Scripture, however, they appear under a different aspect: they are made compatible or at least not in conflict with the monotheistic concept.

Traces of magic are evident in the following few examples: The snake was worshiped throughout the Orient as a healing god and was the object of a widespread magic cult; in the Bible he appears in the stories of the Garden of Eden and the brazen serpent. The persistence of this cult is proved by the fact that the serpent had to be destroyed by King Hezekiah to prevent its worship. The Babylonian "Sabbath" is quite likely connected with the magic concept familiar to all Oriental peoples of the unlucky number seven and its multiples. Circumcision was practiced among many primitive peoples and it can probably be explained as an attempt to substitute some bloody rite for human sacrifice. The story of Abraham and Isaac in Gen. 22 is surely connected with the substitution of animal for human sacrifice. Circumcision was prescribed also in Egypt, but only for the priests and upper classes. In Judaism, however, as is repeatedly affirmed in the biblical text, the entire people are regarded as priests, regardless of caste or class; all regulations therefore are imposed equally upon everyone.

The belief in the action of malignant demons (masculine, *shedim*, feminine, *lilit*) which cause insanity, sore throat, asthma and many other ills was prevalent among the Jews. The application of pieces of parchment bearing biblical verses or exorcistic formulae was supposed to aid recovery. A man of God could transfer leprosy from one person to another (II Kings 5:27); with a number of charms the priest could "dry up the thigh and swell the stomach" of the sinful woman after he had made her drink the water in which had been immersed a curse written on a piece of parchment. In epidemics one could obtain relief by sacrificing the sinful person (II Sam. 21:5-6); the prophet Elijah (I Kings 17:21-22) brought a dead child back to life by breathing into its mouth, a rite similar to a Babylonian practice. The proceedings described in Leviticus 14 and the ceremony of the blood of the paschal lamb are founded on analogous practices elsewhere.

In the course of time, after the general acceptance of monotheism, all these beliefs, traditions and customs were absorbed into and filtered through the moral and legislative system of Judaism and the theocratic principle definitely governed the moral, social and political life of the people and the evolution of its medicine. Thus the use of the phylacteries (*tephillin*) and the *mezuzot*, originally ancient apotropaic rites, assumed the character of a religious law of moral importance.

The concept of purity is of eminent importance in biblical legislation. Physical purity is put on a par with moral purity, and it is not admitted that heart and mind can be pure without cleanliness of the body. The aim of Jewish religious precepts, to which the hygienic regulations belong, is purity before God. Hygienic regulations were imposed on the people by law with the authority characteristic of Divine maxims and in the form of religious ceremonies. Some of these regulations existed also in Egypt and in Babylonia, where they had a magic character; but in the Bible the religious distinction between pure and impure is a standard for everyday life. Whoever becomes impure (*tame*) for whatever reason, whether he had committed an evil deed or had contracted a contagious disease, or had touched a corpse, could become pure (*tahor*) with the help of exactly prescribed practices in which bathing was of the greatest importance. The hygienic law of impurity after contact with corpses, of women during and after the menstrual period, of those affected with gonorrhea and leprosy, arise from a purely religious concept. This originally mystic apparatus is important and soon assumes a symbolic character. David prays to God: "Wash me thoroughly from mine iniquity, and cleanse me from my sin" (Ps. 51:4). The sinner is told: "For though thou wash thee with nitre, and take thee much soap, yet thine iniquity is marked before Me" (Jer. 2:22).

This makes it amply clear that the practice of purification signified to the common mind also a cleansing of oneself from the sin of moral transgression. The well-known passage in the Psalms, "I will wash my hands in innocency" (26:6), takes on symbolic significance, and later the purifying bath is transformed into the symbolic baptism.

No Jew could enter the Temple without being pure, that is to say, without having first taken a bath if he had been in contact with impure persons or things or had done anything which made his body impure. Even before reading the Law, which was regarded as a daily duty for every Jew, a bath had to be taken. The same rite was prescribed after every ejaculation.

The people of Israel did not have professional physicians, although an empirical medicine flourished among the Jews as everywhere else. In ancient times there was no physician (*rophe*) even on such occasions as that of embalming Jacob's body. For embalming, Joseph called physicians from Egypt. That is why we can derive only fragmentary information on medical cures and medicines from the Bible. The prophets appear to have acted in some cases as wonder-healers, but it is evident that their healing activity was closely connected with an intense moral and religious suggestion.

Later we find mention of physicians and we learn that they enjoyed great esteem. Jesus, the son of Sirach (180 B.C.E.), says, "Honor the physician according to thy need of him with the honor due unto him because verily the Lord hath created him." The physician is always considered as the intermediary, working with the help and carrying out the Will of God.

The Jewish physician who appears in the pages of the Talmud is not a specialist like the Egyptian medical men of whom Herodotus speaks. The physician of the Talmud prescribes cures for internal diseases, but he is also a surgeon who binds the patient on the table and has with him a bag which contains his instruments. He is able to heal wounds with herbs, to give dietetic prescriptions and to give the patient a potion (*samme deshinta*) for inducing sleep during the operation (Baba Mezia 83b). He opens an abscess and, we are also told, is able to open the skull with a trephine to operate on the brain and to close the wound with the skin of a squash (Tosefta Ohalot 2.6). Amputation of limbs and of gangrenous parts is performed. The physician is expert in the treatment of fractures and it is expected that he be ready to work with knife, plasters, bandages and internal remedies alike.

Gynecological or obstetrical interference of physicians was not admitted,[1e] but midwives (*meyalledet*) played an important role. Some of them are quoted in the Bible; for instance, at the delivery of Rachel (Gen. 35:17) and of Tamar (Gen. 38:28). In the Mishna the midwife is called *hakama*, the "wise woman," like the *sage femme* of the French. Embryotomy was also to be performed by a midwife if a surgeon could not be reached, but not by a pagan because she might kill the child.

Unlike other legislations, the Jewish law holds the physician responsible only if he has intentionally hurt his patient, not if an error occurred. This is commented upon by Pardo, quoted by Preuss, with the observation that "if the physician should be made responsible for every mistake nobody would follow this profession. The judgment and punishment are reserved to God."

There is a clear distinction in the Talmud between the physician, *rophe*, and the bloodletter (*umman*). The latter was considered a worker and had a very low social position. The Talmud regards him unfavorably: he can never become a leader of a community nor take part in the election of king nor High Priest. It may be noted that the profession is despised also among the Arabs. Circumcision, the most frequent surgical operation, was generally practiced by the physician or by a specialist who was called *mahola*, later *mohel*. Circumcision was a religious act of fundamental importance; it was, however, prescribed that children who were sick or bleeders should not be circumcised.

The anatomical knowledge in biblical and talmudic literature was derived only from occasional inspection of corpses and from the examination of the internal organs of slaughtered animals in order to determine their condition. That human dissections should have been practiced in ancient times is very unlikely. The fear of hurting a corpse (*niwwul met*) was certainly the most important reason making dissection impossible. Not even exhumation and inspection of the corpse was permitted. For the same reason embalming was forbidden. A similar attitude is responsible for the custom once general in Egypt of throwing stones at the embalmer as a punishment, after he had performed his work. It is, however, told of the pupils of Rabbi Ishmael (about 100 C.E.) that they boiled the corpse of a prostitute who had been condemned to death, in order to learn what was the number of bones in the human body (B. Bekorot 45a). This method of treating bones seems to have been usual in antiquity, and was expressly forbidden by Pope Boniface VIII in 1301.

In his scholarly work, Preuss has given an exhaustive summary of talmudic anatomy. We may only say briefly that the esophagus, the larynx, the trachea, the lungs, meninges and the genital organs are described, and the spleen, kidneys, liver, heart and intestines are often mentioned. Blood constitutes the vital principle; muscles are referred to as *basar* (flesh) and the tendons as *giddim*. The body was thought to have 248 bones and 365 tendons. One bone called *luz*, placed somewhere in the vertebral column, was believed to be the nucleus from which the body would be reconstructed at the resurrection of the dead. This ossicle, which was said to be indestructible, was searched for by the anatomists of the Middle Ages without success.

It may be noted that, according to the texts, the liver, the origin of the blood, is the most important organ and the center of life. The heart is not the center of the circulation, but the seat of the soul (Aristotelian doctrine). The anatomical and physiological information about the brain is very poor. During sleep, the brain, they believed, could be removed without breaking any bones, through the nose or, according to the Talmud, through the auditive channel.

The importance of dreams was generally accepted. R. Eleazar stated, "There is no dream without significance," and R. Hisda said, "A dream which is not interpreted is like a letter which is not read." In general the opinion of the teachers is against this interpretation of dreams which, however, are given prominent place in the Bible and Talmud. Very interesting is a statement by R. Joshua b. Hananja that all dreams can be realized according to their interpretation and that for any dream there are not less than twenty-four interpretations which may be correct.

The popular view of etiology of diseases was analogous to that of the Babylonians and Egyptians. The belief in the stars was widespread as was the belief in the influence of the evil eye (*ayyin ha-ra*), which also is probably of Babylonian origin, and is widespread in our times, too, especially among the Mediterranean peoples.

It was generally believed that a mortal disease lasted five days. In therapy the incantation (*lahash*) played an important part, but it was considered part of the occult practices of which no sign can be found in the Talmud. Amulets and charms were very much in use and were not forbidden, probably because this practice was too deeply rooted in the traditional belief of the people. What we know of the spread of epidemic diseases in biblical and later times proves that the idea of contagion, its dangers and the need to overcome them by isolation was well known to the Semitic peoples. In the story (I Sam. 5:1-2) of the capture of the Ark of the Covenant by the Philistines, who carried it to the temple of Dagon, is found the description of an epidemic of bubonic plague (their punishment for the desecration), and when the Philistines decided to return the Ark they offered at the same time a symbolic gift of five golden emerods and five golden mice to the God of Israel. Here is remarkable evidence of the importance attributed to rodents in the spread of the plague in very ancient times. In another epidemic (II Kings 19:35) we are informed of the mortality caused when the angel of the Lord killed 185,000 of Sennacherib's soldiers (705-681 B.C.E.). In the story of this pestilence, which is referred to by Herodotus (II, 141), the rat also plays an important part. In fact, according to Egyptian tradition, the Assyrians were decimated by the god Ptah, who was represented in the temple of Thebes with a rat in his hand. It is probable that the importance attributed to animals as transmitters of disease also had a magic origin.

Leprosy received considerable attention in the biblical books. The Hebrew word for leprosy is *tsaraat*. The number of writings on this subject and of commentaries on the thirteenth chapter of Leviticus, where the diseases are described, is so great that we may easily believe that many discussions took place in order to identify the disease. All the descriptions of the symptoms and of the sanitary measures justify the conclusion that leprosy is meant. Preuss closes his study on the subject with the statement that it is at least a probable identification: we have to admit, however, that the term was often used for other clinical phenomena such as psoriasis, eczema and various inflammations of the skin, perhaps even syphilis. The person suspected of being a leper was brought to the priest; if he found that the *nega*, the affected place, was white and appeared to be deeper than the surrounding skin, he declared that it was really *tsaraat* and that the patient was impure. Note that the symptomatic signs here quoted are the same that the Arabian physicians, especially Avicenna, describe as characteristic of leprosy. It is the white sign, *morphoea alba*, which is recognized as such plus the fact that the hair on the spot turns white.

Among the other more frequent diseases in biblical times were dysentery, dropsy, apoplexy, and mental diseases like Saul's. That certain venereal diseases were common in Judea is apparent from the strict hygienic regulation for those with an "issue" (gonorrhea?). According to certain interpreters, the biblical account of the plague of Baal-Peor should be regarded as the story of a syphilis epidemic as a result of the Hebrews' visit to the brothels of the Midianites. The terrible disease killed twenty-four thousand people. This interpretation, however, is not at all sufficiently proved.

Other diseases like *shehim* (universal eczema), the disease of King Hezekiah (pharynx abscess?), the *baale raatan* (leprosy) are difficult to identify. The information about their symptoms, their course and their recovery is neither clear nor the same in the different accounts; only hypothetical suppositions, therefore, can be advanced.

The sect of the Essenes, which was formed about 150 B.C.E.,[2a] deserves to be mentioned. The Essenes were Jews who lived a monastic life; they included the *Therapeutae* and *Hemerobaptists*, and it seems that the former particularly practiced medicine in some mild form of suggestion. Some believe that the name "Essene" is derived from the Aramaic *Asa* (he healed), corresponding to the Greek Therapeutae. In the therapy of the Essenes prayers and pious formulae were very important and we may compare this medicine with the Christian conventual medicine which arose in the Middle Ages at the time of the foundation of the monasteries.

The Essenes were considered saints, wonder-healers who cured by faith and by words. They practiced medicine in order to perfect the soul and make it more accessible to Divine truth and Divine health. By conjuration they drove hostile spirits out of the patient's body. The Mishna (Bekorot 4:4) refers to Teudas, who was acquainted with conditions in Alexandria as a worthy physician, and Josephus (*De Ant. Jud.* VIII, 2:5) describes the cure of a possessed person in the presence of the Emperor Vespasian by Eleazar, an Essene. A root allegedly recommended by King Solomon and endowed with healing properties was introduced into the nose of the sick man. The Essene pronounced the name of the wise king and a magic formula and the patient recovered. The laying on of hands was practiced and amulets were used.

It is interesting to note that in the Talmud some animal products, in some kind of primitive opotherapy of magical origin, are prescribed. A man bitten by a mad dog was given the omentum of the dog to eat; parts of the liver and the spleen of animals were prescribed for diseases of that organ.

From many biblical passages it is clear that the art of the apothecary was not unknown to the ancient Hebrews. In Ex. 30:22-26 we read: "The Lord spoke unto Moses, saying, 'Take thou also unto thee the chief spices, of flowing myrrh five hundred shekels, and of sweet cinnamon half so much, even two hundred and fifty, and of sweet calamus two hundred and fifty and of cassia five hundred, after the shekel of the Sanctuary and of olive oil a hin. And thou shalt make it a holy anointing oil, a perfume compounded after the art of the perfumer.' "

Mandrake also was a very popular remedy among the ancient Hebrews and it was generally believed to be useful in promoting conception (Gen. 30:14). Nitre was employed as a cleansing agent and oil was used to dress wounds, bruises and sores (Is. 1:6). Many remedies, especially ointments, are referred to by Roman authors as being used by Jews.[3]

Jewish philosophers and physicians participated actively in the flourishing science of Alexandria and, at the time of the Ptolemies, enjoyed a great popularity. The Greeks were then inclined to admire these strange people and to accept them in the schools, in the public discussions, and in the professions; but in the first century c.e. anti-Semitism began to manifest itself and in the Christian empire it took on the form of a social persecution, despite the fact that Julius Caesar and the early Roman emperors followed the policy of the Hellenistic princes to patronize the Jews and grant them full liberty. Jews adopted Greek as their mother tongue and Jewish students inherited the intellectual legacy of Greece.[4a] The inner conflict of the Jewish-Hellenistic intellectual world is reflected in the work of Philo.[5a]

Biblical-talmudic literature permits us to trace the evolution of medical thought among the Jews from fundamental magical beliefs and conceptions common to all primitive peoples to an empirical and religious medicine. How great the influence of Greek medicine was is difficult to determine. The Talmud, as already observed, is a collection of discussions and of laws and their interpretation but not of medical doctrines. We may, therefore, pass only a general judgment on the practice of medicine and believe that the Jewish physicians of those days accepted the diagnostic rules and therapeutic means prescribed by Greek medicine, but did not care too much for the clinical doctrines or the theoretical scientific explanations that were the characteristic elements of Greek science. Jewish physicians acknowledged the facts, but were cautious and skeptical in adopting doctrines which appeared to them heterodox from the point of view of their strong religious faith, whose central belief was expressed by the words of Divine revelation, "I am the Lord, that healeth thee" (Ex. 15:26).

In his memorable speech at the International Medical Congress in Rome (1894) on "Morgagni and Anatomical Thought," Rudolf Virchow said: "In the Middle Ages the Jews and the Arabs certainly had a definite influence on the progress of medical doctrine. Recent discoveries have brought to light Hebrew manuscripts which demonstrate with how great a diligence and scholarship the Jewish physician of the Middle Ages was active in the preservation and development of medical thought."

The role played by the Jews during the Arab conquests of the Mediterranean is an impressive one in the history of the Middle Ages and the pre-Renaissance.[6a] In contact with the Arabs, among whom they were respected physicians, teachers and counselors, Jews were perhaps the only aliens able to understand the language and the psychology of the people whose victorious banners flew over southern Europe for six centuries. The Jews enjoyed complete freedom in their professional and intellectual activity. They became the advisers of sultan and caliph and once more played the historic role to which they seemed destined by the geographical position of their native country, and by their constant relations with different races and creeds as a result of war, persecution, dispersion and exile. These events had surely given the Jews their peculiar orientation of thought, for they had to adjust themselves to different conditions, laws and customs, and to adopt or reject new beliefs. Theirs was the passionate desire to seek out the true and the best everywhere, as far as possible to placate hostile powers and conciliate opposing opinions. They were, or tried to be, according to the biblical prescription, the seekers and teachers of truth, always fighting with others and themselves for their beliefs. They were acquainted with Greek philosophy and medicine and had felt deeply the influence of the Alexandrian schools. To the Arabs, a people of warriors and fanatic believers whose contact with Western civilization was a violent one at the outset, the Jews gave the first lessons in classic philosophy and science.

At first not only difference in religion but also difference of language was the chief difficulty in the evolution of a Jewish medical literature. The Jews in the Diaspora used Hebrew in their writings, but always needed new words for their scientific vocabulary. These they took from the language of the country they inhabited; and thus the glossaries or dictionaries arose. Later, however, when the Jews in exile forgot the Hebrew language, or used it only in their prayers and in their religious studies, it was necessary for the teacher and scholar who had to address a larger public to write in the language of the country; hence the fact that for the most part Jewish physicians, among them the most illustrious like Maimonides, wrote their medical works in Arabic.

In the evolution of Arabic medicine, the study of classical medical authors went hand in hand with philosophy, and both subjects were entirely free from any religious influence. Thanks to the meticulous researches of Moritz Steinschneider, we now know how great was the service of Jewish translators to science. In their hands was the light of ancient scientific knowledge and by adding it to Arabic culture they saved Greek science for the Occident. The most important classical writings in philosophy, astronomy, mathematics and medicine were translated from Greek into Arabic. Hardly fifty years after the conquest, a Babylonian Jew translated a medical work from Syrian into Arabic.[7] In the latter half of the seventh century Masarjawaih translated many medical texts. These were later retranslated by other Jewish scholars from Arabic into Hebrew and Latin. The activity of Jewish physicians among the Arabs had a decisive influence on the progress not only of Arabic but, later, of Western medicine also.

Although the bulk of Jewish Arabic scholarship consisted of translation from and assimilation of Greek works, it did far more than that. They not only transmitted ancient knowledge, but also contributed to the creation of new knowledge.

The most remarkable Jewish medical writers were Isaac Israeli (850-950 C.E.) and Moses Maimonides (1135-1204). The first was physician to the Caliph Obaid Allah and wrote philosophical works on the elements. According to Harry Friedenwald, Israeli's medical works were the greatest contributions of Arabic Jewish physicians. His full name was Abu Yakub Ishak ibn Suleiman al Israeli, and his works, soon translated into Hebrew and Latin, had widespread fame. He was known among the Arabs as Israeli, in the Western medical world as Isaac Judeus. His works were translated into Latin by Constantinus Africanus, the learned monk who was said to be of Jewish origin. Israeli's most famous books, which are frequently referred to as classics, and which served as textbooks at the school of Salerno, were the books on Urine and Fever, the Opera Isaaci Judaei *"medicorum monarcha,"* were published in Latin in Lyons (1515).

Moses Maimonides (Abu Imram Musa ibn Maimun), born in Cordova in 1135, fled to Fez in 1148 because of the persecutions by the Almohades; later he went to Palestine and finally to Cairo, where he settled in 1165 and soon became famous as philosopher and physician. He was the physician of Saladin and his son, and head of the Jewish community of Egypt; he died in 1204 and was buried in Tiberias. As George Sarton says, his influence was far reaching in space and time. He occupied a prominent place among the great thinkers of the Middle Ages and the forerunners of scientific medicine. That he was the greatest exponent of a new trend of thought is shown by the influence of his work on Albertus Magnus and Thomas Aquinas. He practiced medicine with intelligent observation of his patients, with love and faith, and strictly followed the moral precepts of the Bible. His fame as a healer is still a living tradition throughout the Orient. Even today his synagogue in Cairo is considered an especially sacred shrine, the sick go there to pass the night in order to speed their recovery. And to his tomb at Tiberias, on the shore of the Sea of Gennesaret, a pilgrimage of the sick takes place even at the present time. Many places in different countries enjoy similar fame, but this is the only case in history where the physician himself is regarded, after his death, as a wonder-healer.

This is not the place to estimate the importance of Maimonides as philosopher and religious writer.[8a] We may only say that his profound comprehension and fervid admiration of the scientific achievements of the Greek philosophers and physicians, and, on the other hand, his firm belief in the teachings of the Law, led him to attempt a conciliation between Aristotle and the Bible. This is evident also in his medical works, in his fight against astrology and superstition, in his deep understanding of the importance of a psychological therapy, in his high conception of the duties of the physician. To understand and with a free mind to discuss new currents of thought without abandoning the laws and the traditional beliefs of the Jewish people caused perpetual conflict in the soul of Jewish scholars at all times. In his stupendous activity as commentator of the sacred books, as revered judge in all religious problems, and at the same time as teacher and physician, Maimonides followed the example of the prophets and the great Rabbis. In the evolution of scientific thought in the Mediterranean, which was the center of civilization for twenty centuries, the work of Moses Maimonides had a decisive influence.

Among the distinguished medical translators we may mention the following: Moses ibn Tibbon (*c.* 1283), a Provençal physician who translated many works of Maimonides and Rhazes; Nathan Ha-Meati of Cento (Italy), who lived in Rome (1229-1283) and translated, among other books, the *Canon* of Avicenna and the *Aphorisms* of Hippocrates with the *Commentaries* of Galen. Hasdai ibn Shaprut, minister to the caliph of Cordova (*c.* 960), with the aid of a Greek monk translated Dioscorides into Arabic.

Faraj ben Salim was one of the most prominent translators of the thirteenth century. He was very likely connected with the school of Salerno, and must have been in close touch with Charles of France, who ruled Sicily from 1266 to 1285. The Latin translation of the medical work by the Arabic Ali ibn Jazla, which was published in 1532, was dedicated to the king. Faraj was one of the first Jewish doctors to translate from the Arabic directly into Latin. (One of the most popular translators was Gerard of Cremona, who put into Latin the *Canon* of Avicenna [a book which vied in popularity with Aristotle's and Galen's works] and the treatise on surgery by Abulcasis, which was widely read in the Occident until the end of the Renaissance.) The influence of Jewish physicians in Spain and their activity in the schools of southern France (Montpellier), perhaps also in the school of Salerno which many Jewish students attended, was of far-reaching importance.

During the Middle Ages, when dogmatism and Scholasticism hampered the evolution of Western medicine, there occurred an interesting development in Jewish medicine. On the one hand, in certain circles mysticism began to be cultivated with a renewed vigor, and in the *Zohar*, the mystic's Bible, so to speak, appeared its most significant expression. Elsewhere in the present work, the nature of the *Zohar* is discussed.[9a] For our immediate purpose, however, and from one point of view, the work may be described as a mystic-medical book. According to the *Zohar*, the soul, invisible and imperceptible, has its seat above the cortex and governs life through the organs which are divided into two regions separated by a "heaven," the diaphragm. Through channels the Divine grace flows to all parts of the body, but the function of the organs ceases when sin stops the flowing of grace. Different pulses are described and mystically connected with the four elements. A supreme importance is attributed to generation: mysticism and the erotic are closely connected, and each organ receives mystic significance.

Another form of mystic medicine originated in the traditional trust of the devout in the counsel of holy men whose sayings have been preserved for centuries by pious Jews in the East and by the Hasidim. These mystical tendencies were not without influence on Jewish medicine: they introduced the medicine of the so-called wonder Rabbis, who were the revered advisers and medical counselors. Their cures, however, were generally limited to moral or hygienic prescriptions and to the use of certain prayers, formulae or cryptograms. The work of the wonder-healers flourished whenever superstition or belief in the occult was rampant. Generally their medical system was of only the mildest sort; its suggestive therapy was often educational, always fantastic, but certainly not dangerous.

Medicine among the Jews in Eastern Europe, especially in Poland, followed the same mysticism up to our time. In a book published by Jacob Koblenz (Offenbach, 1788) many wonder remedies are recommended, among them incantation with formulae in Hebrew and Yiddish. Throughout the Middle Ages certain prayers and biblical passages were very popular as remedies. The Psalms were often prescribed as cure. In the *Shimmush Tehillim*, which was often printed, we find passages which have to be recited to hasten delivery, passages for protection against eye diseases, against fever. Psalm 22:21 was believed to be especially efficacious against dogbite.

In 1720 a book, *Toledot Adam*, was published whose authors were said to be Elia baal Shem, Joel baal Shem and Simha Rofe; the work contains a great number of cabbalistic prescriptions. The name *baal Shem* was given to those who were believed to be cabbalistic wonder-healers. The most famous of them was the "Besht," Israel baal Shem Tob, the founder of modern Hasidism. It is evident that a continuous line leads from the mystic therapy of the Essenes to the therapeutic system of the wonder practices popular in the East up to the present.

In the schools of the Mediterranean countries, especially in Italy and France, Jewish physicians had always played an important role. The condition of the Jews in the Middle Ages had been one of great hardship and persecution, their activities were restricted; nevertheless, they had maintained an almost continuous line of medical practitioners. Friedenwald, who has written an interesting chapter on this period of Jewish medicine also, says that the history of the Jews in the Diaspora has been the longest in Italy, lasting over more than two thousand years. Already by the end of the fourth century c.e. the Jews had attained great prominence and many of them were official physicians, *archiatri*. Thereafter many church councils forbade Christians to call upon Jewish physicians or be medically treated by them.

However, many exceptions were made. In 1220 Pope Honorius III took under his papal protection Azzachus Avembenist of Barcelona, Jewish court physician to the king of Aragon. Pope Martin IV had at his court a Jewish physician who was a pupil of Rabbi Nathan of Montpellier and his example was followed by many Popes. The attitude of the Popes toward the Jew varied at different times, but in general we can say that the Jewish physicians continued in their prominent position.

In the thirteenth and fourteenth centuries Jewish physicians enjoyed the protection of the rulers and great fame even in Catholic Spain. One of these physicians was Judah Alfachar (d. 1235). He had the title of *Nasi* (Prince) at the court of Ferdinand III in Toledo, and held an important position not only as physician, but also as collector of revenues. Another was Sheshet Benveniste, physician and diplomat at the court of Aragon, with the same position and title. José Orabuena (fourteenth century) was the physician of the king of Navarre and for a long time the treasurer of the court. Both Samuel and Judah ibn Wakar were physicians who enjoyed the confidence of the ruling family.

In many Italian cities, especially in Ferrara, Mantua, and Genoa, many Spanish and Portuguese refugees were received and many Jewish physicians granted the privilege of practicing medicine.

The part that Jewish scholars and teachers played in the old schools is an important one. According to Theodor Puschmann, medicine was probably taught in the ancient Jewish academies of Tiberias, Sura and Pumbedita;[10a] in general, however, medicine was learned by a student serving as apprentice to a physician. Sometimes schools of higher learning grew out of a private undertaking. Dr. Harry Friedenwald quotes a prospectus, published in 1564, by David Provençal and his son Abraham, for a Jewish university to be established in Mantua where not only the sacred laws, but also Latin, logic, philosophy and mathematics were to be taught. Both father and son were physicians. It is not known whether this project was realized, but we do know of an early Jewish school in Paris where medicine was taught; in the fourteenth century, it is said, this school rivaled the university. Many medieval rabbis were physicians as well. The Gaon Hai in his *Moral Admonitions*, about 1000 C.E., urged the study of medical writings.[11a] There were teachers who had a large number of pupils and conducted private schools in which medicine also was taught.

The school of Salerno plays an important role in the history of medical teachings. Salvatore De Renzi tells the well known story of its foundation by four physicians: a Greek, a Latin, an Arab and a Jew (Elinus), each teaching in his own language. This is almost certainly a legend, but it is probably founded on ancient tradition. The Jews played an important part in medical education at this time; Donnolo, who practiced medicine in the tenth century, enables us, as George Sarton says, "to realize how the so-called school of Salerno gradually came into existence. Such men as Donnolo created in southern Italy that focus of medical syncretisms and eventually of medical teaching."

Among the Salernian teachers Benvenutus Grassus (Grapheus) deserves to be mentioned. His book on ophthalmology, translated into English by Casey Wood of Chicago, was very much studied and commented upon in the ancient universities. Benvenutus is believed to have come from Jerusalem and is described by Sarton as the most famous non-Moslem oculist of medieval times. Julius Hirschberg believes that he was Jewish, and in a Parisian codex his name reads "*Biem Venu Raffe.*" This name, Hirschberg observes, is very likely only a slight change from the Hebrew *Ha-Rophe.*

His book, *De oculis eorumque egritudinibus et curis,* was the most popular Latin textbook on the subject, as is shown by the number of copies which have been preserved in Latin, English, French and Provençal (twenty-two manuscripts and eighteen printed editions). It also had the distinction of being the first printed book on ophthalmology (Ferrara, 1474). Benvenutus makes frequent reference to his own anatomical studies on the structure of the eye, and his books constituted a notable advance over the work of the Arabic authors. For five hundred years it was regarded as the classical text on ophthalmology.

Salernian uroscopy found in Isaac Judeus, whom we mentioned above, its classic master. According to his book, the urine was carefully examined for color, density and content. For deducing some extremely important conclusions, the different kinds of clouds and precipitates which form after standing for a time were observed. Though this method had no diagnostic value, it was employed for centuries.

In France, in many cities near the Spanish border, where the influence of the Arabic-Jewish physicians was more deeply felt, there were Jewish schools where medicine was taught. Rashi (Rabbi Solomon ben Isaac, 1040-1105), born in Troyes, famous commentator of the Talmud, had a remarkable influence on scientific thought. At Lunel there was a flourishing medical school where Judah ibn Tibbon taught. These schools certainly had an influence on the University of Montpellier, which was perhaps as old as Salerno and for many centuries a leading medical school. Jean Astruc (1684-1766), who studied medicine in Paris and wrote a history of the medical school of Montpellier, stressed the importance of the Jewish participation in the early years of the university.

The first Jewish teacher of Montpellier, Jacob ben Makir ibn Tibbon (Prophatius Judeus), who lived from 1236 to 1304, was, according to Astruc, regent of the university for a long time. Among the outstanding Jewish doctors at Montpellier were the five doctors of the Saporta family, the first of whom, Luis, came from Lerida in Spain, lived first in Arles, then in Avignon, and became professor at the faculty in Montpellier (1506-1529). He was Charles VIII's physician and died at the age of 106. His great-grandson Jean was graduated in 1572 and became professor in 1577 and vice-chancellor in 1603. The Saportas were Marranos[12a] and for this reason were not admitted to municipal office. Friedenwald has suggested that Jean Astruc was also of Jewish origin. It is in any case interesting that the tradition of Jewish instructors and their influence on the development of medical studies at Montpellier survived so long. In the hall of the faculty there is a plaque in honor of Nathan ben Zechariah, master of the medical school in the thirteenth century.

After the Spanish victories and with the end of Arab domination in the Mediterranean, during the renaissance of art and science, the great migration of the Jews began. Among the Jews expelled from Spain were physicians and these now went to the Orient, especially to Constantinople, and to Italy and France.[13a]

The first universities were founded at the end of the thirteenth century; they were under the permanent supervision and control of the Catholic Church, and in 1431 the Council of Basel decreed that no Jew should receive a university degree. However, in many cases Jews were admitted as students to the medical schools, obtained a degree, and sometimes also were permitted to lecture.

With the Bull of Pius IV (1565), it was decided that no Jew should be admitted to any examination for the doctorate. The Venetian Senate, however, eager to protect freedom of learning and teaching at Padua, named a procurator who had the power to grant the degree regardless of the candidate's religion. The non-Catholics had recourse to the Counts Palatine, who had obtained the privilege of conferring academic degrees from the emperor. In 1616 the Venetian Senate decreed the foundation of a collegium which conferred degrees by authority of the Venetian state. Padua had the largest number of Jewish students, not only from Italy, but from foreign countries. Ismar Elbogen, in his article on Padua in the *Jewish Encyclopedia*, says that from 1517 to 1619 eighty Jews obtained the medical degree at Padua, and that in the next century there were about 150. At other universities, *e.g.*, in Rome and Ferrara and Siena, Jewish medical students were admitted and received their degrees.

This is not the place to enumerate all the Jewish physicians who had a part in the history of the ancient universities. Some names should be given, however, particularly those whose works were very popular in the medical literature of the Renaissance and are still considered remarkable contributions to medical progress.

Most interesting was Amatus Lusitanus, born in Castello Branco, Portugal. His parents were Marranos. He studied medicine in Salamanca, went back to Lisbon and later left Portugal for Antwerp. His reputation was so great that he was invited by Duke Hercules d'Este II to occupy the chair of medicine at the University of Ferrara (1540-1547). He lectured on Hippocrates and Galen, enjoyed the friendship of colleagues and scholars and participated in the dissections performed by the famous anatomist Canano. He later went to Ancona, where he finished his first *Centuria* in 1549. Amatus was often called to other cities as consultant; in May, 1550, he was invited to Rome to treat the newly elected Pope Julius III and later to attend the Pope's nephew, the ruler of Ancona. He spent several months in Rome and was very successful. In April, 1551, he finished his *Centuria II*, which was dedicated to Cardinal d'Este. In May, 1551, he dedicated his translation of Dioscorides to the Senate of Ragusa, where he wished to be appointed as city physician. His life was extremely adventurous, and it may be cited as an example of the persecution and the restrictions of Jews and Marranos at this time. In 1555 Pope

Paul IV was elected, and new decrees were promulgated forbidding Jewish physicians to treat Christian patients and ordering the yellow badge for all Jews. The Inquisition began its ruthless program, a great number of Marranos were arrested and subjected to torture, many burned at the stake. The house of Amatus was broken into and all valuables, including books and manuscripts, were looted.

Amatus repaired to Pesaro, where the Duke of Urbino was very friendly toward the refugees; from there he went to Ragusa, where his fame was soon established. But the persecution was not yet ended. In 1558 he left Ragusa for Salonica, where he found a large practice, and wrote the *Centuria VII*. It is believed that he died in 1568 of the plague that was raging in the city. His great work, the translation and comments on Dioscorides, was published in 1553 and contained many criticisms of the book by Matthioli, a famous pharmacologist, who replied to the criticisms in a violent way.

The medical writings of Amatus are interesting chiefly because they cite a great number of case histories, followed by discussion in the form of a dialogue between himself and other scholars. In therapy Amatus stressed the importance of proper diet and general hygiene; he describes more than twenty surgical cases and made an important contribution to the surgical treatment of empyema. He reveals in all his work an extensive knowledge of medical literature and a fine power of observation. He was emphatic in his opposition to superstition and magical treatment. In the history of the discovery of the valves of the veins, Amatus, who worked in Ferrara with the famous anatomist Canano, played an important part.

Another of the great physicians in the medicine of the Renaissance was Abraham ben Samuel Zacutus, also known as Diego Rodrigo, born in Salamanca about 1452. After the expulsion of the Jews from Spain he fled to Portugal and later to Tunis, where he was taken prisoner. He was not only a well-known physician, but also an author of astronomical and historical works of which the *Almanach Perpetuum* and the *Astrolabe* are the best known. It is certain that Vasco da Gama, the first navigator who made the voyage around the Cape of Good Hope, and had a long consultation with Zacuto before leaving, utilized his books during the navigation.[14a]

His great-great-grandson, well known under the name of Zacutus Lusitanus, born in Lisbon in 1575, took the doctor's degree in Salamanca in 1596 and went to Amsterdam in 1625. He published two interesting books of medical history, but he was considered chiefly as a great clinician. He was one of the first to describe blackwater fever, and made an important contribution to the knowledge of syphilis. His *Opera Omnia* were published in Lyons in two large volumes (1642-1644) and were dedicated to Louis XIII of France.

Jewish physicians were among the pioneers in the East Indies. The most illustrious of this group was Garcia da Orta, born in the last years of the fifteenth century in Elvas, Portugal. He studied medicine in Salamanca, then became professor of logic in Lisbon and in 1534 finally sailed for India. He lived in Goa, where he carried on extensive study of medicinal herbs. His work, *Colloquios dos simples e drogas e cousas medicinae de India*, appeared in 1563 and was immediately recognized as the first and most important contribution to the knowledge of Indian flora. The *Colloquios* had a great influence on the study of tropical medicine and of pharmacology. Da Orta's life was one of great affliction: he was tried as a Marrano by the Inquisition, but judgment was pronounced twelve years after his death. In Portuguese literature he is recognized as a most distinguished representative of the natural sciences.

To the same group of medical pioneers in the East Indies belongs Cristoval d'Acosta, a Marrano who was born in Mozambique in about 1515. He embarked for India in 1568 and stayed there four years. He devoted himself to botanical studies and tried to complete the work of his predecessor, Garcia.

Of medical importance in the sixteenth and seventeenth centuries was the family de Castro, of Spanish and Portuguese origin. Many physicians belonged to this family, the first, and one of the most distinguished, being Rodrigo de Castro (1550-1627). He was the author of a book on gynecology, *De Universa Muliebrium Medicina* (Cologne, 1603), which went through many editions.

One of the physicians in this family deserves special mention. Orobio de Castro, born in Portugal in 1620, studied philosophy and medicine in Seville, became professor of philosophy and later took up medical practice. He was very well known and had a large family. He was denounced to the Inquisition by a servant, who had been whipped for stealing, and was thrown into prison and tortured. The story of his suffering, quoted by Friedenwald, is found in the history of the Inquisition by Philipp van Limborch, who had it from Orobio's own mouth: "A linen garment was put over his body and drawn so very close on each side that it almost squeezed him to death. When he had overcome this torture and persisted in his refusal to confess, they tied his thumbs so very tight that the blood spurted out from under the nail." The whole procedure was repeated for a long time and always with new instruments. Finally he was condemned to perpetual banishment. He left Spain, went to Toulouse and then to Amsterdam, where he publicly reverted to Judaism, took the name Isaac and became one of the leaders of the community.

From the Renaissance up to modern times, that is, to the epoch of the Emancipation,[15a] Jewish physicians practiced medicine all over Europe, as we have seen, in great numbers and often with success; however, everywhere, with the exception of Italy, they were persecuted and interrupted in their activity. Some acquired great fame and were also physicians and counselors to kings and princes; sometimes they also had important positions and special privileges; but these were always exceptional cases. In general their life was insecure and it was not possible for them to have an important part in research and in teaching because admission to the great hospitals, the medical schools and general practices was either entirely forbidden or permitted only sporadically for short periods and under the protection of some enlightened ruler.

In the seventeenth century, when religious struggles were raging in Germany, the Italian universities were the only ones where Jewish students could obtain the doctor's degree. For a long time Padua was the school to which they came from all countries of Europe. The first Jewish student, a certain Bonacosa, was inscribed in Padua's medical school in 1255. Elijah Delmedigo (1460-1497) was one of the first among the famous Paduan professors; he taught also in Florence and Perugia. But it was in the sixteenth or seventeenth century that Jews from Germany, Austria and Poland flocked in great numbers to the university. For two centuries all Jewish doctors permitted to practice in Germany and Austria held their degrees from Padua.

It was only in 1782, after the so-called Act of Tolerance by the Emperor Joseph II of Austria, that Jewish students were admitted to the Austrian universities and as candidates for the doctor's degree in the medical schools. However, even when other German universities—such as Giessen, Halle, Goettingen—opened their doors to the students it was very difficult for them to be admitted to the academic profession. Jewish doctors were often referred to as "Italian doctors" because most of them had studied in Italy, and it was only at the beginning of the nineteenth century that a change occurred, that they were free to practice and were given the opportunity to become assistants and professors at the universities.

In the nineteenth century, when emancipation of the Jews was proclaimed after the French Revolution, Jewish students began to attend universities in ever-increasing numbers, and their love for medical studies became intense. Although medical students and professionals faced all kinds of hardship, which made it difficult and sometimes impossible for a Jewish scholar to attain a chair at a university, many distinguished scholars appeared in every branch of medical science.

It is not the purpose of this chapter to list the names of all the eminent physicians who exerted a decisive influence on medical progress. We wish merely to call to the attention of the reader the fact that some specialties, such as immunology, clinical medicine, otology, ophthalmology and psychiatry, seem to be the fields in which the talents of Jewish scholars were particularly noteworthy. In all branches of medicine, however, we find Jews who are prominent.[16a] Especially in the German and Austrian universities there was a growing number of Jewish teachers and students during the era of Enlightenment. In the first part of the nineteenth century three outstanding scientists contributed to the progress of clinical medicine; Moritz Heinrich Romberg (1795-1873), the founder of modern neuropathology who became professor in Berlin in 1838, Robert Remak (1815-1865), professor in Berlin (1859), the founder of microscopic anatomy of the nerves, and Ludwig Traube (1818-1876), who ranks among the greatest clinicians of the period.

Jacob Henle (1809-1885) was among the most famous teachers at German universities. Already in 1840 he postulated the existence of micro-organisms as the cause of contagious diseases. Hermann Lebert (1813-1878), professor in Zurich (1853) and Breslau (1859), was among the first to use the microscope for pathologic-anatomical investigations. One of the greatest clinicians and brilliant teachers of the Vienna school was Heinrich von Bamberger (1822-1888), who taught in Vienna (1872) and was the teacher of Edmund von Neusser. His textbook on diseases of the heart is considered classic. Ludwig Lichtheim (1845-1928), professor in Berlin and Koenigsberg, first described subcortical aphasia, which is named after him; Ottomar Rosenbach (1851-1907) was called to Berlin in 1893 and described the reflex neurosis named after him, as well as the sign of Rosenbach.

Oscar Minkowski (1858-1931) was the founder of modern metabolism research to which Adolf Magnus-Levy (b. 1865) brought an outstanding contribution. Georges Hayem was professor of clinical medicine in Paris (1893-1911) and first described the blood platelets (1878).

In psychiatry Joseph Breuer (1842-1925) was, with Sigmund Freud (1856-1940), the founder of the revolutionary doctrine of psychoanalysis: certainly one of the most famous scientific teachings of the nineteenth century. Cesare Lombroso (1836-1909) gave a new impulse to the study of delinquency and his doctrine has had a mighty influence on legislation in modern times. Abraham A. Brill (1874-1948) of Columbia University was the advocate of psychoanalysis in America and contributed to the development of the doctrine.

In pediatrics Edward Heinrich Henoch (1820-1910) and Heinrich Finkelstein (b. 1865) were leaders in the progress of modern pediatrics in Germany; Max Kassowitz (1842-1913) did basic work on hereditary syphilis and rickets; Bela Schick (b. 1877) is universally known for research in the fields of diphtheria and scarlet fever. The pioneer of pediatrics in America was Abraham Jacobi (1830-1919), and among prominent American pediatricians are men like Isaac Arthur Abt (b. 1867), professor at Northwestern University; Abraham Levinson, with his studies on cerebral spinal fluid; Henry Koplik (1858-1927), the founder of a

Children's Pavilion at the Mt. Sinai Hospital in New York, discoverer (1896) of the initial spots in measles (Koplik spots); and Alfred Fabian Hess (1875-1933), with his splendid studies on rickets and scurvy.

Among the founders of modern neurology were Moritz Benedikt (1835-1920) and Moritz Rosenthal (1833-1889) of Vienna. Emil Redlich (1865-1930) discovered the pupillar phenomenon that is named after him. Otto Marburg (b. 1874) of Vienna and New York, pathology of the nervous system, Arnold Pick (1851-1924), with his investigations of the anatomy of the brain, and Ludwig Edinger (1855-1918) are considered among the most eminent research workers and teachers in this field. Hermann Oppenheim (1858-1919) of Berlin was the first to give attention to post-traumatic neurosis.

In dermatology and syphilology the names of the founders of the Viennese school of dermatology, Ferdinand von Hebra (1816-1880) and Moritz Kaposi (Kohn) (1837-1902) immediately come to mind. Paul Gerson Unna (1850-1929), professor in Hamburg, won great fame through his anatomical and biochemical works in the field of skin pathology.

Among the great surgeons of the nineteenth century Anton Woelfler (1850-1917), a pupil of Billroth, was the first to perform gastroenterostomy (1881). To the Vienna school belong also Robert Gersuny (c. 1844-1924) and Julius Schnitzler (1865-1939). James Israel (1848-1926) in Berlin was a leader in urologic surgery and in this field Otto Zuckerkandl (1861-1921) was an outstanding teacher. Mario Donati (b. 1879), professor of surgery at the University of Milan, is generally recognized as the leading surgeon in Italy.

Among the most distinguished gynecologists were Ernst Wertheim (1864-1920) and Joseph Halban (1870-1939), and more recently Bernhard Zondek (b. 1891), whose name became famous through the Aschheim-Zondek reaction (1927).

Among the great ophthalmologists are the names of Hermann Cohn (1838-1906), professor in Breslau, and Harry Friedenwald (b. 1864) of Baltimore who is well known also for his splendid work in medical history. A leader of scientific otology was Adam Politzer (1835-1920), professor in Vienna, founder of a famous school to which disciples came from all over the world. The best known among the pupils of the Vienna school were Heinrich Neumann (1873-1939) and Robert Bárány (b. 1876), professor at Upsala. Among the prominent representatives of laryngology are Karl Stoerk (1832-1899) of Vienna and his pupil M. Hajek (1861-1941), a brilliant surgeon who accomplished a fundamental work. Sir Felix Semon (1849-1921) occupied an important rank among English laryngologists.

Modern physiology was enriched by the work of Rudolph Heidenhain

(1834-1897), Moritz Schiff (1823-1896) of Frankfort, professor in Florence, and Jacques Loeb of Chicago (1859-1924). Among the great research workers in general and experimental pathology were Salomon Stricker (1834-1898), professor of experimental pathology in Vienna, and Arthur Biedl (1869-1938), professor at the German university in Prague, whose book on endocrinology (1910) is of fundamental importance. The revolutionary current of thought that upset the fundamental conceptions in therapy was determined by three great scholars: Carl Weigert (1845-1904), Paul Ehrlich (1854-1915) and August von Wassermann (1866-1925). Weigert introduced new staining methods and wrote a new page in the history of the pathology of the tissues; Ehrlich discovered the doctrine of immunobiological relations and was the founder of chemotherapy with the introduction of Salvarsan (1910) in the therapy of syphilis, marking a new era in the history of the struggle against that disease. Wassermann's work on toxins and antitoxins was one of the most important contributions to the science of immunity. The reaction that is named after him made his name famous. Still another, Fernand Widal (1862-1929), is well known for the reaction of typhoid fever (1896).

In 1908, together with Metchnikoff, Ehrlich received the Nobel Prize. Robert Bárány received it in 1945, and Otto Meyerhof in 1923 for his work on the physiology of the cell. In 1930 the prize was awarded to Karl Landsteiner of the Rockefeller Institute in New York for his discovery of the blood groups, and in 1931 to Otto Warburg for his work on the respiratory ferment. Otto Loewi of Graz, and now of New York, received the prize in 1936 for his outstanding work in biochemistry.

In the field of the history of medicine two great Jewish scholars did very important work as teachers and leaders: Charles Singer (b. 1876)[17a] of London published a great number of studies on the history of medicine in antiquity and the Middle Ages, and was the leader of the modern English medical historical school, and Max Neuburger (1868–1955), professor of the history of medicine in Vienna, then in London, brought a new impulse to historical studies with his classic book on the history of medicine, with the foundation of the institute for the history of medicine in Vienna, and with a great number of historical works illustrating the relation between the great school of Vienna and the progress of medicine in other countries.

The consequences of the spread of anti-Semitism in the past decade and its terrifying development after the rise of Hitler in Germany, and of the occupation of so great a part of Europe by the victorious Nazi armies, are well known. Jewish professors and physicians who in all the occupied countries had held prominent positions were jailed or exiled; the activity of the medical schools in Germany, in Poland, in France, in Italy and in the Balkan countries was halted; the books of the Jewish scholars were burned. It was a fight which threatened to destroy freedom of science and of opinion, but for many reasons it concentrated first on the Jews, their lives and their activities as professionals and teachers. The end of the war with the victory of the United Nations has changed the situation, but the loss is irreparable. The work that was accomplished by Jews in the European countries was destroyed or wiped out. At the same time, however, what had occurred in the Middle Ages was repeated. The persecuted Jews found a haven partly in Palestine, where scientific medicine began to rise and flourish, partly in other countries, especially in the United States. Just as in the Renaissance Jewish scholars and physicians found a shelter in Italy and the possibility of learning and teaching in the Italian universities, so during World War II a great number of them came from Germany and the occupied European countries to the United States and began here the reconstruction of their life and of their work.

Once more, as in ancient times, during the struggles in the Mediterranean countries and the Arab conquests, the Jewish scholars have been the intermediaries of scientific thought between the East and the West and have upheld freedom of teaching and of learning.

To summarize, then: The evolution of medical thought among Jews followed the line of development to be observed among other peoples, from mystic and magic to empiric and sacerdotal, with this important difference, that the moral and ethical influence of monotheism always predominated in Judaism. The moral and sanitary laws assumed the character of religious prescriptions, and it was among the Jews that hygienic laws were imposed and accepted with the authority of divine commands.

Despite long centuries of persecution in various countries, in two great epochs, during Arab supremacy in the Mediterranean and the Renaissance in certain cities and under certain conditions, the study and practice of medicine flourished. This development of medical studies culminated in the nineteenth century after the Emancipation. In certain periods and regions, particularly in the Orient where Jews were segregated and hounded, the intensive cultivation of traditional mystical beliefs led to a development of medicine like that of the Essenes, the cabbalists, the Hasidim. Note, however, that even when magical practices are suggested and accepted as an escape from misery, as an expression of hope in supernatural salvation, this magic is always practiced with words and scripts, with formulae and sayings, and never degenerates into cruel or obscene acts—a rather frequent and sometimes characteristic phenomenon among other peoples. The mystic medicine of the Jews always had a metaphysical, I might say a literary, character; it involved essentially a subtle discussion and interpretation of words and letters, symbolic signs and numbers. There is not a trace of black magic and its attendant practices in the history of Jewish occult, suggestive medicine.

The history of medicine among the Jews reflects the history of the Jewish people, its sufferings, its struggle for liberty and religious freedom. In this distress the Jews return to the pure virtue of the faith that heals, and which represents the highest and last hope of sufferers. What contri‑ bution the Jews made to the science and practice of medicine was made through the centuries by thousands and thousands of believers, of scholars, of martyrs, of teachers and of humble practitioners, obedient to the moral law that constitutes the basis of the Jewish religion. They were inspired by a passionate desire for knowledge and longing for the truth. The Jews have been called the People of the Book: they have been in medicine as in many fields of intellectual activity diligent scholars, great searchers and learned teachers, able to command the respect and the esteem of their pupils and their patients even during the most difficult conditions of their own lives.

NOTES

[1a Throughout this chapter there is material on persons mentioned also below, cf. Charles Singer "Science and Judaism."]

[1b Cf. above Judah Goldin, "The Period of the Talmud (135 B.C.E.-1035 C.E.)," pp. 141 f.]

[1c The Talmud often refers to children born by Caesarian section, i.e., the law that forbids circumcision of such a child on the Sabbath.]

[2a Cf. ibid., pp. 116-117.]

3 Celsus, Lib. V., 19-22.

[4a Cf. above Elias J. Bickerman, "The Historical Foundations of Post-biblical Judaism," p. 93.]

[5a Cf. above Alexander Altmann, "Judaism and World Philosophy," pp. 957 f.; see also above Ralph Marcus, "Hellenistic Jewish Literature," pp. 1107 f.]

[6a Cf. above Cecil Roth, "The European Age in Jewish History (to 1648)," pp. 222-224.]

7 Steinschneider, M., Arabische Literatur. Introd.

[8a Cf. Altmann, op. cit., pp. 972 ff.]

[9a Cf. above the chapter by Abraham J. Heschel, "The Mystical Element in Judaism."]

[10a Cf. Goldin, op. cit. pp. 178 ff.]

[11a Cf. above Julius B. Maller, "The Role of Education in Jewish History," p. 1245.]

[12a Cf. Roth, op. cit., p. 236.]

[13a Cf. Singer, op. cit., pp. 1402 ff.]

[14a Cf. above Anita Libman Lebeson, "The American Jewish Chronicle," p. 447.]

[15a Cf. above Roth, "The Jews of Western Europe (from 1648)," p. 264.]

[16a Cf. Singer, *op. cit.*, pp. 1424 f.]
[17a Cf. Singer, *op. cit.*]

BIBLIOGRAPHY

The most exhaustive treatise on the history of Jewish medicine is the book of Julius Preuss, *Biblisch-Talmudische Medizin* (Berlin, 1911), which is up until now the most authoritative work on this subject. The history of Jewish hygiene has been dealt with accurately by Max Grunwald (ed.), *Die Hygiene der Juden* (*mit Bibliographie*) (Dresden, 1911). Mystic medicine of the Cabbalists has been studied by Karl Preis, *Die Medizin in der Kabbala* (Frankfort, 1928). An important contribution to the history of Jewish physicians in ancient times and in the Middle Ages has been made by Harry Friedenwald, *The Jews and Medicine* (Baltimore, 1944, 2 vols.), in which the author throws light upon the work of great scholars, translators, and research workers. An account of the development of ancient Jewish medicine is summarized in Maurice B. Gordon, "Medicine among the Ancient Hebrews," in *Isis* (Bruges, 1941), Vol. 33, Pt. 4. For the history of circumcision see J. Almkvist "Zur Geschichte der Circumcision," in *Janus* (Leyden, 1926), Vol. 30:86, 152, and D. Schapiro, "La Péritomie; étude générale et particulière," in *Janus* (1923), Vol. 27:161, 241, 259 and 1924, 28:120, 193. On the conception of pathology see Adolphe Lods, "Les idées des Israélites sur la maladie, ses causes et ses remèdes," in *Beihefte zur Zeitschrift fuer die Alttestamentliche Wissenschaft*, 40 (Giessen, 1925), pp. 181-193. The prescriptions for contagious diseases have been studied by E. W. G. Masterman, "Hygiene and Disease in Palestine in Modern and in Biblical Times," in *Palestine Exploration Fund, Quarterly Statement* (London, 1918), pp. 13, 56, 112, 156, and 1919, p. 27; also Georg Sticker, *Vorgeschichtliche Versuche der Seuchenabwehr und Seuchenausrottung* (Zurich, 1924). Among the older historians whose works deserve to be consulted, see Thomas Bartholin, *De Morbis Biblicis miscellanea medica* (Frankfort, 1672), and Richard Mead, *Medica sacra* (Amsterdam, 1749). Other subjects of Jewish medicine have been treated by L. Kotelmann, *Die Ophtalmologie bei den alten Hebraeern* (Hamburg und Leipzig, 1910); Max Neuburger, *Die Medizin im Flavius Josephus* (Vienna, 1919); Ludwig Ventianer, *Asaph Judaeus* (Strassburg, 1916-1917, 2 vols.). On the plague see Otto Neustaetter, "Where did the Identification of the Philistine Plague (I Sam. 5 and 6) as Bubonic Plague Originate?" reprint from *Bulletin of the History of Medicine* (Vol. XI, No. 1, Baltimore, 1942, pp. 36-47). The subject of the ritual food prescription among the Hebrews has been studied by S. I. Levin, and E. A. Boyden, *The Kosher Code of the Orthodox Jew* (Minneapolis, 1940).

CHAPTER 32

SCIENCE AND JUDAISM

By Charles Singer

1. THE GREEK FOUNDATIONS OF SCIENCE

Science has been defined as a search for judgments on which *universal* assent is attainable. Nevertheless, despite this universal element, there is a relation between science and certain particular phases of civilization. The association of science with Judaism is a special case of a general rule, for only in certain periods in the millennia of Jewish history and only in certain localities has there been scientific development. Association of science with Judaism has never been worldwide. In considering these special occurrences we must often dwell on individual achievements; yet much more significance should be attached to those aspects of Jewish thought which have favored the growth of scientific ideas. For this consummation we must await an adequate sociological history of the human vehicles of Judaism.

The first step toward the scientific attitude must be the realization that Nature works in regular and ascertainable ways. Barbarous men, children, even animals, show trust in Nature. They behave as though confident that day will succeed night, that the moons will wax and wane, that summer heat will follow winter cold, that the processes of life will run in certain cycles. But to accept Nature's ways is very different from seeking systematically to know her ways. That form of inquiry appears only late and is always exceptional. It is first clearly discernible among the Greeks of the sixth century B.C.E. Without some consideration of science among them its course among the Hebrews cannot be intelligible.

The Greeks, it has often been remarked, had no sacred writings. The forwardness of their science contrasts with the backwardness of their religion. At a very early stage they concluded that the world is subject to laws that are ever further discoverable. This was the *scientific idea*. Their science and ours grew out of it.

Before the close of the sixth century B.C.E. Greek thinkers were seeking universal applications of conceptions derived from their science. They distinguished as a universal principle *physis*, a word which survives in *physics, physiology, physical,* and *physician.* Physis meant at first growth or development, the essential element of all existence. This, it was seen, always follows definite rules, notably those of development and dissolution, coming into being and passing away, generation and corruption. By transference physis came to be regarded as this rule of change itself, and so something near to what we now call a *natural law*.

As knowledge grew, natural laws were traced more widely. Men tried to discern what lay behind them. It was inevitable that some should see in these laws a common active element. Physis was thus given an independent existence. It was, in fact, more or less personified. Had the religion of the Greeks grown with their other activities, physis would perhaps have reached the rank of a god.

The change in intellectual outlook initiated by Socrates (470-399 B.C.E.) was as fundamental as the spiritual revolution heralded by the Unknown Prophet of the last chapters of Isaiah. Socrates was skeptical as to the validity of all human knowledge, and his thought turned away from physical philosophy. His predecessors, concentrating on the physis of the sensible universe, had developed a system of physics. But his interest, like that of the Hebrew prophet, was in conduct. Seeking guidance for right conduct he concluded that man's soul partook of the Divine. He rejected the whole structure of the physicists and regarded as futile all attempts "to pursue knowledge for its own sake"; instead he stressed "practical wisdom" (*phronesis*), leading to right action. It was *phronesis* against *physis*. Phronesis also tended to personification under various names.

From the conflict between the followers of the Socratic revolution and the physical philosophers arose the main streams of Greek thought. One of them leads on to Plato and to the *doctrine of ideas*. Its ultimate development was the complete indifference to worldly happenings of certain later "Neoplatonists." The physical philosophy, on the other hand, often assumed dogmatic forms, as with the followers of Epicurus (342-270 B.C.E.), the title in Rabbinic writings for the most refractory type of paganism. It is significant that both the Neoplatonic and Epicurean schools ultimately became inimical to science, while neither was friendly to current religion. The development of both science and religion is thus historically associated with other systems of thought which chose a middle way. For science this was the path of Aristotle and his successors which drew heavily on the physical philosophers. For religion it was that of the great Judeo-Christian system of thought, which borrowed not a little from Neoplatonism.

"That nothing," says Aristotle in his *Metaphysics*, "comes to be out of that which is not, but everything out of that which is, is a doctrine common to nearly all the natural philosophers." Only if this is so is investigation of the material universe worth while. Such a view would have found itself in immediate conflict with a religion that had reached the coherent and vocal level of that of the Hebrews. As it was, the inevitable clash among the Greek-speaking peoples was deferred until their philosophy was confronted with Judeo-Christian thought.

But within the philosophic realm itself there was from the first a tension. As this increased it burst its bonds and ultimately brought ancient philosophy to an end. In a world in which, to use the phrase of Lucretius (*c.* 60 B.C.E.), "nothing is ever begotten of nothing by divine will," it must be that all things act by rules inherent in everlasting matter. What, then, is left that is our real conscious selves?

The question was variously answered. Christians and Jews, as well as those who hovered between the creeds of these, were in agreement in giving the answer—"man's immortal soul." But the Stoic, the most "religious" of the philosophic schools, could, like the Epicurean, only reply with the saintly emperor, Marcus Aurelius (C.E. 121-180): "Thou hast subsisted as part of the whole. Thou shalt vanish into that which begat thee, or rather thou shalt be taken again unto its Seminal Reason, by process of change." Such thinkers could take little interest in Nature. In our day men learn Nature's ways to control her, but that time was not yet. Epicurus would have us know only so much about her as would remove all fear of supernatural interference. Stoic and Epicurean alike show a flagging scientific curiosity. Men were weary of the world. Why seek to know more of Nature, the pitiless, the tyrannical, the irresistible machine? It is better to forget her demonic majesty. We are on the brink of the "Dark Ages." Let us return, then, to the Hebrews and their ideas on Nature.

2. THE BIBLICAL CONCEPT OF NATURE

The earlier parts of the Old Testament know nothing of natural law. Natural events, and especially the more dramatic and destructive, thunder and whirlwind, drought and flood, plague and famine, reveal God expressing Himself. "The voice of the Lord is upon the waters: the God of Glory thundereth" (Ps. 29:3). Even in a less anthropomorphic setting natural events are still acts of Him:

> Who hath measured the waters in the hollow of His hand,
> And meted out heaven with the span,
> And comprehended the dust of the earth in a measure,
> And weighed the mountains in scales . . . ?
> I form the light, and create darkness;
> I make peace and create evil;
> I am the Lord that doeth all these things.
>
> (Is. 40:12, 45:7 *c.* 540 B.C.E.)

Such a work as Job of the fourth century B.C.E. shows a definite development. The author dwells on the wonder and intricacy of the rules by which God governs His world. *His* world! If Job does not comprehend them, how can he hope to grasp their purpose?

> Dost thou guide the heavens to know the laws,
> Dost thou establish the dominion thereof in the earth? (Job 38:33.)

These laws are invoked as proof of the power, wisdom and goodness of God, for exactly the same reason as in the famous *Bridgewater Treatises* of more than two thousand years later. The recognition of the natural laws in Job is an echo of the main preoccupation of Greek thinkers when the book was being written.

In the later "Wisdom literature," the contact with Greek thought has become quite evident.[1a] The general features of physical philosophy have been grasped and the concept of the relation of God to the material world has become modified. The laws of nature are now administered by the elusive Wisdom (*Hokmah*) or the awesome Word (*Memra*).

The gracious form of the one or the stern features of the other are almost as difficult to discern as those of *Physis*, whom they both in part resemble. Wisdom has divine attributes, being omniscient and omnipresent. "She reacheth from one end of the world to the other and ordereth all things aright" (Wisdom 8:1). The Word is specially responsible for the catastrophic events. "While all things were in silence . . . Thine Almighty Word leaped down from heaven as a fierce man of war and brought Thine unfeigned command as a sharp sword and filled all things with death" (Wisdom 18:12-16).

This new turn of thought has become self-conscious and polemic. It is set against Greek physical philosophy, wherein various "first principles" had been adopted. Thales proposed "water," Heraclitus "fire," Pythagoras the "circling stars," Anaximenes "air," other philosophers a subtle world essence, or *pneuma*, "winds," while astrological science, coming in from Babylonia, claimed the actual complex mathematical order of the heavenly bodies as the motive power of all things. The Wisdom of Solomon, written by an orthodox Jew in Alexandria about 100 B.C.E., inveighs against all these:

> Surely vain were all men in their natures,
>   and without perception of God
> Who could not, from the good things that are seen,
>   know Him that is.
> Neither by giving heed to the works
>   did they recognize Him who hath wrought them,

But either fire [Heraclitus], or wind [the Pneumatists]
    or the swift air [Anaximenes],
Or circling stars [Pythagoras], or raging water [Thales],
    or the lights of heaven [the astrologers]
They deemed the gods which govern the world.

(Wisdom 13:1-2)

3. Nature in Later Jewish and Judeo-Christian Thought

Much of the pseudepigraphic and apocalyptic literature written by Jews of the later pre-Christian or first post-Christian centuries shows the same tendency. This may be traced in the Book of Jubilees, the Apocalypse of Baruch, the Book of Enoch, and the New Testament Book of Revelation.

That this movement, even under philosophic guidance, became indifferent to or contemptuous of scientific spirit is shown by the Alexandrian Jewish thinker Philo, contemporary of Jesus. His trend was Neoplatonic and away from the study of phenomena. He represents a separation of religious Judaism from an interest in phenomena. Judaism and physical philosophy have diverged completely.[2a]

Philo was a conscious "philosopher" in the Greek sense. He betrays this in several ways not found in earlier Jewish writings. The biblical record and Rabbinic doctrine treat God as a separate and very personal existence outside the world, which He had produced by definite acts and continues to guide. But the God of the Hellenist Philo is without emotions or attributes and consequently without name—changeless, imperceptible by man, self-sufficient, simply existent. This God of the Platonic idea could not act upon the world, or create or guide it, though He might set it going once and for all. The old Hebrew view was as incompatible with that of Philo as with that of the Stoics.

Under these circumstances Philo resorted to a new form of an old device. He introduced an existence between God and the world. Physis, Phronesis, Wisdom, the Word (*Memra*) were previous attempts. Philo's device was the Logos. They have now become a regular pantheon! Any of them must turn men's thoughts away from phenomena. Logos and the Memra have other parallels in Rabbinic literature and their further development appears clear enough in the Gospel of St. John, in Acts and in other New Testament works. Science cannot live at close quarters with any of these divine emanations. Judeo-Christian thought lost interest in Nature and her phenomena.

There was yet a further reason for the "flight from phenomena" in later Jewish as in early Christian thought. Since the Socratic revolution some Greek thinkers had regarded the material universe as essentially without worth. They opposed *Nous,* mind, Soul or Spirit to *Hyle,* Brute Matter. The idea of the worthlessness of the material world could be made to fit Hebraic doctrine and the biblical story of the Fall of Man. The view could and did thus enter Jewish and Judeo-Christian thought. Though Philo, like other early Jewish and Judeo-Christian writers, seeks to avoid the conclusion that the world is evil, his efforts, like theirs, are not very successful. His claim, like theirs, is verbal, not real. The "sins of the flesh" became a theological commonplace which passed over naturally, along with the *Logos,* into Christian thought. It is a main theme of apocalyptic literature, Jewish, Christian and intermediate.

Paul's teaching was greatly influenced by this idea, which he extended to include a physical basis of sin. "We know that the Law is spiritual; but I am carnal, sold into the power of sin" (Rom. 7:14). Christianity thus followed Judaism in turning away from phenomena, if for an allegedly different reason. Paul does not conceal his contempt for Greek physical philosophy. It is not so much false as trivial and irrelevant and, before the fearful issue of salvation, therefore impious.

Another common Judeo-Christian thought emphasized this contempt. The end of the world was at hand. Now in much Greek physical philosophy this world is one of a long series. Its end is but the beginning of another like to it, re-formed from its "elements." But in the Judeo-Christian conception the end of the world must involve the destruction of the elements themselves. "The day of the Lord will come as a thief. At that time the heavens will pass away with great violence and the *elements* will be dissolved with heat, and the earth and the works that are in it will be burned up" (II Pet. 3:10) [author's italics]. With that in mind who could regard phenomena? Belief in an imminent Messiah was as deadly for science as was the apocalyptic vision. The combination of the two was instantly fatal. "The day of the Lord" rang the death knell of Greek science. We see it most dramatically in that Jewish work in the New Testament known as Revelation. Judaism, having approached the scientific view of the world, led or escorted Christianity in a retreat therefrom. Opportunity for reunion was not to come again to Judaism for a thousand years and to Christianity for longer.

4. Nature in Rabbinic Thought

Thus Jewish thought for the first nine centuries of the Christian era is almost entirely devoid of the scientific element.[2b] A certain amount of calendarial debate and discussion on well-worn lines of the physical bases of purity rules covers most of the area. Many have vainly searched the Talmud for evidence of scientific interest or scientific method. The excursions have been unfruitful. Those who have written on science and

medicine in Rabbinic literature have merely shown that such studies
have left some faint trace on Jewish life in talmudic times. What they have
not shown is that science took any part, either integral or incidental, in
Rabbinic *thought*. It could not have been otherwise. The basic conception of
Torah is that every phase of knowledge must be brought into relation with
or drawn from an existing and accepted system. Science can exist and
even flourish *by the side of* any thought-world, religious, mystic, even
magic, but it cannot exist *within* any world but its own. Any attempt to
force it to do so is rapidly fatal to it. While science could and later did
develop in the same civilization as Torah, it could not and did not take
root in a mind or a culture already fully occupied by that concept. A
quotation on natural law from the Talmud itself illustrates this incompatibility or rather impossibility:

"*Give ear, ye heavens* (Deut. 32:1). God said to Moses, 'Say unto
Israel; Consider the heavens which I made to serve you, Have they ever
failed in their duty? [*lit.*, changed their nature.] Does not the sun rise
in the east and give light to the inhabitants of the earth? It rises and sets
with regularity (Eccl. 1:5), nay, more, it rejoices in doing its Creator's
will (Ps. 19:5).' *And let the earth hear My mouth's words* (*Ibid.*).
'Consider the earth which I created for your service. Has it ever changed
its nature? Have you ever sown wheat, and has it yielded barley? Or does
the cow not thresh and plough? or the ass not bear his load and walk?
Does not the sea observe the limits which I have assigned to it? (Jer.
5:22). If *these* have not changed their nature, these which, unlike you,
were created neither for profit nor for loss; if, unlike you, when they do
well, they receive no reward, if when they sin, they are not punished:
they have no care for their sons and daughters, yet these have not changed
their nature: but you if you do well, you receive reward, if you do evil,
you receive punishment, and you have care for your sons and daughters.
How much more ought you in no wise to change your characters? [*i.e.*,
from good to bad, in view of Deut. 32:5, 'You have corrupted yourselves.']' "[3]

Nature, as thus represented, elicits no curiosity and commands no more
affection than a machine. There is no hint of the infinite variety and beautiful complexity of the physical world, still less of its exploration as a continual delightful adventure. No scientific interest could be evinced by those
whose lives were passed within the talmudic universe of discourse. Scores
of Greek names occur in the Talmud, but not one is of a man of science.
Even Aristotle is unmentioned. Saadia Gaon (882-942), founder of
Rabbinic philosophy,[4a] who had read some Aristotelian works in Arabic,
avoids naming him. The discussion of secular science was for many
centuries resisted by Rabbinic authority.

Philosophy and science ultimately obtained entry into Israel via Islam.

Christendom was some two hundred and fifty years behind Israel and received the gift largely through Israel. Science, having reached Israel, was certainly seized upon and developed with astonishing vigor. Medicine was followed with particular zeal and success. On this point certain observations should be made on which we shall need to enlarge later.[5a] First, in the Middle Ages science among Jews was almost confined to the Mediterranean area. Second, in Spain, where science first and mostly flourished among Jews, science obtained a foothold before talmudic studies came fully to occupy the Jewish intellect. Third, Jewish devotion to medicine can be explained partly as surrogate for Jewish interest in conduct, partly as a way of livelihood for those interested in science, partly as a result of social pressure which excluded Jews from other professions. There is, in fact, hardly a Jewish scientific personality before the nineteenth century that did not practice medicine.

The question remains why within Judaism scientific interest declared itself only on certain occasions. These were (a) within Islam and neighboring countries from the tenth to the thirteenth century with a trailing off into a mainly translatory period from the thirteenth to the fifteenth; (b) as part of the Marrano incident in the sixteenth century and (c) in northwestern Europe for about a hundred years from shortly before the mid-nineteenth century. The answer must cover not only these phenomena but also certain others, notably the substantial absence of the scientific element within Judaism at other times and places, the late entry of science into the Jewish orbit, the intensity of Jewish application to certain sciences, and the character of the non-Jewish cultures associated with the three main scientific outbursts among the Jewish people. Discussion of these matters is best deferred till the incidents themselves have been reviewed.

5. HEBREW-ARABIC SCIENCE

Until the ninth century scientific interest is hardly encountered in Jewish writings. Only the Egyptian astronomer Masha alla ("What God wills," c. 770-820), known to Latins as Messahalla, has left any impression on later ages. He was the first Jewish man of science (if he was a Jew) to write in Arabic. There is little evidence that before him Jews were especially prominent even in medicine. The great scientific movement within Judaism arose as part of the renaissance of learning in the Arabic-speaking world.

The Arabic language was cultivated by Jews as a consequence of the Saracen conquests. From the mid-ninth century it was familiar to all who dwelt in Moslem lands. Arabic writing rapidly replaced Aramaic, which from about 300 C.E. till that time had been used for both secular and sacred purposes. For centuries scientific works were written by Jews in

Arabic. Yet while Jews spoke Arabic throughout the Islamic world they did not everywhere develop science. The overwhelming Jewish interest was talmudic throughout the Asiatic Arabic-speaking world. Science took no root there. But the Talmud did not effectively reach the West till the tenth century and by then science was established among the Jews of Tunis and Egypt and was appearing in Spain.

In Spain, Arabic continued in general use among Jews, even in the Christian zone, till the end of the twelfth century. Spanish Jews preserved some living acquaintance with the language till the fourteenth century. Even then, when Arabic had ceased to be spoken by Spanish Jews, it was still used for learned purposes by Western Jewish scholars. But from the beginning of the thirteenth century, the output of original literature in Arabic by Jews ceased to have value. Original scientific works in Hebrew, however, continued to appear, while Jews were actively translating into Latin from both Arabic and Hebrew until the sixteenth century.

We must not expect in the Hebrew-Arabic scientific literature that vast variety and range associated in the twentieth century with the word "science." The experimental and the biological sciences were absent from the whole Western medieval scheme, both Latin and Arabic. In effect we meet but three kinds of works that can be called scientific: (a) cosmological, passing into philosophy, (b) mathematical often associated with astronomy and astrology, and (c) medical with rare excursions into biology.

Science of its very nature tends to become superannuated. The cosmology of the Middle Ages is now an interesting fossil that has left some quaint remains in our language. But our own mathematical and medical systems are natural outgrowths of the mathematical and medical systems of the Latin Middle Ages, which were in their turn not only influenced by the Hebrew-Arabic material but were actually founded and based upon it and extended very little beyond it. The transmission of this material and its development were largely the work of Jews. Indeed, it is fair to present medieval European mathematics and medicine as special developments of the Hebrew-Arabic system. The cosmological systems of the Latin Middle Ages also bear constantly the impress of Jewish thoughts.

6. The Kairouan School, Ninth and Tenth Centuries

Of the departments in which Jews have attained distinction, medicine comes first. The ancient Jewish contribution to hygiene, both social and individual, has often and rightly been stressed. But, although highly important, it was not made by the scientific method or presented in the scientific spirit. Therefore, it does not concern us here. But during certain periods from the ninth century Jews have contributed to scientific medicine to a degree out of all proportion to their numbers.

This phenomenon is first observable in Tunis under a local dynasty that ruled from Kairouan for more than a century from 800. One of these sultans invited to his capital the Egyptian Jewish (?) physician Isaac ibn Amram (d. 908). His writings show a definite scientific interest. He had Jewish pupils and a most distinguished Jewish successor, Isaac ben Solomon Israeli (c. 855-c. 955), Isaac Judeus of the Latins. He is the first Jewish scientific figure whose life course is known.

Isaac Judeus, like Isaac ben Amram, who was perhaps his teacher, was born in Egypt and like him may have received direct some remnant of the Greek scientific tradition of Alexandria. He practiced as an oculist in Egypt where he served the sovereign. Later at Kairouan he was physician to several of its rulers. A Moslem historian describes him as a man of the loftiest character and worthy of the highest respect, for, though much occupied about the court, he was quite indifferent to wealth and personal advancement. He lived childless and unmarried—a most unusual thing among medieval Moslems or Jews—and died at over a hundred.

This able and saintly man wrote many philosophical treatises. That *On Definitions* introduced some of the favorite terms of the Latin Scholastics which they adopted from it. Isaac's larger philosophic work expounds Aristotelian physics. Beside these he wrote *On Diet, On Urine, On the Pulse, On Simples,* and above all his great book *On Fevers.* This last, perhaps the best clinical treatise of the Middle Ages in any language, was widely read until the seventeenth century.

Isaac's medical works early influenced the Latin West. His pupil's pupil was Constantine the African, who began life in a Jewish environment at Kairouan. When that city was sacked by the Bedouins in 1057 he made his way to Sicily. There he became the Oriental secretary of the Norman invader, Robert Guiscard, who afterward conquered Salerno, in the shin of Italy. At Salerno, alone in Christian Europe, there was the remnant of a medical school in the reawakening of which Jews had some part. Constantine spent the last ten years of his life as a monk at Monte Cassino, turning into Latin the writings of Isaac and of one of Isaac's pupils. They were the first Arabic medical works to be translated into Latin and introduce the long supremacy of Hebrew-Arabic medicine in Latin Europe.

Isaac's *On Fevers* was, for centuries, the constant companion of every European physician and was, in fact, one of the most genuinely useful in his library. Isaac's work influenced the Persian Avicenna (987-1037), whose vast *Canon of Medicine* was and is extremely popular among the Arabic-speaking peoples. Through it certain of Isaac's views can be traced throughout the world, for the *Canon* was early translated into every literary language, and several times into Hebrew.

The centuries from the tenth to the twelfth are the flowering time of the scientific movement within western Islam. In this Jews had a large share. Science had come to Spain in the ninth century, when the life of Spanish Jews was still isolated from that of their fellow countrymen. The entry of Jews into science opens, as might be expected, with medicine.

7. THE IBERIAN SCHOOL, TENTH TO TWELFTH CENTURIES

Of medical writings of classical antiquity the most popular, during the first Christian millennium, was that *On materia medica* of the Asiatic-Greek Dioscorides (first century C.E.). In 948 the Byzantine emperor sent to the Spanish caliph a finely illustrated manuscript of this work. Since no one in Spain knew Greek the caliph asked the emperor for an interpreter. In 951 he sent him a learned monk Nicholas who gave open instruction in Greek at Cordova to many physicians and scholars. Among them was the Andalusian Jew, Hasdai ibn Shaprut (915-970).[6a] He joined Nicholas in translating the Dioscorides manuscript into Arabic. These two were thus the first Westerners to introduce Greek writings directly to the Arabic-speaking world. Their version of Dioscorides still circulates in the Orient.

Ibn Shaprut was a man of great and varied activity. The shift of the Jewish intellectual center from Babylonia to Spain came in his time and was largely his work. He is the first of the brilliant Jewish scientific school that lasted till the thirteenth century. He was also instrumental in establishing talmudic study in Spain (*c.* 945).

A member of the scientific school initiated by Hasdai was another Andalusian—Jonah ibn Biklarish ("man of Biclar" or Valleclara) of Almeria. About 1080 he produced a dictionary of drugs in Syriac, Persian, Greek, Latin and "vulgar barbarian" (Spanish). It is the earliest of its kind. Jonah was one of the first Jewish scholars to learn Latin, which, it must be remembered, took with Christians the place of Hebrew with Jews. His knowledge of Greek probably reached him in a direct tradition from his fellow countryman and coreligionist ibn Shaprut.

A very different figure was Jonah's contemporary, Moses Sephardi. He was born in 1062 at Huesca in Aragon, then in Moslem hands. In 1096 Pedro I recovered it for the Christians and it became the Aragonese capital. Pedro was succeeded in 1104 by his brother Alfonso to whom Moses became physician. In 1106 Moses was baptized as Petrus Alfonsi (Alfonso's Peter), Alfonso being godfather. He wrote two astronomical works and another which makes a plea for astronomical observation. Alfonsi visited England, became physician to Henry I, and was intimate with Walcher, prior of Malvern, an ardent astronomer. In 1120 Walcher issued a work which introduces the use of degrees, minutes and seconds and contains certain exact observations. All are in the Arabic manner and had evidently been learned from Alfonsi. This represents the first impact of Arabian learning in England.

A figure as important for Jewish culture as Hasdai ibn Shaprut was the

Catalan Abraham bar Hiyya (d. *c.* 1150), known to the Latins as Savasorda, that is, *Sahib al schurta,* "chief of the police," which was his office. Until his time the Sephardic and the Ashkenazic Jews had been almost isolated from each other. They were in geographical but not social contact on the frontier between Catalonia and Provence. In 1112 these territories came under one ruler. Thus Savasorda could contact the Provençal Jews, among whom Arabic was unknown. To them he opened secular studies by translating Arabic scientific works into Hebrew. He was the first Arabic speaker to prepare works specifically for a non-Arabic speaking audience. Writing always in Hebrew, he and his successors gave to that language a special interpretive value which it retained for centuries. His chief scientific work was an encyclopedia of mathematics, astronomy, optics and music. In it he wrote: "I have not entered on this work of my own wish or for my own honor, but because in all the land of France there is no book on these sciences in the holy tongue. Therefore I have summarized what follows from the Arabic." A treatise by him on practical geometry (1116) was translated into Latin by his friend Plato of Tivoli (1145) as the *Liber embadorum.* It is the first introduction of Arabic trigonometry and mensuration to the Latin West and contains the oldest table of chords in a Latin work. It made a special impression on Leonardo of Pisa, the ablest mathematician of the Middle Ages, who embodied large sections of it in his *Practical Geometry* (1220).

Savasorda also left a treatise *On the Form of the Earth* which was turned into Latin and French. He wrote in 1123 the first Hebrew treatise devoted to the calendar and also Hebrew astronomical tables based on Ptolemy. His *Scroll of the Revealer* is an extensive treatise on the courses of the stars, treating Arabic astronomy with understanding and acuteness. In it he concludes that the Messiah will come in 1358! Savasorda, with his Christian friend, Plato of Tivoli, translated at Barcelona a whole series of Hebrew and Arabic works into Latin (1133-1145). The most important of them was Ptolemy's *Quadripartitum.*

The famous Abraham ibn Ezra (1092-1167), poet and scholar, was born in Toledo. In 1140 his life was devastated by the conversion of his son to Islam. Thenceforth he led a wandering life, first in Italy, where he composed many works, and then in Provence, where he was enthusiastically received. In 1158 he went to London, where he wrote an account of the intellectual state of the Jews in England. After much journeying he died at Calahorra in northern Spain. He has permanent importance as a forerunner of biblical criticism, and Spinoza derived much from him. Ibn Ezra seconded Savasorda in translating Arabic writings into Hebrew, thus opening secular literature to his coreligionists and especially to the Ashkenazim outside Spain. His wanderings helped to distribute manuscripts of his works.

Among Abraham ibn Ezra's scientific achievements is the introduction into Hebrew science of a decimal system of numeration with place value for the integers. This he did through his commentary on al-Kwarizmi's tables (Narbonne, 1160). He made certain other real additions to mathematics. Several of his astrological treatises became extremely popular. Among the works that he translated into Hebrew from Arabic were two treatises on astrology by Messahalla (Lucca, 1148). Incidentally, ibn Ezra provides some important information as to the passage of the decimal place-value system from Indian to Arabic mathematics.

The advent of Latin translations of Arabic scientific works aroused the emulation of Latin Christians. A number sought a knowledge of Arabic. All worked with Jewish aid. The pioneer was Adelard of Bath (c. 1090-1150) who visited both Spain and the Sicilies. His great achievement is the Latin translation of the astronomical tables of al-Kwarizmi. They included a table of sines and, with Savasorda's *Liber embadorum* of about the same date, introduced Arabic trigonometry to the Latin world. Adelard also made a version of Euclid. His popular *Natural Questions* is a compendium drawn from Arabic sources and largely from a debased "Aristotelian" work. The French-Jewish scribe Berachiah Ha-Nakdan (Benedictus Punctator), who was in Oxford in 1194, translated it from Latin into Hebrew. It was the first work so treated. This Hebrew version has since been translated into English. Parts of it have thus passed from Greek into Syriac, from Syriac into Arabic, from Arabic into Latin, from Latin into Hebrew and from Hebrew into English!

Throughout the medieval period the Latin West was eagerly seeking the treasures of Arabic learning. Jews, as translators and interpreters, played an overwhelming part in this effort. The best known of the native Spanish translators was Johannes Hispalensis, whose Arabic name, ibn Daud (ben David), was corrupted by the Schoolman into Avendeath (c. 1090-1165). He was born at Toledo, soon after that city fell into Christian hands (1085). He translated a whole host of astronomical and astrological works, among them those of Albumasar (786-886) of Bagdad, of Omar ibn al-Farrushan (d. c. 932) the Persian, of Thabit ben Kurra (826-901) the "Sabian" of Harran, of Messahalla (d. 815) the Jew of Egypt, of Messahalla's pupil Albohali (d. 835), of Alfraganus (d. c. 880) of Fargan in Transoxania, and the *Centiloquiam* of Ptolemy (c. 180). Avendeath provided an appreciable proportion of the mathematical, astrological and astronomical works in the medieval Latin library.

Notable among Avendeath's versions was the pseudo-scientific, pseudo-Aristotelian *Secretum secretorum*. This extremely popular work he prepared for a Spanish queen. There are copies and variants in hundreds of manuscripts in many languages, Hebrew included. It influenced serious scholars, and Roger Bacon wrote a commentary on it.

Most important of Avendeath's translations is the *Liber Algorismi de practica arismetrica*. This is an elaboration by Avendeath of an elaboration by a Moslem writer of the work of the Persian Muhammad ibn Musa al-Kwarizmi (fl. *c.* 830). In it our so-called *Arabic* numerical notation, in which the digits depend on their position for their value, is fully used in a Latin work for the first time. It is professedly based on Hindu knowledge. The "Arabic" numerals displace the clumsy Latin forms. The method was but slowly accepted. The whole of modern mathematics may be said to date from this translation but incorporation into our system was hardly complete until the sixteenth century. The word *algorism*, used in the Middle Ages for what we now call arithmetic, conceals the name al-Kwarizmi, *i.e.*, "the man of Khiva."

The most active translator from the Arabic was Gerard of Cremona (1114-1187). As a young man he came to Toledo to acquire Arabic that he might read Ptolemy's *Almagest*. He remained for life and superintended the translation of no less than seventy-one works, many, such as the *Canon of Medicine of Avicenna*, of great length. He worked with a whole school of Arabic-speaking Jews and Christians. They translated many scientific works by Jews such as Messahalla and Isaac Judeus. Perhaps the oddest work from his school is that of "Alchandrius." It is an astrological treatise which contains a number of Hebrew words. It seems based on a very early pre-Arabic original showing remnants of the ancient classical astrology. It may be the earliest scientific work of Jewish origin.

8. Maimonides. Second Half of the Twelfth Century

Contemporary with the twelfth-century Jewish movement in science in Spain and the West there was in Africa a comparable activity, for which Jews were almost entirely responsible. Several were physicians to the caliphs and published genuine clinical observations—a very unusual thing at that time. The letter of one to Saladin (d. 1193) has survived. Incomparably the most important of this school was the great thinker Maimonides, with whom Jewish philosophy culminates.

Moses ben Maimon, called Maimonides (1135-1204), was born at Cordova, and educated by a learned father and Arabic masters. When he was thirteen Cordova fell to the fanatical Almohades. Maimonides fled and, after wandering in Spain, Morocco and Palestine, settled in Cairo (1155) where he passed the rest of his life. He was a very successful physician and was attached to the court. His works, both medical and philosophical, became widely known, not only among Arabic-speaking peoples, but also among the Latins and Jews. He used Arabic for nearly all his writings.

Maimonides held that there can be no conflict between truths discerned by reason and those inculcated by revealed religion. The former are to be sought primarily in the Aristotelian writings, the latter in the Torah. He was convinced that both written and oral Torah contain philosophical material which harmonizes with Aristotle. We can here discuss neither his philosophical nor his religious views,[7a] but we are concerned with his presentation of the structure of the world. This had a share in determining both Latin and Jewish beliefs. With certain closely similar schemes it provided the framework within which alone medieval science could develop. It is set forth in his *Guide for the Perplexed*.[8a]

The universe in the Maimonidean-Aristotelian system is spherical, with earth fixed in the center, and the heavens revolving round it. The matter of our world is composed of the four elements, *earth, air, fire* and *water*. These, however, are not seen in their pure form on our imperfect globe. Each has in it an admixture of the other three. The three lighter elements tend to range themselves in concentric hollow spheres around the spherical earth. *Earth* being heaviest is naturally lowest, that is, at the center. Remove it from the center and its natural motion is in a straight line toward its own place, that is, downward toward the center; hence gravity. *Water* is next heaviest; its natural place is just above earth; like earth it tends toward the center. Above the water, which laves earth's surface, is the hollow sphere of *air*, concentric with that of earth and water. The natural motion of air is opposite to that of earth and water, straight outward, that is, upward, toward the circumference of the world. It cannot, however, go beyond the sphere of the lightest and purest element *fire*. The natural place of this is outside the other elements but like air it tends outward, that is, upward. Fire, too, forms a hollow sphere, the *Empyrean*.

All things formed by combination of the elements in this our lower world are subject to generation and decay. While nothing here is permanent, there is yet no annihilation, for all material change is but recombination of the four elements. Causes of all this generation and decay are the motions of the heavenly bodies that occupy spheres outside the sphere of the outermost element. Lowest of these heavenly bodies is the moon, next the other planets, next the fixed stars. The heavenly bodies are composed of a fifth substance, something purer than the elements, namely, the *quintessence* or *ether*. Heavenly bodies differ from things composed of the four elements in that they are not subject to generation, save at the Creation, or to decay, save at the final consummation and then at God's will. Their only change is *movement*, but this movement differs from that of things in our lower world and notably of the elements there. These have their natural movement of falling or rising in straight lines, but the heavenly bodies circle eternally round the center, for the circle is the perfect figure. They are set in a series of concentric transparent spheres which revolve and carry them in their movement:

> For ever singing as they shine
> The Hand that made us is Divine.

The world thus pictured is finite in time as well as in space. God Himself set the outermost sphere in motion, or rather is the eternal cause of its motion. Similarly each of the many circular motions, of which the composite movements of the heavenly bodies are the resultant, is produced by its own proper mover, which is pure form or spirit. Hence the absurdity of astrology, for it is these spirits, acting under God, that cause the movements of the stars and not *vice versa*.

One aspect of the physics of Maimonides affected scientific development. Maimonides perceived that the difference between belief in an eternal and belief in a created world may ultimately be resolved into a difference between belief in impersonal mechanical law, as an explanation of the universe, and belief in an intelligent being acting with a particular design. Maimonides admits that Aristotle's resolution of all motions below the lunar sphere in terms of an impersonal mechanical law is successful. It is in the outer spheres that Aristotle fails, though we need not follow Maimonides into details of his failure. Yet, since outer and inner spheres are intimately connected, failure in explaining the one involves failure in the other. The mechanistic view of the world, which excludes free will, miracle and efficacy of prayer, must, he claims, therefore be rejected.

For the mechanistic hypothesis Maimonides substitutes the intelligent purpose and design so dear to the heart of Galen (130-200 C.E.), physician to the philosopher-emperor Marcus Aurelius (121-180 C.E.). With the works of Galen, Maimonides, as a physician, was very familiar. For Maimonides, as for Galen, *design*—God's plan—is expressed in *natural law* and continues to be directed by intelligence. That there were rules of wide application in nature Maimonides fully realized; that these rules depended for their working on certain underlying series of events he also accepted. But ultimately these rules depended, he held, on the action of an intelligence working to intelligible ends. By avoiding the enormous claims of Galen that these ends were wholly known or immediately discoverable by man, he leaves far more room for scientific discovery than does Galen and far less room for the comparable claims of astrology.

The actual scientific efforts of Maimonides do not compare in profundity with his philosophic studies. They can, perhaps, hardly be expected to exhibit great originality—a quality to which his age attached a negative value—but they do nevertheless reveal him clearly as a highly competent, sensible, trusted and effective physician. He knew no Greek and relied entirely on Arabic versions of Galen and Aristotle and on Arabic writers who in their turn relied on Galen and Aristotle. His medical writings have exercised much influence on both Eastern and Western medicine. It is reasonable to claim for them that they kept Hebrew-Arabic medicine sane and levelheaded. Most of his medical works have been translated into both Hebrew and Latin.

Maimonides must have been a very busy man. He thus describes his day's work in a pleasant letter written in 1199, a vivid picture of the life of the best type of medieval physician:

I dwell at Fostat but the sultan at Cairo; these places are two Sabbath days' journey [about one mile and a half] from each other. My duties to the sultan are very heavy. I have to visit him daily early in the morning; and when he or any of his children, or inmates of his harem, are indisposed I dare not leave Cairo, but must spend most of the day in the palace. If any of the royal officers fall sick, I must attend them. Hence I usually go to Cairo very early in the day, and can hardly return to Fostat until afternoon. Then I am tired and hungry. I find the antechambers filled with people, Jews and Gentiles, nobles and common people, judges and bailiffs, a mixed multitude, awaiting my return.

I dismount from my animal, wash, and beg my patients to bear with me while I eat, the only meal I take in the day. Then I attend to my patients, write prescriptions and directions for them. Patients come in and out till nightfall, and sometimes, I assure you, until two hours and more in the night. Sometimes I converse with and prescribe for them while lying down from sheer fatigue, and when night falls I am so exhausted that I can scarcely speak.

Thus none converse with me [on religious matters] except on the Sabbath. Then the whole congregation, or at least most of them, come to me after the morning service, when I advise them as to the work of the week. We study together a little until noon, when they leave. Some return and read with me after the afternoon service until evening prayers. Thus I spend the days. I have related to you only a part of what you would see if you were to visit me.

Late in the twelfth century Maimonides received an inquiry from the Rabbis of Provence asking his views on astrology. He replied in Hebrew that he regarded it as superstition. This attitude was rare in the Middle Ages, for astrology then stood for rationalism. Astrology was therefore often condemned as impious but seldom for the reasons that Maimonides gave. Though he wrote no work on astronomy, his views on the subject can be traced in his other works. They were conservative, rejecting the doctrine of epicycles as contrary to the view of Aristotle.

Almost exactly contemporary with Maimonides was ibn Ruschd (1126-1198) of Cordova, Averroës of the Latins. He held the office of a judge but studied and practiced medicine. He was a Moslem and his writings earned him the bitter enmity of orthodox Moslems, just as those of Maimonides were long abhorrent to orthodox Jews. Averroës had immense influence on Jewish thought.[9a] The opponents of Averroës regarded him as a Judaizer. The general contents of his writings were similar to those of Maimonides though his opinions were very different. The works of Averroës, like those of Maimonides, were almost immediately translated into Hebrew. The widely read Latin versions of Averroës were rendered not from Arabic but from Hebrew. Averroan works and doctrine were forbidden in the universities and regarded by the church as presenting the utmost spiritual danger.

9. PROVENÇAL AND SICILIAN TRANSLATORS, THIRTEENTH CENTURY

The end of the twelfth century and the death of Maimonides (1204) saw the close of the brilliant period of Spanish and Egyptian Jewish science. There were several important figures in the centuries to come though none to measure by Hasdai ibn Shaprut, Abraham bar Hiyya and Maimonides. Nevertheless, the demand for translations from Arabic and Hebrew increased with the development of the universities. Jews played the main part in providing these. Why, then, did their original output fall in quality and quantity?

The full answer is complex but the major factors are plain enough. The thirteenth century was the great period of foundation of universities. Those at Palencia, Valladolid, Salamanca, Lerida and Coimbra in the Iberian Peninsula and, outside it, Paris, Montpellier, Salerno, Bologna, Padua, Naples, Rome, Oxford and Cambridge all began effectively in the thirteenth century. From all these Jews were excluded. As the learned output of the universities rose, that of the Jews fell in relative importance. Jews were thrown back on their own resources. Moreover, the Inquisition was established in Spain and the position of Spanish Jews was steadily deteriorating.[10a] The Jews of Provence and Italy were losing such hold as they had on the Arabic language. Outside the Mediterranean area secular science had hardly reached any Jewish group. Among the Ashkenazim, outside France and Italy, talmudic studies remained all-absorbing. The Golden Age of Jewish science was over.

Prominent among the translators of the Silver Age were members of the Provençal family Bene Tibbon of Spanish origin. Samuel ben Judah ibn Tibbon (c. 1160-1232) of Lunel and Marseilles[11a] introduced Aristotle to Hebrew readers by his Hebrew version of the *Meteorology* from the Arabic. He made it at sea during a voyage from Alexandria (1212). He also rendered a commentary on Galen, but he is chiefly remembered for his diffusion of the Maimonidean philosophy in the West and his development of the Hebrew philosophical language.

Jacob Anatoli (c. 1194-1256) of Marseilles was a disciple and son-in-law of this ibn Tibbon. The Emperor Frederick II invited him to Naples (1231), where he possibly met Thomas Aquinas and certainly Michael Scot. Anatoli turned the work of Averroës into Hebrew and thus took the first step toward Averroistic heresy among both Jews and Latins. Equally influential was the help that he gave to Michael Scot (d. c. 1235)

to render into Latin a conflation of the great biological works of Aristotle,
the first work of ancient biological science that became available to the
West.

In the same region and period there worked the Sicilian Moses Farrachi
(Ferrachius). He was specially employed as one of a band of Jewish
translators by Charles of Anjou (1220-1285). His great achievement is his
Latin version (c. 1275) of the enormous *Liber continens*, a medical work
by Rhazes (d. 932). Another Jewish Sicilian translator, Moses of Palermo,
was engaged by Charles to learn Latin. He afterward translated a veterinary work from Arabic.

The most active of all the translators from Arabic into Hebrew was
Moses ben Samuel ibn Tibbon of Marseilles. In addition to Aristotle's
philosophical works, he translated many mathematical and medical treatises
including Geminus's *Introduction to Hipparchan Astronomy* (Naples,
1246), Euclid's *Elements* (Montpellier, 1270) and Theodosius of Bi-
thynia's *Spherica* (Montpellier, 1271), medical works by a pupil of Isaac
Judeus 1259), Rhazes's *Antidotary* (1257), Avicenna's *Canticum* (1260),
and many others.

10. CASTILIAN AND ARAGONESE ASTRONOMERS AND CARTOGRAPHERS, THIRTEENTH CENTURY

In Spain there were some noteworthy translations from Arabic in the
thirteenth century. Alfonso X of Castile (1252-1284), called "the Wise,"
came to the throne when the transference of Eastern thought was very
active. He directed the translation of some of this material into the vernacular and so influenced the development of the Spanish language. He was
himself an author, interested in philosophy and astronomy, and employed
a number of Jewish translators. The most remarkable scientific work of his
reign was the so-called *Alphonsine tables*. These lists of planetary movements are the basic documents of modern astronomy and continued in repute
for centuries. They were prepared under the wise king's direct command
between 1262 and 1272 by two learned Jews of Toledo, Judah ben Moses
Cohen, a physician, and Isaac ben Sid, a synagogue precentor. They are
based on the tables of a Cordovan astronomer of the eleventh century
and the last edition for practical use appeared at Madrid in 1641! They
were consulted by Kepler and Galileo. The tables on which they were
based were themselves rendered into Spanish by another Jewish translator
for Alfonso X.

The preface of the Alphonsine tables tells that, since computed positions
often differ from those observed, the king had collected instruments and
directed observations to be taken at Toledo. The writers, Moses Cohen
and Isaac Hazan, therefore observed the sun for him through an entire
year, particularly at the equinoxes and solstices, and at the middle of the

signs of Taurus and Scorpio, Leo and Aquarius. They also observed conjunctions of planets both with each other and with fixed stars, and took observations of lunar and solar eclipses. Both authors produced many other important astronomical, mathematical and mechanical works in Spanish, and constructed many astronomical instruments.

Alfonso's patronage of learning was copied by his neighbors, the monarchs of Aragon. The Jew Astruc Bonsenior of Barcelona was secretary and interpreter to King Jaime I of Aragon (1208-1276) in his campaigns. His son Judah Bonsenior became interpreter to Alfonso III (reigned 1265-1291) and Jaime II (reigned 1291-1327). In 1287 Alfonso III took him on his expedition to Minorca. In 1294 Jaime II arranged that he review the translation into Spanish of all Arabic business documents.

A scientific department in Aragon that was largely officered by Jews was that of mapmaking. For Aragonese merchants sailing books of the Mediterranean known as *portolani* were prepared. These contained descriptions of coasts, harbors, anchorages and so forth. Toward the end of the thirteenth century they began to be provided with charts. The *portolano maps* give the outline of the Mediterranean and have the directions of and distances between different ports. The best were made in the island of Majorca, where an important school of Jewish mapmakers sprang up. They relied largely on the Arabic geographers.

At Las Palmas in Majorca the Jew Cresques drew up in 1375 the first map that set forth the discoveries of Marco Polo. This was sent as a gift from the king of Aragon to Charles VI of France. Cresques long continued his cartographical activities. In 1419 he was summoned to Portugal by Prince Henry the Navigator (1394-1460), to assist in establishing an astronomical observatory.

11. RISE OF NORTH ITALIAN SCHOOL, THIRTEENTH CENTURY

By the mid-thirteenth century the two original gates of entry of Arabic science into Europe—the Spanish Peninsula and the Sicilies—were ceasing to function. In the former, organized into Christian kingdoms, the vernaculars Catalan, Castilian and Portuguese began to be used even for learned purposes. The cultural and political importance of the Sicilies was waning. The universities of north Italy and France had determined the intellectual centers of gravity. Islam was in retreat in the West, and at its heart had sustained the irreparable blow of the Mongol invasion and sack of Bagdad (1227). The great period of translation from the Arabic was past although the process continued for centuries. Yet the prestige in Europe of Arabian science was still undiminished. Padua had become an important medical school, linked to Venice, the portal of Eastern trade, and Paduan learning had stamped itself on the philosophical and medical thought of Italy and soon spread to Montpellier.

Jews were numerous at Padua and there one of them, Bonacosa, made the first important north Italian contribution to the library of Arabic-Latin medical translations, the *Colliget* (Arabic *Kulliyyat, i.e.,* "General [medical] rules") of Averroës (1264). It was long studied at Padua and the last edition appeared there in 1560. It was translated twice into Hebrew.

Another product of the Paduan Jewish school was a Latin translation from the Hebrew version of the *Theizir* (Arabic *Taysir, i.e.,* "Aid to health"), of the Spanish Moslem, Avenzoar (d. 1162), written for his friend Averroës. It was widely read in Hebrew, whence it was turned into Latin by the Jew Jacob of Capua, an immigrant from the south. He also rendered into Latin from Hebrew the *Hygiene* of Maimonides, and a book of Indian stories, the so-called *Kalilah wa-Dimmah.* This collection became extraordinarily widespread, largely through Jewish agency. It is said to have been translated into thirty-eight languages and to have passed into about one hundred and eight editions. The English version was derived from the Spanish, which was taken from Latin, which was taken from Hebrew, which was taken from Arabic, which was taken from Pehlavi, which was taken from Sanskrit!

Another strange document of the Paduan school is the most popular of all the medieval books on remedies, the *Canones generales* of "Mesue." This is the name of a well-known Arabic medical writer, but the book is a compilation from the Hebrew. At the end of the thirteenth century one Samuel ben Jacob of Capua, son of the above, composed this drug list, or part of it, in Hebrew. From this the Latin version was prepared. It became very popular and was printed scores of times, the last occasion being in 1581. It was the chief pharmaceutical work of the Renaissance and has influenced the modern pharmacopoeias, including that of England.

A translator who links north Italy with north Spain and south France was Abraham ben Shemtob of Tortosa, whose father, Shemtob ben Isaac of Marseilles, was a well-known translator into Hebrew from Arabic. In 1290, with the Christian Simon Cordo of Genoa, Abraham produced in Latin the popular drug list associated with the name of *Serapion junior.* This mysterious figure is unmentioned by the Arabic historians. He was invented, perhaps by Cordo and Abraham, to cover a work of miscellaneous Arabic and Hebrew origin. *Serapion* was frequently printed. It, too, has influenced the modern pharmacopoeias. The partnership between Cordo and Abraham Shemtob produced several other medical translations.

12. FRENCH CHRISTIAN AND JEWISH HEBRAISTS, THIRTEENTH AND FOURTEENTH CENTURIES

In southern France, Jews were particularly active in the practice of medicine, notably at Avignon. There were many Jewish physicians at

Montpellier, which had been a medical center since the early twelfth century. In the thirteenth century it received a new medical tradition from Bologna and Padua. In 1263 John of Brescia, who had migrated to Montpellier from Bologna, collaborated with the Jew Jacob ben Makir in translating from Arabic into Latin certain important astronomical tables.

This Jacob ben Makir (d. 1308) was born at Marseilles, studied at the great talmudic seminary in Lunel, married the daughter of Moses ben Samuel ibn Tibbon and practiced actively as a physician at Montpellier. After assisting John of Brescia he busied himself in presenting the philosophy of Maimonides in Hebrew. He is best known for a Hebrew work that he wrote in 1288 on the astronomical quadrant, into which he introduced certain improvements. The form he advocated was known as the "Jewish quadrant" (*quadrans judaicus*). This important work was turned into Latin no less than three times, on the first occasion by an Englishman, who was making a stay at Montpellier about the year 1308, and on the second occasion about 1314 by the Christian Hebraist Armengaud of Montpellier. The well-known surveying instrument usually called *Jacob's staff* is probably named after this Jacob ben Makir. The first description of it that we have is, however, by his countryman and coreligionist Gersonides. An *Almanach* of Jacob ben Makir was used by Dante in the *Divina Commedia*.

Jacob ben Makir made many translations of scientific works from Arabic into Hebrew, such as Euclid's *Elements* and Alhazem's *Astronomy*, the works of Autolycus and of Menelaus *On the Sphere*, and Aristotle's *De partibus animalium* and *De generatione animalium* in the version of Averroës. His work was appreciated in both Latin and Hebrew circles and he is quoted by Copernicus and Kepler.

With Jacob ben Makir is associated the equally accomplished Christian Hebraist and physician Armengaud Blasius of Montpellier (d. 1314). He rendered many Hebrew works into Latin including writings of Maimonides. He was always helped by Jacob ben Makir or by his pupils. In 1305, while at Barcelona in attendance on Jaime II of Aragon, he occupied his spare time in Latinizing from the Hebrew the very curious *Cantica* of Avicenna and the medical work of Maimonides *On the Treatment of Poisoning*. His reliance on Hebrew rather than Arabic for these works exemplifies a widespread practice in the Scholastic ages. The reciprocal relationship of Jacob ben Makir and Armengaud is typical and was much commoner in the later Middle Ages than appears on the surface.

In 1305 Armengaud was displaced in his attendance on Jaime II by Arnald of Villanova (1235-1311), than whom few medieval figures would give a better opportunity to a romantic writer. Arnald, after a youth of hardship, studied at Naples and Salerno, traveled in Italy, Sicily, France and Spain and taught at Montpellier. Both there and at Barcelona he was associated with Armengaud. He was one of the earliest European alchemical writers and he also wrote voluminously on philosophical subjects in a heretical vein. He had some knowledge of both Hebrew and Arabic, and had ample access to those who had such knowledge. He was medical adviser to the papal court both at Rome and at Avignon, was employed as ambassador on more than one special mission, and he ended a very eventful life at sea. He translated from the Arabic a work of Avicenna on the heart and from the Hebrew a work of Avenzoar on diet. Both were effected with Jewish help. On the other hand, Arnald's own works were much read in Hebrew into which language about ten of them were translated.

By the second half of the thirteenth century activity in translation from Arabic had spread northward, and had reached Paris and Flanders. The earliest patron of these northern translators of whom we have tidings was the Fleming, Henri Bate (c. 1244-1310), a disciple of Albertus Magnus (1206-1280) at Paris. He was intimate with William of Moerbeke (d. 1285), the translator from the Greek employed by Thomas Aquinas (1227-1274). Bate received an ecclesiastical benefice at his birthplace at Malines in 1273. Next year a French Jew, one Hayyin, translated into French works of Abraham ibn Ezra in Bate's house at Malines. These influenced Bate's later writings, notably a treatise on the astrolabe, produced in 1274 on William of Moerbeke's suggestion. Bate later went to Italy and translated other works of ibn Ezra at Orvieto (1281 and 1292). Other works of ibn Ezra were translated by the heretical Paduan professor Peter of Abano (1250-1318), one of the most picturesque of the Scholastics whose natural death saved him from a more violent one, for his body was exhumed and burned.

During the first half of the fourteenth century the French Jews displayed much philosophic and scientific activity. The leading representative of this movement is Levi ben Gerson, known as Gersonides (1288-1344).[12a] He lived at Avignon and Orange, and is important in the general history of philosophy and especially for the thought of Spinoza. He was a courageous man of outstanding scientific ability, but as a writer Hebrew was his only medium. The extent, variety and depth of his knowledge bear testimony to the qualities and possibilities of medieval Hebrew literature.

Gersonides was an enthusiastic Aristotelian, who fearlessly interpreted what he regarded as the view of his master in opposition alike to current Judaism and to the Averroism of the schools. He regarded himself as a complete rationalist and his philosophy was largely banned by his own people. His work that most stirred the world in which he lived was astronomical. A passage from it dealing with "Jacob's staff" was translated into Latin in 1342 during his lifetime by order of Pope Clement VI as *The Instrument That Reveals Secrets*. Later the whole work was Latinized. It demonstrates the falseness of the current view that all the heavenly bodies move round the same center. It thus in a sense leads on to Copernicus. It deservedly enjoyed a high reputation and was still esteemed in the seventeenth century, when Kepler was at pains to secure a copy. Kepler quotes Gersonides several times and refers to three separate works by him.

Mention should perhaps here be made of the very important French Hebrew fourteenth-century writer Hasdai Crescas. He had nothing to say on science in the modern sense but he is philosophically important as opposing Aristotle as represented by Maimonides. Thus he anticipates the reaction against Aristotle that later introduced the scientific movement to the Latin world.[13a]

13. DECLINE OF HEBREW-ARABIC SCIENCE, FIFTEENTH AND SIXTEENTH CENTURIES

In the later fourteenth century the long decline of the Jewish scientific intellect began. The political and social conditions of Jews were steadily deteriorating, culminating with the expulsion from Spain, Sicily and Sardinia in 1492. Yet it was long before the Hebrew-Arabic element that had already entered Latin thought began to lose importance. The main philosophical reading of the West continued to be affected by Hebrew-Arabic literature far into the time of printing, and even to the seventeenth century. In this connection it must be remembered that the revival of Greek learning affected science much later than literature and philosophy.

Among the later Jewish translators of the period of decline, mention should be made of Elijah Delmedigo (1463-1497) of Padua. A good Hebrew, Latin and Italian scholar and a physician as well, he applied himself to philosophy and took part in the activities of the university. Padua, alone among the universities, occasionally granted a medical degree to Jews and that from as early as 1409. Among Elijah Delmedigo's students was Pico della Mirandola (1463-1494), at whose request some of his translations were undertaken. Delmedigo's writings are mostly Latin renderings of various treatises by Averroës. He also produced original philosophical works. He differs from Pico in having a strong bias against cabbalism.

In contrast to Delmedigo is Judah Verga of Lisbon, where he died under torture in 1490. He was a cabbalist but his secular work was of an exclusively scientific nature. Among his scientific writings, which are all in Hebrew, is a description of an astronomical instrument which he invented to determine the sun's meridian. The account of it was written at Lisbon about 1457.

It may seem strange that cabbalistic and scientific learning should occur in the same individual. In fact, however, this was often the case. Thus Guglielmo Raimondo of Girgenti, who was converted to Christianity in

1466, and later became a bishop, had both these interests. From him we have a translation of an astronomical work of the Arab mathematician Alhazen of Basra (965-1038). The dedication cites the Talmud and ibn Ezra. About 1477, Raimondo also prepared a number of eclipse tables.

A similar combination of interests was exhibited by Paolo Ricci, a converted Jew of German origin who acted as physician to the Emperor Maximilian. He translated cabbalistic treatises from Hebrew and later became professor of medicine at the University of Pavia. He is mentioned favorably by Erasmus. In 1519 he issued the only edition that we possess of the medical treatise of the Spanish physician, Albucasis (1013-1106).

Bonet de Lattes was of a family from Lattes near Montpellier and he himself was from Carpentras. He achieved an excellent reputation for himself as a physician and was medical attendant to two successive Popes, Alexander VI (d. 1503) and Leo X (d. 1513). In 1493 in a work dedicated to Pope Alexander VI he described in Latin an astronomical instrument for taking solar and lunar altitudes and thus determining the hour. It gained much popularity. A pleasing description of Bonet, his house, his instruments and his mode of life has been left by a Christian scholar who visited him at Rome (1507). Some remains of this house were recovered half a century ago.

By the sixteenth century translation of scientific works into Latin directly from the Arabic had ceased, but translation into Latin from Hebrew continued, mostly in the spirit of the New Learning. The last of the Jewish translators who can rightly be termed medieval, Jacob Mantino (d. 1549), was also connected with Padua. He was born in Spain, whence, on the Expulsion, his parents brought him as an infant. He studied philosophy and medicine at Bologna and Padua, and devoted most of his life to translation into Latin. He settled in Venice and attracted the attention of Clement VII as well as that of many scholars. His eventful life was marked by office as physician to Pope Paul III and by disputes with the Messianic visionary, Solomon Molko (1500-1532).

Mantino rendered into Latin from Hebrew works of Averroës, Gersonides, Maimonides and Avicenna. He is best remembered, however, as editor of the monumental standard Latin edition of Averroës published at Venice in 1552, soon after his death. It was the basis of the Averroistic philosophical school that flourished among Christians and Jews at Padua well into the seventeenth century and had some distinguished exponents. William Harvey (1578-1657), discoverer of the circulation of the blood, was affected by it. The ultimate representative of the medieval Hebrew-Arabic movement in Italy was the Averroist, Cesaro Cremonini (d. 1637), professor of philosophy at Padua till his death.

The decline of what we may call the Hebrew-Arabic-Latin scientific movement is contemporary with the advent of a Jewish element in the new

"Renaissance" of science. The movement was short lived. It is illustrated by the careers of two Jewish astronomers, Abraham Zacuto and Joseph Vecinho who were involved in the explorations of Vasco da Gama and Columbus. So far as Hebrew-Arabic science in the Iberian Peninsula is concerned, theirs is a swan song.

Abraham Zacuto (1450-1510) taught astronomy at the universities of Salamanca and Saragossa. Leaving Spain he settled in Lisbon as astronomer to John II. He was consulted on the expedition of Vasco da Gama, whose vessels were fitted with astrolabes designed by him and provided with improvements that he introduced. In 1473, while still at Salamanca, Zacuto wrote in Hebrew a *Perpetual Almanac*. This was translated into both Latin and Spanish by his pupil Vecinho and issued in 1496 at Leiria in Portugal by a Jewish printer. Manuscript copies of it were carried in the fleets of Vasco da Gama, Cabral, João de Nova, and Albuquerque.

This Joseph Vecinho was also in the service of John II of Portugal, who sent him to the coast of Guinea to measure the solar altitude. When the plan of Columbus for Western exploration was laid before King John he submitted it to a committee of five, of whom Vecinho was chief. The other members were the Bishop of Ceuta, the court physician, the German cartographer Martin Behaim, and a Jewish mathematician named Moses. The committee reported against the expedition but Columbus retained a high respect for Vecinho and wrote in the margin of one of his books: "In the year 1485, the king of Portugal sent Master Joseph, his physician and astronomer, to determine the altitudes of the sun throughout Guinea, all of which he performed. He reported to the king, in my presence, that he found the Island of Idols near Sierra Leone to be exactly five degrees distant from the equator. Afterward the king often sent to Guinea and other places, and always found the results accord with those of Master Joseph." In another marginal note Columbus states that during voyages to Guinea he had taken solar altitudes of the sun, which always agreed with those of Vecinho.

Columbus (1446-1506) had, in fact, much intercourse with Jewish men of science and was acquainted with Zacuto as well as with Vecinho. Almost the first financial assistance that he secured was from the Jewish statesman and Bible commentator, Isaac Abrabanel (1437-1508), and in his will Columbus left a legacy to a Lisbon Jew. At least five Jews accompanied him on his first expedition, especially as interpreters. The first landing was effected on October 15, 1492, and on November 2, Columbus sent out his first expedition on American soil. It consisted of two men, one the Jew Luis de Torres. Torres was one of the first Europeans to tread American soil and the first to experiment with the effects of tobacco, using himself as guinea pig. He settled and died in Cuba.

Many have thought that Columbus was himself of Jewish origin and

there is much to support that view. One point that might be made is that
Columbus, though born and bred in Genoa, never employs an Italian word
in any of his documents. Spanish is the only vernacular that he uses. This
language was and is the lingua franca of Mediterranean Jews. For a
Genoese to write only Spanish would in itself suggest a Jewish origin.

This is perhaps the place to mention the remarkable figure of Pedro
Nunes (*c.* 1492-1577). He was born of a Marrano family in Portugal and
studied medicine at Lisbon and mathematics at Salamanca. He went to the
East Indies as an official in 1519 but was soon recalled as professor of
philosophy at Lisbon. In 1529 he became cosmographer royal. In 1544 he
was called to the chair of mathematics at Coimbra. Nunes devoted himself
to investigation of figures and lines on spheres other than "great circles."
He is a founder of scientific navigation and his *Treatise on the Sphere*
(Lisbon, 1537) and *On the Art and Science of Navigation* have an
assured place in the history of cartography. He himself escaped the direct
attentions of the Inquisition but his grandchildren paid the penalty.

14. THE MARRANO EPISODE[14a]

In the world of intellect the persecution of Jews in Spain had certain
surprising implications, some of which have been insufficiently recognized.
Toward the end of the Jewish Iberian period there was, especially in
Portugal, a remarkable number of Jewish writers touched by the spirit of
the New Learning. The works of Judah Verga (d. 1490), Abraham Zacuto
(d. 1510) and Joseph Vecinho (d. *c.* 1495) were the swan song of Jewish
science in the Peninsula. With the migration their tradition was continued
by such men as Elijah Delmedigo (d. 1497), Abraham de Balmes
(1423-1523) and Jacob Mantino (d. 1549). But from then onward
Jewish science, outside medicine, is mute until the nineteenth century. No
important Jewish name appears in scientific literature, except in medicine,
for nearly three centuries. The revival is not then with the Sephardim but
with the Ashkenazim of Central Europe. This very fact adds significance
to the immense number of physicians of the Marrano migration.

For much of the sixteenth, seventeenth and even the eighteenth
centuries an astonishingly high proportion of important physicians of
Europe was of Marrano descent. The phenomenon needs explanation,
which is not yet perhaps fully forthcoming. Many factors may be suggested. Doubtless it was an advantage to possess the full clinical tradition
of the Hebrew-Arabic medical system. Social pressure certainly left few
avocations open to foreign refugees. Perhaps the mental detachment that
comes of insecure social position may not be without its uses to the medical
observer. Surely a natural channel of the Jewish tradition will always be
humane social service. Assuredly it was no small thing to acquire early a

respect for learning. Moreover, the minds of the Marranos were free in a sense in which those of professing Jews were not, for their very circumstances and history implied release from Rabbinic limitations.

There is something to be said for all these as factors of the intellectual outburst, which was almost exclusively among those of Sephardic and Iberian origin. The period coincides with the movement of the center of gravity of the Latin intellect from the Mediterranean area to the northwest. Thither the Marranos largely followed it. The northern Ashkenazim, however, were still in a pre-Scholastic stage. They were neither in a social nor an intellectual position to develop secular studies and there is no significant scientific figure among them before the nineteenth century. The determining elements in the outburst of Marrano intellectual activity will be a matter of opinion. The general situation bears resemblance to that of the Jews of Central Europe during the past hundred years. A culture hunger is aroused by the breakdown of the Rabbinic environment. This is most easily satisfied by the rising enthusiasm for science in a changed social milieu. The New Learning of the sixteenth century was to the Marranos what the New Science was to central European Jewry.

In both cases importance must be attached to the freeing of the mind from talmudic preoccupation. This sounds like a truism since a mind preoccupied by any line of thought obviously cannot at the same time admit another line. But it is a special feature of talmudic preoccupation that it tends to occupy the whole area of thought as do few other studies; for the Talmud is not only a subject of study, it is a habit of thought, a cast of mind, a way of life. The practical test lies in the historic record. Very few if any talmudists have made contributions to science. Why should this be? The answer must be in terms of Jewish sociology or psychology where it cannot be followed in this place.

It is difficult to give a picture of the medical activity of Marranism as a whole. It represents no definite school. The groups with which we are concerned are almost entirely disconnected. It is precisely this division among themselves that prevented the Marranos from developing a separate religion and so from having a history in any proper sense. But an account of the lives of a score of Marrano physicians over these three hundred years reveals the impetus of a remarkable intellectual movement working itself out until it becomes extinct in the nineteenth century. Not all the figures here selected are of great medical eminence. Some are selected as helping to complete the patchwork picture of the Marrano intellect. Some, too, were not Marranos themselves but descendants of Marranos.

Belonging to the first generation of the migration were two physicians bearing the name Leo, whose widely different careers illustrate the diversity of the Marrano activities. The better known was Leo Hebreus or Judah Abrabanel (c. 1470-1535), son of the famous statesman Isaac

Abrabanel. In 1492 his son was taken from Leo and baptized and he himself was expelled from Spain. He practiced in Naples and was physician to the successive kings of the "Sicilies." That realm being invaded, he sought a home successively at Venice, Corfu and Genoa, where his famous *Dialogues of Love* was written (1502) for his friend the philosopher Pico della Mirandola. Leo was a Neoplatonic dreamer and his work is a discussion between *Sophia*, Wisdom, and *Philo*, Love. Despite its esoteric character it contains matter of medical interest and Leo's medical services were always highly esteemed. The book is an Italian classic. It was printed nineteen times in the sixteenth century and has been translated into many languages, including Hebrew and English.

The other Leo, less known to fame, was a pioneer in a different sense. He was of Venice, and ventured to Russia in 1490 in the train of an ambassadorial mission to Moscow, the first Western European medical man to enter Russian territory. He was called to treat a local prince, who unfortunately died. The physician was accordingly executed and Russia had naturally to wait some time for her next Western medical adviser.

Francisco Lopez de Villalobos (1472?-1549) was one of the very few great physicians who remained in sixteenth-century Spain. His surname is that of a place near Zamora but it is uncertain whether he was born there or at Toledo. He studied at Salamanca, was much occupied about the court of King Ferdinand (1509-1516) and of the Emperor Charles V (1518-1542), retiring at the age of seventy. He came early under suspicion of the Inquisition and was incarcerated for eighty days but managed to clear himself. He was forced on later occasions to be a witness to the burnings of heretics. Villalobos has a definite place in the history of medicine. He provided the clearest early account of syphilis in the form of a poem published at Salamanca in 1498. He wrote other important medical works which are still of interest.

Dionysius Brudo (*c.* 1470-*c.* 1540), son of a medical man, occupied an excellent post as physician to the crown in Lisbon. He was a controversialist on bloodletting, the method of which was a subject of violent debate at the time. In 1534, despite his eminence, he found reason to leave suddenly for Antwerp and a pension from the crown ceased to be paid him. His Jewish sympathies had been discovered. His son Manuel Brudo is said to have declared himself a Jew at Venice. Manuel practiced in England for a time about the year 1540. A work by him on the treatment of fevers (Venice, 1544) was widely read. It contains many references to his English cases and his English experiences and to English customs.

Although not medically important, one of the more remarkable of the Marrano physicians was another member of the London Marrano group, Hector Nunez (*c.* 1520-*c.* 1595). He was born at Evora, graduated at Coimbra, came to England about 1550 and joined the minute colony of Judaizing Marranos in London of whom there were about a hundred.

He became their leading spirit during the reign of Catholic Mary (1553-1558), despite the rigidly anti-Jewish attitude of her husband, Philip of Spain. Hector had widespread connections in the government and continued to enjoy the confidence of Elizabeth's great ministers, Burleigh and Walsingham. He was the first Jew or Marrano to be admitted as a fellow of the Royal College of Physicians (1554). He was esteemed within the college, holding the title of censor in 1562 and 1563. The college books show that he was still living in 1589 but that he was not then in England.

The most striking medical figure of the sixteenth century was the Belgian professor at Padua, Andreas Vesalius (1514-1564), founder of the study of anatomy. For both of his anatomical works (1538 and 1543) he had Jewish assistants. He speaks of the chief of these in the most cordial way as his friend and guest. He needed their help to explain to him the meaning of Arabic and Hebrew anatomical terms.

Of the medical men of the sixteenth century few were better known in their own time than Juan Roderigo who usually called himself Amatus Lusitanus (1511-1568).[15a] He was born at Castello Branco in Portugal, son of Marrano refugees from Spain. He took a medical degree at Salamanca and practiced for a while in Lisbon. About this time complaints were raised in the Cortes that almost all physicians and apothecaries were "New Christians," that is, Marranos. There was much truth in this. Anticipating the entry of the Inquisition into Portugal (1536) Amatus left for Antwerp. There he established a reputation based partly on his *Index to the Remedies of Dioscorides* (1536). In 1540 he was called to the chair of medicine at Ferrara, then one of the most tolerant places in Europe. It was a center for anatomical study, a subject entirely neglected in Spain and Portugal. At Ferrara he performed a considerable number of dissections and witnessed more. He was invited to become court physician in Poland and town physician in Ragusa. Owing to some miscalculation concerning the latter he moved to Ancona (1547), where he carried on a very successful practice and wrote the first of his seven *Centuriae* (1549) of medical observations. This was issued at Rome in 1551 during a long visit there. In 1555 decrees issued by the new Pope, Paul IV, placed restrictions on medical practice by Jews and Marranos. A number in Italy were arrested by the Inquisition and twenty-four burned at the stake. Amatus fled first to Pesaro and then across the Adriatic to Ragusa. Finally he reached Salonica, 1558. There he wrote his *Centuria VII* (1561) and died some years later.

Amatus wrote an important book on *materia medica* (Venice, 1552) that contains many original botanical observations. The works by which he is rightly remembered, however, are his *Centuriae*. These are clinical records of actual cases, the first major collection of the kind ever made, and are of great historic and scientific importance.

Garcia da Orta (1498-1568) was one of the most distinguished medical men of the sixteenth century. He studied at the universities of Salamanca and Alcalá. In 1534 he sailed for India and settled finally at Goa. He was the pioneer of the study of tropical diseases and one of the fathers of botanical science. His valuable and interesting *Colloquies on the Simples and Drugs of India* (Goa, 1563) was the first book printed in that country. It is still consulted as the earliest authority on the subject. Da Orta traveled much in India and his observations were outstanding. One of his famous sayings expresses the true spirit of science: "In Spain I would never have dared to affirm anything contrary to the Greeks and particularly to Galen, but in India, free from convention, in the midst of luxuriant vegetation, it matters little what Dioscorides, Pliny, Avicenna and Galen have said. Do not frighten me with them. I have seen." What was in effect an illustrated edition of Da Orta's book was produced in 1578 by another Marrano, Cristoval d'Acosta.

Many of Garcia da Orta's relatives suffered from the Inquisition and his sister was burned at the stake in the year of his death. In 1580 the Inquisition found that he was a Jew and ordered his remains to be burned. He had been dead for twelve years.

Continuity of medical tradition in a Marrano family is illustrated by the Saportas. The Catalonian Luiz Saporta was born at Lerida (*c.* 1460-1565). After nine years of medical practice there he left for Provence and started practices first at Arles, then at Avignon, and then at the ancient university town of Montpellier. He did much military service, received many signs of royal approval and is said to have died at Marseilles, age 106. His son Louis Saporta II (*c.* 1490-*c.* 1580) took his degree at Montpellier and practiced at Toulouse, where he acquired a great reputation, dying at the age of ninety. His son Antoine Saporta (*c.* 1510-1573) was born at Montpellier, took his medical degree there in 1531, became professor of medicine there in 1540, dean in 1551 and chancellor in 1566. His son Jean Saporta (*c.* 1550-1605) also became professor there (1577) and later vice-chancellor (1603).

Rodrigo de Castro (1546-1627) came of a well-known Marrano medical family, many members of which, including his own brother, suffered from the Inquisition. He was born at Lisbon, educated at Salamanca and practiced first at Evora and then at Lisbon. He earned a great reputation and was offered a post in India to continue the work of Garcia da Orta. He decided, however, to leave Portuguese territory, fearing the inquiries of the Holy Office. He settled in Hamburg about 1590 and there became one of the most respected and sought-after physicians in northern Europe, being called upon to attend a number of sovereigns and high notables. De Castro's own reputation was greatly increased by his steady refusal to leave his post in plague-time. About the beginning of the seventeenth century the very small band of Marranos in Hamburg began openly to profess the Jewish religion. Official sanction was given to their residence in 1611. De Castro wrote two books of considerable medical importance, one the earliest original modern treatise on gynecology and the other on the relation of the doctor to the state. He had two sons who also were physicians.

At the end of the sixteenth century the grand dukes of Tuscany sought to attract a higher type of professor in reorganizing the University of Pisa. One of their captures was a young man named Galileo Galilei. For the medical department distinguished Marranos were available. Among those secured was Estevão Rodrigues de Castro (1559-1637), a native of Lisbon. He was a prolific writer who made pioneer observations in pathology. A gifted teacher, he was called in 1615 to Padua, the leading medical school of the time. He was followed at both Pisa and Padua by Antonio Rodrigues da Fonseca (d. 1632), another native of Lisbon and also a voluminous writer, whose achievement lay in having helped to check the practice of excessive bleeding.

Abraham Zacuto (1575-1642) the Portuguese (Lusitanus) came of a long line of physicians, perhaps the longest on record, for his great-grandfather of the same name was already the third of his line. Our Zacutus was born at Lisbon, studied at Salamanca and Coimbra and took his degree at Siguenza. After practicing for thirty years (1596-1626) in his native town with noteworthy success, he was forced to flee and headed for Amsterdam. He joined the Jewish congregation there and at once began a long and voluminous series of publications which ended only with his death. Zacutus was a strong medical conservative. Although he had passed beyond the "Arabist" phase he was obstinately Galenist in the mood of the previous generation. Living till almost the middle of the seventeenth century this attitude was certainly backward but he was nevertheless an excellent clinical observer. His work on the infectious diseases is still occasionally consulted and he was one of the first to describe the deadly blackwater fever.

A physician who is immortalized for adventitious reasons is Dr. Ephraim Hezekiah Bueno (d. 1665). He came of a Spanish family that included many physicians. His father, Joseph Bueno, arrived in Amsterdam from Bordeaux, where he had taken a medical degree, and was a doctor of good repute. Ephraim was very friendly with Manasseh ben Israel, whose first work he published, but he will always be remembered by the delightful picture of him by Rembrandt known as "The Jewish Doctor." His features represent the best Spanish type, with gentle, pitiful, sadly thoughtful eyes; a typical Sephardi. Beneath the contemporary engraving by Lyrius is inscribed, "A second Avenzoar, distinguished in medicine and a pupil of a distinguished father." He was a kind and charitable man, an efficient doctor and a good son of the synagogue.

John Lumbrozo (d. 1665) was a refugee from Portugal to Holland. Thence in 1656 he came to palatinate of Maryland, where he practiced medicine with much success. In 1663 he secured letters of denization. He was the first Jewish inhabitant of Maryland of whose faith there is documentary evidence. One of the earliest trained practitioners there, he was probably the earliest ex-Marrano to practice medicine in the territory of what is now the United States. His career is of interest in relation to the development of religious toleration in Maryland. After two years of undisturbed quiet as a recognized Jew, as a consequence of his own indiscretion zealots obtained his arrest for "blasphemy," that is, for denying the doctrine of the Trinity. He was released under the general amnesty proclaimed a few days later by the Protector, Richard Cromwell.

Balthasar Orobio de Castro (1620-1687) was the child of Marrano parents living in Seville. He studied at Alcalá and became a teacher of philosophy at Salamanca. Later he studied medicine and practiced successfully at Seville, attending relations of the king. He was denounced by a servant to the Inquisition as an adherent of Judaism, but persistently denied the truth of this through two years of imprisonment and torture. In view of his later history it is evident that this treatment turned him toward Judaism in at least the sense that it turned him against Christianity. On his release he left Spain (1663) and became professor of medicine at Toulouse. Finally he migrated to Amsterdam (1666), where he embraced Judaism openly. There he practiced medicine until his death. He is known chiefly for his theological writings and for his friendship with Spinoza. His wife died at Amsterdam in 1712. Members of his family continued to be victims of the Inquisition far into the eighteenth century. An Orobio de Castro was writing medical works at Amsterdam toward the end of the nineteenth century.

Fernandez Mendez (c. 1645-1725) was born in Portugal and was graduated from Montpellier in 1667. He reached London in 1669 and became physician in attendance on Queen Catherine of Braganza (d. 1705). In 1687 he was admitted a fellow of the Royal College of Physicians. He married a lady of the migration, a Jewess, and a child was born to them in the royal palace of Somerset House. He was one of those in attendance on Charles II in his last illness. There is no reason to suppose that Mendez was a man of any special medical ability. The fact that the queen should choose this ex-Marrano illustrates the poorness of non-Jewish medical personnel in Portugal. The great tradition of Marrano medicine was itself petering out.

Daniel da Fonseca (1667-c. 1745) was born in Portugal. His grandfather had been burned as a Marrano and his father escaped as one when Daniel was only eight years old. He was baptized, brought up in the Catholic faith and entered the priesthood, nevertheless secretly adhering

Tab eclipfis luminariuz et primo de fole

numer⁹ annornz	nomina menfinz	dies	digiti	feria	hore	minut	finis eclipfis hore	minu
1493	octob	10	9	5	0	0	1	20
1502	septeb	30	8	6	17	28	19	12
1506	Julii	20	3	2	1	49	3	3
1513	martii	7	4	1	23	49	1	9
1518	Junii	7	10	2	18	22	19	17
1524	fannaz	23	9	2	3	12	4	6

Tabla de eclipfib⁹ lnne

1494	septeb	14	17	1	17	5	2	33
1497	fannaz	18	17	4	3	50	7	18
1500	noueb	5	13	5	10	17	13	30
1501	maii	2	10	1	15	33	19	6
1502	octob	15	14	7	10	15	12	9
1504	februa	29	16	5	10	47	14	13
1505	ang⁹	14	15	5	5	42	9	6
1508	Junii	12	23	2	15	21	19	0
1509	Junii	2	7	7	9	29	2	3
1511	octob	6	13	2	9	11	2	25
1514	fannaz	29	16	2	14	20	16	3
1515	fannaz	19	15	7	5	0	6	42
1516	Julii	13	14	1	10	0	12	30
1519	noueb	6	20	1	5	50	6	48
1522	septeb	5	15	6	11	22	12	4
1523	martii	1	17	1	7	30	9	14

A PAGE FROM THE *Almanach Perpetuum* OF ABRAHAM ZACUTO, LEIRIA, 1496

Christopher Columbus used Zacuto's computations. As is well known, Columbus learned from them of the moon's eclipse on February 29, 1504 (listed in the page above), and used the information to overcome the hostility of the Indians on the Island of Jamaica.

to the Jewish religion. This being suspected, he fled to France, where he studied medicine. He then made his way to Constantinople, where he openly embraced Judaism, practiced medicine, successfully obtained the confidence of high officials and showed himself consistently pro-French and anti-Austrian. He was appointed physician to the French embassy and later to the sultan himself. He retired about 1730 to Paris, where he spent his last years in the delightful society of the salons, a friend of Voltaire, who regarded him as the only Jewish philosopher.

Samuel Nunez (c. 1680-c. 1750) was a Marrano physician of great distinction who was born in Lisbon, where he was educated and practiced in high circles. He was denounced to the Inquisition, however, and he and his family were imprisoned. His services were in such demand that he was released but had to submit to the permanent residence in his house of two officers who would make certain that he did not relapse into Judaism. He succeeded in persuading the captain of an English ship to take his family and himself to England secretly. There they joined other Marranos and a small party of German Jews. They set sail in 1733 for Georgia. Despite attempts to prevent them from settling, most of them, protected by Oglethorpe, were able to remain, Nunez among them. He became a substantial landowner and was an ancestor of Mordecai M. Noah.

Jacob de Castro Sarmento (1691-1761) was born at Braganza, studied at Evora and Coimbra, taking his medical degree in 1717. He left his country to escape the Inquisition, settled in 1720 in London, was admitted to the Royal College of Physicians in 1725, became a fellow of the Royal Society in 1729 and of the college in 1739. He was one of the earliest advocates in England (1721) of the protection against smallpox by "variolation," that is, by inoculation with a mild form of the disease (to be distinguished sharply from vaccination, which came into use eighty years later). It is possible that he may have brought the idea with him from Portugal as he did a preparation of quinine, which he introduced. He published in Portuguese in London a work of some importance on mineral substances used in medicine (1731-1758). He openly professed Judaism and equally openly corresponded with Jesuits on scientific matters. He always retained his connections with Portugal and translated Newton's works into Portuguese. He left the synagogue in 1758.

Of the later Marranos perhaps the most important scientifically was Jacob Rodrigues Pereira (1715-1780). He was born in Spain of Marrano parents. On his father's death his mother was in danger of denunciation to the Inquisition. She and her son fled, settled in Bordeaux and embraced Judaism. From about 1737 on, the young man devoted himself to the experimental study of deaf-mutes. He thus slowly elaborated a method of teaching them to speak and gradually his method was accepted. His achievements have been generally acknowledged in modern times and his scientific reputation now stands very high. His interest in deaf-mutes was inherited by his great-grandson.

It would be very easy to extend this description of the pageant of Marrano life with a whole series of romantic figures. It would be equally easy to include in our illustrative list many scores of physicians distinguished in their day but short of eminence. Again the series might be made to include many theologians or other thinkers who, in the Jewish manner, had practiced for a time as physicians or had medical degrees. But by the mid-eighteenth century the Marrano impetus was failing. The migration had ceased. The Iberian Peninsula had become, as it remains, the most backward and illiterate region of Western Europe. The Marranos themselves were largely absorbed in the general population. The Jewish people of the eighteenth century, whatever their interest in the sociologist and social historian, provide little for the historian of science.

15. A Hundred Years of Central Europe

The role of Jews in the drama of modern scientific progress has been noteworthy in several Western countries. In central Europe it has been overwhelming and a discussion of the entire situation would be interminable. Here the consideration of the historical elements must suffice, omitting contemporary figures. Moreover, in order to keep within reasonable limits, we must confine ourselves, for the most part, to the German-speaking region. In that area Jews have played an ever-increasing part in intellectual life. Something must, therefore, be said of the history of Central European science, which is, in effect, German science. Furthermore, the German-speaking area is the effective center of the modern Jewish people. It is true that by the beginning of the twentieth century the relative importance of the German language and of German culture from the Jewish standpoint was rapidly declining. Nevertheless, Germany remained, until the rise of Nazism, the center of Jewish intellectual life.

A characteristic of German cultural history is the lateness of its scientific development. The great scientific movement of the sixteenth, seventeenth and eighteenth centuries, beginning in Italy, spread to northwestern Europe. For a long time the German area was little affected by it. There were a few eminent early German scientists but no outstanding school of scientific thought in a German environment. The real German scientific contribution was scarcely begun until the end of the eighteenth and did not reach impressive proportions until the nineteenth century. The first important native school of scientific thought was the mathematical, astronomical and physical movement linked with the great names of Karl Friedrich Gauss (1777-1855), and Wilhelm Eduard Weber (1804-1891) and associated largely with Goettingen.

Both this tardy arrival and rapid development are rendered partially understandable by the history of the universities and of the technical industries of Germany. German scientific technique has, like German learning, always been in the hands of university professors. The brilliant amateur, so frequently a figure in French and English science, has seldom appeared on the German scene. On the other hand, a significant role has been played by the "doctoral dissertation," a feature always greatly stressed in German university life. Until well into the nineteenth century German custom demanded that these dissertations, like lectures, be formal and in Latin. When this tradition, with its associated turgid absurdities, was finally abandoned, the system so developed as to provide German professors with what were, in effect, considerable staffs of trained but unpaid assistants. The officers of German universities have always been under state control and, given judicious state support, it was easy for a professor to introduce a high degree of organization into research.

Neither institutes nor organizations create science. Men of science are unique and beyond all valuation. Looking back upon the history of science as a whole, taking into consideration the proportion of people in Europe who use the German tongue, the high state of their material culture, and realizing that a large proportion of German scientific writings are products of non-German or part-German influences, it may fairly be said that Germans have been distinctly less successful than several other peoples in producing creative work of the first rank. But the situation in the second half of the nineteenth century had special features. Much of the significant scientific advance in German in that period was related to skilled co-operative effort. There are phases in the development of the sciences for which a high degree of organization is especially favorable. Such a phase was traversed for certain sciences between the years 1860 and 1920. It happened to coincide with the industrialization of Germany. The rise of industrialism and the development of great scientific institutes were of mutual assistance, notably from 1882 to 1907, when the extremely able Friedrich Althoff reigned tyrannically in the Prussian Ministry of Education.

In the later nineteenth century private benefaction in the United States, England and France had not yet enabled research to be organized on anything like the scale that we see today [1946]. Moreover, universities in these countries shunned industrial contacts, sometimes even depreciating the sciences. Hence the German universities had advantages in certain disciplines. In Germany many scientific departments, ably officered and with numerous highly trained and well-disciplined staffs, were in a position to concentrate directly on specific problems to a degree unknown elsewhere. All this fitted the state-directed industrialization under the Prussian hegemony, some of the profits from which were skillfully diverted to the needs of fundamental research. The development of scientific interests among Jews in Germany must be considered with this background in mind.

The nineteenth- and twentieth-century outburst of Jewish intellect reveals both contrasts and parallels to that of the earlier Marrano episode. In contrast it was almost entirely among Ashkenazim, for Sephardic activity has progressively waned. Its external accompaniments were those liberating, liberalizing, humane forces that both produced and emerged from the French Revolution. The atmosphere of this emancipation was totally different from the extreme Catholic nidus that bred the Iberian Marranos. Moreover, the political emancipation of Jews in central Europe resulted, and was designed to result, in their assimilation to the normal social environment.[16a] This, too, was quite unlike the designedly extrusive process of the Spanish and Italian Inquisitions. Furthermore, the Emancipation coincided with and was partly dependent on a general recession of the power of the churches.

Despite these differences in origin, the two movements had analogous features. Both arose among people in whom the breakdown of talmudism had left the tension produced by a spiritual vacuum. It is not remarkable that in the resulting cultural hunger the intellectual products should bear traces of this. The Marranos, like their later counterparts, carried some residue of the old Jewish culture and, like them, they had not quite completely absorbed the culture of their environment. The double maladjustment, not so great as to constitute a spiritual conflict of the gravest kind, was yet enough to give an independence of approach, a philosophic detachment to the entrant into the newly accessible scientific field. This was certainly an advantage. An impartial outlook is a significant part of the equipment of the man of science. The circumstances that may induce it are worthy of further attention from the social psychologist.

It is not easy to depict the rise of science as a part of the history of western European Jews. Science, in the modern sense, is truly no part of their heritage. How could it be rooted in the history of a people to whom the renaissance of literature and of learning, of art and of science, had brought nothing except heavier bonds? The Renaissance has little place in Jewish history. On the other hand, the development of science itself cannot be said to be distinctive of any people. How could it be, since science is, of its nature, universal? It is neither Jewish nor Christian, neither national nor racial, but a product of a particular philosophic outlook. If we use language exactly we cannot speak at all of Jews or of Judaism in science. We do so in this place only by making several elipses and assumptions.

As with the Marrano episode, we can thus but present an imperfect panorama, emphasizing here and there those activities in which Jews have especially distinguished themselves. And even for such a partial account of the part that Jewish individuals have played in science it is necessary to correlate the record with that of the admission of Jews to universities.

In the sixteenth century the only university to which Jews had any easy access was Padua. In the seventeenth, Leyden began to take its place both in scientific eminence and in the freedom with which religious tests were waived. This great Dutch school achieved even greater prominence in the eighteenth century. In the central European universities professing Jews could hardly obtain admission until the mid-nineteenth century, while important posts, and notably full professorships, were almost entirely denied to them until well into the twentieth century. In the ancient English universities it was not possible for a Jew even to take a degree until the passing of the Universities Test Act in 1871.

Under these circumstances there arose in the German-speaking countries a movement closely resembling Marranism. Among nineteenth-century Jews, as among Christians, only a small proportion were "believers" in any profound sense. Many, both of Jewish and of Christian parentage, to whom religion meant little, found the formal profession of Christianity no unbearable strain on the conscience. In all countries, but especially in the Germanic, facile "converts" passed readily enough into the prevailing formal Christianity. Naturally they carried with them some elements of their traditional habits of thought. Of such persons it may be said that, except for the fact that their environment was happier and safer, their spiritual outlook did not and does not differ vastly from that of the earlier Iberian Marranos.

But while these German Marranos differ in some respects from their neighbors of non-Jewish origin, these differences did not and do not unite them. They have no common outlook. These nominal Christians of Jewish origin represented, and still represent, no organized or effective movement. As with the Iberian Marranos, their separateness was the result of external pressure rather than of internal force. This absence of internal force, this failure of and even resistance to organic development, has been the real basis of the Jewish tragedy. Even Jewish nationalism is basically of external origin, part of the nationalist pandemic that has swept the world for a century. Moreover, the withering of the religion, the only possible unifying element in the Jewish intellectual revival, happened to be contemporary with certain scientific developments. Jewish emancipation coincided with an era of enormous scientific advance, the result of extreme fragmentation in the scientific field resulting from the natural product of increasingly complex techniques. As with the finest craftsmanship, the very exercise of technique provided an outlet for self-expression. The frustrated and culture-starved German Marranos eagerly occupied this new field. They gave to it a certain spiritual significance that they drew from their half-forgotten religious heritage.

There is another and contrasting side to this scientific movement corresponding to the natural variety of character found in every social aggregate. Those of the reflective type sought immediate substitutes to fill the religious gap. They rapidly became part of the philosophic movement at the German universities. With this we are hardly directly concerned, except for the significant effect it had on the scientific movement itself. In fact, some of the greatest Jewish exponents of science in the early nineteenth century were men of the widest scientific grasp. Let us glance at the effects on Jews of these new sources of inspiration.

Before World War II Jews formed roughly one per cent of the population of Europe, which was roughly five hundred millions. But the Jewish five millions was far from evenly distributed. In the Iberian Peninsula it was next to nothing. In Scandinavia it was about one-tenth of one per cent. In parts of Russian and Rumanian territory it was a hundred times as much. The special area of Jewish intellectual success, though not of density of Jewish population, was German-speaking. In that region Jews formed about one in a hundred of the entire population. To a lesser extent Italian-speaking Europe, with a Jewish population of about one in a thousand, presented similar phenomena. These were less marked in the French- and English-speaking worlds. For obvious reasons Jewish intellectuals played hardly any part in the old Russian Empire and Rumania. Jewish scientific development was thus confined to a relatively small part of the European area in which Jews were settled.

These phenomena are capable of comparatively simple historical and demographic explanation. Jewish activity in the scientific realm has been particularly notable in the mathematical and medical fields. Mathematics relies less on apparatus and on organization than do other departments of science. In its development the solitary worker is less handicapped than in most departments. Those debarred from normal social, literary and scholastic contacts naturally throw themselves into this most abstract discipline. Jewish addiction to medicine again requires little explanation. Its pursuit is in the full Jewish tradition. Moreover, the social developments of the time and the constitution of the universities made it simpler for Jews to enter this than any other profession.

But when all is said there remains an essential something that is a real source of wonder. A people scattered, disunited, numerically less than one of the smallest nations of Europe, has for a century provided from an effective German-speaking population of some two millions an ever-increasing proportion of the best scientific exponents in central Europe and Italy. Put the matter numerically and in the roughest way. In pre-Nazi Germany Jews formed about three-quarters of one per cent of the population. Of distinguished German mathematicians, physicists and medical researchers, they provided something like thirty times their due proportion, for at least twenty-five per cent of these were Jews. In Italy, where the Jewish population was only one per thousand, Jewish intellectual supremacy was even higher in certain departments. Well above fifty per cent of the distinguished Italian mathematicians were Jews.

We turn to glance at some individual achievements in the different sciences, beginning with mathematics.

Karl Jacobi (1804-1851), son of a Jewish merchant of Potsdam, was the first prominent German mathematician of Jewish origin and among the greatest mathematicians of modern times. A prolific writer and able teacher, he profoundly influenced the entire realm of mathematical thought of his age; there is hardly a branch upon which he did not leave an imprint. His greatest contribution was his development of the theory of elliptic functions. Very important was his work on the theory of numbers and of determinants and, especially, of functional determinants ("Jacobians"), of the calculus of variations, of differential equations and of the theory of mechanics. In the last two fields his achievements form the basis of modern mathematical physics.

Jacobi's pupil Leopold Kronecker (1823-1891) of Liegnitz in Silesia entered the business world but by the time he reached his early thirties had saved enough to give all his energies to mathematics. He became the recognized leader of the "Berlin school." His chief work was on the theory of numbers. His theory of equations was based on the idea of the theory of groups of Galois. Kronecker tried to "arithmetize" the whole of mathematics.

Among the greatest mathematicians of all time, whose ideas revolutionized the whole area of mathematics, was Georg Cantor (1845-1918). Though born at St. Petersburg, he was of German origin, speech and culture and spent nearly the whole of his life in Germany. Despite the greatness of his achievement he was a tragic figure. Misunderstood by his contemporaries and exhausted by the struggle to defend his views, he passed into depression mounting to insanity. It would be hardly possible to overestimate the value of his idea of sets or aggregates, which is fundamental to the study of the philosophical foundations of mathematics. Of prime importance, too, is his notion of transfinite numbers by which he overcame the *horror infiniti* of his predecessors. The notations of the so-called "transfinite cardinal numbers," represented by the Hebrew symbol ℵ, remains his monument. The whole of modern analysis and theory of functions is based on Cantorian principles and his activity marks a period in the history of mathematics.

A distant relation to his namesake was the German scholar Moritz Cantor (1829-1920) who wrote an unsurpassed history of mathematics and organized much research in the subject.

At the age of eighteen, Hermann Minkowski (1864-1909) of Alexotas in Lithuania submitted his solution of a problem in the theory of quadratic forms to the Academy of Sciences at Paris. It earned the Grand Prix des Sciences Mathématiques. He became a professor at Goettingen, long a leading mathematical center. His introduction of the new notion of geometrical illustration into the theory of numbers created the so-called "Geometry of Numbers" and made his reputation international. No less important were his works relating to the new mechanics of Albert Einstein. His name must always be connected with the scientific revolution of the theory of relativity of time and space.

Felix Klein (1849-1925) was the recognized head of the Goettingen "universalists." He was a model professor both as teacher and as organizer of research. During the last forty years of his life his was the foremost mathematical influence in Germany. His many-sidedness is especially noteworthy. He held that all the various geometries should be regarded from the standpoint of the theory of groups. He was a very able propagator of Georg Friedrich Bernhard Riemann's theory of functions and his own researches in allied departments are of lasting value. A strong adversary of one-sided specialization, he dealt with all the branches of mathematics, seeking to link them more closely and to treat them as a unit. Klein played an important part in the planning and editing of the famous *Mathematical Encyclopedia*, and its success is largely due to his fascinating personality.

In addition to such men, whose genius is admittedly of the highest rank, there were and are scores of very eminent German-Jewish mathematicians whose distinction cannot yet be estimated. It is not possible here to list even their names. Of special interest, however, is Emmy Noether (1882-1936), the very gifted daughter of the well-known mathematician Max Noether (1844-1922). She was one of the most brilliant modern algebraists and perhaps the ablest woman mathematician since Hypatia. Through her numerous works she gave a new direction to the theory of algebraic fields, initiated by Evariste Galois and developed by Richard Dedekind and Kronecker. She laid down the foundations of the theory of ideals, of great importance in modern algebra. Expelled by the Nazis, she found refuge in the United States, where she died soon after her arrival.

Luigi Cremona (1830-1903), one of the outstanding Italian mathematicians, was the founder of the modern "synthetic" geometry. The "Cremona transformation" has proved of importance. In addition to this achievement, he was a senator and minister of education. Another Italian, Vito Volterra (1860-1940) was largely instrumental in the creation of a new branch of mathematics, the theory of integral and differential equations. He stands among the great mathematicians of modern times. Tullio Levi-Civita (1873-1942) died in the Vatican during World War II, having been dismissed in 1938 from his professorship in accordance with the Fascist anti-Jewish policy. With Gregorio Ricci (Curbastro) he laid the foundations of absolute differential calculus. This, as Einstein has recognized, made possible the formulation of the mathematical theory of general relativity. Levi-Civita's work in mechanics and theoretical astronomy is no less valuable. Gino Loria (1862-1954) has contributed greatly to the theory of curves and is of the highest distinction as a historian of mathematics. Federigo Enriques (1871-1945) earned great regard as a mathematical philosopher. There have been several other eminent modern Italian-Jewish mathematicians. When one recalls that only one Italian in a thousand is a Jew, the contemporary existence of at least five eminent Italian-Jewish mathematicians is, in itself a matter, of note.

Several of the most prominent figures in French mathematics have been of Jewish origin. The most notable are Georges Halphen (1844-1889), Paul Appel (1855-1930) and Jacques Hadamard (1865-   ). In general Jewish eminence in mathematics have been a special feature of the German scene. In the English-speaking world, however, a mathematician of the first rank was James Joseph Sylvester (1814-1897). As a loyal Jew he was unable to take a degree at Cambridge and still less to hold a fellowship. Nevertheless, he adorned the chair of mathematics successively at London, at the Royal Military Academy, Woolwich, at Johns Hopkins and at Oxford. In brilliance of conception, in acuteness of penetration, in fluency and richness of expression, Sylvester has had few equals among mathematicians of any age or nationality. At an earlier date Benjamin Gomperz (1779-1865) of London, though occupying no official position, helped to lay the foundation of modern vital statistics.

Success in astronomy usually demands official status and Jews, especially in the German zone, have thus been more handicapped than in mathematics. Nevertheless, there have been among them some able exponents of astronomical science.

One of the greatest of all astronomers, Sir William Herschel (1738-1822), was born at Hanover, his family being of remoter Jewish origin, and settled early in England. His discovery of the planet Uranus in 1781 brought him immortality. He conducted valuable researches on double stars, nebulae and star clusters and is the founder of modern stellar astronomy. His theory of the general structure of the universe still holds the field. His sister Caroline (1750-1848) was his very able research assistant, detecting some remarkable nebulae and many comets. His son Sir John (1792-1871) has a rank among astronomers second only to his father.

Wilhelm Beer (1797-1850), brother of the well known Parisian musician Giacomo Meyerbeer, having secured a competence in business, devoted himself to astronomy. With Needler he produced a great chart of the moon which marked an epoch in works of its kind. The Viennese Maurice Loewy (1833-1907) settled in Paris and with the support of Urbain Jean

Joseph Leverrier made researches on comets and on the photosphere of the sun. He became president of the French Academy of Sciences and, as so often, German loss was the world's gain. Samuel Oppenheim (1856-1928), a Moravian, president of the Astronomical Society of Vienna, was a master of astronomical calculations. His writings are devoted to the motion of stars, double stars and calculation of orbits of comets.

Despite the early death of Karl Schwarzchild (1873-1916)—the result of service in the German army during World War I—he was one of the greatest astronomers of his day. As a schoolboy he published two articles on determination of orbits. In later years he originated in photographic photometry a new method depending on measurement of density of star images. He introduced the use of a color index for stars, which has yielded information on their spectral types and surface temperatures, and is well remembered for his *Goettinger Aktinometrie*, a catalogue of 3,500 stars completed in accordance with his newly invented method. No less influential have been his mathematical study of star movements and of the structure of the solar system and his contributions to physical theory, especially in optics.

A German-Jewish astronomer who had a remarkable career was Hermann Goldschmidt (1802-1866) of Frankfort. After years in his father's warehouse he migrated in 1836 to Paris, where he earned distinction as a painter. In 1847 he turned to astronomy and in 1852 discovered a minor planet which he called Lutetia, the ancient name of Paris. He continued his researches and revealed the presence of fourteen previously unknown asteroids. Of Jewish origin also was Adolf Marcuse (1860-1930), who made numerous astronomical expeditions and, like Fritz Cohn (1866-1921), was director of the Royal Observatory at Berlin. German-Jewish astronomers who worked in Switzerland were Adolf Hirsch (1830-1901) of Neuchâtel, remembered for his services to the International Commission for Measurement of the Earth, and Rudolf Wolf (1816-1893) of Zurich, the accepted historian of astronomy.

Experimental physics, even more than astronomy, is dependent on that free access to a laboratory which only university status can provide. Nevertheless, many Jews have distinguished themselves in this field. The earliest was Moritz Jacobi (1801-1874), brother of the great mathematician. He was an architect but devoted much attention to the electrical deposit of metals, or electroplasty. The first Jew elected to the Prussian Academy of Sciences was Peter Riess (1805-1883), who devoted himself to the study of frictional electricity. But during the second half of the nineteenth century the number of German-Jewish physicists became so large that we can mention only a few of fully recognized distinction.

Eugene Goldstein (1850-1930) of Gleiwitz (Silesia) was one of the most skillful experimental physicists of modern times. His name is especially associated with the discovery of gamma rays. Great scientific men cannot be arranged in order of merit. Yet it is safe to say that Heinrich Hertz (1857-1894) is among the ten physicists of most influence during the past hundred years. He wrote little during his short life but every line was significant. He measured the length and velocity of electromagnetic waves and showed that they are the result of transverse vibration and are subject to reflection, refraction and polarization, like those of light and heat. He demonstrated that electromagnetic oscillations are propagated with the same velocity as light and finally demonstrated the electromagnetic nature of light. He adumbrated the principles of wireless and of X rays. It is pitiful to recall that Hertz's pupil, successor and literary executor, Philipp Lennard, himself a recipient of the Nobel Prize, shamed his old age by devoting himself to violent anti-Jewish Nazi propaganda directed largely against the teacher whose works he had edited and whose biography he had written.

Outstanding work in solar physics was done by Ernst Pringsheim (1857-1917) of Breslau. Certain other of his investigations led naturally to the quantum theory later enunciated by Max Planck.

Lise Meitner (1878-) of Vienna is among the small band of great women physicists of whom Madame Curie is the best known. Like hers, Lise Meitner's name is connected with radioactivity. She is especially remembered for her discovery in 1918, along with Otto Hahn, of the element protoactinium with atomic number 91. Her name will always be connected with the development of the theory of atomic energy.

Jews played a large part in the development of the classical physics of the nineteenth century. It may fairly be said that their contributions to the physics of the twentieth century based on relativity have been overwhelming in proportion to their numbers. The mention of Albert Einstein, Niels Bohr, James Franck, Ludwig Hertz must suffice. At the time of the Nazi seizure of power the general development of theoretical physics was greater at Goettingen than in any other university in the world. The dismissal of teachers under the "Aryan" edicts left the two great institutes of physics in that university almost entirely depopulated.

Few Jewish physicists distinguished themselves in the classical period outside the German zone. The most eminent was probably the American Albert Michelson (1825-1919), whose parents were driven from Germany when he was two years old. Between 1879 and 1882 Michelson made measurements of the velocity of light. In 1886, along with Edward Williams Morley, he made experiments on the relative motion of ether and matter, showing that the ether within a transparent medium is carried forward when it moves, but at a lesser velocity. In 1887 he had suggested the wave length of sodium light as a standard unit. This was put into effect in a very delicate experiment performed by him in Paris in 1892.

Since this unit depends only on the properties of vibrating atoms it is probably one of the most constant dimensions in nature. In 1900 he showed that spectral lines are tripled when the radiations emanate in a magnetic field. Michelson was the first American to be awarded the Nobel Prize.

Jews have perhaps been less successful in the practical development of physical principles than in investigating the fundamental properties of matter. In other words, they have excelled more in pure than in applied science. Nevertheless, there have been some very eminent inventors among them.

Siegfried Marcus (1831-1897) of Mecklenburg, a very gifted and versatile inventor, produced the first electrical instrument for regulating temperature and the first effective means of estimating earth movements. He is, however, particularly remembered as father of the internal-combustion engine, of which he constructed a model in 1864. By 1875 he had made a practical engine which he was able to drive in the streets of Vienna, where it was still preserved in 1937. The scheme of lighter-than-air dirigibles was first developed by the German David Schwarz, who built his first airship at St. Petersburg in 1892. His patents were afterwards purchased from his widow by Count Zeppelin.

Philip Reiss (1837-1874), born in poverty near Frankfort, began experiments on hearing apparatus in boyhood which ultimately developed into what was in effect a telephone (1861). This was exhibited in 1864. It was on his principle that Alexander Graham Bell and Thomas Edison perfected their device (1876). Emil Berliner (1851-1929) of Hanover settled in the United States in 1870 and there developed several inventions, among them the microphone.

Hermann Aron (1845-1913) was professor at the Artillery School at Berlin and developed an effective electrometer (1888). Leo Arons (1860-1919) was a picturesque figure who was dismissed from his post at Berlin University (1899) because of his Socialist sympathies. He did much to advance the practical applications of electricity. Notably he invented the first mercury vapor lamp (1896). Gabriel Lipman (1845-1921) of Luxembourg passed his scientific life in Paris, where he held a chair of physics. His development of color photography earned him a Nobel Prize in 1908.

Arnold Berliner (1862-1939) was put to death by the Nazis. A man of extraordinary scientific versatility, he rendered great services to German science as editor for many years of *Naturwissenschaften*, a journal for the general exchange of scientific views.

Chemistry was for long largely extra-academic. Thus Jews had opportunities that were denied them in physics. An early Jewish arrival in the chemical field was Heinrich Magnus (1802-1879), a pupil of Berzelius at Stockholm and of Gay-Lussac in Paris. He made many technical contributions of importance, perhaps the most significant being his determination of the coefficient of expansion of gases. He described a large number of new compounds, one of which, his "green salt" (a platinum-ammonia compound), is still known by his name. He ultimately became rector of Berlin University.

Charles Gerhardt (1816-1857) of Strasbourg was a pupil of Justus von Liebig and did most of his scientific work in Paris. He has a distinguished place in the history of chemistry, for his name is associated with the doctrines of valency and of chemical equivalents. He developed the molecular theory and made the first effective classification of organic compounds.

There is nothing more remarkable in the history of modern Germany than the rise of her chemical industry. Without this she could not have become a great power. There were so many and such able chemists of Jewish origin associated with this process that it is safe to say that without them her industrial development would have been impossible.

Adolf Frank (1834-1916) was the founder of the potash industry of Germany. He instituted the first potash factory (1861) at Stassfurt near Magdeburg, obtaining it from the local mineral deposit. Until then potash had been extracted from ashes burnt in or under pots, hence the name. With the Polish Jew, Nikodem Caro (1871-1935), he took the first step toward the nitrogen-fixation industry by forming calcium cyanide from nitrogen and calcium carbide. This industry was to be epochal not only for Germany but for the world.

Equally important for German economic development was Adolf von Bayer (1835-1917), professor at Munich whose mother was a Jewess. Just as Frank founded the German heavy chemical industry so did Bayer found that of fine chemicals. He was one of the foremost organic chemists of his day, the discoverer of the phthalein class of dyes (1874) and the first to synthetize indigo (1878). Synthetic indigo came entirely to take the place of the natural product. His patents passed to the Badische Anilin und Soda Fabrik, which formed the nucleus of the giant I. G. Farbenindustrie. Other patents absorbed by that combine were those of Heinrich Caro (1834-1910) of Poznan, the discoverer of methylene blue and of many other aniline dyes and of Carl Liebermann (1842-1914) of Berlin, who made important discoveries among the aniline compounds. German chemical industry was, in fact, substantially based on Jewish genius and Jewish enterprise.

The name of Victor Meyer (1848-1897) of Berlin is one of the greatest in the history of organic chemistry. At Heidelberg he was the favorite pupil and personal assistant of Robert Wilhelm von Bunsen. He succeeded Friedrich Woehler at Goettingen (1882) and Bunsen (1889) at Heidelberg, where he died by his own hand. His comprehensive researches on nitro compounds of the fatty series, upon isonitrous compounds and upon thiophene are among the most remarkable of the nineteenth century. The method he devised for estimating vapor density has become standard.

To give an account of all the German chemists of Jewish origin would be to write an appreciable part of the history of German chemistry from about 1860 onward. There have also been many distinguished Jewish chemists outside the German zone, but only a few can be mentioned here.

Henri Moissan (1852-1907) of Paris is remembered for several achievements. He succeeded in isolating fluorine, long a main problem in chemistry. He invented the electric furnace for very high and steady temperatures, which is known by his name. He demonstrated the nature of the diamond by producing it artificially.

Another brilliant chemist was the Englishman Raphael Meldola (1849-1915). He made the first oxazine dyestuff (Meldola's blue, 1879) which has become important for cotton dyeing, and worked much on naphthalene and azo compounds. He was very versatile, took much interest in biology, was a friend and correspondent of Charles Darwin and experimented with the coloration of animals.

A rather special place is occupied by Edmund Lippmann (1857-1942) of Vienna. He was the leading authority on the chemistry of sugars and the sugar industry and introduced the strontium process into sugar refining. He extended his researches into the history of the subject and finally became an authority on its alchemical aspects.

The name of Fritz Haber (1868-1934) will always be associated with the opening up of new industrial possibilities by a practical method of nitrogen fixation, the "Haber process" for the synthetic production of ammonia. It proved of the utmost importance to Germany's supply of nitrates both for agricultural and for military purposes. Nevertheless, in 1933 he was forced by the Nazis to leave Germany. This great benefactor of his country died in exile while Germany made war with the processes he had invented.

Richard Willstaetter (1872-1942) of Karlsruhe, a very great biochemist, discovered several forms of chlorophyll in plants. He demonstrated relationships between this green coloring matter and the red coloring matter in the blood of animals. He also produced the anesthetic avertin.

Mineralogy, as a science, has few exponents but among them the most distinguished were several who were Jewish. The first of them, the Parisian Armand Lévy (1794-1841), who spent many years in England, was a skilled mathematician and did much to introduce mathematical notation into crystallography. Harry Rosenbusch (1836-1914) of Heidelberg became head of a new school that dealt with the microscopy of minerals. Auguste Michel Lévy (1844-1911) of the Collège de France and of the French geological survey was among the founders of the modern science of petrography. Edward Suess (1831-1914), born in London, son of a German merchant, was long professor of geology in Vienna. His monumental *Face of the Earth* (1885) has been translated into many languages and gone into many editions. Many tendencies in modern geology have stemmed from it. Victor Goldschmidt (1853-1933), for many years a professor in Heidelberg and afterwards at Oslo, was one of the greatest exponents of crystallographic science. He introduced the binocular goniometer. His monumental work summarized the knowledge of the subject and his home became the recognized meeting place of the crystallographers of the world. His son succeeded him as professor of crystallography at Oslo.

Turning to biology, it might be thought that age-old urbanization of Jews would deprive them of interest in what were primarily countrymen's subjects. That this has not proved to be the case is doubtless due to the fact that the traditional Jewish attitude toward medicine has always involved contact with the problems of living things. In fact, since the German universities have been opened to them Jews have always been prominent in biology.

The name of Nathaniel Pringsheim (1823-1894) is especially connected with the study of algae. He demonstrated the reproductive processes of many kinds and showed that they were exhibited in an alternation of sexual and asexual generations (1856), both of which he elucidated. He produced a classic work on the life of the fern (1862) and later turned to plant physiology, doing much to explain the action of chlorophyll (1874). He subsequently demonstrated that light itself may have a lethal effect on plants (1879).

Ferdinand Cohn (1828-1898) of Breslau, a pupil of Johannes Mueller, was a peculiarly skilled microscopist particularly interested in the minute fungi. As author of the first monograph on bacteria he is the father of bacteriology. He rendered a great service by his encouragement of an unknown young man, Robert Koch (1843-1910). The latter's demonstration of the relation of anthrax bacteria to the disease was publicized by Cohn (1876); it contained the first evidence of the production of a specific human disease by a known species of bacteria.

Perhaps the most influential botanical teacher of the nineteenth century was Julius Sachs (1832-1897) also of Breslau and professor for many years at Wuerzburg. After applying himself to the study of the structure of forms of plants he turned to physiology and from 1857 became immersed in the problems of nutrition. He became convinced that chlorophyll is not diffused in tissues but is contained only in special bodies, the "chloroplasts." He showed that sunlight plays the decisive role in determining their action in reference to the absorption of carbon dioxide. Further, chlorophyll is formed only in light and, moreover, in different variations of light the process undergoes different degrees of activity. Sachs's researches covered every aspect of botany and he became a kind of botanical dictator.

Edward Strasburger (1844-1912) worked at Bonn, where he laid the foundations of the knowledge of the phenomena of nuclear division (*Mitosis*, 1875), clarifying the relation of nuclear changes to the sexual process. He was an encyclopedic botanist and his textbook is still in common use. Demonstrating that the chromosomes are individually recognizable and traceable from cell to cell (1905-1908), he thus laid the foundations of the modern science of genetics.

Approaching the medical field we are overwhelmed with names. From the beginning of the nineteenth century the number of distinguished Jewish names in the German-speaking countries have progressively increased in this their own traditional field. During the century interest became most intensely focused on the minute analysis of structure and its correlation with function. In this field Jews played a particularly prominent part.[17a]

The earliest influential Jewish figure in this movement was Karl Friedrich Canstatt (1807-1850) of Ratisbon, who made a study of the finer structure of the eye. Perhaps his greatest discovery was his pupil at Erlangen, Robert Virchow, accounted with Henle the founder of modern pathology.

Jacob Henle (1809-1885) of Fuerth near Nuremberg was the greatest German microscopic anatomist of his time and one of the greatest anatomists of all time, comparable only to Vesalius. He was professor of anatomy at Zurich (1840), Heidelberg (1844) and Goettingen (1852). His achievements in his special field were enormous and his work in histology was the first of its kind. He was a most versatile genius, for he was a poet, artist, orator and a very great teacher. And he was in his way a prophet, for he saw, as in a glass darkly, the microbic origin of infectious disease.

Benedikt Stilling (1810-1879), a skilled surgeon, introduced a new technique for the microscopic examination of the nervous system in the manipulation of which he was extremely expert. Structures in the nervous system are still identified by his name. He also instituted important advances in nervous physiology.

Ludwig Traube (1818-1876) of Ratibor worked in Berlin for thirty years, and was a founder of experimental pathology and of the scientific investigation of the action of drugs. He was an outstanding clinician and a particularly successful teacher. Gustav Valentin (1810-1883) of Breslau accomplished much in the physiology of muscle and nerve and in the digestion of carbohydrates. Gottlieb Gluege (1812-1898) of Brakel in Westphalia migrated to France and was thence called to Brussels. He did excellent physiological work, wrote the first treatise of pathological histology (1839-1841), began the study of parasitology and gave the earliest account of the essential cause of trichiniasis.

Robert Remak (1815-1865) of Posen worked in Berlin, where he had a distinguished reputation as a microscopist. His most eminent service was perhaps to demonstrate the true nature of the multiplication of cells. In 1842, long before Pasteur and Koch, using himself as guinea pig, he showed that certain skin diseases are caused by microscopic organisms. He was also a pioneer in electrotherapy.

Moritz Schiff (1823-1896) of Frankfort began as a zoologist and turned afterwards to physiology, which he taught at Florence and Geneva. He was a man of restless energy, almost prophetic insight and infinite originality, who covered too many fields to be a complete master of one. He anticipated Pavlov in the conception of conditioned reflexes, Claude Bernard in that of vasodilator nerves and much later work on the thyroid. He was a pioneer in many aspects of brain physiology and his experiments in the artificial production of diabetes via the nervous system (1856-1859) are classics.

Rudolph Heidenhain (1834-1897) of Breslau is especially associated with the interpretation of secretion in cellular terms. His research projects on the secretion of various organs and his stains and methods of staining are daily recalled in every biological laboratory. Julius Conheim (1839-1884), while professor at Breslau, revealed the true nature of suppuration, proving that the corpuscles of pus are formed from those of the blood. Despite his short life his contributions to pathological knowledge were numerous and very important.

Hugo Kronecker (1839-1914) of Liegnitz in Silesia, professor of physiology at Berne in 1885, distinguished himself particularly by his work on the fatigue and recovery of muscle, by his proof that the heart muscle can pass into a tetanic state and by his investigation of the mechanism of swallowing. He invented many ingenious physiological devices, and he is especially remembered for his demonstration that the heart's motto is "all or none," that is, that it will either contract to its fullest extent or not at all.

Carl Weigert (1845-1904) was perhaps the most eminent microscopic anatomist of the later nineteenth century. He introduced many new methods and was responsible for the highly important technique of bacterial staining which is one of the most valuable aids to modern scientific medicine. He also greatly added to the knowledge of the structure and function of the nervous system.

Elie Metchnikoff (1845-1916) was a Russian half-Jew who worked most of his life in Paris. His most important experiments, begun on the water flea, showed how amoeboid cells act as scavengers in the body, engulfing and digesting solid particles and notably bacteria. He showed that inflammation is accompanied by the gathering of swarms of these scavengers or policemen to the site of the injury.

Oscar Minkowski (1858-1931) brother of the mathematician, demonstrated the relation between the pancreas and diabetes and thus led to the study which culminated in the discovery of insulin.

Jacques Loeb (1859-1924) left Germany for America in middle life and ultimately became head of the department of experimental biology at the Rockefeller Institute. His research projects were of varied character. Many of them were designed to demonstrate that much "vital" action can be explained as response to chemicals or physical stimuli and do not involve the intercurrence of "mind."

These are hardly more than a random sample of those of central European Jewish origin who made distinguished contributions to nineteenth-century medicine. The mind of any well-informed medical man will react to the names of the members of this list.

The most characteristic development of modern medicine is the interest in the vast complexity of the functions and minute parts of the body and their reactions to its environment and especially to the organisms of disease and to their products. In this field the Jewish contribution is overwhelming. There is Alexander Besredka (1870-1940) of the Pasteur Institute, Ludwig Brieger (1849-1919), who initiated the study of toxins, Albert Neisser (1885-1916), discoverer of the gonococcus, Albert Frankel (1848-1916) and Carl Friedlaender (1847-1887), discoverers of the organism causing lobar pneumonia, Fernand Widal (1862-1929), elucidator of the nature of blood reactions, Paul Ehrlich (1854-1915), the greatest of biochemists, who made chemotherapy a science, Waldemar Haffkine (1860-1930), introducer of protection against plague and cholera, Alexander Marmorek (1865-1923), whose serum provides protection against streptococcal infection, Casimir Funk (1884-   ), one of the discoverers of vitamins and originator of the name, Ernst Salkowski (1844-1923), father of clinical pathology.

In the investigation of the functions of the nervous system a high place is taken by Wilhelm Erb (1840-1921), who introduced electrodiagnosis by induction, revealed the significance of the knee jerk and, along with his contemporary Hermann Oppenheim (1858-1910), described many unrecognized pathological conditions.

Anatomy, in the old sense of the term, is regarded as one of the "completed" sciences. Such significant contributions as were made to it in the past generations were largely the work of Jews, among them the Viennese Julius Tandler (1869-1910), last of the great anatomists, and Emil Zuckerkandl (1849-1910), also of Vienna, whose account of the structures of the parts of interest to otorhinologists is likely to remain the standard work of reference.

Space fails even for the names of eminent exponents of clinical practice of central European origin, but we mention Wilhelm Ebstein (1836-1912) of Goettingen, and the great authorities on drugs Matthias Liebreich

(1838-1908) of Berlin, Oswald Schmiedeberg (1838-1921) of Dorpat, and Moritz Romberg (1795-1893) of Berlin.

Psychology in its medical applications may be said to be almost a Jewish science. Since our list must be brought to an end we do so with the names of Alfred Adler (1870-1937) of Vienna, Viktor Adler (1852-1918) of Prague, Sigmund Freud (1856-1939) of Vienna, and Bernard Hollander (1864-1934) of London. These men have not only introduced new methods of treatment but they have changed the whole direction of medical thought, practice and education. They have done more, for they have taught us a great deal about ourselves and changed the outlook of modern philosophy.

As one contemplates the galaxy of talent at which we have but glanced, two reflections arise. First, it is a tragedy for the Jewish people that the stream of life and thought that this implies has been broken. The break is more than that of the inevitable death of individuals, for the stock from which they have arisen has ceased to reproduce itself adequately. This is a loss to humanity as well as to the Jewish people. And secondly, it is a tragedy for the German people that, at the urging of a perverted outcast, it has extruded from its body politic a main source, perhaps *the* main source, of its claim to respect from the world of intellect. So far as the products of the intellect are concerned we must write *Germania fuit,* for henceforth German will be a language of secondary importance in the field of learning.

The intellectual future of the Jews themselves must depend, in this writer's opinion, upon many factors that are at present indeterminable, but most of all on one that *is* determinable. We live in a world in which religions and religious sanctions are breaking down. Religion is the one link that can unite the Jewish people. The problem is whether the Jewish religion can or cannot develop in a non-Jewish environment as one of the great world religions. If it can, the future of a special Jewish intellectual atmosphere is secure. If it cannot, Judaism will continue as a fossil fragment of the ancient Syrian civilization and, like other fossils, it will slowly but surely disintegrate.

NOTES

[1a Cf. above Elias J. Bickerman, "The Historical Foundations of Post-biblical Judaism," pp. 97-99; see also above Robert Gordis, "The Bible as a Cultural Monument," pp. 808-813.]

[2a Cf. above Alexander Altmann, "Judaism and World Philosophy," p. 957; see also above Ralph Marcus, "Hellenistic Jewish Literature," pp. 1107 ff.]

[2b Professor Saul Lieberman, the authority on Judaism in the Hellenic period, finds that "many parallels exist between the rabbinic natural science and that of the Greeks and the Romans of that time" (the first four centuries). He cites discussions of many natural phenomena—botanical, zoological and biological—comparing the concepts of the Rabbis and their contemporary scholars in other cultures. Professor Lieberman concludes that in natural science there were "great similarities between the methods, behavior, practices and notions prevalent among Jews and gentiles alike." However, he cautions that "no definite opinion can be pronounced until all that the Rabbis said about it is collected." See his "The Natural Science of the Rabbis," in *Hellenism in Jewish Palestine*, New York, 1950, pp. 180 ff. The editor of the present work is indebted to Dr. Solomon R. Kagan for questioning the opinion expressed by Dr. Singer.]

³ *Sifre, Deuteronomy, Haazinu*, 306, f. 131 a. (Quoted from Montefiore and Loewe, *Rabbinic Anthology*, London, 1938.)

[⁴ᵃ Cf. above Judah Goldin, "The Period of the Talmud (135 B.C.E.-1035 C.E.)," pp. 194 ff.; see also Altmann, *op. cit.*, pp. 966 ff.]

[⁵ᵃ Cf. also the chapter above by Arturo Castiglioni, "The Contribution of the Jews to Medicine."]

[⁶ᵃ Cf. above Cecil Roth, "The European Age in Jewish History (to 1648)," pp. 222-223.]

[⁷ᵃ Cf. Altmann, *op. cit.*, pp. 972 ff.]

[⁸ᵃ Cf. above Abraham S. Halkin, "Judeo-Arabic Literature," pp. 1143-1145.]

[⁹ᵃ Cf. Altmann, *op. cit.*, pp. 974-977.]

[¹⁰ᵃ Cf. Roth, *op. cit.*, pp. 237 ff.]

[¹¹ᵃ Cf. Halkin, *op. cit.*, p. 1146.]

[¹²ᵃ Cf. Altmann, *op. cit.*, p. 975.]

[¹³ᵃ Cf. *ibid.*, pp. 975-976.]

[¹⁴ᵃ Cf. Roth, *op. cit.*, p. 236.]

[¹⁵ᵃ Cf. Castiglioni, *op. cit.*, pp. 1366-1367.]

[¹⁶ᵃ Cf. above Roth, "The Jews of Western Europe (from 1648)," pp. 264-265.]

[¹⁷ᵃ Cf. Castiglioni, *op. cit.*, pp. 1369 ff.]

BIBLIOGRAPHY

General Works

For the general scientific background: Charles Singer, *Short History of Science to the Nineteenth Century* (Oxford and New York, 1941, and later editions). For an objective study of Judaism and the Jewish people in world history: A. J. Toynbee, *A Study of History* (*abridgement by D. C. Somervell*) (Oxford and New York, 1946). For estimate of the contribution of Judaic thought to modern civilization: Edwyn R. Bevan and Charles Singer (eds.), *The Legacy of Israel* (Oxford and New York, 1927, and subsequent editions). For a general account of the contribution of Jews, as distinct from Judaism, Cecil Roth, *The Jewish Contribution to Civilization* (Cincinnati, 1940). Much material is to be found in that mine of well-arranged learning, George Sarton, *Introduction to the History of Science* (Baltimore, 1927).

Specialized Works

For the Rabbinic attitude toward nature: C. G. Montefiore and H. Loewe, *A Rabbinic Anthology*, selected and arranged with Comments and Introduction (London and New York, 1938). The entire Hebraeo-Arabic period with bibliography is treated by Aldo Mieli in *La Science Arabe et son rôle dans l'évolution scientifique mondiale* (Leyden, 1938). The specifically Hebraic aspect of Arabic science is treated with superb comprehensiveness, but for reference only, in Moritz Steinschneider, *Die hebraeischen Uebersetzungen des Mittelalters und die Juden als Dolmetscher* (Berlin, 1889-1893). For the translation of this literature into Latin, etc., Moritz Steinschneider. *Die europaeischen Uebersetzungen bis Mitte des 17 Jahrhunderts* (Vienna, 1904-1905), also only for reference. For the Marrano episode: Cecil Roth, *A History of the Marranos* (Philadelphia, 1941). For the Central European century: Louis Gershenfeld, *The Jew in Science* (Philadelphia, 1934); Ernst Heppner, *Juden als Erfinder und Entdecker* (Berlin, 1913); Felix A. Theilhaber and Ernst Heppner in *Juedisches Lexikon*, Vol. 2, cols. 462-467 (Berlin, 1928); *L'Apport d'Israel à la Civilisation: Conférence donnée à l'Hotel de la Paix, à Lausanne, le 8 fevrier, 1939, sous la Présidence de M. le Prof. Henri L. Miéville*, containing "La Médecine" by Professor Dr. Maurice Muret, and "La Philosophie et les Sciences," by Marcel Reymond (Lausanne, 1939); H. Newman (ed.), *The Real Jew, Some Aspects of the Jewish Contribution to Civilisation* (London, 1925), containing "The Jew and Scientific Research," by S. Brodetsky, "The Jew and Medicine," by Lester Samuels, and "The Jew and Chemistry," by Philip Blackman; Madison C. Peters, *Justice to the Jew* (London, 1899), Ch. VII: "The Jew in the Sciences."

For Medicine

Harry Friedenwald, *The Jews and Medicine* (Baltimore, 1944, 2 vols.), Sidney Osborne, *Germany and Her Jews* (London, 1939), Ch. 3: "The Jews as Physicians"; Ch. 4: "German Jews as Scientists and Inventors." Felix A. Theilhaber, *Schicksal und Leistung, Juden in der deutschen Forschung und Technik* (Berlin, 1931). *Cahiers Juifs*, Alexandria-Paris, Nos. 5-6, September-November, 1933: *L'Apport des Juifs d'Allemagne à la Civilisation Allemande*, contains "Le Progrès des Sciences Naturelles," by Horace Goldie, "Médecine, Chirurgie, Pathologie," by Ernst Fraenkel, "Mathématique, Physique," by Bernard Kwal and "Techniciens et Inventuers," by E. Aisberg. *The Jewish Review*, No. 5, June-September (London, 1933). *The Jewish Contribution to Modern Life and Thought in Germany* contains "The Physical Sciences," by H. Levy; "Applied Science," by F. Adler, and "Medicine," by Samson Wright.

CHAPTER 33

JUDAISM AND THE DEMOCRATIC IDEAL

By Milton R. Konvitz

JEWISH AND DEMOCRATIC IDEALS

In this chapter we shall take as the essence of the democratic ideal the belief in equality. An explication of this belief in equality leads to cultural and religious pluralism; to constitutional government, with effective checks on the agencies of government; a wide and equitable distribution of property; universal education and emphasis on reason, rather than superstition and force, as instruments of social control and progress; freedom of speech, freedom of the press, and freedom of assembly.

Just as a sharp distinction must be made between the accidental and the essential aspects of democracy, so the same distinction must be made among the various aspects of Judaism. Judaism, too, has had its highest insights, which, though they may have been conditioned by historical events, deserve perpetuation on their own account. On the other hand, like all other social institutions, Judaism has frequently needed to accommodate itself to the accidents of time and place in ways which did not at all times exhibit its own highest ideals. As in the case of democracy, it is the deeper motivation, the profounder insights, rather than the superficial aspects, that have kept alive Judaism as a way of life and as a philosophy of life.

Living in the middle of the twentieth century, we, of course, face problems radically different from those faced by the prophets thousands of years ago, or by the great Rabbis responsible for the Babylonian and Palestinian Talmuds.[1a] Freedom of speech must mean something sharply different to a people with a press than it did to a people who prohibited reduction of their learning to writing. This means only that the branches of democracy are different; the root is the same: it is the same wherever and whenever people live together in a community, wherever and whenever people constitute a society. The problem of human freedom is always the same: though at one time, to achieve more of it, we must fight a civil war to abolish economic and physical slavery; at another time we must fight to abolish racial distinctions in immigration policy; at one time, to achieve more of freedom, we must carry on a fight for woman suffrage; at another time the fight is against the white primary and the poll tax;

1430

at one time the fight is for freedom to teach Torah in Jabneh; at another time the fight is for freedom to teach the theory of evolution in Tennessee. The scenes change; the characters and the plot are pretty much the same. This does not mean, necessarily, that the history of mankind can be written in terms of the history of liberty. We are not here concerned with the degree of truth in a Crocean philosophy of history. All we mean to say is that, whatever liberty may have meant at different times in the history of mankind, its essential character, as we have stated it, has been always pretty much the same. The struggles have been variations on a theme. The theme has been: human equality and freedom.

THE DEMOCRATIC IDEAL: RACIAL AND NATIONAL EQUALITY

Almost at the outset of our discussion we must face the obvious question of the consistency of the concept of the chosen people with the democratic ideal. How can a people that considers itself elected of God as His special inheritance, find its institutions and ideals consistent with democracy? Some have met the question by a denial that Jews today consider themselves God's chosen people.

This is one answer. Most Jews, however, assert that, when rightly understood, there is no inconsistency between the doctrine of the chosen people and democratic ideals. The doctrine of the chosen people may lead to exclusiveness, physical and spiritual isolation, haughtiness of spirit; but this happens only when the doctrine is adhered to by a person with a narrow heart and mind, who has no real comprehension of the meaning and utility of the doctrine. When taken on a higher ground, it is said, the concept has great value in furthering the ideals of both Judaism and democracy.

An excellent statement of this point of view is to be found in the philosophical writings of Rab Saadia Gaon.[2a] "All creatures are His creatures," said Rab Saadia Gaon, "and we may not say that He has taken to Himself one to the exclusion of the other or to a greater degree than another." For, "if God hath chosen but one man and one city, who would remember the rest of mankind?"

In the same way, said Rab Saadia Gaon, we must consider allusions to God as the God of Abraham, Isaac and Jacob. "For when the Psalmist exclaimed 'O Lord, the portion of *mine* inheritance and *my* cup,' did he alone want to possess the master of the worlds?"

"We hold," said Rab Saadia Gaon, "that He is the God of all mankind" and that "the worth of each man and his lot are equally precious before Him." The doctrine of the chosen people to Rab Saadia Gaon was nothing more than an expression exalting and praising God; for he who feels himself especially touched by God's love describes himself as the recipient of God's grace and special favor. But it carries no implication that God does not stand in the same loving relationship to all men, and that others may not designate that relationship in the same or similar terms.

It is probable that today most Jews accept the doctrine of the chosen people as the Jews' explanation of the possession by them "of a spiritually unique literature and philosophy." The Jews are the chosen people only because God has chosen them from among all peoples to give them the Torah.[3a] The supreme treasure is not the Jewish people but the Torah; and the former are important in God's universal scheme only as the recipients and bearers of this great treasure. Israel was selected and made the custodian of the Torah only so that he might share his inheritance with all other men. It is the duty of Israel to be the model and guide to all nations; but this he can accomplish only by living in accordance with the dictates of the Word of God in the Torah. In brief, Israel was "chosen" only in the sense that he was selected by God to transmit the Torah to all the peoples of the earth—to be a light unto the nations. When the Exile was considered from this standpoint, the Rabbis said that it was not intended as a punishment of Israel, but as an opportunity to spread the Word of God among the nations of the earth: the Jews are deprived of a home and the security it offers because they are God's servants. Viewed in this light, the doctrine of the chosen people offers the Jews no privileges denied to others; on the contrary, it imposes on them a mission, loyalty to which must bring them suffering, humiliation, agonies of pain and death; the Jew must suffer persecution, so that of him one might say in truth: "He is despised and rejected of men; a man of sorrows, and acquainted with grief." In this aspect, the doctrine implies no superiority inherent in the Jewish people, apart from the superiority that is attached to one who is charged with the duty to carry an important message. It is the message and not the messenger that is superior; so that one might speak really of the *Chosen Message* rather than of the *Chosen People*; the people are not endowed with superiority, but charged to be humble; humility, rather than riches or glory, must clothe them.

This interpretation of the concept points away from the particularism that is frequently charged against Judaism, and points to the universalism of which the Prophets were the leading spokesmen. Judaism, then, is a universalistic religious faith. Its truths are not to be kept under lock and key. In the first place, the truths of Judaism are to guide the Jewish people at every step and at every moment: Israel must obey God's law; he must strive to attain the purposes of mankind, as directed by God, *within his own community*. But he must do more: he must strive to attain that purpose in the *entire community of mankind*. If the Jew is particularistic at all, it is only that he wants to make of himself a *worthy* messenger, *one who himself lives by the message he carries*.

Jews, it has been said, are actually "an ethnic group with a universalistic religious faith which transcends the values of a single people but which they are forced to use as an instrument of survival in an alien world." This is the irony of Jewish existence: devotion to a universalistic faith marks the Jews off as a "peculiar" people, a "chosen" people! But God's "covenant" with this people is binding on God only so long as Israel himself observes the letter and spirit of the "covenant." To quote from Reinhold Niebuhr:

> The first religious apprehension of a universal and unlimited moral obligation was achieved in prophetic monotheism, which had its inception in the prophet Amos's conception of a universal history, over which the God of Israel presided as sovereign but of which the history of Israel was not the center and end. Amos thought of the "Holy One of Israel" as a transcendent God who would both use and reject the special mission of Israel in his universal designs and who could taunt his own people with the words, "Are ye not as children of the Ethiopians unto me?"

This is not, I submit, only a Christian's view of the mission of Israel; it is the view of Israel, the view of Israel's prophets. The "chosen people" are not at the center of the world; they are charged with the duty to live by, and transmit, the highest moral ideals, in deep humility and in a spirit of charity. But God's ways are inscrutable; the Torah was written in the words of man, so that man might understand it, but there are errors and sins at every step and in every moment of the life of a mortal man; there is the finiteness of the intelligence, and the contingency of the will. Who, then, knows what is the ultimate truth? or what is the way or the plan of God? All one can do is walk humbly; and if one does this, he may trust that he is walking humbly with his God.

This is what is meant by the doctrine of the chosen people. Admittedly, it is a statement of ideals and not a description of the way Jews live. To live by these ideals would make it very dangerous to be a Jew. But during the past thousands of years many Jews have lived dangerously. The ideal, at any rate, is not an impossible one; and even if it were, it might, from the moral point of view, still be a relevant one.

When men are judged by any empirical test they are not equal: some are richer than others, some wiser, some swifter, some more beautiful. Yet the essence of democracy is equality. Men reject the empirical tests and assert their equality notwithstanding the evidence adduced by their eyes and ears and other senses. "All men are created equal," said Jefferson in the Declaration of Independence; and he had no footnote references to statistical tables by way of documentation. The belief in equality is a transcendental belief, if you wish; it makes an assertion which may be true only in the world of noumena. But no matter: it is the cornerstone of the democratic faith and the essence of moral idealism. "The basis of democratic development," says Harold Laski "is therefore the demand that the system of power be erected upon the *similarities* and not the *differences* between men." Here we have the clue to the problem of democracy: differences are not to be eliminated, for it is good that one man paint better than another, that one woman cook better than does her neighbor, that one surgeon operate better than another; yes, and even that one man legislate better than another. But the system of power (political power, economic and social power) must be based on the similarities and not on the differences between men. The demand for equality manifests itself in many relations: there is the demand for equal suffrage; for economic equality; there must be no privilege by birth; there is the demand for educational equality; there must be equality in participation in the results of social developments and improvements; equality before the law (real and not merely formal equality).

At bottom the democratic faith is a moral affirmation: men are not to be used merely as means to an end, as tools; each is an end in himself; his soul is from the source of all life; a man is born "trailing clouds of glory behind him"; no matter how lowly his origin, a man is here only by the grace of God—he owes his life to no one but God. He has an equal right to pursue happiness: life, liberty and the pursuit of happiness are his simply by virtue of the fact that he is a live human being. He has his place in the sun, and neither the place nor the sun was made by men.

This faith finds its essence in what Henry Michel called the "eminent dignity of human personality." One of the chief sources of this faith is in the wellsprings of Judaism.

It may be possible to arrive at the philosophy of equality within the framework of secular thought, as, *e.g.*, in the systems of John Dewey and Bertrand Russell and in socialist Marxism. Within the framework of a religious system, however, it is probably impossible to arrive at the philosophy of equality in the absence of a belief in ethical monotheism.

For as long as one believes in the existence of a multiplicity of gods, each expressing his own biases and partialities, loving his friends and hating his enemies, and no one supreme god above all others, there is no room provided for accommodation of the beliefs in the fatherhood of God and the brotherhood of man. In ethical monotheism, however, these beliefs are basic. Judaism conceived of God as the creator and ruler of the entire universe: "In the beginning God created the heavens and the earth." He created Adam and Eve, from whom all mankind have sprung. Humanity lives, therefore, in "One World"; one world in every sense of the term; the laws of physical nature are the same everywhere; the laws of human nature are the same everywhere: the heavens and the moral law are the same everywhere.

Not only are the physical laws the same everywhere, but the laws of righteousness too. For God is not only *ehad,* One, but He is God "sanctified in righteousness." He is the judge of all the earth, as Abraham said, and cannot act unjustly. "Thou art not a God who hath pleasure in wickedness; evil shall not sojourn with Thee; Thou hatest all workers of iniquity." God, as the prophet said, wants to loose the fetters of wickedness, to undo the bands of the yoke, to deal bread to the hungry, to cover the naked, to shelter the homeless—He wants to see all this, and more, accomplished—but through the free agency of man.

Implicit and explicit in the ethical monotheism that is Judaism are, then, the beliefs in the fatherhood of God and the brotherhood of man. Thus Malachi cried out: "Have we not all one Father? Hath not One God created us?" Thus is posited the fatherhood principle. But in the same breath the prophet added: "Why do we deal treacherously every man against his brother?" The fatherhood and brotherhood principles go together; they are inseparable: if two men have the same father, are they, then, not brothers?

"God," said the Rabbis, "is on the watch for the nations of the world to repent, so that He may bring them under His wings." When the nations will accept the reign of righteousness, the Kingdom of God will have become established; and God wants this to happen above all else.

The most graphic expression of the fatherhood of God and the brotherhood of man is the statement in the Bible that man was created in the image of God. The Rabbis did not tire of creating homilies on this figurative expression of the oneness of the human family. Thus, R. Joshua b. Levi said: "When a man goes on his road, a troop of angels proceed in front of him and proclaim, 'Make way for the image of the Holy One, blessed be He.'" The following passage from the Mishna is especially revealing of the universalism of Judaism:

Only one single man was created in the world, to teach that, if any man has caused a single soul to perish, Scripture imputes it to him as though he had caused a whole world to perish; and if any man saves alive a single soul, Scripture imputes it to him as though he had saved a whole world. Again, but a single man was created for the sake of peace among mankind, that none should say to his fellow, "My father was greater than your father"; also that the heretics should not say, "There are many ruling powers in heaven." Again, but a single man was created to proclaim the greatness of God, for man stamps many coins with one die, and they are all like to one another; but God has stamped every man with the die of the first man, yet not one of them is like his fellow. Therefore every one must say, "For my sake was the world created."

In another passage there is the same emphasis on the transcendent importance of human life, any man's life:

"By ten sayings the world was created." To teach you that him who fulfills one command, or keeps one Sabbath, or preserves one human life, the Scripture regards as if he had preserved the whole world. And him who commits one sin, desecrates one Sabbath, and destroys one human life, the Scripture regards as if he had destroyed the whole world.

It is related that Ben Azzai quoted the verse from Genesis, "This is the book of the generations of Adam," and remarked that this is the greatest principle in the Torah. The same point was made by Rabbi Akiba but in a different statement. He said that the greatest principle in the Torah is "Love thy neighbor as thyself." Rabbi Tanhuma put the matter in a third way. He said that one should not say to himself, "Because I am despised, so may my neighbor be cursed with me"; for if one acts in this way he despises a being made in the image of God.

In the Talmud the question is raised why man was created a solitary human being, why were there not created several Adams and several Eves at one time? The answer given is this: "So that it might not be said that some races are better than others."

The injunction against shedding blood is repeated frequently in the Bible and in the writings of the Rabbis, and the law was declared that the life of one man may not be sacrificed to save the life of another man. The law is illustrated by the following passage from the Talmud:

A man came to Raba and said, "The prefect of my town has ordered me to kill so and so, or he will kill me." Raba said, "Let him kill you; do you commit no murder. Why should you think that your blood is redder than his? Perhaps his is redder than yours."

In the Midrash it is stated that the falling of rain is an event greater than the giving of the Torah, for the Torah is for Israel only, but rain is for the entire world. According to the Mekilta, however, even the Torah is for the entire world: "The Torah was given in the wilderness and in fire and in water. As these three are free to all the inhabitants of the world, so are the words of the Torah free to all the inhabitants of the world."

Are only the righteous among Israel the elect of God? Not at all; for righteousness, like sin, is the great leveler; the sinners among Israel are no better off than the evil ones among the non-Jews; and the righteous Israelites are not preferred to the righteous among the non-Jews. "The just among the Gentiles are the priests of God," says the Midrash. "I call heaven and earth to witness that whether a person be Jew or Gentile, man or woman, manservant or maidservant, according to his acts does the Divine Spirit rest upon him." Just as the acknowledgment of idolatry is a repudiation of the Torah, so repudiation of idolatry is an acceptance of Torah.

The injunctions in the Bible relating to the treatment of a brother were not construed as being directed only to the treatment of Israelites (though all Israelites are brothers) but of all mankind (for all men are brothers). Thus it was said: "The heathen is thy neighbor, thy brother. To wrong him is a sin." The point is made graphically by the following incident in the Midrash:

Simeon ben Shatah was occupied with preparing flax. His disciples said to him, "Rabbi, desist. We will buy you an ass, and you will not have to work so hard." They went and bought an ass from an Arab, and a pearl was found on it, whereupon they came to him and said, "From now on you need not work any more." "Why?" he asked. They said, "We bought you an ass from an Arab, and a pearl was found on it." He said to them, "Does its owner know of that?" They answered, "No." He said to them, "Go and give the pearl back to him." "But," they argued, "did not Rabbi Huna, in the name of Rab, say all the world agrees that if you find something which belongs to a heathen, you may keep it?" Their teacher said, "Do you think that Simeon ben Shatah is a barbarian? He would prefer to hear the Arab say, 'Blessed be the God of the Jews,' than possess all the riches of the world . . . It is written, 'Thou shalt not oppress thy neighbor.' Now thy neighbor is as thy brother, and thy brother is as thy neighbor. Hence you learn that to rob a Gentile is robbery."

In the same spirit it is said in the Talmud that an idolator who studies the Torah is like the High Priest; that a non-Jew who lives a godly life is like the High Priest. It is related that Rabbi Judah told the Emperor Antoninus that he would have a share in the world to come even though he was a non-Jew; for all men have a share in the world to come as long as they desist from acts of violence. In the spirit of Simeon ben Shatah the Talmud states:

In a city where there are both Jews and Gentiles, the collectors of alms collect both from Jews and Gentiles, and feed the poor of both, visit the sick of both, bury both, comfort the mourners whether they be Jews or Gentiles, and restore the lost goods of both.

The Bible begins the story of man not with the birth of Abraham but with the creation of Adam and Eve; and the Rabbis said that Adam was made from dust gathered by God from the four corners of the earth, so that no people should later be able to say that he was made from the dust gathered only in their own corner of the world. And wherever one turns in the writings of the Jews this motif of equality, the fatherhood of God and the brotherhood of man, appears irresistibly. Thus, at the Passover *seder* a drop of wine is to be spilled from the cup at the mention of each of the ten plagues with which the Egyptians were afflicted, the

reason being, say the Rabbis, that one's cup of joy cannot be full as long
as there is suffering somewhere in the world. And Purim, when the names
of the sons of Haman, as they are hanged, are read in the synagogue, the
reader must try to read them all in one breath; for it is painful to consider
the torture of even Haman and his sons. Again, at the Passover *seder* the
head of the household reads of the drowning of the Egyptian hosts in the
Red Sea; and the Rabbis comment on the passage by relating that when
the drowning was taking place, angels in heaven commenced to sing the
praises of the Lord, but He rebuked them, saying, "My children are
drowning, and you would sing!"

These sayings of the Rabbis are in the spirit of Amos, who cried out:
" 'Are ye not as children of the Ethiopians unto Me, O children of Israel?'
saith the Lord. 'Have I not brought up Israel out of the Land of Egypt?
and the Philistines from Caphtor, and Aram from Kir?' " (9:7).

So, too, according to Isaiah, The Lord says: "Blessed be Egypt My
people and Assyria the work of My hands, and Israel Mine inheritance"
(19:25). And when Jeremiah speaks of the afflictions that must be visited
upon the sinful people of Moab, he says that God wails: "Therefore will
I wail for Moab; yea, I will cry out for all Moab; for the men of Kir-heres
shall my heart moan" (48:31). And the Book of Jonah, which occupies
so prominent a place in Jewish ritual, relates of God's concern for the
salvation of the inhabitants of the city of Nineveh—a city of Gentiles, not
of Jews.

It is clear, we believe, that Judaism, or the ethical monotheism elaborated by the Old Testament and the Rabbis, posits as one of its fundamental precepts the equality of all men before God: all men who share
righteousness share the grace of God. And righteousness is not considered
from the standpoint of ritual observance: works of benevolence, says the
Talmud, form the beginning and end of the Torah; or, as Micah expressed
the truth:

> Wherewith shall I come before the Lord?
> And bow myself before God on high?
> Shall I come before Him with burnt-offerings?
> With calves of a year old?
> Will the Lord be pleased with thousands of rams,
> With ten thousands of rivers of oil?
> Shall I give my first-born for my transgression,
> The fruit of my body for the sin of my soul?
> It hath been told thee, O man, what is good;
> And what the Lord doth require of thee;
> Only to do justly and to love mercy
> And to walk humbly with thy God (6:6-8).

THE DEMOCRATIC IDEAL:
SOCIAL AND POLITICAL EQUALITY AND FREEDOM

That the ideals of equality and freedom which one finds at the heart of Judaism were not projected merely for "the end of days," but were principles of daily conduct, becomes clear when one examines some of the institutions that are characteristic of Judaism. In their relations with Gentiles the Jews could speak of equality and freedom only as ends to be achieved after a long struggle: both the Jews and the non-Jews will need to realize the nature of righteousness and strive for it together before they lie down together in equality, no one a lion and no one a lamb, but all children of the One Father, brothers who have issued from the same source of life. The ideal was always there; Israel could preserve itself only by loyalty to its universalistic religion; its mission was never to be treated lightly, let alone forgotten; and every opportunity was to be taken advantage of to elicit from the non-Jew a blessing for the One God, and thereby to bring him closer to righteousness. The incident about the pearl found on the Arab's donkey dramatically illustrates the consciousness of the obligation to win adherents for God and His ethical laws. That is what *Kiddush ha-Shem* means. The same awareness of this mission is illustrated by the dictum in the Talmud that to cheat a Gentile is even worse than to cheat a Jew, for besides being a violation of the moral law, such conduct brings Israel's religion into contempt and causes a *Hillul ha-Shem* (a desecration of the Name).

In relations among themselves the Jewish people had an opportunity to give the ideal of equality "a local habitation and a name." The keystone of the Jewish community was the precept that "all Israel are responsible for one another." The Rabbis relate that when Moses summoned all Israel before God, he said, "Your captains, your judges, your elders." But God made him add the words: "all the people of Israel." This passage receives clarification by the statement of the Rabbis that Moses did not stop with "all the people of Israel," but went on to add: "your little ones, your wives, and the stranger that is in thy camp"; for, said the Rabbis, "God's mercies are on male and female alike, on the wicked equally with the righteous, as it says, 'From the hewer of thy wood to the drawer of thy water.' All are equal before God; hence it says, 'All the people of Israel.' " Rabbi Akiba said that even the poorest in Israel are looked upon as freemen who have lost their possessions, "for they are the sons of Abraham, Isaac and Jacob." In other words, all *men* are equal because all are the children of Adam and Eve; all *Israelites* are equal because all are the children of Abraham, Isaac and Jacob—not to mention Adam and Eve.

The hereditary character of the priesthood in ancient Israel[4a] has led to the charge that Judaism recognized a class of privileged persons whose rights were obtained by birth: a hereditary aristocracy. But this is due to a misunderstanding. The priests were not permitted to consider themselves the heads of the community; they were a class whose status was determined by function; they were servants of God in a special sense; but being such servants, they carried obligations rather than privileges. People were not to stand in superstitious fear of them; they had no superior spiritual powers. The Rabbis had freed themselves from almost every trace of sacerdotalism. The priesthood was maintained because the Torah required it; but it was not the priests who blessed Israel; it was God Who bestowed the blessing; the priests were not intermediaries, like angels or saints.

It says at the end of the priestly benediction, "and it is I that will bless them." One might think that if the priests choose to bless the Israelites, then they are blessed, and if they do not choose, they are not blessed. Therefore it says, "And it is *I* that will bless them. *I* will bless my people."

Nor did the Rabbis themselves constitute a privileged caste. Three crowns were recognized, the crown of the Torah, the crown of the priesthood, and the crown of the kingdom.

Aaron was worthy of the crown of the priesthood and obtained it, David was worthy of the crown of the kingdom and obtained it. The crown of the Torah remains, so that no man shall have the pretext to say: "If the crown of the priesthood and the crown of the kingdom were yet available, I would have proved myself worthy of them and have obtained them." For the crown of the Torah is available for all. For God says: "Of him who proves himself worthy of *that* crown, I reckon it to him as if all the three were yet available, and he had proved himself worthy of them all. And of everyone who does not prove himself worthy of the crown of the Torah, I reckon it unto him as if all three crowns were yet available, and he had proved himself worthy of none of them."

The crown of the Torah is not inherited; it was worn by men who earned their living by cobbling shoes, weaving flax or making candles. Ben Azzai said: "If any man humiliates himself for the Torah, eats dry dates and wears dirty clothes, and sits and keeps guard at the doors of the wise, every passer-by thinks him a fool, but at the end you will find that all the Torah is within him"; and if the Torah is within him, he may wear the crown of the Torah. A famous passage in *Pirke Abot* is the following:

This is the way that is becoming for the study of the Torah: a morsel of bread with salt thou must eat, and water by measure thou must drink, thou must sleep upon the ground, and live a life of trouble, the while thou toilest in the Torah. If thou doest thus, "Happy shalt thou be and it shall be well with thee"; happy shalt thou be in this world, and it shall be well with thee in the world to come. Seek not greatness for thy self, and crave not honor more than is due to thy learning; and desire not the table of kings, for thy table is greater than theirs, and thy crown greater than theirs; and faithful is He, the master of thy work, to pay thee the reward of thy labor.

As water is priceless, said the Rabbis, so is the Torah priceless; and as water is free for all, so is the Torah free for all. But the Torah was also compared to wine: as wine cannot keep in vessels of gold and silver, but only in cheap earthenware vessels, so the words of the Torah are preserved only in him who makes himself lowly. "The greater the man," says the Midrash, "the humbler he is." Man, especially one who wears the crown of the Torah, must be as humble as is God Himself; wherever you find the greatness of God, there, too, you will find His humbleness. For "God loves nothing better than humility." Said Rabbi Johanan: "The words of the Torah abide only with him who regards himself as nothing." The Torah was not to be used as an ornament with which one might adorn himself; nor was it to be used as a spade with which to dig; knowledge of the Torah was its own reward; it is only to study the Torah that God created man: study of the Torah is his purpose, his end, his happiness and his reward.[5a] "Do the words of the Torah for the doing's sake; speak of them for their own sake. Do not say: 'I will learn Torah so that I may be called wise, or sit in the College, or gain long days in the world to come.' " Nor may one charge fees for teaching the Torah; for the words of the Torah are free; God gave the Torah free: "he who takes a fee for the Torah destroys the world."

The humility with which the greatest of the three crowns was to be worn is illustrated by the following incident related in the Talmud:

One day, at the close of the fig harvest, Rabbi Tarfon was walking in a garden, and he ate some figs which had been left behind. The custodian of the garden came up, caught him, and began to beat him unmercifully. Then Rabbi Tarfon called out and said who he was, whereupon they let him go. Yet all his days did he grieve, saying, "Woe is me, for I have used the crown of the Torah for my own profit." For the teaching ran: "A man must not say, I will study so as to be called a wise man, or rabbi, or an elder, or to have a seat in the College; but he must study from love. The honor will come of itself."

The Rabbis did not constitute a caste; they generally were not supported by the community but had to carry on a trade or calling from which they might support themselves and their families: "I call heaven and earth to witness," says the Midrash, "that every scholar who eats of his own, and enjoys the fruits of his own labor, and who is not supported by the community, belongs to the class who are called happy; as it is written, 'If thou eat the fruit of thy hands, happy art thou.' " They were teachers, but received no compensation for their teaching; they had to make a living by spending a part of their day in some occupation for which there was a monetary reward: "He who occupies himself with the study of the Torah only is as if he had no God." A man was counseled to spend as little time as possible, however, at his trade or work: only long enough to earn sufficient money to keep body and soul together. It was the duty of everyone to study the Torah at some time during each day: at least two ordinances in the morning and two in the evening; but the more study, the greater the reward (in the world to come). "If a scholar engages in business and is not too successful, it is a good omen for him. God loves his learning and does not want to enrich him." The greatest calumny was to call one an *am ha-aretz*, a boor; to be poor was to be blessed, but to be ignorant was to be cursed. No *"mitzva"* was greater than study: the study of the Torah was superior to all other things—all other things except one: teaching Torah. "He who learns receives but one-fifth of the reward that goes to him who teaches."

It is evident, then, that the crown of the Torah did not carry with it social privileges: the most learned man still needed to continue at his cobbler's bench or carpentry work. On the contrary, it imposed the obligation to teach. The social ideal of Judaism was a community of scholars, where all would be companions. This is what it means to have been created in the image of God: to fulfill the obligation or commandment to study the words of God. This commandment was imposed on *every* Jew equally; it had to be fulfilled by himself, and not by a surrogate.

The schools were commanded not to engage in strife one with the other. Tolerance in scholarly dispute was an obligation. "If a scholar has no *derek eretz* [good taste, refinement], he is lower than an animal." It is related that Rabbah would open his discourse with a jest, and let his hearers laugh a little. For years the schools of Hillel and Shammai[6a] maintained a dispute over a matter of law, finally a Voice descended in Jabneh and cried out: "The words of both are the words of the Living God, but the decision should follow the School of Hillel." It was asked, why, if the words of both are the words of the Living God, was the decision granted to Hillel's school? The reply was: "Because the members of the school of Hillel are amiable of manner and courteous; they teach the opinions of both schools; and furthermore, they always give the opinion of their opponents first." This teaches, said the Rabbis, that whoever abases himself is exalted by God. One was not to assume that the Divine Wisdom rested with him alone and that those who differed from him uttered words of no worth. One was to be a constant fount of tolerance and humility; one must be conscious of the relativity of his own statements even when, or perhaps especially when, the statements related to ultimate truths; for one was always subject to error and sin; all statements of truth were subject to finiteness and contingency. "One says its meaning is this, and another says its meaning is that. One gives such an opinion, his fellow a different one. But they all were given from one shepherd—that is from Moses, who received the teaching from Him who is One and unique in the world." This spirit of tolerance, mutual respect, profound religious humility, is perhaps best expressed in the following favorite saying of the Rabbis of Jabneh:

I am a creature of God and my neighbor is also His creature. My work is in the city and his is in the field. I rise early to my work and he rises early to his. He cannot excel in my work and I cannot excel in his. But perhaps you say, I do great things while he does small things. We have learnt that it matters not whether a man does much or little, if only he directs his heart to heaven.

Judaism is not merely a matter of beliefs and ceremonies, it is a way of life; and the economic aspect of human existence was not a matter of indifference to the prophets and Rabbis. The Bible was not considered a mere theological treatise; it was viewed as a document with the greatest social significance; for in its teachings one could find the ways by which to enter into intimate relation with God, and find joy and freedom in His service; also the ways by which to enter into proper social relations, so that the perfect social order, the kingdom of heaven, might be established on the earth. Today we might be tempted to say that one aim was religious while the other was social; but Judaism would reject the distinction. Judaism recognizes no profane virtues; all virtues are sacred; the social function is as religious as the religious function is social. "Rabbi Judah said in the name of Rab: 'A man is forbidden to eat anything until he has fed his beast.'" Was this considered a religious law or a social law? The distinction would not have been comprehensible to either Rabbi Judah or Rab. In Judaism all duties are divine commands. While several duties appear to be arbitrary, nearly all are expressed in laws which our conscience recognizes as obligatory on free will. Economics and ethics are the same; ethics and religion are the same.

In a word, there was no distinction between the social conscience and the religious conscience. The study of the Torah was chiefly the study of social relations, individual and communal problems. The Torah taught that "if two men claim thy help, and one is thy enemy, help thy enemy first"; and the same Torah taught that "he who gives food to a small child, must tell its mother"; and the same Torah taught that one must permit the poor to glean after the reapers, and that one must not take interest on a loan.

Perhaps it was the experience of the Israelites in Egypt that compelled them to project the ideal of social equality and freedom. For in Egypt they saw that when great wealth and political power are in the hands of the same group, the welfare and happiness of the rest of the people are greatly imperiled. Political and economic power must be spread out among all, with little if any disparity in the distribution. If this is not accomplished, and men are unjustly exploited—used as mere means and not as ends; when it is forgotten that every man bears the image of God—physical, spiritual and social pestilence will spread, and insurrection will follow, shaking the community to its very foundations. Masters cannot exploit their workers and God should not see. The excessive wealth of the masters leads to luxury; derived through injustice, wealth breeds further injustice; luxury corrupts what may have been left untouched by the injustice of exploitation. In the end the system collapses; blind injustice leans against the pillar of its palace and is destroyed with it.

Furthermore, as Charles Foster Kent has well pointed out, the experience of Moses showed him that violence does not avail in correcting industrial evils. The only true method is that which he used:

Education and organization of those industrially oppressed; clear presentation of their claims and rights; patient, persistent agitation in order to educate public opinion; and efficient organization to protect their interests.

The Israelites did not win their freedom merely to duplicate among themselves the system they had rejected. They were to build their own community on a basis of moral idealism, ethical religion and social justice. There was to be in the Promised Land no form of political or industrial oppression; for always the Jews were commanded to remember, at every turn, in every crisis, at every temptation to commit an injustice: "Remember that thou wast a slave in the land of Egypt, and that the Lord thy God brought thee out from there by a mighty hand and an outstretched arm." Future generations, after the exodus from Egypt, were commanded to look upon themselves as though *they*, and not merely their forefathers, had been rescued from the hand of the Egyptian taskmaster. The *freshness* of their freedom was constantly to be before their eyes.

Moreover, they were commanded to remember in humility that it was not by their own strength that they won their freedom, but because God is One Who watches over the poor, the fatherless, the afflicted, the helpless, the outcast: He is a just Judge; He loves justice and mercy and righteousness, and requites evil with evil. God has created a world in which the moral law is as implacable, as impersonal, and as imperative as is a physical law: there is no escape from it.

In ancient Israel the atmosphere was a thoroughly equalitarian one: all were practically equal and free. Each was represented in the council of the clan or tribe.[7a] While slavery was tolerated (it is to be remembered that the United States retained this institution until only three generations ago), the harshness of the master-servant relationship was in many ways mitigated. The biblical fugitive-slave law, unlike the laws passed by Congress before the Civil War, protected the fugitive; for in Deuteronomy it is provided:

Thou shalt not deliver to his master a bondsman that is escaped from his master unto thee. He shall dwell with thee in the midst of thee, in the place which he shall choose within one of thy gates, where it liketh him best; thou shalt not wrong him (23:16-17).

While the institution of private property was recognized, and there were laws against theft, clear recognition was given to the fact that property is fundamentally a social object, that property is subject to social control, that society may direct as to how much property a man may possess, how much of his income he may retain for his own use, for how long a period he may divest himself of title to property allotted to him, and so on. Thus it was provided that "when thou comest into thy neighbor's vineyard thou mayest eat grapes until thou have enough at thine own pleasure . . . when thou comest into thy neighbor's standing corn, thou mayest pluck ears with thy hand . . ." (23:25-26). Among the first laws to protect the rights of laborers are those found in the Bible. The Sabbath was instituted as a social institution, as a day of rest: "in it thou shalt not do any manner of work, thou, nor thy son, nor thy daughter, nor thy man-servant, nor thy maid-servant, nor thine ox, nor thine ass, nor any of thy cattle, nor thy stranger that is within thy gates . . ." (5:14). Wages were to be paid promptly:

Thou shalt not oppress a hired servant that is poor and needy, whether he be of thy brethren, or of thy strangers that are in thy land within thy gates. In the same day thou shalt give him his hire, neither shall the sun go down upon it; for he is poor, and setteth his heart upon it; lest he cry against thee to the Lord, and it be a sin in thee (24:14-15).

The well-off were forbidden to oppress the impoverished citizen:

No man shall take the mill or the upper millstone to pledge, for he taketh a man's life to pledge . . . When thou dost lend thy neighbor any manner of loan, thou shalt not go into his house to fetch his pledge. . . . And if he be a poor man, thou shalt not sleep with his pledge; thou shalt surely restore to him the pledge when the sun goeth down, that he may sleep in his garment, and bless thee (24:6,10,12-13).

Bankruptcy laws were instituted, so that a man shall not be borne down by his debts forever, but shall, instead, have an opportunity for a fresh economic start. "At the end of every seven years shalt thou make a release" (15:1); the creditor shall not exact the debt from his debtor. At the same time, he who hath must not close his heart to the importunities of him who hath not, and say to himself that "the seventh year, the year of release, is at hand" (15:9), and refuse to lend to the poor; for if this happen, God will hear the cry of the poor man, and the rich man will be guilty of a crime. "Thou shalt surely give him and thy heart shall not be grieved when thou givest unto him" (15:10). The owner of the land was not to think that the land was *really* his, to do with as he pleased;

for the land is the Lord's; and the Lord commanded that every seventh
year the land must lie fallow; it must not be abused, lest it become a waste
place, and all the land a dustbowl. A share of a man's income had to be
turned over to the communal authorities for the relief of needy persons.
Even when a man builds a house for himself, he must take into consideration the duties he owes his neighbors; he must make a parapet for
his roof, so that no one will fall from it.

Time and again the prophets cried out against the economic inequalities
that resulted in loss of freedom, injustice and oppression. Men became too
rich and too powerful for their own and the community's good. Such rich
men were declared enemies of the people and the chief sinners against God.
The accumulation of such wealth and the exploitation it entailed were
condemned in the strongest terms possible:

> Because they sell the righteous for silver,
> And the needy for a pair of shoes,
> That pant after the dust of the earth on the head of the poor,
> And turn aside the way of the humble . . .
> And they lay themselves down beside every altar,
> Upon clothes taken in pledge,
> And in the house of their God they drink
> The wine of them that have been fined (Amos 2:6-8).

Amos foretold such as these what their destiny would be:

> Hear this word,
> Ye kine of Bashan, that are in the mountains of Samaria,
> That oppress the poor, that crush the needy,
> That say to their lords, "Bring, that we may feast."
> The Lord God hath sworn by His holiness:
> "Lo, surely the days shall come upon you,
> That ye shall be taken away with hooks,
> And your residue with fish-hooks . . ." (4:1-3).

Isaiah brought severe charges against the oppressors of the common man:

> It is ye that have eaten up the vineyard;
> The spoil of the poor is in your houses.
> What mean ye that ye crush My people,
> And grind the face of the poor? . . . (3:14-15)
> Woe unto them that join house to house,
> That lay field to field
> Till there be no room and ye be made to dwell
> Alone in the midst of the land! (5:8).

Just as Judaism posits the ideals of social equality and economic equality,
so, too, it posits political freedom and equality. Israel was to be a holy
nation, each Israelite was to be a member of "a kingdom of priests, a
holy nation." God alone is ruler over Israel. What need is there of a king?

No one was permitted to make laws for the nation; for God had given His Torah to His people Israel—to every Israelite; there was no room left for a king. Not even David or Solomon[8a] could abrogate the laws of the Sabbath, or of the seventh year, or make oppression of the needy just. Israel was different from all other peoples: its legislation came from God. If a king cannot make laws, of what use can he be? God was the Lawgiver, the Ruler and the Judge. When the Jews asked Samuel to appoint over them a king, he told them of what use a king could be:

"This will be the manner of the king that shall reign over you: he will take your sons and appoint them unto him, for his chariots, and to be his horsemen; and they shall run before his chariots. And he shall appoint them unto him for captains of thousands, and captains of fifties; and to plow his ground, and to reap his harvest, and to make his instruments of war, and the instruments of his chariots. And he will take your daughters to be perfumers, and to be cooks, and to be bakers. And he will take your fields, and your vineyards, and your oliveyards, even the best of them, and give them to his servants. And he will take the tenth of your seed, and of your vineyards, and give to his officers, and to his servants. And he will take your men-servants, and your maid-servants, and your goodliest young men, and your asses, and put them to his work. He will take the tenth of your flocks; and you shall be his servants" (I Sam. 8:11-17).

The Jews never forgot this lesson of Samuel's; even though they took upon themselves the yoke of a kingship, they would not tolerate oppression and despotism. The king was to be a servant of the people and not their master; he was to rule under God and not as a substitute for Him. Thus the Jews became a "rebellious" people; for they would not tolerate a tyrant even if he were of the seed of David. When Solomon died, the northern tribes rose in protest against a perpetuation of oppressive measures by Rehoboam, whom Solomon had nominated as his successor.[9a] It is related that Rehoboam and the Israelites met at Shechem, where he was asked if he would make lighter their yoke. The king took counsel with the old men who had served Solomon, and they said to him: "If thou wilt be a servant unto this people this day, and wilt serve them, and answer them, and speak good words to them, then they will be thy servants forever" (I Kings 12:7). The king would not follow their advice; he "gave no heed to the people." When the Israelites saw that he disregarded their petition, they said to him:

> "We have no portion in David
> Neither have we inheritance in the son of Jesse;
> Everyman to his tents, O Israel" (II Sam. 20:1).

Even if it meant breaking up the kingdom, Judaism's democratic ideals had to be asserted and reasserted. Thus it was throughout Israel's history in Palestine. The people, and sometimes the prophets speaking for the people, constantly submitted the moral presuppositions of the ruling caste to scrutiny and re-examination. The freedom of the private moral judgment was always kept alive. When Ahab, misguided by Jezebel, his queen, showed his disloyalty to the democratic ideals, a popular uprising ended his dynasty. Elijah spoke for the conscience of Israel.[10a] When Naboth refused to sell his vineyard to the despotic king, and the king, through a perversion of justice, had him murdered, Elijah spoke out against the king, and when the king heard his words, "he rent his clothes and put sackcloth upon his flesh and fasted, and he lay in sackcloth, and went softly" (I Kings 21:27). For the king knew that he could reign only under and within the law; and he was not above the Torah.

And this brings us to our final point, namely, that no people can be free, no democracy can continue to exist, if the rulers selected by the people do not consider themselves bound by the law. There must be limitations on rulers if the individual's rights are to be preserved. The citizen's rights are measured by the restrictions on government. There must, in other words, be a constitution which defines clearly how far the government may go in this matter or that delegated to its authority. Israel had such a constitution in the Torah. No one was above it. Only under the Torah could kings rule and judges judge. As God is righteous, so must the king be; as God defends the weak, so must the king. Only justice is the foundation of a people's happiness and stability. Psalm 72 expresses this thought:

> Give the king Thy judgments, O God,
> And Thy righteousness unto the king's son;
> That he may judge Thy people with righteousness,
> And Thy poor with justice . . .
> May he judge the poor of the people,
> And save the children of the needy,
> And crush the oppressor . . .
> He will have pity on the poor and needy,
> And the souls of the needy he will save.
> He will redeem their soul from oppression and violence . . .

This, in part, is the picture of the ideal king.

Indeed, how could Israel view the status and function of government otherwise; for does not God Himself govern in accordance with law? Judaism is a law-centered religious civilization. All that God does, said Rabbi Akiba,[11a] He does by justice; "the procedure in the heavenly court is governed by law as in an earthly court." The day has twelve hours, said Rabbi Judah in the name of Rab, and in the first three God sits and busies Himself with the Torah! God Himself is bound by the Torah, by His own laws. He made the world "by law," not arbitrarily. Why, then, should He not spend His time teaching the Torah to the righteous in heaven? When Moses went up to heaven, he found God sitting and weaving crowns for the letters, little flourishes on some letters of the Torah to ornament the Scroll of the Law. The imagination of the Jewish folk could devise no occupation more worthy of God than the writing and study of His own Torah; because Israel found such a delight in the Law: "But his delight is in the law of the Lord; and in His law doth he meditate day and night" (Ps. 1:2). The ordinances of the Lord are to be desired more than gold, yea, than much fine gold; they are sweeter than the honey and the honeycomb. "I have rejoiced in the way of Thy testimonies . . . I will delight myself in Thy statutes." The Lord's commandments apply to every significant act in life; as Rabbi Phineas said, one must think of the commandments when one builds a house, when he makes a door, when he buys new clothes, when his hair is cut, when his field is plowed, when his field is sowed, when the harvest is gathered, "even when you are not occupied with anything, but just taking a walk . . ." And the commandments are for *all* the people to observe: "All are equal before the law. The duty of observance is for all. For the Torah is the 'inheritance of the congregation of Jacob.' It does not say 'priests' or 'Levites' or 'Israelites,' but 'the congregation of Jacob.' " No one can be above the Law—whether he wear the crown of Torah, or the priestly crown, or the royal crown— because all men are equal, all are equally bound by the Law and subject to it, alike at every point; more than this, the world itself is subject to the Law; God made the world in accordance with the Law. Is not then even God Himself bound by the Law? "God created the world by the Torah: the Torah was His handmaid and His tool by the aid of which He set bounds to the deep, assigned their functions to sun and moon, and formed all nature. Without the Torah the world falls." The same Torah sets bounds to man's greed, man's injustice; assigns functions to this man and that, and forms civilization.

Without law there is no freedom. Unless a people meditate on the statutes and delight in the Law, they will not be able to walk at ease; unequal strength will lead to unequal justice; and when justice is dead, said Kant, it is better not to be alive. If Judaism projects a *rechtlichbuer-gerliche Gesellschaft*, it is to be borne in mind that this law-centered society is also an *ethischbuergerliche Gesellschaft*, for the law is within as well as without; and at the center of the ethico-legal system is the injunction of God: "For unto Me are the children of Israel slaves; they are not slaves unto slaves."

Not all democratic institutions were foreseen by the prophets and Rabbis; such agencies are evolved by societies of men as the need for them is felt to be irresistible even by those who would prevent their emergence. But the spirit, the inner values, the energies of democracy are right at the very heart of Judaism.

NOTES

[1a Cf. above Judah Goldin, "The Period of the Talmud (135 B.C.E.-1035 C.E.)," pp. 172-179.]

[2a Cf. *ibid.*, p. 194.]

[3a Cf. below Louis Finkelstein, "The Jewish Religion: Its Beliefs and Practices," pp. 1752-1754.]

[4a Cf. above Robert Gordis, "The Bible as a Cultural Monument," pp. 790-791.]

[5a Cf. Finkelstein, pp. 1743 ff.]

[6a Cf. Goldin, *op. cit.*, pp. 129-133.]

[7a Cf. Gordis, *op. cit.*, p. 803.]

[8a Cf. above William Foxwell Albright, "The Biblical Period," pp. 24 ff.]

[9a Cf. *ibid.*, pp. 29 f.]

[10a Cf. *ibid.*, pp. 34 f.]

[11a Cf. Goldin, *op. cit.*, pp. 156-158.]

BIBLIOGRAPHY

The literature on the subject is meager. Following are a number of essays suggested for further reading:

BOKSER, BEN ZION, "Democratic Aspirations in Talmudic Judaism," in *Science, Philosophy and Religion* (Second Symposium), published by the Conference on Science, Philosophy and Religion. New York, 1942.

———, "Rabbinic Judaism and the Problem of Egoism," in *Conflicts of Power in Modern Culture* (Seventh Symposium), ed. by Lyman Bryson, Louis Finkelstein and R. M. MacIver, published by the Conference on Science, Philosophy and Religion. New York, 1947.

BURROWS, MILLAR, "Democracy in the Hebrew-Christian Tradition: Old and New Testaments," in *Science, Philosophy and Religion, op. cit.*

FINKELSTEIN, LOUIS, "The Beliefs and Practices of Judaism," in *The Religions of Democracy*, by Louis Finkelstein, J. Elliot Ross and William Adams Brown. New York, 1941.

———, "Foundations of Democracy—Hebrew Sources: Scriptures and Talmud," in *Foundations of Democracy*, ed. by F. Ernest Johnson, published by The Institute for Religious and Social Studies. New York, 1947.

———, "The Ideal of Religious Liberty—A Jewish View," in *Wellsprings of the American Spirit*, ed. by F. Ernest Johnson, published by The Institute for Religious and Social Studies. New York, 1948.

KAPLAN, MORDECAI M., *The Future of the American Jew*. New York, 1948. Chapter 15 on "Basic Values in Jewish Religion."

A number of pamphlets in the series *Popular Studies in Judaism* published by the Tract Commission of the Union of American Hebrew Congregations and the Central Conference of American Rabbis, Cincinnati, are relevant:

CRONBACH, ABRAHAM, *The Social Outlook of Modern Judaism.*
FELDMAN, ABRAHAM J., *Contributions of Judaism to Modern Society.*
HELLER, BERNARD, *The Jewish Concept of the Chosen People.*
SCHULMAN, SAMUEL, *Jewish Ethics.*
TARSHISH, JACOB, *Judaism and Socialism.*
WITT, LOUIS, *Judaism and Democracy.*

CHAPTER 34

THE INFLUENCE OF THE BIBLE ON ENGLISH LITERATURE

By David Daiches

I

It has long been a commonplace among teachers of English in British universities that a proper understanding of English literature is impossible without a thorough knowledge of the Bible and of the Latin and Greek classics. These have been the great twin sources of inspiration for English writers at least from the latter part of the sixteenth century, and to a lesser degree and in a somewhat different way in earlier centuries also. Both these influences operated in a twofold manner: they were used rhetorically, as a teacher of style and literary devices of all kinds, and they also provided a set of stories and ideas which were incorporated, in an infinite number of ways, into the content of the later literature. While the Latin and Greek classics exerted this twofold influence on all the literatures of Europe, it was only in English literature that we find the Bible working similarly in both ways—and this because only in England was there produced a translation of the Bible acclaimed by successive generations as among the very greatest masterpieces of that country's literature. "Among the greatest" is perhaps too mild a phrase, for, while the Authorized Version of the Bible is generally ranked with the works of Shakespeare by literary critics, there can be no question that of the two the Bible has always been the more widely read and the better known among the English people as a whole. The fact, therefore, that the English Bible existed as a great literary work in its own right, as well as constituting a popular source of stories and moral ideas, meant that in England the Bible had a rhetorical, or purely literary, influence in addition to its influence as a rich storehouse of tales and ethical principles. In other European countries the Bible had only the latter kind of influence, for its translation into the vernacular never achieved the position among national literary masterpieces that was achieved by the English translation of the Bible known as the Authorized, or King James, Version.

It is true that in the seventeenth century it is often impossible to distinguish the rhetorical from the ideological influence of the Bible, for familiarity with the diction of the Authorized Version came to be regarded by many as implying an acceptance of certain religious doctrines. There are occasions when the experienced reader can infer from the kind of biblical English used by a writer (for there are many kinds of biblical English) to what particular Protestant sect he belonged. It is also true that in the eighteenth century it is sometimes difficult to distinguish a writer's use of the classics as a source of imagery and other stylistic devices from his acceptance of certain Greek or Roman ideals. In other words, though both the Bible and the classics have two distinct kinds of influence on English literature, there are periods when enthusiasm makes a writer deliberately exhibit one kind to show that he has also been affected by the other. Yet this is true of only certain limited periods, for on the whole it can be fairly said that both the Bible and the classics have had a con-tinuous stylistic influence even in quarters where agreement with the ideas expressed in the models imitated has been of the slightest.

That a Protestant people, encouraged by all the religious controversies of the Reformation to turn to the text of the Bible as their main weapon of attack and defense, should come to know the Bible well is easy enough to understand. But the full extent of the purely *literary* influence of the Bible on English literature can only be explained when we realize the number and variety of literary forms that the Bible contains.[1a] A writer like Milton thought of the Bible both as the fundamental document of his religion and as a collection of literary models comparable on aesthetic grounds with the great classics of Greece and Rome. History, short story, lyric, epic, ode, elegy, tragedy, comedy—these are all displayed in some form in the Old Testament. If we think for a moment of the differences in style and literary form between the simple narrative of Exodus, the lyrical directness of the Psalms (which themselves display a wide variety of poetic expression), the slow-moving, plangent eloquence of the fortieth chapter of Isaiah, the poetic elegies of Jeremiah, the variety of narrative styles shown in the Books of Kings, Ruth, Jonah and Esther, the extraor-dinary quality of the Book of Job (which Milton called a "brief epic")— to mention only a few examples—we can see how the Bible struck the imagination of a generation of writers still wrestling with the problem of literary "forms" and the kinds of style appropriate to different kinds of subject matter. This is what makes the seventeenth century such a pivotal period in English literature; for it was during this century that the struggle was waged with equal intensity both on the religious and on the literary plane. Whereas in many other European countries the religious struggle was fought out on the battlefield, in England it was on the whole a battle fought with texts and pamphlets, and each side produced its triumphs, which include Hooker's *Laws of Ecclesiastical Polity* at the end of the sixteenth century and Bunyan's *Pilgrim's Progress* in the latter part of the seventeenth century—neither of which books could have been written if there had been no English Bible.

It should be remembered that, although it was the acceptance of the Authorized Version as the definitive English translation that made possible the tremendous literary influence of the English Bible, that influence was already beginning to be exerted long before 1611, for the style of the Authorized Version—a style already antique when that translation was made—had been building up for generations, from Tyndale's earliest efforts in 1525, through the work of Coverdale and others for almost a century before the Authorized Version was published. English biblical prose was not born in the seventeenth century: indeed, by the time the Bible of 1611 appeared the people long had fairly fixed ideas of the kind of language appropriate for the English Bible, and they judged—and accepted—the Authorized Version accordingly. Coverdale's Bible, Matthew's Bible, the Great Bible, the Geneva Bible, the Bishop's Bible—each of these versions had played its part in developing biblical English. By 1604, when the Authorized Version was begun, the standard of style had long been set, and the only problem that remained was that of greater accuracy of rendering.

There is another point to be remembered. The achievement of the English biblical style was taking place during the very period when modern (*i.e.*, postmedieval) English literature was entering on its first great phase. When we talk of "the Bible and Shakespeare" (a collocation of a kind possible only in English literature) we are referring to two different kinds of English literary achievement; we are referring also to two contemporary achievements. The Authorized Version was being prepared during the period when Shakespeare was producing his final masterpieces. This was the fine flower of generations of noble experiment with style and language, in both poetry and prose. The fact, therefore, that English Bible translation was fortunate enough to grow up with this great phase of English literature helped both to ensure that it would profit to the utmost from the exciting literary experimentation that was taking place at this time and to produce a counterinfluence from the Bible translation already achieved on the secular literary works being produced. Thus the fanatical attitude of the more extreme Puritan sects to the letter of the biblical text as they understood it was tempered by the simultaneous consideration of the English Bible as a secular document, which contained important lessons for the writer and the literary critic. If this happy conjunction had not taken place, the Puritan suspicion of the arts would have done more damage in England than it actually did. Just as the medieval Church combined sacred and secular activities in the Miracle Plays (which brought the Bible into literature in a very different manner from the way in which it entered literature after the Reformation in England), so the seventeenth-century Puritan was led, often in spite of himself, to an appreciation of literary art even while denouncing the arts as pastimes of the devil. Milton, artist and Puritan, is the great symbolic figure here, but it is also worth considering whether the extraordinary work of Spenser—Platonist, Protestant, and at the same time a "poet's poet"—or the poetry of a Puritan such as Andrew Marvell could have existed were it not for the resolution of Puritanism and aesthetics made possible by English Bible translation. Only in the work of that Greek Puritan, Plato, the poet who denounced poets, is a similar phenomenon to be observed.

2

Before the sixteenth-century English Bible translation had brought the Bible to the people as a literary as well as a religious document, the ordinary Englishman, like his contemporaries all over Europe, had a sporadic knowledge of the Bible from pictures in stained-glass windows, sermons which quoted and elaborated biblical texts, and popular biblical paraphrases. In medieval Europe, therefore, the Bible could be known only for its stories and its doctrine, never for its literary qualities. Even the translations of single biblical texts made by individual members of the clergy in sermons were always made in the preacher's own words, not in the words of such translations as existed. Translations of the Bible did exist in Europe in the Middle Ages, but at least until the end of the fourteenth century they were translations made for individual members of the nobility or by some solitary scholar for his own private use, and they never achieved any circulation. The Church, during this period, took the view that ordinary folk should not read the Bible themselves, but should have appropriate portions of the Vulgate (Jerome's Latin version, the authorized text of the Church) interpreted to them by properly trained experts. "It was not without reason that Almighty God decided that Holy Scripture should be secret in certain places, lest, if it were clearly apparent to all men, it might perhaps be little esteemed and be treated disrespectfully," wrote Pope Gregory VII to the king of Bohemia in 1179 in a letter refusing the latter's request that his monks might be allowed to recite the divine office in Slavonic. It was this principle that underlay the persecution of sects like the Waldensians in southern France and the Lollards in England, both of which groups advocated the rendering of the Bible into the vernacular so that it could be understood by the people. Innocent III's letter to the archbishop of Metz in 1199 made the same point as Gregory had made earlier. Innocent was concerned with another heretical Bible-reading sect, the "Vaudois," and he expressed the view that "the secret mysteries of the faith ought not to be explained to all men in all places," stating his fear "lest any simple and unlettered person should presume to attain to the sublimity of holy scripture." In concluding his letter Innocent asked the archbishop to find out the social and educational status of those who indulged in vernacular Bible reading, the implication being clear that permission to read a translation of the Bible would depend on the status and intentions of the reader. The local applications of this theory (later embodied in the *Decretal* of Gregory IX and thus becoming of universal canonical application) made it clear that the clergy as a whole understood it to imply a general prohibition of biblical translation as such, particularly when any popular circulation was aimed at.

The Anglo-Saxon church in early medieval England, though it had formally accepted the Roman discipline at the Synod of Whitby in the seventh century, never wholly lost those qualities of humanitarian common sense and quiet individualism characteristic of the Celtic church which had been originally responsible for the conversion of Britain. The limited but definite interest in Bible translation in England during Anglo-Saxon times derives to some extent, perhaps, from these qualities. Bede is said to have translated the Gospel of St. John into English, though it has not survived. More definite evidence is the ninth-century *Vespasian Psalter*, which contains the Psalms in Latin together with an Anglo-Saxon "gloss," or literal word-for-word translation, written above. Such a translation was not, of course, intended for the general reader: it was to assist the less well educated of the clergy. The *Paris Psalter*, another Anglo-Saxon version of the same period—the time of King Alfred—contains a slightly different Latin text of the Psalms together with an Anglo-Saxon version, in parallel columns. It is also significant that in the preface to the code of laws drawn up by King Alfred there is an Anglo-Saxon translation of chapters 20 to 23 of Exodus—the account of the giving of the Law to Moses and of the Ten Commandments. Anglo-Saxon versions of the Gospels also exist, the earliest (if we exclude the "glosses") probably dating from the year 1000.

The most famous name in Anglo-Saxon Bible translation is that of Aelfric, abbot of Eynsham, who is known for his interest in promoting the translation of the Bible among English scholars. His sermons are full of biblical texts, translated by himself, and he produced the Anglo-Saxon *Heptateuch*, a somewhat abbreviated version of the first seven books of the Old Testament. Aelfric seems to have been the first English translator to have made some attempt to achieve an appropriate literary prose style for his biblical translations.

In an age when the distinction between literature and scholarship was obscure, and secular literature as a worthy contemporary activity had not yet achieved recognition, it was inevitable that a high proportion of written works should be biblical or at least religious. It should be remembered that by far the great majority of literary works produced in the Middle Ages are religious works. Thus we cannot infer from the Anglo-Saxon record any real "influence" of the Bible on literature, for literature in its modern sense was not yet adequately differentiated from any other activity of "clerks." And when we find numerous paraphrases of Bible stories, such as the Anglo-Saxon poems *Genesis, Exodus* and *Daniel*, attributed to Caedmon, we must not forget that these works were produced by the clergy primarily as religious documents and not by secular poets as "literature." The authors of these poems wrote for the instruction and edification of the tiny minority of the population who read them, and not, as the seventeenth-century religious poets wrote, in order to produce works of art which were at the same time religious in content and feeling. It is of course true that many religious documents were not written as "art" though they have later come to be regarded as such. The Bible itself, as the sixteenth- and seventeenth-century English critics were so excited to discover, contains many individual works of literary art, though it is doubtful, to say the least, if they were originally produced as such. But if we are to deal with "influences" at all we must first distinguish the factor that influences from that which is influenced. In an age when writing is the prerogative of the clergy and art is to a large extent (though by no means wholly) a by-product of religion, the question we are discussing becomes chiefly one of terminology.

The position becomes a little clearer in the Middle English period, for an age which produced the medieval lyric, the romances, and the works of Chaucer and his followers can hardly be said to have been without an ideal of secular literature. It is thus possible to make some useful generalizations about the influence of the Bible on English literature from the beginning of the thirteenth century to the middle of the fifteenth. As in Anglo-Saxon times, we have in this period a considerable number of biblical paraphrases, but we also have a variety of secular works which make use of biblical story for purposes of illustration or embellishment and, in addition, some ostensibly religious works which deal with biblical themes in a purely secular manner. There are, too, religious poems such as *The Pearl* which, like the religious poetry of the seventeenth century, were written as works of literary art rather than as religious documents. In the main, however, we are able to say that during this time a general knowledge of biblical story, acquired by the people through nonliterary means, had made it possible for writers to refer to biblical characters in their works with confidence that the significance of the reference would be apparent not only to those who could read the work but also to the much larger number of those to whom the work was read. The more picturesque of the Old Testament stories were frequently so used, sometimes with dramatic effect. While in the Middle Ages, as in later times, the more emotional type of religious poetry drew its inspiration more from the New Testament than from the Old, the Old Testament was the main source for secular writers in search of effective analogies and images, as well as the paraphrasers.

To the medieval Englishman, as to his contemporaries throughout Europe, the Bible was a Latin book[2a]—the Vulgate—and all translations were of course made from the Vulgate, not from the original texts. Neither Hebrew nor Greek was to any extent known in medieval Europe—Greek was acquired in some degree by a few scholars, and the merest rudiments of Hebrew only by the tiny minority of clerics who found Jewish teachers.

It was in the Middle English period that it first became clear that the historical portions of the Old Testament were—at least the earlier parts—fairly widely known and were accepted as authentic history. Thus almost all the medieval histories that are more than chronicles of individual reigns begin with the Creation and accept the Book of Genesis as their starting point. At some stage or other in their narrative these histories link up the story of the nation with which they deal with the biblical account—just as in the romances of this period there is so often a link with Greek and Roman history. The link with the Bible in the medieval histories is in a sense closer than that with the classics in the romances, for the Vulgate was accessible and known, while the texts of Homer and Virgil were known only by repute and even those who referred to these ancient writers had the vaguest ideas of the contents of their works. Indeed, Virgil throughout most of the Middle Ages was known simply as an ancient magician—and this in spite of the fact that his "Messianic" eclogue had long been interpreted by the Church as a prophecy of the coming of Christ and he had therefore won for himself a special place among the classical writers. The "matter of Rome" with which so many of the medieval romances dealt is very difficult to associate with anything found in the Latin or Greek writers, and though the story of Troy haunted the medieval imagination in an almost uncanny fashion, it is not the story that Homer told or Virgil used, but a series of strange, passionate incidents in which figures who are casually mentioned only once by Homer play the dominant parts. But the origins and nature of medieval romance are hardly relevant to this discussion. All we need point out here is that the link between medieval romance and the classics (best exemplified, perhaps, by the characters of Troilus and Cressida and their development up to Chaucer) is less direct than the link between medieval history and the Bible. These medieval histories were almost all written in Latin, however, and cannot be said to be wholly a part of English literature.

The influence of the narrative portions of the Old Testament is thus to be seen in Middle English writing and the Latin works of the period in several ways. Bible characters and events are used for purposes of comparison and illustration. And in the histories biblical events are actually used in the opening portions. There are also paraphrases and glosses of parts of the Bible, including two versions of the Psalms. One might add a less tangible kind of biblical influence, an intense moral feeling about justice and retribution, which one finds in such works as Chaucer's *Pardoner's Tale* and which pervades much of *Piers Plowman*. Such a feeling is directly or indirectly traceable to the Hebrew prophets (though the prophets were little known in the Middle Ages), just as in certain medieval devotional works the influence seems to be that of the Psalms together with parts of the New Testament. But here we come to cases in which we are dealing with the influence of Christianity rather than of the Bible, and this raises questions far beyond the scope of this chapter. There is, however, yet another direct kind of biblical influence noticeable in Middle English literature and conspicuous in such poems as *Cleanness* and *Patience*, in which biblical stories (taken of course from the Vulgate text) are woven almost whole into the narrative. While the function of the biblical stories in these poems is illustrative, the author is not content merely to allude to the story by way of example but proceeds to tell it in his own words. Thus *Patience* illustrates the nobility of that quality by giving a versified version of the story of Jonah.

Finally, before proceeding to say something about actual biblical translations in the Middle English period, we must touch on the most striking of all examples of the use of biblical story in medieval English literature. This is to be found in the Miracle Plays, which, having their origin in antiphonal chants as part of the church service, developed into crude ecclesiastical dramas and finally into full-dress though primitive plays more secular than religious in feeling. The plays as they eventually developed are often lively, if naïve, dramatizations of scriptural story. Some show a boisterous humor and even a flagrant coarseness that testify to the extent to which they had moved away from the spirit of their origins. *Noah and the Flood*, one of the best known, exists in various forms, the version in the Wakefield group being full of lively humor while that in the Chester Cycle contains humorous and realistic details of animal life combined with more serious religious scenes. The famous quarrel between Noah and his wife in the Wakefield *Noah* is a purely original, realistic treatment of an aspect of the Bible story done in contemporary terms. The later the date of these plays the more the elements of humor and realism have ousted the original religious feeling, the mid-fifteenth-century Wakefield Cycle being the furthest advanced on this road. The plays of the late fifteenth-century Coventry Cycle, however, revert to a serious didacticism, drawn almost entirely from the New Testament. The most effective of all the Miracle Plays is the Brome play, *Abraham and Isaac*, a genuinely dramatic version of the biblical story maintaining a high level of serious expression without any contemporary comic relief.

These, then, are the ways in which the influence of the Bible manifested itself in medieval English literature without benefit of any vernacular version. The Bible thus made use of by writers was the Vulgate, a text accessible to all who could read Latin—that is, to the greater number of the relatively large class of "clerks," all of whom were members of the clergy—but inaccessible to the unlearned. The story of the fight for Bible translation, which arose in England in the fourteenth century, shows that even at this period there were forces working for the extension of biblical knowledge among the people. These forces eventually produced a wholly new situation as far as the influence of the Bible on English literature is concerned.

3

The first complete English version of the Bible was the direct result of a challenge to the authority of the Church in matters of practice and doctrine. John Wycliffe, who instigated if he did not actually translate the Vulgate in the early 1380's, was moved by his determination to make the original source document of Christianity available to the people. This attitude, which was to become one of the main elements in Protestant thought, regarded the Bible as the final court of appeal in matters of doctrine. The orthodox view had been that it was the duty of the priests to explain selected scriptural passages in their sermons, relating parts of the Bible story in their own words and adding "the usury of their own minds," i.e., the moral to be drawn. Wycliffe and the movement with which he was associated took the view that the people ought to have direct access to the Bible themselves and ought not to be dependent on the fancy interpretations of preachers—"for some by rhyming, and others by preaching poems and fables, adulterate in many ways the word of God." If the Bible was to be generally accessible, it had to be translated into the vernacular.

We need not here go into Wycliffe's social and theological theories, which led him to formulate his demand for Bible translation and to take steps himself to satisfy that demand. Suffice it to say that Wycliffe and the Lollard movement, which spread many of his ideas, argued for Bible translation that the people might have ready access to the one original source of their religion, and that out of this movement developed the two translations of the Bible from Latin into English associated with Wycliffe's name. The Church opposed the Lollard attitude as it had opposed that of the Waldensians and other groups in Europe who had advocated vernacular Bible translation on a large scale. The Wycliffite translations, like the Lollard movement in general which developed the Wycliffite tradition, remained suspect as heretical, and as late as 1528 Sir Thomas More condemned them as such, though ignorant of their nature. The immediate climax of the controversy about Bible translation was reached in 1408 when the provincial council at Oxford forbade the translation of the text of the Bible into English without specific episcopal license.

The literary quality of the Wycliffite translations is not impressive: the second is better than the first, less literal and wooden, but even it hardly constitutes a great monument of English prose. These two versions, especially the later one, enjoyed a certain popularity, as the number of surviving manuscripts prove, though their popularity cannot, of course, compare with that of later printed Bibles (the Wycliffite versions were made before the age of printing) made after the principle of vernacular translation had been generally accepted.

The Lollard heresy was suppressed at the beginning of the fifteenth century, but the idea that the Bible, as the one original source of Christianity, should be available to the people in their own language did not die. As the criticism of the Church that was eventually to bring about the Reformation spread in England as elsewhere, the demand for Bible translation also grew. The Church shifted its ground somewhat in the face of this growing demand and began to object to the Wycliffite translations because they were erroneous rather than because they made the Bible readily accessible to the public. When Sir Thomas More, for example, was discussing Bible translation in 1528 he made it clear that in his view the Church could only have condemned the Wycliffite versions if they were textually corrupt and contained heretical notes, and he accordingly assumed that these versions did in fact have these faults. Thus there had been a radical shift in orthodox opinion some time before More wrote: earlier, the opinion had been that the text of the Bible should not be made accessible to ordinary people, who were not qualified to interpret it properly, while the later view was that translations for whatever purpose were permissible if they were accurate and contained no heretical notes. This change was the measure of the success of the growing popular demand.

The development of large-scale Bible translation in England is bound up with the development of the Reformation, and the development of the Reformation is in turn inseparable from the growth of the "New Learning." The revival of the study first of Greek and then of Hebrew in the fifteenth century and later made available a critical apparatus for the examination of the original texts of the basic documents of Christianity. This put a new weapon in the hands of the reformers and they lost no time in using it. The work of Reuchlin and Erasmus—who fought obscurantism in the Church without leaving the fold—made the scholarship of the Renaissance available to the zeal of the Reformation, and from this marriage the Golden Age of English Bible translation was born.

The story of that Golden Age has been often told. William Tyndale, profiting by recent developments in Greek and Hebrew studies, began his work on Bible translation from the original texts in 1524 and spent the rest of his life in this activity. He was unable to do his work in England, and for thirteen years worked secretly in exile until he was brought back to England by a trick and burned as a heretic in 1536. Tyndale was an open reformer and attacked not only the abuses of the Church but its doctrine. His zeal for Bible translation was bound up with his interest in Church reformation and his theological ideas; like Wycliffe before him, he wished to have the one original source of Christianity laid open to all. "I defy the Pope and all his laws," Tyndale is said by Fox to have declared, "and if God spare my life, ere many years I will cause a boy that driveth the plow shall know more of the scripture than thou [a 'learned man' to whom he was talking] dost." Tyndale was here echoing words which the humanist Erasmus had uttered earlier in his *Exhortation to the Diligent Study of Scripture,* a work which Tyndale translated.

Tyndale translated the whole of the New Testament and a considerable portion of the Old, and his work is the foundation on which all subsequent English Bible translation is built. Shortly after his death the atmosphere in England grew more favorable to Bible translation. While the rise of humanism and the Renaissance movement in general had put new and stronger weapons in the hands of those who argued in favor of Bible translation, and helped to produce a series of significant changes in European thought and culture, the invention of printing had enabled these changes to develop with unprecedented rapidity and had also made it increasingly difficult for the authorities to prevent the circulation in large numbers of prohibited works. The abuses of the Church, the new attitude to religion that was in part produced by these abuses, the rediscovery of forgotten aspects of the ancient world, the development of a new Greek and Hebrew scholarship and the invention of printing—these were the factors that combined to speed the pace and improve the quality of English Bible translation. At the time of Tyndale's death his victory was already assured.

In England the situation was further helped by the changing political situation. Henry VIII found the Reformation helpful in his personal difficulties, and throughout the many changes in the theory and practice of Church government in England for which he was responsible the cause of the English Bible steadily progressed. In 1530, while strongly condemning Tyndale's translation and prohibiting Bible translation, Henry nevertheless affirmed his intention of providing for an authorized translation when the time was appropriate. Five years later the first complete printed English Bible appeared, the work of Miles Coverdale, a man inspired by the same ideals as Tyndale but milder in his views and more compromising in character. This was not the authorized version for which the English bishops were preparing, but Coverdale assumed that his work would be acceptable to the king. A later edition of Coverdale's Bible, published in 1537, bears the legend: "Set forth with the Kynges moost gracious licence." The main battle had been won, and the 1537 quarto edition of Coverdale's Bible was the first "authorized version" of the Bible in English. Henceforth the fight was to be concentrated not on the right to translate but on the improvement of the translation.

Coverdale's was not an original translation from the Hebrew and Greek but a version derived from later Latin and German versions. Though his style lacked the fine simplicity of Tyndale's, it was smooth and free flowing and contributed substantially to the rhythms of later English renderings. From now on translations followed closely on one another's heels. The same year that Coverdale's first authorized version appeared saw the publication of Matthew's Bible, also "set forth with the King's most gracious licence," and strongly supported by the bishops. Matthew's Bible was a composite version, made up of Tyndale's translation of as much of the Old Testament as he had translated, Coverdale's translation of the remainder of the Old Testament and Tyndale's New Testament. It was this Bible that was the basis for the series of revisions that culminated in the King James, or Authorized, Version of 1611. Its imperfections were freely admitted by the bishops, even though Archbishop Cranmer promoted it as strongly as he could, and the Great Bible, a revision of Matthew's Bible made by Coverdale at the instance of Thomas Cromwell, was published in April, 1540. By this time public Bible reading had become widespread and the readings were often accompanied by scenes almost riotous in their enthusiasm. Thus we find that, while the Great Bible was ordered to be set up in every parish church, provisions were made against the misuse of Bible reading, readers being enjoined not to read "with loud and high voices" or in a disputatious frame of mind, but "humbly, meekly and reverently."

By this time citations of biblical texts in English were freely used to challenge specific practices of the Church. Fox, for example, tells the story of a young man refusing to kneel down before the crucifix and quoting from the Bible in justification, "Thou shalt not make any graven image, nor bow down to it, to worship it." The English Bible was rapidly becoming a familiar part of the ordinary Englishman's intellectual equipment. Further, while in the Middle Ages only the Psalms and the more picturesque narratives were generally known of the Old Testament, from this time on the Hebrew prophets, almost unknown earlier, began to influence men's minds and imaginations.

The Great Bible ran into many editions, but there were continuous suggestions of a further revision. On the death of Edward VI the progress of English Bible translation was temporarily halted. Queen Mary was a

Catholic, and on her accession the printing of vernacular Bibles in England came to an abrupt stop. Many of the Protestants most interested in Bible translation went into exile, and it was at the colony of these exiles at Geneva that the next English translation of the Bible was made. The Geneva Bible, published at Geneva in 1557, was a thorough revision of the Great Bible after the original texts with the help of such other versions and aids to translation as had recently appeared on the Continent. The most accurate and scholarly English translation yet made, the Geneva Bible is not in the direct line of succession of the Authorized Version, though it was fairly heavily drawn upon by the King James translators. On the whole, the Geneva translators sacrificed style to accuracy, and there is a pedantic flavor about the work, particularly noticeable in the spelling of proper names.

The accession of Queen Elizabeth marked a reversion to middle-of-the-road Protestant policy. The Great Bible was once again ordered to be set up in churches (the Geneva Bible, being the work of more extreme Protestants who were considerably to the "left" of Elizabeth's Anglican Church, was not officially recognized). In 1568 the Great Bible was superseded by a further revision made by a company of bishops, and hence known as the Bishops' Bible. This version was not, however, altogether successful. A combination of the work of different revisers working with little common policy or discipline, it is patchy and uneven, and in accuracy considerably behind the Geneva Bible, which continued to be the most popular translation in England until after 1611. Finally, when James I ascended the throne in 1603 he appointed a company of learned men consisting of the most competent Hebrew and Greek scholars available (excluding, however, those who were definitely antagonistic to the Anglican Church) to prepare a great new revision. This work, begun in 1604 and completed seven years later, after meticulous and carefully co-ordinated labor, has remained *the* English Bible ever since. There have been more scholarly versions made in the past three-quarters of a century, but none has rivaled the Authorized Version of 1611 in literary quality and none has had the great literary influence of that extraordinary work.

It has often been remarked that the Authorized Version was the work of a syndicate, yet is a total work of art with all the marks of individual genius. This mystery becomes less baffling when we realize that the diction of the English Bible was forged in almost a century's experimentation and was an organic and not a mechanical development. The Authorized Version was the culmination of that development. And when we further realize—as has already been noted—that this development took place during the most brilliant experimental period in the whole history of English literature, we can understand something of what lies behind the diction of this translation.

By the time the Authorized Version appeared the English Bible had been accepted for several generations as the great basic document of English civilization. Theologians, moralists, philosophers, poets, political thinkers and economists turned to it for inspiration, for historical facts, arguments, images, principles and theories. The extent to which the great debate on the nature of political freedom, which raged in England throughout the Civil War and indeed throughout almost the whole of the seventeenth century, drew its inspiration from biblical sources has never yet been fully appreciated by political historians. Anyone who has studied the debates in the Long Parliament and the innumerable pamphlets and tracts of a sociologico-religious or politico-religious nature that fell in a tremendous flood from the printing presses of the period cannot have failed to notice the underlying biblical inspiration. There was an inspiration both in style and in ideas. The various Puritan sects which advocated different types of democratic organization and whose discussions of the nature of liberty contributed more than has yet been conceded to the development of British democratic ideals, were trying to apply biblical principles to the modern world. And though with the Restoration this kind of activity subsided, its effect was by no means lost, and it continued in a milder form throughout subsequent ages. It might further be pointed out that behind the American Constitution and the American Bill of Rights lies the English Bill of Rights of 1689 and all those theories of individual liberty so fiercely debated by Puritan students of the Bible in the seventeenth century and later, given more polished and equable form in the writings of philosophers such as Locke. The influence of the English Bible here will bear much further investigation.

4

We have not mentioned all the English translations made before the Authorized Version, nor have we discussed in any detail the kinds of biblical style developed between 1523 and 1611. A full treatment of these aspects of the subject would require a volume. The main point for our present discussion is that the Authorized Version represents at the same time the culmination of almost a century's work in English Bible translation and one of the greatest literary masterpieces in the language. This twofold aspect accounts in part for the strength of its influence. For a great body of Protestants, both Puritans and Anglicans and, later, a variety of nonconforming sects, the English Bible was the authentic voice of God and could be appealed to, quoted, and directly and indirectly referred to in innumerable ways. Hundreds of biblical texts in the Authorized translation became proverbs and household words in English homes. And though there was a great deal of what their opponents called "canting" among

Puritan quoters of the Bible, among the majority of the people such quotation became a natural embellishment of serious speech. And while the English Bible was working among the people this way and enriching popular speech, which in turn enriched the speech of writers like Bunyan, literary men irrespective of religious belief were assimilating its stylistic riches. The English Bible thus came into English literature both directly and indirectly—indirectly through its influence on popular speech and directly through the conscious utilization of biblical rhythms, images or diction by writers from Milton to Ruskin and beyond.

That this influence was making itself felt before the Authorized Version had become the accepted translation is made clear by the attitude toward the Bible of writers who used other versions. Shakespeare, for example, used the Geneva version, drawing upon it freely for illustration and allusion and taking for granted that his audience would immediately see the references. In this he was typical of a host of writers of his own time and later who often achieved some of their most brilliant effects by such use of biblical sources. The actual vocabulary of the English Bible introduced many new words and familiarized many others which had been in little use previously. Nothing exercises a developing language more effectively than its use in translation. Words and phrases such as "loving-kindness," "tender mercy" (both first introduced by Coverdale), "beautiful" (not found before Tyndale) and numerous others, both gentle and stern, pastoral and passionate, realistic and highly figurative, entered into the English literary language through English Bible translation. The rich imagery of the Song of Songs, the melancholy lyricism of *Kohelet*, the pithy aphorisms of Proverbs—their influence is everywhere in English prose and poetry. In one short piece alone, David's lament for Jonathan, there are half a dozen phrases that have become part of the English language: "how are the mighty fallen," "in their death they were not divided," "swifter than eagles, stronger than lions." One could write a volume on the influence of the Book of Job alone, and a whole treatise on the use of the word "shepherd," both as noun and as verb, deriving from the first verse of Psalm 23. The use of the words prompted by the Bible does not confine itself to the serious use of the original context: the treatise on the use of "shepherd" would have to take up, for example, the ironic and humorous use of the term as applied by Tony Weller to the Reverend Mr. Stiggins in Dickens's *Pickwick Papers*. Too much "canting" by Puritans led to a secondary use of such words, an ironical use which, though only indirectly attributable to the Bible, has had a great deal of influence on English speech and in English fiction.

As far as actual influence on style is concerned, the Psalms, the Prophetic books and the "Writings" had much more influence than the Pentateuch, whose narrative style is extremely primitive (any number of short sentences linked by "and") and whose influence manifested itself through the use of biblical stories rather than through any imitation of rhythm or cadence. But the passionate rhythm of the Hebrew prophets is to be found in much nineteenth-century prose, just as the cadences of the Psalms can be found in both prose and poetry in that century. And as there is some evidence that the translators of the Authorized Version made an attempt to preserve something of the Hebrew rhythm (or what they conceived to be the Hebrew rhythm) in their English rendering, especially in the Prophets, the link with the original text here is more definite than might be thought.

Seventeenth-century English literature is so rich in works showing biblical influence of every kind that it is impossible to deal with this influence in short compass. Though the prose of the period is often more influenced by Latin and Greek models than by the prose of the English Bible, and writers like Robert Burton, Sir Thomas Browne and Jeremy Taylor turned to the classics for their literary inspiration, biblical influence on the poetry of the period and on the controversial tracts on religious and political subjects was continuous. But here, as we have seen, it is difficult to separate religious from purely biblical influence: the two become so intertwined in the religious poetry of the century (and so much of the best poetry of the century was religious) that one cannot isolate the influence of the Bible as a book from that of the Bible as the source document of the Christian religion. Yet in the poetry of George Herbert, for example, there is found that combination of gravity and simplicity which, as a quality of *style*, clearly owes something to English biblical prose. A line like, "But thou shalt answer, Lord, for me," could not have been written if the Psalms had never been translated into English. As a rule it is in those poets whose emotion is more restrained and whose passion is under control that the biblical influence is most clearly discernible: we can see it in Herbert but not in Crashaw, in Vaughan and Marvell more than in Donne. And we can see it in a different sense in the great satires of Dryden, which drew on biblical characters and incidents with a confidence that amounts to nonchalance.

Milton perhaps more than any other English poet was conscious of the twofold value of the Bible—its moral teaching and its literary qualities. Though by no means a typical Puritan, he had the typical Protestant attitude toward the Bible as the final court of appeal for all Christians: "Let them chant what they will of prerogatives, we shall tell them of Scripture; of custom, we of Scripture; of Acts and Statutes, still of Scripture . . ." He also recognized the number of literary forms contained in the biblical writings, and deliberately modeled his own *Paradise Regained* on the Book of Job. A humanist as well as a Puritan, a lover of the Latin and Greek classics as well as the Scriptures, Milton was able to reconcile the religious and the aesthetic aspects of the Bible just as he reconciled classical with biblical imagery. Early Christian practice had long established the tradition of retaining classical gods as Christian devils, and Milton saw the advantages of this combination for poetic expression. As a result, he gives us, from his earliest period, examples of combined biblical and pagan allusions done with complete confidence:

> Peor, and Baalim,
> Forsake their Temples dim,
>   With that twice batter'd god of Palestine,
> And moonèd Ashtaroth,
> Heav'n's queen and mother both,
>   Now sits not girt with tapers' holy shrine,
> The Lybic Hammon shrinks his horn,
> In vain the Tyrian Maids their wounded Thammuz mourn.
>
> And sullen Moloch, fled,
> Hath left in shadows dred,
>   His burning Idol all of blackest hue;
> In vain with cymbals ring,
> They call the grisly king,
>   In dismal dance about the furnace blue;
> The brutish gods of Nile as fast,
> Isis and Orus, and the Dog Anubis haste.
>   —Ode on the Morning of Christ's Nativity—The Hymn

Throughout all of Milton's prose and poetry Bible names and images recur. The fact that his greatest works are on biblical themes makes this the more appropriate. But in general the style as such is influenced more by classical than by biblical models, though in *Paradise Regained* and *Samson Agonistes* he deliberately cultivated a less ornate style closer to at least one kind of biblical style than to that of classical epic.

John Bunyan's use of the Bible was more direct and more naïve than that of Milton. He adopted the Bible's simpler narrative style, making frequent use of the actual language of the Authorized Version. Bunyan's clear prose narrative played its part in the simplification of English prose that went on in the late seventeenth and the early eighteenth century, and thus we can trace some connection between biblical English prose and the prose of Sir William Temple and Joseph Addison, which in turn laid the foundations for generations of later English prose writers.

The growth of hymn writing in the eighteenth century, attributable in large measure to the Wesleyans, did not, as might have been expected, bring the language of the English Bible more and more into English diction, for hymns were by nature nonbiblical—they were the alternative to Scripture reading and biblical paraphrases, using more everyday speech and, often, exhibiting more sentimental attitudes. Even the hymns of William Cowper, often based on specific biblical texts, can hardly be said to be in any sense biblical in their language except for the actual references to the texts used. On the whole, the influence of the English Bible in the eighteenth century took the form of unconscious assimilation of the images and expressions of a familiar text. The direct and conscious influences were almost always classical—and because they were so direct and conscious not always so happy in their results, perhaps, as the less deliberately sought influence of the Bible. At any rate, it is worth remembering that the style of Johnson and Gibbon and the less successful styles of their imitators are classical and not biblical in their inspiration, though, of course, by this time no writer (and least of all Johnson) could have written at length in prose without displaying in his work some of the effects of generations of Bible reading.

"Generations of Bible reading"—the phrase is worth pondering. For the English, perhaps more than any other people in Europe, were Bible *readers*. The Bible was read, both silently and aloud, in innumerable families throughout the country from the late sixteenth century until the late nineteenth, and even today there is much more knowledge of the English Bible among the people of Britain than there is in the United States, in spite of the fact that there are in the latter country whole areas and communities where a lively evangelical tradition has kept Bible reading very much alive. The effect of this continuous Bible reading among the people of Britain was to acquaint all classes with a vocabulary and a number of literary styles (for, as we have noted, the Bible has many styles) that were constantly working on both the spoken and the written English language.

The English poets of the eighteenth and nineteenth centuries drew as naturally on the English Bible for imagery and allusion as if the book had been an original English masterpiece bearing the same relation to later literature as the *Iliad* and the *Odyssey* did to later Greek writing. Some, like Byron, drew deliberately on Old Testament stories and ideas. Among the nineteenth-century prose writers Ruskin was perhaps the most influenced by the Authorized Version. He was brought up to read it regularly, and he more than once testified to the effect this reading had on his literary taste and prose style. Knowing much of the English Bible by heart, he wrote, "it was not possible for me, even in the foolishest times of youth, to write entirely superficial or formal English." Ruskin was also one of those who was profoundly influenced by the ideals of social justice proclaimed by the Hebrew prophets, and in this he was typical of his age, for as the nineteenth century advanced there was a distinct tendency to turn away from those aspects of the Bible which had most

influenced earlier writers and to dwell on those books which had been less
dwelt on previously. The tendency was, as far as the Old Testament was
concerned, away from Law and toward the Prophets. Isaiah, Amos, Hosea
and Malachi became more popular than the Pentateuch and the historical
books, and their words were often consciously echoed by the increasing
number of those who were preoccupied with the problems of social and
economic reform. Among English writers and thinkers today this tendency
continues to be strong, and there are many who, while turning away from
the more specifically theological formulations of religious doctrine, have
sought inspiration for a creed of humanistic reform from the passionate and
noble utterances of the Hebrew prophets. Among adherents of all religious
faiths and of none, the Bible thus continues to exert influence, and to the
various kinds of influence the English Bible has had in the past—influence
as a source of images and symbols, as a source of literary forms, as a series
of models in prose style, as a storehouse of moral and religious ideas—
there is now to be added its contribution toward the formulation of a
dynamic social philosophy.

Brief though this discussion has been, and few and sketchy as have been
the illustrations of the argument, enough has perhaps been said to make
clear the extraordinary way in which the Bible has worked in English
literature. Because English Protestantism drew equal strength from the
humanistic scholarship of the Renaissance and the individualism of the
Reformation, insisting equally on broad learning and on the popularizing
of the fruits of that learning, the English Bible became at the same time
a moral and an aesthetic force. That strange but significant old Hebrew
phrase "the beauty of holiness" thus found a new interpretation in the
history of English literature, whose development illustrated time and
again that wisdom and beauty were bound up with each other. There was
a classical ideal at work here too, the Socratic identification of virtue with
knowledge and the implied Platonic association of the aesthetic with the
moral. In a sense it can be said that the English tradition at its best and
most characteristic always tended to interpret the Bible in the light of
classical humanism, and thus to avoid pedantry in its view of either.
English literature is, on the whole, moral without being didactic and
humanistic without being pagan. In the first of these qualities it differs
from the German, and in the second from the French. It is not extravagant
to see the basis of this English *via media* in the fact that the Bible became
known to Englishmen in a book which was regarded at the same time as a
great religious and a great literary document. Thus the Puritan read it
for its doctrine and fell under its literary spell, and the skeptic read it as a
work of art and imbibed its morality. Which of the two profited more is a
question that can be debated forever.

NOTES

[1a Cf. above Robert Gordis, "The Bible as a Cultural Monument," pp. 816 f.]

[2a Cf. below Frederick Lehner, "The Influence of the Bible on European Literature," pp. 1472-1473.]

SELECT BIBLIOGRAPHY

BAIKIE, JAMES, *The English Bible and Story: Its growth, its translators, and their adventures.* London, 1928.

BOWEN, FRANCIS, *A Layman's Story of the English Bible considered in its Literary and Secular Aspect.* New York, 1885.

BUTTERWORTH, CHARLES C., *The Literary Lineage of the King James Bible, 1340-1611.* Philadelphia, 1941.

COOK, ALBERT, S., *Biblical Quotations in Old English Prose Writers.* London, 1898.

———, *The Authorized Version of the Bible and its Influence.* New York, 1910.

DAICHES, DAVID, *The King James Version of the English Bible.* Chicago, 1941.

DEANESLEY, MARGARET, *The Lollard Bible and other Medieval Biblical Versions.* Cambridge, 1920.

GRIERSON, SIR HERBERT, *The English Bible.* London, 1943.

LOWES, JOHN L., "The Noblest Monument in English Prose," in *Essays in Appreciation.* Boston and New York, 1936.

McAFEE, CLELAND B., *The Greatest English Classic: a Study of the King James Version of the Bible and its Influence on life and literature.* New York and London, 1912.

McCLURE, JAMES G., *The Supreme Book of Mankind: The Origin and Influence of the English Bible.* New York, 1930.

McCOMB, SAMUEL, *The Making of the English Bible, with an Introductory Essay on the Influence of the English Bible on English Literature.* New York, 1909.

MOULTON, RICHARD G., *The Literary Study of the Bible.* Boston, 1899.

NOBLE, RICHMOND, *Shakespeare's Biblical Knowledge.* London and New York, 1935.

POLLARD, ALFRED W., *Records of the English Bible.* Oxford, 1911.

SANDS, P. C., *Literary Genius of the Old Testament.* Oxford, 1924.

WESTCOTT, BROOKE F., *A General View of the History of the English Bible* (3d. ed. rev. by W. A. Wright). London and New York, 1905.

WORK, E. W., *The Bible in English Literature.* New York, 1917.

CHAPTER 35

THE INFLUENCE OF THE BIBLE ON EUROPEAN LITERATURE

By Frederick Lehner

It is nothing new to consider the Bible not only as a religious document but also as a great work of literature, an anthology containing historical reports, poetry, short stories, one philosophical drama and illuminated, apocalyptic writings. As literature, it follows the laws of all great literary works: it is a creation of lofty imagination, and it influences writers of the following generations and centuries to appropriate from its content whatever they decisively may feel as new, startling, impressive, stimulating thought and provoking imagination. Indeed, as an anthology of literature, as a source of stories, forms and ideas, the Bible became bread and meat for centuries to come. To be exact, the Bible did not enter the mind of continental Europe as a Jewish document; it became influential as a part of the Old and New Testament, and it took centuries before its specific essence was recognized. First it became a part of the intellectual property through the channels of Christianity.

Thus it was not the Hebrew original—even though the study of the original never was discontinued—it was not even the first Latin translation that created the miracle, that interested nations in Hebrew stories and history and philosophy; it was rather the Latin version of the Hebrew Bible by Jerome (fifth century) that helped the Oriental tales to shine and sparkle in a new setting. At first, of course, its influence was not wide, but when the monasteries sent out missionaries to win over native tribes to Christianity, especially in the eighth, ninth and tenth centuries, the Jewish legends went along with the Christian legends. Soon the Hebrew report about the Creation replaced the report of the Icelandic saga, the story of the tree Yggdrasil. Soon the tragic stories of the Fall, the First Murder, Sodom and Gomorrah, the Flood, the Tower of Babel appeared in many variations, sometimes distorted, more naïve than the original. Then the first epics and plays about Joseph were written, about Moses, Judith, Solomon, Daniel, Susanna and the Elders. Topics and forms abounded. And soon we can perceive several different trends. We can see how topics were discovered and used, how the Psalms became an essential part of the Christian service, how the many apocalyptic dreams in the Bible provoked new utterings and new mystical outbursts, far from the mystical world of Jerusalem.

What could the Bible offer other than what was offered by the other major traditions or legacies of imagination, fiction and folk lore? The four great traditions which influenced and formed European literature in its various manifestations were the Hebrew, the Greek, the Germanic and the Celtic. The Germanic tradition (*Edda*) and the Celtic (*Les Chevaliers de la Table Ronde*) appeared and disappeared again, as well as the Hebrew and the Greek, but they did not have the general appeal, the great and persistent influence on *all* Continental literatures; they did not have the extraordinary and absolute value of the Greek and Hebrew legacies. These two, certainly, were responsible for the spirit of Western civilization; they served as its pillars of beauty and intellectual strength. They formed our world, though in different ways, sometimes alternately, sometimes together, and each according to its special essence, inherent in its spiritual body. If "the governing idea of Hellenism is spontaneity of consciousness,"[1] that of Hebraism is strictness of conscience. Where one legacy stated the problem, the other made it ethical. "It is in the confluence of the Hellenic stream of thought with the waters that flow from Hebrew sources that the main direction of world's progress is to be sought."[2] In this report we are concerned only with one part of the problem. We shall try to observe the influence of the Bible on Continental European literature, to follow this influence, and to analyze its aspects and importance.

Such an influence can be found in many regions and sections of what we call literature. We can easily discover that certain stories, topics, tales of the Bible were taken out of their (religious) context, and told, retold, changed in many curious ways. There is, however, to begin with, the problem of the language itself, a fact that should not be neglected.

In an essay contained in the Oxford *Legacy of Israel*,[3] Laurie Magnus cites good English material to make this point clear. He quotes a poem by Matthew Arnold (*Sohrab and Rustum*) and another poem by Alfred Lord Tennyson (*Ulysses*), and shows rather clearly that, when we analyze their language, the structure of their thoughts, the images and similes, we discover that the Oriental poem by Arnold owes its poetical structure to Greece, while the Greek poem by Tennyson is full of biblical echoes.

This influence of the Bible on the interior construction of a poem, the molding of its expression, the selection of its comparisons, for instance, can be exemplified by the authors of other nations as well: Dante, for instance. In general it can be said that from single words to images, from images to the entire mode of the expression, from expression to topics, philosophy— every kind of influence can be detected in the European languages and literatures. "Sodom and Gomorrah," to cite some examples, the "Tower of

Babel," the "Hueter meines Bruders," "the keeper of my brother," the "calf of gold," a whole world of words, images and ready-made thoughts have remained alive and have been added to the languages of Germanic, Romance and Slavic roots as well. Magnus, in his contribution to the *Legacy of Israel*, proves even more, on the same level. He shows how not only in English, but in other languages as well, "the Hebrew simile has become naturalized." To explain his point he states that the Greek writer compares one element with another, and elaborates the second. The Hebrew simile elaborates the first element as it speaks of it in terms of the second. ("*He* shall be like a tree, *his* leaf also shall not wither.")[4] And the Continent imitates the example.

The historical development of this phenomenon follows a common trend. Often-quoted material influences our thinking to the very expression of thoughts: the Bible, obviously, was often quoted. And as this material found its way to European minds, first mostly through the medium of Latin, the perennial language of the Church, the phenomenon of this influence became genuinely visible only with the Reformation, when Luther's Bible in the German vernacular created the German *Schriftsprache*. This translation and the King James Version[4a] in English-speaking countries and the corresponding efforts in France, in Italy and in Spain popularized the original text and wording of the New and the Old Testament in a tremendously successful and efficient way. The original text became known not only to scholars or priests, not only to educated laymen, but to everyone who could read. And not only certain basic books dealing with scientific topics became afterwards a "Bible" whose pronouncements were law; the Bible itself became a "Bible" in this respect and was consulted, quoted and understood. Let us now proceed to its influence on topics.

The so-called *Wiener Genesis*—the manuscript is of the twelfth century —is the oldest of the many religious poems written in the Austrian Carinthia and based on the Bible.[5] It was written because the Roman Church demanded in its *Breviarium* that the *lectiones* during the time from Septuagesima Sunday to Tuesday after Quadragesima be based on chapters 1 to 14 of Genesis.[6] Thus the poem, as it was preserved for us in the different manuscripts, contained especially two lessons, the Creation and the Fall. (Another chapter, however, added to those two, deals with Cain and Abel, and others with Noah, with Abraham, with Isaac and his sons, and with Joseph in Egypt.) To the same epoch, about 1220, belong two other manuscripts, two epics about Exodus, as described in the first fifteen chapters of the Second Book of Moses.[7] The poem followed the text of the Itala. We have also a separate poem dealing with Moses, a Balaam, two Judiths (mostly to be found among the manuscripts of the Vorau monastery), a *Lob Salomos*, the *Juenglinge in dem Feuerofen*, fragments of a book about the Maccabees, an Esdras, an Isaiah, and a Song of Songs translated in 1276 by Brub von Scombeck, constable of Magdeburg.

These stories and poems taken from the Hebrew Bible were also stories in the medieval tradition. Wherever there was an opportunity to adjust the foreign context to the surrounding European and Christian world, it was done. When the plants of Paradise were described, the poet found his material in the description of a model garden as it was given in Charlemagne's *Capitulare de Villis*.[8] In the *Exodus* we have an elaborate presentation of a medieval army, even the grasshoppers, frogs and flies were enemy armies and described as such. But to summarize, if we take the German epics mentioned above as an example of what happened in all civilized districts of continental Europe, we may correctly conclude that an essential part of the Hebrew Bible was known to every educated man of the twelfth century. But it came to him as a part of the Christian legacy, and the ethical or philosophical content of the Jewish stories was taken purely as a forethought of what was expressed with greater clarity in the Gospels of the New Faith. At any rate, this first approach proved not only stimulating; it was also carried over as a durable element into European literature.

The topics from the Hebrew Bible, of course, were not only chosen by the monks in Austria and Franconia, who described them in hymns or epics or songs. In France, too, the Bible attracted creative minds. If we follow the report given by Bédier and Hazard, we learn that translations of parts of the Bible in prose or in verse, poems taken from this or that chapter of the Scriptures were done in the twelfth century.[9] There are translations of the Psalms, the first of them in the first half of that century; there is a version in verse of Genesis (by Everat for the Comtesse Marie de Champagne) from 1190. In the same year the Hebrew and the New Testament were put into verses by Herman de Valenciennes; and other attempts of this kind followed. And here and there in Europe the *fratres* imitated the French and German example.

In the twelfth century, however, another type of literature, *the drama*, also discovered the treasures hidden in the Hebrew Bible. The oldest drama written in French dates from the twelfth century. It is called *Représentation d'Adam*[10] (author unknown), and again we are back to our topic. This *mystère*, as the religious tragedies were called, presents first the *Paradis terrestre*, then the Temptation and the Fall of Adam and Eve. We see the murder of Abel, after which the prophets parade by and announce the arrival of the Messiah. It is a lively play, and really dramatic, truly medieval and truly French, especially in the scenes of the temptation. This play, however, was only a beginning. The end of the development can be found in the *Cycle de l'Ancien Testament,* a compilation into one great work which was made in the course of the second half of the fifteenth century.[11] The opus is composed of fifty thousand verses. This play was performed in Paris in 1542 by the *Confrères de la Passion* in the Hôtel de Flandres, and proved to be a great success. "*L'entrée coûtait deux sous par personne; et une loge, trente sous pour toute la durée de la représentation qui remplit environ vingt séances.*"[12] But this tradition was stopped by the Arrêt du Parlement de Paris (November 17, 1548), which banned *all* religious plays from the stage, including the *Mystère du Vieux Testament*. Nevertheless, it was not very long before the specific value of the topic overcame the ban, and the colorful and thrilling stories of the Bible reappeared on the stage, this time no more as *mystère* nor as *moralité*, but as plots of Renaissance tragedies, climaxed in *Les Juives* by Robert Garnier (1580) and in *Esther* by Jean Racine (1688-1689). Before we proceed to describe this change and new life, however, we have to see what happened in other European countries, especially in Spain.[12a]

In the Iberian Peninsula there was no parliament that forbade the performance of religious plays. The great flowering of these plays was never interrupted by decree. Unfortunately, we do not know too much about their beginnings. But we do know that in the first half of the sixteenth century Diego Sanchez wrote a *Farsa de Salomón*, a *Farsa de Isaac*, a *Farsa de Abrahám, de Moysén, del Rey David*, topics chosen again because of their "close symbolic relationship to Christ's sacrifice."[13] In the second half of the century Micael de Carvajal wrote a *Tragedia Josephina* which deals with the sale of Joseph by his brothers, with his stay in Egypt and the death of Jacob. The most important document, however, is the great Codex at the Biblioteca Nacional (1550-1575) containing ninety-six religious plays, twenty-six of which deal with material taken from the Hebrew Bible.[14] If we look into details, two of these plays treat Adam, one treats Cain and Abel, three deal with Abraham, four with Jacob, two with Joseph and three with Moses, the lawgiver. The ratio is, as we see, twenty-six to ninety-six; that is to say, one-fourth of the entire corpus was taken from the Hebrew Bible, which proves how useful the plots seemed to be for dramatists, and how well they lent themselves to the special treatment of playwrights. We find here, for instance, an *Aucto de los hierros de Adán*, and an *Aucto de la lucha de Jacob con el ángel*, or an *Aucto de la deposório de Moysén*, an *Aucto del rey Nabucdonosor cuando se hizo adorar*, an *Aucto del sueño de Nabucdonosor*, religious plays with familiar topics. And here, too, the subjects correspond to the *lectiones* in Septuagesima, Sexuagesima and the Quadragesima season of the Catholic service, as we had observed when we looked into the epics of the German Middle Ages. And at the time when the religious epic in Central Europe began to lose its appeal, when the religious drama reached its climax in

Spain with Lope de Vega and Calderón de la Barca, the religious epic found its most perfect fulfillment in Italy; the Bible proved again to be a stimulating force demanding respect, offering stories, characters and philosophical insight even into the modern life of the fourteenth century.

If we follow Vossler in his *Medieval Culture*,[15] which is an introduction to Dante and his times, we are soon convinced that the great Italian poet considered the Bible not only a religious document. It was not only Divine truth for him; it was Divine poetry as well. The *Divine Comedy* may be called a summary of the ethical, religious and aesthetic tendencies of the Middle Ages ("the voice of ten silent centuries"). Thus we find in it all the features that belong to such a representation. And the Bible meant for Dante not only the specifically Christian, but the Hebrew Scriptures as well. We find here indeed an extreme reverence for the word and the letter of the Hebrew legacy, we find an almost jealous effort to extract from the pictures in the biblical stories and from their poetic contents more or less general philosophical concepts. We find also that Dante deduced from them moral commandments, and we find mystical significance. It is again Vossler who points out the tremendous influence of the language of the Bible in Dante's work.[16] He shows how Dante's memory was full of biblical reminiscences and pictures. And, true, the Bible is the most-quoted book in his writings. "He [Dante] had it in his head and heart better than many professional clerics."[17] Dante took over unchanged whole sentences, figures, comparisons, similes, especially in his early works. In the *Divine Comedy* this method, this *hantise*, reached its climax. Dante presents the whole cast of the Bible; he presents Adam and Eve, Cain and Abel, Abraham, Rachel, Rebecca, Sarah, Isaac and Esau, Jacob and his sons, the kings, the prophets, the Maccabees, Esther, Ruth, and so on. He presents Cain in the first part of the poem, in *Inferno*, then he lifts him up into *Purgatorio* and we meet the sinner finally even in *Paradiso*, Dante's heaven. But this lavish use of heroes, patriarchs, personages from the Hebrew Bible must not obscure the fact that here again the Jewish men and women are taken from the Christian Bible, of which the Old Testament is a part. Their presence has to be justified. Dante does this very soon, in the beginning of the poem. He crosses a rather Greek landscape in order to enter the Inferno, and among the first people he meets there are the great persons belonging to Jewish antiquity. They are to be found in the first Circle already, in the Limbo, or the borderland of the Unbaptized.[18] It is true, admits Dante, that they have their merit, but to have merit is not enough so long as you have not been baptized. Thus we meet the shades of the First Parent, of Abel, of Noah and Moses, of Abraham, David, Israel with his father and his children and Rachel. If anything is comforting in this picture it is this: we meet them in good company, for soon after them we see Homer, the sovereign poet,

Horace, Ovid, Lucan, Plato, Socrates, Orpheus, Hippocrates and Saladin. And when Dante uses some striking picture taken from the Hebrew Bible, Jacob's dream, for example, he soon shapes the tale into a new form, and the ladder into heaven becomes a representation of contemplative monasticism. But the beginning of the poem is pure Jeremiah. There is the wilderness in which we find ourselves, "midway upon the journey of our life"; there is the lion out of Jeremiah's forest ("which will slay them"); there is the wolf of Jeremiah of the evening ("which will spoil them"); there is the leopard ("which shall watch over their cities") and "everyone that goeth out thence shall be torn to pieces." A good example of the method Dante used to transform the biblical picture and text is given in the passage quoted by Vossler to prove the same point. Of the mysterious tree in Paradise, he says:

> Two shoots from this plant first appear on the sixth cornice of the Purgatorical mountain: first, as actual means of punishments, second, as magical mouthpieces of moral admonition and warning. Thirdly, we find on the summit of the mountain the tree of knowledge itself, as a comprehensive allegory, full of philosophic, ethical, and political instruction. All the transformations from sensuous materialization to moralizing, and even to intellectualizing, are here passed through, and according to its needs the Biblical tree receives the most varied and marvelous environment.[19]

Dante, however, not only quoted and transformed the Bible and transplanted its content into the ideas and symbols of the medieval world. His work reveals also that in his soul there slumbered a more deeply rooted affinity with that part of the biblical tradition which comes from the Prophets. He starts with Jeremiah, as we saw. He possessed not only the voice but also the spirit of a prophet himself.[20] This "inward genuineness" was certainly one of the reasons why Dante often attained a real prophetic style of his own

> which is both classic and thoroughly Florentine, wherein the Hebrew elements acquired fresh and eloquent life and were all but recognizable. The single sermon of wrath, *Ahi serva Italia, de dolore ostello*, suffices to convince us that the Old Testament prophets' language of moral indignation is the mightiest of all artistic treasures which the Bible bestowed upon our poet.[21]

In Chapter 1 we meet the four apocalyptic beasts of Jeremiah. In the fourteenth canto of *Inferno* we have Nebuchadnezzar's dream. In *Purgatorio* 29 we meet Ezekiel, in *Paradiso* 15, Isaiah. They certainly live in Dante's work, as stimulants and even more. In his *Divine Comedy*, then, the influence of the Bible reached its climax, as far as the medieval approach is concerned. But with Dante and some minor disciples the trend to quote the Hebrew Bible, to transform its stories and to interpret them so that they might prove the events in the New Testament, also came to an end.

The reason for this change has to be sought in the general development religion went through in the sixteenth century, when the Renaissance introduced Luther's Reformation and Protestantism as its religious counterpart. Not only in Germany, but in France and England also, the ideas of Protestantism proved to be a liberating force.

Through the Reformation the Bible became common property and the new era of its influence can now be detected. Especially in German-speaking countries, where Luther's translation was a sensational event, the social group of the *Buerger* could now read the story of the Creation, of Joseph and of Moses in the vernacular. In the mind of Luther the different tales of the Bible did not have the same value, so that he in a sense overlooked their importance for writers and poets. Thus he was enthusiastic about the Fifth Book of Moses, but he was less interested in the Book of Proverbs. The reason for this is obvious. The *Liber Proverbium Salomonis* is for him *"ein schoenes Buch, denn darim sieht man, wie es in der Welt zugeht"* (a beautiful book, for one can see in it what the world looks like). Further, he disliked the Books Ezra, Judith and Tobias, while Job again was classified as a *"sehr gutes Buch."*[22]

At any rate, his translation proved to be influential and stimulating, even more than his remarks in letters or in his *Tischreden,* although these remarks also opened the way to deeper understanding and appreciation. And to those who believed that the Old Testament was entirely superseded by the Gospels, he answered in clear language: "Ob aber jemand wollte vorgeben, das alte Testament sei aufgehoben und gelte nicht mehr . . . antworte ich: Das ist nicht so . . ." (If someone should think the Old Testament discarded and of no further value, I say: It is not so.)[23] There was no religious epic of importance, however, in the sixteenth century, and it took almost two hundred years before Protestantism in Germany dared to follow the English example given by Milton. Only as late as 1748 was Klopstock ready to publish the first part of his *Messiah.* The reason for this is easy to detect. The people could now read the thrilling stories in the vernacular, and there was no immediate need to rewrite them as tales or poems. The drama, on the other hand, was strongly influenced through Luther's translation and also by his remarks. Translation included not only the Greek but the Hebrew of the Bible. The dramatists, however, ostensibly preferred the Jewish tradition, as these stories could easily be adapted to modern sixteenth-century life.

In France, as we have seen, the presentation of medieval religious plays was forbidden by law; the ban struck also the *mystère* of the Old Testament. In Spain, on the other hand, the Golden Age of the drama, of Lope de Vega and Calderón de la Barca (who used very few tales from the Hebrew Bible), kept the Bible more than ever on the stage. But these authors closely followed the medieval tradition in which the Old Testament had to "prove" the New. In Germany now, through Luther, and after him without interruption, the dramatists of the laymen's *Buergerspiele* and the writers of the laymen's school theater, in colleges and universities, with enthusiasm and almost incredible haste, appropriated the rich material offered to them by the Bible in the vernacular. All reports show conclusively that now, as no outspoken religious purpose stood behind the undertaking, and nothing had to be proved but moral, ethical issues, the authors of the *Schuldrama*, of the *Buergerspiele*, preferred the colorful tales of the Hebrew Bible to all the other material at their disposal. It is almost unbelievable, notes one authority, to observe what material was taken as a pretext for a drama. The Fall, of course. Then the first murder, the story of the Patriarchs, Moses, the Judges, Susanna and the Elders, the three men in the fiery furnace, the golden calf. In these dramas, certain characters had become typical of certain problems: passionate and criminal love appeared in Joseph; the mad passion of old men for a young woman was depicted in Susanna; harmonious life in the bosom of the family was presented in Rebecca, in Tobias. But there were also Judith and Holofernes, and another Joseph by a Dutch educator, and another Susanna in German and Latin. In brief, after Luther the dramatists preferred the biblical stories above all; they liked the interesting plots as they found them in the new translation of the Old Testament. The Hebrew Bible became secularized.

But there is also another reason why Luther is featured in this report. He translated not only prose and the historical parts of the Bible, he also translated the Psalms and contributed thereby to a renewal of Hebrew poetry.

His translations of certain psalms were not the first. We have already mentioned French attempts to put Hebrew poetry into the vernacular. From the tenth century we have a free Bavarian translation (or adaptation) of Psalm 138, a poem written in the *althochdeutsch* vernacular. No other part of the Bible was taken over so completely and so uniformly as the Psalms: from the beginning they were a part of the Christian service. What Luther added was a new, strong and productive emphasis, a new evaluation of this part of the Bible. And the genuine poetical feeling of his translation in the vernacular transformed certain Hebrew songs (Psalm 46:6: "Eine feste Burg ist unser Gott . . .") into German poems of unusual brilliance. That is to say, before Luther the songs in the Church (including the *Stabat Mater* and the *Dies Irae*) were influenced by Solomon's psalms. Luther brought the tradition closer to the Bible when he tried his hand at Psalms 2, 14, 46, 67, 124, 128, 130. And there was Clément Marot in France, who published a very successful, but poor translation of the Psalms (1541, *Trente Psaumes de David;* 1543, *Cinauante Psaumes*). The Huguenots especially praised him for his work, for the songs *"qu'ils entonnaient en marchant au combat."* The Huguenots needed a hymnbook. This explains the vogue, the immense success of the book. But it was read by the Catholics also. And, according to Bédier, the courtiers at the court of Navarre and the court of France hummed the *Chants de David*, even though the Sorbonne banned the translation. Thus it became a part of the Protestant liturgy, it deeply influenced the develop-ment of French poetry in the following centuries, and was followed by another translation, that of Théodore de Bèze (1563). The Catholics soon tried to compete: Le Baïf's attempt dates from 1578. And there were the German Protestant and Catholic poets in the seventeenth century following his example. A new sphere of influence remained active.

The very program of French classicism—the next trend in modernism—seemed to exclude biblical topics; Greek costumes (more than Greek thoughts and philosophy) outlawed all else. All the more, therefore, is it interesting to see how the Jansenist Jean Racine came back to the Bible when he wrote *Esther* for Madame de Maintenon's school for girls in Saint-Cyr. In *Esther* the play follows the Bible closely, except for the smoother, less bloody ending of the French tragedy. It is a hymn to Israel, and not merely superficially, for it owes its plot as well as its style and philosophy to Hebrew tradition. It is true, the *chœur des Israélites* is a chorus in the manner of Greek tragedy. It follows the tradition and the purpose of Greek drama, but the philosophy and the wording come from the Hebrew legacy, from the Psalms. And when we analyze this chorus we find, for instance, the very words of Psalm 121. But the *Esther* of Racine shows still another interesting change. The biblical story is related to prove its own objective, its own philosophy, not—as in the Middle Ages—to prove Christianity. The process of secularization has gone so far that there is not the slightest allusion to another religion. The play is, furthermore, the perfect amalgamation of Greek form and Hebrew content. The king in the play, however, is Louis XIV.

In the eighteenth century, the Protestants, that is to say, Klopstock, Bodmer, Herder and Goethe, lead us to another and different sphere of influence. The reasons for this change are rather complex. As we saw, there was a readiness to reinterpret the Bible, a readiness that came from Luther and the Reformation. But there was also the influence of Jean Jacques Rousseau, whose social philosophy found its way even into the field of literature. The *"retour à la nature"* in literature meant indeed a new flowering of folklore, of original poetry and ideas, an attitude which soon was used in respect to the Hebrew Bible. Rousseau was—in the beginning—less successful with this idea in France than in Germany. The German disciples of Rousseau—Herder above all, and with him the outstanding disciple of Herder, namely Goethe—looked at Hebrew folk lore with new eyes. They were no longer interested in the Bible as a religious document (overcoming thereby the Middle Ages, and Luther too), they discovered in the secularized text the loftiest piece of "original" literature. Goethe was so much enchanted by the Bible, so strongly influenced by its stories and ideas, that he asked his father's permission to study Hebrew in order to be able to read the Bible in the original. Remarks about his interest in the Hebrew text abound in his work. The *Jahrmarktsfest in Plundersweilen* includes a playlet dealing with Haman, Mordecai and Esther. In *Dichtung und Wahrheit*, his autobiography, sixty-year-old Goethe expresses rather extensively and in clear words how deeply he is and was influenced by the Bible, meaning the Hebrew text. The same can be said about certain paragraphs in the novel *Wilhelm Meisters Lehrjahre*. The influence continued the older the poet and thinker himself grew, as we can see in the appendix to the *Westoestlicher Divan*, where Goethe's admiration for the Hebrew contribution is expressed. The debt to a great influence reached its climax in the greatest drama the poet conceived. The final stage of Faust's life and his death is clearly developed after the greatest model in the Bible, after Moses' last years and death. The lawmaker Faust closely follows the lawmaker Moses in his last experiences, and the end of Faust's life and his salvation is certainly influenced by the Bible on the highest, the spiritual, level.

All over Europe they soon followed Goethe, even in France where the Age of Enlightenment drove religion underground. A student of details and catalogues will easily find how strong was the influence of the Bible on the French writers, poets and dramatists in the nineteenth century. He has only to search the work of Chateaubriand, Lamartine, Alfred de Vigny, Victor Hugo. The characters, whom Chateaubriand borrowed from the Bible, are no more the *belles infidèles* of Robert Garnier or Racine; they are taken from the Bible itself. The words of the young Eudore in *Les Martyrs* come directly from the Song of Songs: "*Que vous êtes belle, mon amie . . . que la myrrhe et l'aloès couvrent votre lit embaumé!*" And finally, according to a subtle remark of the French poet, André Spire, "*la découverte de la valeur de la Bible par Chateaubriand fut l'origine d'une profonde transformation de la langue littéraire française.*"[24] And Lamartine writes: "*Lorsque mon âme enthousiaste ou pieuse ou triste, a besoin de chercher un écho à ses enthousiasmes, à ses piétés, ou à ses mélancholies . . . je n'ouvre ni Pindare, ni Horace, ni Hafiz . . . j'ouvre les psaumes et j'y prends les paroles qui semblent sourdre des siècles et qui pénètrent jusqu'au fonds de l'âme des générations.*" And in his tragedy *Saul*, and in other works of inspiring importance, Lamartine rediscovered the lyrical *élan* of the prophets: "*La Providence divine est toujours présente, la pitié pour les pauvres et les déshérités, les appels des opprimés à la miséricorde et à la pitié de Dieu.*"[25] And Alfred de Vigny left six biblical poems among the thirty he wrote.

Thus, a student of literary influences will find biblical themes, quotations from biblical material, interpretations of certain tales, biblical similes, images and characters in the works of Michelet, Quinet, Lamennais, James Darmesteter (*La Légende Divine*), Leconte de Lisle. He will discover the unbroken influence of a great legacy in the poems and works of French symbolists, Remy de Gourmont (*Lilith*), Gustave Kahn, Edouard Dujardin. In Germany—where the harvest is less abundant than in France—he will find Hebbel's *Judith*, Gutzkow's *Koenig Saul* and Otto Ludwig's *Makkabaeer*, to mention only writers and plays of great importance.

In France the twentieth century witnessed the *Saül* of André Gide, a play sparkling with intellect; so, too, we have *Judith* by Jean Giraudoux, where the biblical story lends itself to a brilliant play of sophisticated spirit. We have *Samaël* by André Spire, a serious philosophical fantasy. And we have *La première famille* by Jules Supervielle, a biblical farce, surrealist in style, full of that *esprit gaulois*. We have tragedy, comedy, farce. The great Viennese Jewish dramatist and poet, Richard Beer-Hofmann, published his biblical tragedies (*Jaakobs Traum, Der junge David*), which enjoyed great success. Stefan Zweig wrote his *Jeremias*. We could point furthermore to the influence of Hebrew poetry—I mean the Psalms—on two French Catholic poets, Péguy and Claudel. But there I should first mention the influence of the Psalms on the *vers libre* of Walt Whitman, and on other forerunners of Claudel. At any rate, we hear an echo from Solomon in the *Grandes Odes* of Claudel, in his dramas, and in the *Mystère d'Eve* by Charles Péguy.

Thus we have reached the climax of a development which began with an old French play, an old German epic. The old sacred story is employed not merely for its narrative, as in the period before Luther; it is adopted not only as a form convenient for moderns. Its potentialities as a symbolic frame for a twentieth-century idea or problem are discovered. We turn, therefore, to Thomas Mann's *Joseph* novel. What could a writer of the twentieth century find in the Bible? In a former work Thomas Mann had described successfully the rise and fall of a nineteenth-century bourgeois family; in another novel he described the intellectual, moral and political situation of Europe before the 1914 war. His style was patterned after the style of Goethe, dramatist, novelist and poet of the eighteenth and the early nineteenth century, and his world was seen with the eyes of a naturalist, that is to say, with the eyes of a man who reveals even romantic feelings as "natural" as possible; and his imagination found its expression and its symbols in the intellectual language of a modern twentieth-century thinker. What could he find in the Bible? Well, in a later work he intended to describe, above all, the problems of the twentieth century. He looked around for some *durable* material in which to express his ideas. And as he looked he could find no more adequate a frame for his picture than the one he discovered in the Bible: the adventures of young Joseph, Joseph in Egypt, Joseph the Provider. The reason for this choice was, of course, not superficial; it was a special and inescapable one. In his own words: "The selection of the Old Testament subject was certainly not mere accident." He found in the story of Joseph and his brothers something which could not be expressed in another material, which could not be presented through another symbol, in the same defiant spirit, with the same convincing clearness. The defiant spirit states: "To write a novel of the Jewish spirit was timely, because it seemed untimely,"[26] a remark which reveals more of the author's mood than of his search for a creative theme. And Thomas Mann knows this as well as we do. As a creative spirit he has to follow his own rules, his own inner law. Therefore, he adds to his first statement, that he did not intend to write a hymn of a tradition, a political tract or a religious essay. He was influenced by a great legacy, he was overwhelmed by it, but he was not sold to it. Thus his story follows the report in Genesis, in Thomas Mann's own words, only "with semijocular faithfulness, and often it reads like an exegesis and amplification of the Torah, like a Rabbinical Midrash," and "all that is Jewish, throughout the work, is merely foreground, only *one* style element among others, only one stratum of its language . . ."[27] But even if we do not overlook the self-imposed limitation expressed in these words, we see that such an approach to the original story, to the original spirit of the sacred text, has never been undertaken or dared before. The *Wiener Genesis* was a Hebrew report, but did not show Jewish spirit at all; and Racine's *Esther* celebrated in a Jewish story the glory of King Louis XIV. The Jewish spirit was only the setting, the décor, the costume in those works. Here we discover that it is at least one stratum of its language. And when Thomas Mann was asked what "made [him] turn to this remote, out-of-the-way subject and induced [him] to transform the biblical legend of the Egyptian Joseph into a broad cycle of novels," he answered that he was "delighted" when he read the original, which means that his imagination was caught by the text. Then, "a preliminary probing and productive searching began in [his] mind as to what it would be like to renew and reproduce this charming story in fresh narrative with all the modern means."[28] This final success and reawakening of a centuries-old story would not prove very much if this reawakening were a single fact. Thomas Mann, however, helps us here, too, when he reveals how "almost immediately, these inner experiences [mentioned above] significantly associated themselves with the thought of a tradition: the thought of Goethe, in fact, who relates in his memoirs *Truth and Fiction* how he, as a boy, had dictated the Joseph story to a friend and, in doing so, had woven it into a broad narrative . . ." As an explanation of this youthful and premature adventure, the sixty-year-old Goethe observes, "This natural story is highly amiable, only it seems too short, and one is tempted to carry it out in all its details." And it seems also to be revealing of the attitude of a twentieth-century man who is influenced by the Bible.

"As a man," confesses Thomas Mann, "and as an artist, I must somehow have been in readiness to be productively attracted by such subject matter, and my Bible reading was not mere chance." This readiness has to be explained more elaborately.

The various stages of life have different inclinations, claims, tendencies of taste—as well as abilities and advantages. It is probably a rule that in certain years the taste for all purely individual and particular phenomena, for the *individual case,* for the "bourgeois" aspect, in the widest sense of the word, fades out gradually. Instead, the typical, the *eternally human, eternally recurring, timeless,* in short, the *mythical steps into the foreground of interest.* For, after all, the typical is already the mythical, in so far as it is pristine pattern and pristine form of life, timeless model and formula of old, into which life enters by reproducing its traits of the unconscious.[29]

How far we have come! To take an illustrious example: the Jewish story of Joseph and his brothers appeared and reappeared again and again, as stimulating form and thought-influencing material in European—French, Spanish, German and Italian—literature. It was an epic in the twelfth century in Germany; a play in the thirteenth century in France and Spain; its characters appeared in Italian and Portuguese works of literature; it was a *moralité* in the Germany of the Protestant Reformation, then again (Goethe), and finally an opera and a ballet and a novel. In brief, it was a sacred story in the original text and became a symbol of humanity in the provisional present form.

By this the circle is rounded again. The Bible, a religious work, has proved its inspiring value in the field of literature, too, as an influence on language, images, thought, as a storehouse for fairy tales, moral stories, ethical legends, as a model for new forms in poetry, and as a gold mine for mythical symbols. Its lasting charm has worked on the greatest occasions—in the *Divine Comedy,* in the *Esther* of Racine, in Goethe's *Faust,* in Mann's *Joseph*-novel—as a genuine, sparkling and influential source of inspiration.

NOTES

[1] E. R. Bevan, and C. Singer (eds.), *The Legacy of Israel,* p. 504.
[2] *Ibid.,* pp. 540 f.
[3] *Ibid.,* p. 483.
[4] *Ibid.,* p. 486.

[4a Cf. above David Daiches, "The Influence of the Bible on English Literature," p. 1464.]

5 P. Piper, *Die geistliche Dichtung des Mittelalters*, pp. 87 ff.

6 *Ibid.*, pp. 91-191.

7 *Ibid.*, p. 194.

8 *Ibid.*, p. 12.

9 J. Bédier and P. Hazard, *Histoire de la littérature française illustrée*, I, 4.

10 L. Petit de Julleville, *Le Théâtre en France*, p. 3.

11 *Ibid.*, p. 19.

12 *Ibid.*, p. 71.

[12a For the development in English literature cf. Daiches *op. cit.*]

13 J. P. Crawford, *Spanish drama before Lope de Vega*, pp. 41 ff.

14 *Ibid.*, pp. 142-147.

15 *Medieval Culture*, II, 99.

16 *Ibid.*, II, 100.

17 *Ibid.*, II, 100.

18 Dante, *Divine Comedy* (Inferno, canto IV).

19 K. Vossler, II, 103.

20 Dante, canto I.

21 Vossler, *op. cit.*, p. 104.

22 *Luthers Werke* (ed. Buchwald), VII, pp. 191, 195.

23 *Ibid.*, VII, 241.

24 *Pour la Victoire*. New York, March 13, 1943.

25 *Ibid.*, quoted by André Spire.

26 Thomas Mann about his *Joseph*-novel (printed report of a lecture delivered at the Library of Congress), p. 17.

27 *Ibid.*, p. 18.

28 *Ibid.*, p. 5.

29 *Ibid.*, p. 7.

BIBLIOGRAPHY

BEDIER, JOSEPH, and HAZARD, PAUL, *Histoire de la littérature française illustrée*. 2 vols. Paris, 1923-1924.

BEVAN, EDWYN R., and SINGER, CHARLES (eds.), *The Legacy of Israel*. Oxford, 1927.

CRAWFORD, J. P. WICKERSHAM, *Spanish drama before Lope de Vega*. Philadelphia, 1937.

PETIT DE JULLEVILLE, LOUIS, *Le Théâtre en France*. Paris, 1923.

PIPER, PAUL, *Die geistliche Dichtung des Mittelalters*. Berlin, 1888. Vol. 3.

ROTH, CECIL, *The Jewish Contribution to Civilization*. Cincinnati, 1940.

VOSSLER, KARL, *Medieval Culture*, An Introduction to Dante and his times. 2 vols. New York, 1929.

III

THE SOCIOLOGY AND DEMOGRAPHY
OF THE JEWS

CHAPTER 36

WHO ARE THE JEWS?

By Melville J. Herskovits

I

The problem of drawing definitions precise enough to permit the setting up of acceptable and workable categories of human types has from the earliest days plagued students of man. As in the other natural sciences, the difficulty arises primarily out of the fact that in nature categories are never sharply differentiated from each other. Rather, we find that one type merges imperceptibly into the next. The definitions by means of which delimitation is sought, though in a broad sense inherent in the materials, in their precise statement lodge primarily in the mind of the student. It follows, then, that unless there is agreement as to where the lines of demarcation are to be drawn, the validity of a classification will be a subject of endless debate.

The differentiation of human groups according to their physical characteristics for the most part stands where taxonomy, the science of classification, stood in the other biological sciences at the turn of the century. It will be recalled that until then, the attention of biologists was so focused on the need to distinguish species from species, subspecies from subspecies, race from race, that there was little consideration of problems of a more dynamic character. It is hardly necessary to repeat here how, when Gregor Mendel published his findings concerning the mechanisms of heredity in 1865, the discovery was to all intent ignored, and continued so for almost four decades.

It is important that we understand why classification presented the difficulties it did and resulted in long debates between specialists, since the point is crucial for any discussion of human types. In essence, it was because the attention of students was so centered on the problem of differentiating types that the factor of variation was quite neglected. Yet, in truth, we know today that there is no "real" type specimen of any living form except by agreement, since no two examples of a given class are exactly alike. They can only be said to approximate each other more closely than either will resemble a form that belongs to a different category.

Nor is this all. Classifications based on measurements and description have classically employed the end products of a process of change that for the group is described in their biological evolution and for the individuals is encompassed by the processes of their hereditary endowment and the influence of the natural setting in which they live their lives. But it is these dynamic problems, involving change, that bulk so large in the thought of present-day biologists and have brought the revolutionary concepts of the nature and functioning of the organism, and of the reasons for the rise and maintenance of the many different forms, to be distinguished in the plant and animal world, that are today basic in the biological sciences.

In the study of human physical type, the fact of variability is, in the main, today taken into account; but what may be termed the genetic point of view is by no means as prevalent as its importance in the study of the lower forms would seem to warrant in the study of man. It is true that the difficulties of method in the study of human genetics are so great as to be discouraging; yet with the proper biometric techniques they can and are being attacked, on the basis of statistical analysis rather than through the laboratory controls it is possible for animal geneticists to maintain. Even to recognize the approach as valid when applied to man is fruitful, however. A race becomes not an aggregate of individuals, but an aggregate of genetic lines that breed true to produce certain types. Conventional studies of race—something which, perverted to serve racist rather than scientific ends, has caused such misery in the world—become almost pointless; it is studies of local types, population formation, stability of physical traits under crossing and the plasticity of the organism under different environmental conditions that come to have meaning and lead to significant results for the study of human biology.

Yet a serious complicating factor faces the human biologist that the student of other forms need not take into account. This arises from the fact that man is the only member of the biological series who possesses speech, and who can use tools. This in turn induces an element operative in the case of none other than the human animal, the factor of culture. Man is the only culture-building animal that exists in the world, and the multitude of differing ways of life he has devised as a result of differing traditions have influenced his physical types in their ultimate form by protecting him against the elements, giving him a stable habitation, assuring him the kinds of food his tradition demands, and above all in setting up conventions which, all unconsciously, function as controls over his mating and make for social rather than natural selection. It is significant that the only types that resemble man in living under such conditions are the domesticated animals, and they alone are as variable in physical form, species for species, as is the species *homo sapiens*. Nor is it without further significance for an understanding of the nature of human racial differences that the traits in which these animals vary most markedly are the characteristics of coloring, size, hair form, among others, the very traits that, since they comprehend the outstanding differences between men, have been most employed in differentiating human races.

2

Of all human groupings, there is none wherein the problem of definition has proved to be more difficult than for the Jews. Even when all possibilities seem to have been exhausted—race, people, nation, religion, cultural entity, historic group, linguistic unit—we find students casting about for other, more precise, more comprehensive designations. That this is a fact does not mean that it is the less important to continue the search for adequate delimitation, for though the establishing of categories can never be an end of scientific investigation, it is an essential beginning.

It is instructive to set forth some of the attempts that have been made to draw definitions of the term "Jew." Thus Haddon and Huxley (1936) say:

Ripley, in his classic *Races of Europe* (1900), concludes by affirming that "the Jews are not a race but only a people after all." We believe him to be right. The Jews can rank neither as nation nor even as ethnic unit, but rather as a socio-religious group carrying large Mediterranean, Armenoid and many other elements, and varying greatly in physical characters. Like many other groups its members are held together by external pressure of various kinds, partly by a long historic memory, partly by a sense of common suffering, partly by a religion. These factors, acting through long ages, have produced a common consciousness which is relaxed when the pressures are relaxed and intensified with the reverse process.[1]

Coon (in 1939), in one of the most elaborate studies of human taxonomy that has been published to date, gives his concept of what constitutes Jews in the following terms:

... the Jews form an ethnic group; ... like all ethnic groups they have their own racial elements distributed in their own proportions; like all or most ethnic groups they have their "look," a part of their cultural heritage that both preserves and expresses their cultural solidarity. And since the ethnic solidarity of the Jews is remarkable for its strength and constancy, so the Jewish look seems to be one of the most noticeable and most easily distinguished of characteristic facial expressions found within the family of white people.[2]

In a subsequent consideration of the problem (in 1942), he states:

... not only are the Jews different to a measurable degree from the other people among whom they live, but they are a *population*, just as the Volhynians and Swabian villagers are populations. The Jews, therefore, are not a race ... They are a group of people as united biologically as is the average intermarrying social or geographical unit found among white peoples; they have racial peculiarities which serve to differentiate the majority of them anthropometrically from their non-Jewish compatriots and neighbors.[3]

Krogman (1945), after pointing out that "centuries of injustice and of rigorous competition" have forced the Jew so to "compensate . . . by a tremendous drive," says, "this fact . . . has given him a set of behavioral attitudes and responses that are often characteristic to the point of recognition and group definition . . . [but] that . . . are *cultural, not biological.*" He summarizes his position with the statement: "A Jew belongs not to a race but to a Jewish community."[4]

Seltzer (1939), presents this definition:

For our purpose we shall define the word Jew to include all individuals of the so-called "White" races of mankind who, by virtue of family tradition, do practice or whose ancestors did practice the religion of Judaism.[5]

This is in line with Parr's conclusion (1934), based on the study of blood types, that: "There is serological evidence that the Jews are a religion rather than a race."[6]

Wider in its limits is the racio-religious definition implicit in the categories set up by Joseph Jacobs, in an early study of the anthropometry of the Jews aimed at describing what he held to be a Jewish race, and presented in a paper read before the Royal Anthropological Institute of London (1886).[7] In a table giving the numbers "of various classes of persons now living, who may claim to be Jews by religion or by birth, or both," he includes:

A. Jews both by religion and by birth
     Ashkenazim, Sephardim, and Samaritans (?)
B. Jews by religion, but not by birth
     Falashas of Abyssinia, Karaites of the Crimea, Kaggatouns, etc., of the Sahara, Beni-Israel of Bombay, and the Cochin Jews of Cochin
C. Jews by birth, but not by religion
     Chuetas or Anussim of the Balearic Islands, the Maiminen of Salonica, and the G'did al Islam of Khorasan.

He adds, "Besides this, there exist a large number of persons, mostly in Europe, who have Jewish blood in their veins as Jewish converts . . . especially . . . in Spain."[7a] He insists that "The anthropology of Jews can never be satisfactorily settled till careful examination of these various data has shown their resemblances and differences. From the common qualities of classes A and B we can determine qualities due to religion; from those common to A and C, but differing in B, we might draw valuable conclusions as to the influences of race," and expresses regret that because "for the second and third classes we have practically no data to work with," such analyses must be deferred. In all this we find adumbrated a recent dictionary definition of the Jew: ". . . any person of the Hebrew race or whose religion is Judaism."[8]

All the definitions that have been cited, while recognizing the existence of both biological and cultural factors, have because of their anthropological character been directed primarily at the problem of whether or not the Jews comprise a racial entity. Students who approach the problem from the sociological point of view, however, are likewise no clearer or more agreed on proper terms to be employed. A case study of this conflict in definition is to be had in the summary given by Max Weinreich (1945) of replies received by the Yiddish Scientific Institute from social scientists to a questionnaire concerning the desirability of having the classification of "Jew" on United States Immigration and Naturalization Service forms retained or deleted.

Bram (1944), in a discussion of the problem of definition, notes that "countless attempts to place the Jews in clear sociological categories have still left them an undefined social phenomenon," and documents his statement with these examples:

Louis Wirth has said that "the elementary question as to whether the Jews are a race, a nationality or a cultural group remains unsettled." Other writers who have tried to find a proper definition for them have expressed the difficulties in very characteristic terms. They refer to the Jews as "an unusual type of nationality," "a social anomaly," "a peculiar people." Talcott Parsons considers them "a unique social phenomenon," Carl Mayer calls them "a chimeric people" leading "a life of unreality."[9]

Kennedy (1942), striving for preciseness in characterizing the group status of the Jews in the United States, says: "The Jews are a religio-national group occupying the status of a quasi-caste in American society." Earlier in his paper, after stating that "our focus can shift at once from the biological to the social and cultural plane," he provides the basis for the "religio-national" element in the definition just quoted in these terms:

We see then that the Jews manifest traits characteristic of a nationality in their common traditions, common patterns of ideas and behavior, and common ethnocentrism or consciousness of kind, and that these transcend whatever other nationality affiliations they may assume. Most of these traits are closely intermeshed with their religion, so much so that some readers may insist that it is enough to call them a religious group rather than stress the point of nationality. . . . The issue can be resolved by designating the Jews as a "religio-national" group.[10]

It must be clear from this sampling of the many attempts that have been made to define the term "Jew" and to arrive at some formula to describe those who are to be placed in the category of Jews that there is certainly no agreement. The failure to obtain a consensus of opinion would seem to derive, in part at least, from the difficulty of drawing a definition when the very terms that must apparently be employed so lack preciseness. What, for example, is an "ethnic group"? It is obviously not a race, yet it is stated to have subracial status, with certain distinguishing physical characteristics and certain ways of life. And how does an "ethnic group" differ from a "people," or "a socio-religious group," terms accepted by students of competence who specifically state that Jews are neither to be ranked "as nation or even as ethnic unit"? What does it mean to say they are a "population," or that they are those who belong to "a Jewish community" or that they are a "religio-national group"? What, even, does it mean to state that Jews are "a religion," when the views of the nature and functioning of the universe held by those included in a Jewish "ethnic group," "population" or "community" are so heterogeneous that, as one Jewish wit has said, "Where there are two Jews, there are three opinions!"

Let us refer to certain broad principles in the scientific study of man that may help us understand the dilemma in which those who would define the term "Jew" have found themselves. Outstandingly, it is essential to remember the basic fact that, though man is both a biological and a culture-building animal, and that while these two aspects may and on occasion do interact, man's physical type and his culture represent different dimensions of his existence which must be regarded as independent even when they are interrelated variables. Physical traits are inherited through the genetic mechanism that determines the limits within which a given form, in its development, will eventuate in the kind of adult human being it proves to be. Culture, on the other hand, in all its many manifestations, is learned, and is thus of a different order of causation.

But if we turn not only to the definitions that have been cited, but also take into account the many others that have been drawn and continue to be heard, we find that they almost invariably attempt to encompass both dimensions of man, physical and cultural. That is, Jews are held to have delimitable physical traits, like other groups we designate as nations, or peoples, or tribes, or races; and they are also held to be marked by certain beliefs, or habits, or traditions, or points of view, or values that mark them off from other peoples. Hence any attempt to draw a logically valid definition, it is felt, since it must describe as well as delimit, has to include two terms which, because they vary independently, rarely, if ever, exhibit a one-to-one correspondence. We may merely refer to the categories of Joseph Jacobs that have been cited, to realize that no such order of correspondence holds for the Jews.

It is instructive to scrutinize the following description of the Jews of

Cochin, India, with the definitions that have been cited, in their two-dimensional form, in mind:

At present the Jews of Cochin number, in all, some fourteen hundred. As are their Hindu neighbors, the Jews are divided into castes which do not intermarry or interdine with each other. There are three Jewish castes . . . The white Jews, who are at the head of the Jewish caste hierarchy, range in skin color from a pale white to a medium brown . . . The skin color of the other two castes is like that of the natives of Cochin, ranging from a light brown to a deep brownish-black. The white Jews have their own synagogue, where the brown Jews are also allowed to worship. The black Jews, who are by far the most numerous, have seven synagogues.

The life of the Cochin Jews is conducted strictly according to the precepts of the *Shulhan Aruk*, the orthodox codex. While the mother tongue of the children is Malayalam, the Dravidian dialect of the country, yet all, boys and girls alike, learn to read Hebrew; the men whose single garment is a waist-cloth, inevitably have a small skullcap of gaily colored cloth perched atop their heads, from which two earlocks often drop; rice and curry, the diet of the South Indian, is also their staple food, but meat curries are never mixed with milk curries. An orthodox Jew from Warsaw or the Bronx might find the Sephardic liturgy of the Cochin synagogues a bit odd at first, but the devotion of the Cochin Jews to Jewish law and learning would soon make him feel at home.[11]

The matter of definition is especially baffling because there is enough similarity in physical type between enough Jews to permit the development of a stereotype that in the minds of the laity receives daily reinforcement and even justifies certain scientific classifications for certain Jewish sub-groups. There is, also, enough of a least common denominator of belief, a certain minimum of traditionally accepted values, a certain sense of historic continuity held by enough Jews to make these aspects of Jewish life loom large in the minds of those concerned with definition. Yet whether on the level of physical type or of culture, the exceptions remain, exceeding any limits that can seemingly be drawn. This is undoubtedly the reason why it is far easier to say what Jews are not than to describe what they are.

Even so tentative a discussion as that of Bram does not elude the common dilemma. Admitting the "picture of the Jewish people" to be "one of heterogeneity . . . of a changing people interacting with diverse national societies and whose social identity is constantly subjected by both sides to fluctuating interpretations," he still frames his concept of his task as an understanding of "the problems of social and ethnic identity" of the Jews. "The two extreme groups," he says, with insight, "those who want to be Jewish and those who cannot escape being Jewish, have, for a common denominator, only common ancestry and the recurrent hostility of the surrounding world."[12]

In the remainder of this chapter we shall attempt to describe the physical characteristics and trace the differentiation of the various types of Jews that have been distinguished, and to raise again the question of their unity, referring to anthropometric analyses except where cultural— that is, historical—factors must be taken into account to explain the observed facts. As for the delimitation of the Jewish groups with which we are concerned, we shall face our dilemma in the only way possible, by utilizing the flexibility and realism of an operational definition to permit us to follow the data wherever they lead. In the manner of a definition advanced some years ago (Herskovits, 1927) which stated, "A Jew is a person who calls himself a Jew or who is called Jewish by others,"[13] we shall seek to describe the antecedents and physical traits of those who, over the world, are held to be Jews.

3

There is today general agreement among anthropologists that the Jews, in their biological and historical antecedents, stem primarily from that special type of the Mediterranean subrace of the Caucasoid race—or, as others put it, of the Mediterranean race included in the Caucasoid stock of *homo sapiens*—formed several thousand years ago in the eastern littoral of the Mediterranean Sea.[13a] The most recent findings have been summarized by Krogman (1945), who describes the "historic nucleus of Jewish origins" as follows:

The earliest Jews in their Euphrates homeland soon mixed with the Canaanites of the lowlands, the Amorites of the highlands, and with the Hivites, Amalekites, the Kenites, the Egyptians and the Hittites—mostly long-headed peoples, but round-headed peoples as well. By about 2000 B.C., the "Semitic Empires" of Palestine centered the Jews in western Asia Minor.[14]

Some disagreement exists among students as to the component populations from whom the early Jews were derived. Haddon (1925)[15] designates partial Hittite descent as the source of the "so-called 'Jewish' nose" thus accepting von Luschan's position[16] which is unacceptable to Coon (1939).[17] Seltzer,[18] on the other hand, lays stress (1939) on the influence of the "Iranian Plateau type" described by Field (1935) whose significance he maintains derives largely from the fact that "the most outstanding feature of this race is its nasality." He therefore holds that the Jews are the descendants of early inhabitants of Palestine "predominantly of Mediterranean stock with a definite element of the convex-nosed Iranian Plateau type."[19]

The modern descendants of these early Jews achieved their dispersal in three historic periods, until their final expulsion from Palestine. Coon[20] gives these as, first, the period of the captivity of the Jews in Babylonia beginning 586 B.C.E.,[20a] when considerable numbers were removed to the East, to Mesopotamia and Iraq, where they took root and where, as in Iraq, their descendants live to the present. The second dispersion was during the period of Hellenistic influence, from the time of Alexander and continuing through the Byzantine Empire,[20b] when substantial centers of Jewish population were established in Egypt, Syria, Asia Minor, the Crimea and the Balkans. The third and final distribution of Jews, throughout the Roman world, was a long process, covering more than two centuries. It was primarily in a westward direction, and when it ended the Jews were not only established in Rome itself, but had taken part in the settlement, along with Romans, of Spain, France and Germany west of the Rhine.[20c]

In most discussions of Jewish types, two principal groups have been distinguished, the *Ashkenazim,* or German, Russian and Polish Jews, and the *Sephardim,* the Spanish and Portuguese Jews, as Fishberg (1905)[21] puts it. These latter, in the Balkans, are also called "Spanioli," after the dialect they use, which is derived from the Spanish their ancestors spoke before their expulsion from Spain in 1492, and which distinguishes the Sephardim from the Ashkenazim, who speak Yiddish, a tongue based on German. This dual designation has attained prominence only because so much attention has been given to European Jews. It will be remembered that the first category of Jacobs[22] includes, besides these two, the Samaritans, though they are queried. Today, however, the Samaritans, said by Coon to be "generally supposed to represent the indigenous Palestinian Jewish strain more faithfully than any other,"[23] are held to appertain to a third category, the *Oriental* Jews, who inhabit Palestine, the Yemen, Iraq, Iran, Turkey and the Caucasus.

Krogman (1945)[24] holds that the Oriental Jews are in physical form closest to their "Mediterranean prototype," then the Sephardim, then the Ashkenazim. The most striking anthropometric differences, however, are between the first two, on the one hand, and the third. The resemblance between Oriental and Sephardic Jews is such, indeed, that Coon (1939), while distinguishing them, says, "On the whole the Jews of the entire Mediterranean racial belt, from Persia to Morocco, and including those whose ancestors once lived in Spain, are remarkably constant in their racial unity."[25]

The differences between these groups and the Ashkenazim is customarily discussed in terms of variations in head form, the trait that has been most studied by anthropologists. In recent years this problem has been posed as the "brachycephalization" of these Central European Jews—that is, their conversion from a long-headed Mediterranean type to a short-headed form that characterizes the Alpine subrace of Caucasoids. Such a formulation, which assumes an aboriginal long-headed type (though there are difficulties here, as in the case of the Nablus series of Samaritans discussed by Huxley [1905], who found much short-headedness among them), was first sketched in terms of this process of brachycephalization by Dixon (1923).[26] Later Coon made of it a principal point of his study of European "races" (1939), stating that the study of what he terms "the brachycephalized Jews" of Asia and Central Europe is "an intimate part of the problem of Central European brachycephaly."[27]

"The contrast between the Ashkenazim and the Sephardim," writes Krogman (1945),[28] "is really one between an Alpo-Dinaric (or Armenoid) and a Mediterranean racial type." He cites F. Wagenseil's figures (1923), which show an average in the ratio between length and breadth of the head of male Spanish Jews to be 78.1, as against 82.5 for male Russian Jews, the figures for females being 78.9 and 82.4, respectively. This means that the Spanish Jews are strikingly longer headed than the Russian Jews measured, since the lower the ratio the longer the skull in relation to its breadth. This is also seen in the distribution of this ratio, the *cephalic index*, when all the members of each series, irrespective of sex, are considered together:

	Spanish Jews (Per cent)	Russian Jews (Per cent)
Long-headed	19.7	1.0
Medium-headed	65.5	29.0
Short-headed	14.8	70.0

Comparable results are to be found in a table given by Fishberg (1911)[29] for the head form of Jews of differing areas, which may be rearranged to afford greater clarity than in the original:

	Yemen (Per cent)	No. Africa (Per cent)	"Jews in Europe" (Per cent)	Caucasus (Per cent)
Long-headed	71.80	25.97	2.89	—
Medium-headed	24.35	57.15	48.65	10.80
Short-headed	3.85	16.88	48.45	89.20

Similar findings are at hand for a trait of a quite different order, blood type, despite the fact that, according to Parr, from whose work these data are taken, any general "correlation between blood types and anthropometric features . . . can hardly be justified." As an example of this, he says, "Recently we examined twenty-eight members of an American Jewish family of three generations and found that the blood type percentages (O, 17.8, A, 82.1) would give a race index of infinity, distinctly different from the race index for the group (1.85), yet these twenty-eight people are beyond question typical of their race."

It is impossible here to explain in detail the serological techniques or genetic assumptions underlying the study of blood groups, but relative percentages of the four types (O, A, B and AB) for Ashkenazic and Sephardic Jews, Arabs (who are long-headed Mediterraneans) and Armenians (short-headed Alpine-Dinaric types), suggest how basic are the distinctions between the two categories of Jews, and how close is their taxonomic affiliation with the subraces represented by these two other non-Jewish populations:[30]

Population	Blood-group			
	O	A	B	AB
Arabs	43.6	32.4	19.0	5.0
Sephardic Jews	41.1	28.5	23.4	7.0
Ashkenazic Jews	37.2	34.1	18.1	10.6
Armenians[a]	27.0	53.0	14.0	6.0
Armenians[b]	36.3	40.3	16.6	6.8

[a] 653 cases, typed by Parr.
[b] 380 cases, typed by Kossovitch.

It is thus not strange that students, in the light of these and the many other facts concerning differences in physical type, no longer regard the Jews as a "race." With this has also gone the tendency of earlier days to speak of Jews as "Semites." The word "Semitic," it is now realized, describes a linguistic phenomenon, so that at most Jews might be termed descendants of one of the "Semitic-speaking peoples" much in the way that, for want of a better designation, the inhabitants of the heart of the African continent, a heterogeneous grouping of local types, are referred to as "Bantu-speaking peoples." The lack of validity of such a phrase as "Semitic race" is to be seen from the following statement by Ariëns-Kappers (1934):

The expression "Semitic race or races" . . . is one of the most inappropriate expressions occurring in anthropology, just as confusing as the word Aryan. Although taken in the biblical sense it means to indicate people that are mutually related (being all descendants of Sem) practically the term only indicates people that speak a Semitic language . . . What then is the anthropological meaning of the expression "Semitic people"? None at all.[31]

This would seem to put a capstone of specific refutation on the structure of critical analysis exemplified in von Luschan's Huxley Memorial Lecture for 1911:

Combinations of Philology with Anthropology have in former times, especially through Friedrich Mueller and his school, often led to serious mistakes. One spoke of Aryan races instead of people with Aryan languages, and one went so far as to speak of Aryan skulls and of Aryan eyes, so that Max Mueller formally protested against the intrusion of linguistics into ethnology, stating that one might just as well speak of a brachycephalic grammar as of an Aryan skull.[32]

Granting, then, that the Jews are no race, but in the main belong to sub-races of the Caucasoid grouping of mankind, we may in so far as possible sketch the types that are envisaged by students of human taxonomy. The Sephardim and Oriental (Mediterranean) Jews, according to Coon (1939),[33] are brunet in coloring of hair and eyes, and "brunet-white" in skin color. Two subtypes are distinguished, both slender, but one heavier than the other. One has a short and moderately broad face, the other a face long and narrow. The nose type of the former is short and straight "with a tip of medium thickness and nasal wings usually medium, seldom compressed or flaring"; of the latter, the nose is "extremely long with compressed wings, the nasion depression slight, the nasal tip somewhat depressed, the nostrils highly set on the sides," with convex nasal profile, and a high, but not unusually high nasal bridge. The fact that the Sephardic and Oriental Jews are as distinctly Mediterranean as they are, that they are no more heterogeneous than they are, is undoubtedly caused by the fact, also recognized by most students, that they have lived among peoples who belong to this same subrace, and with whom they could mix without unduly disturbing any physical characteristics that marked their forebears among the early Israelites.

To describe any single set of physical traits that mark off the Central European Jews is quite another matter. The relative homogeneity of the Mediterranean type of Jew gives way, in Europe, to a divergence of type that makes it necessary to set up a series of local forms, each for separate analysis, rather than envisage any single category. Seltzer has indicated the complexity of the task in no uncertain terms. "The Ashkenazic Jews are extremely composite in physical characteristics," he says, "which indicates a very heterogeneous racial background."[34] A favorite quotation employed by Fishberg[35] from Renan, "Il n'y a pas un type juif, il y a des types juifs," to underscore the results of his study of the physical form of European Jews, aptly summarizes the matter. Boas's statement (1923), that "the assimilation of the Jews by the people among whom they live is much more far-reaching than a hasty observation might suggest,"[36] implies the mechanism whereby the marked variation in physical type within the category of European (Ashkenazic) Jews may have been brought about, as well as why this division stands in such striking contrast in homogeneity when compared to the Sephardic and Oriental Jews in this respect. We must, therefore, next address ourselves to the significance of this.

4

Homo sapiens constitutes a single species,[37] and its members, as with all other similar categories in the animal world, whatever their subspecific (racial) affiliation, are mutually fertile. This biological fact has been implemented in the historical development of the human race by the widespread amount of intermixture that has occurred between all groups of men who have come into contact. Not only on the level of crossing between representatives of those major aggregates of mankind we term races has this been continuous, but also between subracial types and groups of smaller order, such as local communities. So universal has this been over the ages man has been on earth, even in early prehistoric times,[38] that it takes on the aspect of an axiom in the study of man when we say that any two human groups, whatever their differences in physical type or way of life, will under contact produce offspring of mixed parentage. This is why anthropologists have rejected the concept of a pure human race as a fiction, why it is stated that man is the most mongrel of all animals.

In the case of the Jews, this fact of mixture between peoples in contact is given almost a laboratory demonstration. If, as seems reasonable to assume, the early Jews were a Mediterranean type whose dispersion took them into areas where they were in contact with indigenous populations also of Mediterranean stock with whom they mixed, then the mixture with these other Mediterranean populations would result in the maintenance of type and the relative homogeneity in physical traits that marks the Sephardic and Oriental Jews as compared to the Ashkenazic Jews, who mingled with Alpine, Nordic and Dinaric populations. As Coon has put it (1942):

Among the Ashkenazim one can pick out Palestinian types that could readily be drawn from the courts of Solomon and David; Nordics to delight the eye of Julius Streicher, if he were to see them without their passports; Alpines who could yodel in any Hofbrauhaus; and Dinarics who could be Tyrolese skiers or Parisian policemen.[39]

We can see how, statistically, this is manifest by citing some comparisons that have been made between Jewish and non-Jewish populations living in the same countries. Fishberg, whose studies even today provide the most inclusive documentation for questions of the physical anthropology of the Jews, has several tables that show how average head form, expressed as cephalic index, is manifested among Jews and non-Jews living together:[40]

	Jews	Non-Jews
Lithuania	81.05	81.88
Rumania	81.82	82.91
Poland	81.91	82.13
Hungary	82.45	81.40
Little Russia	82.45	82.31
Galicia	83.33	84.40

When the above table is scrutinized it becomes evident that the head form of Jews varies, in the main, as does that of the non-Jewish populations

with whom they are in contact. This is also apparent in a similar table
of average indices for Jews and non-Jews gathered together by Coon
(1942):[41]

	Jews	Non-Jews
England	80.0	78.0 (English urban population)
Bosnia	80.1	85.3
Frankfort	80.8	81.4 (Rhineland)
Karaites, Lithuania	81.0	82.6 (Lithuania)
Lithuania	81.7	
Galicia	81.7	83.5
Poland	81.9	82.9
So. Russia	82.5	83.2 (Ukraine)
Poland	82.8	82.9
Warsaw	82.9	82.0
Ukraine	82.9	83.2
Bavaria	83.5	84.1
Bukovina	84.3	86.3

Here, again, a correlation is apparent. But it is also true, as Coon points
out, that if we compare the range of values in the Jewish column
(80.0-84.3) with that of the non-Jewish (78.0-86.3) the differences manifest among the latter are greater than those among the former. This
brings Coon to the following conclusion: "That the Jews of all European
countries have more in common anthropometrically than do the non-Jews
of these countries." He also feels that "there are no clear general trends
in correspondence between local Jewish and non-Jewish means," but this is
not nearly so evident from inspection of the table as the other, nor is it
supported by Fishberg's data given above.

We must be fully aware of the implications that lie in the fact that only
cephalic index has been considered in these tables, since the form of the
head is but one of many traits used in analyzing relations between populations, traits which do not by any means always vary in the same way. Thus
Fishberg, many years ago, found that the hair and eye color of Jews was
distinctly darker in both characters than of non-Jews in the same country
(1905),[42] a finding confirmed recently by Morant (1939).[43] On the other
hand, when comparative figures for stature are given[44] they confirm "in a
striking manner the similarity of the stature of the Jews to that of their
non-Jewish neighbors."

Let us approach the matter from another point of view, and consider
the degree of variation found within European Jewish and non-Jewish
populations. For this, we may abstract from a table presented by Coon
(1942)[45] the statistical constants that indicate variability (technically, the
mean square deviations, or *sigmas*) of the series of Eastern European Jews

measured by Fishberg, of seventy-nine series "chosen from many parts of the world" by Howells, and of an average of six series of "small, geographically unified, isolated village communities" in Germany, for various traits:

Group	St.	H.L.	H.B.	F.H.	F.B.	N.H.	N.B.	Av., 6 Meas. in mm.
E. European Jews	6.6	6.1	5.5	6.6	6.2	4.0	3.0	5.2
"79 Series"	5.8	6.2	5.2	6.4	5.3	3.8	2.9	5.0
6 German Series	5.7	6.0	5.8	6.7	5.5	4.0	3.0	5.2

Group	Cephalic Index	Facial Index	Nasal Index	Av. 3 Indices
E. European Jews	3.2	5.8	8.1	5.7
"79 Series"	3.4	5.1	7.8	5.4
6 German Series	3.2	5.0	6.7	5.0

(St., stature; H.L., head-length; H.B., breadth of head; F.H., facial height; F.B., facial breadth; N.H., nasal height; N.B., nasal breadth; Cephalic Index, ratio between length and breadth of head; Facial Index, ratio between height and width of face; Nasal Index, ratio between height and breadth of nose.)

This table is presented by Coon to show that the variation within Jewish groups is no greater than in non-Jewish populations, so that "the Eastern European Jews measured by Fishberg deserve the rank of a biological population as truly as do most central and eastern European communities united, as the Jews are not, in space."

The problem of relative variability of Jews and non-Jews may be attacked from a dynamic point of view which is often overlooked. This approach, devised by Boas (1916) is essentially an analysis in terms of the genetics of population formation, and can be stated simply, and in summary, as follows: A population is composed of a series of family lines, the end results of which are at any given moment its individual members, some of whom are related more closely than others, some quite unrelated. These individuals differ in their physical traits from one another, but less so when they are related than when they are not. Gross variation of a population is thus to be divided into the *variability of family lines*, manifest in the differences between families, and *fraternal variability*, or the average range of variation found to exist within the families that make up this population. The lower the former the more inbreeding there has been; the lower the latter the more homogeneous the stock from which the population was derived. Free mating in a population of mixed origin would thus produce high family *and* fraternal variation; an inbred community descended from the same stock would have low values.

Comparative findings, which include Eastern European Jews, are in-structive; they concern cephalic index:[46]

	Variability of family lines	Variability within families
Potenza, Italy	2.41	2.52
Central Italians	2.39	2.72
Bohemians	2.37	2.61
Worcester, Mass.	2.36	2.36
East European Jews	2.29	2.52
Scottish	2.17	2.66
New York mixed Negroes	1.85	2.93
Blue Ridge Mountaineers	1.85	2.09
Chippewa Indians	1.77	3.32
Bastaards (So. Africa)	1.26	2.52

Inbreeding among the Blue Ridge mountaineers, New York Negroes, and an Indian tribe with mixed ancestry, caused by geographical and sociological isolation, give low values for variation of family line, while free inter-mingling of short- and long-headed Italians, or absence of selective factors in such a city as Worcester, Massachusetts, makes for high values. It is interesting that the Jews occupy a middle position in the variability of their family lines, but that they show a higher figure for fraternal variation both in comparison with their own family variability and with such an inbred population of homogeneous ancestry as the Kentuckians.

Yet this is what we should expect on the basis of what we know about the biological history of the Jews. With a tradition of endogamy and under pressure from outside their own group Jews have inbred more than the surrounding populations. Yet the "axiom" of crossing as a result of contact, the historical fact of proselytizing which brought non-Jews into the Jewish religious group, the gradual lifting of discriminatory legislation during the nineteenth century, made for interbreeding between Jews and non-Jews that gives those called Jews—to say nothing of those non-Jews of partial descent from families called Jewish—anything but a homogeneous ancestry. Hence we find that Jewish populations differ from each other as do those among whom they live, yet that each has a degree of homogeneity that comes from a tradition of marriage within the group reinforced by majority pressures; and with this, an overall variability that has completely denied scientific validity to the concept of a "Jewish race."

What of the "Jewish look"? Is it "nasality," as Seltzer claimed (1939), thus giving present-day assent to Jacobs's thesis expressed in 1886? Or is it some "quality of looking Jewish,"[47] some "characteristic facial expres-sion" that still makes of the Jews, for all their anthropometric heterogeneity and historical divergence of derivation, a recognizable unit?

Stereotypes die hard. "Nasality" was considered, and dismissed as an identifying trait of the Jew many years ago. Topinard's conception of the "hooked," or aquiline, nose as Jewish was later analyzed by Fishberg (1905),[48] who gave the following figures for nasal profile in Jews of European origin living in New York City:

	Males (Per cent)	Females (Per cent)
Straight	58	59
Hooked, aquiline	14	13
Retroussé (snub)	22	14
Flat and broad	6	14

The aspects of the trait that figure in the stereotype may, of course, be other than profile—Fishberg himself felt that it might be a matter of "nostrility." But to date no device for measuring this exists, so that, on the basis of other studies, and until data to the contrary are presented, it can be regarded as a stereotypical rather than typical "Jewish" characteristic.

Is the "Jewish look" contained in the gestures the Jew employs when he talks? That Jews "talk with their hands" is a fundamental element in the Jewish stereotype, and one that is not easily susceptible of objective analysis. The study made by Efron (1941) does, however, throw considerable light on the matter. With the aid of an artist and using motion pictures, he analyzed the gestures of Italians and Jews, dividing each group into "assimilated" and "traditional" categories. The findings demonstrate how little validity there is in the assumption that the Jewish type is to be described in terms of patterns of gesturing:

Both from the standpoint of number of people gesturing and of frequency and manner of gesticulation in those people who do gesture, the assimilated Eastern Jews and the assimilated Southern Italians in New York City (a) *appear to differ greatly from their respective traditional groups,* and (b) *appear to resemble each other.*[49]

The quality of "looking Jewish" was again tested in an ingenuous study begun by the late Franz Boas two decades ago [1926] and carried on with the co-operation of various universities over the country. Its purpose was to discover how far racial or national origin could be determined through inspection. Freshmen, grouped in sections of large classes, were asked during the first week of sessions, before they knew one another, to indicate on forms provided for the purpose their places of birth, that of their parents and grandparents, the language they spoke at home, their "race"—however they might wish to define this term—and its characteristics as they conceived them. Then each student, in turn, called by number only, stood before the class while his fellows wrote what they thought his origin to be, their degree of certainty in drawing this judgment, and why they classified him as they did.

The results of this study were never published, but in conversation Professor Boas stated that at one of the New York colleges forty per cent of the Italians were taken to be Jews, and the same percentage of Jews were adjudged Italians. This would seem to argue that if there is a "Jewish look" it is also in a large number of cases an "Italian look"—quite possible, since South Italians, like stereotyped Jews, are of Mediterranean stock. Midwestern judgments, where the northern European population is predominant, were also of interest. Some of the replies from students at Northwestern University may be given. One lad of Scottish birth was designated as belonging to all Northern European groups, and to be of French and Italian origin as well; three blond Jews were similarly assigned, while four brunet non-Jews, only one of whom was of southern European origin, were designated as Jews by some of their fellows.

5

It is thus apparent that it is neither race, nor such an aspect of physical type as nasality, nor a "Jewish look" that affords terms in which the question "Who are the Jews?" is to be answered. In some regions some aboriginal Mediterranean traits have been retained, but by no means everywhere. In like manner, language, culture, belief all exhibit so great a range of variation that no definition cast in terms of these concepts can be more than partial. Yet the Jews do represent a historic continuum, have survived as an identifiable, yet constantly shifting series of groups. Is there any least common denominator other than the designation "Jew" that can be found to mark the historical *fait accompli* that the Jew, however defined, seems to be? It is seriously to be questioned. A word can mean many things to many people; and no word, one may almost conclude, means more things to more people than does the word "Jew."

NOTES

[1] J. S. Huxley and A. C. Haddon, *We Europeans; a Survey of "Racial" Problems*, (New York and London, 1936), p. 147.

[2] Carleton S. Coon, *The Races of Europe* (New York, 1939), p. 442.

[3] *Ibid.*, "Have the Jews a Racial Identity?" in *Jews in a Gentile World* (Isacque Graeber and Stewart H. Britt, eds.) (New York, 1942), p. 35.

[4] Wilton M. Krogman, Anthropology, physical (ms. of article prepared for the *World Encyclopedia Institute*, 1945).

[5] Carl C. Seltzer, "The Jew—His Racial Status," in *Harvard Medical Alumni Bulletin*, Vol. 13, No. 3, 1939, p. 68.

[6] Leland W. Parr, "Isohemagglutination Studies on Near East Race Groups," in *An Introduction to the Anthropology of the Near East in Ancient and Recent Times* (Amsterdam, 1934), p. 195.

[7] Joseph Jacobs, "On the Racial Characters of Modern Jews," in *Journal of the Royal Anthropology Institute*, Vol. xv, 1885, pp. 24-25 (London).

[7a] Cf. above Cecil Roth, "The European Age in Jewish History (to 1648)," p. 236.]

[8] Webster's Collegiate Dictionary, 1943, s.v. "Jew."

[9] Joseph Bram, "The Social Identity of the Jews," *Trans. N. Y. Acad. of Sci. Ser.* II, Vol. vi, No. 6, 1944, p. 194.

[10] Raymond Kennedy, "The Position and Future of the Jews in America," in *Jews in a Gentile World*, op. cit., pp. 419-420.

[11] David G. Mandelbaum, "The Jewish Way of Life in Cochin," in *Jewish Social Studies*, Vol. I, 1939, p. 424.

[12] Bram, op. cit.

[13] M. J. Herskovits, "When Is a Jew a Jew?" in *Modern Quarterly*, Vol. iv, No. 2, 1927, pp. 109-117.

[13a] Cf. above William Foxwell Albright, "The Biblical Period," pp. 3 ff.]

[14] Krogman, op. cit.

[15] A. C. Haddon, *The Races of Man and their Distribution* (New York, 1925), p. 25.

[16] Felix von Luschan, "The Early Inhabitants of Western Asia," in *Jour. Roy. Anth. Inst.*, Vol. xli, 1911, p. 244.

[17] Coon, op. cit., p. 435, n. 41.

[18] Seltzer, op. cit., p. 72.

[19] Henry Field, "Arabs of Central Iraq, their History, Ethnology and Physical Characters," *Anthropology Memoirs* (Field Museum of Natural History, Chicago), Vol. iv, 1935.

[20] Coon, op. cit., pp. 435 ff.

[20a] Cf. Albright, op. cit., pp. 31 ff.]

[20b] Cf. above Elias J. Bickerman, "The Historical Foundations of Post-biblical Judaism."]

[20c] Cf. Roth, op. cit.]

[21] Maurice Fishberg, "Materials for the Physical Anthropology of the Eastern European Jews," in *Annals New York Academy of Sciences*, Vol. xvi, No. 6, Pt. II, p. 157.

[22] Jacobs, op. cit., p. 24.

[23] Coon, op. cit., p. 439.

[24] Krogman, op. cit.

[25] Coon, op. cit., p. 443.

[26] Roland B. Dixon, *The Racial History of Man* (New York and London, 1923), p. 174.

[27] Coon, op cit., pp. 638 ff.

[28] Krogman, op. cit.

[29] Fishberg, op. cit., p. 50.

[30] Parr, op. cit., pp. 188-189.

[31] C. U. Ariëns-Kappers, *An Introduction to the Anthropology of the Near East in Ancient and Recent Times* (Amsterdam, 1934).

[32] Von Luschan, *op. cit.*, p. 244.

[33] Coon, *op. cit.*, p. 440.

[34] Seltzer, *op. cit.*, p. 74.

[35] Fishberg, *op. cit.*, p. 160; also Fishberg, *The Jews: a Study of Race and Environment* (London and New York, 1911), p. 506.

[36] Franz Boas, "On the Variety of Lines of Descent represented in a Population," in *American Anthropologist* (Lancaster, Pa.), (n.s.), Vol. xviii, No. 1, 1916, p. 5

[37] Cf. Th. Dobzhansky, "On Species and Races of Living and Fossil Man," in *American Journal of Physical Anthropology* (n.s.), Vol. ii, No. 3, 1944, pp. 254-255.

[38] Cf. Franz Weidenreich, "The Skull of Sinanthropus Pekinensis; a Comparative Study on a Primitive Hominid Skull," *Palaeontologia Sinica* (Lancaster), (n.s. D.) No. 10, 1943, pp. 238 ff.

[39] Coon, "Have the Jews a Racial Identity?" p. 32.

[40] Fishberg, *op. cit.*, p. 52; also *ibid.*, "Materials for the Physical Anthropology of the Eastern European Jews" (p. 164) for more detail and for sources.

[41] Coon, *op. cit.*

[42] Fishberg, *op. cit.*, p. 269.

[43] G. M. Morant, *The Races of Central Europe, a Footnote to History*, (London, 1939), pp. 80-83.

[44] Fishberg, *op. cit.*, pp. 186-187; Morant, *op. cit.*, pp. 72-74.

[45] Coon, *op. cit.*, p. 36.

[46] Boas, *op. cit.*; also Herskovits, *The American Negro, a Study in Racial Crossing* (New York, 1928), p. 28.

[47] Coon, *The Races of Europe*, p. 441.

[48] Fishberg, *op. cit.*, p. 257.

[49] David Efron, *Gesture and Environment* (New York, 1941), p. 136.

BIBLIOGRAPHY

ARIËNS-KAPPERS, C. U., *An Introduction to the Anthropology of the Near East in Ancient and Recent Times*. Amsterdam, 1934.

BOAS, FRANZ, "On the Variety of Lines of Descent Represented in a Population," in *American Anthropologist* (Lancaster), (n.s.), Vol. xviii, No. 1, 1916, pp. 1-9.

———, "Are the Jews a Race?" *World Tomorrow*, Vol. vi, No. 1, 1923, pp. 5-6.

BRAM, JOSEPH, "The Social Identity of the Jews," *Trans. N. Y. Acad. of Sciences* Ser. II, Vol. vi., No. 6, 1944, pp. 194-199.

COON, CARLETON S., *The Races of Europe*. New York, 1939.

———, "Have the Jews a Racial Identity?" in *Jews in a Gentile World* (Isacque Graeber and Steuart H. Britt, eds.), pp. 20-37. New York, 1942.

DIXON, ROLAND B., *The Racial History of Man*. New York and London, 1923.

DOBZHANSKY, TH., "On Species and Races of Living and Fossil Man," in *American Journal of Physical Anthropology* (n.s.), Vol. ii, No. 3, 1944, pp. 251-265.

EFRON, DAVID, *Gesture and Environment*. New York, 1941.

FIELD, HENRY, "Arabs of Central Iraq, their History, Ethnology, and Physical Characters," *Anthropology Memoirs*, Vol. iv. Field Museum of Natural History, Chicago, 1935.

FISHBERG, MAURICE, "Materials for the Physical Anthropology of the Eastern European Jews," in *Annals New York Academy of Science*, Vol. xvi, No. 6, Pt. II, 1905, pp. 155-297.

———, *The Jews: a Study of Race and Environment*. London and New York, 1911.

HADDON, A. C., *The Races of Man and their Distribution*. New York, 1925.

HERSKOVITS, M. J., "When Is a Jew a Jew?" in *Modern Quarterly*, Vol. iv, No. 2, 1927, pp. 109-117.

———, *The American Negro, a Study in Racial Crossing*. New York, 1928.

HUXLEY, J. S., and HADDON, A. C., *We Europeans; a Survey of "Racial" Problems*. New York and London, 1936.

JACOBS, JOSEPH, "On the Racial Characters of Modern Jews," in *Journal Royal Anthropological Institute*, Vol. xv, 1886, pp. 23-56.

KENNEDY, RAYMOND, "The Position and Future of the Jews in America," in *Jews in a Gentile World, op. cit.*, pp. 418-432.

KROGMAN, WILTON M., Anthropology, physical (ms. of article prepared for *the World Encyclopedia Institute*), 1945.

VON LUSCHAN, FELIX, "The Early Inhabitants of Western Asia," in *Jour. Roy. Anth. Inst.*, Vol. xli., 1911, pp. 221-244.

MANDELBAUM, DAVID G., "The Jewish Way of Life in Cochin," in *Jewish Social Studies*, Vol. i, 1939, pp. 423-460.

MORANT, G. M., *The Races of Central Europe, a Footnote to History*. London, 1939.

PARR, LELAND W., "Isohemagglutination Studies on Near East Race Groups," in *An Introduction to the Anthropology of the Near East in Ancient and Recent Times, op. cit.*, pp. 178-196.

SELTZER, CARL C., "The Jew—His Racial Status," in *Harvard Medical Alumni Bulletin*, Vol. 13, No. 3, 1939, pp. 67-75.

WAGENSEIL, F., "Beitraege zur physischen Anthropologie der spaniolischen Juden und zur juedischen Rassenfrage," in *Zeitschrift fuer Morphologie und Anthropologie*, (Stuttgart), Vol. xxiii, 1925, pp. 33-150.

WEIDENREICH, FRANZ, "The Skull of Sinanthropus Pekinensis; a Comparative Study on a Primitive Hominid Skull," in *Palaeontologia Sinica* (n.s. D), No. 10. Lancaster, Pa., 1943.

WEINRICH, MAX, "Summary and Conclusions," in *The Classification of Jewish Immigrants and its Implications* (Yiddish Scientific Institute), pp. 106-154. New York, 1945.

CHAPTER 37

SOURCES OF JEWISH STATISTICS

By Uriah Zevi Engelman

There are two sources of Jewish population statistics: the government population census and the researches of private Jewish agencies. Not all government censuses collect Jewish statistics, while the private Jewish statistical agency, wherever it was organized, proved a poor substitute for census taking. As a result, Jewish population statistics are incomplete and defective.

The governments that gather Jewish population statistics do so by means of the general religious census of individuals. Its aim is to enumerate, individually, the members of each separate creed. The individual religious census usually makes up part of the general population census and is taken simultaneously with it. The question bearing on religion appears in the form of a separate item on the general population schedule. It is addressed to every individual, who is asked to state his religion in his own words, irrespective of whether or not he attends a church, belongs to it, or observes all its tenets.

A deep-rooted antagonism, however, against the inclusion of a religious query on the population census prevents many governments from collecting statistics about Jews as well as about other religious groups in their countries. This antagonism is very common in democratic countries, and is shared by legislators, census statisticians, liberals of all types and leaders of religious minorities. It is based on the conviction that religion is the intimate, private concern of an individual and must suffer no public probing by census takers. The opponents also claim that the individual religious inquiry will not only violate the principle of freedom of conscience but, by arousing in the enumerated a suspicion of bias, will have an adverse effect on the accuracy of the answers to all questions on the schedule. Leaders of religious minorities advance added reasons against the individual religious census. They are afraid that information gathered about them by the census will be interpreted in an unfavorable light, or that in the presentation of the final census reports they will not be allowed proper space, that their numbers will be published under a miscellaneous heading or be thrown into the total of some major creed.

Historically, these fears are justified. In the past, in most autocratic countries, the religious census was frequently followed by the enactment of antiminority legislation.

The situation is, of course, different in the modern democratic state. The census is no longer feared as the source of discriminatory legislation. The religious question on the schedule, phrased simply "What is your religion?" allows the individual to state the particular creed he believes in, while the final published tables classify the answers as given on the original schedules.

And, finally, the answers to the religious question on the population schedule in all democratic countries are optional. There is no penalty for refusing to answer the question, while the answers to the other items on the schedule are obligatory.

But old suspicions die hard. There are at present many countries where a direct, even though optional, request to state religious profession is considered undesirable. Great Britain, France, Belgium, Spain, Portugal and Italy belong to this category of states. The United States and most countries of South and Central America are in this group. The United States, however, independently of the general population census, collects information about the membership, property and expenditures of the organized churches. Canada, on the other hand, regularly gathers information about Jews through its decennial religious population census.

The U.S.S.R. forms a notable exception. It collects comprehensive statistics about Jews, not by means of the religious item on the schedule but by the question on the ethnic background of the enumerated.[1]*

In Asia, Jewish population statistics are gathered for the Russian-Asiatic provinces and Palestine. Most of the other countries in Asia conduct no censuses at all.

In Africa, official statistics on the Jews are available for Egypt, British South Africa, Algiers, Tunis and Tripoli. Australia and New Zealand also gather Jewish statistical information in connection with their general population censuses.

The scope of the published government-population statistics of Jews varies greatly. Russia, Germany, Poland, Palestine have, in the past, given a comprehensive demographic description of Jewish population numbers, male and female, urban and rural distribution, occupations, age groupings. Switzerland and Canada classified the Jewish inhabitants by sex and by rural and urban residence only.

The Census of Religious Bodies

The United States conducts a unique religious census, not of the religious profession of every individual but of the membership and wealth of organized denominations. The survey is not general, it reaches only those who are officially affiliated with some house of worship. The source of the data is secondary; it is either supplied by the head of the organization or copied from denominational sources. This census is known today as the Census of Religious Bodies. It was first instituted in 1850 under the name of the American Census of Social Statistics, and for five decades was taken simultaneously with the general population census. At the turn of the century, however, it was detached from the latter and has since been carried on separately during the intercensal interval, on the sixth year of each decade (1906, 1916, etc.).

At the first three censuses of 1850, 1860 and 1870 the religious inquiries sought to determine the number of houses of worship, value of church property and number of sittings for each denomination. Under the last heading, the census was to record the number of seats for individuals in church structures and halls hired for worship, or the number of people they could accommodate.[1] It was only in 1890 that statistics on communicants or membership were collected for the first time.[2] And as members or communicants, the instructions of 1890 considered "all those, without distinction of sex, who were permitted to partake of the Lord's Supper in denominations observing that sacrament and those having full privileges in denominations like the Friends, the Unitarians and the Jews";[3] in a word, affiliated, dues-paying members. Obviously, since not all Jews are affiliated synagogue members, the Census of Religious Bodies could not claim to have enumerated all Jews in the land.

In order to realize how inadequate the Census of Religious Bodies was as a general census of the Jewish population, one need but state that for 1906 it reported 101,457 and in 1916 it reported 357,135 members of Jewish congregations. The Jewish population for these years respectively was estimated at fifteen and ten times these figures.

In 1926 the Census of Religious Bodies extended the definition of a member of a Jewish synagogue to include "all persons of Jewish faith, residing in communities where there was a congregation."[4] This definition also held for the census of 1936. It substituted population statistics for church membership. The latter it ascertained, not through a government-conducted, general population census but through private efforts, which involved a variety of scientific and pseudo-scientific calculation methods.

PRIVATE SOURCES OF JEWISH STATISTICS

There are few Jewish statistical research organizations in the world. There was one in Germany. Vilna was the seat of the Yiddish Scientific Institute (YIVO), which had a valuable statistical section. Following the occupation of Vilna by the Nazis, the YIVO was transferred in 1940 to New York City. The Jewish Agricultural Association in czarist Russia engaged in extensive statistical studies. The Jewish communities of France and England made sporadic attempts at organizing statistical bureaus. In Canada the American Jewish Congress recently established one. In the United States the American Jewish Committee for a number of years in the past helped support the Jewish Statistical Bureau.

The private Jewish statistical research bureau has proved useful for intensive studies of population data published by governments. However, it turned out to be a defective instrument for carrying out enumerations of large population groups. For this task extensive and expensive machinery is needed so that everyone in the country may be reached. Such machinery the private Jewish bureau lacks. Nor does it command the authority to enforce general compliance with its requests. Whenever, therefore, a private research agency attempts a canvass of a widely distributed population it must resort to estimates. These may range from mere guesses to elaborate statistical studies based on one or more demographic factors. Thus, in some places, the number of Jewish births, deaths, marriages, or the number of people affiliated with synagogues was used as a statistical clue in determining the Jewish population; in others, the proportion of popular Jewish names in the city directory (Cohen, Levy), the number of absentees in the public schools on the High Holy Days, or the number of contributors to the Jewish Federation was used as a basis for estimating the number of Jews.

The main agency for estimating the Jewish population in the United States is the Jewish Statistical Bureau, whose findings are published in the statistical section of the *American Jewish Year Book* and in the United States Census of Religious Bodies. For a number of years the Jewish population statistics for separate cities and states were personal estimates by prominent residents. The total Jewish population was then arrived at by combining these estimates. Joseph Jacobs, one of the earliest pioneers in the field of American Jewish statistics, rightly considered these estimates as little better than guesses because "few persons are aware how large a few hundred of human beings bulk in the real or imaginary eye."[5]

In 1910 an improvement was made in the method of evaluating the Jewish population in the United States. The improvement consisted in determining the percentage increase in the population of fifty cities—by comparing their estimated Jewish populations in 1907 and 1910—and then assuming that the entire Jewish population in the country had grown proportionately. It is obvious even to the least statistically trained that basing one estimate upon another may be but a compounding of errors. A more earnest attempt at estimating the Jewish population in America was made by Joseph Jacobs in 1914. Realizing that estimates even by well-informed people might be misleading, he conducted the inquiry "on as many divergent lines as possible, so that the figures to which they all

converge may be reasonably supposed to vary but little from the truth."[6]
These lines were: (1) the number of Jewish immigrants, (2) the census
data bearing on "mother tongues" of the "foreign white stock," including
Yiddish, which was spoken by a large number of Jews who migrated to this
country, and (3) estimates of the Jewish population by the Industrial
Removal Office for a number of cities to which it had been planning to
direct immigrants.

In 1917 Dr. Alexander Dushkin[7] made a new contribution to the
techniques of estimating the Jewish population in the United States. He estimated the total number of children in New York City on the basis of attendance statistics on the High Holy Days and on a sample study of
Jewish names in the continuous school census kept by the Bureau of Attendance of the Board of Education of New York City. Having determined the number of Jewish children of elementary school age (five
through fourteen), he then assumed that its proportion to the total Jewish
population of New York City is similar to that given by the United States
Census Bureau for the general elementary school population of the city in
relation to the city's general population.

This method, which came to be known as the Yom Kippur absentee
method, was later used in estimating the Jewish population in a number
of cities. The major defect of this method is that it assumes that the Jewish
child age distribution is similar to that of the general population: an assumption entirely unwarranted by Jewish demographic experience.

In 1926 the Jewish Statistical Bureau took a new step in the development of American Jewish statistics. It undertook a comprehensive survey
of the Jewish population in connection with the Census of Religious Bodies,
which adopted for that census (1926) an enlarged definition of what
constitutes a member of a Jewish congregation. According to this definition,
as pointed out above, all Jews living in localities having one or more
congregations were reported as synagogue members.

Dr. Harry S. Linfield, director of the Jewish Statistical Bureau, who
was in charge of the population survey, was also appointed United States
government special agent to gather Jewish religious statistics for the 1926
Census of Religious Bodies. In making the two surveys, Dr. Linfield
utilized most of the techniques for estimating the Jewish population that
were in vogue at the time. The Jewish population of the cities of New
York, Newark, Boston, Detroit, Philadelphia, St. Louis, was estimated on
the basis of school attendance on the Day of Atonement; of Cleveland and
Pittsburgh, on the basis of a roster of all Jewish children prepared by local
social workers. The estimates were supplemented and corrected in the light
of government census statistics bearing on the number of people who reported Yiddish or Hebrew as their mother tongue.

The number of Jews in the remaining fifty-seven cities of 100,000 population or over and in the 219 cities of 25,000-100,000 population was determined "chiefly on the basis of the local estimates, examined in the light of the number of Jews that reported Yiddish or Hebrew as their mother tongue in the census of 1920, and in the light of the number of Jewish children enrolled in the religious schools of the respective cities."[8]

Before 1927 estimates of the number of Jews in the country were made only for states and divisions. But in 1926, for the first time, Dr. Linfield used a statistical method for sampling "the 15,700 incorporated cities, towns and villages of the various sizes and the 45,000 rural unincorporated areas in the country"[9] to determine how many of these had Jewish residents and what the number of such residents was.

The use of many methods does not of course assure the accuracy of a survey. If each method is defective, the survey must necessarily suffer from the sum total of all the defects. And that the methods used for determining the Jewish population in 1926 and later in 1936 were defective becomes apparent when one considers that they were based on (1) guesses (personal local estimates), (2) estimated child population, and (3) random sampling.

The defectiveness of the data is not the only criticism one may advance against the statistics gathered by the Jewish Statistical Bureau. Another equally important objection is their very narrow scope. These statistics only offer totals for states, cities and other geographical divisions. There is no classification by sex, age groups, civil status, occupations, etc. Consequently, the data are of little value as material for social, economic and demographic studies. The lack of any significant body of sociological information about the Jewish group in America can be traced directly to deficient and meager Jewish demographic statistics.

In the past decade, a serious attempt has been made to correct the defective American Jewish statistics. Under the auspices of the Conference on Jewish Relations, organized by Morris R. Cohen, censuses, based on total or partial counts of the Jewish population, were made for a number of cities. These censuses were the first to gather information on sex and age distribution, marital status, occupations, size of family, etc. These studies have been published in a volume of *Jewish Population Studies*, which is the first important work on Jewish demography in America.

The Biblical Period[9a]

The Bible is one of the earliest repositories of statistical data. It contains records of three major censuses taken of the ancient Hebrews. The first two were ordered by Moses: one, at the foot of Mt. Sinai, a year and a month after the Exodus; the second, after forty years of wandering in the desert. The third was ordered by King David.

Dr. Salo W. Baron painstakingly scrutinized the statistical data in the Bible.[10] He examined the figures mentioned more than once in the original Hebrew Scriptures and in the early translations, and found few discrepancies. He also analyzed the factors that could possibly influence Jewish population growth in antiquity: infanticide, polygamy, slave economy, economy of scarcity, spread of disease, size of families, famine, wars. This analysis and the inner consistency discovered in the figures, he rightly concludes, testify to the accuracy of the biblical census population statistics. King David's census, which related to adult males able to bear arms, would indicate, according to Professor Baron, a total population well over four million in the days of the Kings. But since the enumeration was made with a view of ascertaining both the number of people in the military class and those subject to taxation, Professor Baron thinks the census included also people of non-Jewish tribes. Deducting the latter, he arrives at an estimate of a Jewish population of 1,500,000-1,800,000 in the days of the Kings.

About one hundred years before Professor Baron, Moreau de Jonnés, a famous statistician and member of the French Academy of Science, analyzed the statistical records in the Bible and found them trustworthy. "Mankind," said Moreau de Jonnés, "may take pride in realizing that more than 4,000 years back, in a remote corner of Asia, there lived a small nation which gathered population statistics of great scientific accuracy, and for the very reasons modern nations do it today, for the purpose of governing the country, conducting wars and regulating the people's economy."[11] The Jewish population of Palestine in the days of King David, according to his estimate, numbered 3,757,000. His reasoning sheds interesting light on Jewish population trends of that period.

According to the biblical record, four hundred and thirty years elapsed from the time Jacob arrived with his "seventy souls" in Egypt, until the enumeration at the foot of Mt. Sinai. During this period Jacob's family grew to be a people of apparently 1,500,000. They lived in peace, in a salubrious place, and had an abundance of food. It was an increase of one person per every 430 individuals a year. Many European countries in the nineteenth century enjoyed a rate of increase twice or three times as high. Only as we go back into antiquity, when modern arts and sciences were unknown, do we encounter the slow rate of increase of Israel in Egypt. During the forty years of wandering in the desert the Jewish population declined slightly. Scarcity of food, plagues and civil war, it seems, destroyed that part of the population which comes from an excess of births over deaths. During the centuries between the conquest of the land and the reign of King David, the population more than doubled to 3,757,000 individuals. The annual proportional increase was one person per 770, or about one-half of the relative increase recorded by them in Egypt. France within an equal period tripled her population, and England increased her population sixfold. In Canaan the Jews were no longer primitive shepherds. They were soil cultivators and city dwellers. They had a well organized military and civil organization. And this, apparently, retarded their rate of natural growth as much as high standards of living do today.

THE CLASSICAL PERIOD

During the millennium following the reign of King David the little country of Palestine was twice completely devastated, several times overrun by invaders, ravaged by prolonged wars of extermination and laid waste by civil strife and bloody revolts.[11a] While no authoritative figures are available, the writer estimates that in the first century of the Common Era, the Jewish population, according to various authoritative estimates, numbered between five and seven millions. This population increase was made possible because: (1) Jews encouraged population growth. (2) They were a useful, productive and valuable economic element in Roman society. Hence, Jews were allowed to live in relative security. (3) They voluntarily migrated and spread over the lands and islands of the Mediterranean Basin. Especially numerous were these migrations during and following the Hellenistic period. (4) Greek and Roman rulers valued Jews as colonists for their skill, industry and dependability; frequently they were employed for opening up new territories. (5) The Jewish practice of ransoming captive brethren and Jewish proselytizing [a practice characteristic of this period] also were factors in the growth and spread of the Jewish population. (6) Last but not least, Jews manifested a remarkable ability to resist assimilation. This resistance was rooted in their deep loyalty to a nomocracy, to a book of laws, and it was not confined to any one locality. Such loyalty was everywhere to be seen.

In the classical world, the Jews formed between eight and ten per cent of the population. It was the highest density ever achieved by a large Jewish population group scattered over so wide a territory. Had the Jews retained today the same proportion to the total population, there would have been more than ten times as many Jews in the lands that were once part of the Roman Empire. And this empire, it is well to recall, did not include Russia, Poland and the United States, where today the majority of world Jewry is to be found.

THE FEUDAL PERIOD

In the centuries following the breakup of the Roman Empire, the Jewish people was decimated. These were centuries of vast population movements.[11b] In their wake cities shrank in size, decayed, ceased to be

centers of population, government and trade. Commerce vanished, government disintegrated and all orderly means of communication broke down.
The Jews found their old urban occupations, trade and crafts, no longer
serviceable for earning a living. Together with the non-Jews who formerly
lived in cities, they now settled on the land. For about five or six centuries
the soil became the chief and almost only source of livelihood for the
Jewish population. But this radical occupational readjustment resulted in a
severe dwindling of their numbers. The non-Jewish population was relatively less affected by this change, since it had had a very small urban
element in the classic world.

How much the Jewish population declined during this period we have
no way of telling, until we come to the twelfth century, and read the
diaries of Benjamin ben Jonah of Tudela, a Jewish traveler, who preceded
Marco Polo by a century and a half. According to his testimony and
additional information which he did not include in his report, the Jewish
population in the then known world was probably less than a million and
a half.[12] But the decline still continued in the coming three centuries.

From the evolving manorial economy, the Jews were gradually eliminated. They were removed from the soil, shut out of the guilds, and
barred from all lucrative economic occupations offered by church and
monastery, the only great medieval employers of labor. The Jews were
thus forced to gain a living outside the manorial economy. This meant
earning a livelihood through trade in goods and in money. But trading
in the medieval period was a nonsanctioned, highly hazardous occupation.
Besides, there was little of it. Medieval trade did not require the services
of a large middle class. Even if it were largely in Jewish hands, trading
could support only a small number of people. The fact is, however, that
non-Jewish merchants—Syrians, Armenians, Lombards, Portuguese—outnumbered the Jews. The Jewish masses had no big share in medieval trade.
Removed from soil and manor, they could find no means of gaining sustenance and, as a result, their numbers diminished.

It was at this time also that the Crusades, and the intolerance they
unleashed, played havoc with the Jewish population.

THE PERIOD OF COMMERCIAL EXPANSION

Extinction loomed real on the Jewish horizon. This danger was partly
offset. Jews married early, and meticulously observed a sanitary religious
code of life which probably reduced mortality rates among them. These
measures, however, were of little avail. Jewish populations continued to
decline as long as they were treated as superfluous within the social-
economic body of the countries they inhabited. This decline reached its

nadir by the fifteenth century. On the entire European continent there were probably fewer than 300,000 Jews; in the entire world there were fewer than a million, most of whom were concentrated in the Near East. But the following century marked a turn of affairs.[12a] Crusades were ended and with them the wanton destruction of Jewish life. The feudal order, which forced the Jew into the interstitial zone of feudal economy, had about spent itself. There was a vigorous revival of city life, a substantial increase in the volume, variety and number of commodities for trade. A large trading class was emerging. The highly restrictive town economy, in which the Jew was considered an alien intruder, yielded to a system of intercontinental trade with international trading corporations and exchanges where the Jew was accepted as a member. The importance of commerce and handicrafts for the development of a country had become apparent even to the most backward ruler. Increasingly, countries were being linked closer to each other. It was an interlinking due to the greater mutual dependence of trades and markets. This was of tremendous influence on the growth of Jewish population in the next few centuries. The Jews, whom feudal disabilities a few centuries ago had forced to engage in trade, now found themselves in the vanguard of an evolving commercial era. Their expulsion from any one place could no longer be the sole concern of a ruler's or class's arbitrary whim. A massacre, an expulsion of the Jewish trading group, might disrupt the normal economic activities of a city, and might unfavorably affect its relations with other commercial centers. The period of expulsions was ended; the era of readmission had begun. One of the first effects of the Commercial Revolution was to check the decline of Jewish population.

Another favorable demographic factor at this time probably operated within the Jewish, as contrasted with the general population. Medieval cities had been nests of disease. Yearly, they had had a large excess of deaths. Only by drawing on the countryside population had the cities been able to grow in size and replenish their losses.

The Jews lived in the unsanitary medieval cities because they were forced off the land in the early feudal period. During the centuries they probably developed a relative biologic immunity to the city. And it was at this time that the city took on added importance.

The expanding commercial activity on the Continent naturally resulted in a sudden increase of aggregate wealth. Such an increase, according to demographic experience, has always been correlated with an increase in population growth. And what happened generally happened to Jews too. They shared in the increase of aggregate wealth; their population also increased. According to available fragmentary information, Jewish numbers probably more than doubled by the time the Commercial Revolution had become the Industrial Revolution. It has been estimated that at the end of the eighteenth century the Jewish population of the world was between two and two and a half millions.

JEWISH POPULATION IN THE NINETEENTH CENTURY

During the nineteenth century the Jewish population increased more than fourfold. This large increase, part of a general increase of world population, was the consequence of technical, industrial, economic and social processes, partly initiated and partly accelerated by the advance of industrial capitalism.

TABLE 1

Jewish Population Growth in the Nineteenth Century

Year	Population
1800	2,500,000
1825	3,280,000
1850	4,750,000
1880	7,650,000
1900	10,600,000

Source: Jacob Lestschinsky, "Die Umsiedlung und Umschichtung des juedischen Volkes im Laufe des letzten Jahrhunderts," *Weltwirtschaftliches Archiv*, Jena, 1929, II, Band 30, p. 155.

What were these processes? Among others, they were the rise in the number, prestige, differentiation and power of the middle classes; the shift in the center of economic activity from village to town; the enormous increase in the opportunities for gaining a livelihood—a consequence of the

TABLE 2

Growth of Jewish Population

1825-1900

Countries	1825	1850	1880	1900
Western and central Europe	458,000	693,500	1,044,500	1,328,500
Eastern and southeastern Europe	2,272,000	3,434,000	5,726,000	7,362,000
Europe	2,730,000	4,127,500	6,770,500	8,690,500
America	10,000	65,000	250,000	1,175,000
Asia	300,000	320,000	350,000	420,000
Africa	240,000	250,000	280,000	300,000
Australia	1,000	2,000	12,000	17,000

Source: *Schriften fuer Wirtschaft und Statistik* (in Yiddish), Juedisches Wissenschaftliches Institut, Berlin, 1928, Band I, p. 6.

introduction of mass production; the division of labor and the vast development of transportation and communication; the abolition of the legal limitations on Jewish marriages; the vast improvement in the sanitary conditions of city life; the opening up of new centers for colonization, especially in North America.

Political emancipation played a minor part in the expansion. The major increase in the Jewish population occurred in eastern Europe, which remained politically unemancipated. The countries that abandoned anti-Semitism as a state policy in the nineteenth century, the highly industrialized western countries and the Americas, shared only indirectly in the growth of the Jewish population by accepting the population overflow from eastern Europe.

How Fast Did the Jews Multiply?

The fourfold increase of the nineteenth-century Jewish population, remarkable as it seems, was in keeping with the general population trends of the period.

The nineteenth century was one of tremendous population expansion. "For half a million years since mankind rose up on its hind legs and made a bid for world supremacy . . . its natural increase was so slow that in the year 1800 there were less than 850 million people."[13] But in 1938 there were over two billion people in the world. In 138 years mankind not only exceeded the growth achieved by it in the preceding half million or million years, but had added more people to the human total than in the entire previous span of its existence. Dr. Henry Pratt Fairchild rightly considers these figures the most amazing statistics in the world, while all other statistics "may quite accurately be regarded as mere embroideries upon this great central pattern."[14]

When the Jewish population increase is compared with another that might be analogous, namely, that of the English-speaking peoples—who, like the Jews, are distributed over several continents—one finds that the Jewish rate of natural increase in the nineteenth century was quite slow. A United States Census report is revealing on this point.

The population of Great Britain in 1712 is estimated to have been but 9,000,000. During the succeeding century, the eighteenth, Great Britain contributed from the small population the stock which formed the larger part of the white population of the United States in 1790, and which increased by 1900 to approximately 35,000,000 souls. In 1801 the population of the United Kingdom was 16,200,000, by 1900 it had increased to 41,000,000. But during the nineteenth century the mother country also contributed, even more freely than she had contributed during the eighteenth century to North America, to the population of the United States and to that of a score of younger colonies

. . . It is possible that a population growth similar in character may have occurred upon a small scale in connection with some of the colonies established
by ancient cities along the Mediterranean, but in magnitude there appears
to be no parallel in history for this population achievement of the British race
from 1700-1900.[15]

Nor does the growth of Jewish population seem exceptional when compared with the growth of separate countries, as is shown in Table 3.

TABLE 3

	1580	1680	1780	1880
England	4,600,000	5,532,000	9,561,000	35,002,000
Prussia	1,000,000	1,400,000	5,460,000	45,260,000
Russia	4,300,000	12,600,000	26,800,000	84,440,000
France	14,300,000	18,800,000	25,100,000	37,400,000

It is well to note that the world population increased also prior to the
sixteenth century, "an increase of possibly 33 per cent in one hundred years
was reached by the seventeenth century and of 50 per cent by the
eighteenth."[16] The Jewish population following the disintegration of the
Roman Empire declined until almost the sixteenth century.

THE HINTERLAND OF JEWISH POPULATION GROWTH

A population as a whole may grow only by an excess of births over
deaths; in any one specific area, however, it may increase by an excess
of births and a difference between immigration and emigration. Viewing
world Jewish population as a unit, one learns the remarkable fact that
practically its entire natural increase during the nineteenth century was
supplied by those in eastern Europe. This area comprised the Ukraine,
White Russia, Lithuania, Poland, Rumania, Galicia and Hungary. It
constituted the hinterland of Jewish population expansion. It served as a
reservoir of people, the kind of reservoir which in all countries the rural
communities provide. Culturally, it was backward; socioeconomically, it
was just about to emerge from an economy based on serfdom. It had, in
the nineteenth century, higher Jewish birth and death rates, a higher rate
of natural increase, and a lower standard of living than any of the other
Jewish population groups of western and central Europe, or America.

The advance of industrial capitalism into this hinterland, the introduction of the steel plow, the opening up of numerous small factories, the
increase in trade, resulted in augmenting the opportunities for livelihood.
These opportunities were not followed by an increase in individual well-
being but by a large expansion of the population and a sinking standard of
living. It seems that as soon as the frontiers of starvation were pushed

back the area left open was filled by new births. For once Malthus's theory was vindicated! This experience of the Jewish hinterland was not unique. It followed the pattern set by England and other European countries in their early stages of capitalist development.

And as the pressure for bread and space became acute in the hinterland, its population pushed out into the western countries and overseas, replacing with its members the dwindling urban Jewish communities.

TABLE 4

Showing Absolute and Relative Increase of Jewish Population in the Countries of Western and Eastern Europe, 1825-1900[17]

	1825-1850 Absolute Increase	Percentage Increase	1850-1900 Absolute Increase	Percentage Increase
Western Europe	235,000	51.3	635,500	91.7
Eastern Europe	1,162,000	51.1	3,928,000	114.4

The figures in Table 4 do not reveal the full extent of the natural increase of the Jewish population in western and eastern Europe. To determine the natural increase of the Jews in eastern Europe one must add to its given population the number of the east European immigrants and

TABLE 5

Growth and Distribution of the Jewish Population in the Hinterland

1825-1900

Country	1900	1880	1850	1825
Prewar Russia	5,175,000	3,980,000	2,350,000	1,600,000
Poland without Posen	1,325,000	1,005,000	575,000	400,000
Ukraine, New Russia, Bessarabia	2,200,000	1,600,000	925,000	625,000
Lithuania, White Russia	1,450,000	1,225,000	800,000	550,000
Other provinces of Russia	200,000	150,000	50,000	25,000
Galicia	811,000	687,000	450,000	275,000
Hungary	852,000	638,000	352,000	200,000
Rumania	267,000	200,000	130,000	80,000
Bukovina	96,000	67,500	15,000	8,000
Bulgaria	34,000	20,000	10,000	7,000
Other provinces of southeastern Europe	92,000	77,000	52,000	35,000

Source· *Schriften fuer Wirtschaft und Statistik, op. cit.,* p. 6.

their descendants, who lived at the time in western Europe, in the Americas and in the other countries. What their number was one cannot tell precisely. But that it was large may be gauged from this: By 1900, more than one million East European Jews had settled in the Americas, and about a quarter of a million in western Europe and other lands. Eastern Europe, on the other hand, received no Jewish immigrants.

Similarly, in order to evaluate the natural increase of west European Jews in the nineteenth century, one would have to add, on the one hand, about 250,000 west European Jewish immigrants and their descendants who migrated to America and other countries and, on the other hand, deduct at least 200,000 east European Jews who settled in western Europe.

NINETEENTH-CENTURY VITAL BALANCE SHEET

Leroy Beaulieu makes a pointed observation in his book *Israel Among the Nations* in regard to Jewish population growth in the nineteenth century. "They [the Jews] bring fewer children into the world, but they bring more of them to maturity. It would seem as if, with their characteristic cleverness at calculations, they have instinctively solved the difficult problems of population in the manner most advantageous to themselves and most satisfactory to the economists." This observation held true for every country in Europe, as is shown by Tables 6 and 7.

The Jewish birth rates in the eastern countries of nineteenth-century

TABLE 6

Jewish and General Birth Rates in Europe at the End of the Nineteenth Century

Place	Year(s)	Jewish Birth Rates	General Birth Rates	Jewish Birth Rates Lower by
Rumania	1896-1900	40.1	40.1	—
Galicia	1895-1900	40.4	44.3	3.9
Bulgaria	1891-1895	37.5	37.5	—
Russia	1896-1897	35.9	50.2	14.3
Budapest	1891-1900	29.5	34.6	5.1
Vienna	1900	22.2	31.7	9.5
Prussia	1900	19.4	36.2	16.8
Hamburg	1900	19.1	28.8	9.7
Frankfort on the Main	1900	18.0	30.3	12.3
Trieste	1891-1900	17.2		
Padua	1891-1900	13.2		

Based on the following sources: B. Bienstock and S. Novoselski, *Dvijenie Eureiskavo Naselenia v Europeiskoi Rossii*, Petrograd, 1915; Robert R. Kuczynski, *The Balance of Births and Deaths*, The Institute of Economics, The Brookings Institution, New York, 1928, II; Jacob Lestschinsky, "Probleme der Bevoelkerungs Bewegung bei den Juden," *Metron*, Padova, 1926, VI; *Zeitschrift fuer Demographie und Statistik der Juden*, 1905; *Blaetter fuer Demographie, Statistik und Wirtschaftskunde der Juden*, Berlin, 4.

Europe were higher than in the western countries. This difference increased with the distance from the hinterland. The physical distance was probably of minor importance. The major cause for the differential was the higher degree of modernization in the western lands. In all countries, the Jewish birth rates were much lower than those of the general population.

TABLE 7

Jewish and General Death Rates at End of Nineteenth Century

Country	Years	Jewish Death Rates	General Death Rates	Jewish Death Rates Lower by
Bulgaria	1891-1895	23.1	27.9	4.8
Rumania	1896-1900	21.4	27.4	6.0
Galicia	1895-1900	20.8	28.4	7.6
Russia	1900-1904	16.7	31.0	14.3
Warsaw	1901	18.2	21.6	3.4
Hungary	1896-1900	16.8	27.6	10.8
Prussia	1900	14.9	21.7	6.8
Vienna	1900	12.9	20.7	7.8
Trieste	1891-1900	17.6		

Based on the following sources: Kuczynski, *op. cit.*; Bienstock and Novoselski, *op. cit.*; *Mouvement de la Population de la Ville de Varsovie*, Publié par le Service Statistique de la ville de Varsovie, Varsovie, 1902; Lestschinsky, *Metron, op. cit.*; *Zeitschrift fuer Demographie und Statistik der Juden*, 1905, Heft 5, Heft 6.

The Jews, who, historically, became urbanized earlier than their neighbors and were more sensitive to the inroads of industrialization, led the decline in Europe both in birth rate and in death rate. Jewish death rates began to decline much sooner than their birth rates. The difference in birth rates between Jews of the western countries and of the hinterland, held also for death rates. The Jews of eastern Europe had higher birth rates, they also had higher death rates. As in the case of birth rates, the Jewish death rates were lower than those of the general population.

Jewish Population in the Twentieth Century

The great increase in mankind's population in the nineteenth century was, in Dr. Fairchild's words, the resultant, among others, of man's ability to "spread himself over the entire globe without breaking up into more than one species." In the twentieth century, the Jews literally found themselves spread throughout the world, yet, on the whole, retained their spiritual ties with one another.

Between 1900 and 1938, according to the estimate of Dr. Arthur Ruppin, in his book *Jewish Fate and Future*, the Jewish world population increased from 10,600,000 to 16,717,000.

But in the twentieth century new demographic tendencies became apparent, whose origin could be traced to the latter part of the nineteenth century and whose cumulative effect was a sharp slowing up of the rate of increase. The Jewish population felt the impact of these influences both earlier and more strongly. As a highly urbanized minority, living most of the time under severe social pressures, it developed a higher sensitivity to social change than did other urban groups. This higher sensitivity was revealed in its continued lead in the twentieth century of a decline in birth rates; in its being first to mark a sharp rise in death rates in a number of countries; in its rate of natural increase and in the size of its families, which were shrinking faster than those of the general population.

The Drying Up of the Reservoir of Jewish Population Growth

Early in the twentieth century it became clear that many Jewish communities in western, northwestern, southern Europe, and also in America, could not continue to maintain themselves through natural increase. Their birth rates were declining, their death rates rising; intermarriage increased, and the Jewish proportion in the total population diminished. The Jewish population of these countries, however, was replenished and in fact increased through immigrants. Yet as the twentieth century advanced the hinterland lost its function as a reservoir for supplying Jewish people.

Wars, revolutions, secession meant dismemberment for Jews; a sinking rate of natural increase reduced the relative Jewish population density in the entire area and its separate provinces, even before the outbreak of the Second World War.

In the Soviet Union, which comprised the major part of the hinterland, the Jewish population was subjected to economic and intellectual influences which weakened its historic consciousness of uniqueness as an ethnic group.

Before the First World War half the world Jewish population lived in Czarist Russia, where it formed 4.2 per cent of the population. In the Soviet Union in 1926 it numbered 2,600,000, and had a relative density of 1.8. The Jewish density of the Soviet Union will continue to sink because the Jewish rate of natural increase is lower than that of the other population groups. Thus in 1926, for the entire territory of all the Soviet Republics, the rate of natural increase for the White Russians was 26.91, for the Ukrainians, 24.31, for the Great Russians, 22.64, and for the Jews, 14.97. Also the growing number of mixed marriages is an added factor in diminishing the Jewish proportion in the population of the Soviet Union.

This latter fact is especially significant, since, according to a study made by the present writer, there is a direct relationship in the Soviet Union between the rate of natural increase and the density of the Jewish population, and an inverse relationship between Jewish population density and intermarriages.[18]

Poland and Rumania, the other two important sections of the hinterland, were occupied for over four years by the Nazis. Most of the Jews in this area were slaughtered. Not much better is the situation in Austria, especially in Galicia, or in Hungary. Eastern Europe as a hinterland of world Jewry has thus ceased to exist. It is questionable whether the Jewish communities outside the hinterland will be able to maintain themselves by natural growth.

Table 8

Jewish and General Birth Rates in the Twentieth Century

Countries	Year	Jewish Birth Rates	General Birth Rates	Jewish Birth Rates Lower by
Rumania	1901-1905	32.6	39.5	6.9
	1930	15.8	35.8	20.0
Bulgaria	1904-1907	34.2	43.2	9.0
	1930	20.2	30.1	9.9
Poland	1928	20.4	26.5	6.1
	1933	18.7	26.5	7.8
Galicia	1901-1902	38.1	43.9	5.8
	1928	20.8		
Lithuania	1925	15.9	29.6	13.7
	1928	17.1	28.7	11.6
Hungary	1896-1900	33.9	38.5	4.6
	1929	12.0	25.8	13.8
Prussia	1900	19.4	36.2	16.8
	1929	9.1	19.1	10.0
	1931-1935	6.1	18.0	11.9
Vienna	1900	22.2	31.7	9.5
	1929	6.5	9.4	2.9
Amsterdam	1899-1900	25.2	30.4	5.2
	1919-1922	19.2	21.7	2.5
Leningrad	1910-1913	17.6	27.7	10.1
	1920	17.2	21.8	4.6

Tables 8 and 9 based on the following sources: Jacob Lestschinsky, "Probleme der Bevoelkerungs Bewegung bei den Juden," *op. cit.; Information de L'Office Central de Statistique,* Varsovie, 1932, XX, Fasc. 2; *Résultats Généraux du Recensement de la Population dans le Royaume de Bulgarie,* 1926, I; *Lietuvos Respublica, Statistikos Biuletenis* (Statistics of the Lithuanian Republic), Kaunos, 1928-1929, 6, 56; *Zeitschrift fuer Demographie und Statistik der Juden,* 1905; Arthur Ruppin, *Sociologia shel Hayehudim,* Tel-Aviv, 1931-1932; *Idem, The Jews in the Modern World,* London, 1934; *Idem, Jewish Fate and Future,* London, 1940; Kuczynski, *op. cit.,* I, II; *Digest of Jewish Statistics,* published by the Jewish Statistical Bureau of New York, I and II.

Twentieth-Century Vital Balance Sheet Birth Rates

During the first three decades of the twentieth century, both Jewish and general birth rates declined in all the lands for which statistics are available. In the hinterland the Jewish birth rates declined faster and in the western countries slower than the general birth rates. As a result, during the first three decades the differential between the Jewish and the general birth rates widened in the hinterland and was narrowed outside of it. As in the nineteenth century, the birth rates were lower the farther the country was from the hinterland.

In eastern Europe Jewish death rates declined during the first three decades of the present century; in western Europe they rose. They were lower than the general death rates in all countries, except for Prussia, where the Jewish death rates were higher than those of the general population.

In the nineteenth century, east European Jews had higher death rates than their coreligionists in the western countries. In the twentieth century the situation has been reversed. Interesting to note is this: the countries farthest from the hinterland now have the higher death rates; in the nineteenth century this was true of the countries in the hinterland.

TABLE 9

Death Rates of Jewish and General Population in the Twentieth Century

Country	Year	Jewish	General	Jewish Greater or Lower by
Rumania	1901-1905	21.2	25.7	−4.5
	1930	10.1	19.7	−9.6
Poland	1927	11.2	19.6	−8.4
	1933	10.0	14.2	−4.2
Bulgaria	1904-1907	13.7	21.9	−8.2
	1925-1928	11.1	18.5	−7.4
Budapest	1925	13.4	17.2	−3.8
	1929	15.0	18.8	−3.8
Vienna	1900	12.9	20.7	−7.8
	1929	13.2	14.4	−1.2
Prussia	1900	14.9	21.7	−6.8
	1929	15.4	12.9	+2.5

Iɴᴛᴇʀᴍᴀʀʀɪᴀɢᴇs

Intermarriage has become a serious factor in reducing Jewish numbers in politically emancipated countries. Two circumstances contributed to that. The Church withdrew the medieval ban against mixed marriages; more-over, cultural assimilation, which follows political emancipation, leads frequently to mixed marriages. In many cases intermarriage is a prelude to baptism.

Assimilation affects Jewish population growth in yet another way. The upper professional, intellectual, artistic and financial classes are usually unable by their reproductive powers to maintain their ratio to the population as a whole. This gap in the upper ranks creates a movement from the lower classes into the upper ones. But in the upper economic and professional classes the influence of assimilation is unusually strong. That influence sometimes insulates the members from all Jewish influence, and may even result in intermarriage and baptism.

Julius Drachsler pointed out in his *Democracy and Assimilation* that in America a high degree of mental and social assimilation coexisted with a low proportion of intermarriages. Whether this is still so today we do not know; in Germany, however, assimilation always went hand in hand with mixed marriages and baptism. During the past three decades of the twentieth century there were in Germany 109,544 homogeneous marriages and 37,507 mixed marriages. The latter formed 34.2 per cent of all endogamous marriages.

In the Soviet Union, the number of mixed marriages increased from 2,987 in 1924 to 3,198 in 1925, and to 4,361 in 1926. The number of homogeneous Jewish marriages during the same period decreased by 800.

The rate of Jewish intermarriages in the Soviet Union varies inversely with the density of the Jewish population. White Russia has the highest Jewish population density, 8.2 per cent of the total White Russian population, and the lowest record of Jewish mixed marriages. In 1926 it reported sixty-five mixed per thousand Jewish homogeneous marriages. In the Ukraine, where Jewish density is slighter, 5.4 per cent of the Ukrainian population, the rate of Jewish mixed marriages was 106 in 1926. The highest rate of Jewish intermarriages was reported for the European part of R.S.F.S.R. (Russia Proper) where the density of Jewish population is only 5 per cent of the total population of the republic. In 1926, for every thousand unmixed Jewish unions there were 532 that were intermarriages.

In Hungary the number of mixed Jewish marriages formed over 32 per cent of the homogeneous ones. Thus during the years 1931-1933 there were in Hungary 9,420 endogamous marriages and 3,059 mixed Jewish marriages. In Bohemia the number of Jewish marriages has been rapidly mounting. During the first year after World War I, ten out of every hundred marriages were contracted out of the fold. In 1927, 300 mixed against 500 homogeneous marriages were reported. In Austria mixed marriages formed 24 per cent of all Jewish marriages of 1929-1931.

Likewise, Switzerland has reported a growing number of intermarriages. The ratio of mixed per every thousand homogeneous marriages has increased from 57 in 1888 to 74 in 1900, to 97 in 1910, to 132 in 1920, to 190 in 1930.

In Copenhagen, for the 1889-1899 decade, the average yearly number of intermarriages was sixty-eight for every hundred unmixed marriages; the average rose to eighty-two for the 1900-1905 period.

URBANIZATION OF JEWS

Jews massed into cities earlier than other population groups and at a faster tempo. In the Middle Ages, Jews settled first in cities along the trade routes. Later, in eastern Europe, where navigable rivers were few and roads bad, each district was economically self-sufficient and had its own markets. Jews, who were artisans and small traders, spread very thinly over the countryside because no one village could support more than several of them.

The church records of the number of Jews in the 5,019 villages of the diocese of Olck for the year 1775 offer a graphic illustration of the wide distribution of the Jews in the eighteenth century.

TABLE 10

Distribution of the Jewish and Non-Jewish Rural Population of the Diocese of Olck[19]

	Number of Villages	Number of Christian Inhabit.	Aver. No. of Christian Inhabit. per Village	Number of Jewish Inhabit.	Aver. Number of Jews per Village
Olck	595	33,332	56	2,460	4.1
Maszovien	2,688	129,467	48.1	10,332	3.8
Rawa	44	3,172	72	114	2.6
Wyszogorod	176	9,222	52.4	1,211	6.9
Dobrzyn	365	24,631	67.4	1,235	3.4
Wizk	265	17,408	73.2	1,486	5.6
Zawskrzyn	595	20,464	34.4	1,052	1.7
Zakzosczyn	291	15,197	52.2	904	3.1

In the nineteenth century Jews shared fully in urbanization, which had become a universal concomitant of the Industrial Revolution and the rapid development of modern means of transportation and communication.

In the hinterland, which in the nineteenth century contained more than 60 per cent of Jewish world population, this movement was accelerated by anti-Jewish legislation, which barred Jews from rural areas. Jewish urbanization entailed moving from villages and smaller towns to larger ones. But at the end of the nineteenth and the first decades of the twentieth, it entailed moving to the capitals and the large industrial centers of the world. "One may thus speak," aptly remarks Professor Salo Baron, "of the metropolization rather than urbanization of the Jewish people."[20]

In 1925 more than a fourth of all Jews in Europe and America lived in the fourteen cities with a million population or more, while only 5.7 per cent of the total population of the two continents lived in them.

Before the outbreak of the Second World War this process was so far advanced that more than half the world's Jewish population lived in forty-two cities having 100,000 inhabitants or more; each had upwards of 50,000 Jewish residents; while 35 per cent of the world's Jewish population lived in communities with more than 100,000 Jews. In America only 21.7 per cent of the total population lived in cities of more than 100,000 people, while 83.7 per cent of the Jewish population lived in such cities.

The urbanization of the Russian population, coming in the wake of the five-year industrialization periods, was phenomenally rapid. During the years 1928 to 1932, Russia's city population increased 40 per cent. Jewish participation in this urbanization process was equally amazing.

Urbanization retards population growth. In the cities birth rates are lower, death rates higher, families smaller and the population "older" than in the rural areas or in the smaller towns. Many cities have only an apparent natural increase—apparent because migration has resulted in a population whose age composition is favorable to low death rates and high birth rates.

But for many, if not most, urbanized Jewish communities of the world, even before the outbreak of World War II, there was no longer an apparent natural increase. For these there was an actual natural decrease.

Of all Austrian Jews 91.9 per cent were in Vienna. For the decade 1928-1938 the city's Jewish birth rates were insufficient to balance the yearly number of Jewish deaths. Likewise Budapest, which contained more than half of Hungary's Jews, registered 2,526 more Jewish deaths than births for 1931-1932. The situation was similar in most European capitals and large cities.

The major portion of the Jewish populations of England and France was in London and Paris. London had, in 1932, a natural increase of only two per thousand population and Paris recorded even a lower natural increase. Since Jewish birth rates were everywhere lower than those of the general population, one may safely assume that Jews did not share in the small surpluses recorded by either capital. And this trend is prevalent not only in the old capitals of Europe, it is asserting itself also in the United States. There are no birth or death statistics for American Jews. However, the several studies of the size of the American Jewish family and of the age composition of the Jewish population, recently made for a number of cities, tell that their Jewish population is not reproducing itself.[21]

THE EFFECT OF THE DECADE 1936-1946 ON JEWISH POPULATION NUMBERS[21a]

World War II cut into Jewish population in a double sense. It killed, literally, millions of Jews, and it contributed to the aggravation of the dysgenic demographic trends that were observable before its outbreak.

The European phase of the war was waged in an area which contained almost 60 per cent of world Jewish population. The actual annihilation of the Jewish population was one of the main ideological and military objectives of the German Nazified war machine. And this objective was to a large extent achieved.

Eugene M. Kulisher estimated in his study *The Displacement of Population in Europe* that by the beginning of 1943 over four million Jews were expelled, deported and uprooted. The number perished is variously estimated from 25 per cent and up.[22] But during the years 1943 and 1944 the toll mounted. As the Nazi machinery of death was forced to roll back under blows of the Allied armies, it slaughtered or carried off the surviving Jewish populations.

But wars, massacres, expulsions are aberrations of an age. They do not decide the ultimate destiny of a population. The latter is determined, in the long run, by the vital processes, which work constantly and persistently at shaping its size, course and composition; upon these processes wars are only superimposed.

At the beginning of the war, there was a general rise in the number of first and second births, but a decline in the number of consecutive births. The average size of the family has not been materially altered. And the low Jewish birth rates of the prewar period will probably sink still more. A further decline will of necessity be followed by a rise in the death rates and the fast "aging" of the population.

NOTES

[1] "At the census of 1870 the inquiry headed 'number of churches' was divided into two parts (*a*) number of church organizations and (*b*) number of church edifices. This was done because on the previous two censuses it was not possible to feel assurance in any particular case whether church organizations or church edifices, were returned." (*U. S. Census of 1870*, 9th census, Vol. I, "Population and Social Statistics," [Washington, 1872], p. 502.)

[1*] On the 1926 U.S.S.R. population census schedule, the question used for gathering information on the multi-national character of Soviet society was "narodnost" (an ethnographic category); in 1939 the question was "natsionalnost" (nation). The wide difference in the terms used on the two censuses makes the statistics hardly comparable.

[2] At the census of 1880 statistics of religious bodies were collected but never published. Dr. Henry Randall Waite, who was at the time head of the Department of "Statistics of Churches, Schools and Libraries" ascribes "this misfortune for which there is no excuse . . . to the failure of appropriations; also to an indisposition on the part of the then superintendent of the Census (Colonel Seaton) to give to these statistics the attention . . . they should have received." (*Lutheran Quarterly*, [Gettysburg, Pa.] Vol. XIX, No. 3, July, 1889, pp. 413-414.)

[3] *A Compendium of the Ninth Census*, (Washington, 1872), p. 261.

[4] *Jewish Congregations,* Statistics, History, Doctrine and Organization, Census of Religious Bodies, 1926 (U. S. Government Printing Office, Washington, 1929), p. 6.

[5] Joseph Jacobs, "Jewish Population of the United States," Memoir of Bureau of Jewish Statistics of the American Jewish Committee (*The American Jewish Year Book,* 1914-1915), pp. 339-378.

[6] *Ibid.*

[7] Alexander M. Dushkin, "A Statistical Study of the Jewish Population of New York," *The Jewish Communal Register of New York City, 1917-18* (New York, 1918), pp. 77-79.

[8] Harry S. Linfield, *The Jews in the United States,* A Study of their Number and Distribution (New York, 1929).

[9] *Ibid.*

[9a For background material cf. above William Foxwell Albright, "The Biblical Period."]

[10] Salo W. Baron, *Uklusei Yisroel bimei hamelakim* (Population of Israel in the days of the Kings), in *Abhandlungen zur Erinnerung an Hirsch Perez Chajes* (Vienna, 1933).

[11] Alexandre Moreau de Jonnés, *Statistique des peuples de l'antiquité, les Egyptiens, les Hébreux, les Grecs, les Romains, et les Gaulois,* 2 vols. (Paris, 1852).

[11a Cf. above Judah Goldin, "The Period of the Talmud (135 B.C.E.–1035 C.E.)," and Elias J. Bickerman, "The Historical Foundations of Postbiblical Judaism."]

[11b Cf. above Cecil Roth, "The European Age in Jewish History (to 1648)."]

[12] Benjamin of Tudela, *The Itinerary of Rabbi Benjamin of Tudela,* translated and edited by A. Asher, 2 vols. (London and Berlin, 1840-1841.)

Benjamin of Tudela's data add up to 989,475. For five places which he visited he gives no figures, stating only that he found there Jewish congregations. His data for western Asia are probably exaggerated; on the other hand, he did not include in his itinerary the Jewish communities of central Europe, of Russia and of Poland.

[12a Cf. above Roth, "The Jews of Western Europe (from 1648)."]

[13] Edward M. East, *Mankind at the Crossroads* (New York, 1923), p. 66.

[14] Henry Pratt Fairchild, *People, The Quantity and Quality of Population* (New York, 1939), p. 3.

[15] *A Century of Population Growth from the First Census of the United States to the Twelfth, 1790-1900.* United States Bureau of the Census (Government Printing Office, Washington, 1909), p. 91.

[16] W. S. Rossiter, "The Adventure of Population Growth," *Journal of the American Statistical Association,* March, 1923, p. 563; see also A. B. Wolfe, "Fecundity and Fertility of Early Man," *Human Biology,* 1933, Vol. 5; pp. 35-60.

[17] Jacob Lestschinsky, "Das juedische Volk im Wandel der letzten hundert Jahre" (in Yiddish), in *Schriften fuer Wirtschaft und Statistik* (Juedisches Wissenschaftliches Institut, Berlin, 1928), Band I, p. 10.

[18] Uriah Z. Engelman, "Vital Statistics in the Soviet Union in 1926," in *American Journal of Sociology*, Vol. XXXVIII, No. 3, November, 1932, pp. 437-440.

[19] Konotacya Parafii I, Handschrift 806, S. 651-673, quoted from *Zeitschrift fuer Demographie und Statistik der Juden* (Berlin, 1919), pp. 61-64.

[20] Salo W. Baron, *A Social and Religious History of the Jews*, 3 vols. (New York, 1937), II, 226.

[21] ". . . The Buffalo Jewish Family is so small as to be below the size necessary for the perpetuation of the Jewish group." *A Study of the Size of Families in the Jewish Population of Buffalo*, University of Buffalo Studies, (Buffalo, 1938), Vol. XVI, No. 1.

"Although the percentage composition of the Jewish population is such as is associated with a positive crude rate of natural increase, the net reproduction rate of 64 for native and 68 for foreign-born Jewish women forecasts a decrease in the future."—A. J. Jaffe, *A Study of Chicago Jewry Based on Death Certificates*, p. 144. *Jewish Social Studies*, Publication No. 3, Edited by Sophia M. Robison, Conference on Jewish Relations, New York, 1943.

[[21a] Cf. above Arieh Tartakower, "The Decline of European Jewry (1933-1953)."]

[22]

Jewish Losses in Nazi-Occupied Countries of Europe

Country[1]	Jewish Population September 1939	Number of Jews Lost	Percentage of Jews Lost
Poland	3,300,000	2,800,000	85.0
Soviet Union (Occupied area)	2,100,000	1,500,000	71.4
Rumania	850,000	425,000	50.0
Hungary	404,000	200,000	49.5
Czechoslovakia	315,000	260,000	82.5
France[2]	300,000	90,000	30.0
Germany	210,000	170,000	81.0
Austria	60,000	40,000	66.6
Lithuania	150,000	135,000	90.0
Holland[2]	150,000	90,000	60.0
Latvia	95,000	85,000	89.5
Belgium[2]	90,000	40,000	44.4
Yugoslavia	75,000	55,000	73.3
Greece	75,000	60,000	80.0
Italy[2]	57,000	15,000	26.3
Bulgaria	50,000	7,000	14.0
Miscellaneous[3]	20,000	6,000	30.0
Totals	8,301,000	5,978,000	72.0

[1] Considered within prewar borders.

[2] Figures for Holland, France, Belgium and Italy include refugees.

[3] Denmark, Estonia, Luxembourg, Norway, Danzig.

Balance Sheet of Extermination, by Jacob Lestschinsky, Jewish Affairs, Vol. I, No. I, Feb. 1, 1946, issued by the Office of Jewish Information, American Jewish Congress.

BIBLIOGRAPHY

ENGELMAN, URIAH ZEVI, "The Need for Jewish Population Statistics," in *Menorah Journal* (New York), November, 1927, pp. 464-479.
A discussion of the methods used in collecting Jewish population statistics.

LESTSCHINSKY, JACOB, "Das wirtschaftliche Schicksal des deutschen Judentums," in *Schriften der Zentralwohlfahrtsstelle der Deutschen Juden*, No. 7. Berlin, 1932.
An analysis of the social-economic position of German Jews prior to the advent of the Nazis.

LINFIELD, HARRY S., *The Jews in the United States*. New York, 1929.
A study of the distribution of the Jewish population in America by larger and minor divisions.

RUPPIN, ARTHUR, *Sociologia shel Hayehudim* (Hebrew), 2 vols. Tel-Aviv, 1931-1932.
The most comprehensive sociological study of the world Jewish population.

——, *The Jews in the Modern World*. London, 1934.

——, *The Jewish Fate and Future*. London, 1940.
Dr. Ruppin's books in English offer in condensed form the material contained in the *Sociologia shel Hayehudim* and brought up to date.

Tzentral'noye Izdatelstvo Narodov USSR (Russian). Documents and Studies about the Jewish population. Moscow, 1929.
Based on the data of the 1926 census of U.S.S.R.
Much demographic statistical material is found scattered in various publications in several languages.

The American Jewish Year Book. Published by the American Jewish Committee, Philadelphia, 1899- .

Blaetter fuer Demographie, Statistik und Wirtschaftskunde der Juden (Yiddish). Berlin, 1923-1925.

The YIVO Blaetter. Schriften fuer Yiddischen Wissenschaftlichen Institut. New York, 1939- .

Zeitschrift fuer Demographie und Statistik der Juden. Vols. 1-15. Herausgegeben vom Bureau fuer Statistik der Juden. Berlin, 1905-1919.

CHAPTER 38

JEWISH MIGRATIONS, 1840-1956

By Jacob Lestschinsky

1. MIGRATIONS IN GENERAL AND JEWISH MIGRATIONS IN PARTICULAR

It is doubtful whether certain historians and sociologists are correct in saying that the whole of world history is contained in the history of mass migrations. No one will deny, however, that migrations play a colossal role in human affairs—and this is especially evident in the period of capitalism.

One need only glance at the American continent, at its weighty role in human history from the beginning of the nineteenth century to the middle of the twentieth, to appreciate the significance of migration. The immense growth of this continent has revolutionized the lot of all the peoples of the world. At the beginning of the nineteenth century, there were on this continent hardly twenty million people, representing no more than 2½ per cent of world population; now this continent numbers almost three hundred million people, practically 15 per cent of the world's population. When these figures are properly understood, however, it is clear that they signify much more than 15 per cent of the life, the conditions, the perpectives of the world.

From Europe alone, during the past century and a half, sixty-five million people have migrated into the various American countries. These sixty-five million have become hundreds of millions, of which the United States received approximately half. And the transplanting of sixty-five million people from the most civilized and cultured region of the world to an almost free and uncultivated area altered the appearance of the earth, changed the entire trend of world history. The center of gravity of world history shifted from Europe to America. The American continent has about 75 per cent of the world's iron supply, 80 per cent of the nickel supply, 60 per cent of the copper and naphtha supplies, 35 per cent of the coal, and about 50 per cent of the cotton supplies. So much for material wealth. Now, it can be safely assumed that, as far as spiritual-cultural resources are concerned, the center is also shifting to America, primarily, of course, to the United States. Thousands of European leaders of the highest positions in art and science have settled during recent years in the Americas, mainly in the United States. The destruction of the cultural institutions of Europe and the pauperization of Europe as a whole make, therefore, for a new distribution of power, not only in the political and economic sense, but also in the spiritual and cultural sense.

The destruction of Europe is the fault of the European peoples, but the extraordinary progress of the American continent is the work of those same peoples—of those splinters of the European nations who were compelled, for various economic, political, and religious reasons, to leave their old homes and seek their happiness across the sea. Splinters of scores of nations of aged Europe revealed on the virgin soil of the new continent new strength, almost entirely unsuspected in the forsaken Old World. The nations of course remained where they were, on their historic territories; but they sent off their youngest, most energetic, and most creative children to the Americas. The fate of these nations was henceforth bound up not with the fortune of their émigrés, now identified with new national groups, but with the development of the American continent. Even for Englishmen, who of all peoples furnished the greatest number of emigrants, the national center remains on the European isle. The United States is an English country in language only; it does not belong to the English people. Nationhood is a much broader concept than language. In the United States the number of people of British descent is perhaps not less than in England itself. And without a doubt, the number of people of Irish descent in the States is greater than in Ireland. Yet the homeland remains the national home, the national center of the *Volksgeist*. The same is true of all other European nations. Each may have given huge numbers to the American peoples—from ten to twelve million Italians, eight to nine million Poles, and so on; nevertheless, they remained as nations, as national groups, in the old home, in historic Europe.

Regardless of the absolute or relative number of the various European peoples in the New World, they do not feel themselves to be Englishmen, Germans, Frenchmen, Swedes, Italians, Spaniards, Poles. They regard themselves as Americans, as Americans of the United States, as Argentinians, as Brazilians, as Mexicans, and so on. Despite their European descent the immigrants are unable to resist the pressure of their new countries. Memories of origin soon yield to the need to strike root in a new world.

The nature of the émigré's ties with his native land varies. Such ties are either strong or weak, of long or short duration, depending upon the well-being of the "old country." Hence the paradox that immigrants from highly developed countries, Swedes, Englishmen, Norwegians, Danes, are less closely attached to their mother countries than immigrants from backward, impoverished lands, Poles, Ukrainians, Lithuanians, Letts, etc. Apparently the former, children of rich and free peoples, are confident of the survival of their original national groups; when they migrate they cease to worry about the future of their historic group. On the other hand, the latter emi-

grants, children of poor and less free peoples, take with them the unrest of
their early homes and even in their new country bear for quite a long time
the yoke of battle for freedom for the native land.

Many additional factors, of course, determine the degree of affiliation to
the new land and new people. One must also take into account time, distance, remigration, cultural kinship between land of origin and new land,
and a host of other influences.

As with Christians, so with Jews—and yet this is not altogether true.
The position of Jews is peculiar, unique, so that certain phenomena acquire
a new dimension, a new character, in their case. The intensity of Jewish
migrations; the concentration in certain regions, on the one hand, and,
on the other, a vast dispersion over the whole world; the consequences of
migration for the fate of the entire people, for those remaining in the
old country and those in the new settlements; adaptation to new cultural
environments and attachment to the older heritage—externally all these
are no different from what confronts all or many Europeans; essentially,
however, the case is very different with the Jews.

Of sixty-five million people who emigrated from Europe, in a century
and a half about four million were Jews. This represents about 6 per cent
of the entire emigration from Europe. The percentage of Jews in Europe
at the beginning of the nineteenth century was not more than 1½, never
more than 2. The intensity of Jewish emigration was, therefore, three to
four times as great as that of the general emigration from Europe. If we
consider only those sections of Europe from which Jews emigrated, i.e.,
middle eastern and southern Europe, the intensity of Jewish emigration
is not three to four times, but six to seven times as great as that of the
general emigration. Western and northern Europe (France, England, the
Scandinavian countries, Belgium, Holland, and Switzerland) had so few
Jews at the beginning of the nineteenth century that for Jews they became
lands of immigration, although there was quite an exodus of non-Jews
from these countries to America. It is safe to say that the sixty-five million
who migrated from Europe during the past century and a half comprise
a third of Europe's population at the beginning of the nineteenth century,
while the approximately four million Jewish migrants outnumber the total
Jewish population of the world at the beginning of that century. Even if
we grant that not all of the four million were from Europe (two to three
hundred thousand were Sephardic and Arabic Jews from middle eastern
Asia and North Africa), there would still remain about three million and
seven to eight hundred thousand Jewish emigrants from Europe: this is
still greater than the number of Jews in the entire world at the beginning of
the nineteenth century.

No other people among all the immigrants into the various American
countries so concentrated itself in urban centers, especially in the large

cities, as did the Jews. In the United States, 98 per cent of the Jews live in urban centers, 86 per cent in cities of more than 100,000 population; 58 per cent are in three of the largest cities (New York, Chicago, and Philadelphia) and 43 per cent are in one city, New York. Approximately the same is true in all countries where Jews have migrated. And yet none of the other migrating European peoples spread itself out over as many continents and isles. The Vienna community, in its migration report for the year May, 1938, to May, 1939, listed eighty-four countries to which 104,000 Viennese Jews had gone. There is now actually no corner of the world where a Jew cannot be found. This is, however, a result of the past hundred years, and especially of the past ten to fifteen years, when the need for new places of settlement was constantly on the increase, for the gates of the formerly hospitable lands where Jews had concentrated in the first stages of their great migrations were being closed more and more tightly.

Regardless, however, of the world-wide nature of Jewish dispersion, the center of the Jewish people shifted from one continent to a second—from Europe to America. And if for a thousand years the Jews were first an Asiatic-European people and later a European-Asiatic people, they have become, as a result of the migrations of the last hundred years, an American people.[1a] If in the past two to three hundred years the bulk of Jews was found mainly in the sphere of Slavic-Arabic culture, now the majority of the Jewish people finds itself in an English sphere of influence.

Table 1 will illustrate the organic transplanting of the center of the Jewish people, and at the same time reveal the relative growth of the new center, as a result of the catastrophe that befell European Jewry.

TABLE 1. *The Number of Jews on the European and American Continents at Different Times during the Past Hundred Years*

YEAR	EUROPE		AMERICA	
	Absolute Numbers	Percentage of World Jewry	Absolute Numbers	Percentage of World Jewry
1840	3,950,000	87.8	50,000	1.1
1900	8,800,000	80.0	1,200,000	11.0
1939	9,500,000	56.9	5,540,000	33.2
1945	3,000,000	27.3	6,000,000	54.6

The American continent, which a hundred and five years ago had one seventy-ninth the Jewish population of Europe, now has twice as many Jews as the latter. From one per cent of the Jewish people, American Jewry jumped to more than half the entire Jewish population. The first three lines of the table show clearly the results of the migrations—as we shall see later, from 1840 to 1945, in round numbers, about 3,300,000 Jews (approximately 85 per cent of all Jewish migrants) migrated into all American countries. Through natural increase, the 3,300,000 immigrants became more than five and a half million. The fourth line shows the results of the European catastrophe. Although the absolute number of Jews on the American continent increased little from 1939 to 1945, in all about 460,000, and although that increase is the result more of natural increase than of immigration, still the relative weight of American Jewry increased. What was formerly one-third of world Jewry has now become more than half of the Jewish people. This is due to the destruction of six million Jews on the European continent.

The important fact, however, is that Jews are now an American people. We must also take into account the fact that the Jews of America have a natural increase of approximately fifty thousand per year, while European Jews in the next ten to fifteen years will undoubtedly suffer a biological decline, for the mortality rate of the physically and mentally wearied European Jews will certainly be high. It is impossible to hope for many births, because the material conditions in which European Jews find themselves make family life impossible. And no matter how small immigration into American countries may be, there will still be some Jews immigrating and large numbers in flight from Europe. The conclusion is inescapable: in the next ten years European Jewry will lose numbers heavily, and there will be an increase of American Jews. Quantitatively, therefore, Jews are becoming decidedly an American people.

Parallel with a world-wide dispersion, as we noted, a concentration of Jews has taken place. The chief concentrations are in American countries, particularly the United States, Canada, and Argentina. In these three lands live 5,700,000 of the 6,000,000 American Jews; in other words, 93 per cent of all Jews on the American continents. More than 87 per cent of all American Jews live in the United States alone. But Jews migrated not only to the Americas; they migrated to many other lands, only two of which may be characterized as centers—Palestine and South Africa. Of approximately more than 600,000 Jewish migrants to countries besides America, about 400,000 (easily two-thirds) went to Palestine and about 75,000 to South Africa. Of all the countries admitting Jewish immigrants, the Americas included, the United States takes first place and Palestine second. Of course, in the past one hundred years, the United States admitted seven times as many Jewish immigrants as Palestine; but Palestine received a greater number of Jewish immigrants than all the other countries. Since Palestine exerts more of a spiritual than an economic or political influence, it figures prominently immediately after the great "quantitative center" of the United States.

We have been contrasting Europe with America. Actually, however, Jews on each continent had a specific area which could be regarded as their center. In America it has been the United States, and in Asia it has been

Palestine. In Europe it was the eastern part of the continent. This region was almost a territorial center for Jews for several centuries. Till the middle of the twentieth century, in those countries which lie between the rivers Vistula, Niemen, Dvina, Dnieper, and Danube (Poland, Ukrainia, White Russia, Lithuania, Latvia, Hungary, Rumania, Slovakia, and Carpathia), there lived about seven million Jews; eight million if we include Russia proper. The Jews in all these lands were geographical neighbors and, until the First World War, the great majority belonged to two empires—Russia and Austria. To geographical proximity and common citizenship are to be added common language, traditions, and habits. These people had behind them a history and legacy of many centuries and together constituted, until World War II, the principal quantitative and spiritual center of world Jewry. But it would be an error to think that Hitler alone destroyed that center. Its decline had begun much earlier.

Table 2 reveals how emigration caused the decline of eastern Europe as a center, and how, as if directed by a national providence, it prepared

TABLE 2. *The Development of the Three Centers of World Jewry*

PERIODS	EASTERN EUROPE*		U.S.A. & CANADA		PALESTINE	
	Absolute Numbers	Percentage of World Jewry	Absolute Numbers	Percentage of World Jewry	Absolute Numbers	Percentage of World Jewry
1840	3,200,000	71.1	40,000	0.9	10,000	0.2
1900	7,400,000	67.3	1,100,000	10.0	50,000	0.5
1939	7,000,000	41.9	4,900,000	29.5	480,000	2.9
1945	1,000,000	9.1	5,400,000	49.0	580,000	5.3

* Figures exclusive of the Jews in Russia proper.

two substitute centers: the quantitative one in the United States and the spiritual one in Palestine. (We have added Canada to the States, because Canadian Jewry is an integral part of the North American Jewish center.)

For the first three periods, the results of the migrations are conclusively expressed—the relative importance of the East European Jewish center continued to decline. From 1900 to 1939 even the absolute numbers of Jews in that historic center decreased. Relatively, its weight fell from over 71 per cent in 1840 to a mere 42 per cent in 1939. The decline was a significant one, but despite that, this center still played an enormous role in the life of the entire Jewish people. It was this center which supplied the human material for the upbuilding of Palestine and the spiritual and political leaders for Israel in all countries. The Hitler catastrophe completely liquidated this center. Of seven million before the war, there remained only one million. This remnant, however, is broken physically and spiritually, and most likely it will exert all its efforts to leave Europe. The migrations that brought millions of Jews to America and hundreds of thousands to Palestine saved, therefore, the Jewish people from oblivion. Thus the significance of migration for the fate of the Jewish people is unique; for no other people has migration played so decisive a role. Elsewhere emigration eased the economic conditions of the masses, often distracted them from political revolt; in the case of Jews it made survival itself possible. For all other peoples, despite migration, national centers remained in their original European countries; so far as Jews were concerned, the situation in this respect was entirely different. Even now no one can tell how the development of the two new immigration centers will proceed: to what extent the Palestinian spiritual center will become quantitatively strong and to what extent the American center will assume also spiritual leadership in Jewish life. The Jewish people is today at the crossroads; both immigration centers are still young.

Although in speaking of Asia we have concerned ourselves only with the *Yishuv* in Palestine, we must add that in Soviet Asia during recent years a great number of Jews have been admitted. One hundred years ago, there were no more than several hundred Jews in Asiatic Russia. Today the region must contain about half a million. While this increase is a result of migration, it does not enter into our account, for this migration is within the confines of the Russian state. We are here concerned only with transoceanic movements. If we were to include in our survey the migrations within the borders of Europe and within the boundaries of any one state, we would have to conclude that in the past hundred years about six million Jews changed their place of habitation—more than twice the number of Jews in Europe at the beginning of the nineteenth century. About half a million Jews migrated from eastern Europe to England, France, Germany, Austria, Belgium, and the Scandinavian countries. Several hundred thousand migrated from the Russian-Ukrainian, Russian-White Russian and Russian-Lithuanian provinces to South Russia (the provinces of Kherson Ekaterinoslav, Bessarabia, and Taurien). In the twenty-five years after the Russian Revolution and the abolition of the Pale of Settlement, about half a million Jews migrated from Soviet Ukrainia and Soviet White Russia to the central areas of Russia proper.

At present there are half a million Jews in Asiatic Russia. In Biro-Bidjan, however, which has the right of a Jewish autonomous district, there are no more than 25,000 Jews, newcomers from 1928 to 1939. This may be inconsequential, but Biro-Bidjan is already assuming the character of a center. The remaining Jews of Soviet Asia are scattered over many districts, cities, and villages. Of the half million, about 225,000 were already in Asia prior to World War II; the remainder are Jews evacuated in 1940-1941 and stranded there.

2. MIGRATIONS AS A FACTOR IN JEWISH HISTORY

The historic common fate of the Jews, manifest in various countries under various economic, political, and cultural conditions, was once again affected by these migrations. The stronger the ties between the Jewish communities of various lands, the easier was reunion. The Jews of the various East European countries, of Russia, Poland, Galicia, Rumania, Carpathia, etc., who had already begun to adjust themselves to various foreign tongues and cultures, very soon banded together in the American countries. This was more difficult for the younger generation, because it had already adopted another language, the language of *its* native country. Disregarding the language question, however, we must definitely assume that even between German Jews and East European Jews an amalgamation has taken place. And in the most recent tragic years, there is a marked tendency on the part of Sephardic Jews to declare their oneness with the larger communities of the Ashkenazim. This could happen only through the coming together in the lands of immigration.

One hundred years ago, on the steamers traveling to the New World there had already taken place a commingling of Jewish migrants from Germany and North Africa, Poland and England, Lithuania and Hungary, etc. Especially colorful was the meeting of Jews on the ocean liners in the past ten to twelve years. Never before in the sufficiently sad history of the Jews had there come together so many hunted and harried Jews from so many different countries and from so many different social and cultural levels. They fled from practically all the countries of Europe—and the exceptions can be counted on the fingers of one hand. Jews with earlocks and *sisit* prominent, and Jews whose fathers had already forgotten that they were the seed of the Patriarchs, fled together. Ships with financiers of Vienna and Paris and poor shopkeepers and artisans from Poland and Rumania; ships with rich land magnates from Hungary and uprooted beggars and peasants from the Carpathians; rich manufacturers from Warsaw and Lodz and beggarly junk peddlars from the Galician villages; professors and artists and scientists along with old fashioned *heder* teachers and modern Hebrew pedagogues from Poland and Lithuania—this kaleidoscopic mass testified, on the one hand, to the fact that not one or two European countries, but almost all of Europe was in the throes of a profound social and economic convulsion and, on the other hand, that "all Israel are brethren," that in a violent age Jews of all groups are victim, and there is "neither wisdom nor shrewdness" which can prevail against anti-Semitism.

"All Israel are brethren and all Jews are responsible for each other"—in transit, and in the first difficult years of adjustment to the new life this becomes clear for all the scattered individuals. No matter what Jews live in this or that remote land, or how small the settlement happens to be, when Jewish immigrants arrive the care for their lives and the provision for their support begin at once. There is even concern over the immigrants' conduct, for it is often but too true that the common fate that Jews share is more the result of anti-Semitism than of national interests.

The longer a Jewish community is settled in a country, the deeper, obviously, is its attachment to that country, to its language and culture. This has generally meant that that particular community also drifted away from other Jewish communities. Such isolation from other Jews, however, is interrupted as soon as immigration gets under way on a large scale. An awareness of kinship is once again established.

An excellent illustration of this phenomenon is provided by the development of Yiddish. Jews came to the Germanic countries in very small groups, often family by family. Naturally, to be able to communicate with the local population, they were forced to adopt the language of the land. But they did not take over the language mechanically. Instead they transformed and adapted it to their own religious and national requirements. They punctuated German with Hebrew words and concepts. Nevertheless, the structure of this adopted language and its whole spirit remained very close to the original idiom of the surrounding alien environment. Had the Jews remained in Germany uninterruptedly it is doubtful whether the language would have acquired the typical form and spirit that it acquired in the Slavic countries. When Yiddish finally departed from its original source and became an independent vehicle of expression it experienced a noteworthy development.[2a] Jews of Germany came to Poland in great numbers and found there most favorable conditions for remaining isolated in culture and language from the environment, and for developing further the language they had brought with them. Though the first Jews in Slavic countries had begun to adopt the languages of their neighbors, the new large migrations of German Jews put a halt to that cultural assimilation. Yiddish then became the language of the East European Jews, even of those who had previously used Slavic languages.

As a result of conditions that prevented the Jews from taking root in any one country for long, two significant facts emerged. On the one hand, Jews could not altogether lose their identity, the process of assimilation never became thoroughgoing. On the other hand, whatever Jews did adopt from their environment they integrally converted into their own; that which had been foreign became organically an element in their culture.

What we have said of language is true in other respects, too. Any number of alien customs and forms found themselves naturalized in Jewish life.

So long as the religious tradition was strong in Jewish life, the Jewish immigrant, for his own well-being and happiness, had to participate actively in the life and habits of the Jewish community to which he had come. Not only did his new neighbors make possible the *minyan* which he required for public prayer, not only did the community own the cemetery where he would have to purchase his burial plot, but daily and in a thousand ways he was dependent upon his new milieu. Hence integration in the community was the only choice open to the immigrant, and migration reinforced a sense of kinship.

In our own day, however, the story is entirely different. A generation had grown up which had no knowledge of Yiddish. These Jews spoke the language of their respective countries; and although in the recent upheaval they all met in flight and their fate was the same, the Hungarian Jews did not understand the Rumanian, the Rumanian could not understand the Polish, the Polish could not understand the French. Since piety had languished, there was little the religious tradition could do to emphasize for the immigrants their interdependence. True enough, in the haven of refuge the German Jew came closer to the Polish and Lithuanian Jew, estranged Hungarian and French Jews showed deeper interest in Jewish affairs than they had in their native lands. But in this era of assimilation migration ceased to achieve positively what it could accomplish in days gone by.

3. The Causes of the Jewish Migration 1840-1946

If one studies the migrations of the nineteenth century, one is amazed by what at first appears paradoxical: the modern period of emigration begins much earlier and is of longer duration in the wealthier countries than in the poor lands. And by "wealthier" we mean not only material riches, but cultural resources, resources which contribute to the individual's initiative and enable him to risk danger in search of happiness and fortune. The greatest number of emigrants came from the wealthiest continent, Europe. Of all European countries, the richest (England, Germany, Sweden, Norway) supplied the greatest mass of emigrants, numerically and relatively. And emigration from these countries began much earlier than from the poorer East European countries.

This phenomenon can be observed also in the case of Jews—the Jews of Russia in the time of Nicholas I certainly suffered more politically and were economically poorer than the German Jews; yet Jewish mass emigration began first from Germany; only later did it occur in the poverty-stricken ghettos of eastern Europe.

Poverty, apparently, is not alone sufficient to dislodge masses and set them into movement. Indeed there is a poverty so acute that it makes one indifferent and resigned. To be sure, those who emigrated from the rich countries were the poorer elements; nevertheless, they had lived where horizons were broader, concepts loftier, knowledge of the world greater than in the backward countries of eastern Europe, where feudalism reigned until late in the nineteenth century. At a time when the feudal lords of Russia and Poland were still beating their serfs to death, there was already in England a complete legal code concerning obligatory support of poor families by the civic communities.

The industrial machinery which, at the beginning of the nineteenth century, was responsible for the well-known English unemployment sharpened the appetites of the masses for better living conditions. Decades passed before this machinery had like effect on the appetites of the eastern and southern European masses, before it gave them the mental initiative, cultural courage, and self-confidence necessary to pull up stakes. Only then did the great emigrations from those countries of Europe, where the number of Jews was great, occur.

Here are some figures to tell the story: 6,700,000 Europeans came to the United States from 1820 to 1870. Of these immigrants only seventy thousand, i.e., 1 per cent, were from eastern and southern Europe, although these countries had one-third of the entire European population. From 1870 to 1930, 25,558,000 European immigrants entered the States; fourteen million, or 54 per cent, were from eastern and southern Europe.

The partition of Poland in the second half of the eighteenth century and, simultaneously with it, the decline of business and urban life in general shook the foundations of Jewish life. Before the partition, fully half the entire Jewish people lived in Poland, from two-thirds to three-quarters of all Ashkenazic Jews, in other words, of all European Jews. The poverty of the Jewish masses in the Polish towns of that time was so serious that the Polish government was forced to establish commissions to find some means for its alleviation. Solomon Maimon, in his autobiography, paints a vivid picture of that tragedy. The Jewish masses were not only materially poor, but culturally they were provincial, backward. The few rich *arendars* (lease holders) and merchants who traveled to the Leipzig fairs and had some knowledge of the distant world were an inconsequential percentage of the Jewish population. Yet the Jewish masses exhibited initiative, and we find that in 1776, 1777, and 1778 several Polish communities appealed to the consulate of the recently founded New Russian province (later the provinces of Kherson and Ekaterinoslav) for permission to emigrate and settle there. This was fully forty years before the colonization program was organized by the Russian government, after it acquired great numbers of Jews from partitioned Poland. Jewish migration to New Russia from the erstwhile Polish districts began, then, before the Russian government took the initiative.

But at approximately the same time—only a few years later—a German Jew turned to the President of the Continental Congress with a request for land for a large group of Jews who wished to emigrate from Germany to America. The letter was first made public in the June, 1783, number of the German journal *Deutsches Museum;* it appeared in pamphlet form in 1787, in Frankfort and Leipzig as *Schreiben eines deutschen Juden an den Amerikanischen Presidenten.* The author of the work remained, unfortunately, anonymous, but the document, which portrays, on the one hand, the tragic situation of the German Jews and, on the other, the desire to emigrate, presents great interest and we shall permit ourselves to quote from it at length.

After the writer has expressed his joy at the peace which the States have at last made with England, and after observing that the States have so much land that even after a hundred years it will probably not be as thickly populated as Germany, he goes on to say:

Your religion cannot prohibit you from leaving these deserts to us for cultivation; besides, for a long time you have been tolerating Jews near you. Whether policy might forbid you that, I do not know. At all events you have the legislative power in your hands, and we ask no more than to be permitted to become subjects of these thirteen provinces, and would gladly contribute twofold taxes for their benefit, if we can only obtain permission to establish colonies at our own cost and to engage in agriculture, commerce, arts and sciences. Do we not believe in the same God as the Quakers do? Can our admission become more dangerous and precarious than that of the Quakers? Supposing that two thousand families of us would settle in a desert of America and convert it into a fertile land, will the old inhabitants of the provinces suffer by it? Let the conditions be stated to us, gracious President, under which you will admit us; we will then consider whether we can accept and keep them.

You would be astonished, most mighty President, at the perseverance of a German Jew, if you could witness it. The great, nay, perhaps the greatest part of them, spend almost their whole life on the highway in the pursuit of retail business, and the trader consumes for his own person nothing but a herring and a penny loaf; the nearest brook or well has to supply his drink. All that he earns besides he conscientiously lays aside in order to bring it home on Friday to supply food and clothing for wife and children. During these one and a half days when he enjoys somewhat better food and rests in the bosom of his family he forgets the wretched life which he is compelled to take up again on the next Sunday. And would you believe it, this wretch, who has to strain all his wits to convert a capital of fifty florins nearly as many times during the year, if he wants to live by it with his family, is nevertheless not infrequently envied by many Jews? . . . Granted that a Jew has at last become possessor of a capital that would suffice to support a family, still he will not be able to marry the woman he loves. Most of the time and in most of the German provinces he is obliged to acquire protection money for a sum which reduces his property to a half or a third. But love overcomes this difficulty too. He strains his energies anew, again completes his capital and then seeks permission to marry. If he obtains it, the experience just described is repeated, for he has to pay dearly for this permission, and the expenses of a wedding are not less among the Jews than among the Christians.[3]

A few German and even Polish Jews were in the States as early as the eighteenth century. Newport, which in the second half of the eighteenth century had the largest Jewish community in America (over a thousand of approximately three thousand Jews), certainly included Ashkenazic Jews. But they were few in the literal sense of the word; one can hardly speak of migration of European Ashkenazic Jews before the nineteenth century. Jewish migration into the United States and the other Americas until after the Napoleonic Wars was Sephardic, though in absolute numbers the Sephardim did not represent a large mass. In relation to the total number of American Jews, however, they were the largest majority, and the period up to 1820 bears their stamp.

Mass emigration of Ashkenazic Jews began in the years following the Napoleonic Wars. It is perhaps characteristic that within eight years there appeared in Russia two Yiddish translations of Joachim Heinrich Kampfe's famous work, *The Discovery of America*: the first, *Zafenat Paaneah*, by the well-known *Maskil*, Chaim Horowitz, in 1817; and the second in 1823 by the Hebrew writer, Mordecai Aaron Ginsburg.[4a]

The history of the Jews in Europe in the first half of the nineteenth century reveals two developments. On the one hand, political reaction grew stronger in Germany and Russia, the two countries with the majority of European Jewry. Ruined and impoverished by the Napoleonic Wars, which, for the most part, were fought in those regions where masses of Jews were concentrated, these countries let loose on the Jews unremitting restrictions and persecutions. In 1827 the Russian recruiting policy began, the military conscription of Jewish children for twenty-five years, which practically meant conversion. Several years later came the edict driving the Jews out of the border provinces. In 1845 recruiting of Jews was made law in Poland also. Russian Jewry was in a quandary. Philippson, the editor of the German *Allgemeine Zeitung des Judentums*, wrote a series of articles about the frightful plight of Russian Jewry, in which he said: "The persecutions have reached that borderline where even human cruelty must end—unless one were yet to take the slaughtering-knife into one's hands. The victim—Jewry—stands at the brink of the grave, its blood already flows."[5] In Germany, the *hep-hep* pogroms of 1818 and 1819[6a] were accompanied by a spread of anti-Semitic literature, which called for new restrictions and renewed expulsions.

On the other hand, in both countries Jewish communities bestirred themselves. The German Jews began to battle mightily for equal rights. Germany was then at the height of its transition from feudalism to capitalism. In this transition Jews played a principal role. In the seventeenth century the Prussian king invited wealthy Viennese Jews to settle in Berlin in order to develop industry and commerce. In Berlin, in the eighteenth century, there was a Jewish community of three (later four) thousand, although Jews had no right of residence in the Prussian capital. Already a significant Jewish bourgeoisie, for whom there was great need, had arisen; so, too, a Jewish professional intelligentsia and a Jewish propertied middle class appeared. Germany's economic development actually dictated equal rights for Jews—Jews were, after all, the biggest and ablest bankers in the country; they created capital funds and organized foreign loans; they first connected Germany with world markets and possessed the initiative necessary to develop the German domestic market.

In Russia also significant economic developments were taking place, altogether opposed to the backwardness of Nicholas's regime. In the provinces of erstwhile Poland commerce was exclusively in Jewish hands. The efforts of the Russian government economically to absorb Polish territory into the Russian Empire was impossible without the participation of Jews, who in many areas were the majority of the urban population and, as already stated, the only tradesmen. Export of grain, which was on the increase and which was necessary for the awakening Russian capitalism, was almost exclusively managed by Jews. Despite the above-mentioned persecutions and pogroms, therefore, there developed in the first half of the nineteenth century large Jewish communities in Warsaw, Odessa, Berdichev, and many other cities. The Jewish village and rural masses threw off their lethargy and began to seek sources of income in the larger cities.

Along with this general awakening, along with the rising discontent with the *status quo* and feverish search for new opportunities in life, began also the stream of migration. The masses of poor, who in the first half of the nineteenth century constituted the outstanding majority of German Jewry, grew more enterprising; in their search for a new life they were prepared for a number of risks. If one brother moved from Posen to Berlin and opened a tailor shop which in ten years developed into a clothing factory, the other brothers also contemplated settling in Berlin. If there were no opportunity for them in that city, they might think of the prospects in England, or other distant lands. The same occurred in Bavaria, where the Jewish masses were poorest, even though the country might already boast of a few wealthy Jewish bankers. Even in Germany there was at that time no strong middle class between upper bourgeoisie and the poor masses; there was only a very narrow margin of more or less wealthy people.

This phenomenon—economic progress of the few along with impoverization of the many to the point where they feel they must move on to other countries—confronts us, *mutatis mutandis*, in every other European country, with this difference, however: elsewhere it appeared about half a century later than in Germany, because there capitalism developed later than in Germany. In Russia, in the Polish provinces, in Hungary, and in all other East European countries capitalism became intensive only in the second half of the nineteenth century. Only then did the great awakening of the Jewish masses take place. In the first half of the nineteenth century, therefore, German Jews emigrated in great numbers but East European Jews in driblets. In the second half of the century the wave of Jewish emigration from Eastern Europe rose higher and higher, while the number of emigrants from Germany decreased.

Because in Eastern Europe capitalism came very late, its development was slow and weak. Here, however, lived the great Jewish masses. The contrast between increasing poverty as a result of a dying feudalism and the new opportunities as a result of a rising capitalism was much greater than in Germany—where Jews were few and capitalism was well advanced. No wonder, therefore, that in the eighties of the nineteenth century—the peak was reached in the first years of the twentieth century—there was little emigration *from* Germany but considerable migration *into* Germany by Polish and Russian Jews.

In contemplating the reasons for emigration, it is not enough to consider the factors that lead one to leave the homeland. One must also take into account the conditions in the lands of immigration, which may attract and also repel newcomers. If the need to emigrate from Europe had not been accompanied by a phenomenal economic progress in America, emigration would certainly not have reached such heights. Toward the beginning of the twentieth century American industry developed so rapidly and impressively that it became one of the most significant factors in attracting all those who wished to quit Europe. The Jewish weaver from Lodz, who earned barely two dollars a week and received a letter from a former fellow countryman or relation saying that in Paterson one earns seven to eight dollars a week and that living costs are only twice as high as they were in the old country, hurried to America even if in Lodz he was sure of work. The same was true everywhere: the letters from the first émigrés were the best agitation for emigration.

One further point. The poor Jew who in 1850 or 1860 knew of the New World and its magnificent opportunities, particularly for his children, often lacked the funds to travel; hence he was compelled to remain where he was though he saw his doom plainly. At the beginning of this century, however, there were already more than one million Jews in the Americas, and they subsidized the emigration of their European kin.

This was particularly the case in Russia, where the greatest concentration of Jews was located.[7a] On the one hand, for the sake of economic interests the czarist government had to make concessions and grant rights of residence in all of Russia to certain Jews, rich merchants, manufacturers of the first and second guilds (a kind of commercial franchise), individuals with an academic training, qualified artisans; on the other hand, it expelled Jews from the villages even in the Pale of Settlement, instituted quotas in the universities and high schools, and interfered with the economic Jewish institutions of mutual and self-help and with Jewish communal and charity institutions. Add to this the fact that in 1871 there was a pogrom in Odessa, in 1881 and 1882 a whole series of pogroms with many dead and wounded, in 1903 the Kishinev pogrom, and in 1905, during the October Revolution, over five hundred pogroms in five hundred places; it becomes clear why emigration from Russia continued and increased.

In Rumania the situation for Jews was no better, if not much worse. In the seventies conditions there were so frightful that the American government deliberately appointed a Jewish public servant, Benjamin Franklin Peixotto, as general consul with a special mission to help the local Jews. And these were the words of President Grant to the consul: "The reports concerning the sufferings of the Rumanian Jews deeply stir our humane sentiments. That which reaches us from Rumania is a chain of malice and barbarity without measure."[8] As is known, Peixotto presented a project for an organized Jewish mass migration from Rumania. Evidently Peixotto found no hope for improvement there. Today it is clear to everyone that the American Jew was far more farsighted than the philanthropists of Paris and Berlin, who discarded this plan and staked the fortune of the Rumanian Jews on the card of the struggle for equal rights.

It would, however, be an error to assume that all classes of the Jewish population were treated equally in Rumania. The Jewish commercial and industrial bourgeoisie, most active in the creation of what little modern economic life Rumania possessed, was generally and for a limited time not disturbed. But at the same time the impoverished Jews were so mercilessly treated that hundreds of them organized in groups and journeyed afoot to Vienna in the hope of meeting with sympathy there and finding the opportunity to emigrate to America.[9]

This dual policy—exploitation of Jewish intellectual forces, Jewish commercial abilities, Jewish psychological awareness, and international connections, on the one hand, and, on the other, driving of the Jewish impoverished masses to despair and emigration—operated only when there was a more or less intensive development of capitalism and an ever-increasing emigration of the broad masses. Capitalism created new sources of income for those who abandoned the villages because there was not enough land for the growing rural population, and emigration drained off those who found no place in the urban economy.

But the crisis of lack of land and employment, already manifest before World War I, grew far more acute after the war. Emigration became less and less possible because countries to which immigrants had come in the past would not admit an unlimited number of new settlers. Such restrictions, however, applied universally and affected non-Jews as well as Jews. What complicated matters for Jews was their specific minority status.

The stream of Jewish emigration from the small towns was accompanied by a corresponding one of the non-Jewish population from villages and hamlets, in all the central and eastern European countries. The number of non-Jews moving from country to town was of course much larger than that of the Jews; but it was smaller in proportion to the total population. The Jews entered business, liberal professions, labor and small industries, established factories, and engaged in domestic and foreign trade, preparing the way for the large numbers of non-Jewish migrants who came to the city, and became part of the culture of the towns. The large group of non-Jews that flocked from the villages entered the factories or became unskilled laborers. The children of large and middle class landowners became public officials, or professionals, with some few entering commerce and industry. But the second generation of the citified non-Jews was more dynamic, businesslike, and ambitious. Yet as a result of the first stage of development, it turned out that in all the lands of Eastern Europe—Poland, Rumania, Hungary, Lithuania, and Latvia (Russia must be excluded, as the First World War led to distinctive situations there) the Jews constituted the majority in trade and particularly in foreign commerce and big business. They also provided between 35 per cent and 50 per cent of the physicians and members of liberal professions, that is, those callings in which personal talent and initiative play an important role.

All the above-mentioned countries became politically independent after the First World War. This gave the ruling national majority a weapon against which the Jews were helpless. In the open market the Jew was victorious, even when the surrounding Christian merchants, artisans, and doctors called for a boycott of their Jewish colleagues; but against the governments' measures, which placed higher taxes on Jews than on Christians, which expelled all Jewish doctors from the national and city hospitals, which limited credit to Jews but granted enormous concessions to Christian entrepreneurs—such official anti-Semitic policies,[10a] which were not merely formal but actual, rendered the Jews helpless.

Added to the general economic crisis and the diminishing emigration was the program of thorough elimination of Jews from all business. The aggressiveness of the general population grew with the encouragement of the governments. Finally force was resorted to: people began to beat Jews in the universities, picket their stores and keep out Christian customers, demolish Jewish market stalls and prevent Jews from coming to the markets and fairs, forbid Jewish stores to open in Christian sections of the city. Then came pogroms, which were everywhere of one pattern and purpose—not so much to kill as to make the lives of the Jews so miserable that they would flee in great numbers. Emigration of Jews was the objective not only of these governments but of numerous elements of the populations, especially those competing with Jewish businessmen. The members of the professional classes, particularly doctors and jurists, led the anti-Semitic agitation that more and more spread over the countries of Eastern Europe; behind them were the merchants; then followed the manual laborers and the youth of all strata, including the peasantry, who had received a modern education.

Thus was created the inferno in which the majority of European Jews lived from 1925 to 1939. With Hitler's rise to power all these governments became either entirely or partly Fascist and therefore more arrogant and aggressive in their anti-Semitic policies. Naturally, that element of the general population which was in the anti-Semitic vanguard until 1933 grew even more violent. In those prewar years Jews did try to find some corner in the world where they might live in peace, but, as is well known, they were not very successful.

What we have tried to describe is that "normal" conditions compelled European Jewry to emigrate in order to survive. To dwell on the result of Hitler's triumph in Germany and the occupied countries in superfluous. Even in Jewish life this is an unprecedented experience; strictly speaking, such a chapter is not of immediate concern.

4. THE EXTENT OF JEWISH MIGRATIONS IN THE NINETEENTH AND TWENTIETH CENTURY AND THE DIVISION OF THE MIGRANTS ACCORDING TO COUNTRIES OF IMMIGRATION

If one wishes to visualize the extent of Jewish migrations in the past hundred years, one must go to the countries to which the immigrants went, for the information about the respective emigrant peoples was, up to the present, scanty. Unfortunately we do not possess official data on the dispersal of immigrants, according to religion, for the whole century. In the United States the rubric "Hebrew" was adopted only in 1899; for Palestine we have official data from 1919, for Canada from 1925; and there is information also for a few small countries, such as South Africa and Australia. These official data include, however, about 70 per cent of all Jewish emigrants. If to the official sources we add the data of ICA on the South American countries and of the philanthropic organizations of the United States on the years until 1899, we get sufficient correct data for over 90 per cent of the Jewish migrants of the past century. For the other countries, the only alternative is a rough estimate.

Tables 3A and 3B give us the total of Jewish migrations for one hundred and two years, in absolute and relative figures. One must remember that until 1914 migration was determined exclusively by the free will of the

TABLE 3A

Jewish Migrants According to Countries of Immigration
1840–1942
Absolute Numbers

Years	U.S.	Canada	Argentina	Brazil	Uruguay	Other Countries of America	South Africa	Palestine	All Other Countries	Total
1840–1880	200,000	1,600	2,000	500	——	1,000	4,000	10,000	2,000	221,000
1881–1900	675,000	10,500	25,000	1,000	——	1,000	23,000	25,000	4,000	764,500
1901–1914	1,346,400	95,300	87,614	8,750	——	3,000	21,377	30,000	10,000	1,602,441
1915–1920	76,450	10,450	3,503	2,000	1,000	5,000	907	−15,000	5,000	89,310
1921–1925	280,283	14,400	39,713	7,139	3,000	7,000	4,630	60,765	10,000	426,930
1926–1930	54,998	15,300	33,721	22,296	6,370	10,000	10,044	10,179	10,000	172,908
1931–1935	17,986	4,200	12,700	13,075	3,280	15,000	4,507	147,502	20,000	238,250
1936–1939	79,819	900	14,789	10,600	7,677	15,000	5,300	75,510	60,000	269,595
1940–1942	70,954	800	4,500	6,000	1,000	2,000	2,000	35,000	10,000	131,954
1840–1942	2,801,890	153,150	223,540	71,360	22,327	59,000	75,765	378,956	131,000	3,916,988

Jewish Migrants According to Countries of Immigration
1840–1942
Relative Numbers

Years	U.S.	Canada	Argentina	Brazil	Uruguay	Other Countries of America	South Africa	Palestine	All Other Countries	Total
1840–1880	90.5	0.7	0.9	0.2	—	0.5	1.8	4.5	0.9	100.0
1881–1900	88.4	1.3	3.3	0.1	—	0.1	3.0	3.3	0.5	100.0
1901–1914	84.0	5.9	5.5	0.5	—	0.2	1.4	1.9	0.6	100.0
1915–1920	85.6	11.7	3.8	2.2	1.1	5.6	1.0	−16.6	5.6	100.0
1921–1925	65.6	3.4	9.3	1.7	0.7	1.7	1.2	14.0	2.4	100.0
1926–1930	31.7	8.9	19.5	12.9	3.7	5.8	5.8	5.9	5.8	100.0
1931–1935	7.6	1.8	5.4	5.5	1.4	6.3	1.9	61.7	8.4	100.0
1936–1939	29.7	0.3	5.4	3.9	2.8	5.5	2.0	28.1	22.3	100.0
1940–1942	53.7	0.4	3.3	4.6	0.7	1.5	1.5	26.6	7.7	100.0
Total	71.5	3.9	5.7	1.8	0.6	1.5	1.9	9.7	3.4	100.0

TABLE 4.　*Average Yearly Migration in Various Periods*

Years	Average Migration
1840-1880	5,393
1881-1900	38,225
1901-1914	114,460
1915-1920	14,885
1921-1925	85,386
1926-1930	34,551
1931-1935	47,650
1936-1939	67,400
1940-1942	43,985
1840-1942	38,029

emigrants and by the laws of the countries of origin. One may say that until 1914 there were no limitations on emigration; even in Russia, where travel out of the country was forbidden and entailed many formalities and difficulties, in actuality the Jewish population was openly and freely allowed to organize and plan emigration. Fortunately also only few and exceptional persons—the sick, criminal, anarchist, and such—were denied admission to the countries immigrants flocked to. Consequently the data of the Jewish emigration until 1914 reflect more or less accurately the emigration needs of Jews. And this was the yearly average:

1840 to 1880	5,393
1881 to 1900	38,225
1901 to 1914	114,460

Such were Jewish migrations under free conditions. Obviously, to understand such migrations fully one must remember that the countries to which immigrants came were at the same time experiencing an economic growth. Now, from the first period to the second, Jewish immigration increased sevenfold while at the beginning of the present century it increased threefold in the short interval of fourteen years. The war years do not enter into our account; the 15,000 emigrants per year indicated merely that the Jewish need even in the dangerous war years was so great that Jews hazarded everything in order to escape the European Gehenna. No sooner was the war over than Jewish emigration spiraled upward—in 1921 into the United States alone came close to 120,000 Jewish immigrants. If we include immigration into Palestine and South America the figure, for the first normal year after the war, is over 150,000. Had it not been for the quotas that were soon enacted, Jewish immigration in the postwar era would have risen higher and higher.

Nevertheless, Table 4, reveals that from 1921 to 1925 there was an average emigration of over 85,000 per year. The fact is that the tragic halt to migrations did not take place before the adoption in 1925 of the second quota system. It was directed principally against East European countries whence came 95 per cent of the immigrants.

From 1926 to 1930 emigration dropped from the more than 150,000 of the year after the war and from the yearly average of over 85,000 during the first five normal years, to less than 35,000 per annum. But despite the crisis in the Americas and the high restrictions that the consulates of all countries established, the Jewish masses, driven to a new low of insecurity by economic persecution and physical attacks, swept aside all migration barriers and penetrated into the remotest corners of the world, particularly into Palestine—a country unprepared economically for a mass immigration, but the land of Jewish dreamers nonetheless. Gradually it received the greatest number of Jewish immigrants, surpassing even the United States.

This is clear to us from Table 3B, which furnished the relative numbers of the different countries. The United States, which, until the end of the nineteenth century took about 90 per cent of all Jewish emigrants, admitted less than 8 per cent from 1931 to 1935—fewer than 4,000 immigrants yearly. In the same five years Palestine admitted an average of 30,000 annually and almost two-thirds of all Jewish immigrants.

Tables 3A and 3B give us a clear picture of the role of the various countries in Jewish migration. Of about four million Jewish emigrants, the United States received more than two-thirds, 71.5 per cent; next comes Palestine, which in the entire period received close to one-tenth (9.7 per cent); third is Argentina, with over 5 per cent of all Jewish migrants. The other countries admitted only small numbers of Jews.

Within larger limits of time, the picture is even more striking. Contrast, for example, Palestine with the United States. We have used round numbers for the sake of convenience.

Years	Total Jewish Migration	Immigration into the U. S.		Immigration into Palestine	
		Absolute	Per Cent	Absolute	Per Cent
1840-1900	985,000	875,000	88.8	35,000	3.6
1901-1925	2,119,000	1,703,000	80.4	76,000	3.6
1926-1942	813,000	224,000	27.5	268,000	33.0
1840-1942	3,917,000	2,802,000	71.5	379,000	9.7

Here we see the development more strikingly. In the past years the United States has taken second place to Palestine in respect to Jewish immigration. In the most tragic years of Jewish history, from 1926 to 1942, the United States admitted only 224,000 Jewish immigrants, only

27.5 per cent of all Jewish immigration, while Palestine admitted 268,000, 33 per cent.

Of great interest is the range of Jewish immigrant dispersion. Here is a table of Jewish immigration into all countries besides the United States, Palestine, Canada, and Argentina:

	Absolute Numbers	Per Cent
1840-1900	36,000	3.6
1901-1925	89,000	4.2
1926-1942	234,000	28.8
1840-1942	359,000	9.2

In general, in over a hundred years, 359,000, less than a tenth of all Jewish emigrants, scattered to tens of countries. Within certain periods, however, the situation is even more tragic. In the sixteen years from 1926 to 1942 more than 28 per cent of all Jewish migrants were dispersed in tens of countries where no firmly established Jewish communities existed.

For a more thorough understanding of the character of the mass of Jewish immigrants, we must analyze all available data on the various countries. Inasmuch as 80 per cent of all Jewish immigration of the past hundred years was taken care of by the United States and Palestine, we shall study carefully the characteristic streams of immigrants into these two countries.

5. THE CHARACTER OF THE JEWISH IMMIGRANT MASS IN THE UNITED STATES

A. JEWISH IMMIGRATION INTO THE UNITED STATES IN THE NINETEENTH CENTURY

Jewish immigration into the United States may be divided into two large periods for a purely technical reason: we possess official and exact information only for the twentieth century. For the earlier period we are obliged to be satisfied with private sources, and therefore with much sparser content.

Nineteenth-century immigration into the United States was made up of two basic streams: (1) the German Jewish, from about 1820-1825 to 1870; it moved slowly and was never very large until 1880, when it was almost completely stopped, though a few businessmen continued to come occasionally for commercial purposes; (2) the East European Jewish, which began a little later than the German; it grew intensive in the middle of the century and immediately after the first large wave of Russian pogroms in 1881 and 1882 developed into a great mass movement.

The tempo of immigration of both German and East European Jews can best be gauged by the rise of the Jewish communities in the States.

The famous traveler, J. J. Benjamin, who traveled through the States in the fifties, lists the founding dates of fifty congregations. The following tables, which we have drawn up, will give the information at a glance.

Year in Which Congregation Was Founded	German Jewish	Polish Jewish	Portuguese Jewish	Others	Total
1730	—	—	1	—	1
1782	—	—	1	—	1
1791	—	—	1	—	1
1802	1	—	—	—	1
1819	—	1	—	—	1
1823	1	—	—	—	1
1828	1	—	—	—	1
1830	1	1	—	—	2
1840	2	1	—	—	3
1841	2	—	—	—	2
1843	1	—	—	—	1
1845	1	—	—	1	2
1846	—	2	—	1	3
1847	1	—	1	—	2
1848	1	—	2	1	4
1849	2	1	—	1	4
1850	2	2	—	—	4
1851	1	1	—	—	2
1852	1	2	—	1	4
1853	1	1	—	2	4
1854	—	—	—	2	2
1855	—	1	—	—	1
1856	—	—	1	—	1
1858	—	1	—	—	1
1859	—	—	—	1	1
	19	14	7	10	50

Here we have in dry figures the tempo of immigration of different groups of Jews. One must not forget that a congregation is not founded by a negligible number of people or heads of families; often it is not founded even when there is the minimum required to create institutions. A cemetery alone—the first thing Jews generally acquire to begin their communal life—does not yet make a congregation. In the eighteenth century only three congregations were founded, all of the Portuguese ritual. But this does not mean that over the country there were not individual or tens of German Jews, even Polish Jews. All it means is that these had thus far not organized into a community. The first German

Jewish congregation was founded in 1802 and the first Polish Jewish congregation in 1819. It is safe to say that this is the time difference that separates the German from the Polish Jewish mass immigration (by "Polish Jewish" we mean all East European Jews). Further, this was the development:

> 1820 to 1830,   4 congregations, of which   3 were German and 1 Polish
> 1831 to 1840,   3 congregations, of which   2 were German and 1 Polish
> 1841 to 1850, 22 congregations, of which 10 were German and 5 Polish
> 1851 to 1859, 16 congregations, of which   3 were German and 6 Polish

The greatest number of congregations of the German ritual were founded between 1841 and 1850. Evidently, then, in the preceding ten or twenty years there had taken place an intensive immigration, and by this time the immigrants had been sufficiently rooted to establish communities. Between 1851 and 1859, however, more congregations of the Polish than of the German ritual were already founded—evidence that in several cities there were enough Polish Jews to found a congregation of their own. And in those last eight years there were founded six "other" congregations, of Hungarian and Bohemian Jews.

Despite the fact, therefore, that the first important period of Jewish migration into the United States was German in character, it is well to remember that other elements also were then present. This is particularly so in the years between 1860 and 1881, when a good many East European, Hungarian and Bohemian Jews arrived. These may even have outnumbered the German Jewish immigrants. Already in 1869, at a conference in Berlin called by the *Alliance Israélite*, the question of East European Jewish immigration was taken up, with particular attention paid to the Jews of Kovno, where a famine was raging. From 1870 on, East European Jews came to the States in ever-increasing numbers, and their great migration should perhaps be dated from then rather than from 1881. This is the record according to the official data of the United States:

Years	From Russia and Poland	From Austria-Hungary
1820-1870	7,550	7,800
1871-1880	52,254	72,969
1881-1890	265,088	353,719

According to official Austrian data from 1881 to 1890, the Jewish emigrants from Galicia constituted 59.7 per cent of the total emigration. In the emigration from Poland and Russia the percentage of Jews was still higher.

On the basis of various calculations, we have reached the conclusions that in general, during the nineteenth century, approximately 850,000 to 900,000 Jews entered the United States. Of these about 750,000–700,000 at the least—were from Eastern Europe and about 150,000 from Germany and the German portion of Austria.

In comparison with the total immigration into the United States, the Jewish immigration was approximately as follows:

1820 to 1870	0.4 per cent
1871 to 1880	2.5 per cent
1881 to 1890	3.8 per cent
1891 to 1900	10.8 per cent

In the first fifty years Jewish immigration constituted less than one-half of one per cent of the total immigration. These were the years of the great migration from western and northern Europe—from England, France, the Scandinavian countries, etc. The percentage of Jewish immigrants rose continually in the last thirty years of the century, until at the end it represented almost 11 per cent of the total immigration. This was the highest percentage point of Jewish immigration. Here it remained, with rare exceptions which we shall discuss below, in the twentieth century.

From the material published in the German Jewish press we get a clear picture of the nature of Jewish emigration from Germany.

For example, the *Israelitische Annalen* (Frankfort) of 1839 (pages 213-214) presents in German the following very interesting and characteristic description of an emigrant group:

Until now we often read reports about Jews emigrating from Bavaria (our neighbor) to the Free States of North America. Now I have something similar to tell you about a community of Royal Wuerttemberg, although the causes and conditions are different.

On Sunday, June the 16th, fifty souls of the Mosaic faith (some of whom were young people who had already started a few weeks ago), left Ebenhausen (a parish eight hours from Stuttgart) to emigrate to the United States of North America.

A large crowd of bystanders had come from far and near, for the leave-taking. There was no eye without tears, all hearts were filled with sorrow, for this time it was not only the young, but fathers of families, women and children. It was really touching and heart-breaking when an old man of eighty (out of whose twelve children eleven will have emigrated), said good-bye to three of his children and fourteen grandchildren, the youngest of whom was two months old.

The cause of this strange happening in Wuerttemberg is partly that, for the past thirty years, many people had left this place to go to the United States, where they found free work and made a good living; those people invited their relatives (who had stayed behind), provided them with the neces-

sary travelling expenses and prepared everything for their arrival across
the ocean.

The religious community here counts 500 Jews. As the number of the
emigrants has grown to be ninety-two souls, this makes one-fifth of the community; it is a situation which presents palpable gaps.

This quotation is rich in content. First, it tells us that for thirty years
Jews had already emigrated from Wuerttemberg. So, too, we learn that
no less than a fifth of the Wuerttemberg population had already migrated
to America, and this in 1839, before the emigration of German Jews became intensive. Our correspondent also tells us that the pioneers of this
emigration did remarkably well in the United States; and they invite relatives and friends and take care of their needs even before the latter arrive
at their new destination. Clearly, then, there were some who did not possess enough for expenses. This is well corroborated by the famous Dr.
Lillienthal, who wrote in the *Allgemeine Zeitung des Judentums* of 1847
(page 24):

We have in this city [New York] a great number of retail merchants who
own business concerns which amount to 100 or 200 thousand dollars—and
these people, upon their arrival six years ago, had not a penny in their
pockets. They first carried 100 to 120 pound packs on their backs all day,
in order to earn a trifle. When they had already earned this "trifle," they
began to peddle goods with horse and buggy. Later they opened small stores
in the villages and now they have concerns in New York which are regarded
highly by all and which have good credit.

The social-economic background of the Jewish emigrants from Germany
is difficult to determine, but there is no doubt that the large majority came
from the commercial class—German Jewry had few artisans. In Prussia,
no more than 7 to 8 per cent of the Jews were artisans; in Posen, about 15
per cent; and in other parts of Germany there were fewer than in Prussia.
Among the emigrants from Germany after the revolution of 1848 there
was already no small number of Jewish intellectuals, but a really great
percentage could not have been educated, for there were not yet many
Jewish professionals in Germany then.

We have a bit more information about the emigrants from Eastern
Europe in the nineteenth century. The minimum of 700,000 Jews who
entered the United States may be divided, according to period, as follows:

1820 to 1870	30,000
1871 to 1880	70,000
1881 to 1890	200,000
1891 to 1900	400,000
Total 1820 to 1900	700,000

Whoever is at all acquainted with the East European scene will agree that, both economically and politically, conditions, in the last ten years of the century, were better than in the entire period from 1820 to 1870; yet in the decade from 1890 to 1900 thirteen times as many Jews as in the fifty years from 1820 to 1870 emigrated. We have already explained this phenomenon: (1) only in the second half of the nineteenth century did the Jewish masses shake off their lethargy and go off in search of better living conditions; (2) the first immigrants were now subsidizing the later emigration.

According to countries of origin, this is how the immigrants into the United States are roughly divided:

From Russia and Congress Poland	72.0 per cent
From Galicia and Hungary	23.0 per cent
From Rumania	3.5 per cent
From South European Countries	1.5 per cent
Total	100 per cent

Already in the closing years of the nineteenth century Jewish immigration into the United States meant not an individual but a family migration, with the intent to settle permanently in the new country. This was the percentage of women:

1886-1888	37.1
1889-1896	44.0

The percentage of children was as follows:

1886-1888	27.9
1896-1898	44.0

Among these East European immigrants the percentage of artisans was certainly higher than among the immigrants from Germany, but even among the former this percentage was not so high as it was to be later, in the twentieth century. The first large wave of East European Jewish immigration included very many vocationless elements, without craft or trade to their name. Here is what one immigrant of the 1880's, who had lived among the masses all his life, had to say:

Happy were they who knew a trade in the old country. The tailors, the joiners and other artisans would obtain employment very quickly. But the bulk of the Jewish immigrants had no vocation.[11]

And there is hardly an exaggeration to the picture which Dr. Hoffman presents in his history of the cloak operators union:

Former Yeshiva students, sales clerks, insurance agents, semi-intellectuals, teachers, bookkeepers, sons-in-law of the well-to-do, storekeepers, merchants, etc., became cloak operators.[12]

We can therefore say that socially the East European Jewish immigration was made up of an enormous vocationless lower middle-class mass, of approximately 25 per cent handworkers, and of altogether common people, porters, wagoners, peddlers, and the like. The percentage of intellectuals was negligible; its influence, however, was great. But we must also remember that among the vocationless lower middle-class mass there were quite a few who had attended not only a good *heder*, where they already studied Talmud, but also a *Yeshiva*. Although this group was without knowledge of worldly matters, it adjusted itself quickly to the new environment and culture, and very quickly, too, learned to speak English. And this group of educated Jews, with talmudic acuteness and Jewish energy, soon began to produce modern intellectuals who became the leaders of Jewish movements and the founders of Jewish institutions. Not a few likewise quit the Ghetto to take their place in the general cultural life of America.

B. JEWISH IMMIGRATION INTO THE UNITED STATES IN THE TWENTIETH CENTURY

Jewish immigration into the United States in the first forty-four years of this century was also made up of two principal streams, the East European and the German. With this difference, however: until 1933, 95 per cent of the Jewish immigrants from Europe were East European; some of course came via Germany and France, England, and Belgium; they may even have been registered as coming from these countries; but in fact they were East Europeans who stopped temporarily in those countries until their funds permitted them to go on. From 1933 on, however, German Jews predominated—at least they represented half of all Jewish immigrants. It is not that East European Jews gave up their wish to emigrate in these terrifying years. On the contrary, they would have given anything to emigrate from Poland, Rumania, Hungary, and the rest of Eastern Europe; but no country would admit them. In this respect the German Jews were fortunate: Germany had a high quota of over 27,000 immigrants per year, while Poland had a quota of only over 6,000, Rumania of barely 377, and Hungary of 869. But even these small quotas could not serve Jews exclusively, for non-Jews, too, were in flight from the Old World. According to law, the consul was not obliged to issue all available visas. The quota figure constituted the maximum at his disposal, and all consuls were dedicated to the proposition that "the more sparing the more praiseworthy."

For technical statistical reasons also we must divide these forty-four years into two periods. Until 1925 the immigration data present an accurate picture of the character of the immigrant mass, they provide us with the individual's sex and age as well as social and economic background. The subsequent data reflect quotas and privileged groups like clergymen, students, and others. In the distribution of visas altogether different factors begin to operate in 1938. Henceforth Jewish immigration becomes more a matter of sheer physical rescue than of economic need. A proper understanding of the normal character of the Jewish immigrant mass requires, therefore, an analysis of the official data up to 1925.

As already observed, Jewish immigrants arrived everywhere with the intent to settle permanently. This was especially true with regard to the United States, to which Jews came not only from Europe but also from other American countries. Yearly, for example, thousands of Jews come from Canada. This is confirmed by official figures from the year 1908 on.

From 1908 to 1925, 1,018,878 Jews entered the States and only 52,585 Jews emigrated, barely 5.2 per cent. Compare this Jewish remigration with the remigration of other European peoples (remigration, by the way, implies not only a departure of people but also the export of funds saved by the immigrant during his sojourn):

TABLE 5. *The Remigration of Various Peoples from the United States (1908-1925)*

Peoples	Absolute	Remigration Percentage Relative to Immigrants
Rumanians	65,554	67.0
Magyars	150,936	64.2
Italians	1,167,407	55.8
Russians	111,903	50.6
Poles	324,493	40.0
Lithuanians	35,513	25.4
Czechs	18,366	21.2
English	161,914	19.0
French	65,104	17.3
Ruthenians	29,124	16.7
Germans	125,738	15.3
Jews	52,585	5.2

Now note: in the case of four peoples, more than half the immigrants returned to their native land; the percentage of remigrants of two of these peoples reached two-thirds. Of six of the twelve peoples more than one-fourth of all immigrants returned. The highest percentage of remigrants are for the agrarian peoples: the role of the American dollar in the Italian or Hungarian village is sufficiently well known. Even one-sixth of the French and English remigrated—three times as much as Jewish remigration. Rumanian remigration was thirteen times as much, Magyar twelve times as much, Italian eleven times as much, and so on.

A serious factor of even greater weight than the export of funds saved is presented by remigration. There is considerable difference in mentality between the immigrant who, from the moment he boards ship on his way to a new country, resolves unqualifiedly to settle in his adopted land and to raise his children there and the immigrant who is ever contemplating return to his native land.

Especially striking in this connection are the data on remigration in the years just after the First World War. Poland, which became independent after the war, shall serve as a model. Polish Jews fought heroically and wholeheartedly for the liberation of Poland. Now, not only Poles and Jews lived in Poland but also Ukrainians. Let us therefore compare the remigration of the three peoples. Between 1919 and 1922 there returned from the United States to Poland:

Peoples	Absolute Numbers	Percentage Relative to Immigrants in the Same Year
Poles	89,959	369.5
Ukrainians	428	56.5
Jews	528	0.5

Truly eloquent figures. Almost four times as many Poles returned to Poland as came from Poland; more than half the number of Ukrainian immigrants went back to enjoy their status as a territorial minority in the resurrected Polish state. What about the Jews? Hardly one-half of one per cent relative to the number of immigrants chose to return to the resurrected Polish state! The pogroms even in liberated Poland during the honeymoon of liberation were hardly an inducement.

One more fact is particularly illuminating. During the critical years 1932-1935, when economic conditions in the United States were difficult and insecure, more people emigrated from than immigrated into the country—138,911. In other words, the natives of Europe were going home, although in the homelands, too, as we recall, livelihood was far from certain. But "there is no place like home," after all. In these very years, however, 13,911 Jews entered the States.

The permanent-settling character of Jewish immigration is corroborated also by the data on the sex and age range of the respective immigrants. Of every hundred immigrants from 1900 to 1925, the percentages of women were:

Jews .... 45.8 per cent
Non-Jews .... 32.9 per cent

The percentages of children under fourteen were:

Jews .... 25.3 per cent
Non-Jews .... 12.3 per cent

Very interesting, too, are the places to which the Jewish immigrant went. These were not always the same and a comparison between 1900 and 1925 reveals the distribution of Jews over the land during those twenty-five years, for one naturally goes to a place where he has relations or *landsleit* (countrymen).

At the beginning of the century hardly one-half of one per cent of all Jewish immigrants went to California and Michigan; in 1925 almost one-tenth went there. Seventy per cent of all Jewish immigrants used to go to New York; in 1925 only half went there. In the case of non-Jewish immigrants the same tendency prevailed, but not in the same proportion.

TABLE 6. *Destination of Jewish and Non-Jewish Immigrants (in Per Cent)*

People	New York	Philadelphia	California	Michigan
Jews:				
1900	70.0	9.7	0.1	0.4
1925	50.4	9.0	4.3	5.1
Non-Jews:				
1900	29.3	21.3	2.9	2.7
1925	21.7	6.3	8.1	8.9

And now for the most important point in the character of the Jewish migrant mass. A country may not only attract a large or small number of immigrants but also affect their professional status. This was certainly true of the United States, which not only absorbed tens of millions but in its melting pot converted huge masses of one profession into another. On the other hand, the majority of immigrants continued at their former occupations even in the New World. The Italian, Polish, Ukrainian peasant was attracted to husbandry or to the kind of labor with which he was more or less acquainted. The skilled German, English, or Swedish mechanic or technician sought employment in heavy industry. The Jewish tailor or cobbler looked for his opportunity in the ghettos of the city, where the manufacture of commonly used articles was concentrated. This has been true of the immigrants of the past fifty years, for American economy had by then been highly developed and the immigrant saw little pioneering to be done. He looked for the path of least economic resistance, for work which resembled what he had done in the Old World. Kinship and friendship also played their part in determining the occupation of the immigrant; and so, too, did United States demand for certain types of labor.

Concretely: (1) In Russia, which contributed more than two-thirds of all Jewish immigrants to the States during the first quarter of this century, a complete revolution in the occupational structure of the Jewish masses occurred in the last quarter of the nineteenth century. The transition from various middleman occupations to labor, especially to handicrafts, assumed mass proportions. This was especially true of the younger generation of the middle class; up to the age of fourteen or fifteen they studied in the small town *heder* and then went to Lodz, Warsaw, Odessa, Ekaterinoslav, Vilna, or Bialystok, to the workshop or factory to learn a trade. These small-town boys and girls formed a large percentage of the Jewish émigrés from Russia at the beginning of the century.

(2) Simultaneously, industry, and particularly the clothing industry, developed intensively. Here are some figures of the number of workers employed by the ladies' garment industry: 1879—25,192; 1899—83,739, more than three times the number twenty years earlier; 1919—165,649, the figure is again doubled, and it is seven times what it had been in 1879. These were the wages that the industry paid out: 1879—$6,661,000; 1919 —$195,296,000, thirty times the first amount. This extraordinary advance in wages, rumors of which penetrated into the ghettos of Russia, Poland, Rumania, Hungary, Lithuania, and Latvia, influenced not only experienced tailors to come to New York, where more than 90 per cent of the clothing factories were then located, but young Jews, too, children of the upper middle class. They now took sewing lessons to be equipped for America.

Let us now look at the occupational structure of the Jewish and non-Jewish immigrants.

TABLE 7. *Occupational Structure of the Jewish and Non-Jewish Gainfully Occupied Immigrants into the United States (1900-1925)*

	Jews		Non-Jews	
Occupational Groups	Absolute Numbers	Percentage	Absolute Numbers	Percentage
Industry	596,043	60.1	1,719,361	14.9
Commerce (Trade)	100,147	10.1	475,822	4.1
Husbandry	24,792	2.4	3,059,798	26.6
Liberal professions	19,620	2.0	261,033	2.3
Unskilled laborers	102,739	10.4	3,760,213	32.7
House servants	123,220	12.4	1,779,218	15.4
Miscellaneous	25,769	2.6	456,111	4.0
Total	992,330	100.0	11,511,556	100.0

Almost two-thirds of all gainfully employed Jewish immigrants belonged to the industrial class, the highly productive class of immigrants. For non-Jews, this group comprised only one-seventh of all gainfully employed immigrants. The percentage of farming and unskilled labor among non-Jewish immigrants was the same as that among Jewish skilled labor. One-tenth of all Jewish and 4 per cent of non-Jewish immigrants were merchants. In general merchants comprise only a small proportion of Jewish immigration—Jews brought to America not only six times as many skilled workers as traders, but also more menial laborers and domestic servants.

Here is a table of the distribution of craftsmen according to branches of industry:

Clothing industry	362,642	60.8 per cent
Lumber and building	84,683	14.2
Metal work	46,336	7.8
Food industries	42,501	7.1
Jewelry and watchmaking	9,582	1.6
Printing	9,282	1.6
Leather workers	8,017	1.4
Miscellaneous	33,000	5.5
	596,043	100.0

The role of the Jewish immigrant mass in the general immigrant mass can be seen from the following table (1900-1925). In percentages Jews represented

Of the total immigrant mass	10.3
Of the industrial immigrants	25.8
Of the clothing workers	48.8
Of the wood workers	16.4
Of the metal workers	12.8
Of the food workers	12.8
Of jewelers and watchmakers	49.7
Of printing workers	34.1
Of the leather workers	41.4
Of shopkeepers and merchants	22.2
Of farm workers	0.8
Of the liberal professions	7.0
Of domestic servants	6.5

This table is instructive. It reveals that one-fourth of all immigrant and skilled industrial labor in the United States was brought by Jews. The many millions of non-Jewish immigrant farm workers and menial laborers became, in large measure, industrial workers because of the intensive development of industry; but for this development on their part the country had to expend energy and funds. Jews, on the other hand, arrived in large measure as industrial workers. For two crafts—tailoring and watchmaking —Jews brought almost half the immigrant craftsmen. Jews constitute less than one-fourth of immigrant merchants and shopkeepers, but more than a third of all printing workers and more than 40 per cent of all immigrant leather workers.

This distribution of the Jewish immigrant mass during the greatest Jewish immigration period not only makes clear what Jews went through in adjusting themselves to the New World and its opportunities, but also belies the widespread notion that immigrant Jews were mostly merchants and vocationless persons. The Jewish immigrant was a laborer, a skilled craftsman, capable not only of keeping himself employed and helping those who remained in the old country, but also of taking his place in industry, which was then in need of skilled labor.

Beginning with 1933 the social structure of the Jewish immigrants changed radically. The entire immigration was stamped with the features of the German Jew's social and economic character. The more than 75,000 gainfully employed Jews who immigrated into the United States from 1933 to 1943 were distributed occupationally as follows:

Trade	31,724	41.9 per cent
Skilled workers	20,798	27.5
Liberal professions	15,047	20.0
Maids and menial labor	4,848	6.4
Miscellaneous	3,180	4.2
Total	75,597	100.0

More than twice the number of those of the first quarter of the century are now in trade. The percentage of persons engaged in the liberal professions is three times what it was, and correspondingly there is a decrease in the percentages of skilled workers, now less than half of the former numbers.

It is still too early to determine the results of the immigration of over 15,000 Jewish intellectuals, hundreds of whom were first-rate scholars, scientists, and artists. In an editorial the *New York Times*, April 9, 1943, declared that in the future chronicle of World War II one of the most glorious pages will have to be devoted to the contribution of the many talented mathematicians who escaped from Germany prior to the war. The influence of tens and hundreds of talented and creative individuals will be manifest in the coming generation.

These are the occupations of over eleven thousand Jewish intellectuals who entered the United States from 1938 to 1943:

Physicians	2,693	24.0
Professors and teachers	1,470	13.0
Lawyers	1,306	11.7
Engineers	1,218	10.9
Clergy (rabbis)	487	4.3
Miscellaneous	4,047	36.1
Total	11,221	100.0

That the doctors were very useful to this country in the war years is beyond a doubt. The contribution also of first-class professors of medicine and world-renowned specialists in various branches of medicine to medical science in America is difficult to appraise. Among the approximately 1,500 Jewish scholars were tens, if not hundreds, of internationally famous mathematicians, philosophers, sociologists, economists, psychologists, natural scientists; their influence in American institutions of learning is already being felt and will be more apparent in later years. Among the more than four thousand various intellectuals there are many first-class writers, poets, actors, journalists, etc.

6. THE CHARACTER OF THE JEWISH IMMIGRATION TO PALESTINE[13a]

According to the table of migrations 379,000 Jews entered Palestine from 1840 to 1942. If we include the immigrants of 1943, 1944, and the first six months of 1945 the total rises to over 400,000. In 1943, 8,507 Jews arrived, 14,500 in 1944, and 8,000 by July, 1945. Since at the end of the First World War there were in Palestine no more than approximately 50,000 Jews, it is clear that more than four-fifths of all Jewish immigrants came in the past twenty-five years. This is the reverse of what occurred in the United States, where the largest number of Jewish immigrants arrived in the first fourteen years of this century.

All the figures given below about the character of Jewish immigration will not be in accord with the data of the above-mentioned table because we have taken the net immigration. The data on sex, age, as well as occupation in the old country, are included in the gross immigration figures, which are those registered by the Palestine immigration office. On the other hand, we have everywhere omitted the unknown rubric and have taken only the exact figures in order that the relative numbers shall correspond more nearly accurately.

Immigration into Palestine took on a mass character only after the First World War. Before that generally only a highly idealistic, ideologically committed element went there, namely, Zionists. The rest were ordinary folk seeking a livelihood, but also possessing a nostalgia for the Holy Land, with its ancient memories, and its rural life.

TABLE 8. *The Distribution of Immigrants into Palestine According to Country of Origin*
1919-1943

Countries	Immigrants Absolute Numbers	Percentage
Poland	139,756	42.2
Soviet Union	30,926	9.4
Germany	44,635	13.5
Rumania	18,737	5.6
Czechoslovakia	10,555	3.2
Lithuania	9,908	3.0
Yemen	9,813	3.0
Austria	9,772	3.0
United States	8,043	2.4
Greece	6,739	2.0
Iraq	5,842	1.8
Latvia	4,982	1.5
Turkey	3,929	1.2
Hungary	3,555	1.1
Miscellaneous	23,430	7.1
Total	330,622	100.0

TABLE 9. *Distribution of Illegal Immigrants According to Countries of Origin*

Countries	Immigrants Absolute Numbers	Percentage
Czechoslovakia	4,557	30.6
Poland	2,450	16.4
Austria	2,187	14.7
Germany	1,714	11.5
Rumania	1,318	8.7
Hungary	1,300	8.9
Bulgaria	769	5.2
Miscellaneous countries	460	3.1
Stateless	132	0.9
Total	14,887	100.0

To be sure, even in the past twenty-five years a goodly number of enthusiastic Zionists left for Palestine. But it is difficult to distinguish these from the large mass of immigrants. Although a majority of the illegal immigrants were young Zionists, illegal immigration became a mass movement only when remaining in one's native land proved even more terrible than sailing on the Black Sea and not being admitted into any port. This is easily seen from Table 9. Polish Jews, who, during normal migration, contributed (Table 8) over 42 per cent of all immigrants, were but little more than 16 per cent of the illegal immigrants. Czechoslovakians, on the other hand, who in normal migration were only slightly more than 3 per cent, constituted almost one-third of the illegal immigrants. The same is true of the Austrians: normally they represented only 3 per cent of the immigrants; among illegal immigrants they were almost 15 per cent.

There are figures in Table 8, however, which remind us that eight thousand and more immigrants went into Palestine from the United States. Considering that the United States was the land to which above all immigrants flocked, the land of which millions of Jews over the world dreamed, eight thousand is no small number.

From Table 8 we see that Palestine is really "a gathering place of the exiles." To it people have come from every corner of the world. Poland and Germany together contributed more than half the entire immigration. From Soviet Russia also came no small number of immigrants; one must remember, however, that this immigration occurred only in the first years after the Bolshevik revolution. Later emigration was prohibited and the prohibition stands to this day.

If we divide the immigrants into Palestine according to historic background, we get the following (in percentages):

Ashkenazim	88.8
Sephardim	5.1
Yemenites	2.9
Miscellaneous	3.2
Total	100.0

The percentage of women among Palestinian immigrants is similar to that of the immigrants into the States—from 1919 to 1942 it amounted to 47.6.

The age groups reveal that a markedly large percentage of young and middle-aged people went to Palestine, in other words, the most able workers and the most productive element of the Jewish people. The following table tells the story for the period from 1919 to 1942:

0 to 9	10.7
10 to 20	21.7
21 to 35	41.8
36 to 50	12.8
51 and over	13.0
Total	100.0

Almost three-fourths of all the immigrants are younger than thirty-five and all of 87 per cent are younger than fifty.

The data on the percentage of women and children among the illegal immigrants testify to the pressure to emigrate and to their choice of Palestine: 33.9 per cent of all illegal immigrants were women and 7.2 per cent, or 1,116, were children under sixteen. When the sword is at your throat you risk everything. Under such circumstances Jews fled from Europe to Palestine. They sought refuge in other countries, too; in these, however, they were not only refused admittance, but it was unthinkable to seek admittance forcibly. Yet this was done in Palestine and several tens of thousands of Jews were thus rescued from the Hitler massacre. Of course, there were many tragedies—the *Struma* with her 700 Jewish passengers drowned, the *Patria* with her 250 passengers drowned, the 1,585 illegal immigrants mercilessly packed off by the English to the island of Mauritius, where they languished for almost five years, from November, 1940, to August, 1945, and many others. Nevertheless, the number rescued is much greater than those sacrificed—who would have suffered far more in the Hitler Gehenna than on the waves of the sea.

The uniqueness of the Palestinian immigrants is even more strikingly brought out by their occupational distribution. The fact that during these years at least several tens of thousands *halutzim* entered Palestine—young people trained especially for agriculture or physical labor of various kinds —itself put a special stamp on the social structure of the immigrants. But even among the immigrants of the recent war years who were running for their lives the percentage of workers was higher than among immigrants into other countries.

TABLE 10. *Distribution of Gainfully Occupied Immigrants According to Their Occupations in Their Native Countries*

Occupation	Absolute Numbers	Percentage
Industry and crafts	38,066	33.0
Building and unskilled labor	23,618	20.5
Agriculture	19,075	16.5
Trade	15,114	13.1
Liberal professions	11,300	9.8
Officials (or executives)	4,364	3.8
Religious leaders	1,906	1.6
Transport workers	1,318	1.1
Miscellaneous	657	0.6
Total	115,418	100.0

The higher percentage (16.5) of those engaged in agriculture—seven times what it is among the immigrants into the United States—strikes one immediately. In addition, one must take into account the fact that in the past ten years the proportion of German and Austrian Jews among the im-

migrants was great, and that in the last five years almost all of the pre-
paratory training in the Diaspora for work in Palestine was all but halted.
Only 13.1 per cent were engaged in trade, almost half of what it was
among the immigrants into the States. The percentage (9.8) in the liberal
professions is high, five times that among the immigrants into the States
during the first quarter of the current century; but it will probably not be
higher than the percentage of United States immigrants in the liberal
professions from 1932 to 1943.

We also possess trustworthy knowledge of the amount of private capital
which Jews managed to rescue in the five war years (1940-1944). In these
years Jewish immigrants brought into Palestine £21,450,000, or over
$85,000,000. The national capital brought into Palestine during the same
period was £12,000,000, or $48,000,000. Private capital, therefore, is al-
most twice as much as public capital. Estimates were also made of the capital
which the refugees brought into the States from the beginning of the war
until 1944. These estimates ran between $800,000,000 and a billion dollars;
but in this figure is also included the wealth of Christian refugees from
France, Belgium, Holland, Norway, and other countries.

7. JEWISH POSTWAR MIGRATIONS AND IMMIGRATION TO PALESTINE*

A. THE IMPETUS FOR THE EMIGRATION TO PALESTINE

With Hitler's death the counting of Jewish victims began and the entire
Jewish people, in all its subdivisions and classes, in all its torn and even
estranged branches, experienced a shock whose effects will undoubtedly
be felt for generations to come.

East European Jewry, the most intensive carrier of all creative Jewish
movements and culture of the past century, lost three-quarters of its members, slaughtered. With them disappeared all the accumulated rich, religio-
ethnic heritage of about 1,000 years—a heritage which had spiritually
nourished the entire Jewish people in all its dispersion, whose deepest roots
probed the most intimate values of the Torah and the Talmud, while its
branches reached out to the most progressive and succulent fruits of idealistic
nineteenth-century European culture.

The European refugees who fervently dreamed of escaping the Vale
of Tears, of leaving the unholy earth saturated with Jewish blood, faced
closed gates in the countries richest in land. And to make the tragedy of
the landless all the more heartrending, the gates of the historic homeland,
the object of Jewish dreams for 2,000 years, were barred even tighter in
the very years of greatest despair. The few admitted from refugee

* This section was written for the present third edition. The first six sections, including
the tables, have been reprinted from the plates of the first edition, 1949.

masses of the D.P. camps served only to emphasize the tragedy of a people
without a home, without its own soil and sky.

In this tragic moment of Jewish existence the historical strength of
Creative Despair, which had often saved the Jewish people from complete
destruction, again revealed itself.

Actually there was a conjunction of two desperate factors in Jewish
destiny. On the one hand, hundreds of thousands of Jews were seized
with a burning desire to leave Europe as soon as possible. These despairing
remnants—parents without children and children without parents, husbands
without wives and wives without husbands, thousands upon thousands of
lone souls, individuals without a relative and without a redeemer anywhere
in Europe—all these dreamed a single dream: to leave the bloody soil of
Europe as soon as they could. Becoming aware, as never before, of the
orphan status of the Jewish people, its homelessness and landlessness, these
masses were prepared to make the greatest sacrifices in the struggle for a
home for the Jewish people—for Eretz Yisrael.

On the other hand, the Jewish *Yishuv* in Palestine, in which so much
Jewish material and, particularly, spiritual effort had been invested, and
which represented the profoundest and most sacred historic aspirations and
dreams of the Jewish group, was facing a dilemma: now or never! Either
the Jewish community was to become a majority in the country, achieve
statehood, and proceed with that salvation which was the heart and the
core of Zionism; or else the Jewish community was to submit to the satanic
power that was making light of the tragedy of an entire people, and remain a minority in the ancestral home, face to face with a majority which
was increasing in numbers, growing politically, and culturally approaching
a ruling position. All the invested stores of energy—physical, material, cultural, and spiritual—would then be lost; all the hopes and aspirations of
a millennium, all the prayers and dreams would be exploded. The Jewish
people would face the darkest moment of its history, without that historical
faith in redemption which has always protected its continuity, the amulet
of survival and continuity in its long, dark Diaspora.

These two historical elements of despair—filled with mighty explosives,
yet also with rich creative powers and aspirations; with profound disappointment in other nations, yet with deep faith in its own people, in its
powers and in its aims—these two elements crossfertilized and strengthened,
complemented and enriched one another. The *ha'apalah,* the "illegal" immigration, was organically turned into the last embittered fight for Palestine, for free immigration which would give every Jew the right to enter
the country.

Despite the terrible tragedy of Europe, whose children had built the
flourishing countries of America, the gates of those very countries were
not open to the war-torn people struggling to escape the European hell.

Surveys even in Holland and Belgium disclosed that between 25 and 30 per cent of the total population hoped to emigrate. Even more difficult was the status of the Jews. The cracks through which Jewish migration was possible were even smaller or nonexistent. All immigration privileges for refugees, except in the United States, were made narrower and more meager for Jews. This meant that the people that had suffered most during Hitler's slaughter had small use of the privileges offered European D.P.'s.

By the middle of 1948 for over 1,500,000 Jews emigration from Europe and Asia-Africa was not merely a matter of economic or political preference, but a vital need, if not a matter of life and death. In those East European countries occupied by Hitler during the Second World War where the local population had played an active role in the massacres of Jews, the returning remnants were met with such vicious hatred that the Jews began to flee in such haste that the boundary officials of Poland or Rumania, for example, in the ensuing confusion "illegally" let out tens of thousands of Jews.

The Kielce pogrom (Poland, July, 1946) was a warning to all East European Jews that not only were their former economic positions occupied, their property, houses and stores, community buildings, and social institutions divided among the non-Jewish population, but they themselves were not wanted.

This pogrom, in a country which was the burial ground for millions of Jews from all the countries of Europe, demonstrates the atmosphere the Jews encountered in Poland, and to a lesser degree in Rumania and Hungary, after the war.

The following quotation is from a report by a Communist who undoubtedly tended to understate the tragedy, for Communists were preaching that staying put to build communism was the proper thing to do.

This was not a night, but rather the day of the long knife. I saw the survivors, was in the Lodz hospital. I looked into their faces that were like minced meat. Not merely to kill the Jews was their intent, but to torture them. "Shoot me. I can't stand it any longer," Joseph Feingold pleaded with the crowd. "No! We won't shoot. Suffer, suffer in agony, accursed Jew!" was the reply. It was a craze for torture, an almost mystical blood-dance of murder, a holy cult of cruelty.

Thus wrote the Communist, B. Mark, in 1946 (*Dos naye lebn*, Lodz, July 12, 1946) and in December, 1956, there was a speech by the Polish Under Secretary of the Interior in which, according to the Yiddish Communist newspaper of Poland, *Folks-shtime* (December 1, 1956), he said:

We are faced with a growth of clearly anti-Semitic acts. There are cases where Jewish children are persecuted by their Polish friends, and even by school teachers. There are instances of the firing of Jewish workers from their jobs. Especially alarming is the case of the murder of the Jewish worker, Khayim Gutkevitch, in Wroclaw.

Ten years after the return of most of the Polish Jews who had been exiled by the Soviet regime to the distant regions of Russian Asia, after ten years of communism, a Jewish worker is killed in the street, because he is a Jew.

The *New York Times* correspondent was right when he cabled on July 27, 1946, that the news of the pogrom in Kielce may have surprised the outside world, but in Poland it came as no surprise at all. We may add, nor was the murder of a Jew in Wroclaw ten years later, in 1956, a surprise, when there were not 200,000 Jews in Poland (as was the case in 1946) but only about 50,000.

The atmosphere in the remaining countries of Eastern Europe was perhaps not as strained, yet was antipathetic enough to produce feelings of anxiety and insecurity in the Jews.

We refrain from discussing the Communist regime as a factor which has in no small measure influenced, and continues to influence, the emigration mood among the Jewish masses.

At the same time, anti-Semitism was growing in the Arab countries bordering Palestine. The more evident it became that a Jewish State was approaching realization, the more dangerous and difficult became the situation in Iraq, Egypt, Syria, and Lebanon. Somewhat less strained, yet difficult, became the situation of the Jewish population in the Arab lands of Africa. There was, in fact, a pogrom in Morocco.

The flight from East European countries was not only to the camps of Germany, Austria, and Italy, but also to West European countries. The emigrants included those who had once lived in western Europe before being deported by Hitler's murderers to Poland or Germany, and those who had relatives living in western Europe who had escaped the Nazi claws. However, even these Jewish groups sought a way of fleeing Europe. The fears of the Hitler era deeply embedded in the majority of the Jews in western Europe, as well as the cold war which produced forebodings of another war, created—among large portions of the Jews in France, Belgium, and Holland, and to some extent among those in England—a mood of panic that drove many to pack their suitcases and search for a refuge far from Europe.

Let us now estimate the number of Jews living around 1948 in those countries from which they hoped speedily to emigrate. There were about 250,000 Jews in the camps of Germany, Austria, and Italy. In the countries under Communist regimes (Poland, Rumania, Hungary, Czechoslovakia, Bulgaria, and Yugoslavia), after large numbers had legally and even more had illegally escaped to the West European camps, there were about 500,000 Jews in 1948. If not all, then at least 90 per cent were anxious to emigrate. In the Arab countries of the Middle East (Iraq, Yemen, Syria, Lebanon, and Egypt) there were about 275,000 Jews, of whom the majority had to emigrate—"had to" and not "wanted to" because this was, in fact, the situation at the time. Finally, in the North African Arab countries, there were about 500,000 Jews, some exceedingly anxious to leave for political and economic reasons.

This mass of about 1,500,000 Jews, though not all to the same degree, was infected with the desire to emigrate, to move out. Certainly there were also aspirations for material well-being; yet the dominating desire, the most intimate dream, was to reach a haven. This was especially the case with the potential European emigrants, who had been through infernal tortures at Nazi hands, and who were either roaming the camps or were held captive in the Communist countries.

This tense situation for large numbers is without doubt one of the most important factors in the founding of the State of Israel and the intensive development of that much neglected and desolate land. The entire potential mass of migrants did not reach its goal, although many, many hundreds of thousands did escape from the unholy soil of Europe and the Asian and African lands where Jewish life was endangered. The mass migrations and regroupings have not only transformed Jewish life spatially, and thereby perhaps changed the destiny of Jews condemned to wander, but have also affected the status of the Jews as a nation. This revolutionary change was possible only because the Jewish people went from wanderings to *aliyah*, from search for cracks in the walls of foreign nations and for tolerance in foreign countries to its own land of salvation.

It goes without saying that the despair just described would not have led to creative and victorious results were it not for the foundation laid by the accumulation of constructive forces in the *Yishuv* and the Zionist organization.

B. THE NEW DISTRIBUTION OF THE JEWISH MIGRANTS (1946-1956)

We have just established that until about 1920 the United States received more than 80 per cent of all Jewish migrants. Until 1914 the United States percentage was close to 90 per cent of the total Jewish migrations. With the introduction of the quota system, the distribution of the Jewish migrants changed radically. Fate was apparently playing a mean trick on the Jewish people: the greater its need for emigrating from Europe, the main source of Jewish mass migrations, the narrower became the entrance to the land that for over half a century had been the main place of refuge for the Jewish masses escaping pogroms and political persecutions, poverty and untold misery.

Beginning with the middle 1920's, Jews were turning, on the one hand, more and more to their historic land, and, on the other, literally to all four corners of the earth. Not only did they flee to all Latin American countries (which possessed a natural attraction due to the proximity of the United States and to such local Jewish settlements as those in Argentina and Brazil) but also to Africa and Asia. However, the Latin American countries soon slammed shut their doors to immigrant Jews. Mass immigration to various desolate areas in Asia and Africa was out of the question. Palestine, later the State of Israel, became the refuge for the wandering Jewish masses.

It would, however, be false to interpret the large stream of Jewish immigrants to Palestine-Israel only through negative factors. Suffice it to mention the incident of the ship *Exodus* that achieved world-wide notoriety. The *Exodus* carried over 4,000 Jewish men and women, old and young, from German refugee camps. The British government did not allow the immigrants to disembark in Palestine. They were sent back to Europe. France permitted them to disembark, but not a soul accepted the hospitality of France. They were all taken back to the German camps. Yet absolutely all managed to reach Palestine. The last party of "illegal" immigrants in this group reached the shores of Haifa on May 14, 1948 (the very day of the Declaration of the State of Israel)!

It would be superfluous to dwell at this point on the *Bilu* or the *halutzim*. They were the founders of those basic settlements that made any immigration possible. When one turns to the huge numbers, the hundreds of thousands of immigrants of the very last years, however, socioeconomic and political conditions must also be taken into account.

TABLE 11. *Distribution of Jewish Migrants According to Country of Immigration (1840–1956)*

Years	Total Immigration	United States & Canada Absolute	Percentage	Palestine Absolute	Percentage	Other Countries Absolute	Percentage
1. 1840–1914	2,595,000	2,330,000	89.8	70,000	2.7	195,000	7.5
2. 1915–1947	1,520,000	690,000	45.4	435,000	28.6	395,000	26.0
3. 1948–1951	870,000	120,000	13.8	715,000	82.2	35,000	4.0
4. 1952–1953	60,000	20,000	33.3	35,000	58.3	5,000	8.4
5. 1954–1956	125,000	15,000	12.0	100,000	80.0	10,000	8.0
Totals	5,170,000	3,175,000	61.4	1,355,000	26.2	640,000	12.4

Table 11 tells, in unmistakable language, the history of the Jewish people over the past fateful hundred and some odd years. Whereas in 1840 there were only 4,500,000 Jews in the world, over 5,000,000 took to the road during the past 116 years. This transformation of the Jewish people through migration and massacre caused a radical change in the geographic distribution of the Jews. The central shift from eastern Europe to the American and Asian continents marks the beginning of a new chapter in Jewish history, consisting of two opposing tendencies: on the one hand, the United States with intensive assimilatory potential; on the other, the State of Israel with intensive nationalizing potential. The table vividly shows the shift of the dominant Jewish concentration process from the United States to Palestine. For over half a century—from 1840 to 1914— the United States and Canada received more than 90 per cent of all Jewish immigrants. The figures of the last three columns, from 1948 to 1956 indicate that Israel received 850,000 Jewish immigrants out of a total of 1,055,000, i.e., 80.6 per cent.

We cannot here discuss fully the assimilatory power of various environments. We shall restrict ourselves to a small table which pictures the three quantitatively largest centers. Russian Jewry comprised the greatest number until World War I. Today America is the largest and Israel the youngest center. A comparison of the figures yields a most interesting picture of the transformations that took place in Jewish life during the past 100 years or so.

TABLE 12. *The Decline and Rise of Jewish Centers in the Past Century*

	Number of Jews in					
	Russia-Poland[1]		United States		Palestine	
Year	Absolute	Percentage[2]	Absolute	Percentage[2]	Absolute	Percentage[2]
1850	2,800,000	62.2	50,000	1.1	10,000	0.2
1900	6,000,000	54.5	1,100,000	10.0	50,000	0.4
1939	6,300,000	38.3	4,700,000	28.1	450,000	4.1
1945	1,800,000	16.3	4,950,000	44.1	564,000	5.1
1955	2,000,000	16.6	5,250,000	43.8	1,590,000	13.3

[1] We have combined the two countries as the bulk of Poland belonged to Russia in the nineteenth century. Moreover, the cross-influences even with Galicia, which belonged to Austria, were intense.

[2] This column gives the percentage out of the total Jewish people. We have reckoned the number of Jews all over the world as follows: In 1850—4,500,000; in 1900—11,000,000; in 1939—16,450,000; in 1945—11,000,000; and in 1955—12,000,000.

Parallel to the post-World War I concentration in America and Palestine went an intensive process of dispersion over the wide world. It is evident from Table 11 that "other countries" received over one-fourth (26.0 per cent) of all Jewish migrants from 1915 to 1947. Dozens of countries were involved—Latin American states, Australia, the Union of South Africa, China, India, the Congo, Angola, and so forth. This process of scattering soon came to a halt. The large majority of the Jewish migrants became *olim* (i.e., went to Israel). Most recently (1956) 80 per cent of the Jewish migrants went to Israel.

In the past eleven years 1945-1956, about 200,000 Jews immigrated to the United States and Canada. There are exact figures only for Canada;

as far as the United States is concerned, recourse must be had to estimates based on reports by HIAS and the Joint Distribution Committee (as official records do not indicate religion). But estimates are close to the facts. Of the 200,000 immigrants within the past eleven years, roughly 40,000 have arrived in Canada and 160,000 in the United States. Inasmuch as nearly 2,000,000 immigrants reached the United States during this eleven-year period, Jewish immigration amounts to about 8 per cent of the total. This is the smallest percentage of Jewish immigrants for the past twenty-five years. It can be explained by the fact that the special laws permitting above-the-quota immigration were meant for the non-Jewish emigrants from Europe. Out of more than 1,000,000 immigrants to Canada for the same period, Jews comprise 40,000, or 4 per cent.

As regards the immigrants to Canada, we have data concerning the countries of emigration for the period of 1945 to 1954. As they are highly instructive we present them here.

TABLE 13.　*Jewish Immigrants in Canada According to Country of Emigration*
(1945-1954)

| | Number of Immigrants | |
Country	Absolute	Percentage
Poland	11,171	27.3
Israel	5,410	13.2
United States	5,193	12.7
England	4,832	11.8
Germany	2,295	5.6
Hungary	1,836	4.5
Czechoslovakia	1,775	4.3
Rumania	1,504	3.7
France	1,462	3.3
Austria	1,029	2.5
Belgium	868	2.1
China	472	1.2
Holland	391	1.0
South America	336	0.8
Miscellaneous	2,431	6.0
Totals	41,005	100.0

This table is interesting in many respects. I would, however, like to emphasize one important fact. The last line, which lists 2,431 immigrants under the column "miscellaneous," refers without doubt to at least a dozen countries. This serves as a good illustration of Jewish dispersion and of the regrouping that is taking place. It is also unquestionable that most of the immigrants to the United States would give a similarly checkered picture. They went, or rather fled, wherever they could. During the war years there were, for example, 20,000 Jews in Shanghai. It is probable that the 472 inhabitants of China that went to Canada were remnants of the Shanghai ghetto, which the Japanese had instituted on the German model. After the war, there was a regrouping. Some went looking for and found their relatives, while others went in search of better fortunes.

Of the various countries that received relatively large numbers of Jewish migrants, Australia and New Zealand accepted around 15,000 Jewish immigrants, i.e., one-half the number of their total Jewish population, in the years 1945-1956.

All twenty of the Latin American countries received not quite 30,000 Jewish immigrants in the years considered above. Even so, many immigrants were forced to resort to actual or pretended conversion. Late in 1956, Brazil promised to admit 1,000 families from North Africa.

South Africa was almost completely closed. The nationalist government that had been in power over the past eight years thought it had done its duty by keeping anti-Semitism in check. The government seemed to believe that it was favoring the existing Jewish population by restricting further immigration of Jews.

Let us turn to the immigration in Israel, which merits a more differentiated and detailed treatment, if only because Israel in the past years has received 80 per cent of all Jewish migrants. Fortunately, here we have copious material that depicts with clarity and in detail all sides of this immigration as a phenomenon that is playing a decisive and revolutionary role in the fate of the Jewish people.

C. THE NUMBER OF IMMIGRANTS TO PALESTINE AND THEIR DISTRIBUTION BY COUNTRY OF ORIGIN

We now turn to a topic which is a sensitive reflection of Jewish group life as a whole. Every detail is representative: the number of immigrants, their countries of origin, their sex and age distribution, their occupations, and many other questions to which we shall devote our study. Thanks to the first-rate material, the picture is clear and precise.

Table 14, divided into two large sections, offers a wealth of material about the geographic origin of the immigrants. This division is natural. The immigration until the founding of the state bore mainly a European stamp. True, it consisted of two very different types of immigrants— *halutzim*, who were not seeking material gains in the land of their ancestors but rather idealistic goals; and persecuted refugees, who fled to Palestine because all other immigration gates were closed or so nearly shut that not all were able to slip through. The latter included German Jewish immigration during the Hitler years. But we are not interested in the reasons for immigration to Israel for given cases, but rather in the physiognomy of the *Yishuv* during various periods.

TABLE 14. *Jewish Immigrants to Palestine by Country of Birth* (*1919-1955*)

Country of Birth	May 1919-1948	May 1948-1955
A. *Asia*		
1. Turkey	8,277	35,278
2. Iraq	7,994	124,896
3. Iran	3,536	27,660
4. Yemen	14,566	45,749
5. Aden	1,272	3,422
6. India	. . . . .	4,869
7. Miscellaneous	5,131	9,786
Total	40,776	251,660
B. *Africa*		
1. Tunisia, Algiers, Morocco	994	98,834
2. Libya	873	32,681
3. Union of South Africa	259	732
4. Miscellaneous	1,907	20,263
Total	4,033	152,510
C. *Europe*		
1. U.S.S.R.	52,350	8,455
2. Poland	170,127	107,787
3. Rumania	41,105	121,968
4. Bulgaria	7,057	38,413
5. Yugoslavia	1,944	7,778
6. Greece	8,767	2,336
7. Germany	52,951	8,692
8. Austria	7,748	2,796
9. Czechoslovakia	16,794	18,943
10. Hungary	10,342	15,056
11. England	1,574	2,240
12. Holland	1,208	1,368
13. France	1,637	3,460
14. Italy	1,554	1,411
15. Miscellaneous	2,329	2,192
Total	377,487	342,895
D. *America*		
1. U.S.A.	6,635	1,815
2. Canada	316	332
3. Argentina	238	1,926
4. Miscellaneous	318	1,589
Total	7,507	5,662
E. Australia and New Zealand	72	163
F. Unknown	22,283	18,807
General Totals	452,158	771,697

Immigration after the creation of the State of Israel took on a very different character. The Asian-African branch of Jewry assumed a major role; most recently it accounts for a majority of all immigrants.

To draw conclusions from Table 14 we must extract from it the pertinent proportions in more concentrated form. First let us take entire continents, on the premise that, no matter how varied the levels of culture in the fourteen countries in which Jews lived in Europe, the European continent represents a certain cultural physiognomy for its entire population. The same can be said in the case of every other continent. We shall return to a deeper and more detailed analysis later in the paper.

TABLE 15. *The Distribution of the Immigrants to Palestine by Continent*

Continent	May 1919-1948 Absolute	May 1919-1948 Percentage	May 1948-1955 Absolute	May 1948-1955 Percentage
1. Asia	40,776	9.5	251,660	33.4
2. Africa	4,033	0.9	152,510	20.3
3. Europe	377,487	87.9	342,895	45.5
4. America	7,507	1.7	5,662	0.8
5. Australia	72	0.0	163	
Total	429,875[1]	100.0	752,890[1]	100.0

[1] The total in this table does not coincide with the total in Table 14 because the "unknown" column is deleted here.

Table 15 makes it clear that in the first period of the creation of the state, the European Jewish inhabitants represented such a vast majority (87.9 per cent) that it is only natural that their stamp marks the foundations of the *Yishuv*. Europe is, to be sure, too broad a term, and we shall narrow the analysis as we go on. If we add to the European Jewish population that of the American, which of course also belongs to the European type of culture, the result is that almost 90 per cent of the old *Yishuv* was made up of European Jewry who offered the necessary physical, material, and cultural energy during the period when the utmost in idealism, resoluteness, and readiness for sacrifice was needed.

The picture of the second group of immigrants, of the immigrants after the founding of the state, is very different.

The European immigrants still made up 45 per cent of the total, and this constituted a relative majority. The other two groups, however—the Asian and African—which are close to one another with respect to both the culture of their immediate neighbors and the relative levels of their own cultures, made up the majority. It is self-evident that the face of the community had to change radically as a result of the immigration after creation of the state.

Let us broaden the analysis of the figures. After all, there are great differences between the Jewish communities of the various countries within each continent, for the general cultural level and the Jewish cultural equipment of the Russo-Polish Jews were not the same as that of the German and Austrian Jews. We now turn to the influence of each of the two principal groups during the first period of the *aliyah*: the East European and West European.

Out of 377,487 European immigrants from 1919 to May, 1948, the period in which the spiritual values of the *Yishuv* began to be formed, nearly 300,000, or over 80 per cent, came from Eastern Europe (Russia, Poland, Rumania, Hungary, and a part of Czechoslovakia). The second period (May, 1948-1955) gives us almost the same picture. The East European immigrants make up more than three-quarters of all the European immigrants.

One clear conclusion follows from this. Wherever one talks about the influence of any particular group, it must be borne in mind that the European immigrants were the first to build the material and spiritual foundations of the *Yishuv*. Moreover, "European immigrants" means, in effect, East European Jews, and in fact mainly the Russo-Polish Jews who were not merely the Guardians of the Walls of the Jewish faith but also the creators of the most modern Yiddish and Hebrew literature, and of both of those social movements that gave the *Yishuv* its particular social flavor.

During the second period of immigration, the Asian and African sectors together composed a majority of the total immigrating mass. This process of surpassing the European immigrants continues to increase. Most recently over 90 per cent of all immigrants have been non-European.

Thus, for example, out of a total of 23,475 immigrants in 1952, there were 16,751, or 71.4 per cent, from Asia and Africa, already quite a large proportion. In 1955, however, out of 36,303 immigrants, 33,736, or 93.0 per cent, were from Asia and Africa. In the first seven months of 1956, out of 30,229 immigrants, 28,321, or 93.7 per cent, were from Asia and Africa.

Although the Jewish inhabitants of Asia and Africa share many characteristics, they are perhaps even more differentiated than East versus West European Jews. They have in common their backwardness with respect to modern European culture, and the fact that they have missed the modern national-political development as Jews experienced by East European and, to a lesser degree and in a weaker form, West European Jewry. On the other hand, these Asians and Africans remained completely faithful to Jewish traditions and were hardly touched by the assimilation processes, which even national-minded East European Jewry had undergone. (We say "hardly" because North African Jewry, particularly Algerian Jewry, did undergo a process of French assimilation.)

Descriptions of Jewish life among the Yemenite Jews, the poorest both materially and with respect to secular culture, are reminiscent of the totally pious life led by Polish Jewry in the middle of the eighteenth century. The *Yishuv* is highly pleased with Yemenite Jewry because of its industriousness as well as its distinctive Jewish culture.

We have purposely taken as examples the most retarded of all—Yemenite—Jewry to show that the increase in the number of immigrants from the backward Asian and African countries need not be alarming. Not all the immigrants from these countries are backward to the same degree. Iraqi Jews, especially those from Bagdad, whose ancestry dates from the Babylonian Exile, had a large percentage of intelligentsia of the type found among East European Jewry, i.e., steeped in specifically Jewish learning, yet cognizant of secular culture as well. The Bagdad Jewish community had an excellent school system which covered all Jewish children of school age, in which not only Jewish but general course subjects were taught thoroughly.

We have discussed the make-up of the two large streams of immigrants. Now let us remember that in questions pertaining to culture it is not so much quantity as quality that is decisive. It is sufficient to glance at Israel's political leaders, and at the spiritual leadership forging the national character of the country, to be convinced that East European Jewry has been dominant.

However an additional factor must be kept in mind. Although the European and Asian-African immigrants undoubtedly play a large role in the life and development of the *Yishuv*, there is a third group which affects all the immigrants—the native-born generation made from the earth and the sky of the Land, whose spirit is reflected in their souls. For them Hebrew is the mother tongue; for them the country's mountains and valleys are hiking areas. This generation, which has displayed its heroism, may yet have the largest influence in the spiritual sphere. Let us now see how large this third factor is.

TABLE 16. *Population of Israel by Country of Birth (1948-1954)*

| | November, 1948 | | End of 1954 | |
Country of Birth	Absolute	Percentage	Absolute	Percentage
1. Israel	253,414	35.5	471,346	31.0
2. Europe and America	392,304	54.9	640,729	42.0
3. Asia and Africa	69,685	9.6	413,934	27.0
Total	715,403	100.0	1,526,009	100.0

The native born and the European immigrants together made up three-quarters of the total population even as late as the end of 1954. From 1948 to 1954, the native-born group declined by only 14 per cent of its previous size (i.e., by 4.5 per cent of the total population), although this was a period when the country received 750,000 immigrants. Natural increase among Israeli Jewry is very high. It comes to twenty-two to twenty-three per 1,000, almost three times as high as among American Jews, and twice as high as among Canadian Jews. If we add the number of native-born to those born in Europe and America, the two add up to as much as 73 per cent, while those born in Asia and Africa only come to 27 per cent, even as late as 1954.

The native-born generation is different—and will grow more so in the future—from the European-American types and especially from the Asian-African types. Nevertheless, it can be affirmed with certainty that it will be the European, and in particular the East European heritage, which will predominate in future. Anyone even but slightly familiar with the poetry and *belles-lettres* of the native-born writers is aware of the influence of European culture in its East European variety, which had organically amalgamated the general European culture with the basic roots of historic Jewry. Anyone cognizant of the directions taken by the most recent Israeli literature will certainly agree that the cultural and spiritual development of Israel is in the direction of the best ideals of European culture, imbued with and transformed by an organic blending of the Bible and the Talmud.

We now have considered the countries from which the immigrants stemmed. The sex and age distributions of the immigrants are highly interesting: the more men and the younger the population, the greater the physical working force and vice versa. Let us now proceed to study this question.

D. SEX AND AGE DISTRIBUTION OF THE IMMIGRANTS

Jewish migration is a family affair. Among non-Jewish migrants the percentage of men is much higher because a man very often migrates only to accumulate a little capital and then return home. The Jewish migrant usually pulls up his stakes when leaving a country. This is always true in the case of immigrants going home to Palestine, and whose sole dream is to become as deeply rooted as possible in the new-old land.

Out of 768,286 immigrants from May, 1948, to the close of 1955 whose sex distribution is known, there were 388,317 males and 379,969 females, i.e., 50.5 per cent and 49.5 per cent, respectively. It is self-evident that each of these intended to remain in the country and to build a new nest there.

Much more important is the question of age distribution. In the first place, the biological future of the population rests here. A higher percentage of children portends a bright biological future; a higher percentage of old people, a biological handicap. Children and old people are a heavy burden to a population, for they are incapable of working. A high percentage of people between the ages of fifteen and fifty-nine is very beneficial to the economy, for such age grouping contributes a high proportion of wage earners.

TABLE 17.   *The Age Distribution of the Immigrants to Israel (May 1948-1955)*

Age Groups	Absolute	Percentage
0–14	225,907	29.4
15–59	487,839	63.5
60–69	36,212	4.7
70 and over	18,323	2.4
Totals	768,281	100.0

This is a healthy distribution of age groups, It is, in general, similar to the age group distribution of Polish Jewry before World War II, considered a biologically normal and healthy community. The percentage of children is high; it is similar to that of pre-World War II Polish Jewry, and is about twice as high as that of German Jewry in 1933. German Jewry was considered a degenerating branch of the Jewish people in which children up to fifteen did not account for more than 13-14 per cent of the total population, while old people accounted for 9-10 per cent. These were old people of over seventy. Old people over sixty years, according to the pre-World War I figures, amounted to 15 per cent.

The number of immigrants completely employable amounts to two-thirds the total number of immigrants. If we add to this the partly employable between the ages of sixty and seventy, the result is somewhat over 68 per cent.

The age pyramid of the present total Jewish population in Israel is very close to the picture just drawn for the immigrants. This healthy pyramid is a result of a startlingly low death rate. The natural increase was 31,316 in 1954, and 33,346 in 1955, i.e., over 20 per cent. The mortality in 1955 was 5.8 per 1,000 among the total Jewish population, and 5.5 per 1,000 in the *kibbutzim*. This is the lowest mortality in the world. Let us, for the sake of truth, add, however, that the death rate is much higher in the temporary immigrant camps: 46.5 per 1,000. We must, on the other hand, remember that there now remain in such camps almost solely the old and invalid.

It is interesting to dwell briefly in Table 18 on the age structure of the immigration in its various periods.

The first line—the years 1928-1931, when there were many *halutzim* —had a high percentage of youth, which makes the fifteen to fifty-nine age group so large. Of this fifteen to fifty-nine age group, 63.5 per cent were young people from fifteen to twenty-nine years old. The second group— 1932-1938—includes a large wave of German Jews with a high percentage

TABLE 18. *Age Structure of Immigrants to Palestine-Israel During Various Periods*
(Percentages)

Years	0–14	Age 15–59	60 and over
1928-1931	13.6	79.8	6.6
1932-1938	18.8	74.5	6.7
1946-1948	13.6	83.4	3.0
1949-1955	29.4	63.5	7.1

of middle-aged people (from thirty to fifty-nine) which enlarged the fifteen to fifty-nine age group. Then came the tragic period when remnants of European Jewry arrived during 1946-1948, without children and without old people. The years 1946-1948 show the smallest percentage of old people, because they were practically all wiped out in the Hitler camps. The percentage of children, too, is as low as 13.6. From 1949 onward there began the mass migration in which Iraqi and Yemenite Jews play a major role. The age pyramid became sound again, with children making up as much as 29.4 per cent. To be sure, there was also a higher percentage of old people, inasmuch as grandmothers and grandfathers were taken along; however, the main fact is the high percentage of children, which augurs well for the future.

We are now approaching one of the central problems in immigration— that of the socioeconomic structure of the immigrants. It is needless to dwell on the centrality of this problem. This is especially important in view of the fact that the immigrants came rushing in by many tens of thousands annually, compared to the relatively slow trickle up to the founding of the state. They did not come to a country with a developed economy, and each group of immigrants naturally sought security in line with its former professions and knowledge. In Israel the socioeconomic structure remained to be shaped. It is true that we are no longer living in an era when an agrarian economy is viewed as the only possibility and necessity for a new country needing to be colonized. In our age industry and agriculture go hand in hand. Conversely, if it be true that man cannot live by bread alone, it is even a greater certainty that without bread he cannot live at all. During the first stages and also in the later developmental stages of the country, virtually to this day, the problem of producing one's own bread, of the country's agricultural output, has been vital.

Let us first take a look in Table 19 at the socioeconomic structure of the immigrants during the past few years, selecting the dates of the mass immigration, 1950-1955.

These data call for comment. First of all, we must explain why we have not, as in most previous tables, used the data as of May, 1948. During

TABLE 19. *The Occupational Structure of the Economically Active Immigrants in Israel*
(1950-1955)

Occupation in the Old Country	Males		Females	
	Absolute	Percentage	Absolute	Percentage
Artisans and industrial employees	35,091	34.0	9,063	49.2
Merchants and salesmen	20,688	20.2	381	2.1
Professionals	7,148	7.0	3,050	16.5
Communication and transportation workers	3,188	3.2	21	0.1
White-collar workers	14,315	14.0	2,882	15.7
Agricultural workers	6,098	6.0	634	3.4
Unskilled workers	8,989	9.0	1,381	7.5
Construction workers	3,447	3.3	23	0.1
Domestics	3,315	3.3	1,004	5.4
Totals	102,270	100.0	18,439	100.0

the first years of statehood the camp immigrants accounted for a very high percentage. The number of economically active among them was low. Almost an entire generation of young people between the ages of ten and twenty had gone through the Nazi camps and were without training for any particular occupation. This same handicap applies to a large proportion of the immigrants in the years represented in Table 19. During the same period, 1950 to 1955, for which the occupations are listed, out of 102,000 immigrants there were also 32,320 "not employed in their occupations," and 17,430 whose "source of income was unknown" (*Shenaton statisti le-Yisrael*, 1956, p. 38, Table 11). We get a picture of a mass that is *déclassé*, which has had to adjust to very different and often physically more difficult occupations than those to which it had been accustomed in the countries of the Diaspora. This is a gigantic problem which the *Yishuv* has assumed and which it is tackling with courage and talent. This revolutionary occupational restructuring is a historical phenomenon which will be recorded in Israeli history as one of its most important achievements. Table 20, on Israel's economically active population, will give some idea of the restructuring process, which is far from completion.

The first thing that strikes one is that the percentage having agriculture as its occupation is three times as large as among the immigrants. This is the most difficult operation that must be, and is being, tackled. Construction and unskilled labor has second place. Here many of the above-mentioned *déclassé* individuals are employed. There is a very large amount of unskilled work to be done in a new country, such as paving highways, planting trees, clearing roads, and, finally, in construction proper, the many unskilled jobs. The percentage of businessmen is almost half the amount found among the immigrants. The percentage of professionals is somewhat

TABLE 20.   *The Occupations of the Economically Active in Israel (June, 1954)*

Occupations	Absolute	Percentage
Crafts and industries	135,900	24.2
Commerce and finance	68,500	12.2
Professions	55,000	9.8
Communication and transportation	35,900	6.4
Officials, administration, and management	110,000[1]	19.6
Agriculture	102,200	18.2
Construction and unskilled labor	53,900	9.6
Totals	561,400	100.0

[1] Personal services, such as those of waiters, hotel employees, barbers, etc., are included in this figure.

higher, and this is natural. What comes as a surprise is the high percentage of professionals among the immigrants: doctors and even lawyers, not to speak of engineers and chemists are welcome guests in many countries where economic conditions are better than in Israel. To sum up, the so-called laborization, about which the East European Jewish intelligentsia had dreamed, is taking place in Israel on a grand scale.

The high percentage of officials and white-collar workers should not come as a surprise. In the first place, the young state still has to learn the techniques of administration, and such training is costly. Secondly, this figure includes all officials of the Jewish Agency and of the central Zionist organization, both working principally in Diaspora countries. The machinery supplying Diaspora Jews with cultural and educational materials will have to grow, because the demand from the Diaspora will undoubtedly increase.

We have listed above the occupational distribution of the immigrants during the years of mass and unselective immigration, 1950-1955. The selectivity factors introduced in the past few years by the Jewish Agency refer only to health and age, but not to occupation. It will therefore be interesting to see what the structure of the immigration looked like in those years when the *halutzim* accounted perhaps not for a majority, but at least for a very high percentage of the immigrants. To take two occupations which have usually been considered opposites in Jewish life, the aspiration was to have fewer storekeepers and merchants, and more peasants and farmers, among Jews.

The first three lines of Table 21 show a high percentage of farmers. To be sure, between 1924 and 1927 the percentage of farmers dropped and there was an increase in the percentage of merchants. This was when the huge middle-class migration from Poland, fleeing from the so-called

TABLE 21. *Percentage of Farmers and Merchants among the Immigrants to Palestine-Israel during Various Periods*

Years	% Farmers	% Merchants
1919-1923	29.9	6.9
1924-1927	19.0	10.3
1928-1931	27.9	4.1
1932-1938	11.6	15.8
1950-1955	5.0	17.9

Grabski wagon, took place: their belongings had been confiscated because they were unable to pay the exorbitant taxes imposed on Jewish store-keepers by the Grabski government. In the remaining two periods the percentage of businessmen immigrants was very small. From 1932 to 1938 a high percentage of the immigrants were German Jews. The role of the farmer sharply declined and the percentage of businessmen shot up. Lower still is the percentage of farmers in the years 1950-1955, when the *halutz* movement was all but forgotten, and when the masses from countries where there had been even fewer Jewish farmers than in Poland began to flood the country. The percentage of farmers among North African Jewry, which has in recent years accounted for over 90 per cent of all immigrants, is much smaller than it was among Polish Jews before the Hitler massacre.

We have up to now discussed only the immigrants. Unfortunately, there have also been emigrants. Some repatriation is a natural phenomenon in all countries of immigration. Suffice it to mention that 5 per cent of the Jewish immigrants used to return to Russia from the United States during Czarist times, when pogroms were frequent in Russia, and when other political difficulties were not lacking. The recent immigrant mass in Israel is different from the Russian emigrants. A large percentage of today's Jewish immigrants have been through infernal Nazi torture, and their adjustment to new situations, even in the land of their ancestors, is beset with greater difficulties than those experienced by any other migrants. To be sure, there is also a certain portion of old settlers who are well established, and even possess some capital, who are leaving Israel in search of peace and happiness elsewhere. But even among this group our tragic times have created such a diversity of motivation for emigration that it would be necessary to examine each individual case separately to find the real reasons for leaving the country. Generally speaking, the number of emigrants is so insignificant that it is not worth discussing at length.

As nearly 700,000 Jews immigrated to Israel during these seven years, the emigrants amount to less than 10 per cent of the total. This is not a high percentage of emigrants in view of the tragic composition of the im-

TABLE 22. *Jewish Emigrants from Israel by Year*

Year	Number of Emigrants
1949	7,207
1950	9,463
1951	10,057
1952	13,000
1953	12,501
1954	7,000
1955	6,000
Total	65,228

migrant mass, and the extremely difficult circumstances facing the settler in Israel. At the same time it is striking that precisely in the years 1954-1955—years of great political tension—the number of emigrants declined. It looks as if that element that could not manage to adjust to Israeli conditions, climatic or economic, has already been skimmed off, and the number of emigrants will diminish still more. During the first half of 1956 fewer than 3,000 emigrants left the country.

NOTES

[1a Cf. above Anita Libman Lebeson, "The American Jewish Chronicle," and Moshe Davis, "Jewish Religious Life and Institutions in America (A Historical Study)."]

[2a Cf. above Yudel Mark, "Yiddish Literature."]

3 Dr. Ch. Kayserling, "A Memorial sent by German Jews to the President of the Continental Congress," *Publications of the American Jewish Historical Society*, No. 6, 1897.

[4a Cf. Mark, *op cit.*, p. 1203.]

5 *Allgemeine Zeitung des Judentums* (Leipzig, 1845), pp. 46-50.

[6a Cf. above Cecil Roth, "The Jews of Western Europe (from 1648)," p. 266.]

[7a Cf. above Uriah Zevi Engelman, "Sources of Jewish Statistics," pp. 1526-1527.]

8 Joseph Kissman, *Studien zu der geschichte fun rumenische yiden in ninezenten yahrhundert* (New York, 1944), p. 22.

9 *Ibid.*

[10a Cf. Roth, *op. cit.*, pp. 273 ff.]

11 Bernard Weinstein, *Yiddische Yunions in America* (New York, 1929), p. 44.

12 B. Hoffman, *Fufzig yahr klokmacher yunion* (New York, 1936), p. 22.

[13a See above Oscar I. Janowsky, "The Rise of the State of Israel."]

BIBLIOGRAPHY

In addition to the official statistical publications of the United States, Canada, Palestine and the Latin-American republics, and the reports of ICA (Jewish Colonization Association) and *Hicem* the following works have been utilized in this study:

The American Jewish Year Book. New York, 1920-1944.
Bulletin of the Economic Research Institute of the Jewish Agency for Palestine. Jerusalem, 1945.
DAVIE, MAURICE R., *World Emigration.* New York, 1939.
Ha-Aliah, ha-Yishuv, ve-ha-Tenuah ha-Tivit shel ha-Oklosiah be-Eretz Yisrael. Jerusalem, 1945, Shenaton, Tel-Aviv, 1945.
JOSEPH, SAMUEL, *Jewish Immigration to the United States from 1881-1910.* New York, 1914.
LESTSCHINSKY, JACOB, *Die anheben fun emigratzie bei yiden in ninezenten yahrhundert.* Berlin, 1929.
——, "Die berufliche Zusammensetzung der juedischen Einwanderung in die Vereinigten Staaten," in *Weltwirtschaftliches Archiv,* January, 1948.
——, "Die juedische Wanderung, ihre Ursachen und ihre Regelung," in *Archiv fuer Wanderungswesen.* Leipzig, 1930.
——, "Dos soziale ponim fun dem Americaner yudentum" in *YIVO Bleter* (Journal of the Yiddish Scientific Institute), Vol. XVII. New York, 1941.
——, "Emigratzie in der kapitalistischer tekufeh" in *Yiddische Ekonomik,* Nos. 2 and 3. Warsaw-Vilna, 1937.
——, "Juedische Wanderungen im XIX. Jahrhundert" in *Internationaler Congress fuer Bevoelkerungsforschung.* Rome, 1932.
——, *Wuhin gen mir?* (*Yiddische wandrungen amol und heint*). New York, 1944.
——, *Yiddische wanderung in die letzte fuenf und zwanzig yahr.* Berlin, 1927.
LEVINE, LOUIS, *The Women's Garment Workers.* New York, 1924.
ROSENBERG, LOUIS, *Canada's Jews.* Montreal, 1939.
TAFT, DONALD R., *Human Migration.* New York, 1936.
TARTAKOWER, ARIEH, and GROSSMAN, KURT, *The Jewish Refugee.* New York, 1944.
Yiddish Scientific Institute, *The Classification of Jewish Immigrants and Its Implications.* New York, 1945.

ESPECIALLY FOR SECTION 7

Shenaton statisti le-Yisrael, Jerusalem, 1953-1954, 1954-1955, 1955-1956.
Yarhon statisti le-Yisrael, Jerusalem, June-October, 1956.
Dape aliyah, Jerusalem, Jewish Agency, Immigration Department, 27-31, 1954-1957.

Keren ha-Yesod, Ha-Magbit ha-Meuhedet le-Yisrael, Jerusalem, 1956-1957.

Jacob Lestschinsky, *Dos natsyonale ponem funem veltyidntum,* Buenos Aires, 1955.

———, *Tefuzat Yisrael leaher ha-Milhama,* Tel-Aviv, Beterem, 1957-1958.

———, "Le-Baayat demuto he-Hebratit-tarbutit shel ha-Yishuv," in *Bitzaron,* New York, 1951-1952.

Information Please, 1956 Almanac, New York, 1956.

American Jewish Yearbook, 1950.

Facts and Figures, Israel Office of Information, New York, 1955.

Rescue, The United Hias Service Information Bulletin, 1954-1956.

Newcomers from Israel, Toronto, 1955.

CHAPTER 39

ECONOMIC STRUCTURE AND LIFE OF THE JEWS
By Simon Kuznets*

I. INTRODUCTORY ANALYSIS

1. Dispersion and Community

The economic structure and life of any group, within a given historical epoch, is largely a matter of its natural and social environment. The dispersion of Jews among numerous societies with different historical and institutional backgrounds suggests wide differences in economic structure and life among the many Jewish communities also. A question arises whether there is any common repeatedly observed feature in their economic life. Are there some social and spiritual characteristics common among the various groups belonging to the world community of Jews?

Consider the nature of the dispersion for recent years. For 1939, when the population of Jews was perhaps at its peak, about 16,600,000, Dr. Arthur Ruppin provides estimates for over seventy-five countries, most of them sovereign states, widely dispersed and with markedly different historical and social backgrounds.[1] In forty-two states the Jewish population was 10,000 or more, and in seventeen it was 100,000 or more. Even the three largest communities—each with more than 1,000,000 Jews—lived in countries that differed sharply in level of economic performance and in social and political structure: Poland, the U.S.S.R., and the United States.

For 1954 the picture is similar.[2] Total Jewish population of the world was estimated to be 11,900,000. In thirty-two separate states and territories the Jewish population was 10,000 or more, in fourteen it was 100,000 or more, and the three largest communities, each with over 1,000,000 Jews, were in the United States, the U.S.S.R., and Israel. Over a century ago (in 1825) dispersion was as wide, even though the world population of Jews was only 3,300,000 and only one country had a Jewish population of over 1,000,000.[3]

How do we identify these communities as Jewish?[3a] (a) They possess a common history from original ancestry in Palestine to a chain of genera-

* I am indebted to Miss Lillian Epstein for assistance in checking and editing the original version of the chapter (available for reference in the Library of The Jewish Theological Seminary of America, New York City) and in preparing the abridged version.

tions through the Diaspora to the present. (b) They share the same religion, *not* shared with others, and participate in a religiously colored community life. (c) They have a feeling of belonging to one group, and each is more responsive to the fate of the others than it is to the fate of most other population groups. (d) Finally, they have a feeling of distinctiveness, often intensified by a discriminatory policy or attitude on the part of non-Jewish groups.

Clearly, this list of characteristics is not exhaustive: in the course of some 2,000 years of Jewish and world history they have led to and been accompanied by other characteristics—demographic, social, and economic. Nor do they provide an infallible method for classifying individuals or groups as Jews. And yet some such characteristics are indispensable for identifying the groups that constitute Jews. Without such identification, how can we count them or study their economic life and structure?

If belonging and distinctiveness, associated with a common history and religion, are the identifying characteristics, groups recognized as Jews necessarily exclude many descendants of the Jews of ancient Israel and Judea and include some nondescendants. The exclusion implies that the group tends toward cohesion and distinctiveness even though some individual members do not fully recognize or share in the feeling of belonging. In a sense, the group is cohesive and distinctive because that is the way we define it:[4, 4a] we would not find such distinctiveness and cohesion if we defined Jews as descendants of ancient Israelites. But this is neither tautology nor circular reasoning: Jews are recognized in the real world by either internally originated or externally imposed feeling of belonging to a distinctive group. The definition thus corresponds broadly to the identification in real life; and from it other characteristics can be deduced. It is to these, more directly relevant to the economic structure and life of the Jews as a minority group, that we now turn.

2. *Minority Status*

We are interested here in the economics of modern Jewry within the past seventy-five years to give us the minimum perspective necessary. For this purpose the most relevant characteristic of Jewish communities is their minority status. With the single exception of Israel since independence, in every country with a sovereign government or some similar mechanism for making independent and authoritative social decisions, the distinctive Jewish group constitutes much less than the majority of the total population.

While minority status is a familiar and obvious feature of the Jewish world community, some of its characteristics should be specified. A brief discussion will go far to suggest and explain some common characteristics of the economic structure of modern Jewry.

A. It need not be stressed that, except in Israel, the Jewish population is a minority within each country of residence. Indeed, even today, the overwhelming proportion of Jewish world population—10,400,000 out of 11,-900,000—has minority status; and as recently as 1939, this was true of all world Jewry. It follows that the economics of the Jews must be the economics of minority groups which strive for cohesion and distinctiveness within larger population masses.

B. The Jewish minorities may be quite large in absolute numbers—in a few cases they are larger than the *total* population of many independent states. The Jewish population of the United States, estimated at 5,200,000, is much larger than the total population of several states in Europe, Latin America, and Asia, and of some semi-independent territories in Africa. But, again with the exception of Israel, even the large Jewish communities are small minorities in the total populations of their countries of residence. In no country in 1954 did the Jewish population constitute more than 4 per cent of the total. The two absolutely large Jewish communities outside of Israel, in the United States and the U.S.S.R., account for only 3.3 per cent and 1.0 per cent respectively of total population. The shares were somewhat higher in the 1930's, when the large Jewish groups in some smaller eastern European countries were still alive. But even then the highest share, outside of Palestine and some freak political units, such as Tangier, was somewhat less than 10 per cent (in Poland). This *small* minority status is significant—particularly for those few Jewish communities that reached large absolute numbers and that are, therefore, most important for our discussion. Within the economic system of a country, a minority group tending toward cohesion and distinctiveness is likely to perform one set of functions if its proportion in total population is less than 10 per cent; and another, if its share is as high as 20 to 30 per cent.

C. If only because their proportions in the totals are so low, little expectation is entertained, either by Jews or by non-Jews, that Jews will ever become a majority, or even a large minority. Even in Israel, Jews attained a majority partly by setting boundaries to promote that end, partly because of the accidents of war and the reaction of the resident Arab population. In all other countries, neither the demographic patterns of natural increase among Jews compared with those for non-Jews nor the prospects of addition by immigration (even if unrestricted) suggest a rise in the share of the Jewish population beyond that of a small minority. In other words, the small minority status is more or less permanent and, therefore, a matter of some importance in the long-term adjustment which the minority group is likely to make in the economic field.

D. The large Jewish minorities of the past century are mostly of recent origin—recent in the history of the countries of residence and the history of the Jews. In many countries Jews have, of course, been living since time immemorial, and are, therefore, among the oldest residents. This is true of many Jewish communities as a whole, particularly where such communities are small and the countries have been too isolated and backward to attract Jewish immigrants. It is also true of some groups within the larger Jewish communities—e.g., the ancestors of some members of the Jewish community in the United States settled in this country in the seventeenth century. But in the fairly large Jewish communities of the recent century, the majority are relatively recent immigrants. In the United States, as well as Canada, Argentina, and Brazil, the bulk of Jewish immigration occurred after 1880. In eastern Europe, the Jewish population migrated largely at the end of the Middle Ages and much of the territorial expansion of the Jews within Czarist Russia occurred during the nineteenth century (out of the area of the original Kingdom of Poland). In the Near East many of the Jews migrated after the expulsion from Spain.

"Recent" may not seem to be an apt description of migrations at the end of the Middle Ages. However, in the present connection the term is used to suggest that the bulk of the Jewish minorities arrived after the economy of the country of destination had reached the point where it was already almost entirely manned by the resident majority; and where, therefore, the economic choices available to the recently arrived minority were limited by established interests. The term also indicates the chronology of these major Jewish migrations in the long stretch of Jewish history. While a full demonstration of the recent origin of Jewish minorities would require detailed documentation and discussion, the well-known facts of history speak clearly for it.

3. The Economics of a Small Minority

Economic and social life has a logic of its own, even if it is not as simple, or as hard and fast, as that of the physical world. The characteristics of a permanent small minority of relatively recent origin that strives toward cohesion in and of themselves imply consequences for its economic structure, dynamics and life.

A. The economic structure of a small, cohesive minority is likely to differ substantially from that of the majority, and hence from that of a country's total population. The validity of this statement can be perceived if we ask the inverse: How likely is a small minority to reproduce, with fair similarity, the full range of the economic structure of the total population? The case is *prima facie* against it, if only because the minority can hardly attain the diversity of the much larger total. But it is particularly unlikely because we assume the minority's desire for cohesion. In economic relations, this desire is naturally translated into a desire for proximity and close links at many levels. The minority, rather than be dispersed, tends to be concentrated in selected industries, selected occupations, and selected classes of economic status.

If this consequence is an indispensable condition of a minority's survival as a cohesive unit, much of the popular discussion about lack of "normality" loses point. If the economic structure of a country's total population is "normal," then, almost by definition, the economic structure of a small and permanent minority must be abnormal. Otherwise the minority will not long survive as a distinctive group. It would perhaps be more appropriate to describe the narrower range of industry, occupation, and status distributions as normal for distinctive small minorities, and an economic structure similar to that of the total population as abnormal.

B. The statements under A, above, apply to any minority, even one whose members can be linked to ancestors resident in the country early in its history. But if a minority is of recent origin, its economic structure is more likely to be concentrated in some sectors. As some sectors will be fully manned by the time the minority enters the country, the range of economic opportunities open to it will necessarily be limited; and even within this range, selection will be limited further by the specific heritage of the minority.

But *how* would the economic structure of the minority differ from that of the total population? The immigrating minority would presumably move into industries that are growing rapidly at the time and where opportunities exist. Such a choice would probably be acceptable to the resident population, whereas competition by an immigrant group in an established industry might meet with objections from the resident majority, which could take the extreme form of legal exclusion.

However, within the growing sectors, opportunities open to the immigrating minority would be at a low economic level, for the latter depends in large part upon the equipment that the minority possesses. And its capital funds or special skills would probably be meager, for mass migration usually follows from the loss of economic position in the country of origin.

C. There is, however, another group of factors—the heritage of the immigrating minority. Here the point that recent origin means recent in the long history of the minority itself bears with particular force. The immigrating minority is conditioned both by its heritage and by the possibility of continued contact with its place of origin and with other kindred groups.

These factors affect the choices that determine the initial economic structure—within the range set by the existing opportunities in the country of arrival. This range is not necessarily fixed: there is always the probability of the minority *creating* previously unperceived opportunities. But either in following already marked out directions or in creating new occupations and industries, the minority is affected by its history.

D. What of the dynamics of the economic structures of small minorities of recent origin? The range of industrial, occupational, and status choices within which a minority is likely to grow is significantly narrower than the range open to a country's total population. Economic growth is accompanied by major shifts in industrial structure, in the relative importance of various occupations, in the proportionate numbers of various economic classes. For total population these secular changes cover the full range of industries, of occupations, and of socioeconomic groups. The distinctive economic structure of a minority of recent origin is concentrated in some sectors and this, in and of itself, limits the range of structural changes that can occur in the process of growth. For example, if the initial economic structure of the minority emphasizes trade and consumer goods manufactures, and underemphasizes agriculture, heavy industry, and professional pursuits, a shift toward agriculture is certainly not likely—if it is a laggard industry in the country's economic growth. And if the growth of trade and light industry for the minority is substantial, reflecting in part the rapid growth of these sectors in the economy at large, the stock of human resources within the minority may not be enough to take advantage also of opportunities in other pursuits. Thus both the initial choices and the permanently small relative size of the minority limit structural shifts.

E. This limited range of structural growth of a minority may be reinforced by another consideration. A small group with permanent minority status may fear possible discrimination, even if there is no legal limitation. If some sectors were originally underrepresented by a minority because of resistance to its entry, even with a rise in its economic status and with increasing numbers, the minority may shun those sectors. In other words, the limited range of structural growth may also be due to the recognition of the *permanency* of minority status and to the fear that discrimination will remain too real to warrant attempts at entry.

F. The narrow industrial-occupational range of a small minority, combined with growth in its numbers, may result in its numerical dominance of some sectors of a country's economy, which may appear to be a *capture* of whole industries. This may in fact be true: concentration in certain industries and pursuits, conditioned originally by limited opportunities and the distinctive heritage associated with recent entry, must, if sufficient growth in numbers is attained, result in dominance within these industries and pursuits. This result can be avoided either by greater dispersion or by constancy or decline of numbers. The former is inconsistent with the desire of a minority to remain a distinct cohesive group; the latter means demographic distortion or refusal to migrate, despite compelling pressure at points of origin and economic and social attractions in the countries of destination.

G. The economic rise of a minority may be significantly larger than that of the total population. This expectation applies to periods of growth of a recent minority—until some time after immigration slackens—and to countries with economic freedom.

First, since the minority is naturally directed to sectors with greater growth potentials, its rate of economic growth should be greater than that of total population. Second, since the immigrant minority tends to occupy the lower rungs of the economic ladder within these sectors, it has a greater opportunity to rise; especially if, because of a long history of adjustments, it possesses equipment which it can use to advantage. Third, an immigrant group is generally more rootless than the resident majority, and can move more freely in adjusting to changing economic opportunities. This last observation is particularly the case of countries where the pace of economic growth is moderate; but is true even of rapidly growing countries, if the minority can adapt itself readily to economic change.

However, once the small minority is established and the immediate effects of recent immigration wear off, these factors no longer operate to produce a greater rise in per capita income. Nor would the hypothesis hold for countries where severe economic and political restraints are put upon a minority, e.g., Czarist Russia. Under such conditions, found for other minorities in other countries, the pressure exercised by the hostile government may counteract the factors noted above and, in fact, depress the rate of economic growth of the minority to levels below those for the majority.

H. The alternatives suggested above for the rise in per capita income of a minority compared with that of the majority carry different implications for trends in the distribution of income within the minority. If members of the minority may be assumed to rise on the economic scale, after arrival in the country of residence, at higher rates than the population at large, within that minority the older residents will be above the new arrivals on the economic scale. Furthermore, these economic inequalities will persist, often accompanied by cultural and other differences, as long as there are large proportional additions to the minority by continuous immigration.

If these additions cease or are reduced, as they usually are in the course of time, the rise in economic levels affects increasing proportions of the minority and may be expected to be relatively greater among the recent arrivals. One would, therefore, expect a reduction in the *relative* economic and income differentials within the minority—a greater lifting at the lower levels than at the already high levels. This process of decreasing economic inequality would presumably be accompanied by increasing cultural homogeneity as the period of residence lengthens and the minority increasingly absorbs common elements of the culture of the country.

In an established minority no such reduction in income inequality can be expected (unless it is part and parcel of a leveling process in the country at large). And if political and other conditions are oppressive and restric-

tive, inequality in the distribution of income and social and cultural differentiation within the minority may even increase, for such restrictions never
affect all individuals equally, and they rarely completely bar the economic
and social rise of some limited groups. The result may be a widening contrast between the high economic and social position of a small group and
the depressed levels of the broad masses of the minority.

II. ECONOMIC CHARACTERISTICS OF JEWS

The comments in Section I apply to the economics of all minorities that
are small, permanent, and recent. Many such minorities can be found—in
the current and more distant past, on almost all continents, and of quite
diverse origin. Italians in Brazil, Indians in some countries in Africa, and
Chinese in many countries of Southeast Asia easily come to mind; and the
economic structures and evolution of all would, I believe, differ from those
of the majorities in their host countries along the lines suggested above.
The economics of Jews is thus one case of many with similar characteristics.
Unfortunately no general study of the economics of minorities is available,
and no comparisons can be made.

Of the specific economic characteristics of the Jews, we attempt to provide information about their industrial and occupational structure and general economic position. Fortunately, much useful compilation, sifting, and
synthesis have already been done by many in the field, notably by Jacob
Lestschinsky, to whom students of the demography and economics of Jews
owe a great debt.[5a]

Comprehensive coverage is not attempted here. With the wide dispersion of Jews, it would require inclusion of many countries for which even
elementary statistical information for total population is lacking. Nor is
it necessary to be comprehensive, for many Jewish communities account for
only insignificant proportions of world Jewry. Furthermore, the distinctive
characteristics of the economics of Jews are found with such conspicuous
regularity in the countries for which data are available that the likelihood
of their being *general* is quite high. We are, therefore, limiting the tables
to the easily available data, which cover the largest Jewish communities and
account for a high proportion of World Jewry. However, in this section
we omit all reference to Palestine and Israel because that area is unique.

Finally, we limit the presentation in Section II to one or two years before World War II—either in the 1920's or the 1930's, going back only
if recent data are lacking. The purpose is to summarize the characteristics
of the economic structure when world Jewry was at its peak and before
the catastrophe that accompanied World War II. It is essentially a cross-
section analysis, with no discussion of the patterns of growth. The latter

will be attempted in Section III for three major Jewish communities in Russia and East Europe, America, and Palestine and Israel.

1. Lack of Participation in Agriculture

In the twelve countries covered here, the proportion of Jews engaged in agriculture is far lower than that of non-Jews or of total population (Table 1). The universality of this characteristic is scarcely to be doubted.[5]

As Jews are a small minority, a lower than country-wide ratio of them engaged in agriculture means a minuscule fraction of the total agricultural population. Thus in Poland, Jews accounted for 0.6 per cent of all gainfully occupied persons engaged in agriculture; in the U.S.S.R. and the United

TABLE 1

Share of Agriculture (Including Forestry and Fishing) in the Gainfully Occupied Population, Jewish, Non-Jewish, and Total, Twelve Countries, Pre-World War II Year

Country (1)	Date of Coverage (2)	Share of Agriculture (%)		Total Adj. to Exclude Women in Agriculture (5)	Jews as % of Total Population (6)
		Jews (3)	Non-Jews (4)		
1. Poland	1931	4.0	66.0	53.4	9.8
2. U.S.S.R.	1939	4.2		52.0	2.1
3. U.S.A	1937–40	2.2	18.0	18.3	3.7
4. Latvia	1930	1.1	68.5	52.7a	4.8(1935)c
5. Lithuania	1937	3.8		67.4(1923)	7.6(1923)c
6. Germany	1933	1.3	24.9	16.9	0.8
7. Czechoslovakia	1930	8.3	35.6	27.3	2.4
8. Hungary	1930	2.7	54.1	48.2	5.1
9. Rumania	1930	4.1	75.6	63.5	4.2
10. Bulgaria	1926	0.5		69.4b	0.85
11. Canada	1931	1.3	28.8		1.5(1941)c
12. Argentina	1935	5.8		23.6(1914)c	2.0

a Average of ratios for 1925 and 1935.

b Averages of ratios for 1920 and 1934.

c The years in parentheses refer to the date of coverage when it is different from that in col. 2.

SOURCES: Col. 3: lines 1, 4, 6, 7, 8, 9, 11 from Nathan Reich, "The Economic Structure of Modern Jewry," *The Jews*, Vol. II, 2nd ed., 1949, pp. 1241 ff. These refer to shares in gainfully occupied population. Lines 2, 3, 5, 12 from Jacob Lestschinsky, "Economic and Social Development of the Jewish People," *The Jewish People: Past and Present*, Vol. 1, New York, 1946, p. 377. Line 10 from Peter Meyer and others, *The Jews in the Soviet Satellites*, Syracuse, 1953, pp. 559–560.

Col. 4: lines 1, 4, 6, 7, 8, 9, 11 from Reich, *op. cit.* Line 3 from Lestschinsky, *op. cit.*

Col. 5: from Colin Clark, *Conditions of Economic Progress*, 2nd ed., London, 1951, particularly pp. 398-399, 419, 420. The figure for the U.S.S.R. (p. 420) has been reduced from 57.8 to allow for overrepresentation of dependents.

Col. 6: all lines, except 10, from Arthur Ruppin, "The Jewish Population of the World," *The Jewish People: Past and Present*, Vol. I, New York, 1946, pp. 350-351. Line 10 from Meyer, *op. cit.*

States this fraction is below 0.2 and 0.5 per cent respectively.

The reasons for this slight participation in agriculture are numerous, and most of them are familiar. Perhaps the major long-standing factors are political and legal limitations, which have prevailed for centuries and date back to times when land ownership and use, the bases of political power, were not accorded to minorities with a religion and historical roots so different from those of the majority. Under such conditions the Jews could hardly acquire experience in agricultural operations, and consequently they had no such skills to carry from one country to another, as other minorities often had. In the past century, when agriculture was open to the Jews, it was no longer a promising industry. Indeed, agriculture is one of the oldest industries—although not without great growth potential in some countries. Other less important factors can be adduced, but one that *cannot* be claimed is the territorial dispersiveness of agriculture: some minorities have devoted themselves to agriculture and yet maintained cohesiveness (e.g., the Amish in this country), even though many of their younger generations have vanished among the urban population.

There is no obvious relation between the share of agriculture among Jews and either the share of agriculture among non-Jews or the share of Jews in the total population. The two largest shares of agriculture among Jews are in Czechoslovakia (largely Carpatho-Ruthenia) and Argentina: in both countries the share of agriculture among non-Jews is relatively low. The smallest shares of agriculture among Jews are in Bulgaria and Latvia, but in both the shares among non-Jews (or total population) are among the highest; and India could be added to this group. Countries with fairly high proportions of Jews to total populations, e.g., Latvia and Hungary, have relatively low proportions of Jews in agriculture; and countries with low proportions of Jews to total population, e.g., Czechoslovakia, Argentina, and the U.S.S.R., have higher proportions of Jews in agriculture than other countries.

If we may assume that the proportions of Jews in agriculture are quite low, the following implication can be suggested. In the underdeveloped countries that operate at relatively low economic levels, the proportion of total population in agriculture is usually quite high, from 50 to 70 per cent; in more advanced economies it is quite low, 20 per cent or less. Hence the urban population is correspondingly low in the underdeveloped and high in the advanced countries. The Jewish minority may constitute a substantial fraction of an underdeveloped country's small urban population; but it *cannot* be more than a small minority of the urban population of an industrialized country. Therefore, the Jews are likely to exercise more important economic functions in an underdeveloped than in an industrialized country. Correlatively, any cleavage and friction between the urban and rural sectors may have a bearing upon the Jewish minority in underdeveloped countries different from that in more industrialized countries.

2. *Industrial Distribution of Nonagricultural Labor*

In Table 2 we compare, for ten countries, the distribution among major industrial sectors of Jews engaged in nonagricultural pursuits with those for non-Jews or for total population. As column 2 shows, almost the entire Jewish working population, but much smaller fractions of the non-Jewish or total working population, are engaged in nonagricultural pursuits: e.g., in Poland, Jews engaged in industry amount to 47 per cent of nonagricultural workers and to about 45 per cent of all Jewish workers; but non-Jews engaged in industry amount to 54 per cent of nonagricultural workers and to only about 25 per cent of all non-Jewish workers.

In all countries but Poland and the U.S.S.R. the largest sector in the industrial structure of the Jewish gainfully occupied population is trade and finance. In all countries without exception its share among Jews is far greater than its share among the non-Jewish or total nonagricultural gainfully occupied population.

The next important sectors are industry and handicrafts and the much smaller public services and the professions. There is some diversity in the relation of the shares of these sectors among Jews to those among non-Jews. In all countries except Canada the share of industry and handicrafts is lower among Jews than among the non-Jews. In three countries, the U.S.S.R., Germany, and Czechoslovakia, the share of public service and professions is higher among Jews than among non-Jews; in one, the United States, it is about the same; in others it is lower. However, for the distribution of the *total* working population rather than nonagricultural, in all countries except Czechoslovakia, the United States, and Germany, the share of industry and handicrafts is higher among Jews than among non-Jews. The same is true of the share of the public services and professions sector, with four exceptions (Poland, Rumania, Bulgaria, and Canada).

The shares of transportation and communication and domestic and personal services are distinctly lower among the Jewish nonagricultural working population than among the non-Jewish or total. In many cases these differences are so striking that, even on the basis of total working population, the shares of these sectors are lower. In other words, despite their greater urbanization, lower proportions of Jews than of non-Jews are engaged in transportation and communication in all countries except Poland and the U.S.S.R., and the same is true for domestic and personal services in all countries for which this sector is shown separately.

The reasons for this distinctive structure for Jews are not far to seek, and will become apparent below when we observe some of the details. In general, trade and finance accounts for such large proportions of the nonagricultural Jewish population because small entrepreneurship is feasible; because heavy capital investment, either in commodities or in personal train-

TABLE 2

Distribution of Nonagricultural Labor Force by Major Sectors, Jewish and Non-Jewish Population Compared, Ten Countries, Pre-World War II Year

Country and Year (1)	Approx. Shares of Nonagric. Workers in Total (2)[a]	Percentage Shares of:					
		Industry and Handi-crafts (3)	Trade and Finance (4)	Transpor-tation and Communi-cation (5)	Public Service and Pro-fessions (6)	Domestic and Personal Services (7)	Other (8)
Poland, 1931							
1. Jews	96	46.7	39.2	3.6	6.3	3.3	0.9
2. Non-Jews	47	53.9	10.3	8.1	13.2	12.0	2.5
U.S.S.R., 1926							
3. Jews	96	44.9	25.8	3.6	18.9	——	6.8
4. Non-Jews	27	45.2	9.2	12.6	18.7	——	14.3
U.S.A., 1940							
5. Jews	98	28.6	51.0	2.6	11.7	6.1	0
6. Non-Jews	82	39.0	25.4[b]	11.2	11.8	12.6	0
Latvia, 1930							
7. Jews	99	29.1	49.2	2.2	13.0	2.0	4.5
8. Non-Jews	47	41.1	11.8	10.6	17.0	10.5	8.0
Germany, 1933							
9. Jews	99	23.5	62.8	0.4	11.8	1.6	0
10. Non-Jews	83	57.1	18.9	6.9	10.4	6.6	0
Czechoslovakia, 1930							
11. Jews	91	27.0	56.8	2.7	10.1	2.1	1.3
12. Non-Jews	73	61.8	12.1	7.2	8.0	8.3	2.6
Bohemia, Moravia and Silesia, 1930							
11a. Jews	—	24.7	61.4	1.7	10.9	1.1	0.3
12a. Non-Jews	—	63.8	12.6	7.0	7.2	7.6	1.9
Slovakia and Carpatho-Ruthenia, 1930							
11b. Jews	—	28.6	53.4	3.4	9.6	2.9	2.1
12b. Non-Jews	—	48.8	8.7	9.4	13.1	13.1	6.8
Hungary, 1930							
13. Jews	97	35.4	49.9	2.2	9.1	1.6	1.8
14. Non-Jews	52	54.3	11.0	6.8	11.4	12.7	3.7
Rumania, 1930							
15. Jews	96	34.8	51.5	2.6	2.9	incl. in (8)	8.2
16. Non-Jews	37	47.5	18.1	10.1	13.4	incl. in (8)	10.9
Bulgaria, 1926							
17. Jews[c]	99	35.3 incl. (5)	55.0	incl. in (3)	6.2	incl. in (8)	3.4
18. Total pop.	31	53.6 incl. (5)	14.4	incl. in (3)	22.6	incl. in (8)	9.3
Canada, 1931							
19. Jews	99	33.3	39.0	2.9	5.7	6.0	13.1
20. Non-Jews	71	27.1	12.4	11.3	10.4	13.4	25.4

[a] Col. 2 derived from Table 1, with additional information on the U.S.S.R. in 1926 from Clark, *op. cit.*, p. 420.

[b] Assigns two-thirds of clerks to trade and credit.

[c] Averages of percentages for 1920 and 1934.

SOURCES: The same as in Table 1.

ing, is not required; and because the conditions under which Jewish minorities have operated for centuries, and which resulted in some ties among them, favored both the acquisition of skills and formation of useful links for the pursuit of trade and finance. Industry and handicrafts, second in relative importance among the Jews, attains its significance for primarily the same reasons. Here again, small-scale activity is possible, requiring neither heavy capital investment, nor dependence upon government monopolies or large corporations, nor as much reliance upon personal relations between the producer and the consumer as is involved in many professions. Finally, the share of the public services and professions sector is a reflection of economic growth because its status is high and can be reached only after sizable investment in personal training. It is not an accident that this share is far lower than those of trade and industry; nor that it is usually lower in underdeveloped than in developed countries, or lower in developed countries where the Jewish minorities are of more recent origin.

The rather low shares of transportation and communication and domestic and personal services are not difficult to explain. As the former is dominated by large corporations or government, the Jewish minority may be discriminated against either legally or tacitly but still effectively. In the domestic and personal services, the demand for more lucrative types of activity depends not so much upon purely economic, objective criteria as upon social and other conventions that a minority, at a low social level, is not equipped to meet. Other important factors here are the low economic levels (of domestic service, in particular) and the separation from one's community, which make the pursuit unpalatable for a member of the minority.

3. *Specialization within Trade and Finance*

The distinctive economic structure of the Jews becomes clearer when we examine the components within the trade, industry, and public and professions sectors. The shares of various industries in the total Jewish population gainfully occupied (including or excluding those in agriculture) will show which branches within a major sector employ substantial proportions of the total Jewish population. The proportions that Jews are of the total gainfully occupied in any industry will show those in which the Jews play a major role.[6]

For the breakdown within the trade sector, we have only illustrative data, but they are quite suggestive and warrant discussion.[7]

A. Within trade and finance, commodity trade is by far the most important branch—certainly when measured by numbers engaged. In Poland in 1921, the total number of Jews in trade and finance was 342,600, about 35 per cent of *all* Jews gainfully occupied and close to 40 per cent of Jews gainfully occupied outside of agriculture. But commodity trade accounted for 288,700 and other types of trade (mostly brokerage, etc.) for another

14,800. In Rumania in 1913, of the total of 33,400 Jews in trade and finance, only 1,200 were engaged in banking, insurance, and money exchange; only 3,500 were engaged in restaurants and cafes; and the balance of over 28,000 were in commodity trade. In Germany in 1907, of some 145,600 Jews in trade, etc., over 125,000 were in commodity trade.

B. There is further specialization among Jews within commodity trade. Some relevant data are available. In Rumania in 1913, of some 20,000 Jews gainfully occupied in commodity trade and distributed by branches, over 17,000 were in four branches—textiles; groceries; wholesale cattle, grain, fish, and vegetables; and retail fruit and vegetables. In New York City in 1937, of the 164,000 Jewish gainful workers in retail trade, food stores and the apparel group (two of the ten branches distinguished) accounted for 107,000.

C. Because of this distinctive structure, the proportion of Jews to the total engaged in some trade industries is high enough to suggest "dominance."

Three aspects of specialization lead to this numerical dominance. The first is the large proportion of Jews in the broad trade and finance sector. If 50 per cent of all Jews are engaged in trade, if 20 per cent of all gainfully occupied are engaged in trade, and if 10 per cent of the total working force are Jews, then the proportion of Jews among all engaged in trade is 25 per cent, i.e. (50 per cent of 10 per cent), related to 20 per cent. The second is the concentration of Jews in certain branches of trade. Thus, if of the Jews in trade and finance, 80 per cent are in retail grocery trade (to use an extreme example), and if the retail grocery trade accounts for 5 per cent of the total gainfully occupied, then the proportion of Jews among all gainfully occupied in the retail grocery trade is 80 per cent, i.e. (80 per cent of 50 per cent of 10 per cent), related to 5 per cent, and they are "dominant" in that field. The third aspect is the regional concentration of Jews. Within any country, there are distinctive regions or urban communities where the Jews are heavily concentrated and where, therefore, their shares in certain sectors and branches may be far above the average for the country as a whole.

There is abundant evidence on this point, of which one example should suffice. In the United States in 1937, Jews were 3.7 per cent of total population; in New York City, they were 28 per cent. In the United States in that year, 9 per cent of the total gainfully occupied in trade were Jews; in New York City, over 41 per cent were Jews. Specialization within trade could readily account for a proportion of Jews in the food stores group of over 58 per cent and in the retail apparel group of 80 per cent.

D. Tentatively, it can be suggested that dominant proportions of Jews might be found in finished consumer goods trade in the larger cities. On the other hand, in producer goods branches the proportion of Jews to the total engaged would be low.[8]

In New York City in 1937, where Jewish gainful workers were over 50 per cent of the total in food stores, apparel, household furnishings and furniture, and drug stores, they were only 12.4 per cent in the automotive group. In Rumania in 1913, where the proportion of Jews to the total was highest in furniture and household furnishings, jewelry, textiles, and leather, it was low (but not lowest) in iron, wood, and chemical products. In Riga, Latvia, in 1924, where 35.1 per cent of all retail stores were in Jewish hands, over 60 per cent of the leather goods, jewelry, notions, tobacco, clothing and shoes, and linen and wool textiles stores were Jewish.

4. *Specialization within the Industry Sector*

In all countries in our sample, industry includes mining, manufacturing, and construction; and also, in some, the nontransportation utilities—water supply, electricity, gas. However, the latter branch is small in terms of number engaged and its occasional inclusion does not affect comparability significantly. In Table 3 mining, chemicals, and the nontransportation utilities (when given) were put into the residual, "other" subgroup. But the detail is sufficient to indicate the specialization of Jews within industry.

A. The most important branch of the industry sector is clothing (including in some countries the much smaller cleaning industry). It employs from about 30 to over 50 per cent of all Jews engaged in industry. In contrast, the proportion of non-Jews in the clothing industry ranges from below 10 to somewhat over 20 per cent. Scattered information suggests that this overrepresentation of Jews is likely to be true of other countries, including the United States and Canada.

B. The next largest branch is the food industry (including drinks and tobacco), the proportion ranging from about 8 to about 20 per cent. In every country in our sample, except Rumania, its share among Jews is larger than among non-Jews.

C. The two other branches of industry whose shares among Jews appear to be larger than among non-Jews are leather (including furs) and printing and paper. These are largely finished consumer goods industries (shoes, fur articles, books, etc.). However, they account for relatively minor fractions of gainfully occupied within industry, whether among Jews or among non-Jews.

D. The shares of textiles, metals, construction, and "other" among Jews engaged in industry are significantly below the shares among non-Jews (or total population). Although the shares of the metal industries among Jews reflect the concentration in the jewelry and precious metal branches, they are on the whole only about half of those among non-Jews.

E. The relatively low shares of the textile branch among Jews are in sharp contrast to the higher shares of the related clothing industries. However, textiles are large-scale, factory-organized industries and in many countries Jews do not have easy access to them. Consequently, they tend to

Table 3

Distribution by Branches within the Industry Sector, Jews and Non-Jews Compared, Selected Countries

Country, date, and coverage	Total Industry (000's)	Total Industry % Shares or Ratios	% Shares or Ratios								
			Food (Incl. Drink and Tobacco)	Clothing	Textiles	Leather	Printing and Paper	Wood	Metals	Constr.	Other
Russia, 1897											
1. Gainfully occupied, Jews	543	100	11.2	46.9	6.4	4.0	2.9	7.8	10.5	7.2	3.2
2. Total attached, Jews	1,754	100	12.9	44.6	5.3	4.1	2.4	8.0	10.7	8.7	3.2
3. Total attached, non-Jews	7,495	100	8.1	17.7	12.3	3.1	1.5	9.3	17.6	17.2	13.3
4. Proportion of Jews in total attached		19.0	27.1	37.3	9.2	23.7	27.4	16.7	12.4	10.6	5.4
Austria, 1910											
5. Gainfully occupied, Jews	132	100	17.9	40.5	6.1	4.5	2.0	7.0	9.9	5.4	6.4
6. Total attached, Jews	325	100	21.9	35.0	5.5	4.5	1.8	8.3	9.7	6.3	7.0
7. Total attached, non-Jews	7,224	100	9.4	16.6	11.6	3.1[a]	1.3[a]	8.7	16.4	14.8	18.0
8. Proportion of Jews in total attached		4.3	9.5	8.7	2.0	6.2	5.9	4.1	2.5	1.9	1.7
Germany, 1907											
9. Gainfully occupied, Jews	63	100	21.9	40.2	5.5	3.7	4.5	3.5	10.0	4.4	6.2
10. Gainfully occupied, non-Jews	11,193	100	9.9	14.9	9.4	1.9	3.6	7.0	18.6	17.0	17.8
11. Proportion of Jews in total gainfully occupied		0.5	1.2	1.5	0.3	1.0	0.7	0.3	0.3	0.1	0.2

	1	2	3	4	5	6	7	8	9	10	11
Rumania, 1913											
12. Wage earners, Jews	17.5	100	7.7	54.7	5.9	3.3	2.1	7.4	9.6	7.3	2.0
13. Wage earners, non-Jews	150	100	12.5	21.7	4.7	3.1	2.0	15.6	17.7	15.6	7.1
14. Proportion of Jews in total wage earners		10.5	6.8	23.8	12.6	11.1	10.5	5.3	6.0	4.9	3.5
15. Proportion of all gainfully occupied Jews in total gainfully occupied		12.2		21.4	14.5	13.2	15.1	6.8	7.0	6.3	
Poland, 1921											
16. Gainfully occupied, Jews	297	100	15.4	46.7	8.2	3.7	2.6	6.6	4.9	4.5	7.4
17. Gainfully occupied, non-Jews	969	100	11.0	20.0	14.5	2.6	2.0	12.1	9.7	9.4	18.7
18. Proportion of Jews in total gainfully occupied		23.5	30.0	41.7	14.8	43.6	28.5	16.8	13.4	12.7	11.4
Czechoslovakia, 1921[b]											
19. Wage earners only, Jews	7.6	100	19.7	31.6	3.9	2.6	6.6	7.9	15.8	3.9	7.9
20. Wage earners only, non-Jews	1,095	100	8.2	9.6	17.4	1.3	3.0	6.8	18.6	12.9	22.2
21. Proportion of Jews in total wage earners		0.7	1.6	2.2	0.2	1.5	1.4	0.8	0.6	0.2	0.2

[a] Paper is included with leather.

[b] The sum of Bohemia, Slovakia, and Carpatho-Ruthenia.

SOURCES: Lines 1–11, from *Zeitschrift fuer Demographie und Statistik der Juden*, February and March, 1906, pp. 9–21 and 43; June, 1911, p. 86; and January–March, 1919, pp. 19 ff. Lines 12–14 from Lestschinsky, *Weltwirtschaftliches Archiv*, Vol. 32, 1930, pp. 582–593 and 595. Line 15, from Ruppin, *Die Soziologie der Juden*, Vol. 1, p. 434. Lines 16–21, same source as lines 12–14.

concentrate in hand trades and small-scale enterprises, with a strong leaning toward individual entrepreneurship.

F. With concentration of Jews in one or two branches within industry, and lack of concentration among non-Jews, the distribution of the former among the several branches is necessarily more "unequal." In other words, the Jewish minority does not have as "balanced" an industrial distribution as the non-Jewish majority.

G. It follows that the proportion of Jews among the total occupied in some branches of industry is far greater than the proportion of Jews in industry as a whole. But even in clothing, the most "overrepresented" branch, Jews are well below the majority of the total engaged. However, it may be that in some narrow divisions of the clothing industry and in some within metals (jewelry, etc.) Jews are the preponderant majority of the total occupied.

5. Specialization within the Public Service and Professions Sector

This sector accounts for moderate proportions of the gainfully occupied, but it is of special interest because of its relative importance to society and the high level of skill required in some branches. Unfortunately qualitative variations within the sector are wide and meaningful, and comparable statistics are rare. Even if we exclude military services, we are left with a variety of skill and economic productivity, ranging from routine clerical jobs to activities of highly trained personnel. The data are at best only suggestive, and Table 4 is limited to a few cases that reveal a range of extremes.

A. The proportion of Jews engaged in public service is likely to be quite low in many countries because of legal restrictions, e.g., in Russia in 1897 and Poland in 1931. But even if no legal limitations exist, the proportion is lower among Jews than among non-Jews, e.g., in Germany in 1907. So long as there is some discrimination and the Jewish minority is reluctant to trust its economic future to the conditions of government service, its share is likely to be moderate and lower than for the majority.

B. These limitations extend into education and culture and the health services. Yet both loom large among the total body of Jews attached to the sector because, despite restrictions, Jews can find employment opportunities in these fields. Specialization may be a factor. If government hospitals and public health offices are restricted, there is a concentration of Jews in private health services.

C. The data given in Table 4 exclude professionally trained persons attached to other industries (engineers, chemists, etc.), and limitation to four professional groups is a simplification. If the distribution were more complete and detailed, the specialization of Jews would be more apparent.

D. There is some semblance of a pattern in the structure of the pro-

TABLE 4

*Distribution within the Public Service and Professions Sector, Jews and
Non-Jews Compared, Selected Countries*

Country and Date	Total (000's)	% Shares and Ratios	% Shares or Ratios				
			Government Service	Attorneys, Notaries, etc.	Religious and Social Institutions	Education and Culture	Health Services
Russia, 1897							
1. Gain. occupied, Jews	72.2	100	3.6	1.5	28.5	52.7	13.5
2. Total attached, Jews	264.6	100	4.2	1.7	33.7	50.3	10.9
3. Total attached, non-Jews	1,704	100	18.7	2.1	44.2	20.3	13.7
4. Proportion of Jews in total attached		13.4	3.9	12.5	12.1	31.3	11.6
Germany, 1907							
5. Gain. occupied, Jews	16.8	100	23.2 (incl. col. 5)		8.1	37.1	31.6
6. Gain. occupied, non-Jews	1,071	100	36.0 (incl. col. 5)		7.4	37.7	19.0
7. Proportion of Jews in total gain. occupied		1.5	1.0 (incl. col. 5)		1.7	1.5	2.6
Poland, 1931							
8. Gain. occupied, Jews	68.3	100	4.6	9.4	15.1	46.0	25.0
9. Gain. occupied non-Jews	497.7	100	35.0	2.6	17.6	30.1	14.7
10. Proportion of Jews in total gain. occupied		12.1	1.8	33.5	10.5	17.3	18.8

SOURCES: Lines 1–4, see source for lines 1–4 in Table 3. Lines 5–7, Ruppin, *Die Soziologie der Juden*, Vol. 1, p. 488. Lines 8–10, Raphael Mahler, "Jews in Public Service in Poland, 1918–39," *Jewish Social Studies*, October, 1944, pp. 290–350, particularly Table VII, p. 288.

fessions themselves (excluding government service) associated with the economic phase of development of a country, and in its effects on the specialization of Jews. It is perhaps not an accident that the proportion of the religious branch is largest in Russia in 1897, distinctly lower in Poland in 1931, and very much lower in Germany in 1907. The high ratio in Russia is due to a large service element connected with synagogues, burial places, and religious schools. By contrast, in Germany because of secularization and the higher professional standards of increasing numbers of Jews, the percentage in the religious branch is low—among both Jews and non-Jews. Similar shifts in the relative importance of education and culture and of the health services also occur, the former falling and the latter rising with the rise in the economic level of the country in general and of the Jews in particular. More detailed data would probably reveal corollary shifts within education from predominance of elementary education, perhaps largely religious, to a greater proportion at the higher levels of education and to broader cultural pursuits.

E. Because of differentiation within the professional categories and because of specialization, Jews are dominant in some categories. In Poland in 1931, Jews accounted for 18.8 per cent of the health services, but for 56 per cent of private physicians. In Hungary in 1920, the proportion of Jews in legal service was 27.5 per cent, but their proportion among lawyers was 50.6 per cent. These examples for single professions with a specific employment status could easily be multiplied.

6. *Distribution by Employment Status*

We have already referred to a trend among Jews toward independent economic activity and away from employee status within large-scale enterprises. This economic characteristic can be substantiated by evidence on their distribution among employers or self-employed (such as artisans, independent professionals, etc.), white-collar or salaried employees, and manual workers.

Table 5 presents the data for the total body of gainfully occupied outside of agriculture, Jews and non-Jews, in six countries.[9] The conclusions are unmistakable. Generally, the proportion among Jews of employers or self-employed is high, ranging from over a third to close to two-thirds of all gainfully occupied outside of agriculture. And, more important, the proportions are invariably much higher than those for the non-Jewish majority. The contrast in Poland, Germany, and Czechoslovakia is particularly striking.

The share of salaried workers among the Jews is far smaller than that of "independents," and sometimes smaller and sometimes larger than the share for non-Jews. In Germany, Hungary, and Czechoslovakia, the share among Jews is larger than that among non-Jews; in the U.S.S.R. and Rumania, they are about the same; in Poland, the share among the Jews is distinctly smaller. The share of salaried workers must be affected by complexes of factors that differ materially from country to country, and probably from time to time; and no general characteristic of Jews with respect to this share can be distinguished. However, as the proportion of working population outside of agriculture is much higher among Jews than among non-Jews, and as there are few salaried employees in agriculture, the proportions of salaried employees may, in terms of population, *including* agriculture, be higher among Jews.

The share of manual workers is far lower among the Jews than among

TABLE 5

Distribution by Employment Status, Gainfully Occupied Population Outside of Agriculture, Jews and Non-Jews Compared, Six Countries

Country and Date	Total (000's)	% Shares				
		Total	Employers and Self-Employed	Salaried Employees	Manual Workers	Not Specified
Poland, 1931						
1. Jews	1,144.5	100	62.2	8.2	26.8	2.8
2. Non-Jews	4,139.5	100	18.2	13.2	59.2	9.4
U.S.S.R., 1926						
3. Jews	929.8	100	38.9	32.9	19.1	9.1
4. Non-Jews	12,794.5	100	17.5	31.0	37.6	13.9
Germany, 1933						
5. Jews	297.3	100	43.1	28.6	7.8	20.5
6. Non-Jews	28,477.6	100	13.0	19.0	47.8	20.2
Hungary, 1930						
7. Jews	207.3	100	35.0	25.3	32.3	7.4
8. Non-Jews	1,719.5	100	16.4	11.0	63.6	9.0
Czechoslovakia, 1930						
9. Jews	152.3	100	42.2	28.2	11.8	17.8
10. Non-Jews	4,821.4	100	12.2	18.0	53.4	16.4
Rumania, 1913[a]						
11. Jews	71.7	100	47.4	21.9	30.8	0
12. Non-Jews	406.0	100	34.2	22.4	43.4	0

[a] Sum of three sectors: trade and finance, industry, and public services plus professions.

SOURCES: Lines 1-10, Lestschinsky, "The Economic and Social Development of the Jewish People," in *The Jewish People: Past and Present*, Vol. I., p. 383. Lines 11-12, based on Lestschinsky, *Weltwirtschaftliches Archiv*, 1930, Vol. 32, p. 593.

the non-Jewish majority. This must follow, for "independents" claim a much larger share among the Jews and the share of salaried employees does not differ equally in the opposite direction. But the disparity in the share of manual workers is significant. In Germany and Czechoslovakia, where the ratio of Jews to gainfully occupied population outside of agriculture is particularly low, the share of manual workers among Jews is also low; and correspondingly, the difference between it and the share among the non-Jews is particularly high.

This comment suggests an aspect of employment status that is not evident in Table 5. In nonagricultural industries the demand for various types of labor differs. Thus trade and finance require few manual workers, whereas some branches of industry require many. Because the economic structure of Jews is noted for greater concentration in trade and in the consumer goods industries, this specialization may, in itself, make for higher shares of "independents" and salaried employees and lower shares of manual workers.

Generally, within trade, within industry, within the public services and professions sector, separately, and for every country, the share of Jews among the total of all employers and independents is higher than the share of Jews among the total of all engaged (Table 6). Again invariably, except for Rumania, where the numbers in public service and the professions are quite small, the share of Jews among all manual workers is lower than the share of Jews among the total gainfully occupied. In other words, the

TABLE 6

Percentage Shares of Jews in Total, by Employment Status within Major Sectors Outside of Agriculture, Six Countries

Industry Sectors and Status Classes (1)	Poland 1931 (2)	U.S.S.R. 1926 (3)	Germany 1933 (4)	Hungary 1930 (5)	Czecho-slovakia 1930 (6)	Rumania 1913 (7)
Total excl. Agriculture						
1. All Jews	21.2	6.8	1.0	10.8	3.1	15.0
2. Employers and independ-ent workers	47.9	13.9	3.3	20.4	9.8	19.7
3. Salaried employees	14.3	7.1	1.6	21.7	4.7	14.7
4. Manual workers	10.9	3.6	0.2	5.8	0.7	11.1
Trade						
5. All Jews	52.3	18.0	3.3	35.8	12.7	31.3
6. Employers and independ-ent workers	65.4	25.4	5.5	41.9	16.8	32.2
7. Salaried employees	30.3	13.9	3.0	47.7	12.1	29.1
8. Manual workers	23.1	8.1	0.3	24.4	3.1	11.4
Industry and crafts						
9. All Jews	19.9	7.2	0.4	7.4	1.3	12.5
10. Employers and independ-ent workers	35.6	11.4	1.3	10.6	4.6	14.3
11. Salaried employees	19.7	8.3	1.4	33.0	3.5	16.6
12. Manual workers	12.9	4.4	0.2	4.8	0.5	11.1
Public service and professions						
13. All Jews	12.0	7.3	1.2	8.9	3.8	3.6
14. Employers and independ-ent workers	43.7	13.3	6.0	34.2	14.9	6.2
15. Salaried employees	10.3	7.1	0.8	7.4	2.8	2.9
16. Manual workers	5.1	3.6	0.3	3.1	1.1	15.5

SOURCE: Col. 7, lines 1–4, are for sum of the three sectors below (see source in Table 5). Cols. 2–6 are based on Lestschinsky, "The Economic and Social Development of the Jewish People," pp. 379–381, 389.

higher shares among Jews of employers and independents and the lower shares of manual workers are found for all three major sectors.

7. Some General Implications

For a clear picture of the economic structure of the Jews, the data are woefully inadequate. In many countries, the basic country-wide statistics do not distinguish Jews. In others, the data are limited to the kind associated with population censuses. This type of information covers the occupational and industrial attachment, but it tells us little about other important aspects of economic structure and life—size and distribution of wealth, size and distribution of income, earnings and savings patterns of minorities and majorities, and the like. No such information is available, barring some exceptional cases (e.g., the religious tax returns in Germany, which are of doubtful value even for the small group covered, let alone for the study of the economics of world Jewry), and none is likely to be collected in the future, except for the Jewish majority in Israel.

If one then asks what the distinctive economic structure of Jews with respect to their industrial, occupational, and employment status means for their over-all economic performance, no unequivocal answer can be given. But some implications can be explored, and we conclude this section by commenting briefly on three general aspects of the economic characteristics of Jews that have been discussed so far: (A) the concentration of Jews in urban communities; (B) the implications for the general level and distribution of income among Jews, compared with those of the majority; (C) the meaning of "dominance" by Jews of selected industries.

A. That Jews are largely city dwellers is a common and familiar fact. But the extent to which Jews have concentrated in the larger urban communities, and the links between this process and "specialization," are not generally realized.

The evidence on urbanization, important for the question of the level of income and to some extent even of its size distribution, can be presented by two brief citations. Both are from a paper by Dr. Lestschinsky published in 1930, and the data refer to the early or middle 1920's:

In the whole world there are nineteen cities, each with over 1,000,000 inhabitants. Five of these—two in China, two in Japan, and one in India—are omitted from the analysis because there are almost no Jews in the respective countries. We are left with fourteen great, million-population, cities in Europe and the Americas. These largest centers of the civilized world were inhabited in 1925 by about 38,000,000 people; among them about 3,500,000 or 9.2 per cent were Jews, whereas the proportion of Jews in the total population of Europe and the Americas was about 2 per cent. Europe and the Americas are inhabited presently by about 665,000,000 persons. Hence, the 38,000,000 inhabitants of the great cities form about 5.7 per cent of the total population. On these great continents there lived some 13,700,000 Jews, of whom 25.4 per cent were settled in the great cities, while the corresponding percentage for non-Jews was less than 4.5 times as small (5.3 per cent). If we calculate the proportion of Jews living in these great cities to the total of Jews in the whole world, the resulting share is 23 per cent.[10]

The concentration in giant cities may have increased after the mid-1920's, as there is a strong tendency in this direction in the United States and the relative weight of United States Jewry has increased appreciably. No elaborate proof is needed to conclude that a high proportion of Jews lives in metropolitan areas with multimillion total population.

Moreover, the Jewish population is concentrated in large Jewish communities. In the same paper, Dr. Lestschinsky shows that of total world Jewry (at that time close to 15,000,000), well over a third lived in thirty-four Jewish communities, each of which comprised 50,000 or more. And over half (55.3 per cent) were estimated to live in Jewish communities of 10,000 or more.

Like many other links within complex social problems, the relation between the distinctive economic structure of the Jews and their concentration in large cities runs both ways. It is impossible to say whether Jews are impelled to large cities because only there can they practice the economic pursuits in which they specialize; whether they concentrate on the latter because they wish to live in large cities; or whether the economic structure and high degree of urbanization are a joint product of some common forces. Perhaps it is not as important to know the cause as to recognize the close association between these two aspects of Jewish life. If community of feeling and cohesion impel Jews to live in groups of a minimum size and if they concentrate in certain branches of trade, consumer goods industries, and independent professions, this minimum group so engaged *must* reside in fairly sizable urban communities. No community (except an artificially set up capital city) can sustain more than a small proportion of its members in highly specialized pursuits. The usual proviso holds, of course, that no legal restraints exist and that desires and strivings can be given relatively free rein. (There are also other noneconomic causes, e.g., the greater anonymity and tolerance of large cities compared with small, but we are concerned here with economic arguments.)

Concentration in large cities, however, affects the economic structure of the Jews. The younger generations will be born in, and immigration will tend to gravitate to, these urban centers. The effect on the younger generation is particularly important. Its horizon and outlook will be influenced by its environment, and those born in large cities will tend to remain within the range of economic and social opportunities offered by them. Those born in smaller cities, with their drive toward pursuits at economic levels higher than those of their parents, may enter the more specialized trade or professional pursuits, and thus further the movement to the large urban centers.

B. Since, in general, per capita incomes of urban groups are higher than those of rural groups—and there is some tendency to gradation by size of city—the average income of Jews should be higher than the country-wide average.

But this differential is only one of many forces that determine the level of income among Jews. Unfortunately, in considering these additional determinants, we get little help from the findings concerning the economic structure by industry, occupation, employment status, or urbanization, if only because they may have different meanings in terms of income yields, particularly for a small minority. For example, let us assume that per capita income in trade is 20 per cent higher than country-wide per capita income and that Jews account for 50 per cent of the gainfully occupied in trade. Can we assume that the per capita income of Jews engaged in trade is 20 per cent higher than the country-wide level? Definitely not, because we also can assume that Jews are likely to be concentrated in some branches of trade or that they are preponderantly owners of small establishments. It is conceivable that the per capita income of Jews in trade is 40 per cent above, and that of non-Jews equals, the country-wide average; or conversely, that the former is equal to, and the latter is 40 per cent above, the country-wide average. There is no way of passing from the industrial and employment status of Jews to the relation between their income and that of the rest of the population, unless we know the specific levels in all branches in which Jews are close to 100 per cent of total occupied and these branches employ close to 100 per cent of the Jewish population. No such data are available and no such conditions exist in any country with a sizable proportion of world Jewry.

This argument also bears upon any inference from the greater urbanization of Jews. Granted that the per capita income of urban population is higher than that of rural, yet in no country do Jews even approach 100 per cent of urban population; they constitute a much smaller fraction—no matter how narrowly we define urban. Hence it is possible for total urban population to have a per capita income above the country-wide, while Jews in cities have an income still higher or appreciably lower. And the per capita income of Jews is likely to be different if only because their economic structure is specific and different.

We can, therefore, only speculate about the income (and wealth) position of the Jewish minorities. These speculations, useful only for channeling further exploration, may be summarized as follows:

First, per capita income of the Jewish minority can be higher than that of the majority if legal limitations upon the economic activity of Jews are relatively minor and the proportion of recent Jewish immigrants is relatively moderate. Under such conditions, the skills and specialization of

Jews in the pursuit of trade, industry, and the professions, concentrated in the larger cities, may well produce a per capita income above the country-wide average. If this situation prevails for some time, the well-known middle-class virtues of the Jews can produce a level of wealth-holding that is also above average.

The underlying assumption that the shares of agriculture producers and of wage earners, both relatively low per capita income groups, are appreciably higher among the majority than among Jews is true in practically all countries for which we have data. But we have no hard and fast criteria for judging the conditions under which the inference was drawn. Whether legal discrimination is minor or major, and whether a given proportion of recent immigrants is moderate or not, are matters of judgment. By dint of study of experience we can infer that the per capita income and wealth of Jews were higher than those of total population during the first decade of this century, and perhaps later, in France, Germany, Italy, the Scandinavian countries, and perhaps even in England. But until further data can be brought to bear on the question, we can only infer that at the end of the nineteenth century in Russia, because of legal limitations, the per capita income of Jews was at best equal to, and probably below, the per capita income of total population; nor can we guess at the comparative levels in the United States at the end of the past century or in the first decade of the twentieth century when immigration added sizable proportions to the resident body of Jews.

Second, the size distribution of income among Jews compared with that of the majority is subject to three influences. First, since there is practically no agriculture and there is only a small proportion of wage earners among Jews, the distribution of their income should be *less* unequal than that of the majority. Second, since a greater proportion of Jews are entrepreneurs and self-employed, the distribution of their income should be *more* unequal than that of non-Jews. For annual returns of "independents" are subject to sizable variations; and the range, on a long-term basis, is much wider for them than for employees whose compensation varies within a narrow one of fixed salaries or wage rates. Finally, where there are large additions by immigration, the differentiation between the more prosperous older residents and the poorer newcomers is likely to be greater for Jews than for the majority, for the proportional additions of immigrants to the latter are likely to be far smaller, and the distribution of the income of Jews should be *more* unequal.[11]

What is the balance of these influences working in opposite directions? It may well be that income and wealth inequality among Jews is wider than that of the urban population and perhaps even than that of total population. This is more likely for countries and periods where continued large immigration or legal restrictions operate to keep the mass of Jews at low economic levels. However, for an established and relatively stable Jewish minority, operating under conditions of economic freedom, the distribution of income is likely to be less unequal than for the majority.

When and if wide inequality in income and wealth prevails, comparisons of *average* per capita income and wealth of Jews with those of the majority lose their significance. Furthermore, whenever it exists, the wide divergence in economic fortunes points up the distinctive characteristics of Jews—forcing the attention of observers, hostile or sympathetic, not only to the few Jews at the peak levels of economic attainment but also to the many more at the poverty and social problem level.

C. Our last comment related to the meaning of "dominance," a subject which has attracted much emotion-charged discussion. If by dominance we mean a high, say, over 50 per cent, proportion of Jews to the total engaged in a given field in a given area, then, assuming a desire for cohesion and specialization among Jews, dominance must exist in some small and narrowly defined economic cells.

But a high proportion to the total engaged in a specific field, in and of itself, is no special advantage. The specialization is partly a result of lack of antecedent experience, partly a result of restrictions. Relatively complete domination by a minority of an industry means that it occupies both the high and the low positions; i.e., profits from the well-managed and successful units and suffers from the poorly managed and economically less productive ones. Consequently, unless the industry *as a whole* represents a highly advantageous sector of the economy, relative to others, no *economic* advantage attaches to the dominance of a minority.

That the particular industries in which Jews tend to be numerically dominant are economically the most advantageous is to be doubted; trade, light consumer goods industries, and even the independent professions can hardly be put in that category. Nor is it clear that, despite the preponderance of employers and self-employed, Jews occupy the most advantageous positions within those industries. Granted the generally higher incomes of owners of large establishments, the numerical basis for the greater share of "independents" among Jews is the masses of artisans and petty traders. The specialization of Jews in the latter pursuits is more a matter of compulsion than of presumptive economic advantage. The fact that with improving economic position and greater assimilation the share of salaried employees among Jews rises—often at the expense of the share of employers and self-employed—is an indication that no lasting economic advantage can be attached to this aspect of dominance. In fact, the high proportion of Jews, based upon numbers, may be interpreted as an economic disadvantage—an overcrowding in one field.

This argument does not bar the possibility of economic dominance of another kind, i.e., the control of assets that may affect some important branches of an economy. No reliable data are available on the share of Jews in the wealth of the countries of their residence, nor is it clear that such data would shed much light. What would it mean if we found that Jews as a body hold, say, 10 per cent of the stocks in the steel industry? Or, for that matter, what would it mean, except for propaganda purposes, if we found that a few Jews have large holdings in copper or aluminum—to the point of constituting a major interest group?

The reason for the questions is twofold. First, Jews may be a distinctive and cohesive minority in their community of religious beliefs or historical heritage and in their patterns of life and work. But it is difficult to view their investments and financial activities (when the latter are *not* their work) as an integral part of their functioning as members of a minority. Indeed, it can be argued that the financial investment activity of Jews as a whole, aside from that involved in their work, is neither distinguishable from that of the rest of the population nor affected by their membership in the minority. This particularly occurs in countries where legal conditions do not compel Jews to act always as possible refugees.

The second reason is that exceptional individual cases hardly matter. That Mr. X, a Jew by some definition, owns an imposing stock of financial claims on the copper industry has little significance in the economic life of the Jewish minority as a cohesive social group. For it is the functioning of the group that is decisive, whereas the attachment and the functioning of an individual are subject to the caprices of fortune and can never have much weight in the life of the minority—unless they enlist the latter through successful leadership. The bearing of this argument can be seen clearly by asking: If Mr. X separates himself from the minority and in the next one or two generations merges into the majority, would we say that the Jewish minority, which at one time, through Mr. X, exercised a major claim on the copper industry, in a decade or two no longer does so?

If this argument is valid, the burden of emphasis in the study of the economic structure of the Jews must be on the basic patterns of life and work of the masses, and not on such peripheral matters as their behavior as investors, or on the conspicuous successes of some small group of individuals who may have attained positions of wealth. Any consideration of dominance of Jews must be related to the proportions of their numbers in the economic activities that absorb the masses of mankind; and in that sense dominance can be achieved only in narrow segments where it is an inevitable result of cohesion and specialization—and carries with it not only economic advantages but also disadvantages. The economic balance is uncertain, but it is likely to be negative as noneconomic factors propel Jews toward pursuits different from those that would normally follow from an economic calculation of potential returns to given ability and resources.

III. Trends and Displacement during the Past Century

Little attention was paid in the preceding discussion to the evolution of the economic structure of Jews. Nor did we consider the shifts in the relative importance of various communities and their effects on that structure. Yet both aspects are of obvious importance. It seems likely that the long-term changes in level and structure of the economic life of Jews within a country, while following to some extent those characterizing the economic life of the majority, would still differ from them. At any rate, it is of interest to see what these changes are within some relatively recent period, long enough to give us some perspective.

Such a review of trends should yield two valuable results. First, we could ascertain whether one pattern of growth is followed by Jewish communities in different countries; and, if so, how this pattern compares with that in the economic growth of the majorities. Second, if the data were available over a long period for all countries in which the Jews were substantial proportions of world Jewry, we could see the long-term shifts in the distribution of the latter among the countries with different levels of income and patterns of growth.

While there are estimates of the number of Jews in several countries extending back over a century, the data on economic life and structure are exceedingly scanty. However, the striking changes and displacements in numbers have alone been sufficient to influence the economic evolution of world Jewry, and scattered data relating to economic structure shed some light on the trends since the end of the past century. It is, therefore, possible, in a sketchy way and by some heroic manipulation of data, to study the broad lines of economic dynamics—at least for the major group of Jews.

This study comprises a review of trends in three Jewish communities (or complexes of such): East European Jews, with primary emphasis on those within the Czarist Russian Empire; Jews in the United States; and the Palestine-Israel Jewish community.

1. Russian and East European Jews

A. Growth and Decline in Numbers[11a]

We begin with this group for two reasons: until about 1880 it accounted for well over two-thirds of world Jewry, and from the first quarter of the nineteenth century it fed, through migration, the Jewish communities in other countries—in particular the United States and Israel.

In 1825, some 2,400,000 eastern European Jews accounted for over 70 per cent of all the Jews in the world (Table 7, Part A). The precise reasons why such a large proportion was concentrated in a relatively narrow area

TABLE 7

Growth of Russian and East European Jewry,
Compared with That of World Jewry

Country (1)	A 1825–1925				
	1825 (2)	1850 (3)	1880 (4)	1900 (5)	1925 (6)
	Absolute Figures (000's)				
Erstwhile European Russia					
1. Congress Poland	400	575	1,005	1,325	1,475
2. Ukraine, U.S.S.R., Bessarabia	625	925	1,600	2,200	2,150
3. Lithuania and White Russia	550	800	1,225	1,450	1,200
4. Other parts	25	50	150	200	460
5. Total (1+2+3+4)	1,600	2,350	3,980	5,175	5,285
6. Galicia	275	450	687	811	740
7. Bohemia, Moravia, Lower Austria	85	130	245	310	375
8. Hungary	200	352	638	852	983
9. Rumania and Bukovina	88	145	267.5	363	420
10. Other East European areas	109	137	154	161	190
11. Total East Europe	2,357	3,564	5,971	7,672	7,993
12. Total world Jewry	3,281	4,764	7,663	10,602	14,800
13. 11 as % of 12	71.8	74.8	77.9	72.4	54.0

	Percentage Changes per Decade				
	1825–50	1850–80	1880–1900	1900–25	1825–1925
14. Erstwhile European Russia	16.5	19.2	14.0	0.8	12.7
15. Eastern Europe	18.0	18.8	13.4	1.7	13.0
16. Non-Eastern Europe	11.0	12.1	31.6	40.2	22.1
17. Total world Jewry	16.1	17.2	17.6	14.3	16.3

Country (1)	B 1925–1954		
	1925 (2)	1939 (3)	1954 (4)
	Absolute Figures (000's)		
1. Poland	2,850	3,300	45
2. European Russia	2,525	2,825	
3. Lithuania	160	155	2,000[b]
4. Latvia	105	95	
5. Estonia	5	5	
6. Hungary	490	403	140
7. Czechoslovakia	360	315	17
8. Austria	300	55	10.6
9. Rumania	900	800	225
10. Other Eastern Europe	204.5[a]	175[a]	63.3[c]
11. Total Eastern Europe	7,899	8,128	2,500.9
12. Total world Jewry	14,831	16,648	11,867
13. 11 as % of 12	53.3	48.8	21.1

[a] Includes Bulgaria, Yugoslavia, and European Turkey.
[b] Total for Soviet Union, including Asiatic Russia. Jews were estimated to be 190,000 in 1925 and 235,000 in 1939.
[c] Includes Albania, Bulgaria, Yugoslavia, and Turkey (including Asiatic).

SOURCES: Part A, Lestschinsky, in *Weltwirtschaftliches Archiv*. Vol. 30, 1929, p. 132. Part B, col. 2, Lestschinsky, in *Zeitschrift fuer Demographie und Statistik der Juden*, 1925, Part 1, pp. 2–3; col. 3, Ruppin, in *The Jewish People: Past and Present*, Vol. 1, pp. 350–351; col. 4, Leon Shapiro, in *American Jewish Year Book*, 1955, pp. 281–283.

on the western boundary of the Russian Empire cannot be reviewed here; yet they have some bearing upon the economic evolution of eastern European Jews and the major Jewish communities that are their offshoots. The historical process by which the Jews were carried from the Mediterranean largely through western and central Europe to this area and were hemmed in, as it were, between the hostile western rear and the hostile eastern front can hardly be recounted here and will be assumed. We also assume that in these areas of concentration, long-standing limitations on pursuits open to Jews resulted in specialization in trade and certain handicrafts. But two aspects must be stressed. First, while legal restriction varied from country to country within the East European area, the dominant proportion of East European Jewry—that within the Russian Empire—was under control of a government that was both hostile to Jews as a minority and none too capable of pursuing an intelligent policy. Consequently there was an ever-present pressure upon the life and economic opportunities of East European Jews. Second, despite this hostility, the majority power, particularly in Russia, exercised sway over a vast empire and, granted its discriminative legislation, protected even the Jewish minority from extensive physical dangers and gave them some chance to grow without being decimated by massacres of the Chmielnicki or Hitler type.

This latter circumstance explains in part the remarkable growth in numbers of East European Jews from 1825 to 1880. The rate was appreciably greater than that for Jews in the rest of the world, and it was greater than that for the total populations of many European countries of the period. On the demographic side it was largely the product of a fairly high birth rate combined with a gradually declining death rate, resulting from the spread of modern medical and health measures; and on the economic side it was largely sustained by the fact that this rapidly growing group was a small minority in a large country with a wide potential of growth.

It is this rise, 3,600,000 Jews of some 4,300,000 additions to world Jewry in 1825-1880, that provided the base for further growth and the reservoir from which, through migration, the other major Jewish communities were either created or strengthened. This migration, westward within Europe or overseas, rose from a trickle before the 1880's to a wide stream before World War I, to continue with interruptions and at a greatly reduced rate up to World War II.

The increase in emigration largely accounts for the decline in the rate of increase of East European Jews from 1880 to 1900. Emigration during these twenty years was about 700,000.[12] To add them all to the recorded population for eastern Europe in 1900 is an exaggeration, as only the *survivors* should be included. On the other hand, if these migrants had remained at home they would have contributed to the natural increase. If, then, 700,000 is the rough adjustment, the total Jewish population in eastern Europe in 1900 would have been 8,372,000; and the rate of increase per decade for 1880-1900 would have been 18.4 per cent, practically identical with the 18.8 per cent for 1850-1880.

It may well be that a similar adjustment for emigration, which was at a much higher rate in 1899-1914 than during the 1880's and 1890's, would erase the decline in the rate of growth of East European Jewry up to World War I. This supposition cannot be tested, for no estimates of Jews in eastern Europe in 1910 or 1914 are available. But whatever the case, the almost complete stoppage in growth for the period 1900-1925 is only partly due to emigration. Hersch's estimate of Jewish emigration for 1899-1925, largely eastern European, is somewhat short of 2,500,000. Even if we add this total to the number of East European Jews in 1925, the resulting 10,500,000 yields a decade rate of increase for 1900-1925 of only 13.4 per cent. Clearly, the ravages of war and revolution have begun to take their toll.

The catastrophic acceleration of the destructive effects of war, revolution, and reaction is too well known to warrant stressing (Table 7, Part B). By 1954, the growth of more than a century was wiped out; and the only consolation is that a number of East European Jews succeeded in settling elsewhere and multiplied rapidly.

B. *Trends in Economic Structure to World War II*

The rapid growth up to the 1880's; then slower but still substantial growth accompanied by large and increasing emigration; and then war and massacres must surely have been due in part to shifts in the economic structure of both the Jews and the majority populations of eastern Europe and, of course, must also have affected them.

Table 8 illustrates the already familiar economic structure of Jewry in Russia and in Austria, largely dominated by Galicia. We find the large shares of industry (mostly handicrafts) and trade; also the negative correlation of the proportion of Jews to urban population with the proportion among Jews of those engaged in trade, and the positive correlation with the proportion among Jews engaged in industry, i.e., largely artisans. Lithuania and White Russia, with the highest proportion of Jews in urban population, have the highest proportion among Jews in industry and the lowest in trade. We stress this point because it was in the provinces with the highest proportions of Jews among the urban population that the pressure to emigrate was the greatest. The Lithuanian-White Russian provinces were the most heavily represented among the Jewish emigrants from Russia to the United States.

The turn of the century falls within the period of substantial emigration. It is significant, therefore, that the few data that exist suggest that the heavy emphasis on industry, shown in Table 8, is *not* observed in the nine-

Table 8

Industrial Distribution of Jews in Russia and Austria, 1897 and 1900

(1)		Russian Empire, 1897					
	Poland (2)	Lithuania and White Russia (3)	Southwest and South (Pale) (4)	Outside the Pale (5)	Total (6)	Austria, 1900 (7)
1. Total no. of Jews (ooo's)	1,321	1,422	2,156	317	5,216	1,225
2. Jews as % of total population	14.1	14.1	9.4	0.4	4.2	4.7
3. Jews as % of urban population	37.7	52.7	31.8			
4. Total gainfully occupied Jews (ooo's)	338	403	591	99	1,431	
% Distribution of line 4 or line 1 for column 7[b] by sectors						
5. Agriculture	1.8	4.1	2.9	2.1	2.9	12.6
6. Manufacture and mechanical pursuits	36.6	43.2	35.0	38.0	37.9	31.9
7. Transportation	2.9	4.1	3.0	1.8	3.2	3.4
8. Trade and finance[a]	31.1	25.6	37.0	26.8	31.6	38.9
9. Personal services[a]	23.6	17.6	16.8	27.6	19.4	6.0[c]
10. Professional services	4.0	5.4	5.4	4.7	5.0	7.2

[a] Hotel, restaurant, and saloon keepers are included with personal services. If they were shifted to trade, the shares for Russia as a whole would become: personal services—17.8; trade—33.2.

[b] Total population including military, nongainfully occupied, and occupations unknown (together about 118,000).

[c] Including unknown occupations (see note b), this would be almost double (with offsetting decreases in other shares).

Sources: Cols. 2–6: from I. M. Rubinow, "Economic Conditions of the Jews in Russia," *Bulletin of the Bureau of Labor*, No. 72, Washington, September, 1907. Col. 7: *Zeitschrift fuer Demographie und Statistik der Juden*, August, 1905, pp. 1–6.

teenth century. According to data for over 500,000 gainfully occupied Jews in the Ukraine, Lithuania, and White Russia in 1818, the share of trade was over 86 per cent; that of artisans, 11.6 per cent; and of agriculture, 2 per cent. Granted the approximate character of these data, the dominance of trade and the small share of industry and handicraft, compared with 1897, cannot be gainsaid. Some data for Galicia in 1820 show that trade accounted for fifty-five per cent of all Jews, industry and handicrafts for thirty-nine per cent, free professions for four per cent, and agriculture for 2.5 per cent.[13] Lestschinsky states that the data cover only sixty per cent of the gainfully occupied and must be quite short of complete coverage of elusive occupations which belong to trade (i.e., agents, brokers, etc.), and that the share of trade must be underestimated and that of industry overestimated. Yet in the census of 1900 for Galicia trade is roughly thirty-two per cent, and industry about twenty-nine per cent of total gainfully occupied Jews.[14] Both shares are lower than in 1820, but here again industry rises substantially relative to trade.

There is consequently some ground for concluding that the economic structure of East European Jews shifted during the nineteenth century from predominant engagement in trade toward proportionately heavier engagement in industry, with some minor diversion to the professions and in some areas, as in Galicia, even to agriculture. Plausible explanations can be suggested. For Czarist Russia there is some evidence that, within the Pale, the proportion of Jews to total population rose somewhat during the nineteenth century;[15] and this increase, in and of itself, might have filled the openings within trade and the overflow may have been channeled into handicrafts. The increasingly severe legislation in the Russian Empire restricting the opportunities for Jews in the countryside—where they functioned primarily within trade—and the resulting greater concentration in cities within the Pale must have limited even further the opportunities in trade. The shift of larger proportions to handicrafts, hailed by some observers as a favorable change toward more "productive" occupations, was more a response to undesirable pressures and limitations than a drive toward more efficient economic activities.[16]

The large share of industry reflects the pressures under which the East European Jews operated, and hence is an indication of their low product and income. This view is reinforced by some direct data on the extent of poverty. The proportion of Jewish families receiving assistance during Passover, according to a survey for 1898 of some 1,200 cities (but excluding some larger cities), was close to 19 per cent, and ranged from 14 per cent in the central provinces of Poland to 22 per cent in the Lithuanian provinces. Similarly striking figures can be cited on the proportion of families that needed charitable contributions of fuel during the winter.[17]

One can conclude that while a substantial proportion of East European Jewry at the end of the century belonged to the petty and middle bourgeoisie, with an income level probably above the average, large groups of Jews were at extremely low levels of income and productivity—artisans in industry, less secure workers in trade, and unskilled labor in personal or "other" services. And the Jewish population at all levels had also to face the possibility of increasingly severe regulations; at least in Russia there was always the danger of tighter restrictions. This combination of circumstances produced a pressure for emigration that gathered momentum as a migration pattern emerged and as the dislocations which gave the initial impetus continued and grew apace.

Emigration, as well as war and revolution, should have affected the economic structure of East European Jews after World War I; yet no such effects are apparent (Table 9). Except for the sharply reduced proportion of trade and the increased proportion of the public service and professions sector among Jews under the new regime in Russia, the changes in industrial composition are within the margin of error of the estimates. (Compare Tables 8 and 9.) If we combine the shares in Table 8, weighting Russia and Austria by the numbers of Jews in each, the share of agriculture around the turn of the century becomes 4.7 per cent compared with 6.4 per cent in Table 9; of industry, 37 per cent compared with 40 per cent; of trade, 33 per cent compared with 35.5 per cent; of public service and professions, 5.5 per cent compared with 10 per cent; and of personal services (largely skilled labor), 17 per cent compared with 5 per cent. Allowing for the effects of the revolutionary changes in Russia, and for some incomparability (particularly in the classification of professions in Poland), one is forced to the conclusion that no significant shifts took place.

While this lack of change may be partly explained by the broad categories used, it is still significant because it covers some three to four decades during which the over-all percentage of Jews to total population declined. The number of Jews barely rose between 1900 and 1925, or for that matter

TABLE 9

Industrial Distribution of Jews in Eastern Europe After World War I

	Poland 1931	U.S.S.R. 1926	Latvia 1930	Hungary 1930	Czecho-slovakia 1930	Rumania 1930	Total
1. Total Jewish pop., average 1925–39 (000's)	3,075	2,888	100	446	338	850	7,721
2. Jewish gainfully occupied (000's)	1,137	947	41	198	140	323[a]	2,786
% Distribution of (2)							
3. Agriculture	4.5	9.3	1.1	3.1	10.8	5.7	6.4
4. Industry	44.5	40.8	28.8	34.3	24.1	32.8	39.9
5. Transport	3.4	3.2	2.2	2.0	2.3	2.5	3.1
6. Trade	37.4	23.3	48.7	48.4	50.8	48.6	35.5
7. Personal services	3.2	0	2.0	1.6	1.8	0	1.6
8. Public services and professions	6.0	17.2	12.8	8.8	9.1	2.8	9.9
9. Others	0.9	6.2	4.4	1.8	1.1	7.7	3.6
10. (7+9)	4.1	6.2	6.4	3.4	2.9	7.7	5.2

[a] Includes nonservice income recipients.

Source: Based largely on Lestschinsky, "The Economic and Social Development of the Jewish People," pp. 377–379.

between 1900 and the 1930's, but total population did. The population of the Russian Empire in 1897 was about 126,000,000.[18] By 1926, the population of the *reduced* area then in the U.S.S.R. was about 148,000,000.[19] In other areas of eastern Europe there were also substantial increases, certainly exceeding the 7 per cent rise from 1900 to 1939 in the Jewish population. However, despite the reduced proportion of Jews, and despite the passage of time which presumably should have brought about an improvement in economic position, no shift occurred in their industrial structure.

Other evidence of the hostility and restrictions under which Jews operated in the newly formed states (with some exceptions, such as Czechoslovakia) suggests that the unfavorable pressures on the economic position and opportunities of Jews continued. In the U.S.S.R. the Pale was abolished and the policy of nondiscrimination instituted; but these changes were accompanied by a drastic redirection of economic activity, which had disastrous effects on the privately managed units in trade and industry, thus bearing far more heavily upon Jews than upon the rest of the population.

C. The Situation Since the 1930's

The destruction of a major proportion of East European Jews during World War II is the overwhelming fact in the postwar situation. As of today, substantial groups exist only within the U.S.S.R., with a much smaller remnant in Rumania. The post-World War II situation is, therefore, largely that of Jews in the U.S.S.R., with those in the satellite countries probably following the same pattern.

Solomon M. Schwarz in *The Jews in the Soviet Union* gives some figures on Soviet Jewry after 1926 and through the 1930's. The main feature of these data is the reduction to insignificant proportions of groups other than wage or salaried employees. In 1926, the proportion among Jews of wage and salary earners was less than 40 per cent. The other big groups were artisans, 19 per cent; traders, 12 per cent; other employers, self-employed, and people without specified occupation, 21 per cent.[20] For 1926, the total number of Jewish wage and salary earners was given as 394,000, implying that the total number of gainfully occupied was close to a million. By 1931, the total number of Jewish wage and salary earners was estimated to be 787,000, almost double the number in 1926.[21] Obviously, as industrialization and the reduction of private enterprise proceeded under the plan, the overwhelming proportion of Jews shifted to wage- and salary-earning status. There are no grounds for assuming that the process has not continued; and hence, except for insignificant fractions, Jews in the Soviet area must be wage or salary employees.

However, some of the specific characteristics of the economic structure of Jews persisted, at least until the late 1930's. In 1939, Jewish wage earners constituted somewhat less than 43 per cent of Jewish workers, the majority being salaried employees.[22] In 1937, in the Ukraine and White Russia almost half (48.3 per cent) of nonfarm Jewish wage and salary employees were in administration, public service, commerce, and communications—a far larger share than for total population. The greater urbanization and the previous concentration of Jews in certain pursuits still influenced their industrial-occupation selection even under the drastically different conditions of a Soviet state.

What of the future of East European Jewry, now all behind the Iron Curtain? Their economic future will necessarily be governed by the demands of the authoritarian states, and may continue to reflect for a while its earlier characteristics. The real question is much wider: Can we still consider the individuals identified as Jews behind the Iron Curtain a lasting minority and part of world Jewry?

At the outset we defined a Jewish minority as a cohesive group with a common historical past and with a minimum freedom to seek contacts with other members and to keep alive the feeling of belonging. This is hardly the place to review the shifts in attitudes of the Soviet state to the Jewish minority; but it is at present, and has been for some time, the policy to discourage and rigidly limit any opportunities for the Jewish minority to act cohesively or to maintain contacts with other countries.[23] If this policy continues for any length of time, the Jewish minority may well disappear as a distinctive group.

A major factor in its survival so far has been the persistence and occasional flare-up of anti-Semitism. Such persistence is not surprising, for the Soviet state has had to rely heavily upon nationalist feelings and has imposed strains upon the population for which internal as well as external scapegoats were needed. Nor has the Soviet state been immune to the propaganda of its neighbors in the West. Thus, even in the Soviet countries, persistence of discrimination, though temporarily prohibited by law, would keep Jews from pursuits in which the majority can demonstrate its hostility. The underrepresentation of Jews in large-scale productive units has for a long time been partly due to the difficulties which the Jews face in working with the hostile majority, and this factor has been operating in Soviet Russia also. In other words, the continuation of hostility is reason enough for the persistence of cohesion among the Jews and for their distinctive economic structure.

But there is little comfort in this consideration. It implies the choice between a combination of discouragement of cultural minority activities with tolerance—which can result in the extinction of the Jewish minority as a separate group—on the one hand, and, on the other, continuation of hostility—which can be used by the authoritarian state to canalize discontent and strain, and may be used without restraint and respect for human life. This is a precarious choice: between complete assimilation and physical extinction.

2. Jews in the United States

A. Growth in Numbers

The Jewish community of over 5,000,000 in the United States is the largest in the world today, and accounts for over four-tenths of the world total. The process by which this community grew has direct bearing upon its economic structure and must, therefore, be reviewed before the economic aspects are discussed. Table 10, devised to bring out some features of this process, suggests several conclusions.[24]

First, the growth has been spectacularly large and rapid. From 250,000 in 1880, or about 0.5 per cent of total population, the Jewish community has grown to over 5,000,000 in 1950, or about 3.3 per cent of the total. The rise was also greater than that of urban population: in 1880, Jews accounted for less than 2 per cent; in 1950, for about 5.2 per cent.

Second, however, Jews remain a small minority of total or urban population and the increase in their numbers is a small fraction of the *total addi-*

TABLE 10

Distribution of Jews in the United States by Period Since Their Arrival

Year	Estimated Number of Jews (millions) (1)	Percentage of Entrants and Their Descendants				
		Preceding 5 Years (2)	Preceding 10 Years (3)	Preceding 20 Years (4)	Preceding 30 Years (5)	Residual Total (Over 30 Years) (6)
1880	0.25					
1885	0.33	16				
1890	0.49	26	38			
1895	0.74	28	47			
1900	0.97	17	40	63		
1905	1.46	28	40	68		
1910	2.11	25	46	68	80	20
1915	2.70	15	36	62	80	20
1920	2.93	2	17	55	73	27
1925	3.44	8	9	42	65	35
1930	3.73	1	9	24	59	41
1935	3.93	less than ½	2	11	43	57
1940	4.23	3	3	12	27	73
1945	4.55	1	4	6	15	85
1950	5.03	2	3	6	15	85

SOURCES: Col. 1: derived from the original estimate of 0.25 in 1880 by application of the rate of natural increase for native-born white, and cumulative immigration. Cols. 2–6: Based upon cumulative immigration from Samuel Joseph, *Jewish Immigration to the United States*, New York, 1914 (for 1881–1910); Hersch, *op. cit.*; p. 409; and *American Jewish Year Book*, several issues (for 1944 to date).

tion to the population. From 1880 to 1920, when the rate of growth was most rapid, the addition of some 2,700,000 Jews constituted less than 5 per cent of the additions to total population and less than 7 per cent of the additions to urban population.

Third, the growth of the Jewish community was largely a matter of immigration. On the assumption that after 1880 net Jewish migration was zero, and that the original body of some 250,000 grew at the same rate as the resident white population, the number by 1950 would have been slightly over 700,000. Roughly speaking, over eight-tenths of the Jewish population today derive from immigrants since 1880.

Fourth, immigration of Jews between 1880 and 1915 was an ever-increasing stream, the immigrant additions forming a constant, rather high proportion of the rapidly growing number of resident Jews. Thus, from 1885 to 1915, Jews who came into the country during the preceding five years were never less than a seventh of the total number of Jews, and at some points were well over a quarter. From 1900 to 1915 the proportion of those who came in during the preceding two decades was more than six-tenths of the resident total.

Fifth, World War I and its aftermath—increasingly severe immigration restrictions followed by isolation of those Jews who were the reservoir of immigration—produced a sharp break. By 1930, the proportion of Jews who came in during the preceding five years dwindled to a few percentage points. And by 1945, the proportion of Jews who themselves, or whose ancestors, came in more than thirty years before was well over eight-tenths of the total.

Sixth, because the estimates of total Jewish population in Table 10 are crude, we cannot tell exactly whether the proportion of Jews to the total population was increasing during recent decades. To measure this proportion accurately one would need recent birth and death rates for Jews, as well as rates of secession from the Jewish community—if the latter is at all important—in addition to precise rates of immigration. Immigration of Jews has continued in recent years, but it may have been more than offset by the possibly lower rate of natural increase of Jews than of total population.

It is, however, reasonable to argue that substantial rises in the proportion of Jews to total population are unlikely. Despite continued immigration, the proportion (using the rough figures of Table 10) increased from 2.8 per cent in 1920 to 3.0 per cent in 1930, to 3.2 per cent in 1940, and to 3.3 per cent in 1950. The suggested retardation in the rise may well continue and be succeeded by a decline.

B. Trends in Occupational Structure

Study of the occupational structure is impeded by absence of comprehensive data and by the heterogeneity in economic structure in the early phases of the period. From 1880 until after World War I, the Jewish community consisted of two distinct elements: the older residents and the descendants of earlier immigrants, who followed one pattern of adaptation to economic life; and the recent immigrants, who came largely from Russia and eastern Europe[25] and whose skills, background, and recent entry spelled a different pattern.

This dichotomy is illustrated in two studies quoted by Nathan Goldberg in his analysis of occupational patterns of American Jews.[26] One study, by Dr. John S. Billings of the Bureau of the Census, deals with some 18,000 gainfully occupied Jews in 1889, four-fifths of whom were immigrants from German-speaking countries and their descendants. The occupational structure of this sample is heavily weighted toward trade—bankers, brokers, wholesalers, retail dealers, collectors, agents, etc., accounting for 62 per cent, to which should be added some of the 17 per cent accounted for by bookkeepers, clerks, etc. Professional service claimed another 5 per cent, so that a residual of only 16 per cent was left for all other sectors, including manufacturing and mechanical pursuits. Another study in 1890 of some 224,000 gainfully employed Jews in three New York City Jewish districts shows that 60 per cent were needle workers, 15 per cent were in other industrial pursuits, 11 per cent were peddlers, and about 13 per cent were retail dealers. The contrast between the concentration of the first group in trade and at upper economic levels and that of the second group in clothing and other consumer goods industries and at the lowest economic levels of trade could not be sharper. It is especially significant, for, according to Table 10, of some 500,000 Jews in the country at the time, close to 40 per cent had migrated during the preceding ten years. Because of their age structure, recent immigrants are an even larger percentage of the labor force, and it is not unreasonable to assume that they accounted for at least 50 per cent and perhaps a higher proportion of all gainfully employed Jews.

We have no other data on the occupational structure of the earlier Jewish settlers at the turn of the century. We would guess, however, that the share of trade and finance ran well over 50 per cent, and that of industry was not higher than 30 per cent; and perhaps 60 and 20 per cent would be more likely levels.

We do have data on the recent immigrants, largely because their arrival aroused attention and official statistics were collected. The information of most interest in the present connection is summarized in Table 11. It relates partly to the occupational structure of Jewish immigrants who indicated some occupational affiliation at the time of entry, and partly to foreign-born who can be identified as Jews because of their country of origin. Neither set of data is precise. Questions addressed to immigrants about occupation do not always elicit accurate answers. And not all foreign-born whites identified in 1900 as having come from Russia were Jews. However, since the Poles and Finns, i.e., those who spoke Polish or Finnish, were eliminated from the figures for foreign-born from Russia (and from Austria-Hungary), the overwhelming proportion of persons covered in lines 5-10 probably were Jews. At any rate, despite the limitations of the data, the broad conclusions suggested by Table 11 are beyond reasonable doubt.

TABLE 11

Occupational Distribution of Jewish Immigrants and of Russian Jews in the United States

Groups	Agriculture	Manufacturing and Mechanical Pursuits	Trade and Transportation	Unskilled Labor and Domestic Service	Professions
Jewish Immigrants					
1. 1899–1914	2.6	65.6	9.2	21.3	1.3
2. 1915–1920	2.3	54.0	21.5	17.7	4.6
3. 1921–1924	3.0	36.3	17.1	38.1	5.4
4. 1931–1932	3.6	31.1	29.2	22.8	13.3
Russian Jews (Russian Foreign-born), Cities with 250,000 Inhabitants or More, 1900					
5. Males (120.1 thous.)	0.5	57.1	32.2	7.0	3.3
6. Females (30.6 thous.)	0.2	69.4	16.7	12.4	1.4
7. Total (150.7 thous.)	0.5	59.6	29.0	8.0	2.9
Foreign-born, Russian, New York State, 1900					
8. Males (73.2 thous.)	0.8	61.2	29.5	5.6	2.9
9. Females (18.6 thous.)	0.2	72.4	12.2	14.0	1.2
10. Total (91.8 thous.)	0.7	63.5	26.0	7.2	2.6

SOURCES: Lines 1–4: from L. Hersch in *International Migrations*, Vol. II, New York, 1931, particularly p. 495, and *The Jewish People: Past and Present*, Vol. I, p. 427. Lines 5–7: Nathan Goldberg in *The Jewish Review*, April, 1945, p. 11, clerks included in trade; public service in professions. Lines 8–10: See source in Table 12.

We can compare the occupational distribution of Jewish immigrants (largely from Russia) with the distribution of Jews in Russia, and with the distribution upon settlement in the United States. While the data in line 1 relate to 1899-1914, they were probably typical of the two earlier decades also. They show that the structure of immigrants was heavily dominated by industry and mechanical pursuits. The share of trade and transportation is, however, moderate. This distribution is quite different from those for Russia in 1897, and for Austria in 1900. (See Table 8.) Two reasons may be suggested: the pressure toward emigration was greatest in those areas where both the proportion of Jews in cities and the share among Jews of workers in industry were highest, and it was easier for an artisan than for a trader to transfer his skill to a new country.

On the other hand, the occupational structure of the Russian Jews even as early as 1900 begins to shift away from that recorded at entry. The share of mechanical pursuits, largely clothing manufactures, remains high, but the share of unskilled labor and domestic service drops sharply; that of trade increases; that of professions rises slightly. While the movement away from industry has not begun, that toward trade and related activities is already apparent.

The occupational structure of Jewish immigrants changed over time (lines 1-4), and after World War I the change was largely due to changes in the country of origin. The shares of commerce and transportation and of the professions increased, and that of manufacturing and mechanical pursuits declined markedly. After 1932, with migration from Germany and countries west of Russia, the occupational composition changed even further in favor of commerce and the professions.

Recalling the dichotomy at the turn of the century, we can see that the trend over time is toward the "old resident" pattern, toward lower shares of industry and domestic and personal service and higher shares of commerce and the professions (including public service). This trend is a composite of several movements that can only be surmised, not measured. The first and most important is the choice by the second generation: the children of the East European Jews, who were predominantly workers in the needle and other crafts, chose to work in different capacities and in other sectors. Second, the foreign-born immigrants themselves probably moved out of industry into trade or even professions. Third, the occupational structure of the successive waves of immigration changed in favor of trade and the professions.

Table 12 reveals the occupational characteristics of both the foreign-born and the second generation (i.e., native-born with one or both parents foreign-born) in 1900 and by country of origin. These data do not distinguish Jews. But we can assume that they were the overwhelming proportion of the Russian-born residing in New York in 1900. While this assumption is not as warranted for those born in Austria and Hungary, the occupational distribution of the first generation is quite similar to that of the Russian immigrants. But even if the groups from Austria and Hungary are mixed, the contrast between the structure of the first and second generations is still illuminating.

The first generation of males is preponderantly in manufacturing and mechanical pursuits, and, within that category, the share of tailors is most substantial (over a quarter of the total for Russia and Austria). The same is true of the female foreign-born of Russian origin, with over 72 per cent in manufacturing, and over 50 per cent concentrated in the needle and related trades. While the shares for female workers of Austrian and Hungarian origin are not as great, they are substantial and the needle trades

TABLE 12

Occupational Distribution of Foreign-Born and Second Generation from Russia, Austria, Hungary, in New York State, 1900

Occupation	A. Male Russia (Except Poland and Polish-Speaking) 1st Gen.	2nd Gen.	Austria (Except Poland and Polish-Speaking) 1st Gen.	2nd Gen.	Hungary 1st Gen.	2nd Gen.
1. Total (000's)	73.2	4.5	34.9	2.4	15.6	1.0
Percentage shares						
2. Agriculture	0.8	0.4	1.5	1.3	1.0	0.4
3. Manufacturing and mechanical	61.2	32.6	59.5	32.9	60.2	36.3
(a) Tailors	28.3	11.2	26.9	4.2	17.1	4.6
4. Trade and transportation	29.5	57.8	23.4	51.8	22.1	51.9
(a) Clerks	2.3	16.6	1.8	14.5	2.2	16.0
(b) Hucksters and peddlers	5.8	1.7	4.3	0.8	2.2	1.1
(c) Retail dealers	11.6	6.5	7.6	6.9	7.5	4.2
(d) Salesmen	3.2	12.5	2.5	8.1	2.8	9.4
5. Professional	2.9	4.4	3.0	7.7	3.2	6.3
6. Domestic and personal	5.6	4.8	12.6	6.4	13.6	5.1
(a) Laborers unspecified	2.9	1.8	6.2	2.7	8.1	2.3
	B. Female					
1. Total (000's)	18.6	2.5	10.3	1.3	6.3	0.7
Percentage shares						
2. Agriculture	0.2	0.1	0.1	0	0.1	0
3. Manufacturing and mechanical	72.4	56.9	46.8	53.6	41.3	59.4
(a) Needle trades and related	54.8	36.3	32.5	31.7	23.0	34.2
4. Trade and transportation	12.2	33.5	7.3	31.1	6.2	29.8
(a) Clerks	1.0	4.1	0.5	2.0	0.6	2.3
(b) Saleswomen	4.5	12.2	3.2	11.4	2.1	8.0
(c) Stenos and typists	1.1	6.3	0.6	7.1	0.9	5.7
5. Professional	1.2	4.1	0.9	6.6	0.8	3.9
6. Domestic and personal	14.0	5.4	44.9	8.7	51.6	6.9
(a) Servants and waitresses	10.8	3.9	39.7	6.5	45.2	5.4

SOURCE: *Reports of the Immigration Commission*, Vol. 28, Senate Document No. 282, 61st Congress, 2nd Session, Washington, 1911, pp. 272, 277, 280, 362, 367, 370. Group 3a in Part B includes hat and cap makers and shirt, collar, and cuff makers.

account for from a quarter to a third of all workers. The shares of trade and transportation are lower; those of professional service are also small.

The second-generation workers are naturally a relatively small group, as immigration from Russia, Austria, and Hungary began to be substantial only in the 1880's. For this reason the second generation is only 6 to 7 per cent of the first for males and slightly over 10 per cent for females; whereas for the older immigrant groups (e.g., the British or German) the same source indicates ratios of 150 to over 200 per cent. Also, this second generation is relatively young. We can assume that the occupational structure of the immigrant parents of the second generation of 1900 was not too different from that of the first generation of 1900, especially as we are dealing largely with Jewish immigrants from Russia and Austria-Hungary. Hence, we can view the differences between the occupational structures of the two generations as shifts away from that of the first generation. Uniformly, the shares of manufacturing and mechanical pursuits, and of tailors in particular, among the males decline quite sharply. The same is true among the female workers from Russia, with a sharp drop in the share of the needle trades; but among the female workers from Austria and Hungary, the sharp drop comes in the shares of servants and waitresses, the shares in the industry rising slightly. Uniformly, for all groups in Table 12 the shares of trade and transportation among the second-generation workers are appreciably higher than among the first; and within this sector the shares of clerks and salespeople rise, whereas those of hucksters, peddlers, and retail dealers decline. The latter movements may, however, be associated with differences in age composition. Uniformly, the shares of domestic and personal service, and particularly of unskilled labor among men and servants and waitresses among women, drop and the shares in the professional pursuits rise from the first to the second generation.

The cumulative effect of the trend is, of course, manifest in the occupational structure of Jews in recent years. The occupational structure is probably not unlike that which prevailed among the older Jewish residents in

TABLE 13

Recent Data (1930's) on Occupational Structure of Jews in the United States

Groups (1)	Agriculture (2)	Manufacturing and Mechanics (3)	Trade and Transportation (4)	Domestic and Personal Service (5)	Professions (6)
1. 61 communities (clerical included in trade)	—	12.4	64.9	7.9	14.8
2. New York City, 1933 (clerical in trade)	—	30.6	55.8	5.3	8.3
3. New York City, 1937 (specified occupations only)	—	36.0	36.9	15.7[a]	11.3
4. Country-wide estimate for 1940	2.0	28.0	52.5	6.0	11.5

[a] Includes amusements. Transfer of latter to trade would shift 2.8 per cent from col. 5 to col. 4.
SOURCES: Line 1: Nathan Goldberg, in *The Jewish Review*, October-December, 1945, p. 172. Other and unknown included in domestic and personal service. Lines 2 and 4: Lestschinsky, "The Economic and Social Development of the Jewish People" pp. 388-390; "The Economic Development of the Jews in the United States," *The Jewish People: Past and Present*, pp. 391-399. Line 3: Reich, *op. cit.*, p. 1244.

the 1880's, trade being dominant and manufacturing and mechanical pursuits being distinctly smaller, perhaps only half of the former (Table 13). The important change has been, of course, the reduction of the industry sector. There has also been a reduction in the share of domestic and personal service. And last but not unimportant, there has been a rise in the share of professional services to a level probably never reached before.

The recent occupational structure of Jews is distinctly different from that for the country at large. The shares of trade and of the professional sector are higher and those of agriculture and domestic and personal service are lower. The share of industry is not too different from that for total population, but the specialization of Jews in the consumer goods industries should be kept in mind. Finally, if only because of this distinctive industrial attachment, the proportion of employers and self-employed among Jews must be larger, and that of wage earners smaller, than among the urban and perhaps even total population. In short, the occupational and employment status structure of Jews in the United States in recent years has the features of an established small minority unhampered by legal restrictions.

C. Trends in Income

Since the 1880's national income per capita in the United States has almost tripled,[27] and there are no grounds for assuming that the Jews did not share in this rise. But other circumstances, peculiar to Jews and perhaps to other small minorities, must have also affected their income. The first is suggested by the origin of the majority of Jews in eastern Europe. At the time of the large flow of migration, the per capita income levels in eastern European countries were appreciably lower than those in the United States. Per capita income in the United States from 1880 through World War I was probably between three and four times larger than that in Russia, and its excess over those in other eastern European areas must have been almost as large.[28] True, the per capita income of Jews in these areas may have been somewhat higher than those for the total populations; but the East European Jews who migrated to the United States were shifting to a country that not only promised large prospective growth but also already afforded opportunity for a substantial rise in earning and income standards.

An illustration of the difference can be cited. In Lithuania and White Russia annual earnings of Jewish artisans around the turn of the century were estimated to range up to the fairly high level of 250 rubles, or about $125 at the prevailing rate of exchange. Earnings of males eighteen years and over in the first decade of the twentieth century, for a sample of about a thousand Russian-born Jewish wage earners, were about $461.[29] Furthermore, the immigrant Jews, and particularly their next generation, could rise on a relative scale within the United States. This probable trend is not only a matter of inference from the economic benefits of increasing assimilation but also can be supported by reference to the occupational structure. The shifts in the occupational distribution of the Jewish community were more marked than those for total population. From 1900 to 1950 the proportion of total labor force engaged in manufacturing rose from over 20 to about 26 per cent, and that in trade and transportation rose from about 14 to about 27 per cent.[30] Among Jews the proportion in manufacturing and mechanical pursuits must have dropped from about 50 to about 30 per cent, and that in trade and transportation must have risen from below 30 to above 50 per cent. These more pronounced shifts among the Jews must have caused their per capita income to rise more than that of total population.[31]

3. Jews in Palestine and Israel[31a]

A. Growth in Numbers

The large Jewish community in what was formerly Palestine and is now Israel is of quite recent origin. In the early 1880's the number of Jews in Palestine was estimated to be between 24,000 and 25,000, and even this small group was the result of a relatively recent influx, as the estimate for 1855 is barely over 10,000.[32] Migration before that time was dominated by religious motives, and the desire to establish a center of economic and social life was of little effect.

The Jewish population in Palestine increased rapidly after 1880, as a result of successive waves of immigration, or *Aliyahs*. The first, from 1882 to 1903, brought 20,000–30,000 immigrants, largely from Russia and Rumania, who suffered from the pogroms in South Russia in 1881 and migrated in fulfillment of Zionist hopes and ideals. By 1900, the number of Jews in Palestine was roughly 50,000. The second *Aliyah*, from 1904 to 1914, brought 35,000–40,000 immigrants. This group also originated in Russia; and while workers active in the revolutionary movement and subjected to the pogroms that accompanied the Revolution of 1905 were in the minority, their participation lent a distinctive character to the second *Aliyah*. By 1914, the number of Jews in Palestine was 85,000, of whom 70 per cent were East European in origin. World War I not only halted immigration but resulted in a reduction in the resident population to well below 80,000. The third *Aliyah*, from 1919 to 1923, was the first response to the Balfour Declaration and brought a large number of *halutzim* prepared to build a new state. It involved about 35,000 immigrants, and by 1923 the number of Jews in Palestine had reached levels above those of 1914. The fourth *Aliyah*, from 1924 through 1931, was due partly to the attraction of Palestine, and partly to economic pressure in Poland and other eastern European countries. Gross immigration was substantial, 82,000 from 1924 through 1931; but there was also considerable emigration, amounting to over a quarter of immigration. By the end of 1931, Jewish population in Palestine was about 175,000.

It is at this point that Table 14 picks up the story. The fifth *Aliyah*, usually dated from 1932 to the end of World War II, was characterized by the influx of Jews from Germany and other areas of central Europe, which previously accounted for only small groups of immigrants to Palestine. But the much larger reservoirs in Poland and Rumania still accounted for the dominant proportion of immigrants.

First, the rate of increase of the Jewish population from 1931 onward, and in fact from a low point immediately after World War I, has been spectacularly large. From 1922 to 1931, the Jewish population more than doubled. From 1931 to 1948 it more than quadrupled. From 1948 to 1954 it more than doubled, the increase occurring almost entirely from 1948 to 1951. These changes put their stamp on the economic activities of the community.

Second, the masses of immigrants included Jews from countries that differed widely in economic and social structure. And even from one and the same country of origin, the successive waves of emigration represented groups with different economic composition and motivation. As a result, Palestine, and particularly Israel, faced the "melting pot" problems in all their complexity, aggravated by the rapidity with which the volume and composition of the mix were changing.

Third, between 1931 and independence, the proportion of foreign-born Jews increased. While the groups born in eastern Europe still predominated (the U.S.S.R., Poland, and Rumania accounted in 1948 for over 60 per cent of those born abroad), communities from other countries in Europe (Germany, Austria, Czechoslovakia, and Hungary) rose to significant dimensions.

Fourth, from 1948 to 1951, composition by country of origin changed even more. Of the total immigration close to half still came from the "western" countries, large groups originating in Rumania, Poland, and Bulgaria. But the other half, from Asia and Africa, meant a huge proportional addition to the "Oriental" Jewish community. As a result, by 1951, the proportions among the foreign-born residing in Israel shifted markedly; and the share of those born in "western" areas dropped from 55 to 47 per cent, whereas the share of those born in "Oriental" areas increased from about 10 to about 28 per cent.

Fifth, the changes from 1951 to 1954, with a relatively small volume of immigration, suggest those likely to occur in the future—provided that immigration will remain a fairly small fraction of the resident population and that most of it will come from the Oriental areas. The proportion of Israeli-born in total population increased from 25 per cent in 1951 to 31

TABLE 14

The Structure of the Jewish Population of
Palestine-Israel, by Country of Birth, 1931-1954

Country of Birth	1931 (18/XI)	1948 (8/XI)	1951 (31/XII)	1954 (31/XII)	Change 1931 to 1948	Change 1948 to 1951	Change 1951 to 1954
		A.	*Absolute*	*Numbers*	(*thousands*)		
1. Total	174.6	716.7	1,404.4	1,526.0	542.1	687.7	121.6
2. Born in Israel	73.4	253.7	353.2	470.8	180.3	99.5	117.6
3. Born abroad	101.2	463.0	1,051.2	1,055.2	361.8	588.2	4.0
Europe, America, and Oceania							
4. Total [a]	81.3	393.0	663.0	641.3	311.7	270.0	−21.7
5. U.S.S.R.	32.6	53.8	57.7	55.1	21.2	3.9	− 2.6
6. Poland	35.9	161.7	243.5	234.1	125.8	81.8	− 9.4
7. Rumania	5.0	56.4	158.3	155.0	51.4	101.9	− 3.3
8. Germany-Austria	1.8	54.4	60.1	56.4	52.6	5.7	− 3.7
9. Czechoslovakia	0.5	17.3	33.9	32.2	16.8	16.6	− 1.7
10. Hungary	0.8	13.7	24.7	23.8	12.9	11.0	− 0.9
11. Bulgaria	1.3	12.6	44.5	44.0	11.3	31.9	− 0.5
Asia							
12. Total [a]	17.3	57.8	289.6	292.9	40.5	231.8	3.3
13. Iraq	4.0	9.0	132.0	131.5	5.0	123.0	− 0.5
14. Yemen-Aden	5.1	16.3	63.9	63.8	11.2	47.6	0.1
15. Turkey	2.2	10.7	41.6	39.0	8.5	30.9	− 2.6
16. Iran	2.8	3.9	25.5	29.3	1.1	21.6	3.8
Africa							
17. Total [a]	2.6	12.2	98.6	121.0	9.6	86.4	22.4
18. Morocco, Algeria, Tunisia	1.4	5.4	44.8	63.9	4.0	39.4	19.1
19. Libya	0	1.3	31.8	32.9	1.3	30.5	1.1
		B.	*Percentage*	*Distribution*			
1a. Total	100.0	100.0	100.0	100.0	100.0	100.0	100.0
2a. Born in Israel	42.0	35.4	25.2	30.9	33.3	14.5	96.7
3a. Born abroad	58.0	64.6	74.8	69.1	66.7	85.5	3.3
4a. Europe, America, and Oceania	46.6	54.8	47.2	42.0	57.5	39.3	−17.8
2a. Asia	9.9	8.1	20.6	19.2	7.5	33.7	2.7
7a. Africa	1.5	1.7	7.0	7.9	1.8	12.6	18.4

[a] Only some of the countries included in the total are listed below.

SOURCE: M. Sicron and B. Gil, *Jewish Population by Sex, Age and Country of Birth, 1931–1954*, Central Bureau of Statistics, Special Series No. 37, Jerusalem, November, 1955, Table 6, pp. 14–15.

per cent in 1954 and will probably rise further. The number of "old" immigrants, largely from the western countries, has declined, both proportionately to total population and absolutely, and this decline will presumably continue. Among the Oriental communities, the oldest immigrant body (from Iraq) declined and will continue to do so in the immediate future, as will other communities from Asia, as further immigration is unlikely to offset the deaths among the aging groups of original immigrants. Jews born in Africa have increased both absolutely and proportionately from 1951 to 1954, and the process may continue under the pressure of Arab nationalism in North Africa.

Sixth, in view of the importance of the combination of western and Oriental areas of origin, it may be well to consider the mix by age groups, as it is the adult groups that bring established economic and social patterns. At the end of 1954, of the total group fifteen to twenty-nine years old, about a quarter were Israeli-born; somewhat over a third were born in western areas; and about two-fifths were born in Oriental areas. If we can assume that the preponderant proportion of the Israeli-born of that age group was western by parentage and training, the mix would be roughly half and half. In the groups over thirty years of age, the composition is more heavily western: those born in western areas account for over two-thirds, the Israeli-born for a few percentages, and those born in Asia and Africa for only a quarter.

There is no intention here to exaggerate the heterogeneity of the successive waves of Jewish immigrants. But we stress it to draw attention to the implication that there were continuously strong integrating elements that helped to overcome heterogeneity of origin and to produce a unified community whose cohesion withstood the test of the war for independence. What were those integrating elements?

Seventh, one obvious element is the selective character of immigration, particularly in the periods before independence. Before World War I, and even through much of the 1920's, when immigration to the more prosperous communities in the Americas and elsewhere was possible, only those interested in the long-term future of Palestine as the locus of a distinctive Zionist-envisaged community migrated to the area. There was a continuous settling in Palestine of Jewish groups whose major motivation was the building of a home and in essence a new economic society; and when this motivation was not strong enough to cope with the difficulties, these new residents emigrated again.

Eighth, an associated element was community of origin of most early migrants. They came largely from those areas in eastern Europe with the greatest concentration of Jews, where the exacerbation of economic and political pressures provided the impetus to emigrate. Granted that only a selected small part of the total stream flowed to Palestine, nevertheless that small part came for decades from eastern Europe. Much of the economic and social structure of Palestine, particularly the blend of social and cultural idealism with economic radicalism, bears the unifying imprint of origin in Russia and contiguous areas. To put it differently, from the 1880's to the 1930's, only in eastern Europe were the elements compelling migration prominent; and only in eastern Europe could sizable groups be found who, given the push, would for idealistic reasons migrate to Palestine. And the thoughts and ideals of this group could not but be affected by this process of preselection and by the intellectual and social milieu of their origin. As these were the earliest and most continuous currents of immigration, they determined the patterns of the Jewish community in Palestine and limited the extent of modification that the more numerous recent arrivals could effectuate.

Ninth, in Palestine before independence, the Jewish community was a minority amid a hostile Arab majority that lived at a much lower economic and social level than the Jews were willing to accept. This situation continued after independence, with the Jews surrounded by Arab countries whose endemic hostility was intensified by their loss of the war. In a sense, unity was imposed on the Jews from the outside. Whatever the differences in country of origin, social and economic views, or any other characteristics that might have divided them, there was constantly the need for unified action in the struggle with the hostile or indifferent Mandate power, and in the attempt, to ward off the threats of neighboring Arab majorities.

Tenth, finally, a strong element of unity was provided by the relations between the Jewish community in Palestine and Israel and world Jewry in the Diaspora. If Zionist idealism was a strong force in determining the migration to Palestine and Israel, it was also a source of strength, as was the general interest of Jews the world over—even those who took no part in Zionist activities. This is not to deny the divisive elements in Zionist activities or among world Jewry that may have contributed to the divisive elements among the Jews in Palestine or Israel. But the elements of unity and strength were far more important and served to reduce the effects of the heterogeneity of country of origin and of social and economic antecedents on the life of the Jewish community in Palestine and Israel.

B. Industrial Structure of the Labor Force

The influences on immigration to and life in Palestine and Israel also affect economic structure. The motivation by Zionist ideals is reflected in the occupational preparation of the immigrants, as well as in the organizational forms, some of them new, that they developed upon settlement. The origin in eastern Europe is reflected in the occupational and industrial pattern of the economy. Coexistence with the Arab majority naturally influenced the economic structure. Finally, the economic relations with Jews in the Diaspora necessarily created distinctive economic conditions to an extent and of a kind not paralleled in any other community of Jews. All these effects become apparent when we consider the industrial structure and the level and structure of income.

The working population was largely determined by the successive waves of immigration, so the industrial structure of the immigrants during the successive periods must be considered first (Table 15). Despite the elements of incomparability in the data, the major distinctive features can be accepted.

First, there is a sharp break in the economic characteristics of the immigrants between 1919-1931 and the later decades. Before the 1930's immigration was heavily dominated by people of working ages, a substantial proportion of whom came with special training and desire to work on the land—work considered essential for a viable and independent Jewish economic community. In 1919-1923 and 1924-1931 the ratio of gainfully occupied to total immigration was close to a half, and the proportion of the labor force reported in agriculture (including those trained to work on the land) was also high. Both ratios dropped sharply as immigration became less selective, all ages and both sexes were fully represented, and the compelling force was the rescue of whole Jewish communities. After 1939 and through 1954, the proportion of gainfully occupied to total immigration remained at the relatively low level of 30 per cent, and the share of gainfully occupied in agriculture dropped to between 4 and 5 per cent.

Second, the high share of agriculture, in striking contrast with the low share among Jewish immigrants to other countries, is significant. While the difference was more in intention than in past experience, it had a marked influence upon the structure of the settlement.

Third, in other respects the industrial structure of migrants to Palestine and Israel is not too dissimilar from that of Jewish migrants to the United States. The proportion of industry, including building construction, is highest—averaging between 35 and 45 per cent—but not as high as in the early immigration to the United States. There are substantial proportions of unskilled labor, although the variations in Table 15 suggest some incomparability in the classification during the successive periods. The share of commerce and transport is rather limited, but increases, with this upward trend paralleling that in the share among the Jewish migrants to the United States. Finally, the share of the professional-religious groups is on the high side—particularly in the early periods—compared with that among Jewish migrants to the United States. Perhaps because of the much smaller absolute volume of immigration to Palestine and because of the idealistic elements involved, it was possible to attract a group of professionally trained persons that, while absolutely small, accounted for a substantial fraction of total immigration.

The occupational-industrial structure of the immigrants is important

TABLE 15

Industrial Distribution of Jewish Immigrants to Palestine and Israel, Successive Periods, 1919–1954

Period	Total immigration (ooo's)	Gainfully occupied or Earners (ooo's)	Col. (2) as % of Col. (1)	% Shares Among Gainfully Occupied							
				Agriculture and Farming	Industry and Handicrafts	Building construction	Unskilled labor	Commerce	Transport	Clerical	Professions and religion
	(1)	(2)	(3)	(4)	(5)	(6)	(7)	(8)	(9)	(10)	(11)
1. 1919–23	35.1	16.6	47.3	29.9	34.8	8.0	6.0	6.9	1.0	2.8	10.6
2. 1924–31	73.4	37.4	51.0	20.6	33.5	6.6	20.0	9.2	0.5	2.4	7.2
3. 1932–39	186.1	50.2	27.5	11.5	31.5	7.6	12.7	17.0	1.1	3.9	14.7
4. 1940–45	40.4	11.7	29.0	4.2	34.6	1.8	13.5	19.6	1.4	9.7	15.3
5. 1919–45	335.1	115.9	34.6	16.3	32.9	6.8	14.2	13.3	0.9	3.9	11.7
6. 1939–45	62.2	18.6	29.9	5.3	36.8		13.1	18.8	2.1	9.4	14.5
7. 1919–47		134.1	29.9	14.9	36.0	6.7	12.7	12.6	6.7	4.2	11.5
8. 1/IX 1948–31/XII 1953		167.0		5.2	41.4	3.7	5.9	15.9	3.5	15.6[a]	8.8
9. 1950–54	394.5	111.6	29.4	5.5	34.8	2.6	8.9	18.1	2.6	18.9[a]	8.6

[a] Includes administrative and service workers, and, in line 9, also a small group of unclassified.

SOURCES: Lines 1–6: *Statistical Handbook of Jewish Palestine*, pp. 101, 111. Lines 7–8: M. Sicron, *Immigration Since the Establishment of the State of Israel*, Falk Project for Economic Research in Israel (MS.), ch. X, Table 1. (Some of the unpublished and manuscript sources relating to economics of Jews in Israel, taken largely from the Falk Project, will have been published since completion of the present chapter. Therefore, recent publications on the economics of Jews in Israel are necessarily omitted.) Line 9: *Statistical Abstract of Israel, 1954/5*, Jerusalem, 1955, p. 37, Table 12.

only in its effect upon the economic adjustment of the population after they were settled in the new country. Was the high share of agriculture among the immigrants followed by a comparatively high share of agriculture in the Jewish labor force in Palestine and Israel? Was the decline in the share of agriculture among the immigrants followed by a decline among the resident Jewish labor force? Was the increase in the share of commerce and transportation among the immigrants followed by an increase among the resident Jewish labor force?

There is some incomparability in the data, and even at best one would encounter difficulties in using the standard industrial classification under Palestine-Israeli conditions. (E.g., the variety of *kibbutzim* and *moshavim* activities affect the division between agriculture and other pursuits.) Yet Table 16 does provide fairly clear and reliable answers to the above questions.

TABLE 16

Industrial Distribution of the Jewish Labor Force, Palestine and Israel, Selected Years, 1931–1955

Industrial Divisions	1931 (18/XI) (1)	1939 (31/XII) (2)	1948 (8/XI) (3)	1954 (VI) (4)	1955 (XI) (5)
1. Total Jewish population (ooo's)	174.6	475.0	716.7	1,505.0	
2. Total Jewish labor Force (ooo's)	66.7	192.0	315.3	517.3	542.3
3. Col. (2) as % of col. (1)	38.2	40.4	44.0	34.2	
% Shares of Industries in Labor Force					
4. Agriculture[a]	18.5	19.3	12.4[a]	15.5[a]	15.5[a]
5. Industry and handicrafts	21.8	19.8	26.5	23.0	22.3
6. Building construction and public works	7.7	7.3	5.3	9.7	8.6
7. Commerce and finance	16.3	19.8	11.6	12.7	14.4
8. Transportation and communication	4.9	5.2	5.3	8.6[c]	8.3[c]
9. Professions and religion[b]	11.1	10.9	9.6⎫	30.5	30.9
10. Government, public, and personal services	7.1	12.5	16.0⎭		
11. Miscellaneous and unknown	12.6	5.2	13.3	—	—

[a] Including in 1948, 1954, and 1955, mining and quarries, amounting to 0.8 per cent, 0.4 per cent, and 0.2 per cent, respectively, of total labor force.

[b] In the 1931 census this included "Physicians, engineers, lawyers, teachers, religion, misc." This classification was not used in 1948. Accordingly, for 1948 we have placed under this heading items under "Medical service, education, and judiciary," and "Religion, culture, and art"; and for 1954, "Health, education, and social culture, etc."

[c] Including "Electricity, gas, water, and sanitary services."

SOURCES: For 1931 and 1939, D. Gurevich, "The Jewish Population," *The Palestine Year Book*, Vol. 2 (1945–46), New York, 1946, p. 135. The 1931 data are based on a census taken by the Palestine Mandatory Government, and the 1939 data on a sample study of the Jewish Agency. For more detailed presentation of the 1931 census, see *Statistical Handbook of Jewish Palestine*, 1947, pp. 66–69. For 1948, "Registration of Population," 8, XI–48, *Statistical Abstract of Israel*: 1952–53, No. 4, p. 29. For 1954, "Labor Force Survey," A. Hovne's manuscript for Falk Project for Economic Research in Israel. For 1955, Labor Force Survey, Israel Central Bureau of Statistics, *Bulletin*, Part B, February, 1956.

Fourth, the share of agriculture in the Jewish labor force was and remains, on the average, at much higher levels than in other countries. Except for the disturbed year 1948, the level is, at the lowest, about a seventh of the total labor force. Nor, taking seasonal considerations into account, is there any significant decline. In November, 1931, the share of agriculture in a labor force of about 67,000 was 18.5 per cent; in November, 1955, the Jewish labor force was over 500,000, and yet the share of agriculture was over 15 per cent. The difference between the two percentages, given the margin of error in the figures, is not significant.

Fifth, there was no rise in the share of commerce and finance, or in the share of that sector combined with transportation and communication—despite the relative increase in the latter after independence, with the employment of Jews by public utilities, which in the Mandate days was not common practice.

Sixth, the only other significant change in the industrial distribution suggested by Table 16 is the rise in the share of the government and public service sector. The increasing need for Jews in these services after independence is obvious.

The structure of the labor force was adjusted to the needs of a diversified Jewish economy with emphasis on all sectors of activity essential to an economy geared to western standards and not conceived as that of a minority dependent upon a neighboring majority. Indeed, such dependence was impossible, since the Jewish minority was not willing to sink to lower levels of economic life, or to specialize in ways that would conflict with Zionist ideals.

This shift from the industrial distribution of the immigrants to that of the settled labor force, obviously meant the conversion of large groups from activities in which they had been engaged before migrating to new types of activity for which they may not have had previous training. This conversion is illustrated by data made available in a sample survey of the labor force taken in June, 1954 (Table 17).

The recent immigrant groups show a larger proportion of the labor force in agricultural and related pursuits—over 19 per cent in the industrial classification and over 18 per cent in the occupational distribution, compared with 11 or 9 per cent for the arrivals before 1949 and the Israeli-born. Yet, as Table 15 indicated, the proportion of the recent immigrant groups in agriculture was fairly low, about 5 per cent; and, on the whole, lower than the proportion among the earlier immigrant groups. Two processes were obviously in force. On the one hand, a substantial proportion of the new immigrants was settled on the land and a smaller proportion was directed to clerical, administrative, white-collar jobs and the skilled pursuits in public utilities. On the other hand, the earlier and older immigrants had begun to shift from agriculture toward the secondary and tertiary sectors of the economy.

Table 17

Occupational and Industrial Structure of Employed Jews, by Length of Residence, Israel, 1954

A. Occupational Structure	Arrivals before 31/XII, 1948, and Israeli-born	Immigrants After 1948	Total
1. Agric. workers, skilled and semiskilled	9.1	12.1	10.5
2. Agric. workers, unskilled	0.6	6.2	3.3
3. Subtotal	9.7	18.3	13.8
4. Manufacturing, handicrafts, construction, skilled and semiskilled	24.4	23.9	24.1
5. Manufacturing, handicrafts, construction, unskilled	8.1	19.4	13.6
6. Subtotal	32.5	43.3	37.7
7. Drivers and transport workers	5.5	2.5	4.1
8. Tradesmen	10.9	9.1	10.1
9. Managers	4.3	1.0	2.7
10. Office workers, excl. managers	17.0	9.1	13.2
11. Liberal and technical professions	13.5	6.2	10.0
12. Workers in services, skilled and semiskilled	6.6	10.5	8.4
B. Industrial Structure			
1. Agriculture, forestry, fishing	11.2	19.2	15.1
2. Manufacturing and handicrafts (incl. mining)	23.8	23.0	23.4
3. Building and construction	8.3	11.2	9.7
4. Elec., gas, sanitary services	2.1	1.8	2.0
5. Commerce and banking	14.3	10.9	12.7
6. Transportation	7.5	5.7	6.6
7. Services	32.8	28.2	30.5

Source: Unpublished study of labor force survey in 1954 by A. Hovne, Falk Project for Economic Research in Israel.

The industrial structure of the Jewish labor force even in Palestine, and more so in Israel, shows a full sweep of economic activities. It ranges from a substantial proportion in agriculture to an even larger proportion in industry, and to substantial shares in all service activities. The pattern is similar to that of economically developed countries.

This diversity can be further illustrated by the distribution among the various industries within manufacturing (Table 18). There is no evidence of heavy concentration in the apparel industries and, to a lesser extent, in the food and other light consumer goods industries. Even in Palestine in 1931, the proportion of the producer goods industries was substantial, accounting for between a fifth and a third of all Jewish workers in industry. This proportion is even larger in Israel in 1952, accounting for between 30 and 40 per cent.

C. Level and Structure of Income

The Jewish community in Palestine and Israel is the only one, as far as I know, for which total product from economic activity has been measured.

TABLE 18

*Distribution of Jewish Labor Force Within Industry, by Industrial
Divisions, Palestine and Israel, 1931 and 1952*

	1931	1952
1. Number employed (000's)	14.5	100.3
% shares		
2. Minerals	not incl.	0.8
3. Food	11.8	18.9
4. Textiles	4.1	9.1
5. Clothing and footwear	20.2	14.9
6. Leather	9.3	1.5
7. Metal		11.8
8. Machinery	13.1[a]	4.8
9. Electrical appliances		3.6
10. Woodwork	15.3	9.4
11. Chemicals	2.2	3.5
12. Stone and cement	2.0[b]	7.0
13. Printing and paper	6.7	4.5
14. Diamonds	0	2.2
15. Miscellaneous	15.2	8.5[c]

[a] "Metalworks and electricity."
[b] "Building materials."
[c] Includes power stations.

SOURCES: For 1931, *Statistical Handbook of Jewish Palestine*, 1947, p. 66. For 1952, *Statistical Abstract of Israel*, 1953-54, pp. 102-104.

Not that the measures of national product are completely reliable. Because such estimates include the products of *all* economic activities and are distributed among industrial sectors, types of use, etc., they are never accurate —not even in countries with rich bodies of statistical data and long experience in the procedures involved. The supply of data for Palestine and even for Israel is not that rich; and, moreover, the variety of new institutional forms renders the application of standard concepts difficult. Nevertheless, some measures do exist and they do reflect the level and structure of economic activity.

First, the first estimate of the income of Jews in Palestine is for 1936, when the community totaled some 370,000 people. The total net income *produced* during that year was estimated to be about £17,800,000 Palestine. Per capita income was about P£48, or $225—about four-tenths of that in the United States.[33] This is a fairly high level on the international scale. Only some fifteen countries (most of them in western and northern Europe, and in their overseas offshoots, e.g., Canada, United States, Australia, New Zealand) were ranked higher in Point Four.[34] This per capita income was larger than that for most countries in southern and eastern Europe, and for almost all countries (except possibly Argentina) in Latin America, Asia, and Africa. And it was much larger than the per capita income for the non-

Jews in Palestine, estimated to be about P£17 in that year. It must be emphasized that this is a measure of *production,* not of capital imports and of payments due abroad.

In 1954, the last year for which relatively complete estimates of national income are available, the Jewish population was 1,500,000, and total population 1,690,000. The national income was estimated to be 1.461 billion Israeli pounds in current prices.[35] It is not clear to what extent the basic data include the product of the Arab minorities, although agricultural product certainly includes it. For the present purposes total income is related to the Jewish population, but we must keep in mind the possible element of exaggeration—which, however, cannot be large.

National income produced per capita of Jewish population in Israel in 1954 is then I£974, or about $263 in 1936 prices.[36] Because the estimates are rough, it is perhaps best to conclude that real income per capita did not change significantly from 1936 to 1954. The estimates, nevertheless, suggest a remarkable economic performance. Despite the war for independence and political perturbations, despite the striking increase in population, and despite the preponderance of immigration from economically depressed areas, the Jewish community in Israel managed to maintain its high 1936 per capita level of output. And that it was a matter of sizable effort is indicated clearly by the available estimates for some intervening dates. P. F. Loftus's estimates for 1944 suggest that per capita income of the Jews rose some 20 per cent from 1936. Daniel Creamer's estimates suggest that per capita income rose about 16 per cent from 1950 to 1954 (using total population figures). This means that in 1950 real per capita income was about 85 per cent of the 1954 level, at least 15 per cent below the 1944 level, and perhaps below the 1936 level. The level in 1949 may have been even lower. In other words, the 1954 per capita product was attained after real per capita product had dropped a seventh to a fifth *below* the 1936 level.

Despite this impressive performance, the disparity between the per capita income of the Jews in Israel and those in other countries which achieved more continuous and uninterrupted growth increased. In 1954, the per capita income of Israel was less than a third of that of the United States. But it was still at a high level on the international scale: several times above those in the neighboring Arab countries, and significantly above the levels in the underdeveloped countries.[37]

Second, the industrial structure of the national income is to some extent predetermined by the industrial distribution of the Jewish labor force. Yet there are some interesting interrelations between the industrial origin of income and the distribution of workers (Table 19).

In 1936, among Jews, income per worker in agriculture was only half of income per worker for the community as a whole; whereas income per worker in industry was a quarter, and that in commerce, finance, and trans-

TABLE 19

Industrial Distribution of National Income, Palestine, 1936, and Israel, 1953

			% Shares and Ratios				
Year	Absolute Totals (1)	Agricul-ture (2)	Manu-factur-ing and Handi-crafts (3)	Contract con-struction (4)	Trans-portation and Communi-cation (5)	Commerce and Finance (6)	Others (7)
1936, Jews							
1. Gainfully occupied (000's)	171	18.7	17.5	8.2	18.7		36.8
2. National income (000's P£)	17,795	9.4	22.0	8.7	25.4		34.5
3. Income per gainfully occupied	104	50	125	107	136		93
(P£) in column 1, and percentage ratios to income per gainfully occupied in columns 2–7							
1936, Non-Jews							
4. Gainfully occupied (000's)	261	62.1	8.4	3.0	12.2		14.2
5. National income (000's P£)	14,540	26.7	13.6	2.2	23.7		33.9
6. Income per gainfully occupied	56	43	16.1	70	191		238
(P£) in column 1, and percentage ratios to income per gainfully occupied in columns 2–7							
1953–54, Jews							
7. Gainfully occupied VI-1954 (000's)	517	13.8 [a]	22.0 [a]	9.1 [b]	8.0	11.9	34.9
8. Net domestic income 1953 (mill. I£)	1,107	12.6	19.8	4.7	9.4	18.3	35.2
9. Income per gainfully occupied (I£)	2,141	91	90	52	118	154	101
in column 1, and percentage ratios to income per gainfully occupied in columns 2–7							

[a] Mining shifted from columns 2 to 3.
[b] For the labor force the category is "building construction and public works."
SOURCES: Lines 1–6: Robert R. Nathan, Oscar Gass, and Daniel Creamer, *Palestine: Problems and Promise*, Washington, 1946, p. 150. Line 7: See Table 1b, column 4. Line 8: Daniel Creamer, *Provisional Estimates of Israel's National Income, 1952–1953*, Central Bureau of Statistics and Falk Project for Economic Research in Israel, Jerusalem, March, 1955, Special Series No. 29.

portation over a third, above the total community average. For the larger non-Jewish labor force in Palestine in 1936 the interindustry differences were much wider—from somewhat over 40 per cent of the community average in agriculture to over 200 per cent in "others," dominated by government and similar services. These wider interindustry differentials among non-Jews were due partly to greater heterogeneity, and partly to the low status of Arab agriculture.

The interrelations in 1953-1954 were distinctly different. While the share of labor force in agriculture among the Jews was slightly lower than in 1936, the share of income was higher. As a result, income originating per worker in agriculture was only about 10 per cent below the country-wide average. This narrowing differential in income per worker raises an interesting question. Perhaps income in agriculture was kept relatively low in 1936 by the competition of Arab agriculture. Perhaps continuous capital investment in agriculture produced a greater rise in productivity per worker than in industry. Perhaps the prices of agricultural products rose more between 1936 and 1953-1954 than those of industrial products, with the internal terms of trade and rates of compensation of productive factors shifting in favor of agriculture.

Another change in income per worker occurred in construction: the relative to the community average dropped from 107 to 52. The estimate for 1953-1954 may be too low, as we have matched income in contract construction with labor force engaged in "building construction and public works." Yet this change may be real; in 1936, Jews engaged in construction may have been at relatively skilled levels, the lower levels having been occupied largely by Arabs. (Note the relatively low per capita income in 1936 among the non-Jews.) In 1953-1954 both skilled and unskilled labor were Jewish, the majority of the latter recent immigrants.

The interindustry differentials in income per worker for 1953-1954 are rather narrow, taking into account the size of the groups within the total labor force; and have narrowed since 1936. More important, in many other countries the interindustry differentials, particularly between agriculture and other pursuits, are much wider. These narrow differentials are probably a major reason for the equality in the distribution of income remarked upon repeatedly by visitors. Sample data on the size distribution of income that will become available in the near future should provide a basis for measuring this equality.

Third, perhaps the most intriguing aspect of the income estimates is the use of income and that of other resources made available from the outside. Table 20 presents a condensed picture of the allocation of domestic income and other resources in 1936 in Palestine and in 1953 in Israel. The broad conclusions stand out clearly, and probably were not much different for other years (except during World War II when contact with other countries was difficult and conditions were affected by military procurement and mobilization). First, both in 1936 and in 1953, ultimate consumption by the Jewish community, private only in 1936 but including government consumption in 1953, absorbed all income produced. In fact, ultimate consumption was slightly *above* income produced—the excess being P£ 360,000 in 1936 and I£ 97,000,000 in 1953. This meant that none of the income produced was available for capital formation. Second, both in 1936 and in 1953 substantial additions to the stock of capital were made. Gross capital formation was about 30 per cent of all resources in 1936 and about 20 per cent in 1953. Third, these additions to capital stock were made possible by

TABLE 20

Allocation of Income Produced and Other Resources Between Consumption and Capital Formation, Jewish Community in Palestine, 1935, and Israel, 1953

A. Allocation for 1936 (Millions of P£)

Available Resources		Uses	
1. National income, at factor cost	17.80	1. Consumer expenditures, factor cost	18.16
2. Indirect taxes	1.76	2. Indirect taxes	1.76
3. Nat. income, market prices (1+2)	19.56	3. Cons. exp., market prices (1+2)	19.92
4. Capital consumption	0.86	4. Net increase in wealth (excl. land purchases)	8.17
5. G.N.P., market prices (3+4)	20.42	5. Capital consumption	0.86
6. Government capital formation	0.62	6. Gross domestic capital formation (4+5)	9.03
7. Net capital imports (Palestine),	7.85		
of which: capital of immigrants (net)	(5.56)		
capital of "national" and religious funds	(1.2)		
currency	(0.8)		
8. Total available resources, gross of capital consumption (5+6+7)	28.89	7. Total uses, gross of capital consumption (3+6)	28.95

B. Allocation for 1953 (Millions of I£)

Available Resources		Uses	
1. National income, at factor cost	1,130	1. Private consumer expenditures, market prices	1,091
2. Indirect taxes, less subsidies	113	2. General government consumption	249
3. National income, market prices (1+2)	1,243	3. Total consumption, market prices (1+2)	1,340
4. Capital consumption (incl. errors and omissions)	111	4. Gross domestic fixed capital formation	331
5. G.N.P., market prices (3+4)	1,354		
6. Net capital imports	317		
of which: transfers and donations	(226)		
borrowing	(91)		
7. Total available resources (5+6)	1,671	5. Total uses (3+4)	1,671

SOURCES: Part A: Nathan, Gass, and Creamer, *op. cit.*, pp. 151 ff., 317. Part B: Estimates by Harold Lubell for the Falk Project for Economic Research in Israel (see 2nd Annual Report).

capital imports. In 1936 the major sources were capital of immigrants (to which a large part of net currency imports should probably be added) and various national and religious funds.[38] In 1953 the major sources were unrequited transfers (grants, donations, etc.) and net capital borrowing.

That the Jewish community consumed slightly more than the total income it produced may at first seem puzzling, considering the high level of per capita income and, at least in 1953, the origin of the bulk of immigration in areas with low living standards. Under such circumstances consumption might be expected to be sufficiently below income produced to leave a margin for internal financing of domestic capital formation. Yet the puzzle is more apparent than real. In 1936, recent immigration was from fairly well-developed economic areas, and the substantial imports of immigrant capital testify to it. And in 1953, given the western cast of the Israeli economy, it would have been impossible to gear the living standards of recent immigrants to the low levels of their countries of origin. It would have widened the social and economic gap between the newcomers and the settled population, and, more important, it would have prevented the integration of the recent arrivals in the country's productive system. If high levels of product were to be expected from the Jewish labor force, the recent immigrants had to be accorded the opportunity of adequate living standards, regardless of whether their productivity yielded sufficient income for such standards.

Given the intent and desire to develop an economy that would yield a relatively high product per capita, a fairly high standard of consumption had to be established. Recent immigrants would, by and large, probably not reach a level of productivity that would yield income sufficient to provide for savings until *after* some years in the country—a period varying from group to group, and even person to person, depending upon previous training and other factors. Hence, at any given time the Jews in Palestine and Israel comprised settled groups whose product was above, and recent groups whose product was below, their consumption. The former just about offset the latter, and this in itself was quite an accomplishment when the proportional weight of the recent settlers was strikingly raised by large immigration.

To the extent that maintenance of a high consumption standard assures a highly productive labor force, it is as much a capital investment as additions to material capital. In that sense, the capital formation or investment problem connected with the rapid growth of the Jewish population was a double one: investing in human capital by maintaining high standards of consumption and investing in material capital to provide sufficient tools per worker. The investment in human capital was met by domestic savings; the investment in material capital was met by capital imports of different types (immigrant capital, private capital investment, public grants, donations, government borrowing), varying in importance from period to period.[39]

The high level of production could not have been maintained without capital imports. If they had not been available, domestic consumption would have had to be reduced to assure a minimum amount of financing for additions to material capital. In either case per capita income produced would have declined: in the former because of the deterioration in the labor force, in the latter because of shortages of material capital.

Against this broad background, the sources of capital imports are not crucial—important as they may be in policy relations between the Jewish community in Palestine and Israel, Jews in the Diaspora, and the world at large. In some past periods immigrants' capital was a major source, but it is not likely to be important in the future unless immigration from economi-

cally advanced countries becomes substantial. In recent years, the important
sources were donations and grants, and partly reparations—although borrowing was also of some magnitude. Whatever the source, an obviously important factor in the past was the large economic potential of the Jews in
the Diaspora. Capital imports of 30 per cent of total available resources
(in 1936 and in the high level years after independence) are about 43
per cent of the national product of Palestine and Israel. But the total income in 1954 was only a small fraction of the total income of Jews in the
Diaspora. In the United States alone, the Jewish community was about
3.3 times as large as that in Israel in 1954; and if the per capita income
of Jews in the United States is conservatively set at the country-wide
average, their total income must have been well over ten times that of
Israel. The *total* capital imports to Israel amount, on that basis, to at most
about 4 per cent of the income of United States Jews, and probably not
much more than 3 per cent. Considering also the Jewish communities in
the other advanced countries, one must conclude that the economic potential
of the Jews in the Diaspora was a vital factor in capital formation in Israel.

IV. Concluding Comments

A summary of the preceding discussion is neither possible nor desirable,
in view of the brief treatment of many topics. But, in concluding, we advance some reflections suggested by the whole sweep of recent changes in the
economic structure of the Jews.

1. The Economic and Noneconomic Elements

In the economics of Jews the noneconomic elements are important
almost to the point of dominance. The very existence of a distinctive and
cohesive minority is in essence noneconomic—which is true even of many
independent sovereign states. Some rational economic principles, e.g., maximization of long-term economic returns, would argue *against* the perpetuation of such a minority, and would affect the attitudes of both the minority
and the majority which *imposes* unity and cohesion on the minority.

Economic calculations based on principles of maximization of long-term
net yields cannot be made with precision and reliability. But it can be
argued that a Jewish minority would, given its personal and material
economic assets, most likely attain (for itself and its descendants) a higher
level of returns if it could act freely in response to perceived economic
opportunities. "Freely" means without regard for any noneconomic motives and considerations that they might have as members of a Jewish
minority.

Much of the preceding analysis lends emphasis to the point that no such
"pure" response is exercised by the Jewish minority, and that in reality a

high economic price has been paid for the sake of preserving its cohesion and identity. This was certainly true of the Jews who went to Palestine when greater economic opportunities were available elsewhere, as well as of the sizable Jewish minorities anywhere in the Diaspora, where proximity to other members of the group and other conditions of social life affected economic decisions.

The hostile or discriminatory policies of the majorities, whenever manifest, are even more irrational economically. Given the kind of human capital that the Jews represent, the majority in any country, if it wished to maximize long-term economic returns, should have not only permitted the Jewish minority the utmost freedom, but in fact should have subsidized any improvement in the economic and social performance of promising individual Jews. Such help in developing contributors to the stock of human knowledge and hence to economic capacity would have been a high-yield investment. If only for this reason, the discriminatory policies of many majorities, often specifically retarding the dynamics of Jewish minorities— from trade into intellectual and professional pursuits, within business corporations, etc.—constitute extreme economic irrationality.

Of course, people do not act on purely rational economic calculations, and the preceding paragraphs are belaboring the obvious. Yet two implications for the analysis of the economics of the Jews follow from this platitude. First, in explaining the economics of the Jews, these noneconomic elements must be explicitly formulated. Only then will the connection between motivation as members of the minority and economic choices and results become clear—a comment which applies equally to the connection between the motivation and actions of the majority and economic and social opportunities made accessible to the Jews. The second and more elusive implication is that the utmost clarity must be sought in formulating the bases for any *appraisal* of the economic structure of the Jews, in any reference to it as "normal" or "abnormal," desirable or undesirable. Since these bases often include a mixture of economic and noneconomic elements, a clear differentiation of these elements will prevent misleading shallow judgments. For what is abnormal or undesirable according to one criterion may turn out to be normal or desirable according to another. Again, this applies to both the economics of the Jewish minority and the policy of the majority.

2. Historical Continuity

My own interest is an understanding rather than appraisal, so my second reflection mirrors the impression of the pervasiveness of historical continuity in any analysis of economic changes among Jews in the recent century. In a sense this is both obvious and inevitable, as we deal with a minority whose heritage stretches over centuries. Changes in its conditions can hardly be understood except as links in a long chain. But it is the major scenes in this historical drama, and the close connection between them, which strike the eye of an observer who stands, as it were, on the outside.

The main point in much of the discussion, the dominance of East European Jewry as the major reservoir of growth during the past century, and the source from which the two largest communities—in the United States and Israel—have been recruited, is clearly one such link. The reasons for the concentration of Jewry in eastern Europe at the beginning of the nineteenth century certainly lie in centuries of earlier history, when the Jews were expelled from western Europe, and were attracted to Poland and neighboring areas by favorable conditions.

But there is even more to this historical interconnection. The favorable position of Jews in Poland and Lithuania for several centuries meant their occupation of certain economic links in the structure of these countries and impeded the formation of a native middle class. The lack of a strong native middle class may, in turn, have been an important factor in the weakness of the Polish-Lithuanian states and may have delayed their evolution to more effective national states—which in other countries was attained by a combination of the feudal nobility with the economically strong middle classes. It seems ironic that, having flourished and grown within the framework of these weaker nobility-dominated states, the Jewish communities in Poland and Lithuania have paid the price of partition and ended up under the domination of one of the most centralized and authoritarian powers in the world.

The above observations may be superficial reflections of the surface of history writ large—and misleading at that. But they do illustrate the kinds of historical continuity that may be perceived in the changing economics of the Jews. And some of the connecting links have been suggested in the preceding discussion, as we analyzed the shift in the industrial structure and income levels of the East European Jewish community, first in its original area, and then in the United States and Israel, where they and their descendants account for the majority of the Jews.

The changing economics of the Jews is at the same time part of world history and part of the responses of the Jewish groups themselves, acting as distinctive and cohesive minorities. And each of these also has long roots in the past. The interplay of the variety of historical forces affecting the economic conditions of Jews is almost overwhelming. Certainly, only the very broad lines can be marked out; and one must always be aware of the depth of the antecedents and the shallowness of the explanations that can be offered and tested.

This applies to the position today. Of some 11,000,000 Jews in the world, about 7,000,000 are in the Western Hemisphere and western Europe. Their economic and social fate is a function of the economic and social fate of these areas and will be governed largely by the possibilities of preserving peace and avoiding a major world war. Another sizable group of Jews, about 2,500,000 is behind the Iron Curtain and its future is partly a function of the internal changes within these authoritarian states, any relaxation in the dictatorship meaning a relief of hostile pressure on the Jewish minorities; and partly a function again of the major course of international relations. The third sizable group of Jews, 1,500,000, is in Israel, an embattled bastion facing Arab hostility and still a potential refuge for the 500,000 Jews in the disturbed areas of North Africa. Here the lines of historical continuity from the not so distant past of nineteenth-century relations between the western powers and the underdeveloped countries of the Arab belt are being played out to ends that can be only dimly perceived. Against this background, the characteristics of and changes in economic structure dwindle to mere details on a canvas in which other factors are more important.

NOTES

[1] See Arthur Ruppin, "The Jewish Population of the World," *The Jewish People, Past and Present,* Central Yiddish Cultural Organization (CYCO), New York, 1946, Vol. I, pp. 348-360, particularly the table on pp. 350-351.

[2] See Leon Shapiro, "World Jewish Population," *American Jewish Year Book, 1955,* Vol. 56, The Jewish Publication Society, Philadelphia, 1955, pp. 291-297.

[3] See Jacob Lestschinsky, "Die Umsiedlung und Umschichtung des Juedischen Volkes," *Weltwirtschaftliches Archiv,* October, 1929, p. 132.*

[3a See above Melville J. Herskovits, "Who Are the Jews?"]

[4] This is apparent in the very methods used for statistical study of Jews. In countries that do not require specification of religious affiliation in their governmental statistics, e.g., the United States, the so-called *Yom Kippur* and burial methods of estimating Jewish population will, by their nature, yield estimates including only persons whose children do not attend school on *Yom Kippur* and those whose dead are buried in accordance with Jewish law. In states requiring religious affiliation data, it may be relatively easy for persons to conceal their belonging. (Even under Nazi conditions such concealment, while difficult, was not impossible.) Our basic information is therefore limited to individuals who share, even if in a minimal way, the feeling of belonging to a distinctive group with a common religion and history.

[4a See above Uriah Zevi Engelman, "Sources of Jewish Statistics."]

[5a Represented in this volume by Chapter 38, "Jewish Migration, 1840-1956."]

[5] Even in India, a country with a relatively small Jewish community of less than 30,000, the proportion in agriculture is only 6.5 per cent, whereas that of total population is about 70 per cent. Jewish population, for 1941, is from

H. G. Reissner, "Indian-Jewish Statistics (1837-1941)," *Jewish Social Studies,* October, 1950, particularly pp. 362-363.

[6] Even if a sector accounts for a large proportion of the total Jewish population, the proportion of Jews to all engaged within it is not necessarily high. In general, Jews can form a dominant proportion in any one sector only under one of two conditions, and usually only if both conditions are met: this sector must account for a *large* proportion of the Jewish population and for a *small* proportion of total population.

[7] In addition to the sources quoted in Table 1, I have used here Jacob Lestschinsky's paper in *Weltwirtschaftliches Archiv,* Vol. 1, Berlin, 1913; Vol. 32, 1930, pp. 563-599; and Arthur Ruppin, *Soziologie der Juden,* Vol. I, Berlin, 1930, particularly chs. 21, 22, and 23.

[8] The data on distribution within trade of Jews in Russia in 1897 merit specific reference because they partly confirm, and partly differ from, the generalization suggested. (See the detailed breakdown reported in *Zeitschrift fuer Demographie und Statistik der Juden,* February and March, 1906, pp. 19-21 and 43.) Credit institutions and restaurants, hotels, and clubs accounted for only 3 per cent of Jews in trade (whether gainfully occupied only or including dependents), and commodity trade accounted for 97 per cent. Also, of the total sector, as much as 44 per cent was in trade in agricultural products, with perhaps more to be added from the vague category of "general" trade (which accounted for another 20 per cent). Producers' goods, such as construction materials and metals, accounted for only 7 to 8 per cent of Jews engaged in trade. In this sense, the data confirm the generalization suggested. However, proportionately to total population engaged in trade, Jews were important in almost *all* branches of commodity trade. Thus, while the ratio of Jews to total (both including dependents) was 54.7 per cent for all commodity trade, it was 60 per cent in construction materials and fuels, and 47 per cent in metals, machinery, and weapons. It may be that the high ratios of Jews in these producer goods branches of trade were associated with the dominance in these sectors of small-scale enterprises; and yet, as will be seen below, even in Russia in 1897, Jews were underrepresented, in comparison with non-Jewish and total population, in the producer goods industries themselves.

[9] The data in Table 5 and in lines 1-4 of Table 6 should have been based, like the entries in Table 2, on gainfully occupied, excluding recipients of non-service income (given for two or three countries). But this adjustment could not be made with the data at hand. However, the effect on the differences in employment status between Jews and non-Jews would be slight.

[10] See *Weltwirtschaftliches Archiv,* 1929, Vol. 30, pp. 147* and 150*.

[11] Migration of poor Jews, while increasing income inequality among Jews in the country of immigration, presumably decreases it in the country of emigration. There is a tendency, however, for immigration to a single country, such as the United States, to account fairly fully for emigration of Jews from several countries. This may result in a net balance in which the increasing effect upon inequality in the country of immigration is greater than the reducing effect in the countries of emigration.

[11a Cf. above Bernard D. Weinryb, "East European Jewry (Since the Partitions of Poland, 1772-1795)"; Arieh Tartakower, "The Decline of European Jewry (1933-1953)"; Lestschinsky, *op. cit.*]

12 This is total Jewish migration, given by L. Hersch for 1881-1898 in his paper "Jewish Migration During the Last Hundred Years," in *The Jewish People: Past and Present,* Vol., I. p. 415. The period is two years short of that from 1880 to 1900, but the figure includes some emigration from areas other than eastern Europe.

13 See Lestschinsky, in *Weltwirtschaftliches Archiv,* 1930, pp. 573-574.

14 See *Zeitschrift fuer Demographie und Statistik der Juden,* August-September, 1907, pp. 114-155.

15 In his *System of Geography* (London, 1853, Vol. I, p. 23), James Bell reports the population of Russia for 1843 (from the *Almanach de Gotha*) by provinces. The total population for the provinces that comprise the Pale, including Poland, is approximated at 20,800,000, and, allowing a 10 per cent rise to 1850, yields a total of about 23,000,000. The number of Jews for this area (see Table 7) was estimated to be 2,300,000 and the proportion of Jews in the total was 10 per cent. For the population of the Pale, including Poland, of 42,340,000 in 1897, the census reported 4,900,000 Jews, or 11.6 per cent. (See I. M. Rubinow, "Economic Conditions of the Jews in Russia," *Bulletin of the Bureau of Labor Statistics,* No. 72, Washington, September, 1907, p. 491.) This increase is significant as it covers a period of substantial emigration.

16 That trade was saturated with Jews is suggested by the fact that *within the Pale,* their proportion to the total engaged in commerce was as high as 72.5 per cent, and in Lithuania and White Russia it was 88.2 and 89.3 per cent respectively. In some provinces within these regions, e.g., Grodno and Minsk, it was well over 90 per cent. (See Rubinow, *op. cit.,* p. 554.)

17 See M. Lawin, in *Zeitschrift fuer Demographie und Statistik der Juden,* January, 1906, pp. 10 ff. In other countries the percentage of families receiving assistance during Passover in the 1890's ranged from less than 1 per cent in the United States to 5.5 per cent in Holland and Sweden. (See Vasili Rosenthal, "Russia—Charities," *The Jewish Encyclopedia,* Vol. X, New York, 1905, p. 539.)

18 See Rubinow, *op. cit.,* p. 490.

19 See Ruppin, *Die Soziologie der Juden,* Vol. I, pp. 91-92, sum of European and Asiatic.

20 See Solomon M. Schwarz, *The Jews in the Soviet Union,* Syracuse, 1951, Table IX, p. 20.

21 See *ibid.,* p. 265.

22 See *ibid.,* p. 267.

23 A striking illustration of this recent policy is a comparison of the articles appearing under the heading "Jews" in two editions of the *Great Soviet Encyclopedia,* the first published in 1932 and the second in 1952. In the first edition (Vol. 24) there are several articles covering over 150 pages, and while naturally reflecting the biases of the authors, they implicitly and sometimes directly recognize the reality of Jews as a cohesive minority with a *raison*

d'être. In the second edition (Vol. 15) all Jews and Jewish culture and problems are dismissed in one article two and a half pages long (supplemented by two more pages on Biro-Bidjan), with a prominent reference to a statement by Stalin that Jews are not a cohesive minority but splinters held together by an ossified religion and some desiccated sentimentalities.

[24] For the description of the estimates see the unabridged mimeographed paper, available for reference at The Jewish Theological Seminary, pp. 81 and 83.

[25] Of the 1,600,000 Jews who immigrated during 1881-1910, 72 per cent came from Russia, 18 per cent from Austria-Hungary, and 4 per cent from Rumania. (See Samuel Joseph, *Jewish Immigration to the United States*, New York, *op. cit.*, 1914, pp. 93-94.)

[26] See *The Jewish Review*, April, 1945, pp. 1 ff.

[27] The per capita in 1874-1883 was $281 in 1929 prices; in 1939-1948 it was $790, also in 1929 prices, and it rose further from 1939-1948 to 1944-1953. For the figures cited, see "Income and Wealth of the United States, Trend and Structure," *Income and Wealth, Series II*, Cambridge, Eng., 1953, p. 55.

[28] See Colin Clark, *Conditions of Economic Progress*, 2nd ed., London, 1951, pp. 46-47 and 191.

[29] For the earnings in Russia, see Rubinow, *op. cit.*, pp. 528-529. For the data on the United States, see *Immigration Commission Reports*, Vol. I, *Abstracts*, Senate Document No. 747, 61st Congress, 3rd session, Washington, 1911, p. 764.

[30] See *Income and Wealth, Series II*, p. 107.

[31] Illustrative measures of the upward movement of per capita income and of the reduced inequality in income are given in the unabridged mimeographed paper, available for reference at The Jewish Theological Seminary, pp. 98-101.

[31a See above Oscar I. Janowsky, "The Rise of the State of Israel."]

[32] These and other figures, for the period before 1948, are from Ruppin, *op. cit.*, pp. 145-148; and *Statistical Handbook of Jewish Palestine, 1947*, edited by A. Gertz, Department of Statistics, The Jewish Agency for Palestine, Jerusalem, 1947, particularly the sections on population and immigration.

[33] For the method of calculation, see the unabridged mimeographed paper, available for reference at The Jewish Theological Seminary, p. 120.

[34] Department of State, Publication 3719, Washington, January, 1950, pp. 113-114.

[35] An estimate prepared by Daniel Creamer, of the Falk Project for Economic Research in Israel, in co-operation with the Central Bureau of Statistics (manuscript in press, 1957).

[36] For the method of calculation, see the unabridged mimeographed paper, available for reference at The Jewish Theological Seminary, p. 122.

[37] For 1949, the United Nations set the per capita income of Israel at $389. (See *National and Per Capita Incomes, Seventy Countries, 1949*, United Nations, Statistical Papers, Series E, No. 1, New York, October, 1950.) Per capita incomes of the neighboring Arab countries were as follows: Egypt—$100; Syria—$100; Iraq—$85; Lebanon—$125. For practically all countries in

Asia and Africa, per capita incomes were well below $300; for many of them, below $100.

The estimates, and particularly the conversion to United States dollars, are subject to wide margins of error. The figure for Israel seems too high. The data used in the text suggest a level closer to $300 than to $400. But even at this lower level, the per capita income in Israel was more than three times that of most Arab countries, and the disparity must have widened significantly after 1949.

[38] For 1936 I assumed that the net capital imports shown in the balance of international payments for Palestine should be attributed completely to the Jewish community. On the other hand, to avoid duplication I omitted a small item for purchases of land. Also in 1936 part of government capital formation was credited to the Jewish community.

[39] Savings of some groups within Palestine or Israel were not necessarily used directly to finance "dissavings," i.e., the excess of consumption over income, of other groups. On the contrary, domestic savings were probably used to finance domestic capital formation, and funds coming from outside were used to finance dissavings of recent immigrants. The references in the text apply to the matching of aggregates of the type involved in Table 20, not of specific sources of savings with specific channels of investment. The latter type of matching is difficult, as funds circulate freely and, once shifted from point of origin to point of use, are merged in a common pool for all uses. In Palestine and Israel the links could perhaps be more clearly traced than elsewhere. It is obvious that the Jewish Agency and related organizations channeled funds from the outside at least partly to sustain consumption levels of recent immigrants during the early periods when their production would inevitably fall short of their consumption requirements.

BIBLIOGRAPHY

BELL, JAMES, *System of Geography*. Vol. I. London, 1853.

CLARK, COLIN, *Conditions of Economic Progress*, 2nd ed. London, 1951.

CREAMER, DANIEL, *Provisional Estimates of Israel's National Income, 1952-1953*. Central Bureau of Statistics and Falk Project for Economic Research in Israel, Special Series No. 29. Jerusalem, March, 1955.

GERTZ, A. (ed.), *Statistical Handbook of Jewish Palestine, 1947*. Jerusalem, 1947.

GOLDBERG, NATHAN, "Occupational Patterns of American Jews," in *The Jewish Review*, Vol. III, No. 1, April, 1945, and Vol. III, No. 3, October-December, 1945.

GUREVICH, D., "The Jewish Population," in *The Palestine Year Book*, Vol. 2 (1945-1946). New York, 1946.

HERSCH, L., "International Migration of the Jews," in *International Migrations*, Vol. II. New York, 1931.

———, "Jewish Migrations During the Last Hundred Years," in *The Jewish People: Past and Present*, Vol. I. New York, 1946.

JOSEPH, SAMUEL, *Jewish Immigration to the United States.* New York, 1914.

LESTSCHINSKY, JACOB, "The Economic and Social Development of the Jewish People," in *The Jewish People: Past and Present,* Vol. I. New York, 1946.

——, "The Economic Development of the Jews in the United States," in *The Jewish People: Past and Present,* Vol. I. New York, 1946.

——, "Die Umsiedlung und Umschichtung des juedischen Volkes," in *Weltwirtschaftliches Archiv,* October, 1929. Also other articles in 1929 and 1930.

MAHLER, RAPHAEL, "Jews in Public Service in Poland, 1918-1939," in *Jewish Social Studies,* October, 1944.

MEYER, PETER, and others, *The Jews in the Soviet Satellites.* Syracuse, 1953.

NATHAN, ROBERT R.; GASS, OSCAR; and CREAMER, DANIEL, *Palestine: Problems and Promise.* Washington, 1946.

REICH, NATHAN, "The Economic Structure of Modern Jewry," in *The Jews: Their History, Culture, and Religion,* Vol. II, 2nd ed. New York, 1949.

REISSNER, H. G., "Indian-Jewish Statistics (1837-1941)," in *Jewish Social Studies,* October, 1950.

ROSENTHAL, VASILI, "Russia—Charities," in *The Jewish Encyclopedia,* Vol. X. New York, 1905.

RUBINOW, I. M., "Economic Conditions of the Jews in Russia," in *Bulletin of the Bureau of Labor Statistics,* No. 72. September, 1907.

RUPPIN, ARTHUR, "The Jewish Population of the World," in *The Jewish People: Past and Present,* Vol. I. New York, 1946.

——, *Die Soziologie der Juden.* Vol. I. Berlin, 1930.

SCHWARZ, SOLOMON M., *The Jews in the Soviet Union.* Syracuse, 1951.

SHAPIRO, LEON, "World Jewish Population," in *American Jewish Yearbook, 1955,* Vol. 56. Philadelphia, 1955.

SICRON, M., and GIL, B., *Jewish Population by Sex, Age and Country of Birth, 1931-1954.* Central Bureau of Statistics, Special Series, No. 37. Jerusalem, November, 1955.

American Jewish Year Book, 1944—date.

Great Soviet Encyclopedia, Vol. 24, 1932 ed., and Vol. 15, 1952 ed.

Immigration Commission Reports, Vol. 28, Senate Document No. 282, 61st Congress, 2nd session, Washington, 1911; Vol. I, *Abstracts,* Senate Document No. 747, 61st Congress, 3rd session, Washington, 1911.

"Income and Wealth of the United States, Trend and Structure," *Income and Wealth Series II,* Cambridge, Eng., 1953.

Labor Force Survey, Israel Central Bureau of Statistics, *Bulletin,* Part B, February, 1956.

National and Per Capita Incomes, Seventy Countries, 1949, United Nations, Statistical Papers, Series E, No. 1, New York, October, 1950.

Statistical Abstract of Israel 1953-54 and *1954-55,* Jerusalem, 1954 and 1955.

United States Department of State, *Point Four,* Publication 3719, Washington, January, 1950.

Zeitschrift fuer Demographie und Statistik der Juden, articles by various authors including Lestschinsky (1925), M. Lawin (January, 1906), and Arthur Ruppin.

CHAPTER 40

THE JEWS OUTSIDE OF ISRAEL, THE UNITED STATES, AND THE SOVIET EMPIRE

By Milton Himmelfarb*

I. Introduction

In the sixth decade of the twentieth century the Jews of the world numbered about 12,000,000,† of whom less than a quarter lived in countries other than Israel, the United States, and the Soviet Union and its satellites. This chapter deals with the contemporary status, rather than with the history, of that quarter of world Jewry.

Some were Ashkenazim and some Sephardim, the latter term having in effect become the designation not merely for Jews with an Iberian tradition, but for all non-Ashkenazim. Nearly all of the Ashkenazim in our minority of the world's Jews were in countries western by geography and culture, and relatively few lived where their ancestors had also lived centuries ago. The Sephardim were mainly in North Africa and Asia.

On the European continent most of the Jewish communities had suffered directly at the hands of Hitler and the Nazis from the early 1930's to 1945. In North Africa and Asia some ancient Jewish communities had almost completely disappeared after the creation of the State of Israel in 1948; the continued existence of others was uncertain, depending in large measure on whether the hostility of the Arab states toward Israel would increase or diminish; in others still, the Jews, living in the midst of populations struggling for independence, hoped that their status would be tolerable after the overthrow of foreign rule, but feared that it might not be.

II. Western Hemisphere

Of the approximately 850,000–900,000 Jews in the Western Hemisphere (exclusive of some 5,000,000 in the United States) in the 1950's, there were about 240,000 in Canada and 630,000 in Latin America and the

* I wish to thank Mrs. Lucy Dawidowicz and Mrs. Hadassah Schultz of the Library of Jewish Information of the American Jewish Committee, and Mr. Leon Shapiro of the Conference on Jewish Material Claims Against Germany, for their generous help.

† This and the other figures cited are approximate and should be understood to have a fairly wide margin of error.

British and Dutch possessions: 360,000 in Argentina, 120,000 in Brazil, 50,000 in Uruguay, 30,000 in Chile, 25,000 in Mexico, 11,000 in Cuba, and the rest in nineteen other countries.

1. CANADA

There were about 240,000 Jews, including some 50,000 who had immigrated after World War II, in a total Canadian population of 16,000,000. They lived in every part of the country and in almost every city with a population greater than 5,000, but four-fifths were in Montreal, Toronto, and Winnipeg, with Montreal alone having two-fifths and Toronto a third.

Somewhat fewer than three-fifths were native-born, the number of Jews in Canada having been 2,400 in 1881 and 16,000 in 1901. Between 1931 and 1951 the number whose mother tongue was Yiddish fell from 150,000 to 104,000, while the number whose mother tongue was English rose from 4,000 to 88,000. (Almost all, in the 1950's, spoke English, and 15 per cent, mostly in Quebec, spoke French, too.) The majority of the gainfully employed worked for wages or salaries, but outside the three cities with the largest Jewish populations the majority were self-employed. The major sources of livelihood were commerce, manufacturing, and the professions. Jewish women had more children than women of British origin, but fewer than women of French or Slavic origin. Intermarriage was rising, being highest where the Jewish population was small. Most of the almost 200 congregations were Orthodox, about 10 per cent were Conservative, and a few were Reform.

In Quebec, where there was no system of state-supported nonsectarian schools, taxes were paid either to a Catholic or to a Protestant school system, with the Jews paying their taxes to the Protestant schools and most Jewish children attending them; but many of the Jewish children of school age in Quebec were enrolled in Jewish day schools, in which Hebrew and Yiddish were taught, among other Jewish subjects, besides the general curriculum. There were Jewish day schools in provinces with a nonsectarian school system as well. Jewish education, including both Hebrew and Yiddish, was also provided in afternoon schools. Few children attended Sunday schools.

The Canadian Jewish Congress was the spokesman for the Jews of Canada in their relations with the government and the general community, besides being the central body for a wide range of Jewish communal matters. In this dual capacity it was recognized both by the Canadian people and government and by the Jews of Canada. Zionism was strong.

2. LATIN AMERICA AND THE BRITISH AND DUTCH POSSESSIONS

Among the 630,000 Jews of Latin America and the British and Dutch possessions, the largest group was of fairly recent East European origin.

On the whole, the Jews of Latin America were prosperous. In many countries the weakness of democracy made them feel insecure. Their main communal problem was how to strengthen Jewish religion and education.

A. Argentina

In Argentina there were 360,000 or more Jews in a total population of 19,000,000. Three-quarters of them lived in Buenos Aires, the capital. About a half were native-born, nearly all of these being the children of immigrant parents. About one-sixth were Sephardim, and the Ashkenazim were divided between a large majority of East European origin and a minority that had arrived during the Hitler period from Germany or the German cultural area.

About 6 per cent were still in the Jewish agricultural colonies, mostly in the provinces of Santa Fé and Entre Rios, founded by Baron de Hirsch in 1889. In 1941 it had been estimated that a little more than 20 per cent of the Jews of Argentina earned their living by agriculture and related trades. In the 1950's it was not expected that the rural Jewish population would continue to decline nearly so rapidly as in the years after 1941; some observers thought that stability had been reached, and others even thought they detected a slight trend back to the country.

The Jewish occupational pattern was much the same as in other parts of Latin America. The East European immigrants were engaged mostly in retail trade—many had started as peddlers, and not all peddlers had yet become storekeepers—and light manufacturing; the native-born children, besides continuing these occupations—but very few went into peddling—were also in the professions and white-collar employment. The German Jews, having arrived with a background of education and experience in a more advanced society than Eastern Europe, and having typically brought with them more capital than the earlier immigrants from Russia and Poland, tended to be on correspondingly higher rungs of the economy. Many Jewish agricultural and commercial credit co-operatives were still in existence, the outgrowth of mutual-aid societies established by the early immigrants.

The early immigrants had also established kehillot, especially in the colonies, and in the cities synagogues and the traditional societies for education, visiting the sick, and mutual aid. From these had grown schools, cultural organizations, hospitals, orphan asylums, homes for the aged, immigrant-aid institutions, Zionist groups, and social and sports clubs. In the mid-1950's there was a Buenos Aires kehilla with a membership of some 50,000, as well as a federation of kehillot for the whole country. DAIA (Delegación de Asociaciones Israelitas de Argentina) was the central organization.

Argentine Jewry was still divided according to origin. Philanthropic and Zionist organizations were East European, German, or Sephardic—or, sometimes, native. The Sephardim were divided according to place of origin (Morocco, Syria, Turkey, the Balkans), language (Arabic, Ladino), and degree of acculturation.

Only a small minority of the estimated fifty to one hundred congregations in Buenos Aires had their own permanent synagogue buildings. *Kashrut* was widely neglected; in Buenos Aires, with its 300,000 Jews, there were no *kosher* restaurants. There were few rabbis, and even fewer capable of attracting the younger people.

Buenos Aires was a world center of Yiddish publishing, but many observers thought the younger generation to be not much more interested in Jewish culture than in religion. Zionism was strong. Emigration to Israel, while not large absolutely, was considerably larger relatively than from the United States.

The major communal effort was directed to Jewish education. There were supplementary and full-time Jewish schools reflecting every ideology from religious to secularist, from General Zionist to Left Poale-Zion, from Hebraist to Yiddishist.

In their relations with the rest of the Argentine people, the Jews of Argentina emerged relatively undamaged from the Péron era.

B. Bolivia

In Bolivia there were about 4,000 Jews in a total population of some 3,200,000. Most were of German origin, having arrived as refugees after Hitler rose to power. Nearly all were engaged in commerce and industry and lived in the two largest cities, La Paz and Cochabamba.

Their dominant Jewish organization was the *Juedische Kultusgemeinschaft*. Their major cultural problems were the same as those of all other small communities: the lack of personnel and facilities for Jewish educational, religious, cultural, and communal matters.

C. Brazil

Brazil, with a total population of almost 60,000,000, had a Jewish population of 120,000, of whom a third lived in Rio de Janeiro and another third in São Paulo.

The modern history of Brazilian Jewry began with a small Sephardic immigration from Turkey and Morocco in the first half of the nineteenth century. In the first quarter of the twentieth century close to 40,000 Jews immigrated, and between 1925 and 1940 close to 50,000. About 30 per cent of all Brazilian Jews were native-born. Quatro Irmãos, an agricultural colony established shortly after 1900 by the Jewish Colonization Association, had a population of 1,500.

Most of the Jews of São Paulo came from Germany, and more of them were engaged in industry than in commerce. In Rio de Janeiro 70 per cent of the Jews were in commerce and 10 per cent in industry, and in the rest of the country nearly 85 per cent were in commerce. The Sephardim, about 10 per cent of Brazilian Jewry, were nearly all in commerce.

A central community organization had long been advocated as a means of counteracting anti-Semitism, fomented largely by Brazilians of German origin, but the heterogeneity of the Jews of Brazil was a major obstacle to creating a central body.

There were several synagogues, with two rabbis in Rio de Janeiro, one in São Paulo, and one in Porto Alegre. A number of Jewish philanthropic and social organizations were also in existence, but were not very active. Zionism was the strongest movement, the United Zionist Organization acting as the central fund-raising body for Israel and also making some allocations for domestic needs. Yiddish was losing ground. In São Paulo there were about twenty day schools attended by a sixth of all Jewish children of school age.

Many Brazilian Jews feared continuing losses to Judaism and the Jewish community from assimilation and intermarriage.

D. Chile

Chile, whose total population was 6,800,000, had a Jewish population of 30,000, the majority of whom lived in Santiago. About 2,000 or 3,000 were Sephardim, and of the Ashkenazim slightly more were East European than German in origin. About one-third were native-born.

The Jews were especially prominent in light industry. The economic rise of Chilean Jewry owed much to the loan funds and similar bank and credit facilities established by immigrants in the 1920's.

The Chilean Jewish community was characterized as perhaps the best organized in Latin America. Its central representative organization was the *Comité Representativo de la Colectividad Judía de Chile*. There were seven or eight local religious kehillot, but religion was not in a flourishing state. Zionism was strong. There were a central board of Jewish education and three day schools, in addition to supplementary schools, but most Jewish children received no Jewish education.

Yiddish and German were increasingly giving way to Spanish. The merging of East European, German, and Sephardic elements into a common Chilean Jewry was proceeding fairly rapidly.

E. Colombia

In Colombia there were 9,000 Jews in a population of 13,000,000. The majority were Germans. Of the East Europeans, most had arrived in the late 1920's and early 1930's. The Sephardim, mainly from Palestine, had immigrated earlier in the century. The largest Jewish community was in Bogotá. Most Colombian Jews earned their living in commerce, light industry, artisan occupations, such as tailoring, and the professions. A number of Sephardim were important in industry.

Community organization, mostly local, was restricted largely to synagogues and the traditional philanthropies. Zionist and pro-Israel sentiment was intense. Jewish education was weak.

F. Costa Rica

In Costa Rica, with a population of 950,000, there were about 1,500 Jews. They were East European, German, and Sephardic—the last mostly from Turkey. A Jewish Center in San José served a variety of Jewish needs. The community was Zionist.

G. Cuba

There were about 11,000 Jews in Cuba, which had a population of 6,000,-000. More than three-quarters of the Jews lived in Havana. The majority were East European, with some Germans who had immigrated shortly before the United States entered World War II, and some Sephardim from Turkey. Most of the Jews were in trade and light industry; there was little left of the relatively large working class of the 1920's and 1930's.

The *Central Israelita* in Havana served as a central representative body. There was much concern with Jewish education. The five synagogues in Havana included a Reform congregation of Jews from the United States.

The Jews of Cuba had the reputation of being exceptionally devoted to Yiddish culture, but Yiddish was weakening. The community was mostly Zionist.

H. Dominican Republic

The Dominican Republic, or Santo Domingo, had a population of 2,400,-000, including about 450 Jewish families. Two-thirds of these lived in or near Sosua, a Jewish agricultural colony established in 1940 as a partial solution to the refugee problem, and about one-third lived in Ciudad Trujillo, the capital. There was a synagogue in Sosua and another in Ciudad Trujillo. Jewish education was weak.

I. Ecuador

In Ecuador, with a population of 3,600,000, there were about 2,000 Jews, mostly from Germany and Austria. They were important in industry. The majority lived in Quito.

Because of the relative homogeneity of the Jews of Ecuador, there was little difficulty in community organization. The *Comité Coordinador de las*

Organizaciones Israelitas de Quito was the central representative body. Jewish education was weak. The community was generally Zionist.

J. El Salvador

In El Salvador, with a population of 2,200,000, there were 200 Jewish families, consisting mostly of Germans who had immigrated during the Hitler period. A kehilla served both religious and Zionist purposes. There was a considerable degree of intermarriage.

K. Guatemala

In Guatemala, which had a population of more than 3,000,000, there were some 1,000 Jews, mostly from Germany. Nearly all lived in the capital, Guatemala City, where they had established a few new industries. They had three kehillot—Sephardic, East European, and German. Only the Sephardim had their own synagogue and there was one teacher available for Jewish education. The community was Zionist.

L. Honduras

Two hundred Jews lived in Honduras, which had a population of 1,700,000. Most of the Jews had come from Germany and more of them lived in the capital, Tegucigalpa, than in any other city. They were chiefly in trade. There was no Jewish education to speak of.

M. Jamaica

There were 1,500–2,000 Jews in Jamaica, which had a total population of 1,500,000. The ratio of Jews to the small white population was about 10 per cent. They were very prominent in the civic and economic life of the island.

The Jewish community had a history going back to the seventeenth century, and most Jews were of old families. Some were Sephardim and some Ashkenazim by tradition. There was one synagogue, resulting from a merger after World War I.

N. Mexico

Of Mexico's total population of 30,000,000, about 25,000 were Jews. Approximately 80 per cent of these lived in the capital, Mexico City, and some observers thought that the proportion was rising. The occupational pattern was much the same as in the rest of Latin America, with most Jewish livelihoods being earned in commerce, light industry, and, to a lesser degree, the professions. It was a prosperous community.

The majority were East European by origin or descent; the second largest element was Sephardic, having the highest rate of natural increase; and then came the Germans. There was also a small, exotic group of Indian

Jews, claiming descent from the Marranos who had been so prominently associated with Mexican history in the first centuries after the Spanish conquest. Separate Ashkenazic and Sephardic community organizations were in existence, but there was also a central representative body, the *Comité Central Israelita de México*. The community was generally Zionist. Few Jews were unaffiliated with some Jewish institution.

Mexico had the best organized and most flourishing Jewish educational system in Latin America. In the mid-1950's about four-fifths of all Jewish children of school age were enrolled in Jewish day schools. These were either secular or religious, but the large majority of students were in the secular schools. Nearly all the Ashkenazic schools taught Yiddish as well as Hebrew, besides the subjects required by the Mexican educational authorities.

O. Netherlands Guiana (Surinam)

Surinam had a total population of 240,000, of whom only a small minority was white, including 1,000 Jews. They lived mostly in the capital, Paramaribo, and many were of old Sephardic families. They had an important place in the economy.

P. Netherlands West Indies (Curaçao and Aruba)

In the Netherlands West Indies population of some 180,000 there were fewer than 1,000 Jews, an important element in the white minority. Most were of old Sephardic families, but there were also about 200 Ashkenazim of more recent origin. The great majority lived on the island of Curaçao, especially in the capital city, Willemstad, where they were very prominent in commerce and finance.

It was said that Mikve Israel, which followed the Sephardic Orthodox ritual, was the oldest Jewish congregation in the Western Hemisphere. There was also a Reform congregation, founded in the middle of the nineteenth century, most of whose members were of the old Sephardic families.

Q. Nicaragua

In Nicaragua, with a population of some 1,300,000, there were about 150 Jewish families, mostly from Germany. Nearly all lived in the capital, Managua, where they maintained a temple, but no Jewish school.

R. Panama

The 2,500 Jews of Panama, with a population of 900,000, were concentrated in Panama City. Many were long-settled, highly assimilated Sephardim. There were three congregations: a Sephardic Reform temple, of which most of the Jews from the United States, as well as from Germany, were members, and which had an American tone; an Orthodox synagogue for Jews from the eastern and southern Mediterranean; and an Orthodox synagogue for Jews from Eastern Europe. The National Jewish Welfare Board, working in Panama because of the presence of American soldiers and sailors, influenced the cultural activities and community organization of Panamanian Jewry.

S. Paraguay

In Paraguay, with a population of 1,600,000, there were about 2,000 Jews, mostly in the capital, Asunción. They were mainly engaged in commerce. The majority were Ashkenazim and had two synagogues, one German and one East European; the Sephardim had two synagogues of their own. There was a small Jewish agricultural colony, founded in 1934, in Colonia Franca. Jewish education was weak. The Jews of Paraguay looked to Argentine Jewry for cultural and communal leadership.

T. Peru

There were 3,000–4,000 Jews in Peru, which had a total population of 9,500,000. The largest element in the Jewish community was East European, followed by the German and by the Sephardic. Commerce was the major occupation. Jewish settlement was concentrated in Lima, the capital.

The East Europeans, Germans, and Sephardim had their own communal institutions, which had autonomous membership in a religious kehilla recognized by the government. Religion and education were not in a flourishing state. Zionism was strong.

U. Uruguay

In Uruguay, with a population of 2,500,000, there were about 50,000 Jews. The very large majority lived in the capital, Montevideo. In their economic history, pursuits, and institutions they closely resembled their neighbors, the Argentine Jews.

Uruguayan Jewry was divided into four communities, East European, German, Hungarian, and Sephardic, federated in the *Comité Central Israelita*, the central representative body.

It was a basically Zionist community. Ideological differences, embodied in social, political, and cultural institutions and reflected in the supplementary Jewish schools, were sharpest among the East Europeans.

V. Venezuela

There were between 5,000 and 6,000 Jews in Venezuela, which had a total population of 6,000,000. Most lived in Caracas. Generally they were prosperous businessmen.

In Caracas there were equal numbers of German and East European

Jews, and a somewhat smaller Sephardic element. Each of the three groups had its own center. Most of the children of the East European immigrants attended a Jewish day school. It was a Zionist community.

III. EUROPE

The countries to be considered here include Turkey but exclude the Soviet Union and its European empire—Albania, Bulgaria, Czechoslovakia, East Germany, Hungary, Poland, and Rumania—and Yugoslavia. Most of these countries had been gravely affected by the war and Hitler, and the Jews in them more gravely still.[1a] In the years after the war, a feature common to nearly all the West European Jewish communities was a desire to rebuild, and more particularly a desire to strengthen their religious, educational, and cultural life and institutions. Equally common was a strongly positive attitude toward Israel, which in several countries was in sharp contrast to the prewar indifference or opposition of significant Jewish elements to Zionism. In nearly every European country the well-being of Jews and Judaism owed much to the continuing help of the American Jewish Joint Distribution Committee; and welfare, educational, and cultural enterprises were financially supported in large measure by German restitution and compensation funds made available through the Conference on Jewish Material Claims Against Germany.

I. GREAT BRITAIN

Great Britain, consisting of England, Wales, Scotland, and Northern Ireland, had a total population of more than 50,000,000, including 450,000 Jews, the largest Jewish community discussed in this chapter. In England and Wales, with a combined population of more than 44,000,000, there were almost 435,000 Jews; there were 15,000 in Scotland (population 5,000,000) and fewer than 2,000 in Northern Ireland (population 1,400,-000). The majority of British Jews, about 280,000, lived in Greater London. The next largest Jewish communities were in Manchester, with 31,000, and Leeds, with 25,000. The rest of the Jews of Great Britain lived in a hundred other cities and towns.

That the figures for the Jewish birth rate and the average size of Jewish families were somewhat lower than the figures for the British population as a whole was due to the rapid rise of a once predominantly immigrant and working-class community to middle-class status. In the East End of London, where in 1900 there were 125,000 Jews and in 1929 there were 85,000, in the 1950's there were only 30,000. The chief economic pursuits of British Jews were commerce, light industry, and the professions. A considerably higher proportion of Jews than of non-Jews were self-employed, were in the professions, or were students in universities.

In 1956 British Jewry celebrated the 300th anniversary of the readmission of Jews to England under Cromwell, centuries after their expulsion in the Middle Ages. The first to benefit had been Sephardim, and both their descendants and the descendants of other Sephardim who settled in England during the next 150 years still occupied positions of honor and leadership at the time of the tercentenary. Ashkenazim began to arrive in England shortly after the readmission, and they were the great majority. Most British Jews were the children or grandchildren of immigrants who came from Russia and other parts of Eastern Europe between 1880 and 1914. A number of German Jewish refugees from Nazism had also established themselves.

British Jewry was well organized and had a strong sense of itself as a community. The Board of Deputies of British Jews, which had its origins in the middle of the eighteenth century, was the central representative body and enjoyed a measure of special recognition by the state. The United Synagogue set the tone of the official Orthodoxy, though its actual jurisdiction did not extend far beyond London and though there were dissident Orthodox groups, besides a number of non-Orthodox synagogues. The Chief Rabbi had considerable authority over the religious life of the community and was generally regarded as its ecclesiastical spokesman and representative. Less official, but probably not less influential, was the weekly *Jewish Chronicle,* the leading English-language Jewish newspaper in the world, which had been in existence for more than a century.

The ("Reform") Association of Synagogues—fifteen, of which six were in London—corresponded in theology and ritual to synagogues of the so-called left wing of American Conservatism. The ("Liberal") Union of Liberal and Progressive Synagogues—seventeen, of which nine were in London—was less traditionalist. Both the Association and the Union belonged to the World Union for Progressive Judaism. The quality of official Jewish life in England was more Orthodox than in the United States, a higher proportion of English than of American Jews were affiliated with the synagogue, and of those affiliated a higher proportion was Orthodox; but most of those who described themselves as Orthodox were not completely observant.

The social services of British Jewry were diverse and numerous. There were boards of guardians, friendly (i.e., mutual-aid) societies, youth services that had originated in the desire of the established elements to further the Anglicization of the newcomers, and the like. These were far less vigorous than they had been a generation earlier, because British Jewry had prospered and become more native and because Great Britain itself had become a welfare state.

At the apex of the Jewish educational pyramid were Jews' College, established in 1855, and a number of *yeshibot.* There were Talmud Torahs, congregational schools, and, increasingly since the end of World War II, day schools and a growing number of secondary boarding schools. The Union of Orthodox Hebrew Congregations, representing a kind of Frankfort Judaism, was especially vigorous in promoting the day and boarding schools. The insufficiency of rabbis and teachers was one of the chief communal problems.

Zionism and pro-Israel sentiment were strong.

Democracy in Great Britain was as firmly established as anywhere in the world and anti-Semitism was therefore weak. The ratio of Jewish members to the total memberships both of the House of Commons and of the House of Lords was several times greater than the ratio of Jews to the total population.

2. IRELAND

The Jews of Ireland, with a total population of 3,000,000, numbered slightly more than 5,000, nearly all of them in Dublin. Most were in commerce and industry, with some in law and medicine.

After Eire's withdrawal from the British Commonwealth in 1949, the Irish Jewish community severed its official connection with the British Jewish community, but in practice the traditional close ties continued.

More than 90 per cent of Irish Jewish families were members of synagogues, nearly all Orthodox. The one Liberal synagogue was closely linked to the Liberal movement in England. The Chief Rabbi was Orthodox. It was a predominantly Zionist community, with a number of adult and youth societies. The central organization was the Representative Council.

More than four-fifths of the children received a regular Jewish education. Of these about half attended Jewish day schools.

Equal rights were guaranteed in law and enjoyed in fact, but in general Irish Jews were socially isolated from the rest of the overwhelmingly Catholic population.

3. NETHERLANDS

In the Netherlands, with a population of 11,000,000, there were 24,000 to 25,000 Jews, 14,000 of them in Amsterdam. The Nazi occupation had taken a greater toll of the Jews in the Netherlands than in any other West European country. Its effects were still to be seen in the excess of Jewish women over men, in the great weakening of the ancient Sephardic element and its institutions, in a Zionist and pro-Israel sentiment far more intense than before the occupation, and in the existence of an unknown but possibly significant number of men and women, born Jews, whose experience of the mortal danger of being Jewish under the Nazis led them to continue denying or concealing their origin. Socially and economically, it was largely a middle-class community.

The central Jewish organization was the *Nederlands-Israelietisch Kerkgenootschap*. There were three religious groupings: Sephardic, Ashkenazic, and Liberal. There was great concern for Jewish education. Zionism was strong.

A continuing reminder of the Nazi occupation, as well as a continuing source of intergroup friction, was the question of the Jewish war orphans. Many Jewish parents, later murdered by the Nazis, had entrusted their children to the care of Christian friends or institutions before being deported. Most of these children were returned to relatives or to the Jewish community after the war, but some had been baptized; and quite apart from religious considerations, some Christian guardians had grown so fond of the Jewish children they had brought up that they could not bear to part with them. There were a number of cases of defiance of court orders for the return of such children to Jewish custody, causing a certain amount of tension and bitterness.

4. BELGIUM

The Jewish population of Belgium, which had a total population of almost 9,000,000, was between 35,000 and 40,000; it had been 80,000 before World War II. Between 20,000 and 25,000 Jews lived in Brussels and 9,000 or 10,000 in Antwerp. There were smaller Jewish communities in Liége, Charleroi, and Ghent. Ostend was a favorite summer resort for Jews from all the countries of West Europe.

In Brussels the major trades in which Jews were engaged were clothing, textiles, leather, fur, and plastics. In Antwerp about four-fifths of the Jews made their living from the diamond industry. A number of Jews were in the medical and legal profession and some were university teachers. A few were in the civil service. Most of the Jews in Belgium were either foreign-born or the children of foreign-born parents. There was little anti-Semitism.

The Jewish communities of Brussels and Antwerp were very different. In Brussels the Jews were rather assimilated, were generally unaffiliated with Jewish institutions, and had a relatively high rate of intermarriage. Antwerp, on the other hand, had probably the most intensely Jewish community in postwar Europe. Orthodoxy was strong and most of the Jewish children attended Jewish day schools.

The officially recognized central Jewish body was the *Consistoire Central Israélite de Belgique*. Like other clergymen, rabbis were officials of the state, receiving their salaries from the government.

5. LUXEMBOURG

There were about 1,000 Jews in the Grand Duchy of Luxembourg, which had a total population of some 310,000. Most of the Jews lived in the capital city, Luxembourg.

The Jews were a middle-class business element. A *consistoire* was in charge of their religious and communal affairs. There was a Chief Rabbi. The main communal concern, as in most of Western Europe, was about Jewish education.

6. FRANCE

France had a population of 45,000,000, including more than 300,000 Jews. Of these, more than half lived in Paris and the surrounding region; 40,000 in Alsace-Lorraine, which, for historical reasons, had a different Jewish communal organization from the rest of the country; 12,000 in and near Lyon, and 9,000 in and near Marseilles.

Most of the "old stock" French Jews, mainly of Alsatian origin, were in business and the professions. Among the immigrants—mostly from Eastern Europe, but with the proportion of North Africans rising as unsettled conditions in Algeria, Morocco, and Tunisia led many Jews to emigrate —there were also workers, artisans, and peddlers. Jews had been prominent in the intellectual and artistic life of France for generations.

Relations between the immigrant and the longer-established Jews were gradually improving, and observers noted a tendency toward the formation of a truly embracing community. Both among the older and the newer Jewish groups there was considerable abstention from Jewish participation and affiliation. The major Jewish organizations were the *Consistoire Central des Israélites de France et d'Algérie*, the *Conseil Représentatif des Juifs de France*, and the *Fonds Social Juif Unifié*. French Judaism was officially Orthodox, with chief rabbis for the country and the larger cities; but there were a few Liberal congregations, too. The dominant communal concern was to provide the education and make available the facilities that would attract the youth to Judaism and the Jewish community, and thus to keep French Jewry from disappearing. The chief problem was the lack of enough qualified teachers, rabbis, and social workers. The effort to keep French Judaism alive included the establishment in Paris of a Jewish center on the American model, the preparation of attractive curricula and books for Jewish education, and the creation of a system of traveling rabbis to care for formerly neglected Jewish communities. In Paris there were a number of training schools, including the *École Rabbinique*. Zionist and pro-Israel sentiment were far stronger than they had been a generation earlier.

The political status of French Jewry could be judged from the fact that in the first ten years after the war, three Jews had been prime minister. But democracy could not be said to be out of danger in France, and the enemies of democracy were also the enemies of the Jews—from the Communists to the semi-Fascist Poujade movement.

7. SWITZERLAND

Slightly fewer than 20,000 Jews lived in Switzerland, which had a total population of 5,000,000. The largest Jewish community, numbering about 6,000, was in Zurich, about 2,400 were in Basel, a little more than 2,000 in Geneva, 1,000 in Lausanne, and about 800 in Berne. Slightly more than half were citizens. Nearly all were in the middle class.

It was an aging community, with deaths exceeding births. There was a high and growing rate of intermarriage.

There were twenty-six local religious communities—some cities having more than one—served by thirteen rabbis. The dominant religious tone was what an American Jew would call Conservative. There were several Orthodox congregations as well, mostly East European. Swiss law forbade *shechita*, so *kosher* meat had to be imported, mostly from France.

The central communal organization was the *Schweizerische Israelitische Gemeindebund*.

8. SPAIN

In Spain, with its population of 30,000,000, there were about 3,000 Jews, including 2,500 in Barcelona and 250 in Madrid.

Few of the adult generation were native-born. Most were Mediterranean Sephardim; some were Ashkenazim from Eastern and Central Europe who had settled there for business or out of necessity.

A discreet exercise of Judaism was tolerated. Without drastic changes in Spain, few Jews were sanguine about the future of a Spanish Jewish community. Their effort was bent to keeping the young people Jewish. Zionist and pro-Israel sentiment was intense.

9. PORTUGAL

Portugal, with its 9,000,000 people, had a Jewish population variously estimated at between 700 and 2,000. Most lived in Lisbon, where they were mainly in commerce. The next largest concentration was in Oporto. Most were Sephardim.

A large number of Portuguese Catholics were said not only to retain the memory of their Jewish ancestry but also to practice a few Jewish rites secretly and to seek out marriages with others like themselves. In the 1930's there had been an attempt to bring about the return of these people to Judaism, but it was not very successful.

10. ITALY

There were about 30,000 Jews in Italy, which had a total population of 48,000,000. Slightly more than half lived in Rome (12,000) and Milan (6,000). Other communities with more than 1,000 Jews were Florence,

Genoa, Leghorn, Trieste, Turin, and Venice. Most Italian Jews belonged to families that had been in Italy for centuries.

Outside of Rome the Jews were economically and socially of the middle class. Roman Jewry was sociologically unique in the western world; though it included almost no recent arrivals from abroad, many of its members continued to live in the ghetto—the old Jewish quarter—and to earn their living by petty trade and peddling.

By a law enacted in 1930 at the request of the Jews and still in force, a Jew had to belong to a Jewish community unless he officially abandoned Judaism, and the Jewish communities had the power to levy taxes. The twenty-three communities were organized in the *Unione delle Communità Israelitiche*, the central representative body of Italian Jewry.

Because of Saturday teaching and the primacy of Catholicism in the state schools, a number of communities maintained separate, full-time Jewish schools, some of them subsidized in greater or lesser measure by the government. In the mid-1950's more than a third of Jewish children of school age were in these schools in Rome, more than half in Milan, and four-fifths in Turin. Since the end of World War II there had been a vigorous effort to strengthen Jewish education, formal and informal. The *Collegio Rabbinico* trained rabbis for the western, latitudinarian kind of Orthodoxy that was the official Judaism of Italy. Though there were a number of Italian synagogues that were liturgically non-Sephardic, Italian Jewry could in general be said to be Sephardic. Pro-Israel sentiment was strong.

11. SCANDINAVIA

Denmark, Sweden, Norway, and Finland had a total population of close to 20,000,000, of whom about 22,000 were Jews. There was a common Scandinavian consciousness among the Jewish communities of these four countries, which was expressed in such forms as a Union of Scandinavian Jewish Youth Associations. Before Hitler most Scandinavian Jews had been in middle-class occupations, Liberal in religion, and concentrated in the capital cities. German immigration before the war and an East European immigration after the war had introduced certain changes, especially in the Swedish Jewish community: a little more Jewish traditionalism, more artisans and workers, and a greater geographic dispersion. (But after the new immigrants had begun to adjust themselves to their new conditions and to seek Jewish association, a number of them moved to the capitals.) Something of the aroused concern for Jewish education evident in the rest of Western Europe was also to be found in the Scandinavian countries. Each Jewish community had its own central organization.

The political and social climate was democratic.

A. Denmark

In Denmark, with a population of 4,500,000, most of the 6,500 Jews lived in Copenhagen.

B. Sweden

About 12,500 Jews lived in Sweden, which had a population of 7,300,-000. The number of Jews was twice as large as before Hitler. Half lived in Stockholm.

Until the early 1950's a Swedish law on the relations between church and state had meant for Jews that unless they chose to be converted to Christianity they must belong to the Jewish community and pay taxes to it; but only citizens could belong. After the abrogation of the law a few Jews withdrew from the Jewish community, but it was expected that this loss would be more than compensated by the noncitizens who would join.

C. Norway

Norway, with 3,500,000 people, had only 1,000 Jews, including post-war immigrants. A third were in Oslo. Before the war the native Jews alone had numbered several hundred more than the postwar 1,000. Norwegian Jewry had suffered more heavily at the hands of the Nazis than the communities of the other Scandinavian countries.

D. Finland

In Finland, with a population of 4,300,000, there were 1,800 Jews, between a third and a half of them in Helsinki. Though Finland had been allied with Germany in the war, it had protected its Jewish citizens and residents against the Nazis.

12. WEST GERMANY

In West Germany, including West Berlin, there were about 17,000 Jews registered with the official communities, besides about 7,000 who were unaffiliated. They lived in nearly eighty cities, but in only four cities were there 1,000 Jews or more. The largest number, between 4,500 and 5,000, were in West Berlin.

It was an elderly community, the average age being forty-five and about 15 per cent living on pensions. Only a minority were German by citizenship, birth, or education. Most of the gainfully employed were in business. There were fewer professional men, proportionately, than in the pre-Hitler days.

The central Jewish body was the *Zentralrat der Juden in Deutschland.* The Jewish communities were largely supported by the so-called church taxes collected and distributed by the government. A number of homes for the aged and similar health and welfare institutions were maintained. There were about ten rabbis, and most of the synagogues were Orthodox. There was much concern for Jewish education and a considerable effort to provide it.

On the whole, the West German government had shown its good will toward the Jews, not only of Germany, but also of the world. With the Conference on Jewish Material Claims Against Germany it had concluded and honored an agreement that was a significant element in the Israeli economy and in Jewish welfare and educational work in countries as far away as Australia. The years after the German defeat in World War II had shown nothing like the appearance of Hitler and his movement in a similar period of time after the German defeat in World War I. Still, memory of the past and occasional experience in the present combined to maintain an attitude of reserve among the Jews: in the old days, their organization was the central association of "German citizens of the Jewish faith"; now it was the central council of "the Jews in Germany"—not even of "the German Jews." The majority were in Germany either because economic opportunities were better there than in the lands to which they could emigrate or because they had found it too hard to adjust themselves to life in other countries.

13. AUSTRIA

Of Austria's population of 7,000,000 about 11,000 were Jews, including an estimated 1,000 unaffiliated with the Jewish community. Ninety per cent lived in Vienna. The Austrian Jews were an aging group: only about one in eight was under twenty-five years of age, and deaths exceeded births.

The central Jewish organization was the *Kultusgemeinde*, to which representatives were elected periodically from lists submitted by the various parties, including the Socialists, the Zionists, and the religious. The Socialists were strongest.

The Austrian government was much more grudging than the German about compensating Jews for their losses under Nazism. Few believed that the Austrian Jewish community had a future.

14. GREECE

In Greece, with a population of approximately 8,000,000, there were about 6,000 Jews, mostly Sephardic, in the mid-1950's; before World War II and the Nazi murders there had been about 75,000 Jews, including more than 55,000 in Salonica. In the 1950's there were fewer than 1,500 in Salonica, and 3,000 lived in Athens.

The age distribution was normal, and births balanced deaths. The major occupations were commerce, light industry, and the professions.

There were a Central Council of Jewish Communities and one rabbi.

15. TURKEY

Turkey had a population of 25,000,000, including 50,000 to 60,000 Jews, nearly all Sephardim. Most lived in Istanbul. The Jewish population had been larger, but more than 30,000 had settled permanently in Israel.

Turkish Jews were engaged mainly in commerce. Increasingly Turkish was replacing Ladino as their vernacular. There was strong state control over the grand rabbinate, as over all religious institutions in Turkey.

The government was essentially authoritarian, and the underlying xenophobia of the population periodically made itself felt against all non-Moslem groups.

IV. THE ARAB LANDS

The creation and existence of the State of Israel, Arab nationalism, the transformation of economics, politics, and social life among the Arabs—all had produced a crisis in the lives of the Jews, nearly all Sephardim, in the Arab lands. From Yemen, in which for many centuries there had been a vigorous Jewish life, almost all the Jews had gone to Israel. Iraq and Libya were left with a very small fraction of the Jews who had lived there. After the Israeli-Egyptian war and the Franco-British attack on the Suez Canal in 1956, Egypt decided to expel some Jews and to make life so difficult for the others that they would not want to stay. In no Arab country could the continued existence of Jews and Judaism be taken for granted.

In North Africa, Tunisia and Morocco had become independent of France (and Morocco of Spain as well) when this chapter was written (1957), and there was rebellion against French rule in Algeria. The political status of the Jews in those countries was largely a by-product of the struggle for independence and of the conflicting aspirations among the Moslem majorities. Poverty, disease, and ignorance were the lot of most of the Jews. In the second half of the 1950's, when North African Jews—especially the more prosperous—felt that they had to leave, they were at least as likely to go to France as to Israel.

Throughout North Africa the J.D.C., the *Alliance Israélite Universelle*, and ORT rendered important welfare and educational services.

1. IRAQ

Iraq had a population of 5,000,000. Before the State of Israel, there had been about 130,000 Iraqi Jews. Nearly all went to Israel, leaving only 5,000 or 6,000 behind, mostly in Bagdad. There did not seem to be much likelihood of a flourishing Jewish community. Anti-Jewish animus was traditional and hatred for Israel was intense. Significant numbers of the remaining Jews were reported to be seeking conversion to Islam.

2. SYRIA

There were about 6,000 Jews in Syria, which had a population of 4,000,-000. Half lived in Damascus, and were mostly poor and uneducated; the third living in Aleppo were more prosperous and better educated.

The rising Syrian chauvinism, together with the intense hostility to the State of Israel, prompted Jewish emigration—to South America, France, Italy, and Lebanon. Few took the circuitous route to Israel.

3. LEBANON

Among the 1,500,000 people of Lebanon—the only Arab country where Christians balanced Moslems—were between 6,000 and 8,000 Jews. Their position was the best of any Jewish community in a country belonging to the Arab League. Lebanese Jewry, uniquely, had actually grown in size since the Arab-Israeli war, as a result of immigration from Syria and Iraq.

Commerce was the chief occupation. Children were educated mostly in the several schools of the *Alliance Israélite Universelle* and the local community.

4. ADEN

The population of British-ruled Aden was about 750,000, including probably fewer than 1,000 Jews remaining after a mass emigration to Israel.

5. EGYPT

The population of Egypt was 23,000,000, including probably 35,000 to 40,000 Jews. Most of them lived in Cairo; formerly large and prosperous communities in Alexandria, in the Delta, and along the Suez Canal had shrunk in consequence of unfavorable economic and political conditions. It was predominantly a commercial community, though with a large number of poor, and had once constituted, together with other non-Moslem minorities, the bulk of the middle class.

Sephardim predominated over Ashkenazim, and there were some Karaites as well.

For a variety of reasons embedded in the modern history of Egypt, most of the Jews, even those born in the country, were not citizens. Culturally they were oriented to Europe, especially France. The Egyptianization of the economy and of society that had been gathering momentum for a number of years was steadily undermining the position and security of all the minorities. The Jews were especially affected because of Egyptian enmity toward Israel. Especially after the Sinai war in 1956, the future of Egyptian Jewry seemed hopeless. Expulsion, imprisonment, and sequestration or confiscation of property seemed to be speeding the day when there would be no significant Jewish community left.

6. LIBYA

After World War II, Libya had a population of something more than 1,000,000, including about 35,000 Jews. By 1952, when Libya became independent, nearly the entire Jewish community had emigrated to Israel. Israel itself attracted them, and fear of how they would fare under Moslem rule in a backward country made them unwilling to remain where they were. Only about 3,500 to 4,000 Jews stayed behind, mostly in Tripoli. They were chiefly small tradesmen and artisans. There was little hope for the continued existence of a Jewish community.

7. TUNISIA

Of the Tunisian population of 3,800,000, about 85,000 were Jews, nearly all Sephardim. About a quarter were French citizens. Four-fifths lived in or near Tunis. They were mostly artisans and small tradesmen. There had been a fairly large emigration to Israel in the years immediately following its creation, but in the second half of the 1950's most Jewish emigrants went to France.

After independence, Tunisia adopted a constitution assuring equal rights for all citizens, but giving primacy to Islam as the Arabic religion. Though the leading elements in the government were western in outlook and opposed to the Moslem theocratic tradition, and though a large measure of communal autonomy was retained, many Jews were worried that the Arab nationalism of Tunisia might entail not only hostility to Israel but also intolerance toward Tunisian Jewry. This led a number of Jews to emigrate.

The Jewish communities were supported largely by government taxes on the meat and wine used by Jews. The decisions of rabbinical courts on matters of personal status (marriage, divorce, inheritance, and the like) were enforced by the government. There was a federation of Jewish communities.

8. ALGERIA

The Algerian population of 10,000,000 was mostly Moslem. There were about 140,000 Jews, nearly all Sephardim, the majority of whom lived in Algiers, Oran, and Constantine. Culturally and economically they were more western than the Moslems and more native than the Europeans. Their major occupations were trade and handicrafts, but there were some professional and business men, too. The Crémieux decree of 1870 had made Algerian Jews French citizens, but it did not apply to the Jews of the Saharan part, who in the 1950's numbered about 1,500. These, with an ambiguous and unsatisfactory civil status, were poor, sick, and uneducated; many were planning to go to Israel.

The civil emancipation under the French had weakened the communal structure and discipline and the attachment to Jewish religion and culture. There was a revival after World War II, with the creation of a *Fédération des Communautés Juives d'Algérie,* the establishment of a rabbinical school in Algiers, and the initiation or strengthening of religious, educational, cultural, and welfare activities.

Jewish emigration, which increased as the rebellion continued, was directed more to France than to Israel.

9. MOROCCO

By 1956, the king (formerly the sultan) of Morocco ruled over his domain, formerly divided into French and Spanish Morocco and Tangier. The Moroccan population was about 10,000,000, including about 200,000 Jews, 10,000 of whom were not Moroccan subjects. More than four-fifths of the Jews lived in what had been French Morocco, 75,000 of them in Casablanca. Most Moroccan Jews earned their living as artisans or small traders. Poverty, disease, and ignorance were prevalent.

The Jewish communities traditionally had a large degree of autonomy in matters of religion, education, and welfare. In the formerly French part there was a council of communities which in effect represented Moroccan Jewry.

Before independence there had been a very large Jewish emigration to Israel. The new government, expressing its Arabic character by opposition to Israel, made emigration to Israel difficult. At the same time it assured the Jews of its benevolent intentions. But since the theocratic character of the Moroccan polity had not been changed and since under Koranic law Jews could be only second-class citizens, the Jews were apprehensive. Their apprehension was heightened by the insistence of some Moroccan nationalist leaders that the Jews should be "integrated" into Moroccan society, which was interpreted as requiring the abandonment of the traditionally separate Jewish educational and welfare institutions and their merger with generally inferior Moslem institutions.

V. NON-ARAB ASIA

There were significant Jewish communities in India (with a branch in the portion of the Indian subcontinent that became Pakistan after the withdrawal of the British), Afghanistan, and Iran. Turkey has been considered under Europe.

I. INDIA

India's population was more than 380,000,000, of whom between 20,000 and 25,000 were Jews. Indian Jewry consisted of three major groups, the Bene Israel, the Iraqis, and the Cochin Jews, besides a few hundred Europeans, mostly German refugees, and some Persian-Bokharan Jews who had arrived during World War II.

The most numerous element were the 16,000 Bene Israel, living in and near Bombay, whose ancestors according to tradition had come to India 2,000 years ago. They spoke Marathi and they were craftsmen, artisans, and skilled workers, as well as civil servants and professional people.

Several thousand Iraqi Jews, living mostly in Bombay and Calcutta, were descended from Bagdadi immigrants, led by the Sassoons, of the early nineteenth century. Their language was Arabic and they were in commerce and small trade.

The Cochin community of southern India, numbering about 2,000 before the State of Israel was established, had been greatly reduced in size by emigration to Israel. Their language was Malayalam.

There were a Central Jewish Board of Bombay, a Jewish Association of Calcutta, and a South Indian Jews' Association.

Each of the three communities maintained its own synagogues, schools, and welfare institutions. A moderate Sephardic-Oriental Orthodoxy was the norm, but the Bene Israel and the Iraqis had a Liberal synagogue as well. Zionist and pro-Israel sentiment was strong.

There was practically no anti-Semitism, and the Bene Israel in particular were well represented in the government service and the judiciary.

2. PAKISTAN

Pakistan's population of about 85,000,000 included only about 700 Jews, mostly Bene Israel, in and near Karachi, who had been separated from the main body of their community when the Indian subcontinent was partitioned to form the states of India and Pakistan.

3. AFGHANISTAN

Among the 12,000,000 people of Afghanistan were about 4,000 Jews, culturally and religiously a branch of Persian Jewry. At one time they had been a considerably larger and more prosperous community, but their size and well-being had been reduced by intermittent persecution for a century, down through the years of Hitler and the Arab-Israeli war. Emigration, mostly to Israel, continued in a trickle.

4. IRAN

After a substantial emigration to Israel, about 80,000 Jews remained in Iran, which had a total population of 21,000,000. About 40,000 lived in Teheran, 15,000 in Shiraz, and 6,000 in Isfahan.

On the whole, Iranian Jewry was poor, badly organized, uneducated, and without equal civil rights. The J.D.C., the *Alliance Israélite Universelle*, and ORT provided needed educational and welfare services.

5. JAPAN

Between 1,000 and 2,000 Jews lived in Japan, which had a population of 90,000,000. Nearly all had come from Europe or the Levant, either for business or as part of a refugee movement. Some were Americans. Relatively few were in Tokyo, most being in the seaports.

VI. Africa South of the Sahara

In this section the Jewish communities of the Union of South Africa, the Rhodesias, the Belgian Congo, Kenya, and Ethiopia are considered.

1. SOUTH AFRICA

There were 110,000 Jews in South Africa out of a white ("European") population of 3,000,000 and a total population of 14,000,000. South African Jewry derived mostly from Eastern Europe in the last quarter of the nineteenth and the first third of the twentieth centuries. It was a prosperous, middle-class, well-educated community. As between the English and the Afrikaner ("Boer") elements, most Jews were culturally and linguistically closer to the English. They lived mainly in the large cities, especially Johannesburg and Cape Town, but there were about 200 organized Jewish communities in all.

The central representative organization was the South African Jewish Board of Deputies. The community was intensely Zionist and noted for the generosity of its support for Israel. The Orthodoxy of the United Synagogue in England was the official norm, but South Africa had its own chief rabbis. Several Liberal congregations were also in existence. There was much concern for Jewish education, and more rabbis and teachers were needed.

The Nationalist government, mostly representing the Afrikaners, was not anti-Semitic, though before it had come into power there was reason to fear that it would be. Most Jews probably shared the general white approval of the government's policy of *apartheid*, the rigorous separation of the races and the exclusion of nonwhites from the franchise; the chief criticism of the government was not that its principle was wrong, but that its methods were too extreme. Among the relatively few whites who disapproved *apartheid*, the Jews were well represented.

Jews were prominent in public life.

2. SOUTHERN RHODESIA

The population of Southern Rhodesia was about 2,300,000, of whom about 160,000 were white, including 6,000 Jews. Most were in commerce.

The two chief Jewish settlements were in Salisbury, the capital, and Bulawayo.

Their central body was the Rhodesian Jewish Board of Deputies (which also represented the Jews of Northern Rhodesia, *q.v.*). There were several synagogues and Zionist, cultural, and welfare societies. Rhodesian Jewry could be considered as a province of the South African Jewish community.

Most were Ashkenazim from Great Britain and South Africa, as well as Eastern and Central Europe. Nearly all the fairly large number of Sephardim were from the island of Rhodes, in the Aegean Sea.

A prime minister of Southern Rhodesia was Jewish, the son of a founder of the synagogue in Gwelo.

3. NORTHERN RHODESIA

The Northern Rhodesian population of 2,000,000 included about 55,000 Europeans, of whom there were more than 1,000 Jews, mostly in commerce.

The Jewish community was an extension of the Southern Rhodesian community. It had several synagogues and a number of other organizations.

4. BELGIAN CONGO

There were 2,000 Jews in the Belgian Congo, which had a white population of less than 100,000 in a total population of 12,000,000 They were prosperous businessmen. Nearly all of them, mostly Sephardim from the island of Rhodes, were in Elisabethville, which had the only synagogue, and Leopoldville. The community was pro-Israel. It tried to assure an adequate Jewish education for its young people.

5. KENYA

The population of Kenya was about 6,000,000, of whom fewer than 50,000 were white. The 1,000 Jews were mostly engaged in commerce. They lived mainly in Nairobi, the capital; others lived in Mombasa and Nakuru. Most were of Central European origin, refugees from Nazism. The Nairobi synagogue had been founded by a few Jews who in the early years of the century were attracted to the country by the British government's offer of Uganda for autonomous Jewish settlement.

6. ETHIOPIA

The Falashas, as the Ethiopian Jews were known, numbered 20,000 to 25,000 in a population of 20,000,000. Racially and culturally like other Ethiopians, they preserved a religion that must have branched off from the main body of Judaism before the Talmud. They knew no Hebrew, their ritual and sacred literature, including the Bible, being in Gheez, an ancient Ethiopian language. Besides being farmers, they had a more specialized economic function as skilled artisans: smiths, weavers, and the like. Since the early part of the twentieth century attempts had been made to link them more closely to the Jews of the rest of the world, to teach Hebrew to some of their promising young people, and generally to help them resist the sustained efforts and pressures to convert them to Christianity.

VII. Australia and New Zealand

1. AUSTRALIA

The Jews of Australia, with a population of some 9,500,000, numbered about 55,000. Nine-tenths lived in Melbourne and Sydney. Immigration had been chiefly responsible for doubling the size of the community during the twenty years after 1937.

Australian Jewry was mostly middle class, prosperous, and well educated. It was a highly organized community, with the Executive Council of Australian Jewry as its central representative organ. In religion it was dominantly Orthodox in the manner of the United Synagogue in England, and it welcomed the influence of the English Chief Rabbi. There were a few Liberal congregations as well. Much effort was devoted to Jewish education in congregational and day schools. Zionist and pro-Israel sentiment was strong.

There was little anti-Semitism, and a number of Jews were prominent in public life.

2. NEW ZEALAND

In New Zealand, which had a population of more than 2,000,000, there were about 4,500 Jews, most of whom lived in the provinces of Auckland and Wellington. They were a prosperous, well-educated community, resembling that of Australia.

Note

[1a See above Bernard D. Weinryb, "East European Jewry (Since the Partitions of Poland, 1772-1795)"; Arieh Tartakower, "The Decline of European Jewry (1933-1953)."]

Bibliographical Note

The indispensable reference work is the *American Jewish Year Book*, published annually in Philadelphia. The *Jewish Year Book*, published annually in London, is not nearly so complete but is useful for Great Britain and the Commonwealth. They have over books, magazines, and newspapers the great advantage that their information is presented regularly and brought up to date systematically. Even so good a book as Israel Cohen's *Contemporary Jewry* (London, 1950) soon becomes outdated, especially in the sections on communities where change is rapid. The *Jewish Chronicle Travel Guide* (London, latest edition, 1957) contains much valuable, concrete information.

Dealing with a part of the world where there has been no sharp break in the continuity of Jewish life lately, fairly recent, and thoroughly competent is Jacob Shatzky's work on the Jewish communities of Latin America (Buenos Aires, 1952) in separate books in Yiddish and Spanish: *Di yidishe yishuvim in Latein-amerike* and *Las comunidades judías en Latinoamérica*. For Europe it may be helpful to consult Nehemiah Robinson (ed.), *European Jewry Ten Years After the War* (New York, 1956). For the Middle East and North Africa the two most informative books produced in the past decade are already, in varying degrees, more of historical than of contemporary interest: S. Landshut, *Jewish Communities in the Muslim Countries of the Middle East* (London, 1950), and André Chouraqui, *Les Juifs d'Afrique du Nord* (Paris, 1952).

Canadian Jewry provides frequent and detailed information about itself in the form of studies, usually processed rather than printed, by Louis Rosenberg of the research department of the Canadian Jewish Congress; his data are found also in the *American Jewish Year Book*. The tercentenary of British Jewry has occasioned the publication of two good books, both dealing as much with contemporary as with historical matters: Maurice Freedman (ed.), *A Minority in Britain* (London, 1955), and V. D. Lipman, *A Social History of the Jews in England, 1850-1950* (London, 1954). A recent history of South African Jewry has useful contemporary information: Gustav Saron and Louis Hotz, *The Jews in South Africa* (Cape Town, London, and New York, 1955).

Outstanding among Jewish newspapers in English is the London *Jewish Chronicle*.

CHAPTER 41

SOCIAL CHARACTERISTICS OF AMERICAN JEWS*

By Nathan Glazer

The purpose of this essay is to describe the social characteristics of American Jews from the time they began to arrive in the territory that was later to become the United States through their 300 years of history in that country. By "social characteristics" we refer to such things as the numbers of Jews, their geographic distribution, occupations, income, education, style of life, and relations with their neighbors. Social groups differ from one another in these and many other characteristics; the sum total of these differences defines the group, whether it be Negroes, Episcopalians, or factory workers. Here we shall try to make the social characteristics of American Jews explicit, to the extent the data available permit. And since prejudice and preconception so often give the misleading impression that a group is characterized by a property which applies only to a small part of it, we shall, wherever we can, depend on statistics describing the whole group or a large portion of it.

Out of this description will emerge the fundamental ground tone of American Jewish life—the tone of respectable, prosperous, "middle-class"† existence, in fact or aspiration. We must leave it to others to document the impact of this tone on the spiritual, cultural, and political life of American Jews. Here, however, we shall try to show by a complete review of the available material that certain common social characteristics do bind together 300 years of American Jewish life.

THE FIRST HUNDRED AND FIFTY YEARS

For the first half of the 300 years of Jewish experience in America, there were so few Jews that it has been possible to track down almost every

---

* The author first wrote much of this material as "Social Characteristics of American Jews, 1654-1954," the article which appeared on pages 1-42 of the *American Jewish Year Book*, 56 (1955), published by the American Jewish Committee and the Jewish Publication Society. In the present chapter the original material has been substantially revised and expanded.

† We use "middle class" to refer both to a social group defined primarily by its occupations (business, the professions, and white-collar work) and to a set of values (emphasizing steady work, sobriety, saving, calculation) which are generally accepted as marking off the middle class from both the aristocracy and the working or lower class. The Jews, as we shall see, are in America a middle-class group in both senses of the term.

scrap of information that exists about each of them; and so much ingenuity and industry have already been expended on this task that we know a great deal about Jewish settlers in the American colonies in the seventeenth and eighteenth centuries. These earliest settlers take us back to the late medieval age of Jewish history. They were members of that quasi-caste of merchants that the Jews, Sephardim and Ashkenazim alike, had largely become by the seventeenth century. In the letters of these first American settlers, we can read of their close connections, both business and personal, with the families they had left behind, in England or the West Indies or Central Europe; of their travels from one colony to another in search of opportunities for trade; of their business ventures, their occasional bankruptcies. Not all were merchants, but there were almost no farmers or common laborers or indentured servants among them; the least of them, the poor butcher or the poor synagogue employee, was always ready to turn his hand to trade if an opportunity offered itself. Aside from the main body of merchants, the only sizable occupational group among the early Jewish settlers was that of artisans. Thus, as Jacob Marcus writes, the 2,500 Jews in the United States in 1790 formed only one class, "a middle class."[1]

Perhaps the most interesting thing about this handful of colonial Jews is that they survived as a group. While some of the communities they established died out, others have lasted to this day. Where they were settled singly, in villages or on the frontier, we know that many took non-Jewish wives, and some became converted themselves. But in the larger settlements—where, by the end of the colonial epoch, the largest Jewish community did not number more than a few hundred—the synagogues had a tight hold on their members, and required strict adherence to the practices of Judaism. Almost every Jew one reads of was a member. It was clearly important for the American Jew of that day to feel part of a community, to be sure, for example, of being buried in a Jewish cemetery; hence, the sanctions of the congregation could effectively control him. The congregation itself was not averse to using powerful disciplinary measures. Spinoza's expulsion from the Amsterdam community in 1656 occurred just two years after a small group of Dutch Jews landed in New York, and the Amsterdam Jews who expelled Spinoza were the friends and relatives of those who founded the first Jewish community in America.

The power of the first congregations of Jews in America was a reflection of the conditions of Jewish life in Europe at that time, where the Jewish community still possessed some governmental functions. Every Jew was as a matter of course, by virtue of birth alone, a member, and the community had disciplinary power over every Jew. In the new land the first synagogues were able to take over the role of the European Jewish communities. The conditions of settlement helped them. These early Jews came alone—their families followed later, if at all. The congregations offered the only possibility for help in difficulties. They were run by the richest and most powerful, who considered themselves responsible for poor Jews, as well as for merchants who had suffered one or another of the misfortunes so common in seventeenth- or eighteenth-century trade. Even the richest of them might be brought down by disaster, as was Aaron Lopez of Newport in the early days of the Revolution. The strength of the synagogue thus reflected not only the social position of the Jews everywhere in the seventeenth century, as a legally separate community, but the dangers facing isolated merchants on a colonial frontier.

It is now believed that Sephardim—Portuguese and Spanish Jews who had spent some time in Holland or England or the West Indies—predominated among the American Jews until about 1735.[2] But even though Ashkenazim—Central and East European Jews—predominated after that time, there was apparently no religious or social struggle between the two groups, as there was to be between the German and Polish Jews (both technically Ashkenazim) 100 and 150 years later. Intermarriage between the two groups was common (perhaps it was not considered intermarriage) and the Ashkenazim accepted the Sephardic ritual in most of the early synagogues.

Perhaps the best contemporary equivalent of the Jewish life of those days is to be found in the small towns, far from any major Jewish settlement, that contain only a few or a few dozen Jews. Such communities either cannot afford to maintain a rabbi or he would not come if they could; the same was the case with our colonial ancestors. (There was not a single rabbi in colonial America.) Again, like Jews in contemporary small towns, colonial Jews clung together to form a community, but there were so few of them that naturally a good deal of their time was spent with non-Jews. And, as in the contemporary small Jewish settlements, intermarriage, whether viewed as a threat or with equanimity, was an ever-present prospect. Because of their small numbers and few types, Jews led a more limited existence in colonial times than they do today—we do not find Jewish intellectuals, secular or religious, in colonial America—but at the same time they were thrust out more into the non-Jewish world than they are today.

THE GERMAN IMMIGRATION

There have been two periods in American history when the steady recruitment from abroad was halted, and the various strands of the American population could settle down to assimilation without the disturbing impact of heavy immigration. The first such period ran from about 1775 to 1815. Immigration, we know, is largely the effect of economic causes—prosperity in the country that receives the immigrants, depression in the country that sends them forth. During this long forty-year period, a sequence of war (in America), depression (in America), and war again (in Europe) kept immigration low. So the Revolution marks a break, not only in American political structure, but also in the history of immigration. When we next take up the story, Jewish immigrants to the United States are coming directly from Germany, and from those parts of central Europe under German cultural influence, rather than, as in the eighteenth century, from the West Indies and England.

From 1800 on, the few German Jews already settled were being supplemented by small numbers of migrants from Germany and the parts of eastern Europe adjacent to it. But in 1836, the first of the mass emigrations that were to characterize European Jewish history for the next 100 years began; the impoverished Jews of the small towns of Germany, particularly in Bavaria, finding it impossible to live under the galling load of special taxes and restrictions and affected by a general slump in trade conditions, began to emigrate to America.[3] Scenes that were, in later years, to become common in Poland, Russia, Rumania, and other eastern countries were first played in the southern states of Germany. We read of communities losing a large part of their young and vigorous people in a single year as these decide to remove to America.[4] The number of American Jews grew rapidly. Estimated at only 15,000 in 1840, there were believed to be 50,000 by 1850 and 150,000 by 1860.[5] Even the great wave of East European Jewish immigration in the twentieth century was not capable of multiplying Jewish population tenfold in twenty years.

If the Jews of the seventeenth and eighteenth centuries can be called "merchants," the immigration of the mid-nineteenth century may well be characterized as that of "peddlers." As Glanz writes: "We [know] that German Jewish emigrants set out to learn new trades before emigration. Nevertheless, upon arriving in America, practically all German Jews began peddling."[6] As a contemporary account puts it—and in the absence of statistics (and often even in their presence) a contemporary is the best guide to reality—"the majority of them became peddlers and petty traders."[7] Joshua Trachtenberg, in his fine history of the Jewish community of Easton, records the predominance of peddlers in this small trading town on the Pennsylvania-New Jersey border: between 1845 and 1855, a good majority of the Jews of Easton were peddlers.[8]

Just as the Arab has many terms for the camel, because it is so important to him, so the mid-century German Jews had many terms for peddling, which was the first step in their efforts to establish themselves. Thus, Rabbi Isaac M. Wise recorded the varieties of basket peddler, custom peddler, pack peddler, wagon baron, and jewelry count. The next stage was a store, and, from all one reads, it did not take many years to progress from pack to store.

The Jewish merchants of the colonial period, with their far-ranging in-

terests, had been found first in one colony, then in another, sometimes on
the frontier, sometimes in the West Indies or England. Their permanent
settlements, however, had been limited to the Atlantic seaboard, the site
of most of the permanent settlements of the American colonies. But the
peddler was, in his way, a pioneer. He needed to establish his own itinerary,
his own circle of customers, and, ultimately, his own store. While the
peddler would naturally think first of a settlement where he already had
a friend or a relative, he would, just as naturally, think next of settling
where there were not too many friends or relatives—even in a town he had
only heard of, perhaps a likely spot some other peddler had passed through,
and where no one was established. The period of the German immigration—between 1830 and 1880—was the period when great numbers of
American towns were established; it was also the period when most of the
American Jewish communities were founded.

So the German immigration became the pioneering immigration in American Jewish history. The traveler Benjamin II (I. J. Benjamin of Rumania),
visiting the small towns of California on the eve of the Civil War, found
large numbers of Jews everywhere.[9] These settlements had been established
just a few years before, and in many cases, one suspects, there was a higher
percentage of Jews among their founders than these towns have today. In
an era when the small trading towns close to or on the frontier played
an important role, Jews were numerous in them.

It is interesting, too, to note that during most of this period we find no
tendency for Jews to concentrate in New York City. In 1825 there were
still only 500 Jews, out of an estimated American Jewish population of
6,000, in New York. By 1848, under the impact of German immigration,
New York's Jewish population had grown to the point where it occupied
the unquestioned first place among the American Jewish communities, with
12,000 or 13,000 Jews, out of a national population of 50,000. From this
point on, New York's Jewish population growth matches that of American
Jewry in general. In 1880, New York's 60,000 Jews made up about 25
per cent of the Jews of the country,[10] the same proportion as in 1848.

This was the great age of expansion for American Jewry, in all areas.
Colonial Jewry had established congregations in five communities—by 1880
there were congregations in almost two hundred communities. Colonial
Jewry had been limited to one class and one occupation. German Jews
were not only peddlers and merchants but also manufacturers, intellectuals,
politicians, and even workers, active in every sphere of American life. For
the first time one finds American Jewish professors, judges, congressmen,
doctors, lawyers; for after the revolution of 1848, many German intellectuals left for America, and there were German Jewish intellectuals
among them.

It was a great age of expansion for American Jewry internally, too. Between 1840 and the 1880's a vast number of Jewish organizations were founded, and that characteristic multiplicity of organizations of all types in American Jewish life became the pattern that was to be maintained from then on. We have already mentioned the great increase in the number of congregations. There were also established philanthropic organizations, Jewish hospitals, fraternal organizations, social clubs, Young Men's Hebrew Associations, and many others. Did this enormous development of special Jewish organizations mean that Jews were withdrawing—or being forced out of—the general social life of the times? As compared with the tiny colonial communities, a greater part of Jewish life was probably conducted within an all-Jewish environment; as compared to the situation established after the great East European immigration, and which exists today, probably a smaller part.

On such a point, of course, one's evidence must be slight and anecdotal, yet it is, I believe, convincing. It is not until the 1870's and 1880's that one begins to find evidence of the exclusion of Jews from areas of American life, and the first reactions of Jews and non-Jews is that of shock and outrage. Clearly Jews had not experienced anything of the sort in America before. "When in 1870 the Arion Society of New York refused to admit a man to membership because he was a Jew, many newspapers carried editorials on this infringement of the American spirit. . . . In 1877, when Joseph Seligman and his family were refused accommodations at the Grand Union Hotel . . . Jewish opinion was upheld by public opinion as well as by the Protestant clergy. Henry Ward Beecher preached one of his famous sermons . . . on this occasion."[11] Bret Harte also wrote a poem on this incident which was printed in a number of leading newspapers. From another source, we discover that it was not until the 1880's that in New York City "private schools began to be closed to Jewish children. . . . Advertisements of summer hotels, refusing admittance to Jewish guests, began to appear in the newspapers." And "in 1893, the Union League Club of New York had refused to admit Jews to membership."[12]

Anti-Semitism, then, both in "Society" and in the social order in general, only began to become a problem in this country, it would appear, after the 1880's.[13] How are we to explain this? One reason for the easy acceptance of German Jews until the 1880's is to be found in the fact that until then there were very few Jews in the country. American society, and probably any other, too, tends to "integrate" a smaller group more successfully than a larger one, socially, politically, and otherwise. A smaller group may be ignored; a larger group must at least be defined—what is its character, what is its weight in society, how is it to be understood in relation to other groups and the whole society? Inevitably, such a process creates discomfort. So when an American ethnic group looks back upon the time when it was relatively small as a golden age of acceptance and integration, it is not deluding itself. The first Italians, the few Negroes in the North before the great migration from the South, the small community of German Jews before the waves of immigration from eastern Europe, did have a less problematic relation to their surroundings.

There were other reasons for the easy acceptance of German Jews in most of American society. Reform Judaism, which by the 1880's had become the religion of the majority of the German Jews in America, was in tune with developments in leading Protestant denominations, and the Jewish religion, in its Reform variant, lost most of its peculiarities. (Indeed, it was to be one of the complaints of those who opposed Reform that it was becoming impossible to distinguish church from synagogue.) Jews had no important special interests in those years that marked them off from the rest of the population. Discrimination and anti-Semitism were not yet serious problems, nor were Jews agitated by Zionism and anti-Zionism until the end of the century.

On the whole, Jews had large families, lived comfortable lives, had servants, entered professions, and met with little discrimination. Those were the days before Americans in general worried much about being respectable —and consequently Jews were more respectable. When the newest multi-millionaire might be some barbarian who had no table manners, it hardly mattered if he were a Jew. Certainly it did not seem to matter in the West, where the few Jews often seemed to become leading citizens.

In short, before 1880 or 1890, there were too few American Jews for them to constitute a problem. Hence, one can understand the feelings of dismay of the earlier German Jewish immigrants as the Russian Jewish immigration, which had spurted upward at the beginning of the 1880's, showed no signs of abating, and indeed grew larger. It is as if a man who has built himself a pleasant house and is leading a comfortable existence suddenly finds a horde of impecunious relatives descending on him. On the other hand, the German Jews did indeed feel themselves to be relatives. They did not say, "What have you to do with me?" but threw themselves into the work of finding homes and jobs for the vanguard of the East European Jewish immigration—despite the unhappiness that some voiced at having to do so.

AMERICAN JEWS AROUND 1880

It is one of those fortunate accidents of history that the first attempt at a census of American Jews was carried out on the eve of the great migration from eastern Europe that was to transform American Jewry. One discovers in this census, conducted by the Union of American Hebrew Congregations in 1877-1879, Jews located in every state in the Union, and in every territory save Oklahoma. More remarkably, they formed a higher percentage of the population in the West than in the Northeast—they formed 1.6 per cent of the population of the West, and only 0.6 per cent of the population of the Northeast.[14]

The bare recital of numbers and places in this survey is elaborated in the report by John S. Billings on the vital statistics of the Jews published in 1890, the only effort to collect social statistics on Jews alone ever made by the United States Government.[15] Ten thousand Jewish families, including 60,000 individuals, the great majority of whom were German immigrants who had arrived in the 1850's, 1860's, and 1870's of the nineteenth century, supplied information on themselves. So Billings's statistics concern the same Jewish population, more or less, as that surveyed in the census of the Union of American Hebrew Congregations. And how well these immigrants had done since they had arrived in the United States as peddlers! Of the 10,000 families, almost 4,000 had one servant, 2,000 had two, 1,000 had three or more. Almost half of the men were in business —as wholesale or retail merchants. One-fifth of them were accountants, bookkeepers, clerks, collectors, agents. One tenth were salesmen. One out of every twenty was in the professions, and there were some who were bankers, brokers, and company officials (2 per cent) and others who were farmers and stock raisers (2 per cent). One out of every eight was engaged in some kind of manual work—there were many tailors, clock and watch-makers and jewelers, cigar makers, butchers, and printers. Perhaps one-half of 1 per cent were laborers and servants, and about one out of every 100 was still a peddler. (As people in lower class occupations, such as peddlers, laborers, and servants, very often do not answer questionnaires, there were certainly more of these than the figures would indicate.)

Jewish families were large—perhaps even larger than the large families of the day. The mothers of these 10,000 families had on the average almost five children. But parents who had been born in the United States had fewer children than those born abroad. Their birth rate was declining with residence in the United States, and in the preceding five years had been below the national average. But their death rate was also far, far below the national average, and at every age their life expectancy was greater. As a result, they were a group that was still growing in numbers.

The East European Jews Around 1900

We have gone into such detail in reporting this study because, as we have said, it permits us to see the German Jewish community at a period when it had settled down to a comfortable middle-class existence, and just before it was transformed by the flood of migration from eastern Europe. There was a fairly heavy immigration from eastern Europe throughout the 1870's. But in the early 1880's, in the wake of a wave of pogroms, a series

of harsh and restrictive decrees, and generally miserable economic conditions, the numbers of East European Jewish immigrants began to spurt
upward. It is estimated that by the end of the nineteenth century (when the
government started keeping records of arriving "Hebrews") 500,000 or
more East European Jews had arrived in the United States; another 1,500,-
000 had come by the time of the outbreak of World War I in 1914; and
still another 350,000 came before national quotas were imposed and the
mass immigration came to an end in 1924. Between 1899 and 1914 more
than 90,000 Jews a year entered the United States, and all but one out of
fourteen stayed on.[16] And, as we know, these immigrants brought their
wives and children with them.[17]

The over-all picture of American Jewry was changed, and its main
features today are those stamped on it by this immigration. American Jews
increased from about 0.6 per cent of the population in 1880 to 3.5 per cent
in 1917—and the proportion of Jews in the population of the United States
has remained remarkably constant since. In 1880, American Jews were a
group fairly well distributed through the land, with a sizable concentration
in New York City; by 1920, they had become a group overwhelmingly
concentrated in the Northeast, with almost half their numbers in New
York. The identification of the Jew in general American folk lore as a
New Yorker dates from the great East European immigration. In 1880,
the Jews made up only 3 per cent of the population of New York City. By
1920, they constituted 30 per cent of its population, and they have maintained a similar proportion ever since.[18]

But the biggest change of all was in the social character of the new
immigrants. The *Jewish Encyclopedia* estimates that during the 1870's
about 4,000 Jews a year came to the United States from East Europe, and
"up to the 1880's the Russian Jews were principally peddlers, shopkeepers,
and manufacturers."[19] In effect, before 1881 it was neither easy nor fruitful to draw a line between "German" and "East European" Jews. The
latter tended to come from the German-influenced parts of eastern Europe,
and followed the same economic pursuits as the German Jews. But this
pattern was upset by the post-1881 immigrants. They became workers,
concentrated in the largest American cities, and particularly New York
City. In 1900, three out of every five of the Russian Jews were engaged
in manufacturing, almost all as workers, and more than half of the workers
—that is, one-third of the Russian Jews—were workers in a single industry,
the manufacture of clothing. One-fifth were in trade—one half as proprietors, another fourth as peddlers. Only one-tenth were in clerical work
or the professions. In comparison, in 1890, ten years before, one-tenth of
the German Jews had been workers, three-fifths had been in trade (if we
include the salesmen), and only a fraction were still peddlers.[20]

Enough has been written about the horrors of the sweatshop and the overcrowding of the lower East Side; I do not plan to add anything on that subject. The interesting question is why the Russian Jews of the post-1881 period did not follow the pattern of those who had preceded them, put packs on their shoulders, and go off to try their luck in the small towns. The explanation is that the immigrant does what is at the moment rewarding, what his training and experience fit him for, and what he can afford to do.

Thus, at a time when new towns were springing up to service vast new farming areas, German Jews went out to service them as peddlers and storekeepers. But when light industry, particularly the industry of clothes making, was taking over some of the functions that had once been taken care of in the home, the new immigrant Jews entered those industries, either as entrepreneurs (the longer-established German Jews) if they had the capital or as workers if they did not (the new East European arrivals).

Nor was this type of work foreign to the experience of East European immigrants. The German Jewish immigrants had been, characteristically, the traders and, to a smaller degree, the artisans of the small towns of Germany. (An artisan is also a merchant.) While some of them were emigrating to America to continue as merchants and peddlers, others were emigrating to the burgeoning German cities to transfer their trading and merchandising activities to a more promising environment. But the Jews of eastern Europe, though they, too, had begun as the traders and artisans of small towns, with the coming of the Industrial Revolution became in ever larger measure workers. For one thing, the Czarist state kept Jews out of some of the most rapidly growing Russian cities, where the best business opportunities existed. For another, the Jews were so impoverished that when they migrated to cities they could take employment only as wage workers. Many East European Jews were thus clothing workers before they came to America. According to the Russian census of 1897, almost one-fifth of the Russian Jews in cities over 100,000 were already working in the clothing industry.

In addition to the opportunities offered by the economic landscape which the immigrant is entering and the economic experience with which he arrives, there is another factor—the individual's economic capacity. The Italian immigrants came to a land which could use farmers and from a land where they had been farmers, but they were so impoverished that they could take work only as day laborers. Similarly, as compared with German Jews peddling declined in importance among East European Jews because many of them were too poor to put up even the minimal stake that peddling required. In 1900, the average Jewish immigrant landed with $9—in that year, the average for all immigrants was $15.[21]

In absolute number, probably as many or more East European Jews as German Jews ended up as peddlers and storekeepers in the small towns of America. But the East European Jewish peddler formed only a very small part of the huge number of East European Jewish immigrants, and most of them became workers in the light industry of the rapidly growing cities; for the clothing trade in America offered an opportunity for an unskilled man to make what was in those days a living wage, even if earned under conditions that, by American standards, were inhuman. On this wage the Russian Jewish immigrant saved, brought over wife and child, and could even often "go into business for himself." For reasons which are not completely clear, Jewish immigrants earned rather more working at the sewing machine than did those of other national groups. Apparently the Jews were pioneers in the "task system," the breaking down of the garment into a number of parts by a team of workers; but the contemporary observers of the time also believed that Jews simply developed more dexterity and worked harder and longer hours. Whatever the reason, there is no question that Jews earned more than did non-Jews.[22]

Horrible as conditions in the clothing industry were, for the immigrant Russian Jews who had lived in abysmal poverty in the Old Country the clothing industry was no trap. They could earn wages high enough to permit a very large number of them to leave the industry, or at least to keep their children from entering it; and they could afford to educate their children. As peddling was no trap for the German Jew, but rather the first rung on a ladder to established middle-class security, similarly, for the Russian Jews, the sweatshop was the first step on the way up. This, in any case, was the way it looked to the dean of American labor economists, John R. Commons, who puzzled over this problem for the Industrial Commission in 1901. He wrote at that time:

The Jew occupies a unique position in the clothing trade. His physical strength does not fit him for manual labor [a common belief of the time]. His instincts lead him to speculation and trade. [Change "instincts" to "experience" and this is true enough.] His individualism unsuits him for the life of a wage earner, and especially for the discipline of a labor organization. [The kernel of the truth in this statement is that, whether because of individualism or not, the Jewish immigrant did not remain a wage earner as long as other immigrants did.] For these reasons when the Jew first lands in this country, he enters such light occupations as sewing, cigar-making, shoe-making, etc. Only about 11 per cent of the Jewish immigrants were tailors in Europe.[23] The reason that so many of them take up that occupation in America, is because the work is light. They begin as helpers and advance to full-fledged mechanics. After they have worked for some time and have learned the trade, they open contractors' shops. They can begin with a capital of $50. From that they go into the wholesale manufacture of clothing. . . .

Jewish women are employed to a much less extent than the women of other nationalities, and their children are kept in school until 15 or 16 years of age. It is quite unusual for Jewish tailors to teach their children their own trade. The younger generation seek other callings. . . . [For this and other reasons] it seems that the future clothing workers in this city [New York] are not likely to be the Jews, but the Italians. . . . The standard of living of all nationalities has been gradually raised after their immigration to this city. Probably the Jewish immigrant changes his standard of living soonest.[24]

This passage is interesting because it was clear, as early as 1900, and to John Commons at least, that the Jewish worker was not like the other workers. Just why this was so Commons did not know, and his explanations (instincts, etc.) are not very convincing. But his observations were right.

The difference between the Jewish and other immigrants could be seen in many other characteristics. In 1890 there were no Russian Jewish almshouse paupers in New York, and the proportion of Jews in penitentiaries was much below their proportion in the population.[25] Jewish families were larger than other families,[26] and the Jewish death rate was considerably lower.[27] The death rate for Jewish children under five was less than half of that for the city as a whole.[28] Further, the Jews enjoyed school, and did well at it: "In the lower schools," an observer for the Industrial Commission wrote in 1900, "the Jewish children are the delight of their teachers for cleverness at their books, obedience, and general good conduct."[29]

Unquestionably, despite Industrial Commissions and Immigration Commissions, though they may have lived five and ten to a room, the Jews throve in their crowded tenements—and in a shorter time than any other group, the Jews left the tenements: "Economic advancement comes to these poverty-stricken Hebrews with surprising rapidity," to quote from the report of the Industrial Commission of 1900. ". . . . Many tenements in Jewish quarters are owned by persons who formerly lived in crowded corners of others just like them. . . ."[30]

From 1900 to the Great Depression

We have described the situation of the East European Jewish immigrants in 1900, at a time when there had been heavy migration at a rate of about 30,000 a year for almost twenty years. Did the same situation prevail during the period between 1900 and the outbreak of the First World War in 1914, when Jewish immigration averaged more than 90,000 a year?

Between 1900 and 1920, it can be argued, more American Jews were engaged in a desperate struggle for existence than at any time before or since. As a result of a long continued and heavy immigration of impoverished elements, the more prosperous part of American Jewry, which had bulked so large in 1880, was, statistically speaking, submerged. Even when expanded, the philanthropic services that had been able to ameliorate the condition of a relatively small number of poor Jews could do little for very large numbers. The Jewish immigrants still maintained a small advantage, in weekly and annual earnings, over other immigrants;[31] but it was a very small advantage indeed. The Jews were scarcely distinguishable from the huge mass of depressed immigrants, illiterate and impoverished, that was pouring into the United States at a rate of 1,000,000 a year before the First World War.

Nevertheless we can see that, hard pressed as they were, the Russian Jewish immigrants were, so to speak, storing up virtues for the future. Thus, we find that more of them than of other groups were learning English.[32] Even more significant as a sign of Jewish preparation for the future were the large numbers that were going to college. When the Immigration Commission surveyed seventy-seven colleges and institutions in 1908, no less than 8.5 per cent of the male student body was composed of first- and second-generation Jews. (Jews at this time made up about 2 per cent of the American population.) Jewish students already made up 13 per cent of those studying for law, 18 per cent of those preparing for pharmacy. But they dared not, as yet, think of such expensive studies as dentistry or medicine. Only 6 per cent of the potential dentists and 3 per cent of the potential doctors were Jews in 1908.[33]

There is no question that the East European Jews who immigrated during 1900-1914 showed the same flexibility and ingenuity as the earlier immigrants from eastern Europe and the still earlier ones who had come from Germany. Yet, in contrast to the German immigrants, it was to be a long time before the majority of East European immigrants would reach the respectable level of trade and the professions. The German Jewish immigrants had risen in the social scale rapidly, and without any great difficulty; the East European Jewish immigrants, for the most part, had to leave it to their children to move beyond the position of wage worker. Sometimes, of course, an immigrant could earn enough money to go into business himself; more often, the small financial advantage that he held over the other immigrants permitted him only to keep his wife out of the factory, or to keep his children in school for a longer time. So, while the proportion of Jewish needle trades workers fell, it remained very substantial; we do not find the majority of them moving out of their occupation in a single generation, as did the German Jewish immigrants who began as peddlers. Most of the Jewish clothing workers of the first decade of the twentieth century remained clothing workers all their lives. But their children had advantages, in terms of better home care and longer period of education, that permitted a great advance in the second generation. The East European Jews who immigrated into the United States required two generations to accomplish what the earlier German Jewish immigrants had done in one.

As a result, the distinction between the generations, between the immigrants and their children, would seem to have been much sharper among the East European Jews than it had been among the German Jews. One can detect this difference as early as 1900, when the Immigration Commission, analyzing the census returns of that year, tried to discover what changes had occurred, between first and second generations, in the pattern of occupations followed by immigrants and their children. In 1900, there were few children of Russian Jewish immigrants who were old enough to have started work. The statistics showed about 15,000 sons of Russian immigrants already engaged in occupations. Almost 10 per cent of the native-born children were already clerks and copyists, as compared with only 2 per cent of the immigrant fathers. Almost another 10 per cent of the children were salesmen, compared with 3 per cent of the immigrant fathers. Almost 20 per cent of the immigrant fathers were tailors, compared with 5 per cent of their native-born children. In 1900, it was, of course, far too early for the professions to play any role, either among the immigrants or their native-born children: 2 per cent of the Russian immigrants were engaged in the professions, and 3 per cent of their children.[34] Many of these immigrants, we know, were not Jewish; yet the striking differences between the occupations of immigrant fathers and sons reflect the changes among the large majority of Jews in the Russian immigrant group.

This, then, was the pattern of social advance that was followed by the East European Jews. The immigrant fathers, on the whole, remained workers. Part of the energy that in earlier stages of American Jewish history had gone into individual betterment seems to have gone into an attempt to better the condition of the entire Jewish working class group, and this attempt was remarkably successful. The garment trades were organized in a series of great strikes before World War I, and became a model of trade union organization, quite confounding Professor Commons's analysis that Jewish individualism did not lend itself to labor organization. The small advantage in wages that dexterity, hard work, and perhaps superior organization of work had won for the earlier East European Jewish immigrants was preserved for the later Jewish immigrant clothing workers by superior labor organization.

Of course, many members of the older generation were not workers: even in 1900, as we have seen, one-fifth of the Russians in large cities, whom we assume to be Jews, were in trade. And when the Immigration Commission surveyed a group of representative immigrants in large cities in 1908, more than one-third of the Jewish immigrants were already in trade.[35] Still, the greatest change in the social characteristics of the East European Jew was reserved for the next generation.

The upward mobility of the immigrant generation was, for the most part, an economic mobility in terms of a better standard of living and higher wages, not a social mobility altering occupation and status. After World

War I and during the 1920's the modest prosperity of the immigrant generation was reflected in a phenomenally rapid desertion of the old congested centers of settlement. In 1916, the lower East Side of New York held, it was believed, 353,000 Jews; in 1930, it held 121,000. Between 1914 and 1920, the number of Russian born (Jewish immigrants) in the old ghetto area of Chicago was more than halved. Of course, other immigrant groups were also leaving their first areas of settlement, but, again and again, we find the Jews, when they follow a common American pattern, doing so more rapidly. Thus the Jews left their first areas of settlement earlier, and in greater numbers, than did other ethnic groups.[36]

It was in the twenties, too, that for the first time the East European Jewish group began to show the characteristic demographic features of the American middle class. The Jewish immigrants around the turn of the century had, as we have seen, larger families than the non-Jews, a higher birth rate and a lower death rate, and in particular a lower death rate for children. So a good part of the huge increase of Jewish population between 1880 and 1927 (from about 250,000 to 4,225,000, though the latter figure is probably somewhat exaggerated) must be due to the fact that Jews had the high birth rate of the poor and the high survival rate of the rich.

The American Jews have never lost their high survival rate. But as early as 1925, when the mass immigration from eastern Europe had just come to an end, the Jews of New York began to show a lower birth rate than the rest of the population. This pattern was to characterize the Jewish population of the United States persistently. In 1925, 8 per cent of the New York Jews were under five years of age, as against 11 per cent of the general population; 9 per cent of the New York Jews were in the five- to nine-year-old group, as against 10 per cent of the general population.[37]

In all this, of course, we are describing changes that took place in American society in general, as well as among the Jews. In the United States as a whole the years before World War I were difficult ones for workers. We find large scale strikes, the organization of trade unions, the growth of a strong Socialist party. The Jews, as workers—and in those years most of the Jews were workers—shared in all these movements. The same improvement that took place in the condition of Jews after World War I also took place throughout American society. The Jewish birth rate dropped faster than the general birth rate in the 1920's; but the general birth rate was nevertheless dropping, too, and the same factors were affecting the birth rate among Jews and non-Jews—the cutting off of immigration, which had introduced a very fertile element into the population, the growing prosperity, and the reduction in the number of the most impoverished.

The changes we have described in the numbers, distribution, and economic characteristics of the Jews as a result of the great immigration from eastern Europe could not help but affect Jewish social life and relations with non-Jews. We have described what appear to have been the easy relationships that prevailed between Jews and non-Jews in the United States in the 1880's. In those days, when Jews were portrayed on the vaudeville stage, they were considered as Germans, and no one bothered to make very fine distinctions. There were not very many Jews, they were not highly visible, and they created no social problems. But after 1900, it was very clear what a Jew was—and he was neither a Russian nor a German. The hints of anti-Semitism which began to affect the well-to-do German Jewish elements in the 1880's and the 1890's had become a set and well-developed pattern by the time of the First World War. Anti-Semitism had also developed a more complete rationale in the rise of the idea of a Jewish "race" with ineradicable characteristics.[38] This notion had little place in America when there existed only a small German Jewish community; but it became quite popular after 1900, and seriously affected the social life of the established German Jewish community, as it found itself excluded from private schools, clubs, and upper class resorts. It also affected the rapidly rising East European group, for the exclusion of Jews from social clubs and social circles spread to some colleges of high status in the 1920's, where quotas were imposed on Jews.[39]

Caught up in a common fate, the German Jews slowly changed, and in certain ways became more "Jewish" than they had been at the end of the nineteenth century. The distinctively Jewish characteristics of the East European immigrants affected German Jewish religion, culture, and politics. The Reform temple, rapidly becoming indistinguishable from a Unitarian church, revised its course. This was not only because the East European Jews, rising, joined the temples and insisted upon a more "Jewish" service; it was also because the East European Jews, by creating a community where there was a continual and intense discussion of Jewish issues from many points of view, made it impossible for an unconscious or half-conscious drift away from Jewish life to continue. With newer Orthodox and Conservative synagogues—quite different from the older established American Orthodox synagogues—springing up on every side, it was not possible for Reform Judaism to remain unaffected. It could have separated itself more sharply from traditional Judaism, or modified its drift; Reform Judaism chose the latter course.

At the same time, the East European Jews brought with them Jewish politics on a large scale—Zionism, Bundism, Yiddishism, all became part of American Jewish life. The vast array of organizations created by German Jews became even greater, for added to all the types that existed in the nineteenth century were to be found, in great number, Jewish political organizations: Zionist organizations, Socialist organizations, Anarchist organizations, nationalist but non-Zionist organizations, and mixtures of all kinds, with their attendant women's auxiliaries and youth groups. Created by the East Europeans, for the most part, some of these organizations—in particular the General Zionist ones—also served as places where East Europeans and members of the German Jewish group met on common ground.[40]

The influence of East European Jews was felt by the older community not only in Jewish but in general politics. Members of the German Jewish community had gone into politics in the nineteenth century and in the early years of the twentieth century. They were generally Republicans, and they were not identified with "Jewish constituencies," for there were too few Jews to form them. With East European immigration, this earlier pattern of Jewish participation in politics changed. The immigrants were more often Socialists and Democrats than Republicans. The dense settlements they formed in the cities created Jewish districts, which were represented in state and national legislatures by Jews. And, as is often the case, these happened to be the more assimilated and prosperous members of the group, and for the Jewish group they were often of the old German Jewish element. Just as German Jewish doctors and lawyers found a ready-made clientele in the immigrant group, so did the few members of the older community that went into politics. After the elections of 1922, these representatives of the Jewish areas, German and East European Jews alike, who had almost all been Republicans before, were almost all Democrats, and representatives elected from Jewish districts since have almost always been Democrats.

One outcome of the growing influence of the East European element in affecting the character of American Jewish life was that tendencies toward assimilation, the complete loss of one's identity as a Jew, seem to have become weaker after 1900. The evidence for this is of the most tentative sort; but it seems fairly clear that the rate of intermarriage between Jews and non-Jews in the United States has been rather lower than in other countries (such as those of western and central Europe) where the Jews have been culturally assimilated to the dominant population.[41] It is less clear, but also likely, that this rate was higher in the nineteenth century, when Jewish communities were smaller and Jews were more closely identified in culture and language with the countries from which they came and with a large non-Jewish element of the population of this country, and, by the same token, less distinctively Jewish. The East European Jew, on the other hand, was distinguished in language and culture as well as religion from the population of the countries from which he came, and more of his values and attitudes were distinctively Jewish. Further, the conditions of American life were less receptive to the assimilation of new elements after 1900. Unitarianism had long since lost its influence. The cult of respectability was growing, and the effort to create an aristocracy of the *nouveau riche,* aped to some extent by those who were less rich, made

American social life more snobbish, more "exclusive," and less open.

But it was not all a matter of rejection by non-Jewish society. By the 1920's there was clear evidence of a desire within the Jewish community— and this desire could be pretty well located within the East European group —to maintain or create an all-Jewish social environment which would insulate Jews, to some extent, from the impact of the general society. American Jewry had created many, many Jewish organizations in the first 250 years of its existence, but they had been created to meet specific and definite needs —religious, philanthropic, cultural. They had had a social function, of course, but this had been, in the consciousness of those who created these organizations, secondary to the immediate need which created them. By the 1920's, many Jewish organizations were being created in which the aim of providing a Jewish social environment was primary. This was the function of the many Jewish Centers which sprang up in the 1920's. Some had been started as settlement houses, with the definite function of Americanizing the immigrant and raising the slum dweller; but as the "ghettos" emptied in the 1920's, more and more became general social centers for the Jewish community. The synagogues of the 1920's, too, more and more aimed at becoming social centers, containing meeting rooms, auditoriums, and gymnasiums. Thus, under the impact of the exclusiveness and anti-Semitism of part of the non-Jewish world and the desire to maintain an all-Jewish social environment on the part of some of the East European element, a new type of Jewish social life was being created in the 1920's.

THE JEWS IN THE 1930's

If the East European Jewish immigrants of 1900-1914 could, on the whole, look forward to no more than a moderate success as workers themselves, their children could contemplate a really startling change from the occupational and social status held by their fathers. These native-born American Jews who were in their teens in the 1920's, and in their twenties in the 1930's, entered the labor market during the greatest depression in American history. But they showed a most amazing ability to find economic openings, and established a community that today consists largely of well-to-do professionals, merchants, and white-collar workers.

Their first move was into white-collar occupations and business—the former often as a preparation for the latter. During the 1930's, they came under the lens of social investigation a number of times. In 1935, the Jewish youth of New York City and Detroit were both the subject of extensive study. It is interesting to compare them with their parents, as well as with their non-Jewish age mates.

In New York, almost one-half of the young people came from homes where their fathers were still workers, one-third from homes where their fathers owned their own businesses or were managers and officials in other enterprises; in one-tenth of the homes the fathers were clerks and in fewer than one-twentieth they were professionals. Here we see the typical distribution of the East European Jewish immigrant group, with a few more businessmen and professionals, and fewer workers, as a result of twenty or thirty years of change. But 60 per cent of the children were engaged in "clerical and kindred" work, and many of them, we may be sure, were headed for independent businesses. The Jewish youth, who constituted 31 per cent of the youth of the city, also constituted 56 per cent of those who had their own businesses or were managers and officials, 43 per cent of those in clerical and sales work, 37 per cent of those in the professions. The Jewish youth had less than their share in skilled and unskilled work (24 per cent), and they made up only one-tenth of those young people who were engaged in unskilled work. Fewer of the Jewish youth were on relief (12 compared to 15 per cent). Many more of the Jewish youth than of the others had had some kind of business and vocational training. It can be said that in bad times the Jewish youth were better off than the others.[42]

In Detroit the situation was much the same. Of the Jewish youth 12 per cent were in the professional and "proprietor, manager, official" category, as against 4 per cent of the non-Jews. Forty-six per cent of the Jewish youth were in clerical work, and only 21 per cent of the non-Jewish. On the other hand, three-fifths of the non-Jewish youth were engaged in semiskilled and unskilled labor, while only one-third of the Jewish youth were engaged in such work. In Detroit, of course, a much larger percentage of the Jewish fathers—almost half—were proprietors, managers, and officials than in New York (in general, the larger the Jewish community, the larger the proportion of Jewish workers). Two-fifths of the Jewish fathers and roughly the same percentage of their sons were workers. But it must be realized that the sons were at the beginning of their occupational careers, and 1935 was the middle of a depression.[43]

The Jewish youth of Detroit were starting out with much more education than the non-Jewish youth; 70 per cent of them had at least a high school education, while only 40 per cent of the non-Jewish Detroit youth had graduated from high school. This, of course, helped explain the head start of Jewish youth. But it also appeared that, no matter what the educational level, Jewish youth did better than the non-Jewish. Thus, of those Jewish young people who had had an elementary school education of eight years or less, 64 per cent were engaged in manual labor; but of the non-Jewish youth who had had an elementary school education or less, 87 per cent were engaged in manual labor. As in New York, in Detroit, too, we find fewer of the young people among the Jews unemployed. "Jewish workers can get jobs younger, to some degree, and hold them at older ages, than [other] Detroit workers. Likewise, unemployment affects them relatively less at the extreme ages."[44]

Thus Jews maintained significant advantages, small as they may have appeared at the time, in a generally stricken community. Because the Jews had, even in large cities, a relatively strong concentration in trade (they formed one-fifth of persons in wholesale and retail trade in Detroit, while making up only one-twentieth of the population), young Jews tended to have relatives who could put young people to work in a business. This is why the Jewish community of the time showed, as a complement to a relatively strong representation in trade in the older generation, a very strong representation in clerical and sales work in the younger generation. The non-Jewish factory worker (in Detroit, more than half the non-Jews, less than one-fourth of the Jews, were in "manufacturing and mechanical work") would tend to have a more limited range of acquaintances who would be likely to know about job opportunities; in any case, the industries that the factory worker and his acquaintances would know about were terribly depressed. In general, in a depression the highly organized branches of industry, such as heavy manufacturing, tend to cut production and employment to keep up prices. The unorganized branches—agriculture and retail trade—tend to cut prices and keep up the number of people employed.

It is this fact that led many observers in the 1930's to take the position that, even though more Jews were technically employed, they were employed at running losing businesses, and were no better off than the unemployed non-Jew. But again, the figures show a different story. In Detroit, the Jewish median income in 1935 was $100 more than the non-Jewish ($1,139 as compared with $1,027). It was true that Jewish clerks and salesmen (the young men and women laboring away in a relative's store at a purely nominal income) earned less than non-Jewish clerks and salesmen, and Jewish workers earned less than non-Jewish workers. But Jewish proprietors earned as much as non-Jewish proprietors and Jewish professionals earned more.[45]

We have gone into such detail on Detroit, first, because we have two excellent studies of the Jews of that city during the depression; but equally important, because it is a representative Jewish community, containing a larger number of workers than most of the smaller Jewish communities, and fewer than the huge Jewish population of New York.

The movement of immigrant children into work as clerks and secretaries, salesmen, and other white-collar workers caused this category to loom very large in almost every study conducted in the middle 1930's. In Buffalo (1938), Detroit (1935), and San Francisco (1938), "clerks and kindred" constituted the largest group when the Jewish working population was broken down by the kind of occupation followed. When the Jewish working population was broken down by the branch of industry (a less useful type of breakdown, unfortunately used more widely in the studies of the 1930's), trade bulked largest—but we know that a large part of those engaged in "trade" were actually clerks and salesmen.

This concentration in white-collar work was particularly evident among Jewish women. This was the age of the Jewish secretary, now disappearing almost as fast as the Jewish manual worker. Thus, one study in 1933 showed large numbers of New York non-Jewish women in domestic and personal work (34 per cent), clerical and sales work (29 per cent), and in professional work (16 per cent); but more than half of the Jewish women—51 per cent—were engaged in clerical and sales work.[46] In other cities this concentration was even greater: In Buffalo in 1938, 78 per cent; in Detroit in 1935, 66 per cent; in Passaic in 1937, 63 per cent of the employed Jewish women were engaged in clerical and sales work.[47]

In this general movement of Jews into nonmanual work in the 1930's, there are two special cases to be explained: the absence of Jews in big organizations, and their great numbers in certain professions:

1. In view of the Jewish youth's consistently better education, one might expect to find a large proportion going into government service. Indeed, during the depression the government service was attractive to all groups, and particularly to Jews. With the rise of an independent civil service it was reasonable for Jews, always looking for kinds of employment where personal prejudice would not touch them, to rush into government work. There was a considerable movement of this kind, and in New York Jewish young women did gradually replace Irish young women in the teaching force. But, despite the attractions of government service, Jewish representation remained small. In seven cities for which this information is given (for 1935-1938) in the volume of studies edited by Robinson, 1 per cent or fewer of the employed Jews were engaged in government work in six cities; in one city, Pittsburgh, 6 per cent of the Jews were in government work (but one suspects an error). For the United States as a whole, almost 4 per cent of the working population were in public employment in 1940. In proportion to their number in the general population, in Detroit in 1935 only three-tenths as many Jews as non-Jews were engaged in government work; in New York City, in 1937, there were two-thirds as many Jews as non-Jews in this work.[48] (Probably rather more Jews, proportionately, tended to work for the federal government than for local government; the picture would be somewhat altered if we had figures for Washington.)

In general, the tendency of Jews was to stay out of the bureaucracies of government and private corporations. In the case of the large corporations, anti-Jewish prejudice played an important role in restricting the number of Jews. In 1937, only one-eighth as many Jews as non-Jews, proportionately, were working in public utilities in New York City.[49] But even where prejudice played no role, or practically none, Jews seemed to prefer occupations where they were less dependent on others and had a chance eventually to be completely independent.

2. We have already pointed out that as early as 1908 there was statistical evidence of the large attendance of Jews in colleges, and their particularly strong interest in studying for the law and pharmacy. Dentistry and medicine were as yet too expensive to attract Jews in large numbers. Ten years later the situation was quite different. In 1918-1919, law was still very popular among Jewish students, but dentistry was hardly less popular, and medicine was even more so.[50] In the early 1930's about one-eighth of the entering classes in American medical schools consisted of Jews; it was only the extension of a subtle discriminatory system in most medical schools that reduced this percentage.[51]

In the middle 1930's, the great interest among Jewish students of earlier academic generations in the "free" professions of law, medicine, and dentistry—professions, it may be pointed out, which do not generally require employment in large organizations—bore fruit in the presence of an amazingly large number of Jews in these professions in most communities. In San Francisco eighteen of every 1,000 gainfully employed Jews were lawyers or judges; sixteen were doctors. Among non-Jews, five out of every 1,000 were lawyers or judges, and five were doctors. In Pittsburgh fourteen out of every 1,000 Jews gainfully employed were judges or lawyers; thirteen were doctors. Among non-Jews, the proportion was four out of 1,000 engaged in each of these professions. The situation was about the same with dentists. In Trenton, there were ten times as many Jews as non-Jews (proportionately) who were doctors; six times as many (proportionately) who were lawyers.[52] In general, a somewhat larger proportion of Jews was in the professions than non-Jews; and in the professions Jews favored medicine, dentistry, and the law, as against such professions as engineering, architecture, and teaching. Very likely these Jewish professionals had a somewhat smaller income than their non-Jewish colleagues (the Detroit evidence, as we saw, showed otherwise); but this was not unusual in view of the fact that few of the Jewish professionals had gone to good schools, many were foreign-born, and few inherited the established practices of parents and relatives.[53]

We have already spoken of the drop in the Jewish birth rate, which, it became evident around 1925, had begun to dip below the general American birth rate. Of course, we speak of the East European Jewish birth rate—the birth rate of the German Jews was already below the general birth rate in the 1880's. It was to be expected that as the middle-class character of the Jewish population became accentuated, the birth rate would drop. The surprising thing, perhaps, was that this lower birth rate was already clear in New York City in 1925 when there was still a very large

Jewish working class. But this is only one of the many middle-class social features that have for a long time seemed to characterize Jews, both as working class and middle class: they have almost always shown less juvenile delinquency,[54] and less adult crime,[55] than the rest of the population; they have generally shown a more stable family life,[56] a higher proportion attending school and for a longer period,[57] and fewer deaths from accident and violence.[58]

The studies of the 1930's reveal a very large drop in the Jewish birth rate. Here we should speak of a persistent feature of Jewish sociology: the great volatility of social movements among the Jews. These reflect the general movements of society, but are more emphatic. Thus, if there is a general movement away from manufactural work, among the Jews it becomes a flight; and when the general birth rate dropped during the depression, the Jewish birth rate plunged downward. Ben B. Seligman has calculated "fertility ratios" in eleven communities where studies were made between 1930 and 1940 (Chicago, Detroit, Passaic, Trenton, New London, Norwich, Minneapolis, Buffalo, San Francisco, Pittsburgh, Erie).[59] The "fertility ratio" is the proportion of children under five per 1,000 persons aged twenty to fifty-four. For United States whites, this figure was 153.5 in 1940; for the ten Jewish communities studied in 1930-1940, it ranged from 81 to 122. On the basis of these and other studies, sociologists were predicting, not long ago, that the Jewish community in the United States would begin to decline. In the late 1930's it seemed fair to conclude that a modicum of relative prosperity had been accompanied by a very rapid drop in the size of the Jewish family.

When we consider the nature of Jewish social life in the 1930's, we find that it reflected the trends introduced by the great East European migration, and which we described above. The Jewish population was concentrated in the largest cities, and within those cities it was further concentrated in almost completely Jewish districts. These were not only the districts of "first settlement," where the impoverished immigrants had settled, for many Jews had moved out of these areas during the prosperity of the First World War and the 1920's. But even the neighborhoods in which the upwardly mobile element settled had Jewish populations as concentrated as the ghettos which had been formed by the immigrants. All kinds of Jewish movements—political, religious, cultural, linguistic—flourished, or at least found adherents, in these areas of "second settlement." The number of Jewish organizations that had come into being staggered the imagination. Statistics reveal more than 3,700 religious congregations alone in 1936. While this figure is not large compared with some other religious denominations, it is enormous in view of the fact that Jews were almost completely an urban population, where congregations are generally much larger than in rural districts and small towns. The number of Jewish congregations, it is clear, reflected the great diversity of interests and experience among the Jewish population, and the ease with which Jews resorted to the creation of formal organizations.

During these years, the East European Jewish population penetrated the organizational and even social life of the older German Jewish community, and the distinctions between them weakened. In the Reform Temples, once entirely German Jewish, one-half the members were of East European origin as early as 1930.[60] On the boards of philanthropic organizations and hospitals, and in the community federation devoted to fund raising for philanthropic needs, the monopoly of the German Jewish element was maintained longer. In these areas, the East European Jewish organizations had generally established their own organizations, but with the passage of time both the older and newer organizations tended more and more to work together and even to merge.

A more important mingling of the two elements occurred in the new organizations called into being by the crisis that began in Jewish life when Hitler gained control over Germany. In the years after 1933, greatly expanded fund-raising organizations were required to move refugees from Germany and other countries that fell under Hitler's sway, and to resettle them in Palestine, the United States, and elsewhere. Other organizations fought Nazism on the political level. In this work the old distinctions disappeared. Thus an organization such as the American Jewish Committee, which had since 1906 acted as the representative of the older element of the Jewish community in defending Jewish rights abroad and at home, lost its character as a German Jewish organization as it expanded to meet the threat posed by Nazism.

In the 1930's, anti-Semitism, which as we have described it up to this point had revealed itself largely in social life, became far more important in the economic and political sphere. The reasons for this are in part to be found in the changes within the Jewish community. As business men and professional men, the older elements were relatively free from any economic effects of anti-Semitism. As workers, the East European immigrants were also largely immune. But as a large proportion of the Jewish population turned, as we have seen, to white-collar work, and was inevitably forced to seek employment in large organizations, discrimination on account of religion became a serious and ever-present threat. This danger was exacerbated by the severe competition for jobs during the great depression. In the 1930's, the defense organizations that had been established in previous years (the American Jewish Committee, 1906; the Anti-Defamation League of B'nai B'rith, 1913; the American Jewish Congress, 1922; the Jewish Labor Committee, 1933) were forced to devote a good deal of their energy to this problem.

White-collar work was not the only channel of upward mobility in which blockages occurred. The medical schools were closed to the great majority of Jewish applicants during the 1930's, and in other institutions of higher education the suspicion that Jewish applicants were meeting discrimination was often aroused, though it was not easy to prove this discrimination actually existed.

Hitler's anti-Semitism found its echo in American politics. It cannot be said that anti-Semitism played a large role in politics during the 1930's, but whatever role it did play was frightening to American Jews, who had seen Hitler grow from a minor agitator to a world threat.

Did these anti-Semitic trends affect Jewish relations with non-Jews? It is hard to say. In any case, the tendency for Jewish social life to be restricted within the Jewish community was probably at its apogee in the 1930's. The old pattern of Jewish integration into the general social life was gone, except for the smaller cities and towns, and there were few Jews there. There was little active hostility to Jews, but Jews lived pretty much to themselves. The Jewish workers generally worked in all-Jewish shops; Jewish white-collar workers often worked in all-Jewish offices; Jewish business men generally had only formal relations with non-Jewish businessmen. This was not a peculiarly Jewish pattern. It was to be found also among the other ethnic groups that made up so large a part of American society. Nevertheless, it raised questions as to the future place of Jews in American society, and encouraged a large Zionist movement which argued that Jews could never be at home except in their own country.

WORLD WAR II AND AFTER

Fifteen years of prosperity have created the Jewish community we know today. The effect of these changes has been to raise the East European Jews —the immigrants of 1880-1924, their children and grandchildren—more or less to the level achieved by the German Jews in 1880. These changes have wiped out most of the occupational and economic distinctions between the two elements and, along with other developments, have in large measure merged the two formerly distinct elements into a single community.

In these fifteen years, the older generation of East European Jewish immigrants, with its large proportion of workers, has been further reduced by the natural effects of age, while the younger generation has risen in the social scale. Perhaps a majority of the younger generation is now composed of business and professional men. This community of business and professional men is a well-educated and well-to-do element of the population— probably as well educated and as wealthy as some of the oldest and longest established elements in the United States.

Outside of New York City, the homogeneous character of Jewish communities is beyond dispute. Between 1948 and 1953 local Jewish communities conducted surveys in fourteen cities—Camden, New Jersey; Charleston, South Carolina; Gary, Indiana; Indianapolis, Indiana; Los Angeles, California; Miami, Florida; Nashville, Tennessee; New Orleans, Louisiana; Newark, New Jersey; the suburbs of Newark (considered as a separate community); Passaic, New Jersey; Port Chester, New York; Trenton, New Jersey; and Utica, New York. This is a fair random sample of the existing types of Jewish communities. It was discovered that the proportion of Jews in the nonmanual occupations (that is, of those working in the professions, as proprietors, managers, and officials, and as clerks and salesmen) ranged from 75 to 96 per cent.[61] For the American population as a whole, the proportion engaged in this kind of work was about 38 per cent of the gainfully employed in 1950. Even if we add to this group the farm owners and tenants, who might be considered a rural social equivalent of the Jewish shopkeeper, we find that only 48 per cent of those gainfully employed in the general population were in nonmanual work or owned and managed farms.

It is only in the largest cities that one finds fairly substantial proportions of Jewish workers. Yet even in New York City two-thirds of the gainfully employed Jews are engaged in nonmanual work. Among the non-Jews of New York (excluding the colored population), only one-half or fewer are engaged in nonmanual work. Though forming 26 per cent of the population of the city in 1952, Jews constituted over 45 per cent of the proprietor and managerial group, 33 per cent of the professional and semiprofessional group, only 6 per cent of the service workers' category, and 19 per cent of the craftsmen, operative, and labor categories.[62] There is still a substantial Jewish working class in New York City; but it must be pointed out that most Jewish workers are of the immigrant generation, and are not being replaced by their children.

The distinction between manual and nonmanual work is today considered a crucial one for determining the social status of individuals and groups. (Of course, there is a considerable amount of movement across the line.) Yet it is also important to know where in the nonmanual group American Jews fall. Here, too, the evidence is decisive: they are high in the group, and an extremely large proportion of them are professionals. Large as this proportion was in the 1930's, it is considerably larger today. Thus, if we compare the fourteen communities that were surveyed in 1948-1953 with another group of ten communities surveyed during 1935-1945 (Buffalo, New York; Detroit, Michigan; Erie, Pennsylvania; Grand Rapids, Michigan; Jacksonville, Florida; New Orleans, Louisiana; Passaic, New Jersey; Pittsburgh, Pennsylvania; San Francisco, California; and Trenton, New Jersey),[63] we find that the proportion of professionals has risen, on the average, from about 11 per cent of the Jewish gainfully employed in the earlier group to about 15 per cent in the later group. One might argue that the two groups of cities are not strictly comparable. However, three of the cities—New Orleans, Trenton, and Passaic—were included in both groups. In New Orleans, the proportion of professionals rose from 15 to 21 per cent of the Jews gainfully employed; in Trenton, the proportion rose from 12 to 19 per cent; in Passaic, there was no change. In 1950, about 8 per cent of the general American population were professionals.

This rise in the proportion of professionals has been accompanied by a fall in the number of Jews engaged in the lower levels of white-collar work —as clerks and salesmen. Comparing our two groups of Jewish communities, we find that in the 1935-1945 group about 36.5 per cent of the gainfully employed Jews were clerks or salesmen; in the 1948-1953 group the proportion was only about 27 per cent. The rapid decline in the numbers of Jewish secretaries and salesmen in recent years is a phenomenon apparent to the naked eye; the available figures support this impression.

What has happened, in effect, is that the great Jewish economic advantage, already perfectly obvious in the 1930's, because of superior education and a higher proportion of self-employed persons, has borne fruit in the fifteen years of prosperity since 1940. The proportions of Jewish doctors and lawyers has probably not risen greatly. (It was very high, as we have seen, in the 1930's.) For one thing, the number of Jewish doctors has continued to be artificially held down by discrimination. The greatest increase in the number of Jewish professionals has been in other categories—there are more Jewish journalists, authors, engineers, architects, college teachers. In short, one finds a rapid rise in the number of Jews engaged in all intellectual occupations in recent years.

One interesting example of this Jewish professionalization is afforded by Charleston. In the middle 1930's, the Jews of Charleston—an element long established in the city, with a relatively low proportion of immigrants —included one doctor, one dentist, several lawyers, two pharmacists, three or four teachers, and one rabbi. In 1948, there were eight doctors, seven dentists, eighteen lawyers, five pharmacists, nine teachers, eighteen engineers, seven social workers, four accountants, three radio commentators, three writers and editors, three artists, an orchestra leader, and four rabbis. All this in a community of fewer than 2,000 persons.[64]

At the same time there has been little sign of change in another of the characteristics of Jewish occupational distribution. The Jews are largely still proprietors of their own businesses—whether they be pushcarts, junk yards, groceries, or factories—rather than managers and executives of enterprises they do not own. There are a number of reasons for this. As we have already said, the American Jew tries to avoid getting into a situation where discrimination may seriously affect him. In a great bureaucracy, he is dependent on the impression he makes on his superiors and, increasingly in recent years, dependent on the degree to which he approximates a certain "type" considered desirable in business. The Jew prefers a situation where his own merit receives objective confirmation, and he is not dependent on the good will or personal reaction of a person who may happen not to like Jews. This independent confirmation of merit is one of the chief characteristics of business, as against corporate bureaucracy. In Abraham Cahan's *The Rise of David Levinsky*, we read how the young immigrant going into business could, despite his accent, produce clothing as good as that produced by longer established Americans, and more cheaply. Only a rare business man would not buy Levinsky's goods because of his accent. But if David Levinsky had been trying to rise to the vice-presidency of a huge corporation, he would certainly have found the going harder.

Closely related to this concentration in the professions and business is what we have called the "Jewish advantage" in education. This has been maintained in contemporary American Jewish life. In New York City a 1952 study showed that 26 per cent of the Jewish male population twenty-five years of age and older had attended college, compared with only about 16 per cent among other white males.[65] We must keep in mind that fewer of the Jews were native-born, and in smaller cities, with smaller numbers of foreign-born Jews, the percentage of those who have attended college is much greater. (In Nashville, Tennessee, for example, 44 per cent of the Jewish males over eighteen had some college in 1949.)[66] Among those aged twenty to twenty-four in New York City, the Jewish rate of school attendance is almost twice as great as that for the non-Jews, excluding the colored population.

We have demonstrated a striking rise in the socioeconomic position of American Jews, concentrated in the years between the 1930's and the 1950's. The statistics available also show that this rise surpasses that for any other immigrant group, and indeed surpasses, for the same period, improvements in the socioeconomic position of long settled groups. A study of American college graduates made in 1947 showed that more Jews than non-Jews became professionals (excluding teachers, who, though professionals, generally have a smaller income than other professionals); more Jews became proprietors, managers, or officials; fewer Jews became any type of white-collar and manual worker.[67] Yet if we were to look at their parents' occupations, we would find that *fewer* of their parents than of the parents of non-Jews had been professionals and proprietors, managers, and officials.[68] This same point is demonstrated in a study of the careers of 1,500 children with high I.Q.s selected from California schools in 1921-1923. When studied twenty years later, the Jewish children showed the same rapid rise, compared with their parents. Of the Jewish children, 57.5 per cent became professionals; of the non-Jewish, 44 per cent. Yet only 15 per cent of the Jewish fathers, as compared with 35 per cent of the non-Jewish parents, had been professionals. In other words, in this group, in a single generation, the Jews had increased their proportion of professionals by close to 400 per cent, the non-Jews only by about 25 per cent.[69]

Does the higher socioeconomic position of the Jewish group, as indicated by the high proportion in the professions and business, also mean greater income for Jews? This is a question that has long been disputed. However, in the 1947 study of Jewish and non-Jewish college graduates, it was found that, on the whole, the Jewish graduates tended to enjoy a higher income than the non-Jewish.[70] The careful researchers tried to determine the cause for this disparity. Knowing that Jews tend to settle in large communities, and that large incomes are more easily obtained in big cities, the researchers held the factor of size of city constant, and compared small-town Jews with small-town non-Jews, large-city Jews with large-city non-Jews. Jews had larger incomes in the small towns, as well as the large cities, and in every size of community in between. The researchers then tried to find out whether the higher Jewish income was a product of the fact that more Jews were concentrated in the professions. But even in the professions, Jews earned more than non-Jews. It appeared that the Jewish superiority in earning power could not be ascribed to any objective social characteristics—at least not to any that had come within the purview of this study.

In fact, the whole body of information on the socioeconomic position of the Jews that we have attempted to summarize in this article leaves us with one unanswered question: What is the explanation for the greater success—measured in the objective terms of income, and the commonly accepted status of different occupations—of the Jews in the United States?

The question is interesting not only in itself but also because its answer will suggest whether we may expect this prosperity to continue. The modern student of social phenomena cannot stop at psychological explanations. We know that Jews get (or used to get) better marks in school. We know that Jews work (or used to work) harder at getting an education. We know, too, that Jews have had the reputation of working hard at their occupations. But what is the explanation for these traits?

Ultimately, social explanations must resort to history and explain a present peculiarity by discovering an earlier one. We think that the explanation of the Jewish success in America is that the Jews, far more than any other immigrant group, were engaged for generations in the middle-class occupations, the professions and buying and selling. It has also been said that the urban experience helped them, but we think that is much less important. For in any case, very large proportions of Jews, German as well as East European, came from small towns and villages that were scarcely "urban." The special occupations of the middle-class—trade and professions—are associated with a whole complex of habits. Primarily, these are the habits of care and foresight. The middle-class person, we know, is trained to save his money, because he has been taught that the world is open to him, and with the proper intelligence and ability, and with resources well used, he may advance himself. He is also careful—in the sense of being conscious—about his personality, his time, his education, his way of life. The dominating characteristic of his life is that he is able to see that the present postponement of pleasure (saving money is one such form of postponement) will lead to an increase in satisfaction later. Perhaps the most significant findings of Alfred Kinsey's study of male sexual behavior was on this point: the person who postpones sexual pleasure, Kinsey discovered, was already essentially middle-class; for even if such a person was now in the working class, he was going to rise into the middle class.

Since the end of the Middle Ages, and particularly since the French Revolution, it has been those with training in the middle-class virtues who have reaped the greatest rewards in society. The world has indeed been open to persons with enterprise and capital, and the United States has been perhaps more open than most countries. The peasant and the worker, no matter what philosophers and moralists have to say about the virtue of manual work, never stand high in society. In primitive society, it is the chief and priest who dispose of the greatest wealth; in feudal society, it is the warrior and churchman; in modern society, it is the businessman and the intellectual. Consequently, it is in modern society that the Jews, who have been stamped with the values that make for good businessmen and intellectuals, have flourished; and it is when society reverts to a more primitive state, where force and those who wield it receive the greatest rewards, that the Jews are again thrust back to a low social position.

But what is the origin of these values that are associated with success in middle-class pursuits? Max Weber argues that they originated in a certain kind of religious outlook on the world, the outlook of Calvinism. There is no question that Judaism, too, emphasizes the traits that business men and intellectuals require, and has done so since at least 1,500 years before Calvinism. We can trace Jewish Puritanism at least as far back as the triumph of the Maccabees over the Hellenized Jews and of the Pharisees over the Sadducees. The strong emphasis on learning and study can be traced that far back, too. The Jewish habits of foresight, care, moderation probably arose early during the 2,000 years that Jews have lived as strangers among other peoples. Other features of Jewish religion and culture tended to strengthen the complex of habits leading to success in trade and the professions. One scholar has argued that the very strong interest of the Jews in medicine, both in ancient and medieval times and today, in the Arabic world as well as the Christian, comes from the orientation of Jewish religion to the good things of this world, conceived not in hedonistic or epicurean, but in sober, moderate, Apollonian terms.[71, 71a]

These are the origins of what we have called middle-class values among Jews. But certainly Jewish economic experience since the beginning of the

Christian era can only have strengthened the bent given to them by religion and culture. Until the nineteenth century the Jews were characteristically a group of traders and businessmen and scholars. (The term professional is hardly applicable to the medieval doctor or teacher.) They included a very large group of artisans, but, in contrast to the Christian artisans, the Jews were not members of guilds and corporations, but rather independent craftsmen and artists; consequently in large measure the Jewish artisans, too, were tradesmen. It is not easy to evaluate, in the creation of a Jewish character strongly influenced by middle-class habits, the relative influence of religion and that of occupations followed for centuries—both influences worked in the same direction.

The Jewish immigrants who came from eastern Europe to the United States during 1881-1924 numbered as many workers, and as many impoverished workers, as any other ethnic group. But they carried with them the values conducive to middle-class success, and they could, under the proper circumstances, easily return to the pursuit of trade and study, and thus to the ways of their fathers and forefathers. What is really exceptional, in terms of the large perspective of Jewish history, is not the rapid rise of these Jews in America, but the degree to which in the Czarist empire and eastern Europe in general, they had been forced out of their age-old pursuits and proletarianized. This process was to a certain extent a response to the Industrial Revolution: everywhere peasants and artisans and small traders were forced to become workers. But in the Czarist empire, where the bulk of East European Jews lived, artificial measures were taken to drive them out of their traditional occupations. Jewish taverns were closed; Jewish students were artificially limited in the schools; Jews were not permitted to live in the expanding capital cities.

As a consequence, then, of governmental anti-Semitism and the Industrial Revolution, the East European Jews arrived in this country either as workers or *Luftmenshen*—businessmen and traders with neither stock nor capital. But they were not, like the other workers who immigrated with them, the sons of workers and peasants, bearing the traditionally limited horizons of those classes. The Jewish workers were the sons—or the grandsons—of merchants and scholars, even though some merchants had only their wits for capital, and some scholars' wits were devoted to feats of memory. This background meant that the Jewish workers could almost immediately, as Commons says, turn their minds to ways and means of improving themselves that were quite beyond the imagination of their fellow workers. Business and education were, for the Jews, not a remote and almost foreign possibility, but a near and familiar one. They, or their friends or relatives, had the necessary experience and knowledge; with the prospect of success beckoning, it became worth while for the Jewish immigrants to work harder and save more than other immigrant groups.

In any case, the pattern of foresight and sobriety so essential for middle-class success was so well established in Jewish life that it was maintained even when there was no prospect of going into business. Jews did not drink; Jewish students were docile, accepting—as lower-class children rarely do—today's restraints for tomorrow's rewards; Jewish workers stayed out of jail. When we look at the working-class Jewish neighborhoods of the great American cities of the 1920's and 1930's, it is clear we are not dealing with ordinary workers. It was not dangerous to walk through the New York slums at night when they were inhabited by Jews. The Jewish workers violated most of the patterns of lower-class behavior, and were in many important ways indistinguishable from the non-Jewish as well as the Jewish middle class. Thus, a study of voluntary organizations in New York City in 1934-1935 revealed, as other studies have, that the higher the class, the larger the number of persons active in organizations. But the Jewish workers break this pattern—more of them belong to organizations than do Jewish white-collar workers.[72] A study in Chicago six years later told the same story: "Whereas among Protestants and Catholics working-class persons belong to fewer associations, among Jews the relationship is reversed."[73] And a study of political activity in New York City in 1945 showed that low-income Jews wrote more often to their congressmen than did even high-income Protestants and Catholics.[74]

In the early 1930's, J. B. Maller compared the social characteristics of the solidly Jewish neighborhoods of New York City with those of the rest of the city. The Jewish neighborhoods were, economically speaking, representative of the city: the average rent in the Jewish neighborhoods was about that of the city as a whole. Yet no matter what statistics we look at, we find a more markedly middle-class pattern of behavior in the Jewish neighborhoods than elsewhere. Thus, the homicide and accident death rates among Jews were half of those for the whole city. (The lower class is much more subject to fatal accidents than the middle class.) The infant mortality rate was lower, the I.Q. of school children higher, the school attendance rate higher, the juvenile delinquency rate less than half of the general city figure.[75]

One more study is worth quoting on this point. In 1935, one out of every ten youths in the city of New York was interviewed. Here is a description of the leisure-time activities of the Jews among them:

The principal recreational activities of Jewish and non-Jewish youth are the same, but more of the Jewish than the non-Jewish had participated in them. . . . More of them had participated in athletic games, had gone swimming, played tennis or golf, attended concerts and lectures. More (though the differences were not so great) had hiked, gone to dances, and visited museums. Fewer had spent any time on manual diversions such as sewing or knitting, or doing carpentering, or putting a radio in condition, or repairing a motor.[76]

What this means is that twenty years ago the Jewish youth of New York City, half of whom, according to this study, came from working-class homes, showed in their leisure-time activities the pattern of the middle class—just as their fathers, who would never be anything but workers, showed a middle-class pattern in their leisure-time activities.

It is one of the great anomalies of American Jewish life, and of American life, that the Jewish immigrants, who, by objective criteria, are eminently suited for personal success and civic responsibility, nevertheless feel themselves apart from the mainstream of American social life. The Jews have been, we have seen, successful in achieving middle-class status, the aim of the overwhelming majority of Americans, and have achieved the good education, the high income, and the materially rich life that go along with it. They are also a civically responsible element of the population: they contribute heavily to Jewish and non-Jewish causes, are rarely found among lawbreakers, and take a serious and intelligent interest in politics. And yet, through a combination of their own wishes and the wishes of other Americans, they lead a life apart, in their own communities.

It is only recently that Jewish social life, and the relations of Jews to other Americans, have come under scientific study. When we have dealt with this matter before in this article, we have had, perforce, to speak on the basis of very general impressions derived from personal accounts. That in colonial times the few Jews had many relations with their neighbors; that in the period after the German Jewish migrations and before the heavy East European Jewish migrations German Jews found acceptance in society, to the extent that they wished it, and to the extent that the looser social relations of most of the United States in that period could be called "society"; that East European migration seriously affected the social position of the established German Jewish element, and played some part in the rise of social anti-Semitism; and that the East European element lived a life almost entirely within its own group as late as the 1930's—all these are impressions, open to challenge. When we consider the present scene, we have more to go on, both in the form of social research and in the ability to consult our own experience.

The general situation is that American Jews, even though in large measure they look like, act like, and feel like other middle-class Americans, have developed a set of parallel social institutions, formal and informal, which greatly limit their contact with other middle-class Americans. This is the case even though the great majority of this population is now made up of native-born Americans. In the third generation, this closed community shows few signs of weakening.

One of the ways it might weaken is by intermarriage. It seems to be a fact, however, that the over-all rate of intermarriage for American Jews is not high, as compared with the rates of other western Jewish communities we have known of. In small towns, there is naturally more intermarriage. But in the large cities, where the overwhelming majority of American Jews live, intermarriage is low. And in small cities, where there is somewhat more intermarriage, the lines between Jewish and non-Jewish communities are so closely drawn that a sizable proportion of those who marry non-Jews bring them into the Jewish community—perhaps as many as half. Even in the large cities, the intermarried couple that lives a life unidentified with Jewish or non-Jewish elements generally finds, after the arrival of children, that some form of identification is demanded.

What is the basis of this closed community? In part, there is allegiance to the Jewish religion; in larger part, allegiance to the Jewish people; in some measure, exclusion by the non-Jewish world. But the antagonism of the non-Jewish world is less significant than the Jewish attitudes which interpret it. One study in a town of 50,000 people, with about 1,500 Jews, shows that whereas only 9 per cent of non-Jews who belonged to mixed organizations (containing Jews and non-Jews) feel differently toward the Jews, as compared to their feelings toward other members, 39 per cent of the Jews who belong to such organizations *think* the non-Jews feel differently toward them.[77]

The fear of exclusion is only one part of the story, though an important one. Perhaps more important in determining the nature of Jewish social life is the desire to maintain the Jewish group. This is expressed, particularly in the smaller Jewish communities where there is more opportunity for meeting with non-Jews, in the form of an almost overwhelming fear of intermarriage—and this fear, we must realize, is almost as intense in the second and third generations as in first-generation immigrants. In the town we have just mentioned, the sociologist describes how contacts with non-Jews are gradually restricted as one gets older and approaches the age of marriage, until by the age of marriage the number of non-Jewish friends is so small as greatly to reduce the possibility of intermarriage.

The structure of Jewish organizational life has, in recent decades, expanded to the point where a Jewish organization exists to parallel almost every non-Jewish one. Thus, Jewish children may go to Jewish nursery schools, school-agers will attend Sunday and afternoon schools, and an ever-growing proportion attend Jewish day schools; the high-school element will be urged to attend dances and participate in other social activities in synagogues, Jewish community centers, and Jewish youth groups. The college element, perhaps least provided for, has all-Jewish fraternities and sororities and Hillel centers. After college, where the opportunity for meeting non-Jews is greatest in contemporary American Jewish social life, the network of associations closes in again. After marriage, there are country clubs, synagogues, charitable organizations, social organizations—all Jewish.

A good part of the motivation for the support of this enormous system of organizations, we could argue, comes from the fear of intermarriage, and the consequent desire to supply a full social life, within the Jewish community, for one's children. The history of intermarriage among American Jews seems to show three periods. In the first, Jews were very much like other (or many other) Americans, there was considerable intermarriage, and it was not a great issue in Jewish life—the colonial period and the period of the domination of the German Jewish element. In the second, Jews were very different from other Americans, had few contacts with them, intermarriage was low, and it was not a great issue because the threat was remote—the period of the East European immigration when most of American Jews were East European immigrants and their children. In the third, Jews are again very much like their neighbors, but intermarriage, even though low, is considered a great threat and carefully guarded against. The difference between the middle-class American Jewish community of today of East European background and the middle-class Jewish community of fifty to seventy-five years ago of German Jewish background in attitudes toward intermarriage and "Jewishness" in general is striking, and it would not be easy to determine just why it exists. But it expresses itself in many spheres. It is reflected, for example, in the fact that the Americanized form of Judaism created by the German Jewish element was a Reform Judaism scarcely distinguishable from Protestantism, while the Americanized form of the old religion created by the East European element is Conservatism, which is scarcely distinguishable from Orthodoxy.

Our story must end at a given moment in time—1956—which is no natural stopping point. While the socioeconomic structure of American Jewry is reaching a certain equilibrium, as more and more Jews join the prosperous middle class by way of business, the professions, and upper white-collar jobs, the social life of American Jews has not reached equilibrium. It is not clear whether the largely closed community of today will be maintained by the next generation; and if it is not, what the attitude of other Americans will be to a greater "integration" of Jews into general social life. And if the present highly developed and highly articulated institutional nexus of Jewish life is maintained, it is not clear how it will be justified, to Jews or non-Jews, and what role it will play in the life of the general society. These questions must be left open in this study.

CONCLUSION

The story we have set out to tell has two addenda, which do not change any part of the main line. Another two migratory waves succeeded the great immigration from eastern Europe. Between 1936 and 1943, about 150,000 Jewish refugees entered the United States from Germany, Austria, Czechoslovakia, and other central European countries that had been overrun by Hitler. The new immigrants were of uniformly high social and economic status and formed a cross section of the prosperous and cultured Jewish communities of central Europe. Naturally, these newcomers had all the difficulties of adjustment of new immigrants, combined with the pain involved in the loss of wealth and position and of familiar cultural surrounding. Many of them—the doctors and scholars, for example—rapidly achieved positions in the New World in every way the equivalent of those they had held in the Old. Others—the lawyers were perhaps the hardest hit—found it more difficult. But today there is no question of the generally high economic and social position speedily achieved by this stratum of the American Jewish population.

An immigration of this size would have had a great impact on the Jewish community if it had come at any time before 1900. But coming as it did, at a time when there were 4,500,000 Jews in the United States, its impact was not great.

After World War II another, and the latest, wave of immigration reached American shores—about 100,000 Jews who had survived Hitler. They came with nothing or less than nothing, but they came to a community that was able to spend tens of millions of dollars to help establish them. Most of them today are workers; many have been helped to start businesses; some are studying. There is no question that these Jews, the remnant of the once populous Jewish communities of eastern Europe, will follow the path of their relatives who were fortunate enough to arrive in the United States before 1924. Most of them will remain workers for the rest of their lives. But the perspective of education and business is as attractive to them, and to their children, as it was to the East European Jewish immigrants of fifty years ago, and in a generation this latest immigration will be merged almost indistinguishably into the whole body of the American Jewish community.

We have again and again emphasized those characteristics in which the American Jews have differed from the "general American population." It is useful to compare Jews with "average Americans" (3.5 per cent of whom are Jewish), because in this way we can define what is characteristic of Jews. But we should realize that the "average American" is even more of an abstraction than the "average Jew." If we were to leave out such underprivileged groups as the Negroes and Mexicans and Puerto Ricans, the Jewish success in economic life we have chronicled would become less striking. If we were to compare Jews with Episcopalians or Presbyterians, we might find that the proportion of Jewish professionals was lower than that of professionals in these high-status denominations. Indeed, one study conducted in Madison, Wisconsin, showed just that. Among the Episcopalians of that city, no fewer than 36 per cent of those gainfully employed were professionals, as compared with 16 per cent among the Jews.[78] And if we were to describe the social life of other American ethnic groups, we would find much that would remind us of American Jewish social life, its peculiarities, anomalies, and problems.

The groups that make up America differ very little from each other in their overt culture. But they do differ greatly from each other in many other respects. The fact of concentration in certain classes or occupations is not peculiar to the Jews; any group in the population which is relatively small, and whose arrival in this country has been concentrated in a relatively short span of time, is likely to have a special socioeconomic distribution, different from that of the abstraction we call "the general population." Two factors will determine what this distribution will be: the character of the group at the time of its arrival, and the structure of economic opportunity in the country at the time of its arrival. We have already shown how Jewish religion and culture and occupational experience fitted the Jewish immigrants for business and the professions; it should now also be pointed out that these nonmanual occupations were expanding greatly during the period of the greatest Jewish immigration, and unskilled manual work and farming were employing a progressively smaller proportion of the labor force. Between 1910 and 1950, the proportion of the population engaged in nonmanual work rose from 21 per cent to 38 per cent. Certainly this offered great opportunity to the Jews. But one had to be of the proper social and psychological constitution to take advantage of it—which the Jewish immigrants were. Hence, while America in general became more markedly middle-class in its occupational structure, Jews became even more so.

There is a general tendency for the ethnic concentration in a single occupation or industry to suffer dilution in time, just as the ethnic neighborhood is gradually dissolved as the second and third generations move away. This means that in the second generation of Norwegians we do not find quite so many farmers, in the second generation of Italians we do not find quite so many heavy manual workers, and so on. This dilution is actually a movement upward, occasioned by the better education and wider knowledge of opportunities available to a native-born generation. But in the case of the Jews, this dilution upward becomes a *concentration*, for the Jews have begun to reach the upper limit of occupational mobility. In order to reflect the heterogeneity of the "general American" population more nearly accurately, it would now be necessary for the Jews to oppose actively their natural inclinations, as well as the natural movement of American society itself, and artificially to attempt to increase the number of farmers and workers and maintain the proportion of office workers and salesmen among them. This is not going to happen, so we may expect the Jewish community to become more homogeneous in the future, as the number of first-generation workers, and the culture they established, decline.

The future of the Jew in the United States does not, to our mind, raise economic problems, and raises only slight political problems; but it does raise social problems and cultural problems which we have at best only hinted at. There does exist a problem of the proper relation between Jewishness and Americanism; there does exist a problem raised by a social life lived almost entirely within a homogeneous Jewish community; there does exist, most significantly, the problem of whether the active communal life of American Jews should embody "values"—other than the value of sheer survival as a distinct group. All these questions are influenced by, indeed to some extent arise from, the social structure of American Jewry. But the answers to them will not be given by studies of social structure, but by the experiences and commitments of individual Jews, and by the history of the Jewish group in America. Our assigned task, and our method, carry us to the threshold of these questions, but do not permit us to go into them.

NOTES

Abbreviations

AJYB—*American Jewish Year Book*
JE—*Jewish Encyclopedia*
JSS—*Jewish Social Studies*
JSSQ—*Jewish Social Service Quarterly*
PAJHS—*Publications of the American Jewish Historical Society*
YAJSS—*Yivo Annual of Jewish Social Science*

[1] My chief source for this section is Jacob Rader Marcus, *Early American Jewry*, 2 vols., Philadelphia, 1951, 1953. Marcus speaks of the middle-class character of the eighteenth-century American Jews in Vol. II, p. 423. On p. 413, a characteristic type of statistic, reflecting the middle-class character of the Jewish community, makes its appearance for the first time in American Jewish history: In 1775 in Newport, Rhode Island, Jews, "though less than 2 per cent of the total number of taxpayers . . . paid 8.25 per cent of the amount collected."

[2] *Ibid.*, Vol. II, p. 390.

[3] Rudolph Glanz, "The Immigration of German Jews up to 1880," YAJSS, Vols. II-III, 1947-1948, pp. 84-85.

[4] "In many a place, out of a Jewish population of 30-40 families, 15-20 people have emigrated." A letter in a German Jewish newspaper, 1839, as quoted *ibid.*, p. 90.

[5] The 1840 population estimate is contemporary, and recorded along with

many other early estimates of Jewish population, in David Sulzberger, "The Growth of Jewish Population in the United States," PAJHS, Vol. 6, 1897. The estimates for 1850 and 1860 are from Bertram Korn, *American Jewry and the Civil War*, Philadelphia, 1951, p. 1, who follows earlier estimates.

[6] Glanz, *op. cit.*, p. 92.

[7] Quoted *ibid.*, p. 93.

[8] *Consider the Years*, Easton, Pa., 1944, p. 125.

[9] I. J. Benjamin, *Three Years in America*, Philadelphia, 1956, Vol. II, *passim*.

[10] These figures are from Sulzberger, *op. cit.*, checked against Hyman Grinstein, *The Rise of the Jewish Community of New York 1654-1860*, Philadelphia, 1945, p. 469. Where there is a large discrepancy in figures, Grinstein is preferred—e.g., the figure of 500 for 1825.

[11] Eric E. Hirshler (ed.), *Jews from Germany in the United States*, New York, 1955, p. 59.

[12] Richard Gottheil, *The Life of Gustav Gottheil*, Williamsport, Pa., 1936, pp. 182, 232.

[13] Oscar Handlin, "How United States Anti-Semitism Began," *Commentary*, Vol. 11, 1951, pp. 541-548.

[14] *Statistics of the Jews of the United States*, Board of Delegates of American Israelites and Union of American Hebrew Congregations, 1880. For the regional distribution, see H. S. Linfield, AJYB, Vol. 30, 1928-1929, p. 159.

[15] John S. Billings, *Vital Statistics of the Jews in the United States, Census Bulletin*, December, 1890.

[16] Sidney Liskofsky, AJYB, Vol. 50, 1948-1949, p. 753.

[17] Samuel Joseph, *Jewish Immigration to the United States from 1881 to 1910*, New York, 1918, pp. 127-132; and C. B. Sherman, *Yidden un Andere Etnische Grupes in die Fareinigte Shtaten*, New York, 1948, pp. 242-243.

[18] These calculations are based on the standard estimates of Jewish population which, since 1900, have been published in the *American Jewish Year Book*.

[19] JE, Vol. XII, p. 369.

[20] The figures for 1900 are Nathan Goldberg's, based on the very likely assumption that persons identified as "Russians" in the census of 1900, in cities of more than 250,000, were almost entirely Jews. See his *Occupational Patterns of American Jewry*, New York, 1947, pp. 12-16.

[21] *Report of the U. S. Industrial Commission*, 1901, Vol. XV, p. 284.

[22] *Ibid.*, pp. 343-369, where shops of different nationality groups are compared. JE, Vol. XII, p. 375.

[23] This figure must be an error. The same volume (p. 301) gives 14 per cent of the Russian immigrants of 1890 as tailors. For 1903-1904, JE, Vol. XII, p. 375, gives 26 per cent. Joseph, *op. cit.*, gives 25 per cent of the Jewish immigrants occupied in 1897-1910 as tailors. Goldberg, *op. cit.*, p. 18, reports that the Russian census of 1897 showed that 17 per cent of Jews in cities over 100,000 were engaged in the manufacture of clothing.

[24] See *Report of the Industrial Commission*, pp. 325-327.

[25] *Ibid.*, p. 480.

[26] Nathan Goldberg, *The Jewish People*, Vol. II, New York, 1948, p. 27, skillfully analyzes census statistics for the number of children born to Yiddish-speaking mothers, and shows that immigrant Jewish women around 1900 were more fertile than native American white women. See too JE, Vol. XII, p. 377, for statement that New York Jews in 1903 had more children than had New York Catholics.

[27] This we will find wherever statistics are available; Goldberg, *Occupational Patterns of American Jewry*, pp. 33-34.

[28] E. Lifschutz, "Jewish Immigrant Life in American Memoir Literature," YAJSS, Vol. V, 1950, pp. 221-222.

[29] *Report of the Industrial Commission*, p. 478.

[30] *Ibid.*, p. 477.

[31] Isaac A. Hourwich, *Immigration and Labor*, New York, 1912, pp. 370-372; and *Abstracts of Reports of the Immigration Commission*, Vol. I, 1911, pp. 367, 368, 764.

[32] *Ibid.*, Vol. I, p. 769.

[33] *Ibid.*, Vol. II, pp. 81-82.

[34] *Ibid.*, Vol. I, p. 827.

[35] Goldberg, *Occupational Patterns of American Jewry*, p. 25.

[36] Nathan Glazer, in Leo Grebler, *Housing Market Behavior in a Declining Area*, New York, 1952, pp. 254, 141; and Louis Wirth, *The Ghetto*, Chicago, 1928, p. 243.

[37] *Jewish Communal Survey of Greater New York, First Section: Studies in the New York Jewish Population*, New York, 1928.

[38] Barbara Miller Solomon, *Ancestors and Immigrants*, Cambridge, Mass., 1956, pp. 172-175.

[39] *Ibid.*, pp. 205-206.

[40] For this impact of the East European element on American Jewish life, see Nathan Glazer, *American Judaism*, Chicago, 1957, ch. VI.

[41] Nathan Glazer, "What Sociology Knows About American Jews," *Commentary*, Vol. 9, 1950, pp. 282-284; Hershel Shanks, "Jewish-Gentile Intermarriage: Facts and Trends," *Commentary*, Vol. 16, 1953, pp. 275-284.

[42] Nettie Pauline McGill, "Some Characteristics of Jewish Youth in New York City," JSSQ, Vol. 14, 1937, pp. 251-272.

[43] S. Joseph Fauman, "Occupational Selection Among Detroit Jews," JSS, Vol. 14, 1952, pp. 17-50.

[44] Henry J. Meyer, "The Structure of the Jewish Community in the City of Detroit," Ph. D. thesis, University of Michigan, 1937, p. 142.

[45] Henry J. Meyer, in Sophia M. Robison (ed.), *Jewish Population Studies*, New York, 1943, p. 127.

[46] Esther Kinzler, "Some Aspects of the Occupational Distribution of Jews in New York City," thesis. Graduate School of Jewish Social Work, New York, 1935.

[47] Robison, *op. cit.*, pp. 41, 124, 31, 33.

[48] *Ibid.*, pp. 14, 31, 41, 66, 78, 104, 122; and Kinzler, *op. cit.*, for New York City.

[49] New York Conference on Jewish Social Relations, *Industrial Classification of Jews in New York City,* New York, 1938, as quoted by Nathan Reich, in Oscar Janowsky (ed.), *The American Jew,* New York, 1942, p. 163.

[50] "Professional Tendencies Among Jewish Students in Colleges, Universities and Professional Schools," AJYB, Vol. 22, 1920-1921, pp. 383-393.

[51] Lawrence Bloomgarden, "Medical School Quotas and National Health," *Commentary,* Vol. 15, 1953, pp. 29-37.

[52] Robison, *op. cit.,* pp. 175, 105, 15.

[53] See Melvin J. Fagen, "The Status of Jewish Lawyers in New York City," JSS, Vol. 1, 1939, pp. 73-104.

[54] J. B. Maller, "The Maladjusted Jewish Child," JSSQ, Vol. 9, 1933, pp. 285-295; Vol. 10, 1933, pp. 157-162.

[55] H. S. Linfield, "Jewish Inmates of the State Prisons of the United States," AJYB, Vol. 33, 1931-1932, pp. 203-211; Nathan Goldberg, "Jews in the Police Records of Los Angeles, 1933-47," YAJSS, Vol. 5, 1950, pp. 266-291.

[56] Thomas P. Monahan and William M. Kephart, "Divorce and Desertion by Religious and Mixed Religious Groups," *American Journal of Sociology,* Vol. 59, 1954, pp. 454-465.

[57] J. B. Maller, "A Study of the Jewish Neighborhoods of New York," JSSQ, Vol. 10, 1934, pp. 271-276.

[58] *Jewish Communal Survey,* p. 20.

[59] AJYB, Vol. 51, 1950, p. 42; Vol. 52, 1951, p. 10.

[60] Union of American Hebrew Congregations, *Reform Judaism in the Large Cities, A Survey,* Cincinnati, 1931, p. 10.

[61] See articles by Ben B. Seligman, AJYB, Vol. 51, 1950, p. 28; Vol. 52, 1951, p. 12; Vol. 54, 1953, p. 14.

[62] These figures are from the data of an important sample study of the population of New York City conducted by the Health Insurance Plan of Greater New York in 1952, as reported in Henry M. Cohen, *Jewish Population Trends in New York City, 1940-1970* (mimeographed), Federation of Jewish Philanthropies of New York, January, 1956, p. 8.

[63] These studies are from Robison, *op. cit.;* Seligman, in AJYB (Grand Rapids, Erie, and Jacksonville), Vol. 51, 1950, p. 28; the information on New Orleans is from Julian B. Feibelman, *A Social and Economic Study of the New Orleans Jewish Community,* Philadelphia, 1941.

[64] Uriah Zvi Engelman, "Jewish Social, Educational, and Religious Developments in Charleston, S.C., 1900-1950," *The Reconstructionist,* Vol. 18, March 21, 1952; and Charles Reznikoff and Uriah Zvi Engelman, *The Jews of Charleston,* Philadelphia, 1950, pp. 263-264.

[65] See footnote 61.

[66] Nashville Jewish Community Council, *Study of Jewish Population, Nashville, Tennessee,* Nashville, 1949, p. 22.

[67] Ernest Havemann and Patricia Salter West, *They Went to College,* New York, 1952, p. 187.

[68] Robert Shosteck, *Five Thousand Women College Graduates Report,* B'nai B'rith Vocational Service Bureau, 1953, Washington, D. C., pp. 8-9.

[69] Louis M. Terman and Melita H. Oden, *The Gifted Child Grows Up*, Stanford, 1947, p. 298.

[70] Havemann and West, *op. cit.*, pp. 187-189.

[71] L. Wallerstein, "The Jewish Doctor," *Commentary*, Vol. 19, 1955, pp. 244-260.

[[71a] Cf. above Arturo Castiglioni, "The Contribution of the Jews to Medicine"; Charles Singer, "Science and Judaism."]

[72] Mirra Komarovsky, "The Voluntary Associations of Urban Dwellers," *American Sociological Review*, Vol. 11, 1946, pp. 686-698.

[73] Herbert Goldhamer, "Some Factors Affecting Participation in Voluntary Organizations," Ph.D. thesis, University of Chicago, 1942, p. 54.

[74] Gerhart H. Saenger, "Social Status and Political Behavior," *American Journal of Sociology*, Vol. 51, 1945, pp. 103-113.

[75] Maller, *loc. cit.*, 1934.

[76] McGill, *op. cit.*, p. 267.

[77] John P. Dean, "Patterns of Socialization and Association Between Jews and Non-Jews," *Jewish Social Studies*, Vol. 17, 1955, pp. 247-268. Much of the discussion on pp. 1726-1728 is based on this article, and on the (as yet unpublished) Riverton Study, conducted by the American Jewish Committee Scientific Research Department in 1952 in an eastern city with a population of 130,000, of whom 8,500 are Jews.

[78] Louis Bultena, "Church Membership and Church Attendance in Madison, Wisconsin," *American Sociological Review*, Vol. 14, 1949, p. 385.

Selected Bibliography

(This is a brief listing of general works on American Jews, intended to supplement the greater body of material referred to in the footnotes.)

Graeber, Isacque, and Britt, Steuart Henderson (eds.), *Jews in a Gentile World: The Problem of Anti-Semitism*. New York, 1942.

Handlin, Oscar, *Adventure in Freedom: Three Hundred Years of Jewish Life in America*. New York, 1954.

Janowsky, Oscar I. (ed.), *The American Jew: A Composite Portrait*. New York, 1942.

Rischin, Moses, *An Inventory of American Jewish History* (Foreword by Oscar Handlin). Cambridge, Mass., 1954.

Robison, Sophia M. (ed.), *Jewish Population Studies*. New York, 1943.

Sklare, Marshall (ed.), *The Jews: Social Patterns of an American Group*. Glencoe, Ill., 1958.

IV

THE JEWISH RELIGION

My impressions comes

CHAPTER 42

THE JEWISH RELIGION: ITS BELIEFS AND PRACTICES

By Louis Finkelstein

INTRODUCTION

Judaism is a way of life that endeavors to transform virtually every human action into a means of communion with God. Through this communion with God, the Jew is enabled to make his contribution to the establishment of the Kingdom of God and the brotherhood of men on earth. So far as its adherents are concerned, Judaism seeks to extend the concept of right and wrong to every aspect of their behavior. Jewish rules of conduct apply not merely to worship, ceremonial, and justice between man and man, but also to such matters as philanthropy, personal friendships and kindnesses, intellectual pursuits, artistic creation, courtesy, the preservation of health, and the care of diet.[1]

So rigorous is this discipline, as ideally conceived in Jewish writings, that it may be compared to those specified for members of religious orders in other faiths. A casual conversation or a thoughtless remark may, for instance, be considered a grave violation of Jewish Law. It is forbidden, as a matter not merely of good form but of religious law, to use obscene language, to rouse a person to anger, or to display unusual ability in the presence of the handicapped. The ceremonial observances are equally detailed. The ceremonial Law expects each Jew to pray thrice every day, if possible at the synagogue; to recite a blessing before and after each meal; to thank God for any special pleasure, such as a curious sight, the perfume of a flower, or the receipt of good news; to wear a fringed garment about his body; to recite certain passages from Scripture each day and to don *tephillin* (cubical receptacles containing certain biblical passages) during the morning prayers.

Decisions regarding right and wrong under given conditions are not left for the moment, but are formulated with great care in the vast literature created by the Jewish religious teachers. At the heart of this literature are the Hebrew Scriptures, usually described as the Old Testament, consisting of the Five Books of Moses (usually called the *Torah*), the Prophets and the Hagiographa. These works, particularly the Five Books of Moses, contain the prescriptions for human conduct composed under

Divine inspiration. The ultimate purpose of Jewish religious study is the application of the principles enunciated in the Scriptures, to cases and circumstances the principles do not explicitly cover.

Because Judaism is a way of life, no confession of faith can by itself make one a Jew. Belief in the dogmas of Judaism must be expressed in the acceptance of its discipline rather than in the repetition of a verbal formula. But no failure either to accept the beliefs of Judaism or to follow its prescriptions is sufficient to exclude from the fold a member of the Jewish faith. According to Jewish tradition, the covenant between God and Moses on Mt. Sinai included all those who were present and also all their descendants. This covenant was reaffirmed in the days of Ezra and Nehemiah, when the people together with their leaders made "a sure covenant to walk in God's law, which was given to Moses the servant of God, and to observe and do all the commandments of the Lord our Lord, and His ordinances and His statutes" (Neh. 10:30). To apply the words used by Scripture in another connection, this covenant has thus been made binding upon the Jews, "and upon their seed, and upon all such as joined themselves unto them" (Esth. 9:27). There is therefore no need for any ceremony to admit a Jewish child into the faith of Judaism. Born in a Jewish household, he becomes at once "a child of the covenant." The fact that the child has Jewish parents involves the assumption of the obligations that God has placed on these parents and their descendants.

This concept of the inheritance of religious traditions does not imply any sense of racial differentiation. The concept derives simply from the belief that a person may assume binding obligations not only for himself, but also for his descendants. Thus anyone who is converted to Judaism assumes the obligation to observe its discipline, and makes this obligation binding on his descendants forever, precisely as if he had been an Israelite, standing with Moses, before Mt. Sinai on the day of the Revelation.

The ancestry of the proselyte, and therefore his "race," are quite irrelevant. Whether he be of Arabic background like Queen Helene, or Roman like Aquila, or Khazar like the members of the south Russian kingdom that became converted to Judaism in the eighth century of the Common Era, or like Obadiah, the well-known Moslem who became a proselyte, or Polish like the famous Count Valentine Potocki of the eighteenth century, his descendants, from the point of view of Judaism, would all be bound by his obligation to follow the laws and customs of Judaism.

On the other hand, in view of the Jewish attitude toward other monotheistic faiths, it is considered improper for a Jew to urge a member of another faith to become a Jew. Indeed, a person who desires to adopt Judaism must be told of all the difficulties inherent in affiliation with the faith. Only a person who persists in his desire to become a Jew, and demonstrates that his desire is based on no mundane motive, may be accepted into the Jewish fold.

Because of the special place that the home occupies in Judaism as a center of religious life and worship, almost co-ordinate with the synagogue itself, Judaism holds it essential that both parties to a Jewish marriage be members of the Jewish faith. There is, of course, no objection to marriage with a sincere convert to Judaism. But it is not possible for the home to function in the manner prescribed by Jewish law unless both husband and wife are of the Jewish faith.

In the case of a mixed marriage, the status of the children is determined by the faith of the mother, as the greatest influence in their lives. The children of a Christian mother are considered Christians; the children of a Jewish mother are considered Jews. The Jewish partner in such a mixed marriage is considered living in continual transgression of Jewish law, but remains, like those who deviate from the Law in other respects, within the fold of Judaism, entirely subject to the duties and obligations placed on other Jews.

While no one outside of the Jewish faith is bound by the rules of Jewish ceremonial discipline, Judaism draws a distinction between the adherents of monotheistic faiths—including Christianity and Islam, which are recognized as each making a distinctive contribution to the realization of the Kingdom of God on earth—and nonmonotheistic faiths. The various regulations Judaism, like early Christianity, established to prevent reversion to paganism, obviously have no application to the relationship between Jews and their neighbors in Christian and Mohammedan countries. A Jew may not enter a building dedicated to idol-worship even to protect himself from inclement weather; and of course he cannot participate in any festivity dedicated to any form of idol-worship.

These ceremonial rules are intended to register a protest against paganism; they do not place the pagan in any inferior position with regard to Jewish law or ethic. According to Philo and Josephus, it is a violation of Jewish law for a Jew to speak with disrespect of the gods of any people, for the verse "Thou shalt not revile God" (Ex. 22:27) is interpreted as applying to all gods. While this interpretation is not accepted in the Rabbinic tradition, it does express the spirit with which Judaism approaches all systems of belief, regardless of the extent of their difference from itself.

This spirit is expressed in the principle that every rule of moral conduct a Jew must observe toward another Jew applies also to relations with persons of other faiths. The laws of justice, kindness, and charity, as well as the obligation to visit the sick, bury the dead, support the needy, must be assumed for all people.

Like other religions, Judaism can be, and indeed has been, practiced under various forms of civil government: monarchical, semimonarchical, feudal, democratic, and totalitarian. Adherents of the Jewish faith, like those of other religions, regard themselves as citizens or subjects of their respective states. In every synagogue prayers are offered for the safety of the government of the country of its location; and in the ancient Temple of Jerusalem daily sacrifices were offered on behalf of the imperial Roman government, as long as Palestine remained under its dominion. This patriotic loyalty to the state has often persisted in the face of cruel persecution. The principle followed has been that formulated by the ancient teacher, Rabbi Haninah: "Pray for the welfare of the government; for without fear of the government, men would have swallowed each other up alive."

Despite this ability to adjust itself to the exigencies of any form of temporal government, Judaism, like other faiths derived from the Prophets, has always upheld the principles of the Fatherhood of God and the dignity and worth of man as the child and creature of God; and its ideals are more consistent with those of democracy than any other system of government.

The most vigorous and consistent effort to formulate the discipline of Judaism in terms of daily life was that made in ancient Palestine and Babylonia. The Palestinian schools devoted to this purpose were founded in the second or third century before the Common Era, and flourished in their original form for six centuries and in a somewhat altered form until the Crusades. The Babylonian schools were founded in the third century of the Common Era and ended the first and most significant phase of their activity about three hundred years later.[2a]

The rules of conduct worked out in the discussion of these academies form the substance of Jewish Law. In arriving at these precepts, the ancient teachers were guided by their desire to know the Will of God. So far as possible they sought to discover His will through an intensive study of the Scriptures. Where Scripture offered no clear guidance, they tried to ascertain His will by applying its general principles of moral right. In addition, they had a number of oral traditions, going back to antiquity, which they regarded as supplementary to the written Law, and equal to it in authority and inspiration.

The high purpose of the discussions made them of monumental importance to Judaism. As a result, they were committed to memory by eager and faithful disciples, until the memorized material grew to such proportions that it had to be reduced to writing. The work in which the discussions were thus preserved is known as the Talmud. As there were two groups of academies, differing slightly from each other in their interpretation of the Law, and widely in their manner of approach to the subject, we have two Talmudim, that of Palestine and that of Babylonia. Both are considered authoritative guides for Jewish Law. Where they disagree, the Babylonian Talmud is, for historical reasons, considered the more authoritative.

THE PLACE OF STUDY IN JUDAISM

It is impossible to understand Judaism without an appreciation of the place it assigns to the study and practice of the talmudic Law. Doing the Will of God is the primary spiritual concern of the Jew. Therefore, to this day, he must devote considerable time not merely to the mastery of the content of the Talmud, but also to training in its method of reasoning. The study of the Bible and the Talmud is thus far more than a pleasing intellectual exercise, and is itself a means of communion with God. According to some teachers, this study is the highest form of such communion imaginable.[3]

Because the preservation of the Divine will regarding human conduct is basic to all civilization, none of the commandments is more important than that of studying and teaching the Law. The most sacred object in Judaism is the Scroll containing the Five Books of Moses. Every synagogue must contain at least one copy of it. The Scroll must be placed in a separate Ark, before which burns an eternal light. The position of this Ark in the synagogue is in the direction of Jerusalem; everyone turns toward the Ark in prayer. When the Scroll is taken from the Ark for the purpose of reading, all those present must rise. No irreverent or profane action may be performed in a room which contains a Scroll, nor may a Scroll be moved from place to place except for the performance of religious rites. From time to time the Scroll must be examined to ascertain that its writing is intact.

The preparation of the Scroll is a task requiring much care, erudition, and labor. It is usually done by a professional copyist called a *sofer* (scribe). The text is written on sheets of parchment, especially prepared for the purpose. Only skins of animals permitted for food, in accordance with Lev. 11:1-9 and Deut. 14:3-9, are used. The whole work is then attached at the beginning and at the end to wooden rods, so that it can be rolled in the form of a scroll.

The ink used in writing must be black, and should be indelible. Before beginning to copy the text, the scribe must say, "I am about to write this book as a sacred Scroll of the Law." He must repeat a similar formula every time he is about to copy the Divine Name, saying, "I am writing this word as the sacred Name."

Like other Semitic languages, Hebrew requires only a consonantal text for reading: the vowels are omitted in classical texts. Hence the Scroll of the Five Books of Moses contains only the consonantal text. This text is fixed by tradition, almost to the last detail. Even such matters as division into paragraphs and sections, and the special size of certain letters, which are particularly large or particularly small, is determined. The texts of all the extant Scrolls are thus virtually identical. Any significant deviation from the traditional text makes a Scroll unfit for use, and must be corrected as soon as it is discovered. No decorations or illuminations are permitted in the Scrolls intended for the public service. Tradition prescribes, however, that certain poetic portions are to be written in verse form and that certain letters shall have little coronets adorning them.

No less important than this homage paid to the Scroll as symbol of the Law, is that paid to the living Law itself. Fully three-fourths of the Hebrew literature produced within the first nineteen centuries of the Common Era, is devoted to the elucidation of the Law. Many of the best minds in Judaism have been devoted to its study. Every parent is required to teach his child its basic elements. Its study is considered vital not only for the guidance it offers in the practice of Judaism, but for liberation from the burden of secular ambition and anxieties. The study of the Law is believed to be a foretaste of the immortal life, for the Sages of the Talmud believed that Paradise itself could offer men no nearer communion with God than the opportunity of discovering His will in the study of the Law.

The Talmud derives its authority from the position held by the ancient academies. The teachers of those academies, both of Babylonia and of Palestine, were considered the rightful successors of the older *Sanhedrin*, or Supreme Court, which before the destruction of Jerusalem (in the year 70 of the Common Era) was the arbiter of Jewish Law and custom. The Sanhedrin derived its authority from the statement in Deut. 17:8-13, that whenever a question of interpretation of the Law arises, it is to be finally decided by the Sages and priests in Jerusalem.

At the present time, the Jewish people have no living central authority comparable in status to the ancient Sanhedrin or the later academies. Therefore any decision regarding the Jewish religion must be based on the Talmud, as the final résumé of the teachings of those authorities when they existed. The right of an individual to decide questions of religious Law depends entirely on his knowledge of the Bible, the Talmud, and the later manuals based on them, and upon his fidelity to their teachings. Those who have acquired this knowledge are called *rabbis*. There is no sharp distinction in religious status between the rabbi and the layman in Judaism. The rabbi is simply a layman especially learned in Scripture and Talmud. Nor is there any hierarchical organization or government among the rabbis of the world. Yet some rabbis, by virtue of their special distinction in learning, by common consent come to be regarded as superior authorities on questions of Jewish Law. Difficult and complicated issues are referred to them for clarification.

To be recognized as a rabbi, a talmudic student customarily is ordained.

A SCROLL IN ITS CASE WITH A CROWN OF THE LAW

This Scroll was made in Spain in the 17th century. The silver case of repoussé, embossed, pressed and cast work was made in Paris about 1860 by Maurice Mayer, court silversmith to Napoleon III.

Traditionally, the authority to act as rabbi may be conferred by any other rabbi. It is usual, however, for students at various theological schools to receive this authority from their teachers. In America, there are several rabbinical schools, each of which ordains its graduates in the manner in which degrees are conferred on graduates of other institutions of learning. At present (1958) the best known of these schools are:

The Hebrew Union College—Jewish Institute of Religion, Cincinnati, New York City and Los Angeles

The Jewish Theological Seminary of America, New York City

Jewish University of America, formerly the Hebrew Theological College, Chicago[4]

Yeshiva University, New York City.[5a]

There is considerable variation among the interpretations of Judaism taught at these seminaries, and consequently there is a considerable difference in emphasis on the subjects included in their respective curricula. This has resulted from the fact that during the second half of the nineteenth century various groups of rabbis, primarily in Germany and America, claimed authority not merely to interpret but also to amend talmudic, and even biblical Law. These rabbis are known as Reform rabbis, and their congregations as Reform congregations. Of the rabbis who adhere to traditional Judaism, some reject any significant innovations from customary practice; these rabbis are called Orthodox. Others maintain that Jewish law is a living tradition, subject to change, but they insist that such changes must be made in accordance with traditional canons for the interpretation and development of Rabbinic law. These rabbis are usually called Conservative.[6a]

The differences between the various groups of American rabbis have not led to any sectarian schism. Although the difference in practice between the traditional and Reform groups is considerable, each accepts the other as being within the fold of Judaism. It is possible for them to do so, because of the principle that even an unobservant or a heretical Jew does not cease to be a member of the covenant made between God and Israel at the time of the Revelation. Only actual rejection of Judaism, by affiliation with another faith, is recognized as separating one from the Jewish community.[7] So long as a follower of the Jewish faith has not by overt act or word and of his own free will declared himself a member of another religion, other Jews are bound to regard him as one of their own faith, and to seek his return to its practice and beliefs.

THE PLACE OF ETHICS IN JUDAISM

The ceremonial discipline is considered obligatory only for members of the Jewish faith, but the ethical element in Judaism is universal in scope.[8u] The commandment against murder is explicitly stated in Scripture to have been revealed to Noah (Gen. 9:5); and therefore applies to all human-kind. By analogy, the commandments against theft, cruelty to animals, sexual license, blasphemy, idol-worship, and the violation of civil justice are considered to be universal. Those who observe these fundamental laws are considered "the righteous of the peoples of the world," who will par-take in the resurrection and in immortality.

One further distinction is made between the ethical and the ceremonial content of Judaism. When faced with the danger of death, one may violate any of the commandments, save only those against murder, sexual license, and idolatry. This rule does not apply in the event of a religious persecution. When a government undertakes to suppress the observance of Judaism, it becomes the duty of the Jew to submit to martyrdom rather than deviate from his faith in even a slight matter.

The duty of accepting martyrdom, either for the ethical Law in the normal course of events or for the whole of the Law in times of persecu-tion, is called *Kiddush ha-Shem* (sanctification of the Name of God). Any violation of this duty is called profanation of the Name of God, *Hillul ha-Shem*. These terms may also be applied to situations that do not call for martyrdom, but where it is possible to increase or lessen respect for religious faith through action. Anyone who through sacrifice and saint-liness brings others to more profound recognition of God "sanctifies" the Name of God. But anyone whose actions bring religion generally and Judaism in particular into disrespect is guilty of *Hillul ha-Shem*. Because of this principle, religious leaders are expected to be particularly careful of their ethical conduct, for even the slightest deviation from propriety on their part naturally casts aspersion on the whole faith. Similarly, any impropriety on the part of a Jew in his relations with members of other faiths tends to decrease respect for Judaism as a faith, and is therefore a "profanation of the Name of God."

The application of the ethical teachings of Judaism to every aspect of daily life has necessarily involved the creation and development of a system of civil law. Like contemporary Christians, the Jews of the talmudic period believed it wrong to resort to the pagan courts of their time for adjudication of civil differences. Not only did the Jewish conception of justice frequently differ from that of the pagans, but the pagan courts were often corrupt, and almost always cruel. The tradition opposing the use of civil courts for adjudication of civil disputes persisted during the Middle Ages. For many centuries secular courts were few and inaccessible, and even in later periods their judgments were generally considered unfair. Only with the enlightenment of the eighteenth and nineteenth century, and the disappearance of the ghettos, have Jews become ac-customed to apply to secular courts of justice for settlement of litigation. However, it is a fundamental principle of talmudic Law that the civil law of a country is binding there, and a Jewish court would necessarily have to take cognizance of the civil law on any disputed point.

The necessity of dealing with civil litigation compelled the talmudic Sages and their medieval successors to give much attention to this aspect of the Jewish Law. Hence, about one-fourth of the Babylonian Talmud, and a proportionate share of later Rabbinic literature, is devoted to questions of civil law. The latest compilation of this law is to be found in the *Hoshen Mishpat*, the fourth volume of Rabbi Joseph Caro's famous code, the *Shulhan Aruk*.

The Jewish civil law is frequently applied even today in the adjudication of disputes arising among religious functionaries, and is sometimes used as a basis for arbitration agreements.

But the Jewish conception of justice transcends the realm of civil law. Justice includes all ethical conduct, as well as philanthropy. Indeed, the word for charity in Rabbinic Hebrew is *zedakah*, or righteousness. Under certain circumstances, talmudic Law actually permits courts to compel a man to do his duty by the community or by individuals, beyond the letter of the law.

As a rule, a Jew is expected to give between one-tenth and one-fifth of his income to charitable purposes. To give less than one-tenth is to fail in duty to the community; to give more than a fifth may involve injustice to his own immediate family. Beyond provision of material assistance for the needy and suffering lies the duty of encouraging them with personal attention and kind words, of recognizing them as personal friends, and above all enabling them to help themselves. In his Code, Maimonides recognizes eight types of philanthropy, arranged according to their merit, as follows: (1) helping the needy to be independent by providing opportunity for work; (2) giving charity to the poor in such a way that neither the donor nor the recipient knows the other; (3) giving charity in such a way that the donor can identify the recipient but the recipient cannot identify the donor; (4) giving in such a way that the recipient can identify the donor but the donor cannot identify the recipient; (5) giving in such a way that the donor and recipient know each other, provided the gift is made before it is requested; (6) giving after a request is made, provided the amount is sufficient to meet the need; (7) giving less than is needed, but with a kindly countenance; (8) giving less than is needed, and without a kindly countenance.[9a]

Judaism lays great stress on the importance of personal ethical relations between friends. The last of the Ten Commandments is a prohibition against "coveting" the blessings of a neighbor. Other regulations warn against talebearing, gossip, envy, and dislike of a neighbor. Any form of vengeance also is prohibited. If a persons says to another, "Lend me your hatchet," and the second replies, "I will not lend you my hatchet today,

because yesterday you refused to lend me your sickle," the second transgresses the commandment, "Thou shalt not take vengeance" (Lev. 19:18).
If the second replies, "I will lend you my hatchet, despite the fact that
yesterday you refused to lend me your sickle," he transgresses the second
half of the verse, "nor bear any grudge." The importance of these commandments in Judaism is such that one of the most distinguished Jewish
scholars of the eleventh century, Bahya ibn Pakudah, devoted a whole
book to their analysis, the *Book of the Duties of the Heart*.[10a] In our own
generation, the famous Rabbi Israel Meir Kahan (better known by the
title of his book, *Chofetz Chayyim*, first published anonymously) devoted
his life to warning against the transgression of these laws of ethical conduct.
During the nineteenth century, there developed under the influence of
Rabbi Israel Salanter (1810-1883) a whole group of students who refrained from conversation over long periods, in order to discipline themselves against the sin of "evil speech."

In accordance with the precept of Lev. 19:17, Judaism considers every
member of the faith responsible for the moral conduct of those neighbors
over whom he is able to exert influence. To see injustice done without
protesting against it is to participate in the injustice. To provoke a man
to anger is to partake of the sin of unjust anger. To permit an opposing
litigant to take a false oath is to share in the transgression of perjury;
just as to listen to blasphemy, gossip, or talebearing is to be a party to them.
The concept is summarized in the teaching of Rabbi Jacob that "a person,
on whose account God has to inflict punishment on another, will not be
admitted into the presence of God" (*Shabbat* 149b). The underlying
principle of this teaching is the doctrine that a victim of injustice falls short
of the ideal of Judaism to the extent that he fails to obtain Divine forgiveness for the person who acted unjustly toward him.

The public confession of sins prescribed for the Day of Atonement
reflects this consciousness that every member of the community is to some
extent responsible for the sins of every other member. The confession lists
not only the sins the average man is liable to commit through oversight,
but also such sins as theft, unchastity and rendering false judgment, of
which the vast majority are usually innocent.

THE BASIC CONCEPTS OF JUDAISM

The central doctrine of Judaism is the belief in the One God, the
Father of all mankind. The first Hebrew words a Jewish child learns are
the confession of faith contained in the verse "Hear, O Israel, the Lord
is our God, the Lord is One," and every believing Jew hopes that as he
approaches his end in the fullness of time he will be sufficiently conscious
to repeat this same confession. This monotheistic belief is subject to no
qualification or compromise.

We owe this monotheism to some of the earliest teachers of Israel who, having discovered that the Lord is One and His name One, devoted their lives to the propagation of this teaching. But the prophets proceeded a step further. To whom shall you compare God, they exclaimed, and what manner of likeness shall you set up alongside Him? This served as a cue to sages and philosophers who pondered over the meaning of God. Through their insight the Jew learned that at most every description of God was a metaphor, due to the limited idiom of man. God is not to be compressed into physical form (He is incorporeal), He is not subject to the boundaries of time, of beginning and end (He is eternal), He cannot be confined by space (He is omnipresent). As one of the talmudic Sages put it, "In God is the universe fixed, not He in it."

True enough, not only the simple but the learned, not only the average but the saintly, have described God as wise, just, long-suffering, merciful; and, depending on the occasion, have appealed to Him because preeminently these attributes are His. When our motives are questioned we call upon Him for support, for in His wisdom He knows the deepest stirrings of our hearts. When we suffer, we invoke His justice. When in haste we sin, we plead for sufferance on His part. Where we have been exacting or rebellious, we cry for His mercy. What, however, does such language suggest? That man in his dependence and helplessness employs as best he may, to the stretching point if necessary, the sounds and vocabulary at his disposal. These terms, and others like them, are the finest human beings have developed. But even at their finest they will not do; they cannot be precise; they are a stammering to which we have simply grown accustomed. God, the nature of God, rises higher than our discourse. As He is the source of wisdom, we call Him wise; as He is the fullness of mercy, we call Him merciful. But the words fall short of His being.

Put thus, monotheism may strike us with the chill of an intellectual premise, necessary for an adequate interpretation of the universe but inaccessible to man, who is matter, transient and earth-bound. Indeed, these are the qualities that forever interfere with our ambition to understand the meaning of God in full. Fragments, approximations of this understanding, have been the privilege of the saintly in every age. Yet the more they beheld the more they saw that their ignorance was endless. It was as though one filled his cup once and again and once more and still again with water from the ocean; the sea was not diminished.

God's uniqueness and transcendence, however, have not discouraged the Jew from the effort to understand Him and cleave to His ways, for Judaism has also told him that the Lord is near unto them that call upon Him; to all that call upon Him in truth, God's proximity and majesty form a speculative paradox only if they are regarded as categories unrelated to man's own awareness of his shortcomings, to his perennial urge to supersede his *status quo* of deed and thought. To the self-satisfied, it is probably true, God is not nigh; otherwise, how could such a one be content? His charity is niggardly, his justice expedient, his patience mannered, when weighed against Him Whose qualities are a contradiction of the imperfect.

The very surpassing nature of God has taught the Jew that God is not only to be revered, but loved, that the Creator of the heavens and earth, and all that in them is, is also his Rock, his Father, his Shepherd, his Beloved. And in order to escape being remote from God he utilizes every phenomenon and occasion to remind him of the Creator and Father of all. This his prayers accomplish for him. A new morning begins; God has created this light, his morning liturgy reminds him. An evening arrives; and the prayers force upon him the realization that God's activity is once more manifest. For every occasion, experience, event, the Rabbis declared, man ought to pray. The sight of the rainbow, the new moon, a shooting star, the sea, a wise man; deliverance from peril; a visit to historic scenes, particularly those related to biblical history; good fortune, tragedy—each has its proper blessing, and these Rabbinic formulations are the Jew's memoranda. Nothing happens but that his thoughts are at once directed to God. Nothing is taken for granted, nothing is ordinary. Everything is alive with the reality of God, at once man's support and dwelling on high.

Man differs from all other creatures in that he is made "in the image of God." Because Judaism denies that God has any physical form, the image of God in this passage refers to man's mind, unduplicated self, individuality. Created in the image of God, all persons must be accorded the respect due to this dignity which the Divine grace has accorded them. There can, therefore, be no differentiation between various human personalities in their status before God. From the time when the prophet Amos declared, "Are ye not as the children of Ethiopians unto Me, O children of Israel" (9:7), until this day, Jewish religious teachers have continuously emphasized this doctrine. To Ben Azzai, the great teacher of the second century, the most inclusive principle of the whole Law is to be found in the verse "In the day that God created man, in the likeness of God made He him, male and female created He them" (Gen. 5:1-2). He considered this verse uniquely important because it expresses unequivocally the equality and dignity of all human beings, irrespective of nationality, sex, color, creed, or genealogical origin.

The discovery of self, of that element in each of us which is absolutely and unmitigatedly singular, is undated, never complete, and the most momentous experience of life. There are men who may recall that as children they never grasped or gave thought to phenomena of their individuality. Who can, however, recall the instant when that knowledge first pressed itself upon him? Dates, let us grant, are sometimes dispensable, and it may not be necessary to recall that exact instant. It is enough that the mature person recognizes the reality of that self. But even in maturity the recognition is only partial, not altogether clear. Though we find it impossible to picture ourselves disembodied, we know that our self is more than our body. That self is not merely our rational being, for this often may withdraw or fail—in sleep or in delirium—while the self, the "I," has not vanished. Yet awareness of our individuality, incomplete as that awareness may be, constitutes the final appeal and justification for our value. It cannot be exchanged.

Again, it is the prophets of Israel whom we must thank for the most vigorous emphasis on the supreme value of each soul *qua* its individuality. They, not alone but most clearly, saw that the classification of men according to color, the accident of ancestry or purely material condition was never more than secondary; and they, too, perceived that the relation of body to self was not definitive and exclusive.

To the prophets and later the Rabbis, the self therefore appeared so precious that they could not believe that it was coterminous with body. Man's body cannot be proxy for his personality; how then can the body determine life span? Even as self is something more than body, so its survival need not depend on body. Bearing in himself the image of God, man is also—Jewish doctrine insists—endowed with immortality. As conceived by most Jewish theologians, immortality implies the endless persistence of the human personality. This personality is believed to find its consummate expression in the ultimate reunion with God, and to lose all concern with the divisions, rivalries and antagonisms characteristic of physical life.

Attainment of this endless communion with God is the highest reward reserved for man, and its loss the greatest punishment he can suffer. The evil of wickedness consists, therefore, not merely in the harm it does a man in his mundane life, but in the fact that it deprives him of immortal existence. There are many Rabbinic authorities who believe, as do members of other faiths, that certain sinful people may attain immortal life, after having undergone temporary suffering after death. It is held in the Talmud that "the punishment of the wicked in Gehenna does not exceed twelve months." According to Maimonides, this punishment consists of the keen awareness by the soul of its failure to utilize its opportunities for the service of God, and is analogous to the shame sometimes felt by adults for unwise and unkind acts in their youth. We might almost say, the "righteous" is he who has refined and perfected his own self (and obviously other selves along with his own) so that there is an entity capable of reuniting with God; there is the "reward." The "wicked" is he who has neglected and demolished his self so that nothing survives the death of his body and there is an emptiness incapable of reunion with anything; God abhors a vacuum, and there is the "punishment." Be that as it may, a fundamental principle in Judaism, formulated as an ethical norm by Antigonus of Socho, one of the founders of Rabbinic Judaism, declares that men "should not be as servants, who serve their Master with the expectation of receiving reward, but rather as servants who serve their Master, without expectation of receiving reward." In other words, the belief in immortal life is accepted as a metaphysical and theological truth. But it is not to be considered a motive for proper conduct. Proper conduct should be based simply on love of God and the desire to see His Will performed in the world.

That the principle of "reward and punishment" cannot be translated into commercial or nursery terms was already demonstrated by the superb author of Job. In what sense the principle is to be understood remains a mystery, and man repeatedly collides with righteous who suffer and wicked who prosper. Unlike Job, most of us are not even granted the dramatic rejoinder that silences without answering all protest. But in some measure we escape utter confusion if we perceive that "reward" and "punishment" are terms often equatable with *result*. Rebellion against the Will of God, contempt for moral law, perversion of personality, cannot have peace, friendship or love as a consequence. These are the harvest, if harvest there is to be, of submission to God's Will, obedience to the demands of morality and integrity. The lines of the philosopher-poet Rab Saadia (882-942 C.E.) express this thought beautifully: "Not Thee, O Lord, have I injured, but myself. For if man sin, wherein doth that affect Thee? And if his transgressions be multiplied, how doth that harm Thee? But alas for the men who have sinned against Thee, and alas for their souls, for they have brought evil on themselves."

The mystery of reward and punishment remains a mystery; its truth is but too often vindicated; and for all that Judaism insists that conduct must be motivated by that love of God the fullest satisfaction of which is found when His Will is done. Many Rabbinic Sages endured personal affliction without murmur, but suffered anguish at the frustration of God's Will in the world through human sin and waywardness.

Because of God's love for men, He has made it possible for them to escape some of the consequences of error and sinful conduct. Most errors can be rectified through earnest repentance. Indeed, repentance sometimes makes it possible for the experience of error itself to become a virtue. The fact that a person has not lived in accordance with the discipline of religion does not, therefore, condemn him to suffering. It merely places on him the obligation to repent of his error and return to God. In this return to God he obtains the same measure of happiness awarded to the "righteous." Repentance, however, cannot always be achieved. If a man injures his neighbor, he will not be able to repent completely or win peace of mind until he has won the forgiveness of his neighbor. Rulers who mislead their people, causing whole nations and races to indulge in wrongdoing, and to that extent deflecting the development of human civilization, cannot repent.

To be effective, repentance must be more than sorrow or remorse; it must include a determination never again to commit the transgression, and a rearrangement of one's way of life so as to avoid the temptation to fall into the transgression. Thus, for example, if a person has been guilty of theft, repentance requires not merely restitution of the stolen article and a determination never to steal again, but also a study of the motives that led to the theft, and an endeavor to prevent them from being effective in the future.

One of the most important stimulants to the good life is the companionship of well chosen friends. It is a duty to select friends with a view to their probable influence on character. But the greatest possible deterrent from evil deeds or evil thoughts, the greatest stimulant to good, is the study of the Torah. It removes from man the temptation to infringe on the rights of others or the commandments of God. "He who faces temptation should diligently study Torah."

It is through the Law, the prophets, and the Holy Writings that God's Will was revealed to man. Literary excellence and wisdom do not belong to Scripture alone and the riches, artistic or intellectual or scientific, available in the world's classics are not to be minimized without grave sacrifice to civilization. But there is an excellence to Scripture which these other works do not share, for in Scripture came the expression of those truths whose nature has and will admit further elucidations, finer expansion, and interpretation—but never displacement. "It hath been told thee, O man, what the Lord doth require of thee: but to do justly, love mercy, and walk humbly with thy God." Time and discipline may teach us profound meanings of these ideals, meanings perhaps unknown to our predecessors. Dynamically, we may discover implications to these commandments which are thus far unsuspected. But that justice, mercy, humility, and other ideals fixed for man's destiny by Scripture are makeshift standards or temporary hypotheses, Judaism has never been even tempted to accept. There is a finality to these ideals, which does not mean that we know everything there is to know; what it does mean is that these ideals do represent the ends of being and ideal grace and that their removal from life is nothing less than blasphemy. Man is eternally obliged to discover fresh possibilities inherent in these ideals, to extend their applicability, and to be their recurrent expositor.

That is why, though other writings may share with Scripture properties of merit in one thing or another, Scripture is unique in its holiness. And that is why works devoted to the analysis and interpretation of Scripture, to its greater fulfillment, that were developed in its spirit, share in a degree its sacredness. Through the insight of the Talmud—the discussions of Scripture in the Palestinian and Babylonian academies, the commentaries on the Talmud, the codes based on these, and all instruction clarifying Scripture—we see light.

This is what Jews mean when they say the Law is immutable. The statement is not intended as a denial of progressive knowledge or illumination, or to affirm that everything had been discovered in antiquity. Much indeed is new under the sun. But the ultimate imperatives of the Holy Scriptures are absolute. They are not prudential or conditional.

The people to whom this revelation was made was the people of Israel, of which only a remnant now survives, known as the Jewish people. The fact that the people of Israel received the Law and heard the prophets does not, according to Jewish teaching, endow them with any exclusive privileges. But it does place upon them special responsibilities. "You only have I known of all the families of the earth," the first literary prophet (Amos) exclaimed, "therefore I shall visit all your iniquities upon you." These responsibilities—to observe the Law, to study it, to explain it, and to be its unwavering exponents—are expressed in the term "The Chosen People." For similar reasons the Hebrew language, in which these permanent ideals were articulated and recorded, is the holy language; and Palestine, the country where the prophets lived and whence spring so many discoveries of these extraordinary men, is the Holy Land.

Virtually every prophet in Scripture has predicted that in the fullness of time man will gain a more complete understanding of God and a reign of justice and peace on earth will be inaugurated. According to the interpretation of this prophecy in the Talmud and later writers, this age of universal peace will be established by a great, but humble teacher of the lineage of David: the Messiah. Reform and many Conservative Jews expect that the Messianic age will come about through the gradual enlightenment of men and through the work of many thinkers and teachers. All agree that the age will be one of profound and universal faith in God, recognition of human brotherhood, and an unprecedented knowledge of the universe. There will be no discrimination between persons because of sex, origin, faith, occupation, nationality, or any other reason. The evils of human origin will have been overcome; those inherent in nature will be mitigated through further knowledge and increased piety. In this world of brotherly love there will be no room for pride in achievement, nor for memories of past bitterness and oppression.

The prophetic tradition, originating in the teachings of Moses, may be considered a continuous endeavor, looking to the fulfillment of this vision. Together with other faiths derived from Scripture, Judaism has a unique contribution to make to the enlightenment of the world. Its special gift consists, in part, in the preservation of the Hebrew language and the original form of the Hebrew Scriptures, as well as in the transmission unchanged of the ethical ceremonial and intellectual disciplines that were native to the prophets and the later Sages.

The increased hatreds and persecution of our day do not weaken the Jew's faith in God and in His prophets, or his conviction that ultimately the age of universal human brotherhood will be established on earth. In the most trying moments of his own and world history, the Jew repeats with assurance the ancient declaration: "Thou are faithful, O Lord our God, and Thy words are faithful. And not one word of Thine shall ultimately remain unfulfilled; for Thou art a great, holy, Divine King."

There is a wide variety of interpretation among Rabbinical scholars, both ancient and modern, with regard to the concepts of Judaism. In some instances, the differences of interpretation are so great that it is difficult to speak of a concept as being basically or universally Jewish or Rabbinic. There are thus a number of concepts, each having its own limited authority and following.

This applies also to a degree to the fundamental beliefs which have been brought together in the best known Jewish creed, that of Maimonides. According to this creed, there are thirteen basic dogmas in Judaism. They are as follows:

1. The belief in God's existence.
2. The belief in His unity.
3. The belief in His incorporeality.
4. The belief in His timelessness.
5. The belief that He is approachable through prayer.
6. The belief in prophecy.
7. The belief in the superiority of Moses to all other prophets.
8. The belief in the revelation of the Law, and that the Law as contained in the Pentateuch is that revealed to Moses.
9. The belief in the immutability of the Law.
10. The belief in Divine providence.
11. The belief in Divine justice.
12. The belief in the coming of the Messiah.
13. The belief in the resurrection and human immortality.

This creed has been incorporated in the Jewish liturgy, in the famous hymn *Yigdal*. Nevertheless, various distinguished authorities, including such teachers as Hasdai Crescas[11a] and Joseph Albo, rejected the classification of the doctrines, and even denied the basic character of some of the doctrines themselves. Because of this divergence of opinion among the most eminent authorities on the subject, traditional Judaism cannot be described as having a universally accepted creed or formulation of its dogmas. This has led to the assertion that "Judaism has no dogmas." The assertion is true only to the extent already indicated. On the other hand, as Rabbi Albo pointed out, the requirement that Jews observe the discipline of the Law implies the belief in God, in Revelation, and in Divine providence.

Orthodox and Conservative Jews have in general followed the example of the ancient and medieval teachers in avoiding any effort to formulate a generally adopted Jewish creed, beyond the informal consensus of opinion found in traditional writings. As a result, there is still wide latitude of interpretation of Judaism among both Orthodox and Conservative Jews.

Reform Jews have tried to formulate a definite platform outlining the principles on which they agree, and which they believe basic to Judaism. The most recent platform is that adopted at a meeting of the Central Conference of American Rabbis (the organization of American Reform rabbis) in 1937. In this platform no effort is made to indicate the way Reform Judaism deviates from the Orthodox or Conservative interpretation of Judaism. And, indeed, the platform does not contain much to which Orthodox and Conservative groups can take exception. It is rather in its implications that by its direct statements that it deviates from tradition.

Known as the Columbus Platform from the Ohio city in which the meeting was held, the statement reads as follows:

In view of the changes that have taken place in the modern world and the consequent need of stating anew the teachings of Reform Judaism, the Central Conference of American Rabbis makes the following declaration of principles. It presents them not as a fixed creed but as a guide for the progressive elements of Jewry.

I. JUDAISM AND ITS FOUNDATIONS.

I. NATURE OF JUDAISM. Judaism is the historical religious experience of the Jewish people. Though growing out of Jewish life, its message is universal, aiming at the union and perfection of mankind under the sovereignty of God. Reform Judaism recognizes the principle of progressive development in religion and consciously applies this principle to spiritual as well as to cultural and social life.

Judaism welcomes all truth, whether written in the pages of Scripture or deciphered from the records of nature. The new discoveries of science, while replacing the older scientific views underlying our sacred literature, do not conflict with the essential spirit of religion as manifested in the consecration of man's will, heart and mind to the service of God and of humanity.

2. GOD. The heart of Judaism and its chief contribution to religion is the doctrine of the One, living God, Who rules the world through law and love. In Him all existence has its creative source and mankind its ideal of conduct. Though transcending time and space, He is the in-dwelling Presence of the world. We worship Him as the Lord of the universe and as our merciful Father.

3. MAN. Judaism affirms that man is created in the Divine image. His spirit is immortal. He is an active co-worker with God. As a child of God, he is endowed with moral freedom and is charged with the responsibility of overcoming evil and striving after ideal ends.

4. TORAH. God reveals Himself not only in the majesty, beauty and orderliness of nature, but also in the vision and moral striving of the human spirit. Revelation is a continuous process, confined to no one group and to no one age. Yet the people of Israel, through its prophets and sages, achieved unique insight in the realm of religious truth. The Torah, both written and oral, enshrines Israel's ever-growing consciousness of God and of the moral law. It preserves the historical precedents, sanctions and norms of Jewish life, and seeks to mold it in the patterns of goodness and of holiness. Being products of historical processes, certain of its laws have lost their binding force with the passing of the conditions that called them forth. But as a depository of permanent spiritual ideals, the Torah remains the dynamic source of the life of Israel. Each age has the obligation to adapt the teachings of the Torah to its basic needs in consonance with the genius of Judaism.

5. ISRAEL. Judaism is the soul of which Israel is the body. Living in all parts of the world, Israel has been held together by the ties of common history, and above all, by the heritage of faith. Though we recognize in the group loyalty of Jews who have become estranged from our religious tradition, a bond which still unites them with us, we maintain that it is by its religion and for its religion that the Jewish people has lived. The non-Jew who accepts our faith is welcomed as a full member of the Jewish community.

In all lands where our people live, they assume and seek to share loyally the full duties and responsibilities of citizenship and to create seats of Jewish knowledge and religion. In the rehabilitation of Palestine, the land hallowed by memories and hopes, we behold the promise of renewed life for many of our brethren. We affirm the obligation of all Jewry to aid in its upbuilding as a Jewish homeland by endeavoring to make it not only a haven of refuge for the oppressed but also a center of Jewish culture and spiritual life.

Throughout the ages it has been Israel's mission to witness to the Divine in the face of every form of paganism and materialism. We regard it as our historic task to co-operate with all men in the establishment of the kingdom of God, of universal brotherhood, justice, truth and peace on earth. This is our Messianic goal.

II. ETHICS.

6. ETHICS AND RELIGION. In Judaism religion and morality blend into an indissoluble unity. Seeking God means to strive after holiness, righteousness and goodness. The love of God is incomplete without the love of one's fellowmen. Judaism emphasizes the kinship of the human race, the sanctity and worth of human life and personality and the right of the individual to freedom and to the pursuit of his chosen vocation. Justice to all, irrespective of race, sect or class is the inalienable right and the inescapable obligation of all. The state and organized government exist in order to further these ends.

7. SOCIAL JUSTICE. Judaism seeks the attainment of a just society by the application of its teachings to the economic order, to industry and commerce, and to national and international affairs. It aims at the elimination of man-made misery and suffering, of poverty and degradation, of tyranny and slavery, of social inequality and prejudice, of ill-will and strife. It advocates the promotion of harmonious relations between warring classes on the basis of equity and justice, and the creation of conditions under which human personality may flourish. It pleads for the safeguarding of childhood against exploitation. It champions the cause of all who work and of their right to an adequate standard of living, as prior to the rights of property. Judaism emphasizes the duty of charity, and strives for a social order which will protect men against the material disabilities of old age, sickness and unemployment.

8. PEACE. Judaism, from the days of the prophets, has proclaimed to mankind the ideal of universal peace. The spiritual and physical disarmament of all nations has been one of its essential teachings. It abhors all violence and relies upon moral education, love and sympathy to secure human progress. It regards justice as the foundation of the well-being of nations and the condition of enduring peace. It urges organized international action for disarmament, collective security and world peace.

III. RELIGIOUS PRACTICE.

9. THE RELIGIOUS LIFE. Jewish life is marked by consecration to these ideals of Judaism. It calls for faithful participation in the life of the Jewish community as it finds expression in home, synagogue and school and in all other agencies that enrich Jewish life and promote its welfare.

The Home has been and must continue to be a stronghold of Jewish life, hallowed by the spirit of love and reverence, by moral discipline and religious observance and worship.

The Synagogue is the oldest and most democratic institution in Jewish life. It is the prime communal agency by which Judaism is fostered and preserved. It links the Jews of each community and unites them with all Israel.

The perpetuation of Judaism as a living force depends upon religious knowledge and upon the education of each new generation in our rich cultural and spiritual heritage.

Prayer is the voice of religion, the language of faith and aspiration. It directs man's heart and mind Godward, voices the needs and hopes of the community, and reaches out after goals which invest life with supreme value. To deepen the spiritual life of our people, we must cultivate the traditional habit of communion with God through prayer in both home and synagogue.

Judaism as a way of life requires in addition to its moral and spiritual demands, the preservation of the Sabbath, festivals and Holy Days, the retention and development of such customs, symbols and ceremonies as possess inspirational value, the cultivation of distinctive forms of religious art and music and the use of Hebrew, together with the vernacular, in our worship and instruction.

These timeless aims and ideals of our faith we present anew to a confused and troubled world. We call upon our fellow Jews to rededicate themselves to them, and, in harmony with all men, hopefully and courageously to continue Israel's eternal quest after God and His kingdom.

None of the basic doctrines of Judaism deals expressly with the teachings, principles or leading personalities of the younger religions derived from it. As Judaism antedates the origin of both Christianity and Mohammedanism, its views regarding both faiths are simply negative: it has not accepted their teachings. This attitude does not, however, prevent Judaism from endeavoring to appraise the significance and value of other faiths as spiritual and moral phenomena. Rabbi Jacob Emden (1697-1776), one of the foremost teachers in the history of Judaism, summarized the general Jewish view regarding Christianity in the following words:

It is, therefore, a customary observation with me that the man of Nazareth wrought a double kindness to the world: On the one hand he fully supported the Torah of Moses, as already shown, for not one of our Sages spoke more fervently about the eternal duty to fulfill the Law. On the other hand he brought much good to the Gentiles (if only they do not overturn his noble intention for them, as certain stupid people, who did not grasp the ultimate purpose of the New Testament have done; in fact, just recently I saw a book from the press whose author did not know himself what he had written; because, had he known what he had written, then his silence would have been more becoming than his speaking, and he would not have wasted his money nor spoiled the paper and the ink uselessly; just as among us are to be found stupid scholars who know not between their right hand and their left in the written, nor in the oral law, but deceive the world with a tongue that speaks arrogantly; but there are highly educated men of intelligence among the Christians, even as there are among the students of our Torah a few outstanding individuals, men of lofty erudition). For he (the man of Nazareth) forbade idol-worship and removed the image-deities, and he held the people responsible for the seven commandments, lest they be like the animals of the field; he sought to perfect them with ethical qualities that are much more rigorous even than those of the Law of Moses (as is well known), a policy that was surely just for its own sake, since that is the most direct way to acquire good traits. . . .[12]

None of the articles of faith in the creed of Maimonides deals with the holiness of Jerusalem, as the Holy City, or Palestine; yet the concept that Jerusalem, as the Holy City, and Palestine, as the Holy Land, have a special relation to the Jews and its religion is fundamental to all Judaism. Every service contains a petition for the welfare of the Holy City and the Holy Land, and it is a basic principle in Judaism that to provide for the settlement of the land of Israel is to fulfill one of the biblical commandments. A Jew seeing a city of Israel in ruins must recite the benediction of bereavement, for every member of the Jewish faith is expected to regard the desolation of the Holy Land as a personal loss.

In the centuries since the destruction of the Second Temple by Titus in 70 C.E. and the gradual diminution of the Jewish population of the Holy Land, many efforts were made to resettle the country, to reclaim its arable soil, to restore its ancient forests and rebuild its cities. The persecution of Jews in Russia and other East European countries toward the end of the nineteenth century gave new impetus to this movement (described elsewhere in this work[12a]). The whole endeavor culminated in the establishment of the State of Israel on the 5th of Iyyar, 5708 (May 14, 1948).

The problems of the new State, political, social, economic, and spiritual are enormous. As an independent State Israel claims allegiance only of its own nationals and inhabitants. But it also had declared that any Jew settling in Israel will be welcomed as a brother and become an Israeli citizen. Established in the Holy Land, the State under Jewish law is entitled to economic support from Jews everywhere. As the first State in almost 2,000 years in which the Jewish Sabbath and festivals are national holidays, and the Hebrew language an official tongue, its establishment clearly opened a new chapter in the history of Judaism and of the Jews. How the discussions of human relations in the Talmud and medieval Jewish writings will be translated into concrete policies, to what extent the solution of internal and external problems of the State of Israel will be affected by the tradition in which it is rooted, whether the civilization fostered in the State of Israel will in any wise differ from that of purely secular countries, how far the very soil of the Holy Land will determine the character of the community, are issues yet (1958) unresolved.

As a modern republic, the State of Israel grants freedom of worship to all its inhabitants. However, the manner in which the State will approach deviations within Judaism itself is as yet not clearly defined. After bitter debate permission was granted to establish in Jerusalem a synagogue modeled after American Reform temples; and there are several synagogues in Israel which follow the ways of American Conservative Jews. Nevertheless, the authoritative spokesmen for the Jewish religion in Israel are all committed in different degrees to what is in America called Orthodox Judaism.

The vast influx of Jews from North Africa, from Iraq, from Yemen, have brought to the State new problems of group relations and of accommodation among differences of traditional practice. Leading Israeli citizens and thinkers hope that the educational system, far more effective in Israel than in most other lands, will ultimately lead to a solution of the problems created by the new situations.

One of the remarkable developments following the emergence of the State was the renewed study of Scripture. Biblical archaeology has a fol-

STATE OF
ISRAEL
MAY 1949

LEGEND

State of Israel
Established by Armistice Agreements
Demilitarized area
Troop withdrawals
Israeli Lines
Arab Legion lines
Railroads

Scale of Miles
0   10   20   30

lowing, both professional and amateur, of truly astonishing proportions. The country is studded with talmudic academies. The discovery of the Dead Sea Scrolls has aroused new interest and concern with the development of ancient Jewish sects. Many of these studies are fostered with special vigor at the Hebrew University in Jerusalem.

Elements of Unity and Disunity in Judaism

From what has been said, it is clear that Judaism is not a unit in any organizational or institutionalized form. There is no person or group of persons to whom the Jewish people everywhere owe obedience, or whose views must be accepted by all Jews as authoritative and binding. The principle set down in Deut. 17, ff., making the Sanhedrin at the Temple in Jerusalem the final authority in the interpretation of Jewish law, lost some of its effectiveness when the Temple was destroyed by the Romans in the year 70, and became completely inoperative as the talmudic academies in Palestine lost their vigor. For a time the successive schools of Jabneh, Usha and Tiberias claimed this authority, but ultimately it ceased to be recognized. Every effort since that time to re-establish some center of authority has failed. At times local groups and even countrywide communities have agreed to recognize rabbinic or lay councils or individuals as their guides. During some periods, scholars and groups of scholars have been accepted over far wider areas. The views of the Geonim (the heads of the Babylonian academies from the seventh to the eleventh century c.e.) were considered binding on most Jewish communities of the Diaspora during that period. Ashkenazic Jews, in general, still follow the ordinances established by Rabbenu Gershom, the Light of the Exile, in the eleventh century, and by "the communities" of the Rhineland in succeeding centuries. Toward the end of the nineteenth century, Rabbi Isaac Elchanan Spektor, the Rabbi of Kovno, won recognition first as the leading guide in Jewish Law in his own country of Lithuania, and then throughout Russia and a large part of the Western world.

While there is thus no central Jewish religious organization, there have been various attempts to create worldwide organizations of Jews for special purposes. The most effective of these was the World Zionist Organization, which was expanded in 1929 through the addition of Jewish non-Zionists, and became the Jewish Agency for Palestine. But even the Jewish Agency did not include representatives of all Jewry, and claimed authority to act on behalf of the Jewish people only in connection with the establishment of a Jewish community and state in Palestine.

Organizations like the American Jewish Committee, the Order B'nai B'rith, the American Jewish Congress (part of the World Jewish Congress) and similar agencies in lands other than America, have arisen to make articulate special requests and wants of the Jewish community. The American Jewish Joint Distribution Committee has become a nationwide effort to provide assistance to Jews in distress abroad. The National Council of Federations and Welfare Funds represents virtually every large fundraising committee in the cities of the United States outside New York and Chicago, and has been constituted by philanthropic agencies throughout the country for mutual discussion of joint problems.

But Judaism seems to resist organization as a denominational group, and preserves the independence of its many diverse elements, despite the common bond of tradition and history. It does not seem likely that in any foreseeable time, any organization will be established approaching the strength and comprehensiveness of Judaism in the times of the Temple. Yet the ties of history make for consciousness of a *Keneset Yisrael* (the congregation of Israel) which Solomon Schechter translated into "Catholic Israel." This mystic, abstract entity existing without organization, power or authority, is the only bond that can be described as uniting the Jewish people.

THE SYSTEM OF BLESSINGS

The fundamental concept of the Jewish ceremonial system is that God continually reveals Himself in nature, in history, and in man's daily life. Each ceremony seeks to emphasize some aspect of this Divine revelation, and thus becomes a special means for communion between man and God. By stressing the common dependence of all men on God, ceremonies strengthen the sense of human kinship. By drawing attention to the phenomena of nature, they help develop man's sense of the aesthetic and increase his joy in the contemplation of beauty. By opening vistas of achievement and satisfaction, they help free him from subjection to material needs and desires, and enable him to fulfill his higher potentialities.

Jewish tradition has evolved the system of ritual blessings as an effective means for achieving continual realization of God's manifestation in the world. According to Rabbinic Law, a Jew is expected to recite a blessing whenever he enjoys any particular aspect of the world.

When he awakes, he thanks God for having created the day, for having granted him the power of sight, for the creation of the earth, for the gift of clothes, for the power to walk, and for the renewal of his strength in sleep. He also thanks God that he is not an idolator nor a slave. Mindful of the severity of woman's lot in the world, and her consequent inability to fulfill some of the rituals, the man recites a benediction that he is male, rather than female; while a woman thanks God that He "has created her according to His Will." The observant Jew also recites some verses from Scripture and a passage from the Talmud. Before doing so, he thanks God for the revelation through the Law, and for the commandment to study the Law.

Before sitting down to his morning meal, he is expected to recite special prayers. At the meal itself, both before and after eating, he recites prescribed blessings. These blessings are repeated at every meal. The blessing at the beginning of the meal is the simple benediction, "Blessed art Thou, O Lord, our God, King of the Universe, Who dost bring bread out of the ground." The blessing after the meal consists of four paragraphs. The first is devoted to thanks to God for supplying all men and indeed all living things with their daily needs. The second is an expression of gratitude for His having caused ancient Israel to inherit the Holy Land. The third is a prayer for the restoration of Jerusalem. The fourth paragraph is a blessing of God for His continued goodness to all men.

When three people eat together, the blessing after the meal is recited in unison. Such a group is popularly called *mezuman* (prepared), because before he begins the person reciting the grace asks whether all are prepared for it. If there is a guest at the table, the recital of the grace is assigned to him. If there are several guests, the most learned is expected to recite it. At the end of the grace, the person reciting it invokes a blessing on his host and the hostess: "May the All-merciful bless the master and mistress of this house, them, and their house, and their children, and all that is theirs; us, and all that is ours, as our ancestors, Abraham, Isaac, and Jacob were blessed."

At every meal attended by three or more persons "words of the Torah" should be spoken. If this is done, the meal becomes sanctified, and "it is as though they have partaken of the table of the Lord," i.e., of a sacrificial meal. In order to fulfill this requirement, it is customary to recite a psalm at every meal. Psalm 137 is recited on weekdays, and Psalm 126 on Sabbaths, festivals, and half-holidays. On festival occasions, and other occasions when it is possible, the recital of these psalms is supplemented by discussions of questions related to religious or spiritual life. To emphasize the sacred character of the meal, one's hands should be washed both before and after it, just as was done at sacrificial meals in the Temple.

In addition to these blessings which are recited virtually every day, there are special blessings to be repeated, such as those for the sight of the trees in the spring, a view of the ocean, a meeting with a friend after a long absence, the appearance of meteors, lightning, the rainbow, the new moon, the sight of strange creatures, the acquisition of new clothes[13] or new possessions, and the reception of good news. On hearing bad news, a special benediction must be recited, accepting the Divine judgment. This benediction, "Blessed art Thou, O Lord our God, King of the Universe, the true Judge," is also recited on the occasion of any bereavement. Finally, there are prayers prescribed for the afternoon and the evening and a concluding prayer at bedtime.

THE SYNAGOGUE AND THE PRAYERS

In ancient times, the center of Jewish worship was the Temple in Jerusalem, where sacrifices were offered in accordance with the prescriptions of the Law. But there were prophets in Israel even in the days of priests, and the prophets frequently organized prayer meetings at which people assembled for devotion and religious exhortation. From these meetings eventually the synagogue was to develop; and subsequently the church and the mosque. As the chief element in the Temple service was sacrifice, so that of the synagogue was prayer. The precedent for prayer was, of course, ancient. Abraham interceded with God on behalf of the people of Sodom. Fearing attack, Jacob uttered the beautiful prayer that contains the memorable words, "I am not worthy of all the mercies, and of all the truth, which Thou hast shown Thy servant; for with my staff I passed this Jordan, and now I am become two camps" (Gen. 32:11). Hannah came to the Temple to petition and praise the Lord. Indeed, Solomon in his dedication service referred to the Temple essentially as a house of prayer in which men would supplicate the Lord.

Even before the Exile, gatherings for prayer were to be found among the people. The Babylonian Exile and the return to Palestine,[14a] however, were especially instrumental in strengthening the synagogue. The institution offered an opportunity not only for pious devotion but for study as well, for it was at these assemblies that Scripture was read and explained. The assembly for worship, which proved of such importance in Palestine while the Temple at Jerusalem still endured, became indispensable when the Temple was destroyed. Since that time, the synagogue has been the sole sanctuary of the Jewish people.

The architecture of the synagogue varies according to country and age. The essential elements of the institution are the Ark containing the Scroll of the Law, a stand for the reader of the service who faces the Ark, and in most traditional synagogues a second stand in the middle of the gathering for the reading of the Law. In a large number of American synagogues, no provision is made for this second stand.

In accordance with the tradition derived from the Temple in Jerusalem, the "court of women" is separated from that of the men in traditional synagogues. It is either marked off by a partition or is situated in a gallery. Again, a considerable number of American synagogues, including most of the Conservative synagogues and all the Reform synagogues, have deviated from tradition in this respect, and permit men and women to sit together.

No human figures may be used in the decoration of the synagogue. However, it is permitted, and has even become customary, to depict on the Ark and elsewhere in the building a lion or an eagle, suggesting the latter half of the Rabbinical injunction: "Be bold as the leopard, fleet as the deer, light as the eagle, and strong as the lion, to do the will of thy Father Who is in Heaven." In many synagogues, the passage is inscribed over the reader's stand. It is also usual to place over the Ark a symbolic representation of the two tablets containing the Ten Commandments. Generally, only the first words of each of the commandments is inscribed on the tablets. The so-called Shield (or Star) of David found in many synagogue buildings, and otherwise in Jewish symbolism, is of unknown origin. But its use can be traced back to Rabbinic times.

In many synagogues, there is to be found over the reader's desk a candelabrum, or two candelabra, symbolic of that which stood in the Temple of Jerusalem. But because it is forbidden to set up in a synagogue an exact replica of the utensils used in the ancient Temple, such candelabra have, instead of seven, eight or nine, sometimes fourteen branches.[15a]

In further deference to the unique sanctity of the Temple, kneeling or prostrating oneself in the synagogue worship is forbidden, except on certain occasions in the services of the New Year's Day and the Day of Atonement. Prayers are said either standing or sitting. It is customary to bow one's head on entering the synagogue and while reciting certain portions of the prayers. In Orthodox and Conservative synagogues, men pray with covered heads. It is considered a violation of custom to perform any act of worship, including study of the Scripture or the Talmud, with uncovered head. This custom derives from that prescribed for the priests of the Temple in Ex. 28:40-42. The custom has been abandoned in most American Reform synagogues.

It has become customary to speak of Reform synagogues and Conservative synagogues, as temples. This change of name does not imply any difference other than those already indicated.

The essential element in the synagogue is, of course, not the building, but the community. Public worship may be conducted in a building or out of doors. But it can be held only in the presence of a congregation, which theoretically consists of a minimum of ten heads of households. For the purpose of prayer, and because of the difficulty in finding ten heads of households in very small communities, ten males (over thirteen years of age) are considered heads of households. The assembly of ten such people is called a *minyan* (quorum) sufficient for public service.

The group that habitually prays together each day develops an astonishing community of interest and personal friendship. It is the experience of many who attend synagogue services regularly that the ties of association between the members of a *minyan* is a source of especial delight. Because the daily attendance at prayer is usually small, each person counts; the failure of anyone to come, because of illness or for any other reason, may disrupt the services. Perhaps in no other relationship of life is the personal worth of the individual—no matter how humble his status—so unmistakable as in this religious worship, which requires ten adult Jews and cannot be performed with a lesser number, no matter how learned, how pious, or how distinguished.

Any adult male Jew may lead the congregation in public prayers. The rabbi participates simply as a member of the congregation. It has become usual in large congregations to appoint a special official to read the prayers, especially those of the Sabbaths and festivals. Such a reader is called a *hazzan*. In some congregations the *hazzan* has a choir to assist him. In Orthodox congregations, this choir consists only of men; in some Conservative and in all Reform congregations, women are also admitted to the choir. A number of passages in the service are traditionally sung by the whole congregation in unison. The tendency of modern Orthodox and Conservative synagogues is to extend this practice to include a much larger part of the service.

In addition to the *hazzan*, the congregation may require the services of a special reader for the Scriptures. He must be able not only to read the consonantal text of the Scroll without the aid of vowels, but must be expert in the traditional system of cantillation of the Scriptures. This system of chanting is of great historical interest, because at least certain parts of it, particularly that prescribed for use on the High Holy Days, are of great antiquity.

The duty of looking after the arrangements for the service, that is, seeing that the Scrolls are prepared for reading, that the prayer books are available for the worshipers, and that the members having special duties during the service know their assignments, devolves generally on a functionary called the *shammash* (sexton).

In addition to these officials, who generally are remunerated for their duties, American Jewish congregations usually have lay officers, a president, one or more vice-presidents, a secretary, a treasurer, and board of directors, upon whom devolves the responsibility for the material well-being of the congregation.

As already indicated, tradition expects every member of the Jewish faith to pray at least three times a day: in the morning, *shaharit;* in the afternoon, *minhah;* and in the evening, *maarib.* On Sabbaths and festivals, an additional prayer is assigned for morning service, called *musaf* (addition), to commemorate the special sacrifices offered on such days at the Temple in Jerusalem. On the Day of Atonement, a fifth prayer is recited at sunset. This prayer, in some respects the most solemn of the year, is called *neilah* (closing), and commemorates the service held at the Temple when its gates were closed at the end of the sacred day.

All these prayers should, so far as possible, be recited at a public service. But if it is difficult to arrange to participate in a public service, they can be recited in private (with omissions of certain portions which belong only to the public service). Most observant Jews attend synagogue services at least on the Sabbaths and holidays; every Orthodox and Conservative synagogue endeavors to arrange for public services also on weekdays.

The essential element in all these services is the prayer called *amidah* (literally, standing, so called because one must rise to recite it). The weekday version of this prayer consists of nineteen paragraphs. But in the original Palestinian form, given it by Rabban Gamaliel II eighteen centuries ago, it contained only eighteen paragraphs; and the prayer is therefore frequently called *shemoneh esreh* (eighteen).

At all services, except the evening service, this prayer is recited twice. It is first recited in an undertone by each individual in the congregation; and then aloud by the reader, on behalf of the congregation. The first and last three paragraphs of the *amidah* are identical for all the services. The first paragraphs consist of confessions of faith in God as the God of the Patriarchs, Abraham, Isaac, and Jacob; as the One Who gives strength to the living and new life to the dead; and as the Holy One, Who has no equal. The final paragraphs include a prayer for the return of God's presence to Jerusalem; an expression of gratitude for all the goodness God has shown; and a prayer for peace.

On the festivals, it is the rule in all Orthodox and in many Conservative synagogues, that the descendants of the ancient Aaronid priests bless the people before the final paragraphs of the public reading of the *musaf amidah*. The formula used in this blessing is that prescribed in Num. 6:22-27, "May the Lord bless thee and keep thee; may the Lord cause His countenance to shine upon thee and be gracious unto thee; may the Lord lift His countenance upon thee and give thee peace."

Before reciting this blessing, the descendants of Aaron who are in the synagogue remove their shoes (as was the custom in the Temple in Jerusalem). The Levites who are present in the synagogue then wash the hands of the Aaronids, who thereupon step forward, face the congregation, and recite the ancient blessing.

The middle paragraphs of the daily *amidah* contain petitions for the fulfillment of various needs for the granting of wisdom, repentance, and forgiveness, for the redemption of Israel, for the healing of the sick, for prosperous years, for the gathering of the dispersed, for the restoration of the Sanhedrin, for the suppression of tyranny, for the protection of the righteous, for the rebuilding of Jerusalem, for the coming of the Messiah, and for the acceptance of prayer.

All the prayers are for the good of the whole community. Petitions for private needs may be inserted in their appropriate place. For example, the prayer for a sick person may be included in the general prayer for the sick of the world.

On Sabbaths and festivals, these petitions for the satisfaction of material wants are omitted; for it is forbidden to consider material needs on such days. On these occasions there is a single prayer for a complete rest on the Sabbath, and for happiness on the festival.

At every service the silent reading of the *amidah* ends with the prayer which begins: "O my God! Guard my tongue from evil, and my lips from speaking guile. To such as curse me, let me be dumb. Let me, indeed, be as dust unto all. . . . If any design evil against me, speedily make their counsel of no effect, and frustrate their intentions."

At the morning and evening services the *amidah* is preceded by the recital of the *Shema* and the various benedictions with it. The *Shema* begins with the verse, "Hear, O Israel, the Lord is our God, the Lord is One" (Deut. 6:4), and includes Deut. 6:5-9, 11:13-21, and Num. 15:37-41. In all services the recital of the *Shema* is preceded by a blessing of God for His revelation in the Law, and is followed by a blessing for His redemption of Israel from Egypt. In the morning, there is also a blessing for the light, in the evening a blessing for the darkness.

Each of the services begins and ends with the recital of the *Kaddish*, an Aramaic prayer for the coming of the Kingdom of God. It is, in effect, a prayer on behalf of the congregation by the reader before he enters on his service and after he ends it. Its essential element is its first section, reading: "May the great Name of God be exalted and sanctified in the world which He created according to His will, and may He cause His Kingdom to come, in your lives and in your days, and in the lives of all the House of Israel; speedily, and in a short time. Amen."

In the course of time, it has become customary to recite this prayer at other parts of the service. Since the Middle Ages, it has been usual also for the observant Jew to recite it at services during the year of a bereavement, and on the anniversary of the death of his parents.

In the morning services held on Mondays and Thursdays (the market days of ancient Palestine, when a larger congregation would be available than on other weekdays), as well as on Sabbaths, festivals, new moons, and fast days, portions of the Five Books of Moses are read from the sacred Scrolls. The readings are so arranged that the whole of the Pentateuch is covered within a year. On Sabbath and festival mornings, as well as at the afternoon services on fast days, selections from the Books of the Prophets are read in addition to those from the Torah. Such a portion is called the *haftarah*, and the person reading it is called the *maftir*.

As stated above, the reading from the Torah is now assigned to a special functionary. In ancient times, the members of the congregation would each in turn perform this duty. In deference to this tradition, it is still customary to call various individuals to read special portions of the Torah, though they merely repeat the words *sotto voce*, while the reading aloud is the duty of the professional reader. There are seven such participants in the Sabbath morning reading of the Torah; six in that of the Day of Atonement, five in those of the festivals; four in those of new moons and the festival weeks; and three at all other services when the Torah is read. Whenever the Torah is read, the first person to be called must be a descendant of Aaron, if there is any in the synagogue. The second to be called must be a Levite, and the others are chosen from the remainder of the congregation. When the prophetic portions are read at the morning services of the Sabbaths and festivals, an additional person is called for that purpose. He may be either an Aaronid, a Levite, or any other Israelite.

There are certain occasions when it is considered an especial obligation to participate in the public reading of the Torah. The most important of these are the Sabbath succeeding a boy's thirteenth birthday; the Sabbath preceding one's marriage; the anniversaries of the death of one's parents; and the Sabbath following one's recovery from illness or escape from danger. It is usual for persons who are thus required to participate in the reading of the Scriptures to be assigned to the *haftarah*. A person recovering from illness or escaping from danger recites a special blessing on the occasion, saying: "Blessed be Thou, O Lord, our God, King of the Universe, Who dost grant kindness to the undeserving, and Who has granted me every good." The congregation, hearing the blessing, responds, "He Who has granted thee kindness, may He ever continue to grant thee kindness." This ceremony is usually performed when such a person is called to read from the Torah in synagogue. But the blessing may be recited, if necessary, simply in the presence of the congregation. Thus a woman after childbirth should, on her first appearance in the synagogue, recite this blessing and receive in return the good wishes of the congregation.

The language of the prayers of the traditional service is for the most part Hebrew. However, a number of prayers are in Aramaic, the vernacular of the Jews in the first centuries of the Common Era in Palestine and Babylonia. At the present time the proportion of Hebrew to some other language (in America, for example, English) will vary with the individual congregation. But everywhere some portions of the public service are read in Hebrew.

According to Rabbinic tradition, it is customary for men to wear a prayer shawl called the *tallit* (garment) during the morning prayers. This prayer shawl is a square or oblong woolen cloth, with fringe at each of its four corners. It is a very ancient garment, probably worn in antiquity as a cloak. The purpose of the fringe (*sisit*) at the four corners is explained in the Bible: "That ye may look upon it and remember all the command-

ments of the Lord and do them . . . and be holy unto the Lord your God"
(Num. 15:39-40). In addition, it is customary for men to don the *tephillin*
(phylacteries) during the morning services on weekdays. These *tephillin*
consist of two boxes of parchment to which are attached long leather straps.
In the boxes are deposited little strips of parchment with the contents of
Ex. 11:16, 13:1-10; Deut. 6:4-9, 11:13-21. The Bible also gives the meaning of this symbol: "And it shall be for a sign unto thee upon thy hand,
and for a memorial between thine eyes, that the Law of the Lord may
be in thy mouth; for with a strong hand hath the Lord brought thee out
of Egypt" (Ex. 13:9). To the ancient Rabbis the *tephillin* on the head,
and on the left arm close to the heart, represented the concentration of the
intellect and the emotion on the Divine. As Maimonides subsequently expressed it: "As long as the *tephillin* are on the head and on the arm of a
man, he is modest and God-fearing; he will not be attracted by hilarity or
idle talk, and will have no evil thoughts, but will devote all his thoughts
to truth and righteousness."

Two of these biblical sections, namely, Deut. 6:4-9 and 11:13-21, are
also inscribed on pieces of parchment which are placed in receptacles, attached by the observant Jew to the doorposts of every room. Such receptacles are called *mezuzot* (literally, doorposts). These inscriptions are
intended to remind man, as he enters home or leaves it, of the unity of God
and of the duty of loving Him.

THE SABBATH AND THE FESTIVALS

While according to the Jewish faith God's presence can be felt at any
time and place, there are times, just as there are places, which through their
associations have come to lead especially to communion with God. Of these
the most important are the Holy Days and the fast days. The Holy Days,
according to the Jewish ritual, are the *Shabbat* or Sabbath, celebrated on
the seventh day of each week, *Pesach* (Passover), *Shabuot* (Pentecost),
Rosh Ha-Shanah (the Jewish religious New Year's Day), *Yom Kippur*
(Day of Atonement), and *Sukkot* (Tabernacles).

In order that these days may be devoted as completely as possible to
the spiritual life, work is forbidden on them. This prohibition includes not
only all gainful occupation, but also household tasks.

As a result of these various prohibitions, the Sabbath and festivals become virtually periods of cessation of all labor on the part of observant
Jews. Because of the difficulties involved in maintaining this rigid discipline
in an industrial society, many Jews otherwise very observant do not refrain
from all labor on the Sabbath. Nevertheless, even among these a large
number set aside the free hours of the day for spiritual contemplation and
for prayer, and mark the Sabbath with the ceremonials devoted to it.

Theoretically, observant Jews should not benefit from the willingness of members of other faiths to perform tasks for them on the Sabbath day. But because of the severity of the winters in northern and central Europe, and the consequent danger of disease, it became customary in the Middle Ages to permit people who were not Jews to kindle the fire for the Jews on the Sabbath. As a result, in time Christian and Moslem boys came to look after the heating of Jewish homes on the Sabbath. In recent centuries, people of other faiths also extinguish lights for Jews on the Sabbath, on the theory that rest is as imperative for health as warmth.

In the Jewish religious calendar, the observance of festivals begins a little before sunset on the preceding day. Because no fire is kindled on the Sabbath, it has been customary from time immemorial for Jewish housewives to conclude all their household arrangements for the day of rest by preparing the lights, which have therefore become known as the "Sabbath lights." The great antiquity of this usage, and the significance that came to be attached to it, have sanctified it, and consequently in modern Jewish homes the Sabbath candles are lit, even though other means of illumination are available and are in use. Many a Jew has tender memories of his mother lighting the Sabbath candles. As their light is not to be enjoyed by her before the blessing, the Jewish mother with her hands over her eyes recites, "Blessed art Thou, O Lord our God, King of the Universe, Who has sanctified us with Thy commandments, and commanded us to kindle the Sabbath lights."

In the absence of the mother of the household, the lights are kindled by someone acting for her. If by chance the lights have not been kindled on a Sabbath, it is customary for her to kindle an additional light before every Sabbath afterward throughout her life.

The beauty and impressiveness of the custom of the Sabbath lights has caused it to be extended, so that similar lights are now kindled also on festivals for which the use of fire is permitted, and when therefore there is no special reason for lighting candles before dark. In kindling the lights on the seasonal festivals the mother recites the special prayer of thanks for life called *sheheheyanu* (Who has kept us alive), "Blessed art Thou, O Lord our God, King of the Universe, Who hast caused us to live, and attain this day."

Evening services are held in the synagogue on the eve of festivals and Sabbaths at dusk. After the services, the members of the family return home for the Sabbath meal. On the table are placed a flask of wine and two loaves of bread. The Sabbath loaf of bread is called by its Hebrew name, *hallah* (plural, *hallot*, or as popularly pronounced, *hallos*). The two loaves of bread are said to symbolize the double share of manna God granted the Israelites in the wilderness on Fridays to provide for the Sabbath (Ex. 16:5). It is customary in many localities to prepare these loaves in an especially attractive form, made of twisted strands of dough. On festivals, the bread is further enriched by a plentiful supply of raisins. (On Passover the bread is replaced by unleavened cakes.) Recalling the ancient Rabbinic custom of setting the table only after the Sabbath or festival has been ushered in, the loaves of bread are covered with a napkin, and remain concealed, while the head of the household takes a cup of wine, and recites over it the blessing called the *kiddush*, or sanctification of the day. This blessing consists of a prayer of thanks to God for the gift of the wine, and then for the gift of the special festival. The head of the household drinks some of the wine, and distributes the rest among the others present. On seasonal festivals, the *kiddush* also includes the blessing *sheheheyanu*, mentioned above. Then follows the ritual washing of the hands, the blessing for the bread, the breaking of the bread, the meal itself, the special hymns of the Sabbath or festival meal, and the blessing after the meal.

In many Conservative and Reform congregations, special services on Sabbath eve are held after the Sabbath meal. These services are intended to enable those men and women who because of modern industrial conditions do not attend the traditional service at dusk to commune with God during the course of the holy day. The ritual used at these services varies considerably. In some congregations it is the usual Sabbath eve service. In others it consists of the hymns sung at the Sabbath evening meal. In virtually all congregations where such services are held it is customary to include a sermon by the rabbi.

The Sabbath and festival morning service are longer than those of the weekdays, and occupy most of the morning hours. As it is considered improper to eat before prayers, traditional Jewish homes do not provide any breakfast on Sabbaths or festivals. The ritual of the noon meal is similar to that of the evening. It includes a blessing over the cup of wine, the blessing for the bread, the breaking and distribution of the bread, the meal itself, and the blessing after the meal.

In observant homes it is customary to arrange for another meal to be served in the late afternoon of the Sabbath day, so as to complete three Sabbath meals. This third meal is called *seudah shelishit* (third meal) or, more popularly and less correctly, *shalosh seudot* (three meals). No wine need be drunk before the third meal, but the blessing for the bread is recited as usual.

In Israel it has become customary within the past generation, as a result of the influence of the famous Hebrew poet, Hayyim Nahman Bialik,[16a] to substitute for the third meal a public gathering, preferably one at which refreshments are served, called *oneg shabbat* (the delight of the Sabbath). The practice of holding such gatherings has become an institution in other parts of the world, and is rapidly being adopted by congregations in the

United States. It is an effort to bring people together on the Sabbath afternoon for a discussion of religious, literary, or ethical problems, while participating in a symbolic Sabbath meal.

The Sabbath is concluded about half an hour after sunset with a blessing called *habdalah* (division, that is, marking the division between the Sabbath and the weekdays). A flask of wine and a box of incense are set on the table, and a light is struck. It seems appropriate that the workaday week should begin with the taste of the wine, the odor of the incense, and the appearance of the light, which, satisfying three different senses, increase man's awareness of his dependence on God for all his needs. The blessing consists, therefore, of thanks to God for the gift of the wine, of the incense, and of the light; and ends with further thanks for the division between the Sabbath and the weekdays. It is customary to let the cup of wine for *habdalah* overflow, as a symbol that the happiness of the week may likewise overflow. It is also customary to use a candle with three or four wicks (resembling an ancient torch) for the light of the *habdalah*.

The same ritual of *habdalah* is recited in the synagogue, in order to provide for those who cannot observe it in their homes. It also concludes the Day of Atonement and, with the exception of the blessing for the incense and the light, all the other festivals.

The rigid prohibition of work on the Sabbath does not, as is frequently believed, make it a day of gloom for the observant Jew. On the contrary, the complete release from all mundane concern, the concentration on the study of the Torah, and the joy in the sense of communion with God, make it a day of great, though perhaps indescribable, delight. To participate in the observance of the Sabbath gives such happiness that one of the prayers added to the blessing after the meal on the day asks that Paradise may be one long Sabbath. As twilight descends on Sabbath afternoon, some feel an ineffable sense of yearning and loneliness, which the mystics among the Jews have characterized as the loss of part of one's soul.

Aside from the Sabbath, the major Jewish festivals are Passover, Pentecost, New Year's Day, the Day of Atonement, and the Feast of the Tabernacles. Each of these is, according to tradition, a day of judgment for all mankind. "On Passover the world is judged regarding its grain; on Pentecost regarding the fruits of the tree; on New Year's Day [and also on the Day of Atonement] all creatures pass before God in review; and on Tabernacles they are judged concerning the rain."

While this consciousness of judgment gives an air of solemnity to all the festivals, the three festivals of the ancient pilgrimages, Passover, Pentecost, and Tabernacles, are primarily periods of joy. The manner in which the joy of the festival is combined with the sense of solemnity and judgment before God is difficult to explain to the uninitiate. The festival prayers, as well as the special melodies which in certain rituals accompany them, reflect a feeling of awe, arising from the sense of communion with God as Judge and Ruler of the universe; yet united with this feeling and permeating it is a sense of confidence that His judgment will be one of mercy rather than severity, as that of a father upon his child. The joy of the festival is thus prevented from becoming one of physical pleasure or self-indulgence. Ideally conceived, it is a joy arising largely from participation in synagogue and home rituals, that bring about a closer communion with God.

The significance of each festival is enhanced through the natural and historical interpretations associated with it. All are intended to increase man's faith in God by reference to His revelation in the natural order and also in the succession of human events. Their symbols are particularly significant in an industrial and commercial civilization, where man tends to be separated from nature; and their reflection of the Divine purpose in history gives one strength in times of international crisis, and fills one with humility in moments of peace and prosperity. The purpose of the festivals may thus be said to place human life in both its cosmic and historical perspectives. They enable man to see himself both as part of nature and as distinguished through the providence of God. Passover, occurring on the full moon of the first month of spring (toward the end of March or the beginning of April), is the great festival of the rebirth of nature, and also commemorates historically the Exodus from Egypt. The concentration of Jews in the cities during past centuries has tended to minimize the agricultural aspect of the Passover. Nevertheless, certain ancient customs emphasizing the seasonal character of the festival are still observed. The first month of spring in Palestine marks the end of the rainy season and the beginning of the dry season. In this dry season the crops are saved from destruction by a heavy dew each night. Hence Passover became a festival of prayer for the dew, and the *musaf* (additional) prayer of the first day of Passover is dedicated to petition for copious dew on the earth. The second night of Passover was celebrated in ancient Palestine as the beginning of the barley harvest. In accordance with Lev. 23:14, no part of the new crop might be eaten before that night, when the first sheaf (the *omer*) was harvested and prepared as a sacrifice to God. While the observance of the sacrifice is impossible today, it is still customary for men of great piety in European communities to avoid eating new grain before the second night of Passover. All traditional Jewish communities mark the second night of Passover as the beginning of the barley harvest in ancient Palestine; and, following a literal interpretation of Lev. 23:15-16, include in the daily evening service an enumeration of the forty-nine days from that night until Pentecost, the festival of the wheat harvest.

But the historical significance of Passover as commemorating the Exodus and the promulgation of the idea of freedom in the world has far overshadowed the agricultural phase of the festival. The ceremonies prescribed for the festival in Scripture and the additional rules established by the Rabbis have as their purpose emphasis on the idea of human liberty and equality. The most obvious characteristic of the festival is the use of the unleavened bread (called *massah*, pronounced *matzah*), the bread of affliction (Deut. 16:3), recalling to each Jew the bondage of his ancestry in Egypt, and emphasizing by inference his equality with the humblest and most oppressed of men. The significance of the custom has become such that it is observed with greater precision than almost any other law in Scripture. Observant Jews abstain on the festival from eating not only any leavened bread but even any food which might conceivably have a taste or trace of leaven. The grain used for *massah* is carefully examined to see whether any of it has become leaven. The examination is usually performed by a rabbi, who takes a sampling. If he finds that none in his sample has become leaven, the contents of that granary may be used for Passover. After the examination, the grain must be carefully guarded against moistening that might cause it to leaven. The mills in which it is ground are carefully scoured and purified from all leaven. The flour is then again guarded from moisture, until it is brought to the bakery. In the bakery, expert mechanics and especially devised machines make it possible to prepare the dough and bake it with such speed that no leavening can take place. No salt and of course no yeast or any material other than flour and water enter into the making of the *massah*. After the *massah* has been baked, it may be ground again into flour (*matzah* meal), which can then be used for making pastries and other dishes for consumption on the Passover.

Traditional observance of the Passover requires that no prepared food such as dried fruits or vegetables shall be used, unless it has been made certain that not a speck of flour attaches to them. For this reason, raisins, prunes, coffee, pepper, and similar foods are used by observant Jews during the Passover only if they are prepared under the supervision of a rabbi. Dried peas or beans may not be eaten under any circumstances. Ashkenazic Jews do not eat rice on Passover, though following the tradition of their ancestors, Jews of Sephardic descent consider it permitted.

Special cooking utensils and dishes are set aside for the Passover week, so that no utensils or dishes which have contained leaven will come in contact with the Passover food. Families which cannot afford a complete set of special dishes may cleanse their metal utensils and certain types of glassware for use during the Passover week. Such cleansing must follow the ritual prescriptions, and should be done only after consultation with a rabbi.

To purify the home from all leaven before the Passover, it is customary on the night before the festival eve to "search the house" for any bread or leaven. In earlier ages, this searching had the practical purpose of discovering such leaven, for in the simple one-room homes of the ancient East it was possible to delay the removal of leaven until the night before the festival. In modern homes, this cleaning naturally occupies several days or even weeks, and the ritual searching for the leaven has become almost a formal custom. Nevertheless, it is observed in most Orthodox and Conservative homes. The head of the household searches for the leaven, removes all he finds, and puts it aside until the next morning, when it must be burned during the first quarter of the day, that is, around 9:00 A.M. After that hour it is forbidden to eat or to own leavened food. As it is usually difficult to destroy all the leavened food in a home and impossible to dispose of all the dishes used for leavened food, many groups of observant Jews transfer the title of their leavened food to the rabbi of the community during the Passover week. The rabbi in turn technically transfers the title to a member of another faith.

On the first and second nights of Passover there is celebrated a unique home service called the *seder* (order), because the whole meal follows a prescribed ritual order. In addition to a festive gathering of the whole family in each household, strangers separated from their families are invited as guests. In communities where the number of strangers is considerable, provision is frequently made for a group *seder* at a public institution.

The poignant beauty of the *seder* service leaves an indelible impression on every Jewish child who participates in it. It is in effect a pageant in which ancient Palestinian life is re-created in as detailed and precise a form as possible. The head of the household (or, at a public celebration, the leader of the service) is provided with a divan on which after the fashion of the ancients he may recline during the meal and the celebration. According to some rituals, he is expected to don a *kittel,* a white linen garment worn in ancient Jerusalem on festive days.

The service followed at the *seder* is described in a special prayer book, the *Passover Haggada*. This book contains directions for arranging the Passover dish to be placed before the master of the house, and detailed instructions for the procedure during the service.

One of the most significant elements in the *seder* is its highly developed pedagogical technique. In order to impress the child, he is urged to observe the various ceremonies and to ask for their explanation. As the service is recited it thus becomes fundamentally a reply to these questions. The child is informed that the celebration is in memory of the Exodus from Egypt; he is told the story of the Israelite bondage; of the redemption of the people through the mercy of God; and is taught to respect the liberty he has inherited through this redemption.

At the end of the Passover meal, which is eaten in the course of the *seder,* the door is opened as a symbol of the entry of Elijah the Prophet. A cup of wine, "the cup of Elijah," is filled, the whole company rise, and cry, "Blessed is he who has come!" The concept that Elijah, the immortal prophet, visits every Jewish home on the Passover eve emphasizes the significance of the festival as a symbol of eternal freedom, as well as memorial of a past emancipation; for Elijah is the prophet who, according to the words of Malachi, will be the precursor of God's establishing His Kingdom on earth, at the end of days.

The *seder* ends with the recital of various psalms, the tasting of a fourth and final cup of wine, the singing of various hymns, and finally with popular songs dating from medieval times. In many communities the head of the household concludes the whole service by reading Canticles (The Song of Songs). The joyful spirit of youth, which permeates that portion of the Bible, seems appropriate for the spring festival; and its allegorical meaning as an epic of God's relation to Israel is particularly fitting for recollection on the festival of the Exodus.

The period between Passover and Pentecost is now observed in many Jewish communities as one of partial mourning, because it is traditionally described as the time when the disciples of Rabbi Akiba, one of the foremost teachers of the Talmud,[17a] died. Except for certain special days within the period, no weddings are celebrated by observant Jews; and they also abstain from listening to music, attending the theater, or other pleasures.

The thirty-third day of this period, called *Lag Ba'Omer* (literally, the thirty-third day of the *Omer*), is a half-holiday, devoted to the celebration of weddings and other festivities. It is sometimes said to be the anniversary of the death of Rabbi Simeon ben Yohai, the foremost disciple of Rabbi Akiba, which is marked in this way as the occasion of his translation to the Heavenly Academy. To this time it is therefore customary in Israel to mark the day with a festive pilgrimage to the supposed grave of Rabbi Simeon in Meron, a village of Galilee.

Pentecost, or *Shabuot* (occurring toward the end of May or the beginning of June), is described in Scripture primarily as the festival of the wheat harvest (Ex. 23:16). But it also commemorates the Revelation on Mt. Sinai, and is therefore the festival of the Ten Commandments. The reading of the Law assigned to it covers the chapter telling the story of the Revelation (Ex. 19:20); the liturgy of the day is also dedicated in part to commemorating this incident. In many Orthodox congregations, the evening of the first night of Pentecost is spent in reading Scriptural passages. Among some especially pious Jews, it is customary to remain awake all night, reading the Bible and the Talmud. In many modern congregations, the first day of Pentecost is celebrated by the confirmation of boys and girls.

The third of the great joyous festivals is that of Tabernacles, or *Sukkot,* marking the coming of the autumn and the late harvests (some time in October), and also commemorating God's protection during the period when Israel dwelt in the wilderness (Lev. 23:43).

Both the seasonal and the historical aspects of the festival are symbolized in the *sukkah*, the booth in which observant Jews eat their meals during the holiday week. This booth is essentially a rustic cabin, with improvised walls, and a covering of leafy branches and twigs instead of a solid roof or ceiling. Both the covering and the walls are usually adorned with vegetables and fruits, in order to emphasize the harvest rusticity of the surroundings.

The festival is celebrated further by the ceremonial of the *lulab*, a cluster of a palm branch, three myrtle twigs, and two willow sprigs. During the recital of the *hallel* (i.e., Ps. 113-118) in the morning service of the festival, the *lulab*, together with a citron, is taken in hand, and at certain portions of the prayer, they are moved to and fro, eastward, southward, westward, northward, upward, and downward, to indicate that God, Who is being thanked for His gifts, is to be found everywhere. At the end of the service, a Scroll is taken out of the Ark, and each of those having a *lulab* marches about the Scroll in a festive procession, commemorating the similar procession about the altar in Jerusalem in the days of the Temple. On the seventh day of *Sukkot* (*Hoshanna Rabba*) there is a special service of prayer for abundant rains. After the usual service of the day, the palm branches are put down, and the willow (symbolic of abundance of rain, because it grows by the river) taken up. With these willow sprigs in hand, the congregation recites various hymns having the refrain *hoshanna* (or, as it was frequently pronounced in ancient times, *hosanna*), meaning "Help, we pray Thee." At the end of these hymns, the willows are beaten against the floor of the synagogue.

Following *Hoshanna Rabba* is the "eighth day of solemn assembly" or, as it is called in Hebrew, *Shemini Azeret*. This festival is intended as a climax for the joyful season, which begins with *Sukkot*. The festival is marked especially by the prayer for rain in the additional (*musaf*) service, which is therefore called *tephillat geshem* (the prayer for rain).

The final, or ninth, day of the autumn celebration (properly the second day of the *Shemini Azeret* festival) is popularly called *Simhat Torah* (the day of rejoicing in the Law). On this day, the last section of the Five Books of Moses, *viz.*, Deuteronomy 34, and the first section of Genesis are read. In celebration of the annual completion and fresh beginning of the reading of the Pentateuch, all the Scrolls of the Law are taken from the Ark and carried about the synagogue in a procession. To enable every member of the congregation to participate in this ceremonial, the procession moves about the synagogue hall at least seven times in the evening, and then seven times more at the morning service. It is also customary in certain rituals for each member of the congregation to participate in the public reading of the Pentateuch on *Simhat Torah*. Immediately before the reading of the last section of the Pentateuch, it is customary in most congregations to call to read from the Torah one of the distinguished members of the congregation together "with all the children" (Hebrew, *kol ha-nearim*), so that even minors may participate in the reading on this occasion.

The person called to complete the reading of the Pentateuch on *Simhat Torah* is called *hatan ha-torah* (bridegroom of the Law, popularly pronounced, *hoson torah*). The person called to read the first chapter in Genesis on that day is called *hatan bereshit* (the bridegroom of the beginning, popularly pronounced, *hoson bereshis*). These offices are usually bestowed on men of especial piety or learning, and are among the highest honors that can be given in the synagogue service.

While on these festivals communion with God is sought through joy, on *Rosh Ha-Shanah* and *Yom Kippur* it is sought through solemnity. They are described as Days of Judgment when all living things pass before God, to stand in judgment for their deeds during the past year. During the month before *Rosh Ha-Shanah* (which usually occurs during the last three weeks of September or the beginning of October) preparation is made for the festival by sounding a ram's horn, or *shofar*, at the synagogue service each morning, and reciting Psalm 27 each morning and evening. Beginning with the Sunday preceding *Rosh Ha-Shanah* (if *Rosh Ha-Shanah* occurs on Monday or Tuesday, beginning with the Sunday of the preceding week), special prayers (called *selihot*) are recited at dawn of each day, beseeching Divine forgiveness for man's transgressions. While only the most pious assemble at the synagogue to recite these prayers each day, many recite them on the first day, and on the day before *Rosh Ha-Shanah*. In some congregations, these prayers are recited at midnight rather than at dawn, to make possible a larger attendance.

The festival of *Rosh Ha-Shanah* itself is particularly devoted to prayers for peace and prosperity for all mankind, and for life and happiness for individual human beings. It also emphasizes the recognition of God as King of the Universe. This phase of the festival is reflected not only in the prayers of the day, but in several of the ceremonials. The *shofar* is sounded before, during, and after the additional morning prayer. The notes sounded by the *shofar* tend to arouse the people to repentance, reminding them that the Kingdom of God can be realized in our hearts and in our personal lives, even in the world in which we live. In the afternoon of the first day of the festival it is customary in many communities to walk to a river bank, as was sometimes done in ancient times at the anointing of a king. This custom is called *tashlik* (throwing), because of the popular belief that it is intended to cast off one's sins into the river.

On the evening of the first day of *Rosh Ha-Shanah* it is customary to eat apples and other fruits, dipped in honey, saying, "May it be Thy will that this year shall be happy and sweet for us." In many localities bread is dipped in honey at all the meals eaten on *Rosh Ha-Shanah,* and during the days following it until the Day of Atonement. On the second evening of *Rosh Ha-Shanah* it is customary to eat new fruit, over which the blessing *sheheheyanu* (Who has kept us alive) is recited.

The ten days beginning with the first days of *Rosh Ha-Shanah* and ending with *Yom Kippur,* are called the "Ten Days of Penitence." It is expected that everyone will observe particularly high standards of ethical and ceremonial conduct during these days. There are special prayers assigned for the period, beseeching continuance of life and peace, and the *selihot* are recited on them as on the days preceding *Rosh Ha-Shanah.*

On the day preceding *Yom Kippur* (the ninth of Tishri) tradition prescribes festive meals. The final meal of the day, eaten before the sundown that ushers in *Yom Kippur,* thus is marked by a peculiar combination of joy and solemnity. Before eating this meal, an oral confession of sins is recited by each person as part of the afternoon prayer. It is also customary during the day to distribute money for charitable purposes. After the meal the head of the household kindles a lamp or candle to burn for twenty-four hours, that is, until the end of the day. The mother kindles the usual festival lights, and the family proceeds to the synagogue.

The Day of Atonement is a season not only for repentance for trespasses against the ceremonial law but more especially for trespasses committed against ethical conduct in relations between men. Forgiveness for these trespasses can be obtained only when the man who suffered wrong pardons the injustice. It is therefore customary for anyone who is conscious of having injured a neighbor to obtain forgiveness before the Day of Atonement.

Men and women may unwittingly injure even those dear to them, including members of their families. Such thoughtlessness may raise a barrier to friendship and love. The eve of the Day of Atonement is considered an appropriate time to remove these barriers; relatives and friends call upon each other or write, offering good wishes for the coming year and either directly or indirectly asking forgiveness for any misunderstanding. Parents and grandparents bless their children and grandchildren. The moving prayer which is recited just before the evening service closes with the words: "I completely forgive anyone who has committed a trespass against me, whether against my person or against my property. . . . May no man suffer punishment because of me. And may it be Thy will, that just as I offer my forgiveness to all my fellows, that I may find grace in their eyes, so that they, too, will forgive my trespasses against them."

The Day of Atonement thus becomes a day for the renewal of bonds of affection and friendship.

The evening service in the synagogue, which must be recited before dark, is called *kol nidre* from its first words (meaning all vows), and is a service of absolution for ceremonial vows. This ceremony is made necessary by the rule of Jewish Law requiring fulfillment of every vow, even at great sacrifice. The vows that the ceremony of *kol nidre* releases are of course only those relating to ritual and custom. Without the consent of his neighbor, no ceremony can release anyone from a vow or promise made to his neighbor.

Because the *kol nidre* opens the service of the Day of Atonement, it is a particularly solemn ceremony. Its melody is probably the best known of all those associated with synagogue services.

The Day of Atonement is the major fast in the Jewish calendar, a day on which all principal sensual pleasures are interdicted. Men of piety also avoid wearing shoes made of leather on this day, particularly in the home or in the synagogue.[18]

The prayers of *Yom Kippur* are so arranged that they continue uninterruptedly from their beginning in the morning until their end in the *neilah* service after sunset. At each service, there is a confession of sin and a prayer for forgiveness. During the additional prayer of the morning (*musaf*) there is a re-enactment of part of the ancient service at the Temple. In its course, the members or at least the elders of the congregation prostrate themselves four times, just as the community gathered in the ancient Temple prostrated itself whenever the Divine Name was pronounced in the service.

The melodies of each of the *Yom Kippur* services follow definite traditions, and are reflective of the mood in which the service is expected to be pronounced. In the course of these services (as well as in those of *Rosh Ha-Shanah*) the Ark is frequently opened for the recital of especially impressive hymns and poems. The service of the Day of Atonement ends with the sounding of the ram's horn, and the joint cry by all of the congregation, "Hear, O Israel, the Lord is our God, the Lord is One."

There is a curious difference between Israel and other countries with regard to the observance of the Jewish festivals. In Israel Passover is observed for seven days, in accordance with the rule set down in Ex. 12:15; outside Israel it is observed for eight days. Similarly Pentecost and *Shemini Azeret* are each observed for one day in Israel, but for two days elsewhere. Moreover, in Israel work is forbidden only on the first and seventh days of Passover, and on the first day of *Sukkot;* outside Israel it is forbidden also on the second and on the eighth day of Passover, and on the second day of *Sukkot.*

The reason for this variation of custom is historical. In ancient times the beginning of the Jewish month was fixed when the authorities of the Temple in Jerusalem observed the new moon. As the lunar month had been accurately measured in antiquity, it was comparatively easy to foretell when the moon ought to appear in Jerusalem. But the first crescent of the new moon was frequently so thin and set so soon after the sun, that it was impossible to be certain that it had actually been observed. Therefore, those away from Jerusalem always had some doubt as to whether the Temple authorities had proclaimed one day or the next as the beginning of the calendar month.

To meet this difficulty, Temple authorities would send out messengers informing distant communities of the precise day they had fixed as that of the new moon. These messengers were able to reach all parts of Palestine in a comparatively short time, but they could not reach the distant communities of Babylonia. Hence the Babylonian Jews were always in doubt as to whether the month had begun on the precise day of the new moon, or the day following. This put them in doubt regarding the exact day of all the festivals. Therefore, in order to avoid any possible violation of a holy day, they observed all the customs relating to each festival for an additional day. In the fifth century of the Common Era, the Jewish calendar was reduced to a fixed computative system, and thereafter no one could be in doubt with regard to the time of a festival. Nevertheless, the Jews outside Israel continued to observe their ancient custom. In Israel, uncertainty regarding the precise period of the festival could occur only with regard to *Rosh Ha-Shanah*, which occurs on the first day of the month. Hence, *Rosh Ha-Shanah* is observed for two days in Israel as well as in other countries. It is not customary to observe the Day of Atonement for two days because it is considered impossible to impose the severity of two successive days of fasting on the whole community. Reform Jews have, in general, abandoned the observance of the second day of the holidays.

In addition to these major festivals, whose celebration is commanded in the Law of Moses, there are two lesser festivals in Judaism, which are occasions of great religious joy and sense of communion with God: *Purim*, the Feast of Esther, and *Hanukkah*, the feast commemorating the rededication of the Temple during the time of the Maccabees.

In accordance with the prescription of the Book of Esther, *Purim* (occurring in the first half of March) is celebrated as a day of rejoicing and thanksgiving, with the exchange of gifts between friends, and charity to the poor. The Book of Esther is read publicly both at the evening and at the morning service. In the late afternoon, a family festival, second in importance only to that of the *seder* service, is usually held. This festive dinner is called the *seudat purim* (*Purim* meal).

Hanukkah (the midwinter festival that occurs in the month of December) is celebrated in commemoration of the purification of the Temple by the Maccabees, after it had been defiled by the Syrian king, Antiochus IV, in the year 168 before the Common Era. Led by Judas the Maccabee, the Jews won amazing victories over outnumbering Syrian armies, and finally reconquered Jerusalem, drove the pagans out of the Temple, and re-established it as a place for the worship of God. The day of the rededication of the Temple was the third anniversary of its first defilement, the twenty-fifth of Kislev, and that day, together with seven succeeding days, is observed as *Hanukkah* (the feast of dedication).

On the first night of *Hanukkah* a candle is lit, and on each succeeding night of the eight-day festival an additional candle is lit, in celebration of the holiday. It is also customary to mark the festival with family meals, games, and the exchange of gifts, particularly within the family.

Besides *Yom Kippur*, there are several lesser fasts in the Jewish calendar. Of these the most important is *Tisha B'ab* (popularly pronounced *Tishoh B'ov*), the ninth day of the month of Ab, the anniversary of the burning of the first and also of the second Temple. In memory of these catastrophes, it is the rule to fast from sunset on the evening before this day until the sunset of the day itself. The Book of Lamentations is recited in the evening, and in the morning a number of dirges record ancient and medieval sufferings of the Jewish people. To increase a sense of bereavement it is customary in many communities to spend the afternoon of *Tisha B'ab* visiting the graves of relatives.

There are several other fasts, less commonly observed, during which food is forbidden only during the day. These are the fast of *Gedaliah* (on the day following *Rosh Ha-Shanah*); the tenth day of the month of Tebet; and the seventeenth day of the month of Tammuz. All these fasts are mentioned in Zech. 8:19. The fast of *Gedaliah* commemorates the murder of the last governor of Judah in the year 586 before the Common Era (Jer. 41:2). The fast of Tebet commemorates the beginning of the siege of Jerusalem by the Babylonians (Ez. 24:1-2). The seventeenth day of Tammuz is the anniversary of the breach in the wall of Jerusalem by the Romans in the year 70.

Partial mourning is still observed during the three weeks between the seventeenth day of Tammuz and the ninth of Ab, the period when Jerusalem was pillaged by the victorious Roman soldiery. No weddings are performed; other festivities and the wearing of new clothes are considered inappropriate. During the last nine days of this period it is customary for many Jews to abstain from meat and wine (except on the Sabbath day).

The Jewish religious calendar begins in the autumn with *Rosh Ha-Shanah*, the festival of the New Year. The names of the months were adopted from the Babylonian calendar and are as follows: Tishri, Marchesvan (frequently called Heshvan), Kislev, Tebet, Shebat, Adar, Nisan, Iyyar, Sivan, Tammuz, Ab, Elul.

The length of the month is fixed by the lunar cycle of twenty-nine and a half days and therefore is alternately twenty-nine and thirty days. The length of the year of twelve months is thus 354 days, though under special circumstances it may be 353 or 355 days. To make up the difference between this period and that of the solar year of 365¼ days, an additional month is added to the year, seven times in a cycle of nineteen years. This additional month is added immediately before Nisan (the month of the Passover) and is called the Second Adar. The additional month is added on the third, sixth, eighth, eleventh, fourteenth, seventeenth, and nineteenth years of the cycle.

Because of the character of the Jewish calendar, the beginning of each month coincides with the new moon, and the first days of the festivals of Passover and *Sukkot* (falling on the fifteenth day of their respective months) occur at the full moon.

Rabbi José ben Halafta, a great scholar who lived in Palestine in the first half of the second century c.e., compiled a history of the Jews, which, following the example of Scripture, opened with the Creation. This book is called *Seder Olam* (The History of the World). Utilizing the chronology of Scripture for its time, and reconstructing postbiblical history as well as he could, Rabbi José arrived at the conclusion that the world was created in the year 3828 before the destruction of the Temple at the hands of the Romans. As by Rabbinic tradition the date of the destruction was placed in the year 67-68 c.e., the Creation according to his calculation occurred in the year 3761-3760 b.c.e., or to be more nearly exact, in September or October, 3761 b.c.e.

The most significant confusion in Rabbi José's calculation was that reducing the whole period from the rebuilding of the Temple by Zerubabel in 516 b.c.e. to the conquest of Persia by Alexander (which he dates 318 b.c.e.) to no more than thirty-four years. Like other Rabbinic scholars he believed that Zerubabel (sixth century b.c.e.), Malachi, Ezra, Nehemiah (all fifth century b.c.e.) and Simeon the Righteous (third century b.c.e.) were all contemporaries.

For many centuries this calculation by Rabbi José was of interest only to talmudic students, who also tried to satisfy a curiosity for historical reconstruction. The usual calculation adopted by Jews in Rabbinic and even post-talmudic times, was that of the Seleucid monarchy, that assumed rule over Syria and Palestine in the year 312 b.c.e. This era is in Jewish literature usually referred to as that of "legal documents," for it was in dating such documents that it generally occurred.

Only when the center of Jewish life was moved from Babylonia to Europe, and the era calculation based on the rule of the Seleucids seemed anachronistic and became meaningless, was it replaced by that based on the calculations of Rabbi José ben Halafta. Though this calculation (making

A HANUKKAH LAMP

This lamp from the home of Mr. and Mrs. Jacob H. Schiff, was a gift from Mrs. Felix
M. Warburg. It is silver with enamel medallions on the base depicting biblical scenes,
and was made at Frankfort in the early 18th century by Johan Adam Boller.

ILLUMINATED MEGILLAH OR SCROLL OF ESTHER (1.19–3.6)

Italian, 18th century

The figures are Vashti, Mordecai, and Esther. The medallions above are of three courtiers.

5719 the equivalent of 1958-1959) is now in universal use among Jews, it has no dogmatic sanction and is in effect simply an arbitrary figure used for convenience and uniformity.[19]

SPECIAL OCCASIONS IN THE COURSE OF LIFE

The occasions of special joy or sadness in human life are, in Judaism, surrounded with ceremonials intended to make them means for closer communion with God. These ceremonials aid the Jew to temper joy with solemnity and sorrow with resignation. When he is happy, the Jew is instructed to think with gratitude of God, Who is the source of happiness; and when he is in grief, he is likewise instructed to look to God, as the source of consolation. Birth, marriage, and death are thus more than incidents in temporal and sensual existence. They are the occasions for thinking more deeply than usual about the meaning of existence, and the relation of man to God.

Every person born of Jewish parents is considered bound to observe the covenant of Sinai, and therefore subject to the observance of Jewish ceremonial. Although mixed marriages are prohibited, the child of a Jewish mother is regarded as a Jew and need undergo no ceremony of conversion to be admitted to the Jewish faith. A member of another faith who desires to be converted to Judaism must (according to traditional ritual) appear before a rabbi and state his desire to be converted. The rabbi will then provide for his instruction in the elements of Jewish law, belief, and practice. Before admitting him to the Jewish fold, the rabbi must warn him of the severe discipline of Judaism and the difficulties involved in adherence to the Jewish faith. If the applicant persists in his desire to enter the Jewish faith, the rabbi will arrange for the ceremony of proselytization. A male applicant must be circumcised. According to the traditional ritual followed by Orthodox and Conservative Jews, both male and female applicants become proselytes by immersion in a pool of running water, declaring that they are performing the ceremony in order to be admitted into the Jewish faith, and reciting as they emerge from the water the benediction, "Blessed art Thou, O Lord, our God, King of the Universe, Who didst sanctify us with Thy commandments, and hast commanded us regarding the ceremonial immersion of the proselyte." Reform rabbis do not include this ritual immersion in their ceremony of proselytization.

In accordance with the prescriptions of Gen. 17:9-14, the son of Jewish parents is circumcised on the eighth day of his life. (The ceremony may be postponed for reasons of health.) Because the ritual of circumcision involves at once a knowledge of surgery and of traditional customs, it is performed by a man especially trained for the purpose, called a *mohel* (one who circumcises). At the circumcision, the father recites the benediction, "Blessed art Thou, O Lord, our God, King of the Universe, Who didst consecrate us with Thy commandments, and hast commanded us to bring this child into the covenant of our ancestor, Abraham." All those present respond, "Just as he has entered the covenant of Abraham, may he also enter into the study of the Law, into marriage, and into good deeds!" The *mohel* or some other person present, then prays for the child's future piety and welfare and that of his mother, and announces his name.

A girl is named at the service in the synagogue on the Sabbath (or any other day when the Torah is read) following her birth, when the father is called to participate in the reading of the Torah. One of those present then prays for the health of the mother of the child, and for the health of the child, and announces its name.

Boys under thirteen and girls under twelve years of age are theoretically not obligated to observe the discipline of the ritual Law. In order to be trained in the Law, they are expected to observe such parts of it as they can without impairing their health. As soon as a child can speak, he is taught to recite simple evening and morning prayers, consisting primarily of the first verse of the *Shema*. When the child reaches school age, he is taught the Hebrew language, the Bible and, as he grows older, advanced Jewish studies. The instruction is given the child by his parents, by a private teacher, or in a religious school. The traditional school devoted to this purpose is called a *Talmud Torah* (the place of the study of the Law). In America, these institutions usually provide instruction for children for either three or five (in some instances, seven or ten) hours per week, after the regular secular school hours on weekdays, and on Sunday mornings. There are also Jewish day schools established in some communities, providing both secular and religious education. These are sometimes called *yeshibot* (singular, *yeshiba* or *yeshiva*, academy). The name *yeshiba* or *yeshiva* is also used for traditional schools of advanced talmudic study in Europe and for similar institutions in America.[20a]

A month before a boy has reached his thirteenth birthday he is expected to begin to don the *tephillin* each morning. On the Sabbath following his thirteenth birthday, he is called to participate in the formal reading of the Torah at the usual synagogue service. The ceremony of which this is part is popularly called *bar mitzva* (son of the commandment, in reference to his obligation to perform the commandments thereafter). Parents frequently arrange a celebration in honor of this occasion.

In many American synagogues similar note is taken when a girl attains the age of twelve, and therefore becomes subject to the commandments. The ceremony which is called *bat mitzva* (daughter of the commandment, popularly pronounced *bas mitzva*) is variously observed in different communities. In some, the girl is permitted to read the prophetic portion in the vernacular. In others, there is simply a family festivity.

Many Conservative and Reform congregations have established, either in lieu of these *bar mitzva* and *bat mitzva* ceremonies or in addition to them, that of confirmation. This ritual is usually observed on Pentecost. Boys and girls from fourteen to sixteen are taught the elements of Jewish faith and history in preconfirmation classes, and are then called to announce their devotion to the faith at a public synagogue ceremonial.

In the traditional marriage service, the ceremony takes place under a canopy (*huppah*), which symbolizes the home established through the marriage.

Judaism regards complete mutual understanding and trust between the bride and the bridegroom as a basic requirement for a valid marriage. A number of ceremonies have been established to give expression to this conception, and there are even several legal forms which emphasize it.

Before the wedding, the rabbi or other person in charge of the ceremony asks the bridegroom whether he undertakes to fulfill all the traditional obligations of a Jewish husband to his wife. These include various provisions for the maintenance of the wife, both during married life and, if the occasion should arise, during her widowhood. As these are civil obligations, a formal agreement must be made to provide for them. On the bridegroom's assenting, the ceremony of *kinyan* (agreement) is performed. This consists of the rabbi's handing the bridegroom an object of value, usually a handkerchief, as a symbolic consideration, to make the bridegroom's acceptance of the conditions of the marriage valid. The rabbi then draws up a document called a *ketubah* (writ, popularly pronounced *kesubah*) detailing these obligations as well as those of the wife. This *ketubah* is witnessed by two observant Jews, neither of whom may be related to the bride or bridegroom. The officiating rabbi, if not a relation, may act as one of these witnesses.

The language of the *ketubah* is Aramaic, the vernacular of the Jews of Palestine during the period when the present text was composed. The document is sometimes artistically decorated; and a number of the *ketubot* preserved in various museums of Jewish antiquities are of great interest to the student of art.

The wedding ceremony itself consists of a series of benedictions, having for their purpose the expression of thanks to God for the institution of marriage and the family, for having implanted His image on the human race, and for the joy of the wedding, and including prayers for the happiness of the bride and bridegroom and for the restoration of Jerusalem. After the first of these benedictions, the bridegroom hands the bride a ring, and says to her in Hebrew, "Thou art sanctified unto me, with this ring, in accordance with the Law of Moses and of Israel." At the end of the ceremony a glass is broken to commemorate the destruction of Jerusalem.

There is a considerable difference between the marriage customs of traditional and Reform Jews. In the marriage service of the Reform group, the canopy and the *ketubah* are generally omitted. The wedding is usually celebrated in the synagogue. The special prayer for the restoration of Jerusalem is omitted. On the other hand, several prayers in English on behalf of the bride and the bridegroom are added. The service ends with the recitation of the priestly blessing (Num. 6:24-26) by the rabbi.[21]

Jewish Law forbids husband and wife to cohabit or to come into physical contact during the period of menstruation or for seven days afterward. At the end of the period the wife is required to take a ritual bath in a pool of running water, or one especially built for the purpose (*mikveh*). A bride also bathes in such a *mikveh* before her wedding. The value of these regulations in preserving Jewish family life and in the prevention of certain diseases has been recognized by various Christian and Jewish writers on genetics.[22]

In Jewish Law marriage can be terminated by a religious divorce (called *get*).[22a] In practice such a divorce is granted by a rabbi only if both parties consent, and have already been divorced in the civil courts. The ritual of divorce is extremely complicated, and is performed only by specially trained scholars. Reform rabbis generally recognize a civil divorce as terminating a Jewish marriage from a religious as well as from the secular point of view, and therefore do not insist on a religious divorce as prerequisite for remarriage of either husband or wife.

There is one instance in traditional Jewish Law in which the death of the husband does not completely break the marriage bond; that is the case of a childless widow, described in Deut. 25:5-10. Biblical Law, as stated in Deuteronomy, requires such a childless widow to marry her husband's brother, so that her first-born son, by the second marriage, may "succeed in the name of the brother which is dead, that his name be not put out of Israel." Later Rabbinic ordinances forbade the performance of such a Levirate marriage, but nevertheless insisted that the widow may not remarry without performing the ceremony of *halitzah*, ordained in Deuteronomy, as alternative to such a marriage.

When a Jew feels that the end of his life is approaching he should confess his sins in accordance with the fixed ritual, making special mention, however, of any sin which he is conscious of having committed, and which is not mentioned in the traditional formula. In his last conscious moments he recites the traditional confession of faith, "Hear, O Israel, the Lord is our God, the Lord is One." Those about him may help him recite the formula by repeating it with him.

According to Rabbinic tradition, the body should be washed after death and dressed in linen shrouds. The universal use of linen shrouds dates back to the beginning of the second century of the Common Era. Rabban Gamaliel II, the head of the Academy of Jabneh and one of the most distinguished scholars and communal leaders of his time,[23a] specifically requested that no elaborate provision such as was then customary be made for his burial, but that he be interred in a shroud like those used for the poor. The custom has been universally adopted by observant Jews to stress further the equality of all men.

The body must be interred in the ground, as soon after death as possible. Cremation is forbidden, as being an implicit denial of the Resurrection.

The funeral service is usually recited in the home of the deceased, though in the case of a person of special piety it may be recited in the synagogue. Because of the conditions of modern urban life, funeral services are sometimes held in rooms especially devoted to that purpose, so-called funeral chapels. The purpose of the service and the ceremonies associated with it is to give expression to the natural grief of the bereaved, and at the same time to inculcate in the bereaved resignation to the Will of God.

The service consists of the recital of one or more psalms and selections of appropriate verses from other psalms. Usually Psalm 16, 23, 90, or 91 is recited. The reading of the psalm may be followed by an address; and the service closes with a prayer for the peace of the soul of the deceased. This prayer is repeated at the grave, and a second psalm is recited, after which the bereaved recite the *kaddish*. Either during the funeral services or immediately before the burial, the person officiating at the ceremonies asks the near relatives of the deceased (husband, wife, son, daughter, father, mother, brother, or sister) each to cut one of his garments. This ceremony is called *keriah* (tearing the garment) and is reminiscent of the ancient Jewish usage of tearing one's clothes in bereavement (see II Sam. 1:11). After tearing the garment, each of the bereaved recites the blessing of resignation to the justice of God: "Blessed art Thou, O Lord, our God, King of the Universe, the true Judge."

During the week after the burial of a relative, near relatives, including husband, wife, children, brothers, sisters, and parents, remain at home. They must not engage in any gainful occupation, unless the income is vital to their subsistence, or unless they will otherwise forfeit their employment. It is customary for friends to visit the mourners to console them, and to arrange community prayers in the house of the deceased. During the whole week of mourning (called *shiva*, seven, i.e., the seven days of mourning) a lamp is kept burning in the house of the deceased. None of the mourners wears any jewels, and mirrors, considered a luxury, are covered. The mourners sit on low stools instead of chairs; they do not study the Law or the Scriptures, save such solemn works as the Books of Job and Lamentations, the dire prophecies in Jeremiah, and the laws of mourning in the Talmud and Codes; and they are forbidden to wear shoes made of leather.

After the completion of the *shiva*, the relatives observe partial mourning for the remainder of the month. They do not don new clothes, and avoid taking part in festivities, or listening to music. On the death of a parent, this partial mourning is observed for a whole year. In order to make grief itself a means for closer communion with God, the bereaved children are expected, during this year of mourning, to be particularly mindful of religious observances, to attend synagogue service regularly, and to recite the *kaddish* at each prayer. Whenever possible, a bereaved son serves as reader of the public prayers on weekdays during this year of mourning. These customs are also observed on the anniversary of the death of one's parents. Such an anniversary is called *yahrzeit* (a German name, because the custom assumed its present form among the German Jews). It is customary, also, to have a light burning at home during the day marking the anniversary of the death of a near relative. This light symbolizes the belief in human immortality, in accordance with the Rabbinic interpretation of the verse (Pr. 20:27), "The spirit of man is the lamp of God, searching all the inward parts." About a year after the death of a relative, the mourners set up a monument marking the place of the grave. At the unveiling of this monument called *massebah* (pillar, popularly pronounced *matzevah*), psalms are read, prayers are recited for the peace of the soul of the deceased, and the *kaddish* is repeated.

THE JEWISH HOME AND THE DIETARY LAWS

Like every other authentic experience, piety cannot stop short of the home. If religion were to be merely ecclesiastical, it would soon cease to be that too. The Psalmist who was told "Let us go up to the house of the Lord" rejoiced because in his own house the reality of God was never forgotten. Throughout Jewish history the attempt to reproduce in the home the order and mood of the place of worship has never been relaxed.

The interrelationship of sanctuary and home has been responsible for at least two significant results. On the one hand, the Jew did not remain a stranger to the ceremonial and purpose of his sacred institutions. On the other hand, his home and home life were transfigured. His residence became a habitation of God.

This sanctification of the home was achieved by a religious discipline whose purpose was constantly to prompt a remembrance of God. The Jew who visited the ancient Temple, for example, readily understood that the elaborate rites, precautions, exactitudes and purifications were the appropriate expressions of the beauty of holiness. "If you were to serve a king of flesh and blood," the saintly Hillel once reminded a guest, "would you not have to learn how to make your entrances and exits and obeisances? How much more so in the service of the King of kings!"

That such fastidiousness was therefore required in God's House the

Jew accepted unquestioningly. The forms reminded him of God. And because they did, and because Israel's teachers tried to prevent the Jew from forgetting God even when he was away from the Sanctuary, corresponding rituals and attitudes were introduced into the Jewish home. Thus the Jewish home became a sanctuary in miniature, its table an altar, its furnishings instruments for sanctity.

In a sense, every detail of home life is an expression of the pattern of sanctity. Jewish homes, for example, are generally expected to contain basic religious texts such as the Bible, usually accompanied at least by the commentary of Rashi, the Talmud, perhaps an abbreviated code (the short *Shulhan Aruk*), some of the magnificent moralistic works, and of course the prayer book—actually one of the most extraordinary anthologies of Jewish classical literature. It is not uncommon to find in a Jewish home an excellent library with volumes handed down from father to son, volumes which reveal constant use.

Similarly, the various family festival celebrations with their rituals constitute activities that bring the Divine message very close to the Jew. It is an insensitive Jewish child who forgets the beauty of the *seder* at Passover, or the kindling of the lights during *Hanukkah*, or the sight of his mother kindling the Sabbath lamps at dusk. These and like activities collaborate to make holiness a familiar emphasis and delight.

Part of the daily pattern of sanctity is formed by the so-called dietary laws. As is well known, Jewish law prohibits the eating of certain foods. These prohibitions are enumerated essentially in Lev. 11, and again in Deut. 14. No vegetable growths are prohibited; but of animal life the Law permits fish having scales and fins, certain types of fowl, and only those quadrupeds that chew their cud and have cloven hoofs. Among the domestic quadrupeds this includes only oxen, sheep, and goats.

According to traditional Judaism, warm-blooded animals may be eaten only if they are ritually slaughtered, i.e., if they are slaughtered in the manner used in the Temple for sacrificial purposes. The knife used in slaughtering must be sharp, and must be examined both before and after slaughtering to be certain that its edge contains no notch, which by tearing the animal's throat might give it unnecessary pain. The animal must not, however, be stunned before slaughtering, for stunning prevents the free flow of the blood, and the absorption of the blood in the meat makes the food prohibited. To ensure the animal's speedy death, the person who slays it must be trained for the work. He must know enough of the diseases of animals to be able to examine the body and to make certain that it was suffering from no serious disease. A person so trained is called a *shohet* (slaughterer). In order to be allowed to perform his duties, he must receive authorization from a rabbi.

After an animal is slaughtered, its lungs are examined to guard against symptoms of various communicable diseases, mainly tuberculosis. The Talmud, its commentaries, and the later codes, contain an impressive amount of veterinary information regarding the symptoms of disease in animals, so that an examination based on this information is a valuable means of detecting disease.

If an animal has been found to be free from serious disease, its meat is declared *kasher* (fit, popularly pronounced *kosher*).

The meat must not, however, remain unwashed for three days. If it does, the surface blood is believed to be absorbed in the tissues, and the food becomes prohibited. After the meat is cut, the various parts are placed in a container of water for half an hour to be cleansed of surface blood. Thereafter the meat is covered with salt, to draw out the blood further, and remains in the salt for at least an hour. The salt is then washed off, and the meat may be boiled. Meat which is to be roasted on a spit need not be soaked in water or salted. Meat from the udder or the liver may be prepared only by roasting.

In addition to the various laws prohibiting certain types of food, there is a rule mentioned thrice in Scripture against seething a kid in its mother's milk (Ex. 23:19 and 34:26; Deut. 14:21). This rule was originally intended, according to Maimonides, to extirpate an idolatrous practice. It is interpreted as prohibiting the cooking or eating the meat of any warm-blooded animal with milk, or a derivative of milk. Hence to serve meat and milk or butter or cheese at the same meal is prohibited. In order to avoid any possibility of a mixture of meat and milk, observant Jews provide themselves with two types of plates, one of which is used only for meat foods, the other only for milk foods. Further, it is customary in many countries not to eat milk dishes for six hours after a meat meal.

THE STATUS OF WOMAN IN JEWISH LAW AND RITUAL

From its beginnings, Judaism has consistently endeavored to proclaim and effectuate the equality of the sexes before God and in society. The first chapter of Genesis describes Adam as created "male and female" (v. 27), and continues to narrate how "God blessed them, and God said unto them, Be fruitful and multiply and replenish the earth and subdue it. And have dominion over the fish of the sea, and over the fowl of the air, and over every living thing that creepeth upon the earth." This description emphasizing the equality of woman and man, is repeated at the beginning of the fifth chapter of the Book.

Though in the general pattern of Mediterranean society, in which Judaism originated, the status of women was definitely inferior to that of men, Jewish law in its biblical and particularly in its postbiblical stages endeavored to overcome this differentiation between the rights of the sexes.

Among the most significant reforms introduced by the talmudic Sages was that providing for the inheritance by orphan daughters, even when they had brothers.

Plural marriage had become virtually obsolete for Jews in Rabbinic times. It was formally interdicted by Rabbenu Gershom who lived in Germany in the eleventh century. As the foremost Rabbinic scholar in the Europe of his day, he issued a decree of excommunication against any Jew who would practice plural marriage (except under a dispensation to be granted by one hundred Rabbis, in cases other systems of law would regard as justifying divorce or annulment of marriage). He also declared an excommunication against anyone who would divorce his wife against her will. With these measures, and those of older times that permitted a wife to apply to a Jewish court for a writ of divorcement under certain circumstances, the status of husband and wife was practically equalized in regard to marriage law.

While formal education in Rabbinics was generally limited to men, provision was often made also for the education of women. During Rabbinic times, and even more frequently in the Middle Ages, some women achieved high distinction in scholarship. In later ages, books were written in Yiddish for the edification and instruction of women; and many achieved an astonishing degree of erudition simply through listening to the learned disquisitions of rabbis on the Sabbaths.

While the service at the synagogue, like that of the priests in the Temple, is conducted by men, what might be called worship at home is largely the prerogative of the wife and mother. Kindling of the Sabbath lights, supervision of the child's education, maintenance of the food laws, and preparation for the festivals are considered especially part of woman's share in Divine worship.

In the latter part of the nineteenth and in the twentieth century Reform Jews and many Conservative Jews abolished the separation of the sexes in the synagogue. In all groups, there is in modern days far greater participation of women in synagogue work and administration, growing provision for the education of girls, and increasing opportunities for women to serve as teachers and school executives. In many congregations, Orthodox as well as Conservative and Reform, women serve on the lay boards of the synagogues and of synagogue organizations. They serve as members of faculties of teachers institutes, and have been known to be admitted as students in rabbinical schools.

PROHIBITIONS OR NEGATIVE COMMANDMENTS

Most of the laws so far described are affirmative commandments. They tell the Jew what he is expected to do on particular occasions. But according to Rabbinical calculation, the greater part of the biblical Law consists of negative regulations or prohibitions. In fact, a Palestinian scholar of the third century maintained that Scripture contains no less than three hundred and sixty-five prohibitions but only two hundred and forty-eight positive injunctions. Since his time these have been variously enumerated; the most important codification being that of Maimonides, in his Book of the Commandments and in the introduction to his Code.

The system of negative commandments is as vital to Judaism as are its positive ceremonials. Some of the prohibitions have been discussed in preceding sections, and are associated with the ceremonial observances themselves. Thus the observance of Passover includes not only eating *matzah*, but also abstention from leaven. Worship of God involves rejection of all idolatry, including rituals which were part of ancient pagan faiths no longer in existence.

Whatever may be the significance of a particular rule—whether personal hygiene, the extirpation of idolatry, the inculcation of gentleness—the whole system of prohibitions has a common goal. It is to make the awareness of God a continuous, uninterrupted experience. Affirmative actions and gestures are, by their nature, limited to stated occasions. Negations are timeless. The positive ceremonial is intended to arouse man's spirit to particular heights; the prohibition prevents him from forgetting God at any time. There is never a time or place when, to quote the Rabbinic phrase, "a person is naked of the commandments." He is always on the alert against possible violation of the Law. He has more prohibitions to guard against on the Day of Atonement than on the Sabbath; and on the Sabbath than on weekdays. But he is never without the possibility of falling into error, and therefore never free from the responsibility of avoiding sin.

It is in his relations with fellow men that a person becomes especially aware of the presence of God; love for them inevitably develops into love for Him. Jews are therefore warned in their Law to beware any infringement of the rights and privileges of others. "What is distasteful to thee, do not to thy neighbor" was the summary of the Law made by the great talmudic teacher Hillel. To develop such sensitivity to others' feelings as to avoid what may give them pain, and to concentrate on what will cause pleasure, is a discipline demanded by Judaism not simply as courtesy and politeness but as the Law of God. It was the apparent purpose of the Lawgiver and his disciples to create a group for whom the service of God would be the principal vocation of life, and all earthly interests an avocation; for whom the presence of God would be so manifest that the trivialities and temptations of mundane existence would appear unimportant.

The very incongruity between the traditional Jewish system of life and one which lays great stress on efficiency, productivity, and abundance is a basic, implicit idea of the faith. The first premise of the Torah is that "man doth not live by bread alone," and that there are joys in the sense of communion with God, in the awareness of His being and His kingdom, of His love and of love for Him, so deep and all-pervading as to make all other experiences of life insignificant. As neither man as a whole nor Jews as a group have reached this stage of sensitivity to the Deity, the hastening of the process leading to it is a primary obligation. Life in accordance with Torah is a preparation for the detachment from material affairs, a means to attain absorption in spiritual ones. Without such absorption, man may seek compensation for his unhappiness and frustration in domination of his fellows; and his very search for earthly goods may become his undoing. Judaism assumes that there are many ways that man can learn to love God, so as to rise above interest in the physical world. But for its adherents, traditional Judaism prescribes the austerity of a system of conduct, involving not only ethics but ceremonial, which it regards as especially inconsistent with material ambition and especially conducive to spirituality.

Love for God

Love for God is thus both the beginning and the end of the Jewish way of life. Awareness of God's Being, the essence of this love, fosters the observance and study of the rituals and commandments, and is itself stimulated by them. The Torah draws Israel nearer to God; and God draws Israel nearer to the Torah. The greater man's love for God the easier his escape from the futilities of earthly temptation and ambition; the more complete his transcendence of his irrational and perverted hungers for immediate and transient goods the easier for him to attain preoccupation with God.

Absorption in God is man's perfection. As man tears himself free from the chains binding him to animal and less than animal existence, he finds himself contemplating the Eternal and the Spiritual; and conversely, as he, by an act of will, focuses his intellect on the transcendent, his reason allies itself with his good propensities to make him more nearly divine.

This interrelation of love for God and perfection of man is a basic postulate of Judaism. "And thou shalt love the Lord thy God with all thy heart and with all thy soul and with all thy might" is alpha, as well as omega of Judaism. That man is capable of loving God gives promise of his future; the future will be fulfilled as man attains increasing love for God and immersion in Him.

This doctrine teaches man humility, but denies his insignificance. He can escape frustration, and perhaps self-destruction, through the discovery that he is a mere incident in the Divine process of creation.

The recognition of that elemental relationship between him and God and the achievement of the humility indispensable to the service of God give him a unique role in the process of creation. "If I labor not to perfect myself, who will perfect me? Yet if I labor only for myself, what am I?" asked Hillel.

The triviality of man, both in his physical being and in his temporal aspirations, is in sharp contrast to the vastness about him. It is tempting to seek escape from responsibility as an instrument of Divine purpose through the illusion that the immensity of the universe and his own physical insignificance are a measure of relative value. Yet in view of the proverbial prodigality of nature no consideration could be more preposterous. Flowers produce millions of pollen grains, so that one may find its way to an ovule; trees bear fruit without number, so that the species may survive through a few. That galaxies and supergalaxies, numbering many millions and containing millions of suns, should derive meaning from the evolution on a minor planet in one of the less important systems, of a sentient creature knowing good and evil, is far from inconsistent with the usual procedures of Creation. If it be true that of all the conglomerations of atoms, man alone has the power to be like God, in his ability to choose his path, fulfilling or resisting the Will of his Maker, he is indeed the ultimate triumph of Creation. The universe as a whole proceeds according to its inexorable laws; in man God has created a being which can obey, because it can also defy; which can attain perfection, not through a process beyond its control, but through one which it itself directs.

Aware of the possibility that he has this unique role in existence, man will find its rejection for the sake of trifling advantages of power and luxury difficult indeed. To know God metaphysically may be consistent with rebellion against Him; but to know Him religiously is not. Men habituated to serve God, out of love for Him, will develop the calm detached resignation of the Stoic, and yet combine with it a passionate desire to see His Will done. They will not hate, but pity, those who have no share in this enterprise, or who, through ignorance or malice, impede it. They will not resent the painful and heart-rending tarriance; nor will they count the cost for themselves or for their fellows. Yet transcendence of life's vicissitudes will not harden their hearts and freeze their emotions. They will have faith in the ultimate fulfillment of the Divine purpose, and in man's proving himself worthy of his Maker. But they will wish to hasten the progress, and they will wish to share in it. They will want the Master to be pleased with their participation, though it is inconceivable that the effort as a whole should fail even without them.

In a world in which mankind as a whole achieved love of God, to live in accordance with Jewish ritual and morals and for the goals Judaism has set will not seem curious and awkward, but natural and rational. Such a world, still finite, still imperfect, still mortal, will yet be a Kingdom of God, because it will be comparatively free from the ills produced through the confusion of men. Those who bring it nearer may be said to accept the Kingdom of God, though its realization be in the distant future. The faith of Israel teaches that this Kingdom will come, in part through the observances and teachings of Judaism itself. Whatever else a Jew may be able to offer to the world, whether in science, art, philosophy, letters, or industry, his supreme contribution is, therefore, that which he can make through the fulfillment of his religious duties, his perfection as a human being, and his development of all-embracing love for God.

NOTES

[1] Without desiring to ascribe to them any responsibility for this statement, the author records with deep gratitude the assistance in its preparation given by colleagues from different schools of Jewish thought. These include Rabbis Max Arzt, Ben Zion Bokser, Samuel S. Cohon, Judah Goldin, Israel M. Goldman, Simon Greenberg, David de Sola Pool, Samuel Schulman, and Aaron J. Tofield.

[2a Cf. above Judah Goldin, "The Period of the Talmud (135 B.C.E.–1035 C.E.)," *passim.*]

[3] Cf. the essay on "Study as a Mode of Worship," by Professor Nathan Isaacs, in *The Jewish Library,* edited by Rabbi Leo Jung, 1928, pp. 51-70.

[4] Dr. Oscar Z. Fasman is now (spring, 1958) president of the Jewish University of America.

[5a Cf. above Moshe Davis, "Jewish Religious Life and Institutions in America (A Historical Study)," pp. 524 f., 540 f., and Simon Greenberg, "Jewish Educational Institutions," pp. 1281-1284.]

[6a For a survey of the Orthodox, Conservative and Reform movements in the United States, cf. above Moshe Davis, *op. cit.*]

[7] The extent to which even conversion to another faith affects the status of an individual within Judaism is a subject of considerable discussion in Rabbinical literature. Many authorities consider such a person a Jew, despite his conversion.

[8a Cf. above Mordecai M. Kaplan, "A Philosophy of Jewish Ethics."]

[9a Cf. above Israel S. Chipkin, "Judaism and Social Welfare," pp. 1066-1069.]

[10a Cf above Alexander Altmann, "Judaism and World Philosophy," p. 971.]

[11a Cf. *ibid.,* pp. 975-976.]

[12] From Jacob Emden's Letter in his edition of *Seder Olam Rabba we-Sutta u-Megillath Taanit* (Hamburg, 1757). A translation of the whole text is given by Oscar Z. Fasman in "An Epistle on Tolerance by a 'Rabbinic Zealot,' " in *Judaism in a Changing World,* ed. Rabbi Leo Jung (New York, 1939), pp. 121-136.

[12a See Ben Zion Dinur, "The Historical Foundations of the Rebirth of Israel"; Itzhak Ben-Zvi, "Eretz Yisrael under Ottoman Rule, 1517-1917"; Oscar I. Janowsky, "The Rise of the State of Israel"; Jacob Lestschinsky, "Jewish Migrations, 1840-1956"; Simon Kuznets, "Economic Structure and Life of the Jews."]

13 This blessing is not recited when wearing leather garments because it is not considered fitting to thank God for life when using material produced at the cost of life.

[14a Cf. above William Foxwell Albright, "The Biblical Period," pp. 45-50, and Elias J. Bickerman, "The Historical Foundations of Postbiblical Judaism," pp. 70 f.]

[15a For further details on the decoration of synagogues throughout the ages, cf. above Rachel Wischnitzer, "Judaism and Art," passim.]

[16a Cf. above Hillel Bavli, "The Modern Renaissance of Hebrew Literature," pp. 907-909.]

[17a Cf. Goldin, op. cit., pp. 156-158.]

18 Shoes or sandals were considered an object of luxury in the ancient Orient. It was therefore considered improper to wear them on days of fasting or mourning.

19 For further discussion of the chronology of R. José, cf. Professor Alexander Marx in the introduction to his edition of Seder Olam (Berlin, 1903), pp. viii ff. and the references there given.

[20a Cf. Greenberg, op. cit., pp. 1269-1271, and 1279-1281.]

21 Rabbi's Manual, edited and published by the Central Conference of American Rabbis (Cincinnati, 1928), pp. 39 ff.

22 For a further discussion and bibliography, see Mrs. R. L. Jung, in The Jewish Library, edited by Rabbi Leo Jung, Third Series, pp. 355-365.

[22a Difficult problems—especially concerning remarriage—confront Jews divorced in civil courts who are unable to obtain a Jewish religious divorce. Therefore in 1952 the Rabbinical Assembly of America asked Professor Saul Lieberman for application of rabbinic scholarship to a serious contemporary ethical problem. He suggested a reformulated ketubah, which has been adopted by the Rabbinical Assembly. In this contract the bride and bridegroom undertake to bring any tensions which may arise in their marriage before a Beth Din (court) of the Rabbinical Assembly and The Faculty of the Jewish Theological Seminary of America, authorizing the Beth Din to impose penalties on either party who fails to respond to a summons issued at the request of the other, or to accept the decision of the Beth Din in regard to divorcement. For the new ketubah to be valid, both bride and bridegroom are thus required to accept its provisions.]

[23a Cf. Goldin, op. cit., pp. 149-151.]

BIBLIOGRAPHY

EPSTEIN, I., Judaism. London, 1939.
FRIEDLAENDER, GERALD, Laws and Customs. London, 1921.

FRIEDLAENDER, MICHAEL, *The Jewish Religion*. New York, 1923.
GREENSTONE, JULIUS, *The Jewish Religion*. Philadelphia, 1920.
JOSEPH, MORRIS, *Judaism as Creed and Life*. London, 1903.
KAPLAN, M. M., *The Meaning of Modern Jewish Religion*. New York, 1937.
PHILIPSON, DAVID, *Reform Movement in Judaism*. New York, 1931.
STEINBERG, MILTON, *Basic Judaism*. New York, 1947.

APPENDIX

"What questions should be answered
in the book on Judaism and the Jews?"

In 1947 the first edition listed the questions raised most frequently in 209 replies to a questionnaire sent in 1946-1947 to scholars and educators throughout the United States.

In preparation for the present edition the same questions were sent to all those on the 1947 list, and to an additional list of some 2,800 leaders representing a cross-section of America.

Detailed statistical analysis of replies both to the 1947 and the 1957 questionnaires, covering comparisons between the replies separated by a decade, is in the files of The Jewish Theological Seminary of America.

The following questions include those from the first edition plus the others raised most frequently in 1957 in the replies of the total group (of 1947 and of 1957). Material in answer may be found in this book, as indicated.

1. What is a Jew?
   Anthropological and biological discussion
   Melville J. Herskovits, Chapter 30.
   Archaeological definition and discussion
   William Foxwell Albright, Chapter 1, esp. pp. 3-6.
   Considered in relation to "New Christians"
   Cecil Roth, Chapter 4, esp. pp. 236-239.
   Anita Libman Lebeson, Chapter 10, esp. pp. 449-450.
   Charles Singer, Chapter 32, esp. pp. 1412 ff.
   Nazi definition
   Cecil Roth, Chapter 5, p. 280.
   Theological and religious discussion
   Louis Finkelstein, Chapter 42, esp. pp. 1739 f., 1745, 1788 ff.

2. What is the Jewish creed?
   Moshe Davis, Chapter 11, *passim.*
   Louis Finkelstein, Chapter 42, esp. pp. 1748 f., 1755 f.
   Is there a distinction between the ceremonial and the ethical in Judaism?
   Mordecai M. Kaplan, Chapter 21.
   Louis Finkelstein, Chapter 42, esp. pp. 1745 f.

What was the origin of the synagogue and its development?
    Simon Greenberg, Chapter 28, esp. pp. 1257 f.
    Rachel Wischnitzer, Chapter 30, esp. pp. 1332 f.
    Louis Finkelstein, Chapter 42, esp. pp. 1767 f.
Is there a systematic Jewish theology?
    Louis Finkelstein, Chapter 42.
Can Jewish theology be modified in the light of changing conditions?
    Louis Finkelstein, Chapter 42, esp. p. 1753.

3. What is the Jewish attitude to marriage with members of other faiths?

Historical
    Bernard D. Weinryb, Chapter 7, esp. p. 348.
Statistics
    Uriah Zevi Engelman, Chapter 37, esp. pp. 1528 ff.
    Milton Himmelfarb, Chapter 40.
    Nathan Glazer, Chapter 41, esp. pp. 1710, 1727-1728.
Theological and religious
    Louis Finkelstein, Chapter 42, esp. pp. 1788 f.

4. Does Judaism seek or accept converts?

Historical
    Elias J. Bickerman, Chapter 2, esp. p. 77.
    Israel Halpern, Chapter 6, esp. pp. 290-294.
Theological and religious
    Louis Finkelstein, Chapter 42, esp. pp. 1740 f., 1788.

5. What is the Jewish attitude toward members of other religions?

Historical and general
    Elias J. Bickerman, Chapter 2, esp. p. 77.
    Israel Halpern, Chapter 6, esp. pp. 290-294, 295-296.
    Bernard D. Weinryb, Chapter 7.
    Oscar I. Janowsky, Chapter 14, pp. 736-740.
    Milton R. Konvitz, Chapter 33.
    Milton Himmelfarb, Chapter 40, esp. p. 1679.
    Nathan Glazer, Chapter 41, passim.
Sense of obligation to non-Jews
    Israel S. Chipkin, Chapter 22, esp. p. 1068.
Theological and religious
    Louis Finkelstein, Chapter 42, esp. pp. 1740 f., 1788.

6. What is the concept of the Chosen People?

    Milton R. Konvitz, Chapter 33, esp. pp. 1432 ff.
    Louis Finkelstein, Chapter 42, esp. pp. 1754 f.

7. What is the attitude of Judaism to Jesus?

Historical discussion
    Judah Goldin, Chapter 3, esp. pp. 137 ff.

Concept of love
Mordecai M. Kaplan, Chapter 21, esp. pp. 1037 f.
Theological and religious
Louis Finkelstein, Chapter 42, esp. pp. 1740 f., 1754, 1759 f.

8. What is the Jewish doctrine of immortality?

Louis Finkelstein, Chapter 42, esp. pp. 1751 f.

9. What is the Jewish concept of a Messiah?

Historical discussion
Judah Goldin, Chapter 3, esp. pp. 137 ff., 190 f.
Cecil Roth, Chapter 5, esp. pp. 250, 259 ff.
In literature
Walter J. Fischel, Chapter 25, esp. pp. 1171 f.
Yudel Mark, Chapter 26, esp. pp. 1197 f.
Theological and religious
Louis Finkelstein, Chapter 42, esp. p. 1754.

10. What are the ceremonials and rituals of Judaism?

General
Louis Finkelstein, Chapter 42.
Circumcision
Moshe Davis, Chapter 11, esp. pp. 542-543.
Arturo Castiglioni, Chapter 31, esp. p. 1355.
Louis Finkelstein, Chapter 42, esp. p. 1788.
Confirmation
Louis Finkelstein, Chapter 42, esp. pp. 1789 f.
Dietary Laws
Moshe Davis, Chapter 11, esp. pp. 542-543.
Louis Finkelstein, Chapter 42, esp. pp. 1793 ff.
Position of women
Judah Goldin, Chapter 3, esp. p. 176.
Jacob J. Rabinowitz, Chapter 16, esp. pp. 837 f.
Louis Finkelstein, Chapter 42, esp. pp. 1795 f.
Sabbaths and holidays
Moshe Davis, Chapter 11, esp. pp. 542-543.
Louis Finkelstein, Chapter 42, esp. pp. 1773 ff.
Wearing of head covering
Louis Finkelstein, Chapter 42, esp. pp. 1768 f.

11. What is the Jewish attitude to marriage and the family?

Bernard D. Weinryb, Chapter 7, esp. p. 348.
Jacob J. Rabinowitz, Chapter 16, esp. pp. 837 f.
Simon Greenberg, Chapter 28, esp. pp. 1255 f.
Nathan Glazer, Chapter 41, *passim.*
Louis Finkelstein, Chapter 42, esp. pp. 1740 f., 1758, 1772, 1788, 1789-1791.

12. Is there a Jewish "unity"?

    Louis Finkelstein, Chapter 42, esp. pp. 1763-1765.

13. What are the divisions in modern Judaism?

    Anthropological and biological
        Melville J. Herskovitz, Chapter 36.
        Jacob Lestschinsky, Chapter 38.
    Historical discussion
        Anita Libman Lebeson, Chapter 10, esp. pp. 465 ff.
        Moshe Davis, Chapter 11, esp. pp. 498 ff., and Section 4, beginning
        p. 512.
    Organizational and communal
        Milton Himmelfarb, Chapter 40.
        Nathan Glazer, Chapter 41.
    Theological and religious
        Louis Finkelstein, Chapter 42, esp. pp. 1758 f.

14. What is the Jewish attitude to the Bible?

    Judah Goldin, Chapter 3, esp. pp. 151 ff.
    Abraham Menes, Chapter 8.
    Robert Gordis, Chapter 15, esp. pp. 783 ff.
    Jacob J. Rabinowitz, Chapter 16.
    Shalom Spiegel, Chapter 17.
    Abraham J. Heschel, Chapter 19.
    Mordecai M. Kaplan, Chapter 21, esp. pp. 1020 ff.
    Israel S. Chipkin, Chapter 22, esp. pp. 1060 f., 1069 f.
    Ralph Marcus, Chapter 23.
    Abraham S. Halkin, Chapter 24.
    Walter J. Fischel, Chapter 25, esp. pp. 1158 f.
    Yudel Mark, Chapter 26, esp. pp. 1193 ff.
    Julius B. Maller, Chapter 27, esp. pp. 1235 ff.
    Simon Greenberg, Chapter 28.
    Rachel Wischnitzer, Chapter 30.
    Arturo Castiglioni, Chapter 31.
    Charles Singer, Chapter 32, esp. pp. 1378 f.
    Milton R. Konvitz, Chapter 33.
    David Daiches, Chapter 34.
    Frederick Lehner, Chapter 35.
    Louis Finkelstein, Chapter 42, esp. pp. 1739 ff., 1742 f., 1753 f., 1772 f.

*15. What is the Jewish attitude to the Dead Sea Scrolls?

    Louis Finkelstein, Chapter 42, esp. p. 1764.

16. What is the Jewish attitude to Revelation?

    Cf. the references re the Bible.

* Question added in third edition.

17. What is the Jewish attitude to the Talmud?

> Judah Goldin, Chapter 3.
> Israel Halpern, Chapter 6.
> Abraham Menes, Chapter 8.
> Abraham J. Heschel, Chapter 19.
> Israel S. Chipkin, Chapter 22, esp. pp. 1064 f., 1068 f.
> Abraham S. Halkin, Chapter 24, esp. pp. 1131 f.
> Julius B. Maller, Chapter 27, esp. pp. 1238 f.
> Simon Greenberg, Chapter 28.
> Rachel Wischnitzer, Chapter 30, esp. pp. 1331 f.
> Arturo Castiglioni, Chapter 31.
> Milton R. Konvitz, Chapter 33.
> Louis Finkelstein, Chapter 42, esp. pp. 1742, 1743 f., 1751 f., 1796.

18. What is the Jewish attitude to rabbinical literature?

> Israel Halpern, Chapter 6.
> Abraham Menes, Chapter 8.
> Abraham J. Heschel, Chapter 19.
> Charles Singer, Chapter 32.
> Milton R. Konvitz, Chapter 33.
> Louis Finkelstein, Chapter 42.

19. What is the Jewish attitude to Philo?

> Alexander Altmann, Chapter 20.
> Ralph Marcus, Chapter 23.
> Charles Singer, Chapter 32, esp. p. 1382.
> Louis Finkelstein, Chapter 42, esp. p. 1741.

20. What is the Jewish attitude to Maimonides?

> Israel Halpern, Chapter 6.
> Abraham Menes, Chapter 8.
> Ben Zion Dinur, Chapter 12, p. 596.
> Alexander Altmann, Chapter 20.
> Abraham S. Halkin, Chapter 24, esp. pp. 1134 f.
> Arturo Castiglioni, Chapter 31, esp. pp. 1360 f.
> Louis Finkelstein, Chapter 42, esp. pp. 1755 f., 1759, 1773 f., 1795.

*21. What is the Jewish attitude to Spinoza?

> Robert Gordis, Chapter 15, p. 791.
> Alexander Altmann, Chapter 20, pp. 979-981, 985, 991-992.

22. What is authority in Judaism?

> Judah Goldin, Chapter 3, esp. pp. 152 ff.
> Israel Halpern, Chapter 6.
> Bernard D. Weinryb, Chapter 7.
> Abraham Menes, Chapter 8.

Moshe Davis, Chapter 11, esp. p. 497.
Itzhak Ben-Zvi, Chapter 13.
Oscar I. Janowsky, Chapter 14.
Abraham J. Heschel, Chapter 19, esp. pp. 942 f.
Mordecai M. Kaplan, Chapter 21, esp. pp. 1025 f.
Milton Himmelfarb, Chapter 40.
Louis Finkelstein, Chapter 42, esp. pp. 1744 f.

23. What is the position of the rabbi in modern Judaism?

Abraham Menes, Chapter 8.
Moshe Davis, Chapter 11, esp. pp. 507 f.
Louis Finkelstein, Chapter 42, esp. pp. 1744 f.

24. What is the place of study in Judaism?

Israel Halpern, Chapter 6.
Abraham Menes, Chapter 8.
Moshe Davis, Chapter 11, esp. pp. 529 f., Section 6, beginning p. 531.
Julius B. Maller, Chapter 27.
Simon Greenberg, Chapter 28.
Louis Finkelstein, Chapter 42, esp. pp. 1743 ff.

*25. What is the Jewish attitude to the teaching of religion in secular or public schools? To the separation of Church and State?

Bernard D. Weinryb, Chapter 7, esp. pp. 326, 330 f., 360 f.
Oscar I. Janowsky, Chapter 14.
Simon Greenberg, Chapter 28, pp. 1267 f., 1270 f.

*26. What is the relation in Judaism between culture, nationality and religion?

Oscar I. Janowsky, Chapter 14.
Hillel Bavli, Chapter 18, pp. 903 f.
Nathan Glazer, Chapter 41.
Louis Finkelstein, Chapter 42, pp. 1741-1742, 1757, 1760.

27. What are the contributions of Jews to the cultural development of civilization?

Abraham Menes, Chapter 8.
Robert Gordis, Chapter 15.
Jacob J. Rabinowitz, Chapter 16.
Shalom Spiegel, Chapter 17.
Hillel Bavli, Chapter 18.
Abraham J. Heschel, Chapter 19.
Alexander Altmann, Chapter 20.
Mordecai M. Kaplan, Chapter 21.
Israel S. Chipkin, Chapter 22.
Ralph Marcus, Chapter 23.
Abraham S. Halkin, Chapter 24.
Walter J. Fischel, Chapter 25.
Yudel Mark, Chapter 26.

Julius B. Maller, Chapter 27.
Simon Greenberg, Chapter 28.
Eric Werner, Chapter 29.
Rachel Wischnitzer, Chapter 30.
Arturo Castiglioni, Chapter 31.
Charles Singer, Chapter 32.
Milton R. Konvitz, Chapter 33.
David Daiches, Chapter 34.
Frederick Lehner, Chapter 35.
Nathan Glazer, Chapter 41.
Louis Finkelstein, Chapter 42.

28. What is the present extent of synagogue affiliation?
 Bernard D. Weinryb, Chapter 7.
 Anita Libman Lebeson, Chapter 10, esp. pp. 476 f.
 Moshe Davis, Chapter 11, esp. Section 7.
 Milton Himmelfarb, Chapter 40.
 Nathan Glazer, Chapter 41.

29. What is contemporary Jewish institutional organization—congregational
 and secular?
 Bernard D. Weinryb, Chapter 7.
 Anita Libman Lebeson, Chapter 10, esp. pp. 479 ff.
 Moshe Davis, Chapter 11, esp. pp. 488-570.
 Oscar I. Janowsky, Chapter 14.
 Israel S. Chipkin, Chapter 22.
 Milton Himmelfarb, Chapter 40.
 Nathan Glazer, Chapter 41.
 Louis Finkelstein, Chapter 42, esp. pp. 1768 ff.

30. How many Jews are there? In the world? In the U.S.A.? In the U.S.S.R.?
 What is the postwar distribution?
 Bernard D. Weinryb, Chapter 7, Section 3.
 Arieh Tartakower, Chapter 9, esp. pp. 428 f.
 Anita Libman Lebeson, Chapter 10, esp. pp. 476 f.
 Oscar I. Janowsky, Chapter 14.
 Melville J. Herskovits, Chapter 36.
 Uriah Zevi Engelman, Chapter 37.
 Jacob Lestschinsky, Chapter 38.
 Milton Himmelfarb, Chapter 40.
 Nathan Glazer, Chapter 41.

*31. What is the occupational distribution of Jews? What is the proportion
 of Jews in agriculture as compared with urban pursuits?
 Judah Goldin, Chapter 3, *passim* and p. 176.
 Cecil Roth, Chapters 4 and 5.
 Bernard D. Weinryb, Chapter 7, Section 3.
 Anita Libman Lebeson, Chapter 10, esp. pp. 461 ff., 475 f.

Oscar I. Janowsky, Chapter 14, esp. pp. 758 ff.
Uriah Zevi Engelman, Chapter 37, pp. 1530-1531.
Jacob Lestschinsky, Chapter 38, pp. 1538-1539.
Simon Kuznets, Chapter 39.
Milton Himmelfarb, Chapter 40.
Nathan Glazer, Chapter 41.

32. What was the Jewish participation in the wars fought by the U.S.A.?
The Revolution
    Anita Libman Lebeson, Chapter 10, esp. pp. 456 f.
The War between the States
    Anita Libman Lebeson, Chapter 10, esp. p. 458.
    Moshe Davis, Chapter 11, esp. p. 547
World War I
    Anita Libman Lebeson, Chapter 10, esp. p. 458.
    Moshe Davis, Chapter 11, esp. p. 547.
World War II
    Anita Libman Lebeson, Chapter 10, esp. p. 458.
    Moshe Davis, Chapter 11, esp. pp. 572 ff.
    Israel S. Chipkin, Chapter 22, esp. pp. 1046 f.

*33. How did World War II and the preceding events affect the Jews?
Bernard D. Weinryb, Chapter 7.
Moshe Davis, Chapter 11, esp. pp. 572-573.
Oscar I. Janowsky, Chapter 14.
Uriah Zevi Engelman, Chapter 27, esp. pp. 1531-1532.
Simon Kuznets, Chapter 39, esp. Part III.
Milton Himmelfarb, Chapter 40.
Nathan Glazer, Chapter 41.

*34. What is the situation of the Jews behind the Iron Curtain?
Bernard D. Weinryb, Chapter 7.
Arieh Tartakower, Chapter 9.
Simon Greenberg, Chapter 28, pp. 1265-1266, 1282.
Uriah Zevi Engelman, Chapter 37, pp. 1527 ff.
Jacob Lestschinsky, Chapter 38, esp. p. 1542 and Section 7.
Simon Kuznets, Chapter 39, esp. Part III.

*35. What is the relation of Jews to Communism?
Cf. the reference re the situation of Jews behind the Iron Curtain.

*36. What are the bases of anti-Semitism?
Cecil Roth, Chapter 5, pp. 273-276, 279-282.
Israel Halpern, Chapter 6.
Bernard D. Weinryb, Chapter 7.
Arieh Tartakower, Chapter 9, pp. 437 f.
Itzhak Ben-Zvi, Chapter 13.
Jacob Lestschinsky, Chapter 38, pp. 1542-1543, Section 7.
Nathan Glazer, Chapter 41, esp. pp. 1699 f., 1714 f., 1717 ff.

*37. What is Zionism? How extensive is Zionism? Is it related to Judaism?
    Bernard D. Weinryb, Chapter 7.
    Anita Libman Lebeson, Chapter 10, pp. 473-475.
    Moshe Davis, Chapter 11, esp. pp. 526-552, 554, 576-577.
    Ben Zion Dinur, Chapter 12.
    Itzhak Ben-Zvi, Chapter 13.
    Oscar I. Janowsky, Chapter 14.
    Hillel Bavli, Chapter 18, esp. Section 5.
    Walter J. Fischel, Chapter 25, p. 1187.
    Jacob Lestschinsky, Chapter 38, esp. p. 1572, and Section 7.
    Milton Himmelfarb, Chapter 40.

38. What is the relation of the Jews throughout the world to Palestine and the State of Israel?
    William Foxwell Albright, Chapter 1, esp. p. 53.
    Anita Libman Lebeson, Chapter 10, esp. pp. 473 f.
    Moshe Davis, Chapter 11, esp. pp. 564, 576-577.
    Ben Zion Dinur, Chapter 12.
    Oscar I. Janowsky, Chapter 14.
    Hillel Bavli, Chapter 18, esp. pp. 904 f., 919 f.
    Israel S. Chipkin, Chapter 22, esp. p. 1045.
    Walter J. Fischel, Chapter 25, esp. pp. 1186 f.
    Simon Greenberg, Chapter 28, esp. pp. 1285 f.
    Eric Werner, Chapter 29, esp. p. 1320.
    Rachel Wischnitzer, Chapter 30, esp. p. 1341.
    Jacob Lestschinsky, Chapter 38, esp. pp. 1541 f., 1571 f.
    Simon Kuznets, Chapter 39.
    Milton Himmelfarb, Chapter 40.
    Louis Finkelstein, Chapter 42, esp. pp. 1759 ff.
    Cf. The references re Zionism.

*39. What is the relation of Jews in Israel to those in other countries?
    Oscar I. Janowsky, Chapter 14.

*40. What is the relation of Israel to other countries?
    Oscar I. Janowsky, Chapter 14.

*41. What is the status of religion in Israel? The relation of religion to the national life?
    Oscar I. Janowsky, Chapter 14, esp. pp. 718 f., 728 f.
    Louis Finkelstein, Chapter 42, esp. pp. 1759 ff.

*42. Is there a religious revival among contemporary Jews?
    Louis Finkelstein, Foreword, p. xxxi.
    Bernard D. Weinryb, Chapter 7.
    Oscar I. Janowsky, Chapter 14.
    Milton Himmelfarb, Chapter 40.
    Nathan Glazer, Chapter 41.

LIST OF ABBREVIATIONS

Am. Jour. Sem. Lang.
    American Journal of Semitic Languages
Annual Am. Sch. Or. Res.
    Annual American Schools of Oriental Research
Antt.
    Antiquities, Josephus
Archiv f. Orientf.
    Archiv fuer Orientforschung
ARN
    Abot of Rabbi Nathan
AZA
    Ahavah Zedakah Ahdut (B'nai B'rith Youth Organization)
b.
    ben (son of)
B.
    Babylonian Talmud
B. B.
    Baba Batra
B. C. E.
    Before the Common Era
Beih. Zeits. Alttest. Wiss.
    Beihefte zur Zeitschrift fuer die Alttestamentliche Wissenschaft
Bell. Jud.
    De Bello Judaico, Josephus
Ber. Saechs. Akad. Wiss.
    Berichte ueber die Verhandlungen der saechsischen Akademie der Wissenschaften
Bull. Am. Sch. Or. Res.
    Bulletin American Schools of Oriental Research
Bull. de l'inst. Français d'Archéol. Orient.
    Bulletin de l'institut Français d'Archéologie Orientale
Bull. Jew. Pal. Explor. Soc.
    Bulletin of the Jewish Palestine Exploration Society

C. Ap.
    Contra Apionem, Josephus
C. E.
    Common Era
CCAR
    Central Conference of American Rabbis
CJFWF
    Council Jewish Federations and Welfare Funds
cod.
    codex
Comp. Rend. Acad. des Inscr.
    Comptes-Rendus de l'Académie des Inscriptions
De Abr.
    De Abrahamo, Philo
De Ant. Jud.
    Antiquitates Judaicae, Josephus
De Cher.
    De Cherubim, Philo
De Conf.
    De Confusione Linguarum, Philo
De Congr.
    De Congressu Eruditionis Gratia, Philo
De Dec.
    De Decalogo, Philo
De Ebr.
    De Ebrietate, Philo
De Fuga
    De Fuga et Inventione, Philo
De Gig.
    De Gigantibus, Philo
De Mig. or De Migr.
    De Migratione Abrahami, Philo
De Mut.
    De Mutatione Nominum, Philo
De Op.
    De Opificio Mundi, Philo
De Plant.
    De Plantatione, Philo
De Post.
    De Posteritate Caini, Philo
De Praem.
    De Praemiis et Poenis, Philo
De Sacr.
    De Sacrificiis Abelis et Caini, Philo